CW01496235

Communication in Business

4th EDITION

Communication in Business

STRATEGIES AND SKILLS

JUDITH DWYER

PEARSON

Education
Australia

Copyright © Pearson Education Australia (a division of Pearson Australia Group Pty Ltd) 2009

Pearson Education Australia
Unit 4, Level 3
14 Aquatic Drive
Frenchs Forest NSW 2086

www.pearsoned.com.au

The *Copyright Act 1968* of Australia allows a maximum of one chapter or 10% of this book, whichever is the greater, to be copied by any educational institution for its educational purposes provided that that educational institution (or the body that administers it) has given a remuneration notice to Copyright Agency Limited (CAL) under the Act. For details of the CAL licence for educational institutions contact:
Copyright Agency Limited, telephone: (02) 9394 7600, email: info@copyright.com.au

All rights reserved. Except under the conditions described in the *Copyright Act 1968* of Australia and subsequent amendments, no part of this publication may be reproduced, stored in a retrieval system or transmitted in any form or by any means, electronic, mechanical, photocopying, recording or otherwise, without the prior permission of the copyright owner.

Senior Acquisitions Editor: Frances Eden
Acquisitions Editor: Joy Whitton
Senior Project Editor: Rebecca Pomponio
Project Editor: Sophia Oravecz
Associate Editor: Caro Cooper
Production Coordinator: Barbara Honor
Copy Editor: Jo Rudd
Proofreader: Robyn Flemming
Copyright and Pictures Editor: Emma Gaulton
Indexer: Sue Hill
Cover and internal design by Nada Backovic
Cover photography: Miriam Fluit, Newcastle University. Photos part of a collection of 150 entitled 'All Things Bright and Beautiful All Things Great and Small' exhibited in ArtExpress 2006.
Typeset by Midland Typesetters, Australia

Printed in China (SWTC/02)

2 3 4 5 13 12 11 10

National Library of Australia Cataloguing-in-Publication entry

Author:	Dwyer, Judith.
Title:	Communication in business: strategies and skills /Judith Dwyer.
Edition:	4th ed.
ISBN:	9780733986383 (pbk.)
Notes:	Includes index.
Subjects:	Business communication.
Dewey Number:	658.45

Every effort has been made to trace and acknowledge copyright. However, should any infringement have occurred, the publishers tender their apologies and invite copyright owners to contact them.

An imprint of Pearson Education Australia
(a division of Pearson Australia Group Pty Ltd)

Contents

Visual preface

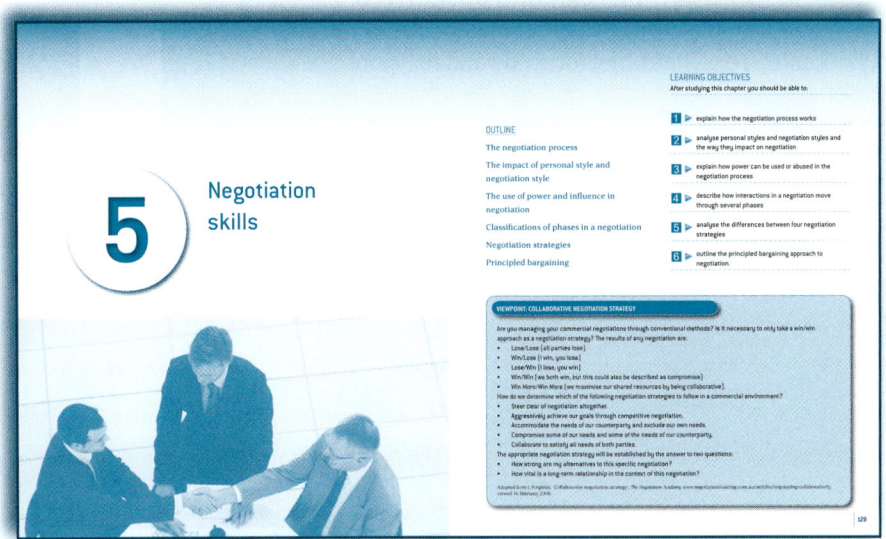

▲ CHAPTER OPENERS

contain a *chapter outline* to provide a framework for reading and study, and *chapter learning objectives* to focus the reader on key concepts.

▲ VIEWPOINTS

to highlight current business practice or points of view.

APPLY YOUR KNOWLEDGE ▷

exercises provide short practical activities that reinforce the theoretical content. They are spread throughout the chapter at strategic study points.

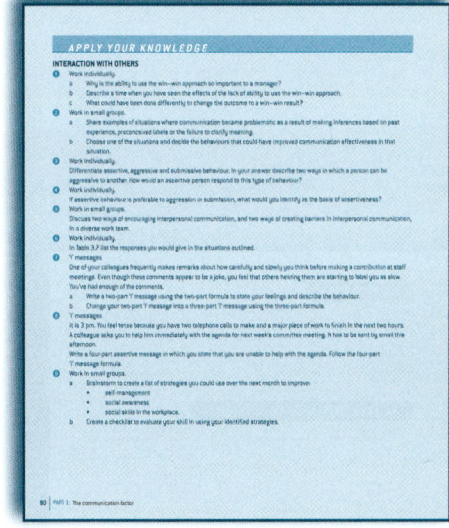

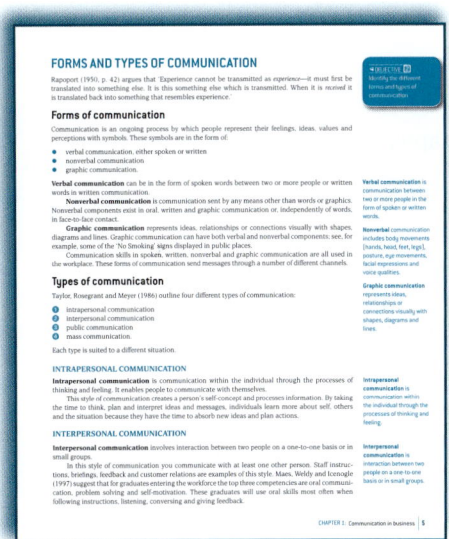

◁ KEY TERMS

are printed in bold the first time they appear, with accompanying **margin definitions** providing an integrated glossary feature to aid comprehension of key terms in context.

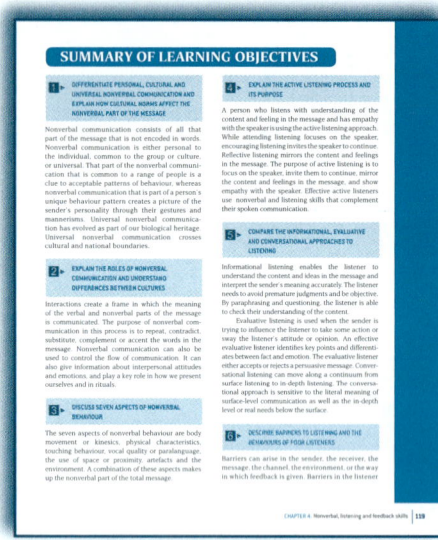

◄ SUMMARY OF LEARNING OBJECTIVES

is a concise overview of the main points in the chapter and an excellent tool for study and revision.

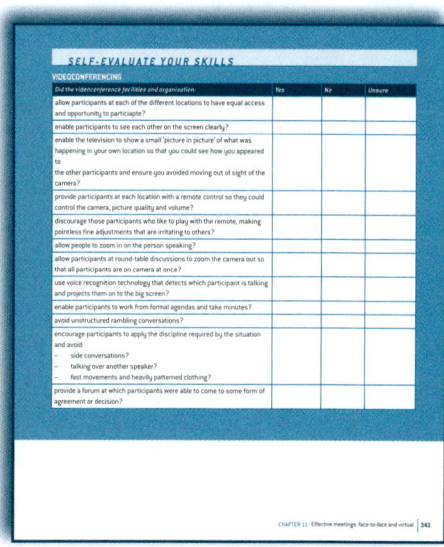

SELF-EVALUATE YOUR SKILLS ►

provides a self-evaluation tool to prompt students to reflect on their communication skills.

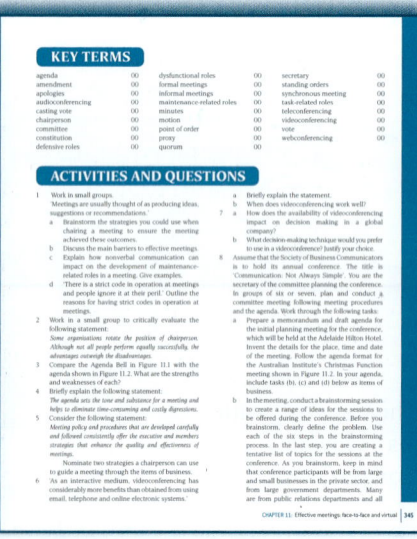

◄ KEY TERMS

are listed at the end of each chapter for reference purposes.

◄ ACTIVITIES AND QUESTIONS

contains graded activities, exercises, role-plays and case studies for further critical analysis and review. The opportunity for group work is highly suitable for student participation and application, whether in study teams or tutorials.

REVIEW QUESTIONS ▷

are short answer questions designed for additional review purposes and to ensure comprehension of the basic theory.

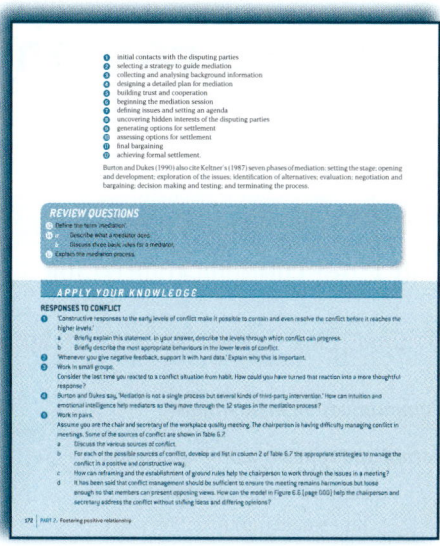

◁ ## EXPLORING THE WEB

requires students to research on the Internet, and verify the accuracy of the information and the source of their research.

◁ ## PROJECT WORK

allows students to apply a selection of the knowledge and techniques presented throughout the chapter.

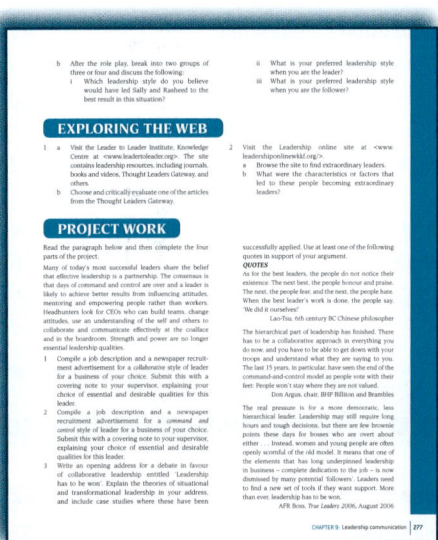

BIBLIOGRAPHY ▷

appears at the end of each chapter, with full reference details for all books and further reading referred to in the chapter.

Detailed contents

CHAPTER 10 TEAM AND WORK GROUP COMMUNICATION 280

CHAPTER 11 EFFECTIVE MEETINGS: FACE-TO-FACE AND VIRTUAL 314

Preface

This fourth edition of *Communication in Business: Strategies and Skills* continues to provide comprehensive coverage of communication strategies and skills in business by linking theory and research with practical skills and examples. The book has a plain English writing style supported by an accessible design that provides a clear how-to guide to help students understand communication principles and apply them in their interpersonal and business interactions. In the business world the trade of goods and services simply cannot happen without an efficient and effective exchange of ideas and information. It is no accident that commerce and communication share the same root word, Latin *commercium*, or trade. Accounting, marketing, retailing, exporting, technology, management, human resource management and property development are all vital branches of the tree of commerce and business, but these branches depend on a strong, well-nurtured and unifying communication system.

The goal of this book is to provide a global communication tool that both expands our knowledge of *what* we can do to interact effectively and provides us with working models to practise and refine *how* well we do it. Opportunities in today's global marketplace can be lost and won in micro-seconds in cyberspace, or in the way we interact with our office colleagues. Practitioners who nurture a strong and efficient communication system as the foundation for work or business realise that communication experiences are cumulative – the helix principle – with past and present experiences influencing the future in ever-widening circles. Communication competence harnesses opportunities and expands business and career opportunities. For example, the manager who wants to introduce a new financial proposal must carry with him or her the knowledge of an effective communication model that will win the support and collaboration of immediate peers, managers and experts, then win new clients and achieve success in the marketplace.

The graduate who wants a challenging and rewarding career must carry with him or her the top ten selection criteria for recruiting graduates in Australia: cultural alignment; values fit; activities including both intra- and extra-curricular; emotional intelligence (including self-awareness, strength of character, confidence, motivation); critical reasoning and analytical skills (problem solving, lateral thinking, technical skills, teamwork skills); passion, knowledge of industry, drive, commitment, attitude; leadership skills; work experience; academic qualifications; and interpersonal and communication skills, written and oral (Graduate Outlook 2006).

Acknowledgments

Communication in Business: Strategies and Skills helps so many readers because it is the product of the collaborative will and high standards set by so many academics and business practitioners.

I am grateful to the reviewers and other experts who have contributed their expertise in shaping the 4th edition of this book. Special thanks are due to Carolyn Swanson whose professional research and advice in Chapters 2, 3, 8, 9, 11, 12 and 15 was invaluable. I would like to thank Elizabeth Morrison, for planning and writing the report 'Proposed New Watering System for Fairways Golf Club'. The report is practical and a valuable example of a long report. My sincere thanks also go to the academics and professionals who shared their expertise in developing the range of quality supplementary materials for this book.

I extend sincere thanks to the many outstanding professionals at Pearson Education Australia, including Rebecca Pomponio (Senior Project Editor) for her support and encouragement, Joy Whitton and Frances Eden (Acquisitions Editors), Emma Gaulton (Copyright and Pictures Editor), Caro Cooper (Associate Editor) and the marketing and sales team. I am exceedingly grateful to Jo Rudd (copy editor) and Robyn Flemming (proofreader) for their care and good judgment in editing, proofreading and making improvements to the text.

Special thanks are also extended to Paul Domoney for supplying computer expertise that made the office run smoothly in the production of this book. I appreciate his advice about current and emerging information technology and its impact on the local and global business world.

Most importantly, I wish to thank my husband, John Burns, for helping me stay focused and for his continuous support, interest and enthusiasm through each edition of the book.

About the author

Judith Dwyer is an acknowledged communication expert, educator and author. She has written 14 books and conducted research and lectured in communication studies for more than 20 years. A longstanding member of the Australian Institute of Management, Dwyer's areas of expertise are communication studies, economics, management and leadership. She consults on and manages a number of industry projects.

Dwyer has a Master of Management (Public) from the University of Technology Sydney, a Bachelor of Economics from the University of New England and a Diploma in Education from the University of Newcastle.

Her fundamental message is that an understanding of people and social processes is more important than our knowledge of facts, but we must research and integrate theory into efficient working practice.

What's new?

This edition has expanded into six parts.

Part 1, The communication factor, gives readers the opportunity to research and carry with them the underpinning knowledge to use an effective communication model.

Chapter 1 Communication in business discusses the role of communication in business, communication models and theories, the importance of ethics, and the increasing significance of technologically mediated communication.

Chapter 2 Intercultural communication discusses the importance of culture, identifies cultural components, outlines barriers to intercultural communication, and discusses comparative value dimensions on which cultures differ and a culture-general approach to communication competence.

Chapter 3 Emotional intelligence, self-awareness and assertion presents the central role of emotional intelligence in emotional awareness. Emotional competence is divided into two categories. The first is personal competence, or managing self (self-awareness, self-regulation and self-motivation). The second is social competence, or managing relationships (social awareness and social skills). Self-awareness, interpersonal communication skills and the ability to value diversity are the foundations of positive professional relationships.

Chapter 4 Nonverbal, listening and feedback skills explains how nonverbal communication and listening that complement one another provide clear and constructive feedback that enhances understanding between individuals, groups and organisations.

Part 2, Fostering positive relationships, highlights the dynamics of interpersonal communication and relationships in negotiation and conflict management, customer service and public relations.

Chapter 5 Negotiation skills covers the principles and processes of negotiation, and examines the stages in a negotiation and ways to negotiate more effectively.

Chapter 6 Conflict management brings concepts of negotiation and conflict management together in an examination of the causes of conflict, discusses how to map and manage a conflict, and presents constructive responses to conflict. Mediation is presented as the response to an intractable conflict.

Chapter 7 Customer service and public relations introduces the features of a valued customer experience, the role of customer relations management, and the importance of communication skills in building positive customer relations. The chapter discusses public relations principles and presents strategies for managing issues.

Part 3, Leading and managing people, discusses interactions across the organisation and between leaders and teams and places new emphasis on knowledge management. It gives readers opportunities to build on skills to communicate effectively in the workplace: in work groups, in teams and in meetings.

Chapter 8 Communication across the organisation covers the interaction of organisational culture, structure and communication channels. Discussion identifies different types of organisational structures and their impact on communication flows. Formal and informal structures are differentiated and the role of small group communication networks is outlined. Techniques to improve organisational communication are presented.

Chapter 9 Leadership communication covers the principles and processes of leadership and focuses on leadership styles, situational leadership, transformational leadership and leadership communication practices.

Chapter 10 Team and work group communication traces the stages of development of groups or teams, identifies roles within a group or team, presents strategies to improve the performance of project, self-managed, cross-functional and virtual teams, and discusses decision making in groups or teams.

Chapter 11 Effective meetings: face-to-face and virtual gives readers opportunities to build on skills to communicate effectively in face-to-face and virtual meetings. The roles of the chair and participants in face-to-face and electronic meetings are clearly defined, and procedures and performance tips are given for video, web, teleconferencing and podcasts.

Chapter 12 Knowledge management and decision making discusses the role of knowledge workers, and presents knowledge-management principles and key concepts as well as decision-making and problem-solving strategies.

Part 4, Finding and communicating information, covers the various aspects of researching, ordering, thinking critically, presenting and communicating information.

Chapter 13 Researching and processing information outlines the research process, discusses academic honesty, business ethics and etiquette, how to find information on search engines, web directories and databases, and how to document sources and prepare a bibliography and list of references.

Chapter 14 Critical thinking: argument, logic and persuasion introduces the concept of critical thinking, argument, logic, fallacies (false argument), the importance of quality, objective evidence, the purpose of persuasion and the characteristics of a persuasive argument.

Chapter 15 Oral business presentations covers different types of presentations, how to plan, prepare and deliver a presentation, and presents strategies to manage challenging audience members.

Chapter 16 Communicating through visuals discusses the role of graphics in reports and written presentations, and how to construct graphics and use visuals in oral business presentations.

Part 5, Writing for results, helps students to develop a strategy to write effectively and efficiently to a proven formula.

Chapter 17 The business writing process presents principles of effective business writing and discusses the advantages gained from composing equitable, efficient and effective business documents, integrating the elements of a plain English writing style and editing according to the principles of plain English.

Chapter 18 Writing business letters, memos and short reports introduces practical strategies to prepare different types of business letters, memos and short reports efficiently and effectively.

Chapter 19 Writing long reports discusses the long report format and explains how to prepare the front matter, body or text and end matter, provides an example of a long report and emphasises the importance of editing long reports.

Chapter 20 Academic writing covers the importance of structuring the content to suit the purpose, writing techniques appropriate to academic documents, how to write an argumentative essay, and how to revise and edit effectively.

Chapter 21 Business messages via electronic media discusses types of electronic media appropriate for business messages, the 3×3 writing process, characteristics of effective email messages, how to communicate via instant messaging, text messaging, blogs and podcasts, and how to manage information overload.

Part 6, Employment communication, focuses on preparing a professional résumé and performing well in an employment interview.

Chapter 22 Finding, applying and being interviewed for a position covers strategies to search for the best position, résumé-writing principles, features of traditional and electronic résumés, the application letter, how to communicate in an employment interview and how to avoid potential problems.

Special learning features

Each chapter of the book is divided into easily recognised learning stages.

Chapter openers include a **chapter outline** to provide a framework for reading and study, and **chapter learning objectives** to focus the reader on key concepts. This is accompanied by a set of **review questions** for each learning objective placed throughout the chapter.

Viewpoints, also at the beginning of each chapter, highlight current business practice or points of view.

Tables and figures, including flow charts and concept maps, are designed for visual clarification of important information. They form a user-friendly reference throughout the chapter.

Key terms are printed in bold the first time they appear, with accompanying **margin definitions**, providing an integrated glossary feature to aid comprehension of key terms in context.

Apply your knowledge exercises provide short practical activities that reinforce theoretical content. They are spread throughout the chapter at strategic study points.

Self-evaluation checklists provide a self-evaluation tool to prompt students to reflect on their communication skills.

A **chapter summary** provides a concise overview of the chapter's main points and is an excellent tool for study and revision.

Activities and questions contains graded exercises and group activities for further critical analysis and review.

Exploring the web encourages students to research on the Web, learn more about relevant areas covered in the chapter, and verify and source the accuracy of their research.

Project work is designed to integrate key chapter concepts.

Supplements

New supplementary material has been designed to complement the book.

Instructor's Resource Manual
The manual includes expanded outlines of topics in each chapter and teaching tips to accompany the learning activities in the text.

PowerPoint Slides
The PowerPoint slides have been developed to distil the key concepts from each chapter of the book.

Australian Video CD
The video suite on CD is a new supplement specially developed to support this fourth edition of *Communication in Business: Strategies and Skills*. The video clips provide a practical point of view of important business communication topics.

Testbank
More than 400 multiple-choice questions and over 60 essay questions are available as a resource for busy lecturers.

The fourth edition of *Communication in Business: Strategies and Skills* provides a solid background in business communication, stimulates critical thinking, and promotes active learning through a variety of features and activities. The supplements accompanying the text are designed to enhance the learning experience through interactive exercises that demonstrate the application of theory to current business practice.

Part 1

The Communication Factor

1

Communication in business

OUTLINE

Communication in business

Forms and types of communication

Characteristics of effective business communication

The role of business communication

Communication models and theories

Ethical behaviour in business

LEARNING OBJECTIVES

After studying this chapter you should be able to:

1 ▷ explain how effective communication builds success in today's business environment

2 ▷ identify the different forms and types of communication

3 ▷ discuss the impact of technology on business communication

4 ▷ outline the role of communication in the workplace

5 ▷ differentiate between communication theories

6 ▷ outline the accepted principles of business ethics.

VIEWPOINT: WHY COMMUNICATION SKILLS ARE SO IMPORTANT

'By successfully getting your message across, you convey your thoughts and ideas effectively. When not successful, the thoughts and ideas that you send do not necessarily reflect your own, causing a communication breakdown and creating roadblocks that stand in the way of your goals – both personally and professionally.

In a recent survey of recruiters from companies with more than 50 000 employees, communication skills were cited as the single more important decisive factor in choosing managers. The survey, conducted by the University of Pittsburgh's Katz Business School, points out that communication skills, including written and oral presentations, as well as an ability to work with others, are the main factor contributing to job success.

Getting your message across is paramount to progressing. To do this, you must understand what your message is, what audience you are sending it to, and how it will be perceived. You must also weigh-in the circumstances surrounding your communications, such as situational and cultural context.'

Excerpt from 'Communication skills', *MindTools Essential Skills for a Successful Career*, www.mindtools.com/CommSkll/CommunicationIntro.htm, viewed 16 February 2008.

Today, business communication is affected by factors such as the globalisation of business, the pervasiveness of technology, increasing diversity in the workforce, changing organisational structures, the increasing value of information and the communication skills of individuals.

Professionals in today's competitive environment need to communicate with people inside and outside their organisation. Successful professionals know and understand the elements and rules of communication. They value diverse points of view and interact easily with people from different cultures, backgrounds, life and career experiences. Their ability to communicate is reflected in the quality and range of their communication skills.

COMMUNICATION IN BUSINESS

OBJECTIVE 1 ▶

Explain how effective communication builds success in today's business environment

Communication is any behaviour—verbal, nonverbal or graphic—that is perceived by another.

Communication is any behaviour—verbal, nonverbal or graphic—that is perceived by another. Knowledge, feelings or thoughts are encoded and sent from at least one person and received and decoded by another. Meaning is given to this message as the receiver interprets the message. A connection is made between the people communicating. Watzlawick, Beavin and Jackson (1967) suggest that people cannot *not* communicate. Even when we ignore another person, something is communicated.

An effective business manager, human resource manager, accountant, financial planner, sales manager or person working in any other occupation is able to communicate and work with others in a purposeful, supportive and flexible manner. Their communication is effective because it achieves the intended outcome. As well as achieving the intended outcome, effective communicators also make connections and build ongoing relationships with others while ineffective communicators raise barriers.

People who are successful at work are not only proficient in their functional and technical areas of expertise. They are also communication-oriented with the ability to demonstrate professionalism, empathy, awareness and concern for others. They use good listening skills, and understand their own concerns and needs. These people are open, approachable and supportive of others.

Employers expect their staff to be competent in a wide range of communication tasks, including:

- communicating with people from different backgrounds, experiences and cultures
- organising ideas and information into knowledge for use by self and others
- expressing and presenting ideas and information accurately and persuasively
- listening to understand others and take actions based on their understanding
- using communication technologies efficiently and effectively
- communicating professionally and ethically.

As you build your communication skills you will be able to complete these tasks effectively and build expertise in higher-level tasks that develop management and leadership skills, such as evaluating performance, building teamwork, coaching, mentoring, facilitating and motivating others.

REVIEW QUESTIONS

1. 'Communication is an interactive process.' Explain briefly.
2. Briefly discuss three factors affecting communication in the current business environment.
3. *a* What are the characteristics of a communication-oriented graduate?
   b How is a communication orientation likely to support them in their career?

FORMS AND TYPES OF COMMUNICATION

◄ OBJECTIVE 2
Identify the different forms and types of communication

Rapoport (1950, p. 42) argues that 'Experience cannot be transmitted as *experience*—it must first be translated into something else. It is this something else which is transmitted. When it is *received* it is translated back into something that resembles experience.'

Forms of communication

Communication is an ongoing process by which people represent their feelings, ideas, values and perceptions with symbols. These symbols are in the form of:

- verbal communication, either spoken or written
- nonverbal communication
- graphic communication.

Verbal communication can be in the form of spoken words between two or more people or written words in written communication.

Nonverbal communication is communication sent by any means other than words or graphics. Nonverbal components exist in oral, written and graphic communication or, independently of words, in face-to-face contact.

Graphic communication represents ideas, relationships or connections visually with shapes, diagrams and lines. Graphic communication can have both verbal and nonverbal components; see, for example, some of the 'No Smoking' signs displayed in public places.

Communication skills in spoken, written, nonverbal and graphic communication are all used in the workplace. These forms of communication send messages through a number of different channels.

Types of communication

Taylor, Rosegrant and Meyer (1986) outline four different types of communication:

1. intrapersonal communication
2. interpersonal communication
3. public communication
4. mass communication.

Each type is suited to a different situation.

INTRAPERSONAL COMMUNICATION

Intrapersonal communication is communication with oneself through the processes of thinking and feeling. This style of communication creates a person's self-concept and processes information. By taking the time to think, plan and interpret ideas and messages, individuals learn more about self, others and the situation because they have the time to absorb new ideas and plan actions.

INTERPERSONAL COMMUNICATION

Interpersonal communication involves interaction between two people on a one-to-one basis or in small groups.

In this style of communication you communicate with at least one other person. Staff instructions, briefings, feedback and customer relations are examples of this style. Maes, Weldy and Icenogle (1997) suggest that for graduates entering the workforce the top three competencies are oral communication, problem solving and self-motivation. These graduates will use oral skills most often when following instructions, listening, conversing and giving feedback.

Verbal communication is communication between two or more people in the form of spoken or written words.

Nonverbal communication is communication sent by any means other than words or graphics.

Nonverbal communication includes body movements (hands, head, feet, legs), posture, eye movements, facial expressions and voice qualities.

Graphic communication represents ideas, relationships or connections visually with shapes, diagrams and lines.

Intrapersonal communication is communication within the individual through the processes of thinking and feeling.

Interpersonal communication is interaction between two people on a one-to-one basis or in small groups.

PUBLIC COMMUNICATION

Public communication
occurs when
an organisation
communicates with a
number of receivers at the
same time.

Public communication originates from one source and takes place when the organisation communicates with a number of receivers.

This communication can be either to receivers within the organisation—for example, in the form of the staff newsletter or intranet—or to others outside the organisation in the form of reports or meetings. Williams (1996) identifies the need for people to think critically and understand their audiences when using persuasion techniques in both internal and external communication in business settings. The three forms of communication—verbal, nonverbal and graphic—are all used by those who have responsibility for communicating effectively within and outside the organisation. Communication is the public face of a company.

MASS COMMUNICATION

Mass communication
contacts an organisation's
public.

Mass communication contacts the organisation's public. This is usually done through the electronic or print media—for example, public relations, annual reports and advertising.

The ability to communicate is a learned behaviour based on skills gained from others and from experience. As experience widens, new learning takes place. The communication style of individuals and organisations develops through using and adapting new techniques. Anyone who believes they can control the communication process is unaware that communication is an intricate, interactive process. The interactions of a number of elements impact on the people communicating. People can do a great deal to influence the communication process, but they cannot control the other person's perception, outlook, values and attitudes. Each of these affects the way communication is received.

REVIEW QUESTIONS

4 Define and give an example of verbal, nonverbal and graphic communication.

5 a Identify four different types of communication.

   b Give an example of each.

CHARACTERISTICS OF EFFECTIVE BUSINESS COMMUNICATION

In a business environment, people are engaged for most of the time in some form of communication activity, such as reading, listening, writing or talking. Business communication is different from academic or literary writing and speaking. It requires precision, clarity and efficiency, because the pressure of time means that business people need to understand and act quickly rather than use time to savour an expression or idea.

**Effective business
communication** is practical
and provides information
that the receiver needs.

Effective business communication has the characteristics shown in Table 1.1. These characteristics apply across all mediums in business. Staff who apply these characteristics communicate well. Their efforts increase an organisation's efficiency by sharing information, responding appropriately and flexibly, contributing to continuous improvement, and participating in activities to achieve organisational goals and objectives effectively. Clear, well-defined messages by leaders, managers, team leaders and team members at all levels in an organisation clarify expectations and eliminate confusion over what needs to be done and by whom. The result is improved motivation and performance.

Technologically mediated communication

OBJECTIVE 3 ▶
Discuss the impact of
technology on business
communication

The last 50 years have seen the introduction and significant expansion of technologically mediated business communication. Telecommunication services transmit written, voice and data messages over short and long distances through a number of mediums including oral communication via:

Table 1.1: Characteristics of effective business communication

Characteristic	Purpose
Clear, concise and complete	To enable your receiver to understand your message easily.
Two-way	To exchange ideas, receive and give feedback to enhance understanding
Factual rather than subjective	To give specific, accurate information rather than your impressions and opinions without supporting facts
Most important information highlighted	To clarify, condense and summarise rather than making the receiver sort through an 'information dump'
Actions identified clearly	To ensure your message is practical and the purpose of your message or instruction and the response you expect is understood by those responsible for acting on your message
Audience-centred approach	To focus on your receiver's interest, their need to understand, and your need to achieve your communication purpose.
Persuasive (when required)	To generate a specific response by offering recommendations and showing the benefits to your receiver (customers, colleagues, suppliers, employers) of adopting a plan of action or responding the way you want them to
Ethical and based on principles of business etiquette	To provide relevant, truthful information and treat others with respect, courtesy and common sense in accordance with the accepted norms of business behaviour

- voice technologies that regenerate a human voice from computer files
- telecommunication services that transmit written, voice and data messages, voicemail and electronic conferences.

Written communication such as word processing, database spreadsheets, fax and graphic applications is also assisted electronically by telecommunication services.

Communication through mobile devices is a bonus to those businesses with staff who are working remotely or travelling between the organisation and its clients or suppliers. Many organisations provide their staff with laptops rather than PCs. The laptops can be carried home, on business trips or to meetings. On returning to the office the laptop is reconnected to the organisation's network connections through a docking station.

Networking advances have enabled businesses to increase their use of instant messaging, wireless networking (Wi-Fi), short messaging services (SMS) and social network services (SNS). Instant messaging enables people to connect virtually and to exchange text information directly without having to go through central email servers. Files are shared and people can work on problems simultaneously. Wi-Fi enables PCs and handheld devices to connect via radio signals with the Internet through wireless access points that extend the reach of the Internet. SMS is a feature of mobile phones that lets you send a text message instead of a voice message to another mobile phone.

Social network services are primarily Web-based and offer various ways for users to interact: discussion groups, messaging, chat rooms, email, videos, blogging and file sharing. Social networking services combine directories of interest groups (such as professional interest groups, social groups or project teams within an organisation) with the means to connect with friends or business associates (usually with self-description pages) or recommender systems. The most widely used social network services in 2007 are MySpace, Bebo and Facebook. Clare Hart (2007, p. 56), executive vice president of the Dow Jones Enterprise Media Group, says: 'Dow Jones is working with clients to create applications

Technology has created new ways to communicate online.

*A **social network service** provides a forum for communities of people who share interests to interact online.*

that combine social networking tools with knowledge management and market intelligence services. The aim is to integrate content from Dow Jones, other third party sources and internal content.' Technological improvements will allow social networking through mobile devices to increase rapidly.

Dawson (2007, <www.futureexploration.net>) comments on one of the five top trends shaping the future: '... on one side, technology has helped create business. But as we have more ways to communicate with each other, we keep adding to our communication load and what we have to get done. The simple summary of business today is to do more with less. If we're not learning how to use the technologies better, we become more and more squeezed. But if we use the way in which we are connected well we can find a solution for this.'

Information technology allows an organisation to apply its knowledge systematically to practical tasks so that relevant data is on hand for decision making. As DeTienne (2002, p. 4) comments, 'what is driving the economy is not information but information plus the knowledge of how to use it'. However, technology-mediated business communication should be kept in perspective as there are some disadvantages to the use of information technology.

First, people need to know how to use the technology efficiently and effectively. Second, technology can cause communication barriers when computers, the Internet, telephones and online social networks are chosen to avoid engaging in personal face-to-face communication with others. Technology is not a replacement for the interaction and support provided by interpersonal contact. Technology used well is an aid to interpersonal communication between individuals within local, national and international organisations. Chapter 21 covers electronic communication.

REVIEW QUESTIONS

6 *a*   Briefly describe the characteristics of effective business communication.

    b   'Nothing much happens in business without communication.' Explain briefly.

7 What is meant by the term 'technologically mediated business communication'?

8 Give examples of three ways businesses can communicate online.

9 Identify two barriers caused by technologically mediated communication, and briefly describe strategies to overcome them.

OBJECTIVE **4** ▷
Outline the role of communication in the workplace

THE ROLE OF BUSINESS COMMUNICATION

Communication is the sharing of ideas, knowledge, feelings and perceptions. It is something that is done by people. The better the communication the more effective the understanding. For business decisions to be effective and relevant, timely and appropriate information has to be obtained and communicated throughout the organisation.

Any organisation is a collection of people. Some have similar backgrounds and life and career experiences. Others have different backgrounds and life and career experiences. Information flow is crucial to any organisation and the better the flow the more successful the company.

Diversity of people and experience is a given factor in the current competitive business environment.

The successful organisation is the one that communicates effectively across the diverse range of people both within and outside the organisation. Increasingly, organisations are interacting nationally and globally with other individuals, clients, suppliers and organisations. Effective business communication bridges the different perspectives of people with diverse life and career experiences by sharing meanings and building understanding.

Effective communicators are honest with themselves and behave ethically towards others. They have the ability to say what they want and need or feel, but not at the expense of others. They are not concerned about getting their own way and winning every time. Nor are they manipulating and managing other people in order to get their own way while pretending to consider and consult with others. Effective communicators avoid a series of quick-fix tricks or techniques. They use their interpersonal listening, speaking, questioning and feedback skills to interact with others courteously and in accordance with the accepted norms of business behaviour. Ineffective business communication dismisses the value of diversity and consequently increases misunderstandings and barriers between people and organisations.

Communication between colleagues

Effective communicators are able to use appropriate communication skills, such as listening, speaking, questioning and offering feedback, as they collect and organise information, give accurate, clear and comprehensive instructions and participate in teams. In business you will need to support other team members and contribute positively to the team dynamics. On occasions you will work cooperatively on a project with team members. On other occasions you will work autonomously towards shared goals and objectives. To complete these tasks successfully, you must also be able to participate in activities and interact in a supportive, efficient and effective way.

People who are able to communicate effectively in the business environment are generally happier in themselves and more effective in the way they handle difficult or tricky situations than poor communicators. They get the best from themselves and other people and are much more likely to achieve outcomes that are satisfying for everyone. They build relationships, are accountable for their actions and embrace new ideas. In today's rapidly changing environment you will be expected to show initiative and enterprise. The emerging challenges require change-management skills, good communication skills and the flexibility to adapt to new situations and technology.

> Colleagues share information and take part in organisational and environmental change.

Communication by leaders and managers

Leaders and managers with the capacity to communicate effectively are able to work directly with people. Consequently, there are fewer hidden agendas and issues are resolved at an early stage before they become long-term problems. Effective communication by leaders and managers leads to fewer direct controls and more understanding, commitment and motivation.

Effective leaders empower and trust others because they realise a high level of motivation builds a successful organisation. David Brown, Managing Director of Hewitt Associates, quoted in Biddle (2007, p. 23) says, 'It is imperative for an organisation to have great leadership, where management genuinely believes in the value of human capital. At least 50% of a CEO's time needs to be focused around people issues. Successful organisations spend a huge amount of time connecting with their people.' Communication from leaders and managers is the means to connect with people and to create understanding, commitment and motivation. Chapter 9 covers leadership.

> Effective communication by leaders and managers leads to fewer direct controls.

CONTROL

Communication can be used by an organisation's management as a means to control procedures and have employees conform to company objectives, directives or work procedures. People within organisations participate in employee assessment schemes, read manuals of procedure for different work tasks and set targets for company plans. People use their communication skills constantly.

Allan Leighton, Royal Mail Chairman, quoted in Wylie (2007, p. 1), suggests that communication is one of the key factors to success. In his view, 'Good leaders have, first of all, to be resilient. Second, they have to focus on the right thing—what's right in the mid term, however painful that is going to be in the short term. And third, good leaders must communicate the message as often as they can, and remember that leadership is not a popularity contest.'

People need to be kept in the communication loop. Anyone who delegates and get things done through other people must give them the information they need to perform their functions. Leaders and managers must be available to receive feedback and to make it very clear what people are doing and why they are doing it.

While people often say how important communication is, it is often ignored. Instead of planning the communication, people assume others will know what needs to be done. The difficulty for leaders and managers is to communicate in a way that achieves a balance between control, motivation and efficiency. Too much control may reduce initiative and actually lead to lower productivity, with less response to what the client wants and more emphasis on what the workers think the managers want. Too little control may cause uncertainty and insecurity.

> The communication loop contains all the messages sent and received.

MOTIVATION

Motivation is a process that directs individual action or behaviour towards a goal.

An organisation's management, including leaders of small teams, can use communication to motivate employees. **Motivation** is a process that directs individual action or behaviour towards a goal. A motivated person is willing to participate in activities. Organisational results are achieved successfully when people want to perform.

Motivation has more to do with effective communication and less to do with 'hype' and trying to inject enthusiasm. The business imperative to create meaning is clear. Leaders and managers must let people know what needs to happen, how it will happen and why. They also need to listen and understand what people within the organisation want, instead of exhorting people over and over again to achieve the business's goals.

Motivation comes from within the person.

A clear alignment between the motive, purpose or reason and the desired result enables people to get on with the necessary tasks to achieve the organisation's goals. By listening to what people want and communicating the desired organisational results, a leader or manager helps employees make the links between their own personal motives and the business goals and activities they undertake. The result is self-motivated employees. Self-motivation towards organisational goals occurs when:

- meaning is created for people
- they understand what needs to be done
- they can connect their activities to things that matter to them.

Employees have a need in varying degrees for achievement, power and a sense of belonging to the organisation.

When an organisation is willing to acknowledge and provide feedback on the achievements of individuals and groups, job satisfaction and performance are improved. Catherine Fox conducted an interview with Mikael Borglund and Denis Spencer, two of Australia's most experienced television executives. In that interview (2007, p. 15) Spencer said, 'I love people, so I think I am a people person. I pride myself [on that], and I like listening to them and getting their ideas and complimenting them for it. It goes a long way these days to compliment people because you get the best out of them.'

Acknowledgment can involve verbal praise or written letters or circulars, or 'thank you' on the organisation's intranet, or podcasts that keep people in the organisation feeling they are an important part of it and that what they are doing is appreciated.

BALANCING NEEDS AND GOALS

Communication is essential to balance the interests and expectations of the organisation with the goals and needs of the employees.

Communication within the organisation has another important role. The interests and expectations of the organisation and the goals and needs of employees need to be balanced. To understand and achieve this balance both employer and employee need to understand one another. Good communication is essential. When this understanding is achieved and the needs and goals of both are compatible, the behaviour required at work to achieve the organisation's goals is satisfying to employees. Possible differences between the needs of the organisation and the individual are highlighted in Table 1.2.

Table 1.2: Organisational and individual goals	
Organisation	**Individuals**
Profit	Good pay
Return on investment	Job security
Employee efficiency	Fringe benefits
Production of quality goods and services	Scope for initative and achievement
Competitiveness	Challenge
Low absenteeism and low turnover of employees	Satisfaction

The organisation needs to convey its viewpoint to employees, and employees must persuade management to appreciate their viewpoint. Slow, inefficient lines of communication may mean dissatisfied customers and demoralised workers. For all these reasons, business organisations need people who are effective communicators and who have effective channels of communication to move information through the organisation efficiently and effectively.

Communication with those outside the organisation

One of the biggest emerging challenges for local, national and global business is the need to balance the interests of large numbers of stakeholders. Businesses interact with a range of external stakeholders including financial, media, government and legislative bodies, citizen action groups, local, national and international clients and suppliers. Effective two-way communication:

- projects the organisation's image and builds positive relationships and goodwill
- is audience-centred and relates to the needs and interests of the organisation's stakeholders
- uses a variety of communication channels (face-to-face, written, technological) to inform stakeholders about the organisation's objectives, policies, standards, products and services
- gathers information to analyse future trends and advise on their likely impact
- avoids communication barriers such as conflict and misunderstanding
- builds local, national and international business relationships.

Effective two-way communication outside an organisation achieves mutual understanding by communicating accurately and in a way that enables the external stakeholder(s) to provide feedback about their needs and expectations. Feedback informs the organisation how well it is meeting these needs and what it needs to do to correct any shortfalls. The outcome is long-term relationships built on trust and goodwill.

Effective two-way communication between an organisation and its external stakeholders creates mutual understanding and acceptance.

REVIEW QUESTIONS

10 What makes a leader's or manager's communication effective?
11 What does effective two-way communication with those outside the organisation achieve?
12 Why do people need to be kept in the communication loop?

APPLY YOUR KNOWLEDGE

THE ROLE OF BUSINESS COMMUNICATION

1 This activity demonstrates the power of the nonverbal form of communication. Work in groups of at least 12 people.
  a The members of the group are to arrange themselves chronologically by age in a straight line, with the youngest at the front and the oldest at the back. The rule is that no one is to use verbal communication (spoken or written).
  b Debrief verbally to verify the group's success in applying nonverbal communication.
  c Discuss the types of nonverbal communication used in the activity.
2 Conduct a small group discussion.
  a Critically evaluate this statement:
    'Communication is to business what the trunk is to the tree.'
  b Present your point of view on the following statement:
    'Communication is a learned behaviour.'
  c Discuss the following statement and give examples of ways in which changes in interpersonal communication skills can impact on individual, team and organisational efficiency and effectiveness:
    'Improved communication skills improve business efficiency and effectiveness.'

3. Work in a small group.

   Differentiate between intrapersonal, interpersonal and mass communication. In your group, brainstorm examples of each type of communication.

4. Work individually.

   a. List the forms of communication you have used in the last week.

   b. What worked well as you used each form of communication?

   c. What problems or issues arose as you communicated? How did you (or can you) overcome these problems?

   d. Which form of communication are you most comfortable using? Why?

5. Work in small groups to prepare a verbal presentation titled 'The Role of Business Communication'.

   a. Plan your presentation by answering the following three questions.

      i. Why does effective communication by leaders and managers lead to fewer controls?

      ii. How can communication balance individual needs and organisational goals in the workplace?

      iii. 'Recognition and acknowledgment are powerful motivators.' How can managers acknowledge and reward employees who have performed well?

   b. Deliver your small group presentation to the larger group.

6. 'One of the most important skills that any person within an organisation needs is the ability to communicate. Without communication your other skills are less useful.'

   a. Explain the meaning of this quotation.

   b. Should an organisation train its staff in business communication skills. Explain your answer.

   c. Why should a business take an audience-centred approach to communication?

   d. Discuss how an organisation of your choice communicates with its stakeholders. Explain the characteristics that make its external communication effective.

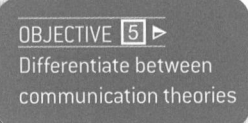

OBJECTIVE 5 ▶
Differentiate between communication theories

COMMUNICATION MODELS AND THEORIES

Communication is a dynamic, interactive process. As people respond, interpret and modify messages, they not only use their intellect to place meaning and structure on the variety of messages received but they also respond emotionally and use their perceptual skills in the interaction. They use their intellectual, emotional and psychomotor skills. Models and diagrammatic representations of how communication works illustrate different views of the process by which people transfer meaningful information. They cannot be regarded as a complete guide: they take the elements that are seen as most significant in the process and place them in an ordered pattern. Their purpose is to explain and classify essential features and regularities in the process.

A communication model is a simplified representation of the main elements in the communication process.

A transmission model of communication

Shannon and Weaver (1949) developed a mathematical communication model based on the work done by Shannon for the Bell Telephone Company. In their view, messages are transmitted from one person to another. Their model is identified as a *transmission model of communication*—communication is represented as a one-way flow. The Shannon and Weaver model has been adapted over the years to form the process models of communication, which show communication as a two-way process (Figure 1.1). In these models, people transmit, receive, interpret and respond to messages with feedback.

ELEMENTS IN PROCESS MODELS OF COMMUNICATION

The seven main elements of the communication process are sender, message, receiver, feedback, channel, context and noise.

Communication consists of several different elements in constant interaction with one another. There are seven main elements:

1. sender
2. message
3. receiver
4. feedback
5. channel
6. context or setting
7. noise or interference.

As communication occurs, sender and receiver interact by encoding/sending and decoding/ receiving messages. **Encoding** means putting the message into words or diagrams or nonverbal signals so that it can be transmitted. The receiver hears, reads or looks in order to **decode**, or interpret, the message.

Communication begins with the **sender**, the individual who reacts to situations from a unique vantage point, interpreting ideas and filtering experiences through their own perception (Figure 1.1). Unique to each individual, and integral to all the communication they engage in, is a background of accumulated attitudes, experiences, skills, cultural conditioning and individual differences that influence how those individuals communicate. If we can expand our view (our perception of events) by being aware of our background and its impact on our perception, then we can choose to send different messages. Consequently, we will be able to operate at a higher level of effectiveness by encoding an idea or feeling in words or signs that are appropriate to our needs and to the needs of the receiver.

The **message** is the idea or feeling transmitted from the sender to the receiver to achieve understanding. It makes a connection between the sender and the receiver and may be made up of signs, words or movement. The tone of voice, inflection, the rate of speech, facial expressions, touching and body movement may be misinterpreted by the receiver, or a poorly constructed message may lead to misunderstanding. The message the sender meant to send is not always the message received.

The receiver decodes or interprets the message to achieve understanding. In doing this the **receiver** also acts as an individual from a unique vantage point, interpreting the idea according to a particular personal perception of the message. This perception is also the result of the receiver's unique background of experiences, beliefs and concerns.

Since **perception** significantly influences communication it is useful to look closely at it. Each person selects, organises and interprets their sensory impressions of their environment. Selection is the art of attending to certain stimuli in the environment while ignoring others. Intense and repetitious stimuli are more noticeable than those that are unchanging or regular. In the perception process, people also organise the stimuli selected in order to create meaning, relationships and patterns. Once the information is organised it is interpreted by referring to past experience, making assumptions, and using expectations and knowledge to interpret the message. Robbins and colleagues (2006, p. 470)

Encoding is putting a message into words, pictures or actions so that it can be sent.

Decoding is interpreting a message to achieve understanding.

The **sender** transmits a message to the receiver.

Messages are ideas or feelings transmitted from the sender to the receiver to achieve understanding.

The message has verbal and nonverbal elements.

The **receiver** decodes or interprets the sender's message to achieve understanding.

Perception is the process by which people select, organise and interpret data in order to give meaning to a message.

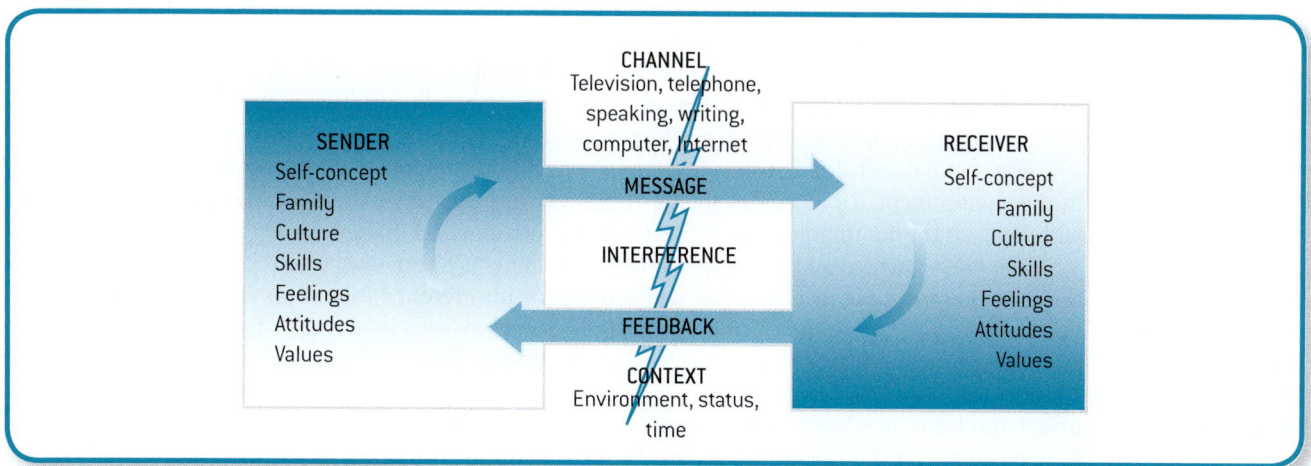

Figure 1.1: The communication process

state: 'A number of factors act to shape and sometimes distort perception. These factors can reside in the *perceiver*, in the object or *target* being perceived or in the context of the *situation* in which the perception occurs.'

Feedback is an essential part of successful interpersonal communication. It is the receiver's response to the sender's message, telling the sender how their message is being received and helping the receiver confirm whether their perception of the message is correct. It can be intentional or unintentional. Feedback:

Feedback is a response to a message, telling the sender how the message is being received.

- provides continuity in the communication
- indicates effective understanding or misunderstanding of the message
- stimulates further communication and discussion.

Leavitt and Mueller (1951) support the view that feedback increases the accuracy of the message in the communication process. Although feedback increases the amount of time needed to send the message, both sender and receiver need feedback. Senders check that the receiver's understanding of the message is correct by asking the receiver to rephrase what has been said and indicating their agreement or disagreement. Feedback is important to the sender because it lets them determine how the message is being received and helps the receiver to understand the message.

Feedback can help or hinder the message and the communication climate. In the workplace most people communicate face-to-face with their leaders, supervisors and colleagues so the ability to provide appropriate feedback can assist the development of effective working relationships.

The **channel** is the communication vehicle for the message.

A communication **channel** is the means or technique used to signal or convey a message; for example, a conversation, letter, telephone call, email, Web page or television program. Communication may pass along more than one channel. For example, an interaction in a meeting may include speaking and listening along a vocal channel, nonverbal gestures received through a visual channel and instructions via a written channel. Messages are sent through channels to communicate affection, control, relaxation, inclusion, escape, pleasure and a variety of other messages.

Messages within an organisation are sent and received through formal or informal communication channels. Four different lines or channels of formal communication are used inside an organisation. An appropriate channel suits the communication purpose, the needs of the sender, the message and the needs of the receiver. Horizontal or lateral channels operate between colleagues at the same level within the organisation's structure, while vertical channels move communication up and down between different levels in the organisation. Diagonal channels flow across the formal vertical channels; for example, a trainee in an organisation notices water flowing on to the stairs and reports this immediately to a senior manager. The water is a hazard that may cause people to slip and fall. Normally, the trainee would speak to their direct supervisor but an immediate report to a senior manager is more effective. These horizontal, vertical (upward and downward) and diagonal flows are discussed further in Chapter 8.

Context is the situation or setting within which communication takes place. It contains three dimensions: physical, social–psychological and temporal.

Context is the situation or setting within which communication takes place, or the circumstances that surround a particular piece of communication. Three dimensions interact in the context. The physical dimension pertains to material nature: the people, places or things in the environment.

The social dimension pertains to human society: companionship, relationships and interactions in the environment. Time factors such as the present, transitory or temporary nature of the context within which the communication occurs make up the temporal dimension.

Noise is an interruption to the message or communication flow that can lead to misunderstanding.

The message received is not necessarily the same as the message sent. Something other than the intended message is received because **noise** or interference interrupts the intended message. Send a message by electronic mail or SMS to a person who is afraid of technology and unable to access the computer screen, and communication barriers will appear through poor choice of channel. Speak face-to-face or write a business letter to this person and the message is easily understood and accepted. Noise or interference that interrupts the message or communication flow between sender and receiver can lead to misunderstanding, or to confused or ambiguous communication.

Communication barriers result in a misunderstanding or misinterpretation of the message. These barriers can be caused by the sender, the receiver, lack of feedback, a poor choice of channel, the wrong context or any other element in the communication model. Even when barriers appear, something is communicated, but the noise or interference distorts the intended message.

Some of the factors that cause communication barriers are:

- inappropriate choice of words
- unsuitable channel
- inappropriate message
- receiver inattention or distractions
- nonverbal communication that does not support the words
- different cultural background and language
- perceptual differences
- poor layout and presentation
- inadequate feedback and inappropriate timing
- deceptive tactics such as exaggerating benefits, downplaying risks or omitting relevant information
- lack of courtesy or knowledge of appropriate business etiquette by sender or receiver.

Recognising these and other causes of poor communication is an important step towards avoiding them. Consider the possibilities shown in Table 1.3.

Communication barriers distort or interrupt the message and its meaning.

Table 1.3: Communication barriers		
Cause of barrier	**Outcome**	**Strategies to avoid barrier**
Differences in perception	People often see and interpret the same event or action in a different way.	Listen carefully. Speak clearly and directly to the other person. Ask questions. Give feedback.
Differences in attitudes and values	People often make different interpretations.	Listen carefully. Speak clearly and directly to the other person. Ask questions. Give feedback.
Inconsistency between spoken and nonverbal communication	Poor communication and confusion because of the ambiguous message.	Match the verbal and nonverbal parts of the total message.
Differences in cultural conventions	Inaccurate or negative inferences about the message.	Develop personal interaction skills based on knowledge of differing questioning and nonverbal conventions between cultures.
Withholding information	Receivers operate with only part of the message, so mistakes are more likely to occur.	Plan and structure the message to include all necessary information.
Dismissing the concerns or point of view of others	The receiver may withdraw.	Listen carefully. Ask questions. Give feedback. Be aware of the other's point of view.

More recent theories

An analysis of different theories shows a long-term change of emphasis in communication theory since World War II, moving from a focus on those who initiate the communication to theories such as Berlo's, which focus on communication audiences.

A human dimension was added to the transmission model of communication in the 1950s and 1960s.

According to Mohan, McGregor and Strano (1992), Berlo's model, although still concerned with the transmission of the message, shows what is happening in human, as distinct from electronic, communication. The six ingredients listed by Berlo (1960) in his model of the communication process (see Figure 1.2) are:

1. the communication source
2. the encoder
3. the message
4. the channel
5. the decoder
6. the communication receiver.

The source, Berlo says, is a person or group of people with a purpose, a reason for engaging in communication. The purpose of the source has to be expressed in the form of a message, which Berlo sees as being translated into a code—a language—a systematic set of symbols structured to achieve meaning. The encoder is responsible for taking the ideas of the source and expressing the source's purpose in the form of a message.

The channel, or medium, carries the message which is then decoded, retranslated and put into a form that the receiver can use. In Berlo's model the channel is related to the five senses: sight, hearing, touch, smell and taste. DeVito (1978) comments that both the source and receiver are treated in essentially the same way, and to study either it is necessary to consider the communication skills of both source and receiver as well as their attitudes, knowledge and social system. Berlo suggests that words do not mean the same thing to all people.

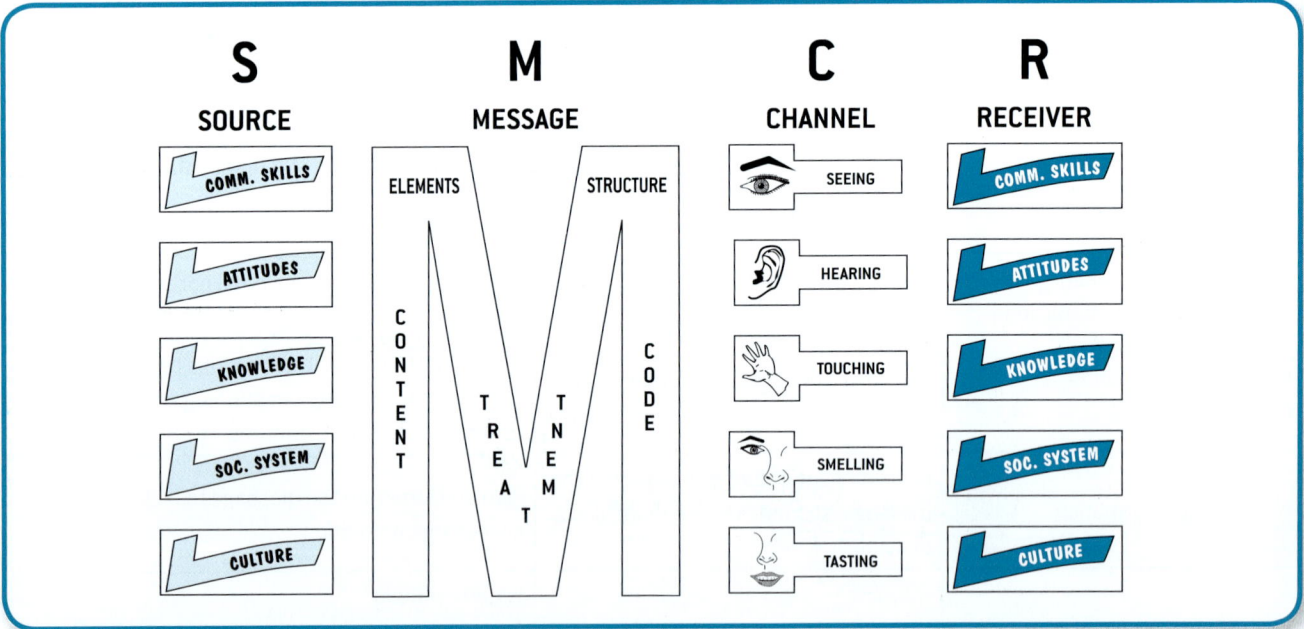

Figure 1.2: Berlo's model of the process of communication

Source: T. Mohan, H. McGregor & Z. Strano, *Logic Social Welfare*, Pearson Education, UK, 1992, p. 30. Reproduced with permission.

Mohan, McGregor and Strano (1992) comment that feedback, a vital element in communication, is not mentioned in Berlo's model, which only depicts a one-way flow.

Wilbur Schramm's two models of transmission theory, outlined in Mohan, McGregor and Strano (1992), reinforced the concept that each person in the communication process is both an encoder and a decoder, and added the concept of a return process—feedback—to determine how the message is being interpreted (see Figures 1.3 and 1.4).

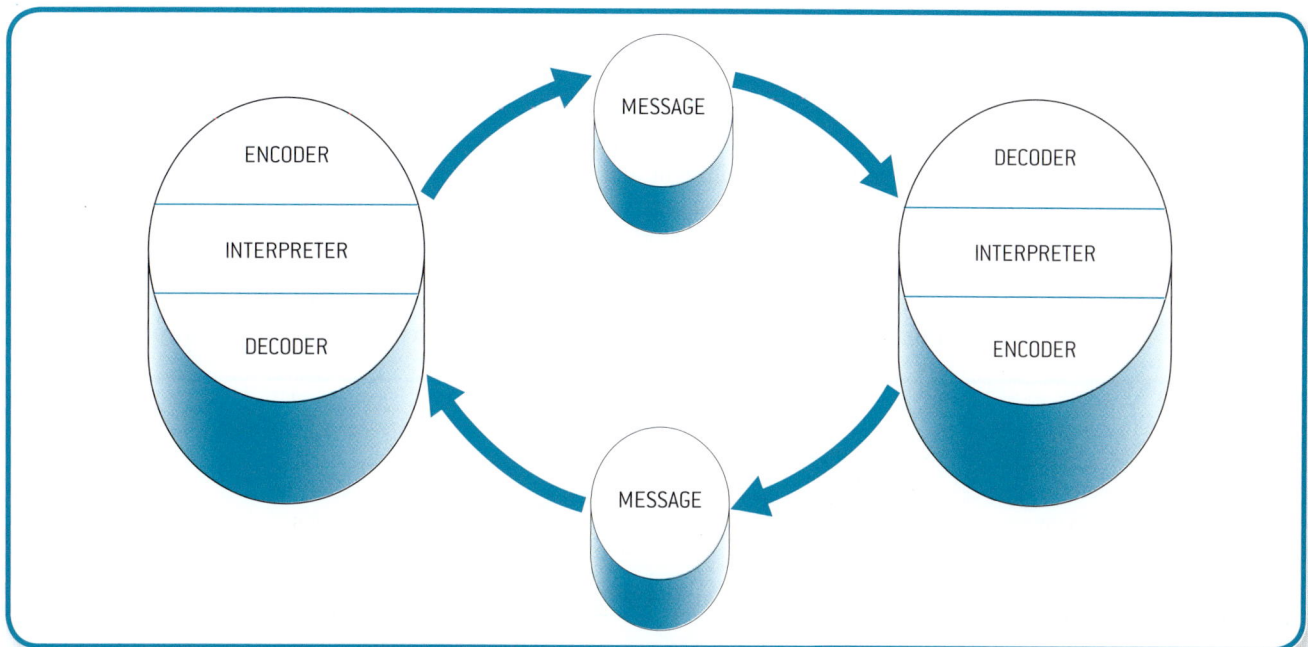

Figure 1.3: Schramm's circular model of communication

Source: T. Mohan, H. McGregor & Z. Strano, *Logic Social Welfare*, Pearson Education, UK, 1992, p. 37. Reproduced with permission.

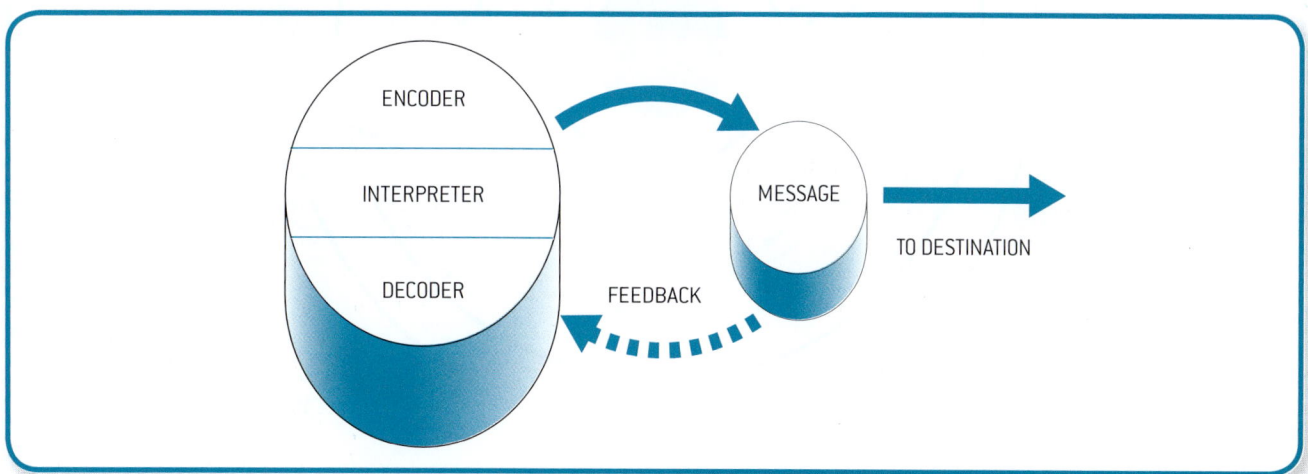

Figure 1.4: Schramm's model of personal feedback

Source: T. Mohan, H. McGregor & Z. Strano, *Logic Social Welfare*, Pearson Education, UK, 1992, p. 37. Reproduced with permission.

In 1970, Barnlund (DeVito 1978, p. 28) emphasised the transactional nature of communication. His process is based on six assumptions:

1. Communication is dynamic; that is, ongoing not static.
2. Communication is continuous.
3. Communication is circular.
4. Communication is unrepeatable.
5. Communication is irreversible: we cannot undo but we can later attempt to qualify or negate it.
6. Communication is complex.

McQuail (1984, p. 31) records that Barnlund says communication 'is not a reaction to something, nor an interaction with something, but a transaction in which man invents and attributes meanings to realise his purposes . . . meaning is something "invented", "assigned", "given" rather than something "received"', and the model he developed sought to incorporate this essential characteristic. Mohan, McGregor and Strano (1992) see the transactional model of communication as two parties responding to a phenomenon or to the environment and bringing to it their own 'receptors' or set of interpretations. The environment, they say, is a central point of reference (see Figure 1.5).

According to Windschuttle and Elliott (1999, p. 8), in the 1970s sociologists and social theorists argued that any communication theory had to include 'the social phenomena of language and culture'. Communication was a process in which a signal was 'encoded' by the sender with the meaning influenced by culture and, in turn, then 'decoded' by the receiver. The focus in this thesis had shifted from the sending

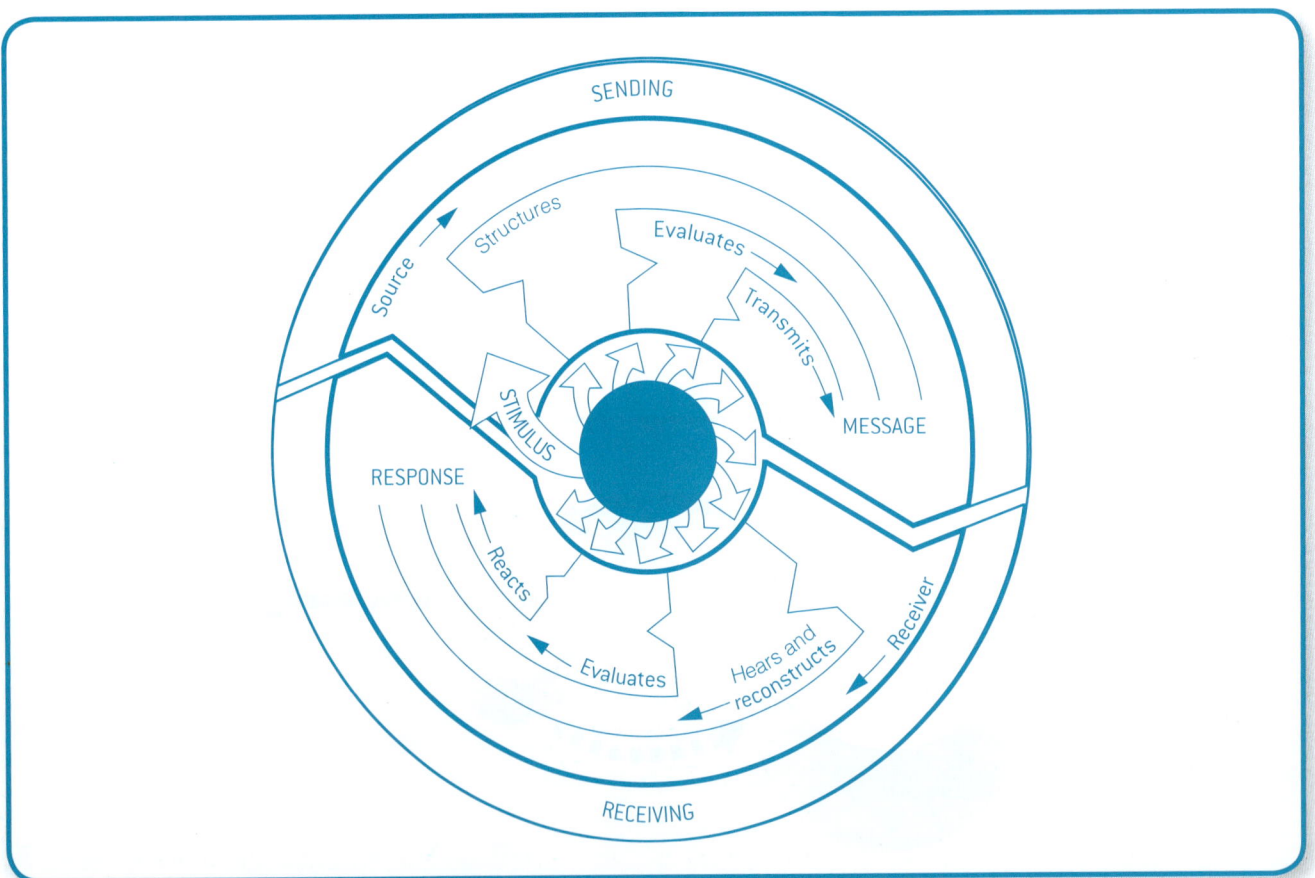

Figure 1.5: The transactional model of communication

Source: T. Mohan, H. McGregor & Z. Strano, *Logic Social Welfare*, Pearson Education, UK, 1992, p. 42. Reproduced with permission.

of the message to the message itself. The 1990s introduced the concept of audience-focused communications with communication theorists recognising that audiences react according to their own expectations and prejudices and never accept precisely what they are told.

West and Turner (2000, p. 5) comment that it is possible to study the communication process even though it is considered dynamic and unique. In 1967, Frank Dance (West & Turner 2000, p. 5) used a spiral, or helix, to depict the communication process (see Figure 1.6). Dance theorised that communication experiences are cumulative and influenced by the past. Present experiences, he argued, inevitably have an influence on a person's future and he emphasised a nonlinear view of the communication process.

Later, in 1996, C. Arthur VanLear (West & Turner 2000, p. 5) also argued that 'because the communication process is so dynamic, researchers and theorists can look for patterns over time'. VanLear said that 'if we recognise a pattern across a large number of cases, it permits us to "generalise" to other unobserved cases'.

An interesting model is presented by Kaye (1994). He used the Russian matouschka doll to demonstrate four interdependent aspects carried by each adult person (see Figure 1.7). The dolls represent the self, the interpersonal, the system and competence. The self is the intrapersonal communication. Kaye says that 'knowing and understanding oneself is a necessary step towards effective self-management'. The interpersonal doll represents the relationships and interactions between people. The third doll represents people-in-systems. Each person works within the systems in their organisation. Communication takes place within the group, team or organisation's culture. Effective communication works within the rules, norms and values. It also takes place within current practices and the formal and informal communication channels.

The fourth doll, communication competence, represents the linkages between our intrapersonal, interpersonal and people-in-systems behaviours. The communication competence reflects our ability to interact and influence others in a variety of contexts. The model allows each of us to disassemble our four dolls and analyse them individually to determine our communication competence in terms of particular strengths or weaknesses at the intrapersonal, interpersonal and people-in-systems level.

The communication process

Barnett Pearce and Vernon Cronen developed the Coordinated Management of Meaning (CMM) theory to understand what takes place during conversations (West & Turner 2000, p. 88). Cronen, Pearce and Linda Harris in 1982 summarised CMM as a theory that 'describes human actors as attempting to achieve coordination by managing the ways messages take on meaning' (West & Turner 2000,

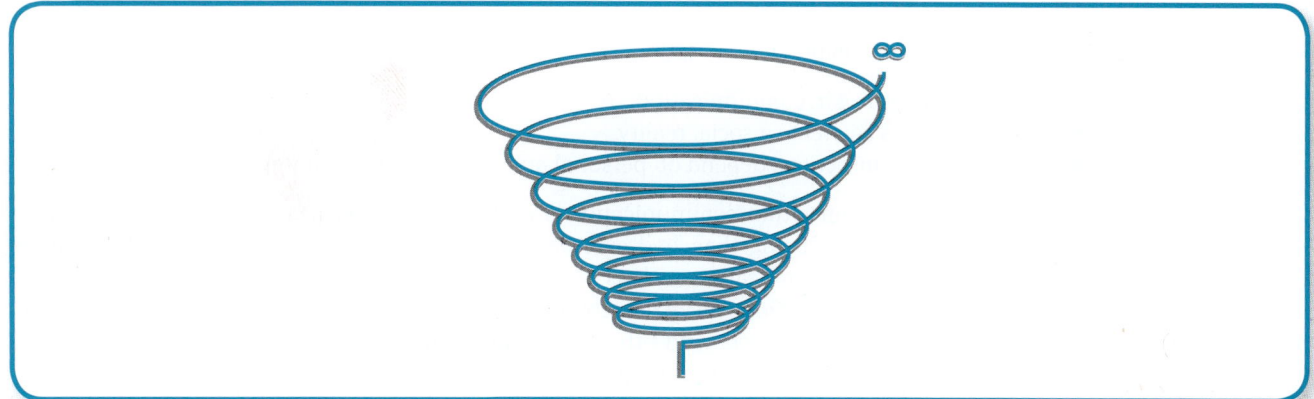

Figure 1.6: Communication as a helix

Source: Adapted from Frank Dance, 1967. Reproduced with permission of the McGraw-Hill Companies. From West, Pr. and Turner, L.H. *Introducing Communication Theory: Analysis and Application*, 2000, p.6, Mayfield Publishing Company, Mountain View, California.

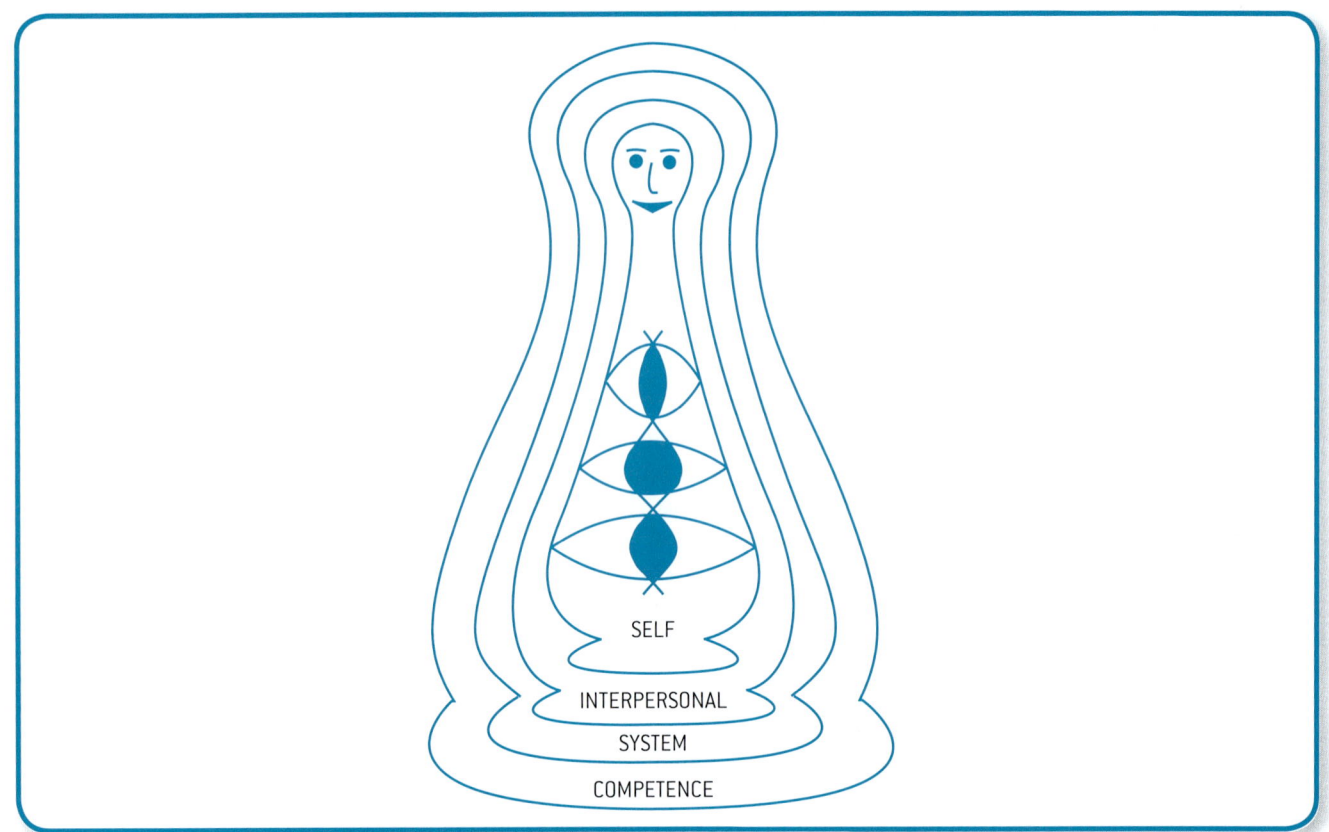

Figure 1.7: The adult communication management model

Source: M. Kaye, *Communication Management*, Prentice Hall, Sydney, 1994, p. 3. Reprinted with permission of Pearson Education Australia.

p. 88). West and Turner (p. 89) state that the theory 'focuses on the self and its relationship to others; it examines how an individual assigns meaning to a message'.

Gerry Philipsen in 1995, commenting on CMM, said: 'The theory is especially important because it focuses on the relationship between an individual and his or her society.' West and Turner (p. 89) believe that, along with the assumption that human beings are capable of creating and interpreting meanings, there are additional assumptions:

- Human beings live in communication.
- Human beings co-create a social reality.
- Information transactions depend on personal and interpersonal meaning.

In 1989 Pearce claimed that 'communication is, and always has been, far more central to whatever it means to be a human being than had ever been supposed' and, as such, he rejected the more traditional models of communication such as the linear model.

Gamble and Gamble (1996) believe that communication is essential in helping people to develop, control and sustain their contacts with others. The **communication process** is two-way and takes place in various situations for different reasons with the potential for many interpretations.

The **communication process** is a two-way exchange of information that encodes and decodes a message.

PERCEPTION

Interpretation of the same message may vary between people depending on their perceptions. This is because individual perception is influenced by experience, attitudes and beliefs, and a range of acquired skills or expectations (see Figure 1.8). For example, one person may perceive the colour blue as cool, peaceful and comforting, while another may perceive blue as old-fashioned and formal. Meaning is influenced by past experience. Even the context of the communication affects perception. Blue may be calming and relaxing one day, intimidating in its formality on another. The way a message is perceived by the sender may be quite different to the way the receiver perceives the message.

Perception is the process by which people select, organise and interpret data in order to give meaning to a message.

Awareness of the varying customs, rules and social behaviour in different cultures reduces the barriers caused by prejudice, stereotypes and discrimination. A group whose culture places rigid rules on who speaks first or last in conversations (with a belief that to look down when someone is talking to you is courteous) would give an impression of discourtesy in a Western country. This perception of discourtesy might lead to a person being excluded from the conversation without knowing why. An unintentional message is received.

Senders and receivers who understand their own cultural filter and accept the cultural filter of others are able to communicate more effectively. They understand that different cultural groups have different rules for the use of humour and irony, courtesies in speech, such as when to say 'please', 'thank you', 'excuse me', and deference to others. Their wider experience enables them to perceive the intended message.

DeVito (1989) identifies three dimensions in the context: physical, social–psychological and temporal. The physical environment contains the tangible or concrete items in the environment. The roles, norms and mores of the society make up the social–psychological dimension. The temporal dimension describes the time in history as well as the position of the communication in the sequence of events.

The same message can have a completely different meaning depending on the situation, since emotions and reactions to ideas and events vary in different situations. For example, the context of an international peace-keeping conference will have different physical, social–psychological and temporal dimensions from the context of a formal meeting in a company office. The communication process will use different language, relationships and authority to achieve the different communication purpose in each context.

Context plays an important part in how a message is encoded and decoded.

THE GAP BETWEEN INTENT AND EFFECT

Weiss (1997) identifies the gap between intent and effect. In this view, communication should not be taken for granted because the message sent is often quite different from the message received. Receivers place their own interpretation on the sender's message.

The message sent is often different from the message received.

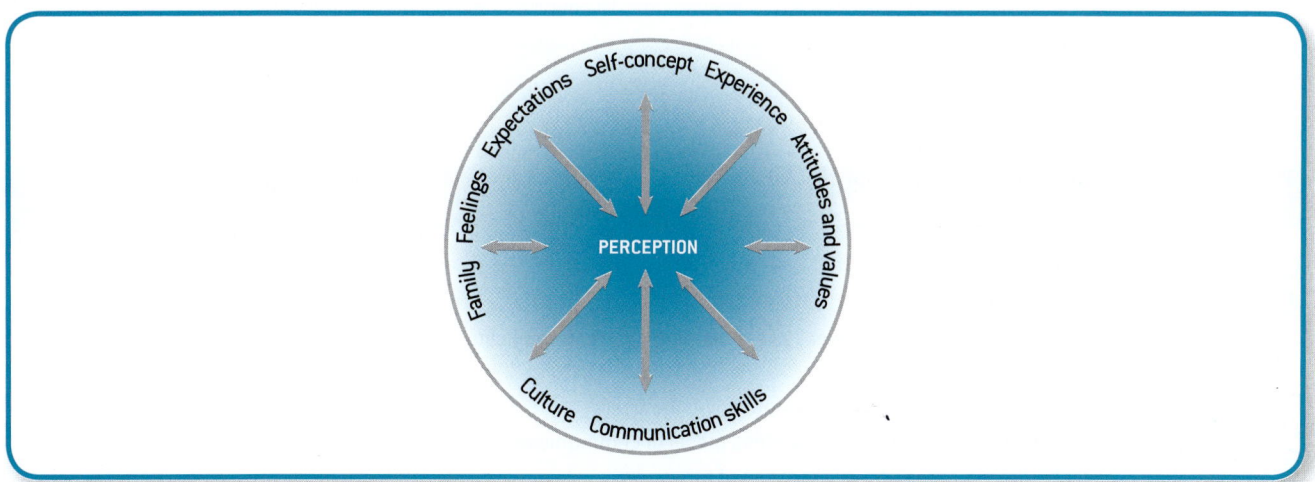

Figure 1.8: The individual

Barriers arise when the sender assumes that the receiver will automatically understand the message. It is impossible for one person in the communication process to control the process, because one person cannot be responsible for someone else's communication style or all the other factors that contribute to communication barriers. Remember to communicate as both the sender and receiver of a message. Cole (1997) states that we can learn more from listening than talking.

As well as considering how we speak as we send a message, and how we listen as we receive a message, we should also recognise the kinds of unspoken messages sent by our nonverbal communication.

EMPATHY

Empathy is the ability to understand and feel as the other person feels.

Good communicators are able to reduce the chance of communication barriers and the associated problems by communicating with **empathy**: a feeling and awareness of the other person and their point of view. A good communicator is able to recognise emotions in others and respond appropriately. Dilenschneider (1996) describes empathy as the foundation for the quality of a relationship. In a satisfying relationship both parties have empathy for the other person's point of view and are also willing to provide appropriate and sufficient feedback to achieve understanding.

REVIEW QUESTIONS

13 a   Define the terms 'sender' and 'receiver' of the message.

    b   Define the term 'message'.

    c   Define the term 'feedback'.

    d   Define the term 'perception'.

    e   Explain the three steps in the perception process.

14 a   'Communication begins with the sender.' What are the remaining six variables at work in the communication process?

    b   As a sender, how do you obtain feedback from your receiver?

    c   How can feedback affect motivation?

15 a   What are two factors that will influence your choice of channel?

    b   Define the term 'context' and give examples of ways in which the context can affect the message.

    c   Give five examples of possible 'noise' in the communication process.

    d   What is wrong with this statement? 'The sender of the message has full control over how it is received and understood.'

16   What is the main difference between the transmission models and the process models of communication?

17   What are the four interdependent aspects carried by each person in the adult communication management model?

18   Explain the term 'gap between intent and effect'. Discuss some of the factors that create the gap between intent and effect.

APPLY YOUR KNOWLEDGE

COMMUNICATION THEORIES

1   Work in pairs.

    a   Briefly discuss the Shannon and Weaver (1949) mathematical communication model.

    b   In your discussion:

       i   identify how the model has been adapted over the years

       ii   explain each of the elements in a process model of communication

       iii   describe the strengths and weaknesses of the model.

② This activity demonstrates the importance of each element in the communication process.

    a   Work in groups of two. Stand back-to-back and conduct a conversation for two minutes. When the two minutes is up, discuss how easy or difficult it was to speak in this way.

    b   Comment on the way nonverbal communication can help two people to talk with and understand one another.

    c   Suggest how knowledge of communication models and theories enables individuals to interact more effectively in their work.

    d   Make a joint verbal presentation of your findings to the large group.

③ Work in small groups.

    a   Discuss Berlo's model of the process of communication, Schramm's circular model of communication and Barnlund's transactional model. In your discussion identify the focus of each theory and the assumptions underpinning each one.

    b   What conclusions could a manager draw from the theories about communication in business?

    c   Report your findings to the large group.

④ 'What people see and feel is a result of the interaction between the situation and their own attitudes, thoughts and ideas.'
In groups of three, discuss this statement. Prepare an outline for a five-minute verbal presentation that identifies four reasons for different perceptions, and explains why two people may perceive the same situation differently.

⑤ Work in small groups.
Use Dance's (1967) model of the communication process as a spiral or helix of cumulative experiences to explain how a person's past experiences can influence their future.

⑥ Work individually to reflect on your understanding of communication theories and principles.

    a   Rate your underpinning knowledge of communication by ticking 'Yes' or 'No' in the checklist below.

    b   In column four of the checklist show how you are able to do each of the activities you ticked as 'Yes' or explain how you will develop the capacity to do those you have ticked as 'No'.

SELF-EVALUATE YOUR SKILL

RATE YOUR UNDERPINNING KNOWLEDGE OF COMMUNICATION

I am able to:	Yes	No	Show how
Use a simplified representation to explain the communication process			
Explain the human dimension added to the transmission model of communication by Berlo (1960)			
Apply Barnlund's (1970) six assumptions to identify the transactional nature of communication			
Analyse the shift by theorists in the 1990s to the concept of audience-focused communication			
Identify Kaye's (1994) four interdependent aspects of communication competence			
Make allowances for the different meanings people assign to messages			
Give and receive appropriate feedback when there is a difference between the intent and effect of a message			

ETHICAL BEHAVIOUR IN BUSINESS

OBJECTIVE 6▶
Outline the accepted principles of business ethics

Fletcher and Brown (2008, p. 203) present a working definition of **ethics** as 'culturally based assumptions as to what is right or wrong'. Guffey (2003, p. 25) comments that one of the most remarkable changes in the world of work involves ethics in the workplace. At one time 'business ethics' was regarded as a joke, but this is no longer the case. Weaver, Trevino and Cochran (1999), in a study of *Fortune* 1000 companies, found that 98% of those surveyed addressed ethical and conduct issues in policy manuals, codes of ethics or some other formal document. Similarly, today in Australia most businesses and government agencies have codes of conduct, values statements and ethics statements that set out the values, principles and standards of behaviour expected from all levels of staff.

Ethics refers to the principles of right and wrong that guide decision making when faced with conflicting responsibilities.

Ethical business communication is legal, socially responsible and in accordance with community standards. For example, privacy and the avoidance of intrusion into personal affairs is an accepted principle in society. There is an expectation that any personal information collected about any individual by a business must be accurate and remain confidential. Privacy laws exist to protect personal information. The laws state that businesses must provide a statement of privacy policy and ask for consent before collecting sensitive data. It is unethical for any business to disclose personal information to third parties.

A code of ethics is a formal statement of an organisation's values and ethical rules.

Many organisations communicate the ethical rules they expect employees to follow in a **code of ethics**. A code of ethics typically provides guidance on:

- what is expected of individual behaviour; for example, punctuality, occupational health and safey (OHS) compliance and dress standards
- how to avoid unlawful or improper behaviour that will harm the organisation; for example, maintain confidentiality of records, avoid misuse of company finances or property, and avoid conflicts of interest
- how to treat customers; for example, provide accurate, factual information, maintain confidentiality, and treat them with respect and courtesy.

An Australian survey of 1200 people by the Institute of Chartered Accountants in Australia (ICAA) found that communication skills and business ethics are valued far more in business leaders than either technical competency or information technology knowledge. An analysis of the survey results showed that the seven most highly valued attributes in New South Wales were:

1. ethical and moral fairness (38.6%)
2. good communication skills (21.8%)
3. innovative and strategic thinking (15.2%)
4. consciousness of providing good service to customers (10.5%)
5. being good at working in a team (9.2%)
6. having a good understanding of computers and the Internet (2.5%)
7. being good at the technical side of the job (2.2%).

Ethical constraints

Ethical constraints affect the way business is conducted. Lehman and Dufrene (2002, p. 18) say that ethics 'refers to the principles of right and wrong that guide you in making decisions that consider the impact of your actions on others as well as yourself'. They also believe that identifying ethical issues in workplace situations can be difficult. Guffey (2003, p. 27) lists five common ethical traps for people trying to achieve correct decisions:

1. *The false necessity trap.* People act from the belief that they are doing what they have to do—that they have no other choice.
2. *The doctrine-of-relative-filth trap.* Unethical actions sometimes look harmless when compared with the actions of others: for example, fudging expenses compared with an overseas junket.

③ *The rationalisation trap.* People try to justify their actions with excuses: for example, 'It's all right for me to arrive late for work or take an extended lunch hour because I don't get paid enough.'

④ *The self-deception trap.* This can happen with job applicants who exaggerate their past work successes or university grades.

⑤ *The ends-justify-the means trap.* Taking unethical actions to accomplish a desirable goal: for example, an insurance company asking staff to work overtime without pay to overcome a backlog of unpaid claims.

Lehman and Dufrene (2002, p. 19) list the main causes of illegal and unethical behaviour in the workplace:

- excessive emphasis on profits
- misplaced corporate loyalty
- obsession with personal advancement
- expectation of not getting caught
- unethical tone set by top management
- uncertainty about whether an action is wrong
- unwillingness to take a stand about what is right.

Figure 1.9 is Lehman and Dufrene's framework for analysing ethical issues. It highlights three decision points based on the illegality of the action, inconsistency with the company's or industry's code of practice, or validation of your personal code of ethics. They also propose a four-step framework for analysing ethical dilemmas after you have identified a possible course of action:

① Identify the legal implications of the alternative and determine whether the alternative adheres to contractual agreements and company policy.

② Determine whether the alternative violates any company or professional code of ethics.

③ Use ethical principles and theories to assess whether the alternative judged to be legal (Step 1) and in compliance with the code of ethics (Step 2) is ethical.

④ Implement the alternative and communicate the decision to the appropriate individuals inside or outside the organisation.

The International Association of Business Communicators (IABC) has developed a Code of Ethics for Professional Communicators 'because hundreds of thousands of business communicators worldwide engage in activities that affect the lives of millions of people, and because this power carries with it significant social responsibilities . . .'. The Code of Ethics for Professional Communicators can be found on the IABC web page at <www.iabc.com/about/code.htm>. It is based on three different but interrelated principles of professional communication that apply throughout the world:

① The professional communication is legal.

② The professional communication is ethical.

③ The professional communication is in good taste.

IABC members are expected to abide by these principles by engaging in communication that is not only legal but also ethical and sensitive to cultural values and beliefs. They must also engage in truthful, accurate and fair communication that facilitates respect and mutual understanding, and adhere to the articles of the IABC Code.

REVIEW QUESTIONS

19 *a* What does a code of ethics typically provide guidance on?

   b Give examples of the type of documents businesses use to address ethics and conduct issues.

20 Define the term 'ethical business communication'.

   Give examples of unethical business communication.

21 Outline strategies you could use to avoid the five common ethical traps identified by Guffey (2003).

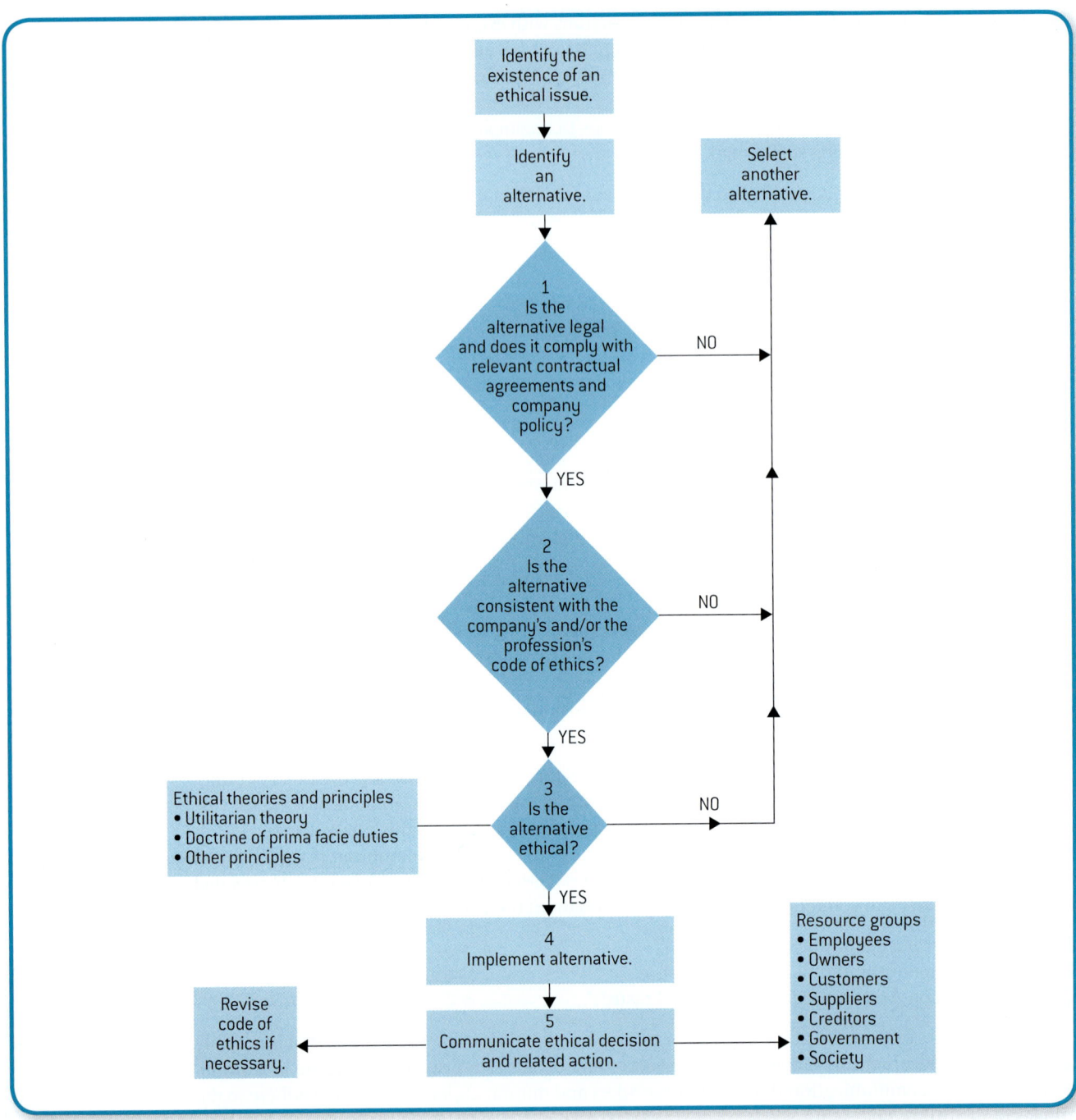

Figure 1.9: Framework for analysing ethical issues

Source: C.M. Lehman & D. Dufrene, *Business Communication Handbook*, 13th edn, p.21, South-Western, Ohio, 2002. Reprinted with permission of South-Western, a division of Thomson Learning: www.thomsonrights.com. Fax 800 730-2215.

APPLY YOUR KNOWLEDGE

ETHICAL COMMUNICATION

 Work individually.

    a   Business decisions involve questions of ethics, of right and wrong. How can Lehman and Dufrene's four-step framework for analysing ethical dilemmas help you present a case against a business decision you believe violates your personal code of ethics?

    b   Briefly describe factors that can make dealing with ethical issues at work a difficult matter.

 Work in groups of three or four.

Businesses are increasingly using the Internet to sell to customers. These business transactions require customers to provide personal information. In the box below, column 1 identifies four ethical constraints in this type of transaction. Column 2 asks four related questions.

    a   In your small group assume you are the manager of a travel agency supplying airline tickets to customers online. As the manager you must answer the question about each of the four ethical constraints. Work together to answer the questions.

    b   Combine with three or four other small groups and present your answers.

    c   What similarities (if any) did you find in the answers from each group?

Constraint	Question
Privacy	What information will the agency need to hold about the client?
Accuracy	How can the agency ensure the information is correct?
Property	Who owns the information? Can it be transferred, and how?
Accessibility	Who is allowed to access this information about the client and under what conditions?

SUMMARY OF LEARNING OBJECTIVES

1 ▸ EXPLAIN HOW EFFECTIVE COMMUNICATION BUILDS SUCCESS IN TODAY'S BUSINESS ENVIRONMENT

Undergraduates studying across a range of occupations cannot complete their degrees without studying business communication. The importance of business communication skills as a requirement of business today is a demonstrated fact. As well as having to adapt to different, more complex situations, business organisations are demanding increasingly specialised professional skill sets, including communication.

Successful organisations need people who can organise ideas and information into knowledge, express and present ideas accurately and persua-sively, listen to others and take actions based on their understanding. Effective communicators interact with a diversity of people from different backgrounds, experiences and cultures, professionally and ethically. Many experienced professionals are now returning to university to improve their professional skills and opportunities for career advancement.

2 ▸ IDENTIFY THE DIFFERENT FORMS AND TYPES OF COMMUNICATION

Successful communication transmits ideas, values and attitudes to others through three different forms of communication: verbal, nonverbal and graphic. Meaning is given to the message as the receiver perceives it—that is, selects, organises and interprets the communication.

The four types of communication are intrapersonal, interpersonal, public and mass communication. People communicate a message using a variety of techniques such as voice, text, action and graphic representation. Many types of technology are now readily available. Communication takes place in a context. It is influenced by past experiences, and current transactions will influence future communication.

3 ▷ DISCUSS THE IMPACT OF TECHNOLOGY ON BUSINESS COMMUNICATION

In the 21st century organisations must make decisions quickly because of the pace and global nature of modern business. Once a decision is made, it may have to be sent anywhere in the world quickly. To be a competitive force in today's economic climate, businesses now use numerous forms of information technology to store, send, receive and present information. Recent advances in voice technologies, telecommunication services, instant messaging, wireless networking, short messaging services and social network services have improved knowledge transfer and the speed of communication.

4 ▷ OUTLINE THE ROLE OF COMMUNICATION IN THE WORKPLACE

Communication is one of the most important skills in the workplace. Effective communication connects two or more people and leads to understanding. It enables individuals to be more effective at work and in their relationships with others. Effective communication also enables leaders and managers to control work procedures, motivate others, and balance the needs and goals of individuals and the organisation. Successful people and successful organisations are often those that communicate effectively. They are able to let other people understand what they are doing and what they require. In their interactions with others, successful communicators effectively use their interpersonal skills while listening, speaking, questioning and asserting themselves, and in their verbal and nonverbal communication.

5 ▷ DIFFERENTIATE BETWEEN COMMUNICATION THEORIES

Communication theories provide an overview of the elements and processes involved in communication. There has been a change of emphasis in the theories from the transmission models in the 1940s to the psychology models in the 1950s and 1960s, to cultural encoding and decoding in the 1970s, to the audience-focused models in the 1990s. Communication theories describe the constant interaction of several elements of communication. The elements most frequently mentioned are the sender, message, receiver, feedback, channel, context, and noise or interference. The process models of communication show the dynamic and interactive nature of communication.

Barriers can interrupt the flow of communication and lead to confusion and misunderstandings. Barriers are caused by the sender, the receiver, a lack of feedback, a poor choice of channel, the wrong context and other factors that interfere with the message.

6 ▷ OUTLINE THE ACCEPTED PRINCIPLES OF BUSINESS ETHICS

Ethics are the principles of right and wrong that provide guidance in choosing between conflicting responsibilities. Ethical business behaviour requires honesty and integrity. Actions taken must be legal, meet any contractual requirements, and be consistent with the company's or industry's code of conduct. Information and disclosure about products and services must be open and truthful. Confidentiality and sensitivity to cultural values and beliefs are essential components of ethical behaviour.

KEY TERMS

channel	14	context	14
code of ethics	24	decoding	13
communication	4	empathy	22
communication barriers	15	encoding	13
communication process	20	ethics	24

feedback	14		
graphic communication	5		
interpersonal communication	5		

ACTIVITIES AND QUESTIONS

1   As the Compliance Coordinator in a large stockbroking firm you are concerned that the latest Australian Securities and Investments Commission (ASIC) standards are understood by managers and staff.

a   Define the purpose of your message clearly.

b   Nominate three communication channels you will use to ensure the message is communicated effectively.

c   Indicate the factors relating to the receiver, channel, message and context that you will take into account in preparing this communication.

d   How you will obtain feedback about the impact of your communication?

2   Each person is to think of someone who is good in their relationships with others at work and then discuss the following:

a   How do these people interact with other people?

b   What are the skills they use?

3   Think of a situation when you tried to communicate with another person, or when someone tried to communicate with you, and it failed. Think about the barriers that interfered with the communication.

a   Outline the situation to the group and tell them why you think it failed.

b   List the reasons for failure identified by your group.

c   Come together as a large group to share the barriers identified by each group.

4   a   Discuss at least three ethical constraints or 'traps' that may affect the way communication in business is conducted.

b   In your view, why would a professional association such as the International Association of Business Communicators (IABC) develop a 'Code of Ethics for Professional Communicators'?

c   What advantages does a code of ethics provide for professional communicators?

d   Outline the main causes of illegal and unethical behaviour in the workplace.

5   In an article in the *Harvard Business Review*, 'Barriers and Gateways to Communication', Rogers and Roethlisberger (1952, p. 47) suggested: 'The major barrier to mutual interpersonal communication is our very natural tendency to judge, to evaluate and to approve (or disapprove) the statements of the other person or the other group.'

a   In small groups discuss this idea using your own experiences to explore its validity.

b   Report your findings back to the large group.

6   Compare and contrast Dance's (1957) depiction of the communication process as a helix with Kaye's (1994) adult communication management model.

EXPLORING THE WEB

1   Check out the resources at *The Times 100 Business Studies Resource Centre* <www.thetimes100.co.uk/index.php>. Log on and choose a case study about communication in business. Read the case study and answer the quiz to improve your business communication knowledge.

2   Visit the St James Ethics Centre site <www.ethics.org.au/about-ethics/ethics-centre-articles/> and find articles on business ethics and codes of ethics and conduct.

a   Explain why companies have a code of ethics.

b   Discuss strategies that enable an organisation to implement a code of ethics effectively.

3   Check out the resources at Business Ethics <www.web-miner.com/busethics.htm> to learn more about ethics in business. Categories of resources include articles and publications, case studies, corporate codes of ethics, professional organisations and associations, and resource centres.

PROJECT WORK

1   Analyse the elements identified in the process models of communication and give practical examples of how each element works. Use the matrix below to identify in column 1 each of the elements. In column 2 give examples of each element. In column 3 describe the interaction of the elements in a real situation you have observed in the past week.

2   Give three examples of barriers to communication in a business or organisational setting. Prepare a one-page description of the situations, the barriers and how these barriers were (or could be) overcome.

3   Identify an example of effective business communication you have observed. Prepare a brief description of the characteristics of the effective communication and its impact on the business or organisation.

Analysis of the communication process		
Element	Examples	Describe the interaction of these elements in a transaction you have observed in the past week

BIBLIOGRAPHY

Adler, R.B. & Rodman, G. 2003. *Understanding Human Communication*, 8th edn, Oxford University Press, New York/Oxford.

Berlo, D.K. 1960. *The Process of Communication*, Holt, Rinehart & Winston, New York.

Biddle, J. 2007. 'Engagement principles', *Management Today*, Australian Institute of Management, September, p. 23.

Chiames, C. 2007. 'Effective employee communication', *Workforce Management*, Vol. 86, Issue 8, April, p. 6.

Cole, J. 1997. 'Last word: spotting communication problems', *Getting Results ... For the Hands-On Manager*, Vol. 42, Issue 5, May, p. 8.

Dawson, R. 'Future Exploration Blog', *Future Exploration Network*, www.futureexploration.net, viewed 19 October 2007.

DeTienne, K.B. 2002. *Guide to Electronic Communication: Using Technology for Effective Business Writing and Speaking*, Pearson Education, New Jersey.

DeVito, J.A. 1978. *Communicology: An Introduction to the Study of Communication*, Harper & Row, New York.

DeVito, J.A. 1989. *The Interpersonal Communication Book*, Harper & Row, New York.

DeVito, J.A. 2001. *The Interpersonal Communication Book*, 9th edn, Allyn & Bacon, Boston.

Dilenschneider, R.L. 1996. 'Social IQ and MBAs: recognizing the importance of communication', *Vital Speeches of the Day*, Vol. 62, Issue 13, April, pp. 404–8.

Fletcher, R. & Brown, L. 2008. *International Marketing: An Asia-Pacific Perspective*, 4th edn, Pearson Education Australia, Sydney.

Fox, C. 2007. 'Beyond the box', *Financial Review—Boss*, October.

Gamble, T. & Gamble, M. 1996. *Communication Works*, 5th edn, McGraw-Hill, New York.

Guffey, M.E. 2003. *Business Communication: Process and Product*, 4th edn, South-Western, Ohio.

Hart, C., 2007. Cited in article from 'MYWORKSPACE', *Financial Review—Boss*, October.

Institute of Chartered Accountants in Australia. 2001. *Brush Up on Your Ethics*.

International Association of Business Communicators, *IABC Code of Ethics*, www.iabc.com/about/code.htm, viewed 19 October 2007.

Kaye, M. 1994. *Communication Management*, Prentice Hall, Sydney.

Leavitt, H. & Mueller, R. 1951. 'Some effects of feedback on communication', *Human Relations*, Vol. 4, pp. 401–10.

Lehman, C. & Dufrene, D. 2002. *Business Communication*, 13th edn, South-Western, Ohio.

McQuail, D. 1984. *Communication*, 2nd edn, Longman, Essex, England.

Maes, J.D., Weldy, T.G. & Icenogle, M.L. 1997. 'A managerial perspective: oral communication competency is most important for business students in the workplace', *Journal of Business Communication*, Vol. 34, Issue 1, January, pp. 67–80.

MindTools.com. 'Communication Skills', *MindTools Essential Skills for a Successful Career*, www.mindtools.com/, viewed 16 February 2008.

Mohan, T., McGregor, H. & Strano, Z. 1992. *Logic Social Welfare*, Pearson Education, UK.

Mohan, T., McGregor, H. & Strano, Z. 2004. *Communicating as Professionals*, Thomson, Melbourne.

Ober, S. 2006. *Contemporary Business Communication*, 6th edn, Houghton Mifflin, Boston.

Pearce, W.B. cited in West & Turner 2000, op. cit.

Philipsen, G. cited in West & Turner 2000, op. cit.

Rapoport, A. 1950. *Science and Gods of Man: A Study in Semantic Orientation*, Harper & Row, New York.

Robbins, S., Bergman, R., Stagg, I. & Coulter, M. 2006. *Management*, 4th edn, Pearson Education Australia, Sydney.

Rogers, C. 1961. *On Becoming a Person: A Therapist's View of Psychotherapy*, Houghton Mifflin, Boston.

Rogers, C.R. & Roethlisberger, F.J. 1952. 'Barriers and gateways to communication', *Harvard Business Review*, Vol. 30, pp. 46–52.

Saia, R. 1997. 'Can we talk here?', *Computerworld*, Vol. 31, Issue 12, 24 March, p. 86.

Schramm, W. 1981. 'How communication works', in J.A. DeVito, *Communication, Concepts and Processes*, 3rd edn, Prentice Hall, Englewood Cliffs, New Jersey.

Shannon, C.E. & Weaver, W. 1949. *The Mathematical Theory of Communication*, University of Illinois Press, Urbana, Illinois.

St James Ethics Centre, www.ethics.org.au/, viewed 20 October 2007.

Stoeger, S. *Business Ethics*, www.web-miner.com/busethics.htm, viewed 20 October 2007.

Taylor, A., Rosegrant, T. & Meyer. A. 1986. *Communicating*, 4th edn, Prentice Hall, Englewood Cliffs, New Jersey.

The Times 100 Business Studies Resource Centre, www.thetimes100.co.uk/, viewed 20 October 2007.

Villiers, A. 2000, 'dear myth', *Management Today*, Australian Institute of Management, November/December, pp. 6–7.

Watzlawick, P., Beavin, J.H. & Jackson, D.D. 1967. *Pragmatics of Human Communication*, Norton, New York.

Weaver, G.R., Trevino, L.K. & Cochran, P.L. 1999. 'Corporate ethics practices in the mid-1990s: an empirical study of the Fortune 1000', *Journal of Business Ethics*, Vol. 18, Issue 3, February, pp. 283–94.

Weiss, D.H. 1997. 'Intent versus effect', *Getting Results ... For the Hands-On Manager*, Vol. 42, Issue 4, April, p. 4.

West, R. & Turner, L.H. 2000. *Introducing Communication Theory: Analysis and Application*, Mayfield Publishing Company, Mountain View, California.

Williams, J. 1996. 'Top business schools see value of communication skills', *Communication World*, October–November, pp. 36–38.

Windschuttle, K. & Elliott, E. 1999. *Writing, Researching, Communicating: Communication Skills for the Information Age*, McGraw-Hill, Sydney.

Wylie, I. 2007. 'A simple plan', *HR Focus*, *The Guardian*, 19 September, p. 1.

2 Intercultural communication

After studying this chapter you should be able to:

1 ▷ explain the concept of culture and differentiate enculturation, acculturation, ethnocentrism and cultural relativism

2 ▷ describe high-context and low-context cultural styles and discuss components of culture relevant to intercultural communication

3 ▷ explain the causes of communication barriers in intercultural communication

4 ▷ discuss the implications of comparative value dimensions for intercultural communication

5 ▷ describe the characteristics of intercultural communication competence and evaluate strategies for developing intercultural competence.

OUTLINE

Definitions of culture

The process of intercultural communication

The relevance of cultural components to intercultural communication

Barriers to intercultural communication

Comparative value dimensions

Intercultrual communication competence

VIEWPOINT: TYRANNY OF DISTANCE STILL RULES

Katrina Nicholas summarises the secrets of success for organisations that manage across different cultures and time zones.

- Understand cultural differences: engaging and motivating employees in Latin America is different to Scandinavia.
- Be open to new ways of thinking. A pre-globalisation mindset inhibits the generation of fresh ideas.
- Strike the right mix between local talent and expatriates to manage and drive offshore operations.
- Use technology to cope with time-zone differences; many chief executives feel like their second home is a Boeing 747.
- Ensure reporting structures are robust so that head office has accurate and up-to-date performance information.
- Communication is key when working across continents and time zones. Sometimes there is no substitute for face-to-face meetings, which cement relationships.

Notable successes in managing across cultures include Rio Tinto, BHP Billiton, Leighton Holdings, Macquarie Group, Resmed, Westfield, Crown, Cochlear and Sonic HealthCare.

Adapted from K. Nicholas, 'Tyranny of distance still rules', *Australian Financial Review*, 7 February 2008, pp. S20–21.

With the increasingly global nature of business and growing diversity within countries, companies need to know how best to interact across national boundaries, manage the diversity of their staff and communicate with a variety of customers from different backgrounds. An understanding of theories of intercultural communication and a willingness and ability to apply them in business enable organisations and people to transcend cultural differences. The statement below highlights the role of mutual understanding and respect in the avoidance of intercultural confusion and tension.

> One has to recognise that, whatever the future may hold, countries and people differ . . . in their approach to life and their ways of living and thinking. In order to understand them, we have to understand their way of life and approach. If we wish to convince them, we have to use their language as far as we can, not language in the narrow sense of the word, but the language of the mind. This is a necessity. Something that goes even further than that is not the appeal to logic and reason, but some kind of emotional awareness of other people. (Jawaharlal Nehru, in Adler, 2002, p. 73)

DEFINITIONS OF CULTURE

OBJECTIVE **1** ▶

Explain the concept of culture and differentiate enculturation, acculturation, ethnocentrism and cultural relativism

Culture is learned social behaviours that develop over time.

Discussions surrounding culture centre on its dynamic and constantly changing nature over time. **Culture** surrounds everything we do and is so pervasive that we are rarely aware of its effects on our lives. Culture is the shared view of the people belonging to that culture. Culture creates patterns of behaviour, patterns of recognition of what is going on and dictates rules about how to behave. Culture is learned behaviour that influences our attitudes and responses to other cultures.

While there are common threads and ideas in discussions about culture, there is no single definition that suits everyone's view of culture. Prem Ramburuth (in Dwyer 2005, pp. 32–33) presents five definitions of culture:

1. Hofstede (2001, p. 4) describes culture as '*the collective programming of the mind which distinguishes the members of one human group from another*'.
2. Hoebel and Frost (1976, p. 6) define culture as an '*integrated system of learned behaviour patterns which are characteristic of the members of a society and which are not the result of biological inheritance*'.
3. Ferraro (2002, p. 19) offers a definition of culture as '*everything that people have, think, and do as members of their society*'.
   The reasoning in these first three definitions is that culture is transmitted and maintained solely through learning, enculturation and group interaction. The notion of 'having' relates to our material possessions; 'thinking' relates to our common values, attitudes and beliefs; 'doing' relates to our commonly accepted behaviours; and the reference to 'society' emphasises our interdependence and the group influence.
4. Samovar and Porter (1991, p. 51) focus on the specific areas of cultural grooming in their definition of culture '*as the deposit of knowledge, experience, beliefs, values, attitudes, meanings, hierarchies, religion, notions of time, roles, spatial relations, concepts of the universe, and material objects and possessions acquired by a group of people in the course of generations through individual and group striving*'.
5. In contrast, Hill (2003) views the determinants of a society's culture as being *the social structure, political system, economic philosophy, religion, language and education.*

Figure 2.1 indicates how these factors interact and influence the norms and values of a society.

The broad culture, or macro-culture, comprises all the arts, beliefs and institutions (legal, governmental, business, educational and social) that characterise an ethnic group, race or nation, while a narrower micro-culture exists within the macro-culture. The micro-culture includes the characteristic attitudes and behaviour operating within a group, organisation or nation. 'Definitions of culture in the literature range from being broad and all encompassing (culture determines everything we do) to narrow and focused (cultivated behaviour associated with refinement as, for example, in appreciation of the arts)' (Ramburuth in Dwyer 2005).

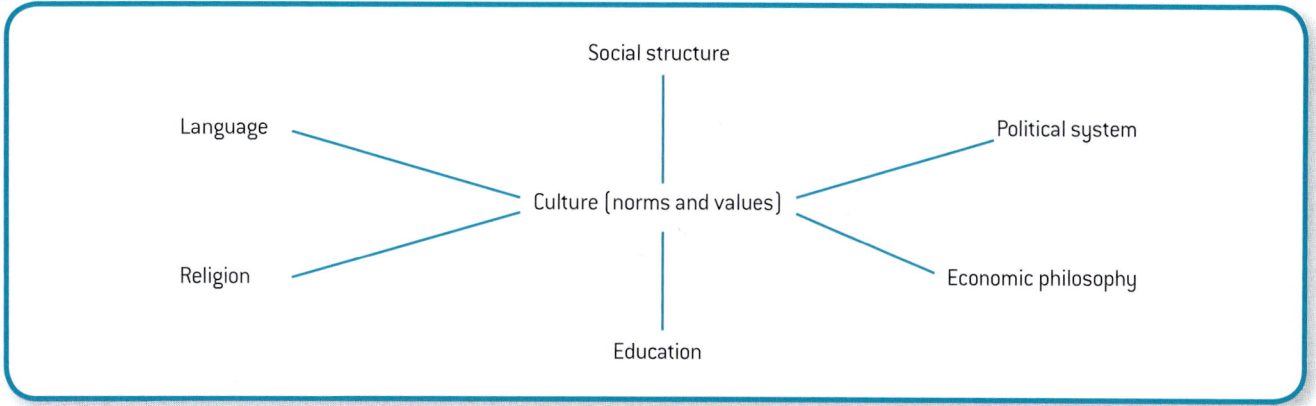

Figure 2.1: Factors influencing cultural norms and values

Source: Adapted from C.W.L. Hill, *International Business: Competing in the Global Marketplace*, Irwin, Chicago, 2003. Reproduced with permission of the McGraw-Hill Companies.

THE PROCESS OF INTERCULTURAL COMMUNICATION

Differences in experiences and culture-specific communication codes and styles all have the potential to impact on intercultural communication and make the process very difficult. Hall (1959) used the term **intercultural communication** to describe the process of communication between people of different cultures. Samovar and Porter (2001, p. 2) reinforce this definition, describing the process as 'the circumstance in which people from diverse cultural backgrounds are engaged in communication'.

To overcome the difficulties, and for effective intercultural communication to take place, there needs to be a *sharing of common meanings* across cultures, as Irwin (1996, p. 22) explains:

> When communication is thought of as the sharing of meanings, what is meant is that each participant in the communication context becomes aware of the meanings about a matter or issue held by the other participant(s). While sharing meanings may bring about agreement it can just as readily and appropriately lead to disagreement. What is important is that communication will lead to clarification and enhanced understanding.

Knapp and Knapp-Potthoff (1987, p. 8) distinguish intercultural and intracultural communication. 'However, there is a crucial difference between intra- and intercultural communication, and that is one related to language. Typically, in intercultural communication at least one of the strangers does not speak the language of the interaction as her or his mother tongue, but is a learner of that language at whatever level of proficiency.' Intercultural communication is the interaction between members of different groups that differ from each other in the knowledge shared by their members and in their linguistic forms of symbolic behaviour.

Sharing common beliefs, values, customs and behaviours helps to facilitate communication among the members of a culture—that is, **intracultural communication**. Ramburuth (in Dwyer 2005, p. 34) discusses how intracultural communication may take place between members of the same dominant culture or co-cultural groups.

> It needs to be remembered that, while cultural groups may be identified by certain common characteristics, there may still be some differences within the groups. Thus, for example, Anglo-Celtic Australians living in major cities such as Sydney or Melbourne may have different perceptions of time, pace of life, political beliefs and attitudes to the environment from those living and working in distinctly rural areas. Similarly, Chinese Australians and Chinese Americans, despite their common Chinese cultural heritage, are bound to have differences influenced

Intercultural communication is the sharing of meanings between individuals of different cultures.

Intracultural communication takes place between members of the same cultural group.

by cultural distance from their original homeland, distance from each other, and exposure to differing processes of socialisation and enculturation.

Three levels of culture

As we have seen, culture derives from the interconnected assumptions, beliefs, values, attitudes, norms and rules shared by a society or group. There are three levels of culture in a society:

1. *The first level is visible.* It encompasses the patterns and behaviour visible in the culture, including technology, buildings, artefacts and behaviour patterns.
2. *The second level is less visible than the first level.* It is made up of cultural communication and describes how people communicate (verbally and nonverbally) as they explain, rationalise and justify what they say and do as a society or group.
3. *The third level is almost invisible* and comprises the ideas, basic assumptions, values and beliefs held by a society. Internalised beliefs and values are assumptions shared by the members of a society. Values evolve from personal experiences and the society's internalised beliefs about what ideals are desirable. Beliefs are derived from personal experience and influenced by the judgment and expertise of trusted others in the culture.

Hall (1990, p. 3) states: '. . . the world of communication can be divided into three parts: *words*, *material things* and *behaviour*. Words are the medium of business, politics and diplomacy. Material things are usually indicators of status and power. Behaviour provides feedback on how other people feel and includes techniques for avoiding confrontation.' He highlights the need to understand culture as a communicative process that involves the use of symbols to shape social reality. The statement 'Culture is communication and communication is culture' has become known as 'Hall's identity':

> Communication rules apply to all levels of behaviour, both verbal and nonverbal as well formal and informal. Some are explicitly coded within the written or spoken language, as in the case of grammatically correct writing or organizational rules and regulations. Most other rules, however, are implicit; they deal largely with the nature of interpersonal relationships, such as involvement and intimacy, status and power, and cooperation and accommodation. . . . non-verbal behaviours reflect the normative cultural rules and elicit specifiable responses with often measurable social consequences. (1990, p. 103)

Enculturation is the socialisation process that we go through as we learn about and adapt to our society (Chaney & Martin 2000).

As part of our socialisation, or **enculturation**, we internalise the rules of interaction within our culture. This is the third, almost invisible, level of culture. Our perception of what is being said in our conversations is affected by the background experience we carry. Perception is determined by our background, which consists of values, attitudes, life concerns, cultural conditioning, skills and other factors. Internalised rules surface in a range of intercultural contexts including business, social and interpersonal contexts. Some of these internalised rules are about:

- courtesies in speech, such as when to say 'please', 'thank you' or 'excuse me'
- politeness—who can speak to whom and who can begin a conversation
- the meaning of 'yes' and 'no'
- humour and irony and their use
- appropriate use of space in terms of proximity
- appropriate use of eye contact
- nonverbal behaviours and their meaning
- deference to others
- use of time.

Context includes all the factors that shape and influence the ways in which we understand an interaction.

For anyone engaging in intercultural communication, the interaction occurs in context. As well as the physical and social setting, the context also includes economic factors, historical factors and perceptions of power. Perceptions of any of these factors vary from culture to culture and have an impact on intercultural communication. This is the first level of culture—the visible level.

Enculturation and acculturation

Intercultural encounters between people of different races, ethnic backgrounds and lifestyles are multiplying. As well as understanding the technical nature of their business transactions, those engaged in international business must also understand differences in the way people think, feel and act.

Hoebel and Frost (1976, p. 58) define enculturation as 'conscious or unconscious conditioning occurring within that process whereby the individual, as child and adult, achieves competence in a particular culture'. Learning about culture can be:

- unconscious (as we absorb and imitate the daily habits, speech patterns and roles of our parents from infancy); or
- deliberate (as we are taught specific manners for greeting people, religious rites and rituals, and reading the Bible, Koran, Torah or other literature).

A member of a culture or sub-culture learns how to use, formally and informally, the patterns of cultural behaviour prescribed by that culture.

Acculturation is the process by which people adjust to the host culture by adopting its values, symbols and behaviour. Acculturation is a multi-dimensional process involving the adaptation of language, cultural beliefs and values of one group (usually the minority group) to the norms and structures of another (usually the majority group). Reasons for difficulties in adjusting to a new culture include:

- conflicting social norms and attempts to retain previous culture
- focusing on differences between own and the new culture
- perceiving differences as weaknesses, rather than adopting a balanced view of the new culture.

Acculturation is an active ongoing process of cultural involvement. People develop new norms of behaviour as they adapt and adjust to the cultural worldviews, customs and traditions of another group. The process may involve direct social interaction or exposure to other cultures through mass media. Rather than abandoning their past for the new culture, people are more likely to accommodate new ideas into their own culture (Chaney & Martin 2000) and try to achieve 'synergy' between the two cultures.

> **Acculturation** is the process of cultural adjustment and adaptation people experience as they move from one culture to another.

Ethnocentrism

Ethnocentrism is the use of one's own culture to interpret all other cultures. Ethnocentric people tend to interpret the actions, customs, values, religion, codes and behaviours of other people using their own culture as a guide. They view their own culture as the 'central' culture and, in interacting and communicating with members of different cultures, use their own cultural norms as the central point of reference.

> **Ethnocentrism** is the belief that one's cultural norms are superior to those of other social groups.

Porter (1976, pp. 6–7) describes ethnocentrism as follows:

> We place ourselves, our racial, ethnic, or social group, at the centre of the universe and rate all others accordingly. The greater their similarity to us, the nearer we place them; the greater the dissimilarity, the farther away they are . . . We tend to see our own groups, our own country, our own culture as the best.

Awareness, knowledge and skills underpin effective intercultural communication. Without awareness, an ethnocentric person may travel the world making no effort to look beyond their own culture or try to understand other cultures. Ignorance prevents interaction with another culture. Rather than interpreting the customs and behaviour of other people by using our own culture as a benchmark, organisations and people have to recognise and apply the symbols of the other culture and be willing to adapt to a new environment. Ethnocentrism is a major barrier to intercultural communication and understanding.

Cultural relativism

Cultural relativism is the recognition of cultural differences and acceptance that each social group has its own set of cultural norms.

Ramburuth (Dwyer 2005, p. 36) says: 'The concept of **cultural relativism** is the opposite to that of ethnocentrism. It is acceptance of the belief that each cultural group has its own set of values, behaviours and symbols and its own code of right and wrong, which are relative to that group.' Cultural relativism recognises that there are differences in the way people from different cultures perceive, receive, interpret and respond to ideas and situations. Cultural relativism accepts that concepts are socially constructed and may vary across cultures, and that what may be considered right and valid in one culture may be frowned on in another culture.

Beamer and Varner (2001) regard this acceptance and understanding of cultural differences as the first step to effective intercultural communication. Cultural relativism, the recognition of cultural differences and acceptance that each social group has its own set of cultural norms, enables us to understand differences in the way people from different cultures perceive, receive, interpret and respond to ideas and situations.

High-context and low-context cultures

OBJECTIVE 2 ▶
Describe high-context and low-context cultural styles and discuss components of culture relevant to intercultural communication

Hall (1976) originally identified the concepts of high context and low context to classify differences in communication styles. From his findings, cultures were classified according to where they fall on a continuum between high- and low-context cultures. In a high-context culture a large part of the message is influenced by the background and basic values of the communicator and implied in the message's context. In a low-context culture the words in the message are explicit, and nonverbal cues have less impact on the intended meaning. In a high-context culture, intercultural business communication and negotiations, in particular, usually proceed slowly. A major purpose of the negotiation in a high-context culture (as well as proceeding to a decision) is for the parties to get to know one another, whereas members of a low-context culture are used to moving quickly to a decision. Without knowledge of the negotiating style in each culture context (high or low), members of either culture may become frustrated; tensions may arise because of a clash of styles and different interpretation of the words and nonverbal components of a message. The characteristics of high- and low-context cultures are shown in Table 2.1.

Since nonverbal behaviour arises from cultural common sense (people's ideas about what is normal, appropriate and effective as communication in relationships), different systems of understanding gestures, posture, silence, emotional expression, touch, physical appearance and other nonverbal cues will exist between high- and low-context cultures. Low-context cultures such as Australia, New Zealand and Canada tend to place less emphasis on nonverbal communication, whereas high-context settings such as China, other Asian and Arab countries convey a significant part of the intended meaning of the communication in the nonverbal components of the message. In a high-context culture, attitudes to time are polycronic, multiple tasks are handled at the same time, and time is subordinate to interpersonal relations. In low-context cultures, attitudes to time are monochronic; 'one thing at a time' and 'time is money' are important concepts and interpersonal relations are subordinate to the time.

Boundary spanners work at the interface of the organisation and in their work cross organisational and/or national boundaries.

People who work across boundaries are defined as **boundary spanners** (Manev & Stevenson 2001). A boundary spanner works at the interface of the organisation and the society or environment of stakeholders surrounding the organisation. Boundary spanners who work effectively have an understanding of high-context and low-context cultures and the capacity to adapt to the different cultural realities of both. Some may become culture brokers who help to negotiate the tensions between cultures and facilitate intercultural interaction. Members of global organisations working in other countries, academics and researchers, public relations staff, salespeople and those who travel on behalf of their company span organisational and national boundaries. Austrade (2008) offers the following etiquette tips to help boundary spanners who do business in China.

- Building up good business relationships (*guanxi*) and trust is very important, so a lot of time will be spent at meetings and banquets with potential business partners.

Table 2.1: Characteristics of high-context and low-context cultures

Type	Characteristics

High-context cultures identify with the group
 	
Example: Chinese culture
	a Sensory involvement is high, with:
	• high-contact touch behaviour
	• close proximity due to low personal space needs
	
	b The message:
	• conveys only a limited portion of the meaning in what is said
	• must also be interpreted in terms of:
	  – how it is being said
	  – where it is being said
	  – body language of the speaker
	
	c Time sense is polychronic:
	• things happen simultaneously
	• time is circular
	• things proceed at their own pace

Low-context cultures identify with the individual. *Example:* Australian culture	a Sensory involvement is low, with: • low-contact touch behaviour • high personal space needs b The message: • words convey explicitly most of the meaning in the communication • nonverbal cues of body language have less impact • status of the speaker is less important in interpretation of the meaning c Time is monochronic: • things happen one at a time and in sequence • time is linear • planning and punctuality are a priority

- The most senior person at the meeting will be introduced first, followed by others in descending order of seniority.
- A handshake is the standard way to greet men and women, whatever their age or seniority. An extra show of courtesy in the presence of an older person will reflect well on you because the Chinese respect their elders.
- Business cards (*ming pian*) are essential in China. Have your card translated into Chinese on the reverse side and present your card with both hands with the Chinese side face up. Spend a few moments examining the business card you are given as a sign of respect, rather than putting it away immediately.
- Know some Mandarin—simple phrases such as '*Ni hao*' (hello), '*Zao shang hao*' (good morning) and '*Xia wu hao*' (good afternoon) can go a long way.
- Surnames are placed first: for example, Mr Yao Ming should be addressed as 'Mr Yao'.
- Do not use your index finger or point when speaking.
- Remain patient and polite—the Chinese do not like to 'lose face', so losing your temper or showing frustration will only set you back.

REVIEW QUESTIONS

1. *a* What do you understand by the term 'intercultural communication'?
   b What is the relationship between culture and communication?
   c How can we promote understanding between different cultures?
2. *a* Distinguish between the terms 'intercultural communication' and 'intracultural communication'.
   b Define the terms 'enculturation' and 'acculturation' and show how they differ.
3. Ethnocentrists view their culture as the 'central' culture. How can we counter ethnocentric beliefs and develop awareness of cultural relativism?
4. *a* Describe the characteristics of a high-context culture.
   b Describe the characteristics of a low-context culture.
   c Discuss the challenges facing a manager who moves from an organisation with a high-context culture to one with a low-context culture.

THE RELEVANCE OF CULTURAL COMPONENTS TO INTERCULTURAL COMMUNICATION

Adaptation to another culture moves through three stages. In the first stage, people take things for granted and are surprised when their expectations are wrong and their approach doesn't work. The second stage involves making sense of new patterns through communication experiences, and the third stage progresses to new understandings of another culture.

Samovar (2006, p. 12) identifies the cultural components of particular importance in intercultural communication as the perceptual elements, patterns of cognition, verbal behaviours, nonverbal behaviours and the influence of context. These elements function concurrently in any interaction and therein lies the importance of learning about culture.

Differing perceptions due to different experiences, backgrounds, attitudes and beliefs can cause people from different cultural backgrounds to interpret the same message differently. Problems in intercultural communication occur because of different ways of thinking and different verbal and nonverbal behaviours between cultures. Rules about acceptable behaviour in different contexts may lead to confusion or misunderstanding. Not only is it valuable to learn about different cultures, it is also important to develop self-awareness because a knowledge of self informs us about the factors that impact on our view of other people and cultures. (See Chapter 3 for further discussion of self-awareness.) Nonverbal behaviours such as tone and pitch of voice, gestures when speaking, and expressiveness or reticence all affect meaning. Often, what is left unsaid and only inferred is more significant than what was said. (See Chapter 4 for a discussion of nonverbal behaviours.) Competent intercultural communicators adapt to perceptual elements, patterns of cognition, verbal behaviour, nonverbal behaviour and the influence of context in business, social and other interactions.

Nonverbal communication consists of all that part of the message that is not encoded in words.

Language

Language and the meaning of words learned within a culture reflect that culture's values and shape its members' view of the world. The way language conveys meaning and the precision of the message varies between cultures. Selection of the right words can have a significant impact on the quality of intercultural communication: for example, formality and the appropriate use of titles is important in a high-context culture.

In some cultures, speakers put the justification first followed by the main point. In other countries, such as Australia, the main point is placed first followed by the justification. In a high-context culture, communication may be ambiguous; in a low-context culture, words carry explicit meaning. One problem encountered by Australian business people in Japan, for example, is whether 'yes' means 'yes' or simply 'I hear what you are saying'. In any culture, language is dynamic and changing over time. When communicating across cultures, awareness of the meaning of words and idiomatic expressions in the language of another culture can prevent communication barriers and their consequences.

Nonverbal communication

Nonverbal cues can be personal, cultural or universal (see Chapter 4). The part of nonverbal communication that is common to a range of people contains clues to acceptable patterns of behaviour, whereas nonverbal communication that is part of a person's unique behaviour pattern creates a picture of the sender's personality through their gestures and mannerisms. Universal nonverbal communication has evolved as part of our biological heritage. Universal nonverbal communication crosses cultural and national boundaries—for example, a smile.

Nonverbal communication is either personal to the individual, common to the group or culture, or universal.

Rules applying to the nonverbal parts of the message are learned from others in the same culture. Some of the many aspects of nonverbal communication influenced by culture are tone of voice, inflection, rate of speech, facial expression, touching, use of space, body movement and dress. Those in the culture share cultural nonverbal communication. Deep feelings such as love and anger can be expressed by words and actions such as a touch, a look, how people stand in relation to one another and by the tone of voice. However, each feeling will have its own nonverbal cues and the cues will vary between cultures.

Nonverbal communication can be classified as:

- *relational nonverbal*, to explain our relationship to others
- *status messages*, indicating our power position to others
- *deceptive nonverbal*, whether a person's nonverbal cues reflect lying or deception.

When deception is involved, the nonverbal part of a message is often more compelling than the contradictory verbal part of the message. The following nonverbal codes may have different interpretations across cultures:

Nonverbal communication is usually learned subconsciously and can sometimes contradict the spoken part of a message.

- *Body movements*—use of body language may be personal, cultural or universal.
- *Eye contact* is more cultural than universal.
- *Facial expression* is emotive and more universal than personal or cultural.
- *Paralanguage*—vocal qualities such as accent, intonation, placement of phrases and tempo are more cultural than universal.
- *Proxemics*—use of space to communicate varies between cultures.
- *Chronemics*—use of time is more cultural than universal.
- *Silence* conveys meaning and is more cultural than universal.
- *Artefacts* are more personal and cultural than universal.

Perception of power

Loden and Rosener (1991) divide the power differential within a culture or society into two dimensions. The first is the primary, more permanent dimension of gender, race, age and sexual orientation. The second, more changeable dimension encompasses educational background, socioeconomic status and marital status. In intercultural interactions, power in either of these two dimensions may be perceived differently. In China an older person is respected for the wisdom their age is thought to have bestowed on them, whereas in Australia age may be viewed with disrespect.

Perception of power is dynamic in intercultural communication, flowing through individuals in various contexts and relationships. In business relationships, people usually communicate from their role within a business or other type of organisation. Within their own society they carry the institutional power offered by their occupancy of that role. Intercultural communication, however, may change the power dynamics a person usually experiences in the employee–employer relations within their own culture. The consequent misunderstandings can cause intercultural communication breakdowns.

Adapting to new cultural contexts

Research conducted by Gudykunst (1985) led to the Anxiety and Uncertainty Management Model. The model suggests that intercultural encounters are characterised by high levels of uncertainty and anxiety, especially when cultural variability is high. Whenever two people meet for the first time, there is uncertainty accompanied by feelings of uneasiness or anxiety. The theory suggests these feelings of anxiety are heightened in an intercultural interaction.

Three key issues impact on the pace and success of adaptation:

1. how much the person wants to become part of the new culture
2. the extent to which the person wants to interact with the new culture
3. ownership of political power.

Intercultural communication is enhanced by the ability to manage anxiety and reduce uncertainty about self and others in the interaction.

Individual differences such as age, race, class, gender, personality, socioeconomic position and other factors all play a role in how a person adapts to another culture. Even an expatriate who has lived and worked overseas for many years may need to readapt to the old culture on return to their country of origin.

REVIEW QUESTIONS

5 a   Briefly describe the relationship between language and culture.

b   Identify three classes of nonverbal communication.

c   Give examples of nonverbal communication codes and describe how they vary between cultures.

d   Identify the two dimensions of power within a culture (Loden & Rosener 1991), and describe how these dimensions may differ between cultures.

6 How can a knowledge of the Anxiety and Uncertainty Management Model improve our understanding of the impact of cultural differences on intercultural interactions?

APPLY YOUR KNOWLEDGE

CULTURAL IDENTITY

1   Identify the components of culture.
What do you consider to be the key components of culture? Using these components, write down a definition of culture. In pairs or small groups, compare definitions and identify similarities and differences. Suggest explanations for these similarities and/or differences.

2   Reflect on your own culture.
Identify some of the key characteristics of the dominant culture to which you belong. Consider commonly held values, beliefs, attitudes, behaviours (social and business), codes of dress, languages spoken, religions and communication styles. What aspects of your dominant culture do you value most? What are some of the commonly held perceptions and misperceptions about your culture, and why have these arisen?

3   Identify other cultures.
Consider the class in which you are studying. Identify culturally different groups based on ethnicity and/or other characteristics, such as gender, age, religion, education, occupation (or part-time occupation if you are full-time students). Develop a profile and understanding of the diversity in your class and the range of co-cultural groups. Working in small groups, discuss similarities and differences within the groups, and why these differences exist. Consider the impact of the differences, how they could be managed to facilitate cross-cultural understanding and the implications for intercultural communication.

Source: Prem Ramburuth, in J. Dwyer, *Communication in Business*, 3rd edn, Pearson Education Australia, Sydney, 2005, p. 35.

BARRIERS TO INTERCULTURAL COMMUNICATION

◄ OBJECTIVE 3
Explain the causes of communication barriers in intercultural communication

Barriers to intercultural communication are created when the behaviour of an individual differs from your own (Chaney & Martin 2000). Failure to recognise and understand the reasons for these differences can cause intercultural confusion, tension and misunderstanding. A number of communication barriers that are relevant to intercultural interactions have been identified in the literature by Hodgetts and Luthans (2003), Deresky (2002a) and Ferraro (2002) (see Figure 2.2).

Ethnocentric behaviour will impede intercultural communication and lead to intercultural misunderstanding, tension and conflict. Attitudes of superiority, and making no effort to understand any views beyond one's own culture, will impede intercultural communication In the workplace, assert Beamer and Varner (2001, p. 17), 'No organisation can afford to go along believing that members of different cultures are all seeking to conform to one culture, or that one day differences will cease to exist. Therefore, the key for business is to find ways for people who think differently to work together.'

Stereotypes and prejudice

Stereotypes come from the natural linguistic tendency to organise phenomena into meaningful categories. In a human social context, stereotyping involves accepting widely held belief systems about particular groups that are usually detrimental to intercultural understanding and communication.

Prejudice is pre-judging with little or no information and creates a negative attitude towards a cultural group. Discriminatory behaviours result from stereotyping or prejudice. Discrimination involves overt actions by nations, institutions, groups or individuals to exclude, avoid or distance another cultural group.

Allport (1954, cited in Berry 2002) postulated the contact model to explain how prejudice can be reduced through exposure to positive experiences and contact with those people a group is prejudiced against. Contact and positive experiences reduce the prejudices and enhance intercultural communication. Berry (2002, p. 374) states '. . . that the groups in contact should have

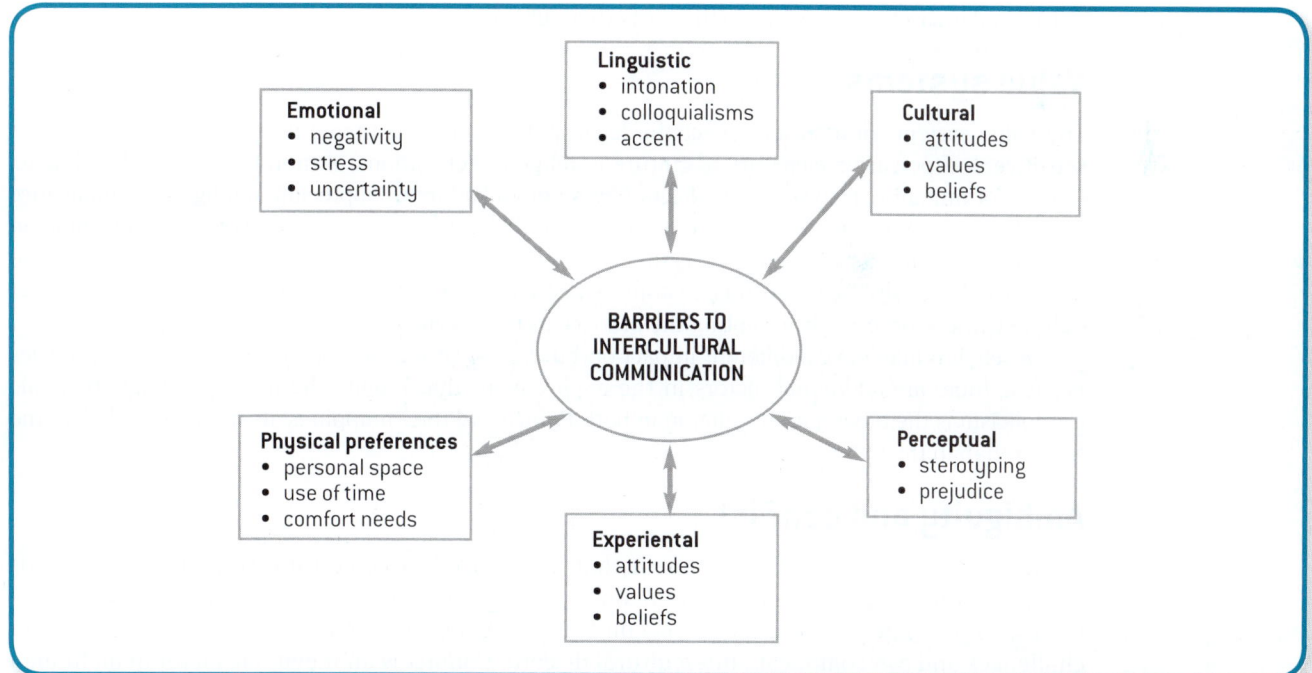

Figure 2.2: Barriers to intercultural communication

roughly equal status; that they should share some common goals; that they should be in contact voluntarily and that there should be some support for the contact (rather than prohibiting it)'. As well as being voluntary, the contact should be ongoing and happen in a cooperative, rather than a competitive, context.

Cultural practices

While a set of practices may not be immediately obvious in intracultural business transactions, there is the opportunity for these practices to cause confusion and misunderstanding when business interactions cross national and cultural boundaries. For example, in Japan, business meetings held during the day can seem to be slow to deal with key issues, whereas after-work drinks and dinners may be more useful as sources of information. The Japanese equate being indirect with being polite. Thus being indirect, such as starting a business meeting with 'small talk', will help to get the meeting off to a good start. Australians can misunderstand this indirectness and interpret it as indecisiveness or non-commitment from the Japanese side. In these situations, it pays to be patient. (www.austrade.gov.au/2008). Products may also carry the characteristics of a culture; for example, an Australian company exporting bathroom accessories to Japan should design a significant quantity in the colour blue, because this is the bathroom accessory colour of preference in Japan.

Social institutions

The norms of a society or culture are the accepted way of doing things. They form the foundation of the cultural process because they show individuals how to become part of the family, education, employment and social, legal and political institutions. Social institutions and their norms determine how people relate to each other, how they manage themselves and what they view as acceptable behaviour. They show how to behave in different roles and identify status within the society and its institutions. Intercultural communication barriers arise when either party demonstrates ethnocentricity rather than cultural relativism. Both parties in an interaction should be aware of differences in behaviour and lifestyle and work towards an understanding, rather than consider their own cultural norms and institutions superior to those of other cultures.

Value systems

The value systems of a society affect the legal, political and economic practices. One of the most sensitive and pervasive elements of culture is religion. Perceptions of morality, immorality, habits, foods, clothing and lifestyle are all affected by religion. Failure to appreciate a religion's significance in a specific culture can easily cause the intercultural communicator to give offence. For example, in an Islamic country during Ramadan, eating between sunrise and sunset is forbidden. Any visitor from another culture who defers to this custom by not eating in public is showing respect for the other culture without necessarily accepting the practice as their own.

A religion may have a different impact on business customs and practices in different countries because there are additional factors in the environment that modify the impact of religion. While Catholicism is the predominant religion in both France and the Philippines, its influence is less in the former than in the latter.

Ambiguity and conflict

Martin and Nakayama (2003) comment that ambiguity in intercultural communication tends to make people respond with a 'default conflict style' that is often counterproductive. Language issues, and different orientations to conflict and conflict-management styles, raise further challenges and can complicate intercultural discord. Conflict is an inevitable factor in all human social interactions.

Augsberger (1995) highlights that conflict is a universal, cultural and individual process. While it can be managed constructively it is not a simple process. He suggests that the four assumptions shown in column 1 of Table 2.2 underpin Western cultural groups' perspective on conflict. Many other cultural groups view conflict as destructive and unproductive for relationships based on spiritual or cultural values. Augsberger (1995) outlines the four assumptions shown in column 2 as typical of this approach.

The responses and actions of different cultures can be evaluated in terms of the culture's context and differences in attitudes, values, emotions, perceptions, linguistics, physical preferences and experiences (see Figure 2.2). Two empirical studies that have improved our understanding of the key dimensions on which national cultures differ are discussed in the next section of the chapter.

> **Intercultural conflict** is a real or perceived incompatibility of goals, values, expectations, process or outcomes between two or more interdependent individuals or groups from different cultures.

Table 2.2: Contrasting cultural assumptions about conflict

Constructive view of conflict	Destructive view of conflict
Conflict is normal and useful.	Conflict is a destructive disturbance of the peace.
All issues are subject to change through negotiation.	Disputants should be disciplined.
Direct confrontation and conciliation are valued.	Confrontations are destructive and ineffective.
Conflict is a necessary renegotiation of contract, a release of tensions and a renewal of relationships.	The social system is not to be adjusted to the needs of its members—its members need to adapt to established values.

REVIEW QUESTIONS

7. Cultural stereotyping is a common practice. What are some of the reasons for stereotyping? How can this practice be changed or minimised?
8. List five barriers to intercultural communication. How can these barriers be overcome?
9. Discuss how ambiguity in intercultural communication can be counterproductive.

COMPARATIVE VALUE DIMENSIONS

Researchers have investigated key dimensions on which national cultures differ (Hofstede 1984, 1991, 2001; Trompenaars & Hampden-Turner 1997). Their research findings help global business managers improve their understanding of cultural differences and cope with workplace diversity.

> ◄ OBJECTIVE 4
> Discuss the implications of comparative value dimensions for intercultural communication

Hofstede's findings

Hofstede (1984) conducted a major study in which he surveyed employees of the multinational IBM Corporation in 67 countries. The findings of the study identified four main dimensions on which cultures differed in terms of their values: power distance, individualism/collectivism, masculinity/femininity and uncertainty avoidance. A brief description of his findings is presented in Table 2.3.

The power distance scores (PD) in Table 2.4 demonstrate the different cultural orientations to power and status in the workplace in 53 countries.

IMPLICATIONS OF HOFSTEDE'S MODEL FOR INTERCULTURAL COMMUNICATION

Hofstede's cultural dimensions provide insight into the influence of culture on the communication process. The findings suggest that the three most feminine countries are Sweden (MAS score of 5),

Table 2.3: Four dimensions of culture

Dimension	How cultures differ	
Power distance is the extent to which less powerful members of a society accept inequality in power and status as normal. A high score (see Table 2.4) indicates a country or culture that accepts inequality in power and status as normal.	*High-power-distance cultures:* • tolerate inequality to a much greater degree than low-power-distance cultures • accept that hierarchies are appropriate and that those in positions of authority are entitled to power and privileges and cannot be challenged or questioned (Irwin 1996) • have managers who tend to prefer autocratic or directive managerial styles • have employees who tend to expect structure and close supervision • expect managers to make decisions with limited employee communication.	*Low-power-distance cultures:* • have flatter hierarchies, less entitlement to privileges and greater equity between different levels of personnel • have managers who tend to adopt participative and consultative leadership styles • have employees who expect to contribute their ideas to the decision-making process • have employees who tend to question or challenge ideas they may not agree with (Lustig & Koester 1999).
Individualism (IDV) refers to the extent to which cultures differ on the bipolar individualism/collectivism continuum. For example, Australia and Western countries such as the United States, the United Kingdom and Canada are highly individualistic cultures, while many South American and Asian countries are more collectivist.	*Individualist cultures:* • assume that people will primarily look after their own interests and those of their immediate family • focus on the 'I' • encourage members to be assertive in their communication styles • express their thoughts and opinions readily • question teachers in the classroom or employers in the workplace • manage rather than avoid conflict and work towards mutual agreement.	*Collectivist cultures:* • belong to and emphasise the 'group' (e.g. the extended family or organisation) • protect the interests of members but expect loyalty in return • focus on the 'we' (Hofstede 1991) • tend not to express their thoughts openly • engage in collective decision making • are more likely to avoid conflict and confrontation to 'save face'.
Uncertainty avoidance (UA) defines the extent to which members of a culture feel nervous about, or are threatened by, situations they perceive as ambiguous, unclear or unstructured.	*People in high-uncertainty cultures:* • are risk averse • maintain strict codes of behaviour • establish more formal rules • tend to be resistant to change.	*People in low-uncertainty cultures:* • take more risks • require fewer structures • are more informal and relaxed • are willing to accept change.
Masculinity (MAS) refers to the extent to which a society adopts male-oriented work values that differ from feminine values (Hofstede 1984). For example, Japan has high masculine values; Sweden and Norway have high feminine values.	*Societies with high masculine values:* • define gender roles more rigidly • distinguish clearly between goals for men and women • show a preference for assertiveness, achievement, ambition, material acquisition and competition in the workplace.	*Feminine societies:* • demonstrate a preference for nurturance and caring for others • demonstrate non-material values and value quality of life • are more flexible and tend to accept 'relatively overlapping' roles for men and women.

Norway (8) and the Netherlands (14); the most masculine country is Japan (95). Ramburuth (2005) discusses the implications of the findings in Hofstede's study (1984):

> Given the differences, it can be expected that when managers or employees from masculine cultures work in feminine cultures, or vice versa, there are bound to be problems in cross-cultural understanding and intercultural communication . . . employees from high uncertainty avoidance cultures (e.g. Japan with a UA Score of 92) will be less likely to be forthcoming in discussions or decision making, and will expect their managers to provide clear and concise instructions in the workplace. This could be problematic if they are working with managers from low uncertainty cultures (e.g. Sweden with a UA Score of 29), who may adopt a more consultative style of leadership and expect input and active participation in discussions and decision making. Differences in levels of uncertainty are bound to impact on the intercultural communication process.

While Hofstede's work (1984, 1991, 2001) provides one of the most comprehensive frameworks for understanding cultural differences in multinational organisations and for identifying the nature and extent of diversity in today's complex workforces, there are some qualifications. Fletcher and Brown (2008) discuss three qualifications. First, Hofstede's study was conducted within a single

Table 2.4: Hofstede's power distance (PD) scores

Country	PD score	Country	PD score	Country	PD score
Malaysia	104	Salvador	66	South Africa	49
Guatemala	95	Turkey	66	Jamaica	45
Panama	95	Belgium	65	USA	40
Philippines	94	East Africa	64	Canada	39
Mexico	81	Peru	64	Netherlands	38
Venezuela	81	Thailand	64	Australia	36
Arab countries	80	Chile	63	Costa Rica	35
Ecuador	78	Portugal	63	West Germany	35
Indonesia	78	Uruguay	61	UK	35
India	77	Greece	60	Switzerland	34
West Africa	77	South Korea	60	Finland	33
Yugoslavia	76	Iran	58	Norway	31
Singapore	74	Taiwan	58	Sweden	31
Brazil	69	Spain	57	Ireland (Rep.)	28
France	68	Pakistan	55	New Zealand	22
Hong Kong	68	Japan	54	Denmark	18
Colombia	67	Italy	50	Israel	13
		Argentina	49	Austria	11

Source: Adapted from G. Hofstede, *Cultures and Organisations: Software of the Mind*, McGraw-Hill, London, 1991. Reproduced with permission by the author.

organisation with the sample consisting of IBM executives in each country. IBM's strong corporate culture could '. . . mask some of the differences between countries' (p. 100). Second, the survey was conducted 40 years ago in the late 1970s and '. . . since that time there have been changes within individual countries and a rise in the globalisation of world trade'. Third, the dimensions of national culture found by Hofstede are '. . . largely Western dimensions and may not be appropriate measures of cultural differences in some Asian countries'. Collectivism does not automatically exclude individualism: '. . . in cultures whose members believe there is no such concept as a single truth . . . uncertainty avoidance may have only limited meaning'. Fletcher and Brown discuss Hofstede's recognition of this shortcoming. He addressed the issue of whether there are other dimensions that might have been overlooked because they are not important in Western cultures in subsequent research with Bond from the Chinese University of Hong Kong. Hofstede and Bond arrived at a '. . . fifth dimension which was initially labelled "Confucian Dynamism" and subsequently "long-term versus short-term orientation" . . . the extent to which cultures exhibit a pragmatic, future-oriented perspective as opposed to a historic short-term view' (p. 108).

Trompenaars' and Hampden-Turner's findings

Trompenaars and Hampden-Turner (1997) conducted a major study in an attempt to measure cultural differences on a global basis. Employees were surveyed across 30 companies. The interviews were divided into 75% with management and 25% with general administrative staff. The study identified five main dimensions on which cultures differed: universalism versus particularism, individualism versus communitarianism, neutral versus affective, specific versus diffuse, and achievement versus ascription. Table 2.5 presents a brief description.

IMPLICATIONS OF TROMPENAARS' AND HAMPDEN-TURNER'S MODEL FOR INTERCULTURAL COMMUNICATION

The first three dimensions in this model are similar to Hofstede's but there are two additional dimensions: the specific versus diffuse dimension and the achievement versus ascription dimension. These two dimensions provide additional empirical findings on which to analyse the degree to which people engage with others. Specific-oriented supervisors or team leaders keep tasks separate from relationships with others, whereas a diffuse-oriented manager intermingles task and relationships. The differences between achievement and ascription cultures affect how status is conferred—by performance against standards or by kinship, title, seniority or some other factor.

Given these differences, it can be expected that when managers or employees from specific-oriented cultures work in diffuse cultures, there are likely to be problems in cross-cultural understanding and communication. Employees from achievement-oriented cultures will have difficulty in accepting status conferred by factors other than performance.

REVIEW QUESTIONS

10 *a* Consider Hofstede's research into cultural differences in the workplace. What are the four main dimensions on which he identified cultural differences?

b How has the research contributed to the understanding of cultural diversity in the workplace?

11 According to research, uncertainty is higher in intercultural encounters than in intracultural encounters. Discuss factors that impact on uncertainty in intercultural encounters.

12 Discuss the advantages global organisations gain from understanding the dynamics of different cultures and intercultural communication.

Table 2.5: Trompenaars' and Hampden-Turner's cultural dimensions

Dimension	How cultures differ	
Universalism versus particularism	*Universalism is about finding broad and general rules:* • when no rules fit, universalism finds the best rule • what is good and right can be applied everywhere.	*Particularism is about finding exceptions:* • a case is judged on its own merits, rather than trying to force-fit an existing rule • obligations imposed by relationships are more important than general rules
Individualism versus communitarianism	*Individualism:* • stresses the rights of the individual • seeks to let each person grow or fail on their own • sees a focus on the group as removing rights of the individual	*Communitarianism:* • stresses the rights of the group or society • sees individualism as selfish and short-sighted • seeks to put the family, group, company and country before the individual
Neutral versus affective	*In neutral cultures:* • expression of emotion is repressed • an impression of objectivity, control and detachment is given	*In affective cultures:* • expression of emotion is open and viewed as natural • emotion is accepted in professional contexts and interactions
Specific versus diffuse	*In specific cultures:* • speakers move straight to the point • activities are often limited to tasks or job-specific activities • less need is felt for relationships and social contact	*In diffuse cultures:* • people discuss business only after relationships have been established • business and professional activities often include maintenance of relationships as well as task completion
Achievement versus ascription	*In achievement cultures:* • status derives from your own achievements • status is gained through performance • people are evaluated on their achievements	*In ascribing cultures:* • status comes from age, gender, kinship, education, connections • status is gained by right, rather than daily performance or seniority • order and security is found in knowing where status is and stays

INTERCULTURAL COMMUNICATION COMPETENCE

A lack of intercultural sensitivity and the inability of negotiators to understand and function in accordance with the norms of a different culture can lead to the failure of business deals and negotiations. Hoecklin (1995, p. 1) emphasises the importance in a business and work environment of learning the value systems of other cultures.

> Working with people whose values and beliefs, not to mention languages and customs, are very different from your own can make for costly misunderstandings and even business failures . . . Ignoring or mishandling differences can mean inability to retain and motivate employees, misreading the potential of cross-border alliances, marketing and advertising blunders, and failure to build sustainable sources of competitive advantage. Mismanaging

◄ OBJECTIVE 5
Describe the characteristics of intercultural communication competence and evaluate strategies for developing intercultural competence

cultural differences can render otherwise successful managers and organisations ineffective and frustrated when working across cultures. When successfully managed, however, differences in culture can lead to innovative business practices, faster and better learning within the organisation, and sustainable sources of competitive advantage.

In researching case studies relating to other issues in communicating across cultures, Ramburuth and Welch (2005) found that many Australian managers encounter difficulty in communicating via email with managers in Asia, due to a lack of familiarity with their hierarchical social structures (e.g. failure to address their emails to managers of the appropriate rank in the organisation). In contrast, managers in Asia found the Australian managers' form of written communication in emails far too informal; they tended to interpret casual greetings and messages such as 'How (are) you going?' and 'Have a good day' as signs of work not being taken seriously. There is potential for cultural confusion at every level of intercultural business communication, requiring ongoing awareness and sensitivity to different ways of communicating across cultures.

Culture-general approach to intercultural communication competence

Intercultural competency is developed through understanding how we perceive and react to cultural rules—not only those of others, but also our own.

The characteristics of an interculturally competent business communicator are similar to those of people who communicate effectively in their own culture. Sensitivity and an orientation towards others to improve understanding and build positive relationships are common to both. Experts point out that there is no fixed list of technical skills that can be developed for general use and transferred across into specific intercultural communication contexts (Chaney & Martin 2000; Hofstede 1991, 2001; Irwin 1996). They advocate instead a broader approach to culture learning and competence. Prem Ramburuth (in Dwyer 2005, pp. 43–44) discusses the issues in overcoming intercultural barriers and highlights the priorities in a culture-general approach to achieving intercultural competence.

Overcoming the barriers to intercultural communication and acquiring intercultural communication competence is no easy task. It requires a great deal of effort and understanding of both one's own cultural norms, values and beliefs and those of people from different cultures. It has become evident that simple lists of 'do's and don'ts' or short 'quick fix' training courses for people travelling, living or working in cultures other than their own are no longer sufficient to achieve the competence required for successful intercultural interaction.

Hofstede (1991) identifies two different approaches to culture learning in the form of *culture-specific* and *culture-general* approaches. Traditionally, the culture-specific approach focuses on acquiring specific knowledge about the 'other' culture. Thus, for example, the business executive who has to work in another country will attempt to learn 'information' about that country (geography, history, customs, language, living conditions, tips on behaviour). While this knowledge and information will be extremely useful, it has limitations in that it does not provide an in-depth understanding of the people and the culture, nor does it provide for long-term intercultural learning.

A culture-general approach to achieving intercultural communication competence adopts a much broader approach to culture learning and focuses on the following priorities:

- the development of cultural awareness and sensitivity, which requires being aware of one's own culture or 'mental software' (Hofstede 1991, p. 232) and of issues of diversity. The emphasis is on having general knowledge and understanding about cultures, cultural environments and core cultural differences. It is more than simply developing 'skills' for survival in a host culture
- the development of cultural and communication sensitivity through being alert to differences in communicating styles and intentions, in verbal, nonverbal and interpersonal communication, and in the interpretation of meanings. This requires a conscious effort to observe the principles of intercultural interpersonal communication

- the development of behavioural flexibility, which requires moving away from cultural 'mindsets' and fixed ways of thinking. It necessitates being able to adapt to intercultural interactions as they occur; it is generally very difficult to predict how an intercultural situation will develop, and to what extent you will understand or be understood in the communication process. The ability to react readily to new and uncertain situations assists in reducing the discomfort, anxiety and stress often associated with intercultural interactions
- the development of an 'other-orientation', which requires the ability to empathise with people from cultures other than your own. It is essential to be able to put yourself into another person's position in order to develop alternative perspectives about a cultural situation or encounter. The ability to empathise with others and other cultures assists in reconsidering preconceptions, overcoming stereotyping and building bridges to intercultural understanding and communication
- taking responsibility for the communication and not assuming that it is the other person's job to communicate effectively with you.

Diversity and intercultural communication

The context of **diversity** covers gender, age, language, ethnicity, cultural background, sexual orientation, religious belief and family responsibilities. Diversity also refers to other ways in which people are different, such as educational level, life experience, work experience, socioeconomic background, personality and marital status. Workplace diversity involves recognising the value of individual differences and managing them in the workplace.

Diversity context covers gender, age, language, ethnicity, cultural background, sexual orientation, religious belief and family responsibilities.

Australia's diversity is reflected in its mixture of cultures, languages, belief systems and values. The Australian Bureau of Statistics' 2006 Census (ABS 2008) indicated that, in a population of almost 21 million, 22.5% of people were born overseas. The official language in Australia, English, was the only language spoken by 78.5% of people counted in the 2006 Census. The remaining 21.5% spoke another language at home. This increasing ethnic, racial, religious and cultural diversity and greater levels of interaction across cultural and national boundaries mean that intercultural communication competence, combined with the willingness and ability to understand and manage differences, has become essential.

The diversity in both national and global interactions is one of the main challenges facing organisations, groups and individuals. Managers who handle diversity successfully create environments that value and utilise the contributions of people with different backgrounds, experiences and perspectives. They exercise leadership and management strategies that accommodate differences in the background, perspectives and family responsibilities of employees, and gather knowledge from the diversity of perspectives to generate new ideas and ways of doing things. The benefits of diversity include increased motivation and job satisfaction, retention of staff, and innovation from the broad range of ideas and insights.

The Diversity Council of Australia (2008) identifies the business benefits of diversity as '. . . access to new ideas and new ways of thinking; language skills; cultural knowledge and understanding; increased business networks; knowledge of business practices and protocols in overseas markets; intelligence about potential new markets'. While increasing diversity has advantages, it also brings challenges for people in understanding and managing differences in culture and communication.

Adler (2002, p. 99) stresses this point in her suggestions for identifying and managing workforce diversity. On the broader level, she advocates transcending 'cultural conditioning', moving beyond stereotypes and premature judging, and generally avoiding ethnocentric behaviours. On a more specific level, she advocates standing back from oneself, developing self-awareness by assessing one's own behaviour and questioning perceptions one may hold of people from different cultures, and then developing greater awareness of those other cultures.

13 *a*   Outline the priorities in the culture-general approach to culture learning.

    b   Discuss the limitations of the culture-specific approach.

14 *a*   Define the term 'diversity'.

    b   What are the business benefits of diversity?

15 *a*   Explain how an understanding of one's own cultural norms, values and beliefs, and those of people from different cultures, improves intercultural communication competence.

    b   Discuss three characteristics of effective intercultural communicators.

APPLY YOUR KNOWLEDGE

CULTURE IN THE WORKPLACE AND CULTURAL COMPETENCE

1   This exercise looks at cultural differences in the workplace and at the implications for interpersonal relations and cross-cultural management.

Work in pairs or small groups of four or five. (Try to ensure you have members from different cultural backgrounds.) Discuss differences in attitudes to work, relationships between senior and junior staff in the workplace (power distance), women in the workplace (masculine and feminine values), and competitive and cooperative practices (individualism and collectivism). How different are your attitudes, values and experiences? How do the differences impact on interpersonal and intercultural relations and communication in the workplace? Discuss strategies for managing these differences.

2   This activity considers how we achieve cultural competence.

In small groups, identify at least five competencies that you regard as relevant for working and communicating across cultures. Explore the different levels of competence among members of the group. Find out:

    a   How many members have lived or worked in another culture, and for how long? What have they learned about the culture? Has the experience changed perceptions they may previously have held?

    b   How many group members speak a second language? Has their language competence proved to be useful in intercultural interactions and communication? Has it been a 'fun' experience communicating in a second language?

    c   To what degree do members feel comfortable/uncomfortable when interacting with people from cultures that are different from their own? What are some of the areas of uncertainty and cultural confusion? What are some of the areas of synergy?

    d   What have been some of the exciting experiences in intercultural interactions? What have been some of the more frustrating and challenging experiences?

    e   What are some of the successful strategies (culture-general or culture-specific) that members have used to gain intercultural competence?

3   a   Use the checklist opposite to self-evaluate your intercultural communication competence.

    b   For those features ticked as 'Unsuccessful', prepare an action plan identifying how you can improve that aspect of your competence. Include a date by which you aim to develop that aspect.

INTERCULTURAL COMPETENCE

Key: VS = Very Successfully, S = Successfully, U = Unsuccessfully

I am able to:	VS	S	U
Accept that each culture has its own set of values, behaviours and symbols, and code of right and wrong			
Think about the impact of the other person's and my cultural values and norms			
Demonstrate openness and respect for others by participating in rituals of greeting and farewell, social and business contact			
Acknowledge differences in use of time, proximity and deference, and adapt in order to achieve goals, objectives and action			
Plan and share clear goals with teams that cross organisational, cultural and national boundaries			
Communicate via the range of communication media and channels that cross cultural and national boundaries			
Aim to achieve clarification and improved understanding in intercultural interactions			
Avoid the ethnocentric tendency to view my own culture as the 'central' culture and the only point of reference			
Appreciate both the diversities and commonalities between myself and those from other cultures			
Learn about differences and take a cultural-relativist approach in my intercultural communication			

Source: Prem Ramburuth, in J. Dwyer, *Communication in Business,* 3rd edn, Pearson Education Australia, Sydney, 2005, p. 44.

SUMMARY OF LEARNING OBJECTIVES

 EXPLAIN THE CONCEPT OF CULTURE AND DIFFERENTIATE ENCULTURATION, ACCULTURATION, ETHNOCENTRISM AND CULTURAL RELATIVISM

Enculturation is the process of learning and absorbing one's own culture both unconsciously and deliberately. Acculturation is the process of adjusting to the host culture by adopting its values, symbols and/or behaviours. Ethnocentrism is the belief that one's own culture is superior to any other. Cultural relativism is the opposite of ethnocentrism: it is the recognition of cultural differences and acceptance that each social group has its own set of cultural norms.

 DESCRIBE HIGH-CONTEXT AND LOW-CONTEXT CULTURAL STYLES AND DISCUSS COMPONENTS OF CULTURE RELEVANT TO INTERCULTURAL COMMUNICATION

In high-context cultures the words in the message convey only a limited portion of the meaning. How and where something is said, and the body language of the speaker, convey a large part of the message. In low-context cultures the meaning of the message is conveyed explicitly in words and the nonverbal message has less impact. There is high sensory involvement, with high-contact touch behaviour in high-context cultures and less sensory involvement in low-context cultures.

The components of culture relevant to intercultural communication are language and the meaning of words, the interpretation of nonverbal behaviours, the influence of context and the perception of power in the interaction. These elements function concurrently in any intercultural interaction.

 EXPLAIN THE CAUSES OF COMMUNICATION BARRIERS IN INTERCULTURAL COMMUNICATION

Hodgettes and Luthans (2003), Deresky (2002a) and Ferraro (2002) identify several common barriers, including linguistic, cultural, physical, perceptual, experiential, nonverbal and emotional factors. Stress has also been identified as a significant barrier. Stress arises from the high degree of uncertainty and threat involved in intercultural communication. Stereotypes, cultural practices, social institutions, value systems, ambiguity and conflict can also cause communication barriers.

 DISCUSS THE IMPLICATIONS OF COMPARATIVE VALUE DIMENSIONS FOR INTERCULTURAL COMMUNICATION

Hofstede (1984) identified four dimensions on which cultures differ in terms of values: power distance, individualism/collectivism, masculinity/femininity and uncertainty avoidance. His work provides one of the most important frameworks for grasping the complexity of intercultural interactions and communication. Trompenaars and Hampden-Turner (1997) identified five dimensions in which cultures differ. Three of these dimensions overlap Hofstede's model. The additional two are the specific versus diffuse dimension and the achievement versus ascription dimension. The findings of the study help global business leaders understand cultural diversity in the workplace,

 DESCRIBE THE CHARACTERISTICS OF INTERCULTURAL COMMUNICATION COMPETENCE AND EVALUATE STRATEGIES FOR DEVELOPING INTERCULTURAL COMPETENCE

Two approaches to intercultural competence are the *culture-specific* and the *culture-general*. The culture-specific approach focuses on learning basic facts and information about the new culture. This is useful but limited. The culture-general approach is much more intensive. It focuses on developing cultural awareness and sensitivity, behavioural flexibility and an 'other-orientation'.

KEY TERMS

ACTIVITIES AND QUESTIONS

1 Describe an incident you have experienced, witnessed or read about that involved miscommunication between people from different cultural groups. Suggest reasons for the miscommunication and ways in which it could have been avoided.

2 'Conscious learning is the easier to see and explain. In its simplest form it involves the ingredients of our culture that we were told about or that we read about . . . However, it is at the second level of learning, the unconscious level, that we learn the bulk of what we call culture' (Samovar & Porter 1991, p. 56). In groups of three, discuss these comments, referring to your own experiences of culture learning.

3   This activity identifies cultural norms and values, and analyses the impact of differences on intercultural communication in social and business contexts.

Find a partner from a cultural group different from your own. Exchange information about elements of culture that are important to both of you (work, family, study, relationships, status, money, marriage). How different are your beliefs, attitudes and value systems? Are you able to understand and appreciate the differences? Use Hofstede's cultural dimensions of individualism/collectivism, power distance, uncertainty avoidance and masculinity/femininity to facilitate understanding.

4   In small groups (3–5), discuss the following case studies. Comment on the cultural confusion or misunderstandings that could arise, and consider strategies for managing the situations.

a   Vincent Choy is a Singaporean manager in an American-owned multinational enterprise in the petroleum industry. He is extremely well educated, having studied and trained in management in Australia, the United States and Singapore. His written and spoken communication skills are of a high standard. He is very concerned at what he sees as the poor standard of written communication in the emails he has been receiving from his colleagues in the United States. He regards their informal style, the colloquial language used, the abbreviations and the 'over-friendliness' as unprofessional and inappropriate for business communication. Is there a basis for his concern?

b   Greetings between friends, family members and colleagues vary from culture to culture. John Langley is a friendly Australian businessman who is new to conducting business in Asian countries. He is eager to impress his customers and, when introduced to a group of Malaysian businessmen and women, firmly shakes hands with them. In greeting Lee Ng, a female member of the group, he gazes directly at her and shakes her hand, holding on to it a little longer while making polite inquiries about her business background. He continues greeting the rest of the group, unaware of Lee Ng's discomfort. Was his manner of communication appropriate, and what assumptions had he made?

c   Australians (Westerners in general) view business cards as a formality and a way of providing relevant information. Asians, on the other hand, regard business cards as a personal reflection of themselves, treating the cards with care and respect. When meeting a Chinese business associate, Peter Mann, an Australian business negotiator, casually accepts the business card given to him, takes a quick glance at it and immediately puts it in his back pocket for safe keeping. How could this action be interpreted?

d   John Dewey was a successful manager in a large multinational corporation in the construction industry in the United States. Because of his success within the company, he was offered a position in the company's subsidiary in Japan. On arrival, he called a meeting of his local managers and sought to get their ideas and input in developing a plan for the future direction of the company. He had always adopted a participative leadership style and believed in involving all his managers in the decision-making process. He was rather puzzled and concerned when he was met with a wall of silence and, despite repeated efforts, received no responses from the Japanese managers. His approach and managerial style had worked in the United States, so why was it not working in Japan?

e   In negotiating business deals, Westerners tend to focus on setting agendas and achieving outcomes in a given time frame, while in many other cultures, such as in Asia, business negotiations move at a much slower pace, with a focus on getting to know the person/s first. Sue Salamander represents a large multinational corporation based in Australia. She is instructed by her parent American company to conclude a major business deal during a brief visit to Taiwan. To make the most of the short time available, she insists on conducting business negotiations during lunch and dinner. Are her actions appropriate in this context? Could she, or should she, have taken a different approach?

f   The notion of being 'on time' and definitions of punctuality vary from culture to culture. Robert Blake, senior manager of CompuSoft Inc., a computer software company in North

Dakota, in the United States, is keen to negotiate a joint venture with Amigo Inc., a software company in Mexico City. Knowing that meetings do not always start on time, Robert Blake arrives half an hour late for his appointment, much to the annoyance of Jose Fernandez, Director of the Board of Amigo Inc. His experience of doing business with Americans was that they were extremely conscious of time and were always punctual, and he had made a special effort to be on time for this important meeting. What is the basis of the misunderstanding and how could it have been avoided?

Source: Prem Ramburuth, in J. Dwyer, *Communication in Business*, 3rd edn, Pearson Education Australia, Sydney, 2005, p. 46.

EXPLORING THE WEB

1 a Visit the *Journal of Intercultural Communication* online at <www.immi.se/intercultural> and *Research and Practice in Human Resource Management* at <http://rphrm.curtin.edu.au>.

   b Find two journal articles that address current issues in intercultural communication.

   c Prepare a 200–300 word evaluative critique for each article.

   d Prepare a brief introduction that identifies the two articles and why you chose them.

2 Visit Diversity Council Australia at <www.dca.org.au> to learn more about diversity.

   a Why does diversity matter?

   b View the latest publications and resources. Choose a current issue relating to diversity and describe its likely impact.

3 View the websites of two organisations that have gone global:

   Nokia at <www.nokia.com.au>
   Oracle at <www.oracle.com>

   a What features do the sites have in common?

   b How do these organisations engage and meet the needs of a culturally diverse audience?

   c What barriers (if any) might either site create or reinforce?

PROJECT WORK

This chapter emphasises the need for intercultural intelligence and empathy to build successful global business relationships. Your project is to design and promote a Going Global Agenda for a specific organisation that will create a positive climate for both global expansion and cultural conditioning. Complete the following four tasks.

1 Compile a Going Global Checklist appropriate to the industry you have selected.

2 Design a Going Global Agenda for the specific organisation you have chosen.

3 Create a PowerPoint presentation to pitch this agenda to a management meeting.

4 Prepare a report to accompany the PowerPoint presentation as back-up notes. This report should explain the detail and rationale for your proposed global agenda and include a recommended action plan.

Some suggestions for your PowerPoint slides and report headings might be:

- Why should we care about going global?
- How we can develop our intercultural advantage?
- Who can help us go global?
- What are some good examples of firms who have gone global?
- When should we think about going global?
- Where should we focus?
- What steps do we need to take for our Going Global action plan?

BIBLIOGRAPHY

Adler, N. 2002. *International Dimensions of Organizational Behavior*, South-Western, Cincinnati, Ohio.

Augsberger, D.W. 1995. *Conflict Mediation Across Cultures: Pathways and Patterns*, Westminster John Knox Press, Louisville, Kentucky.

Austrade. *Tips for Doing Business in China*, last update 7 November 2007, www.austrade.gov.au/, viewed 19 January 2008.

Australian Bureau of Statistics, *Selected 2006 Census Facts and Figures*, ABS, Canberra, www.abs.gov.au, viewed 21 January 2008.

Beamer, L. & Varner, I. 2001. *Intercultural Communication in the Global Workplace*, McGraw-Hill, Boston.

Beamer, L. & Varner, I. 2006. *Intercultural Communication in the Global Workplace*, 4th edn, McGraw-Hill, USA.

Berry, J.W. 2002. *Applying Research Findings Across Cultures*, Cambridge University Press, UK.

Chaney, L.H. & Martin, J.S. 2000. *Intercultural Business Communication*, Prentice Hall, New Jersey, 1998.

Chen, G.M. & Starosta, W.J. 1998. *Foundations of Intercultural Communication*, Allyn & Bacon.

Curtin University of Technology. *Research and Practice in Human Resource Management*, http://rphrm.curtin.edu.au, viewed 21 January 2008.

Deresky, H. 2002a. *International Management: Managing across Borders and Cultures*, Prentice Hall, Upper Saddle River, New Jersey.

Deresky, H. 2002b. *Global Management: Strategic and Interpersonal*, Prentice Hall, Upper Saddle River, New Jersey.

Diversity Council of Australia. *Celebrate Diversity With DCA's Diversity Calendar*, www.dca.org.au/, viewed 21 January 2008.

Dodd, C.H. 1998. *Dynamics of Intercultural Communication*, McGraw-Hill, Boston.

Dodd, P. Interview: 'Difficulties Encountered in Intercultural Business Communication', Sydney, January 1998.

Ferraro, G.P. 2002. *The Cultural Dimension of International Behavior*, Pearson Education, Upper Saddle River, New Jersey.

Fletcher, R. & Brown, L. 2008. *International Marketing: An Asia-Pacific Perspective*, 4th edn, Pearson Education Australia, Sydney.

Griffin, E. 2000. *A First Look at Communication Theory*, 4th edn, McGraw-Hill, USA.

Gudykunst, W.B. 1985. 'A model of uncertainty reduction in intercultural encounters', *Journal of Language and Social Psychology*, Vol. 4, pp. 79–97.

Hall, E.T. 1959. *The Silent Language*, Doubleday, New York.

Hall, E.T. 1976. *Beyond Culture*, Anchor Press, New York.

Hall, E.T. 1990. *Understanding Cultural Differences*, Intercultural Press, USA.

Harris, P.R. & Moran, R.T. 1996. *Managing Cultural Differences*, Gulf, Houston.

Hill, C.W.L. 2003. *International Business: Competing in the Global Marketplace*, Irwin, Chicago.

Hodgetts, R. & Luthans, F. 2003. *International Management: Culture, Strategy and Behavior*, McGraw-Hill, Boston.

Hoebel, E.A. & Frost, E.L. 1976. *Cultural and Social Anthropology*, McGraw-Hill, New York.

Hoecklin, L. 1995. *Managing Cultural Differences: Strategies for Competitive Advantage*, Addison-Wesley, Wokingham, England.

Hofstede, G. 1984. *Culture's Consequences: International Differences in Work-Related Values*, Sage Publications, Newbury Park, California.

Hofstede, G. 1991. *Cultures and Organisations: Software of the Mind*, McGraw-Hill, London.

Hofstede, G. 2001. *Culture's Consequences: Comparing Values, Behaviors, Institutions, and Organizations across Nations*, Sage Publications, Newbury Park, California.

Irwin, H. 1996. *Communicating with Asia*, Allen & Unwin, Sydney.

Jandt, F.E. (ed.). 2003. *An Introduction to Intercultural Communication: Identities in a Global Community*, Sage Publications, USA.

Journal of Intercultural Communication Online, www.immi.se/intercultural, viewed 20 January 2008.

Knapp, K. & Knapp-Potthoff, A. 1987. 'Instead of an introduction: conceptual issues in analysing intercultural communication', in K. Knapp, W. Enninger & A. Knapp-Potthoff (eds). *Analysing Intercultural Communication*, Mouton de Gruyter, Berlin.

Loden, M. 1995. *Implementing Diversity*, McGraw-Hill, USA.

Loden, M. & Rosener, J.B. 1991. *Workforce America! Managing Diversity as a Vital Resource*, Business One Irwin, USA.

Lustig, M. & Koester, J. 1999. *Intercultural Competence: Interpersonal Communication across Cultures*, Harper Collins, New York.

Manev, I.F. & Stevenson, W.B. 2001. 'Balancing ties: boundary spanning and influence in the organisation's network of communication', *Journal of Business Communication*, Vol. 38, Issue 2, pp. 183–205.

Martin, J.N. & Nakayama, T.K. 2003. *Intercultural Communication in Contexts*, 3rd edn, McGraw-Hill, USA.

Martin, J.N. & Nakayama, T.K. 2007. *Experiencing Intercultural Communication: An Introduction*, 3rd edn, McGraw-Hill, USA.

Nehru, J. 2002. 'Visit to the US', in N. Adler, *International Dimensions of Organizational Behavior*, South-Western, Cincinnati, Ohio.

Nicholas, K. 2008. 'Tyranny of distance still rules', *Australian Financial Review*, 7 February, pp. S20–21.

Ong, I.W. & Tan, A. 2007. 'Listening across cultures', *Today's Manager*, June/July, pp. 27–28.

Orbe, M.P. & Bruess, C.J. 2007. *Contemporary Issues in Interpersonal Communication*, Oxford University Press, USA.

Porter, R.E. 1976. 'An Overview of intercultural Communication', in L. Samovar & R.E. Porter (eds), *Intercultural Communication: A Reader*, Wadsworth, California.

Ramburuth, P. 2005. Cited in J. Dwyer, *Communication in Business*, 3rd edn, Pearson Education Australia, Sydney, pp. 32–33.

Ramburuth, P. 2000. 'Cross Cultural and Diversity Management in Australian-Based MNEs: Competencies, Capabilities and Challenges', paper presented at the Academy of International Business (AIB) 2000 Annual Conference, Texas, USA.

Ramburuth, P. & Welch, C. 2005. *Case Book in International Business: Australia and Asia Pacific Perspectives*, Pearson Education Australia, Sydney.

Samovar, L.A. & Porter, R.E. 1991. *Communication between Cultures*, 3rd edn, Wadsworth, California.

Samovar, L.A. & Porter, R.E. 2001. *Communication between Cultures*, 4th edn, Wadsworth, California.

Samovar, L.A., Porter, R.E. & McDaniel, E.R. 2006. *Intercultural Communication: A Reader*, 11th edn, Wadsworth, California.

Sinclair, A. & Wilson, V. 1999. *The Culture-Inclusive Classroom*, Melbourne Business School, University of Melbourne, Melbourne.

Trompenaars, F. & Hampden-Turner, C. 1997. *Riding the Waves of Culture: Understanding Cultural Diversity in Business*, Nicholas Brealey, London.

Young, Y.K. 2001. *Becoming Intercultural: An Integrative Theory of Communication and Cross-Cultural Adaptation*, Sage, USA.

3

Emotional intelligence, self-awareness and assertion

LEARNING OBJECTIVES

After studying this chapter you should be able to:

1 ▷ describe the role of emotional intelligence in building relationships and improving performance

2 ▷ explain how self-concept, self-disclosure, self-esteem, self-regulation and self-motivation contribute to personal competence

3 ▷ explain how the interpersonal qualities of positiveness and empathy contribute to social competence

4 ▷ distinguish assertive, aggressive and passive behaviours, and identify reasons for using verbal assertion

5 ▷ describe how valuing diversity and networking improves social awareness and social skills in business interactions.

OUTLINE

Emotional intelligence

Self-awareness

Interpersonal competence

VIEWPOINT: WHAT IS EMOTIONAL INTELLIGENCE?

'When considering effective leaders, most of us can quite readily think of examples from the sporting arena with comments such as "performs well under pressure", "sets very high standards for him/herself and the team", "makes the most of his or her ability always giving 100%" and "a good team player". In simple terms these are all characteristics of emotional intelligence.

Goleman describes a model of emotional intelligence comprising four domains—self-awareness, self-management, social awareness and relationship management. The first two of these domains are personal. The second two domains are social and concern a person's ability to manage relationships with others. Social awareness covers empathy, for example, in the ability to consider employees' feelings in the process of making intelligent decisions either on a one-to-one basis or as a group. Relationship management covers the ability to communicate, influence, collaborate and work with colleagues.'

Excerpt from S. Davies, 'Emotional intelligence and leadership', *CEO Forum Group*, www.ceoforum.com.au, viewed 17 February 2008. Reproduced with permission from CEO Forum Group.

The success of a business organisation depends largely on the behaviour of the people in it. Currently, many claims are being made that emotional intelligence 'may be the best predictor of success in life'. Mayer (1999) suggests that, until these claims can be substantiated through research, 'emotional intelligence—if substantiated—broadens our understanding of what it means to be smart. It means that within some of us who are labelled "romantics", "highly sensitive" or "bleeding hearts", serious information processing is taking place'. Allen (2005, p. 19) says: 'Personal and interpersonal skills come under the umbrella of "emotional intelligence" defined as the personal skills, characteristics and competencies that are responsible for the ways in which you behave, how you feel, how you relate to others and how well you perform in the job.'

OBJECTIVE 1 ▶
Describe the role of emotional intelligence in building relationships and improving performance

EMOTIONAL INTELLIGENCE

Emotional intelligence is a different way of being smart. It includes knowing what your feelings are and using your feelings to make decisions in life (Goleman 1998).

Singh (2006, p. 21) states: 'Today it is taken for granted that you have adequate IQ, that is, the technical know-how to do your job. The focus instead is on your EQ—personal qualities such as initiative, empathy, motivation and leadership.' Anyone in business or any other type of organisation with these personal qualities is able to build positive relationships and collaborate with others to get the job done. 'Emotional intelligence is what gives a person the competitive edge' (2006, p. 20).

Hay and McBer (2004) concur: 'Emotional intelligence is more than 85% of what sets star performers apart from the average.' Those with emotional intelligence have the social awareness and social skills to interact effectively in different contexts. In personal, social and business relationships, they are able to communicate well, build satisfying relationships and make effective decisions.

Emotionally intelligent leaders are dependable, take responsibility and solve problems. They are able to cope with the fast-paced business environment, stay calm in a crisis and move on positively from difficult situations. Emotionally intelligent managers are empathetic; they motivate team members and earn respect. They are open-minded and adaptable, appreciate diversity, and handle stress positively. Learning to recognise emotions and to empathise with others, developing high self-esteem, managing emotional upsets and anger are all emotional skills that managers should learn (Singh 2006, p. 73).

In any context, our relationships are built through our *interpersonal communication*. Interpersonal communication is usually based on the fulfilment of two broad types of needs: other-directed needs and self-directed needs. The relationship is built as these needs are fulfilled.

In 2006 a survey of Australian employers found that the qualities employers were looking for in graduates included emotional intelligence (self-awareness, strength of character, confidence and motivation), teamwork skills, leadership skills, interpersonal and communication skills. Other selection criteria included cultural alignment, activities (intra and extra-curricular), academic qualifications, work experience, critical reasoning and analytical skills, problem solving, lateral thinking, technical skills, passion, knowledge of industry, drive, commitment, attitude and values fit (Graduate Careers Australia, 2006). The key selection criteria of Australian employers include not only specialist, technical and functional skills, but also emotional intelligence. In today's business environment, emotional intelligence and competence are related positively to job performance at all levels.

Emotional awareness

Emotions are reactions to an object or event. They are intense feelings that are directed at someone or something. Weiss and Cropanzano (1996, pp. 20–22) discuss six basic emotions: anger, fear, sadness, happiness, disgust and surprise. While other words are used to describe emotions, these six emotions are universally accepted. An emotion is experienced when we are conscious of a feeling such as joy, sorrow or love. People who know how they feel and are able to label that feeling with words have **emotional awareness**. Hein (2003, p. 1) states: 'At its highest level it means being able to predict our feelings in advance.' He identifies six levels of emotional awareness:

Emotional awareness means knowing specifically how you feel.

1. feeling the feeling
2. acknowledging the feeling
3. identifying the feeling
4. accepting the feeling
5. reflecting the feeling
6. forecasting feelings.

Hein (2003) describes emotionally sensitive people as those who are aware of their feelings and are able to acknowledge those feelings. Acknowledgment of negative feelings can lead emotionally aware people to their cause and possible solution. By identifying negative emotions with words, it is possible to think about the feeling, accept it and become more in control. The next level, *reflecting*, enables people to learn about their feelings, identify those feelings and take actions in response to them. The ability to forecast feelings lets us make decisions that will avoid negative feelings and lead to long-term satisfaction and happiness. How often have you said, 'I know I'm going to regret this' or 'I know I will feel better if I . . .'. Those who listen to their inner messages are able to make better decisions.

Mayer (1999, p. 1) defines **emotional intelligence** as 'the capacity to reason with emotion in four areas: to perceive emotion, to integrate it in thought, to understand and to manage it'. Those who operate in the first area and *perceive* emotion are able to identify emotions in faces, music and stories. The second area, *emotional facilitation of thought*, allows people to associate emotions with other mental sensations such as taste and colour. The third area, *emotional understanding*, comes from knowing those emotions that are similar or opposites and understanding the messages they convey. Those who operate in the fourth area, *emotional management*, know the implications of social acts on feelings and are willing to regulate emotion in self and others.

> **Emotional intelligence** is the capacity to reason with emotion.

Emotional intelligence competency clusters

The way we respond to people, environmental demands and pressures is called emotional intelligence. The level of emotional intelligence varies between people. Goleman (1996, cited in O'Neil 1996) stated:

> Emotional intelligence is a different way of being smart. It includes knowing what your feelings are and using your feelings to make decisions in life. It's being able to manage distressing moods well and control impulses. It's being motivated and remaining hopeful and optimistic when you have setbacks in working towards goals. It's empathy; knowing what the people around you are feeling. And it's social skill—getting along well with other people, managing emotions in relationships, being able to persuade or lead others.

He defined this further in 1998: '. . . emotional intelligence is the capacity for recognising our own feelings and those of others, for motivating ourselves and for managing emotions effectively in ourselves and in others.'

Emotional competence frameworks divide **emotional competence** into two broad categories:

> **Emotional competence** is the capacity to manage self and relationships effectively.

1. *personal competence*, which is reflected in our self-awareness and self-management
2. *social competence*, which is reflected in our social awareness and relationship management.

Goleman, a proponent of the application of emotional intelligence to business, describes five emotional components—self-awareness, self-regulation, motivation, empathy and social skill (Goleman 1998, p. 88). These essential components are classified under the headings *personal competence* and *social competence* in Table 3.1.

Controversies surrounding emotional intelligence

Proponents of emotional competence view it as a learned capacity and believe it matters twice as much as IQ plus technical skills combined. Emotional intelligence is still a relatively new concept, however, and further research and evaluation of findings is needed to tighten up some of the concepts (Grubb & McDaniel 2007).

The current use of emotional intelligence measures in organisational settings for selection and promotion raises at least three issues. First, it needs to be acknowledged that many emotional intelligence tests are 'unvalidated or poorly validated' (Sternberg 2003, p. xii). Goleman (1995, 1998) identified two issues pertinent to learning more about emotional intelligence. Learning about emotional intelligence will promote prosocial behaviour and a positive ethical outlook in most people. However, there are no doubt instances of Machiavellian types who use emotional intelligence abilities, such as empathy, and the social skill of persuasion 'to lead people astray or manipulate them' or to 'clamber over others to the top of the ladder'.

Furthermore, without a specific theory or framework of emotional competence, leaders and managers may give staff vague or confusing feedback on issues relating to emotional competence, 'people skills' or 'leadership style'. In order to improve on any ability relating to emotional as well as technical competence, people need realistic feedback about their abilities as well as their progress.

Table 3.1: Emotional competencies—the basis of emotional intelligence	
Personal competence: Managing ourselves	
Self-awareness	*Emotional awareness:* Recognising our emotions and their effects
	Accurate self-assessment: Knowing our strengths and limits
	Self-confidence: Sureness about one's self-worth and capabilities
Self-regulation	*Self-control:* Managing disruptive emotions and impulses
	Trustworthiness: Maintaining standards of honesty and integrity
	Conscientiousness: Taking responsibility for personal performance
	Adaptability: Flexibility in handling change
	Innovativeness: Being comfortable with and open to novel ideas and new information
Self-motivation	*Achievement drive:* Striving to improve or meet a standard of excellence
	Commitment: Aligning with the goals of the group or organisation
	Initiative: Readiness to act on opportunities
	Optimism: Persistence in pursuing goals despite obstacles and setbacks
Social competence: Managing relationships	
Social awareness	*Empathy:* Sensing others' feelings and perspective and taking an active interest in their concerns
	Service orientation: Anticipating, recognising and meeting customers' needs
	Developing others: Sensing what others need in order to develop, and bolstering their abilities
	Leveraging diversity: Cultivating opportunities through diverse people
	Political awareness: Reading a group's emotional currents and power relationships
Social skills	*Influence:* Wielding effective tactics for persuasion
	Communication: Sending clear and convincing messages
	Leadership: Inspiring and guiding individuals and groups
	Change catalyst: Initiating or managing change
	Conflict management: Negotiating and resolving disagreements
	Building bonds: Nurturing instrumental relationships
	Collaboration and cooperation: Working with others towards shared goals
	Team capabilities: Creating group synergy in pursuing collective goals

Source: Adapted from Goleman (1998), Emotional Intelligence Consortium (2008).

REVIEW QUESTIONS

1 *a*   Define the terms 'emotional intelligence' and 'emotional competence'.

    b   Briefly explain the six levels of emotional awareness.

2 *a*   Goleman says a successful manager must master five key areas of competency to develop emotional intelligence. Identify each area, giving an example of how the skills involved can enhance workplace performance.

    b   Identify the characteristics of managers you believe to be 'emotionally competent'.

3   Discuss at least one argument against the use of emotional intelligence as a predictor of successful performance in business.

SELF-AWARENESS

How people see themselves—their self-concept—will influence the way they relate to others, their capacity or readiness for self-disclosure, their ability to give and receive feedback in interpersonal relationships, and their level of emotional intelligence. It is useful, therefore, to begin this intrapersonal competence section of the chapter by considering how people can become more self-aware and develop a more positive self-concept. Intrapersonal communication is communication with oneself. It is a mental process internal to the communicator. The individual is both sender and receiver. Intrapersonal communication activities include self-talk, daydreaming, speaking aloud, writing, and making gestures while thinking.

Self-concept

A factor that has a significant impact on interpersonal behaviour and relationships is **self-concept**, which comes from past experience and interactions with others. From our numerous interactions in a variety of contexts (home, university, work, leisure) we establish our self-concept and our identity. Part of that identity is created, sustained and changed by our interactions with others. Self is not 'a solid, given entity that moves from one situation to another. It is rather a process, continuously created and recreated in each social situation that one enters, held together by the slender thread of memory' (Berger 1967, p. 124). Our self-concept is defined and maintained by our relationships. Our skill in communicating and interacting with others makes an important contribution to our self-concept, and our self-concept impacts upon our effectiveness in interpersonal communication. While some people have a positive self-concept, with positive 'self-talk' and feelings about themselves and self-acceptance, others have a negative self-concept, use negative 'self-talk', and feel inadequate and inferior.

The way others act towards us can enhance or decrease our self-concept. Putnis and Petelin (1999) say that it is possible to distinguish three elements of self-concept:

1   the perceived self—our view of ourselves

2   the desired self—what we would like to be

3   the presented self—our public behaviours.

DEVELOPING A POSITIVE SELF-CONCEPT

A person with a positive self-concept is self-directed and able to communicate effectively. Carl Rogers (1961) described people with a positive self-concept as fully functioning individuals able to make decisions for themselves about what they want to do. Fully functioning people are open to experience and accepting of themselves because they can:

- identify themselves clearly
- define themselves positively
- behave effectively in different situations.

> **OBJECTIVE 2**
> Explain how self-concept, self-disclosure, self-esteem, self-regulation and self-motivation contribute to personal competence

Intrapersonal communication is the active internal involvement of the individual in the symbolic processing of messages.

Self-concept is the mental image or idea that people have of themselves.

Fully functioning people are self-directed and able to make choices for themselves.

These dimensions are expanded in Table 3.2.

According to Hall and Gardner (1970, p. 534), Carl Rogers believed that for 'healthy integrated adjustment' people had to be continually assessing their experiences 'to see whether they require a change in value structure. Any fixed set of values will tend to prevent the person from reacting effectively to new experiences. One must be flexible in order to adjust appropriately to the changing conditions of life.' Singh (2006, p. 23) believes, 'It is not possible to feel comfortable at the workplace if you are not comfortable in your own skin.'

The behaviour of people with a positive self-concept flows from their perception of past and present experiences and from the personal meanings attached to those experiences. They are self-aware and their positive self-concept arises from positive self-evaluation, self-esteem, self-respect and self-acceptance. They are able to build open relationships and a positive communication climate. They are able to respond flexibly and behave effectively in different situations. They are aware of their own feelings and able to acknowledge the feelings of others.

Self-disclosure

People may learn a lot or very little when they speak to others. It depends on how much information they are willing to disclose about *themselves*.

Self-disclosure involves showing reactions and feelings about the present situation and giving any information about the past that affects this reaction. This openness comes from an acceptance and appreciation of self. Self-disclosure can lead to increased self-awareness and self-understanding.

Self-disclosure does not mean that people have to reveal intimate details about their past. It means letting the other person know their feelings and reactions to the current situation. Ideas and feelings are shared. Self-disclosure provides feedback to others on the effect of their behaviour. The amount of self-disclosure is affected by the communication climate. In a positive climate, people disclose more; in a negative climate, they disclose less.

Before self-disclosing, think about the reasons and motivation for the self-disclosure. Disclosure at an appropriate time enables the other person to give open and honest responses and to self-disclose if they so desire. Self-disclosure at an appropriate time and in the right context can lead to an improvement in:

> **Self-disclosure** involves revealing feelings and reactions to the present situation.

Table 3.2: Three strategies used by those with a positive self-concept		
Clear identification of self by:	*Positive definition of self by:*	*Effective behaviour by:*
Gaining insight into my own behaviour	Valuing myself and acknowledging the parts that make up the total self	Communicating my attitudes, values and feelings
Identifying influences that have shaped me so far	Being confident in my abilities and skills	Responding to others without judging or patronising them
Knowing my needs	Taking responsibility for my own behaviour	Seeking feedback from others
Knowing my wants	Building my self-esteem	Listening to the ideas and feelings of others
Being aware of my feelings	Being optimistic	Disagreeing without disrespect for the values of others
Being aware of my interpretations	Discussing my positive qualities	Building open, positive relationships without boasting

- communication skills
- self-awareness
- self-confidence
- relationships.

On the other hand, self-disclosure can be threatening because people feel they may:

- expose a weakness
- be ridiculed
- lose self-control
- damage a relationship
- appear inadequate
- have the self-disclosure used against them
- face personal and social rejection.

Self-disclosure and feedback increase understanding and lead to more open communication. Closer and more satisfying relationships can be established. Lewis and Slade (1994, p. 101) define self-disclosure as the intentional disclosure of personal information about yourself to someone else, usually in a one-to-one situation. They comment that 'the higher degree of trust in the relationship, the more likely it is that self-disclosing behaviour will be considered appropriate'. They state that people with a positive self-concept are more likely to be open and self-disclosing. Research has also shown that there are differences in self-disclosure between men and women—women are much more likely to disclose more about themselves. Jourard (1974, p. 224) says that an essential factor in people disclosing themselves to others is the perception that the other person is trustworthy. Security and self-esteem are also important factors. However, he also comments that some people feel more secure disclosing themselves to strangers.

DeVito (2000, pp. 81–82) lists various factors that affect self-disclosure: group size, liking, receiver relationships, age, dyadic effect (the reciprocal effect), competence, personality, topics, culture and gender. He believes that self-disclosure is significant because of the rewards it gives. 'Self-disclosure may bring self-knowledge, increase your ability to cope, improve communication and increase relationship depth' (p. 83).

A further concept considered by Lewis and Slade (1994, p. 102) is **self-presentation**—that is, the way you choose to present yourself when communicating. We have specific identities that we choose in any given situation. Lewis and Slade comment that '[t]he choices we make about self-presentation are also linked to the preservation and enhancement of our self-esteem'. This concept is linked with the idea of **self-monitoring**: that is, the conscious attempt to project a particular image. Self-monitoring depends on how you perceive yourself, and whether you are a high self-monitor or a low self-monitor. DeVito (2000, p. 167) defines self-monitoring as 'the manipulation of the image that you present to others in your interpersonal interactions'. High self-monitors adjust their behaviour according to feedback from others.

Self-presentation is the way you choose to present yourself in a specific context.

Self-monitoring is the manipulation of the image that each person presents to others in their interpersonal interactions.

Factors impacting on self-concept

Lewis and Slade (1994, p. 99) define self-image as 'how a person perceives themselves at a particular time' and an individual's self-concept as 'the set of relatively stable perceptions they hold of themselves'. Self-esteem they regard as 'the extent to which we approve of and accept ourselves' (1994, p. 100); it is the evaluative part of the self-concept—the negative and positive judgments we make about ourselves.

The development of self-concept as a result of experiences as a child and in the teenage years is explained by two complementary theories, *reflected appraisal* and *social comparison*. Reflected appraisal theory argues that self-concepts are formed as a result 'of receiving both approving and critical feedback from "significant others" with whom we grow up'—for example, parents, siblings, peers, friends, workmates. Lewis and Slade point out that as we grow older we are more likely to be selective in accepting others' evaluation and 'the importance of these appraisals we get from others in forming our self-concept changes' (1994, p. 100). We tend to accept appraisals that are based on competency: for example, from a lecturer or from close friends, rather than acquaintances. In support of this theory, Gamble and Gamble (1996, p. 50) comment:

> If people who are important to you have made you feel accepted, valued, worthwhile, lovable, and significant, you have probably developed a positive self-concept. On the other hand, if those who are important to you have made you feel left out, small, worthless, unloved, or insignificant, you have probably developed a negative self-concept.

They point out that self-concept is the mental picture you have of yourself and is 'easily translated into the faces or masks you wear, the roles you play, and the ways you behave' (p. 51).

Social comparison theory differs in that it maintains that our self-concept is shaped by our choosing particular reference groups with which to compare our performance. We may compare our athletic prowess against other athletes, or other competencies in discussion with various groups. In some groups we may consider ourselves superior and in others we may feel inhibited and inferior.

Beebe and colleagues (1999, p. 38) believe that self-concept 'is your subjective description of who you *think* you are—it is filtered through your own perceptions'. They say that self-concept can be viewed as 'the labels we consistently use to describe ourselves to others'. Who you are, they say, is shaped by learned constructs that are reflected in your attitudes, beliefs and values, as shown in Table 3.2.

Suh (2002, p. 1378) comments, 'All individuals have multiple views of themselves.' Research into Western cultures shows that 'people with a more consistent self-view had a more clear self-knowledge, were more assertive and, most notably, had self-experiences that were less affected by the perspectives of others'. Suh's conclusion was that, to achieve optimal psychological functioning, a person needs to have a consistent self-identity across the different spheres of experiences (p. 1389).

Self-esteem

Esteem is the regard or favourable opinion in which a person is held by others. Self-esteem is respect for self.

Self-concept is also affected by self-esteem. Our self-esteem is based on self-respect and respect for others. It is enhanced by the esteem received from others. **Esteem** was identified by Maslow (1954) as a higher-order need after the satisfaction of physiological security and social needs (see Figure 14.2 in Chapter 14).

Wilson (1972, pp. 162–3) comments that 'Maslow regarded "esteem needs" as the need for a "stable, firmly based, high evaluation of themselves, for self-respect . . . and for the esteem of others"'. Lane (1987, p. 66) asserts that an essential requirement of effective relationships with others is the acquisition of esteem, and 'to satisfy our esteem needs we have to see ourselves as worthy and be recognised by others as worthy'. The ability to communicate effectively is enhanced by the acquisition of the traits of high self-esteem, such as expecting to be well received by others, being able to express opinions readily, confident in one's perceptions and reactions, and able to realistically assess one's social skills and personal characteristics.

According to Lewis and Slade (1994, p. 101), 'People with positive self-esteem are likely to think well of others, while those with poor self-esteem will be likely to evaluate others negatively'. Further, the expectations that people hold are likely to influence the outcomes of their interpersonal interactions. This effect is known as the *self-fulfilling prophecy*. It can be seen in interviewing situations—those who expect to perform badly will often do so. Lewis and Slade point out that 'people with positive self-esteem are more likely to evaluate their own performance favourably, to work harder for authority figures who demand higher levels of performance, [and] are also more inclined not to feel threatened by others who hold superior social positions'. Gamble and Gamble (1996, p. 51) concur that 'if you feel you have little worth, you probably expect to be taken advantage of, stepped on, or otherwise demeaned by others. When you expect the worst, you usually get the worst.' DeVito (2000, p. 78) agrees that 'success breeds success'. He further comments that 'increasing your self-esteem will help you function more effectively in school, in your interpersonal relationships, and in your career'.

The Johari window

An approach to understanding our self-concept is offered by the **Johari window**, named after the theory's originators, Joseph Luft and Harry Ingram. This model divides the elements that make up each person's self-concept into two broad categories:

1 the areas of yourself known to you—labelled as *self*
2 the areas of yourself known to others—labelled as *others*.

The **Johari window** explains the two broad divisions (further divided into four sections) that make up our self-concept.

The Johari window is used to divide these two categories further to make four sections. These are shown as four small windows in the Johari window (Figure 3.1):

- public arena
- blind spot
- hidden area
- unknown area.

The *public arena* involves those areas known to yourself and to others. Free and open communication takes place in these areas. The *hidden area* involves the things you are aware of but hide from others. You build a front or a cover for hurts, disappointments and weaknesses, avoiding self-disclosure to others. Self-image or self-concept is created from the information in the public arena and the hidden area, the two areas known to you. Details disclosed to others are in the public arena, while those things you know about yourself but will not disclose to others are hidden.

The *blind spot* covers those areas unknown to yourself but known to others. You are unaware of some of your actions and feelings, while others perceive and know how you react. This window suggests that each person has a blind spot—that is, no knowledge of certain characteristics, even though others may identify them from the public arena. The *unknown area* covers those aspects of yourself about which you and others are unaware. This window holds the unknown reasons for certain behaviours.

Self-disclosure leads to an increase in what others know about you and reduces the size of the hidden or undisclosed area. It occurs when a person is willing to be open with another person.

When feedback is received from others it leads to understanding; the size of the blind area is reduced and the size of the open area or public arena is increased further. In situations where people self-disclose to others and receive feedback from them, the known area in the window increases, while the unknown and blind areas decrease.

Self-regulation and self-motivation

As well as being self-aware, emotionally competent people are self-regulating and self-motivating. They are able to keep disruptive emotions and impulses under control and to maintain standards

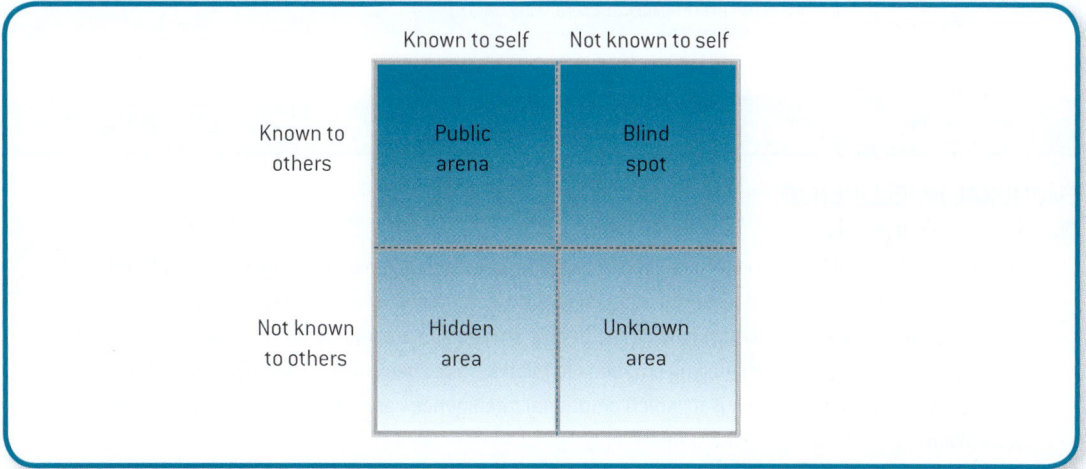

Figure 3.1: The Johari window

of honesty and integrity. They are comfortable with new information, able to adapt to change, show initiative, and commit to organisation or group goals.

The complexity in the modern workplace requires flexible and adaptable responses to changing situations or obstacles. Adaptability includes:

- being objective and relying on the facts of the issue
- following a process or procedure, rather than reacting emotionally
- responding thoughtfully and appropriately to the situation
- managing challenging and stressful situations
- applying a reality check as you solve problems
- exercising self-control and persistence in pursuing goals.

Applying a reality check means being able to use data and information to give a response within workplace parameters. These parameters may include legal and organisational requirements. They may also include budget restraints, resource capability and time constraints.

Stone (2003, p. 670) states: 'The challenge for every employee is to find the level of stress that stimulates productivity without damaging health.' He also points out that, to avoid the adverse effects of stress, employees must learn to 'switch off'. Relaxation can be learned. When time is managed badly, it can lead to stress. The ability to manage time can be learned. Workplace stress can be a positive force encouraging change and leading to improved performance. However, it can also be destructive, creating barriers to performance and leading to burnout. Stone (2003, p. 672) suggests: 'Employees can live with stress quite happily if they plan, keep a balance between work and leisure and practice stress-reducing exercise and habits regularly.' Clearly, stress that improves your performance is useful, while stress that lowers your performance is not.

REVIEW QUESTIONS

4 **a** Explain the term 'self-concept'.

b What are the three elements of self-concept?

c How might an individual develop a more positive self-concept?

d Briefly explain how 'reflected appraisal' and 'social comparison' impact on self-concept.

5 **a** How can self-disclosure lead to increased self-awareness and self-esteem?

b Why is self-disclosure a gradual process in a relationship?

6 **a** What are the four parts in the Johari window? Explain what they represent.

b Briefly explain how the size of the different parts can be increased or decreased.

APPLY YOUR KNOWLEDGE

EMOTIONAL INTELLIGENCE

1 Work in small groups.

O'Neil (1996) describes emotional intelligence as 'being able to manage distressing moods well and control impulses. It's being motivated and remaining hopeful and optimistic when you have setbacks in working towards goals. It's empathy, knowing what the people around you are feeling. And it's social skill—getting along well with other people, managing emotions in relationships, being able to persuade or lead others.' Read the quote and discuss ways in which emotional intelligence can improve performance in the workplace.

2 Work individually.

Explain the three strategies used by people with a positive self-concept.

3 Work individually.
  a Write on six different pieces of paper different answers to the basic question: 'Who am I?' Each separate piece of paper should contain descriptors of how you see your many and varied roles.
  b Give the number six to the role you would be most willing to discard. Continue numbering the roles, making number one the role you would least like to discard.
  c What insights does this activity give you in analysing your current roles?

SELF-EVALUATE YOUR SKILL

HOW EFFECTIVE IS YOUR INTERPERSONAL COMMUNICATION?

Key: VS = Very Successfully, S = Successfully, U = Unsuccessfully

Rate your awareness of self by completing the following

Are you able to:	VS	S	U
Listen to your feelings?			
Identify your feelings accurately?			
Identify the influence of past experiences and interactions with others on your view of self?			
Accept responsibility for choosing to use your relationship skills?			
Receive feedback about your current relationship skills?			
Accept and appreciate yourself?			

Rate your ability to self-disclose by completing the following

Are you able to:	VS	S	U
Show your reactions and feelings about the present situation?			
Give information about the past that affects this reaction?			
Speak for yourself assertively?			
Own your thoughts and feelings?			
Provide feedback to others on the effect of their behaviour?			
Match and deepen the level of intimacy of disclosures?			

Rate your ability to start and build relationships by completing the following

Are you able to:	VS	S	U
Make opportunities to meet people and network?			
Initiate conversations and cope with shyness?			
Take risks to continue contact?			
Use appropriate self-disclosure?			
Express openness and show empathy?			
Use supportiveness, show positiveness and demonstrate equality?			
Improve and develop your relationship skills?			

INTERPERSONAL COMPETENCE

OBJECTIVE 3 ▶

Explain how the interpersonal qualities of positiveness and empathy contribute to social competence

Interpersonal communication is an interaction between two people on a one-to-one basis or in groups.

Studies into emotional intelligence highlight the importance of personal competence—being emotionally self-aware and having self-regulation and management skills. They also highlight the importance of social competence—being socially aware and demonstrating social skills. People who are personally and socially competent build positive, constructive relationships. This section of the chapter focuses on the **interpersonal communication** skills that build social competence.

Proponents of emotional intelligence focus on emotional competence in two broad categories: personal competence and social competence. The research findings of those studying emotional intelligence and the findings of those researching the general qualities and specific interpersonal skills of interpersonally effective people are remarkably similar. DeVito (1989) presented two models—a humanistic model and a pragmatic model—to show the general qualities and specific interpersonal skills of an effective communicator.

The *humanistic model*, which is based on the principles of humanist psychologists such as Abraham Maslow and Carl Rogers, shows the five qualities that people need in order to operate effectively in interpersonal relationships. The *pragmatic model* emphasises the specific interpersonal skills that lead to satisfying interpersonal relationships. People who operate effectively in interpersonal relationships at work and elsewhere display the five qualities supported by the five specific interpersonal skills shown in Table 3.3. They are personally and socially competent.

Interpersonal skills are about how we manage relationships—social competence. Spitzberg and Cupach (2002, p. 573) list other overlapping terms that are employed to describe interpersonal skills: social skill, interpersonal competence and communicative competence. In personal, social and business relationships, people who are socially competent are able to communicate well, build satisfying relationships and make effective decisions. They have a service orientation and anticipate, recognise and meet customers' needs. They are able to develop others, are aware of organisational power relationships, and have the drive to meet internal standards of excellence. Business organisations search for leaders, managers and staff with the qualities to operate effectively in a fast-changing

Table 3.3 Features of interpersonal effectiveness	
Qualities	**Interpersonal skills**
Openness is the capacity to respond frankly and spontaneously to people and situations, and the ability to acknowledge one's personal feelings and thoughts.	*Confidence* is the ability to feel comfortable with the other person and the situation. A confident person is able to take the initiative assertively.
Empathy is the ability to understand and feel as the other person feels. An empathetic person hears the unsaid and understands the other person's thoughts and feelings.	*Immediacy* is the sense of contact a person receives from the one communicating. It refers to what is happening 'here and now'.
Supportiveness is the ability to supply descriptive and spontaneous feedback to another person in a provisional or tentative manner—this shows a mind open to other ideas and indicates a willingness to change an opinion.	*Interaction management* involves finding a balance between the sender and the listener as each acts on the other. In an effective interaction, both parties are satisfied. The verbal and nonverbal communication is appropriate to the context.
Positiveness refers to the ability to communicate in a confident way while also acknowledging the other person.	*Expressiveness* refers to involvement, both as sender and receiver, in the interpersonal interaction, giving appropriate and informative feedback.
Equality refers to situations where each person in the interaction is recognised as worthwhile and with something to contribute.	*Other-orientation* is the ability to attend to and fous on the other person, seeing the situation from the other person's point of view.

business environment. Colloquial phrases suggest that business organisations need people who are able to confront threats head on, think outside the square, push the envelope, be open-minded and curious about the business environment, and take advantage of new opportunities. People drive an organisation's success.

Spitzberg and Cupach (2002, p. 567) use a syllogism to underline the importance of interpersonal skills. 'Interpersonal skills are vital to the development of human relationships; human relationships are vital to personal well-being; therefore interpersonal skills are vital to well-being.'

Burjoon and Hoobler (2002, p. 281) say that nonverbal signals are 'essential ingredients in the interpersonal communication mix'. Research shows that nonverbal signals carry a 'significant and often dominant portion of the social meaning in face-to-face interchanges'. Nonverbal signals are not merely auxiliaries to the verbal communication. (For further details, see Chapter 4.)

A positive and inclusive climate

The **communication climate** is created by the way people feel about each other. In a positive communication climate, people interact confidently and courteously. Their relationships are built on openness, honesty and trust, which come from the goodwill felt towards one another. People are willing to speak with others, listen carefully, ask questions and offer feedback. Information and ideas are conveyed accurately.

A negative climate makes it difficult for people to give and receive information and to take action, because it is hard to communicate. People feel uncomfortable and unwilling to interact. They are unwilling to ask questions or offer ideas and feedback, and are more inclined to wait and see what happens. The accuracy of the communication declines, and interpersonal relationships are less effective, in a negative communication climate.

In an inclusive workplace environment, interactions are positive and lead to satisfactory outcomes for all involved. People are willing to communicate and listen to the perspective of others. There is a win–win approach that focuses on meeting interests and collaborating to get things done.

The **win–win approach** to communication is about concentrating on the needs and interests of the people communicating. It is not about judging others and taking a position. Rather than winning positions or gaining victories over the other person, the win–win approach lets people gather or give information in a way that creates a positive communication climate and conveys accurate information. The communication is more likely to get things done and to maintain and build goodwill because each person understands the needs and interests of the other. The win–win approach is discussed more fully in Chapters 5 and 6.

In the win–win approach, behaviour focuses on interests. It is easier to interact supportively with good listening, speaking and nonverbal communication skills when people have similar interests and concerns. However, by using empathy we can manage interactions with those who have dissimilar interests and concerns.

Empathy

Empathy comes from the Greek word for *passion* and also relates to the German word *Einfühling*, meaning *to feel with* (Beebe et al. 1999, p. 146). Whereas sympathy is saying you are sorry and offering support to someone who is feeling bad, empathy goes one step further. Empathy means that you try to perceive the world from another's perspective; you attempt to feel what someone else feels (Beebe et al. 1999, p. 147). Empathetic people are able to:

- attend to what is said
- maintain objectivity and distance
- recognise nonverbal cues about the feelings of others
- understand the content of the message
- understand the feelings in the message
- communicate their understanding to others.

Communication climate refers to the tone of the relationship, as expressed by the verbal and nonverbal messages between people.

The **win–win approach** aims to satisfy the needs and interests of both parties in the situation.

Empathy is the ability to understand and feel as the other person feels.

Beebe and colleagues (1999, pp. 158–9) state that empathy is a *collection of skills* that helps you to predict the response of others. Goleman (1998), in his book *Working with Emotional Intelligence*, refers to the role and importance of emotions in developing empathy. His research found that those who are sensitive to others and are other-oriented—that is, emotionally intelligent—have better interpersonal relationships.

Empathy enhances the communication climate. The tone of the communication is positive and the communication is about what is happening now. Communication is about the needs and interests of the people taking part.

Assertive behaviour

OBJECTIVE 4 ▶
Distinguish assertive, aggressive and passive behaviours, and identify reasons for using verbal assertion

Assertive behaviour is based on high self-esteem and an acceptance of self.

Aggressive behaviour is based on domination and often leads to conflict.

Submissive behaviour is based on accepting the opinions of others without asserting one's own point of view; comes from low self-esteem.

Effective communication is based on a person's willingness to communicate empathy for the other person and their skill in adjusting their communication approach to suit the other person and the situation in a way that also recognises their own needs and rights. Those who behave assertively are acknowledging both their rights as individuals and the rights of other people. This is the ideal attitude to have at work and in our everyday lives. **Assertive** people tend to demonstrate open, expressive and relaxed behaviour. They are able to build honest, fulfilling relationships. Such people feel comfortable with themselves and with others, and are able to satisfy their own needs and the needs of others.

When the occasion demands, assertive people can disagree, stand up for their own rights, and present alternative points of view without being intimidated or putting the other person down. Assertive people can select suitable behaviour for each situation and recognise when their own behaviour is assertive, aggressive or non-assertive.

The assertive person is confident and can communicate openly. Although assertive people want to be heard and acknowledged, they are able to accept that others may have different perceptions and opinions. They are generally respected and liked by others. In contrast, **aggressive** people may try to win at all costs, even to the point of humiliating others. They are often in conflict and may be disliked by others. At the other end of the scale, **submissive** people are unable to assert themselves or promote their point of view. They are worried, anxious and lack confidence, and may be disliked because of their insecurity. Table 3.4 contrasts the characteristics of *assertive*, *aggressive* and *submissive* behaviour.

Table 3.4: Characteristics of assertive, aggressive and submissive behaviour

Assertive	Aggressive	Submissive
Is self-enhancing of others	Is self-enhancing and dominating of others	Is self-denying
May achieve desired goal	Achieves desired goals regardless of others	Does not achieve desired goals
Has a positive self-concept	Devalues the contribution of others	Feels hurt or anxious often
Makes decisions for self	Makes decisions for others	Allows others to make the decisions
Is expressive	Is expressive	Is inhibited
Feels comfortable with and equal to others	Feels uncomfortable with and superior to others	Feels uncomfortable and of less worth than others
Is able to present a point of view and accept a different point of view	Is able to present a point of view and may try to impose it by dominating	Is unable to present a point of view

VERBAL ASSERTION SKILLS

As people communicate at work, they select from a number of relationship skills. Communication skills that manage an interaction and achieve a balance that satisfies both parties include assertion, 'I' statements, active listening, appropriate nonverbal behaviour, feedback and feedforward. This section of the chapter deals with verbal assertion skills, including 'I' statements. Chapter 4 covers listening, nonverbal communication, feedback and feedforward skills.

Butler-Bowden (2007, p. 36) states: 'The whole point of assertion statements is to produce a change without invading the other person's space. There is no power or coercion involved as the focus is on a result.' Skills in verbal assertion are useful, for example, when a team leader gives team members a first look at the plans to enter a new market segment. Verbal assertion skills enable the team leader to counter objections, gather new ideas, engage in decision making and generally promote the proposed change. In an effective performance appraisal, manager and employee apply the relationship management skills of self-awareness, self-management, situational awareness and assertion. The quality of their interpersonal skills creates a positive communication climate that encourages open, honest exchanges rather than defensive, self-protective responses.

> Assertive verbal statements achieve a result without using power or coercion.

A practical, verbal, assertive strategy to use in a situation where you are required to give either positive or negative feedback on performance is the Flag–Example–Benefit process (Cole 2005, p. 395). Shown in Figure 3.2, the Flag–Example–Benefit process demonstrates to the other person your openness and willingness to engage assertively in conversation. The three steps are explained in Table 3.5. Using these three steps will enable you to give powerful assertive feedback designed to change behaviour and improve performance. Positive feedback encourages the other person to continue the behaviour you describe. The process also provides a way of giving assertive but negative feedback constructively.

'I' statements

A useful technique to demonstrate assertion and show openness with others is the **'I' statement** or **'I' message**. 'I' statements are a way of sharing emotions and letting others know how their behaviour is perceived and how it affects you. One of the most effective ways to begin assertive statements is to say 'I feel . . . when . . .'. For example, the message may be: 'I feel annoyed when you don't let me know you will be late.' People can express their needs and wants with an 'I' message. It shows their personal involvement plus a willingness to share their feelings. It also lets them own their own

> **'I' statements/messages** are assertive statements that help to send a clear message.

> 'I' statements can have two, three or four parts.

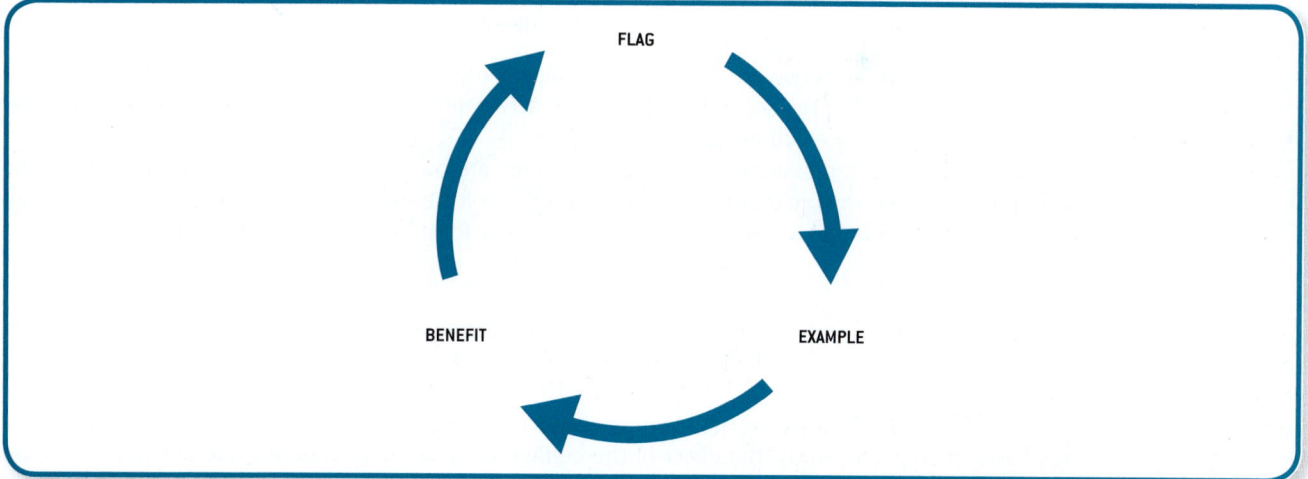

Figure 3.2: The Flag–Example–Benefit process

Table 3.5: Using the Flag–Example–Benefit process to give assertive positive and negative feedback	
Component	*Example of assertive, positive, constructive feedback*
Flagging what you are about to comment on	I liked your last monthly report.
Providing an **example** of what you are actually commenting on	I thought the way you ordered the information and used graphs was professional.
Outlining the **benefit** enables you to be specific and constructive	You highlighted progress to date and detailed next month's activities in a way that made the contents easy to understand.
Component	*Example of assertive, negative, constructive feedback*
Flagging what you are about to comment on	I thought you began the negotiation well by separating the people from the problem.
Providing an **example** of what you are actually commenting on	I think you could have engaged more positively by focusing more on the interests and finding common ground, rather than taking a position. Once a position is taken, it is difficult to generate different possibilities.
Outlining the **benefit** enables you to be specific and constructive	Focusing on interests would have let you and the others in the negotiation work together to generate a range of options. It is then possible to choose together the option that best meets the interests of the negotiators.

reactions. Rather than blaming or holding the other person responsible, the 'I' statement links the other person's behaviour to the reaction.

'I' messages can be used to express both positive and negative feelings; they may talk about behaviour that is acceptable and pleasing, or behaviour that is unacceptable and displeasing. Because 'I' messages dealing with behaviour that is unacceptable are more difficult to express, this section focuses on their construction.

An 'I' message can have two, three or four parts (see Table 3.6). In a two-part 'I' message, the speaker's feelings are owned and the behaviour that is causing the feeling is described in concrete terms. The formula in a two-part 'I' message is:

FEELINGS + BEHAVIOUR

Following this formula, a two-part assertive message could be: 'I feel angry when the dirty clothes are left in the bathroom.' In the second part, take care to *describe* the *behaviour* of the other person rather than interpret, judge or evaluate it.

In a three-part 'I' message, the speaker's feelings are owned, the behaviour that is causing the feeling is described in concrete terms, then the effect of the behaviour on you (that is, the consequences for you) is stated in concrete, factual words. The formula in a three-part 'I' message is:

FEELINGS + BEHAVIOUR + EFFECTS

The statements may occur in any order. Following this formula, a three-part assertive statement could be: 'I feel annoyed when you don't let me know you will be late, because I'm unable to reschedule my timetable.'

In a four-part 'I' message, the feelings are owned, the behaviour that is causing the feeling is described in concrete words, the effect of the behaviour is stated in concrete, factual words, and an alternative acceptable behaviour is offered. The formula in a four-part 'I' message is:

FEELINGS + BEHAVIOUR + EFFECTS + ALTERNATIVE ACCEPTABLE BEHAVIOUR

Table 3.6: Three formulas for 'I' statements		
Two-part 'I' message	**Three-part 'I' message**	**Four-part 'I' message**
Feelings	Feelings	Feelings
+	+	+
Behaviour	Behaviour	Behaviour
	+	+
	Effects	Effects
		+
		Alternative acceptable behaviour

Following this formula, an assertive message could be: 'I feel annoyed when you don't let me know you will be late, because I'm unable to reschedule my timetable. I would like you to ring me and let me know you will be late.'

The fourth part of the message is used to suggest, initially, an alternative acceptable behaviour. It may also be used to negotiate a behaviour that is acceptable to both people by using Dewey's reflective thinking process, which is detailed in Table 12.7 in Chapter 12.

OWNING YOUR REACTIONS

Part of being able to give successful 'I' messages is 'owning your reactions'. This means being able to recognise and identify your feelings. One way to own your reactions is to use the following two-part feedback formula:

1. Describe the other person's behaviour.
2. Describe your reaction to it.

In this way you link the other person's behaviour with your reaction. If you say, 'When you shout, I feel afraid', instead of 'When you shout, you frighten me', you are describing your reaction to their behaviour, rather than blaming them or holding them responsible for your reaction.

Successful 'I' statements communicate in a non-threatening way that is acceptable to the other person. They do not blame or interpret the other person's conduct. Aggressive statements often start with 'You make me feel . . .' and blame the other person for their behaviour and your feelings. Once you become skilled in using 'I' messages, you will frame them in your own words and may omit the words 'feel', 'when' and 'because'. 'I' messages are particularly useful when people need to give and receive information and reach agreement.

Valuing diversity

Business leaders, managers and staff interact with people from many different nations, organisations, cultures, and social and educational backgrounds. Robbins, Millett and Waters-Marsh (2008, p. 16) state: 'Workforce diversity means that organisations are becoming more heterogeneous in terms of gender, race and ethnicity—in other words, there are more differences than there are similarities among members of the organisation.' With the increasing globalisation, interaction across cultures and diversity of Australia's population it is important for leaders, managers and staff to match their personal and social competence to today's complex business world.

The creation of business environments capable of adapting to, and interacting positively with, people from different backgrounds leads to improved business results, increased motivation and job satisfaction. Misunderstandings and the consequent communication barriers will occur in organisations that ignore

◄ OBJECTIVE 5
Describe how valuing diversity and networking improves social awareness and social skills in business interactions

Workforce diversity describes the characteristics of difference between individuals, including culture, age, belief systems and values, gender, race and religion.

the increasing diversity instead of accepting and promoting it. Individuals without the willingness or confidence to accept and manage cultural differences in their interactions will experience communication barriers.

Agar (2006, p. 20) says: 'Problems in communication are rooted in "who you are", in encounters with a "different mentality", "different meanings", a "different tie" between language and consciousness.' A sharing of common meanings across cultures through an understanding of the knowledge system, beliefs, values and behaviours of each culture helps to overcome these problems. Adler (2002, p. 99) discusses standing back from oneself, developing self-awareness by assessing our own behaviour and questioning perceptions we may hold of people from different cultures. Avoiding judgments based on preconceived biases and labels makes it possible to understand what is really happening in an interaction.

Each individual, regardless of culture, background or experience, has a *role repertoire*: a number of roles that are constantly and competently performed. Goffman (1955, 1959) postulated role theory: 'social interaction can best be understood as a kind of theatre in which a great deal of effort is expended in maintaining socially approved identities, or "faces".' Goffman states that to 'be out of face' or to 'lose face' is 'to present aspects of the self which conflict with the approved role'. Most communicators attempt to maintain their own and others' faces and avoid potentially threatening or embarrassing interactions. This maintenance of face is particularly important in business interactions across national and cultural boundaries.

Maintaining face is particularly important in business interactions across national and cultural boundaries.

Confusion and misunderstandings can arise because of interpersonal barriers both verbal (volume, accent, idioms and choice of words) and nonverbal (tone, clothes and artefacts, eye contact, body language, proximity and gestures). Mor Barak (2005, p. 180) says: 'Trust and respect are often conveyed through nonverbal rather than verbal communication ... Clothing has long been used to communicate rank, mourning, occasion and even season. ... Clothes are an extension of the body and closely relate to the person's age, socioeconomic status, and national origin.' Barriers can arise in interpersonal transactions across cultures because of semantics. Different words have different meanings.

Mor Barak (2005, p. 232) says the main barriers to inclusive practices at work '... have to do with managers' and employees' attitudes and behaviours. Specifically, prejudice (biased views) and discrimination (biased behaviour), either overt or covert, are at the core of barriers for implementing inclusive policies at the workplace'. Identifying and managing workforce diversity requires an organisation and its people to transcend 'cultural conditioning' by moving beyond stereotypes and premature judging and generally avoiding ethnocentric behaviours (Adler 2002, p. 99). A useful tool in this process is a *diversity policy* that identifies its purpose, key diversity issues for the organisation and commitment to action.

After designing its diversity policy, management must promote, explain and interpret the policy across the organisation through a range of communication channels. Leaders, managers and staff need to know how cultural norms in the workplace operate to regulate, repress, tolerate and celebrate diversity. Promotion of cross-cultural skills and acceptance of diversity is enhanced through consultation and training and development activities. Development of cross-cultural communication skills and awareness improves interpersonal competence, collaboration, negotiation, problem solving, relationships and working towards collective goals.

How can a business promote and support cultural diversity? First, by respecting culturally diverse approaches to business around the globe. Second, by encouraging a critical and open awareness of inappropriate ethnocentric and gender-biased language, assumptions and stereotypes. Inclusive policies and practices enable organisations to cultivate opportunities through diverse people and let people know they are valued and accepted.

Stereotyping and generalising marginalise groups and create communication barriers.

Networking

Networking is the process of building and maintaining interpersonal professional contacts.

Networking is viewed as a very important and often critical aspect of a professional business career. Networking builds business reputations, widens contacts, provides up-to-date information and develops interpersonal skills in social interactions. A network can contain satisfying personal relationships, and casual and work acquaintances. A work-based network is built on the informal communication network discussed in Chapter 8.

A network may include members of professional associations, government agencies, other companies, consultants and suppliers. Forums and communities of practice provide the opportunity to network. (See Chapter 12 for more on communities of practice.) Professional associations have been formed to promote professional development and meet social needs. The value of networking is the opportunity to pursue professional interests and develop relationships outside your direct connections at work.

Simple tactics that keep a network active include attendance at professional, student and work functions, and joining an appropriate organisation that will give you a wide range of contacts. Keep an address file that is easy to use, and have lunch or meet informally with people every so often to maintain contact.

People who are aware of how they speak, dress and carry themselves as they interact within a network will become more effective networkers. Metcalf (1997) says that the way a person shakes hands sends a message. While an extended hand with the palm down is a dominant signal, a shake with both hands, or holding the other person by the hand or elbow is seen as an attempt to create a false sense of intimacy. A handshake held too long may be interpreted as threatening. A power grip handshake is a widespread means of expressing congratulations, contractual agreement, farewell or greeting (Givens 2008). Over half the communication in face-to-face meetings is nonverbal. A large part of the message is conveyed by posture, hand and body movement, and eye contact.

An ability to watch for the nonverbal cues of others—facial expression, tone of voice, hand movements and energy level—will help you to interpret the other person's message empathically and to build satisfying relationships within the network. Michaels (2008) suggests, 'Remember too that you are part of a network. That's a responsibility that shouldn't be taken lightly. Actively help make contacts, referrals and connections for your network.'

> A community of practice is a group of people joined by a common interest who engage in a process of social learning and collaboration.

REVIEW QUESTIONS

7 *a* What are the essential requirements for interpersonal effectiveness?

    b Explain the concept of 'interaction management'.

8 Why is empathy not synonymous with sympathy?

9 Contrast the likely outcomes from a positive communication climate with those of a negative communication climate.

10 Contrast assertive, aggressive and submissive behaviours.

11 Identify the steps and explain the purpose of the Flag–Example–Benefit process.

12 *a* What does an 'I' statement do?

    b What does a 'you' statement do?

13 *a* What are the characteristics of a diverse workforce?

    b Why are organisations engaging in practices to manage workplace diversity?

    c What is the purpose of a diversity policy, and how can it be implemented across an organisation?

14 *a* Discuss four ways in which confusions and misunderstandings can occur between individuals in the workplace.

    b Identify the main barriers to inclusive practices as discussed by Mor Barak (2005) and explain how they can be overcome.

15 *a* Define the term 'professional network' and give an example of a network that supports your profession.

    b What advantages are gained by networking?

INTERACTION WITH OTHERS

1   Work individually.
    a   Why is the ability to use the win–win approach so important to a manager?
    b   Describe a time when you have seen the effects of the lack of ability to use the win–win approach.
    c   What could have been done differently to change the outcome to a win–win result?

2   Work in small groups.
    a   Share examples of situations where communication became problematic as a result of making inferences based on past experience, preconceived labels or the failure to clarify meaning.
    b   Choose one of the situations and decide the behaviours that could have improved communication effectiveness in that situation.

3   Work individually.
    Differentiate assertive, aggressive and submissive behaviour. In your answer describe two ways in which a person can be aggressive to another. How would an assertive person respond to this type of behaviour?

4   Work individually.
    If assertive behaviour is preferable to aggression or submission, what would you identify as the basis of assertiveness?

5   Work in small groups.
    Discuss two ways of encouraging interpersonal communication, and two ways of creating barriers in interpersonal communication, in a diverse work team.

6   Work individually.
    In Table 3.7 list the responses you would give in the situations outlined.

7   'I' messages
    One of your colleagues frequently makes remarks about how carefully and slowly you think before making a contribution at staff meetings. Even though these comments appear to be a joke, you feel that others hearing them are starting to label you as slow. You've had enough of the comments.
    a   Write a two-part 'I' message using the two-part formula to state your feelings and describe the behaviour.
    b   Change your two-part 'I' message into a three-part 'I' message using the three-part formula.

8   'I' messages
    It is 3 pm. You feel tense because you have two telephone calls to make and a major piece of work to finish in the next two hours. A colleague asks you to help him immediately with the agenda for next week's committee meeting. It has to be sent by email this afternoon.
    Write a four-part assertive message in which you state that you are unable to help with the agenda. Follow the four-part 'I' message formula.

9   Work in small groups.
    a   Brainstorm to create a list of strategies you could use over the next month to improve:
        • self-management
        • social awareness
        • social skills in the workplace.
    b   Create a checklist to evaluate your skill in using your identified strategies.

Table 3.7: Sympathy versus empathy

Situation	Respond with sympathy	Respond with empathy
A colleague informs you that she has lost her briefcase containing the CD with the accounting figures she needs for month-end.		
A colleague phones to tell you that a longstanding friend has been involved in a serious accident.		
A relative tells you that he has been made redundant.		
Your friend tells you that her uninsured car has been stolen.		

SUMMARY OF LEARNING OBJECTIVES

1 ▷ DESCRIBE THE ROLE OF EMOTIONAL INTELLIGENCE IN BUILDING RELATIONSHIPS AND IMPROVING PERFORMANCE

Emotionally intelligent people are responsive to others and able to use their own personal and social competence to express their expectations and values. Researchers have concluded that success is related to more than general intelligence (IQ). Successful people are emotionally intelligent (EI). They have the personal and social competence to develop positive personal, social and work relationships, and to interact easily.

Knowing specifically how you feel is defined as emotional awareness. It operates on six levels—feeling the feeling, acknowledging the feeling, identifying and accepting the feeling, reflecting on and forecasting feelings. Emotional intelligence is the capacity to perceive emotion, integrate it in thought, understand it and manage it. People with emotional awareness and emotional intelligence have the capacity to communicate, set goals and plan effectively. They build positive relationships with family, friends and work colleagues.

2 ▷ EXPLAIN HOW SELF-CONCEPT, SELF-DISCLOSURE, SELF-ESTEEM, SELF-REGULATION AND SELF-MOTIVATION CONTRIBUTE TO PERSONAL COMPETENCE

Self-concept is how we see ourselves. It is defined and maintained by our relationships. A positive self-concept contributes to effective interpersonal communication and behaviour. People with a positive self-concept are aware of their own feelings and able to acknowledge the feelings of others. The Johari window is helpful for understanding self-concept. It defines four areas of the self-concept: public arena, hidden area, blind spot and unknown area.

Self-disclosure is personal openness. It involves revealing feelings and reactions during conversations with others. It can lead to increased self-awareness and understanding. Some people may find self-disclosure threatening. Self-disclosure is most likely when there is a climate of trust.

Self-esteem is based on self-respect and respect for others. It involves confidence and understanding and plays a large part in effective communication and satisfying relationships.

Emotionally competent people are also self-regulating and self-motivated. They are able to control their impulses and emotions and to adapt readily to changing situations. They can manage stress in the workplace and show initiative.

 3 ▷ EXPLAIN HOW THE INTERPERSONAL QUALITIES OF POSITIVENESS AND EMPATHY CONTRIBUTE TO SOCIAL COMPETENCE

Positive and supportive communication boosts confidence and builds self-esteem. Confident people are able to perform better in their jobs. There is an equality in their interactions, because they are seen as worthwhile individuals with something to contribute to the workplace interaction. The communication climate is positive, and people with good listening, speaking and nonverbal communication skills build satisfying personal, social and work relationships.

Empathy is created when people use the win–win approach and self-disclosure. Interpersonal effectiveness is demonstrated by those who have the qualities of openness, empathy, supportiveness, positiveness and equality. Their interpersonal skills include confidence, immediacy, interaction management, expressiveness and other-orientation. People in a relationship with a positive communication climate feel accepted and valued.

 4 ▷ DISTINGUISH ASSERTIVE, AGGRESSIVE AND PASSIVE BEHAVIOURS, AND IDENTIFY REASONS FOR USING VERBAL ASSERTION

Assertive people take responsibility for their actions and respect the rights of others. Their perception of messages is usually correct, and their approach to people is motivated and confident. Assertive behaviour demonstrates a high degree of openness, empathy, supportiveness, positiveness, confidence and the ability to be 'other-oriented'. It avoids both aggressive and submissive behaviour.

Verbal assertion skills include the Flag–Example–Benefit process and 'I' messages. 'I' statements share your emotions and let others know how their actions are affecting you. They can have two, three or four parts. Part of using 'I' messages is 'owning your reactions'.

 5 ▷ DESCRIBE HOW VALUING DIVERSITY AND NETWORKING IMPROVES SOCIAL AWARENESS AND SOCIAL SKILLS IN BUSINESS INTERACTIONS

With increasing globalisation and movement of people around the world, organisations are becoming more heterogeneous in terms of gender, race and ethnicity. Workforce diversity describes the characteristics of difference between individuals, including culture, age, belief systems and values, gender, race and religion.

Networking means establishing and maintaining a wide range of helpful and supportive contacts. Networking builds business reputations, provides up-to-date information and knowledge, and develops interpersonal skills in social interactions. It is a critical aspect of a professional business career.

KEY TERMS

ACTIVITIES AND QUESTIONS

1 a In small groups, critically evaluate this statement.

Emotional intelligence means you are able to understand and take action in response to your emotions or the emotions of others.

  b Record and share examples of situations where you have used the personal competencies or social competencies identified in Table 3.1 on page 64.

  c Identify the outcome in each situation and describe how these competencies improved your communication effectiveness.

2 Create a checklist that a member of a work team could use to self-assess their emotional competence at work. Use the checklist below as a guide and complete the bullet points.

Emotional competence checklist	Yes	No
I am able to demonstrate emotional self-awareness by: • understanding . . . • applying . . .		
I am able to manage self and emotion by: • understanding . . . • applying . . .		
I am able to motivate self and others by: • understanding . . . • applying . . .		
I am able to develop others and accommodate diversity by: • understanding . . . • applying . . .		

3 a In small groups, think of five people whom you consider to be good examples of being adaptable and self-regulating. You may think of world leaders or people from your workplace.

  b How would you describe their emotional intelligence?

  c Share your insight with other groups, and identify those qualities you consider to be adaptability skills.

4 a How can interpersonal skills help you in your relationships with others?

  b Nominate one behaviour pattern that interferes with your interpersonal effectiveness.

  c Name one technique you could use to alter and improve this behaviour.

5 a Use the Web (or your library) to find articles about assertive and submissive behaviour.

  b In the table on the next page, differentiate between assertive and submissive behaviour by creating a list of assertive behaviours and a list of submissive behaviours.

  c Use the table to conduct a survey (over the next week) of the number of times you see or engage in each of these behaviours by placing a tick against the type of behaviour in columns 2 and 4.

  d Submit at least two articles you used to find examples of the behaviours; and the survey results (that is, the table completed).

6 Assume you are team leader. Prepare a briefing paper for a new team member explaining the diverse nature of the team. Outline typical factors that can cause confusion and misunderstanding in diverse workplaces, and detail how to enhance interpersonal communication and build positive relationships within the team.

Assertive behaviour	Survey result	Submissive behaviour	Survey result

EXPLORING THE WEB

1 Learn more about emotional intelligence by visiting 'businessballs.com, emotional intelligence EQ' at <www.businessballs.com/eq.htm>.
   a Choose two of the free materials on emotional intelligence provided to the site by Daniel Goleman.
   b Prepare a 250-word evaluative critique for each article.
2 Review these chapter-related websites to learn more about self-awareness, assertiveness, interpersonal communication and networking:

- 'Johari Window' at <www.businessballs.com/johariwindowmodel.htm>
- 'Assertiveness.com' at <www.assertiveness.com>
- 'Improving Assertive Behaviour' at <www.coping.org/relations/assert.htm>
- 'A Model of Effective Communication' at <www.coping.org/dialogue/model.htm>
- 'My Referral Network' at <www.myreferralnetwork.com.au>

PROJECT WORK

You work for a large global organisation. Your Head of Division is a proponent of emotional intelligence (EI), arguing that EI makes a significant contribution to the success of any organisation. In the last divisional meeting, he announced that an EI training program would be introduced across the Division.

After the meeting the Head of Division directs you to investigate EI training programs promoted on the Web and in professional journals. You are to inform him of your research findings in a short report.

1 Research your report.
   a Begin your research by gathering general information about emotional intelligence from 'The Consortium for Research on Emotional Intelligence in Organisations', Emotional Competence Framework <www.eiconsortium.org/research/emotional_competence_framework.htm>.
   b Conduct additional specific research into the learning objectives or outcomes of EI training programs on the Web or elsewhere. Note that you must reference your sources of information.
2 Write the short report.
   a In the introduction to the report, discuss the need for managers and staff to have:
      i personal competence—the ability to manage themselves, and
      ii social competence—the ability to manage relationships (refer to Table 3.1 Emotional competencies—the basis of emotional intelligence).

b The body of the report should detail the reasons for the growing interest in and acceptance by business leaders of the role of EI abilities in the success of individuals and organisations. The body of the report must also identify the learning objectives or outcomes to include in the training program.

c The final section of the short report should include your conclusions and recommendation(s).

BIBLIOGRAPHY

Adler, N, 2002. *International Dimensions of Organizational Behaviour*, South-Western, Cincinnati, Ohio.

Adler, R., Rosenfeld, R.B. & Proctor, R.F. 2003. *Interplay: The Process of Interpersonal Communication*, 9th edn, Oxford University Press, USA.

Agar, M. 2006. 'Culture blends', in L. Monaghan & J. Goodman (eds), *A Cultural Approach to Interpersonal Communication: Essential Readings*, Blackwell Publishing.

Allen, K.L. 2005. *Study Skills: A Student Survival Guide*, John Wiley & Sons, UK.

Assertiveness.com. www.assertiveness.com, viewed 10 January 2008.

Beebe, S.A., Beebe, S.J. & Redmond, M.V. 1999. *Interpersonal Communication: Relating to Others*, 2nd edn, Allyn & Bacon, Needham Heights, Massachusetts.

Beebe, S.A., Beebe, S.J. & Redmond, M.V. 2007. *Interpersonal Communication: Relating to Others*, 5th edn, Allyn & Bacon, Needham Heights, Massachusetts.

Berger, P. 1967. *Invitation to Psychology*, Penguin, Harmondsworth, UK.

Bishop, S. 2007. *Develop Your Assertiveness*, 2nd edn, Kogan Page, London.

Bolton, R. 1987. *People Skills*, Prentice Hall, Sydney.

Burjoon, J.K. & Hoobler, G.D. 2002. 'Nonverbal signals', in M.L. Knapp & J.A. Daly, *Handbook of Interpersonal Communication*, 3rd edn, Sage Publications, California.

Businessballs.com, emotional intelligence EQ, www.businessballs.com/eq.htm, viewed 10 January 2008.

Businessballs.com, Johari Window, www.businessballs.com/johariwindowmodel.htm, viewed 10 January 2008.

Butler-Bowdon, T. 2007. *50 Psychology Classics: Who We Are, How We Think, What We Do, Insight and Inspiration from 50 Key Books*, Nicholas Brealey Publishing, London.

Canary, D.J. & Stafford, L. 1993. *Communication and Relational Maintenance*, Academic Press, San Diego.

Cole, K. 2005. *Management: Theory and Practice*, 3rd edn, Pearson Education Australia, Sydney.

Consortium for Research on Emotional Intelligence in Organisations, www.eiconsortium.org, viewed 14 January 2008.

Consortium for Research on Emotional Intelligence in Organisations, *Emotional Competence Framework*, www.eiconsortium.org/research/emotional_competence_framework.htm, viewed 14 January 2008.

Cook, M. 1971. *Interpersonal Perception*, Penguin, Harmondsworth, UK.

Davies, S. 'Emotional intelligence and leadership', CEO Forum Group, www.ceoforum.com.au, viewed 17 February 2008.

DeVito, J.A. 1989. *The Interpersonal Communication Book*, 5th edn, Harper & Row, New York.

DeVito, J.A. 2000. *Human Communication: The Basic Course*, 8th edn, Longman, New York.

DeVito, J.A. 2003. *The Interpersonal Communication Book*, 10th edn, Allyn & Bacon, USA.

DeVito, J.A. 2006. *The Interpersonal Communication Book*, 11th edn, Allyn & Bacon, USA.

Dilenschneider, R.L. 1997. 'Social intelligence', *Executive Excellence*, Vol. 31, Issue 12, March, p. 86.

DuBrin, A.J. 2007. *Human Relations for Career and Personal Success: Concepts, Applications and Skills*, 8th edn, Prentice Hall, Upper Saddle River, NJ.

Dunn, D.M. & Goodnight, L.J. 2008. *Communication: Embracing Difference*, 2nd edn, Allyn & Bacon, USA.

Edwards, C. 1997. 'Communication breakdown', *Inside Business Australia*, March, pp. 44–46.

Emmerling, R.J. & Goleman, D. 'Emotional intelligence: issues and common misunderstandings', Consortium for Research on Emotional Intelligence in Organizations, 2003, www.eiconsortium.org/research/ei_issues_and_common_misunderstandings.htm ,viewed 12 January 2008.

Forgas, J.P. 1986. *Interpersonal Behaviour*, Pergamon Press Australia, Sydney.

Fernando, M. 2003. 'To thine own self be true', *Management Today*, October.

Gamble, T.K. & Gamble, M. 1996. *Communication Works*, 5th edn, McGraw-Hill, New York.

Givens, D.B. *The Nonverbal Dictionary of Gestures, Signs and Body Language Cues*, Centre for Nonverbal Studies Press, Washington, 2008, http://members.aol.com/nonverbal2/diction1.htm, viewed 2 January 2008.

Goffman, E. 1955. 'On face-work: an analysis of ritual elements in social interactions', *Psychiatry*, Vol. 18, Issue 2, pp. 13–31.

Goffman, E. 1959. *The Presentation of Self in Everyday Life*, Doubleday & Co., Garden City, New York.

Goleman, D. 1995. *Emotional Intelligence*, Bantam Dell Publishing Group, New York.

Goleman, D. 1998. *Working with Emotional Intelligence*, Bantam Books, New York.

Goleman, D. 2005. *Emotional Intelligence: Why It Can Matter More Than IQ*, 10th edn, Bantam Books, New York.

Graduate Careers Australia. 2006. *Graduate Outlook 2006: A Snapshot*, GCA.

Grubb, W.L. III & McDaniel, M.A. 2007. 'The fakability of Bar-On's emotional quotient inventory short form: catch me if you can', *Human Performance*, Vol. 20, Issue 1, pp. 43–59.

Hall, C.S. & Gardner, L. 1970. *Theories of Personality*, 2nd edn, John Wiley & Sons, New York.

Hay & McBer. 2004. 'Who needs emotional intelligence', Hay Group Emotional Intelligence Services, http://ei.haygroup.com/about_ei.

Hein, S. 'Emotional awareness', www.eqi.org/aware.htm, viewed 25 June 2003.

Johnson, D.W. 1993. *Reaching Out: Interpersonal Effectiveness and Self-Actualization*, 3rd edn, Prentice Hall, Englewood Cliffs, New Jersey.

Jourard, S.M. 1974. *Health Personality: An Approach from the Viewpoint of Humanistic Psychology*, Macmillan Publishing, New York.

Knapp, M.L. & Vangelisti, A.L. 1992. *Interpersonal Communication and Human Relationships*, 2nd edn, Allyn & Bacon, Boston.

Lane, L.L. 1987. *By All Means Communicate*, Prentice Hall, New Jersey.

Lawrence, H.V. & Iswell, A.K. 1995. 'Feedback is a two-way street', *Training and Development*, Vol. 49, Issue 7, July, pp. 49–52.

Lewis, G. & Slade, C. 1994. *Critical Communication*, Prentice Hall Australia, Sydney.

Luft, J. 1970. *Group Processes: An Introduction to Group Dynamics*, 2nd edn, Mayfield, Palo Alto, California.

Maes, J.D., Weldy, T.G. & Icenogle, M.L. 1997. 'A managerial perspective: oral communication competency is most important for business students in the workplace', *Journal of Business Communication*, Vol. 34, Issue 1, January, pp. 67–80.

Maslow, A. 1954. *Motivation and Personality*, Harper & Row, New York.

Mayer, J.D. 1999. 'Emotional intelligence: popular or scientific psychology?', *APAMonitor Online*, Vol. 30, Issue 8, September, p. 1.

Mehrabian, A. 1971. *Silent Messages*, Wadsworth Publishing Co., California.

Metcalf, T. 1997. 'Communicating your message: the hidden dimension', *Life Association News*, Vol. 92, Issue 4, April, pp. 18–21.

Michaels, S.A. *Networking Your Way to Greater Success*, http://ezinearticles.com/?Networking-Your-Way-To-Greater=Success, viewed 28 May 2008.

Mor Barak, M. 2005. *Managing Diversity: Toward a Globally Inclusive Workplace*, Sage Books, USA.

My Referral Network, www.myreferralnetwork.com.au, viewed 10 January 2008.

O'Neil, J. 1996. 'On emotional intelligence: a conversation with Daniel Goleman', *Educational Leadership*, Vol. 54, Issue 1, September.

Putnis, P. & Petelin, R. 1999. *Professional Communication: Principles and Applications*, Prentice Hall, Sydney.

Robbins, S.P., Millett, B. & Waters-Marsh, T. 2008. *Organisational Behaviour*, 5th edn, Pearson Education Australia, Sydney.

Rogers, C.R. 1961. *On Becoming a Person: A Therapist's View of Psychotherapy*, Houghton Mifflin, Boston.

Sandberg, R. 2007. 'The costs of conflict', *Management Today*, Issue 37, August, pp. 18–20.

Singh, D. 2006. *Emotional Intelligence at Work: A Professional Guide*, 3rd edn, Response Books, Delhi.

Spitzberg, B.H. & Cupach, W.R. 2002. 'Interpersonal skills', in M.L. Knapp & J.A. Daly, *Handbook of Interpersonal Communication*, 3rd edn, Sage Publications, California.

Steiner, C.M. 1974. *Scripts People Live*, Grove Press, New York.

Sternberg, R.J. 2003. Preface to G. Matthews, M. Zeidner & R.D. Roberts, *Emotional Intelligence: Science and Myth*, MIT Press, Boston.

Stone, F. 2003. *The Essential New Manager's Toolkit*, Kaplan, USA.

Suh, E.M. 2002. 'Culture, identity consistency, and subjective well-being', *Journal of Personality and Social Psychology*, Vol. 83, Issue 6, December, pp. 1378–91.

Tools for Communication. *A Model of Effective Communication*, www.coping.org/, viewed 10 January 2008.

Tools for Relationships. *Improving Assertive Behaviour*, www.coping.org/, viewed 10 January 2008.

Weiss, H.M. & Cropanzano, R. 1996. 'Affective events theory', in B.M. Staw & L.L. Cummings, *Research in Organizational Behavior*, Vol. 18, JAI Press, Greenwich, Connecticut.

Wilson, C. 1972. *New Pathways in Psychology: Maslow and the Post-Freudian Revolution*, Taplinger Publishing Company, New York.

4

Nonverbal, listening and feedback skills

How satisfied are you with ...

The overall quality of service provided

Your overall experience

Services as you wanted

Your overall experience with our company

Ability to provide you a good value for the money

The comfort and friendliness of the facility

OVERALL SATISFACTION

	very satisfied	satisfied	neutral	dissati

CMario Ragma Jr.

After studying this chapter you should be able to:

1 ▷ differentiate personal, cultural and universal nonverbal communication and explain how cultural norms affect the nonverbal part of the message

2 ▷ explain the roles of nonverbal communication and understand differences between cultures

3 ▷ discuss seven aspects of nonverbal behaviour

4 ▷ explain the active listening process and its purpose

5 ▷ compare the informational, evaluative and conversational approaches to listening

6 ▷ describe barriers to listening and the behaviours of poor listeners

7 ▷ describe how to provide constructive feedback.

OUTLINE

Types of nonverbal communication

The role of nonverbal communication

Aspects of nonverbal communication

The listening process

Barriers to listening

Constructive feedback

VIEWPOINT: CULTURAL NEGOTIATION BOUNDARIES

There is a common belief that over two-thirds of negotiation effectiveness is established through the process of nonverbal communication. We can gain considerable enlightment into an individual's attitudes and feelings through their body language. Facial expressions and other physical gestures can express a great deal about our emotions and state of mind. However, these physical cues could be misinterpreted during intercultural negotiations.

Common areas of misunderstanding are:

- *Facial expressions and eye contact*—many Asians and Africans offer respect by looking down and avoiding direct eye contact. Europeans and North Americans consider the avoidance of eye contact as a lack of attention and regard it as being disrespectful.
- *Sounds and other actions*—clearing the throat, fidgeting, perspiration or hand wringing display apprehension; sideways glances, rubbing one's eyes, touching and rubbing of the nose or buttoning the coat while drawing away may imply or create suspicion.

Negotiators must learn to understand and recognise differences in the use of nonverbal cues so as not to misinterpret the body language of clients, especially those from other cultural backgrounds, as this could have costly repercussions.

Points selected from M. Spoelstra, 'Cultural negotiation boundaries', *The Negotiation Academy*, www.negotiationtraining.com.au/articles/negotiating-global-borders, viewed 18 February 2008. Reproduced with permission from The Negotiation Experts. The Negotiation Experts offer negotiation-related resources on www.negotiations.com. You can find in-depth articles, Q&A's, cartoons, book reviews, definitions and more.

There are few situations where words alone send the message. In any meeting, negotiation or conversation the nonverbal communication accompanying the words reinforces and adds meaning to them. **Nonverbal behaviour** shows our feelings either consciously or unconsciously. Our capacity to communicate nonverbally affects the quality of our intimate, social and working relationships.

Nonverbal behaviour is any movement or position of the face and/or body.

The total message is made up of words and actions. The actions, or nonverbal communication, has the greater impact on how the receiver interprets the message. Consequently, nonverbal communication plays a significant role in reaching shared understanding in our intimate, social and working relationships. Those with the ability to send clear nonverbal messages are able to communicate more easily than those who are inexpressive in their nonverbal communication. People with the ability to decode the nonverbal communication of others find it easier to gain shared understanding than those who are unaware of the role of nonverbal communication.

In reality, the nonverbal aspects of communication are so intermingled with the verbal that it is difficult to separate them. People combine the verbal and nonverbal messages and the context in which the communication takes place and interpret the total message. Nonverbal communication conveys a range of positive and negative cues and signals. Reactions to the nonverbal communication of others have an impact on liking and disliking, and the way in which we respond and relate to one another.

The total message incorporates the words, the nonverbal behaviour and their meaning.

The appropriate use of nonverbal communication and the ability to receive nonverbal communication accurately are two of the skills demonstrated by successful business communicators. They are skilled because they are able to integrate the nonverbal with the verbal and contextual information to form the total message.

Listening is the interpretative process that takes place with what we hear. Through listening, we store, classify and label information. Listening, therefore, involves attention, interpretation and understanding. Listening to another person takes time and effort. There is a difference between hearing and listening. Hearing is a physical process. The ears receive sensations or stimuli and transmit these to the brain; for example, a loud, sudden or unfamiliar sound catches our attention.

Each day a great deal of time in business is spent listening to and talking with others. Listening serves two broad purposes in this process:

1. As a sender of a message, listening to the receiver's answers provides feedback on how the other person has interpreted the message.
2. As a receiver of a message, listening to the information from the other person is essential in understanding the meaning.

TYPES OF NONVERBAL COMMUNICATION

OBJECTIVE 1 ▶
Differentiate personal, cultural and universal nonverbal communication and explain how cultural norms affect the nonverbal part of the message

Nonverbal communication consists of the part of a message that is not encoded in words. The nonverbal part of the message tends to be less conscious and reveals the sender's feelings, likings and preferences more spontaneously and honestly than the verbal part. If the verbal message does not match the nonverbal communication there is a tendency to believe the nonverbal part of the message.

In working towards more effective communication in business, particularly in interpreting the nonverbal part of the message, it is helpful to consider three types of nonverbal message:

1. personal to the individual
2. common to a group of people or culture
3. universal to humankind.

Nonverbal communication is sent by any means other than words or graphics.

To assist in understanding nonverbal communication, Givens (2008) has compiled a *Nonverbal Dictionary of Gestures, Signs and Body Language Cues*. The items in this dictionary have been researched by anthropologists, archaeologists, biologists, linguists, psychiatrists, psychologists, semioticians and others (including Givens) who have studied human communication from a scientific point of view. The dictionary defines every aspect of nonverbal communication, from 'Adam's-apple-jump' to 'zygomatic smile'.

Personal nonverbal communication

Personal nonverbal communication is the use of nonverbal actions in a way that is personal or unique to that person. Givens (2005) points out:

> . . . each of us gives and responds to literally thousands of nonverbal messages daily in our personal and professional lives—and while commuting back and forth between the two. From morning's kiss to business suits and tense-mouth displays at the conference table, we react to wordless messages emotionally, often without knowing why. The boss's head-nod, the clerk's bow tie, the next-door neighbour's hairstyle—we notice the minutia of nonverbal behaviour because their details reveal (a) how we relate to one another, and (b) who we think we are.

Givens believes that 'nonverbal messages are so potent and compelling because they are processed in ancient brain centres located beneath the newer areas used for speech'. Nonverbal cues, he asserts, are produced and received below the level of conscious awareness.

Conditioning in the developmental years of childhood and identification with others who are trusted and respected influences personal nonverbal communication. Over time, people develop preferences for certain patterns of nonverbal communication based on experience. A person's style of dress or image is a form of communication personal to the individual. Statements about self are made through appearance and clothing.

In this type of nonverbal communication the meaning is unique to the person sending the message. One person may laugh through nervousness or fear of crying, while another person may cry. Douglis (1996) suggests that emotional responses, gestures and body language are the manifestations of the energy used in personal interactions. For example, someone may work while talking, while another person may work in silence.

Accurate interpretation of the nonverbal messages comes from knowing the person and their pattern of interpersonal communication, both verbal and nonverbal.

> **Personal nonverbal communication** is the use of nonverbal actions in a way that is personal or unique to a person.

> Everyone has their own unique nonverbal signals.

Cultural nonverbal communication

Cultural nonverbal communication is characteristic of, or common to, a group of people. Cultural groups may evolve on the basis of nationality, gender, age or religion. Nonverbal communication is learned unconsciously by observing others in the society or group. Attitudes, beliefs, values and norms regulate communication (verbal and nonverbal) and interactions between those in the culture.

Social influence is the process by which others affect our perceptions, attitudes and actions. People learn the meaning of nonverbal behaviours and their acceptability through direct instructions or by modelling and imitating the behaviour of others in the group to which they wish to belong. In order to belong, they share and conform to the attitudes, beliefs, values and **norms**, and follow the group's patterns of behaviour as they interact and communicate.

In Aboriginal culture, for example, eye contact is less acceptable than in European culture. Another example is that, in general, women feel free to touch each other, whereas men are often more self-conscious about touching each other. The rules learned as children about nonverbal messages create a level of consensus on which the group agrees. Although the influence of others in a society is strong enough to create cultural norms, it is almost invisible. Acceptable patterns of behaviour are established and modified by the responses of people within the society or group.

> **Cultural nonverbal communication** is rule-governed behaviour learned unconsciously from others in the culture.

> **Norms** are rules of behaviour agreed upon within a group or society.

> The behaviour of members of a society is used as a standard against which individuals measure their own behaviour.

STRATEGIES TO BRIDGE CULTURAL DIFFERENCES

As cultural background influences the way people send and receive nonverbal messages, it is important to consider the cultural factors in the message, as well as interpreting the message within its context. Inconsistencies between the verbal and nonverbal messages of someone from another culture may be acceptable norms within their culture. By acknowledging cultural differences it is easier to understand the intended message.

Beebe, Beebe and Redmond (2008, pp. 110–19) list the following nine strategies or skills to help bridge differences in background and culture.

1. Seek information about the culture.
2. Ask questions and listen effectively.
3. Develop a third culture (based on an understanding and inclusion of elements from two other cultures).
4. Tolerate ambiguity.
5. Develop mindfulness.
6. Avoid negative judgments about another culture.
7. Be flexible.
8. Become other-oriented.
9. Adapt your communication to others.

(Refer to Chapter 2, 'Intercultural Communication'.)

Universal nonverbal communication

Universal nonverbal communication refers to body movements common to humankind, such as a smile or tears.

Universal nonverbal communication is behaviour that is common to humankind. Morris and colleagues (1979) found that some gestures are highly localised in a culture, while others cross national and linguistic boundaries. A person smiling with outspread arms and upturned, open hands communicates welcome universally. Universally, facial expressions and gestures are indicators of emotion. Darwin (1872) suggested that emotions have evolved as part of our biological heritage. An emotion such as displeasure or puzzlement is expressed through a pattern of muscular facial movements that we call a frown.

Universal nonverbal messages often show happiness, sadness or deep-seated feelings; for example, a smile or tears. Their basis is physiological change related to emotions, rather than rituals stylised by a society. Douglis (1996) suggests that emotional responses, gestures and body language are manifestations of the energy used in personal interactions. According to Metcalf (1997), the universal sign for a person withholding their true feelings is putting one or both hands to the face. While an adult may rub the mouth, upper lip or nose with one finger, a teenager may cover the mouth. Children who are less experienced than adults or teenagers at sending and interpreting messages will cover their faces.

Random behaviour may distract but does not change the meaning.

Occasionally, nonverbal behaviours such as a sneeze are unrelated to the verbal message. A sneeze is simply random behaviour. Unrelated nonverbal communication can distract from the verbal message, although it has little effect on the meaning of the verbal part of the message.

Givens (2005) asserts that body-language signals can be learned behaviour, innate behaviour or a mixture of both. He lists the eye-wink, thumbs-up and military-salute gestures as examples of learned signals and the eye-blink, the throat-clear and facial-flushing as examples of inborn or innate signals. Laughing, crying and shoulder-shrugging he considers to be 'mixed', because, although they orginated as innate actions, cultural rules have later shaped their timing, energy and use. Other researchers are in disagreement about the nature–nurture issue, some believing that most or all gestures are learned.

REVIEW QUESTIONS

1.
   a Define the term 'nonverbal communication'.
   b It is often said that 'Silent language speaks'. Explain.
   c List three of your personal nonverbal actions.
2. 'Any nonverbal communication needs to be seen against related cultural norms.' Explain this statement.
3. Identify two strategies that help you to adapt your communication in order to bridge the differences in background and culture.

NONVERBAL CUES

1 Work individually.

  a Define and give examples of personal, cultural and universal nonverbal communication.

  b Explain the conventions of greeting in your culture.

  c List the main gender differences between the rule-governed behaviour for sitting and walking. In your answer, compare the socially acceptable ways in which arms, legs and the body are used when men sit and when women sit.

  d Assume that two people are standing side-by-side and will touch by one placing a hand on the other person's shoulder or arm. Given the social rules of etiquette in your own culture, who would touch whom first in the following situations?
  - college principal and student
  - company director and new employee
  - interviewer and interviewee.

  e Using examples from your own experience, list two nonverbal behaviours that express satisfaction and two nonverbal behaviours that express dissatisfaction.

2 Work in pairs.

  a Discuss a situation when interpreting nonverbal messages through your own gender and cultural rules caused miscommunication.

  b Describe the results of the miscommunication.

  c Suggest strategies you could use to bridge the differences between background and culture.

  d Report back to the large group.

3 Working in small groups, brainstorm the ideas presented in the following statement to develop lists of:

  a up to ten examples of nonverbal communication that strengthens or reduces the impact of verbal communication

  b up to ten examples of specific meanings in relationships that can be conveyed nonverbally.

  'Nonverbal communication strengthens or reduces the impact of verbal communication. It conveys specific meanings in relationships and transmits our emotional content and our attitude to others.'

4 Work individually.

  Givens (2008) points out that 'each of us gives and responds to literally thousands of nonverbal messages daily in our personal and professional lives—and while commuting back and forth between the two'.

  a Compare and contrast the kind of nonverbal messages you give in your professional life and your personal life.

  b What in Givens' view makes nonverbal messages so potent and compelling?

  c Considering that some cultures are contact cultures and others are non-contact cultures, what kind of communication problem would be likely to arise when individuals from each type of culture interact?

  d How can an understanding of Givens' view help an organisation and its representatives conduct business transactions overseas?

THE ROLE OF NONVERBAL COMMUNICATION

The *total message* contains spoken words and nonverbal communication. Birdwhistell (1970) says that 35% of meaning comes from the verbal part of the message and 65% from the nonverbal part. Words alone are not enough to convey the message. Nonverbal communication adds meaning and modifies or changes the spoken words. Six ways of doing this are shown in Table 4.1.

  Birdwhistell (1970) claimed that the average person actually speaks for a total of only 10 to 11 minutes daily and that the standard spoken sentence takes only about 2.5 seconds. He estimated also that verbal components carry about one-third, and nonverbal components carry about two-thirds, of the social meaning of the situation. Mehrabian (1971, p. 44) comments that a person's nonverbal behaviour communicates feelings or attitudes more than words. His equation is:

◄ OBJECTIVE 2
Explain the roles of nonverbal communication and understand differences between cultures

The total message contains both verbal and nonverbal components.

Table 4.1: Nonverbal communication

Purpose	Examples
Repeating	Pointing when giving directions.
Contradicting	Looking at your watch and backing away while telling someone, 'I'm very interested in what you're saying.'
Substituting	Using facial expressions as a substitute for words, to show pleasure, disappointment and a range of emotions.
Complementing	Modifying, emphasising or elaborating words in a way that conveys attitudes and intentions; e.g. a person who disrespects another may stand in a casual way or use a tone of voice that conveys a lack of respect when talking with this person.
Accenting	Moving the head and hands to emphasise parts of the verbal message; e.g. shaking the head as you say 'No'.
Controlling the flow of information	Nodding the head or changing position can indicate to the speaker to continue or to give the other person a turn.

Total feeling = 7% verbal feeling + 38% vocal feeling + 55% facial feeling

Argyle (1983) confirms that research shows that 'the non-verbal style had more effect than the verbal contents, in fact about five times as much; when the verbal and non-verbal messages were in conflict, the verbal contents were virtually disregarded'.

The ability to send clear nonverbal messages facilitates communication.

Mehrabian (1971, p. iii) states that 'people who have a greater awareness of the communicative significance of actions not only can insure accurate communication of their own feelings but also can be more successful in their intimate relationships, in artistic endeavors such as acting, or in work that involves the persuasion, leadership, and organisation of others'.

Argyle (1983) identified four different nonverbal communication roles:

1. communicating interpersonal attitudes and emotions
2. self-presentation
3. rituals
4. supporting verbal communication.

From birth we see and read messages sent by nonverbal communication. It is an innate part of our social behaviour 'used for negotiating interpersonal attitudes, while the verbal channel is used primarily for conveying information' (1983, p. 44). The self-presentation role conveys information about our self-concept, image and feelings. Artefacts such as badges, clothes and hairstyle send information about the self nonverbally. The patterns of behaviour used in rituals and ceremonies, such as university graduations, school speech days, engagements and weddings, confirm social relationships and send messages about status or changes in status (such as undergraduate to postgraduate). The role of nonverbal communication in supporting verbal communication is shown in vocal cues such as timing, pitch, resonance, rhythm and articulation. They support the verbal message.

Nonverbal learning is the extralinguistic transmission of cultural knowledge, practices and lore.

Givens (2008) presents the concept of **nonverbal learning** as the act of gaining knowledge or skills apart from language, speech or words. A great deal of knowledge in business, from how to dress to making a major public presentation on behalf of your organisation, is gained by watching, imitating and practising the nonverbal communication of someone who knows. Givens highlights the importance of nonverbal directions at airports, shopping malls and theme parks, and on the roads. They are linked nonverbally via international graphic symbols in a pictorial format to show people where they are and where they need to go.

Verbal and nonverbal contradictions

Most nonverbal communication is clear and easy to understand, but on occasions the nonverbal part of the message may be ambiguous and confusing. The message is two-edged because the facial and vocal expressions, postures and gestures do not match the words. The percentages for the three components that make up total feeling in Mehrabian's (1971) formula (see page 94) show that facial expressions have the greatest impact on the message. The cues in the vocal qualities have the next greatest impact. The experiment shows that, when we are resolving the general meaning of an inconsistent message, words make up the smallest percentage of the message.

Usually, nonverbal communication is not consciously observed unless it causes some confusion or doubt in the receiver. Sometimes, it is possible to ignore confusing nonverbal communication, but on other occasions it must be acknowledged or even confronted; for example, the verbal message may convey agreement, while a range of nonverbal signals—such as pitch of voice, facial expression or the body held back—indicates lack of agreement or even ridicule. It is useful to check the meaning when you:

The nonverbal message can sometimes contradict the verbal components.

- are in doubt
- are uncomfortable with the communication, or
- will have to make a decision on the basis of the total message.

Different meanings between cultures

Nampo (2002) points out that the Japanese place greater reliance on nonverbal communication to convey meaning and that they 'tend to use nonverbal expression to tell emotional things and what they are unwilling to say aloud'. Similarly, the Japanese infer what others want to say from their nonverbal expressions. Nampo refers to a study by Matsumoto (1985) of the facial expressions of Japanese and Americans. The results show that the Japanese express their feelings less than the Americans, particularly negative feelings such as anger, fear and sadness, and are also poorer at reading facial expressions.

BODY MOVEMENT

Nampo refers also to direct eye contact, which in Western culture implies confidence or sincerity. In Japan, eye contact is often seen as a gesture of defiance or challenge. Research by Archer and Archer (2001) shows that Japanese people may shift their eyes or look down in order to show respect to another person. Similarly, Japanese often smile to conceal embarrassment, pain or distress, and in an uncomfortable situation will give a nervous laugh or awkward smile in order to conceal their emotions. Japanese also consider it rude to overtly express one's emotions in public. Archer and Archer point out that 'the poker face is used to cover up negative emotions as well as used as a shield to protect one's privacy'.

Direct eye contact has different meanings in different cultures.

Gestures are also very different from country to country. In Nampo's opinion, 'It is better not to use gestures in Japan as one might mistake the correct meaning of the signal or use them at inappropriate times' (see Table 4.2).

DISTANCE AND TIME

Because of Japan's high-density population, the Japanese show great respect for the personal space of others. They consider it rude to cross between two people or intrude into another's personal space in order to move through a room. They also rarely touch one another when they are communicating, nor do they show any signs of affection or emotions in public.

In Japan, time is highly valued. Adhering to schedules and being punctual are very important to the Japanese. Research shows that Japanese workers prefer to plan their time carefully, concentrating on one project at a time rather than multitasking.

Table 4.2: Signs of communication between Japanese people	
Sign	**Meaning**
Pointing to one's nose or touching the nose	Me
Nodding one's head up and down. (This should not be mistaken as a 'yes' gesture. It means that one is listening, not necessarily agreeing.)	Listening
Fanning one's hand back and forth in front of the face as if to indicate 'no' or to fan away flies	Negative
Pointing the index fingers up from the temples (mimicking a devil with horns)	Anger
Criss-crossing the index fingers or tapping the index fingers together	Fighting
Forming a circle with the thumb and index finger	Money
Waving the hand in a back-and-forth motion with the fingers pointed downwards	Come here

Source: Adapted from A. Archer & S. Archer, *A Beginner's Guide to Japan: Non-Verbal Communication,* 2001. Reproduced with permission.

SILENCE

Silence can be just as important as what is said.

Silence is important to the Japanese. Silence allows you to understand what has been communicated and provides an opportunity to respond in a considered way. The Japanese consider that silence, or what is not said, can be just as important as what *is* said. Capper (2000) states that, as Japan is identified as a high-context culture in which much background information is shared, there is not the need for an explicit, detailed explanation in conversation.

AMBIGUOUS NONVERBAL BEHAVIOUR

Nonverbal behaviour has a strong impact on any business communication. The accuracy with which nonverbal communication is interpreted and its value in adding understanding to the message depends on the ability of the sender to express the intended message accurately, and the ability of the receiver to interpret the message accurately.

Listeners should check the meaning of ambiguous nonverbal messages.

The total message is made up of words and nonverbal behaviour. Listeners who are in doubt about the meaning of nonverbal behaviour should check it out with the speaker. The total message is understood more easily by following a four-step process: hear the words, see the nonverbal behaviours, check the meaning with the sender when the verbal and nonverbal messages are different and consider the context or setting.

Context is the situation or setting within which communication takes place.

Nonverbal communication in business always exists in a **context** or framework. The context often determines the meaning of the nonverbal behaviour. On different occasions the same nonverbal gesture may have a completely different meaning because of its context. Nonverbal behaviour separated from its context and the spoken words that accompany it is almost impossible to interpret with any accuracy.

REVIEW QUESTION

4 What are the roles played by nonverbal communication?

OBJECTIVE 3 ▶
Discuss seven aspects of nonverbal behaviour

ASPECTS OF NONVERBAL COMMUNICATION

People communicate nonverbally with body movement and with personal relationship behaviours. They rely heavily on nonverbal communication to transmit the message and to modify, change or complement the verbal communication. Nonverbal communication is more powerful than verbal communication in conveying emotions, attitudes and reactions. Charles Darwin published the first scientific study of nonverbal communication in 1872 in *The Expressions of the Emotions in Man and Animals*. Since then there has been considerable research into nonverbal cues. Discoveries in neuroscience funded during 1990–2000, the 'Decade of the Brain', have provided a clearer picture of nonverbal communication. Body language has come of age in the 21st century as a science to help us understand what it means to be human (Givens 2005).

Theoretical writings and research break nonverbal communication into the seven main areas shown in Figure 4.1.

Body movement, or kinesics

Body movements, such as those of the hands, head, feet and legs, and posture, eye movements and facial expressions all affect the message. Forgas (1986, pp. 153–8) regards eye contact as one of the most powerful and most common nonverbal signals.

Hassin and Trope (2000) demonstrated that personality information conveyed in faces changes the receiver's interpretation of the verbal information. They showed also that the perception of facial features and, accordingly, the perceived similarity between faces is changed by information about personality. One of the consequences of reading faces was that 'strong verbal information changes the perception of face and, hence, the physiognomic information derived from it' (p. 848). They concluded that it was possible, over time, that 'verbal and nonverbal information might change the physiognomic information conveyed by one's face and, hence, "untrap" it' (p. 850).

Forgas (1986) comments that 'we learn to unconsciously notice the size of other people's pupils, and interpret the observable changes in pupil size as indications of positive or negative attitudes on the part of our partner(s)'. He also cites the following results of research (p. 157):

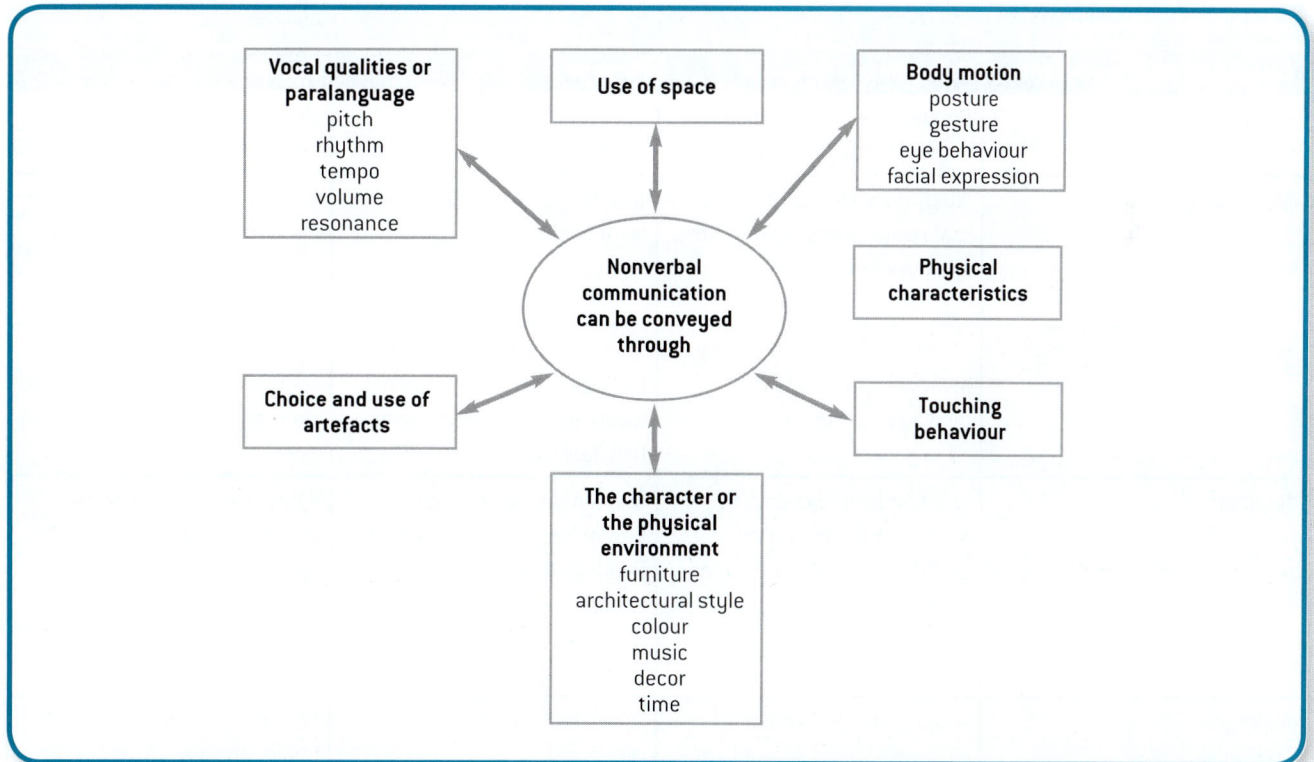

Figure 4.1: Seven areas of nonverbal communication

In a typical two-person conversation, people look at each other about 61 per cent of the time, and their gaze coincides (mutual gaze) about 32 per cent of the time (Argyle and Ingham 1972). Mutual gaze lasts on the average only about one second, while each individual gaze is usually about three seconds long. The same person will look more when listening (75 per cent of the time), than when speaking (41 per cent of the time).

Movements of the hands, arms, feet and head are closely oriented with the spoken words. They convey messages about emotions, feelings and attitudes. Body posture—the way a person stands, leans forward or back, moves the head—has an impact on the message. A person leaning forward, pointing and shaking a finger at someone is seen as trying to dominate the other person. Holding the head high may project arrogance, while fear and uncertainty are suggested when the head is held down low. Fiddling with jewellery, pens or a paperclip may convey nervousness and insecurity. The way we sit or stand can show attitudes such as friendliness or hostility and emotional states such as relaxation or tension. Leaning forward indicates curiosity and interest, and direct eye contact shows confidence. The way body movements are received by others, and the type of response or feedback, determines how the communication will flow.

Knapp (1978) presented Ekman and Friesen's five main categories of body movement: emblems, illustrations, effective or feeling displays, regulation and adaptors. These are explained in Table 4.3.

Physical characteristics

Physical characteristics such as body shape, general attractiveness, body and breath odours, weight, and hair and skin colour are important parts of nonverbal communication. Our physical appearance sends a message about our age, sex and occupation. Someone who dislikes physical exercise and works in an office all day will have a different physique to that of a champion weight-lifter. Because

Table 4.3: Body movement

Category of body movement	Definition	Purpose	Example
Emblems	Emblems are nonverbal acts learned through imitation.	To reinforce or replace the words.	The nonverbals for 'OK' are a nod or a smile.
Illustrators	Illustrators are nonverbal acts that relate to and illustrate the spoken word.	To accentuate or emphasise a word or phrase.	A nod of the head and wave of the arm in a certain direction, accompanying the statement 'over there'.
Affective or feeling displays	Affective displays are changes in facial expressions that display emotion.	Unconscious displays reflect feelings, whereas intentional expressions can disguise or hide feelings.	Facial expressions and eye contact; for example, a smile to express happiness.
Regulators	Regulators are nonverbal acts, such as head nods, that regulate communication between people.	To maintain and control the flow of speaking and listening. Regulators indicate whether to continue, repeat, elaborate or change from speaker to listener.	A head nod to encourage another person to continue speaking.
Adaptors	Adaptors are nonverbal acts performed unconsciously in response to some inner desire.	To display instinctive responses.	Scratching an itchy ear or raising the arms in shock or horror.

people react and respond to physical characteristics, they are influential in determining the responses in interpersonal encounters. First impressions and images of others can be associated unconsciously with past experiences of people with similar physical characteristics.

Touching behaviour

Stroking, hitting, holding or guiding the movement of another person are examples of touching behaviour that communicates nonverbally. Each one adds a different meaning to a message. Touching usually signals interest and leads to a response from the person being touched. Some of our touching behaviour is ritualistic; for example, touching when saying goodbye to friends after an extended holiday in your home. Most people in our culture engage in a hug, kiss, touch on the arm or handshake.

Touching behaviour varies between cultures.

Touching can console or support the other person and show feelings such as affection, sexual interest or dominance. Hand gestures demonstrate feelings and put thoughts and words into movements. A handshake, for example, can suggest dominance or equality. A pat on the arm can convey intimacy or control.

Vocal qualities, or paralanguage

Paralanguage is that part of language associated with the use of the language, but is not the word system. It comprises the voice qualities and vocalisations that affect *how* something is said, rather than *what* is said. Voice qualities include pitch range, pitch control, rhythm control, tempo, articulation control and resonance.

Paralanguage is how something is said.

Vocalisations also give clues to the total message (see Table 4.4).

Other vocal qualities include tone of voice, rate of speaking and voice inflection. A tired person, for example, will speak more slowly than usual; a disappointed person may speak with a flat tone; the tone of voice of a person excited about a coming holiday reflects this excitement. A higher voice pitch than usual is interpreted as dishonesty or discomfort. A salesperson who speaks too quickly may be greeted with suspicion. Someone who raises their voice at the end of a sentence may sound uncertain and less authoritative than one who ends a sentence with a lower voice pitch.

Use of space, or proximity

Proximity refers to nearness in place. It is influenced by the nature of the encounter, the type of relationship, and cultural factors such as gender and nationality. As well as varying in formal, informal and intimate contexts, the use of space indicates how people feel about their role and status.

Proximity means nearness in place.

ORIENTATION

Hargie, Saunders and Dickson (1981), elaborating on Hall's theory of proxemics, refer to another aspect of nonverbal behaviour that should be considered—that is, the angle at which one person interacts with another (orientation)—as it also affects the communication pattern. The authors say

Table 4.4: Vocalisations	
Type	**Example**
Vocal characterisers	Vocal characterisers include laughing, crying, sighing, yawning, clearing the throat, groaning, yelling, whispering.
Vocal qualifiers	Vocal qualifiers include intensity, such as too loud through to too soft, and pitch level, from too high to too low.
Vocal segregates	Vocal segregates are sounds such as 'Uh huh', 'Um', 'Uh', and 'Ah', silent pauses, and intruding sounds from the environment.

that orientation, which refers to the position of the body, should be examined in tandem with proximity because 'it has been found that there is an inverse relationship between them; that is, direct face-to-face orientation is linked to greater distance and sideways orientation is linked to closer distance'. They cite Sommer's (1969) and Cook's (1971) studies on seating behaviour, which indicate that 'a side-by-side position is considered to be co-operative in nature, while a face-to-face orientation usually conveys intonations of competitiveness'.

DISTANCE

Acceptable personal distance varies between cultures.

Hall (1969) identified four distances that people maintain between themselves and others. These four distances form an invisible space (or bubble) around a person's physical being.

1. Intimate distance is 0 to 18 inches (0–45 cm). Intimate distance allows close physical contact and is most often used in close emotional relationships.
2. Personal distance is 18 inches to 4 feet (45–120 cm). Personal distance is used when people interact and share personal concerns in less intimate relationships. Hall suggests that personal distance allows people to interact but at the same time keep the other person 'at arm's length'.
3. Social distance is 4 to 12 feet (1.2–3.6 m). Social distance is used in impersonal and more formal interactions. This distance is likely to be used at work and in situations where less intimate and private feelings and information are communicated.
4. Public distance is 12 feet (3.6 m) to out of sight. The public distance of 12 feet (3.6 m) to the limit of sight makes it difficult for people to communicate. They are able to avoid interaction until they move closer.

How people use their own personal space and the space of others defines the relationship; it communicates and reflects the way they feel towards others. It also varies between cultures. In a business transaction, for example, Oriental, Nordic, Anglo-Saxon and Germanic people are comfortable with just over a metre or more of personal distance. They feel discomfort when strangers intrude into this personal space. On the other hand, Latin, Arab and African people can meet a stranger and feel satisfied with only half a metre of personal space. An understanding and respect for the cultural norms of others improves our perception and interpretation of the way others use space.

Lindgren (1973) confirms that research has demonstrated that physical appearance plays an important role in social attraction; however, he points out that other factors are also important, 'the most notable being interpersonal similarity in attitudes and values'. He further points out that 'the effect of such similarity on attraction can be demonstrated by such behavioural measures as the distance separating pairs of individuals as they stand together'. Lindgren states that when we meet strangers, appearance is the indicator we are most likely to use to make an assumption about their attitudes and values, and we then use this assumption as a basis for our 'decisions to approach or avoid strangers'. Mehrabian (1971, p. 1) agrees that 'people are drawn toward persons and things they like, evaluate highly, and prefer; and they avoid or move away from things they dislike, evaluate negatively, or do not prefer'. He refers to this as the *immediacy principle*.

Artefacts

Artefacts are objects that convey nonverbal messages.

Artefacts are objects used to convey nonverbal messages about self-concept, image, mood, feelings and style. Many artefacts are common to the group, but it is possible to use an artefact such as style of dress as a form of communication that is personal to the individual. Perfume, clothes, lipstick, glasses and hairpieces project the personal style as well as the mood of the wearer. They are an important and highly visible part of nonverbal communication. They also make a statement about image and may create a positive or negative first impression.

Colours create an impression. In Western culture, a navy blue suit conveys more authority than a light brown suit. McCoy (1996) suggests that both men and women can wear navy blue, black, grey or burgundy to project a formal image. The general rule of a white shirt or blouse and a dark suit for formal occasions still applies. Neutral colours such as beige, corn and khaki are cooler colours to use for summer professional clothes.

The choice of clothes reflects the mood, the occasion and a person's attitude to the occasion. A police badge, an army uniform, a university lecturer's gown and an Italian suit are all appearance signals. Some of these artefacts reflect power or nonpower in a situation. If a plain-clothes police officer shows a police badge at an accident there is an immediate perception of authority by those who see the badge.

By deciding not to trouble about personal appearance or clothes, a person is still communicating. Others will form a first impression and read this message as part of the nonverbal communication.

Environmental factors

Environmental factors can influence the outcome of a communication. For this reason, organisations spend time designing office space, factory layout and the sales area, and plan for conferences carefully. The ideal environment puts people at ease and matches their expectations; an unsuitable environment can produce 'noise' that acts as a barrier and interferes with communication.

Certain instincts, such as the need for privacy, familiarity and security, should be satisfied. Careful design of the workplace can help to meet these needs and in so doing improve communication, productivity and morale. Natural and artificial light, colour, temperature, tables, chairs, desks, lounges, plants, sound, artwork, magazines, and floor and wall coverings all have an impact on people's perception of the organisation.

In the workplace, attention to punctuality or a disregard for it can be a powerful nonverbal communicator. A disregard for punctuality may, like a sloppy appearance, merely reflect a casual attitude. However, a deliberate decision to keep a contact waiting may be a way to communicate a negative message. While punctuality is a matter of courtesy, attitudes towards its importance vary between cultures. To be kept waiting for a business appointment on a tropical island will not have the same significance as a similar delay in some European countries where punctuality is highly regarded.

This discussion of the seven aspects of nonverbal communication provides a theoretical analysis. However, to consider them in isolation is artificial. In practice, what is sent as a total message is a cluster of nonverbal cues in association with the spoken words.

Environmental factors such as setting and context can influence the outcome of communication.

REVIEW QUESTIONS

5 *a*   What are the seven aspects of nonverbal communication?
   b   List and give an example of each of the five main categories of body movement.
   c   What is the purpose of each?
6 'Paralanguage will often determine the message being sent.' Briefly explain. In your answer give examples of three vocalisations and discuss their impact on the message.
7 *a*   Briefly explain the four types of space that dictate the rules of proximity in a society or culture.
   b   Give an example of an occasion when space conveyed a nonverbal message, and discuss the impact of that message.
8 What part do artefacts play in nonverbal communication?

APPLY YOUR KNOWLEDGE

COMMUNICATION WITHOUT WORDS

1. Work in small groups.

    'Nonverbal communication can complement, enhance, replace or contradict verbal communication.' Discuss this statement in a small group and provide examples of situations in which each has happened.

2. Work individually.

    a What is the purpose of each of the five main categories of body movement identified by Ekman and Friesen?

    b What other areas of nonverbal communication would you consider before interpreting a message?

    c Is it being manipulative to manage your own nonverbal behaviour?

3. Work in pairs by standing together.

    While person A stays still on exactly the same spot, person B places themselves comfortably in relation to person A. Person B, who has made the decision on comfortable distance, then says what made them choose their position. Person A, who is standing still, then talks about how they feel—that is, whether person B is standing too close, the angle, the amount of contact, the impact of height difference, gender issues, body size and body space.

4. Work in small groups.

    a Identify and give some practical examples of the aspects of nonverbal communication that can cause barriers to effective intercultural communication.

    b In what ways can you prevent these barriers?

    c Develop a plan to improve your interpersonal skills in a way that will improve your effectiveness as a business negotiator in another culture of your choice.

5. Work in small groups.

    a Discuss the four different nonverbal communication roles identified by Argyle (1983).

    b Brainstorm to create a list of examples of each of these roles.

    c In which of the four nonverbal communication roles do you feel most comfortable?

    d In which of the four roles do you feel least comfortable?

    e What actions could you take to make yourself feel more comfortable in that role?

6. Work as a large group (15–20 people).

    The purpose of this activity is to identify different aspects of nonverbal communication and to experience the effect of a stress situation in a controlled environment.

    Walk the circle

    a Place as many chairs in a circle as there are people in the group. Add two extra chairs to the circle.

    b Each person in the group sits on a chair in the circle. A chair on each side of the circle is left empty. The rest of the activity is conducted in silence.

    c Each person takes a turn to stand up, walk across the circle to the first empty chair, sit down, then stand up and walk to the other empty chair and sit down and then return to their own chair. The rest of the group observes the person walking between chairs. Only one person should be moving at any time.

    d When each person has 'walked the circle', discuss as a large group:

        i observations and impressions about the way people used nonverbal communication such as eyes, pace, posture, facial expressions and other movements

        ii the messages received from the nonverbal communication

        iii how people felt about 'walking the circle' in silence in front of others.

THE LISTENING PROCESS

DeVito (2001) lists two studies—using adults as subjects (Rankin 1929) and using college students (Barker et al. 1980)—which showed that listening occupied more time than any other communication activity. The column graph in Figure 4.2 shows the ratios for the two groups.

The ratio varies from 45% (adults) to 53% (college students), with speaking, reading and writing accounting for only 55% and 47%, respectively. Lane (1987), while reporting similar figures (45% listening, 30% talking, 16% reading, and 9% writing), cautions: 'The percentage figure on listening can be misleading . . . it means simply the time spent in silence while someone speaks' (p. 28).

While hearing is a passive process, **listening** is a conscious, knowing response to the message. The listener hears sounds, interprets those sounds, and attaches meaning to the sounds in the message. Hirsch (1986) divided the cognitive components of listening into the ten parts shown in Table 4.5.

> **Listening** is a conscious, knowing response to a message.

Whatever the listening purpose, concentration and a deliberate effort to be interested in the speaker's message will increase listening *effectiveness*. The key to effective listening in any context is active participation. Hargie and colleagues (1981) state that 'in interpersonal interaction the process of listening is of crucial importance' (p. 168). DeVito (2001) comments that, as well as being physically alert, even more important is mental alertness: 'As a listener, participate in the communication interaction as an equal partner with the speaker, as one who is emotionally and intellectually ready to engage in the sharing of meaning' (p. 58).

> **Effective listening** occurs when the listener understands the sender's intended message.

A listener who really understands the sender's intended message is an effective listener. An effective listener can match the listening approach—active, informational, evaluative or conversational—to the listening purpose.

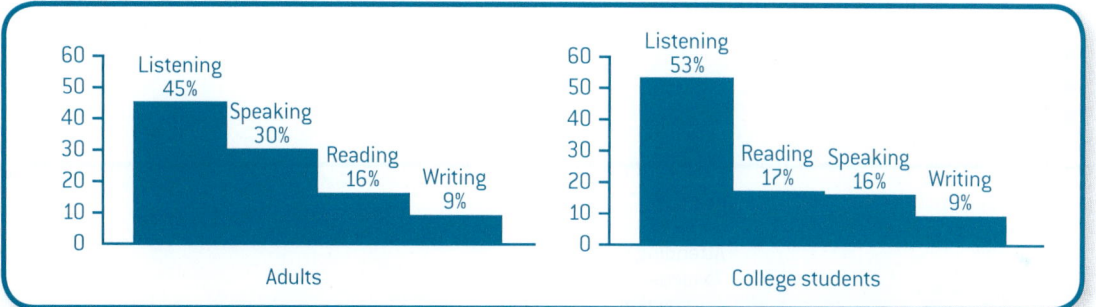

Figure 4.2: Time spent listening

Source: Adapted from J. DeVito, *The Interpersonal Communication Book*, 9th edn, Allyn & Bacon, Boston, MA, p. 54. © 2001 by Pearson Education. Adapted by permission of the publisher.

Table 4.5: Listening: Cognitive components
• Making the physiological and neurological connections
• Interpreting the sounds
• Understanding the sounds
• Assigning meaning to the sounds
• Reacting to the sounds
• Receiving some sounds and ignoring others selectively
• Remembering what was received
• Attending to the sounds purposely
• Analysing the information presented
• Filtering communication information on the basis of past experiences

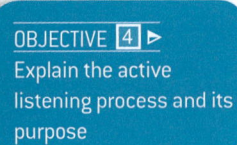
OBJECTIVE 4 ▶

Explain the active
listening process and its
purpose

Active listening

DeVito (2001) identifies three types of listening—listening for enjoyment, for information and to help—and comments that 'Unlike hearing, listening is an *active* rather than a passive process. Listening does not just happen; you must make it happen' (p. 54). Bolton (1987) describes active listening as a cluster of attending, encouraging and reflecting skills used together in order to pay attention to the content and feelings that comprise the whole message. The purpose of each of these skills is shown in Figure 4.3. The *active listening* approach is used when a listener wants to help the sender solve a problem, or to understand the content and feelings in the message. The listener listens actively and with empathy.

Active listening is an
approach in which the
listener relates back to the
speaker the content and
feeling in the message.

Active listening focuses attention and provides feedback, allowing speakers to express their feelings and identify the real cause of those feelings. Attending, encouraging and reflective listening are techniques that allow the listener to give the speaker their full attention until the speaker is able to communicate the real message. The real message can only be understood if listener and speaker are able to bring out the underlying feelings.

Sometimes a listener will use only one of these types of listening skills. On another occasion they might use all in combination. Each type of listening is a set of behaviours or skills. Individually, they allow the listener to focus on the speaker, invite the speaker to continue, give feedback or show empathy with the speaker. These skills are used together in the active listening process.

The following strategies provide the feedback that will encourage the speaker to continue.

FOCUS ON THE SPEAKER

Attending listening
focuses on the speaker by
giving physical attention.

In **attending listening**, listeners focus on the speaker by giving their physical attention to the other person. They use their whole body to provide feedback that assures the speaker of their total attention. Some ways of offering this feedback are:

- eye contact
- posture
- body movement.

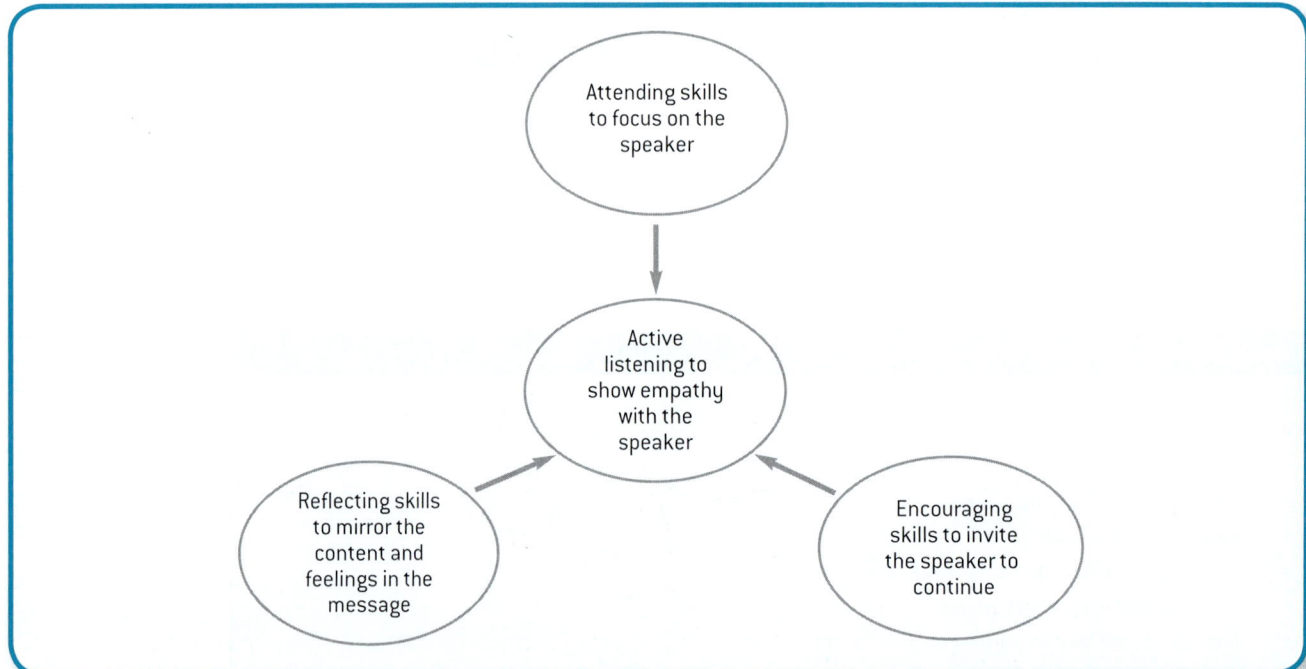

Figure 4.3: Three integrated active listening skills

A capacity to ignore distractions, and an understanding of the impact of moving into the personal space of others and the impact of the environment, also improve the quality of attending listening skills. The six factors in Table 4.6 help listeners to give their complete attention to the speaker.

INVITE THE SPEAKER TO CONTINUE

Encouraging listening indicates that the listener is willing to do more than listen. Encouraging listening invites the speaker to say more and to disclose their thoughts and feelings, but without pressuring them. It is their choice, so let them decide. They may be experiencing feelings of ambivalence about whether to talk or to keep their feelings private. Continue to give attention by using eye contact and an open posture, and give them the opportunity and freedom to disclose. For example, if the speaker seems upset or annoyed, a listener might say something like, 'You seem to be upset about the discussion with that last client. Would you care to talk about it?'

Minimal and brief spoken responses let the speaker know the listener is listening and encourage them to continue. Some of these responses are 'mm', 'hmmm', 'yes', 'I see', coupled with attentive posture. Other nonverbal cues such as head nodding and facial expressions convey the listener's interest to the speaker without attempting to control or divert the conversation away from the area of interest.

A *pause* or *silence* allows the speaker time to consider, reflect and decide whether to continue the conversation. As a listener, use this time to attend and watch the body movement of the speaker. This can give the listener clues to the total message, both the content and the feelings in the conversation. Allow silences and give the speaker time to think.

By asking open questions the listener encourages the speaker to share more personal feelings and thoughts. An example of an open question is: 'How did you go about collecting the files?' An example of a closed question is: 'Did you collect the files?' Whereas open questions encourage the

Encouraging listening invites speakers to disclose their thoughts and feelings.

Minimal and brief responses encourage the speaker to continue.

A pause or silence gives the speaker time to reflect.

Open questions allow the sharing of more personal feelings and thoughts.

Table 4.6: Attending listening	
Factor	**Techniques**
Eye contact	• Use supportive eye contact. • Focus eyes on the speaker without being intimidating. • Show sensitivity and occasionally shift the gaze from the other person's face. • Avoid staring directly at the speaker for long periods, as the speaker may feel uncomfortable.
Posture	• Use open posture (i.e. not folded arms or crossed legs) to attend to the other person. • Lean slightly forward towards the speaker in a relaxed way. • Face the person squarely.
Body movement	• Avoid moving about a lot. • Avoid fiddling with objects, crossing or uncrossing legs, signalling or speaking to passers-by. • Stay still and concentrate on the speaker.
Personal space	• Create a comfortable distance between listener and speaker—comfort in the use of physical distance depends on culture and personal preference. • Avoid moving into the speaker's personal space.
Environment	• Create an environment without distractions or interruptions. • Remove any physical barriers between listener and speaker. • Establish an environment where both people can feel relaxed.
Avoid distractions	• Face and maintain contact with the speaker. • Ignore distractions, rather than turning away. • Stop and focus your attention on the other person.

speaker to answer at greater length and in more detail, closed questions usually lead to a 'yes' or 'no' answer.

Avoid 'why' questions because they can make the other person defensive. Instead of encouraging the speaker to explore their actions, a 'why' question encourages them to justify their actions. The speaker may feel threatened because the 'why' question sounds as if the listener disapproves of their actions.

By asking open questions about what, when, where, how and who, the listener is able to help the speaker to be more specific, precise and revealing. Although encouraging questions let the other person know the listener is interested in talking with them, they do not necessarily show that the listener understands. To show understanding, change encouraging questions into reflective statements that clarify and summarise the other person's words without interrupting the flow of words or thoughts. Reflective statements are discussed in the next section.

MIRROR THE CONTENT AND FEELINGS IN THE MESSAGE

Reflective listening restates or mirrors to the speaker the feeling and content in the message. It shows the other person that the listener has heard and understands the intended message exactly. Several techniques for providing feedback in reflective listening are set out in Table 4.7.

SHOW EMPATHY WITH THE SPEAKER

While reflective statements mirror the feelings and content in the message, active listening goes one step further. Active listening pays attention to the speaker's content and emotion. It mirrors the content and feelings, and also communicates to the other person that the listener understands the problem from their point of view. Active listening builds **empathy** with the other person and creates positive interpersonal relationships. It is a technique that lets the speaker either confirm or correct the feedback from the listener. Active listening also helps the other person to reach their own decisions and form their own insights.

The process of active listening involves actively participating in the conversation with the other person. Examples of listening responses are set out in Table 4.8. Active listening is a conscious attempt to empathise with the other person in terms of the content and feelings, and to let the other person express and recognise those feelings. For example, a response by the listener, 'You seem to be feeling down about this . . .' allows the speaker to agree or disagree and thus provide further clarification.

When listeners use active listening, they are giving the other person all their attention in order to understand the issues from the other person's perspective or point of view. As well as communicating their understanding of the other person, active listeners also enable the speaker to find their own understanding and insights. The speaker, given the opportunity to talk to an active listener, is able to find their own satisfactory resolution or answer to the issue of concern.

Attending, encouraging and reflective listening are separate listening skills, which are combined as people interact with one another. As well as using each of these skills, an active listener demonstrates completeness when they understand the speaker's full intended meaning. Active listening is a more intense form of listening than informational or evaluative listening.

Informational, evaluative and conversational listening

The *informational listening* approach is used when the listener wants to understand the ideas and content in an informative message. The *evaluative listening* approach is used when the listener wants either to accept or reject the ideas in a persuasive message. The *conversational listening* approach is used when the listener wants to share and respond to the different levels of meaning in the messages of others.

Reflective listening restates to the speaker the feeling and content in the message.

Empathy is the ability to understand and feel as the other person feels.

Active listening occurs when the listener pays attention to the whole message—that is, the content *and* the feeling.

Completeness in active listening is achieved by listening for feelings as well as content, and asking questions to ensure understanding.

OBJECTIVE 5 ▷
Compare the informational, evaluative and conversational approaches to listening

Table 4.7: Feedback in reflective listening

Technique	Description	Example
Paraphrasing focuses on the content rather than the feelings and helps to achieve accurate understanding of the content.	• Restate the essential part of the message concisely in your own words. • Listen for the main ideas and the direction of the message and mirror the content to the speaker. • Agree or disagree with what was said and then rephrase the message. • Avoid repeating the other person's statements word for word.	Respond with phrases such as 'You're saying that . . .' or 'I see, you would say that . . .' These help you to paraphrase the message.
Reflective statements reflect feelings from the message and help the speaker to focus on the feelings.	• Express in brief statements the essential feelings you received from the message. • Let the speaker know you understand their feelings. • Respond to a statement such as, 'I thought I would have got that last promotion. Seems like I miss out every time.'	Respond with phrases such as 'It's really discouraging' or 'You seem to be feeling discouraged.'
Clarifying statements establish with the speaker that the listener's understanding is correct.	• State clarifying remarks in terms of the feelings, rather than as criticisms of the speaker. If the listener's understanding is inaccurate, the speaker will then rephrase what they said. • Give feedback to the speaker and show your understanding of the message. • Take the guesswork out of communication.	A listener who feels confused by what the speaker has said can use such phrases as 'Could you repeat that? I don't think I understood' or 'Could you give me an example of . . .? I'm not sure I followed what you said.'
Summarising lets the other person know the listener understands their thoughts and feelings.	• Present relevant points again to give accurate feedback and tie the conversation together. • Restate, in a condensed way, the most important points in a long conversation. • Use at the end of a discussion in order to conclude and give direction.	Respond with phrases such as 'So far we've covered . . .' or 'Your main concerns seem to be . . .'

Paraphrasing is restatement by the listener of what was said, using different words.

Reflective statements let the speaker know that the listener understands the underlying feelings.

Clarifying statements confirm the listener's interpretation of the message, enabling the speaker to confirm as correct or add more information.

Summarising is used in listening to restate in a condensed way the most important points.

INFORMATIONAL LISTENING

Effective **informational listeners** concentrate on the message and look for key points. Their goal is to understand and retain the speaker's message. The key points are related to what has been said and what may be coming. Rather than being distracted by the first few ideas or impressions, an effective listener focuses on the structure. Informational listening is used by listeners who want to understand the content accurately.

An ineffective informational listener makes premature judgments or assumptions. Much information is lost because the listener decides they know everything the speaker is going to say. By the time the first few sentences are spoken, the listener has stopped listening. Some of the information is missed or distorted when the listener does not ask questions because they are relying on the speaker to give all the information.

An effective informational listener responds to what the speaker is saying, not to their own attitudes and feelings. The goal is to think about and understand the other person's thoughts and

Informational listening is used when the listener wants to understand the content, thoughts and ideas in the message.

Table 4.8: Examples of listening responses

Type of response	Examples
Attending	'I hear you . . .' 'I see . . .' 'Oh . . .' 'Uh hmmm . . .'
Encouraging questions	'I'd like to hear how you feel.' 'Would you like to talk about it?' 'You'd like to talk further?' 'Perhaps you'd like to tell me?'
Reflective statements	'You really dislike some . . .' 'Sounds as if you're really . . .' 'It's really exciting . . .' 'You feel it is a good idea . . .' 'You seem to be feeling discouraged . . .'
Clarifying questions	'I think you're saying . . .' 'Could you give an example . . .?' 'I feel a bit confused. Could you repeat that?'
Active listening: empathy	'I understand how you feel.' 'You seem to be feeling upset about this.' 'I see. It really means that . . .' 'On another occasion you'd like . . .'

ideas, rather than to react instinctively to emotive words or ideas. Their listening is a response to the present situation and the speaker, rather than a reaction based on past experience.

An informational listener focuses on the content. By paraphrasing, or restating, the sender's message the listener is able to check their own understanding of the information. The effect of focusing on the content is to understand accurately and fully what the other person is saying. By avoiding reacting to any emotive words used by the speaker and reflecting on the content in the message, the listener is able to double-check their understanding of the information. Rather than simply parroting the speaker's words, the listener restates the message in their own words as accurately as possible.

Questioning verifies the listener's understanding of the information. The listener is able to clarify understanding and at the same time gather additional information by asking open and reflecting questions. Once the listener feels their understanding is clear, a summarising statement can be used to restate the most important points.

A great deal of the information in a verbal message can be lost because of distractions in the physical environment, such as noisy equipment, flickering lights or uncomfortable seating. Other distractions, such as an ill-prepared, unskilled or uneasy sender, using unclear and verbose language, will detract from the information in the message. Resist distractions in order to avoid poor informational listening and the consequent misunderstandings, inaccurate responses, costly errors and loss of goodwill.

EVALUATIVE LISTENING

Evaluative listening is used to accept or reject an idea.

Evaluative listening enables you to think critically and ask questions to evaluate and understand the meaning of the message. Evaluative, or critical, listening is a useful approach in business when the sender is trying to influence the listener to change an attitude or take some action they would not normally take. Think about the message and its implications for you and your organisation. Has anything been left out? What is the speaker's point of view? Are they a credible source or contact?

Evaluative or critical listeners are able to make reference to past statements of the speaker or another person in order to show their understanding and interest in continuing the interaction. The evaluative listener can also ask related questions to follow up on the speaker's message. To gather and evaluate more ideas, the listener asks questions or makes statements that are related to the speaker's comments. However, Brownwell (2002, pp. 230–1) recommends separating fact from opinion and thinking about any bias that might colour the way the information is presented.

Listen for factual, relevant and up-to-date information, and use sound reasoning techniques to think about the ideas. Listen to gather information about and understand the logic of the argument, the quality of the evidence and the validity of the conclusion. Is the speaker presenting a fact or an emotional appeal? Are they using generalisations and appeals to feelings, rather than factual information? The answers to these questions help the listener to distinguish facts, opinions, beliefs and prejudice.

Effective evaluative listeners skip unnecessary words and focus on the key words that contain the main ideas. The key words highlight the structure around which the speaker has presented their ideas and argument, and help the listener choose the most important words as they make an evaluation of the message. By using these techniques the listener is able to make an informed, reasoned choice as they either accept or reject the ideas.

> Effective evaluative listeners identify key points and differentiate between facts and emotions.

Provide feedback

An evaluative listener focuses on facts and information relevant to their needs and gives feedback by:

- paraphrasing the speaker's meaning
- asking questions to verify their understanding of the speaker's message
- giving immediate, appropriate and clear feedback.

A listener who gives effective feedback is active. Rather than passively receiving the message, the listener uses verbal and nonverbal behaviours to show their interest. As they gather facts and information, effective evaluative listeners participate in the interaction in order to understand fully the other person's meaning.

CONVERSATIONAL LISTENING

Effective conversational listeners acknowledge differences in perception and avoid communication barriers caused by past experiences and background. They also have an awareness of the steps or phases in a conversation.

> The information we take in, the part of the message we choose to listen to, and the response we give all result from our perception.

Phases in a conversation

Research by Reardon (1987, p. 101) suggests that conversations move through five steps or phases:

1. initiation phase to exchange greetings and open the channels of communication
2. rule-definition phase to determine the purpose of the interaction and the time it will take
3. rule-confirmation phase to gain agreement about the purpose and time
4. strategic development phase to discuss the actual topic of the conversation
5. termination phase to say farewell or to move on to another topic—that is, start another conversation.

Conversational listening occurs in conversations with a variety of purposes or only one. The nature of the conversation determines its purpose. A social conversation with a friend about next weekend is different from a business conversation with a salesperson about a new car. Conversations are dynamic interactions between the speaker(s) and the listener(s).

> **Conversational listening** involves both surface and in-depth listening skills.

Show attentiveness and interest

Regardless of a conversation's purpose, listeners who reach a shared understanding with the speaker have listened attentively and shown interest in the whole message. They listen to and balance the meaning in the surface message and any in-depth message. DeVito (2001) states: 'Whatever a person says is, in part, a function of who that person is. Listening for those different levels means attending to those self-referential messages' (p. 62). Sometimes a **self-referential statement** may need no more than surface listening and minimal verbal reinforcement by the listener.

Self-referential messages are statements that refer to the speaker.

Strategies for conversational listening

Effective conversational listeners use the following strategies:

- Find the general theme among the facts and details in the message.
- Use any inconsistencies in the message to infer the real meaning.
- Listen for any gaps or omissions from what is being said.
- Observe the verbal and nonverbal parts of the message.
- Focus on the statements that refer to the speaker.

In conversational listening, don't try to find, or place too much emphasis on, deeper hidden meanings at the expense of the surface meaning. The listener's interpretation may be wrong and could stop the conversation mid-track or even offend the speaker. Effective conversational listeners engage with the speaker and listen to the different levels of meaning in the message. Their response is appropriate in that it meets the needs of the speaker, the purpose of the conversation, and the needs of the listener in the context of the particular interaction.

By listening well, a listener is able to avoid directing and leading, blaming, judging or being insensitive to the other person. Rather than feeling the need to be responsible for others or being in confrontation with others, an effective listener is accepting of, and accepted by, others. Skill in listening lets them enjoy the company of others as they listen for pleasure, information, to help others or to interact in a work group.

REVIEW QUESTIONS

9 a Give a definition of listening.

  b Think of a person you regard as a good listener, and then think of one who is a poor listener. Identify three aspects of their listening techniques that make them either a good listener or a poor listener.

  c Give some examples of why listening skills are important in business.

  d What common characteristics, if any, exist in your examples?

10 a Identify three examples of nonverbal feedback you might use in attending listening.

  b Briefly explain two of the strategies used in encouraging listening.

  c What is the purpose of reflective listening?

11 a How can a listener show empathy with the speaker?

  b How is completeness achieved in active listening?

12 Differentiate active, informational and evaluative approaches to listening.

13 a Describe the characteristics of poor informational listeners.

  b What is the likely impact of poor informational listening in a business negotiation?

14 a What is the role of critical thinking and questioning in evaluative listening?

  b Briefly explain two strategies used in conversational listening.

ATTENDING AND ENCOURAGING LISTENING

1 Work in pairs to practise attending and encouraging listening skills. Take turns to act as speaker and listener.

As the speaker, choose a controversial topic on which you hold a very definite position, or a topic you feel strongly about, and speak to your listener about this for three minutes. Use familiar, comfortable language you both normally use and understand.

As the listener, use the following guidelines to focus your listening.

a   Show your interest in the speaker by your body movement. Face the speaker. Make eye contact. Lean forward, keeping an open posture.

b   Notice the speaker's body movement. This may indicate the feelings underlying the spoken message.

c   Use feedback to invite the speaker to continue by using minimal responses.

d   Ask as few questions as possible. However, if you do ask questions, use attending and encouraging questions. (Some examples are shown in Table 4.8 on page 108.)

At the end of this exercise, discuss with one another your effectiveness as listeners. Refer to points (a) to (d).

2 *Paraphrasing: Quick quiz*

Answer True or False to the following statements.

Paraphrasing by the listener:	True	False
focuses on the content rather than the feelings		
allows the speaker to add new information		
lets you listen carefully		
shows the other person they are unimportant		
mirrors to the speaker what they have just said		
lets the listener ignore the speaker		
helps the listener to understand or confirm information		
lets the speaker exaggerate		
means that the listener always agrees with what the other person said		
helps to avoid mistakes		
means they repeat word-for-word (mimic or parrot back) what the other person said		

BARRIERS TO LISTENING

DeVito (2001), citing the research by Nichols (1961), lists the following obstacles to effective listening:

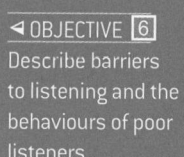

◄ OBJECTIVE 6
Describe barriers to listening and the behaviours of poor listeners

- preoccupation with self
- preoccupation with external issues
- sharpening; that is, the tendency to reconstruct messages so that 'they reflect your own attitudes, needs, and values'
- the friend-or-foe factor, which reflects our attitudes towards the speaker
- hearing what's expected
- the law of least effort; the practice of listening to messages that require little effort and avoiding those that require us to expend energy.

Further obstacles listed by Hargie, Saunders and Dickson (1981) are *dichotomous listening*, which occurs when 'an individual attempts to assimilate information simultaneously from two different sources' (p. 174), and *inattentiveness*, not only on the part of the listener but also the speaker, who may either consciously or unconsciously confuse, distract or mislead the listener(s).

In business you will listen to the team leader or manager for instructions about what you are to do. Ineffective informational listening means you will miss the main point, forget the message, or be unable to determine what you are supposed to do in response to the message. Mohan, McGregor and Strano (1992) comment: 'Even at the purely informational level, it has been claimed that 75 per cent of oral communication is ignored, misunderstood or quickly forgotten' (p. 311). They list the causes of ineffective listening as assuming a topic will be boring, allowing the speaker's personality or mannerisms to overpower the message, poor concentration, poor comprehension and passive listening. They also list internal factors affecting listening, such as threat of excessive control, beliefs and ideas, wishes and desires, fear and its effects, and expectations of people and events.

Barriers in the listener

Barriers interfere with the message.

The **barriers** may come from the listeners themselves when a part of their own background interferes with their perception of the speaker or the spoken message. Barriers may also come from any one of the elements in the communication process; that is, sender, receiver, message, channel, environment or ineffective feedback. Listening is made easier when the speaker is able to send a message that is clear and unambiguous. It is also made easier when the listener avoids the barriers listed below.

Often the most significant barriers to listening are present within the listener. Some examples are:

- boredom or lack of interest
- the listener's dislike of the personality or physical appearance of the speaker
- a desire to change, rather than accept, the speaker
- a tendency to make early conclusions or to listen only for the pause when the speaker can be interrupted
- the intrusion of the listener's own values or attitudes
- a tendency in the listener to judge the speaker
- a perception by the listener that the speaker lacks credibility
- preoccupation with other matters
- lack of common ground
- nonverbal communication that displays inattention or judgment of the speaker
- listening with the same style regardless of the situation
- the listener's tendency to hear only that part of the message they agree with.

Everyone succumbs to some of these unhelpful approaches occasionally. A number of these barriers are caused by habitual behaviours learned from childhood. To break old habits is difficult. No matter how skilled the speaker is at speaking or communicating the message, if the receiver does not listen then communication will fail.

Table 4.9 gives examples of barriers to listening and their impact on the receiver.

Behaviours displayed by poor listeners

Gamble and Gamble (1996) describe six behaviours demonstrated by poor listeners. In their words, people use these behaviours to 'unlisten'. Table 4.10 identifies the purpose of these behaviours.

Poor listening in business situations leads to problems. In business the rule is to listen to understand. Robbins (2006, p. 633) cites research that shows, 'The average person normally speaks at a rate of 125 to 200 words per minute. However, the average listener can comprehend up to 400 words per minute.' Idle thoughts about holidays, sporting events, children and next weekend

Table 4.9: The impact of a listener's ineffective verbal response

Example of a barrier	Receiver's response
Ordering, directing or commanding: 'Stop it or else . . .' 'You must do this . . .'	Resentment
Warning and threatening: 'You'd better do this or else . . .'	Anger
Lecturing or preaching: 'It's in your own best interest to do this . . .'	Resistance
Judging, criticising: 'I think you've gone too far this time . . .'	Offence
Disagreeing: 'I think you're totally wrong . . .'	Put-down
Blaming: 'It's all your fault . . .'	Defensiveness
Name calling: 'You're stupid . . .'	Distress
Using ridicule or sarcasm: 'Someone like you is not expected to know . . .'	Hurt

Table 4.10: Poor listening behaviours

Behaviour	Purpose
Nodders	To imitate listening by pretending to use attending listening skills while thinking or day-dreaming about something else
Ear hogs	To express their ideas and monopolise the interaction by interrupting and dominating
Gap fillers	To make up for what is missed or misinterpreted by manufacturing information in order to give the impression that they heard it all
Bees	To zero in on parts of the message by listening only to the parts that interest them
Earmuffs	To avoid information they would rather not deal with by acting as if they are not listening at all and sidetracking or distracting the speaker
Dart throwers	To attack what the speaker has to say by waiting for them to make an error and then criticising or cross-examining them

create distractions. Move the meeting, negotiation and other business activities forward by taking responsibility for your listening.

One of the reasons for poor listening behaviours is conditioned responses learned from people such as parents, relations or teachers in childhood. Another is the deliberate intention to manipulate or hurt the other person. In emotional situations, people may 'unlisten' because of the pressures or stress in the situation. Sometimes a person may simply choose not to listen because they are tired or uninterested, or dislike the other person. To maintain a high involvement in listening all the time is impossible. People need time to rest their mind; however, when they decide to listen they need to engage actively in the listening process. Listening does not just happen; the listener needs to make it happen.

By listening both for the words and the feelings and receiving the message accurately, listeners are able to give feedback that helps the understanding of both speaker and listener. A good listener ensures that the way in which feedback is given is appropriate to the needs of the receiver and the situation.

REVIEW QUESTIONS

15 List four barriers to effective listening caused by the listener.

16 a Briefly explain four behaviours displayed by a poor listener.

    b What is the role of feedback in the listening process?

17 Think about your own ineffective listening behaviours. Choose two and decide how you could improve these behaviours. Practise using them over the next week.

OBJECTIVE 7 ▶

Describe how to provide constructive feedback

Feedback is the receiver's response to a sender's message—the connecting, continuing or completing link.

CONSTRUCTIVE FEEDBACK

At work, people need **feedback** in order to know how well they are doing their tasks and to understand that their work contributes to their team's and organisation's goals. Cole (2005, p. 388) says: 'The right kind and amount of information at the right time maintains high productivity and lifts average and low productivity. It helps people feel supported, valued and encouraged. It develops people and teams.' Constructive feedback lets others know what they are doing well and how they could improve. Regardless of whether the feedback is positive or negative, the total feedback message—words, nonverbals, questioning and listening—should always be constructive.

Feedback is given by, and received from, the speaker, the listener and the physical environment. We select only a small proportion of feedback from the large volume received in our daily interactions because only a limited amount can be filtered into our consciousness. What a listener chooses to listen to, understand and interpret as you give feedback affects how they respond to the feedback.

In an organisation, appropriate and constructive feedback creates a positive communication climate, which in turns creates an open and encouraging organisational climate. In contrast, a rigid or competitive environment can make most people reticent or hesitant to communicate and provide ideas. How feedback is given, and the type of feedback, have an impact on interpersonal relationships and the communication climate in an organisation.

Types of feedback

Different types of feedback used within organisations and businesses are informative feedback, immediate and specific feedback, positive feedback and negative feedback. Table 4.11 shows the purpose and strategies used to achieve each of these types of feedback.

Feedback should be constructive rather than destructive. It is destructive, for example, to bring up past behaviour and grievances. Deal with the current situation; for example, say 'We agreed to take turns answering the telephone—it's your turn' instead of 'You always expect me to answer the telephone'.

Performance feedback

When giving feedback about performance, formally or informally, follow the BAT MICE formula (Cole 2005) set out in Table 4.12. Try not to judge, evaluate, approve or disapprove of the statements, feelings or attitudes of the other person, because these reactions create barriers instead of increasing understanding about what is really happening in the situation. By giving and receiving feedback, it is possible to understand the expressed idea, opinion or attitude from the other person's point of view. By acknowledging, owning and expressing feelings as feedback, a relationship is built on trust and openness.

Feedback about performance shortfalls or gaps helps people understand how to improve their performance; it describes constructively what needs to be done and to what standard.

Table 4.11: Types of feedback

Type	Purpose	Techniques
Informative feedback	To show understanding and to reinforce positive behaviour or results	• Provide factual information about the situation and use effective listening skills. • Focus on the content of the message; identify the other person's purpose and main ideas by rephrasing or summarising. • Withhold judgment and empathise with any unexpressed feelings. • Share perceptions and feelings about the message.
Immediate and specific feedback	To describe what has been done, or needs to be done, rather than judging or threatening the other person	• Keep feedback clear, specific and tied to actual behaviour; e.g. 'This file could do with a tidy up' instead of 'Your files are always untidy'. • Avoid abstract, vague and sweeping statements. • Respect the other person's right to respond. • Take the time to listen, and acknowledge their response.
Negative feedback	To correct and change unsatisfactory behaviour or results	• Provide definitive, responsive feedback. • Orient the feedback on the task; don't criticise the personal characteristics of the other person. • Give feedback at an appropriate time and place. • Only include behaviour that the receiver is able to change, and only what the receiver can handle at the time.
Positive feedback	To acknowledge the role and contribution of the other person —positive feedback encourages the repetition of behaviour	• Provide timely feedback in an appropriate context. • Be specific about the behaviour and listen to the other person's response. • Invite feedback from the other person: 'What do you think about my suggestions?' The feedback flow becomes an open-ended two-way process.

Table 4.12: The BAT MICE approach to performance feedback

Formula	Actions
BALANCED	Build self-esteem by being both positive and constructive.
ACTIONABLE	Give examples and provide feedback about something the other person is responsible for.
TIMELY	Provide feedback at the most appropriate time and in the appropriate context.
MEANINGFUL	Keep to the point, describe actions, the standards required and specific information about good performance or performance shortfalls.
'I' LANGUAGE	Say 'I' rather than 'you' to minimise defensiveness, resistance and arguments.
CONSTRUCTIVE	Aim to be helpful, not hurtful, by using objective neutral words when giving positive or negative feedback about performance.
EMPATHIC	Keep your comments to the facts and be aware of the other person's point of view.

IMPERSONAL AND GOAL-ORIENTED FEEDBACK

When giving feedback about performance, positive or negative, keep it impersonal and goal-oriented.

When providing constructive negative feedback about performance, focus on the behaviour that needs improvement rather than on the personal characteristics of the person receiving the feedback. Follow the six-step process set out below.

Step 1

Plan by thinking before you give feedback about the behaviour that should be highlighted and how you can help the other person.

Step 2

Explain why the performance is below the required workplace standard and the impact of the low performance. Sandwich the feedback by:

- starting the session with positive comments
- finishing with positive, motivating comments to build morale, self-esteem and willingness to improve.

In between, describe clearly the specific goal that isn't being met, or the behaviour and actions that are or are not happening. Avoid judgmental and subjective words and body language. Provide tangible examples or representative observations to avoid the anxiety caused by vague criticism – if you don't have examples, you are providing criticism rather than feedback.

Step 3

Specify the level of performance that must be met.

Step 4

Allow time for feedback dialogue between you and the other person. Seek their feedback, allowing them to agree, disagree and provide their perspective. Discuss what might be preventing them from meeting the performance standard and what can be done to help them achieve the required level.

Step 5

Agree on follow-up time frames and actions. Document any action items and give a copy to the other person.

Step 6

Follow up with ongoing feedback to let the other person know how they are progressing.

The six-step process enables you to direct the feedback towards the performance shortfalls and to identify the required level of performance. In the discussion, avoid 'dumping' your frustrations about what has or hasn't happened on the other person, by focusing on ways to improve performance. Positive phrases such as 'That could work if . . .' or 'Let's try this and then check the results against . . .' enable you to provide clear, complete, concise, correct and courteous information as part of the feedback process. At the same time, use nonverbal cues that demonstrate patience rather than impatience. As you give feedback, the verbal and nonverbal parts of the message should complement each other.

On occasions when you hear feelings as well as content in a message, in-depth listening to both content and feelings will help you give feedback that reflects the meaning accurately. An in-depth listener hears the paralanguage in the message in the tone, volume, pitch, rhythm, speed and resonance. A listener can engage in **verbal following** by using probing questions to move beneath the surface.

Verbal following probes more deeply into what the speaker has said.

As you give feedback, ask questions related to the speaker's message and follow up on the meaning of the message in order to gain a shared understanding of the speaker's ideas. Check the nonverbal messages being sent, for example, by your stance. Body orientation sends a message about the relationship between you and the other person. Standing at a 90° angle to the other person as you give or receive feedback indicates a cooperative stance, while facing the other person directly may indicate intimacy or aggression. Nonverbal behaviour, such as smiles, head nods, an attentive posture and eye contact, demonstrates the listener's involvement and interest. One nod gives the speaker permission to continue. Alternatively, rapid nods by the listener may indicate a wish to speak (Fiske 1990; Givens 2008). As you give feedback, the receiver's impression of you and their response to the feedback is affected by their perception of your verbal and nonverbal communication. The ability to give feedback well enhances your performance and credibility in the workplace.

By practising and using feedback skills well at work, people come closer to understanding the verbal, nonverbal and *undercurrent messages* sent by others. In addition, they gain a closer understanding of their own communication and of how to communicate well.

> Undercurrent language is the hidden part of the message and may contain feelings and/or content. There is something in the message the person wants to conceal or is unable to convey.

Feedforward

Appropriate, constructive **feedforward** says something about the message yet to be sent. DeVito (2000, pp. 16–17) says that feedforward can carry out four functions in the communication process:

> **Feedforward** is information sent before the main message.

1. It opens the channels of communication and focuses attention on the coming message.
2. It previews the message to be sent by giving and receiving advance information.
3. It disclaims or denies a connection with the statement to follow.
4. It places the receiver of the message in a specific role, requiring them to respond in a certain way.

Feedforward previews the message and opens the channels of communication. It allows a person to say something about the message before it is sent; for example, a smile indicates that the message will be pleasant or contain good news. Feedforward also lets the other person know what to expect from the message before it is sent.

Appropriate feedforward is brief and clear. The receiver will be side-tracked and have doubts about the sender's motives if feedforward takes too long. Appropriate feedforward is followed through; for example, a smile followed by an angry response is inappropriate.

Feedforward can disclaim the main message when the sender feels it might offend the receiver or reflect badly on them. They might disagree, for example, by saying, 'I'm not really expert in the area but . . .'. In this way, they express their disagreement by using the feedforward part of the message to indicate the coming disagreement. At the same time, the speaker lets it be known that the listener can reject the message without rejecting the speaker. How often do you hear, placed before a message the sender feels may be poorly received, a disclaimer such as 'I'm not a racist but . . .'?

Another way to prepare the receiver for the message is to *altercast*; that is, to cast or place the person in a specific role and ask them to respond from that role—for example, 'If you were a rock musician, how would you feel about jazz?' Alternatively, speakers can place themselves in another role to show their point of view—for example, 'If I were a rock musician, I would have little time for jazz.'

In some cases, feedforward helps the sender to present a differing point of view. In others it restricts the receiver's response or manipulates them into doing something—for example, 'You're my brother. You've got to help me move my furniture into my new flat.' A knowledge of feedback and feedforward increases awareness of the constant flow of communication between people. In this flow, feedback takes place *after* the message has been sent, while feedforward occurs *before* the main message is sent.

REVIEW QUESTIONS

18. a   Identify four types of feedback used in organisations.
    b   Explain the purpose of each type and suggest an appropriate technique to use when giving each type of feedback.
19. a   Outline the BAT MICE formula (Cole 2005).
    b   Why should feedback be kept job-related and impersonal?

APPROACHES TO LISTENING

1 Work individually.

    a   'Avoid "why" questions because they can make the other person defensive.' Briefly explain this statement.

    b   What is the role of feedback in the listening process?

2 Work individually.

    a   What is the main purpose of:

        i   encouraging listening?

        ii   reflective listening?

    b   Define the term 'paraphrasing' and explain its purpose as a listening response.

    c   Define the term 'clarifying question' and explain its purpose as a listening response.

    d   Define the term 'summarising' and explain its purpose as a listening response.

SELF-EVALUATE YOUR SKILL

HOW GOOD A LISTENER ARE YOU?

I am able to listen effectively by:	Very sure	Sure	Unsure
paying attention to the whole message			
focusing on the speaker and inviting them to continue			
mirroring the content and feelings in the message			
participating actively and showing empathy			
concentrating and looking for key points in the informational listening process			
applying logic and critical thinking skills in the evaluative listening process			
applying the five phases in conversational listening			
using complementary verbal and nonverbal communication			
recognising and checking ambiguous nonverbal messages			
avoiding jumping to early conclusions			
avoiding any prejudgment and defensiveness			
avoiding any poor listening behaviours			

SUMMARY OF LEARNING OBJECTIVES

 DIFFERENTIATE PERSONAL, CULTURAL AND UNIVERSAL NONVERBAL COMMUNICATION AND EXPLAIN HOW CULTURAL NORMS AFFECT THE NONVERBAL PART OF THE MESSAGE

Nonverbal communication consists of all that part of the message that is not encoded in words. Nonverbal communication is either personal to the individual, common to the group or culture, or universal. That part of the nonverbal communication that is common to a range of people is a clue to acceptable patterns of behaviour, whereas nonverbal communication that is part of a person's unique behaviour pattern creates a picture of the sender's personality through their gestures and mannerisms. Universal nonverbal communication has evolved as part of our biological heritage. Universal nonverbal communication crosses cultural and national boundaries.

 EXPLAIN THE ROLES OF NONVERBAL COMMUNICATION AND UNDERSTAND DIFFERENCES BETWEEN CULTURES

Interactions create a frame in which the meaning of the verbal and nonverbal parts of the message is communicated. The purpose of nonverbal communication in this process is to repeat, contradict, substitute, complement or accent the words in the message. Nonverbal communication can also be used to control the flow of communication. It can also give information about interpersonal attitudes and emotions, and play a key role in how we present ourselves and in rituals.

 DISCUSS SEVEN ASPECTS OF NONVERBAL BEHAVIOUR

The seven aspects of nonverbal behaviour are body movement or kinesics, physical characteristics, touching behaviour, vocal quality or paralanguage, the use of space or proximity, artefacts and the environment. A combination of these aspects makes up the nonverbal part of the total message.

 EXPLAIN THE ACTIVE LISTENING PROCESS AND ITS PURPOSE

A person who listens with understanding of the content and feeling in the message and has empathy with the speaker is using the active listening approach. While attending listening focuses on the speaker, encouraging listening invites the speaker to continue. Reflective listening mirrors the content and feelings in the message. The purpose of active listening is to focus on the speaker, invite them to continue, mirror the content and feelings in the message, and show empathy with the speaker. Effective active listeners use nonverbal and listening skills that complement their spoken communication.

 COMPARE THE INFORMATIONAL, EVALUATIVE AND CONVERSATIONAL APPROACHES TO LISTENING

Informational listening enables the listener to understand the content and ideas in the message and interpret the sender's meaning accurately. The listener needs to avoid premature judgments and be objective. By paraphrasing and questioning, the listener is able to check their understanding of the content.

Evaluative listening is used when the sender is trying to influence the listener to take some action or sway the listener's attitude or opinion. An effective evaluative listener identifies key points and differentiates between fact and emotion. The evaluative listener either accepts or rejects a persuasive message. Conversational listening can move along a continuum from surface listening to in-depth listening. The conversational approach is sensitive to the literal meaning of surface-level communication as well as the in-depth level or real needs below the surface.

 DESCRIBE BARRIERS TO LISTENING AND THE BEHAVIOURS OF POOR LISTENERS

Barriers can arise in the sender, the receiver, the message, the channel, the environment, or the way in which feedback is given. Barriers in the listener may be due to boredom, a difference in values between speaker and listener, or a lack of interest. A failure to listen causes mistakes and misunderstandings in our relationships in personal, business or other contexts. Poor listeners pretend to listen, monopolise the interaction, misinterpret, sidetrack and distract others, zero in on only part of the message and attack, criticise or cross-examine the speaker. These behaviours make it hard to understand and think about the implications of the message for you, your team and your organisation.

7 ▷ DESCRIBE HOW TO PROVIDE CONSTRUCTIVE FEEDBACK

At work, people need feedback about their performance and acknowledgment of their efforts. Feedback is the connecting, continuing or completing link in the communication process. The four types of feedback are informative feedback, specific feedback, negative feedback and positive feedback. Constructive feedback can be positive in the case of work well done; constructive negative feedback is about shortfalls in performance and how to make improvements. Constructive feedback is impersonal, goal-oriented, balanced, actionable and timely.

KEY TERMS

ACTIVITIES AND QUESTIONS

1   The purpose of this activity is to consider how the nonverbal part of the message can be managed.

   a   Form into groups of four and read the information in the next two paragraphs.

   Once you understand the meaning of the other person's communication you may decide to deliberately use body orientation, space and power symbols to manage a person who is using the context, verbal communication or nonverbal communication against you.

   Assume you are called into a colleague's office. He begins to criticise your contribution at the last committee meeting. You feel you have been put down deliberately and decide that the next time you meet him you will call him into your office and ensure that the way you stand, sit or move—that is, your nonverbal communication—will allow you to meet on equal ground.

   b   In your groups, discuss this question:

   How could you use the seven aspects of nonverbal communication to manage the context and the verbal and nonverbal communication of a person whom you feel is putting you down deliberately?

2   Work in small groups to discuss the following research conducted by Argyle and Ingham (1972) and cited in Forgas (1986).

   In a typical two-person conversation, people look at each other about 61% of the time, and their gaze coincides (mutual gaze) about 32% of the time. Mutual gaze lasts on average only about one second, while each individual gaze is usually about three seconds long. The same person will look more when listening (75% of the time) than when speaking (41% of the time).

a What are the implications of Forgas's findings for the use of eye contact in business?

b Think of an interaction you have been part of when an error was made in the use of eye contact. What was the cause? What could have been done to avoid it?

c Report your findings in a large-group discussion.

3 *Workshop:* Using nonverbal communication appropriately.

The object of this activity is to increase your skills in the use of nonverbal communication so that you give your message confidently and courteously; that is, you express assertion. To increase your awareness of the nonverbal behaviours that express assertion, you are asked to role-play aggressive and passive behaviours as well as assertive behaviour. Some of the nonverbal behaviours that indicate assertiveness, aggression and passivity are listed in the 'Self-Evaluate Your Skill' checklist on page 122.

Procedure

a Divide into groups of three. Nominate Person A to be Jenny, the team leader. Person B is James, a team member. Person C is the observer. Jenny asks James to meet her at 4 pm. James responds with the question: 'What will we be discussing?' Jenny and James make up a dialogue and play out their roles.

b The role of Jenny is to be played in three different ways:
- in an assertive way
- in an aggressive way
- in a passive way.

Person C, the observer, uses the Self-Evaluate Your Skill checklist to give Person A feedback on how successfully they use assertive, aggressive and passive nonverbal communication as they play the role of Jenny.

c All three people in the group should take a turn playing the roles of Persons A, B and C.

d Discuss the activity in the group as a whole by answering the following questions.

i Did you find it easy to use your nonverbal communication to show assertive, aggressive and passive behaviour in the role play?

ii How well did each of you use behaviour that showed assertion, aggression and passivity nonverbally?

iii Are there other ways to show assertion, aggression and passivity nonverbally?

iv What effect did each of the three ways of communicating nonverbally have on the person playing the role of James?

v What were your reactions and feelings about the activity?

4 a 'Active listening goes one step further than mirroring the content and feelings.' Explain this statement.

b When is active listening most useful?

c List four benefits of using active listening skills.

5 *Attending, encouraging and reflective listening*

Form into groups of three to practise listening skills. Allocate the roles of Speaker (A), Listener (B) and Observer (C). Rotate each role so that you take a turn at all three roles. A speaks, B listens and responds, C observes and assesses the listener's effectiveness using the 'Listening Skills' checklist on page 123.

The speaker makes the following statements one at a time. The listener responds to statement (a) by paraphrasing, statement (b) by clarifying, statement (c) by reflecting feeling, and statement (d) by reflecting meaning.

a 'I keep getting all the worst assignments in this section, and I just don't think it's fair!'

b 'We have clients complaining every day about errors in delivery or late deliveries. If you can't meet the order, you should let us know so that we can notify the client.'

c 'It's not my job. Someone else can do it.'

d 'What you expect from this job is unrealistic. The time needed to complete all the tasks varies and I can't control the number of tasks. How am I supposed to get my job done?'

Observing guidelines

Observe the speaker and listener. Note when each listening skill has been used by placing ticks in the appropriate boxes in the checklist. Decide whether the skill was used successfully, moderately well or poorly.

Discuss your observations with the speaker and listener.

6   *Role play: Active listening*

Form into groups of five. Nominate one person to play the part of Susan and one to play the part of Jacob. The other three act as observers.

Susan   You have walked past the supervisor's office and witnessed Jacob, your colleague, presenting your report to the supervisor. You heard the supervisor say to him, 'You have done an excellent job.' You are angry because Jacob has presented your work as his own. You go to his office and wait for him.

Jacob   You have taken Susan's report to the supervisor. The supervisor puts it aside and begins to discuss progress on the project you started last week. This project is now ahead of schedule. He says, as you are about to leave, 'You have done an excellent job.' You go back to your office to find Susan waiting for you.

Observers   The observers are to complete three tasks.

a   Use the 'Active Listening Role Play' checklist on page 123 to assess the listening skills used by Jacob as he responds to Susan's anger.

b   List any barriers created by either Susan or Jacob.

c   Lead a discussion as a group of five and give feedback to the people playing the roles of Susan and Jacob. Suggest alternative responses they might have used.

7   Work in small groups to discuss and record the following issues in detail.

a   Why are the skills of active listening and giving effective feedback so important to the leader of a small to medium-sized organisation?

b   Are the skills of active listening and giving performance feedback constructively as important to the leader of a large corporation? Give reasons for your answer.

c   Describe a time when you have seen the effects of giving feedback on performance destructively rather than constructively. What were the outcomes?

d   Are current changes in the business world placing more or less demands on a leader to use their interpersonal skills effectively? If more, what actions would you recommend to increase a leader's effectiveness? If less, why?

e   Make a small group presentation to report your findings to the large group.

Self-evaluate your skill						
Nonverbal behaviour	**Assertive**	**Y/N**	**Aggressive**	**Y/N**	**Passive**	**Y/N**
Posture	Upright and relaxed		Leaning forward		Shrinking away	
Head	Firm and comfortable		Chin pushed forward		Head down	
Eyes	Direct and regular eye contact		Staring, often piercing or glaring		Glancing down with little eye contact	
Face	Appropriate, courteous and friendly expression		Rigid and set		Hesitant, even smiling when upset	
Voice	Confident with appropriate speed, pitch and volume		Loud, fast and dramatic		Soft, trailing off at ends of words or sentences	
Arms/Hands	Relaxed, moving easily and reflecting the verbal message		Controlled sharp gestures with fingers pointing and jerky movements		Still or slow, not reflecting the verbal message	
Movement/ Walking	Confident and measured pace appropriate to the context		Overly confident and heavy or fast, deliberate, hard		Slow and without confidence, or fast and uncertain	

Self-evaluate your skill			
Listening skills (see Question 5)	**Successfully**	**Moderately well**	**Poorly**
Paraphrased			
Clarified			
Summarised			
Reflected feelings			
Reflected meanings			
Used attentive body language			
Encouraged the speaker			
Maintained eye contact			

Self-evaluate your skill			
Active listening role play (see Question 6)	**Yes**	**No**	**Unsure**
1 Did the person playing Jacob use			
a body posture and position			
b eye contact			
c facial expression			
that conveyed to you a feeling that Susan was being listened to?			
2 Did Jacob use			
a words			
b tone of voice			
c rate of speaking			
that you felt comfortable with?			
3 Did Jacob provide enough encouragement for Susan to continue, either by			
a minimal but positive responses, or			
b supportive body movement?			
4 Did Jacob use helpful questions?			
5 How would you rate Jacob's listening skills? Satisfactory Good Very Good Excellent			

EXPLORING THE WEB

1   Learn more about nonverbal communication by visiting the *Nonverbal Dictionary of Gestures, Signs and Body Language Cues* <http://members.aol.com/nonverbal2/diction1.htm> and browsing some of the entries in the dictionary.
  a   What is the nonverbal world?
  b   Explain the principle of nonverbal independence.
  c   What percentage of our communication is nonverbal? What makes it difficult to verify the figure?
  d   How does posture impact on the message?

2   Learn more about listening in the workplace by visiting 'Active Listening' at <www.jobaccess.gov.au/joac/advice/jobrequirement/active_listening.htm> and 'Listening for Information' at <www.aligningaction.com/listen.htm>.
  a   What is the purpose of active listening in the workplace?
  b   How can you make improvements in your motivation and listening habits?
  c   Compare and contrast active listening and informational listening.

PROJECT WORK

The first five parts of this project require you to research and plan a major presentation titled 'The Impact of Nonverbal and Listening Skills on Communication in the Business Environment'.

1   Find three researchers—past or present (other than those mentioned in the chapter)—who specialise in nonverbal communication. Which types of nonverbal communication do they focus on? Briefly summarise the main points of their findings.

2   Find examples of the types of nonverbal communication that are specific to a foreign culture and compare these to your own culture. Analyse how the nonverbal communication of both cultures could impact upon business dealings between the two.

3   Find several different websites on body movement or kinesics (e.g. body language). Compile a list of ten ways you can use this type of nonverbal communication to your advantage in a business environment.

4   Find an article or website that gives details on how to be an effective listener. Briefly summarise the content and compare it with the information in this chapter.

5   Find a specific example of how barriers to listening have adversely affected a group of people or an organisation. What were the barriers? What was, or could have been, done to overcome them? How effective in eliminating the barriers was/would have been this intervention?

6   Write and deliver your presentation.

BIBLIOGRAPHY

Archer, A. & Archer, S. 2001. *A Beginner's Guide to Japan: Non-Verbal Communication*, www.shinnova.com/, accessed 3 July 2003.

Argyle, M. 1983. *The Psychology of Interpersonal Behaviour*, 4th edn, Penguin Books, Middlesex, England.

Australian Government Job Access. *Active Listening*, www.jobaccess.gov.au/, last updated 12 October 2007, viewed 2 January 2008.

Barker, L., Edwards, R., Gaines, C., Gladney, K. & Holley, F. 1980. 'An investigation of proportional time spent in various communication activities by college students', *Journal of Applied Communication Research*, Vol. 8, pp. 101–9.

Beebe, S.A., Beebe, S.J. & Redmond, M.V. 2008. *Interpersonal Communication: Relating to Others*, 5th edn, Pearson International Edition, USA.

Birdwhistell, R.L. 1970. *Kinesics & Content*, University of Pennsylvania Press, Philadelphia.

Bolton, R. 1987. *People Skills*, Simon & Schuster, Sydney.

Bordone, R.C. 2007. 'Listen up! Your talks may depend on it', *Negotiation*, May, pp. 9–11.

Brownell, J. 2002. *Listening*, 2nd edn, Allyn & Bacon, Boston.

Capper, S. 2000. *Nonverbal Language and the Second Language Learner: Some Pedagogic Considerations*, http://langue.hyper.chubu.ac.jp/, viewed 8 July 2003.

Cole, K. 2005. *Management Theory and Practice*, 3rd edn, Pearson Education Australia, Sydney.

Cook, M. 1971. *Interpersonal Perception*, Penguin, Harmondsworth, UK.

Cousins, R.B. 1996. 'Active listening is more than just hearing', *Supervision*, Vol. 57, Issue 12, December, pp. 14–15.

Darwin, C. 1872. *The Expression of the Emotions in Man and Animals*, John Murray, London.

DeVito, J.A. 2000. *Human Communication: The Basic Course*, 8th edn, Longman, New York.

DeVito, J.A. 2001. *The Interpersonal Communication Book*, 9th edn, Allyn & Bacon, Boston.

DeVito, J.A. 2007. *The Interpersonal Communication Book*, 11th edn, Pearson Education, USA.

Douglis, P.N. 1996. 'Human energy: key to expressive photos', *Communication World*, October/November, p. 43.

Ekman, P. 1985. *Telling Lies: Clues to Deceit in the Marketplace, Politics and Marriage*, Norton, New York.

Engleberg, I.N. & Wynn, D.R. 2007. *The Challenge of Communicating: Guiding Principles and Practices*, Allyn & Bacon, USA.

Fiske, J. 1990. *Introduction to Communication Studies*, 2nd edn, Methuen & Co, London.

Forgas, J.P. 1986. *Interpersonal Behaviour*, Pergamon Press Australia, Sydney.

Gamble, T.K. & Gamble, M. 1996. *Communication Works*, 5th edn, McGraw-Hill, New York.

Gilsdorf, J. 1997. 'Metacommunication effects on international business negotiating in China', *Business Communication Quarterly*, Vol. 60, Issue 2, June, pp. 20–37.

Givens, D.B. *Nonverbal Communication*, http://members.aol.com./, last updated 2005, viewed 2 January 2008.

Givens, D.B. 2008. *The Nonverbal Dictionary of Gestures, Signs and Body Language Cues*, Center for Nonverbal Studies Press, Washington, http://members.aol.com/, viewed 2 January 2008.

Hall, E. 1969. *The Hidden Dimension*, Doubleday, New York.

Hargie, O., Saunders, C. & Dickson, D. 1981. *Social Skills in Interpersonal Communication*, Croom Helm Ltd, London.

Hassin, R. & Trope, Y. 2000. 'Facing faces: studies on the cognitive aspects of physiognomy', *Journal of Personality and Social Psychology*, Vol. 78, Issue 5, pp. 837–52.

Hirsch, R.O. 1986. 'On Defining Listening: Synthesis and Discussion', paper presented at the Midwestern Psychological Association Annual Conference, Chicago.

Knapp, M.L. 1978. *Essentials of Nonverbal Communication*, Holt, Rinehart & Winston, USA.

Knapp, M.L. & Daley, J.A. (eds) 2002. *Handbook of Interpersonal Communication*, 3rd edn, Sage Publications, California.

Knapp, M.L. & Miller, G.B. 1985. *Handbook of Interpersonal Communication*, Sage Publications, California.

Kneidinger, L.M., Maple, T.L. & Tross, S.A. 2001. 'Touching behavior in sport: functional components, analysis of sex differences, and ethological considerations', *Journal of Nonverbal Behavior*, Vol. 25, Issue 1, Spring, www.wkap.nl/.

Lane, L.L. 1987. *By All Means Communicate*, Prentice Hall, New Jersey.

Lindgren, H.C. 1973. *An Introduction to Social Psychology*, 2nd edn, John Wiley & Sons, New York.

McCoy, L. 1996. 'First impressions', *Canadian Banker*, Vol. 103, Issue 5, September/October, pp. 32–36.

Marchetti, M. 1996. 'Talking body language', *Sales and Marketing Management*, Vol. 148, Issue 10, October, p. 46.

Matsumoto, D. 1985. *Accuracy of Facial Expressions*, Miyazaki International College, Miyazaki, Japan.

Mehrabian, A. 1971. *Silent Messages*, Wadsworth Publishing Company, Belmont, California.

Metcalf, T. 1997. 'Communicating your message: the hidden dimension', *Life Association News*, Vol. 92, Issue 4, April, pp. 18–21.

Mochal, T. 2006. *Follow these six steps when providing constructive performance feedback*, http://articles.techrepublic.com.com, 8 August, viewed 10 January 2008.

Mohan, T., McGregor, H. & Strano, Z. 1992. *Communicating! Theory and Practice*, 3rd edn, Harcourt Brace, Sydney.

Morris, D., Colleett, P., Marsh, P. & O'Shaughnessy, P. 1979. *Gestures: Their Origins and Distribution*, Jonathan Cape, London.

Nampo, H.2002. *Nonverbal Communication Travel Guide*, University of Montana, 29 November, www.golum.riv.csu.edu.au/, accessed 3 July 2003.

Nichols, R. 1961. 'Do we know how to listen? Practical help in a modern age', *Communication Education*, Vol. 10, pp. 118–24.

Ong, I.W. & Tan, A. 2007. 'Listening across cultures', *Today's Manager*, June/July, pp. 27–28.

Pease, A. & Pease, B. 2005. *Body Language: How to Read Others' Attitudes by Their Gestures*, Orion, London.

Rankin, P. 1929. 'Listening Ability', Proceedings of the Ohio State Educational Conference's Ninth Annual Session (cited in DeVito).

Reardon, K.K. 1987. *Interpersonal Communication: Where Minds Meet*. Wadsworth Publishing Company, Belmont, California.

Robbins, S.P., Bergman, R., Stagg, I. & Coulter, M. 2006. *Management*, 4th edn, Pearson Education Australia, Sydney.

Rowley, R.D. *Listening for Information*, www.aligningaction.com/, last updated 11 August 2001, viewed 2 January 2008.

Scherer, K.R. & Ekman, P.K. 1985. *Handbook of Methods in Nonverbal Behavior Research*, Cambridge University Press, New York.

Seiler, W.J. & Beall, M.L. 2007. *Communication: Making Connections*, 7th edn, Allyn & Bacon, USA.

Sommer, R. 1969. *Personal Space: The Behavioral Basis of Design*, Prentice Hall, Englewood Cliffs, New Jersey.

Spoelstra, M. 'Cultural negotiation boundaries', *The Negotiation Academy*, www.negotiationtraining.com.au/articles/ negotiating-global-borders, viewed 18 February 2008.

Stawar, T.L. 1997. 'How good are you at telling when someone is lying?' *Manage*, Vol. 49, Issue 1, August, pp. 22–24.

Trenholm, S. & Jensen, A. 2007. *Interpersonal Communication*, 6th edn, Roxbury Publishers, USA.

Young, S. 2007. 'Speak easy: the power of quality questions and the art of listening', *Public Relations Tactics*, Vol. 14, Issue 3, March, p. 23.

Part 2

Fostering Positive Relationships

5 Negotiation skills

Photo: Jacob Wackerhausen

LEARNING OBJECTIVES

After studying this chapter you should be able to:

1 ▷ explain how the negotiation process works

2 ▷ analyse personal styles and negotiation styles and the way they impact on negotiation

3 ▷ explain how power can be used or abused in the negotiation process

4 ▷ describe how interactions in a negotiation move through several phases

5 ▷ analyse the differences between four negotiation strategies

6 ▷ outline the principled bargaining approach to negotiation.

VIEWPOINT: COLLABORATIVE NEGOTIATION STRATEGY

Are you managing your commercial negotiations through conventional methods? Is it necessary to only take a win/win approach as a negotiation strategy? The results of any negotiation are:

- Lose/Lose (all parties lose)
- Win/Lose (I win, you lose)
- Lose/Win (I lose, you win)
- Win/Win (we both win, but this could also be described as compromise)
- Win More/Win More (we maximise our shared resources by being collaborative).

How do we determine which of the following negotiation strategies to follow in a commercial environment?

- Steer clear of negotiation altogether.
- Aggressively achieve our goals through competitive negotiation.
- Accommodate the needs of our counterparty and exclude our own needs.
- Compromise some of our needs and some of the needs of our counterparty.
- Collaborate to satisfy all needs of both parties.

The appropriate negotiation strategy will be established by the answer to two questions:

- How strong are my alternatives to this specific negotiation?
- How vital is a long-term relationship in the context of this negotiation?

Adapted from J. Potgieter, 'Collaborative negotiation strategy', *The Negotiation Academy*, www.negotiationtraining.com.au/articles/negotiating-collaboratively, viewed 16 February 2008. Reproduced with permission from The Negotiation Experts. The Negotiation Experts offer negotiation-related resources on www.negotiations.com. You can find in-depth articles, Q&A's, cartoons, book reviews, definitions and more.

Negotiation is a process in which communication between the parties follows conventions such as who will speak first, who has the power, and who will disclose preferred outcomes. *Effective* negotiation requires those in the process to understand the conventions and realise that they are in the process of negotiating. The parties will have to deal not only with any preconceived positions, but also with the issues and the people: their feelings, perceptions and frame of reference. One or both parties may have to change their position. Throughout the negotiation process the balance of power may shift as each party attempts to tilt it via submissive, argumentative, overbearing or manipulative behaviours. By promoting a constructive climate, negotiators can achieve a negotiated agreement.

Negotiation is a social skill in the same way that cooperation, conflict resolution and discussion are social skills used in interactions in our intimate, personal and working relationships. A successful negotiator is able to use empathy appropriately. Empathy is the ability to see the situation from within the other person's frame of reference. To be a successful negotiator, you need to put yourself in the other person's position to show them you have a clear understanding of their needs and concerns. You also need to choose appropriately from negotiation styles and strategies and personal style to generate solutions, design options, select the most appropriate solutions and reach a negotiated outcome.

THE NEGOTIATION PROCESS

OBJECTIVE 1 ▷
Explain how the negotiation process works

Negotiation is a process in which two or more parties try to resolve differences, solve problems and reach agreement. It is an interactive process between two or more people. Robbins and colleagues (2006, p. 793) define negotiation as 'a process of bargaining in which two or more parties who have different preferences must make joint decisions and come to an agreement'.

Negotiation is a process in which two or more parties try to resolve differences, solve problems and reach agreement.

Putnis and Petelin (1999) list four characteristics in a negotiation process (see Table 5.1). They cite Fisher and Ury's (1983) definition of negotiation: 'back-and-forth communication designed to reach an agreement when you and the other side have some interests that are shared and others that are opposed' (p. xi).

Mohan, McGregor and Strano (1992, p. 370) define negotiation as 'a procedure by which people who wish to come to an agreement, but disagree about the nature of the agreement, try to work out a settlement in which each party gives and receives at a level tolerable to both'. Mastenbroek (1993) regards negotiating as a 'particular social skill to be distinguished from other social skills such as "cooperation" and "fighting"', although he also states that 'the three approaches are not clear-cut' and could be thought of as 'a continuum' (p. 84). He regards negotiating as the proper strategy if there are different, sometimes even contrasting, interests and if, at the same time, the two parties are interdependent in a way that an agreement would yield advantages for both of them. Letting things drift or fighting are disadvantageous for both of them.

In his case study, 'Enterprise Bargaining and the Process of Negotiation', Fells (1995, pp. 218–19) says: 'Negotiation itself is viewed as a process of reaching a point of agreement through

Table 5.1: Characteristics in a negotiated process	
Characteristic	**Feature**
There is an ultimate goal of settlement.	Negotiations would be viewed as unsuccessful if no settlement is achieved.
There is competition for divergent ends.	Negotiation parties have divergent objectives which at first appear incompatible.
There is interdependence amongst parties.	There must be cooperation if the objectives are to be reached.
There are norms of interaction.	Negotiations are characterised by particular kinds of speech and action.

Source: Adapted from P. Putnis & R. Petelin, *Professional Communication: Principles and Applications*, Prentice Hall, Sydney, 1999, pp. 241–2. Reproduced with permission.

a sequence of activities including the preparation and statement of positions, exploring options and trading concessions.' The study suggested that 'strong motivation to reach agreement and inherently competitive interaction can have results that meet the needs of the parties'.

An effective negotiation deals with the issues, needs and interests of both parties.

Some of the features in a negotiation situation are:

- dealing with the issues
- dealing with the relationships
- moving through different phases
- trading-off to maintain the relationship
- making decisions
- handling the parties' differing perceptions of the situation
- dealing with high levels of uncertainty
- working with balances/imbalances of power
- representing others
- handling matters of ego and 'face'
- following a procedure.

Effective negotiators recognise the patterns of behaviour in a negotiation and understand how the negotiation process works. They know which strategies are likely to be productive and can alter non-productive behaviour to deal with awkward issues.

Effective negotiators are able to promote a constructive climate.

The personal qualities of a good negotiator

Each negotiation style and the personal qualities of each negotiator have an effect on the relationships between the people involved and the likelihood of them achieving or not achieving their goals. Their personal qualities affect the way in which they state their case, organise the information, make proposals, discuss the issues and acknowledge the interests of the other party. They are able to promote a constructive climate by reducing tension and avoiding hostility and overbearing behaviour. Their personal qualities also affect the negotiation strategy they adopt. Effective negotiators usually have good communication skills, are able to create a positive communication climate and have some of the personal qualities listed in Table 5.2.

Table 5.2: Personal qualities of a good negotiator

Quality	Strategy
Ability to plan	Plan before negotiating; identify their own position and that of the other person or party
Capacity to think clearly under stress	Aware of their stress level and know how to deal with it
Ability to be practical	Able to be clear, flexible and solution-oriented; focused on the 'big picture' and interests
Capacity to communicate well	Listen, question, give feedback and speak clearly in the negotiating process
Competency in their subjects	Know the content and are expert in the issues
Ability to act assertively and with integrity	Approach the issue assertively and confidently and negotiate with empathy
Ability to identify the interests of each party	Separate the people from the problem; focus on the interests of both parties to work things out
Capacity to identify standards	Ensure that the result is based on some objective standards
Willingness to follow up	Aim to check agreement and take follow-up actions

REVIEW QUESTIONS

1. Define the term 'negotiation'. Why do people negotiate?
2. Identify the characteristics in the negotiation process.
3. What does effective negotiation require those in the process to do?
4. What are the personal qualities of a good negotiator?

OBJECTIVE 2 ▷
Analyse personal styles and negotiation styles and the way they impact on negotiation

THE IMPACT OF PERSONAL STYLE AND NEGOTIATION STYLE

Whenever people come together to negotiate, they bring their own *personal style* to the situation. These personal styles affect the way they communicate and handle the conflict. Hellreigel's (1988) classification of interpersonal styles identifies five different styles or ways of handling negotiation and conflict (see Table 5.3). This classification recognises that personal style can help or hinder the negotiation and can cause, prevent or resolve conflict. People who can recognise the type of personal style being used by others in the negotiation process will be more able to separate the real message from the way it is delivered. This skill helps them to receive the message and to respond clearly.

Personal style affects the way an individual negotiates.

In addition to personal style, the parties involved in the negotiating process may use one or more of the *negotiation styles* shown in Table 5.4. A skilful negotiator is able to identify each of the five negotiating styles and recognise the style being used by the other person.

Negotiation style has an impact on the outcome.

Figure 5.1 illustrates how each of the negotiation styles has an effect on relationships and on the achievement of goals. It also shows that each preferred style is matched by the most likely conflict resolution strategy. Negotiators who understand the different styles and strategies, and their preferred style, are in a position to choose another style that is suited to the situation and their intended result, rather than always using their preferred style. The negotiation option chosen is influenced by the context of the negotiation and each party's range of personal communication and negotiation skills.

Table 5.3: Personal negotiating styles	
Type	**Description**
Self-denying	Self-denying people may be difficult to negotiate with as they are introverted and reticent in providing information, especially feedback. Feelings and ideas are hidden from others.
Self-protecting	Self-protecting people use diversionary tactics such as discussing other people or side-tracking to other issues. Diversionary tactics are used to hide true feelings and ideas.
Self-exposing	Self-exposing people wish to be the centre of attention. This attention can be demanded by speaking loudly, speaking over others, using attention-seeking body movements, and ignoring feedback and the views of others.
Self-bargaining	Self-bargaining people will show their feelings and ideas if others show theirs first. These people wait until they are led into negotiation. They can open up and negotiate when others initiate the process.
Self-actualising	Self-actualising people are ideal negotiators because they want to have information and feedback from the other person. This information and feedback is presented constructively to aid the negotiation process and to achieve goals and results that are effective without any conflict.

Table 5.4: Negotiation styles		
Negotiation style	**Explanation**	**Outcome**
Compromise	Compromise is the settlement of differences through concessions by one or both parties. When the settlement meets the needs and goals of both parties, both are satisfied with the outcome. Alternatively, when the solution meets the needs and goals of only one party, the other party is dissatisfied with the outcome.	win–win or win–lose or lose–win
Collaboration	Collaboration results when people cooperate to produce a solution satisfactory to both. It helps interpersonal relationships and explores new ideas. Permanent solutions and commitment to these solutions result. On the other hand, it is time-consuming and each party needs to have negotiation skills to be able to participate in a collaborative negotiation style.	win–win
Competition	Competition occurs when one party negotiates to maximise its results at the expense of the other party's needs. One party gains the advantage over the other. Although it is quick and can be used as a counter against another person who always uses this style, it is bad for interpersonal relationships. The solution is likely to be temporary as there is no commitment from the other party and the issue will occur again. Competition is a negotiation style that leaves the person who loses in a difficult situation.	win–lose
Accommodation	Accommodation is a negotiation style where one party is willing to oblige or adapt to meet the needs of the other party. It is a useful option for negotiation on minor matters as the result can go one way or the other. However, the negotiating parties may not bother to look for creative, new solutions. In this form of negotiation, points of view are easily swayed.	lose–win
Withdrawal or avoidance	Withdrawal means one party retracts its point of view or backs away from the situation, causing the negotiation to be broken off. The situation is unsatisfactory as negotiation stops before either party is able to find an acceptable solution. Dissatisfaction may lead to conflict in the future.	lose–lose

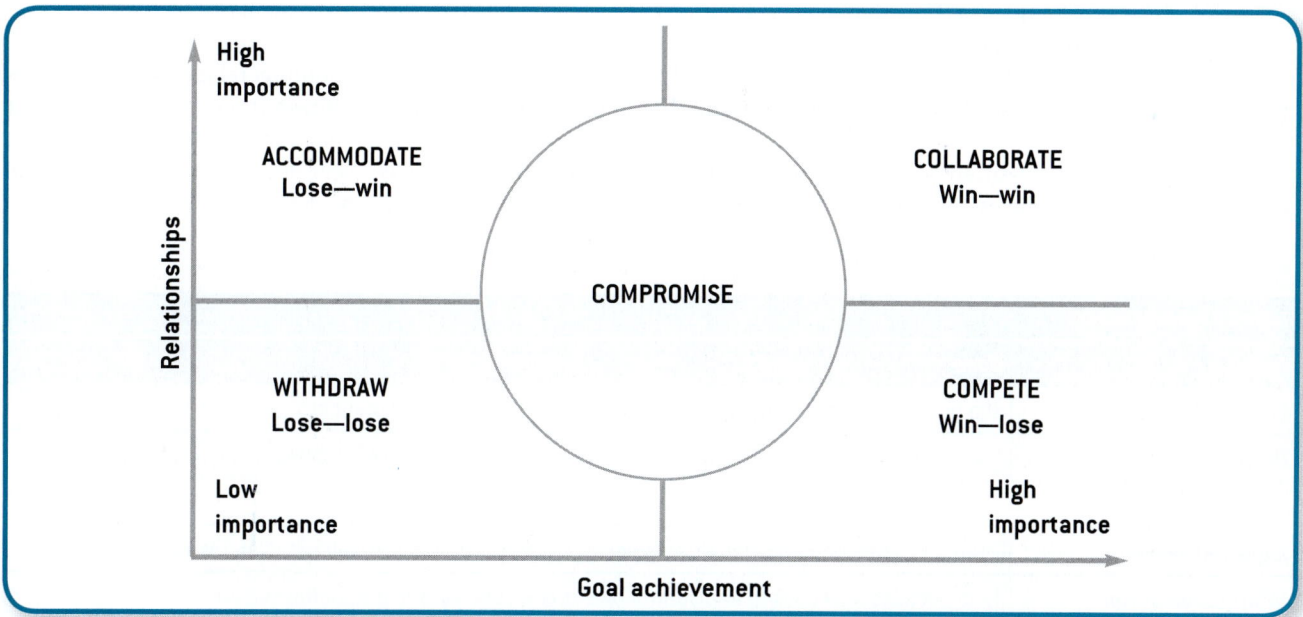

Figure 5.1: The probable impact of negotiation styles and conflict resolution strategies on relationships and goal achievement

Psychological barriers

Psychological barriers may arise in the negotiation process.

Psychological barriers may arise during the negotiation process, belonging to either party (see Table 5.5). Be aware that people may have some of these feelings and 'listen' for their effects. Look for signs of them in the other party, and communicate effectively to ease or lower these barriers.

Table 5.5: Psychological barriers to negotiation

- Fear of being taken for a ride
- Guilt about wanting to be assertive
- Feeling intimidated by so-called powerful people
- Fear of losing face with the boss or colleagues
- Wanting to be liked
- Need to be 'nice'
- Fear of conflict or confrontation
- Lack of self-confidence

REVIEW QUESTIONS

5 List and define five different personal styles used in negotiation.

6 Briefly explain the likely outcome from each of the negotiation options or styles.

THE USE OF POWER AND INFLUENCE IN NEGOTIATION

OBJECTIVE 3 ▶
Explain how power can be used or abused in the negotiation process

An organisation delegates **power** to people to get the job done. Power may be used to influence and, in some cases, to control people. It can also be used to bring about change. Power can be exerted over one person or a group by another person or group. Power used well achieves effective communication and positive results. Negotiating power is the ability of the negotiator to influence the behaviour of another.

Each person has power and can enjoy power. People who are aware of the way in which they use power and are able to use it properly will have an impact on decisions and actions throughout the negotiation. The exercise of negotiating power has both benefits and costs and it can be used to punish or benefit.

Abuse or misuse of power leads to mistrust. A positive negotiating relationship enhances negotiating power. Power is a useful tool in the negotiation process; however, misuse or abuse your power, or refuse to use it correctly, and the likely result is tension and conflict. Negotiating power is enhanced by legal support, company and personal knowledge, skill development and adequate resources. Six types of power noted by Raven (1993) are shown in Table 5.6.

Power is the capacity to influence, the possession of delegated authority, or an ability to take action.

Table 5.6 Types of power

Type	Base
Legitimate power	The organisation has invested power and authority in the position held.
Reward power	The holder has the opportunity to control resources and to give or withhold things wanted by others.
Coercive power	Exercised when a person compels others to behave in a certain way.
Expertise power	Vested in a person's knowledge, aptitude and ability—others are willing to defer to expertise.
Information power	Held because of access to and control over organisational and other information.
Referent power	The holder is respected, admired, liked or personally identified with by others.

All these power bases will be found operating in any workplace, either singly or in combination. Perception of what power is and how it should be used varies between people and organisations. Acknowledgment of power and deference to it is based on people's perception of it. The holder of power, particularly over the allocation and use of resources, must be willing and able to use that power to ensure decisions are taken and actions implemented. If the holder refuses, or is unable to do this, conflict will arise simply because processes that are essential to the running of the workplace do not take place.

Rather than depending solely on their power source in the organisation or their personal power, effective negotiators develop strategies that achieve results. They use ideas to resolve the situation and communication skills to present these ideas without overlapping into conflict.

REVIEW QUESTIONS

7 Identify six different types of power.
8 Contrast coercive and referent power.
9 How can power be used in negotiation?

CLASSIFICATIONS OF PHASES IN A NEGOTIATION

◀ OBJECTIVE **4**
Describe how interactions in a negotiation move through several phases

In a negotiation session the interactions between the parties move through different phases to reach an outcome. A negotiation can be divided into three main phases. The *introduction* initiates the negotiation and establishes the climate. The *main body* is the working part of the negotiation in which issues are identified and problem solving takes place as the parties move towards a negotiated agreement. In the *concluding phase*, the parties reach a negotiated agreement, resolution or other outcome.

Five phases of interaction

There are different classifications of the phases in a negotiation, aiming to explain the interactions. Mohan, McGregor and Strano (1992, p. 376) list five phases in a negotiation session:

A negotiation session moves through several phases to reach an outcome.

1 *Introduction phase*: positions are stated, data exchanged, the climate is developed and responses are sought.
2 *Differentiation phase*: open conflict of views and demands evolves, issues are raised and debated, the range of the negotiation is established, the atmosphere is less tentative and restrained.
3 *Integration phase*: active reconnoitring occurs, there is close and active analysis of detail, concessions are made, deadlocks occur and are broken.
4 *Settlement phase*: final offers are made and accommodation arrived at; a draft agreement may be drawn up.
5 *Post-settlement phase*: agreement is implemented and compliance is monitored by both parties; mutual esteem and respect by each party may be communicated.

A five-phase procedure

Rose (1987, pp. 23–47) identifies a set of five phases used by experienced negotiators:

1 Clarify wants.
2 Put forward proposals.
3 Bargain.
4 Gain agreement.
5 Follow up.

Experienced negotiators use the wants phase to build the relationship in the opening face-to-face discussions. Wants are those things the negotiators believe they could, should and must get from the negotiation. The *wants phase* includes three segments: rapport, context and wants. Rose states: 'The purpose of the Wants phase is to reduce the area of difference between the parties. Before negotiation, the range of possible options had no boundaries' (1987, p. 29). Clarification of wants in the first phase makes it easier to move on to the proposal phase.

The purpose of the *proposal phase* is 'to probe the Wants of each party to see where each will move and where they won't' (1987, p. 31). Negotiators use the 'if/then' technique as they make two-sided proposals. The party putting forward the proposal states the condition first, followed by the specific proposal; for example, 'If you give me a good price for the trade-in of my current vehicle, I will consider your price on the new vehicle.' Successful negotiators avoid running two or more proposals together. They make one proposal, stop and wait for the response. When the other party says 'No' or uses silence, they restate their proposal or ask the other party for an alternative proposal.

The *bargain phase* involves the exchange of concessions. In this stage, the parties move from the 'if/then' to the 'I will if you will' phase. Any concessions made or received should be specific and clear.

In the *agreement phase*, agreement is reached item by item based on bargains made in the previous phase. Items and issues should be packaged so that only one part of the package is given away if concessions have to be made to reach further agreement. Once agreement is reached, Rose suggests that the parties 'summarise agreements in writing, if possible . . . [and] get an "in principle" agreement if a firm conclusion cannot be realised' (1987, p. 42).

The *follow-up phase* monitors the results and actions that come out of the agreement. Performance of both parties is checked and the results are reviewed against wants.

Greater understanding of the phases allows negotiators to work through the phases and gain the best possible outcomes for both parties. Outcomes do not just happen. They are reached by identifying wants and general interests. The negotiators use their negotiation styles, personal styles and negotiation strategies to generate solutions, design options, select the most appropriate solutions and reach a negotiated outcome.

REVIEW QUESTIONS

10 Describe three main phases in a negotiation.

11 a   Identify three segments in the wants phase (Rose 1987).

   b   What is the purpose of the wants phase?

   c   Distinguish the proposal, bargain and agreement phases.

   d   What is the purpose of the follow-up phase?

APPLY YOUR KNOWLEDGE

NEGOTIATION STYLES

1   Work in small groups.

   a   List some recent negotiations in which you have been involved.

   b   Discuss your reasons for negotiating in each of these situations.

   c   Were the needs and concerns of each party taken into account?

   d   Which interpersonal negotiation style did you use?

   e   Choose one of the negotiations from your list and decide which of the five negotiation styles was used in the negotiation.

   f   Was it used effectively or ineffectively? Give reasons for your answer.

2   What is the purpose of the different classifications of phases in a negotiation?

3   a   Identify the most likely personal style of a person using each of the statements in Table 5.7.

   b   In the third column, rewrite the statement to reflect a self-actualising style.

Table 5.7: Power at work

Statement	Likely personal style	Self-actualising statement
Could you please lay out your position first?		
Are you here simply because you need to be seen to be negotiating?		
We can agree on some of those points; however, there are also some sticking points. Our needs are . . .		
Remember the time we won the Maiklin contract. Things went smoothly then.		
Instead of talking, just listen to me. I want you to know . . .		

NEGOTIATION STRATEGIES

◄ OBJECTIVE 5
Analyse the differences between four negotiation strategies

Negotiation is a process in which two or more people (or parties), with common or conflicting interests, discuss ways of resolving an issue. Although negotiation has a specific purpose—to reach agreement—not all negotiation achieves this aim. Any attempt to negotiate and reach agreement must consider the differences between these four strategies:

1. win–win strategy
2. win–lose strategy
3. lose–win strategy
4. lose–lose strategy.

Each strategy has a different result. In the first strategy both parties win; in the second and third, one party wins and one loses; and in the fourth strategy, both parties lose.

WIN–WIN STRATEGY

A **win–win strategy** occurs when both parties are satisfied with the settlement negotiated. It is a process that seeks to meet the needs of both parties, rather than to win a position or gain victory at one party's expense. A situation of win–win is hard to achieve. Those using the win–win strategy use a cooperative approach throughout. They use assertive communication, 'I' messages, effective verbal and nonverbal communication, and listening. These skills are discussed in Chapter 3.

In a **win–win** situation, both parties are satisfied with the settlement negotiated.

Successful negotiation is achieved when both parties concentrate on problem-solving strategies and communicate well to achieve a win–win result. The win–win approach negotiates the situation on its merits. Any bargaining is based on the interests of the parties. As a result, each party is more likely to be committed to the outcome negotiated from a win–win approach than an outcome negotiated from a win–lose or lose–win approach.

WIN–LOSE STRATEGY

A **win–lose strategy** occurs when one party is satisfied and one is dissatisfied. At least one of the negotiators is competing with the other. Those using the win–lose strategy use an aggressive approach. They want a clear winner and a clear loser. Cooperative negotiators who trust aggressive negotiators to

In a **win–lose strategy**, one party is satisfied and one is dissatisfied with the settlement negotiated.

work towards a negotiated agreement are likely to lose because the focus is on the aggressive negotiator's issue and their need to win.

In the win–lose situation, the focus is on one party's problem to the exclusion of the other's until one side gives in or is defeated. People who adopt this strategy often use a confusing presentation or a dominant speaking style and body movement. This style invites the other person to be just as difficult, or to withdraw in order to avoid the conflict arising out of the situation.

LOSE–WIN STRATEGY

In a **lose–win strategy**, one party withdraws or makes too many concessions, while the other party wins.

A **lose–win strategy** is found in a situation in which one party is dissatisfied and the other is satisfied. One party withdraws or makes too many concessions, while the other party wins. Those using the lose–win strategy use a submissive approach. They are likely to lose because they defer to the interests of the other party rather than assert their own needs and interests.

In an extreme case, the win–lose and lose–win styles of negotiation can lead to a deadlock followed by the lose–lose situation. Deadlocks can occur when either one or both parties find their needs are not being satisfied by the negotiations.

LOSE–LOSE STRATEGY

In a **lose–lose** situation, both parties are dissatisfied with the negotiated result.

The **lose–lose strategy** occurs when the objectives of both parties are too rigid, or when both parties are unable to collaborate or are unaware of the opportunity to do so. Two aggressive negotiators are likely to achieve a lose–lose outcome. Two submissive negotiators are likely to achieve a lose–lose outcome. This no-win situation means that both parties walk away from the negotiation dissatisfied. When agreement cannot be reached, a third party may arbitrate and make the decision for both parties. Both sides may lose.

REVIEW QUESTIONS

12　Define and briefly explain the terms 'win–win strategy', 'win–lose strategy', 'lose–win strategy' and 'lose–lose strategy'.

13　Explain two factors that can prevent negotiators reaching an agreement.

14　How does the win–win approach make people into partners and not opponents?

OBJECTIVE 6 ▶
Outline the principled bargaining approach to negotiation

PRINCIPLED BARGAINING

In any negotiation, people are dealing not only with the issues but also with other people who have emotions and different backgrounds and viewpoints. Negotiation occurs because of a conflict of positions. In order to agree on a position, negotiators usually engage in positional bargaining. Those negotiators who argue from positions of 'only what they want' are positional bargainers. A negotiation based on **positional bargaining** usually 'trades off' the relationship to gain the position or 'trades off' the position to maintain the relationship. The relationship and issue are mixed together.

Positional bargaining negotiates from positions only, rather than interests.

Principled bargaining negotiates by identifying interests, rather than taking positions. It looks for mutual gains wherever possible.

In contrast, the **principled bargaining** process developed by Fisher and Ury (1981) aims both to deal with the issue and maintain a good working relationship. In their view, negotiation should separate the people from the problem and identify the interests of both parties. By identifying the interests, rather than taking positions, principled negotiators are more productive and gain better outcomes than positional bargainers because they are willing to ask questions, listen and seek solutions.

Chapter 6, 'Conflict Management', presents strategies that can be used in negotiation to design options and respond constructively. The principled negotiation method takes time, energy and commitment to reach an agreement that satisfies interests without disadvantaging either party. The four elements in the principled negotiation method are shown in Table 5.8.

Table 5.8: The principled negotiation method	
Element	**Purpose**
People	To separate the people from the problem
Interests	To focus on interests rather than positions
Options	To generate a variety of possibilities before choosing an option
Criteria	To ensure results are based on some objective standard

To implement the principled negotiation method, negotiators need to:

- state their case well
- organise their facts well
- use fair procedures
- be aware of the timing and speed of the talks
- avoid abusing power
- assess the others' needs properly
- be sensitive to those needs
- have patience
- not be unduly worried by conflict
- be committed to a win–win philosophy.

Negotiators who recognise the human aspect of negotiation understand the need to deal with the person as well as the issue. They are willing to engage in principled bargaining because they realise that in any negotiation there are two interests—the substance of the negotiation and the relationship between the people negotiating. The process or steps followed in principled negotiation are discussed next.

Planning for the negotiation

Before negotiating, take the time to plan carefully and thoughtfully. In the planning stage, think about the purpose of the negotiation and how to address problems and interests, rather than personalities. Thoughtful negotiators concentrate on the negotiation issues. Effective negotiators aim to gather information in the planning stage that helps them to:

- provide the other party with information relevant to the issue or transaction
- make sure that information presented is accurate and objective
- develop and maintain good relationships with the other party
- think about interests and options, rather than positions
- consider the other party's point of view.

Defining the issues

Set the climate for the meeting by exchanging greetings and aim to establish trust and confidence. Sociability helps to establish a tension-free atmosphere.

Experienced negotiators review proceedings leading up to the meeting and iron out any differences in 'facts' and perceptions before they start to negotiate. Both parties' broad interests and feelings are confirmed, and listening skills are used to identify areas of agreement and to establish some rapport with the other party. The intention is to establish some common ground before moving into areas of difference.

In the discussion, define the issues and specify in detail what is to be resolved. Link issues where appropriate to the other party's objectives, and focus on interests rather than positions. Deal with one issue at a time. Attempt to stay with the issue rather than generalising into other situations, passing judgment on the other person, or confusing the other person's personality with the issue that needs to be negotiated.

If the other person says more than can be comprehended or sounds confused, paraphrase the message received to check that interpretations and understandings are correct. It is also useful to summarise the content, ideas and feelings being communicated. This clarifies the understanding of both parties.

Start by asking for what you want, but accept that your wants may have to be modified. The intention is to collaborate with the other party in order to produce a solution that is satisfactory to both. Remember the phrase 'If/then . . . '. Separate the people from the issue. Try to generate as many options as possible, as this gives both parties room to move as they negotiate to a solution.

Throughout the discussion, summarise the points to confirm understanding, particularly where complex issues are involved. Take the time to agree on what has been negotiated. Unless agreement is fully understood by both parties, the settlement may not last.

Separating the people from the problem

Negotiators who are able to differentiate between the people and the problem are able to treat them separately. As a result, the negotiation is more likely to be based on accurate perceptions of one another's interests without emotions getting in the way of the issue. Rather than wrangling over what each side will or will not do, principled negotiation decides the issues in the interests of both parties.

A negotiated agreement reached by principled bargaining satisfies three criteria:

1. It should be a wise agreement, if possible.
2. It should be efficient.
3. It should improve, or at least not damage, relationships.

Interests are the desires and concerns of the people negotiating. In the words of Fisher and Ury (1981, p. 42): 'Your position is something you have decided upon. Your interests are what caused you to decide.' The problem is defined in terms of the interests—each side's needs, desires, concerns and fears—rather than the positions of each party.

Using objective criteria

Principled bargaining recognises that the parties need to reach an agreement by negotiating and by using objective criteria. Standards such as precedent, accepted community practice, market value, tradition or procedure are examples of objective criteria. Objective criteria are fair and independent of either party's will. Interest rates for a commercial loan are set based on the financial industry standards for that particular type of loan. The potential borrower and the financial institution's representative negotiate the size of the loan, the amount of deposit, the term of the loan and any special features, against the objective standards and the interests of both the borrower and the financial institution.

Using fair procedures

Conflicting interests are avoided when fair procedures are used. For example, an outcome that is independent of will and that uses fair procedures is to divide a bottle of soft drink between two children by asking one child to pour the drink into two glasses and the other child to choose the one they would like to drink. Neither can complain about unfair division. The potential for conflict is reduced by using the principled bargaining process. Rather than competing and clashing because of raised emotions or personality issues, the principled bargaining process focuses on common interests and the variety of options.

Finding common ground and options

Common ground is where both parties find they have the same interest.

Some people decide on their position before they come to the negotiating table. Consequently, they focus on their position in opposition to the other party's position, instead of attempting to find *common ground* and options that will satisfy the needs and wants of both parties. When people negotiate from their selected position rather than from their interests, they tend to lock themselves into those positions. The process then becomes competitive and oppositional, rather than collaborative.

The purpose of the negotiation is to satisfy the underlying interests of the people involved. Sometimes these underlying interests are not met; for example, a goal may be too rigid. In this situation a negotiation based on interests will make it difficult to find common ground and reach a satisfactory conclusion. On some occasions it may be necessary to settle for less than the original goal, because the principled negotiation method can give at least three different outcomes. The first is the negotiated agreement you want; the second is the best alternative to a negotiated agreement; the third is the worst alternative to a negotiated agreement.

BATNA

BATNA stands for the 'Best Alternative To a Negotiated Agreement'. Sometimes, one of the parties may not be able to negotiate an agreement that meets their goal. It is important in this case to have a BATNA. The BATNA is the option that will take place if negotiation leads to no agreement. It will occur independently of the other party. Remember, the reason that both parties negotiate is to achieve something better than what they would have achieved without the negotiation. If agreement cannot be achieved by negotiation, the alternative action to be taken is identified in the BATNA.

BATNA is the best alternative to a negotiated agreement.

WATNA

WATNA stands for the 'Worst Alternative To a Negotiated Agreement'. If the negotiator has less power than the other party, they may have to think about a WATNA. Because the other person has the legitimate power, or the negotiator wants the relationship to continue as it is, they may decide on less than the preferred outcome. They might have to modify their goal in order to maintain the relationship, to acknowledge power, or to achieve a realistic rather than an unrealistic goal. They may even decide not to negotiate, because they feel they cannot achieve something better by negotiating. Braham (2003, p. 2) says: 'Don't drop below your bottom line; you'll feel bad about yourself and the deal afterwards, and you may not follow through on your commitments.' Knowing your BATNA and WATNA not only lets you know what you find acceptable—and unacceptable—from the range of options; it also provides you with substitute or alternative actions you can take when a negotiated agreement is impossible or less satisfactory than the alternatives.

WATNA is the worst alternative to a negotiated agreement.

By identifying the BATNA and WATNA, negotiators are exploring the alternatives available if a negotiated agreement is not possible. Rather than accept an unsatisfactory outcome from the negotiation, they are in a better position to say 'no' to the negotiation and to take the alternative actions identified in the BATNA or WATNA.

By using the principled bargaining approach to negotiation, both parties are able to negotiate more effectively. The approach enables them to solve the problem in such a way that both parties win. Clearly stated needs and goals, and the focus on interests rather than positions, allow each party to think about and evaluate the other's needs and goals and areas of common interest.

Integration and finalisation of the areas of agreement and outcomes is the last step in the process. Agreements, outcomes and actions are reviewed, revised, improved and implemented.

NEGOTIATION

	Yes	No	Unsure
Are the other party's needs being met?			
Are your needs being met?			
Is your negotiation style appropriate in this context?			
Is the environment appropriate or adequate for the negotiation task?			
Is your body movement accepting and cooperative, or is it demanding and threatening?			
Are you willing to identify the needs of the other party?			
Do you check achievements and aim to build on them?			
Are your goals realistic?			
Does common ground exist between you and the other party?			
Do you negotiate the issue, not the people?			

REVIEW QUESTIONS

15 What is principled bargaining?

16 How does finding common ground help the negotiation?

17 Why should you determine your BATNA and WATNA before you negotiate?

APPLY YOUR KNOWLEDGE

NEGOTIATION TOOLKIT

McDonald (2003) has compiled a toolkit for negotiation that was inspired by a talk by Sam Jeffries, chairperson of the Murdi Paaki Regional Council, at the NSW Premier's Department's Strategic Projects Conference held in December 2002.

McDonald comments that 'negotiation moves beyond compromise. It promotes a collaborative approach in which parties pool resources to solve a problem to their best advantage.' Based on a variety of sources, McDonald suggests using the steps and strategies shown in Table 5.9 in the negotiation process in order to achieve outcomes that are agreeable to all parties.

Table 5.9: Steps in the negotiation process

Steps	Strategies
Preparation	Do your homework. Know as much as possible about: • yourself and the other parties • each party's BATNA. Can either party walk away from the negotiations? • your settlement range • your options and the pros and cons of each • the other party's reputation and negotiation models.
Create an appropriate climate and environment for meeting	*Physical:* The location, venue and seating arrangements should be neutral, non-threatening, calming and supportive. *Verbal:* Use appropriate, understandable language. Use interpreters if necessary. *Time frame:* Be flexible and don't rush to an outcome.
Establish the ground rules	*Behavioural:* Do not interrupt. Take turns. Respect the other party. Do not use abuse. *Procedural:* Clarify roles. *Substantive:* What can be discussed and decided? Ensure confidentiality and privacy. Seek permission to speak to the media.
Adopt conflict-resolution strategies	Commit to a win–win solution. Fight fair. Manage your emotions. Be honest. Get your facts right. Focus on the issue, not the person. Maintain the relationship. Use empathy. Identify unfair tactics and deal with them. Use active listening. Use a variety of questioning techniques. Make it possible for parties to back down at any stage without feeling humiliated.
Confirm the authority the participants have to negotiate	Check that all participants have the authority to negotiate a mutually acceptable agreement and to see that it is implemented.
Identify the non-negotiables	What can the meeting discuss and decide? What is not negotiable?
Identify the issues and agree on them	Clarify the areas of disagreement. Divide the issues into parts. Address a less difficult aspect when stuck. Throughout the process, refocus on the issues and try to resolve them based on what is fair for all parties. Explore best and worst alternatives to negotiating an acceptable agreement.
Clarify, and then explore, each party's needs and wants/interests and positions	Wants are not the same as needs. Explore why the parties have these needs/wants—it may end the conflict. Base the negotiation on the basic needs and true interests of the parties.

Steps	Strategies
Find the common ground and establish a common purpose	You will now have defined the scope of the dispute and set a more balanced tone for the negotiation. If possible, establish some objective fair standards against which your final solution can be judged.
Explore the options	Suggested options must satisfy the parties' needs. Be as inventive and creative as possible in suggesting and exploring all options.
Discuss possible solutions, including their viability	Which solutions address most of what you all want? Which come closest to creating a win–win situation? Review common ground.
Select areas of agreement and commit to them	Make clear agreements. Check that all parties understand and confirm these agreements.
Record the agreements	Ensure that all parties have copies of the record of agreements.
Decide on follow-up action and the time frame	Negotiators will need to report outcomes to other stakeholders. If there is media interest, decide who will be the spokesperson/people. Decide on a time for implementation of the agreement.

Source: Adapted from R. McDonald, *Negotiation Skills—A Communitybuilders Toolkit*, www.communitybuilders.nsw.gov.au, viewed 3 July 2003. Reproduced with permission.

1. Identify the steps in the negotiation toolkit that enable the parties to separate the people from the problem.
2. How does the process in the negotiation toolkit help the parties to focus on interests, rather than positions?
3. Contrast compromise and collaboration negotiation styles, and describe how the negotiation toolkit promotes the use of a collaborative style.
4. Think back to a time when you negotiated ineffectively. Explain how establishing the ground rules—behavioural, procedural and substantive—might have helped you negotiate more effectively.

SUMMARY OF LEARNING OBJECTIVES

 EXPLAIN HOW THE NEGOTIATION PROCESS WORKS

Negotiation happens in a context and moves through several phases. It is a process in which communication between the parties follows conventions such as who will speak first, who has the power and who will disclose preferred outcomes. The personal styles and the negotiation styles adopted by the negotiators are part of the process. The issues, positions, interests and options are the substance of the negotiation. In any negotiation there is an ongoing interaction between the process, interpersonal behaviours and substance of the negotiation. To achieve an effective outcome from negotiation, each party has to be able to exchange information in ways that establish trust and confidence. A range of listening, questioning, speaking and nonverbal communication skills are used in each stage of the negotiation process. Effective negotiators usually have good communication skills.

 ANALYSE PERSONAL STYLES AND NEGOTIATION STYLES AND THE WAY THEY IMPACT ON NEGOTIATION

Personal styles can help or hinder a negotiation. Self-denying, self-protecting and self-exposing styles make it difficult for one party to view the interests and issues from the other party's point of view. On the other hand, people who use self-bargaining and self-actualising styles are able to open up and let the other party know their interests and issues. Once both parties understand one another, it is easier to negotiate to meet their mutual interests.

The five different negotiating styles or options are: compromise, collaboration, competition, accommodation, and withdrawal or avoidance. Those who withdraw have little chance of achieving their goals or of building relationships. Those who compete are more likely to achieve their goal, but at the expense of the relationship between those negotiating. Those who compromise are less likely to achieve their goals, but more likely to maintain relationships with the other negotiating party. Those who collaborate are most likely to be effective in achieving mutually acceptable goals and in maintaining a relationship with others in the negotiation process.

3 ▷ EXPLAIN HOW POWER CAN BE USED OR ABUSED IN THE NEGOTIATION PROCESS

Power is the capacity to influence, the possession of delegated authority or an ability to take action. Six types of power are: legitimate power, reward power, coercive power, expert power, information power and referent power. Power used effectively achieves positive results. The abuse or misuse of power can cause insecurity, anxiety and conflict.

4 ▷ DESCRIBE HOW INTERACTIONS IN A NEGOTIATION MOVE THROUGH SEVERAL PHASES

There are three broad phases in a negotiation. The introduction is the initiating phase. The main body is the working part of the negotiation in which issues are identified and problems solved. In the concluding phase, the parties reach a negotiated agreement, resolution or some other outcome. Prescribed in this chapter are three different classifications of the phases in a negotiation to illustrate a range of possible interactions.

5 ▷ ANALYSE THE DIFFERENCES BETWEEN FOUR NEGOTIATION STRATEGIES

Each negotiation strategy is named after the likely outcome from its use: win–win, win–lose, lose–win or lose–lose. The strategy or way people communicate in a negotiation influences the process and the outcome. By observing and analysing a negotiator's speaking, questioning, listening and nonverbal communication, you can recognise their preferred negotiation strategy. Before a negotiation, it is also worth identifying your own preferred negotiation strategy—what you want to communicate and how you will communicate it in the negotiation. People who are genuine respond with openness and honesty in the negotiation process. A positive regard for self and the other person communicates warmth and acceptance of them. Negotiators who have respect for themselves are able to show respect for others. Their verbal and nonverbal communication is open, confident, and oriented to the needs and concerns of both parties in the situation.

6 ▷ OUTLINE THE PRINCIPLED BARGAINING APPROACH TO NEGOTIATION

The principled negotiation method acknowledges two factors in negotiations—the substance of a negotiation and the relationship between the people negotiating. This method of negotiation has four elements: people, interests, options and criteria. The principled negotiation method aims for a wise agreement, if possible; it is efficient and is designed to improve—or at least not damage—relationships.

KEY TERMS

ACTIVITIES AND QUESTIONS

1 a What are the three criteria in the principled bargaining approach?
   b List the four elements in the principled negotiation method.
   c What is the purpose of each element?
   d Why is it important to distinguish between the issue and the people?

2 Do you accept the underpinning principle of the principled negotiation method that people can be separated from the problem in a negotiation? Explain your answer.

3 a Briefly describe the five different negotiating options.
   b What is the likely outcome from each?

4 Edward De Bono (2000, p. 254) states: 'Negotiations range from the usual adversarial and confrontational mode to a cooperate mode in which both parties seek to design a way forward.' Are there ways to shift adversarial and confrontational negotiators to cooperative and collaborative modes of negotiation? Identify the differences between the adversarial and the cooperative modes of negotiation. Include examples in your answer.

5 a What do you understand by the term 'positional bargaining'?
   b What are the barriers to a win–win outcome in positional bargaining?
   c Do you agree with the statement 'All negotiations should use the principled bargaining method'? Explain your answer.

6 Choose two personal qualities of a good negotiator and explain how these personal qualities affect the communication climate in a situation of negotiation.

7 a Over the next four weeks, keep a journal of your negotiations. In the journal, identify under the following headings what you did or the strategies you used to differentiate between:
   • the substance—what you are negotiating about
   • the process—how you negotiate
   • the psychological factors—who is negotiating.
   b In your journal, decide:
   • how well you negotiated each issue
   • what you will do differently next time
   • what your greatest strength is in a negotiation situation.

EXPLORING THE WEB

1 Review the chapter-related article on the website, 'Family Living Program Conference Collaborative Negotiation—A Creative Process for Resolving Turf Issues', at <www.uwex.edu/ces/flp/community_building/collnegotproc.html>.

   a The author, Rossing, suggests that 'Negotiating collaboratively is not easy'. What makes negotiating collaboratively difficult?

   b When should outside help be brought into a negotiation?

   c What problems arise when parties in a negotiation focus on positions?

2 Visit <http://hbswk.hbs.edu/item/5013.html> to view a question-and-answer session about research entitled 'What Perceived Power Brings to Negotiations'. The research was undertaken by Professor Kathleen McGinn of Harvard University and Rebecca Wolf of Princeton University.

   a What can managers and other professionals learn from this research when they find themselves in negotiations?

   b What is the meaning of the phrase 'integrativeness of agreements'?

PROJECT WORK

1 Research two contrasting approaches to negotiation: competitive positional-based negotiation and problem-solving interest-based negotiation.

2 Write a report that compares and contrasts these two approaches to negotiation.

Use an introduction, body, conclusion and bibliography in your report. Include the following headings in the body of the report:

- characteristics of each approach
- assumptions in each approach
- risks of each approach
- probable impact on relationships of each approach.

BIBLIOGRAPHY

Acland, A.F. 1990. *A Sudden Outbreak of Common Sense*, Hutchinson, London.

Albrecht, K. & Albrecht, S. 1993. *Added Value Negotiating, The Breakthrough Method for Building Balanced Deals*, Richard D. Irwin, USA.

Bolton, R. 1987. *People Skills*, Simon & Schuster, Sydney.

Braham, B. & Associates. *Negotiation Tips*, www.bbraham.com/, viewed 3 July 2003.

De Bono, E. 1986. *Conflicts—A Better Way to Resolve Them*, Penguin, London.

De Bono, E. 2000. *The De Bono Code Book*, Penguin Books, London.

Fabry, J.B. 1968. *The Pursuit of Meaning*, Harper & Row, San Francisco.

Fells, R. 1995. 'Enterprise bargaining and the process of negotiation', *Journal of Industrial Relations*, Vol. 37, Issue 2, June.

Fisher, R. & Brown, S. 1988. *Getting Together*, Houghton Mifflin.

Fisher, R. & Ury, W. 1981. *Getting to Yes*, Penguin Books, USA.

Fisher, R. & Ury, W. 1983. *Getting to Yes: Negotiating Agreement Without Giving In*, Hutchinson, London.

Forgas, J.P. 1985. *Interpersonal Behaviour*, Pergamon Press, Sydney.

Frank, M.O. 1987. *How to Get Your Point Across in 39 Seconds—or Less*, Corgi Books, UK.

Harris, T.A. 1973. *I'm OK You're OK*, Avon, New York.

Hellreigel, D., Slocum, J.W. & Woodman, R.W. 1988. *Organizational Behavior*, 4th edn, West Publishing Company, St Paul, USA.

Lax, D.A. and Sebenius, J.K. 2006. *3D Negotiation*, Harvard Business School Press.

Luvmour, S., Luvmour, J. & Hill, S. 1990. *Everyone Wins*, New Society Publishers, USA.

McDonald, R. *Negotiation Skills—A Communitybuilders Toolkit*, www.communitybuilders.nsw.gov.au, viewed 3 July 2003.

Mohan, R., McGregor, H. & Strano, Z. 1992. *Communicating! Theory and Practice*, 3rd edn, Harcourt Brace, Sydney.

Porter, J.N. & Taplin, R. 1987. *Conflict and Conflict Resolution* (a sociological introduction with updated bibliography and theory section), University Press of America, Latham.

Potgieter, J. 'Collaborative negotiation strategy', *The Negotiation Academy*, www.negotiationtraining.com.au/, viewed 16 February 2008.

Putnis, P. & Petelin, R. 1999. *Professional Communication: Principles and Applications*, Prentice Hall, Sydney.

Raven, B.J. 1993. 'The bases of power: origins and recent developments', *Journal of Social Issues*, Vol. 49, pp. 227–51.

Robbins, A. 1988. *Unlimited Power*, Simon & Schuster, UK.

Robbins, S., Bergman, R., Stagg, I. & Coulter, M. 2006. *Management*, 4th edn, Pearson Education Australia, Sydney.

Rose, C. 1987. *Negotiate and Win*, Lothian Publishing, Melbourne.

Rossing, B. 'Collaborative Negotiation—A Creative Process for Resolving Turf Issues', Family Living Program Conference, www.uwex.edu/, viewed 8 November 2007.

Stark, M. 'What perceived power brings to the negotiations', Q&A with Kathleen L. McGinn, published 26 September 2005, Harvard Business School Working Knowledge for Business Leaders, http://hbswk.hbs.edu/item/5013.html, viewed 10 November 2007.

Steiner, C.M. 1974. *Scripts People Live*, Grove Press, New York.

Tillett, G. 1991. *Resolving Conflict*, Sydney University Press, Sydney.

Ury, W. 1991. *Getting Past No*, Business Books, UK.

Williams, G.R. 1993. 'Style and effectiveness in negotiation', in L. Hall (ed.), *Negotiation: Strategies for Mutual Gain: The Basic Seminar of the Harvard Program of Negotiation*, Sage Publications, California.

6

Conflict management

Photo: Brad Killer

LEARNING OBJECTIVES

After studying this chapter you should be able to:

1 ▷ distinguish several approaches to conflict

2 ▷ discuss the causes, benefits and costs of conflict

3 ▷ explain how mapping a conflict helps determine its cause

4 ▷ interact constructively in conflict situations by using assertion, active listening and framing questions

5 ▷ discuss the role of mediation in resolving deep-rooted conflict.

VIEWPOINT: SOFTLY, SOFTLY

United States author, mediator and leadership thinker, Mark Gerzon, comments: 'Most of us run a mile from conflict in the workplace and that's not a good thing. By ignoring or repressing friction points on the job, we risk having the problem harden into cold conflict. Cold conflict that receives no attention is . . . hard to identify or flush out in the open so it can be very tricky to deal with—but deal with it we must. Conflict is part of the human condition.' Handling conflict needs to be built into the way companies operate.

Even in newer, flatter workplaces that use horizontal teams rather than hierarchical top-down orders, conflict happens. Gerzon says: 'The most successful companies are rewarding that friction. It's about productivity and not paralysing. Creative companies deal with conflict through brainstorming, problem solving and saying . . . we want the best ideas.'

Adapted from an interview conducted by Catherine Fox with Mark Gerzon, 'Softly, softly', *Australian Financial Review—Boss*, 29 February 2008, pp. 50–53.

Although most people wish for a life without stress, conflict happens; and, as it is inevitable, it is worth approaching it positively. Wade (2003, p. 1) describes conflict as 'the actual or perceived competition of interests. That is, one interest apparently will gain priority over another interest. An *interest* is something that a person subjectively considers to be important.' Excessively long hours, rudeness, colleagues who don't listen, and physical or emotional bullying are some of the reasons for conflict at work. Conflict handled well can reduce irritations, misunderstandings and crisis, improve awareness of self and other people, and bring about change.

The way that conflict is handled can lead to positive or negative results. Potential conflict may be ignored or avoided in the short term, but if this avoidance continues and the conflict escalates into a bigger issue, people develop hostile feelings towards one another. Some of the symptoms of conflict are tensions, no desire to communicate, slipping productivity, absenteeism, falling morale, argumentative conversations, name calling, formal complaints about behaviour, and disastrous meetings.

Conflict arises when needs are not met. Those needs can be physical, financial, social, educational, intellectual, recreational or spiritual, tangible or intangible. However, even in a situation of conflict, it is possible, by finding areas of common ground, to remove some of the differences and to emphasise the similarities while tackling the conflict and working towards the solution.

UNDERSTANDING CONFLICT MANAGEMENT

OBJECTIVE **1** ▶
Distinguish several approaches to conflict

Conflict is a clash of opinions, values, needs or goals.

Everyone will experience conflict at some time. **Conflict** occurs whenever two or more people, teams or groups have differing wants and goals and one party interferes with the other's attempts to satisfy their wants or goals. Why manage conflict? A capacity to manage conflict is an important skill to possess because conflict handled well can be positive and constructive, while conflict handled poorly can be negative and destructive. Avoidance or denial of conflict in the short term allows it to escalate into deep-rooted conflict in the long run.

The language of conflict resolution

Conflict resolution requires the parties to examine the problem and seek to resolve it in a way that meets the interests of both.

Burton (1987, p. 4) says that deep-rooted conflicts between people occur in 'organisations as they do in personal relationships. They may be conflicts motivated by ambition, personal dislikes, authority relationships and others that are common where people are working together within an organisation.' There is a great deal of confusion about the nature of conflict resolution. Burton defines some of the key terms in Table 6.1. This chapter is about conflict management, how parties can manage conflict and move towards a solution without escalating the conflict or giving away interests.

Positive conflict management stimulates change and clarifies ideas and objectives. Challenging the accepted way of doing things creates innovative ideas and leads to new ways of doing things. It is constructive. Conflict that is either avoided or continuous is destructive. It creates ill feeling, tension and stress.

Approaches to conflict

Conflict can be either approached or avoided.

A variety of considerations influence the way we handle conflict. What we want, how we feel, our view of the situation and the likely consequences of the strategies we use all impact on the way we approach a conflict.

Lewin (1935) showed how the tendency to deal with conflict by either approaching or avoiding it (or using a combination of both) leads to three general approaches to conflict:

1. approach/approach conflict
2. avoidance/avoidance conflict
3. approach/avoidance conflict.

Table 6.1: Definitions of key terms in conflict management

Term	Definition
Facilitation	A process in which a facilitator seeks to help the parties arrive at a common definition of their relationship, define their separate goals, facilitate analysis and discover options that meet the needs of all.
Mediation	A process in which a mediator either makes mandatory proposals or moves back and forward between the parties and tries to help them arrive at agreed compromises.
Negotiation	A process in which two or more parties try to resolve differences, solve problems and reach agreement.
Settlement	A process arrived at by a mediator offering a compromise that differs from a resolution.
Resolution	A process that develops from an analysis of the total situation by the concerned parties to meet all their needs.
Conflict management	A process in which the parties attempt to manage the conflict and move towards a solution without escalating the conflict or giving away their interests.
Conflict resolution	A process that seeks to resolve the problem, even though this requires change.

Source: Adapted from J.W. Burton, *Resolving Deep-rooted Conflict*, University Press of America, Lanham, 1987, pp. 7–8. Reproduced with permission.

Approach/approach conflict occurs when people are attracted to two appealing but incompatible goals at the same time. Conflict arises as the person makes a choice between the two goals. The tendency towards avoidance/avoidance conflict occurs when a person is faced with two undesirable or threatening alternatives at the same time. Approach/avoidance conflict occurs when a person is attracted to and repelled by two alternative wants at the same time. Examples of each type of conflict are given in Table 6.2.

The chosen approach to conflict is influenced by personality, cultural background and communication skills.

Our personality, cultural background and communication skills influence our approach to conflict. Shy people are likely to avoid conflict. People of Asian origin are likely to avoid conflict in front of others because of the need in their culture to 'save face'. Christie (2001, p. 4) points out that this arises from a respect for superiors as well as a fear of 'loss of face'. Communication skills such as assertiveness, empathy and active listening enable people to approach conflict and gain productive outcomes.

Table 6.2: Approaches to conflict

Type	Example
Approach/approach conflict	A career woman aged 36 and her partner are thinking about having their first child in the next 12 months. At work, she is offered a major promotion to Associate Director. Internal conflict arises because both goals are appealing but may be incompatible.
Avoidance/avoidance conflict	A student who dislikes both study and failure is threatened by both. Internal conflict arises because the student wants to avoid both study and failure. The student who has an avoidance/avoidance tendency will try to escape both.
Approach/avoidance conflict	A private consultant who has severely damaged one of the discs in his lower back has to rest for three weeks after an operation or risk further damage to his back. Because the consultant needs an income, he is attracted to the idea of going back to work early but repelled by the risk of further damage to his back.

Conflict styles

Donohue and Kolt (1992) stress that 'People need communication skills to listen to others, develop proposals and bargain about interests' (p. 29). Kilmann and Thomas (1975, cited in Donohue & Kolt) used two dimensions—concern for own interests and concern for the interests of others—to illustrate the five different conflict styles people may use when approaching conflict (see Figure 6.1).

1. *Avoiding style* indicates low concern for both their own and the other's interests.
2. *Accommodating style* indicates a low concern for their own needs and high concern for others.
3. *Competing style* indicates a high concern for own needs and low concern for others.
4. *Collaborating style* indicates high concern for both.
5. *Compromising style* indicates some concern for both their own and the other's needs.

During a drawn-out conflict all five styles may be needed because no one style suits every interaction.

Donohue and Kolt (1992) regard timing and planning as two important parts of productive conflict management and warn against rushing into a dispute and saying anything that comes to mind. They also believe that confronting problems when intense emotions are involved is counterproductive. Kuhn and Poole (2001) examined the relationship between group conflict-management styles and the effectiveness of group decision making in two large United States organisations. Their findings suggest that decision making in groups with integrative conflict-management styles is more effective than in groups that use confrontation and avoidance styles of conflict management. Integrative styles aim to bring together the needs and interests of both parties.

Types of conflict

There are four main types of conflict: internal, external, realistic and unrealistic. Any one of the four types of conflict can have positive or negative results. The nature of the result depends on the way in which the conflict is handled.

INTERNAL CONFLICT

Internal conflict occurs within a person and is caused by an unsatisfied need or an unresolved experience or emotion.

Internal conflict exists when a need is not met or when someone is unable to come to terms with a past experience or feeling. Emotions may contribute to conflict within the individual. A person who is feeling run down, for example, from having to work, attend courses, sit for an examination and consider their next assignment, may find internal conflict is triggered. Emotions are experienced because the person is conscious of feelings such as anger. Internal conflict occurs when the feeling is felt. This is the first level of emotional awareness identified by Hein (2003).

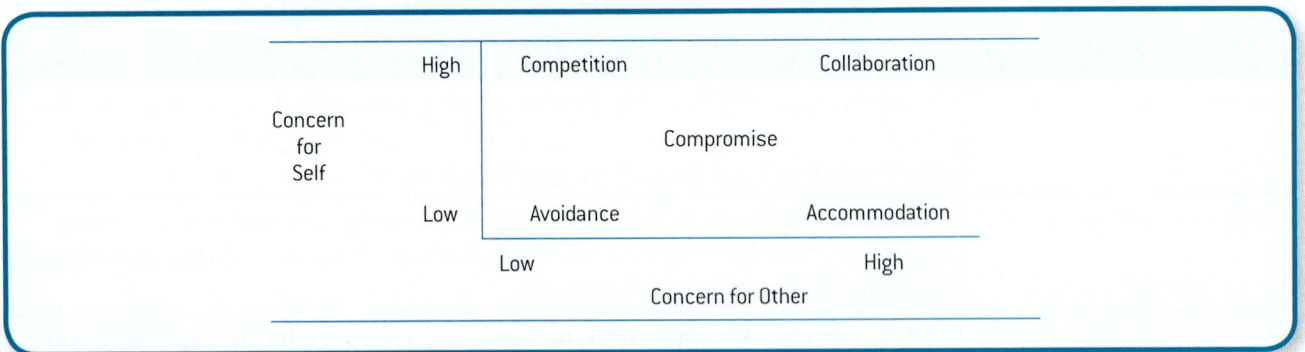

Figure 6.1: Kilmann and Thomas: Conflict styles

Source: Kilmann & Thomas, cited in W.A. Donohue & R. Kolt, *Managing Interpersonal Conflict*, p. 30. Copyright 1992 Sage Publications, California. Reproduced with permission of Sage Publications Inc.

Hein identified another five levels of emotional awareness—acknowledging the feeling, identifying the feeling, accepting the feeling, reflecting the feeling and forecasting feelings. Those who are willing to link this emotional awareness to what is happening have emotional intelligence—the capacity to reason with emotion as well as objective information. They can deal with internal conflict themselves, or perhaps with the careful listening and understanding of a friend they can recognise the source of conflict and use techniques to handle it.

EXTERNAL CONFLICT

External conflict occurs between people. This type of conflict can lead to unpleasant incidents and so cause bad feelings. A misunderstanding between co-workers can leave people feeling uncomfortable with each other. Identifying negative emotions with words, accepting them and reflecting on them makes it possible to link them to their cause.

External conflict occurs between people.

An empathic person is able not only to acknowledge and identify the feeling (i.e. have awareness of their own emotions), but also to help others identify their emotions by using their listening skills to attend to and mirror the feelings in the conflict situation. By using emotional intelligence in conjunction with conflict-resolution skills at the time the conflict occurs, there is a chance to discuss, air and resolve the external conflict.

REALISTIC CONFLICT

Realistic conflict is conflict that can be resolved if people are willing to use effective strategies and negotiation skills. It can lead to positive results. One person may wish to see a film, while his partner wants to visit relatives. An employee values consultative management, whereas her manager wants speed, efficiency and top-down management. Their different interests may lead to conflict. Are they both willing to resolve the difference or let it escalate into a major incident? Once opposing needs are acknowledged, people are able to deal with the conflict realistically, understand one another and move forward to a new situation.

Realistic conflict is conflict that can be resolved if people are willing to use effective strategies and negotiation skills.

UNREALISTIC CONFLICT

Unrealistic conflict cannot be resolved because the parties are unwilling to change their attitudes. There is no room for negotiation because this type of conflict is based on differences in values and attitudes. A longstanding manager values the company's traditions and stability. A new manager wants to introduce modern practices, continuous improvement and change. No amount of negotiation will resolve the conflict. Unrealistic conflict can arise from ignorance or traditions. Prejudice can lead to hostility that neither negotiation nor conflict resolution can alter.

Unrealistic conflict cannot be resolved because the people involved are unwilling to change their attitudes.

REVIEW QUESTIONS

1. Distinguish three approaches to conflict.
2. Identify five conflict styles.
3. a   Explain the difference between internal, external, realistic and unrealistic conflict.
   b   Give an example of a clash of values that can cause unrealistic conflict.

CAUSES OF CONFLICT

◄ OBJECTIVE 2
Discuss the causes, benefits and costs of conflict

Conflict arises in every organisation. Competition for scarce resources, misunderstandings about assigned tasks, conflicting priorities, and different performance criteria between sections or positions can cause clashes, opposition and arguments.

Wade (2003, p. 14) commented that 'Before intervening to assist a person involved in conflict, a skilled helper or representative should make some attempt to determine:

- the causes of the conflict
- the degree of escalation which has occurred.'

Wade believes that, unless a correct diagnosis is made, the wrong intervention can occur. There are many helpful models that can assist in diagnosing the causes of conflict. He regards Christopher Moore's 'circle of conflict', a diagrammatic representation of the causes of conflict (known colloquially as 'Moore's pizza'), as being particularly useful. Moore identified five overlapping categories of conflict:

1. data conflict
2. interest conflict
3. relationship conflict
4. structural conflict
5. value conflict.

For each of these categories, Moore lists the possible causes of the conflict (see Figure 6.2). These vary from issues relating to misinformation and lack of information, to competitive interests, emotional clashes and ideological differences. Determining the cause or causes by using Moore's circle can assist in making a correct diagnosis.

Robbins and colleagues (2006, p. 500) discuss three different views of conflict within organisations: 'One view argues that conflict must be avoided, that it indicates a problem within the group. This is called the traditional view of conflict. A second view, the human relations view of conflict, argues that conflict is a natural and inevitable outcome in any group and need not be negative; rather, it has the potential to be a positive force in contributing to a group's performance. The third and most recent perspective proposes that not only can conflict be a positive force in a group but also that some conflict is *absolutely necessary* for a group to perform effectively. This third approach is called the inter-actionist view of conflict.' Dynamic organisations take the interactionist approach to conflict because they realise that conflict is a predictable social phenomenon. The goal of organisational leadership is not to eliminate conflict but to channel and use it as a positive force.

Productive outcomes

Effective management of conflict reduces petty irritations and improves awareness of self and others.

The benefits of conflict management are the opportunity to clarify issues, generate new ideas and get feelings into the open. Effective conflict management can improve a work group's performance. Differences about how to do a task can stimulate discussion and new ideas and solve problems. Conflict management can force us to learn more about ourselves and develop our relationships with others. While conflict management has benefits, the harm that conflict can cause should not be minimised. Putnis and Petelin (1999, p. 38) state: 'Our aim should not be to deny or avoid conflict, but to develop techniques to manage it and so minimise the destructive power that conflicts can unleash.'

DeVito (1992, p. 344) says: 'The major value of interpersonal conflict is that it forces the individuals to examine a problem and work toward a potential solution. If productive conflict strategies are used, the relationship may well emerge from the encounter stronger, healthier, and more satisfying than before.' Donohue and Kolt (1992, p. 26) comment that the 'natural tendency is to try to avoid conflict as long as possible'. Often this is not possible, and Donohue and Kolt list three decisions that must then be made:

1. whether or not to confront
2. when to confront
3. how to confront.

In their view, confrontation generally works better than avoiding conflict. They believe that 'When people can discuss their problems, and they want to continue the relationship, confronting conflict appears to be generally productive' (1992, p. 29). They list six points to consider when deciding whether to confront the conflict (p. 33):

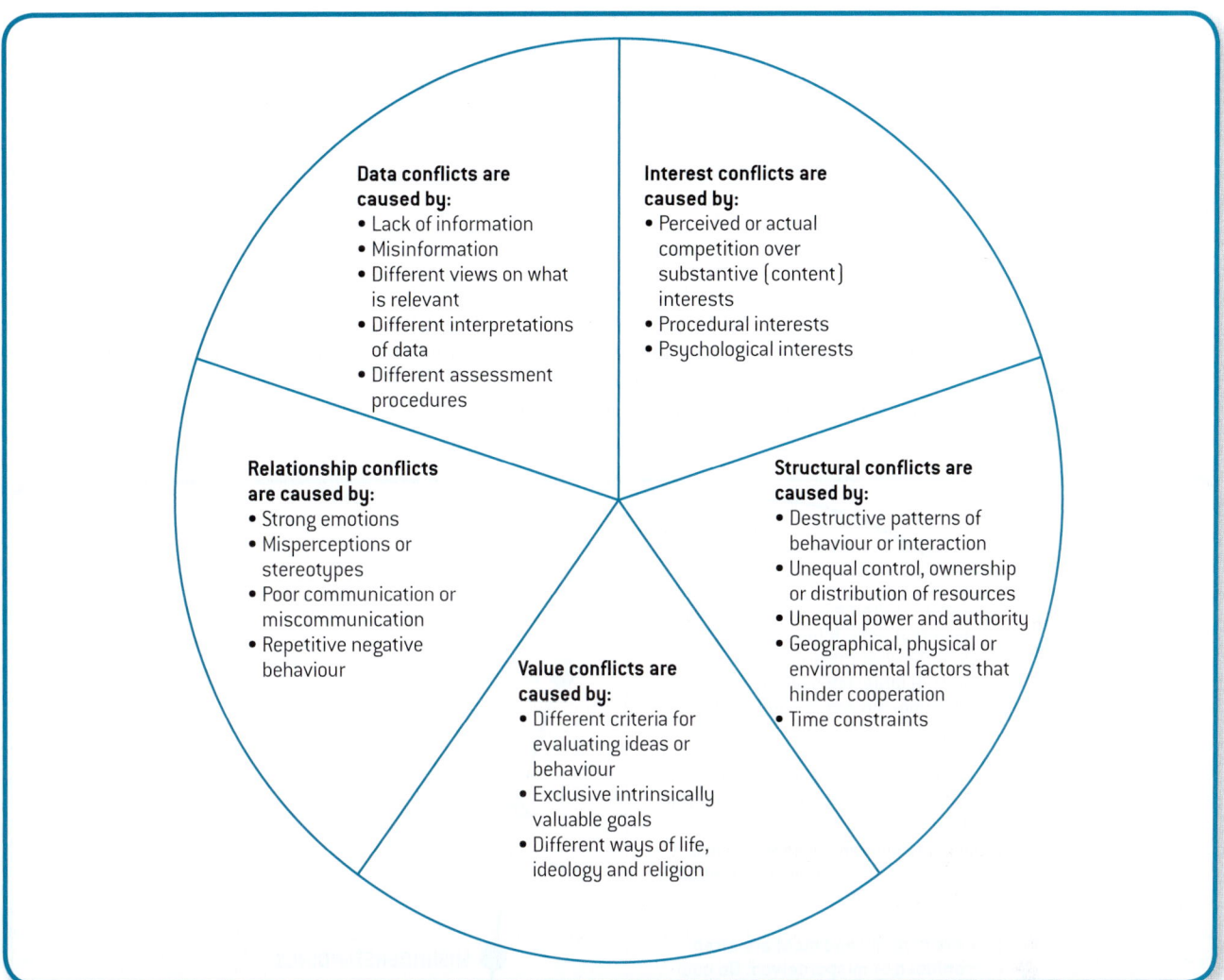

Data conflicts are caused by:
- Lack of information
- Misinformation
- Different views on what is relevant
- Different interpretations of data
- Different assessment procedures

Interest conflicts are caused by:
- Perceived or actual competition over substantive (content) interests
- Procedural interests
- Psychological interests

Relationship conflicts are caused by:
- Strong emotions
- Misperceptions or stereotypes
- Poor communication or miscommunication
- Repetitive negative behaviour

Structural conflicts are caused by:
- Destructive patterns of behaviour or interaction
- Unequal control, ownership or distribution of resources
- Unequal power and authority
- Geographical, physical or environmental factors that hinder cooperation
- Time constraints

Value conflicts are caused by:
- Different criteria for evaluating ideas or behaviour
- Exclusive intrinsically valuable goals
- Different ways of life, ideology and religion

Figure 6.2: Moore's pizza

Source: C. Moore, *The Mediation Process: Practical Strategies for Resolving Conflict*, 2nd edn, copyright Jossey-Bass Publishers, San Francisco, 1996. This material is used by permission of John Wiley & Sons Inc.

1. Is your relationship with this other person important to you?
2. Is the issue in dispute important to you?
3. Do you become verbally aggressive during conflict?
4. Do you look for ways to use a collaborative conflict style in resolving your disputes?
5. Is there limited time available to deal with the problem?
6. Do you fear for your personal safety if you confront the other person?

Levels of conflict

Conflict moves through a number of different levels before it reaches the crisis level. At the first level, people experience **discomfort**, a feeling that things are not quite right. At the next level, an **incident** occurs. Emotions are not running high yet, but something has come between the people concerned. People who are alert to the feeling of discomfort and aware of the incident are able to use their communication skills to

Discomfort is a level of conflict where things do not feel right.

Incident level is where a short, sharp exchange has occurred, causing a slight irritation.

Misunderstanding is a level of conflict where motives and facts are often confused or misperceived.

Tension is a level of conflict where relationships are weighed down by negative attitudes and fixed opinions.

Crisis is a level of conflict where behaviour and normal functioning are affected.

clarify the problem at this level before the situation escalates into a **misunderstanding**. A misunderstanding can occur between individuals or groups and interfere with their relationship. The misunderstanding could be about facts or about the goals or intentions of the parties involved.

Tension arises as a result of the misunderstanding. When people feel anxious about talking, working or coming into contact with each other, emotions run high. Negative attitudes and the likelihood of a negative response—an outburst of anger, complete withdrawal and avoidance of the other party—will lead to a crisis.

Crisis is the fifth level of conflict. The crisis may be over destructive patterns of behaviour or unequal power and authority. In conflict situations, emotions may escalate the conflict. Attempt to defuse the emotions with active listening and empathy before trying to think and work through the problem. By staying alert to the signs of discomfort and incidents (the first and second levels of conflict), a person is able to use the most appropriate conflict-resolution strategy before the conflict moves to higher levels.

The five levels of conflict are illustrated in Figure 6.3.

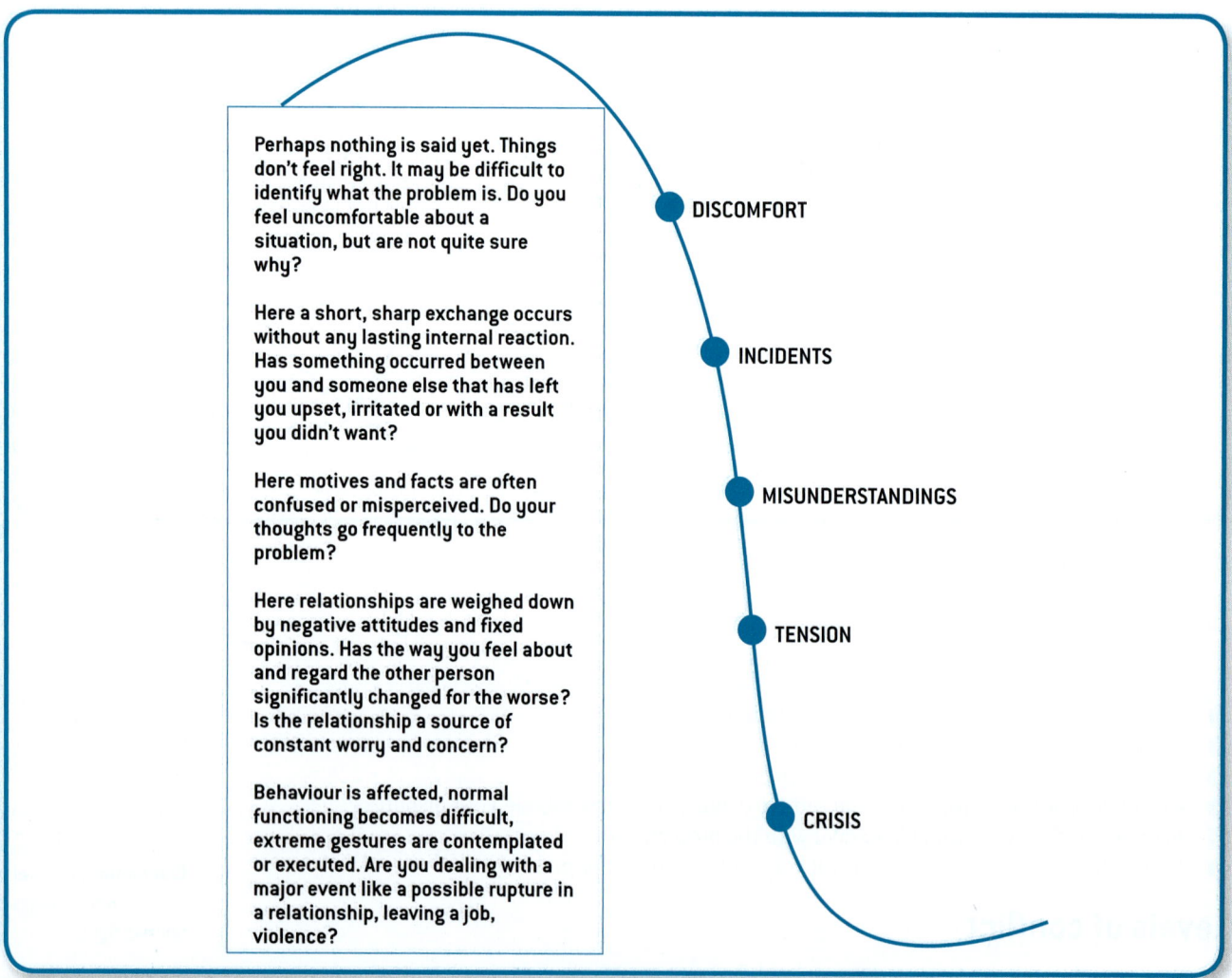

Perhaps nothing is said yet. Things don't feel right. It may be difficult to identify what the problem is. Do you feel uncomfortable about a situation, but are not quite sure why?

Here a short, sharp exchange occurs without any lasting internal reaction. Has something occurred between you and someone else that has left you upset, irritated or with a result you didn't want?

Here motives and facts are often confused or misperceived. Do your thoughts go frequently to the problem?

Here relationships are weighed down by negative attitudes and fixed opinions. Has the way you feel about and regard the other person significantly changed for the worse? Is the relationship a source of constant worry and concern?

Behaviour is affected, normal functioning becomes difficult, extreme gestures are contemplated or executed. Are you dealing with a major event like a possible rupture in a relationship, leaving a job, violence?

DISCOMFORT

INCIDENTS

MISUNDERSTANDINGS

TENSION

CRISIS

Figure 6.3: Levels of conflict

Source: Copyright. The Conflict Resolution Network, PO Box 1016, Chatswood, NSW 2057, Australia, Ph: (02) 9419 8500; email: crn@crnhq.org; website: www.crnhq.org. Reproduced with permission.

REVIEW QUESTIONS

4 Describe the five overlapping categories of conflict identified by Moore (1996).

5 What are the benefits of conflict?

6 Explain each of the levels of conflict.

APPLY YOUR KNOWLEDGE

THE MEANING OF CONFLICT

1 Work in pairs to discuss conflict.

    a   What does the term mean to you?

    b   How would you describe your behaviour in a conflict situation?

2 Work in pairs.

    a   Think of a conflict that was handled in a *destructive* way. Discuss the likely outcomes when a conflict is handled in this way, then complete column 1 of Table 6.3 below.

    b   Think of a conflict that was handled in a *constructive* way. Discuss the likely outcomes when a conflict is handled in this way, then complete column 2 of Table 6.3.

Table 6.3: Likely outcomes

Handling conflict in a destructive way	Handling conflict in a constructive way
1	1
2	2
3	3
4	4

3 Discuss a conflict situation from your recent experience.

    a   What level did the conflict reach?

    b   Identify each level through which the conflict moved.

    c   What was the final outcome of the conflict?

4 How can conflict be positive?

5 How does the capacity to differentiate between the four types of conflict help a person deal with conflict?

6   a   Moore's 'circle of conflict' represents five overlapping causes of conflict. Describe the fives causes and give an example of each.

    b   Do you agree with Wade's statement that it is important to identify the cause of a conflict and the degree of escalation that has occurred before intervening to assist a person in conflict? Justify your answer.

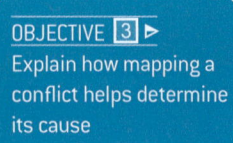
MANAGING CONFLICT

Three needs should be addressed when negotiating a conflict. First are the substantive needs, which concern the cause of the conflict, the issue, the perceived incompatible differences or the problem that needs to be solved. The second needs are procedural, which relate to the process of addressing the substantive needs. They include the *ground rules* that ensure all parties feel included in a meaningful way and the processes that will be used to meet interests, design options and reach agreement. The third needs are psychological. Psychological needs include a safe, positive environment in which people are willing to risk communicating their differences, concerns and potential similarities honestly.

Ground rules are statements about how the parties will treat one another in the conflict negotiation.

Mapping the conflict

A map is a useful way of finding the cause of a conflict. Clarification and agreement about the cause enable both parties to focus on interests rather than diversions or misperceptions. The cause may be a difference in facts, goals or values, or in methods of taking action. A map allows all parties to see the whole picture—their perception of the conflict, the other person's perception and the issues involved. An example of a **conflict map** is shown in Figure 6.4.

A **conflict map** is a useful tool for finding the cause of a conflict.

There are four steps involved in mapping a conflict, each with a specific purpose. These are outlined in Table 6.4.

Generating solutions and design options

Needs are the major requirement of each party in a situation.

After the major *needs* and *concerns* of each party have been decided (from the map), the most suitable solution or set of solutions will be seen more easily. The course of action to take must acknowledge available resources and time constraints. When the most suitable solutions are not obvious, further options for action will need to be generated. One way to do this is to expand the number of issues that relate to the underlying interests of both parties by shifting from specific interests to more general interests.

Concerns are issues that engage a person's attention or interest.

A number of different strategies are used to design the *options* before actions are taken. Some of these are to:

Options are alternatives from which the appropriate choice can be made.

- brainstorm to generate options (see Chapter 11)
- use Dewey's reflective thinking process (see Chapter 12)
- use the decision-making agenda (see Chapter 12)
- divide or 'chunk' the problem into small pieces
- use a trial-and-error approach.

Selecting and acting on the most appropriate option

Before the most appropriate option is selected it is important to link similar or complementary options developed in the brainstorming session. The simplest way to do this is to join similar options

Table 6.4: The four steps in mapping a conflict	
Step	**Purpose**
1 Define the issue.	To gain a clear idea of the issue/s to be mapped
2 Identify who is involved.	To identify and group together the people with shared needs and concerns
3 List the major needs and concerns of each party.	To implement the win–win approach and generate appropriate solutions
4 Read the map.	To draw together common threads and highlight points of special concern or importance.

In the centre circle, define briefly the issue, the problem area or the conflict in neutral terms that all would agree on and that don't invite a 'yes/no' answer, e.g. 'Filing', not 'Should Sal do filing?'

In the sectors of the large circle, write the name of each important person or group.

Write down each person's or group's needs. What motivates them?

Write down each person's or group's concerns, fears or anxieties.

Be prepared to change the statement of the issue as your understanding of it evolves through discussion, or to draw up other maps of related issues that arise.

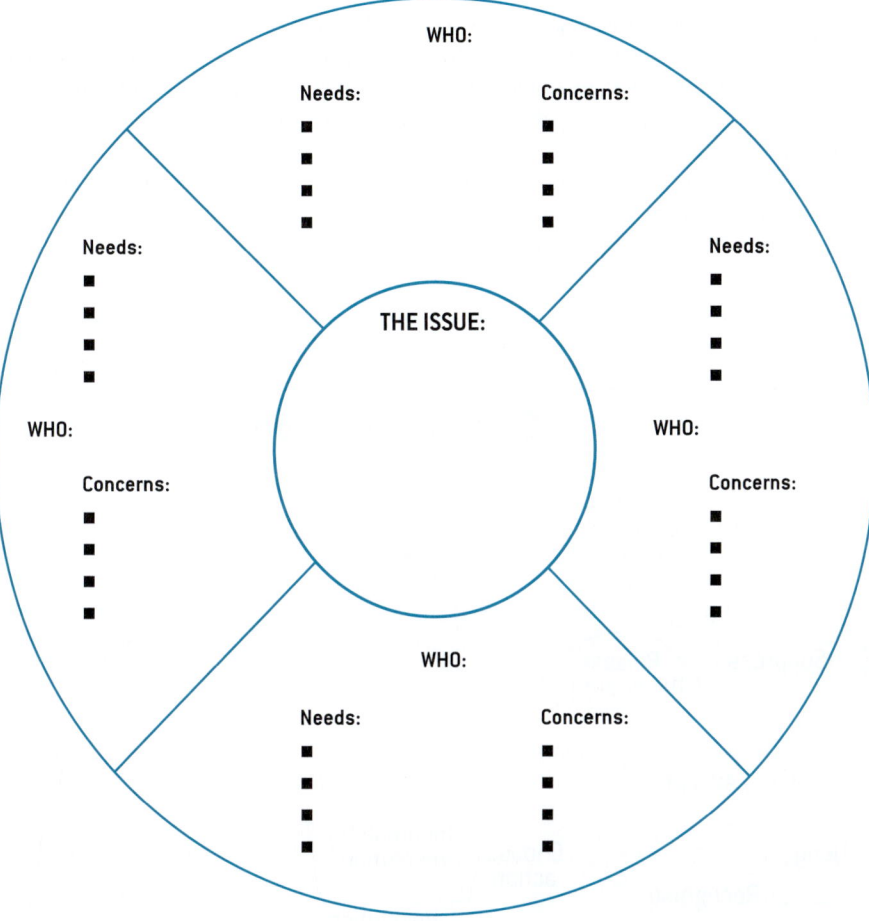

Figure 6.4: Mapping a conflict

Source: Copyright. The Conflict Resolution Network, PO Box 1016, Chatswood, NSW 2057, Australia. Ph: (02) 9419 8500; email: crn@crnhq.org; website: www.crnhq.org. Reproduced with permission.

with a line. Once the similar or complementary options are linked, remove those options that are inappropriate. Analyse those that are left in terms of how well they will meet the need. Then place the options into the order in which they will be implemented. Identify what will be done, how it will be done, who will do it, when it will be completed and the expected results. Set out the actions in an action plan.

An **action plan** is the working document for the implementation of chosen options.

An **action plan** is the working document for implementing the chosen options. Keep the plan realistic and tangible, and identify the time by which the options will be implemented. By acting on the options, it is possible to solve the problems and conflicts experienced by people at work and elsewhere. As changes are introduced, people experience the benefits of the win–win approach to conflict.

Emotional intelligence

A person with **emotional intelligence** is able to manage emotions effectively in any situation.

Intelligence is a general term referring to the ability to learn and to behave adaptively. **Emotional intelligence** as defined by Goleman (1998) is the ability to perceive and identify your emotions and the emotions of others. As well as affecting individual performance and organisational productivity, emotional intelligence affects the way we respond in conflict situations. Emotions such as surprise, fear or anger energise and direct behaviour. The ability to perceive, identify and manage emotions in a conflict provides the opportunity to respond appropriately, build stronger relationships and avoid getting 'hooked' into negative feelings. In a conflict situation, intelligence about our emotions and the emotions of others enables us to diffuse the emotions, control our own behaviour and handle the situation constructively. By diffusing the emotions, we are better able to maintain the relationship and less likely to harm it.

Effective management of emotions maintains a positive atmosphere during conflict negotiation.

The cycle of emotion shown in Figure 6.5 illustrates the difference between effective and less effective management of emotions. Effective management moves from recognition to chosen action and resolution. The cycle of emotion shows the resolution of an issue or problem through a process of:

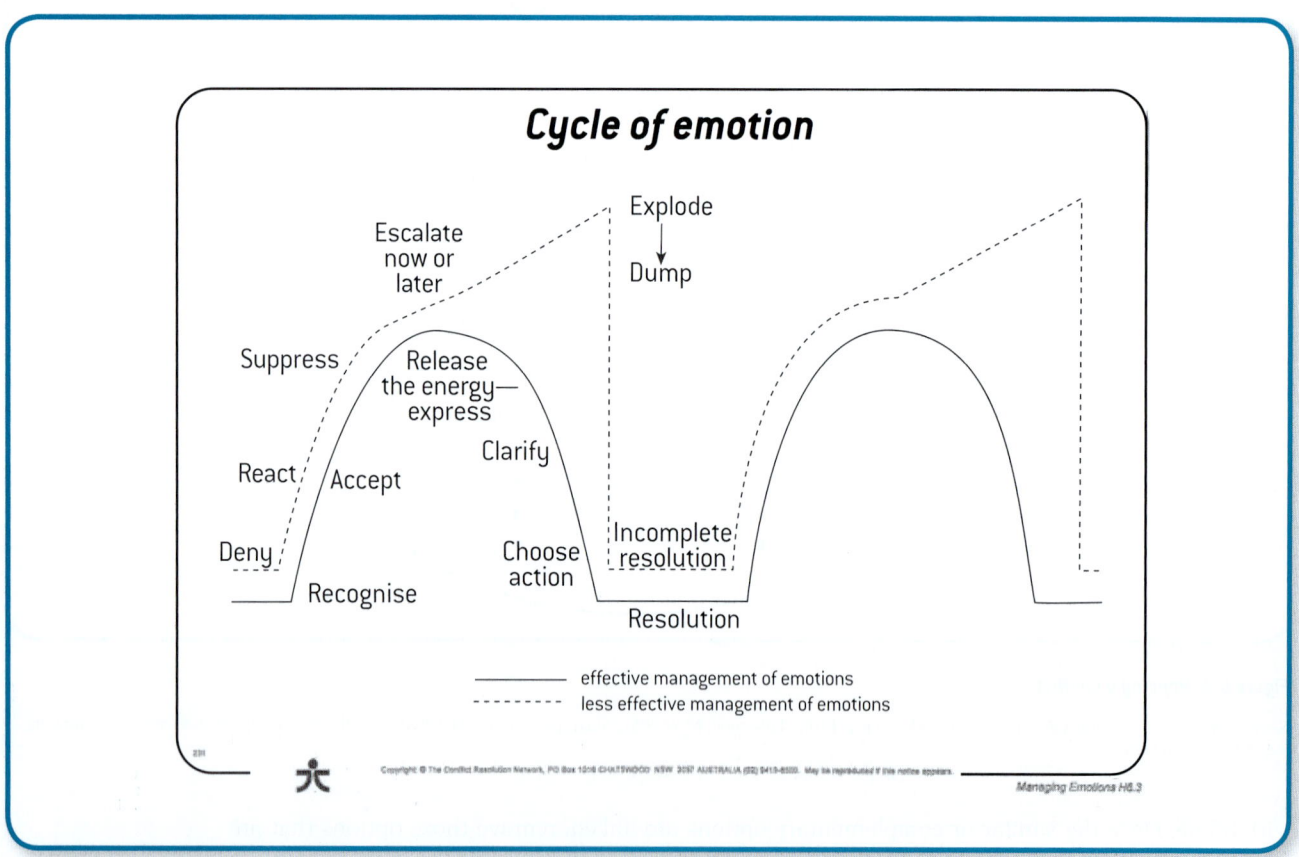

Figure 6.5: Cycle of emotion

Sources: Adapted from materials of The Conflict Resolution Network, PO Box 1016, Chatswood, NSW 2057, Australia. Ph: (02) 9419 8500; email: crn@crnhq.org; website: www.crnhq.org. Reproduced with permission.

- recognising the emotion
- accepting it
- releasing the energy
- clarifying
- choosing action.

Ineffective management moves from denial through to escalation and incomplete resolution of the conflict. Incomplete emotional resolution results in:

- low self-esteem
- poor interpersonal relationships
- rigid and inflexible responses
- stress, either emotional or physical.

A model of conflict resolution

DeVito (1992, pp. 346–9) lists five steps in his model of conflict resolution, shown in Figure 6.6:

1. Define the conflict.
2. Identify possible solutions.
3. Test the solution.
4. Evaluate the solution.
5. Accept or reject the solution.

DeVito (1992, p. 349) also suggests keeping in mind the following law of conflict: 'Any conflict is easier to create than resolve.' He suggests five productive conflict-resolution strategies—openness, empathy, supportiveness, positiveness and equality. These are the general qualities of interpersonal effectiveness, discussed in Chapter 3. By applying these qualities in conflict situations, we have a greater chance of resolving differences and disagreements. DeVito also discusses the following unproductive conflict strategies (pp. 349–53):

- avoidance/redefinition/non-negotiation
- minimisation
- blame
- silencers, such as crying, yelling, screaming
- gunnysacking—the practice of storing up grievances and holding them ready to dump on the other person
- beltlining—knowing the level that can be tolerated and going 'below the belt'
- manipulation
- personal rejection
- force.

The principled bargaining process

Fisher and Ury (1981) developed the principled bargaining process, which does two things. First, it deals with the issue in conflict; second, it maintains the relationship. (Principled bargaining is explained in Chapter 5.) The method works in conflict management because it:

- separates the people from the problem
- focuses on the interests, rather than the parties
- generates a variety of possible options
- ensures that results are based on objective criteria.

Limit the scope of the conflict to the interests of the parties.

By developing procedures—either informal or formal—for dealing with disputes and clarifying the elements of a conflict, both parties are able to focus on issues rather than people, and discuss the issues to reach a shared understanding. The scope of the conflict is limited to the interests of the parties. They are able to give their views and describe their feelings about the issue (or problem), generate possible solutions, and develop and choose a solution. The goal of conflict management and negotiation is not to destroy or dominate the other party; it is to win them over so that they become partners in a shared problem-solving process.

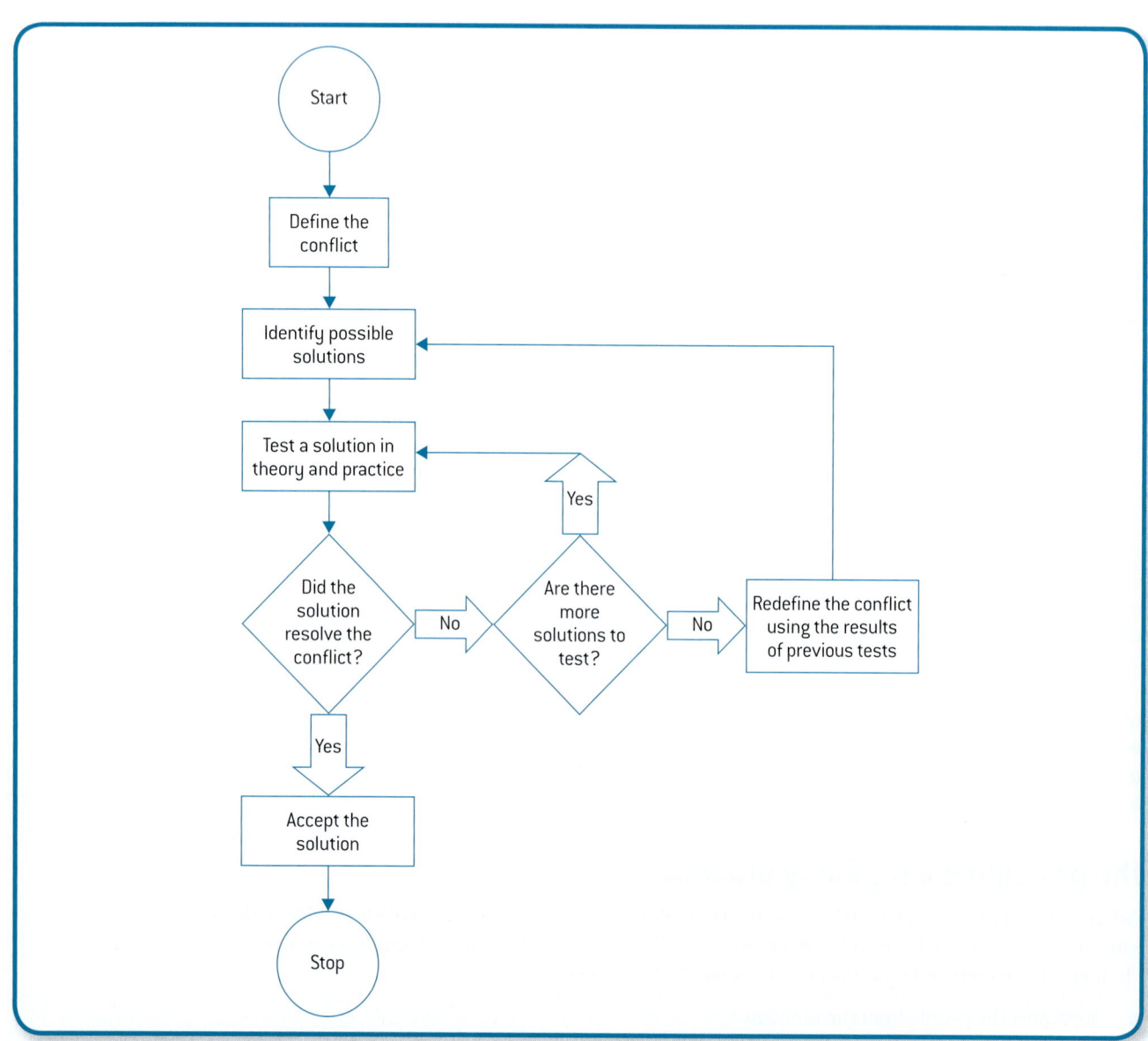

Figure 6.6: The process of resolving conflict effectively

Source: Adapted from J.A. DeVito, *The Interpersonal Communication Book*, 9th edn, 2001. Published by Allyn & Bacon, Boston, MA. © 1992 by Pearson Education. Reprinted by permission of the publisher.

REVIEW QUESTIONS

7 What is the purpose of mapping a conflict?

8 a Explain how an awareness of emotional intelligence and the causes of conflict can help you respond appropriately in a conflict situation.

b Identify the stages in the cycle of emotion.

9 Identify five unproductive conflict strategies.

APPLY YOUR KNOWLEDGE

HOW TO DEAL WITH CONFLICT

1 Work individually.

a How can conflict be positive?

b How can negotiation and conflict overlap?

c Consider this statement: 'Conflict is caused by a clash of opinions, values or needs.' Briefly explain the statement and give an example of a situation in which each of the following results could occur:

- clash of opinions
- a difference of values
- unmet needs.

2 Explain the terms 'substantive needs', 'procedural needs' and 'psychological needs' in a conflict negotiation.

3 How does the principled negotiation process limit the scope of the conflict to the interests of the parties?

4 How does emotional intelligence impact on a conflict? Give examples.

5 Work in small groups.

a Brainstorm to create a list of typical constructive and destructive behaviours in a conflict.

b Choose two destructive behaviours and suggest ways of changing them.

CONSTRUCTIVE RESPONSES TO CONFLICT

◀ OBJECTIVE 4
Interact constructively in conflict situations by using assertion, active listening and framing questions

Responses to conflict are learned early in childhood. These responses become habits and reactions used without thought in adult life. Learning new and constructive ways to handle conflict enables us to respond to it more appropriately, and to focus on the present issue rather than reintroducing past disagreements. A range of behaviours are used as people respond to conflict. Flight, fight and flow behaviours are shown in Table 6.5.

Avoidance is a flight response to conflict. One or both parties disappear. Porter and Taplin (1987) argue that the avoidance approach to conflict is unlikely to end or resolve the conflict. If one or both parties disappear, the conflict lies dormant and is likely to re-emerge in future interactions. On the other hand, the fight response to conflict enables the contact to continue. Both parties can search for ways to resolve the conflict.

When confronted with conflict, some people prefer to use emotional or physical force rather than deal with the issues. Boulding (1962) describes a method of dealing with conflict that he calls *conquest*: one party is defeated, while the other party conquers and becomes the victor. The parties are opposing one another, rather than cooperating to find a solution. Use of the conquest method to resolve the conflict may lead to longer-term problems and conflict because of the ill-will generated by the losses sustained by the defeated party.

Table 6.5: Responses to conflict			
Type	Purpose	Behaviour	Intended outcome
Fight	To be in control and defend a position	Aggressive: manipulation, physical violence, screaming	I win—you lose
Flight	To escape the situation and avoid the results	Submissive: giving in, crying, avoiding, sulking	I lose—you win
Flow	To acknowledge the situation and respond appropriately	Assertive: explaining own perspective/needs, listening, discussing	I win—you win

Sources: Adapted from materials of The Conflict Resolution Network, PO Box 1016 Chatswood, NSW 2057, Australia. Ph: (02) 9419 8500; email: crn@crnhq.org; website: www.crnhq.org. Reproduced with permission.

Flow response

The **flow response** acknowledges the conflict situation and reacts appropriately.

The **win–win approach** aims to satisfy the needs and interests of both parties.

Flow response is another term for the win–win approach to conflict. The **win–win approach** leads to constructive responses to conflict because the needs of both parties are met in an appropriate way. It allow both parties to explore their needs before settling on a solution. People talk, listen and find out what each party wants and needs. The principles underlying the flow response are:

- consideration of own wants and what the other party wants
- belief that both parties' needs can be met without one winning and the other losing
- respect for relationships
- movement towards a solution that meets as many needs as possible
- consultation with others to explore needs and consider all possible options.

Sometimes, the solutions to a problem may be simple and practical. On other occasions, the solutions may be complex and difficult, involving attitude change and the need for commitment from each party. As parties move towards a solution, they may adopt a number of positions: one party may try to change the other party's position, they may change their own position, or both parties may arrive at a compromise.

Figure 5.1 in Chapter 5 shows that each of the identified negotiation styles has an effect on relationships and on the achievement of goals. It also shows that each preferred style is matched by the most likely conflict-management strategy. Those who understand the different styles and strategies, and their preferred style, are in a position to choose another style that is suited to the situation and achieves positive outcomes rather than always using their preferred style.

Empathy is the ability to understand and feel as the other person feels.

In **confrontation**, people are in opposition or feel antagonistic towards each other.

Conflict management and resolution based on *empathy* for the other party, rather than deliberate **confrontation**, establishes a climate where both parties communicate. Both are able to construct a clear agenda and check with the other to see that they are both working from the same agenda, and that the agenda covers the full list of what both parties want.

Conflict resolution occurs when the parties focus on the problem, not individual personalities, and when the responses of both parties show concern for their own wants and the wants of the other party.

Assertive behaviour

Assertive behaviour shows in an individual's way of speaking, listening, questioning and nonverbal signals. This style of behaviour is constructive and helpful when conflict arises, because the needs of both parties are acknowledged and addressed. Both are more likely, through this style of communicating, to understand one another and the situation.

Acting assertively in a conflict situation means standing up for your rights and expressing what you believe, feel and want in direct, honest and appropriate ways that respect the rights of the other person.

Assertive behaviour increases our self-esteem, leads to the development of mutual respect with others and helps us achieve our goals. Assertive behaviour allows people to express how they are feeling in a way that is unlikely to lead to a defensive or aggressive response from the other person.

Non-assertive behaviour is aggressive or *submissive behaviour* that ignores our own rights by failing to express honest feelings, thoughts and beliefs. Non-assertive behaviour can be aggressive when deliberately used to achieve specific goals. An aggressive person usually tries to win at all costs by dominating and humiliating others. Their behaviour shows little respect for others. A submissive person is unable to promote a point of view, even to the extent of ignoring their own needs. They lack respect for self.

Steiner (1974) created the **drama triangle** (Figure 6.7) to illustrate the roles played by a person who uses non-assertive behaviour. People who play the role of the **victim** behave in a helpless manner. They speak and act as if everyone is against them and they are unable to do anything for themselves. In a conflict situation they are unable to act and give up defeated. The victim in this situation is not a real victim, as in a car accident, but is playing the role of a victim and using helpless behaviour in order to have someone rescue them or persecute them.

People who play the role of **persecutor** offer rewards or punishment to those who are acting as if they were helpless and unable to do anything. Persecutors put the other person down, or push or bully them into action. In contrast, people who play the role of **rescuer** offer help and support while denying their own needs. They act like martyrs and may try to protect the victim from the persecutor.

The *submissive behaviour* shown in the **flight response** (Table 6.5) can increase the conflict that the behaviour is trying to avoid. The *aggressive behaviour* shown in the **fight response** widens the differences between the two parties and increases the conflict. Contrast this with the assertive behaviour in the flow response. The flow response is shown in the **success triangle** in Figure 6.8.

Assertion enables people to express their needs and concerns in a conflict situation. When it is used with the win–win approach, with others who also use the win–win approach, the parties are able to consider the needs of one another and move towards a solution that satisfies as many needs as possible.

Assertive statements are used to make people aware of the rights of the speaker while still respecting their rights. If behaviour is aggressive (not respecting the rights of others) or dangerous to themselves or others, the speaker sends clear assertive messages and listens to the message from the other party. The basic 'I' message has three parts:

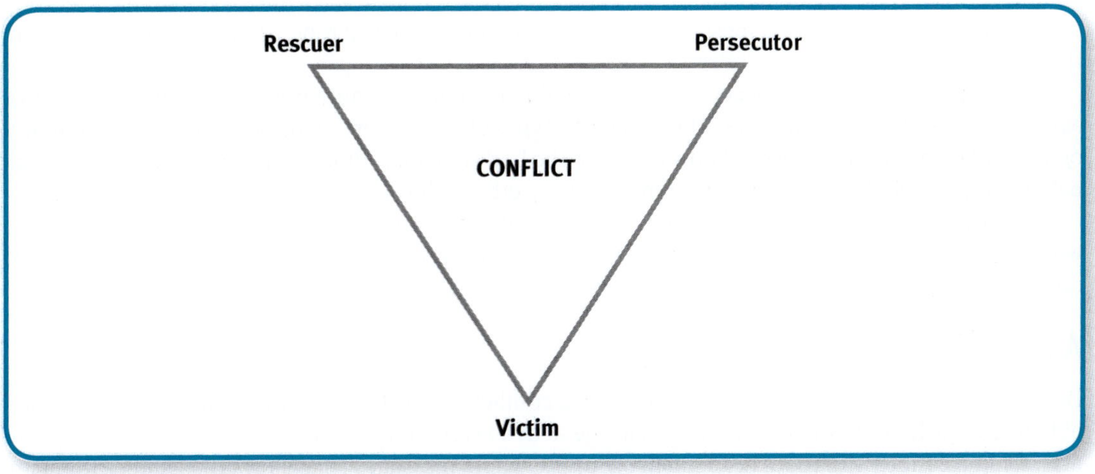

Non-assertive behaviour is aggressive or submissive behaviour that ignores our own rights by failing to express thoughts honestly.

Submissive behaviour is based on low self-esteem.

The **drama triangle** illustrates non-assertive behaviour in which a person plays the role of victim and behaves in a helpless manner.

Victim is a role played in the drama triangle; victims want someone to rescue or persecute them.

Persecutor is a role from the drama triangle; persecutors put others down or bully them into action.

Rescuers in the drama triangle offer help and support while denying their own needs.

The **flight response** is used in a conflict to escape the situation and avoid the results.

Aggressive behaviour is based on domination and often leads to conflict.

The **fight response** is used in a conflict situation to control or defend the position.

The **success triangle** illustrates the flow response, or assertive behaviour, in a conflict situation.

Figure 6.7: Drama triangle

Source: Adapted from C.M. Steiner, *Scripts People Live*, Grove Press, New York, 1974.

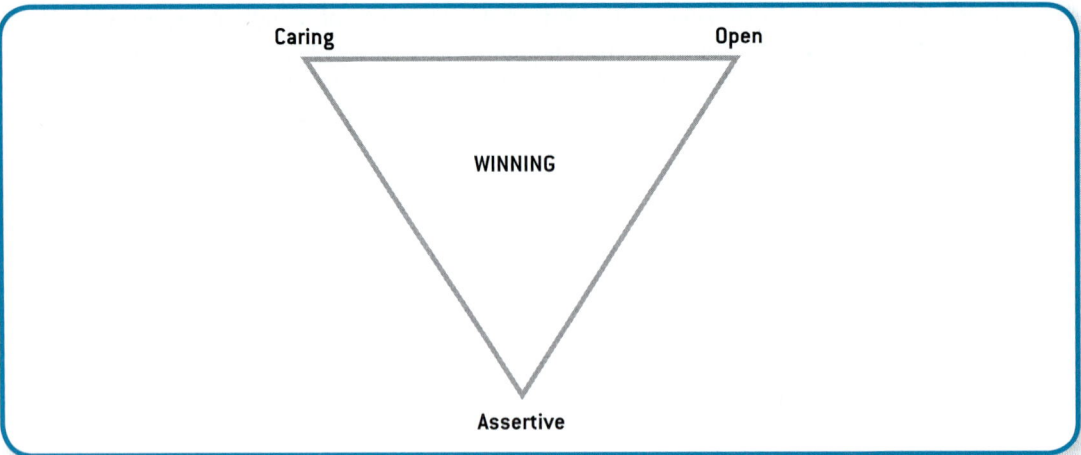

Figure 6.8: Success triangle

Source: Adapted from C.M. Steiner, *Scripts People Live*, Grove Press, New York, 1974.

1. This is what I think, *plus*
2. This is what I feel, *plus*
3. This is how I see the situation.

For example:

1. I know we're really busy.
2. However, I feel stressed when everything is given equal importance.
3. I would like some way of prioritising the work from the most important to the least important.

'I' messages are assertive statements that help to send a clear message, particularly in a conflict situation. As it is a clear statement about what an individual wants or feels, it leads to increased understanding of the situation. (Assertion and 'I' messages are discussed more fully in Chapter 4.)

Nonverbal messages

In a conflict situation, speak in a pleasant way, send appropriate verbal messages to the other person, and match your nonverbal behaviour to the spoken message. Most of the messages we receive from others are based on nonverbal messages. Body movements and vocal tone should be consistent with the spoken message.

Pay attention to the other person's nonverbal behaviours. Identify nonverbal behaviour that is aggressive, assertive or submissive. The checklist, 'Types of Behaviour', on pages 173–4 gives examples of nonverbal behaviour in terms of how we move the body and face. Practise using assertive nonverbal behaviour and avoid aggressive and submissive nonverbal behaviour.

If you can interpret the nonverbal messages as well as the words of the other person, you have two ways of checking the meaning. This feedback is important as people negotiate to remove conflict. Ask questions to check that your interpretation is correct.

Active listening

By listening well, a person is better able to resolve conflict before it reaches the higher levels. They are able to use each of the three components in the active listening process shown in Table 6.6 to listen actively in a conflict situation. Listen actively to the whole message. This allows the listener to relate the total message (content and feelings) back to the speaker. The speaker can then confirm or correct the feedback.

Listen actively to the whole message.

Table 6.6: Three components in the active listening process

Attend to and focus on the other person	Encourage the other person	Reflect or mirror the other person's message
Use eye contact	Use conversation openers	Paraphrase
Face the person and be still	Invite the other to disclose	Clarify or explore
Let them speak	Make brief responses	Reflect feelings
Maintain an open posture	Ask a few questions	Reflect meanings
Be aware of personal space	Pause	Summarise

Listening with empathy helps the listener to identify both content and feelings in the other person's message, and also helps the other person to identify their feelings. One way to create empathy is to use reflecting or mirroring skills; for example, 'I can imagine how upsetting that must have been.' Acknowledge the other party's points and feelings.

PROBING QUESTIONS COMPLEMENTED BY ACTIVE LISTENING

Probing questions complemented by empathic listening can challenge and encourage the parties in a conflict to communicate openly and honestly. For example, 'What did I do that you disliked?' 'What would you like me to do now?' 'How should I start?' 'How would you respond if I did? The ability to stay calm and listen well to the responses in a conflict situation allows a person to accept and respond to the feedback.

When under verbal attack, deal with the other person's anger. Rather than reacting with defensiveness or aggression, or becoming tearful and upset, or retreating into themselves, a person who listens well is able to reduce the emotion in the attack by identifying and acknowledging the emotion accurately. The emotional level is reduced because the speaker feels heard and understood. It is then possible to explore issues and reason more effectively.

Reframing

Reframing is a process designed to create a definition of the cause of the conflict that is acceptable to both parties. Effective reframing increases the potential for collaborative and win–win solutions.

The parties in a conflict have very different perceptions of the issues that are in dispute and the reasons for the problem arising. Mayer (2000, p. 132) states: 'Framing refers to the way a conflict is described or a proposal is worded; reframing is the process of changing the way a thought is presented so that it maintains its fundamental meaning but is more likely to support resolution efforts.' The reframing process enables the parties in a conflict to:

- understand the underlying causes of the conflict
- understand each other's point of view
- think about solutions that will work for both sides.

There is usually a wide disparity in each party's explanation or framing of the dispute. The words are often adversarial and confronting, with blame placed on the other party. Negative qualities can be attributed to the other party and demands made for one party to comply with the other party's demands.

Conflicting frames create tension, argumentative conversations and antagonism which prevent the parties from reaching an acceptable and effective agreement. Effective reframing avoids value-laden language, rephrases strong positions or demands, and removes any bias or judgment. Reframing enables the parties to understand the underlying causes of the conflict in terms of interests and needs, and the conflict can be managed in constructive rather than destructive ways.

Framing is the way in which a party describes, explains or defines a conflict.

Reframing is the process of changing the way a thought is presented.

Reframe the dispute in terms of interests, rather than positions. Asking open-ended, problem-solving questions lets the other party focus on interests, rather than positions. Ask 'why' questions to hear the other party's interests. Check that your 'why' question is probing, rather than accusing, attacking or blaming. If the other person resists, offer alternative solutions and ask 'why not' questions. Introduce new options without directly challenging the other party's position by asking 'what if' questions.

The reframing of a conflict provides a new definition or a new explanation of the conflict. The reframing process is only successful when both parties accept the new definition.

Difficult and longstanding conflicts may require the services of a mediator to reframe and facilitate the parties towards an acceptable solution. Mayer (2000, p. 134) suggests the reframing process is '. . . about changing the verbal presentation of an idea, concern, proposal, or question so that the party's essential interest is still expressed but unproductive language, emotion, position taking, and accusations are removed'. In a difficult conflict, mediators must use language carefully as they reframe problems. The mediation process is discussed in the next section.

Empathy

Despite the fact that we are always communicating, it is difficult to use communication strategies effectively in a conflict situation. Yet, communication is the key factor in the resolution of conflict—without it, no resolution can take place. Empathy is showing that you can feel the other person's needs. The flow response, assertion, active listening and open nonverbal communication are skills you can use to show empathy.

An essential process in a conflict-management interaction is the capacity to generate and promote ideas that do not prejudice either party in any way, and to behave in a way that enables those ideas to be heard. Another is the ability to respond with empathy by placing yourself in the other person's position and moving towards a solution that meets as many needs as possible. Say 'yes' when appropriate, as the word reduces tensions and fosters an atmosphere of agreement.

People who acknowledge a source of conflict and negotiate to remove it often become more aware of one another and of the needs of the other person. They learn a lot about each other and the situation.

EMPATHY BLOCKERS

Empathy blockers have a negative impact on communication.

Empathy blockers tend to have a negative impact on relationships. Barriers arise and increase the difficulties of conflict resolution. Empathy blockers include:

- listening ineffectively
- passing judgment
- changing the topic
- dismissing the speaker's point of view, needs or interests
- giving unwanted advice
- being passive and not giving feedback
- becoming emotionally involved (or 'hooked') by emotive statements
- looking away or past the person.

Empathy blockers result in defensiveness and lowered self-esteem. Conflict is increased, rather than dealt with or resolved, when empathy blockers are used by either party. In contrast, the opportunity to resolve conflict and find new opportunities for collaboration is enhanced when strategies such as active listening, 'I' statements and assertion are used to increase understanding and show empathy.

The Four R Method

Donohue and Kolt (1992, p. 38) comment: 'When in crisis, people are not generally ready for problem solving. They need to have their emotions calmed first to prepare them for this thinking and not feeling transition.' People need time to calm down and start thinking about the problem before they can resolve the conflict. Donohue and Kolt regard it as important to remain sensitive to possible conflict cycles and to avoid patterns that lead to crisis. They suggest (1992, p. 41) the *Four R Method* as a communication strategy for moving out of crisis, because it helps people move away from their emotional concerns.

1. *Receive* the other person's comments without interruption and avoid defensiveness.
2. *Repeat* the other person's comments as objectively as possible.
3. *Request* the other person's proposed ways of dealing with the problem.
4. *Review* the options and decide on the best approach.

REVIEW QUESTIONS

10 a What are the purpose and intended outcomes of the fight, flight and flow responses to conflict?

b What makes assertive behaviour constructive and helpful in a conflict situation?

11 Explain the types of behaviour used in the drama triangle and success triangle.

12 a 'An "I" message is non-evaluative.' Explain the meaning of this statement. Why are 'I' messages used?

b How can appropriate nonverbal behaviour help to resolve conflict?

c Outline the type of listening most suited to conflict management and resolution.

d What is the purpose of reframing?

e How does the Four R Method help in a crisis situation?

MEDIATION

◀ OBJECTIVE **5**
Discuss the role of mediation in resolving deep-rooted conflict

Mediation introduces a trained third party with the skills to listen well and not take sides in a dispute. The mediator guides the mediation process and keeps the parties focused on the issues, moving them towards an agreed solution to the problem. While mediation is used informally in almost every area of human interaction, there has been an increase over the last 15 years in the number of formal mediations taking place in institutionalised settings. Burton and Dukes (1990) refer specifically to mediation in areas such as divorce and custody cases, labour-management relations and council disputes, and point out that 'Many businesses now use mediation internally, as one part of their employee and/or customer grievance proceedings' (p. 28). Mediation, they state, is 'not a single process, but several kinds of third-party intervention'. A mediator may be called in when emotions are high and interfere with the process, a number of issues exist and become confused, or the parties have reached an impasse.

Mediation is a process in which a third party helps disagreeing parties move to an agreement.

Rules for the mediator

Settle (2002) gives three basic rules for the mediator:

1. Take time to build a relationship at the table; this will help them work on the issues.
2. The most powerful tool is your *intuition* about what the parties may benefit from at any given moment, based on your understanding of mediation.
3. Avoid becoming part of the problem.

Settle's article, which can be found at <www.abanet.org/dispute/technics.pdf>, gives tips and techniques on how to overcome an impasse in mediation. A shorter version of the article was published in the section on dispute resolution in *Just Resolutions Newsletter*, January 2003.

Stages in the mediation process

The mediation process has been divided into stages. Moore (1987), cited in Burton and Dukes (1990, p. 31), listed the following 12 stages:

1. initial contacts with the disputing parties
2. selecting a strategy to guide mediation
3. collecting and analysing background information
4. designing a detailed plan for mediation
5. building trust and cooperation
6. beginning the mediation session
7. defining issues and setting an agenda
8. uncovering hidden interests of the disputing parties
9. generating options for settlement
10. assessing options for settlement
11. final bargaining
12. achieving formal settlement.

Burton and Dukes (1990) also cite Keltner's (1987) seven phases of mediation: setting the stage; opening and development; exploration of the issues; identification of alternatives; evaluation; negotiation and bargaining; decision making and testing; and terminating the process.

REVIEW QUESTIONS

13. Define the term 'mediation'.
14. a   Describe what a mediator does.
    b   Discuss three basic rules for a mediator.
15. Explain the mediation process.

APPLY YOUR KNOWLEDGE

RESPONSES TO CONFLICT

1. 'Constructive responses to the early levels of conflict make it possible to contain and even resolve the conflict before it reaches the higher levels.'
   a   Briefly explain this statement. In your answer, describe the levels through which conflict can progress.
   b   Briefly describe the most appropriate behaviours in the lower levels of conflict.
2. 'Whenever you give negative feedback, support it with hard data.' Explain why this is important.
3. Work in small groups.
   Consider the last time you reacted to a conflict situation from habit. How could you have turned that reaction into a more thoughtful response?
4. Burton and Dukes say, 'Mediation is not a single process but several kinds of third-party intervention.' How can intuition and emotional intelligence help mediators as they move through the 12 stages in the mediation process?
5. Work in pairs.
   Assume you are the chair and secretary of the workplace quality meeting. The chairperson is having difficulty managing conflict in meetings. Some of the sources of conflict are shown in Table 6.7.
   a   Discuss the various sources of conflict.
   b   For each of the possible sources of conflict, develop and list in column 2 of Table 6.7 the appropriate strategies to manage the conflict in a positive and constructive way.
   c   How can reframing and the establishment of ground rules help the chairperson to work through the issues in a meeting?
   d   It has been said that conflict management should be sufficient to ensure that the meeting remains harmonious but loose enough so that members can present opposing views. How can the model in Figure 6.6 (page 164) help the chairperson and secretary to address the conflict without stifling ideas and differing opinions?

Table 6.7: Strategies to manage conflict

Sources of conflict	Strategies to manage the conflict
Competition for limited resources	
Difference in expectations	
Perception of 'whose job it is'	
Poor communication	

Non-assertive behaviour
  Aggressive
  Submissive	

Inability to listen	
Disagree with content (facts)	
Lack of empathy	
Difference in goals	
Preconceived opinion of 'who knows best'	

SELF-EVALUATE YOUR SKILL

TYPES OF BEHAVIOUR

Next time you are at a meeting or with a group of people, observe and identify different behaviours, on the basis of the following characteristics, as submissive, aggressive or assertive.

Type of behaviour	Submissive	Aggressive	Assertive
Voice tone			
condescending			
putting down			
criticising			
accusing			
matter-of-fact			
loud			
full of feeling			
sarcastic			
Posture			
attentive			
leaning forward in chair			

Type of behaviour	Submissive	Aggressive	Assertive
involving eye contact			
moving closer to hear			
listening with interest			
puffed up			
slumping down			
super-correct			
Facial expression			
frowning			
excited			
surprised			
eyes downcast			
looking away			
worried			
disapproving			
chin jutting out			
alert			
lip or chin quivering			
tears in eyes			
Body gesture			
hands on hips			
pointing accusing finger			
shrugging the shoulders			
arms folded across chest			
raising hand for permission			
turning away			

SUMMARY OF LEARNING OBJECTIVES

 1 ▷ **DISTINGUISH SEVERAL APPROACHES TO CONFLICT**

Lewin (1935) suggested three approaches to conflict. *Approach/approach conflict* arises when a person is attracted to two appealing but in-compatible goals at the same time. *Avoidance/avoidance conflict* occurs when two undesirable or threatening alternatives are present at the same time. The third type, *approach/avoidance conflict*, results when an alternative has both an attractive and a repellent aspect. The four types of conflict are internal, external, realistic and unrealistic. While internal conflict is *within* the person, external conflict is *between* people. Realistic conflict can be resolved if people are willing to consider their needs and the needs of the other party. Unrealistic conflict cannot be resolved because of differences in values and attitudes.

DISCUSS THE CAUSES, BENEFITS AND COSTS OF CONFLICT

Moore's 'circle of conflict' is a useful way to identify five causes of conflict. Data conflicts are caused by misinformation, a lack of information or different views. Interest conflicts occur because of perceived competition, procedures or psychological interests. Structural conflicts arise from unequal control, ownership or power, time constraints, or environmental factors that hinder cooperation. Value conflicts may be the result of different ways of life, ideology or religion. Relationship conflicts are caused by poor communication, negative behaviour and misperceptions.

In the short term, dealing with conflict can reduce petty irritations, clarify issues, get feelings into the open and improve awareness of self and others. Ignoring conflict can cause friction and decrease mutual understanding. In the longer term, resolution of conflict can improve decision making, cause changes in the way things are done, force people to extend themselves in their work and allow relationships to be more open and ongoing. Avoiding conflict can increase interpersonal hostility and personality clashes, have a negative effect on performance and lead to unproductive outcomes. In dealing with conflict, the aim is to develop strategies to manage it and to minimise any destructive influences caused by unresolved conflict.

3 ▷ **EXPLAIN HOW MAPPING A CONFLICT HELPS DETERMINE ITS CAUSE**

A map is a useful tool for determining the cause of the conflict. The map is used to identify who is involved, their needs and concerns, and the issues. Conflict may be caused by lack of information, misperceptions or stereotypes, different ways of life, ideology or religion, or destructive patterns of behaviour or interaction.

The map helps the negotiators to determine the cause before designing options and exploring ways of satisfying the needs of both parties.

4 ▷ **INTERACT CONSTRUCTIVELY IN CONFLICT SITUATIONS BY USING ASSERTION, ACTIVE LISTENING AND FRAMING QUESTIONS**

Send clear, assertive 'I' messages and listen. Check that nonverbal messages are appropriate to the situation. Feedback should focus on the issue or problem, rather than the person. In the conflict-resolution process, active listening attends to the other person, encourages them and reflects their message. In this way, the listener has empathy for the interests of the other person. In active listening, the whole message—both content and feeling—is heard. Reframing increases the potential for collaboration and agreement by redefining the conflict to clarify the causes and include the interests of both parties.

The challenge is to develop confidence in selecting the communication skill suited to the situation. Conflict expressed and addressed in ways that respect relationships and consider as many needs as possible is positive and constructive, rather than negative and destructive.

 DISCUSS THE ROLE OF MEDIATION IN RESOLVING DEEP-ROOTED CONFLICT

Mediation is a process in which a third party is engaged to help disagreeing parties move to an agreement. The process is used in formal and informal situations. There are many models of the mediation process. The common factor in each is a description of the phases followed in mediation. The phases describe how to set the context, define and clarify the conflict, explore issues, identify options, negotiate and bargain, make and test the decision, gain agreement and conclude the process.

KEY TERMS

ACTIVITIES AND QUESTIONS

1. In groups of three, complete the following tasks:

   a. Read the paragraph here. The interactionist view of conflict is the most recent perspective on conflict in organisations. It suggests that not only can conflict be a positive force in a group, but also that some conflict is absolutely necessary for a group to perform effectively. One conclusion drawn from this theory is that because conflict is a predictable social phenomenon, the goal of organisational leadership should be to channel and use channel conflict as a positive force, rather than trying to suppress or eliminate it.

   b. Brainstorm strategies that organisational leadership can use to channel conflict to achieve productive outcomes.

   c. Is all conflict within an organisation constructive? Give reasons for your answer, supported by examples.

   d. Report your findings to the large group.

2. Work in small groups. Assume a large national company plans to build a processing plant using the natural resources, water, locally produced primary resources and local skilled labour of a small country town.

   a. Discuss the communication approaches that could be used by each of the groups below who have different and equally valid perspectives:
      - promoters of the processing plant
      - local community
      - local government officers
      - local Indigenous population
      - recreational fisher lobby.

   b. In your discussion, decide whether the suggested approaches would avoid conflict, move through conflict, or cause further conflict, and achieve positive or negative outcomes.

   c. Report your findings to the large group in a short verbal presentation.

3. Assume you are Rasheed, the Knowledge Manager in a large organisation. One of your responsibilities is to implement the new Change Management program across the company. Emma, the Operations Manager of one section, is opposing the introduction of the Change Management program. You believe Emma's opposition is based on out-of-date and incomplete information. You feel Emma is finding it difficult to distinguish between facts and opinions and is making selective use of data to support her own position.

   Your needs and interests are to have the first stages of the implementation accepted and in place over the next three months. Your goal is to reach a mutually acceptable solution in an assertive way. You know that Emma can be defensive and may insist that negotiations proceed using the information on which she has based her conclusions. This will present an immediate obstacle to progress, as you will refuse to use the inaccurate information.

   Work in pairs to describe the strategies Rasheed can use to interact constructively in the conflict negotiation. Rasheed wants to:
   - present his needs and interests
   - understand Emma's needs and interests
   - disagree if necessary
   - give feedback
   - negotiate a win–win situation for both of them
   - ensure the results are based on objective criteria.

   Refer to Chapter 3 for more information on assertive messages.

4. In an essay, discuss the Kilmann and Thomas approach to conflict in the workplace (refer to

Figure 6.1). Describe the five different conflict styles the parties in a conflict can use to reduce and manage the conflict. Which styles are likely to be dominant in modern, dynamic workplaces? Why?

5 Isaac (2003) makes the comment that 'Because there are so many variables, there is no one best way of dealing with conflict'. He lists four factors that need to be evaluated before determining a strategy for dealing with conflict:

- the organisational environment
- the situation and the source of the conflict
- personalities and their values
- management styles.

a Discuss these four factors.

b Isaac also says that 'appropriate communication is needed to resolve conflict'. List the factors that you need to consider in order to communicate appropriately in a conflict situation at work.

c Report your findings to the large group.

EXPLORING THE WEB

1 a Check out the resources at *The Conflict Resolution Network* <www.crnhq.org/> to improve your conflict-resolution knowledge.

b Describe the characteristics of the win–win approach.

c What makes an 'I' statement effective?

d How does the mediation process help conflicting parties to move towards solutions?

2 Review the following chapter-related websites to learn more about conflict management and conflict resolution:

a Sage Journals Online: <http://jcr.sagepub.com/> is the *Journal of Conflict Resolution* page. Research past and current articles.

b CRInfo: <www.crinfo.org> contains resources and information about conflict resolution.

c ACR Organizational Conflict Management Section: <www.mediate.com/acrocm/pg5.cfm> has links to articles on conflict management.

PROJECT WORK

Managers with opposing positions

The National Sales Manager and the Financial Controller hold opposing positions. The National Sales Manager wants open credit policies for all preferred, new and marginal customers in order to increase sales. The Financial Controller wants 30-day credit for preferred customers, 7-day credit for new customers, and cash on delivery for marginal customers in order to minimise bad debts. Their disagreement over credit terms has escalated from discomfort to tension. Neither manager will talk to the other. Both are avoiding dealing with the conflict. The General Manager has instructed them to find an agreement that is acceptable to both the Sales and Financial divisions of the company.

a Create a set of ground rules for appropriate behaviour by the managers as they negotiate the issue.

b Identify and explain strategies the two managers can use to negotiate the issue and build an agreement that works.

c Outline constructive responses the managers can use to manage the conflict and facilitate good working relationships.

BIBLIOGRAPHY

Acland, F.A. 1990. *A Sudden Outbreak of Common Sense*, Hutchinson, London.

ACR Organizational Conflict Management Section, www.mediate.com/, viewed 10 November 2007.

Auruch, K., Black, P.W. & Scimecca, J.A. (eds) 1991. *Conflict Resolution: Cross-cultural Perspectives*, Greenwood Press, USA.

Blake, R. & Mouton, J. 1970. 'The fifth achievement', *Journal of Applied Behavioral Science*, Vol. 6, pp. 413–26.

Boulding, K.E. 1962. *Conflict and Defense—A General Theory*, Harper Row, New York.

Burton, J.W. 1987. *Resolving Deep-rooted Conflict*, University Press of America, Lanham.

Burton, J. 1990. *Conflict Resolution and Prevention*, Macmillan, London.

Burton, J. & Dukes, F. 1990. *Conflict: Practices in Management, Settlement and Resolution*, Macmillan, London.

Christie, M.F. 'Some cultural considerations in the globalisation of adult education: an Asia–Pacific case study', Adult Teacher Education and Training, Northern Territory University, www.ntu.edu.au/, viewed 24 August 2001.

Conflict Resolution Network. '12 Skills Summary', www.crnhq.org/, viewed 16 November 2007.

Cornelius, H. & Faire, S. 1989. *Everyone Can Win*, Simon & Schuster, Australia.

Coser, L. 1956. *The Function of Social Conflict*, The Freedom Press, New York.

Coser, L. 1961. 'The termination of conflict', *Journal of Conflict Resolution*, Vol. 5, December, pp. 347–53.

CRInfo. *The Conflict Resolution Information Service*, www.crinfo.org, viewed 11 November 2007.

Dahrendorf, R. 1958. 'Towards a theory of social conflict', *Journal of Conflict Resolution*, Vol. 11, Issue 2, June.

De Bono, E. 2000. *The De Bono Code Book*, Penguin Books, Middlesex, England.

DeVito, J.A. 1992. *The Interpersonal Communication Book*, 6th edn, HarperCollins, New York.

Donohue, W.A. & Kolt, R. 1992. *Managing Interpersonal Conflict*, Sage Publications, California.

Finnegan, R.P. & Monroe, D.K. 1997. 'Defusing loose cannons', *Human Resources Professional*, Vol. 10, Issue 2, March/April, pp. 3–6.

Fisher, R. & Ury, W. 1981. *Getting to Yes*, Penguin Books, USA.

Fisher, R. & Ury, W. 1983. *Getting to Yes: Negotiating Agreement Without Giving In*, Hutchinson, London.

Folberg, J. & Taylor, A. 1984. *Mediation*, Jossey-Bass Inc., San Francisco.

Fox, C. 2008. 'Softly, softly', *Australian Financial Review*, February, pp. 50–53.

Gerzon, M. 2006. *Leading Through Conflict: How Successful Leaders Transform Differences into Opportunities*, Harvard Business School Press, USA.

Goleman, D. 1998. *Working with Emotional Intelligence*, Bantam Books, New York.

Gunderson, T. 1997. 'Staff, it's not my problem', *Restaurant Hospitality*, Vol. 81, Issue 5, May, p. 46.

Hall, C.S. & Gardner, L. 1970. *Theories of Personality*, 2nd edn, John Wiley & Sons, New York.

Hein, S. *Emotional Awareness*, http://eqi.org/aware/htm, viewed 8 July 2003.

Hollier, F., Murray, K. & Cornelius, H. 1993. *Conflict Resolution Trainers Manual: 12 Skills*, The Conflict Resolution Network, Chatswood.

Huseman, R.C., Galvin, M. & Prescott, D. 1991. *Business Communication: Strategies and Skills*, 3rd edn, Holt, Rinehart & Winston, Sydney.

Isaac, L. *Conflict Resolution*, www.leoisaac.com/, viewed 19 June 2003.

Kuhn, T. & Poole, M.S. 'Do conflict management styles affect group decision making? Evidence from a longitudinal field study', *Human Communication Research*, Vol. 26, Issue 4, pp. 558–90.

Lewin, K.A. 1935. *A Dynamic Theory of Personality* (trans. K.E. Zener & D.K. Adams), McGraw-Hill, New York.

Lewin, K. 1948. *Resolving Social Conflicts—Selected Papers on Group Dynamics*, Harper & Row, New York.

Mayer, B. 2000. *The Dynamics of Conflict Resolution*, Jossey-Bass, San Francisco.

Moore, C. 1996. *The Mediation Process: Practical Strategies for Resolving Conflict*, 2nd edn, Jossey-Bass Inc., San Francisco.

Porter, J.N. & Taplin, R. 1987. *Conflict and Conflict Resolution* (a sociological introduction with updated bibliography and theory section), University Press of America, Lanham.

Putnis, P. & Petelin, R. 1999. *Professional Communication: Principles and Applications*, Prentice Hall, Sydney.

Robbins, S., Bergman, R., Stagg, I. & Coulter, M. 2006. *Management*, 4th edn, Pearson Education Australia, Sydney.

Sage Journals Online. *Journal of Conflict Resolution*, http://jcr.sagepub.com/, viewed 11 November 2007.

Sandberg, R. 2007. 'The costs of conflict', *Management Today*, Issue 37, August, pp. 18–20.

Settle, J. 2002. *Tips and Techniques for Helping Parties Move Ahead and Overcome Roadblocks*, May, www.abanet.org/dispute/technics.pdf, viewed 19 June 2003.

Steiner, C.M. 1974. *Scripts People Live*, Grove Press, New York.

Stockwell, R.G. 1997. 'Effective communication in managing conflict', *CMA Magazine*, Vol. 71, Issue 3, April, p. 6.

Tillett, G. 1992. *Resolving Conflict: A Practical Approach*, Sydney University Press, Sydney.

US Department of Justice Office of Justice Programs. 2000. 'Want to resolve a dispute? Try mediation', *Youth in Action*, Issue 15, March, www.uplink.com.au/.

Wade, J. 'Peacemakers and troublemakers—an awkward balance for citizens, lawyers and Christians', Dispute Resolution Centre, Bond University, Queensland, 2001, www.lcf.pnc.com.au/wadepaperPDF, viewed 19 June 2003.

Weinstein, M. 2007. 'Conquering conflict', *Training*, Vol. 44, Issue 6, June, pp. 56–58.

7 Customer service and public relations

LEARNING OBJECTIVES

After studying this chapter you should be able to:

1 ▷ explain the role of strategy, staff and systems in providing a positive customer experience to all customer types

2 ▷ differentiate between four types of customer value

3 ▷ outline the interaction of strategy, process and technology in customer relationship management

4 ▷ analyse skills in customer relations, particularly communication skills

5 ▷ discuss factors that impact on customer defection and retention rates

6 ▷ apply problem-solving strategies to handle customer complaints and difficult situations

7 ▷ identify the groups that make up an organisation's publics

8 ▷ describe different public relations objectives and explain how to plan for them

9 ▷ discuss the role of media releases, news conferences and special events in presenting a positive public image

10 ▷ outline the steps in the strategic management of public relations issues.

OUTLINE

The customer experience

Customer value

Customer relations management (CRM)

Customer relations and communication skills

Customer defection and retention research

Public relations

Media relations

Managing public relations issues

VIEWPOINT: WHY QUALITY MANAGEMENT?

Kotelnikov suggests: 'Past definitions of quality focused on conformance to standards . . . The new definition of quality focuses on achieving "value entitlement". . . which. . . is realized for the customer and provider in every aspect of the business relationship. "Value" represents economic worth, practical utility and availability for both the customer and the company that creates the product or service.'

Quality is made up of a combination of the product or service and the 'add-ons', i.e. packaging, availability, convenience of use and value-adding customer service. Kotelnikov highlights the fact that consumers expect quality by presenting Tom Peters' views: 'Perception is all there is . . . There is only one perceived reality, the way each of us chooses to perceive a communication, the value of a service, the value of a particular product feature, the quality of a product.'

For the customer, says Kotelnikov, 'value entitlement is a rightful level of expectation to buy high-quality products at the lowest possible cost'. For the provider, 'value entitlement is the rightful level of expectation to produce quality products at the highest possible profits'.

Adapted from V. Kotelnikov, *Quality Management a Pre-requisite for Market Success*, www.1000ventures.com/business_guide/mgmt_quality.html, viewed 14 February 2008.

Customers are people or organisations that purchase goods (tangible artifacts) or services (intangible processes) from others.

Public relations is the term used for activities concerned with the image of an organisation and the positive public acceptance of this image.

An organisation's publics are internal and external and include all those affected by its operations—customers, general public, shareholders, government, media, suppliers, employees, activist groups, financial community and distributors.

OBJECTIVE 1 ▶
Explain the role of strategy, staff and systems in providing a positive customer experience to all customer types

B2C is the term for business-to-customer interactions one-to-one between two or more people.

B2B is the term for business-to-business interactions between businesses, government departments and other organisations, rather than with individuals.

Co-destiny relationships are built when buyers, sellers, customers and providers partner in strategic alliances.

Over the last two centuries, growing economies have progressed through a sequence of stages: from agricultural to manufacturing, to a services and knowledge economy. Figure 7.1 illustrates this progression.

In our current knowledge and service-centred economy an organisation that focuses on client service provision from the client's point of view, rather than from its own, is able to provide quality customer service and retain its customers. It is well on the way to achieving its objectives. An organisation achieves quality customer service by clearly defining the types of customers it has. It also finds out about their needs and expectations and communicates regularly with its customers. It designs its customer service around the things a customer values and continually improves that service. The words 'client' and 'customer' have the same meaning in this chapter.

Public relations is different from customer relations. **Public relations** deals with the image of the firm or the organisation's range of publics, whereas customer relations deals specifically with the satisfaction of needs and the provision of service. Terpstra and Sarathy (cited in Fletcher & Brown 2008, p. 608) suggest: 'The publics of the firm are broader than the market it serves and include all those affected by the firm's operations—customers, general public, stockholders, government, media, suppliers, employees, activist groups, financial community and distributors.' **Publics** are those groups that have actual or potential interest in, or impact on, an organisation's ability to achieve its objectives. Organisations communicate with their publics to achieve mutual understanding about specific objectives.

THE CUSTOMER EXPERIENCE

Types of customers

Current thinking about types of customers has expanded the traditional view to include the following:

- **B2C (business-to-customer) interactions** usually occur as one-to-one transactions.
- **B2B (business-to-business) interactions** occur between businesses, government departments and other organisations, rather than with individual customers. B2B transactions build close relationships between organisations that may lead to partnering and **co-destiny relationships**. These relationships depend on effective communication and coordination inside an organisation, between it and its partners, and with other stakeholders (Thorne 2005; Papassapa & Miller 2007).

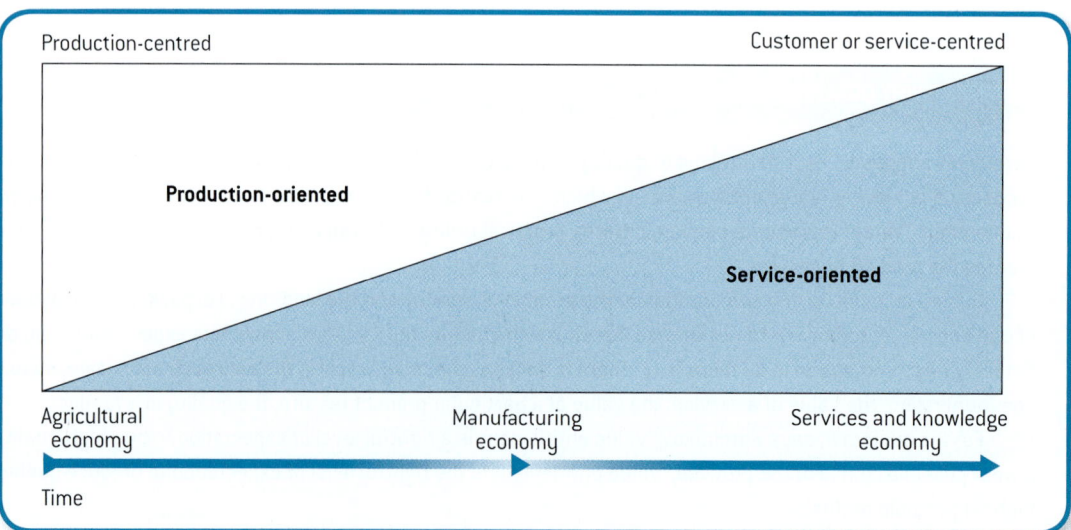

Figure 7.1: Progression of service orientation over time

- **P2P (peer-to-peer) interactions** take place when individuals buy directly from one another with minimal assistance from a business—for example, on auction sites such as e-Bay.

P2P is the term for peer-to-peer interactions without direct mediation of an organisation or business.

The increasing focus on services and knowledge has been accompanied by technological advances and an increasing number of communication channels. The communication channels with customers include face-to-face communication, customer relationship management databases, market research surveys, telephone contact, newsletters, customer briefings, advertising and marketing on television, radio and newsprint, focus groups, networking, product launches, wire service distribution of information, podcasts and blogs, and Internet services.

Meeting customers' expectations

A positive customer experience meets the customers' expectations of quality service, short and reliable delivery times, and innovative policies that respond quickly to their needs and expectations. Customer loyalty is built by organisations that are able to provide customers with positive experiences. Features of a positive customer experience include a pleasant environment, friendly, well-groomed and informed staff with helpful supervisors, speed in providing the service, willing assistance and courtesy.

A relationship based on customers' needs cannot be established unless the organisation's most senior management, and managers at other levels in the organisation, support the rest of the staff in their efforts to provide quality service. The organisation as a whole must have a clearly identified customer service vision or goal.

The **customer experience** is the perception that results from all the interactions that a customer has with an organisation's products, services, people and processes. Positive customer experiences flow from a service culture that meets the customers' needs and expectations. An organisation's **service culture** reflects the service strategy, the application of its systems to meet customer needs, and the interactions of its people or staff with the organisation's customers. A **quality management** approach to client service involves everyone in the organisation in company-wide quality improvement. The Government of South Australia Office of Consumer and Business Affairs (2008) states: 'Providing the necessary management leadership is crucial to developing a customer service culture, irrespective of the number of staff employed by the business . . . To put it simply—staff don't create the service provided by a company, they deliver it. In fact about 80% of the service delivered from a business stems directly from the company's processes, systems and policies.'

Good client service happens when an organisation's strategic vision, training, support systems and incentives are designed to deliver products and services in a way that integrates the staff with the systems and policies that optimise the customer's experience with the organisation. As a result, the organisation's culture focuses on the delivery of quality service.

Strategy (the *what*) is a vision of what quality customer service involves and how to deliver it. The strategy includes the development of plans and procedures to make the vision a reality. Systems (the *how*) are ways of doing things to achieve the strategy—in other words, how the plans and procedures are applied. Staff (the *who*) are the people who use the systems to realise the quality customer service vision. An organisation's managers and staffs create and follow the plans and procedures to make the service happen. However, before you can develop a strategy, you need to know what features of your service your customers value.

Apart from staying in business, the ultimate aim of quality customer service is to provide satisfaction to customers. What are their needs and expectations? What is it about your service that they need, want and value? Providing value for the customer—that is, meeting and exceeding their needs and expectations, is termed customer value. The customer satisfaction model in Figure 7.2 can be applied by managers and staff to provide customers with the service they value. All employees need the willingness, capability and confidence to use the organisation's customer service strategy and the systems supporting it effectively to meet the needs of internal and external customers. Interactions with customers include B2C, B2B and minimal P2P interactions.

Customer experience is the perception customers gain from their interactions with an organisation's products, services, people and processes.

Service culture is the way in which service is offered across an organisation.

A **quality management** approach to client service involves everyone in the organisation in quality improvement.

Customer satisfaction means providing value by meeting and exceeding customers' needs and expectations.

Before planning to provide customers with a positive experience that satisfies their needs and expectations, the organisation must have:

- a knowledge of the product and market demand
- an understanding of the clients' needs and wants
- a commitment to the organisation's goals and strategies
- a capacity to put into place workable practices to establish a quality customer service culture
- an ability to access the funds and necessary resources to maintain the customer service culture
- a willingness to decide what should be done differently
- a capacity to review and improve client service
- an opportunity to let customers know about the improved customer service and products.

By understanding its client base, and their expectations and perceptions, an organisation is able to provide its clients with the expected level of service. Clients are now seeking quality service with short and reliable delivery times and innovative policies that respond quickly to their needs.

When the product and price in one organisation are similar to those of another, it is the quality of the service that makes the difference. Smith (1998, p. 55) defines **customer service** as 'meeting the needs and expectations of the customer as defined by the customer'. This means knowing what your customers want and what they expect, and providing this to them on a consistent basis.

Customer service means meeting the needs and expectations of the customer as defined by the customer.

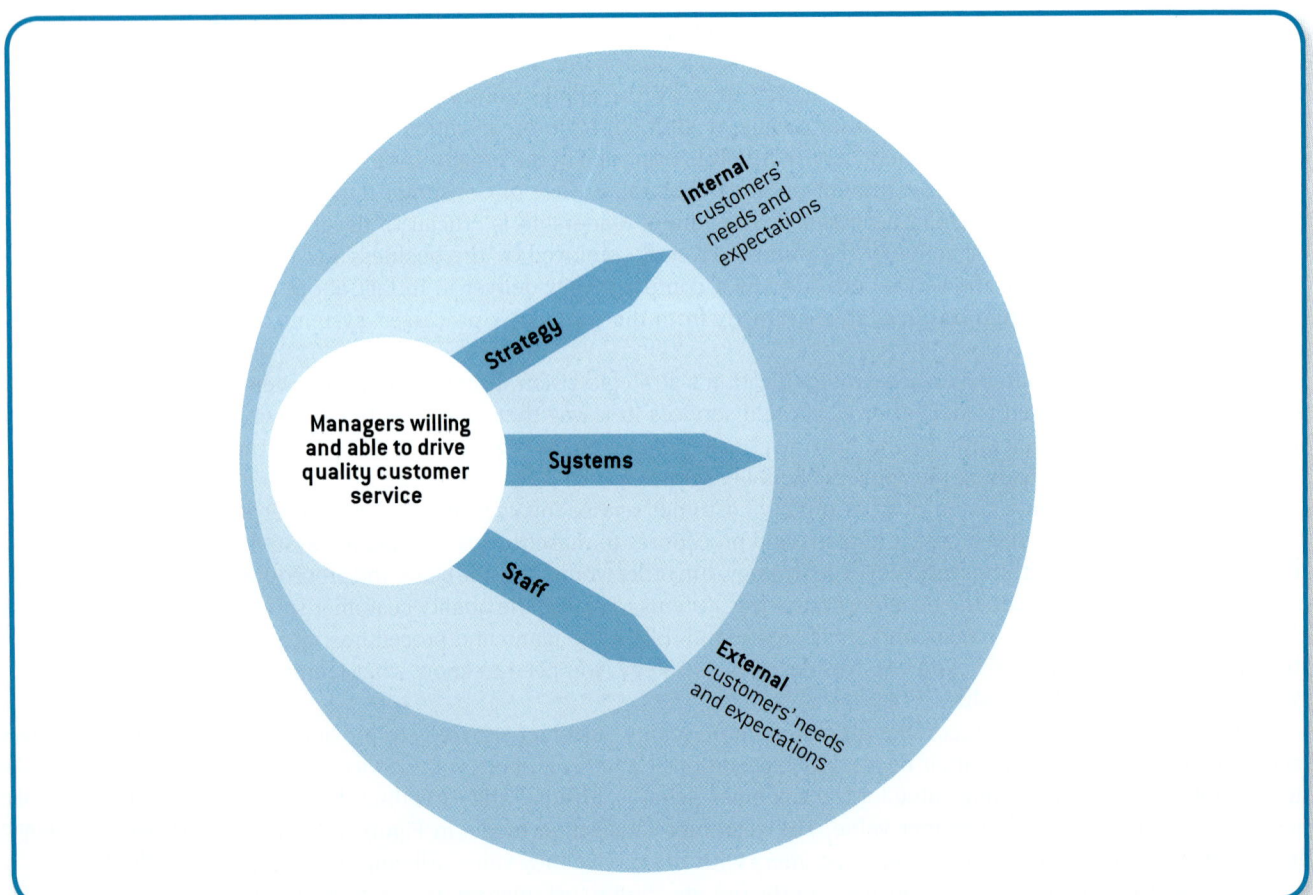

Figure 7.2: Customer satisfaction model

Preparing a valued customer experience

The customer experience is based on a range of strategies designed to provide service around the things that provide customer satisfaction. By building the customer service around the customer's needs and expectations, the organisation has more opportunities to provide service. The following steps help to create customer satisfaction:

- Ask clients what they value by using surveys, listening to their comments and asking questions.
- Set the customer service goal.
- Decide on the strategies to achieve the goal.
- Decide on the service needed to give the customer value.
- Decide how the organisation will let customers know about the improved customer value package.

An experience that satisfies customers brings together product quality and customer service. This concept highlights the need not only to have a quality product, but also to be able to provide quality service to the customer. By bringing together the product and service into a quality package, the organisation is able to satisfy its customers.

A total service package addresses the needs and expectations of customers.

Obtain regular, reliable feedback from your customers about their needs and your service.

REVIEW QUESTIONS

1. What is the best way to establish a relationship with a client?
2. Define the terms 'client needs' and 'client expectations'.
3. Outline four ways in which an organisation can meet customers' needs and expectations.

APPLY YOUR KNOWLEDGE

CLIENT SERVICE

1. a. Define the term 'customer experience'.
   b. Explain the role of strategy, staff and systems in providing a positive customer experience.
2. a. Working in groups of three, think of the worst experience of service that you have each received. List four features that made it bad.
   b. Take it in turns to discuss the experience with the other two people in the group. They should rate each experience on the scale below and then choose one person's experience as the 'worst' example of service.

Service	Poor	Very poor	Worst
Experience of Person 1			
Experience of Person 2			
Experience of Person 3			

   c. List the three features that make it the worst experience. As you focus on the group's experiences of poor service, list as many reasons as you can why clients become upset.
3. In groups of three, consider a business or government department that you regard as successful.
   a. List five factors that contribute to its professional image.

b   Identify one of its services and decide whether the organisation provides average, good or superior service.

4   In your group, discuss and compare the impact of positive and negative service on:
a   the image of an organisation
b   the staff of an organisation.

CUSTOMER VALUE

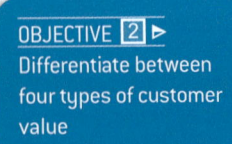

OBJECTIVE 2 ▶

Differentiate between four types of customer value

Albrecht (1992) identifies four levels of **customer value**:

1. basic
2. expected
3. desired
4. unanticipated.

The four types of **customer value** are basic, expected, desired and unanticipated.

By classifying customer value in this way, an organisation is able to focus on customers' needs and identify what gives them satisfaction. Table 7.1 elaborates on the four levels of customer value.

Building customer satisfaction models

Provide the expected level of service consistently by identifying the standard customers expect.

A customer satisfaction model provides customers with the service they value (see Figure 7.2 on page 184). By identifying the standards expected by customers and building these into the way customer service is offered, organisations are able to provide the expected level of service consistently and the desired and unanticipated levels of service when required. Rosen (1997, pp. 98–99) states: 'Building a customer-satisfaction model is relatively easy . . . what's more important is not collecting the data but what you do with it.' He lists ten steps in building a customer satisfaction model:

1. Set standards for providing customer service.
2. Communicate standards to management and employees.
3. Collect customer feedback.
4. Realise you can never reach 100% satisfaction.

Table 7.1: Levels of customer value

Level	Description
Basic service	The most basic service or product offered to your clients. This service is the organisation's reason for being; e.g. to supply newspapers.
Expected service	The expectations that clients have about the manner in which the service will be delivered. It is the service level that the customer expects as a right.
Desired service	The value-added service, i.e. a superior or excellent level of service. This results from the preparedness and capacity of employees in the organisation to offer clients more than they expect. Provision of 'desired service' increases satisfaction but, in the long run, clients may become used to it and see it as 'expected service'.
Unanticipated service	Everything that can be added to the desired service in the future. Once customers become used to superior levels of service they may raise their expectations and expect more. Thus there is a need to look for opportunities and ways to provide different and better service to the client, i.e. 'unanticipated value'.

5. Respond to *all* customer complaints and develop ongoing dialogue with dissatisfied customers to win them back.
6. Analyse results monthly.
7. Compare results with those of the previous month and year to measure improvements.
8. Share results with management and employees.
9. Tie results to performance reviews.
10. Reward employees for excellence.

To establish an effective plan to focus on customer service, Smith (1998, p. 57) says that you need to start with a 'self-assessment that, when completed honestly, will begin to point out opportunities for improving your customer service efforts'. She lists a five-point scale for assessing how you rate on customer service. To understand customers' requirements, she suggests accessing various sources of information from within the organisation, the service company, employees, internal data and the customers themselves by reviewing complaints and surveying. To deal effectively with customers, Smith suggests sharpening the skills (communication and problem solving) necessary for dealing with customers and educating staff.

Measuring customer satisfaction

Chisholm (1998, p. 305) states: 'Delivering customer service requires that managers continually survey customers for feedback and promptly respond to it.' He comments that, whereas in the past telephone interviews and postal mail questionnaires were used to survey customers, '[t]oday, the Internet is enabling customers to provide feedback more easily, quickly, cheaply, and accurately than ever before'. Wilkerson (1997, pp. 69–82) also concentrates on measuring customer satisfaction and suggests a four-step quality measurement system:

1. Identify your customers using a worksheet.
2. Conduct research on customer expectations and satisfaction: what your customers expect from you and how well you are currently satisfying these expectations.
3. Identify and measure the process outcomes or deliverables that lead to customer satisfaction: you should see an improvement in customer satisfaction once you have improved service levels.
4. Improve your performance of factors that drive the quality of those deliverables.

Rosen (1997) lists the following tools for measuring customer satisfaction:

- comment cards
- one-on-one interviews with customers
- focus groups
- direct sales calls
- employee feedback
- customer advisory panels
- third-party research
- 1-800 customer service line
- interactive Internet site
- quarterly surveys of customers.

When questioned by F. John Reh (2003) on how to quantify and measure customer satisfaction, Dianne Booher, President of Booher Consultants, Inc. an international communications training and consulting firm, offered several measures:

Optimise the customer experience by researching and measuring customer satisfaction.

- scorecards showing the decrease in written and oral customer complaints
- the number of additional referrals generated from current customers
- increase in the repeat business of current customers
- faster response time/turnaround time on orders

- increased productivity
- less rework on customer projects.

Continuous research helps the organisation to stay in touch with the needs and expectations of customers. Ask questions, send out surveys and listen. Try to use the win–win approach in which the needs and interests of both parties are met as you gather information about customer satisfaction. As needs are met, customer loyalty is built. Customers will return to an organisation that offers them a quality product combined with quality service that is centred on their needs.

REVIEW QUESTIONS

4. List and explain the four types of customer value.
5. Describe three factors that contribute to effective customer relations.
6. List three measures an organisation can use to quantify and measure customer service.

OBJECTIVE 3 ▶
Outline the interaction of strategy, process and technology in customer relationship management

Customer relations management (CRM) is a combination of strategy, process and technology used to manage customer interactions.

CUSTOMER RELATIONS MANAGEMENT (CRM)

In September 2000, *Government Computer News* defined **customer relations management (CRM)** as a combination of 'strategy, process and technology to manage customer interactions'. It described CRM packages as including at least one of the following items:

- *collaborative CRM*, which covers voice calls, fax, email, collaborative browsing and Internet chat
- *operational CRM*, which covers front- and back-office data systems and IT infrastructures and consolidates disparate databases and systems
- *business process CRM*, which provides automation rules for transacting business
- *analytical CRM*, a collection of tools where data is combined with logical rules and turned into business insight.

Optimising the customer experience

Many companies have invested heavily in customer relations management, but Kilborn (2003, p. 38) states that up to 80% of companies have failed to make it work. The reason he advances for the failure is that customers 'still expect "corner shop" service no matter what channel or combination of channels they choose, and no matter when'. Customer service is no longer confined to customers buying in a shop during normal trading hours. Call centres and the Internet now provide a 24-hours-a-day, seven-days-a-week service. Kilborn comments, 'The effective implementation of customer relationship management requires more than automation of systems. The focus must be on optimising the customer experience.' Effective customer relationships are 'about inspiring loyalty through dealing fairly and effectively with each person'.

CRM focuses on building long-term customer relationships.

Kilborn (p. 39) believes that 'technology does not itself improve customer loyalty' and warns against technology-focused CRM. Technology may improve processes and achieve short-term operational cost savings, but there is no guarantee that it will achieve 'the more profitable, long-term customer relationships' that can be gained from customer-focused CRM. In Kilborn's opinion, 'A true CRM solution treats each customer as an individual, not a category' and companies need to 'supplement CRM software with customer intelligence to gain insight into customer value and loyalty'.

CRM technology

Upton (2001) agrees with Kilborn:

As corporations tighten their operational belts and strive to maintain or improve their bottom lines, they are turning to customer relationship management (CRM) software. But software alone does not transform a corporation into a customer-centric entity. Becoming customer centric requires more than a skin-deep makeover . . .

Customer Relations Management (CRM) in Europe 2001 (2003) concurs:

> It's one of the great ironies that while IT fashion suggests that multi-channel CRM is all the rage, the harsh reality is that many—if not most—early adopters who adopt such strategies have seen little or no success in achieving the goals they set out to achieve. Analysis from the Gartner Group suggests that the real price of achieving cost savings is reduced customer satisfaction . . .

Irrespective of the warnings from analysts, in 2001 European marketers stated that in the years to 2004, 'marketing automation applications will be the fastest-growing segment of the market' (CRM in Europe 2003). Similarly, in 2006 William Band from Forrester, an independent technology and market research company, anticipated '. . . spending on CRM application licenses will generally increase about 2 percent to 3 percent a year through 2008. Going along with that, total spending on vendor offerings, including maintenance and services, will increase about 5 percent to 6 percent a year for the period' (TMCNET 2006). At the same time, companies will focus on extracting more value and capability out of previous CRM spending commitments.

Governments at all levels are becoming more involved in CRM technology. Gamlen (2003) comments, 'As the pace of the Modernising Government agenda increases, support for electronic service delivery is becoming an increasingly essential prerequisite' and 'eGovernment is forcing a radical re-evaluation of the role played by websites, Intranets and customer service teams'. Many government departments are using the Internet to provide community information services, or are developing or redesigning existing customer service capabilities to provide customer service through call or contact centres.

Effects on customer service

The Internet and email have changed the way customers relate to customer service. Dianne Booher, of Booher Consultants, Inc., commented in an interview that 'the email mindset makes it even easier for customers to spread out their dissatisfaction'. She also considers that good customer service is different on the Internet:

> . . . the primary difference is that you have difficulty in building rapport with customers because there are fewer occasions of real-time interaction. A second difference is that customers seem to be more fickle and hostile because they can choose to remain anonymous . . . First impressions about how user-friendly your site is, for example, get translated to how user-friendly your products and services are in general. (Interview with F. John Reh, 2003)

Booher also believes that customer service is dependent on three things:

1. customer-friendly policies set by the organisation's executives
2. training offered to the staff
3. the attitude of the staff to their own organisation, generated by the way their company treats them.

Booher elaborates on what happens if any of these are 'out of whack':

- If executives don't actually know/see how their policies get executed on the frontline, they're often shocked to discover the actual results of how the policies get carried out.
- If people aren't trained on specifics (not just smile and use people's names), they don't know how to build customer loyalty even when they want to.
- If employees get pushed around or treated unfairly, they 'get even' by doing things to drive customers away (act sullen, air your dirty linen, forget to call back or follow up).

Booher warns against publicising intentions to improve customer service: 'Fix it and then brag.' If customers' high hopes are dashed, they may become hostile and disappointed. She comments: 'The first step is to fix the problem, train the staff to deliver better service, and THEN announce the change to your customers as you set about proving it to them.'

REVIEW QUESTIONS

7 Define the term 'customer relationship management'.

8 What factors are driving the uptake of CRM?

9 What are the disadvantages (if any) of CRM?

OBJECTIVE 4▶
Analyse skills in customer relations, particularly communication skills

CUSTOMER RELATIONS AND COMMUNICATION SKILLS

Robbins and colleagues (2006) state that the customer absorbs the organisation's output. Customers who know what is in it for them when they use the products or services offered by an organisation are likely to become satisfied customers. Organisations exist to meet the needs of customers.

Carlzon (1987) identified the *moment of truth* as the customer's first impression of an organisation. The moment of truth creates a lasting impression, so the communication skills used to greet the customer, provide the service and show interest in the customer are important. The challenge for staff providing service of a consistently high quality is to use their communication skills and the communication channels shown in Figure 7.3 appropriately. In order to deliver quality customer service, staff within an organisation must be able to communicate effectively with the customer.

A customer's first impression is lasting.

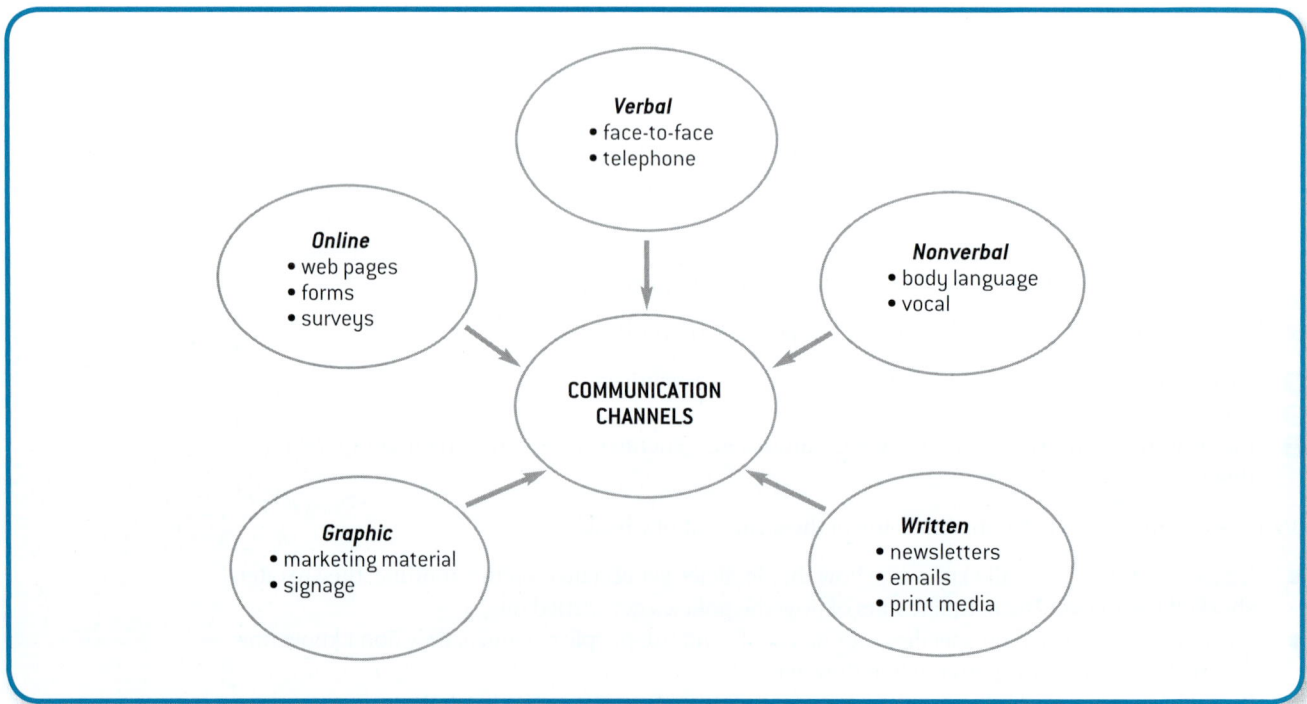

Figure 7.3: Customer service communication channels

Creating a positive impression and goodwill

Using positive and effective communication will create a positive impression and establish goodwill between the organisation and its customers. Good communication strategies are detailed in Table 7.2. Customers have expectations. When a couple go to a restaurant for a meal, they have expectations for the evening. It is unlikely they would have the same expectations when they dine at a very expensive restaurant as they have when they go to McDonald's. Effective communication skills at the moment of truth influence the customer's impression of the quality of service. A quality interaction between customer and service provider is the basis of quality customer service.

USING ACTIVE LISTENING SKILLS

Let the customer know what you have understood by saying, 'What I hear you saying is . . .'. The customer then has the opportunity to agree or to give further information if they see the need. This is paraphrasing, or feeding back, to the customer an understanding of their message. How to use active listening in customer service is set out in Table 7.3.

However, use the technique carefully. Saying 'What I hear you saying is . . .' after every second answer is likely to irritate the customer. Ask for clarification by saying, 'Could you tell me a little more about what went wrong?' Or follow on from the customer's response by asking a probing question. For example, if a customer says, 'I really liked what you did last time', respond with a probing question: 'What did you like last time?' Be open and honest in the interchange and aware of the customer's feelings as well as the content spoken. (Chapter 4 covers active listening, as well as other listening techniques that are useful in customer relations, more fully.)

Harrison (2002) stresses the importance of the voice when dealing with customers: 'Your voice is the most multifaceted customer service tool in your toolkit. Your voice can convey concern, care and compassion. It can alternatively convey boredom, neglect or contempt.' He says that the challenge is to ensure that the voice reinforces the service you are delivering through words and actions. He comments that many telesales and customer service representatives have a mirror on their desks, first

Table 7.2: Creating a positive first impression	
Strategy	**Communication skills**
Greet the customer and show empathy	Greet and recognise customers with a smile. Say 'good morning' and address people by their correct name whenever possible. Always acknowledge a customer's presence and aim to create: • empathy • an understanding of their position • a recognition of their needs • a feeling of comfort • a perception that they are special.
Focus on the customer's needs	Communicate with positive statements. Show respect for the customer's opinions, values and experience. Question and listen to hear their expectations.
Use appropriate verbal and nonverbal behaviour	Ensure that you use complementary verbal and nonverbal messages. Look at the customer as you speak and listen. Demonstrate confidence and professionalism by showing respect for both customer and self, and by using assertive behaviour.
Meet the customer's expectations	Use communication skills to meet the customer's expectations, because customers are most aware of their expectations when their needs are not satisfied. Solve any existing problems and prevent further problems.

Table 7.3: Active listening in customer service
A ttentive to the customer
C oncentrate on the issue, not the person
T arget key points
I nvestigate with questions
V erify the customer's needs
E nergise your response

as a reminder to smile and, second, to confirm that they are smiling when they glance at it periodically. Smiling loosens up the jaw and this is conveyed through the voice.

A pleasant voice tone, effective intonation and empathic emotion create a positive impression.

Harrison also states that it is important to consider the inflection in your voice—which words are emphasised or accentuated. Different messages can be sent depending on the placement of the accent. He further comments, 'Using a pleasant tone, effective intonation and empathic emotion, your voice can go a long way toward helping customers feel heard, valued and cared for.'

Addressing customer needs and expectations

One of the best ways to avoid problems is to make sure the product or service delivers the results promised by the organisation and expected by the client. By asking the customers for feedback, staff are able to check that the results meet their expectations. Some strategies that address the customer's needs and expectations are listed below.

- Survey to gather information on customers' needs and their expectations of service.
- Give information to customers about the organisation's activities.
- Develop a culture of excellent customer service, and raise staff awareness of it through communication, staff training and development.
- Plan to meet customers' needs and expectations.
- Create a set of customer service performance standards.
- Review the customer service outcomes and be willing to improve the service.

Listen to feedback and take action.

To get an organisation operating effectively with a focus on customer service, communication is vital. Haswell (2001) states, 'By asking customers for their thoughts, listening to their feedback, and implementing targeted actions, you are able to address the real needs of your customers.' Communication skills identified as essential to customer relations are questioning and listening. The verbal and nonverbal aspects of each of these must complement one another. Monitor the interaction between customers and the organisation to check that these communication skills are used effectively. They are the key to quality customer service.

UNDERSTANDING CUSTOMER NEEDS

Stewart (1996, p. 137) says that, although patterns of past behaviour have been used as indicators of future performance, 'past performance is not necessarily a reliable indicator of future activity'. He proposes a research program 'designed specifically to yield information on the attitudes and needs that underlie customer behaviour that have thus far determined the measures of lifetime value'.

The research method proposed is based on RRATE, the five key drivers of service performance, a tool outlined by Berry, Bennet and Brown (1989, cited in Stewart 1996):

- **R**eliability
- **R**esponsiveness
- **A**ssurance
- **T**angibles
- **E**mpathy

'With a deeper understanding of the qualitative issues of customer attitudes, expectations and perceptions, you can begin to focus marketing activity . . . however, you must retain the flexibility in your strategy, operations and culture to focus not only on the present—you also have to shape the organisation's future' (Stewart 1996, pp. 142–3).

Strategy, operations and culture may need to change in response to present and future changes.

Even with the best of intentions, barriers to communication can occur. Be aware of the customer's requirements and strive to avoid communication barriers by:

- keeping staff and clients informed of any changes in products, services or procedures
- having sufficient staff to handle customers' needs
- training staff well
- treating customers with respect and sincerity.

REVIEW QUESTIONS

10. Explain two listening skills and two questioning skills that can help to resolve a customer complaint.
11. Explain four aspects of nonverbal communication you can use to help you establish a customer's needs.
12. Identify five key drivers of service performance.

CUSTOMER DEFECTION AND RETENTION RESEARCH

◄ OBJECTIVE 5
Discuss factors that impact on customer defection and retention rates

Rosen (1997, pp. 91–100) says that, according to TARP (Technical Assistance Research Programs) research on customer defections, the reasons customers walk away are:

- 3% move away
- 5% develop relationships with other companies
- 9% leave for competitive reasons
- 14% are dissatisfied with the product or service
- 68% quit because of indifference by the owner, manager or some employee towards the customer
- 1% die.

Additionally, 'Research suggests that only 4 per cent of dissatisfied customers complain and that they will tell 8 to 10 people about their dissatisfaction' (1997, p. 97). He suggests that this amounts to a considerable amount of lost revenue.

Harrison (2001) comments that research has shown that 'many unhappy customers never take the time to let us know we didn't meet their expectations'. He says that if the customer's last impression is unfavourable, often it may be the last transaction you have with them. He emphasises that 'in customer service, it is often the last impression that leaves the aftertaste'. His advice is to 'make sure your last impression is sweet. Find ways to leave your customers feeling valued, cared for and happy to have patronised you. Strive to leave them with smiles on their faces.' Harrison believes that on many occasions we neglect to thank customers for their business or to check that they are happy with their purchases or the services rendered. He suggests a follow-up postcard or phone call to confirm that you have successfully met or exceeded your customers' expectations.

Denham (1998, pp. 20–21) states that an 'American Express/SOCAP *Study of Consumer Complaint Behaviour in Australia 1995*, conducted by TARP Australia, found that 73 per cent of customers did complain about their most serious problem'. The reasons for the remaining 27% not complaining included:

- Fifty-two per cent thought complaining to the organisation would not get results.
- Thirty-eight per cent thought it was not worth the trouble or time.
- The remainder said they did not know where or how to complain.

Denham's summary of the essentials of complaint handling is reproduced in Figure 7.4.

Goodman (1998, p. 17) says: 'In many companies, management believes that customer service is a necessary nuisance.' He points out that, on average, customer loyalty will drop by about 20% if a customer has encountered a problem. This translates into losing one customer in five and the amount this customer was worth. This reduction in loyalty is called 'market damage' by TARP. 'Market damage is the loyalty and revenue lost because of customer-perceived service and quality problems' (1998, p. 18). Research also shows that handling a customer's problem satisfactorily will result in a level of loyalty approaching those who had no problem and '[I]n many industries, a complaining customer whose problem is solved becomes more loyal than a customer with no problem' (1998, p. 20).

Stewart (1996, p. 144) suggests that a research program should cover three key stakeholder groups:

Minimise market damage by handling a customer's problem satisfactorily.

Effective research gathers information from customers, employees and competitors.

1. *Customers*: defection and retention research to determine the 'loyalty hooks' and what the customer perceives the organisation does to add or detract.
2. *Employees*: attitudinal research to determine if employees are accurately reading and meeting customers' expectations and perceptions.
3. *Competitors*: benchmarking to learn about the successes and failures of competitors.

Stewart (1996, p. 148) states that research shows it is not possible to forecast rates of customer retention from levels of customer satisfaction: 'Between 65 per cent and 85 per cent of customers who

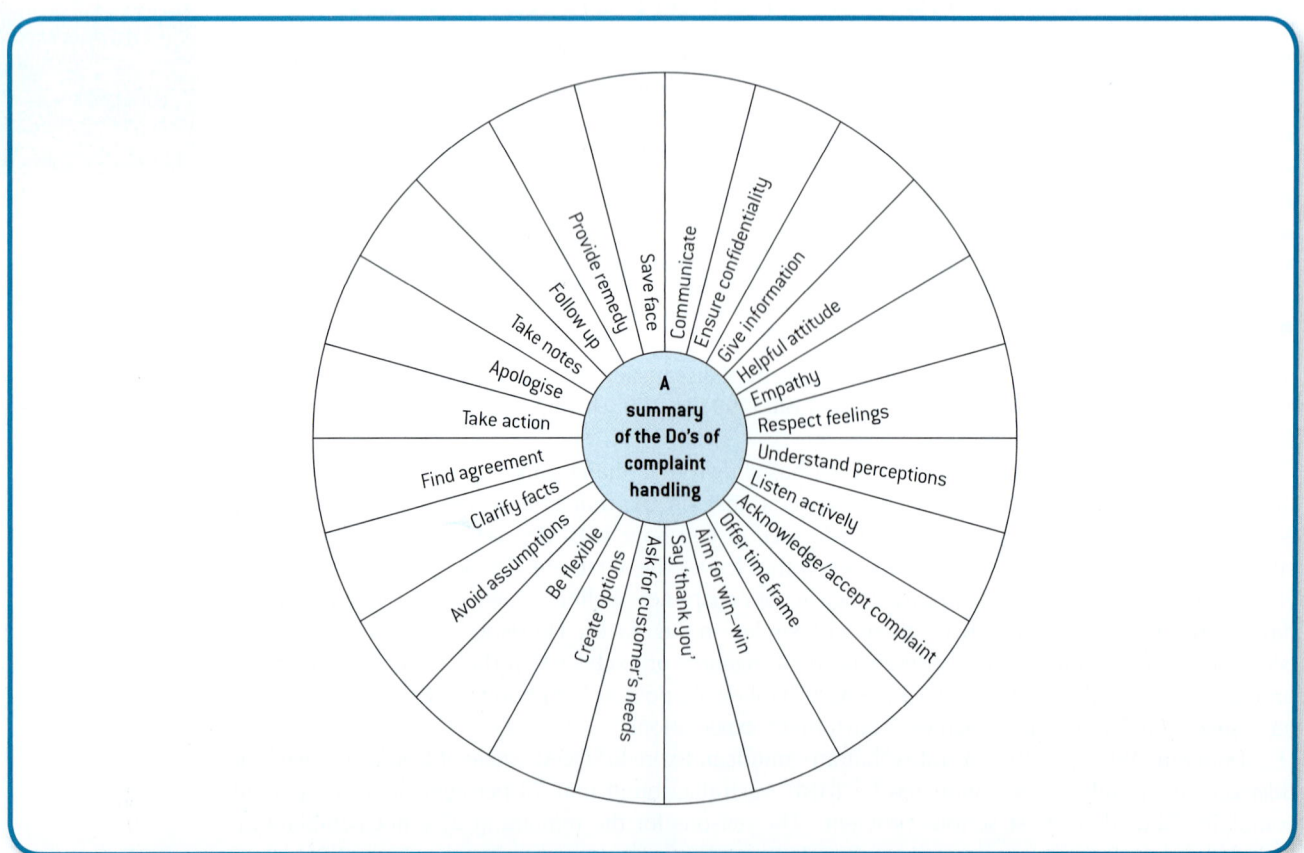

Figure 7.4: A summary of the Do's of complaint handling

Source: Reproduced from J. Denham, *Handling Customer Complaints* with the permission of Pearson Education Australia Pty Limited. Copyright 1998 Prentice Hall Australia Pty Ltd.

defect say they were satisfied or very satisfied with their former supplier.' In the motor vehicle industry the rates are even higher. According to Stewart, 'This is because satisfaction monitors do not consider a customer's alternatives (your service may be good but your competitor's may be better).'

Babin, Babin and Boles (1999, p. 91) studied 'consumer attitudes toward a product, salesperson, and retailer as possible antecedents of purchase intentions' when buying a new car. The research showed that '[f]rom a retail standpoint, the salesperson is clearly the key to winning customers' attitudes and business. The strong relationship between salesperson and retailer attitude makes it unlikely that a consumer would consider a dealership further once a bad interaction with a salesperson is experienced.' However, they pointed out that the person might possibly buy the particular make of car on offer but at a different dealership.

Turner and Reisinger (2001), researching the shopping satisfaction of domestic tourism as distinct from international tourism, found that the main attributes domestic tourists sought were 'value', 'display' and 'uniqueness', and that, when attained, these attributes caused satisfaction in shopping. The dimensions of satisfaction were 'cost', 'product display' and 'shop presentation', the latter being defined as 'clean, conveniently located, attractive shops with well presented sales staff' (p. 25). They concluded: 'For domestic tourists retailers will find competing on price more difficult and the focus should probably be to link value and uniqueness within a high service environment (shop and staff presentation and produce display).'

Problem solving

Sometimes an organisation's staff will have to deal with *customer complaints*. Some complaints will be justified, others will not. All complaints need to be addressed and resolved in a way that maintains the customer's goodwill. The intention is to turn customer complaints into goodwill and future business.

Deal with a complaint by using negotiation and conflict-resolution skills. Acknowledge that the complaint is justified and solve the problem. Because the customer's need or expectation has not been met, there is no point in hedging or asking them to take further action on their own behalf. The role of staff is to solve the problem and avoid further ill feeling. When a complaint is unjustified, acknowledge it and the customer's grievance and ask the customer the reason for the complaint. Two strategies for dealing with complaints and solving the problem are shown in Table 7.4.

◄ OBJECTIVE 6
Apply problem-solving strategies to handle customer complaints and difficult situations

A customer complaint is an expression of dissatisfaction with a good or service.

Professionalism offers quality service to all customers.

Table 7.4: Customer complaints: Two approaches to problem solving
The PAIR approval strategy
P Placate: listen, empathise, respond with concern
A Attend: to the complaint
I Investigate: circumstances, details of the incident
R Resolve: decide on action to take
The five-step method
1. *Listen:* be open-minded; remember, this is not a personal complaint against you.
2. *Respond:* show concern and empathy and apologise for any inconvenience. Remember, the customer may be embarrassed about complaining; put yourself in their position.
3. *Decide on action:* what factors will influence you here—the justice of the complaint, the company policy? When uncertain, seek advice from your supervisor.
4. *Take action:* act promptly.
5. *Follow up:* confirm that the problem has been solved and the customer is satisfied.

Consulting customers

Customers are entitled to accurate information.

By consulting or guiding customers with professional advice about the organisation's products or services, staff members can avoid difficult situations and reduce the number of complaints. Before service is provided, explain the purpose and outcomes of any procedure, the principal steps, and the order in which these steps take place. This consultation with the client helps to prevent anxiety or stress. Obtain feedback from the customer in terms of their comfort, feelings and perception of expected outcomes.

Give precise instructions to staff and accurate information to customers. Acknowledge customers' expectations, but state what can and cannot be delivered. Deal with unrealistic customer requests confidently and without aggression. It is better to state clearly and courteously that it is not possible to fulfil the request than to make a promise that cannot be kept.

REVIEW QUESTIONS

13 *a* Identify three reasons for customer defections.

b Describe how an organisation can retain its customers.

14 Identify three 'do nots' of complaint handling.

15 Describe two barriers to effective customer service.

16 Nominate the steps in handling a customer complaint.

17 What is the PAIR approval strategy? When is it used?

18 Outline the five-step method of handling customer complaints.

APPLY YOUR KNOWLEDGE

WHAT IS CUSTOMER VALUE?

1 a Work in small groups to discuss the following statement: 'Students are the customers of the institution within which they study and learn.'

b Albrecht (1992) identified four levels of customer value. Two of these were the *expected* and *desired* levels of service. Work in a brainstorming session to create a comprehensive list of what the customers value in your institution at these two levels of service.

c How could universities identify the standard of service expected by their customers?

2 Work in pairs.

a Develop a presentation for delivery at a professional development day for new staff in a large banking institution. The topic of the presentation is 'Dealing with Dissatisfied Clients'. In particular, mention:

- how to solve problems
- how to use the five-step method
- what to avoid in providing client service
- features of client service the bank encourages.

b Deliver the presentation to the large group.

3 Break into two groups. Organise a debate with the other group using either of the following topics.

- 'Customer relations management (CRM) really doesn't affect middle managers once their organisation implements CRM.'
- 'Once a customer satisfaction model is developed, strategy doesn't affect managers. Service delivery is their main focus.'

4 Work in small groups.

a Discuss the value of identifying client needs and expectations.

b What simple steps can be taken by an organisation to identify client needs and expectations?

c How can an organisation's staff solve customer problems?

d Report back to the large group.

PUBLIC RELATIONS

Public relations is concerned with creating the organisation's public presence and influencing its publics to take some course of action. For example, an organisation's ability to obtain funds is affected by its financial publics—its shareholders, banks and other financial institutions; hence the organisation issues annual reports and maintains formal and informal contacts with them. While the annual reports use one-way communication from the organisation to its publics, formal and informal contacts at meetings, conferences and business lunches allow two-way communication to occur. This two-way communication between the organisation and its publics is used to achieve mutual understanding and public acceptance of the organisation.

Two-way communication between an organisation and its publics allows the organisation to understand its publics' expectations and the community to understand the organisation's overall goals and objectives. An organisation's community relations officer uses two-way communication to attend meetings, listen to others and answer questions. Consequently, both the organisation and its publics are able to reach a mutual understanding. Most publics, particularly 'activist' publics such as environmental groups, 'want the organisation to be persuaded equally as often as they are persuaded' (Hunt & Grunig 1994, p. 9). Two-way communication is used in public relations to satisfy this want effectively.

Organisations adopt either an upfront approach to public relations or a behind-the-scenes approach. An upfront approach is taken by organisations that want their public relations efforts to be visible in the community. An organisation that appoints a community relations officer to work in the community is using an upfront approach. Some of the duties of the community relations officer are to answer enquiries about the organisation and conduct promotional activities such as Open Days. An *upfront approach* uses two-way communication to give people knowledge and allow them to ask questions and gather information from the experts in an organisation.

By contrast, a *behind-the-scenes approach* to public relations is less visible. For example, a Public Health Unit could conduct a telephone survey of its local publics to determine if they know about the unit and the services that it provides. The survey would also gather information about where the local publics go to access health information, and ask about their knowledge of infectious diseases, or asthma and its triggering factors.

In both the upfront and behind-the-scenes approaches an organisation's objective is to achieve a higher public profile. The approach chosen is the one most appropriate to the particular publics, their needs and expectations, and the type of products or services offered by the organisation.

Stakeholders are individuals or groups who are affected by the behaviour of the organisation. They make up the organisation's various publics; for example, customers, shareholders, suppliers, distributors, community groups, environmentalists and government are all part of an organisation's public. Organisations need to know which publics they want to reach and the responses they want from them.

Planning public relations

According to Fletcher and Brown (2008, p. 586), public relations is '. . . a non-personal form of communication based on conveying messages to many "publics" (stakeholders) or exchange partners designed to create a favourable image for the organization'. Public relations communication is about generating goodwill to enable an organisation to survive. In their view, 'Public relations does not lead to immediate sales, but improves cumulative favourable awareness' (p. 609).

The long-term aim of public relations is to create a favourable image and at the same time to communicate a message that is retained and accepted by the receivers. Successful public relations messages influence community attitudes and cause changes in behaviour of an organisation's publics. Public relations messages convey information about an organisation's objectives, policies, standards, products and services.

◄ OBJECTIVE 7
Identify the groups that make up an organisation's publics

Two-way communication creates mutual understanding between an organisation and its publics.

Public relations manages the organisation's reputation with its various publics or audiences.

Stakeholders are those individuals or groups affected by the behaviour of the organisation.

◄ OBJECTIVE 8
Describe different public relations objectives and explain how to plan for them

The role of public relations is to:

- relate to the needs and interests of the organisation's publics
- inform the publics about the organisation's products and services
- establish and maintain communication with the media and its audiences
- avoid conflict and misunderstanding
- build positive relationships and goodwill
- project the corporate image
- build relationships with the media
- research public opinion and advise on how to influence it
- analyse future trends and advise on their likely impact
- plan formal programs and campaigns
- manage public relations strategically.

Baskin, Aronoff and Lattimore (1997, pp. 6–7) point out that some definitions emphasise the communication function of public relations. Whereas it has always been necessary for public relations practitioners to be excellent writers and speakers, in the 21st century 'the practitioner now must also be able to communicate effectively in cyberspace' (1997, p. 6). They point out that the tasks might include 'Production of a media release, an annual report, an employee magazine, or an electronic newspaper . . . Other tasks include the creation and management of campaigns to achieve awareness of an issue or change opinions about a subject' (p. 7).

Baskin and colleagues also state that, although debatable, it is often considered part of the role of public relations to exert influence on public opinion. They list the following three objectives of public relations practitioners in developing their strategies:

1. to maintain favourable opinions
2. to create opinion where none exists, or where it is latent
3. to neutralise hostile opinion.

Public relations practitioners 'are basically responsible for assimilating and communicating information between an organisation and its environment' (Baskin et al. 1997, p. 12). They must also maintain 'effective relationships with the media representatives who publish or broadcast information about the organisation and its publics' (p. 14).

Public relations can be used as a tool to overcome community objections. Beder (1999) comments, 'Many government agencies and corporations conduct public consultation exercises for the purpose of gaining community acceptance for hazardous facilities or undesirable developments.' She criticises these actions as being 'not aimed at genuine participation in decision making' but rather 'a public relations exercise that seeks to manipulate public opinion and perceptions. PR tools for communicating risk, categorising "publics", dealing with intractable opponents, and fostering trust are all utilised under the guise of public participation.'

Determining public relations objectives

Public relations aims to increase the organisation's profile. Formal public relations programs with clear objectives that focus on promoting the whole organisation need to be prepared in order to highlight the organisation's presence, image, products and services.

The wide variety of *public relations objectives* include:

Public relations objectives aim to gain public acceptance of the organisation.

- explain and interpret the organisation's policies, practices and type of business operation to its publics
- explain and interpret to management the opinions and attitudes held by the public towards the company
- guide management to decision making that presents a positive image to the organisation's publics

- personalise the company by presenting a recognisable image with which its publics can identify
- manage potential issues between the organisation and its publics before conflict emerges
- remove the cause of any problems affecting the organisation's publics
- encourage and persuade public acceptance of the organisation's presence, image, products and services
- focus on the type and quality of service given by the organisation.

The capacity to listen to, appreciate and respond to an organisation's publics is the key to building mutually beneficial relationships with them. Effective public relations is more than one-way communication from the organisation to its publics. Public relations operates at a higher level when it is two-way (Grunig & Hunt 1984). Rapid developments in technology enable an organisation to send and receive public relations messages via many channels.

Customer and other stakeholder perceptions about an organisation's product or service are gathered through market research surveys conducted face-to-face, on the Internet through forms, blogs and email, via company mailouts and by telephone. The data gathered is used to design campaign strategies that meet the organisation's goals and the expectations of its customers and other publics. The techniques used in campaigns include product launches, press conferences, media seminars, press releases, press kits, podcasts, wire service distribution of information, Internet placement, entertainment product placement (television, events, celebrity), speechwriting and establishing partnerships.

Allert and Zawawi (2000) suggest that, when writing an effective strategic communication plan, writers must be aware of the principles of effective communication. The plan must be:

- open and honest
- two-way and responsive
- receiver-oriented
- timely
- clear and consistent
- comprehensive.

Budgeting is also an important factor. They state that without successful and efficient budgeting and thorough scheduling, a public relations plan cannot succeed. In their view, plans in a similar format to business and marketing plans are more readily accepted by others.

Very large organisations can have a number of images. For example, AMP's financial public will have different perceptions of the organisation than its citizen-action public and internal public. Before an organisation decides on a public relations plan, it needs to identify its image and organisational goals and objectives. Research must be undertaken to check opinions, attitudes and reactions to an organisation from a range of its publics. Once these facts are analysed and evaluated, a course of action is planned. The research results may be positive, in which case only small changes will be made. However, the research may reveal negative attitudes, in which case changes and corrections should be made to policies and procedures in order to improve goodwill.

Public relations objectives are developed in the planning stage.

Once the research data is collected, it is analysed and the changes are implemented. Constant research and fact-finding gives feedback on the organisation's impact and how the public perceives the organisation and its decision makers.

The public relations communication experts use their skills to produce the messages. A great deal of effort is put into writing, editing and designing graphics and audiovisuals for public relations materials. Joint activities where organisations collaborate, such as a telethon, allow organisations to influence a range of publics. A telethon is a fundraiser. A national television station, the oncology unit of a metropolitan hospital and the community, for example, may combine to raise money for cancer research and to equip the hospital with specialised equipment and resources. This exercise is a fundraising activity that must also have a public relations aspect. The planning steps carried out by the public relations units of the hospitals and television station in this type of activity are shown in Table 7.5.

Table 7.5: A community public relations program—planning steps

- Survey to determine public likes, dislikes, preferences or objections to the planned program.
- Choose a suitable means of communication to inform people in the community of the program.
- Create a time plan or schedule for special events, local advertising, broadcasts and other communication.
- Seek the opinion and cooperation of staff.
- Advertise and publicise in the daily newspaper and on radio and television.
- Invite opinion leaders, the public and others to open-houses to see the organisation's activities.
- Have employees promote the organisation with speeches at local civic lunches, professional societies, school assemblies, church groups and social service organisations.

Implementing a public relations plan

Communication tools such as news releases, media interviews, news conferences, special events and brochures are used to reach an organisation's publics.

In addition to using its own network of contacts the organisation will make contact with the media—radio, television and newspapers—to get its message across. Communication skills such as questioning, listening, speaking, nonverbal communication and negotiation are all used in the implementation stage. Public relations must be implemented by someone high enough in the organisation's structure to possess a total picture of the organisation and with the power to allocate resources to the campaign. In the implementation stage, the aim is to reach and to influence positively each part of the organisation's publics. Without resources the campaign cannot be implemented.

A successful organisation has identified a part of the marketplace and then operated in that marketplace to satisfy the needs and expectations of its customers and potential customers. The effective public relations campaign is directed at the market. In this process, rather than focusing on the organisation by saying, 'What do we want as a company?', it is far more effective to focus on the existing and potential publics by asking, 'What does our public want?' Then the campaign is directed at filling the publics' need in a way that satisfies them. Effective public relations recognises and acknowledges these needs.

The media provide communication channels that reach large numbers of people, e.g. television, radio, newspapers, magazines, Internet.

For example, McDonald's maintains a public image of quality, value, service and cleanliness. Fast food success is based on consistent quality and value for money. Anyone who visits a McDonald's outlet knows before they enter that a meal will be provided at that level of service, quality and price. At any outlet, service is fast and friendly in modern, clean facilities. The decoration identifies the fast food outlet via posters, colours, brand names and even layout. Job functions are organised, with each member of staff understanding and completing these tasks with a minimum of fuss to maximise customer service.

Internal communication

In-house communication, such as internal publications, intranets, conferences, teleconferencing, seminars and meetings, provide an opportunity to let staff (i.e. the organisation's internal publics) know management's policies, procedures and attitudes. Staff are able to exchange information and give feedback to management on their perception of the organisation.

A cooperative workforce contributes to public relations and is responsible for the delivery of the standard of service to customers. Survey employees to determine their perception of working in the organisation. Identify areas of satisfaction and discontent and suggested areas of improvement. Many employees welcome the opportunity to participate in decision making and to share information. This open approach improves employee relations and removes much of the potential for industrial relations problems, as the needs of both the employer and employee are addressed. The flow of communication is two-way.

REVIEW QUESTIONS

19 **a** What is public relations?

  b How would you distinguish between 'customer service' and 'public relations'?

20 What does two-way communication between an organisation and its publics aim to achieve?

21 **a** Describe the difference between an upfront approach and a behind-the-scenes approach to public relations.

  b What is the purpose of each?

22 List and briefly explain four public relations objectives.

23 What are the objectives and likely outcome(s) from a successful formal public relations program?

24 How does a cooperative workforce contribute to public relations?

MEDIA RELATIONS

> **◄ OBJECTIVE 9**
> Discuss the role of media releases, news conferences and special events in presenting a positive public image

External communication channels are used in media relations. Johnston (2000, p. 228) says: 'Dealing with the media is a critical part of the public relations practitioners' profession.' This incorporates writing news releases, compiling media kits, and advising senior personnel about how to work with the media.

Johnston (2000, pp. 209–11) recommends understanding what makes news so that the media gatekeepers will not reject the material. In order to make news the public relations person has to prepare a story with *news value*. Johnston lists various elements that may give a story news value: impact, conflict, timeliness, proximity, prominence, currency, human interest, the unusual and money. She also recommends knowing newspaper and magazine deadlines. She comments that '[t]he most flexible of all deadlines is in radio news updates. Because radio news people are constantly putting together news bulletins—either hourly or half-hourly—they can receive news as close as 10 minutes before deadline' (p. 211). Similarly, it is important to know the hierarchy that exists in newsrooms, and the names and roles of the journalists in the various departments.

> 'News value' is the term used to describe the criteria for making news.

News releases

A **media release** makes an announcement. It can be sent to a range of publics including financial, government, citizen-action, local, general and internal. The media release's purpose determines to which public it is sent. A media release aims to attract attention. Changes in personnel, expansion, opening a new operation or moving to a new site can be announced as a media release. The message is kept concise and factual and written in the style of standard journalism. The order of information is:

> A news release (or **media release**) aims to attract attention. It may be made in the press, on radio or television, or via some other channel of communication.

1 a lead or opening paragraph that summarises the main facts—who, what, where, when, why and how

2 news of secondary importance

3 reiteration and explanation.

Writing style and presentation—the size of paper, letterhead, double spacing, wide margins—all have an impact on the organisation's image and public relations.

A publishable news release has the characteristics of a news release written by a journalist. Johnston (2000, p. 215) concurs with this point: 'The central rule of writing news releases is to write, where possible, in news style.' She recommends analysing how both the print and broadcast media use stories. News stories should attempt to answer the six basic news questions: who, what, where, when, why and how.

Bovee and Thill (2005, pp. 202–3) recommend keeping the following points in mind when writing a news release:

- 'make sure your information is newsworthy and relevant . . .
- put your most important idea first . . .
- be brief: break up long sentences and keep paragraphs short
- eliminate clutter such as redundancy and extraneous facts
- be as specific as possible
- minimise self-congratulatory adjectives and adverbs . . . the media professionals will be interested in the news on its own merits.'

The news release should look professional with good-quality word processing on A4 paper, double spaced. Letterhead is desirable but not essential. 'For Immediate Release' should be printed near the top of the first page, followed by a creative headline. Edit the news release for correct grammar and spelling. Incorrect grammar and spelling will affect your credibility negatively. Maintain factual accuracy and use the inverted pyramid to order the information. Place the most important information and quotes from key staff, customers or subject matter experts first, followed by less important details. The inverted pyramid allows the story to be cut from the bottom. Johnston (2000, p. 215) points out that 'a poorly written release, which does not adhere to the inverted pyramid style, is more likely to be discarded'. Remember to clear your quotes for public release, and to include the date on which the news release is written and the name, address and telephone number of a contact person.

Web Wire, a press-release writing service, comments (2008), 'A press release is a written communication that purports to report on an event, circumstance or occurrence by a third party, and is provided to the news media for the purpose of promotion. Business, organizational or personal press releases are different from a news article in that a news article is a compilation of facts developed by journalists and then published as news content within a given media outlet.' The press release must be written in the third person, and is most effective when less than 500 words (generally, two to three paragraphs). The first paragraph should grab the reader's attention and contain the most relevant information. Paragraphs two and three should contain more detail and keep to the point. The concluding paragraph restates and summarises the key points of the press release. End with the characters '###' or type 'END'.

> Never use capitals, with the exception of FOR IMMEDIATE RELEASE, EMBARGO or END. Spell out & or % and abbreviations such as 'St', 'Vic' and 'Qld'. Never use underlining. When in doubt about what to do, contact the group to whom you are sending the press release and ask for advice. (Webwire 2008)

Media interviews

Maitland (1999, p. 14) comments that, in contrast to news releases, 'interviews almost guarantee that you're going to get your message across—the media wouldn't waste their time if they weren't going to run the interview in some way'. Maitland warns that journalists might have their own agenda and what you say will be interpreted by them. Macnamara (1996) lists seven tools for successful media interviews (see Table 7.6).

News conferences

Maitland (1999, p. 14) suggests that news conferences 'can be scheduled into a PR campaign—and are often hugely effective . . . you control the message that is being put across; and can support it with product displays and examinations'. Johnston (2000, p. 221) states that media conferences are usually held to allow for wide dissemination of a story, to give all media access to the news at once and to allow journalists to ask follow-up questions.

Important elements to consider are: having plenty of time to plan; and preparing and checking that everything is in place. Some news conferences should be called immediately; for example, in the event of a mine collapse or explosion. Johnston (2000, pp. 222–5) lists the following points to consider:

A news or media release should be written in an inverted pyramid; that is, key points in the first part of the story with information following in descending order of importance.

In a media interview, decide the main point, keep to the 'must say' items and avoid 'red herrings'.

Table 7.6: Tools for successful media interviews	
1 Set your objectives.	Decide the main point that you or your organisation want to make about the topic under discussion.
2 Set your frame of reference.	Determine your audience: comments that have little or no relevance to their audience will be unlikely to be used by editors, news directors or program producers.
3 Work out your 'must say' items before an interview, as well as a few 'would like to say' items to use if time allows.	Prioritise 'must says' to get the message across in the interview, irrespective of the journalist's questions.
4 'Bridge' from the journalist's questions to your 'must says'.	Link (or bridge) from what the journalist asks to what you want to say. Bridging—10 seconds addressing the journalist's question and 30 seconds saying what you want to say—allows you to get your message across.
5 Express your 'must says' as stand-alone statements.	Avoid misquoting and misreporting by the media by using stand-alone statements for your main message.
6 Reiterate your 'must says' two or three times if possible.	Ensure the journalist understands them and reports them accurately.
7 Avoid 'red herrings'.	Keep the 'must says' in sight and avoid 'red herrings' that take you in another direction. 'Bridge' back to your 'must says'.

Source: Adapted from J.R. Macnamara, *How to Handle the Media*, Prentice Hall Australia, Sydney, 1996, pp. 40–61.

- when to hold the news conference
- who to invite
- how to invite: fax, mail, email
- where to hold the conference
- how to set it up
- supplying visuals
- keeping a list of costs
- after the conference, contacting absent media.

Special events

Some businesses decide to use a special event as a public relations exercise instead of regular advertising. Special events that are suitable for this purpose include:

- displays and exhibits, such as national and trade fairs
- meetings and conferences
- telethons
- promotions to customers
- sponsored community events, such as 'Surfest' or 'Model for Life'
- sponsored associations, such as Westpac Regional Rescue Helicopter Operations.

Prepare and promote a special public relations event in the following order:

1. Know why the organisation is staging the special event. Define clear objectives and the intended outcomes; for example, an association supporting a Regional Rescue Helicopter Operation may look for fundraising and increased awareness of public safety.
2. Name the event in a way that suits the organisation's public image.

3. Choose the date and invite the guests.
4. Consider and organise transport, parking arrangements, and procedures for reception and registration of participants.
5. Decide on the type of refreshments.
6. Seek the advice and cooperation of others who may be affected; for example, the local community. (In the case of the Regional Rescue Helicopter Association, it would contact its financial, media, citizen-action, local, general, internal and government publics.)
7. Create a program that supports the objectives and complements the image of the organisation hosting the special event.
8. Use publicity that reaches the target audience and supports the special event and the public presence of the organisation.

Each organisation has a direct impact on its employees, customers and shareholders. Whether it communicates to its publics consciously or unconsciously, the perception and interpretation of this impact is the organisation's public relations. Liaison with government departments, other community activities, educational endeavours, and sponsorships for the arts and sporting activities are all part of public relations.

Plan a campaign around the main public relations objective and use a unique blend of facts and communication media to achieve persuasive communication in the campaign.

REVIEW QUESTIONS

25 Describe three techniques used in public relations campaigns.
26 a   What six basic news questions should a media release attempt to answer?
   b   Why does a news release use the inverted pyramid structure?
27 How can an organisation gather information about stakeholder perceptions of its products or services?
28 What is the purpose of a special event?

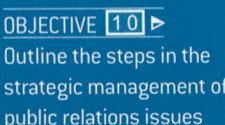

OBJECTIVE 10 ▶
Outline the steps in the strategic management of public relations issues

MANAGING PUBLIC RELATIONS ISSUES

When stakeholders organise to do something about the consequences of an organisation's actions, a **public relations issue** arises. The organisation's communication objective should be to achieve mutual understanding by communicating accurately and in a way that leads to agreement between the stakeholders and the organisation. When the process is built on negotiation and collaboration, neither the organisation nor the stakeholders are forced to make the choice as to who is right. This is because the negotiation process separates the people from the problem and focuses on interests, rather than positions. Both parties can generate a variety of possibilities before choosing an option. This ensures that results are based on some objective standard. The principled bargaining method of negotiating is described on pages 138–41.

A **public relations issue** arises when stakeholders form groups because an organisation's actions impact on them.

Organisations that manage issues effectively over the long term use two-way ongoing communication with stakeholders to create mutual understanding and build a stable relationship. Hunt and Grunig (1994) identify seven steps in the strategic management of public relations:

1. Build a stable long-term relationship—stakeholder stage.
2. Research to identify and segment the publics—public stage.
3. Anticipate issues and manage the organisation's response to them—issue stage.
4. Develop objectives.
5. Plan formal programs and campaigns.
6. Implement the programs and campaigns.
7. Evaluate the effectiveness of the programs in meeting objectives.

Organisations that research the environment and their own and their publics' behaviour are not only able to develop clear objectives and plans, but are also able to identify any issues that are likely to have consequences for their publics before the plans are put into practice. The potential for conflict is reduced.

Identifying and controlling PR issues

A public relations issue is usually defined as something longstanding or predictable that impacts on an industry or product category. Air pollution and other environmental damage, for example, are often linked in the public's mind to coal mining or the production of steel or chemicals. This is an ongoing issue for these industries. Many of the companies in these industries anticipate and manage the issue in order to minimise the threat of pollution and subsequent loss of their public reputation. Advances in media technology mean that when a crisis occurs, a company is immediately in the spotlight locally, nationally and even internationally.

There are three main ways in which public relations helps companies to equip themselves to handle issues and minimise the possibility of a crisis (see Table 7.7).

Effective management of issues helps to minimise or even mitigate the risk of a crisis. If a crisis occurs, it must be managed because of public scrutiny and the resulting negative financial, political, legal and government impacts and perceptions. Examples of crises include a hazardous material leak, damage to the environment, fire, accident, hostile takeover of a company, copyright infringement, natural disaster that disrupts product or service delivery, malicious rumour, legal actions and product recall. The benefits of managing a crisis effectively include:

> In public relations, issue management is the process used to align organisational activities and stakeholder expectations.

> The role of public relations practitioners is to identify the issue, deal with it, and communicate with stakeholders ethically and transparently.

> A crisis is an abnormal situation or public perception that is beyond the scope of everyday business and threatens the operation, safety and reputation of an organisation.

Table 7.7: Strategies for handling PR problems	
Steps	**Strategies**
1 Identify the level of risk the issue poses for the company.	• assessing the monetary or economic risk • assessing the risk to reputation that might flow from the media, government and other stakeholders
2 Scan and monitor the environment actively.	• specialists reading regular science journals to keep up to date and take action before the issue arises • subject matter experts gathering competitor intelligence from advertising, trade shows, annual reports and other public documents • installing environmental scanning and monitoring systems to track an issue through the variety of communication mediums such as newspapers and digital broadcasts on a daily basis to provide advance warning of a potential problem • building rapport continuously with key stakeholders
3 Manage, rather than try to ignore or avoid, the issue.	• developing a position on the issue in order to take immediate action that pre-empts public concern should the issue arise • taking an assertive problem-solving approach, rather than hiding defensively and hoping the issue will go away • building bridges with key influencers and acting in a manner that builds goodwill and the organisation's reputation as an ethical and proactive entity • ongoing management of issues because of the speed at which issues can overtake an organisation • communicating an accurate version of the crisis in accordance with organisational guidelines and legal requirements to all relevant stakeholders • providing a free flow of information during the life of the crisis

- demonstrated corporate social responsibility through compliance with organisational, regulatory and ethical requirements
- improved capacity to better manage future serious incidents
- increased analysis by decision makers of the short-term consequences and long-term effects of actions
- increased staff awareness of their roles and expectations within the organisation
- improved capacity of all stakeholders to prepare and manage risk
- enhanced reputation, goodwill and reduced risk of post-event litigation.

High-transparency organisations have effective flows of information upwards, downwards and horizontally.

Low-transparency organisations have ineffective flows of communication, resulting in strong internal and external grapevines.

Public relations practitioners are better equipped to handle and control crises and issues in a high-transparency organisation than in a low-transparency organisation. In a **high-transparency organisation** there is free-flowing information and communication and a willingness to handle any problem or crisis proactively. The levels of trust are high, and mistakes are seen as learning opportunities. By contrast, a **low-transparency organisation** has poor internal and external flows of information and a tendency to ignore, rather than manage, problems or crises. The levels of trust are low, and mistakes are seen as excuses for punishment (Jahansoozi 2006; Welch & Rothberg 2006).

REVIEW QUESTIONS

29 a   Define the terms 'public relations issue' and 'public relations crisis'.
   b   Why do companies identify and control public relations issues?
30   What benefits are gained from managing a crisis effectively?
31   Explain the difference between a high-transparency and a low-transparency organisation.

APPLY YOUR KNOWLEDGE

PUBLIC RELATIONS

1   'The effective public relations campaign is directed at the market.' Explain this statement by using examples from companies that, in your view, have achieved the objectives of their public relations policy.

2   Work in small groups to analyse a public relations crisis.
   a   Discuss the factors that caused the crisis.
   b   Decide whether the organisation demonstrated corporate social responsibility in the management of the crisis.
   c   What could the organisation do to minimise the risk of a future crisis?

3   Work in small groups.
   a   Outline the planning steps in a community public relations project.
   b   Briefly describe the purpose of a media release in a community relations project.
   c   Identify three general points that a media release should contain.
   d   How could the organisers of the community relations project use the checklist below?
   e   How could the organisers determine whether their community public relations project had been effective?
   f   Report back to the large group.

PLANNING A PUBLIC RELATIONS PROGRAM

Have you:	Yes	No	Unsure
Identified the purpose?			
Decided on the objectives?			
Chosen the most appropriate communication channel?			
Created a schedule?			
Sought the cooperation of those involved or affected?			
Analysed the proposed program to check that the results will be positive?			
Planned in a way that will emphasise the unique or special features of the organisation?			
Allocated sufficient resources to achieve the intended outcomes?			

SUMMARY OF LEARNING OBJECTIVES

 EXPLAIN THE ROLE OF STRATEGY, STAFF AND SYSTEMS IN PROVIDING A POSITIVE CUSTOMER EXPERIENCE TO ALL CUSTOMER TYPES

An organisation has both internal and external customers. Current thinking differentiates three types of customer interactions. B2C (business-to-customer) interactions occur on a one-to-one basis. B2B (business-to-business) interactions take place between businesses, government departments and other organisations, rather than with individual customers. P2P (peer-to-peer) interactions involve buying or selling without the direct mediation of an organisation.

Customer experience for any type of customer is the perception that results from all the interactions that a customer has with an organisation's products, services, people and processes. A service culture is built on the service strategy and the people or staff in the organisation's systems.

 DIFFERENTIATE BETWEEN FOUR TYPES OF CUSTOMER VALUE

Customer value is classified as basic, expected, desired and unanticipated. Basic value is simply providing the product or service; expected value meets the quality of service expected by the customer; and desired and unanticipated value exceed the value expected by the customer, giving a superior level of service. Customers constantly monitor the value of the service they receive.

Plan to create a pleasant environment with friendly and informed staff who provide courteous and efficient service. The working relationship flows from the interaction of the three ingredients in the service package: the service strategy; the staff of the organisation; and the organisation's systems, which are focused on the needs and expectations of the customer. A successful organisation asks clients what they value. It then sets customer service goals and decides on strategies to achieve the goals and deliver value to customers. The staff communicate and consult with the clients, and solve their problems.

 OUTLINE THE INTERACTION OF STRATEGY, PROCESS AND TECHNOLOGY IN CUSTOMER RELATIONSHIP MANAGEMENT (CRM)

CRM aims to build and improve customer loyalty. CRM software packages manage an organisation's interactions with customers by integrating strategies, processes and technology. Effective CRM builds long-term relationships with customers and requires more than helpful technology. It requires strategies and processes that optimise the customer experience by focusing on customers and meeting their expectations. Individual and organisational behaviours impact on the message received by the customer.

4 ▷ ANALYSE SKILLS IN CUSTOMER RELATIONS, PARTICULARLY COMMUNICATION SKILLS

A courteous approach combined with active listening by staff as they provide customer service enables them to meet customers' requirements. In a customer service situation the concept 'active listening' is described as ACTIVE: **A**ttend to the customer, **C**oncentrate on the issue, **T**arget key points, **I**nvestigate with questions, **V**erify customers' needs, and **E**nergise your response. Acknowledging the customer, listening with empathy, providing feedback, and using appropriate verbal and nonverbal communication enable staff to offer quality service to the customer.

5 ▷ DISCUSS FACTORS THAT IMPACT ON CUSTOMER DEFECTION AND RETENTION RATES

Customers leave because they develop relationships with other companies, move elsewhere, are dissatisfied or feel the owner, manager or staff are indifferent to their needs. The major barriers to customer satisfaction are lack of support for customer service by management, customer service staff with too little knowledge about the product and its features, too few staff, poor communication skills, and lack of respect and courtesy towards the customer. When customers find less than the expected value, they may leave the relationship. Loyal customers stay because they feel valued and have their expectations met.

6 ▷ APPLY PROBLEM-SOLVING STRATEGIES TO HANDLE CUSTOMER COMPLAINTS AND DIFFICULT SITUATIONS

If a customer expresses confusion or dissatisfaction, deal with and resolve the problem. Two problem-solving strategies are the PAIR approval strategy and the five-step method. Use these to satisfy the customer's needs and expectations. After dealing with a customer complaint, it is useful to review the problem in order to learn from it.

7 ▷ IDENTIFY THE GROUPS THAT MAKE UP AN ORGANISATION'S PUBLICS

An organisation's publics are the stakeholders, individuals or groups, who are affected by the behaviour of the organisation. Employees, customers, shareholders, suppliers, distributors and the general public are all part of an organisation's publics. An organisation engages in two-way communication with the aim of creating mutual understanding between itself and its publics.

8 ▷ DESCRIBE DIFFERENT PUBLIC RELATIONS OBJECTIVES AND EXPLAIN HOW TO PLAN FOR THEM

Public relations increases a company's profile by presenting a recognisable image with which its publics can identify. The main goal of public relations is persuasion. Public relations practitioners have three main objectives: to maintain favourable opinions; to create opinion where none exists; and to neutralise hostile opinion. Effective objectives work together to gain public acceptance of the organisation's presence, image, products and services.

9 ▷ DISCUSS THE ROLE OF MEDIA RELEASES, NEWS CONFERENCES AND SPECIAL EVENTS IN PRESENTING A POSITIVE IMAGE

The media release and the special event bring an organisation to the notice of its publics. A media release is free and provides an organisation with the opportunity to give positive information to its publics. News conferences allow for wide dissemination of information. An effective special event generates publicity and builds public goodwill.

10 ▷ OUTLINE THE STEPS IN THE STRATEGIC MANAGEMENT OF PUBLIC RELATIONS ISSUES

The seven steps in the strategic management of public relations issues are: build a stable, long-term relationship; research to identify and segment the publics; anticipate issues and manage the organisation's response to them; develop objectives; plan formal programs and campaigns; implement the programs and campaigns; and evaluate the effectiveness of the programs in meeting objectives.

KEY TERMS

ACTIVITIES AND QUESTIONS

1. Work in small groups to workshop your responses to the following challenges. Present your responses as summary points that you could use in a newsletter to staff.
   - working in a manner that supports an organisation's vision, service strategy and systems
   - communicating effectively with clients
   - building customer satisfaction models
   - measuring customer satisfaction.

2. Develop a presentation to your senior manager who is undertaking a fact-finding exercise about the level of client service in the organisation. She has asked you to include your answers to the following:
   a. How can an organisation determine and exceed the expected level of service?
   b. What types of individual and organisational behaviours contribute to a positive customer experience?
   c. What techniques can an organisation use to measure customer satisfaction?

3. An organisation communicates its policies internally and externally. Give examples of ways in which this happens.

4. Kilborn (2003) states that estimates have shown that up to 80% of companies have failed to make customer relations management (CRM) work. What reasons does he advance to explain this failure?

5. a. What opportunities does the Internet provide for companies to optimise customer experience?
   b. Outline customer services strategies that companies could use to complement their online customer service.

6. Working in small groups, assume you work for a large organisation in an industry of your choice.
   a. Design a customer complaints-handling policy for the organisation.
   b. Compare it with the actual customer complaints-handling policy for a similar organisation.

7. a. In small groups, discuss the public relations goals of the organisation for which you work or in which you study.
   b. Identify the groups who make up that organisation's publics.
   c. Name one company you consider has a positive public relations image and discuss the factors that contribute to that positive image.

8. In recent times, communities have attached growing importance to respect for the environment. In small groups, discuss the evidence you have of this concern in public relations programs.

9. Read the following quote from the *Sydney Morning Herald* and then briefly explain three features of good public relations.

   In fact, everyone and every organisation has 'public relations'. It is never a question of whether you have it, the question is only if your Public Relations is good or bad.

10. Find three media releases issued by different organisations. Draft a skills checklist of ten or more elements of a good media release, as outlined in this chapter. Evaluate the media releases according to the checklist and determine a final score for each. Then, ignoring the scores, which one do you think is most effective and why?

EXPLORING THE WEB

1 Learn more about press releases by visiting Web Wire Press Release Format Guidelines <www.webwire.com/FormatGuidelines.asp> and the Concept Marketing Group <www.marketingsource.com/pressrelease/releaseformat.html>.

   a Why is a press release written in the third person?
   b Why are the 'Five W's' placed in the first paragraph?
   c What is meant by the 'inverted pyramid'?
   d What does the final paragraph do?
   e What are the elements of a good press release?

2 Learn how to handle customer complaints by visiting the Government of South Australia Office of Consumer and Business Affairs 'Handling Complaints' web page <www.ocba.sa.gov.au/businessadvice/customers/complaints.html>.

   a What are the characteristics of an effective complaints-handling system?
   b Prepare a set of tips for new staff titled 'How to Handle Complaints Effectively'.

3 What is involved in public relations crisis management?
   • PR Influences.com.au <www.prinfluences.com.au/> provides free articles and opinions on a variety of public relations topics.
   • Free Management Library <www.managementhelp.org/crisis/crisis.htm> has a wide range of free articles providing information on crisis management from a variety of perspectives.
   • Browse the Web to gather information and analyse how organisations are approaching current public relations crises.

PROJECT WORK

1 Assume you work for a large bank, insurance company or any organisation of your choice. The company's Client Services Manager has asked you to prepare a document titled 'Customer Relations Guidelines' for use across the company. In the document include:
   • the organisation's customer service vision and a description of how to deliver the service or product and build relationships with the customer
   • a description of the essential components of the customer experience the organisation wants to deliver to the customer
   • how the customer service strategy, systems and staff focus on the delivery of quality customer service
   • how to handle customer complaints.

2 Assume the Client Services Manager has approved your guidelines and now asks you to collaborate with him and the Human Resources Manager to prepare an internal public relations program designed to influence staff to implement the new customer relations guidelines in a timely and effective manner.

   Prepare the public relations plan. Ensure it is designed to achieve mutual understanding of the guidelines and acceptance of them by the organisation's internal publics. Your public relations plan should contain clear objectives with practical strategies that will support implementation of the plan.

BIBLIOGRAPHY

Albrecht, K. 1992. *Customer Service: The Only Thing That Matters*, Harper & Row, USA.

Allert, J. & Zawawi, C. 2000. 'Strategy, planning and scheduling', in Jane Johnston & Clara Zawawi (eds), *Public Relations: Theory and Practice*, Allen & Unwin, Sydney.

Anderson, K. & Kerr, C. 2002. *Customer Relationship Management*, McGraw-Hill, USA.

Babin, L.A., Babin, B.J. & Boles, J.S. 1999. 'The effects of consumer perceptions of the salesperson, product and dealer on purchase intentions', *Journal of*

Retailing and Consumer Services, Vol. 6, Issue 2, April, pp. 91–97.

Band, W. 2006. *Trends 2006: Customer Relationship Management*, Forrester.

Baskin, O., Aronoff, C. & Lattimore, D. 1997. *Public Relations: The Profession and the Practice*, Brown & Benchmark Publishers, USA.

Beder, S. 1999. 'Public participation or public relations?', in B. Martin (ed.), *Technology and Public Participation*, Science and Technology Studies, University of Wollongong, Wollongong, pp. 169–92.

Bivins, T. 2005. *Public Relations Writing: The Essentials of Style and Format*, 5th edn, McGraw-Hill, New York.

Bovee, C.L. & Thill, J.V. 2005. *Business Communication Today*, 8th edn, Pearson Prentice Hall, Pearson Education International, USA.

Carlzon, J. 1987. *Moments of Truth*, Harper & Row, Australia.

Chisholm, J. 1998. 'Using the Internet to measure customer satisfaction and loyalty', in R. Zemke & J.A. Woods (eds), *Best Practices in Customer Service*, HRD Press, Amherst, USA.

Concept Marketing Group. 'Press release example and template', www.marketingsource.com/, viewed 1 January 2008.

Customer Relations Management (CRM) in Europe 2001, 2003. Paul Budde Communication Pty Ltd.

Deming, W.E. 1982. *Out of the Crisis*, Cambridge University Press, Cambridge, Massachusetts.

Denham, J. 1998. *Handling Customer Complaints*, Prentice Hall Australia, Sydney.

Fairhurst, G.T. 'Echoes of the vision: when the rest of the organisation talks total quality', *Management Communication Quarterly*, Vol. 6, pp. 333–71.

Fletcher, R. & Brown, L. 2008. *International Marketing: An Asia-Pacific Perspective*, 4th edn, Pearson Education Australia, Sydney.

Gamlen, J. 2003. 'A customer relationship management architecture is the key to eGovernment', *eGov monitor Weekly*, 12 May, wwwegovmonitor.com, viewed 10 July 2003.

Get the Word Out. www.getthewordout.com.au/, viewed 10 July 2003.

Goodman, J. 1998. 'Quantifying the impact of great customer service on profitability', in R. Zemke & J.A. Woods (eds), *Best Practices in Customer Service*, HRD Press, Amherst, USA.

Government of South Australia Office of Consumer and Business Affairs, *Handling Complaints*, www.ocba.sa.gov.au/, last modified 29 November 2007, viewed 1 January 2008.

Gronroos, C. 2007. *Service Management and Marketing: Customer Management in Service Competition*, 3rd edn, John Wiley & Sons, England.

Grunig, J. & Hunt, T. 1984. *Managing Public Relations*, Holt, Rinehart & Winston, USA.

Guth, D.W. & Marsh, C. 2006. *Public Relations: A Values-driven Approach*, 3rd edn, Pearson/Allyn & Bacon, Boston.

Harrison, C. 'Last impressions', *Customer Service Newsletter*, August 2001, www.craigspeaks.com/last_impressions.htm, viewed 9 July 2003.

Harrison, C. 'The voice of customer service', *Customer Service Newsletter*, March 2002, www.craigspeaks.com/voice_of_customer_service.htm, viewed 9 July 2003.

Haswell, R. 'Viewpoint: asking for feedback is just the beginning', *Customer Support Magazine*, January 2001, www.CustomerSat.com, viewed 20 February 2001.

Hendrix, J.A. 2007. *Public Relations Cases*, 7th edn, Wadsworth, Belmont, California.

Hunt, T. & Grunig, J.E. 1994. *Public Relations Techniques*, Harcourt Brace College Publishers, USA.

Jahansoozi, J. 2006. 'Organisation–stakeholder relationship: exploring trust and transparency', *Journal of Management Development*, Vol. 25, Issue 10, pp. 942–55.

Jefkins, F. 1994. *Public Relations Techniques*, 2nd edn, Butterworth Heinemann, Oxford, England.

Johnston, J. 2000. 'Media relations', in J. Johnston & C. Zawawi (eds), *Public Relations: Theory and Practice*, Allen & Unwin, Sydney.

Kilborn, R. 2003. 'Off the shelf or made to measure', *Management Today*, January/February, pp. 38–39.

Kotelnikov, V. *Quality Management a Pre-requisite for Market Success*, www.100ventures.com/, viewed 14 February 2008.

Lei, D. & Greer, C. 'The empathetic organization', *Organizational Dynamics*, Vol. 32, Issue 2, pp. 14–65.

Lovelock, C. & Wirtz, J. 2006. *Services Marketing*, 6th edn, Prentice Hall, USA.

McKenna, E. 2001. 'Over 281 million served: agencies begin to adopt a business approach to customer relationship management', *Federal Computer Week*, 14 May, www.fcw.com/fcw/articles/2001/0514/tec-crm-05-14-01.asp, viewed 10 July 2003.

Macnamara, J.R. 1996. *How to Handle the Media*, Prentice Hall Australia, Sydney.

Maitland, I. 1999. *Perfect PR*, International Thomson Business Press, London.

'Multi-channel CRM—hype or reality?', *CRM Forum*, 27 February 2003, http://222.egov.vic.au, viewed 10 July 2003.

Papassapa, R. & Miller, K.E. 2007. 'Relationship quality as a predictor of B2B quality', *Journal of Business Research*, Vol. 60, pp. 21–31.

Pearson, C.M. & Clair, J.A. 'Reframing crisis management', *Academy of Management Review*, Vol. 23, pp. 59–76.

Reh, F.J. 'Good customer service is no longer enough', *Management*, http://management.about.com/library/weekly/aa042699.htm, viewed 9 July 2003.

Robbins, S.P., Bergman, R., Stagg, I. & Coulter, M. 2006. *Management*, 4th edn, Pearson Education Australia, Sydney.

Rosen, J. 1997. 'Customer complaints', in S.A. Brown (ed.), *Breakthrough Customer Service*, John Wiley & Sons, Canada.

Smith, S. 1998. 'How to create a plan to deliver great customer service', in R. Zemke & J.A. Woods (eds), *Best Practices in Customer Service*, HRD Press, Amherst, USA.

Springston, J.K. 2001. 'Public relations and new media technology: the impact of the internet', in R.L. Heath (ed.), *Handbook of Public Relations*, Sage Publications, California.

Standards Australia. *Complaints Handling*, Australian Standard AS4269-1995.

Stewart, M. 1996. *Keep the Right Customers: The Key Steps to Profitable Customer Retention*, McGraw-Hill, Berkshire, England.

Swartzlander, A. 2004. *Serving Internal and External Customers*, Prentice Hall, Upper Saddle River, New Jersey.

'The lowdown on CRM', *Government Computer News/CGN.com*, Vol. 21, Issue 29, 23 September 2002, www.gcm.com/21_29/buyers_guide/20063-1.htm, viewed 10 July 2003.

Thompson, H. 2004. *Who Stole My Customer? Winning Strategies for Creating and Sustaining Customer Loyalty*, Pearson Prentice Hall, Upper Saddle River, New Jersey.

Thorne, K. 2005. 'Designing virtual organizations? Themes and trends in political and organizational discourses', *Journal of Management Development*, Vol. 24, Issues 7/8, pp. 580–608.

Timm, P.R. 2007. *Customer Service: Career Success Through Customer Loyalty*, 4th revised edn, Pearson Education, Upper Saddle River, New Jersey.

TMCNET, 'Forrester sees Three Drivers to CRM Growth in 2006', www.tmcnet.com/, 3 March 2006, viewed 4 January 2007.

Turner, L.W. & Reisinger, Y. 2001. 'Shopping satisfaction for domestic tourists', *Journal of Retailing and Consumer Services*, Vol. 8, Issue 1, January, pp. 15–27.

Upton, M. 2001. 'Not by CRM alone: mind-set required for customer centricity', *CIO.com*, eBusiness Trends, 29 November, http://subscribe.CIO.com/, viewed 10 July 2003.

Warner, J. 2002. *Customer Service Commitment Profile*, HRD Press Inc., USA.

WebWire, 'Press release format guidelines', www.webwire.com/, viewed 1 January 2008.

Welch, T. & Rothberg, E.H. 2006. 'Transparency: panacea or Pandora's box?', *Journal of Management Development*, Vol. 25, Issue 10, pp. 937–41.

Wilkerson, D. 1997. 'Measuring customer satisfaction effectively', in S.A. Brown (ed.), *Breakthrough Customer Service*, John Wiley & Sons, Canada.

Zeithmal, V.R. & Parasuram, A. 2004. *Service Quality*, Marketing Science Institute, USA.

Part 3

Leading and Managing People

8

Communication across the organisation

Photo: Lisa Gagne

LEARNING OBJECTIVES

After studying this chapter you should be able to:

1 ▷ describe how culture is created within and communicated across an organisation

2 ▷ discuss the role of organisational communication

3 ▷ describe formal and informal communication channels

4 ▷ differentiate organisational structures and explain the impact of different structures on organisational and interpersonal interactions

5 ▷ understand the advantages and disadvantages of an informal organisational structure

6 ▷ describe the patterns of interaction in small group networks

7 ▷ discuss strategies that can improve organisational communication.

VIEWPOINT: RELATIONSHIPS RULE AS COMPANIES MAKE SLOGANS REAL

Corporate vision statements, clear articulation of a company's values and development of a strong corporate culture are becoming more common as companies realise work gets done through effective relationships. Alignment of jobs with company goals and an appealing organisational culture supports the development of fully functioning effective relationships and helps to attract and retain talented staff. In an organisation with a strong culture the Chief Executive, key employees and direct reports all embody the organisation's values.

Companies with a strong corporate culture include 'Fedex . . . known for absolutely, positively doing whatever it takes, Lexus for the pursuit of perfection, Apple for innovation and design, PepsiCo for appealing to the younger generation and Wal-Mart for always low prices'. Marianne Broadbent, Managing Director of Edward W. Kelley & Partners, comments: 'Having values which no one actually practices can be very damaging . . . If they're not evident among the senior executive team then people see it as very hypocritical, something they are just paying lip service to.'

Adapted from K. Nicholas, 'Relationships rule as companies make slogans real', *Australian Financial Review*, 7 February 2008. pp. S12–13.

An insight into how communication happens across an organisation may be gained by identifying organisational, individual and cultural factors that are favourable or unfavourable to communication flows in the organisation. How do present organisational characteristics shape the organisation's operations and performance, the behaviour of people and the flow of communication? When analysing an organisation's structure and communication flows the following questions need to be answered.

- How many divisions, departments or sections are there?
- How specialised is work carried out in each area?
- What is the degree of formality or informality within the organisation?
- To what extent do people conform to rules and regulations?
- What is the formality of communication flows?
- How free are people to make decisions?

The answers to these questions give an indication of structure and culture. A company can attempt to improve the effectiveness of communication between individuals and sections within the company, and with others outside the organisation, either by developing better communication methods within the existing organisational structure or by changing the organisational structure and culture.

ORGANISATIONAL CULTURE

OBJECTIVE **1** ▶
Describe how culture is created within and communicated across an organisation

An organisation's culture is the common understanding among members as to what the organisation is and how its members should behave. Bartol and colleagues (2008, p. 76) define **organisational culture** as a 'system of shared values, assumptions, beliefs and norms uniting members of an organisation'. Organisational cultures vary, and analysis of the culture gives an insight into the impact these factors have on the ability of staff to respond and communicate. Answers to the following questions give some understanding of an organisation's culture and its similarities to, and differences from, other organisations.

An **organisation's culture** is a pattern of shared assumptions and beliefs; members learn about appropriate behaviours and share them with new members.

- How do leaders and managers communicate with and support their team members?
- What value is placed on individual initiative?
- Does management take into account the impact of decisions and outcomes on people in the organisation?
- How are new ideas encouraged?
- Does the organisation tolerate and reward innovation and risk, or does it enforce the status quo?
- How are rules and regulations used to control employee behaviour?
- Are work activities organised around teams rather than individuals?

Robbins and colleagues (2008, p. 584) discuss three ways in which culture is created. 'First, founders hire and keep only employees who think and feel the same way they do. Second, they indoctrinate and socialise these employees to their way of thinking and feeling. And, finally, the founders' own behaviour acts as a role model that encourages employees to identify with them and thereby internalise their beliefs, values and assumptions.' An established culture is sustained through selection practices, the actions of top management, socialisation and communication.

Communicating culture

Learning about an organisation's culture is reinforced through stories, rituals and language shared in meetings, company newsletters, on intranets, in blogs and podcasts, and even in national newspapers.

Culture is communicated and learned through stories, material symbols, language and rituals. Stories about an organisation's beginnings, history, rule-breaking, successes and mistakes are embedded in its culture. Robbins and colleagues (2008, p. 589) state: 'These stories anchor the present in the past and provide explanations and legitimacy for current practices.' As an organisation's culture and behaviours change, new stories are created and told and retold. Stories and myths form images of an organisation that help to shape its culture, communicate its values and encourage people to behave appropriately in the future.

Unique terms and ways of using words occur in all occupations and organisations. Accounting and other professions abound with acronyms: for example, BAS (Business Activity Statement), ASIC (Australian Securities and Investments Commission) and ASX (Australian Securities Exchange). Those using the technical language, jargon and acronyms are identified with the culture of the organisation and the profession. The language creates a common understanding.

Observable material symbols include the layout of buildings, size of offices, dress codes, travel by air, chauffeur-driven vehicles and other tangible symbols of power, importance and culture.

Rituals are standardised techniques and behaviours common to a group or an organisation. The Australian Apprenticeship System is an example of a ritual followed as part of the culture of employment for qualified tradespersons. The person is initiated into the trade as an indentured apprentice to an employer with the relevant trade qualification and experience. The apprentice works in the trade a certain number of days per week and is released to study for the required hours in a Registered Training Organisation over the required number of years. On completion of the apprenticeship requirements the person achieves a Trade Licence and is able to gain employment as a fully qualified tradesperson. Other examples of rituals are specific organisational promotion, assessment and reward systems.

By developing and communicating new stories, changing material symbols and varying routines and rituals, an organisation can change its culture.

REVIEW QUESTIONS

1. Define the term 'organisational culture'. Give examples of how culture is communicated.
2. Why do cultures vary between organisations?
3. *a* Give an example of an Australian sporting ritual and a business ritual.
   b What is the purpose of rituals?

WHAT DOES ORGANISATIONAL COMMUNICATION DO?

Communication takes place within an organisation for a number of direct and indirect reasons. Primarily, it is necessary for passing information between people working in the same company and between the company and other organisations. However, communication—written, oral and even nonverbal—is also used by management to direct and motivate employees, evaluate their performance and to manage and share knowledge.

Development of theories

While early organisational theorists such as Taylor (1911) and Weber (1947) suggested that communication systems in organisations were used for the exercise of authority, coordination and control, these early theories did not take into account the human relations aspects in organisations. The emphasis was on organisational structure and individual behaviour, supported by formal, hierarchical and planned communication. The communication purpose was task-oriented, to increase production and efficiency. The emphasis was on communication as a tool, used to achieve work efficiencies within a static and closed system, rather than on how people communicate in an organisation.

Since the early 20th century, 'behaviourists'—a group of psychologists and sociologists—have been researching human behaviour in organisations. The 'human relations movement' gained notice in the 1930s. Maslow (1954), McGregor (1960) and others took into account the human relations aspects and attempted to explain how and why individuals in organisations behave as they do.

The knowledge management scholars Drucker (1973), Lave and Wegner (1991), Schank and Abelson (1977) and others have been researching the impact of the rapid developments in information and communications technology on work. The evolving knowledge economy is changing how people

◄ OBJECTIVE 2
Discuss the role of organisational communication

Communication can control and motivate those working in an organisation.

Good organisational communication achieves understanding that balances the needs of the individual and the organisation.

work and how organisations are valued. The communication purpose is knowledge-oriented: to increase knowledge acquisition, applications and services. The emphasis is on communication as a tool to achieve strategy, capture and utilise knowledge, support collaborative and cross-functional teams, and facilitate effective problem solving and decision making.

Purposes of workplace communication

Four communication purposes are described in Table 8.1. The difficulty for management is finding a balance between control, motivation, efficiency and effectiveness. Too much control may reduce initiative and lead to lower productivity, with less response to what customers want and more emphasis on what employees think management wants.

People have a need, in varying degrees, for achievement at work, power and a sense of belonging to the organisation. Acknowledgment and feedback to individuals and groups on their achievements leads to increased job satisfaction and improved performance. When understanding between employer and employee is achieved and the needs and goals of both are compatible, the behaviour required at work to achieve the organisation's goals is satisfying to the employee. The possible differences between the needs of the organisation and the individual are highlighted in Table 8.2.

Leaders and managers need to convey their point of view to employees, and employees must persuade leaders and managers to appreciate their point of view. For all these reasons, business organisations need effective communication channels. Slow, inefficient lines of communication may mean dissatisfied customers and demoralised employees.

In Chapter 1, 'Communication in Business', each variable in the communication process is outlined. In this chapter, it is important to identify the direction of communication flow (channels) in an organisation before discussing the characteristics of an organisation's structure and some of the communication problems that can arise within an organisation.

Table 8.1: Purpose of communication in the workplace	
Purpose	**Description**
Control	• Communication can be used by an organisation's management to monitor performance in relation to company objectives, directives or work procedures. • For this purpose, management may use employee assessment schemes, manuals of work procedures or company plans that set targets for each section.
Motivate	• An organisation's management, including supervisors of small groups, can use communication to motivate employees. • Acknowledgment can involve verbal praise, letters or memorandums that keep people in the organisation feeling that they are an important part of it and that what they do is appreciated.
Balance needs and goals	• The interests and expectations of the organisation, and the goals and needs of people working there, need to be balanced. • To achieve this balance, both employer and employee need to understand one another: good communication is therefore essential.
Manage knowledge	• The explicit known and retrievable knowledge is shared via policies, procedures and processes. • Tacit knowledge embedded in an organisation's culture can be difficult to communicate because it is the 'know-how' held by experienced individuals. • Communication within the organisation has an important role to play in sharing 'know-how' about customer expectations, sales trends, production methods and strategic directions.

Table 8.2: Organisational and individual goals

Organisational goals	Individual or group goals
Profit	Good pay
Return on investment	Job security
Employee efficiency	Fringe benefits
Control of work	Self-direction
Production of quality goods and services	Scope for intiative and achievement
Competitiveness	Challenge
Low absenteeism and low employee turnover	Satisfaction
Ability to access capable, skilled people	Acknowledgment of work

REVIEW QUESTIONS

4. Discuss three purposes of communication in an organisation.
5. What is the purpose of communication in a knowledge economy?
6. Identify the possible differences between the needs of the organisation and the needs of the individual.

ORGANISATIONAL COMMUNICATION CHANNELS

◄ OBJECTIVE 3
Describe formal and informal communication channels

There is much evidence to show that the way a business is structured can have a major impact on how communication takes place and on its effectiveness. It is useful, therefore, to look at the business environment in general and then at specific organisational communication channels.

Formal communication channels

All organisations set up their own formal or approved channels whereby employees communicate with one another. Any communication is at least two-way. In an organisation there is a multiplicity of ways in which communication can take place.

Formal communication channels convey official, approved information.

Downward communication takes place when a message is sent from the top down to a lower level of an organisation—for example, organisation policies, procedures and practices. Upward communication flows from the lower levels of an organisation to the higher decision-making ones. In some organisations there is a tendency for supervisors to filter or even stop upward information, particularly bad news. Lateral or horizontal communication refers to communication at the same or similar level within an organisation—for example, the marketing, production and distribution divisions. Diagonal communication occurs between the lower level of an organisation and a higher level in a flow between different departments or divisions. The purpose and examples of each are set out in Table 8.3.

The four formal communication channels are upward, downward, lateral and diagonal.

Robbins and colleagues (2008) pose the question: 'Why would there be a need for horizontal communications if a group or organisation's vertical communications are effective?' (p. 366). In their view the role of horizontal communication is to save time, facilitate coordination and expedite action. Horizontal communication channels are often created to short-circuit the hierarchy imposed by vertical channels. Lateral communication, as far as management is concerned, can be either positive or negative. It can be beneficial if strict adherence to the formal vertical structure impedes the transfer of information, but

Table 8.3: Communication flows in formal channels

Flow	Purpose	Examples
Downward channels	<ul><li>Information communicated downwards may change if say, a large document needs to be simplified, or at the discretion of supervisors who withhold what they see as unnecessary information.</li><li>Information may increase on the path down an organisation as supervisors feel the need to add to it so that it is more relevant to their section.</li><li>The message may be distorted or lose its original intention.</li></ul>	Instructions, guidelines or feedback to managers and staff at the lower levels of the organisation in the form of policy statements, meetings, intranet messages or face-to-face meetings.
Upward channels	<ul><li>Can be difficult to achieve successfully; often impeded by the egos of supervisors, a lack of incentive to put forward ideas, poor responses to previous upward communication.</li><li>Managers may feel upward communication challenges their authority.</li></ul>	Production reports, financial information, complaints, ideas for improvements, in the form of one-on-one meetings or suggestion systems.
Lateral or horizontal channels	<ul><li>Often involves open conflict as different divisions battle for a share of the organisation's resources or the CEO's attention.</li><li>Modern organisational structures, such as project and team-based structures, are set up with formal horizontal communication channels.</li></ul>	Highly organised in the form of regular meetings between sections heads, newsletters and standard forms. May also be irregular such as formal letters of complaint or telephone calls.
Diagonal channels	<ul><li>A head of a division may agree with a lower-level supervisor of another division on a matter that will then be put to the supervisor's own Head of Division.</li><li>Informing the relevant supervisor of your actions or obtaining permission can avoid possible barriers to effective communication.</li><li>Management may try to stop the diagonal direction of communication because it threatens control.</li><li>In most organisations informal communication develops to speed up decisions.</li></ul>	Relates to coordination of tasks:<ul><li>information sharing and</li><li>managing conflict in the form of face-to-face meetings, task forces, committees, telephone conversations.</li></ul>

it 'can create dysfunctional conflicts when the formal vertical channels are breached, when members go above or around their managers to get things done, or when bosses find out that actions have been taken or decisions made without their knowledge' (Robbins et al. 2008, pp. 366–7).

Figure 8.3 (page 226), showing the pyramid organisation structure, indicates how each of these four directions of communication flow in a tall, formal organisational structure.

PROBLEMS ARISING FROM FORMAL ORGANISATIONAL COMMUNICATION

When a company or government department starts to get into trouble, whether from a failure to sell its product, industrial disputes or something else, the idea that the root of the problem may be a failure in communication is often the last area to be examined, if at all. Yet, usually, the communication aspect of the situation should be the first to be examined. Poor organisational communication has the potential to cripple a company; at the very least it can mean that productivity and performance are way below what they could be. The following three features can cause communication problems or barriers in an organisation:

Good formal organisational communication improves productivity and performance.

1. Management is too centralised.
2. There are too many management layers.
3. The organisation structure is too complex.

A company with a centralised and very hierarchical management structure may appear to provide its leaders with control and thus the ability to get everyone in the organisation to follow standard procedures and work patterns. However, the more supervisors a company has, the greater the possibility that messages from the top will be distorted, ignored or misunderstood on the way down.

The more layers of management, the greater the time spent in formal communication. This may mean a lot of time on the part of the decision maker and a lot of paper floating around the system. The more formal and structured the organisation, the greater the chance that informal ways around the paperwork will develop. This can be a problem. The more centralised the control within an organisation, the more sections within it that are far from the centre, both geographically or in terms of power and influence. Employees are not aware of what is going on, and central management really knows very little about the activities of the outlying sections.

Communication in a business costs time and money, yet many companies and government departments do not have a clear policy on it or regular evaluation of the level and nature of communication within their organisation.

> The more complex the organisation, the more complex the communication within it and the greater the opportunity for communication barriers to develop.

Informal communication networks

Apart from formally established lines of communication, there are **informal networks**. The informal structure in an organisation is composed of the links between individuals and whole sections of a company that bypass the formal structures in the decision-making processes. Informal means of communication include telephone conversations between managers that smooth the way for a committee decision, and other quick ways of passing work from one section to another. Whatever form it takes, the informal contact between employees in an organisation can be as important as the formal links.

Informal communication networks may flow in several directions within the organisation. Four examples of these networks are:

> **Informal networks** are communication links between individuals and sections that bypass the formal structures in an organisation.

1. the single strand
2. the gossip chain
3. the probability chain
4. the cluster chain.

The *single strand network* consists of a long chain of people who each pass the message to the next person. It is the least frequently used method. In the *gossip chain*, one person tells all the others. This is also used infrequently. Another way of passing information is on a random basis, with one person arbitrarily telling another person who then tells one or two others. This is known as the *probability chain*. The most commonly used network is the *cluster chain*, where one person tells two or three people, who in turn keep the information to themselves or pass it on to two or three others (Figure 8.1).

THE GRAPEVINE

Within groups and departments, gossip travels along the **grapevine**. Robbins and colleagues (2008, p. 370) discuss three main characteristics of the grapevine:

> The term '**grapevine**' describes the way gossip travels through the workplace.

1. It is not controlled by management.
2. It is perceived by most employees as being more believable and reliable than formal communication from top management.
3. It serves the self-interests of those in the group.

They refer to research that found that 'only 10 per cent of the executives [in that study] . . . passed the information on to more than one other person', stating that 'this suggests that while many

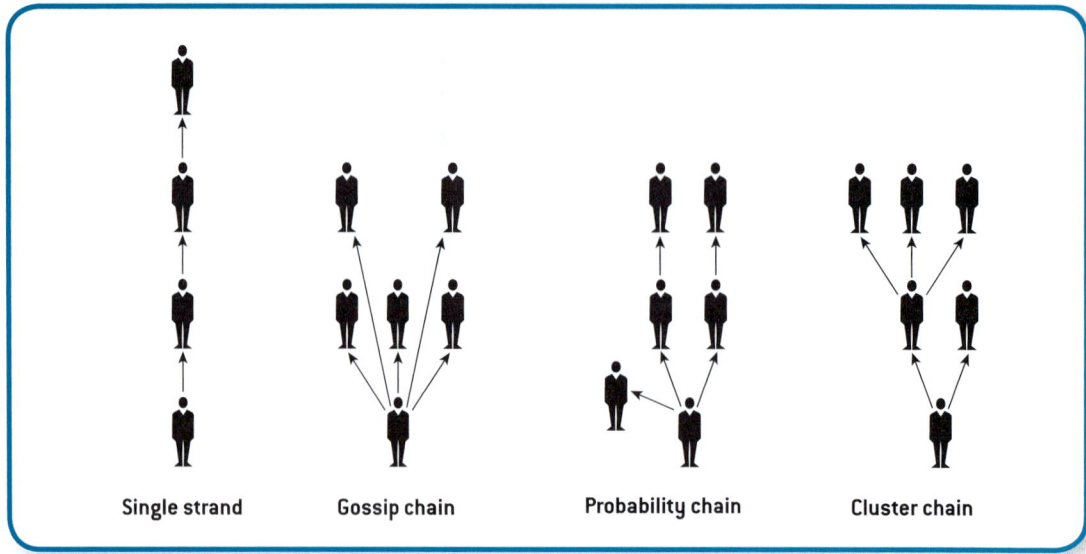

Single strand   Gossip chain   Probability chain   Cluster chain

Figure 8.1: Informal communication networks

people participate in the grapevine, only about one person in ten in an organisation is the centre of the grapevine' (2008, p. 370). They also comment that evidence indicates that about 75% of the information carried by the grapevine is accurate.

Robbins and colleagues conclude that the grapevine 'is an important part of any group or organisation communication network and is well worth understanding' (2008, p. 371). As only about 10% of people actively pass on information to a number of others, it seems possible, from a management perspective, to analyse grapevine information and predict its flow.

REVIEW QUESTIONS

7 Distinguish formal and informal communication channels. Give examples of each.
8 Discuss problems arising from formal organisational communication.
9 *a*   Define the term 'informal communication network'.
   b   Describe four types of informal networks within an organisation.
   c   Describe the characteristics of the 'grapevine'.

APPLY YOUR SKILLS

ORGANISATIONAL CULTURE AND COMMUNICATION

Work in small groups.

1   Recall a time when communication between you and another person broke down in an organisational context. Share your memory of this situation.
   a   Discuss and compare the barriers to communication in each situation.
   b   Identify where these happened—in the formal or informal organisation.
   c   Discuss the consequences of the communication failure.
   d   Suggest ways in which your communication skills could have been used more effectively.
   e   How could the organisation have promoted more effective communication?

2
a   In small groups, discuss the factors that maintain and determine an organisation's culture.
b   Describe how culture is learned and communicated across an organisation.
c   Share your findings with other groups.

3
a   In small groups, contrast the sort of information and knowledge that is communicated through vertical and horizontal channels of communication.
b   Give examples of the types of communication used in vertical channels (e.g. conversation, written reports) and horizontal channels of communication.

4   In large groups, conduct a brainstorming session to create as many examples as possible of the types of communication used in vertical, horizontal, lateral and diagonal channels of communication.

FORMAL ORGANISATIONAL STRUCTURES

While it is not the purpose of this book to examine the impact of an organisation's structure on its overall effectiveness, the structure does have a major effect on the communication that takes place and so it warrants consideration here.

An **organisation's structure** is the way in which different groups are linked together to get the job done. It involves:

- reporting relationships
- range of duties
- ways decisions are made
- communication flows within the organisation.

The organisational structure shown in Figure 8.2 is an example of the specialisation of functions and the **hierarchy** that can occur within a tall, formal organisation. It shows the organisation's framework. Every organisation has its own specific structure, but it is possible to identify a number of features that enable us to classify several structures. Every organisation has formal and informal structures and communication channels. An understanding of the organisation's structure and communication flows will help you to understand how the organisation operates. It also helps in understanding the organisation's culture, climate and cohesiveness.

Characteristics of the formal organisational structure

An analysis of the way in which characteristics are combined in an organisation can help you to decide what type of organisation is operating; for example, is it a bureaucracy (see page 224), a large/small business, or an organisation with a tall/flat structure? The formal structure of an organisation is characterised by three important features, described in Table 8.4. The levels of complexity, formalisation and centralisation in an organisation, and their interaction, determine the nature of the organisation. An organisation's structure impacts on the way people interact and communicate with one another. The hierarchy, specialisation of functions and how job tasks are done varies among organisations. The greater the number of job functions and titles in an organisation, the greater the complexity. The more sections, departments or divisions in the organisation, the more complex it becomes because there is more differentiation between members' jobs and more levels between the least powerful members of staff and senior management. The two extreme structures are *tall* and *flat*.

While all organisations have a formal and an informal structure, the formal structure is deliberately developed to provide official links between people in the organisation. The better the communication, the stronger and more effective the links. An organisation's formal structure may be complex, as shown in Figure 8.3, with many departments and levels of managers in a highly structured bureaucratic system. Or the organisation may have a much simpler formal structure, such as that shown in Figure 8.4 on page 226.

◀ OBJECTIVE 4
Differentiate organisational structures and explain the impact of different structures on organisational and interpersonal interactions

Organisational structure shows the specialisation of functions.

Hierarchy is an organisational system that moves through a number of levels.

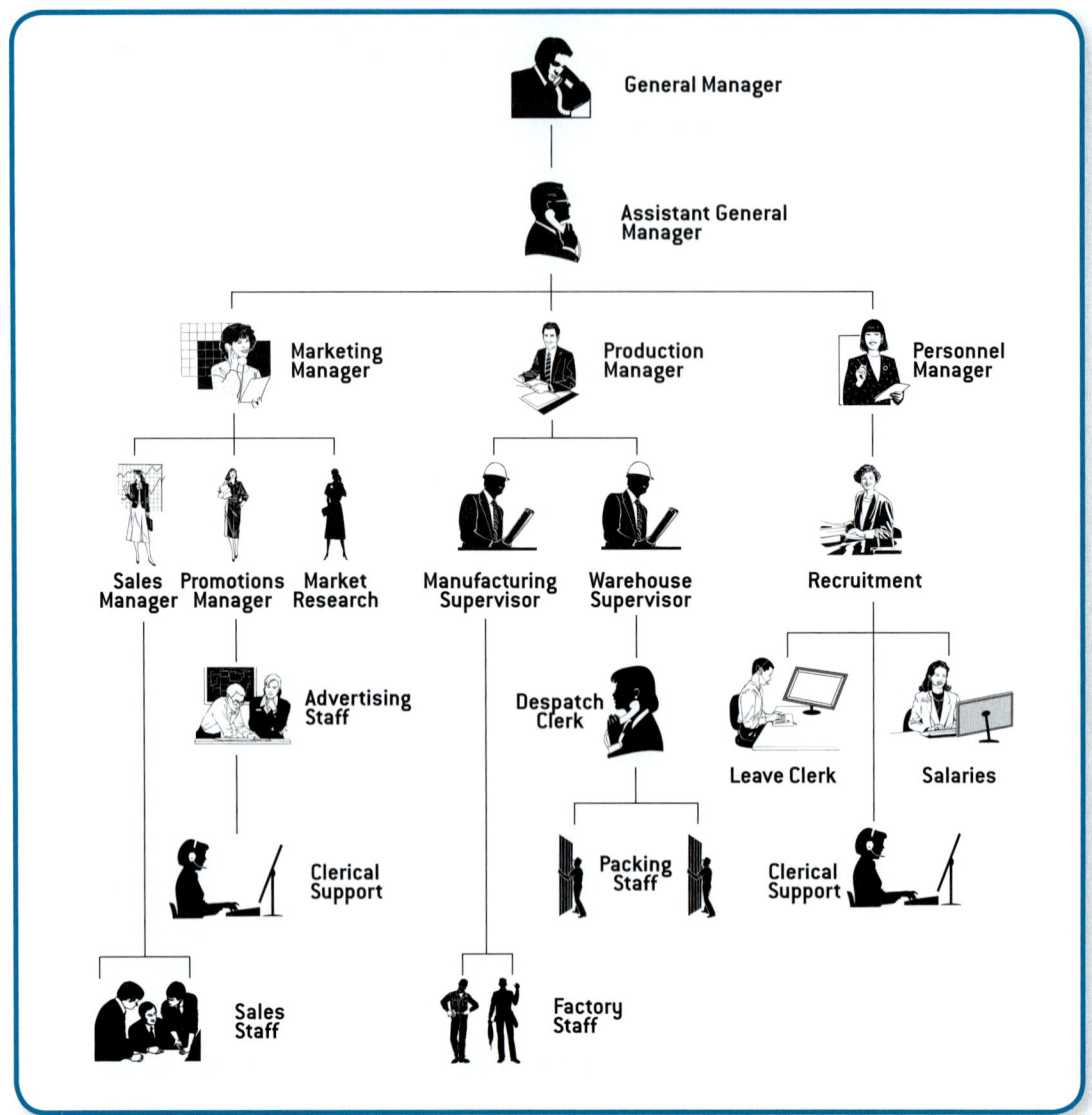

Figure 8.2: Organisation chart

Bureaucratic structure

A **bureaucracy** is a system characterised by division of labour, a clearly defined hierarchy, and detailed rules and regulations.

A **bureaucracy** has a traditional, hierarchical management system. Bureaucratic structures may be functional, divisional or a hybrid of both. Bartol and colleagues (2008, p. 350) define a functional structure as a 'type of departmentalization where positions are grouped into functional (or specialization) areas'. The organisation that combines positions on the basis of similarity of expertise, skills and work activity has a functional structure. A large global bank may design the organisation's structure around the three functions shown in Figure 8.5.

In a bureaucratic structure the organisation is complex, with many different levels of management. Formalisation is usually high, with standardisation of the job through a number of rules and regulations. Decision making is usually highly centralised, with decisions requiring the approval of senior management. This structure has been established largely because it is how managers think they can retain control over

Table 8.4: Features of an organisation

Feature	Description
Complexity is a factor of the number of sections, departments, individual job functions and titles in an organisation.	• An organisation with a tall structure is one with many different levels of management (Figure 8.3). This type of structure is often found in large public sector corporations and in some large companies that are trying to meet the demands of a very large market or public service. • Flat structures exist in organisations that have few levels of management, so that there may be only one or two decision makers to negotiate with in order to reach the managing director or boss. • The number of levels (i.e. whether the organisation is tall or flat) affects organisational communication. The effectiveness of communication will depend on how well managed the organisation is and the extent of horizontal links.
Formalisation is the existence of firmly structured lines of communication, authority and control within an organisation.	• The more an organisation determines the exact work functions of its employees, the more formalised it is. • Formalisation refers to the standardisation of the job, the number of rules and regulations, policies and procedures (written and unwritten). • How many rules and procedures have to be followed is affected by the amount of formalisation. • Low formalisation in a job means that employees have a high degree of independence and discretion in the job, and a high degree of control over their work. • High formalisation means little control or independence and, therefore, little power.
Centralisation is the process of locating all the decision making in an organisation at the highest level.	• The effectiveness of communication also depends on where the decisions are made. • Some organisations, usually those with tall structures, are highly centralised, with just about all important decisions requiring the approval of senior management. • Many junior managers are unable to make decisions, so they use email, memos, short reports or submissions to ask for a decision. • Other organisations, usually those with flat structures, are decentralised. Decisions are made at lower levels.

Complexity is a factor of the number of sections, departments, individual job functions and titles in an organisation.

Formalisation in an organisation is the existence of firmly structured lines of communication, authority and control.

Centralisation refers to the degree of decision-making power located at the highest level.

the whole organisation. The tall, formal, rigid hierarchy can lead to slow decision making and difficulties in responding to change. Figure 8.5 is an example of a bureaucratic functional structure.

Rigid procedures are used by bureaucratic organisations to ensure standardisation, meet compliance requirements and provide security, particularly those organisations with an external board of directors and shareholders. Employees communicate formally, copy colleagues in on emails, and seek back-up and reassurance for decisions and actions. Rigid bureaucracy can leave employees feeling stifled and under pressure to perform. It inhibits the flexibility and freedom to make decisions that are an integral part of knowledge and network structures.

Simple structure

A simple structure is less complex, with few levels of management (see Figure 8.4). Staff communicate directly with managers and have more autonomy than those in a bureaucratic structure. There are

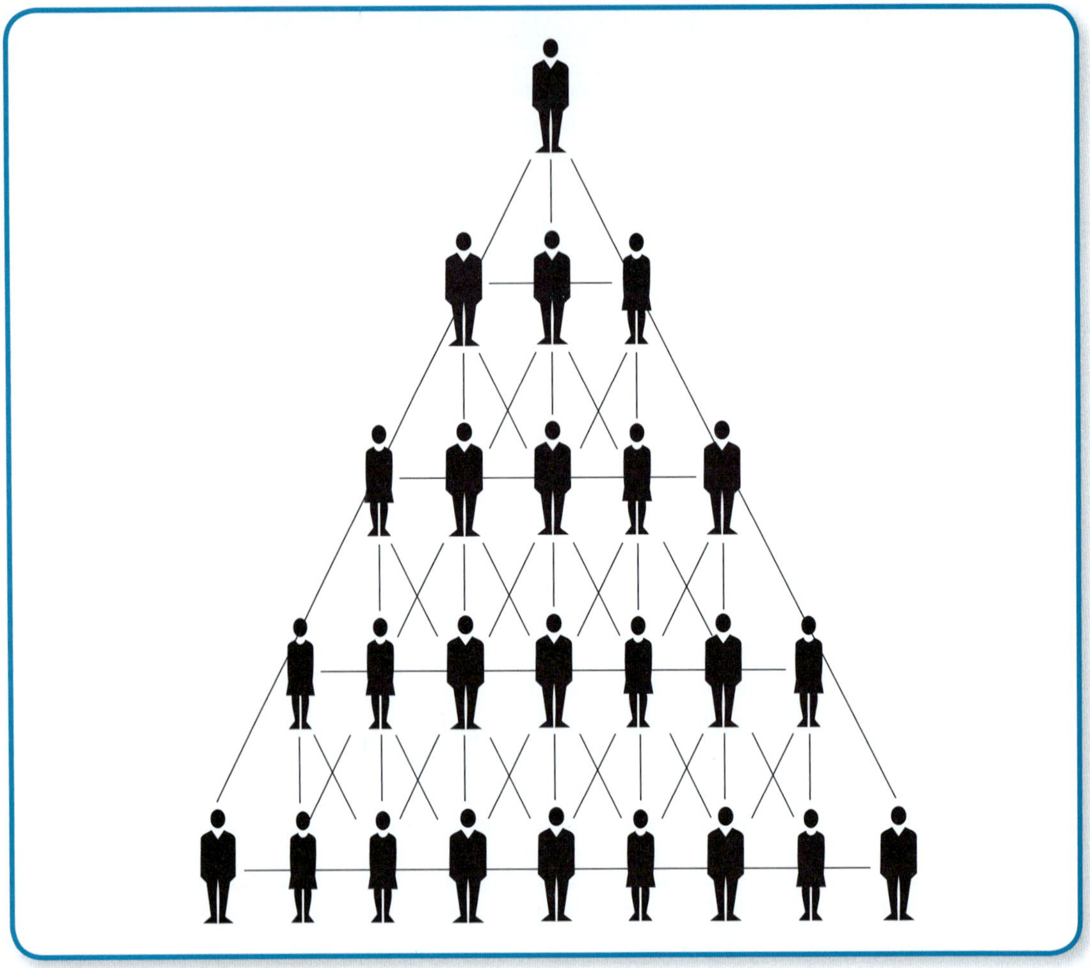

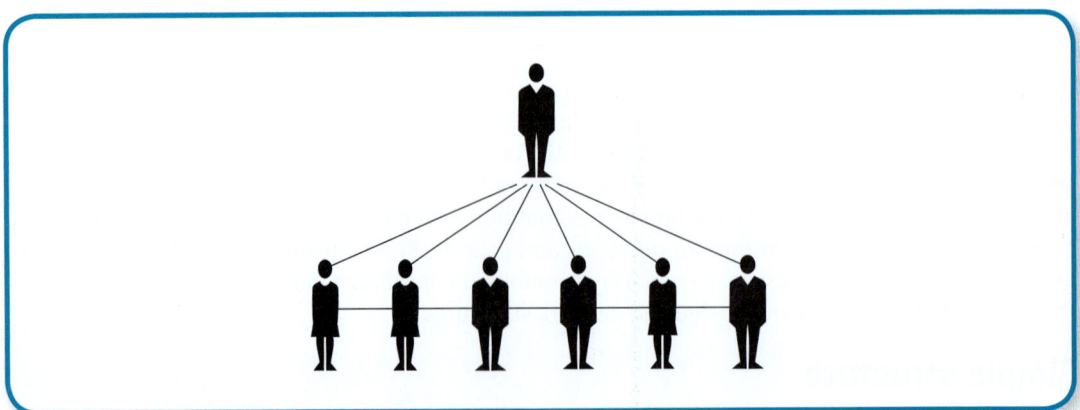

Figure 8.3: Formal, highly structured organisation

Figure 8.4: Formal, lightly structured organisation

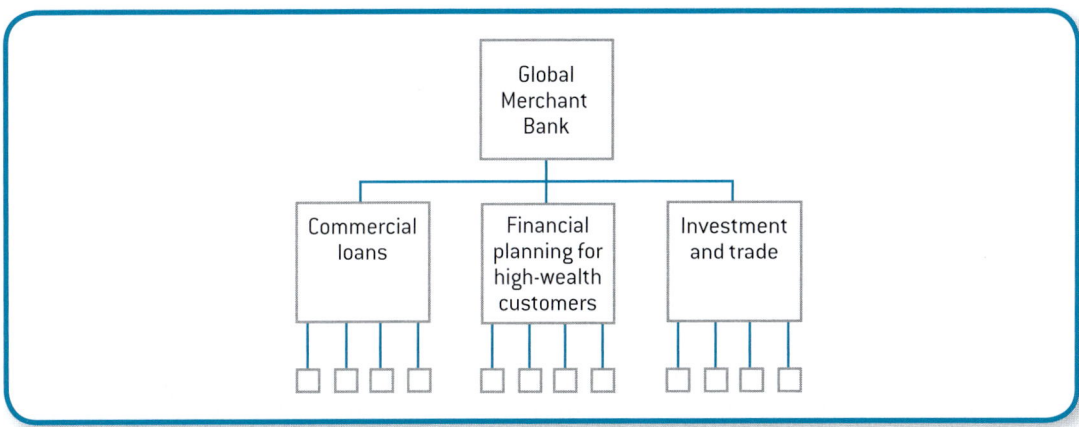

Figure 8.5: Bureaucratic functional structure

fewer decision makers to negotiate with. Employees have discretion in the job, and a high degree of independence and control over their work. Formalisation is low, and employees are given more autonomy and independence to get the job done. Power is decentralised and people are accountable. Communication channels are more informal and faster than those in a bureaucracy. Simple structures can create a less rigid and questioning environment than a bureaucratic or matrix structure.

Matrix structure

The **matrix** organisational structure links together divisions, departments, functions and people in horizontal and vertical relationships. An organisation chart for a matrix organisation reveals the vertical operational responsibilities and horizontal linkages that facilitate the coordination and smooth interaction of employees and communication systems.

A matrix structure is complex and formal but has flatter tiers than a bureaucratic structure. A matrix organisation enables quicker and more efficient decision making. It is both functional and divisional at once, with:

- one vertical command chain, and
- one horizontal command chain.

A **matrix** is a hierarchical, functional, departmentalised structure where people report through two chains of command.

The matrix structure is complex to administer because of the two chains of command. The dual authority in a matrix structure leads to centralised decision making because major decisions must be approved by functional and divisional managers. To perform well, matrix organisations need managers and staff with strong interpersonal and communication skills and the ability to:

- handle potential confusion over authority and responsibility
- participate in group problem solving and decision making
- commit to organisational goals and work in accordance with the organisation's formal rules
- negotiate conflicts caused by the need for groups to interact and report both horizontally and vertically.

A basic matrix structure is shown in Figure 8.6. The matrix structure and reporting lines are designed to focus on business functions, rather than the status of staff. The structure is a complex one in which staff report to two matrix bosses (Bartol et al. 2008, p. 359). An individual or team will have a functional reporting line and a divisional reporting line—hence, two chains of command. In Figure 8.6 the three managers—office buildings, residential complexes and hospital buildings—represent divisional units operating horizontally. The four directors—construction services, marketing, human resources and finance—represent the functional departments operating vertically.

The matrix structure leads to greater administrative complexity at lower levels. Characteristics of successful matrix organisations include a focus on both the functional and divisional dimensions, collaboration and cross-functional decision making when required, rapid coordination of resources in response to change, and the capacity to share functional resources flexibly across products, services or projects. Miner (2006, p. 240) says, 'The value of the matrix form is inherent in its potential for greater flexibility in responding to environmental pressures.'

Organisations that decide to adopt a matrix structure go through several structural changes (Davis & Lawrence 1977; Bateman & Snell 2007; Bartol et al. 2008). Stage 1 is the traditional structure, usually functional, with management and power flowing from the top down through the organisation. Stage 2 moves through a temporary overlay of positions created to manage specific projects (project managers) and to ensure collaboration with other departments and teams. Stage 3 occurs when the temporary overlay of managerial positions operates permanently. In Stage 4 the mature matrix managers have equal power. These stages are illustrated in Figure 8.7.

An organisation may choose to move to a matrix structure to give stronger project or product coordination, improved environmental monitoring or flexible use of human resources. The key to efficient decision making and performance is cooperation and communication between functional and divisional managers.

The effectiveness of a matrix structure depends on the interpersonal competence of leaders, managers and staff. Matrix structures and the organisation's culture should enable managers and teams to collaborate. With its vertical and horizontal command chains a matrix organisation requires

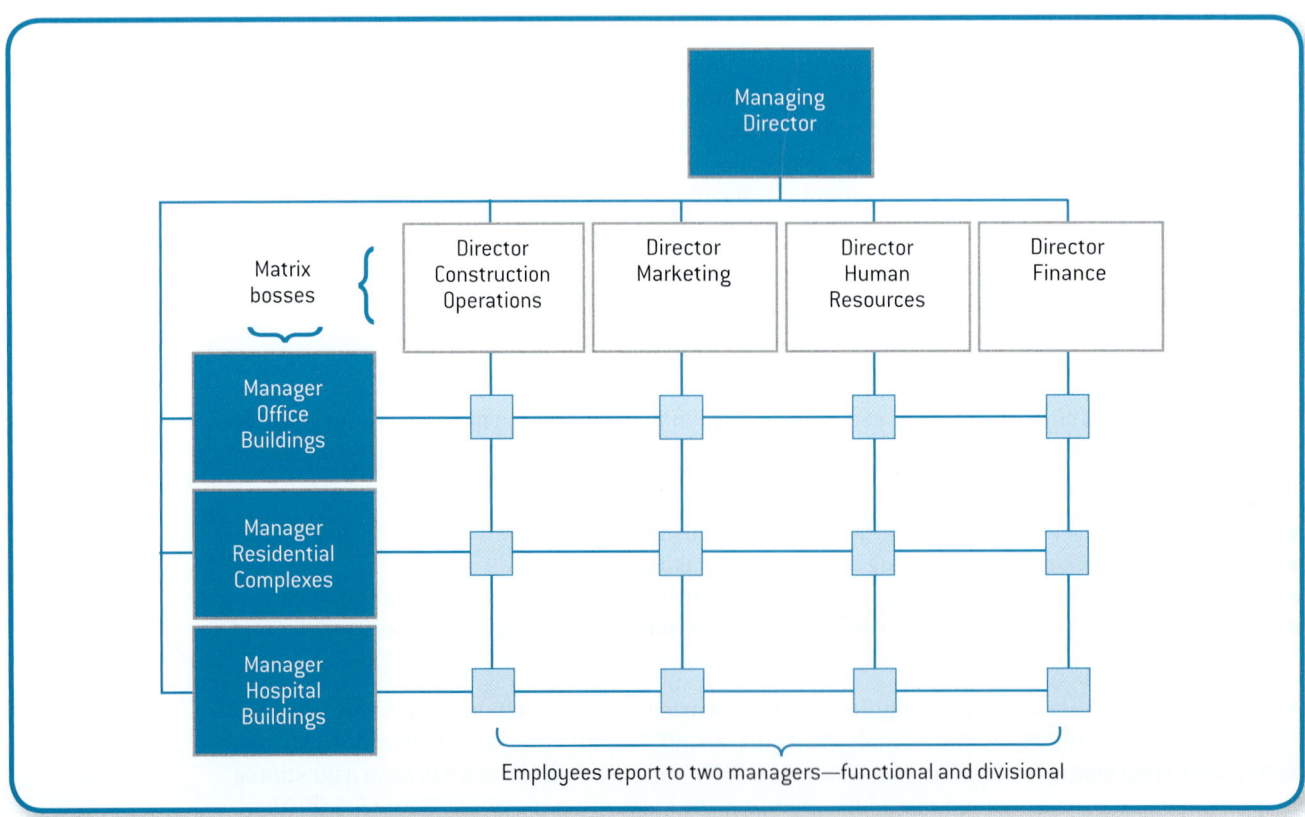

Figure 8.6: Basic matrix structure for a development and construction company

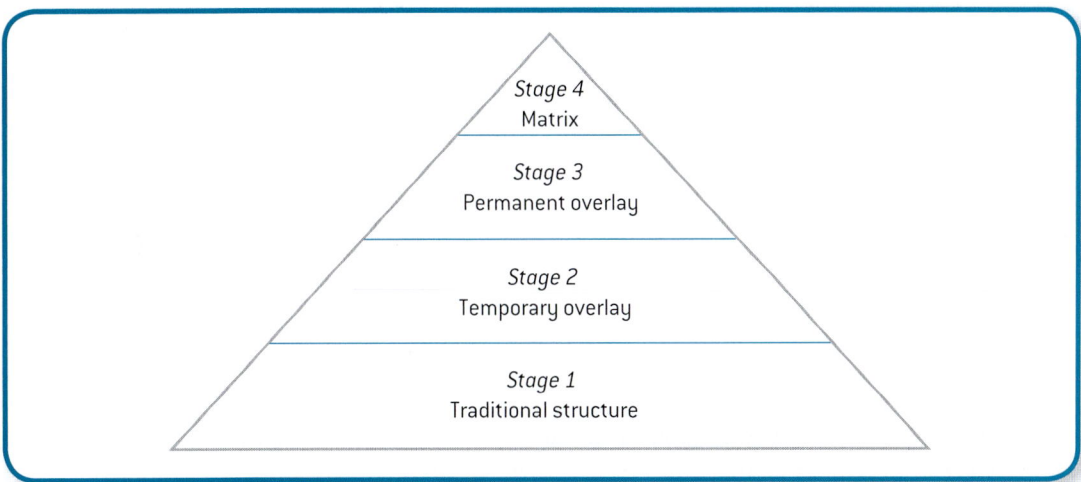

Figure 8.7: Stages of matrix development

leaders with the communication skills to motivate and influence employees to perform within the complex structure.

Evidence suggests that changes in organisational culture may be needed as the matrix structure evolves to support the increased need for collaborative decision making. Managers and their staff may need special training, especially in interpersonal skills, to be able to function effectively. A mature matrix structure is not needed by many organisations, but temporary and permanent overlay stages are quite common in the form of permanent and cross-functional teams (Bateman & Snell 2007).

Knowledge management structure

The knowledge management structure is not complex. It is usually flat, with very few levels of management and only one or two decision makers to negotiate with in order to reach the Chief Executive Officer. Low formalisation gives knowledge workers a high degree of autonomy, discretion and control over their work. Decisions are usually decentralised. Staff are able to apply their knowledge to all activities and are empowered to make decisions relating to work activities. The structure and culture support the development of informal communication networks.

The knowledge management structure enhances the flow and amount of communication. Consequently, information is transferred between people faster than in a traditional structure. Communication and the opportunity to interact with key personnel is essential in a knowledge organisation. Cross-functional and collaborative teams may operate as face-to-face or virtual teams in a knowledge organisation. Figure 8.8 shows the type of activities undertaken in a knowledge management structure.

Social networking analysis (SNA) is the mapping and measuring of relationships and flows between people and groups within an organisation. SNA is an activity that enables organisations with a knowledge management structure to identify key leaders and subject matter experts. The organisation is then able to set up mechanisms such as communities of practice to enable leaders and experts to pass on their knowledge to others.

Boundaryless structure

Boundaryless organisations are not temporary. They are long-lasting and dynamic organisations that evolve from more traditional structures in response to the pressures of emerging globalisation, strategic alliances, and technological and supply interdependence. The reduction of boundaries improves information flow, reduces response time, and facilitates problem solving and decision making

Knowledge management organisational structures comprise knowledge groups or teams of knowledge workers.

Social networking analysis (SNA) is the mapping and measuring of relationships and flows between people and groups within an organisation.

Boundaryless organisations are organic, with communication flowing through predominantly horizontal channels of communication.

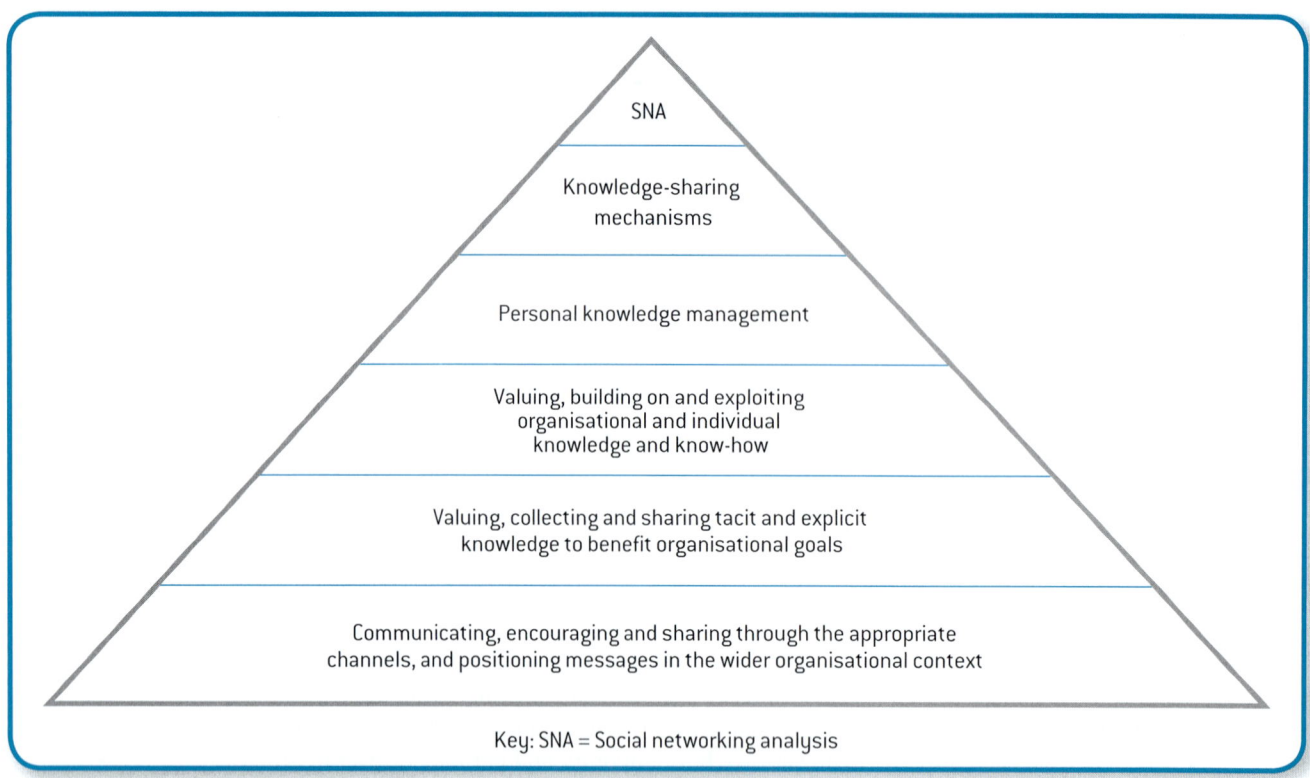

Figure 8.8: Activities undertaken in a knowledge management structure

(Robbins et al. 2008; Bartol et al. 2008). The boundaryless organisation has the ability to redirect flows of information and decisions, uses of power and feedback within the hierarchy. Robbins and colleagues (2008, p. 556) describe boundaryless organisations as those seeking '. . . to eliminate the chain of command'; they 'have limitless spans of control, and replace departments with empowered teams'. They seek to eliminate vertical and horizontal boundaries within and between organisations.

Complexity is less than in traditional structures because the removal of vertical boundaries creates a flatter structure and many horizontal communication links. Formalisation is lower and decisions are decentralised, often being made in cross-hierarchical teams. With their flatter structures, boundaryless organisations can attract strong, self-reliant workers. The introduction of cross-functional teams reduces the horizontal boundaries between functional departments. Rotation of specialists between functional areas creates generalists with a better understanding of what happens elsewhere in the organisation.

A significant amount of communication in a boundaryless organisation happens via networked computers. Sheizaf and Gilad (2003), for example, report that findings from an experimental study of the role of electronic mail in the operation of supply chains indicated a significant correlation between email used to share information up the supply chain and net team profit. The conclusion was that the use of email and the sharing of information online enabled teams to perform well.

Network structure

Bartol and colleagues (2008, p. 364) highlight the virtual nature of the networked structure and discuss how it acts as '. . . virtually one organisation'. They give the example of Benetton, which 'contracts production to about 350 small firms, getting economies of scale by buying materials from all of them'.

Network structures contract out many functions to other independent firms and coordinate and communicate through IT networks.

To operate successfully, networks require clear and specific expected business outputs and the time frame to deliver the output. They also require support for the network process and recognition from senior management of the relationships created by the network. The visibility and free flow of information to all members of the network and the means to communicate among them must therefore be guaranteed.

One disadvantage of network structures is that the lack of rigid tiers of management makes it difficult for those with ambition to identify a clear promotion or career path. The lack of promotional opportunity can lead to frustration and staff turnover. Another disadvantage of these new flat structures is that employees may feel there is no leadership or support when problems arise.

These new and emerging structures are organic and usually exist in younger industries where attitudes to employment are often perceived to be more liberal. A flat management structure allows the organisation to form flexible, dynamic, interdisciplinary teams to meet the production and customer requirements. Communication channels in organic organisations are predominantly horizontal and tend towards the use of informal networks. Conventional channels are often bypassed. This is increasingly prevalent with the trend towards electronic communication. Accountants, for example, no longer need to spend days in meetings deciding on the financial status of a company. A software package can do the analysis in a matter of minutes. In some organisations, once you log on to your personal computer, everyone in the company knows you are at work and can send you reports or messages via email.

Organic organisations operate in a dynamic, flexible environment.

REVIEW QUESTIONS

10 a Describe three features of an organisation.

    b What impact does a high level of complexity, formalisation and centralisation have on the flow of communication in an organisation?

11 Identify and define six types of organisational structure.

12 What is the value of the traditional organisational structure?

13 a What is the value of the matrix form of organisational structure?

    b Identify the stages of matrix development.

14 a Identify the type of activities undertaken in a knowledge structure.

    b What type of negotiation, conflict management and listening skills would be essential in a knowledge management structure?

INFORMAL ORGANISATIONAL STRUCTURES

◄ OBJECTIVE 5
Understand the advantages and disadvantages of an informal organisational structure

People in an organisation establish, within a group or between groups, links or networks of communication that are not formally recognised or legitimised. These informal links operate separately from the official lines in the formal structure. In the formal structure of the organisation, relationships are clearly defined. Each member knows what is expected, the task to be performed and the number of items to be produced. However, most organisations do not function in this way. People tend to do the jobs they prefer and help the colleagues they like. Some members within a group will accept help but will not reciprocate, while others will not offer or receive help but tend to work alone. The spontaneous links that arise between individuals as a result of these patterns of behaviour constitute the informal organisational structure.

An informal organisational structure comprises communication links or networks not formally recognised or legitimised.

Advantages of the informal structure

Informal networks will not appear on any organisation chart but they can have as much impact, or more, on the way the organisation functions as the recognised and established communication system. The main advantages of the informal organisation are:

Informal networks have advantages and disadvantages.

- faster action
- higher productivity
- more job satisfaction
- easier release of tension
- easier feedback.

Informal communication networks convey information within the informal organisational structure.

When an employee in one department needs help to complete a task or solve a problem, members of the informal structure or network in other sections can use their authority or power to assist. This avoids the delay of going 'through the right channels', thus speeding up the communication process. When the goals of formal management match the needs of the informal organisation, employees will take the initiative or be more responsive to delegation. This can create trust between management and employees and lead to higher productivity. Job satisfaction is related to the social environment. The informal organisation can create a climate that fosters morale and job satisfaction and, in turn, productivity.

The informal network allows employees to release tension and frustration with other members of their informal network without directing this at management and risking their jobs. An important advantage of the informal network is that it provides feedback for management. If management is sensitive to the 'grapevine', it can obtain information on how employees feel about the organisation, management and the work. Most managers would have employees they trust to provide them with this kind of informal feedback.

Disadvantages of the informal structure

The informal links or networks of communication are not so clearly defined. As well as advantages, the informal organisation has the following disadvantages:

- conflict
- resistance to change
- conformity to the informal group's standards
- rumours.

When the goals of the informal network are different from those of the formal organisation, conflict can occur. Changes in technology and competition are requiring organisations to alter many aspects of their operation, conditions, work output and efficiency measures. The informal organisation will tend to resist any changes that are perceived to threaten the existing structure. Some changes, for example, may mean the loss of staff and the introduction of new work practices. Employees are often unaware of the effect of the informal organisation on the way they work, conforming to the standards or goals of the informal organisation without question.

Rumour is unsupported or untrue information that arises in the informal communication network and is therefore the greatest disadvantage. Individuals tend to select the part of the message that is important to them and add further details or withhold information, thus distorting the communication.

The informal organisation is inevitable. To deal with it, management should recognise its inevitability and influence its direction. It will do this by being aware of rumours, replacing rumours with fact, providing adequate information via formal channels, and creating conditions that support the goals of both groups.

REVIEW QUESTIONS

15 What is the purpose of the informal organisational structure?

16 What are the characteristics of an informal organisational structure?

17 What are the advantages of the informal structure?

FORMAL SMALL GROUP COMMUNICATION NETWORKS

◀ OBJECTIVE 6
Describe the patterns of interaction in small group networks

While the direction of communication within an organisation affects the format and effectiveness of that communication, we must also consider the impact of the **communication networks** that are established. Five of the most important formal communication networks that develop in business and government organisations are discussed here. (Figure 8.9 shows four of them.) They are:

1 chain network
2 Y network
3 wheel network
4 circle network
5 all-channel network.

In a *chain communication network*, information is passed from one person in a line of authority to the next employee above or below that person. The *Y network* is really an upside-down or reverse Y. It traditionally represents two, three or more levels where the employees at the lowest level report to a supervisor who reports further up the organisation to a manager. A four-level Y diagram is shown in Figure 8.9.

Communication networks are patterns of communication established among employees who work closely together in a small group.

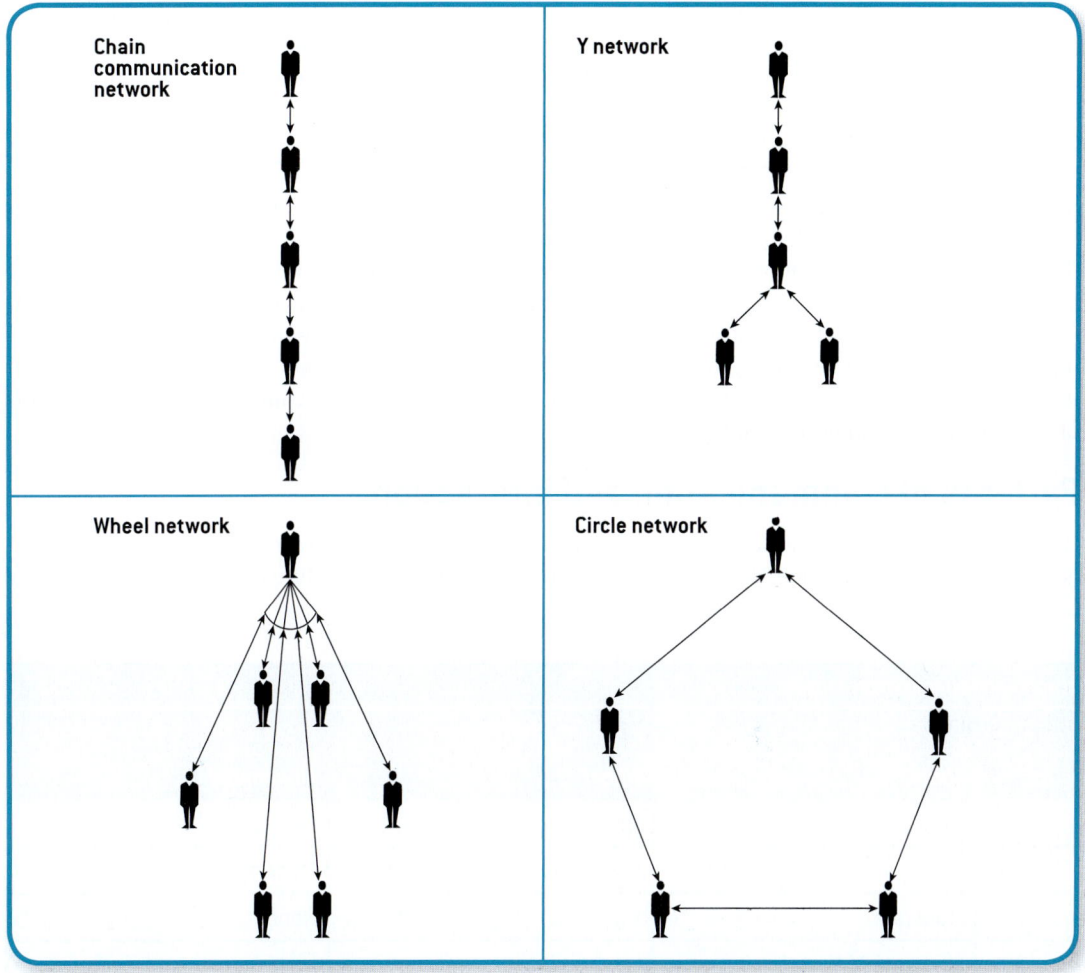

Chain communication network

Y network

Wheel network

Circle network

Figure 8.9: Formal communication networks

A *wheel network* exists when there is a supervisor with a number of subordinates reporting directly to the supervisor without consultation or links with each other. Thus, in some firms a sales manager may have a number of salespeople who report directly to the manager but are isolated from each other except for the annual or monthly get-together. The spokes of the wheel are not really connected.

The *circle network* is a three-level hierarchy of supervision with the lowest level of employees communicating directly with each other and with the person on the next level. That level then reports directly to a higher level. Communication also occurs downwards between the levels. In the *all-channel network*, which is more an ideal than a reality, every member of the organisation is able to communicate directly as an equal with every other member. Some committees are examples of all-channel networks.

Robbins and colleagues (2008) analyse the three common small-group networks—chain, wheel and all-channel—and state: 'The *chain* rigidly follows the formal chain of command . . . The *wheel* relies on a central figure to act as the conduit for all of the group's communication . . . The *all-channel* network permits all group members to actively communicate with each other' (p. 369).

Dawson (1996), commenting on early research on efficiency (defined as arriving at a correct solution to a problem speedily) in three main networks—wheel, circle and all-channel—says that 'repeated experiments show the wheel pattern to be the most efficient' (p. 196). She says that in repeated experiments it was found that informal hierarchies usually emerged in both the circle and all-channel networks, which suggests that 'whether communication is upwards, downwards or across, hierarchies will emerge, usually reflecting the relative power and interests of the parties involved' (p. 196).

Robbins and colleagues (2008), however, show that the varying effectiveness of the three groups differs on speed, accuracy, emergence of a leader and member satisfaction. Table 8.5 demonstrates that the wheel structure facilitated leader emergence, the all-channel structure led to high member satisfaction and the chain structure resulted in better accuracy. They concluded that 'no single network will be best for all occasions' (p. 370).

Wood and colleagues (1998) depict the all-channel or star communication network as a *decentralised* communication network—that is, a group communication network in which all members communicate directly with one another (interacting group). The wheel or chain communication network is referred to as a *centralised* communication network—that is, a group communication network 'in which all communication flows through a central person who serves as the "hub" of the network' (coaching group) (p. 309). A restricted communication network operates in sub-groups (counteracting groups) that disagree with some aspect of overall group operations such as goal achievement or labour–management disputes. Figure 8.10 shows the interaction patterns, characteristics and diagrams of the communication networks.

Patterns of communication and interaction

Business organisations consist of people who work together to achieve common goals. At least, that is the theory. But, in practice, the organisation may be affected by the failure of everyone in it to agree

Table 8.5: Small-group networks and effectiveness criteria			
	Networks		
Criteria	**Chain**	**Wheel**	**All-channel**
Speed	Moderate	Fast	Fast
Accuracy	High	High	Moderate
Emergence of a leader	Moderate	High	None
Member satisfaction	Moderate	Low	High

Source: S.P. Robbins, T.A. Judge, B. Millett & T. Waters-Marsh, *Organisational Behaviour*, 5th edn, Pearson Education Australia, 2008, p. 370. Reproduced with permission.

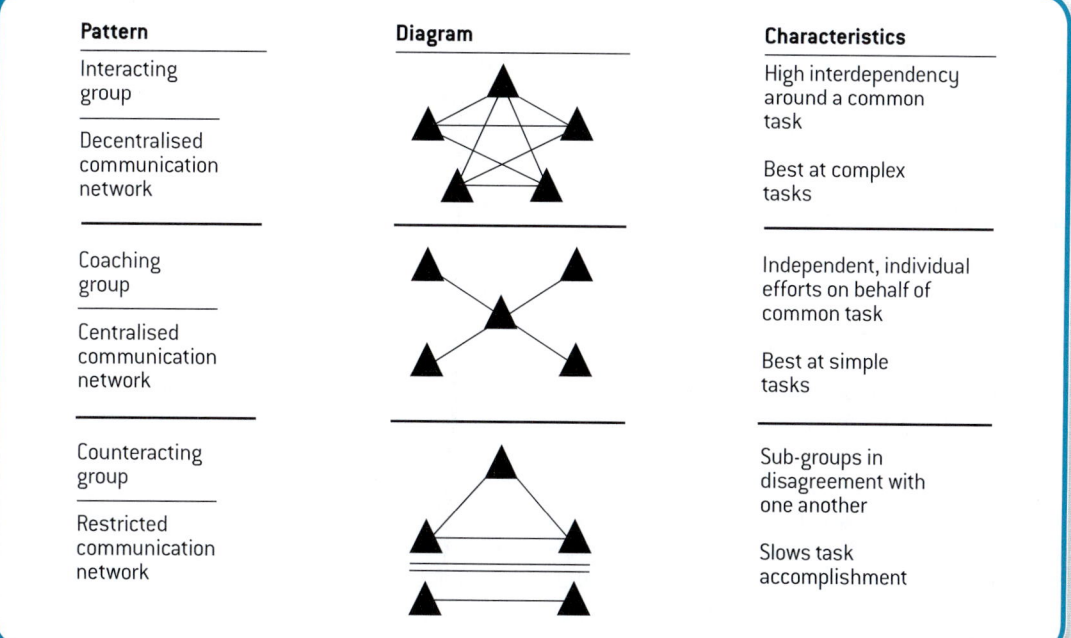

Pattern	Diagram	Characteristics
Interacting group		High interdependency around a common task
Decentralised communication network		Best at complex tasks
Coaching group		Independent, individual efforts on behalf of common task
Centralised communication network		Best at simple tasks
Counteracting group		Sub-groups in disagreement with one another
Restricted communication network		Slows task accomplishment

Figure 8.10: Interaction patterns and communication networks often found in groups

Source: J.M. Wood, J. Wallace, R. Zeffane, J.R. Schermerhorn, J.G. Hunt & R.N. Osborn, *Organisational Behaviour: An Asia Pacific Perspective*, John Wiley & Sons, Brisbane, 1998, p. 309. Reprinted with permission of John Wiley & Sons Australia.

with or work towards the common objectives. Organisations are the systems by which individuals cooperate so that there can be the specialisation of functions and skills to provide goods or services to customers.

Daniels and Spiker (1987) assert that 'there are at least two different ways to think about the structure of organisational communication' (pp. 82–83). One is the traditional definition of communication structure—that is, 'to define structure as a system of pathways through which messages flow—the so-called lines of communication in an organisation', as defined by Goldhaber (1986) and Koehler, Anatol and Applbaum (1981). The second way is to analyse the communication structure—the patterns of interaction among people who comprise the organisation. The structure therefore depends on who communicates with whom. **Communication structure** can be regarded as a system of channels or patterns of interaction among the organisation's members.

An organisation's **communication structure** reflects the communication channels and pattern of communication across the organisation.

NETWORK ANALYSIS

Daniels and Spiker (1987) focus on the patterns of interaction among organisation members (the communication network) using the technique of network analysis. **Network analysis** provides a picture of the patterns of interaction that define an organisation's communication structure. They (p. 96) refer to Albrecht's and Ropp's (1982) description of the ways in which this picture can be obtained.

Network analysis identifies patterns of interaction, cliques, and the connectedness and openness of groups.

- Ask organisation members to report the interactions that they have with one another (self-report surveys).
- Make direct, first-hand observations of interaction patterns (naturalistic observation).
- Unobtrusively 'capture' interaction episodes on audiotape or videotape or from other records in the organisation (constructive ethnography).
- Conduct non-directive interviews with members to obtain information that may help to explain and interpret interaction patterns.

Daniels and Spiker use diagrams of network structure to reveal network roles and relationships (see Figure 8.11). Each circle represents a person and 'the lines connecting the circles are the linkages that show who communicates with whom' (1987, p. 98). In this network, A is a *liaison* person who links the different groups but is not a member of the groups. B and C are *bridge links* between the two groups. D is an *isolate*, not linked to any other member in the network and with little overall contact.

Daniels and Spiker list four uses of network analysis:

1. to make it possible to determine whether the actual communication structure corresponds with the expected channels, group structures and member roles
2. to identify liaison and bridge links that seldom appear on formal organisational charts
3. to identify the isolates
4. to identify new or 'hidden' network structures.

By uncovering and comparing all the different networks that comprise any given system of organisational communication, we are able to understand the influence of communication on every aspect of organisational life.

Lewis (1987, p. 53) defines network analysis as 'a tool to help a manager (or communication researcher) analyse communication flows and patterns'. He comments that network analysis can identify cliques and the specialised roles of members and also measure the connectedness and openness of groups. Similar to Albrecht and Ropp (1982), his diagram (shown in Figure 8.12) identifies the

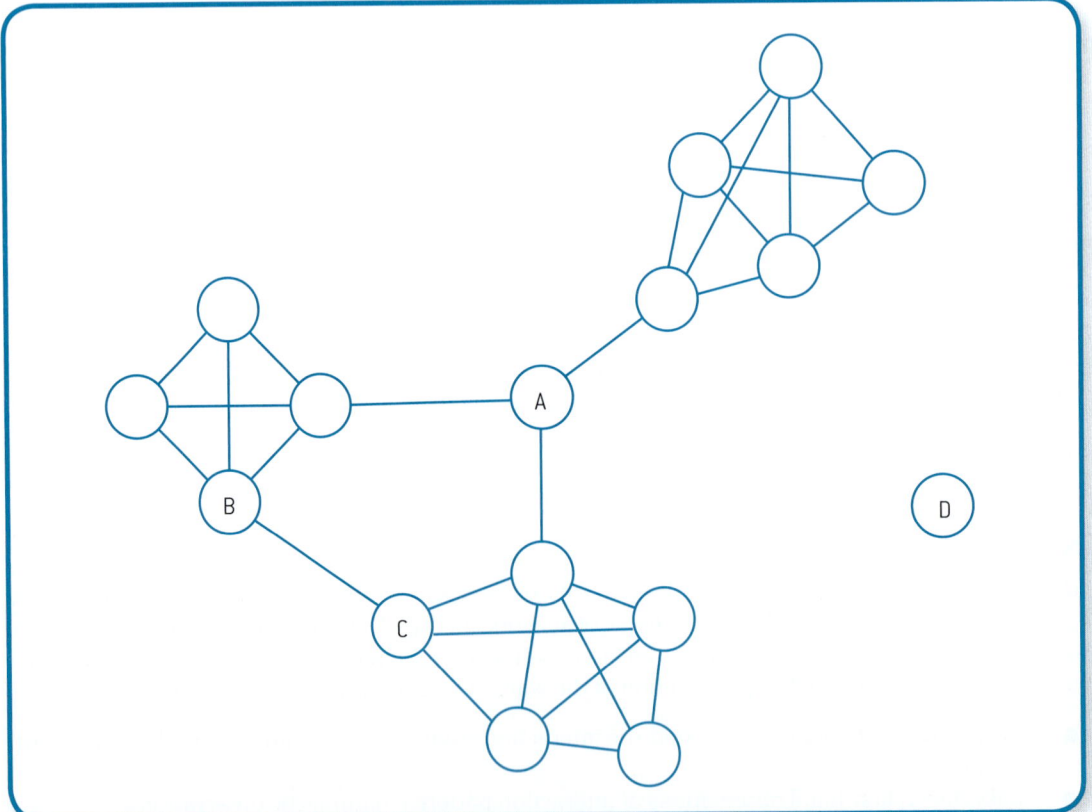

Figure 8.11: A communication network

Source: T.D. Daniels & B.K. Spiker, *Perspectives on Organisational Communication*, Wm. C. Brown Publishers, Dubuque, Iowa, 1987, p. 97. Reproduced with permission of the McGraw-Hill Companies.

liaison and isolate people but also shows the various cliques and gatekeepers. He defines a gatekeeper as 'the person who has the power of controlling the message flow' (1987, p. 53). In the diagram, the gatekeeper is the person who receives information from the liaison person and then decides whether or not to pass it on. Lewis says that 'the challenge to management is to recognise who does not get information and to fill the gaps, to supply good information to the liaisons, and to avoid excessive gatekeeping tendencies' (1987, p. 54).

Hansen's 1999 research dealt with the question of why some sub-units or sections in an organisation can share knowledge among themselves but others are not able to. The research results suggest that weak ties between project teams enable the team to gather useful knowledge from other teams. However, weak ties between project teams or sub-units impede 'the transfer of complex knowledge, which tends to require a strong tie between the two parties to transfer. Having weak interunit ties speeds up projects when knowledge is not complex but slows them down when the knowledge to be transferred is highly complex' (p. 82).

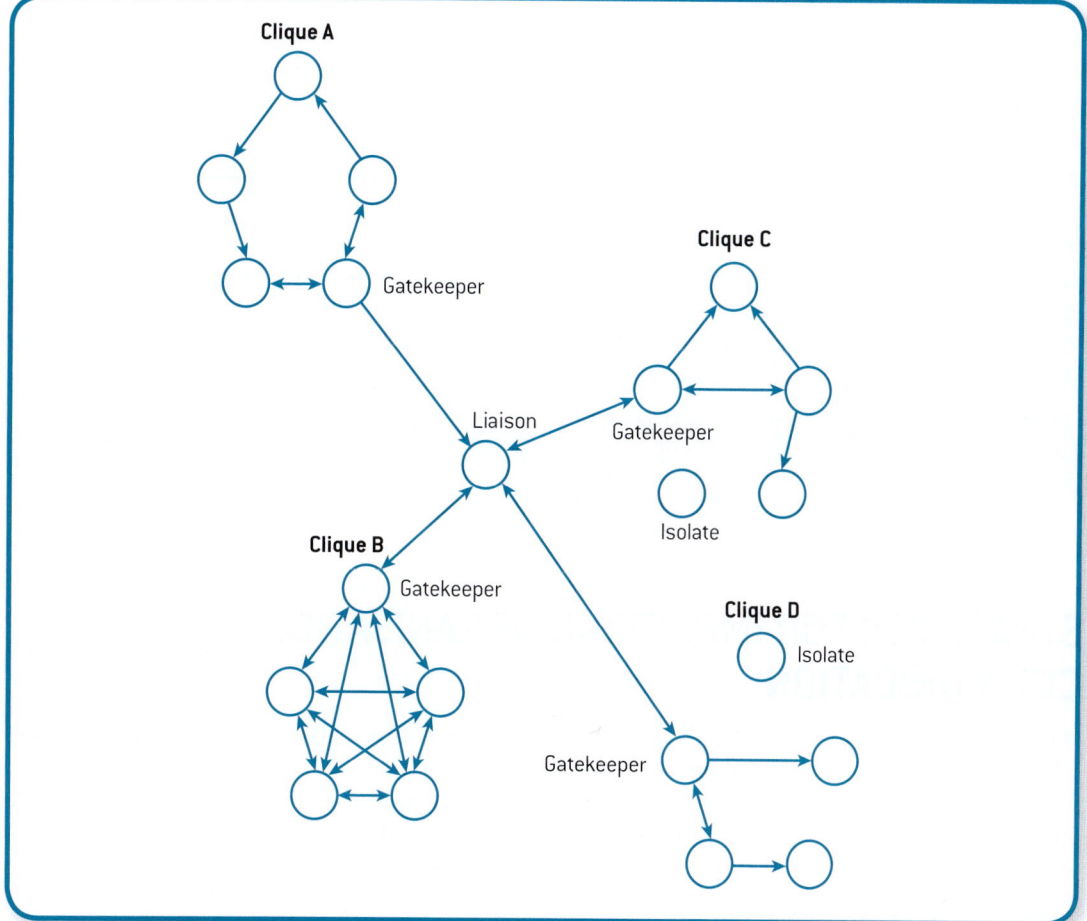

Figure 8.12: Network analysis of one department

Source: P.V. Lewis, *Organisational Communication: The Essence of Effective Management*, John Wiley & Sons, New York, 1987, p. 54. Reprinted by permission of Pearson Education, Inc., Upper Saddle River, New Jersey.

18 In which type of organisational structure would you expect to find:
- a chain-of-command small group network
- a wheel small group network
- an all-channel small group network?

19 a Which network did Dawson (1996) identify as most efficient?

b What was Robbins and colleagues' (2008) view of the effectiveness of small group networks?

20 What is the purpose of network analysis?.

APPLY YOUR SKILLS

FEATURES OF AN ORGANISATION

1 a Construct a diagram of a chain communication network and a circle network. What are the main differences between the two? Name an organisation that you think uses either one of these networks.

b In the diagram, highlight the leader of each network.

2 a Of the five formal communication networks identified on page 233, in which would you prefer to work? Why?

b Which of the above types of communication network would you prefer to use as a leader? Why?

3 a Lewis (1987) defines network analysis as 'a tool to help a manager (or communication researcher) analyse communication flows and patterns'. Describe four different uses of network analysis.

b Critically discuss the significance of the connectedness and openness of groups to the flow of communication and transfer of information in an organisation.

4 Work in small groups.

a Discuss the ways in which a manager can improve communication in a large organisation. In particular, discuss the informal structure and networks and the grapevine.

b Robbins and colleagues (2008) conclude that the grapevine is an important part of any organisation's communication. When would the grapevine serve the manager well in improving communication? What problems could it cause for the manager?

c Report your findings in a verbal presentation to the large group.

OBJECTIVE 7 ▶
Discuss strategies that can improve organisational communication

Mechanistic
organisations operate in a stable, highly structured environment.

STRATEGIES FOR IMPROVING ORGANISATIONAL COMMUNICATION

Organisations operating in a stable, highly structured environment make greater use of organisation charts, rules, policies and job descriptions. Such organisations are labelled **mechanistic**. In contrast, organisations that operate in a dynamic, highly flexible environment may have few organisation charts and few job descriptions or standing plans. These flexible organisations—termed **organic**—are able to adapt quickly to meet the demands of the changing business and workplace environment, whereas a mechanistic organisation is rigid and slow to react. Table 8.6 compares the two types of organisation.

Apart from the impact of the organic or mechanistic nature of an organisation on communication flow, other features of organisational structure can encourage or inhibit communication. The next section considers how some organisational structures may encourage more effective communication than others.

Changing organisational structures to enhance communication

With increasing world competition, businesses must deliver results. In order to deliver results, they must seek ways of incorporating fast and accurate decision making into their existing structure. This has meant improving the:

- flow of communication
- amount of communication
- accessibility of key personnel involved in decision making.

In general, it seems that the less centralised a company is—that is, the fewer the levels of management—the better the conditions for effective communication. Some of the structural changes made by management to improve the scope and quality of communication in the organisation are discussed here.

DEVELOPING STRONG HORIZONTAL CHANNELS WITHIN TRADITIONAL STRUCTURES

Traditionally structured organisations that have attempted simply to delay change, to reorganise or to downsize have found it difficult, if not impossible, to improve communication and speed up decision making. Instead of the intended change, the result is often confusion and lack of morale among employees.

Historically, the traditional formal structure had been adequate to respond to the marketplace, but, as the business environment became more dynamic, the rigid structures and hierarchical channels of communication were unable to cope with the need for information, speedy decision making and the expectations of personnel. Informal networks grew to cope with the need for speed and information. The value of informal networks has been recognised by management, with many organisations advocating an informal environment to foster creativity and reduce bureaucracy within the traditional structure.

Organisations are moving towards building their informal communication network into a formal structure to allow for increased flow of information, focus and dynamic response to change. Communication within these networks, between levels and across sections, can develop strong horizontal channels based on business functions rather than the status of staff.

Organic organisations have low formalisation, horizontal communication and coordination, participative decision making, and are responsive to changes in the environment.

In traditional structures, strong horizontal channels based on business functions rather than the status of staff improve communication flows.

Table 8.6: Mechanistic and organic structures	
Mechanistic structure	**Organic structure**
Description • static, rigid, vertically oriented, pyramid-shaped • uses rules, policies, procedures • decision making concentrated on top • authority based on position • elaborate control system • rigid communication channels	*Description* • fluid, dynamic, ever-changing • flattened shape • horizontally oriented • collaboration • decision making at all levels • authority based on expertise • communication flows based on current needs
Best used when • goals are well known and long-lasting • there is a stable, reasonably simple environment • technology is simple and well understood • workforce appreciates high degree of routine and structure	*Best used when* • tasks are uncertain • environment is complex and ever-changing • technology is changing and not the same for all tasks • workforce is creative and innovative

CREATING AUTONOMOUS/SEMI-AUTONOMOUS WORK GROUPS

Autonomous or **semi-autonomous work groups** have responsibility for decision making and achieving results.

Sections or groups in an organisation that are provided with general objectives and targets by senior managers and then left to decide the work process themselves are termed **autonomous** or **semi-autonomous work groups**. This autonomy extends both to making the decisions involved and achieving the end result. These groups have considerable control over their work. An organisation's communication flow can be improved by the use of autonomous sections within it, with each held responsible for the group's work.

Theoretically, members of an autonomous work group should communicate directly and clearly with each other. However, there is always the possibility of group conflict unless they are united in their goals and have the human relations and communications skills needed for this type of work situation.

FREE-FORM STRUCTURES

Free-form structures encourage communication and interaction because an individual or group is given almost total freedom to complete the task.

A **free-form structure** exists when an individual or group is given almost total freedom by the company's top management, usually to complete a given task. A free-form structure is simple, with few layers of management and may even be boundaryless. Decision making is in the hands of those doing the work. In some situations a free-form structure may lead to improved communication, though it is doubtful if an entire organisation could be based on it. While free-form structures are very rare in Australia and New Zealand, they are occasionally used in high-technology industries.

THE 'NEW' NETWORKS

'New' networks are empowered to make decisions and knowledge is shared along all channels of communication.

The **'new' networks** in major international and national companies affect how decisions are made and who makes them. Those who are affected by changes become relevant in the decision-making process. Members of the 'new' networks or teams are empowered to talk openly, build trust, enhance the quality of decisions and evaluate problems from the customer's and company's perspective rather than the narrower functional or sectional view. Those who are affected by the changes resulting from decisions are then empowered to lead and make decisions. Employees or managers in this type of group are able to make decisions and solve problems in a more focused way.

Information is shared via computerised information systems, electronic mail, regular meetings, and video and telephone conferences with other people in the network; sub-networks are formed to perform particular tasks. In other words, employees take an active part in the decision-making process.

Members of networks are selected from across the organisation's functions, locations and levels of hierarchy. People are selected who have the skills and backgrounds suited to the purpose of the project team or network. Selection criteria are business skills, communication skills, motivation and decision-making skills.

The communication flow in most large organisations tends to be incomplete and sequential and thus open to distortion or manipulation. In a network, information must be communicated visibly and simultaneously. Sharing information openly by using all means, including electronic, allows evaluation of information, focus on performance, understanding across sections and the sharing of a variety of viewpoints.

These days, some organisations are willing to move away from the traditional structure towards autonomous or semi-autonomous structures, free-form structures or the 'new' networks. One of the real advantages of the 'new' network is that members are able to understand the organisation's aims and participate in achieving these aims. Another advantage is an increase in information flow and communication within the organisation.

The role of emotional intelligence in communication

Emotional intelligence is the capacity to reason with emotion.

Organisations are now considering the implications of emotional intelligence (EI) and its role in improving communication and current practices. Lane and Duignan (2004) state that 'organisations want to know how concepts of emotional intelligence relate to current systems for management and staff development, behavioural skills training, competencies and performance management systems'. In their view, 'addressing emotional intelligence within an organisation is directed at enhancing staff and leadership comfort and competence at communicating'. Effective organisations place great value on the development of their people, high levels of service and quality.

Communication skills operate at both the organisational and individual level. At the organisational level, an organisation shares its vision and values. Lane and Duignan (2003) state: 'Organisations where there is a close alignment between organisational and individual purpose at the emotional level will have a strategic advantage over those organisations where this is not the case. This is demonstrated by the emphasis on developing shared vision and values.' Organisations share information about policies, procedures and behaviours. Emotionally intelligent organisations have systems, procedures and practices that enable staff not only to achieve their goals, but also to use their creativity. The systems and practices are supportive and cooperative, rather than oppositional and destructive.

Emotionally intelligent individuals are able to acknowledge the role of subjectivity and intuition, as well as objectivity and logic, in business decision making. They address the emotional aspects of human behaviour as well as the objective and logical, observable and specific behaviours. At the individual level in the workplace, people build relationships, communicate ideas and interact with others to get the job done. Top-performing organisations characteristically have staff with high levels of motivation, morale and trust. The leaders and managers of emotionally intelligent organisations are willing to acknowledge emotional intelligence and have the willingness and confidence to encourage and support staff to be proactive and innovative. The focus is on productive, positive outcomes.

> Effective communication builds a positive communication climate.

Promoting communication skills

The creation of 'new' networks leads to a better flow of communication because they incorporate the advantages of the informal network into the formal structure. This statement is based on the assumption that, given the right climate, access to technology to provide information and the ability to communicate across distances, individuals within the 'new' network are willing and able to communicate better. This is not necessarily true. Managers and employees do not always have the ability, or the necessary organisational and interpersonal skills, to communicate effectively. Promoting effective communication within an organisation requires staff who are willing and able to undertake the activities shown in Figure 8.13. Managers and staff with these capacities are able to communicate well and enhance the organisation's climate. It is therefore the organisation's responsibility to ensure that staff have adequate access to training that will promote better communication. At the same time, individuals will want to work at improving their own communication skills. To communicate openly, people share with others their intentions, feelings and needs relevant to their work.

Problems are solved when and where they happen. Organisational actions are discussed, planned and readjusted on the basis of the needs of the organisation and the customers. Good communicators are involved as members of the team in group and intergroup discussions to gain perspectives and move towards agreement and cooperation. Good communicators show interest in the work, take the initiative for getting information, services and necessary resources, and move towards responsibility for effecting the goals and directions of the organisation. They are also able to set, discuss and reinforce high standards, define problems and attempt to reach mutually acceptable solutions, and to generate and discuss all the identified alternatives. Effective meetings, workshops and conferences all generate participation. Chapter 11 discusses these strategies in more detail.

> Managers and staff who communicate effectively are able to provide feedback that is descriptive and specific and to listen actively, directly confront differences and circulate information.

Effective communicators provide acknowledgment and recognition to others for their achievements; clarify the goals and purposes of group discussions and meetings; experiment with new ways of approaching a task; and check organisational needs and goals to see how they match the goals and needs of people in the organisation. They are able to build a positive communication climate that fosters morale, trust and motivation. They provide training when necessary and delegate tasks based on ability. Effective workplace communicators are able to create messages that get results.

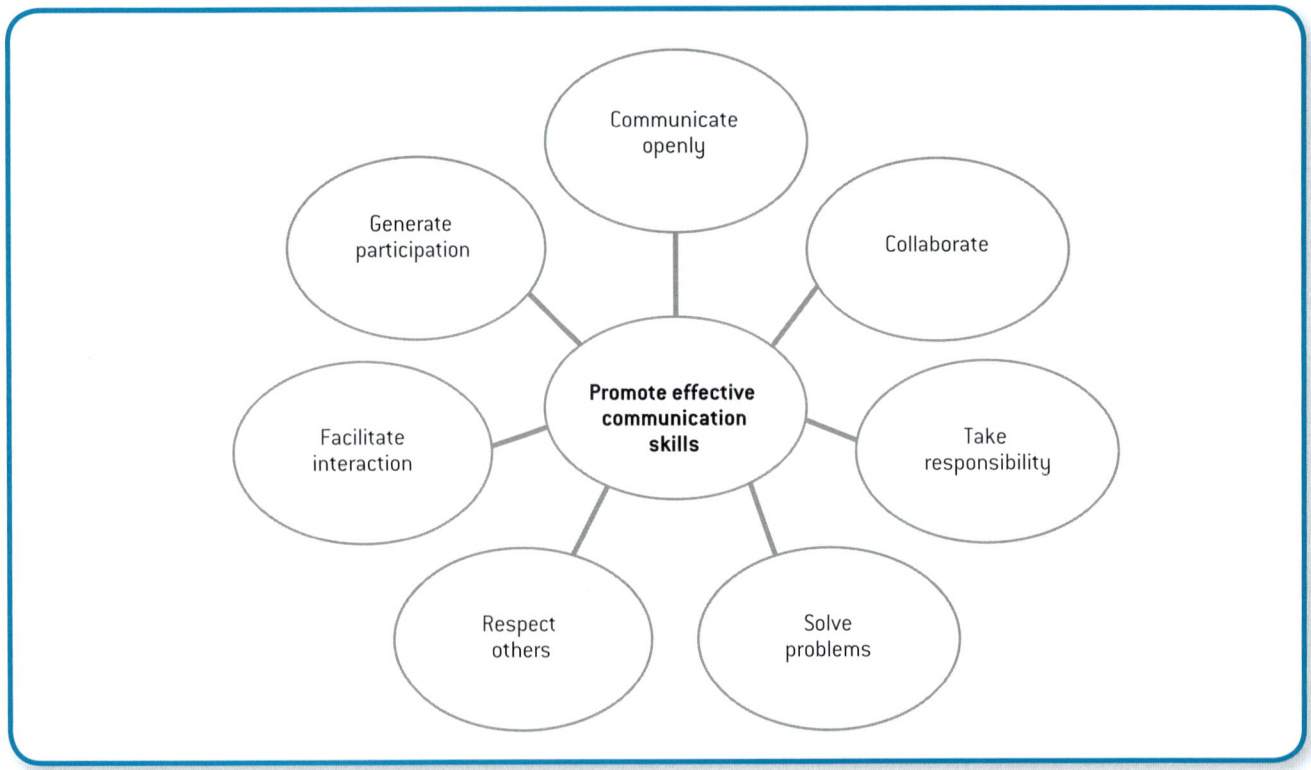

Figure 8.13: Promoting effective communication skills across the organisation

REVIEW QUESTIONS

21 Identify strategies that organisations can use to improve the flow of communication, amount of communication and accessibility of key personnel.
22 How can traditional structures build strong horizontal channels of communication?
23 What is the purpose of addressing emotional intelligence in an organisation?

APPLY YOUR SKILL

ORGANISATIONAL STRUCTURE

1. a Compare and contrast two features of a mechanistic and an organic structure.
   b In which organisational structure would you like to operate: an organic or a mechanistic structure? Briefly outline two reasons for your choice.
   c When is a mechanistic structure best used? Give an example of an organisation that appears to have a mechanistic structure.
   d Scan the business section of a national newspaper. From the articles, identify an organisation that is likely to be mechanistic. What are two features of a mechanistic organisation that are likely to exist in this organisation?
2. a Why are organisations moving towards building the informal network into the formal structure?
   b How does a free-form structure differ from traditional structures?

c　What do you envisage are the advantages for any organisation that moves from a traditional to a free-form structure?

d　Consider some of the organisations to which you belong. Identify the vertical flows of communication upwards and downwards that you have observed or shared in those organisations. What advice would you give to a new member of the organisation about using the vertical flows of communication effectively.

3　a　Rate your organisational communication skills by ticking V, S, or U in the self-evaluation checklist.

　　b　For those items where you ticked the U box, decide how you will improve your skills in that area.

SELF-EVALUATE YOUR SKILL

ORGANISATIONAL COMMUNICATION

Key: VS = Very Successfully, S = Successfully, U = Unsuccessfully

I am able to:	V	S	U
work effectively in the organisation's culture			
match my individual goals to the organisation's goals			
use upward and downward communication channels			
use horizontal and diagonal communication channels			
deal with problems caused by formal communication			
interact in the informal communication networks			
identify the features of the formal organisational structure			
behave appropriately in the organisation's informal groups			
show interest in work and take the initiative			
communicate positively			

SUMMARY OF LEARNING OBJECTIVES

 DESCRIBE HOW CULTURE IS CREATED WITHIN AND COMMUNICATED ACROSS AN ORGANISATION

An organisation's culture is its system of shared values, assumptions, beliefs and norms. It is created first by the founders and owners who hire and keep employees; second, new employees learn about how things are done in the organisation from others; and, third, owners, leaders, managers and others in the organisation act as role models that encourage others to identify and internalise their beliefs, values and assumptions. Culture is communicated and learned through stories, material symbols, language and rituals.

 DISCUSS THE ROLE OF ORGANISATIONAL COMMUNICATION

The main purposes are control, motivation, knowledge management, and balancing the needs and goals of the organisation and its people. When understanding between the organisation and its employees is achieved, the needs and goals of both are compatible. Open organisational communication and sharing of knowledge enables people to focus on the achievement of organisational goals and objectives.

DESCRIBE FORMAL AND INFORMAL COMMUNICATION CHANNELS

The effectiveness of communication and the influence of communication in an organisation are affected by the formal and informal communication channels. Formal channels are approved channels by which communication flows in four directions: downwards, upwards, horizontally and diagonally. Informal communication channels or networks are links between individuals and sections that bypass the formal channels. Communication flows informally across the organisation through four networks: the single strand, gossip chain, probability chain and cluster chain.

DIFFERENTIATE ORGANISATIONAL STRUCTURES AND EXPLAIN THE IMPACT OF DIFFERENT STRUCTURES ON ORGANISATIONAL AND INTERPERSONAL INTERACTIONS

Organisations may have a formal or informal structure, or a combination of both. The type of organisational structure can be analysed by identifying the level of complexity, formalisation and centralisation of functions and relationships. A bureaucratic organisation is highly complex and formalised with centralised decision making. There are many departments and levels of management. A matrix organisation is formal, with two chains of command: horizontal and vertical. A simple structure has less complexity, formalisation and centralisation than the bureaucracy or the matrix.

Network and knowledge management structures provide autonomy for decision making and actions. The focus is on initiative and control of work by the people doing the work. Knowledge management and network organisational structures require clear and specific expected business outcomes and time frames to operate successfully.

UNDERSTAND THE ADVANTAGES AND DISADVANTAGES OF AN INFORMAL ORGANISATIONAL STRUCTURE

An informal organisational structure has a number of established links or networks of communication that are not formally recognised. Advantages offered by the informal structure are faster action, higher productivity, more job satisfaction, earlier release of tension and easier feedback. The disadvantages of the informal structure include potential for conflict, resistance to change, conformity to the informal group's standards, rumours and gossip.

DESCRIBE THE PATTERNS OF INTERACTION IN SMALL GROUP NETWORKS

Small group communication networks, such as the chain, Y, wheel, circle and all-channel networks, carry messages between those who work closely together in small groups in the organisation. Small group networks allow people to communicate and participate openly, collaborate, take responsibility, solve problems, respect others and facilitate interaction.

DISCUSS STRATEGIES THAT CAN IMPROVE ORGANISATIONAL COMMUNICATION

An organisation can change its structure to enhance the flow and level of communication. In traditional structures the development and support of strong horizontal channels will speed up decision making and the sharing of knowledge. By establishing autonomous or semi-autonomous work groups, free-form structures and new networks, decision making and control over work can be moved to the level of the people doing the work. Organisations can address emotional intelligence to enhance leadership comfort and competence in communicating. Organisations that promote communication skills find improvements in relationships and productive, positive outcomes. The capacity to achieve goals is improved and the organisation is more able to respond to change and meet challenges.

KEY TERMS

ACTIVITIES AND QUESTIONS

1   As well as the formal downward and upward communications systems, interpersonal communication and informal communication systems operate within an organisation. Elton Mayo, Douglas McGregor, Rensis Likert and Chris Argyris were some of the theorists who focused on the human elements—human relations, interpersonal communication and informal communication systems. In their view employee relationships impact on production.

Evaluate this quotation by:
   a   outlining the norms, values and behaviours that characterise an organisation of your choice.
   b   explaining how this organisation's culture and structure will help or hinder its efforts to meet challenges over the next two to three years.

2   Write a short report explaining how an organisation's structure helps it to achieve its goals and objectives. In your report, define the terms *complexity, formalisation* and *centralisation*. Compare and contrast the role of the formal organisational structure and the informal organisational structure.

3   Visit a large retail store of your choice and then answer the following.
   a   Does the organisation have a tall structure or a flat structure?
   b   Would you describe the store as a mechanistic or organic structure? Justify your answer.
   c   Describe two horizontal communication channels or links in the organisation.
   d   Choose one department in the store—fashion, furnishings, menswear or any other of your choice. Draw your impression of the organisation chart for this store, from the Managing Director to the particular department you have chosen. Follow the organisation chart in Figure 8.2.
   e   Design three questions you could use in a survey of the retail store's staff to determine their view of the level of formality in the organisation.

4   Find a case study that provides information about organisational communication. Briefly outline the main points. Is the organisation formally or informally structured? Analyse the types of communication channels or flows mentioned in the case study in terms of control, motivation, knowledge management, and balancing needs and goals.

5   Does emotional intelligence have a role in business? Justify your answer.

6   Prepare a checklist of all the communication approaches and strategies you could adopt to communicate effectively from the position of Manager of Customer Service to all stakeholders involved in customer service in an organisation with a network structure.

7   Work in small discussion groups.
   a   Contrast bureaucratic and matrix organisational structures with knowledge management and boundaryless structures.
   b   What factors have led to the emergence of knowledge management, boundaryless and network structures?
   c   What are the communication challenges presented by the newly emerging structures?

8   a   Prepare a set of questions to use in an interview with the CEO of a large transport company, National Distribution. National Distribution has a traditional organisational structure. Your questions should focus on:
      i   the main purposes of communication in National Distribution
      ii   the characteristics of National Distribution's organisational structure
      iii   the communication channels used by the CEO
      iv   the problems (if any) arising from the formal and informal communication channels within National Distribution
      v   the need (if any) to improve communication within National Distribution.
   b   Assume that the CEO is pleased with your interview and asks you to prepare a discussion paper titled 'The advantages of introducing semi-autonomous work groups at National Distribution'. Prepare the paper.

EXPLORING THE WEB

1. Visit 'How to Build an Organisational Culture that Creates a Volunteer Mindset' <www.changeperform.com.au/cultural_change_process.html> to learn more about organisational culture.
   a. Why do people accept the common culture within the organisation?
   b. What must happen before an organisational cultural change process can occur?
   c. What does cultural change involve?
   d. What roles do senior managers and line managers play in a cultural change program?
2. To learn more about the impact of the grapevine on organisational communication, visit 'I Heard it Through the Grapevine' <www.hymncds.com/> and 'Managing the Grapevine' <www.analytictech.com/>.
   a. How can the grapevine help an organisation to manage and share knowledge? Give practical examples.
   b. Where is the grapevine located in an organisation, and how is the word spread?
   c. What factors typically affect the grapevine?
   d. Should managers participate in the grapevine? Give reasons for your answer.
   e. How can an organisation's management manage the grapevine?

PROJECT WORK

Prepare an investigative report titled 'Organisations of the Future'. Your report should address the following four questions.

1. Why do some organisations have traditional structures, while others have the new emerging structures?
2. What are the forces that cause or determine the communication channels in traditional structures and the newer structures?
3. What are the factors currently influencing organisations, and what are the likely characteristics of future organisations?
4. How will continuous improvements in online technology impact on communication in future organisations—within the organisation, with other organisations, with customers and suppliers?

Note: Use a business report format and include a bibliography.

BIBLIOGRAPHY

Albrecht, T.L. & Ropp, V.A. 1982. 'The study of network structuring in organisations through use of method triangulation', *Western Journal of Speech Communication*, Vol. 46, pp. 162–78.

Bartol, K., Tein, M., Matthews, G. & Sharma, B. 2008. *Management: A Pacific Rim Focus*, McGraw-Hill Australia, Sydney.

Bateman, T.S. & Snell, S.A. 2007. *Management: Leading and Collaborating in a Competitive World*, McGraw-Hill/Irwin, New York.

Brooks, I. 2006. *Organisational Behaviour: Individuals, Groups and Organisation*, Prentice Hall, United KImgdom.

Capon, C. 2004. *Understanding Organisational Context: Inside and Outside Organisations*, Prentice Hall, United Kingdom.

Charan, R. 1991. 'How networks reshape organizations—for results', *Harvard Business Review*, September–October, pp. 104–15.

Cook, P. *I Heard it Through the Grapevine*, www.hymncds.com/creative/grapevine.htm, last updated 1 April 2005.

Crozier, M. 1991. 'The boundaries of business: the changing organization', *Harvard Business Review*, July–August, pp. 138–40.

Daniels, T.D. & Spiker, B.K. 1987. *Perspectives on Organizational Communication*, Wm. C. Brown, Dubuque, Iowa.

Davis, S.M. & Lawrence, P.R. 1977. *Matrix*, Addison Wesley, Reading.

Dawkins, J. 'Corporate responsibility: the communication challenge', *Journal of Communication Management*, Vol. 9, Issue 2, pp. 108–19.

Dawson, S. 1996. *Analysing Organisations*, 3rd edn, Macmillan Press, London.

Drucker, P.F. 1973. *Management: Tasks, Responsibilities, Practices*, Harper & Row, New York, 1973.

Feldman, K. *How to Build an Organisational Culture that Creates a Volunteer Mindset*, www.changeperform.com.au/cultural_change_process.html, viewed 27 November 2007.

Goldhaber, G.M. 1986. *Organizational Communication*, 4th edn, Wm. C. Brown, Dubuque, Iowa.

Hansen, M.T. & Johnson, S.C. 1999. 'The search-transfer problem: the role of weak ties in sharing knowledge across organisation subunits', *Administrative Science Quarterly*, Vol. 44, Issue 1, March, pp. 82–111.

Hoffer, S.J. 1986. 'Development efforts', *Journal of Applied Behavioral Science*, Vol. 22, pp. 447–94.

Kanter, R.M. 1991. 'Championing change', *Harvard Business Review*, January–February, pp. 119–30.

Koehler, J.W., Anatol, K.W.E. & Applbaum, R.L. 1981. *Organizational Communication: Behavioral Perspectives*, 2nd edn, Holt, Rinehart & Winston.

Lane, C. & Duignan, P. 'Relating emotional intelligence to managerial competencies, skills and behaviours', www.navigate.co.nz/newsrere.html, viewed 25 June 2004.

Lave, J. & Wegner, E. 1991. *Situated Learning: Legitimate Peripheral Participation*, Cambridge University Press, New York.

Lewis, P.V. 1987. *Organizational Communication*, John Wiley & Sons, New York.

McAleese, D. & Hargie, O. 'Five guiding principles of culture management: a synthesis of best practice', *Journal of Communication Management*, Vol. 9, Issue 2, pp. 155–70.

McGregor, D. 1960. *The Human Side of Enterprise*, McGraw-Hill, New York.

Maslow, A. 1954. *Motivation and Personality*, Harper & Row, New York.

Miner, J.B. 2006. *Organizational Behavior 2*, M.E. Sharpe, Armonk, New York.

Mishra, J. 1990. 'Managing the grapevine', *Public Personnel Management*, www.analytictech.com/mb119/grapevine-article.htm, viewed 28 November 2007.

Nicholas, K. 2008. 'Relationships rule as companies make slogans real', *Australian Financial Review*, 7 February, pp. S12–13.

Robbins, S.P., Judge, T.A., Millett, B. & Waters-Marsh, T. 2008. *Organisational Behaviour*, 5th edn, Pearson Education Australia, Sydney.

Schank, R.C. & Abelson, R.P. 1977. *Scripts, Plans, Goals and Understanding: An Inquiry into Human Knowledge Structures*, Lawrence Erlbaum, Hillsdale, New Jersey.

Sheizaf, R. & Gilad, R. 2003. 'Information sharing as enabler for the virtual team: an experimental approach to assessing the role of electronic mail in disintermediation', *Information Systems Journal*, Vol. 13, Issue 2, pp. 191–206.

Taylor, F.W. 1911. *Principles of Scientific Management*, Harpers, New York.

Weber, M. 1947. *The Theory of Social and Economic Organizations* (ed. Talcott Parsons, trans. A.M. Henderson & T. Parsons), Free Press, New York.

Wood, J.M., Wallace, J., Zeffane, R., Schermerhorn, J.R., Hunt, J.G. & Osborn, R.N. 1998. *Organisational Behaviour: An Asia-Pacific Perspective*, John Wiley & Sons, Brisbane.

9 Leadership communication

Photo: Wolfgang Ar

1 ▷ outline leadership tasks and activities, and discuss behaviours common to most managers

2 ▷ identify early approaches to leadership and discuss current theories

3 ▷ distinguish three broad leadership styles and the types of power available to a leader

4 ▷ discuss the key influences in a situational leadership model

5 ▷ describe the characteristics of, and outcomes from, transformational leadership

6 ▷ identify leadership communication practices and explain the purpose of, and differences between, mentoring and coaching.

OUTLINE

VIEWPOINT: NINE SOURCES OF LEADERSHIP INFLUENCE

Johannsen states: 'In politics, a sphere of influence is typically defined as the cultural, economic, military or political influence a state exerts over another state. Similarly, powerful leaders have a sphere of influence used to influence the people around them.' French and Raven (1959) identified five sources of leadership influence—reward, coercive, legitimate (authority), referent (charisma) and expert power. Ongoing research has postulated nine sources of leadership influence through:

1 charisma that causes followers to identify with the leader
2 vision to motivate to accomplish
3 authority based on the legitimate leadership position
4 relationships based on trust, empathy and reciprocity
5 coaching, showing and mentoring followers
6 persuading and raising the desire to take action
7 motivation through positive reinforcement
8 punishment to decrease undesired behaviour
9 expertise, depth of knowledge and credibility.

Johannsen concludes: 'A leader's influence is like singing—if one only belts out one note there's no song. But if you have nine notes, the song sounds like real music.'

Adapted from M. Johannsen, *Nine Sources of Leadership Influence*, www.legacee.com, viewed 12 February 2008.

Leadership styles are changing in response to increasing diversity in the workplace and the variety of communication channels now available for almost instant global interaction. The command-and-control leadership methods of the 20th century are inefficient in the fast-changing technology world. The pressure now is for leaders to display more democratic and less hierarchical leadership than in the past. A collaborative approach creates a motivating environment that encourages people to assume responsibility and exercise leadership in their area of operations.

The terms 'leadership' and 'management' have different meanings. **Leadership** is the process of influencing groups and individuals towards the achievement of an organisation's vision and objectives. **Management** is the process of planning and coordinating work activities and tasks so that they are completed efficiently and effectively with and through other people. Leaders focus on people and the long-term view; they inspire trust and innovate. Managers focus on systems and controls and the short-term view.

A **leader** achieves the organisation's goals through the work of others without relying on his or her position power. Effective leaders have the ability to influence others through communication. They are able to adapt their leadership style to any changes within the group and to the tasks of the organisational environment. Organisations require leaders who are capable of adapting and of communicating effectively in order to build a high-performance culture. Leaders make things happen through people. Effective leaders have both the skill and flexibility to support people to achieve the organisation's objectives. Their interactions give direction, build trust, inspire and motivate others. The focus in this chapter is on the way leaders can influence followers, and the communication practices they can use to build motivation, confidence and commitment to achieve the organisation's vision and objectives.

LEADERSHIP ROLE AND TASK REQUIREMENTS

The role of a leader can be very complex. Its complexity will vary with the size of the group, the tasks facing the group, the length of time the group is together, and the expectations of both the organisation and the group. A person elected by a committee to be its chairperson for a meeting will have a different role from a long-term supervisor of a group. The leader of a large public-sector organisation will have different problems from an employer leading a workforce of six people.

Whatever the size or complexity of the group, every leader influences the behaviour of followers at work in a more or less positive or negative way. House (1971) argues that a leader's most important role is to motivate others, and that this is achieved through rewards, desired goals and clarifying paths. As they carry out their leadership tasks, the challenge is to try new leadership skills and strategies and to apply those that improve the effectiveness of the group.

Leadership tasks

The perceptions of followers can have an impact on a leader's ability to perform the leadership role and tasks effectively. First, there may be a difference in the followers' and leader's perceptions of power and the type of power used by the leader. Second, the followers' perception of the relationship between them and the leader affects the leader's ability to lead. And, third, their perception of how much can be achieved in that situation affects the followers' willingness to perform and the leader's ability to lead and influence. What followers perceive in terms of tasks, skills and resources is not always the real situation, but it is their perception and the basis for their behaviour. Often, it is a person's *perception* of reality, rather than reality itself, that leads to a particular form of behaviour.

The fact that the leader has influence means that a leader does something to affect the performance of others and to produce results. A leader's capacity to influence others—that is, to affect performance and achieve results—is a factor of the leader's aptitude for leadership and their willingness to fulfil a range of activities. Some of the activities required of a leader are:

- motivate the group
- organise it

Leadership is related to interpersonal behaviour, the process of communication and the capacity to motivate.

Leadership is the process of influencing groups and individuals towards the achievement of an organisation's vision and objectives.

Management is the process of planning and coordinating work activities and tasks so that they are completed efficiently and effectively with and through other people.

A **leader** achieves the organisation's goals through the work of others without relying on his or her position power.

A leader influences followers to achieve the organisation's goals.

Leadership tasks are performed at all levels through an organisation.

OBJECTIVE 1 ▶
Outline leadership tasks and activities, and discuss behaviours common to most managers

- direct its activities
- cope with any unexpected developments
- develop group cohesiveness and the right climate for work
- consult with others
- counsel members
- ensure the group achieves the right objectives
- ensure effective communication within the group and between the group and the rest of the organisation.

Many of these activities involve workplace interaction and interpersonal communication between the leader and team or work group members. These activities can be classified into different tasks. As the tasks are done by the group, a social system develops. While this is happening, the leader completes the six leadership tasks set out in Table 9.1. Each of these tasks requires a leader to develop open communication, effective listening skills, and the ability to give and receive feedback. A leader without these abilities finds it difficult to direct, change or influence others because the followers are unable to understand where the team or group is going and what it hopes to achieve. A **team** is a work group with a charter or reason for being.

Management behaviours

After half a century of research there is a body of evidence on activities that are common to all or most managers (Hales 2001, p. 50). These involve:

- acting as a figurehead, representative or point of contact for a work unit
- monitoring and disseminating information
- networking
- negotiating with a broad constituency
- planning and scheduling work
- allocating resources to different work activities
- directing and monitoring the work of subordinates
- specific human resource management activities
- problem solving and handling disturbances to work flow
- innovating processes and products
- technical work relating to the manager's professional or functional specialisation.

Hales asks, first, what behaviours are distinctly what managers do and no one else does and, second, why managers do what they do. Almost all researchers have shied away from trying to answer the question, *Does managerial behaviour make a difference?* Hale states: 'what is missing is an examination of the behaviours that actually connect the skills and traits that constitute competencies with performance outcomes—in other words, an indication of what "competent" managers actually do' (p. 52). Until now, 'a top-down organisational perspective has predominated with managerial impacts assessed in terms of the performance of the organisation, sub-unit or work group for which the manager is responsible'. In other words, there is a belief that managerial behaviour is effective when it brings about desirable organisational outcomes—for example, employees work 'better', resources are used more efficiently, there is more effective delivery of goods and services, and stakeholder needs are met more accurately. Hales warns against a circular logic 'which says that managers of highly performing organisations must, perforce, be "effective" and vice versa'. Further studies are needed to assess whether, in fact, managerial behaviour affects the work group or organisational performance.

Harvie (2003) refers to Dr Jim Bright, an organisation psychologist with the University of New South Wales, who says: 'People in leadership have to show their long-term commitment to an organisation, decide what are desirable values and demonstrate that behaviour on a regular basis.' Bright warns against leaders using simplistic strategies and short-term interventions to achieve increased productivity. 'You can create novelty but not really inspire culture long-term . . . In the end you need a

Leadership is a highly dynamic, changing process in which leaders influence others to take action in a variety of contexts and changing circumstances.

Leaders with management skills enable staff to complete task functions.

A **team** is a work group with a charter or reason for being.

Table 9.1: Leadership tasks

Task	Leadership skills

Developing a vision and setting goals
Leaders have an impact on the climate and culture in their work group because they have influence and the scope to achieve results. Effective leaders know how they want things to be. They have a **vision** of what the group is doing and will do in the future.
	Ability to:
	• communicate that vision in a way that is understood and accepted by others in the group because followers need to:
	  — see how the vision for their group fits in with the organisation's vision or mission statement
	  — understand how it relates to them and how their efforts will complement the organisation's vision and contribute to the organisation itself
	• establish and clarify goals and priorities and work with followers to:
	  — achieve common understanding
	  — achieve successful outcomes
	  — gain commitment to the goals or, at least, acceptance that the tasks being completed are consistent with the goals
	• motivate followers to achieve goals by acknowledging and providing a sense of inclusion in the group to individual followers.

Making jobs meaningful Effective leaders develop clear lines of communication and ways for people to account for their contributions.	Ability to: • enable group members to understand their responsibilities and tasks, and acknowledge their contribution to the group's efforts • provide variety and challenge to group members • adapt jobs to the individual styles of the members, their abilities and willingness to perform • provide the opportunity for training and development if members demonstrate a lack of knowledge or ability • take an integrated and cohesive approach to the task to achieve its intended results • communicate with followers about what needs to happen so they know what they are doing and are able to do it in a purposeful way.

Giving feedback
Effective leaders acknowledge and give attention to the members of the group—that is, provide feedback on performance—in order to develop a team of people who have a sense of belonging to the group.
	Ability to:
	• provide positive and negative feedback about performance constructively by:
	  — focusing on behaviour
	  — observing factual information instead of hearsay or gossip
	  — giving feedback for a specific event or behaviour
	  — making it timely—that is, close to the event
	  — giving negative feedback in a private setting
	  — delivering it in an open and appropriate way
	• give feedback that is relevant and of value to the receiver in order to affect their willingness and ability to work within the group
	• recognise accomplishments and reinforce behaviour that will lead to further satisfactory performance
	• avoid focusing on characteristics of the person or behaviours long past
	• reward or discourage the specific behaviour that is causing success or failure, rather than 'dumping' past frustrations on the other person
	• avoid hidden agendas such as 'pay-backs'.

A **vision** is a clear view of what is to be done, now and in the future.

Feedback should be relevant and let the follower know how the message has been received by the leader.

Developing teamwork Effective leaders work with team members in the context of the organisation's culture to build trust, cooperation and compatibility.	Ability to: • promote teamwork in the achievement of goals • empower and encourage followers to be involved • consult to gather ideas from team members and work with them to implement the ideas • use rewards constructively to encourage the desired performance from group members and increase satisfaction and productivity • provide tangible rewards (bonus, time in lieu) and intangible rewards (verbal feedback) as appropriate • make a connection between the person's efforts and the reward, to encourage the desired behaviour again • encourage and recognise the activities and involvement of both leaders and followers.
Representing and supporting members Effective leaders provide the link between the work group and higher management by representing and, at the same time, supporting team members.	Ability to: • define tasks and motivate employees to achieve the group's goals • provide guidance about what actions to take and how to have personal needs met (to feel valued and respected, to be heard and able to participate) • be a source of help and guidance by praising, supporting and participating with followers to show recognition and acceptance of their efforts • remove potential communication blocks • support followers by making it possible for them to be involved in problem solving and decision making • listen to and seek the ideas and opinions of team members, and take action on the basis of their ideas • discuss and agree to workable solutions that fit in with the goals of the team • communicate clearly the organisation's needs and expectations and, on occasion, present team members' needs to higher management • see both sides of a situation, match these, and provide information relevant to team and organisational priorities.
Counselling members Effective leaders provide advice, reassurance, a release for emotional tension, guidance for retraining or refocusing of goals, and a link to other agencies or resources.	Ability to: • discuss poor performance using the BAT MICE formulae (see Chapter 4) • use active listening to help the other person understand their feelings rather than acting as counsellor (see Chapter 4) • discuss work-related problems caused by frustration, conflict or stress to try to eliminate or reduce them; or refer to a professional counsellor; or link the person into an agency or other resource with the skills to help.

Teamwork is built on shared objectives, supportive relationships and a sense of commitment.

raft of contingent management policies to encourage a healthy culture.' Jeremy Aitken, the director of Tri-Learning Corporation, also highlights the fact that 'it is important for managers to tell the team what they have discussed off-line, otherwise there can be a perception of a hidden agenda'. Aitken believes it is important that there is a movement away from management control and non-management victim-like status. Managers need to delegate authority, and non-managers need to hassle for more responsibility, to break this nexus of master/servant. Managers who delegate authority, make jobs meaningful, develop teamwork, and empower and acknowledge team members' performance are able to do more than manage. They are also able to motivate, influence and lead others to achieve results.

Communication by leaders, managers and followers

Cohesion is the level of common purpose and commitment to the team among members.

Task-related functions focus on the output.

Maintenance-related functions focus on how people relate to each other.

A leader communicates ideas and shows how the task completed by the group contributes to the organisation. In addition, a leader needs to develop group **cohesion**, a sense of belonging and inclusion that allows members to satisfy their needs and objectives. Hence, when leaders and followers are working together in a group to perform a particular task, they carry out two basic functions—task-related functions and maintenance-related functions (Table 9.2). **Task-related functions** or behaviours focus on the task to be achieved, the problem to be solved or the group purpose. Designing a new product, planning an advertising campaign or hiring new staff are all task-related functions that aim to get the task done. **Maintenance-related functions** focus on what is happening in the group, the way members listen and relate to each other, and the behaviour developments within the group.

Although many task and maintenance-related functions are performed by the leader of a group, other members of the group also perform them. The leader of a group should be able to distinguish between task-related and maintenance-related functions and carry them out effectively. These functions are discussed in Chapter 10.

In an established group, leader and members become used to one another's communication styles. A leader's predominant or preferred style may be either task-oriented or people-oriented. The preferred leadership style may determine the amount of effort put into task-related or maintenance-related functions. The most effective leader of group discussions or activities is one who ensures there is effective use of task functions and that group-maintenance functions are carried out (Table 9.2). The problem is to ensure they are used at the right time and in the right way. Thus, the leader has to balance task-related functions (which include questioning and seeking opinions) with preserving harmony and good morale in the group.

The key to good group leadership is good communication. This is not just the ability to let the group know what the leader wants, but includes listening skills and the ability to ensure that the goals of the group are met with the maximum contribution from everyone in the group.

Table 9.2: Examples of task-related and maintenance-related behaviour by leaders	
Task-related behaviour	*Maintenance-related behaviour*
Setting goals	Communicating
Planning and organising	Providing feedback
Controlling	Supporting
Directing	Interacting
Meeting deadlines	Listening

REVIEW QUESTIONS

1. Define the terms 'leader' and 'team'. List four tasks completed by a leader.
2. What do competent managers do?
3. Briefly outline the differences between task-related and maintenance-related leadership functions.

LEADERSHIP TASKS

1   a   List three situations in which you act or have acted as a leader.

       b   Name three people who have, in your opinion, been successful leaders.

       c   List six behaviours that made these people successful leaders.

       d   'Our values affect the way we react.' What does this mean?

       e   Identify two ways in which you can develop your leadership potential.

2   In groups of six discuss the topic 'Leadership tasks'. Choose a group leader. The purpose of the discussion is to identify three practical ways in which a leader can complete each of the six leadership tasks (see Table 9.1). The leader is to:

- start the discussion with a brainstorming session
- maintain harmony among the group by helping members to see opposing viewpoints
- ask questions and clarify ideas
- organise the discussion
- conclude by summarising the main points.

As you discuss the topic, create a list of three practical ways to complete each of the six leadership tasks. When you have finished, compare your list with those of other groups.

3   Work in small discussion groups.

       a   In what ways are good communication skills necessary to being an effective leader?

       b   What are good leadership communication skills?

       c   Identify common communication barriers experienced by leaders and followers.

       d   How could these barriers be overcome?

THEORIES OF LEADERSHIP

> ◀ OBJECTIVE 2
> Identify early approaches to leadership and discuss current theories

Academic discourse is based on inquiry into new fields of study and on evaluating and questioning what has gone before. While this chapter is about leadership communication and the factors that impact on how leaders communicate, a brief synopsis of prior leadership theories provides the context for current approaches.

Evolution of leadership theories

Leadership theories have evolved from the work of the early pioneers of leadership research. Table 9.3 presents a very brief introduction to the evolution of these theories. While the focus of this book is business communication, a better understanding of what is happening now is gained from acknowledging what has gone before.

A brief summary of some of the research into leadership styles is presented here. Lewin's research with democratic, authoritarian and laissez-faire leaders showed that laissez-faire groups were not productive. While both of the remaining groups resulted in good productivity, democratic leadership produced the better-quality work. Democratic leadership was the most effective in terms of group climate (Lewin, Lippitt & White 1939).

The intense interest in human relations and interpersonal behaviour in the 1950s and 1960s saw the emergence of the 'functions' school of leadership. Industrialists were advised to consider the 'human factor' in their organisations, particularly in training people for managerial roles. Employers were encouraged to include employees in decision making so that they would feel part of the organisation. This led to the contingency theory. Researchers isolated two main categories of leadership functions. The first category is those that have to do with the group's task (asking for or giving information, providing evidence, maintaining procedures, recording ideas). The second category is

Table 9.3: Evolution of theories of leadership	
Theory	
1 **Traits** (1927)	The first serious effort to explain leadership was based on the idea that leaders possess innate qualities that others do not have or have to only a limited degree.
2 **Styles** (1939)	Kurt Lewin believed there were different types of leadership and that each one had a specific effect on group productivity and climate.
3 **Situations** (1945)	Discounting the trait and style theories, this theory presupposed that 'there are no universal leadership traits, but that the qualities important in a leader will vary with task and situations' (Phillips 1986).
4 **Functions** (1955)	The 1950s and 1960s was a period of intense interest in human relations and interpersonal behaviour. 'Industrialists were advised to consider the "human factor" in their organisations, particularly in training people for managerial roles' (Phillips 1986). Additionally, employers were encouraged to include employees in decision making so that they would feel part of the organisation. This led to the fourth theory: 'leadership was not a person but a group'. Researchers isolated 'two major categories of leadership functions: those that have to do with the group's task (asking for or giving information, providing evidence, maintaining procedures, recording ideas), and those that have to do with interpersonal climate in groups (balancing participation, relieving tension with jokes, and seeking compromises)' (Phillips 1986).
5 **Contingencies** (1964)	Fiedler (1967) claimed that 'leadership involves a match between a person's given style and the requirements of a situation'. He concluded that 'leaders who have a relationship-orientated style are most effective in situations where they have moderate amounts of power, but leaders who are task-oriented are most effective in situations that accord either very little or very much power to the leader'.
6 **Adaptive approach**	Unlike previous theories, the adaptive approach regarded 'leading as a highly dynamic, changing process' and every leadership situation as unique, calling for behaviours specifically tailored to the circumstances and people involved. Phillips (1986) comments that 'the name *adaptive approach* stems from the basic assumption that effective leadership is essentially adaptive to particular circumstances, members, and tasks and to changes in all these aspects of problem-solving'.
7 **Triadic leadership** Zand (1997, pp. 22–23)	'Leadership in the new world has three dimensions: processing knowledge, building trust, and using power sensitively.' The dimensions are connected and interact with each other. 'When leaders have and use relevant knowledge, people trust them and grant them power because they have confidence that the leaders know what they are doing.'
8 **Functional versus genetic approaches to leadership** Jesuino (1996, pp. 93–127)	Leadership is a 'motivational function providing direction and energy to a group'. It is 'exercised through power and influence aimed at the locomotion of groups and organisations toward the achievement of their own objectives and goals'. Jesuino refers to two different theoretical approaches to describe and explain leadership processes: the functionalistic and the genetic.
9 **Charismatic leadership** Crant & Bateman (2000, pp. 63–76)	Crant and Bateman researched the relationship between proactive personality and perceptions of charismatic leadership. They departed from previous research by 'assessing leadership perceptions from above—that is, the leadership attributions made about managers by managers' bosses'.

10 **Transformational and transactional leadership**	Robbins and colleagues (2006, p. 580) differentiate two types. A transformational leader 'inspires followers to transcend their own self-interests for the good of the organisation'. Transactional leaders 'guide or motivate their followers in the direction of established goals by clarifying role and task requirements'. In their view, transformational and transactional leadership are not opposing styles. 'Transformational leadership is built on top of transactional leadership.'

those that have to do with interpersonal climate in groups (balancing participation, relieving tension with jokes, and seeking compromises).

Phillips (1986, pp. 78–99) outlined the theories of leadership proposed between 1927 and 1986 (refer to Table 9.3, points 1–6). He viewed them as:

- being a static conception of leadership based on an unchanging set of circumstances
- neglecting the individual's potential to influence factors relevant to gaining and implementing leadership
- neglecting communication, 'the crux of leadership'.

These three deficiencies led to the development of the adaptive approach. Phillips lists the following leadership requirements necessary in the adaptive approach:

- *Sustaining leader acceptability:* leaders are engaged in an ongoing effort to satisfy members and must stay in tune with the group's needs.
- *Analysing member needs:* leaders must realise there is great diversity in what people want in a leader—from authoritarian, directive leadership to democratic—and adapt their actions to both the group and individual needs.
- *Analysing situations:* leaders need to analyse and adapt to their particular situations: recognise competition, time pressures, records of successes and failures.
- *Inspiring commitment:* leaders need to persuade each member of the group to be as committed and effective as possible.
- *Behavioural flexibility:* leaders are expected to provide basic organisation for the problem-solving process, summarise deliberations, suggest causes and consequences of decisions, resolve conflict, test consensus, record agreements, delegate responsibilities and supervise tasks.

Transformational leadership is a style that motivates followers to perform beyond normal expectations by taking people beyond self-interest, and raising motivation and moral commitment to concentrate on higher-level goals.

Transactional leadership is a style linked to goal achievement in which leaders motivate followers to perform at expected levels, agree on goals, focus on compliance, achievement and rewards, and engage in rational problem solving.

Triadic leadership (Zand 1997) suggests that the interactions of its three dimensions—processing knowledge, building trust and using power sensitively—lead to trust in the leader. The results of the trust granted to leaders are disclosure of knowledge and acceptance of the leader's use of power. Using this knowledge, leaders guide their followers towards superior results. Zand comments that 'knowledge, trust and power are tightly coupled, circularly reinforcing each other'. Leaders still have the right to give orders, but their effectiveness now depends on the knowledge and trust of others. Without access to important knowledge, leaders make poor and ineffective decisions, and without trust there is a lack of commitment from staff to carry out the decisions. 'Leaders may have formal powers, but without knowledge and trust they become martinets, leading people on meaningless forays.' Zand states that 'when leaders attempt to enforce traditional leadership in the new knowledge organisations, they impede the flow of information, discourage creativity, inhibit adaptation, and undermine productivity'.

Jesuino (1996) refers to functionalism, in which goals have already been defined and where leadership's role is to provide direction and energy to achieve them. From the genetic perspective, goals do not pre-exist the group action. According to the functionalistic approach, influence is an outcome of power, which differs from the genetic approach in which influence is a way of acquiring power. In the latter approach, although convergence is common to both, innovation is more likely.

Crant and Bateman (2000) commented that little research had been done until recently on charismatic leadership, in the mistaken belief that it was a rare phenomenon. But, they state, charismatic leadership is often found in varying degrees in managers. They found that a manager's proactive personality (i.e. the ability to identify opportunities and act on them, show initiative and effect change) was positively associated with their supervisor's ratings of their charismatic leadership.

Robbins and colleagues (2006, p. 580) suggest that the transformational leader 'is capable of having a profound and extraordinary effect on their followers ... transformational leadership is more than charisma since the transformational leader attempts to instil in followers the ability to question not only established views but those views held by the leader'. **Transactional leaders** clarify role and task requirements to guide or motivate their followers to achieve goals at the desired level of performance. Transactional leaders usually have a laissez-faire leadership style and engage in rational problem solving and communication with followers to achieve mutual goals. They have a 'hands off', low-people-orientation style of leadership and motivate followers to perform activities to expected levels. Transformational leaders have a participative style of leadership. They interact with, empower and inspire followers to achieve above expectations by concentrating on achievement and self-actualisation. Spreitzer, De Janasz and Quinn (1999) examined the relationship between psychological empowerment and leadership and found that empowered supervisors were seen by followers as more innovative, upward influencing and inspirational. Bartol and colleagues (2008, p. 497) state: 'The concept of transformational leadership revolves around transforming organisations, as well as individuals, to produce significant and positive change.'

This section concludes with a brief summary of the emphasis placed on various aspects of leadership.

- *Classical school of management*: the assumption that managers are rational and economic in their decision making. The three classical approaches were:
  — scientific management
  — administrative principles
  — bureaucratic organisation.
- *Human relations school*: the need to deal with technical problems, and to recognise and deal with labour and social problems.
- *Leader traits and behaviour*: the individual characteristics and behaviour of the leader as the central factor in leadership performance. The division of leadership into task and people orientation was a major development in this approach.
- *Contingency or situational leadership models*: situational models are about transactional leadership, a pragmatic style that is concerned with the transactions between leader and followers. The situational models suggest there is no one type of leader best suited to all situations. Leadership style and the characteristics of the situation in which the leader works both affect the leader's effectiveness. Fiedler (1987) also identified *situational control*—the degree to which the situation lets the leader influence group members. Situational control, or how favourable/unfavourable a situation is to a leader, is affected by:
  — leader–member relations, i.e. the atmosphere in the group
  — task structure, i.e. how well the requirements of the task are known, how many ways there are to complete the task, and how well the group understands the task
  — leader position-power, i.e. how much authority and the type of power held by the leader. House's (1971) path–goal theory emphasises the leader's capacity to increase motivation: leader effectiveness depends on ability to motivate. This theory suggests that the leader motivates by delivering or withholding rewards/punishments, clarifying the paths to reach the incentives, and removing obstacles/pitfalls to make it more satisfying to follow the paths to the goals.

In addition to motivating others, the leader's presence or behaviour must provide something more than what is already in the situation. If the group can manage without the leader, or if the leader's behaviour is unsuited to the needs of the group and the situation, the leader may actually be a hindrance rather than a motivating force.

Hersey and Blanchard's (1982) Situational Leadership® model considers the interaction of

Transactional leaders clarify role and task requirements to guide or motivate their followers to achieve goals at the desired level of performance.

leadership style, the characteristics of the followers, and the relationship between task and relationship behaviour. The model is discussed more fully later in the chapter.

- *Charismatic and transformational models:* Martin Luther King, Jr and Mahatma Gandhi are examples of charismatic leaders. Transformational leaders have a more participative style of leadership than the laissez-faire, 'hands-off' leadership style of transactional leaders. They interact with, empower and inspire followers to achieve above expectations by concentrating on achievement and self-actualisation. They foster a flexible and open structure and are aware of the strategic implications of organisational and team initiatives. Their style means they are capable of transforming people and organisations. Mintzberg (1999) suggests that quiet leaders and managers can inspire people and build a culture of independence.

REVIEW QUESTIONS

4 List four current theories of leadership.

5 *a* Briefly describe the differences between the traits, styles and situations theories of leadership.

b What is the difference between the contingencies theory of leadership and the adaptive approach to leadership?

6 Define the terms 'transactional leadership' and 'transformational leadership'.

LEADERSHIP STYLES

◄ OBJECTIVE 3
Distinguish three broad leadership styles and the types of power available to a leader

Most leaders have a preferred leadership style by which they influence the performance of followers or members of a team or group. **Leadership style** is the consistent pattern of behaviour adopted by a leader. Changing roles and responsibilities in an organisation may require leaders to change their leadership behaviour. The ways in which the leader uses power, and the behaviours he or she demonstrates, identify the style of that person's leadership. A number of possible styles have been suggested for leaders.

Leadership style is the consistent pattern of behaviour adopted by a leader.

A leader's style may be directive, supportive or in between the two. It is not easy to change a preferred leadership style, but leaders who can adapt their style are able to be effective in a range of situations. Leadership styles have been the subject of study for many years. On the basis of findings from these studies, researchers have divided leadership styles into two distinctive sets of behaviour, or a combination of them:

1 directive behaviour
2 supportive behaviour.

Leadership styles can be further divided into three general categories:

1 authoritarian
2 participative
3 laissez-faire.

Each style, used effectively, enables a leader to motivate his or her followers to reach organisational goals. **Motivation** is a process that directs individual action or behaviour towards organisational goals. No one style of leadership is the most effective (see Figure 9.1). Each style has advantages and disadvantages.

Motivation directs individual action or behaviour towards a goal.

Authoritarian leaders

Authoritarian leaders determine the policies and work of the group, with little discussion or input from group members. They direct others from above. The authoritarian leader assumes all the power, holds the key information, and maintains overall control of what goes on in the group. The group members are informed and report back to the leader. An authoritarian leader makes and announces the decisions and accepts total responsibility for implementing and enforcing policy and rules.

Authoritarian leaders determine the policies and work of the group, with little discussion or input from group members.

Communication in a group that is dominated by an authoritarian leader is usually in one direction, from the leader to the group. Two-way communication, from leader to members and from members to leader, is limited to immediate tasks. An authoritarian leader usually makes decisions that are task-oriented and in the interests of the organisation ahead of the interests of the leader or the group. While an authoritarian leader may save time and avoid some of the problems of democratically run groups, such a leader may also find poor group motivation, few ideas, and group members who only work to the rules.

Authoritarian leaders may find that the lack of communication means the members of the group live in a world of crisis, unaware of what is really happening in their section or group. As Vroom and Jago (1988) suggest, authoritarian leadership methods require different skills from participative leadership styles. A leader must be intelligent enough to make high-quality decisions, and be able to identify alternatives, seek and disseminate information, and make relevant choices or decisions. He or she also needs to inspire others.

Participative leaders

Participative leaders share decision making.

Participation means 'to take part'. People participate when they contribute. **Participative leaders** encourage group members to take an active role in decision making in the organisation. They are goal-oriented. These leaders delegate authority, encourage feedback, discuss objectives, and provide the chance for members to satisfy their esteem and self-actualisation needs. The group is part of the decision-making process. A two-way exchange of information flows from the leader to the members and from the members to the leader, and between the members themselves. A number of communication channels are used, and greater emphasis is placed by the participative leader on regular meetings and one-to-one discussions with group members.

The participative leader manages others but asks for ideas before making decisions. Opportunities for contributions are more obvious under participative leadership. An effective participative leader is able to delegate more tasks and decision making, because members who have the skills and are willing can become more involved in organising their own work. As members become more involved, the leader needs to move from concentrating on management and decision making to promoting teamwork, and supporting and cooperating with members. The participative leader often directs from the centre and delegates some of the leadership tasks to group members.

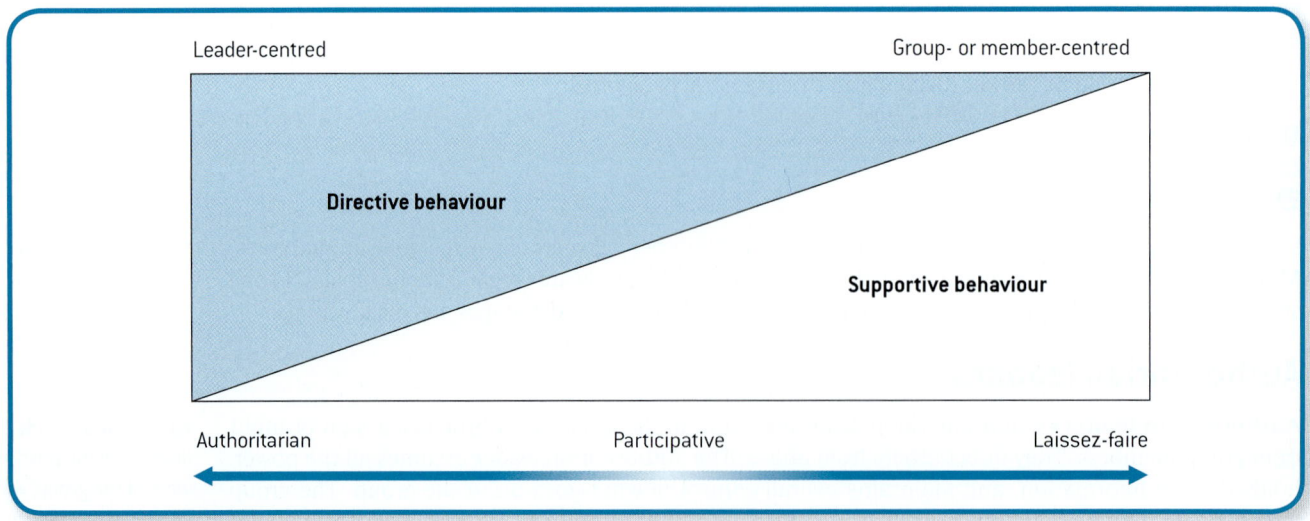

Figure 9.1: Leadership styles

Laissez-faire leaders

The **laissez-faire** or permissive leadership style is at the other end of the leadership spectrum from the authoritarian leader. This is the leader who has a policy of non-interference. This leadership style effectively lets the group run itself.

While there may be some specialised and highly motivated groups that operate well with this leadership style, generally the lack of unity and direction in a permissively led group will soon become obvious. Other people in the group will emerge as leaders, and all the problems that occur in a work environment where there is no clear leadership will appear, unless the group has the skill to operate as a self-managed group.

Communication between the leader and members in a laissez-faire group can be either unclear and limited, or clear, effective and purposeful. When it is unclear and limited, it causes frustration and poor performance as people are unsure where they fit in the group and, consequently, their input may be limited. When a laissez-faire leader is effective, communication flows well between the leader and members, and between members. It is clear and purposeful. Members have a sense of belonging to the group and a clear direction.

An effective laissez-faire leader may coach and support the members. The members are expected to make decisions, while the leader coordinates and supports their activities. As a result, members are more involved and are able to see the reasons for what happens at work and the way in which things happen. In contrast, ineffective laissez-faire leaders simply delegate in an attempt to remove themselves from any responsibility for coaching, supporting or taking part in decision making. Because the leader is ineffective, members may feel resentful as they are expected to take too much responsibility.

Figure 9.2 shows the flow of communication between leader and group members for the authoritarian, participative and laissez-faire leadership styles. There is no one best way to lead: a leader with any one of these styles can be an effective leader. However, the ability to communicate with others is the common factor demonstrated by effective leaders.

A leader who is comfortable letting others take responsibility for part or all of the project is able to empower members by creating a sense of ownership in the project or task. In addition, an effective leader needs the communication skills to offer help without removing responsibility from the followers, to provide coaching when necessary, and to help clarify ideas, directions and expectations. In return, the followers need to be willing and able to take part if the sharing of responsibility is to be successful.

It is unusual to find a completely authoritarian leader or a totally laissez-faire leader. Leadership styles tend to fall somewhere between these two extremes. Many leaders deliberately use a range of leadership styles to suit the particular situation. Others have a style that is probably not even thought out and which varies according to the situation and perhaps even the mood of the leader. Whichever style of leadership is used, and whether it is a conscious or unconscious choice, it affects group performance and the motivation of members.

MOTIVATION

One feature that almost all successful leaders in business seem to have in common is the ability to motivate people to work towards achieving objectives. Many leaders rely on formal directions and control to motivate. Others seem to be able to get the most from the people working with them without ordering them about or threatening them if the task is not completed.

Table 9.4 lists the characteristics of motivation in organisations. What does all this mean to a leader? The difference between the two extreme approaches to motivation—task and job-centred, or people and employee-centred—arises from different assumptions about what makes people at work do things, and from the confidence and ability of the leader to communicate with the group. Choice of leadership style and impact as a leader will depend on the beliefs leaders hold about others, the way they prefer to behave and the components in the situation.

Laissez-faire leaders have a policy of non-interference and let the group run itself.

Leaders empower others by creating a sense of ownership in the task.

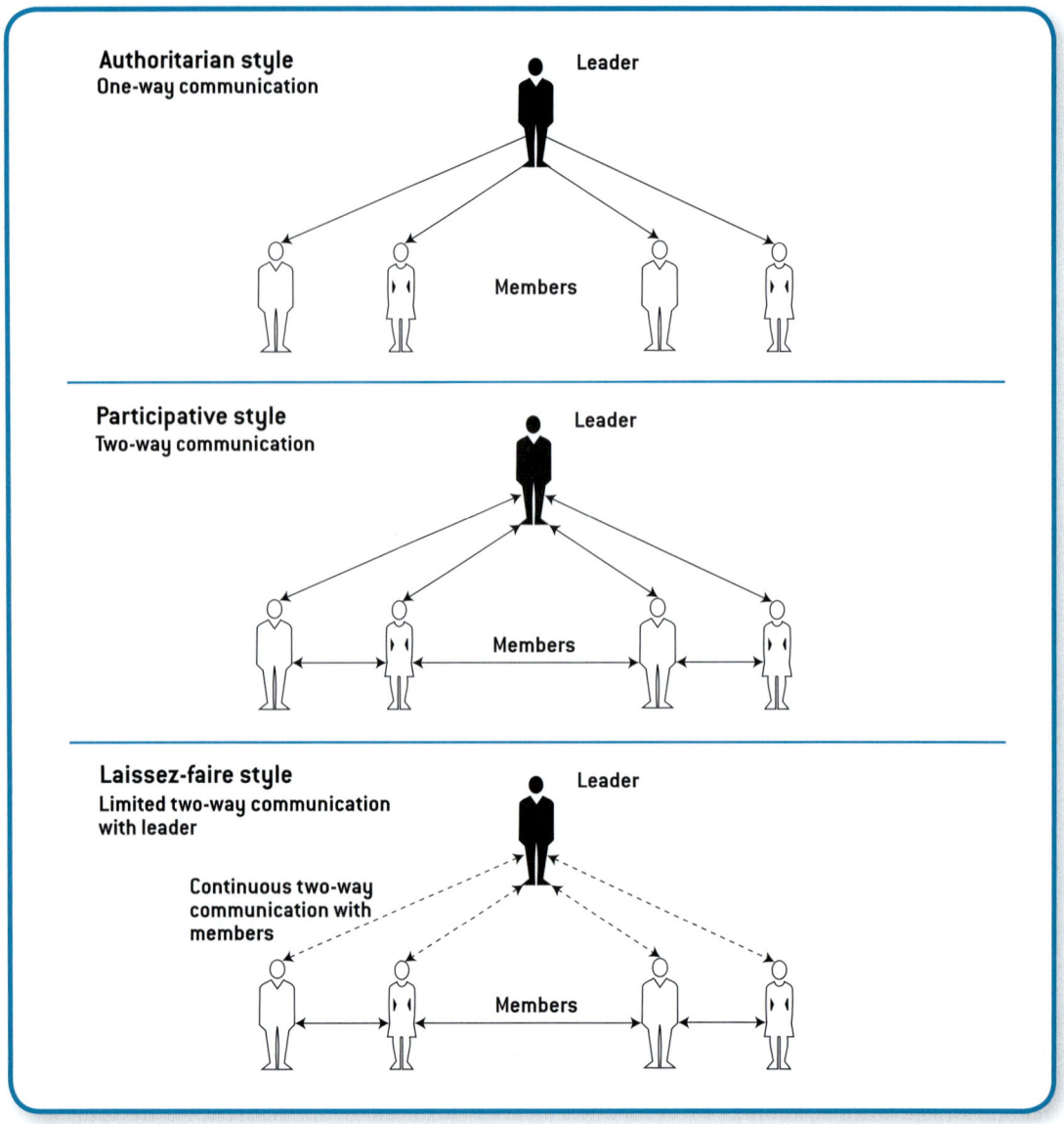

Figure 9.2: Different leadership styles and the flow of communication

Table 9.4: Characteristics of motivation in organisations	
High motivation	**Low motivation**
High performance	Apathy
Consistent results	Indifference
Energy, enthusiasm, determination	High absenteeism
Cooperation	Lack of cooperation
Willingness to accept responsibility	Unjustified resistance to change

Leadership and power

Power is defined as the capacity to influence, the possession of delegated authority or an ability to act. Power thus involves more than personal power; it also involves positional power delegated by the organisation to leaders to get the job done. Leaders can draw on six main types of power (Raven 1993):

1. **Legitimate power**, held because the organisation has given power and authority to the position held by the leader.
2. **Reward power**, held because the leader has the opportunity, through the control of resources, either to give or withhold things wanted by others—the leader can use reward power well to reinforce effective behaviour, or badly to manipulate the behaviour of others.
3. **Coercive power**, held when a leader compels others to behave in a certain way—followers may become resentful and do only the minimum to get by.
4. **Expertise power**, held because of the leader's knowledge, aptitude and ability—others are willing to defer to expertise power.
5. **Information power**, flowing from the leader's access to and control over organisational information, particularly how much information is conveyed by downward channels.
6. **Referent power**, from being respected, admired, liked or personally identified with by others—team members are motivated and follow directions willingly.

Leaders use a combination of the six types of power. A leader who uses reward power or coercive power in a way that deprives members of something they need is likely to lose the ability to influence the group. Members may only tell the leader what the leader wants to hear. By flattering the leader, particular members may ingratiate themselves. Others may submit and conform to the leader's will, while others may become rebellious and defiant or withdraw in an attempt to escape the leader's abuse of power. Group members may compete with each other for the leader's attention or blame one another when problems arise, rather than working towards solutions. Communication barriers develop.

Communication between leaders and followers is more likely to be clear, open and two-way when leaders consult with their followers. A consultative approach is based on a capacity to seek information, consider advice from others and make plans with others. It is based on cooperation and the satisfaction of mutual needs.

When exercising their power, leaders need to consider the sources of their authority and how to use their power effectively. As well as relying on the six sources of power listed above, leaders may be given authority by company management, be elected by other employees, or emerge as the person that the others in a group allow to take the leadership role. In any one of these situations, an effective leader is able to influence behaviour and achieve results in a way that meets the needs of the group as well as the needs of the organisation. In the case of an ineffective leader, there is a significant and important gap between the official title and the actual performance of leadership. Neither the needs of the group nor those of the organisation are met. The intended results are not achieved because the leader is unable to perform the leadership tasks well.

Power is the capacity to influence, the possession of delegated authority or an ability to act.

Legitimate power is held because the organisation has given authority to that position.

Reward power is the capacity a leader has to give positive benefits or rewards to others.

Coercive power depends on the ability to punish others when they do not engage in desired behaviours.

Expertise power is held because of a person's knowledge, aptitude and ability.

Information power results from having access to, and control over, the distribution of important information about organisational operations and future plans.

Referent power flows from being respected, admired, liked, or personally identified with by others.

REVIEW QUESTIONS

7. What is the difference between a directive leadership style and a supportive leadership style?
8. List three characteristics of:
   a. an authoritarian leader
   b. a participative leader
   c. a laissez-faire leader.

◄ OBJECTIVE 4
Discuss the key influences
in a situational leadership
model

SITUATIONAL LEADERSHIP

By identifying the various components of the situation, it is easy to see that there is more in a situation than just the characteristics of the leader and the members or followers, and their level of motivation. An interaction is taking place between leaders and followers. In addition, both leaders and followers have their own levels of motivation, willingness and aptitude for the tasks. Situational leadership is a form of transactional leadership.

According to the Hersey and Blanchard model (1993), performance flows not only from the leader's knowledge, skills and experience, but also from the followers' experience, skills and willingness to do the task. All need to have the necessary knowledge, experience and skills to do the job. The situation in which leaders and followers operate is not always the same.

The large number of studies attempting to isolate the key situational influences on leadership are known as the *contingency theories of leadership*. The Hersey and Blanchard **Situational Leadership®** **model** considers the interaction of leadership style, the characteristics of the followers, the relationship between task and relationship behaviour, and the situation. It is the only contingency theory of leadership presented here.

Hersey's and Blanchard's
Situational Leadership®
model identifies the key
situational influences.

(Situational Leadership® is a registered trademark of the Center for Leadership Studies, Escondido, CA. All rights reserved.)

The style of the leader

The Situational Leadership® model classifies leader behaviour into two broad categories: relationship behaviour with followers, and task behaviour with followers. In Figure 9.3, relationship behaviour is shown on the vertical axis and task behaviour on the horizontal axis. The four quadrants on the graph identify four different combinations of relationship and task behaviour demonstrated by leaders. The curved line running through the four quadrants identifies four different styles of leadership; these emerge as leaders match their leadership style for each task to suit the readiness levels of their followers:

1. *S4 Delegating*: involving low relationship behaviour and low task behaviour between the leader and the follower.
2. *S3 Participating*: involving high relationship behaviour and low task behaviour between the leader and the follower.
3. *S2 Selling*: involving high relationship behaviour and high task behaviour between the leader and the follower.
4. *S1 Telling*: involving low relationship behaviour and high task behaviour between the leader and the follower.

A leader demonstrating either S3 or S2 behaviour places emphasis on supportive relationship behaviour. In addition, the leader using the S2 type of behaviour includes more task behaviour, while the S3 leader is less directive on tasks.

A leader demonstrating S4 or S1 behaviour places less emphasis on supportive behaviour and relationship skills and, in terms of S4, little emphasis on task behaviour or directive skills. The S1 leader is highly directive on task.

Effective leaders identify the followers for a particular task and vary their leadership style to meet the followers' needs. A leadership style of telling, for example, suits a new employee with a low level of skill. As the level of competence increases, the leadership style of selling is adopted. When the person becomes highly competent, the supporting or delegating style of leadership is most appropriate.

The readiness of the follower

Besides identifying leadership behaviour, the Situational Leadership® model also identifies follower readiness. The term 'readiness' applies to the follower's readiness in each situation, rather than the

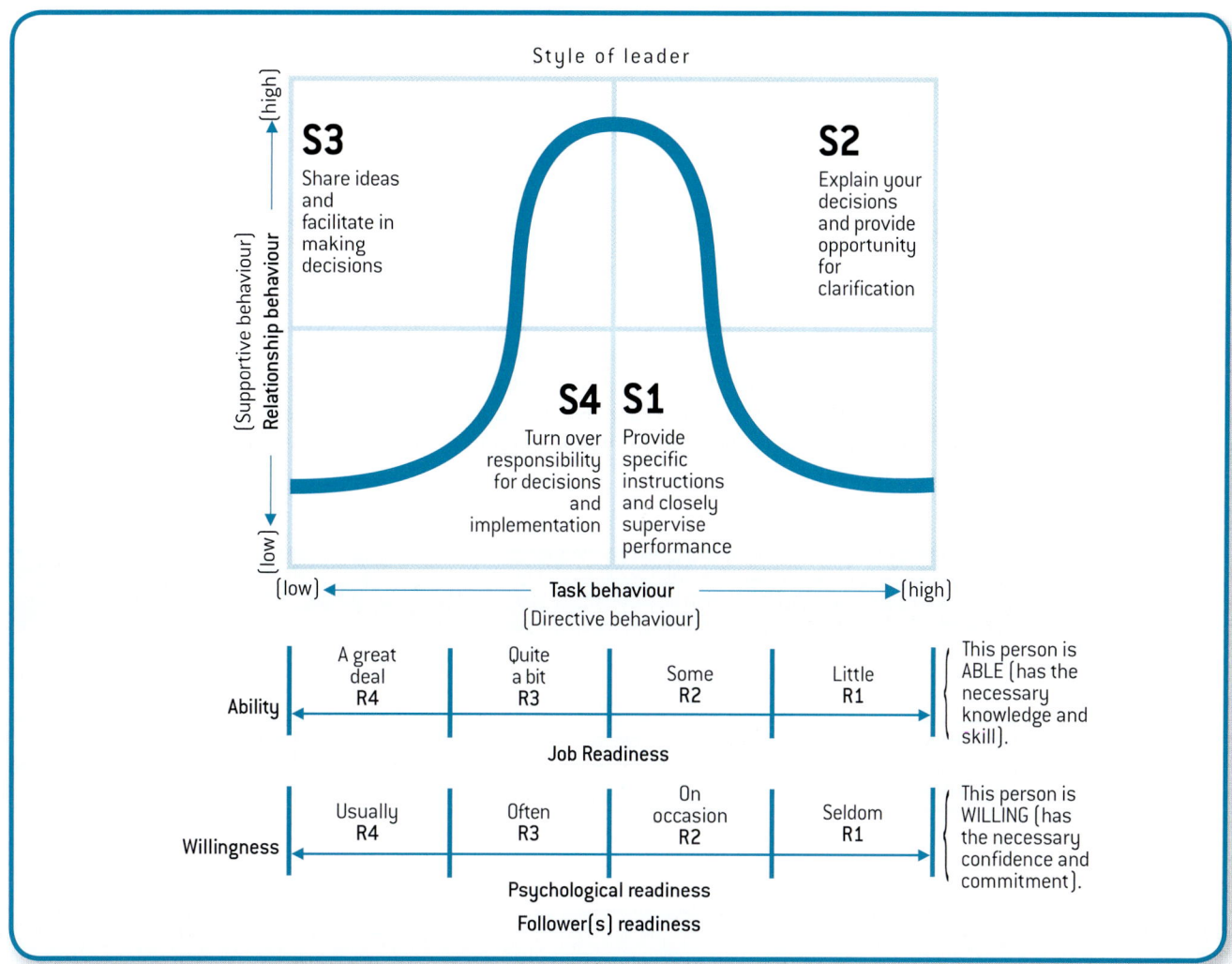

Figure 9.3: Situational Leadership® model

Source: P. Hersey, K.H. Blanchard & D.E. Johnson, *Management of Organizational Behavior: Leading Human Resources,* 8th edn, © 1993, p. 291. Reprinted with permission of The Center for Leadership Studies, Escondido, CA. 92025. All rights reserved.

follower's total readiness. The follower's readiness for a task is shown on a continuum from R4, R3, R2 to R1. Two characteristics are used to identify the level of readiness to complete the task:

1. ability
2. willingness.

The Situational Leadership® model finds that different followers have different combinations of these two characteristics and different levels of readiness and capacity to complete the tasks. The four different levels of follower readiness are:

1. *R4 Willing*: confident, and with the ability to perform the task
2. *R3 Unwilling*: insecure, and with the ability to perform the task
3. *R2 Willing*: confident, and without the ability to perform the task
4. *R1 Unwilling*: insecure, and without the ability to perform the task.

Followers demonstrating either R4 or R3 behaviour are able to direct their own behaviour, whereas R2 or R1 followers need to be directed by the leader. Hence, leaders need to be able to adapt their style of leadership to the situation and to the followers within their group. The leadership behaviour is matched to the readiness of the followers. As a result, no one particular style of leadership is the best. The decision to vary the style from leader-directed to task-directed depends on the readiness level of the followers.

Given that a leader has the influence and power to initiate action and take decisions, it is worth mentioning the decision styles suited to each level of follower readiness. These decision styles are shown in Table 9.5.

Successful situational leadership recognises and creates an effective combination of leadership style, the follower's readiness level and the situation. Note that if a leader decides to change his or her leadership style, it is best to do this gradually. A change that is too dramatic can cause suspicion or resistance, as people may feel threatened by the new style.

Leaders must work with others and, by their leadership style, affect the ability and willingness of others to perform. They also need to establish the support mechanisms required to let others develop their aptitude for the tasks, perform to their maximum ability, and develop the confidence to match their level of willingness.

Table 9.5: The leader's decision style is matched to the follower's behaviour

Leader behaviour	Decision style	Follower behaviour
S4 Delegating	Made by follower	Willing, confident, able
S3 Participating	Made by leader and follower	Unwilling, insecure, able
S2 Selling	Made by leader in consultation with follower	Willing, confident, unable
S1 Telling	Made by leader	Unwilling, insecure, unable

REVIEW QUESTIONS

9 Define the term 'situational leadership' as used in the Situational Leadership® model. List the four styles of leadership identified in this theory.

10 The Situational Leadership® model classifies leader behaviour into two broad categories. What are these categories?

11 *a* What does a leader's decision to vary his or her leadership depend on?

b Why should leaders who vary their leadership style establish support mechanisms for their followers?

OBJECTIVE **5** ▶
Describe the characteristics of, and outcomes from, transformational leadership

TRANSFORMATIONAL LEADERSHIP

Bartol and colleagues (2008, p. 496) state: 'Transactional leaders motivate subordinates to perform as expected.' Transactional leaders view leadership as a transaction between leader and follower. Rather than stimulating change in followers, their focus is on goal achievement. The focus is on leading and supporting followers to identify goals, complete task responsibilities and follow rules. Transactional leaders monitor and provide feedback about processes, outcomes and standards, and avoid intervening unless performance falls below the expected level. Rewards are linked to performance levels. While transactional leaders build confidence and understand the needs of followers, their style of leadership has a lower people orientation than the transformational style.

Behaviour of transformational leaders

Transformational leaders have the ability to evoke strong emotions in their followers. Followers identify with, and tend to trust, admire and respect their transformational leader. Transformational leaders are able to influence others and provide inspiration and motivation. They provide intellectual stimulation and give acknowledgment and consideration to followers. The behaviour of transformational leaders influences and transforms followers by:

- increasing their awareness of task importance and value
- focusing their interest on team or organisational goals, rather than their immediate self-interest
- concentrating on the higher-order needs of achievement and self-actualisation (Bass 1983; Hater & Bass 1988).

Transformational leaders foster a flexible structure and open culture. Transformational leaders also articulate a vision and direction for team goals and activities. They display values that followers either embrace or reject, and motivate people by raising their awareness of the importance of the task. Their style of leadership is capable of transforming people and organisations.

Transformational leaders exercise a high degree of expertise and referent power to inspire, engage and challenge their followers. They model and support with their time, interest and resources, engage with and develop others, and take responsibility for communicating with others in their own sphere of leadership. Their influence may be through stirring appeals or through quieter methods, such as coaching, mentoring and facilitating.

> **Transformational leaders** have the ability to evoke strong emotions in their followers. They value results and relationships, and are aware of the strategic implications of initiatives and able to integrate them with the overall vision.

Four dimensions of transformational leadership

Tracey and Hinkin (1998, pp. 220–36) refer to transactional leaders as emphasising 'work standards, assignments and task-oriented goals'. They suggest that *transformational* leadership comprises four dimensions:

1. idealised influence (behaviour that results in follower admiration, respect and trust)
2. inspirational motivation (behaviour that provides meaning and challenges to followers' work and arouses team spirit)
3. intellectual stimulation through new ideas, encouraging creativity and innovation
4. individual consideration by acknowledging needs, delegating tasks and treating others with respect.

The referent power of transformational leaders is high. Some are described as charismatic, while other transformational leaders may have a quieter approach. Both types have a 'hands-on', people- and task-centred approach that enables them to interact closely with followers. Individual consideration may be given in the form of face-to-face meetings, telephone conversations or one-on-one mentoring.

The research of Sosik and Godshalk (2000, pp. 365–90) examined linkages between mentor leadership behaviours, the perception of the mentoring functions by recipients and job-related stress. They defined *job-related stress* as an 'uncomfortable and undesirable feeling experienced by an individual required to deviate from normal or desired functioning in the workplace'; *mentoring* as 'a deliberate pairing of a more skilled or experienced person with a lesser skilled or experienced one' to achieve specific competencies; and *leadership style* as 'acts or behaviours exhibited by the mentors which influence protégés'. The findings show that mentor *transformational leadership* is associated with increased mentoring functions and reduced job-related stress; mentor *transactional contingent reward* leadership increases receipt of mentoring functions to a lesser degree; and *laissez-faire* leadership has a negative relationship.

Tracey and Hinkin's work (1998) on transformational leadership supports the current research of Sosik and Godshalk outlined above. They state: 'Without a doubt, there is something unique about transformational leadership.' They suggest that future research should 'examine the process by which transformational leaders exert their influence'.

Quiet words of management

Quiet managers strengthen the cultural bonds between people by treating them as respected members of a cohesive social system.

Mintzberg (1999) presents the view that 'Quiet managers don't empower their people—"empowerment" is taken for granted'. Rather than managing by putting someone or something in to fix the problem (management by intrusion), quiet managers change what needs to be changed steadily rather than thrusting change upon followers. They trust followers to take responsibility for ensuring serious changes take hold. Mintzberg identifies the 'quiet words' of managing as:

- 'inspiring', by creating the conditions that foster openness and release energy
- 'caring', by not slicing away problems, by preventing and fixing problems, knowing how and when to intervene
- 'infusing', by changing things slowly, steadily and profoundly, rather than thrusting change upon followers dramatically and in superficial episodes
- 'initiating', by finding out what is going on in the organisation, connecting with those at the base and all levels, rather than parachuting directions down from the top levels.

In his view, while leaders and managers stay disconnected from the rest of the organisation, their strategies and directions will not reach 'the floor' of the organisation. Instead, their disconnectedness will create a culture of dependence that has no real knowledge of the organisation's strategy and direction. A culture of independence is built when '. . . management blends into the daily life of the corporation'. People across the organisation understand, accept and can pursue actively initiatives that support current strategies and even lead to the evolution of new strategies. 'Leadership works because it is legitimate, meaning that it is an integral part of the organisation and has the respect of everyone there' (Mintzberg 1999).

REVIEW QUESTIONS

12. List four dimensions of transformational leadership.
13. Explain the statement, 'Quiet managers don't empower their people—"empowerment" is taken for granted' (Mintzberg 1999).

OBJECTIVE 6 ▶
Identify leadership communication practices and explain the purpose of, and differences between, mentoring and coaching

LEADERSHIP COMMUNICATION PRACTICES

Every leader has the prerogative to control their organisation, department, section or team. On occasions, power (legitimate, reward, coercive, expert, information and referent) must be exercised as part of the leadership role. However, effective leaders do more than exercise their control. Effective leaders are skilled in the tasks that need to be achieved, and in the interpersonal skills needed to convey the messages that help complete the tasks, maintain the group and support their followers.

Effective interpersonal communication and behaviours by leaders enhance working relationships and clarify roles, expectations and standards.

Leaders, managers and followers need to consider the communication factor in their organisation, particularly training people in the interpersonal communication needed for their workplace roles. Additionally, current leaders are being encouraged to develop their mentoring, coaching and facilitating skills. Leaders with high-level interpersonal skills are effective in their work and relationships with others. However, leadership is increasingly viewed as a shared task and partnership between followers and leaders. Both need to be able to communicate well.

While the expectation is that leaders will achieve results through their people, often they are promoted to a leadership role because of their technical expertise without the interpersonal people skills to match. A leader demonstrates effective interpersonal communication by:

- informing followers and others about things happening in the organisation
- listening genuinely to followers about successes, concerns or issues
- modelling behaviour that supports the organisation's and team's vision and strategies

- presenting followers' views and concerns upwards through the organisation
- involving stakeholders in decision making and problem solving
- consulting with relevant stakeholders about changes or issues.

Effective leaders communicate powerful messages by sending signals about the organisation. Signals in this context are defined as activities that build the organisation's culture and teamwork. Congratulating people for their presentations in meetings, describing values the leader finds important at formal and informal occasions, motivating through encouragement, mentoring and coaching, and applying effective facilitation skills in meetings, briefings and functions are all leadership signals about what is valued.

Good communication skills are included in the position descriptions of almost all leaders, managers and supervisors because good communication is one of the attributes of good leaders. Leaders use their communication skills to conduct annual performance reviews and regular informal and work progress reviews with staff. Communication is a major factor in the way in which they lead the group towards the attainment of goals and help in the process that leads to completion of these goals.

A leader who is aware of the communication process recognises the seven elements involved and is able to understand where in the communication process communication is going well and where communication barriers occur (see Chapter 1). They use a variety of communication channels as they fulfil their communication responsibilities within their sphere of activities, especially with their own staff.

Communication responsibilities are fulfilled via face-to-face, written and online communication. The communication responsibilities may include holding regular face-to-face team briefings for staff who report directly to the leader, holding periodic workshop or team sessions on staff communication, setting aside a regular time for staff to raise concerns or new ideas, organising a minimum number of staff recognition activities within their area, developing an internal communication strategy or organising annual stakeholder attitude surveys (Harrison 2008). Mentoring those with less experience and coaching others informally during conversations or in formalised coaching/training sessions are common leadership communication practices.

In the emerging democratic and less hierarchical organisational environments, transformational leaders and managers value empowerment of staff. The leadership style is empowering because they use effective communication practices to develop 'good decision-making ability in subordinates, as well as guiding, coaching and inspiring them' (Bateman & Snell 2007; Bartol et al. 2008).

Mentoring

Mentoring is a relationship in which those with experience and knowledge facilitate and support those with less experience and knowledge. It is a useful skill for leaders. The mentoring process supports career development, improves individual performance and transfers corporate information and knowledge. As mentoring is a deliberate pairing of a more skilled or experienced person with a lesser skilled or experienced person, it is a very useful support tool. Godshalk and Sosik (2000) discuss the psychosocial support and career development functions performed by mentors and focus on the impact of transformational leadership behaviour on the quality of the mentoring relationship.

Mentoring is a relationship in which those with experience and knowledge facilitate and support those with less experience and knowledge.

Regardless of the mentor's style of leadership, one of the key factors in a successful mentoring relationship is communication. Mentors and mentorees who interact using good speaking and listening skills in the early stages of the mentoring process are able to clarify and gain agreement on the process and goals that will enable the mentoree to grow and develop. Goals are identified, an action plan is created, and commitment is gained from both mentor and mentoree.

Mentoring can be either formal or informal. A leader can organise a formal structured program of mentoring that lets mentoree and mentor know what the mentoring program is about. An informal mentoring program leaves individuals and their managers to self-select the areas to include in the mentoring program. The characteristics of formal and informal mentoring programs are shown in Table 9.6.

Formal in-house mentoring programs are designed to enhance communication and collaboration and to foster an open environment where knowledge is transferred from experienced to less experienced

Table 9.6: Characteristics of formal and informal mentoring programs

Formal	Informal
A formal mentoring program:	An informal mentoring process:
• has a mentoring program coordinator (usually)	• requires mentor and mentoree to take a proactive approach
• depends on an agreement between mentor and mentoree	• depends on an agreement between mentor and mentoree
• defines the goals and identifies the approach in a mentoring action plan	• is often impromptu and therefore unplanned
• identifies standards against which the results and benefits of the program will be measured	• is able to measure the results when mentor and mentoree take the time to decide on the intended results
• has fixed schedules	• has flexible, even open schedules
• gives feedback to mentoree and program coordinator	• provides feedback to the mentoree throughout the mentoring relationship
• is supported by the organisation.	• employs informal communication channels.

staff. Effective programs improve individual motivation, performance and innovation by sharing corporate knowledge and exposing mentorees to organisational values, relationships and business processes. As well as gaining a broader view of their work and how it supports the organisation's vision and objectives, a mentoree develops problem-solving skills, self-confidence and insights about themselves.

An organisational culture that supports mentoring and coaching focuses on solving problems, rather than on laying blame.

Mentors also benefit from an effective mentoring program. They gain a better understanding of the needs of followers, other staff and the organisation. Mentors share their knowledge and expertise with others and gain a fresh perspective on their work and the value of helping others. A mentoring program also provides them with the opportunity to develop staff competence and the potential resources for assistance on future projects. Aviation Safety Foundation Australia (2008), for example, has established the Aviation Safety Mentor Program '. . . on the premise that accident and incident rates could be reduced by encouraging members of the aviation community to improve their attitudes toward safety by refreshing aeronautical knowledge and by improving aeronautical skills. A critical component of this process is the transfer of skills and shaping of behaviours from selected mentors to their associated protégés'.

Organisations support formal mentoring programs because of their benefits. Robbins and colleagues (2008, p. 444) say: 'Successful mentors . . . present ideas clearly, listen well, and empathise with the problems of their protégés.' Formal mentoring programs provide support for high-potential staff and developmental opportunities for minorities in a company to develop their organisational knowledge and career paths. Other benefits include improved safety and risk management due to the increased confidence and competence of staff.

Mentors and mentorees need to develop and use communication skills to interact effectively in their mentoring relationship. Those with effective interpersonal skills are able to create a balance in their interaction that allows them to fulfil their roles in the relationship. Open and supportive complementary verbal and nonverbal messages and constructive feedback (refer to Chapter 4) allow both parties to achieve results and build a positive mentoring relationship.

The leader who mentors a staff member is taking an interest in and being responsible for the development of that person. Both mentor and mentoree are contributing to the development of a learning organisation. Rather than overestimating or underestimating what can be achieved, mentor and mentoree should agree on realistic goals and work together towards the intended outcome. Mentoring provides a useful framework to:

● develop skills and support people in rapidly changing work environments
● provide developmental working experiences

- increase productivity for the organisation
- improve organisational communication
- improve succession planning and encourage career planning
- enhance insights into the organisation as a whole
- increase personal and professional networks.

Stern (2002, p. 57) maintains that 'the best mentors are listeners rather than instructors, sympathetic allies when big decisions need to be made'. He lists the following attributes of a mentor (p. 59):

What a mentor will do for you

- Listen to you carefully
- Get you to analyse your situation systematically
- Encourage you to be honest and realistic about your goals and ambitions
- Compare your situation to others in your own experience
- Reassure you that you are not alone
- Help you accurately assess your abilities and potential
- Find other helpful people for you to talk to.

Leaders who mentor staff are acting as role models. They use their communication skills to consult with mentorees about their commitment and desire to be part of the mentoring process. The communication style is open regardless of whether it is one-to-one communication with a mentor or across the organisation. Team leaders, managers and other staff need to understand what happens in the mentoring process and its place in the organisation's processes. Communication is a critical success factor because the mentoring process is interactive and dynamic, and one in which mentor and mentoree self-disclose in terms of their job roles and activities (see Chapter 4). Both parties' expectations need to be realistic, achievable and clarified to minimise clashes or disappointment due to false expectations.

Coaching

Coaching is a method of directing and instructing people with the aim of achieving some goal or developing specific skills that produce results. The purpose of coaching is development, growth and performance improvement. Robbins and colleagues (2006, p. 780) state: 'Effective managers are increasingly being described as *coaches* rather than as *bosses*. Just like coaches, they are expected to provide instruction, guidance, advice and encouragement to help employees improve their job performance.' In their coaching role, leaders and managers aim to develop and inspire people to achieve their best.

Coaching can be informal, such as a coaching conversation with a staff member, or more formal, such as during an appraisal conversation or a formalised coaching/training session. Informal and formal coaching discussions ensure the commitment, clarity, competence and confidence of the follower in the conduct of their job. The coaching conversation is aligned to ongoing organisational needs and the needs of the role. Leaders coach on the job one-to-one or in small groups and engage interpersonally by:

- explaining and clarifying
- respecting the contribution of all
- giving credit for achievements
- providing encouragement
- problem solving
- providing feedback
- demonstrating and modelling desired actions and behaviours.

Those being coached need opportunities for skills guidance, practice and reflection. In their coaching role, leaders not only guide but also tutor, train, empower, counsel, communicate and manage the performance of the person they are coaching. Coaching opens up communication channels and increases job satisfaction, confidence and capability. It also increases staff retention because of the developmental

Coaching is a method of directing and instructing people with the aim of achieving some goal or developing specific skills that produce results.

Obstacles to coaching—lack of time, low priority, lack of coaching skills—are overcome when an organisation identifies coaching as a priority and allocates the necessary time and resources.

Table 9.7: Skills checklist: The basic steps of coaching

Step	What to do
1 **Determine** the training need and the desired outcome	Identify and document the problem: • observe the team member on the job • look through the team member's performance records • consider the outcomes of a formal performance appraisal program. State the desired outcome clearly.
2 **Explain** the process	Describe clearly to the team member: • what the coaching process will involve • what it is designed to achieve and why • when coaching will take place • how long each session will last • what resources will be required.
3 **Demonstrate** the desired behaviour or task	Do it quickly. Do the task or demonstrate the behaviour at the normal pace expected on the job. **Do it slowly:** • break the task or the behaviour down into small sections • carefully demonstrate each section • clearly explain what you are doing and *why*.
4 **Practise** the desired behaviour or task	Do it with them. The team member should practise the task or behaviour with you at their side or assisting. **Let them go:** • arrange to observe only • encourage the team member to practise the task or behaviour as often as possible.
5 **Feedback**	*Monitor* the team member's performance. *Correct* any variations from the expected standard. *Avoid* destructive criticism; encourage and motivate. *Listen* to problems the team member may want to talk about, or any suggestions he or she may have. *Acknowledge* the team member's progress and achievements.

opportunities. Coaching enables people to achieve better results with less effort and less need for corrective actions. The purpose of coaching is to encourage learning, rather than compliance or imitation.

Coaching is often a formalised training process that follows five basic steps:

1 determining the training need and the desired outcome
2 explaining the process
3 demonstrating the desired behaviour or task
4 practising the desired behaviour or task
5 feedback.

Use the skills checklist in Table 9.7 to evaluate your skill in applying the basic planning steps before you conduct a coaching program or session. A coaching plan is a useful way to document what will happen, as well as being a useful guide and checklist.

A process approach to coaching provides a step-by-step guide that slowly produces real behavioural change, but it takes time and commitment from the leader and those being coached. People perform at their best in the coaching process when they are appropriately challenged. Too much stretch causes stress; too little produces boredom. Coaching should encourage people to ask questions and develop their own answers with the help of the coach as required. The person being coached is the expert in their work. Their focus throughout the coaching is on solutions in terms of what is happening now, what is wanted in the future and how to achieve it. The coach's focus throughout the coaching is on encouragement and trusting the other person to move forward through the process.

REVIEW QUESTIONS

14 'Communication is the crux of leadership.' Do you agree or disagree? Give reasons for your answer.

15 Briefly explain a leader's mentoring function.

16 What do leaders do in their coaching role?

APPLY YOUR KNOWLEDGE

STYLES OF LEADERSHIP

1 Contrast authoritarian leadership and participative leadership.

2 Work in small groups to discuss the statement, 'Participative styles of leadership lead to increased job satisfaction and higher performance.'

a   What is it about this style of leadership that leads to increased job satisfaction?

b   Does the participative style always lead to higher performance? Justify your answer.

3 Think of a leader of a section or group with which you are familiar and describe the way that person motivates the group. What do you think are the strengths and weaknesses of their approach?

4 a   Read this paragraph.

When a decision is needed, an effective leader does not just fall into a single preferred style, such as using transactional or transformational styles of leadership. In practice, as they say, things are not that simple. Factors that affect situational decisions include motivation and capability of followers.

b   What other factors within a particular situation can affect the leader's choice of style?

5 Work in small groups.

a   Reflect on the communication practices identified in the checklist below. Self-evaluate your skills.

b   Discuss the practices with your group, and choose by consensus the six that contribute most to effective leadership.

c   Individually self-evaluate your skill in all the communication practices by ticking 'yes', 'no' or 'unsure'.

d   For one of the practices you have ticked with a 'no' or 'unsure', prepare a plan of action to improve your skill in that communication practice.

SELF-EVALUATE YOUR SKILL

COMMUNICATION PRACTICES

I am able to:	Yes	No	Unsure
communicate goals, task importance and value			
listen genuinely to successes, issues and concerns			
present followers' views upwards through the organisation			
inform followers about things happening in the organisation			

continued

I am able to:	Yes	No	Unsure
conduct regular workplace progress review meetings			
hold periodic team sessions on staff communication			
participate and interact with followers formally and informally			
focus the followers' interest on team or organisational goals			
involve stakeholders in decision making and problem solving			
develop an internal communication strategy			
conduct annual formal and regular informal reviews with followers			
set aside regular available time for staff to discuss their concerns			
build a supportive informal mentoring relationship			
conduct informal coaching conversations			
participate effectively in formal mentoring and coaching programs			
organise a minimum number of annual staff recognition activities			
participate in internal and external networks			
consult to gather ideas, and acknowledge the contributions of others.			

SUMMARY OF LEARNING OBJECTIVES

 OUTLINE LEADERSHIP TASKS AND ACTIVITIES, AND DISCUSS BEHAVIOURS COMMON TO MOST MANAGERS

The leader relies on, and taps the resources of, team members in a way that focuses the energies of the group on achieving the intended results. It is therefore necessary to motivate, organise and direct the group, and to cope with any unexpected contingencies. Leaders consult, counsel, develop group cohesiveness and ensure the group achieves the desired objectives. Leaders develop a vision, make jobs meaningful, give feedback, represent, develop teamwork and engage in management activities when necessary. Effective communication is a significant factor in good leadership.

 IDENTIFY EARLY APPROACHES TO LEADERSHIP AND DISCUSS CURRENT THEORIES

Theories of leadership have described leaders in terms of their traits, styles, the situation, functions, contingencies of a situation, the capacity to adapt in dynamic, changing circumstances, and the transactional, charismatic and transformational approaches. Current theories such as the transactional, situational, transformational leadership and quiet management theories describe leadership in terms of motivations and ability to influence and cause change in the new organisations.

 DISTINGUISH THREE BROAD LEADERSHIP STYLES AND THE TYPES OF POWER AVAILABLE TO A LEADER

There are several styles or approaches to leadership. Participative leaders are willing to share the leadership role with others, delegate decision making and make the work environment as supportive as possible. Authoritarian leaders focus on the task and direct others towards the achievement of the task. Laissez-faire leaders have a policy of non-interference and allow the group to run itself. The choice of style or approach will depend on the leader, the group dynamics, the task, time constraints and many other factors. No approach seems to be effective in all situations.

A leader may use six types of power: legitimate power, reward power, coercive power, expert power, information power and referent power.

 DISCUSS THE KEY INFLUENCES IN A SITUATIONAL LEADERSHIP MODEL

The Situational Leadership® model suggests that performance flows from the leader's knowledge, skills and experience, but also from the follower's experience, skills and willingness to do the task. Motivation, commitment and confidence also impact on the situation. In the situational model, leaders motivate followers to perform as expected. Their focus is on leading and supporting followers to identify goals, complete task responsibilities and follow rules. They build confidence in and understand the needs of followers, but avoid intervening unless performance falls below the expected level. Rewards are linked to performance levels.

 DESCRIBE THE CHARACTERISTICS OF, AND OUTCOMES FROM, TRANSFORMATIONAL LEADERSHIP

Transformational leaders have the ability to evoke strong emotions in their followers. They are able to influence others and provide inspiration and motivation, intellectual stimulation and individual consideration. Transformational leaders influence and transform followers by increasing their awareness of task importance and value, focusing their interest on team or organisational goals rather than immediate self-interest, and concentrating on the higher-order needs of achievement and self-actualisation.

 IDENTIFY LEADERSHIP COMMUNICATION PRACTICES AND EXPLAIN THE PURPOSE OF, AND DIFFERENCES BETWEEN, MENTORING AND COACHING

Effective leaders communicate powerful messages by sending signals about the organisation. Examples are congratulating people for their presentations in meetings, describing values the leader finds important on formal and informal occasions, and motivating through mentoring and coaching. Mentoring is the deliberate pairing of a more skilled or experienced person with a less skilled or experienced person; it is a very useful support tool. Mentoring can be a formal organisational process or an informal arrangement between mentor and mentoree. Coaching is a structured process that helps to build employee skills and can be formal or informal.

KEY TERMS

ACTIVITIES AND QUESTIONS

1. Describe the differences between a leader's role and the role of members in a group. How is the role of a leader similar to the role of members?

2. Working in small groups, discuss the five leadership requirements identified by Phillips as necessary in the adaptive approach to leadership. Brainstorm to identify the communication skills needed by a leader who uses the adaptive approach to leadership.

   a. Identify three leadership styles.

   b. Briefly describe the most important aspect of each style.

c   Differentiate between personal power and position power.

d   Who should control a team—the leader or the followers? Justify your answer.

3   Work in groups of three.

a   How does the style of leadership affect the flow of communication between the leader and the group?

b   'People skills are more important to a manager's progress than intelligence, decisiveness or job skills.'
What does this statement mean?

c   Prepare a list of six communication skills that help leaders use their 'people skills'.

d   Compare effective and ineffective nonverbal communication you have observed in leaders.

e   As a group leader, you notice that two members seem to be withdrawing from the group. To maintain group cohesion, you wish to draw these people back into the group. In your group of three, decide on a strategy that would help you to do this.

4   Think of a group you are involved in at work or in your studies.

a   Identify the group leader.

b   Briefly explain this person's approach to leadership.

c   Name three ways in which group members participate in the group.

5   a   Differentiate between supportive and directive behaviour by a leader by nominating three supportive behaviours and three directive behaviours.

b   Give examples of two situations suited to supportive behaviour and two situations suited to directive behaviour by the leader.

6   Work in small discussion groups.

a   What is the difference between a transformational and a transactional leader?

b   Transformational leadership does not replace transactional leadership; it supplements it. Describe how transformational leadership supplements transactional leadership.

c   Prepare a short group presentation to your colleagues titled 'Characteristics of transformational and transactional leadership'.

7   *Leadership workshop*
Brad Haynes is the Senior Supervisor of the Commercial Cleaning Division in a large national cleaning services firm. Brad reports to the Divisional Head, Sally Helman. The Commercial Cleaning Division is formally subdivided into Office Cleaning Services and the smaller but specialised Household Cleaning Services. Sofia McGregor is the Junior Supervisor in the Household Cleaning Division, supervising the small but specialised section responsible for cleaning the homes of elderly clients. Sofia reports directly to Brad, as their responsibilities lie within the same division. Both Brad, and Sofia have experienced much difficulty with the supervision of the Household Cleaning Section. Company guidelines are clear on lines of communication: staff members communicate within their own group and with their immediate supervisor to make decisions and solve problems.

One experienced staff member, Tracey, from the small specialised section, refuses to communicate with either Sofia, her direct supervisor, or Brad, the more senior supervisor. Instead, Tracey ignores the company guidelines and goes around Sofia and Brad to the Divisional Head, Sally. Sally listens to Tracey and makes decisions with her without consulting Brad or Sofia, the senior and junior supervisors. This means Brad and Sofia are often unaware of the decisions and feel undermined. Sally's style of leadership leaves them feeling powerless and that their leadership is ineffectual. They have, in fact, lost control of the section.

As a consequence, barriers in communication arise and constant arguments and problems occur between Tracey and her immediate supervisors, Sofia and Brad. The problems become so severe that Sally Helman takes them to the Director, Rasheed Masood. Without consulting Brad and Sofia, Rasheed and Sally decide to remove the control of the smaller, specialised section from Sofia and Brad for a three-month trial. All staff from both sections are given a memo to attend a meeting called by the Director. 'You are directed to be at a meeting on 9 March at 10.30 am in the Conference Room.' No agenda is provided.

Staff from both sections and Brad and Sofia are in attendance. The Director, Rasheed, chairs the meeting while the Divisional Head, Sally, takes the minutes. It is announced by Sally that the two sections, Office Cleaning Services and Household Cleaning Services, will be separately supervised and administered in the future. Tracey is to supervise the Household Cleaning Services section. Brad and Sofia are devastated and humiliated by the decision, particularly the manner in which the decision is made and announced in front of their staff.

a   In groups of seven or eight, role-play the section

of the meeting in which the announcement about changes in leadership is made. Prepare a script for each of the characters. Place emphasis on their reaction to the situation.

b   After the role play, break into two groups of three or four and discuss the following:

i   Which leadership style do you believe would have led Sally and Rasheed to the best result in this situation?

ii   What is your preferred leadership style when you are the leader?

iii   What is your preferred leadership style when you are the follower?

EXPLORING THE WEB

1   a   Visit the Leader to Leader Institute, Knowledge Centre at <www.leadertoleader.org>. The site contains leadership resources, including journals, books and videos, Thought Leaders Gateway, and others.

b   Choose and critically evaluate one of the articles from the Thought Leaders Gateway.

2   Visit the Leadership Online site at <www.leadershiponlinewkkf.org/>.

a   Browse the site to find extraordinary leaders.

b   What were the characteristics or factors that led to these people becoming extraordinary leaders?

PROJECT WORK

Read the paragraph below and then complete the four parts of the project.

Many of today's most successful leaders share the belief that effective leadership is a partnership. The consensus is that days of command and control are over and a leader is likely to achieve better results from influencing attitudes, mentoring and empowering people rather than workers. Headhunters look for CEOs who can build teams, change attitudes, use an understanding of the self and others to collaborate and communicate effectively at the coalface and in the boardroom. Strength and power are no longer essential leadership qualities.

1   Compile a job description and a newspaper recruitment advertisement for a *collaborative* style of leader for a business of your choice. Submit this with a covering note to your supervisor, explaining your choice of essential and desirable qualities for this leader.

2   Compile a job description and a newspaper recruitment advertisement for a *command and control* style of leader for a business of your choice. Submit this with a covering note to your supervisor, explaining your choice of essential and desirable qualities for this leader.

3   Write an opening address for a debate in favour of collaborative leadership entitled 'Leadership has to be won'. Explain the theories of situational and transformational leadership in your address, and include case studies where these have been successfully applied. Use at least one of the following quotes in support of your argument.

QUOTES

As for the best leaders, the people do not notice their existence. The next best, the people honour and praise. The next, the people fear, and the next, the people hate. When the best leader's work is done, the people say, 'We did it ourselves!'

Lao-Tsu, 6th century BC Chinese philosopher

The hierarchical part of leadership has finished. There has to be a collaborative approach in everything you do now, and you have to be able to get down with your troops and understand what they are saying to you. The last 15 years, in particular, have seen the end of the command-and-control model as people vote with their feet: People won't stay where they are not valued.

Don Argus, chair, BHP Billiton and Brambles

The real pressure is for a more democratic, less hierarchical leader. Leadership may still require long hours and tough decisions, but there are few brownie points these days for bosses who are overt about either . . . Instead, women and young people are often openly scornful of the old model. It means that one of the elements that has long underpinned leadership in business—complete dedication to the job—is now dismissed by many potential 'followers'. Leaders need to find a new set of tools if they want support. More than ever, leadership has to be won.

AFR Boss, *True Leaders 2006*, August 2006

Indeed, the best managing of all may well be silent. That way people can say, 'We did it ourselves.'

Henry Mintzberg, 'Managing quietly', *Leader to Leader*, Vol. 12, Spring 1999

Leaders must be able to adjust their leadership style to the situation as well as to the people being led. Leaders are not limited to one style in a given situation and, with the nature of the battlefield today and tomorrow, being able to adopt appropriate styles will influence soldiers' success.

Major George W. Yeakey, US Army, rtd, *Military Review*, January–February 2005

BIBLIOGRAPHY

Aviation Safety Foundation Australia. *Aviation Safety Mentor Program*, ASFA, http://aviationsafety.org.au, viewed 8 January 2008.

Bartol, K., Tein, M., Matthews, G. & Sharma, B. 2008. *Management: A Pacific Rim Focus*, McGraw-Hill, Sydney.

Bass, B.M., 1983. *Organizational Decision Making*, Irwin, Homewood, Illinois.

Bateman, T.S. & Snell, S.A. 2007. *Management: Leading and Collaborating in a Competitive World*, McGraw-Hill/Irwin, New York.

Chen, J-C. & Silverthorne, C. 'Leadership effectiveness, leadership style and employee readiness', *Leadership and Organization Development Journal*, Vol. 26, Issue 4, pp. 280–8.

Conger, J.A. & Kanungo, R.N. 1987. 'Toward a behavioural theory of charismatic leadership in organizational settings', *Academy of Management Review*, Vol. 12, pp. 637–47.

Conger, J.A. & Kanungo, R.N. 1994. 'Charismatic leadership in organizations: perceived behavioral attributes and their measurement', *Journal of Organizational Behavior*, Vol. 15, Issue. 7, pp. 439–52.

Crant, M.J. & Bateman, T.S. 2000. 'Charismatic leadership viewed from above: the impact of proactive personality', *Journal of Organizational Behavior*, Vol. 21, Issue 1, February, pp. 63–75.

Farrelly, K. 2003. 'Follow the leader', *Sydney Morning Herald*, 'My Career', 29–30 March, p. 1.

Fiedler, F.E. 1967. *A Theory of Leadership Effectiveness*, McGraw-Hill, New York.

Fiedler, F.E. & Garcia, J.E. 1987. *New Approaches to Effective Leadership: Cognitive Resources and Organizational Performance*, Wiley, New York.

French, J.R.P. & Raven, B. 1959. 'The bases of social power', in D. Cartwright (ed.), *Studies in Social Power*, University of Michigan Press, USA.

Gerzon, M. 2006. *Leading Through Conflict: How Successful Leaders Transform Differences into Opportunities*, Harvard Business School Press, USA.

Godshalk, V.M. & Sosik, J.J. 2000. 'Does mentor-protégé agreement on mentor leadership behavior influence the quality of a mentoring relationship?', *Group and Organization Management*, Vol. 25, Issue 3, September, pp. 291–314.

Goleman, D. 1995. *Emotional Intelligence*, Bantam Books, New York.

Goleman, D. 1998. *Working with Emotional Intelligence*, Bantam Books, New York.

Hales, C. 2001. 'Does it matter what managers do?', *Business Strategy Review*, Vol. 12, Issue 2, Summer, pp. 50–58.

Harrison, K. 'What you can do to improve managers' communication skills', *Cutting Edge PR*, www.cuttingedgepr.com, viewed 5 January 2008.

Harvie, J. 2003. 'People power', *Sydney Morning Herald*, 'My Career', 1–2 March, p. 1.

Hater, J.J. & Bass, B.M. 1988. 'Superiors' evaluations and subordinates' perceptions of transformational and transactional leadership', *Journal of Applied Psychology*, Vol. 73, pp. 695–702.

Hersey, P. & Blanchard, K.H. 1982. 'Attitudes; behaviour; leadership styles; self-concept', *Training and Development Journal*, Vol. 36, Issue 5, May, pp. 50–52.

Hersey, P., Blanchard, K.H. & Johnson, D.E. 1993. *Management of Organizational Behaviour: Leading Human Resources*, 8th edn, Prentice Hall, Englewood Cliffs, New Jersey.

Hersey, P., Blanchard, K.H. & Johnson, D.E. 2001. *Management of Organizational Behavior: Searching Human Resources*, 8th edn, Prentice Hall, Englewood Cliffs, New Jersey.

Herzberg, F. 1966. *Work and the Nature of Man*, World Publishing, Cleveland.

House, R.J. 1971. 'A path-goal theory of leader effectiveness', *Administrative Science Quarterly*, Vol. 16.

House, R.J. 1974. 'Path-goal theory of leadership', *Journal of Contemporary Business*, Autumn.

Human Synergistics International. 2003. *Leadership/Impact®*, 2002, www.humansyn.co.uk/news_articles/features/leadership_impact, 15 June.

Jesuino, J.C. 1996. 'Leadership: micro-macro links', in E.H. Witte & J.H. Davis (eds), *Understanding Group Behavior*, Lawrence Erlbaum Associates, New Jersey.

Johannsen, M. 'Nine sources of leadership influence', www.legacee.com/info/leadership/influence.html, viewed 12 February 2008.

Kellogg Foundation. *Leadership Online*, www.leadershiponlinewkkf.org, viewed 4 January 2008.

Lewin, K., Lippitt, R. & White, R.K. 1939. 'Patterns of aggressive behavior in experimentally created "social climates" ', *Journal of Social Psychology*, Vol. 10, pp. 271–99.

Luthans, F. 1986. *Organizational Behavior*, 4th edn, McGraw-Hill, New York.

McGregor, D. 1960. *The Human Side of Enterprise*, McGraw-Hill, New York.

Maslow, A. 1954. *Motivation and Personality*, Harper & Row, New York.

Mintzberg, H, 1999. 'Managing quietly', *Leader to Leader*, Vol. 12, Spring, pp. 224–30.

O'Neil, J. 1996. 'On emotional intelligence: a conversation with Daniel Goleman', *Educational Leadership*, Vol. 54, Issue 1, September.

Phillips, G.M. 1986. *Group Discussion: A Practical Guide to Participation and Leadership*, 2nd edn, Harper & Row Publishers, New York.

Raven, B.H. 1993. 'The bases of power: origins and recent developments', *Journal of Science Issues*, Vol. 49, pp. 227–51.

Reed Business Information. 2002. *Aussie Bosses Fear Failure, Attack and Criticise: Study*, 16 August, www.dialinfolink.com, 15 June 2003.

Robbins, S., Bergman, R., Stagg, I. & Coulter, M. 2006. *Management*, 4th edn, Pearson Education Australia, Sydney.

Robbins, S.P., Judge, T.A., Millett, B. & Waters-Marsh, T. 2008. *Organisational Behaviour*, 5th edn, Pearson Education Australia, Sydney.

Sosik, J.J. & Godshalk, V.M. 2000. 'Leadership styles, mentoring functions received, and job-related stress: a conceptual model and preliminary study', *Journal of Organizational Behavior*, Vol. 21, Issue 4, June, pp. 365–90.

Spreitzer, G.M., De Janasz, S.C. & Quinn, R.E. 1999. 'Empowered to lead: the role of psychological empowerment in leadership', *Journal of Organizational Behavior*, Vol. 20, Issue 4, July, pp. 511–26.

Stern, S. 2002. 'Someone to talk to', *Management Today*, July, pp. 56–59.

Taylor, F.W. 1911. *Principles of Scientific Management*, Harpers, New York.

Tracey, J.B. & Hinkin, T.R. 1998. 'Transformational leadership or effective managerial practice', *Group & Organizational Management*, Vol. 23, Issue 3, September, pp. 220–36.

21st Century Leadership Communication, Melcrum Research, United Kingdom, 2007.

Vroom, V.H. 1964. *Work and Motivation*, Wiley, New York.

Vroom, V.H. & Jago, A.G. 1988. 'Managing participation: a critical dimension of leadership', *Journal of Management Development*, Vol. 7, pp. 32–42.

Zand, D.E. 1997. *The Leadership Triad*, Oxford University Press, New York.

10 Team and work group communication

Steve Vanhorn

OUTLINE

Characteristics of effective work groups or teams

Types of work teams

The development of a group or team

Communication practices

Advantages and disadvantages of groups or teams

Roles within a group or team

Factors affecting group or team performance

Decision making in groups or teams

LEARNING OBJECTIVES

After studying this chapter you should be able to:

1 ▷ describe the characteristics of project teams, self-managed work teams, cross-functional teams and virtual teams

2 ▷ describe the stages of group and team development in an organisation

3 ▷ identify communication practices and describe their impact on teamwork

4 ▷ outline the advantages and disadvantages of group decisions

5 ▷ discuss the roles that can emerge within a work group or team

6 ▷ identify and explain factors that influence work group and team performance

7 ▷ describe several group decision-making techniques.

VIEWPOINT: COMMUNICATE, EDUCATE AND TRAIN

For any organisation and its teams, dealing with change is an essential competence for survival. In an interview with James Nelson, Anne Deering, Vice President of the international consulting group of A.T. Kearney, identifies four factors that enable companies to envision their future. These are different thinking, challenging current practices, building the right team and creating a safe environment. In her view the common characteristics of companies that are managing change well are leading from the top, setting aggressive targets, resourcing for success, managing for results and empowering teams. She suggests companies should 'empower teams to make decisions and act as they see fit. You have entrusted them with the future of the firm, so show you mean it . . . build awareness at all levels . . . communicate, educate and train'.

Adapted from J. Nelson, 2006, 'Managing organisational change', *Management Today*, November/December.

A work team is a group whose members work together on a particular task to achieve common goals. The team has a charter, or reason for being, and is formed for the achievement of organisational goals. A team is effective when its members understand the team's purpose, goals, tasks, results, individual roles and responsibilities, and possess the skills and experience to accomplish their task. The team's communication practices and protocols enable members to get the job done and at the same time build rapport and relationships.

Regardless of the type of team—project team, self-managed work team, cross-functional team or virtual team—its role is to make decisions, plan, achieve goals, reflect on and assess its own performance and, when necessary, to plan again. Some of the many processes that are operating as a team completes a task are problem definition, problem solving, goal setting and creative thinking. Backgrounds, ideas, personalities and expertise are shared as a team works together. As a result the decisions, productivity and outcomes achieved by a team are enriched.

CHARACTERISTICS OF EFFECTIVE WORK GROUPS OR TEAMS

A work team's effectiveness is evaluated by considering two dimensions. The first is the issue of what it does: the outcomes in terms of production, service provided or costs. The second is the issue of how it achieves those outcomes: the behaviours of group members in terms of teamwork, cooperation, new thinking and initiative. The characteristics of effective teams include clear goals, relevant skills, mutual trust, unified commitment, good communication, negotiating skills, appropriate leadership, and internal and external support (Shaw, Duffy & Stark 2000; Robbins and colleagues 2008). A work team's effectiveness is demonstrated by the quantity and quality of its outputs, how the members interact in the achievement of team goals, and the capacity of the team to fulfil its charter now and adapt to ongoing change.

Managers and leaders achieve a great deal of their productivity through working with groups or teams. The number of changes currently affecting organisations make it unlikely that any one person will have the full set of skills needed to complete every task. Rather than depend on one person to have all these skills, a work group is formed to complete the task. In this way a range of skills is pooled. Once team members can relate to one another and make connections between their knowledge and that of others in the group, the team is able to perform effectively.

Theorists have presented a number of definitions of a group. Bertcher (1994, p. 3) defines a group as:

> . . . a dynamic social entity composed of two or more individuals. These individuals interact interdependently to achieve one or more common goals for the group or similar individual goals that each member believes can best be achieved through group participation. As a result of this participation, each member influences and is influenced by every other member to some degree. Over time, statuses and roles develop for members, while norms and values that regulate behaviour of consequence to the group are accepted by members.

This contrasts with Baird and Weinberg (1981, p. 5), who offer a simpler definition of a small group: 'A small group is an entity of three to fifteen persons who perceive themselves to be a group, possess social structure, interact to satisfy group and individual goals, and share a common fate.' Golembiewski (1962) stated that a small number of individuals with a common set of values or norms, interdependent roles and status is a small group. Norms are shared by group members. Robbins and colleagues (2006, p. 493) suggest: 'Norms dictate things such as work output levels, absenteeism, promptness and the amount of socialising allowed on the job.' Norms are the acceptable standards, expectations or 'rules' that 'regulate' and foster uniform member behaviours within a group or team (Goodman, Ravlin & Schminke 1987; Hogg & Reid 2006).

In this chapter the discussion centres on how work groups and teams complete their tasks: the process by which they operate. Communication, involvement, and commitment to the group and team goals are important parts of that process.

TYPES OF WORK TEAMS

The words 'team' and 'group' are frequently used interchangeably, since on many occasions they share almost identical characteristics. However, while a team can always be loosely classified as a group, a group may not conform to the more specific criteria for a team. The key identifiers of a **team** are that members are operating within a charter; they see themselves as having specified roles, and they see the team as accountable for achieving specified organisational goals. There are four important types of teams: project teams, self-managed work teams, cross-functional teams and virtual teams.

◀ OBJECTIVE 1

Describe the characteristics of project teams, self-managed work teams, cross-functional teams and virtual teams

Project work teams

Bartol and colleagues (2008, p. 217) state: 'A project is a plan that coordinates a set of limited-scope activities (which do not need to be divided into major sub-components) intended to reach an important, non-recurring goal.' Projects vary in size and scope—from a global launch of a new project to an end-of-school function. Members of a project work team are chosen because their background and experiences are directly useful to the team's purpose—implementation of the project. The members are usually chosen by management and the team is disbanded when the project is completed.

Project teams are usually participative, with members taking part in planning, controlling and improving processes within the team. The information flow is usually open and shared between the members as they complete the range of project duties. Project team leaders usually adopt a coaching and facilitating style, rather than a directive, authoritarian style.

One of the factors common to all project teams is clarity of purpose, achieved by understanding their stakeholders' needs. By clarifying stakeholder needs and expectations, the project team is able to avoid the potential team disablers of confusion, misdirected work and conflicts. Another common factor is an understanding of the team's capability, including the abilities of the team leader and members, the amount of resources available, expected timelines and the know-how needed to support success.

Participative projects enable team members to participate in the planning, controlling and improving processes. From 1969 to 1974 the Swedish Employers' Confederation conducted research into organisation-development work that predicted the likely outcomes from participation projects. Shrives (2003, p. 33) reports: '[T]he research found there were simple and subtle ways of beginning participation projects that did not reinforce management control.' Table 10.1 lists common factors from successful and unsuccessful projects identified in the research. The strategies in column one of Table 10.1 support the members of the project team to participate and take action, rather than waiting for management directives. The strategies in column two are likely to lead to loss of interest in the project and return to the old way of doing things.

A **team** is a group with a charter or reason for being.

A project work team is created to complete a particular task or project.

A participative team is able to take some initiatives and take part in some of the decision making.

Self-managed work teams

A self-managed work team is described by Robbins and colleagues (2006, p. 505) as '. . . a formal group of employees who operate without a manager and are responsible for a complete work process or segment'. **Self-managed work teams** have a high level of control over their work. They are responsible not only for getting the work done, but also for managing themselves. Team members work together to improve their work, handle day-to-day problems, plan and control their work. Hutzel (1992) states that supervisors now teach, coach and facilitate the team to manage itself, rather than assigning, directing and controlling the individuals in the team. The team leader or supervisor who is able to communicate will help the team become self-managed.

Wageman (1997, p. 49) comments that 'self-managing teams are fast becoming the management practice of choice for organisations that wish to become more flexible, push decision making to the front lines, and fully use employees' intellectual and creative capacities'. Autonomous teams have the independence and discretion to determine the procedures and carry out the team's activities. Semi-autonomous teams have less freedom and discretion than autonomous teams but still have a

Self-managed work teams are either semi-autonomous or autonomous with a high level of control over their work.

Table 10.1: Common factors in participation projects	
Successful projects	**Unsuccessful projects**
• The innovations are described in low-key terms as 'new working methods', and everyday terminology is used throughout. • The programs tend to be simple, with only a small number of procedures and guidelines provided in advance. Others evolve from the implementation experiences of staff. • Formal rules of participation and implementation are kept to a minimum, and management guides and supports pilot groups with ideas and written material. • The programs start on a small scale where there is a willingness to try out the new ideas. Initial trial implementations are guided and advised by a central group, but employees need to find their own ways of making the new practices or changes workable in their everyday work. • When some success is achieved, the approaches spread to other areas spontaneously as staff express an interest in the new ideas. Employees are trained to participate in, and lead, participative groups. • The results create more stimulating jobs and improved work delivery. • In time, reference and other groups established at the start of the project cease to operate, but participative employee groups continue to integrate, review and drive change.	• The project is launched and promoted with labels that are 'catchy' and don't make much sense to staff. • An ambitious and comprehensive business case is presented as part of the launch. It describes, in impressive detail, organisational elements and charts. • A large number of consultative groups are formed that are separate from the usual line functions. • There are many rules and guidelines for how the participative process is to be conducted, e.g. frequency of meetings and sharing information. • The entire consultative systems are set up in a fairly short time with a set timeline. • The participation process results in endless discussions, often focusing on trivial improvements to employee facilities. • Ways of doing things are imposed from the top down. • Hidden agendas arise, such as who achieved the successful outcomes or who should be rewarded. • Experiments on actual changes to the way day-to-day work is conducted are supervised by outsiders not familiar with that part of the business. • In the medium to long term the project stagnates and people return to the old ways of doing things.

high level of control over their work. The principle behind self-managing teams is that the teams, rather than managers:

• take responsibility for their work
• monitor their own performance
• alter their performance strategies as needed to solve problems and adapt to changing conditions.

The belief is that this leads to enhancing the company's performance, organisational learning, adaptability and employees' commitment to the organisation. Wageman points out that, although there are many examples showing the value of these groups, some organisations have become disenchanted with the idea as 'managers observe slow and sometimes nonexistent progress in team members' efforts to take on responsibility for decisions that previously belonged to managers' (1997, p. 51). She states that members of a group that is genuinely managing itself show three basic characteristics in the way they approach their work:

1. They take personal responsibility for the outcomes of their team's work.
2. They monitor their own work performance, actively seeking data about how well they are performing.
3. They alter their performance strategies as needed, creating suitable solutions to work problems.

Wageman's research with Xerox Corporation Customer Service teams, concentrating on the design features of each group and the coaching behaviours of group leaders, showed that the seven success factors listed in Table 10.2 were critical for success (1997, pp. 54–57). She also highlights the need for self-managing work teams to be aware of their environment, have an outward focus, be alert to problems, and be prepared to work in new ways in response to what is happening outside the team.

The research conducted by Wageman showed that 'high-quality coaching had much more positive influence on teams that already had the majority of the critical success factors in place' (1997, p. 60). She asserts that leaders have an important role to play but that the role differs over various stages of the team's life. At the beginning, the leader has a designer role—sets the direction, provides the resources, designs the task (critical success factors 1–5)—but after the team is launched, the leader has a midwife role (critical success factors 6–7) and, finally, a coaching role.

Table 10.2: Critical success factors for self-managed teams	
Success factor	**Purpose**
1 Clear, engaging direction	Gives a sense of why the group exists and what it is trying to accomplish
2 A real team task	Requires the members to work together to complete significant tasks
3 Rewards for team excellence	Distributes at least 80% of rewards equally among team members: rewards that are 50/50 individual/group are associated with the lowest team performance
4 Basic material resources	Meets the team's needs for physical materials such as tools, meeting space, access to computing service
5 Authority to manage work	Allows the team and not the leader to make the decisions over basic work strategies
6 Team goals	Enhance team performance, but goals have to be aligned with the team's overall direction, provide a challenge and be completed by a specified deadline
7 Team's norms that promote strategic thinking	Through informal rules, guide team members' behaviour in a way that gives an outward focus and an awareness of their environment

Source: Adapted from R. Wageman, 'Critical success factors for creating superb self-managing teams', *Organizational Dynamics*, Summer 1997, pp. 49–62. Reproduced with permission of Elsevier Science.

As most research on the effectiveness of self-managed work teams concentrated on manufacturing environments, Spreitzer, Cohen and Ledford (1999, pp. 340–63) conducted research into self-managing work teams in the service context. Similar to the research of Wageman, they found that supervisory leadership was not important for these teams' effectiveness; in fact, supervisory leadership was sometimes negatively related to effectiveness.

HOT GROUPS

Hot groups share an attitude of dedication to the task and are goal-focused.

Lipman-Blumen and Leavitt argue that 'today's organisations need, not more teams, but more hot groups' (1999, p. 63). A **hot group** shares an attitude that is dedicated to the task. It is goal-focused, with impassioned managers and employees who are creative and get great things done fast. In their view, organisational survival now demands speed, flexibility and creativity. Hot groups have all three plus challenging tasks and an accompanying sense of mission. Lipman-Blumen and Leavitt (1999, p. 63) quote Bill Gates' description of his programming group in pre-Microsoft days:

> We didn't even obey a 24-hour clock. We'd come in and program for a couple of days straight, we'd—you know four or five of us—when it was time to eat, we'd get in our cars and kind of race over to the restaurant and sit and talk about what we were doing. Sometimes I'd get (so) excited about things, I'd forget to eat. Then we'd go back and program some more . . . Those were also the fun days.

In their view, organisations think 'individual', while hot groups think 'group'. The structures and norms of traditional organisations are different from those of hot groups. Hot groups differ from organisations in that they value freedom and creativity, thrive on uncertainty and change, and prefer spontaneity. Lipman-Blumen and Leavitt believe organisations can encourage and support hot groups by thinking 'group' more and 'individualism' less, letting individualism reign within the hot groups, and providing less routine, control and structure. They feel that organisations should encourage hot groups by emphasising selection, de-emphasising training, loosening controls as much as possible, extending the span of control, avoiding elaborate, individual performance evaluations, avoiding specification of 'proper channels', and pushing the throttle up to full speed periodically.

They conclude: 'the time has come, we repeat, for big, often cold organisations to start seeding, feeding, weeding, and harvesting small hot groups. Hot groups are right for modern organisations.' While hot groups may operate in all types of organisations, they are particularly suited to the dynamic environment of the boundaryless network and knowledge organisations.

Cross-functional teams

Cross-functional teams have members with complementary skills, knowledge and experience to accomplish the team purpose and task.

Cross-functional team members are experts in several specialities who work together on various tasks. Cole (2005, p. 312) says cross-functional teams are usually 'responsible for delivering an entire product or service, from design to manufacturing, marketing, delivery and after-sales service'. **Cross-functional teams** have members with complementary skills, knowledge and experience to accomplish the team purpose and task. Cross-functional teams, in common with virtual teams, have at least three types of members: core, extended and ancillary (Duarte & Snyder 1999). The first is the core team, those members accountable for the results. The second and third are the extended and ancillary members who add 'know-how' and take responsibility for knowledge management and administrative activities.

Cross-functional teams are flexible interdisciplinary teams with members selected from several functional areas.

Parker (2003, p. 4) notes that the 'role of cross-functional teams in using the expertise of many different people is coupled with the task of enlisting support for the team'. He argues that 'cross-functional teams seem to be most effective in companies with fast-changing markets . . . and industries that value adaptability, speed and an intense focus on responding to customer needs' (2003, p. 6). Cross-functional teams are suited to a dynamic and flexible organisation in which teams need to respond quickly to changing circumstances. Experimentation, risk taking and continuous improvement maximise current performance and future performance potential.

Problems arise when the team purpose and goals are unclear or members lack the functional expertise to contribute to the team's work effectively. The leader and team members need the connections and power to influence those more senior in the organisation to accept, implement and follow through to maintain team outcomes.

In common with other types of teams, cross-functional teams must understand their charter and the importance of their common purpose to the organisation's success. The team leader and members need to communicate with one another to build collective understanding about how the team will perform its work and how successful or unsuccessful performance will be defined. Successful cross-functional teams are able to communicate effectively to achieve goals and participate in group processes with a sense of inclusion in the group.

Cross-functional team members come from different functional areas and have different backgrounds, experiences and perspectives. The team must learn to work with this diversity to build trust and teamwork. In this process, team members must be open-minded, motivated, and willing to communicate positively and to think about, rather than discount, the multiple perspectives contributed by people from different functional cultures and backgrounds. In any type of team, flexible and adaptable responses minimise confusion and conflict. Discussion and acceptance of new and diverse ideas lead to better problem solving and decision making.

One of the communication practices designed to support knowledge management across cross-functional and other types of teams is storing data in a central knowledge base. Data gathered from team members working in different functional areas and geographic locations is stored in a common database that automatically identifies the source of information, integrates it with existing information, and updates the compiled information and knowledge. Team members are able to access a common electronic database easily anywhere at any time. Access to collective knowledge saves individuals information-processing and analysis time. A team linked to information and one another by communication technologies avoids the need to travel and meet face-to-face to share knowledge.

Virtual teams

A **virtual team** is a physically dispersed group working across distance, time, organisational and national boundaries, using information technology to interact. Global organisations and alliances with widely dispersed activities increasingly rely on virtual teams as knowledge becomes more specialised (Bateman & Snell 2007; Duarte & Snyder 2004).

Rather than interacting in the physical location of their company's building, virtual team leaders and members collaborate and communicate remotely through communication technologies. Members seldom or never meet face-to-face. Members may be home-based or office-based employees, suppliers, contractors, consultants, specialists and others at various locations locally, nationally or internationally. They may be specialists from different functional areas.

This physical dispersion presents additional communication challenges for the team leader and members as they build a sense of organisational and team identity, commitment and loyalty. Members of virtual teams need to be skilled communicators and have access to organisational and team information and knowledge. They also need to belong to the organisation's formal and informal networks. A culture of familiarity, relationships and trust within a virtual team depends on quality team communication.

Duarte and Snyder (2004, p. 4) state: 'People who lead and work in virtual teams need special skills including an understanding of human dynamics, knowledge of how to manage across functional areas and national cultures, and the ability to use communication technologies as their primary means of communication and collaborating.' They identify four types of culture that can exist in a virtual team; national culture, organisational culture, functional culture and team culture (2004, p. 70). Virtual teams have more complexity than traditional teams because of the complications caused by differences in culture. Cultural differences may mean that virtual team members have different ways of doing things. Knowing how to use this diversity provides a source of competitive advantage.

A **virtual team** is a physically dispersed group working across distance, time, organisational and national boundaries, using information technology to interact.

Because of the complexity of working together through time, distance and organisational boundaries, establishing a clear purpose is especially critical for building an effective virtual team. Lipnack and Stamps (2000, p. 57) state: 'The best predictor of a virtual team's success is in the clarity of its purpose and the participatory processes by which the group achieves it.'

Lipnack and Stamps (2000) present the '90/10 rule' to highlight the relative importance of people and technology in a virtual team's success. The rule suggests that 90% of the team's success flows from the people involved and 10% depends on the technology. People and the relationships they build enable virtual teams to do their work across boundaries.

A virtual team must develop a team identity; it must have the power to achieve its goals, accountability, capability, direction and transparency. A virtual team leader will establish ground rules, develop interaction schedules, and build the team by encouraging and responding to member participation. The leader must be skilled in anticipating relationship difficulties and conflict in order to facilitate team activities (Combs & Peacocke 2007). As well as team building, these activities remove some of the difficulties faced by virtual teams, including lack of awareness of what others are doing or of who is able and available to work on particular issues. An added difficulty may be time zone differences.

By considering practical day-to-day communication, a virtual team can build a sense of team identity and belonging through knowing how the team works. By agreeing to simple ground rules, team members establish routines about how the team will work. Agreement on turn-around time for emails and phone calls, on how to use the media effectively, and how to remain connected to stakeholders and customers improves workflow and satisfaction. Decisions about how information is shared, knowledge managed and documents stored ensures ease of access to the knowledge base. Guidelines about how, and when, to hold meetings, how to give and receive direct feedback, how the team will handle disagreements and how to make decisions further improve group performance.

REVIEW QUESTIONS

1. Contrast the characteristics of a group with those of a team.
2. Differentiate between a project work team and a self-managed work team.
3. Identify the seven critical success factors of a self-managed work team.
4. Explain the characteristics of cross-functional teams. In what type of organisations are you likely to find cross-functional teams?

OBJECTIVE **2** ▶
Describe the stages of group and team development in an organisation

THE DEVELOPMENT OF A GROUP OR TEAM

Work groups and teams emerge in a number of ways. The most obvious is when a team is established as the result of a decision made by management. A group may, however, emerge slowly and evolve into a particular structure.

While the organisation provides the setting for a work group or team, the group itself is the forum within which people interact, relationships develop, and a common approach and goals emerge. Within the group, the tasks necessary to achieve the group's intended results are completed. Each group or team in an organisation is constantly changing and has a clearly defined life cycle. As a group evolves and works towards completing its tasks and achieving its goals, it moves through different stages of development in its life cycle.

Stages of group and team development

Groups may move through five stages: forming, storming, norming, performing and adjourning.

As the group or team forms and gets on with its task, the group structure develops. Its particular structure may evolve slowly or quickly. Table 10.3 describes the four stages of development identified by Tuckman (1965). A fifth stage, the adjourning stage, is also included. The five stages occur in the sequence shown in Table 10.3. While most groups move through the five stages, some groups may overlap stages or even miss out one or two completely.

In the early forming stages, communication is about the team's reason for being, bringing the team together, and defining the tasks and boundaries. In the storming stage, communication is about who has power, who is included and how tasks will be performed. As the team moves into the norming stage, communication is about commitment to the team, clarification of what is to be done, how it will be done, and how to acknowledge good performance or improve team performance if it is below standard. Communication becomes more open and spontaneous as members begin to know and trust one another. In the performing stage, skilful communicators interact to gather information, negotiate, manage conflict, build relationships and focus on getting things done. Their communication facilitates decision making and translates ideas into procedures and actions to achieve the team goals.

The quality of interactions, sharing of information, decision making and team activities at each of the five stages of team development is affected by the team members' skills in collaboration and communication. Table 10.3, column two, describes each stage of team development. Column three lists the typical behaviours at each stage.

Some groups are effective, others are ineffective; some are open to change, others resist change. Effective groups are able to perform, whereas other groups may never pass from the storming stage to the norming stage, or from the norming stage to the performing stage. The five stages discussed here are the general pattern of development. It is not essential for every group to pass through every stage. Particular groups may bypass some stages altogether or experience two or more stages (such as the norming and performing stages) at the same time. Table 10.3, column 3, describes some of the behaviours of members at each stage in the development of a team.

Table 10.3: Stages and behaviours in the development of a group		
Stage	**Description**	**Behaviours**
Forming stage	The forming stage occurs when a group is established and people begin to interact within it. In this early stage, people will spend time: • finding out about each other • looking for inclusion in the group • determining their relative status • recognising the attitudes of others • establishing the real purpose of the group. Often the real purpose of the group will differ from its apparent purpose.	Clarification of goals Commitment to the group's purpose Establishment of relationships Making of tentative contributions Communication between members
Storming stage	When conflict emerges, the group has reached the storming stage: the period in the development of a group when there is considerable conflict and upheaval. This conflict may be about: • the leadership • the group's goals or the way they are being achieved • how individuals perform or feel in the group • issues of inclusion or exclusion and the individuality of some members • personal agendas or a lack of commitment to the group's goals.	Critique of group's performance Presentation of alternative points of view Emergence of conflict over power or leadership Provision of negative and positive feedback Discussion of problems or concerns Resolution of conflict

In the **forming stage,** group members may be uncertain about the group's membership, leadership and goals, so great importance can be attached to the group's leader as members look for support, guidance and direction.

In the **storming stage**, conflict that clarifies ideas and is resolved is a positive force in the group as the team moves through the conflict and becomes more cohesive.

Continued

Table 10.3: Stages and behaviours in the development of a group (continued)		
Stage	**Description**	**Behaviours**
	If the group is operating under management direction as a formalised section in a company, the conflict may be hidden and take the form of either disagreement or a lack of involvement that jeopardises the group's effectiveness.	
Norming stage	As people interact, similarities and differences emerge. A pattern of relationships develops between people. This is the norming stage, the time required for members of a group to start to: • feel part of the group and for a common approach and shared goals to emerge • establish a 'pecking order' • develop relationships • develop a common group approach to tasks • identify goals and the necessary actions and activities needed to achieve them • become cohesive and even tolerant of one another's differences • accomplish work goals. Groups that fail to identify goals or to follow through to achieve goals can become 'bogged down' in activities rather than achievement of goals. They never really emerge from the norming stage and never achieve group identity or a common purpose.	Offering support to other members Problem solving Decision making Improvement of plans Verification of goals Development or extension of skills
Performing stage	Once the group has established its goals, its way of making decisions and its expectations of the contribution of each member, it can proceed with the task. By this stage: • the group's structure and identity are formed • it gets on with the job, but strikes a balance between working and maintaining interpersonal relationships within the group. There can be wide differences in the effectiveness of different groups in completing their tasks.	Improvement in ways of doing things Development of interpersonal relationships Acceptance of delegated tasks Involvement in decision making Achievement of performance
Adjourning stage	The adjourning stage occurs as the group is restructured, the committee wound up or the task force dissolved after completing its objectives. Members: • check achievement of goals • plan for the future • finalise any outstanding tasks or relationship matters • leave the group. Even a group established by a company's management does not last.	Movement away from the group Commitment no longer needed Fading relationships Finalising of tasks as the group disbands

In the **norming stage**, group norms, or acceptable behaviour, attitudes, work patterns and related behaviour, emerge.

The **performing stage** occurs when a group has formed its identity and structure.

The **adjourning stage** occurs as the group is restructured, the committee wound up or the task force dissolved after completing its objectives.

REVIEW QUESTIONS

⑤ List the five stages in the development of a group.

⑥ Name three behaviours typical of each of the different stages in the development of a group.

⑦ Think of a group you belong to and which is important to you. At what stage of development is this group?

COMMUNICATION PRACTICES

◀ OBJECTIVE 3
Identify communication practices and describe their impact on teamwork

At every stage of group development and in every type of team, members engage in formal and informal communication. They apply their interpersonal listening and nonverbal skills, including body language, voice, tone and nuance, to manage team interactions. Communication purposes in a team include:

- establishing a climate of trust and balancing power and authority
- setting goals and agreeing objectives
- allocating tasks and delegating work
- striking the balance between empowerment and accountability
- identifying tactics for monitoring and follow-up
- evaluating and appraising performance
- dealing with poor performance
- overcoming communication barriers and managing conflict.

The fundamentals of communication are still the same in any type of team. Clear communication channels enhance open communication. Common terminology enhances the sharing of information and understanding. Effective communication creates better performance.

At all stages in the development of a group or team, leaders and members communicate. Skills in speaking, questioning, listening, empathy and openness are clearly important to group performance and work relationships.

These skills are applied as team members interact to share ideas and knowledge either spontaneously and briefly, as in a conversation, or planned and lengthy, as in a formal speech or meeting. In these interactions, members should avoid monopolising the discussion or controlling the group interaction as this impedes the exchange of knowledge and ideas. They should also speak fluently, and articulate clearly and dynamically, to help listeners recognise the importance of the message and identify the main points.

Supportive and responsive communication encourages others to offer suggestions and solutions and to be part of the group communication process. Skilled communicators value the way others communicate, problem solve and offer their skills within the group. They are able to acknowledge and benefit from the range of experiences and diversity offered by others within the team.

There are two major categories of work groups in an organisation—formal and informal. A **formal group** is established by management and may consist of a section, a department, a committee, or some other identified and recognised unit. In formal groups, relationships are usually regulated through formal or contractual processes and the group communicates through the formal channels. The board of directors or an occupational health and safety committee are two examples of formal groups. Communication practices within formal groups serve the four main functions discussed by Robbins and colleagues (2008, p. 364) '. . . control, motivation, emotional expression and information'.

An **informal group** is one that is not formally established within the structure of the organisation, but which meets regularly or irregularly about work and communicates along informal channels. They are known as 'interest' or 'friendship' groups and are desirable if they speed up communication

Responsive teams collaborate with other teams, are outward-focused and flexible, allow risks and mistakes, promote group learning and focus on the customer.

Work groups may be formal or informal.

A **formal group** is established by management and is usually regulated through formal or contractual processes.

An **informal group** is one that is not formally established within the structure of the organisation.

and decision making. By contrast, destructive informal groups are undesirable. They form if members are dissatisfied and resist or obstruct team and organisational goals. A number of formal and informal work groups are discussed in Chapter 8.

Teamwork

Teamwork is cooperative effort by the members of a group or team to achieve a common goal.

Teamwork means people work together to accomplish a common goal. It is cooperative work based on collaboration, understanding and sharing of information and resources. Communication methods and activities that promote effective teamwork include:

- delivering verbal and written presentations to share information
- discussing team objectives and ideas, questioning, seeking out the opinions of others, testing ideas in a way that criticises the ideas, not the speaker, and negotiating agreement
- listening to learn, share and promote better ideas, acknowledge concerns and encourage others to contribute
- giving concrete and precise feedback centred on the idea, rather than the person, to avoid threatening the other person
- persuading other members to interact in order to exchange ideas and problem solve
- respecting team members, supporting their ideas, and helping and supporting others to accomplish team objectives
- managing conflict constructively, finding alternative ways of doing things, and modifying course of action as appropriate
- interacting positively, and sharing and participating in team activities
- avoiding a closed group and groupthink by encouraging members to speak out on issues, and accepting and handling criticism and conflict in a positive way
- creating a climate of trust, respect and cohesiveness
- using communication channels such as email, group meetings, document management systems, and progress reports to work together and achieve the team's purpose and goals
- behaving ethically, and maintaining confidentiality and objectivity.

In a study of teamwork, Bacon and Blyton (2002, pp. 13–29) focused on the impact of teamwork on skills and on employee perception of who gains and who loses in teamwork. Advocates of teamwork believe that there are many intrinsic rewards for employees from the adoption of these work practices. In Bacon and Blyton's longitudinal study, employees in teams were involved in broader jobs and responsibilities and were given training to facilitate the changes in responsibility. The study showed that after teamworking was introduced, the craft employees were more satisfied with the training and skills than the production workers, reversing the situation prior to teamworking. Some of the craft workers gained a higher income and team-leader positions, in contrast to the production workers.

Bacon and Blyton listed (p. 27) a number of implications for managers from this study.

1. It is evident that teamworking can produce changes in the job experience and produce increases in various areas of employee satisfaction. Employees were generally in favour of teamworking and the way it led to more varied, skilled and responsible jobs.

2. The introduction of teamworking carried with it substantial training implications, not only to produce a workforce that can accomplish a broader range of tasks within the team, but also to create the level of communication and leadership skills necessary for teamwork to be effective. It is important that employers also realise that employees have expectations in regard to promises made about increased skills and extensive training. If these promises are not fulfilled, there can be negative effects.

3. Teamworking was not equally well received by all employee groups. Those on the lowest grades continued to be the most disgruntled and saw teamworking as providing less benefit to them than to their higher-level counterparts.

Organisations that encourage teamwork need managers and team leaders with the skills to create a positive communication climate. The way managers approach their work and interact with other managers and team members affects the willingness of team members to share responsibilities and be involved in the broader team-based work. The skills needed by managers are the capacity to define roles, set goals, empower team members and acknowledge successful outcomes. The organisation and its managers provide the systems and procedures. When the systems and procedures encourage positive and safe work practices, employee satisfaction is likely to increase. Team members are able to achieve goals, quality outcomes and high levels of service to both internal and external customers. An organisation that provides training and professional development in team skills as it introduces new work practices will enable its staff to handle the greater variety of skills and work involved in teamwork competently.

REVIEW QUESTIONS

8 Identify four team communication purposes and decide which type of medium should be used to achieve the purpose.
9 Define the term 'teamwork'.
10 Identify four communication methods that promote effective teamwork.

ADVANTAGES AND DISADVANTAGES OF GROUPS OR TEAMS

◄ OBJECTIVE 4
Outline the advantages and disadvantages of group decisions

In many firms it seems that the answer to overcoming a problem or completing a new task is to set up a new group or team, or to reform an old one. In determining whether a group decision will be better than an individual decision in a particular situation, a number of issues will be considered.

Advantages

The advantages a group has over someone working alone will depend on the competencies present in the group and its effectiveness. A group can provide and work on more information than one person. This generally means that the quality of the decision making is better.

A group allows a wider range of alternatives and opinions to be considered, and a greater number of attitudes and experiences to be shared. For this reason, groups are often more effective than individuals in evaluating ambiguous situations, promoting unique ideas, recalling information accurately and, consequently, making good decisions.

Empowerment is a key factor in the way a group works. **Empowerment** allows people to make decisions, accept responsibility, and become more self-directed members of a team. To take on power, Field and Malver (1996) suggest that team members need specific knowledge and skills, such as being proactive, dealing confidently with teams and employees, understanding a wide range of data, concepts and terminology, articulating and justifying suggestions and adjusting their own communication style. Robbins and colleagues (2006, p. 591) describe empowerment as involving 'increasing the decision-making discretion of workers. Millions of individual employees and employee teams . . . are developing budgets, scheduling workloads, controlling inventories, solving quality problems and engaging in similar activities that until very recently were viewed exclusively as part of the manager's job.'

Empowerment allows people to make decisions, accept responsibility, and become more self-directed members of a team.

There are five keys to empowerment:

1 sharing information
2 creating autonomy
3 allowing team members to become more self-directed
4 ensuring teams have explicit objectives
5 identifying and communicating the team's accountabilities.

A group involves a number of people in the decision-making process. The more people involved in making the decision, the greater the likelihood of its being accepted and successfully implemented within the company. It is also better for the morale and motivation of the workforce. People usually experience greater job satisfaction working in groups than working alone. Success can depend on the characteristics of the problem. Problems of moderate difficulty have been found to be more effectively handled by a group, whereas relatively simple tasks or problems may be handled more effectively and quickly by one person working alone. Bartol and colleagues (2008, p. 561) suggest: 'Group efforts are increasingly tapped when creativity and innovation are needed for organizational success.'

Disadvantages

While many groups supply the only means of achieving a business objective, they can also have disadvantages. Generally, groups take a lot longer than one person to make a decision and take action. Groups need time to develop a structure and tend to become more effective over longer rather than shorter periods of time. In some situations, this time may not be available.

Members of some groups may be aware of pressures to conform to group norms and attitudes. Members of such a group may resist change. If the group 'culture' is negative—for example, if it is anti-work—then the person who does work hard is made to feel an outcast. More significantly, the functioning of that person may be reduced in this situation to the lower standards and expectations of the group. In many groups, one person or a few people come to dominate activities. The dominant person may not necessarily be the recognised leader or the most competent, but will influence the effectiveness of the group's decision making.

Group decisions may also fail because the formal leader is not able or willing to accept the decisions reached by the group. In this situation, the leader may show open or hidden resistance to the group's decision. Conflict may emerge and continue. If decisions are made by a group, it may be difficult to identify who is actually responsible for the decision or for ensuring that it is carried out effectively. Decisions that are riskier than they should be may therefore be made because the group can avoid direct responsibility if they go wrong. This behaviour is known as 'risk shifting'.

A group can also be a liability for a company when the members maintain the group even when it is clear there is no real need for it. Highly cohesive groups may be unwilling to disagree or to criticise a popular alternative. In the same way, a strong majority may push through a decision before other members are able to point out its weaknesses.

Tight timetables often result in hasty decisions being made without adequate evaluation of the alternatives. Similarly, if members wish to avoid another meeting or want a resolution to close the meeting, they will opt for the most popular solution. Hasty decisions can be prevented by planning and allowing sufficient time to explore alternatives and consequences adequately. Postpone decisions until another meeting if time is up and alternatives have not been fully discussed. When more information is required or other points need to be investigated, adjourn the meeting until this can occur. Avoid hasty decisions by exploring the advantages and disadvantages of all possible solutions. Involve all members in this process to avoid a situation where members support only their preferred option and criticise others.

While there are many advantages and disadvantages of groups, the problems can be minimised and the benefits increased if people in groups, and particularly those who lead them, are aware of methods for improving performance.

REVIEW QUESTIONS

11 What are three advantages and three disadvantages of working in a group?

12 *a*   Define the term 'empowerment'.

   b   Discuss the five keys to group and team empowerment.

13 Discuss two factors that may lower the standards and expectations of a group.

NATURE AND TYPES OF TEAMS

1. Work in small groups to study the stages in the development of a group.

    a   What do you see as the advantages of team leaders and team members knowing and understanding the five stages of team development?

    b   What can team leaders and team members do if their team 'gets stuck' at the forming or norming stage?

    c   What in your experience are the most difficult aspects of team development?

    d   How were these addressed?

2. Work in small groups. It is the year 2099. Assume that your spacecraft with six travellers has crashed into the newly discovered planet of Desolation.

    a   Individually prepare a list of the needs you would want satisfied during your stay.

    b   Individually prioritise your list in order of the most immediate needs.

    c   In your group, discuss the individual lists and priorities. Develop a group list and prioritise.

    d   Discuss with your group how the findings from this activity have implications for overall group development.

3. Work in small groups.

    a   Compare and contrast the features of participation projects that are driven by management control and those that are driven by staff.

    b   Describe the factors that support team performance and participative practices.

4. Work in small groups.

    a   Brainstorm to create a list of communication practices that impact positively on teamwork.

    b   Identify two practices that impact negatively on teamwork.

    c   Describe how team members can minimise or avoid the use of the two negative practices.

ROLES WITHIN A GROUP OR TEAM

◄ OBJECTIVE 5
Discuss the roles that emerge within a work group or team

Individuals in a work group or team take on various roles. A **role** is a set of expected behaviours associated with a position. Work groups or teams have a set of expectations about how members in the group should behave in the group. In a work group, for example, some of the roles played by the leader are different from the roles played by the members. A leader is expected to behave differently from the members. In addition, both formal and informal roles operate and interact within the group.

Within a group, a number of roles are played by any one or all of the members at different times in the group's life cycle. Four general roles that operate within a group are:

1. task-related roles
2. maintenance-related roles
3. defensive roles
4. dysfunctional roles.

A **role** is a way of behaving in a particular situation; a set of expected behaviours associated with a position.

An understanding of the different roles helps to explain some of the interactions that take place within a group. Some roles are constructive, whereas others are destructive.

Task-related roles

Task-related roles are the behaviours needed to focus on the specified goals to be completed as a group achieves its purpose. Some of the task-related functions that take place in a group are briefing others, explaining, instructing and reporting. Members also evaluate their own performance and the performance of others. One of the task-related roles—that of the initiator, for example—starts the

Task-related roles are the behaviours needed to focus on the specified goals to be completed as a group achieves its purpose.

procedures or finds new ways of viewing the problem. Table 10.4 gives examples of task behaviours displayed by group members who may assume any of the seven task-related functions listed.

While various group members may fill some or all of the roles outlined in Table 10.4, effective leaders will direct proceedings so that they remain in control and ensure that the roles are properly performed.

Maintenance-related roles

Maintenance-related roles are the behaviours needed to focus on people and their relationships.

Maintenance-related roles are the behaviours needed to focus on people and their relationships. They facilitate the group process by keeping the group together so that the task can be completed. Two of the maintenance functions carried out in a group are advising and counselling others. Another, that of the harmoniser, helps to maintain the relationships between members by working to avoid conflict and reduce tension. Examples of maintenance behaviours displayed by group members are given in Table 10.5. Team members may assume any of the five maintenance functions. Maintenance-related functions in a group must be performed by, or at least checked by, a task group leader.

Defensive roles

Defensive roles are behaviours intended to protect a group from anxiety when it is unable to function effectively.

Defensive roles are behaviours intended to protect a group from anxiety when it is unable to function effectively. One defensive role—for example, that of the *scapegoat*—is played by a member in an attempt to deflect the group's feelings of failure or incompetence from the group to the scapegoat. The member adopting the role of the scapegoat may do so either consciously or unconsciously.

Another defensive role is that of the *tension reliever* who jokes, fills long silences with chatter or suggests breaks. Sometimes defensive roles help the group; for example, when the tension is increasing and needs to be broken. On other occasions, defensive roles deflect the group from its task.

Table 10.4: Group behaviour: Task-related roles

Function	Example
1 The *initiator* starts the procedure, and defines and organises ideas or solutions.	'Why don't we define the problem and then move on from there?'
2 The *information seeker* draws out facts by asking questions.	'As the Safety Officer, Jill, could you tell us about the problem?'
3 The *information giver* provides facts, hopefully based on expertise.	'The annual report shows production decreased by 2%.'
4 The *opinion seeker* asks questions to discover the views of the group on a particular topic.	'I'm not sure about the proposal. Do you have any thoughts on it?'
5 The *opinion giver* offers useful opinions based on personal experiences.	'One way to overcome the problem might be . . .'
6 The *clarifier* paraphrases, asks how a member's comment was interpreted, and integrates separate ideas to reduce confusion.	'Are you proposing we complete the manuals ourselves, rather than use consultants?'
7 The *summariser* relates the main points and summarises the group's ideas and plans for action.	'So far we have heard from Data Processing, Accounts and Sales. The proposals seem to be . . .'

Table 10.5: Group behaviour: Maintenance-related roles

Function	Example
1 The *harmoniser* seeks to avoid conflict, reduce tensions and mediate differences between members.	'Both suggestions are useful, Sue and Carlos. I think we can combine both in our plan.'
2 The *encourager* ensures everyone in the group participates and gives appropriate recognition to each member's contribution to the task.	'That's a terrific suggestion. You obviously put a lot of work into it.'
3 The *communication facilitator* ensures that group members are communicating effectively with each other and that no one member dominates the discussions or activities.	'That's interesting. I wonder what other people think?'
4 The *interpersonal problem solver* ensures that any conflicts that emerge in the group are quickly identified and solved.	'There appears to be a problem. Let's talk about it.'
5 The *standard setter* suggests norms and standards of behaviour.	'I've noticed the group prefers to keep issues relating to the management structure out of these meetings. Is this a subject to be avoided?'

Dysfunctional roles

Dysfunctional roles are behaviours intended to distract a group from its purpose or to inhibit progress towards its goals. A member playing the role of *blocker*, for example, raises irrelevancies or argues a point for too long, interfering with the group's progress. Other dysfunctional roles are those of the *pessimist*, who expresses gloom and failure; the *aggressor*, who criticises or blames others in a hostile manner; and the *rebel*, who breaks group norms and attacks authority. In addition, the *show-off*, who draws attention away from the group's purpose; the *lobbyist*, who tries to achieve personal goals ahead of group goals; and the *recognition seeker*, who calls attention to himself or herself ahead of the needs of the group, all distract the group from its purpose.

The type of role a person plays is determined by a number of factors. Natural predisposition in personality, self-image, and the impression a person hopes to make on others all have an impact on which role someone will play. So, too, will the expectations and perceptions of others. Factors such as perceived rewards, prestige or power gained from belonging to the group also influence the role played. Preconceived ideas or stereotypes about how a member of a group should act also affect the role. Work groups continually change emotionally, and so the maintenance roles also change. So, too, do the tasks a group is asked to complete. Whenever the external environment changes, the group may feel the impact.

Group performance is the result of a complex interaction between a number of factors. A continuing interaction exists between people and the roles they play within a group. The role played by one person may even vary between tasks. Also, the interpersonal concerns the individuals bring to the group may vary.

Participation techniques

Bertcher (1994, p. 5) believes that a successful group is one where the individuals interact over time to achieve common or individual goals that are valued because each member 'believes that this group

Dysfunctional roles are behaviours intended to distract a group from its purpose or to inhibit progress towards its goals.

Interdependent behaviours are task behaviours related to goal achievement and socioemotional behaviours related to harmonious relations.

can help him or her to achieve them'. To be successful, two kinds of interdependent behaviours must be performed by members:

1. *task behaviours*—related to goal achievement
2. *socioemotional behaviours*—related to maintaining harmonious relations among members while they are working to achieve goals.

Bertcher (1994, p. 16) focuses on the participation techniques shown in Table 10.6, necessary for a group or team to operate successfully.

Bertcher points out that 'groups generally are more successful when members are *homogeneous* with regard to critical descriptive attributes that pertain to a group's goals and *heterogeneous* with regard to critical behavioural attributes, thus providing some balance in participation' (1994, p. 14). He states that the 'best' size for a group may well be a matter of 'trial and error' because, although larger groups are more capable of dealing with complex tasks, problems of interdependence increase and individual members' questions are likely to receive inadequate responses. He believes 'the best size for the successful group depends on the goal of the group, the attributes of the members, the environment in which the group exists, and other variables' (p. 14).

Figure 10.6: Participation techniques

Technique	Purpose
Attending	Letting others in a group know that you are paying close attention to what they say and do
Information management	Asking questions and giving information in a group in order to solve problems, get to know one another, clarify information, and receive and give feedback
Contract negotiation	Working out an agreement on goals for the group and its members, and the ground rules to be used in working towards these goals
Rewarding	Providing payoffs, such as praise, for effort and/or achievement in the group
Responding to feelings	Letting others in the group know that you understand accurately how they feel about a situation, either verbally or nonverbally
Focusing	Keeping a group discussion on track, and highlighting or clarifying what has occurred
Summarising	Pulling together what has been said by group participants for review and as a basis for next steps
Gatekeeping	Achieving a balance of participation in a group by inviting reluctant participants to speak up and limiting active participators
Confronting	Informing a participant, subgroup or the entire group about discrepancies in words and actions so that they can consider these inconsistencies
Modelling	Teaching by demonstration, learning by imitation
Mediating	Attempting to resolve conflicts among participants
Starting	Beginning a group's first meeting and each group meeting thereafter in order to get members relaxed, interested and focused

The term *emotional attachment* denotes how closely an individual identifies with a group (Paxton & Moody 2003, p. 34). Paxton and Moody's research showed that there are increased levels of belonging and morale among those team members who occupy a central position in the team. They concluded that emotional attachment 'corresponds to network position' in the team. The highest levels of emotional attachment were found among members of subgroups that were tight-knit and at the same time had some cross-cutting ties to the rest of the group.

Interpersonal concerns within a group or team

In addition to completing tasks and achieving goals, members relate to one another. Each member brings interpersonal concerns to the group and these concerns become part of the group process as the social needs of individual members emerge. There are three interpersonal concerns within groups. As the group moves through each stage in its development, these concerns usually develop in the following order:

1. inclusion
2. control
3. acceptance.

Good communication by both leaders and members is one of the most important ingredients in dealing with the three interpersonal concerns. It helps members to understand procedures and tasks, to meet their needs and to have their opinions accepted. When everyone communicates well in the group, inclusion concerns are addressed. Individuals feel included: they know if members are treated equally and who is in the inner circle and who is on the outer. Members also know who is in control and how decisions are made. As the group moves through the stages of development, it recognises whether members are treated as equals in decision making or whether someone has a superior or subordinate position in relation to others in the group.

In addition, there is a sense of acceptance by the group. Members know who tends to develop close personal relationships and who is distant. The interpersonal concern for acceptance in the group centres on how people are valued and accepted. When the group values, accepts and respects the contributions of everyone, members feel the acknowledgment of others and a sense of belonging to the group. As a result, they are able to communicate their intentions, feelings and needs as they work within the group, and to acknowledge and accept the contributions of others. In a group with a culture of acceptance, group leaders and members are accessible to one another. No one person monopolises the conversation or the decision making, or interrupts while others are talking. Members are given the space to talk. Others listen to their suggestions and concerns. Respect is given to individuals and the importance of their thoughts and feelings is acknowledged.

As a group nears the adjourning stage, the three interpersonal concerns—inclusion, control and acceptance—become less important. Their disappearance happens in reverse order: the need for acceptance disappears as relationships no longer operate, and the issues of control and inclusion no longer matter as the group's reason for being concludes.

REVIEW QUESTIONS

14. a   Identify four types of roles that can emerge within a group or work team.
    b   Describe how each of these roles can impact on team performance.
15. Distinguish task behaviours and socioemotional group behaviours.
16. Identify three participation techniques and explain their purpose.
17. Describe three interpersonal concerns within a group and their relationship to teamwork.

FACTORS AFFECTING GROUP OR TEAM PERFORMANCE

Group decision making in organisations frequently occurs at regular meetings held in sections or departments. Group decisions are also made by committees and teams whose members are drawn from different sections in the organisation. The way these different groups function and the quality of their decision making are affected by a variety of factors.

Internal group processes

Internal group processes during each stage of problem solving and decision making can affect the group's or team's decision. The ability of members to contribute information and ideas clearly and persuasively, the logical sequence of the discussion and the way conflict is managed all affect the quality of the decision. If the group, and especially the group leader, identify the factors that have a negative impact, then they can be avoided or at least made less significant. Many factors can prevent a group from using information effectively.

SIZE

A key factor influencing a group is size. A group of four to eight people allows everyone to say something at a meeting, even the quieter, less assertive members. Yet it is big enough for a range of specialised skills to be included. The larger the group, the harder it is to manage. It is more likely that subgroups will emerge within the framework of the main group as people seek out others who agree with their point of view. Larger groups tend to be dominated by a few talkative and aggressive members. This can leave the others feeling threatened and dissatisfied.

Consensus is an agreed position.

A larger group can have more collective knowledge and a variety of perspectives, but meetings require more time to reach **consensus**—an agreed position—and have a greater potential for conflict. If a larger group is required, plan to use subgroups or committees. The most effective size for a group will depend on the task and the people involved. Thus, two or three members may be the best size where the task is highly complex and specialised, and 10 or 12 where it is very general.

Moreland, Levine and Wingert (1996) argue that few theorists have analysed group composition very broadly; they tend to focus on just one characteristic of group members, such as their abilities, opinions or needs. Commenting on the best size for a group, they cite the research of Katzenbach and Smith (1993), who suggest 12 as the optimum number for work teams; Scharf (1989), who suggests seven; Parker (1994), who suggests four to six for cross-functional teams; and Nasser (1988), who suggests six to eight for marketing focus groups (p. 25). Their conclusion was that there is no simple way to determine the best size for a group.

Larger groups have advantages such as access to resources, including time, energy, money and expertise. There is more diversity in larger groups and they can perform better as a result. Larger groups are often seen as more legitimate. However, they suffer from disadvantages such as coordination problems, including confusion about task assignments, miscommunications and scheduling difficulties. A loss of motivation, conflict, absenteeism, lower participation levels and less satisfying membership can interfere with performance in larger groups. Moreland, Levine and Wingert (1996) suggest that, instead of worrying about group size, it might be better to concentrate on maximising the advantages and minimising the disadvantages of whatever size a group has reached.

LEADERSHIP

Assuming that the members of a group have the necessary knowledge to solve the problem or make the decision, then its effectiveness will depend on the quality of the group leader. The more the group respects the leader and the less a leader has to rely on formal status in the organisation, the better it will be for the group. The more organised and informed the group leader, the more the group will work together. Finally, the better the human relations and communications skills of the leader, the lower the conflict and the greater the cooperation there will be in the group. Leadership is discussed more fully in Chapter 9. In an interview with Sheedy (2006, p. 8), John Eales identifies the vital components in building strong management teams. Successful managers, he says,

> . . . tend to be very organized and they have a very clear idea of where it is they want to go and where it is they want to take the people they're leading. They can articulate that view extremely well. They have a passion for what they're doing and they can push that passion across to people—they inspire people through their excitement. From my experience, they also show a great interest in their staff as people—they know them as people and not just someone filling a position. That makes a big difference.

MEMBERS

The qualifications, skills and attitudes of the members of a group are central to how well the group performs. If a group has members who are underqualified, uninterested or overconcerned with their own objectives, then discussion and actions will be less productive. Every group member has needs—for example, status, friendship or achievement—which they expect the group to meet. If the individual objectives of group members clash and are left unresolved by the group, then conflict will be created. Individuals can work towards achieving harmony and eliminating power struggles within the group through conflict-resolution techniques such as confrontation, collaboration and **compromise**—the settlement of differences through concessions by one or both parties. This requires both readiness and skill on the part of members.

Compromise is the settlement of differences through concessions by one or both parties.

The maturity and emotional stability of members are also important factors to consider. If members are immature and unstable, behaviour tends to be more disruptive and self-oriented. Group effectiveness will be reduced by attention-seeking and dominating behaviours. As a leader, options include ignoring or suppressing the behaviour, or pointing out the dysfunctional effects on the group and helping the person to change.

GROUP OR TEAM STRUCTURE

The structure of the group or team will also have an impact on its functioning. Following the development stages of a group, members come to occupy a reasonably stable and predictable position within the group. Structure may be determined by skill, competence, status, or cliques and subgroups to which members belong. Positions in the group structure can depend on a combination of formal factors, as well as informal factors such as friendliness and sociability. A consequence of this structure is the channelling of communication. Members close to each other, either formally or informally, communicate more easily and frequently. Whatever their position within the group structure, it is important for members to feel satisfied, to know what is happening, and to feel confident that they can contribute to, and influence, the group's actions.

By choosing the most effective communication network, maximum dissemination of information to all members is allowed and positive feelings about the group will be created. Communication networks are described in Chapter 8, 'Communication across the Organisation'. As a leader, ensure access to communication channels for all members.

The group's size, leadership, membership, environment, group structure and creativity all contribute to its effectiveness and, specifically, to group cohesiveness and climate.

COHESIVENESS

Group **cohesiveness** is the level of common purpose and commitment among members. A group is more likely to be highly cohesive if members have similar values, attitudes and cultural backgrounds. In a cohesive group, members obtain a high level of job satisfaction and feel they are needed. In a sense, they will not let other group members down. Communication flows freely between members in such a group and decisions are rapidly acted on. Hitchcock (1992) suggests two tactics that will increase trust: creating and communicating clear and direct statements of intent and discussing policies openly, particularly those policies that impact on staff. Communication is an important part of the group process.

Group cohesiveness is the level of common purpose and commitment among members.

Group cohesiveness is desirable in a work group when it is accompanied by agreement between the group's and the organisation's goals. It is undesirable when the group's goals work against the organisation's goals. While group cohesiveness is desirable, it is possible for group unity to go too far. If a group is too close, 'groupthink' can occur.

GROUPTHINK

Groupthink prevents disagreement, constructive criticism and full assessment of alternatives.

Janis (1971) describes the concept of groupthink as the situation where no one in the group challenges the ideas of the group or wishes to be seen to be out of step with the rest of the group. **Groupthink** refers to faulty decision making in a group. The desire for unanimity prevents disagreement, constructive criticism and full assessment of alternative information and courses of action. Hence, groupthink impairs the group's performance because group members would rather make poor decisions than risk independent comments that could lead to them being stereotyped as outside the group. Groups suffering from groupthink fail to consider objectives or research adequately, do not consider alternatives and may take unnecessary risks. Groupthink leads to the selective evaluation of information. It may even lead members unwittingly to look after their own interests rather than those of the company or government department that employs them.

Groups suffering from groupthink display the following characteristics:

- the illusion of invulnerability
- a tendency to stereotype outsiders unfavourably
- a readiness to ridicule critics
- a failure to express doubt because of 'self-censorship' and social pressure by other members
- an illusion of internal harmony, maintained by avoiding disagreements.

Groupthink can be avoided if members are aware of the potential problem and, as either leader or member, attempt to increase critical evaluation of alternatives. A group that is able to express opinions, differing points of view and new ideas usually has a more open and accepting climate than a group experiencing groupthink or any other form of excessive cohesiveness.

CLIMATE

Climate is the atmosphere created by the cohesiveness of the group or team.

The **climate** of a group refers to the atmosphere created by the cohesiveness of the group or team. When the level of cohesiveness is high without being excessive, and the group has a common commitment to the task, then the general attitude and atmosphere tend to be very good; the climate is positive. If, on the other hand, there is dissatisfaction, a lack of unity and low morale, the climate is negative and the group will inevitably be less effective. At all stages in the development of a team, the climate or tone of communication reflects the quality of the communication in the team.

Supportive communication is genuine, spontaneous and empathetic.

Supportive communication is genuine, spontaneous and empathetic. It considers both the needs of the receiver and the need to solve the problem or complete the task. It is non-evaluative, and creates a positive communication climate that encourages people to offer suggestions and solutions and to be part of the team process.

ENVIRONMENT

However well motivated the work group is, the physical surroundings will have some impact on its performance. Poor physical conditions mean low status, low concentration and less motivation. The physical environment can influence group processes. Poor seating arrangements, for example, can result in separation between people. They cannot all see each other and are unable to communicate effectively. Some seating arrangements may mean that an individual member can block another speaker by sitting forward, whereas other arrangements may create a formal climate or emphasise differences in status. Generally, a round or U-shaped seating arrangement is considered best for meetings (see Chapter 11, 'Effective Meetings').

A group also needs adequate time and a quiet environment to perform. Although there is always the danger of the group expanding its activities to fill the time available, make sure there is sufficient time and schedule meetings in quiet locations with minimum distractions and interruptions.

INTERVENTION AND GROUP PERFORMANCE

Wooley (1998) studied the main and interactive effects on group task performance of two types of intervention (interpersonal versus task-focused) administered at two different times (the beginning versus the temporal midpoint of work). The results showed that time and content of intervention interact to affect group task performance. The groups that received a strategy intervention at the midpoint of their work performed significantly better, regarded the intervention as more helpful, and rated their performance on the task as being more successful than those in the other groups. The findings also suggested that, rather than examine the effect of intervention on the group's task, its structure and its readiness for intervention, 'a more fruitful way to proceed is to identify the conditions under which different types of interventions will be helpful within the context of the group's structure, the task they are working on, and the point of time in the group's life' (p. 45).

WORK GROUP MOODS

Larsen and Diener (1992) developed the circumplex model of mood shown in Figure 10.1, illustrating the range of moods that can be shared by group members. Work groups can move through moods from a state of high activation to pleasant, low activation and unpleasant moods. Some of the feelings associated with each mood are shown on the outside of the circle.

Jordan and Lawrence (2005) conducted a study with 241 participants over eight weeks to explore the relationship between team members' negative mood and team processes (social cohesion, workload sharing, team conflict) to determine if negative mood has a detrimental effect on team performance via team processes. They found that negative mood impacted on conflict in teams, team social cohesion and team workload sharing. They drew the conclusion that negative mood influences team processes and, as a consequence, team performance.

Work team enablers

Cooperative relationships are built when a team knows its charter and has the power, accountability, knowledge and skills to achieve its purpose successfully. Each work team must have a common understanding of expectations, individual and shared roles, and be able to build rapport and relationships.

Cooperative relationships help work teams to develop efficient workplace practices. **Work team enablers** are the key to developing positive and efficient communication and cooperation within and between teams. The impact of work team enablers on performance is shown in Figure 10.2.

The **work team enablers** are the key to developing positive and efficient communication and cooperation within and between teams.

POWER

For a team to develop and work well, it must have power. That power is given by the team's charter (reason for being). The team leader and each member must be clear about the team's role and their own role. They must also understand the authority held by their team. The three sources of team power are:

1. personal power held by each team member
2. positional power delegated by the organisation to the team leader or any other team member
3. situational power determined by environmental factors and team interactions.

Any one of these three sources of power can influence the way the work team develops.

ACCOUNTABILITY

The term 'accountability' describes the team's responsibilities. Each work team has a mandate—that is, an authorisation, an order or a contract to perform its particular duties. A mandate, or clear definition of the work team's role and each team member's role, is vital for everyone involved to perform their

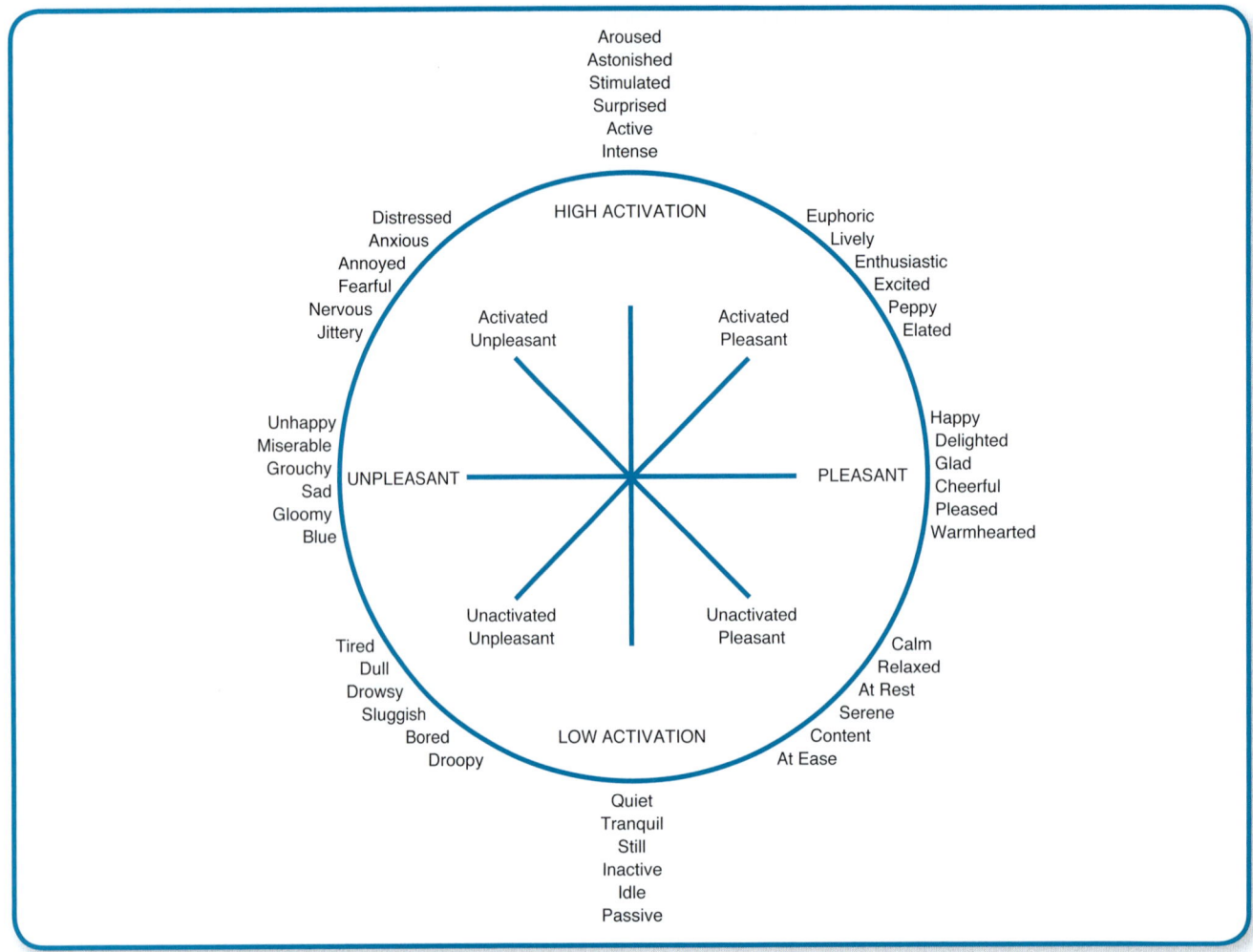

Figure 10.1: The self-report circumplex model of mood

Source: R.J. Larsen & E.E. Diener, 'Promises and problems with the circumplex model of emotion', in M.S. Clark (ed.), *Review of Personality and Social Psychology: Emotion and Social Behaviour*, pp. 25–29. Copyright 1992 Sage, Newbury Park, CA. Reprinted by permission of Sage Publications Inc.

work tasks, singly and cooperatively.

As well as the team as a whole being accountable, the team leader and each member is individually accountable.

CAPABILITY

The team's operating structure is the framework in which the individual team members' capabilities are used. The operating structure enables the organisation, its teams and its individuals to meet legislative, industry, market, customer, operational and personal requirements. A team needs an operating structure for its collective achievement.

The team's operating structure also affects its functioning and how people feel about belonging to it. Team members who know what is happening and feel confident can contribute to, and influence, the team's outcomes. They are able to work productively through the combination of individual and team capabilities.

The operating structure supports the efficient and effective accomplishment of team goals .

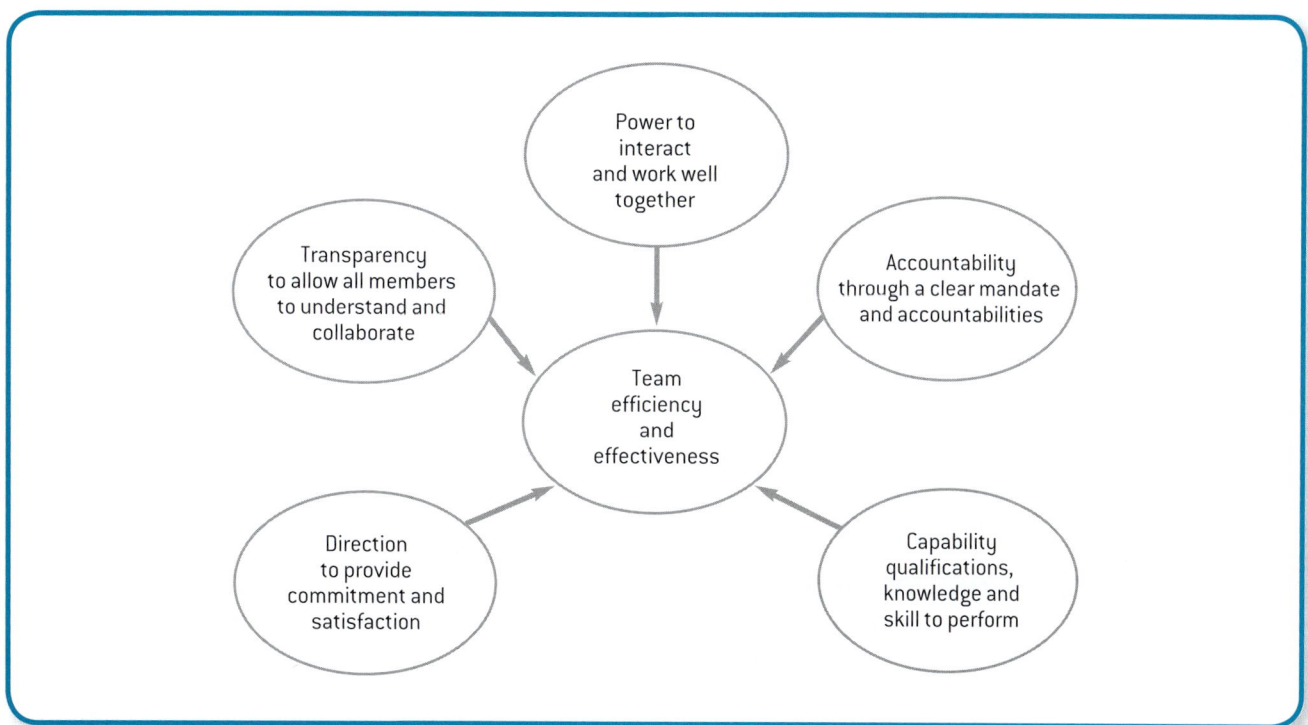

Figure 10.2: Impact of work team enablers on performance

DIRECTION

Direction is the line the team works along to reach its goals. Sometimes these goals are simply to complete the team's day-to-day activities. Other goals may be longer term: for example, changing to new team systems and ways of doing things. If the direction and goals are clear, it is easier for the team to complete its activities.

TRANSPARENCY

With transparency each member can participate and trust one another's capacity to get the job done. Transparency helps individuals to contribute information and ideas clearly, to work towards establishing harmony, and to minimise power struggles and conflict in the team. A *high*-transparency team has free flow of information and high levels of trust. A *low*-transparency team has ineffective flow of information and low levels of trust.

Transparency means access to information that enables all members of a team to understand what is happening in the team.

REVIEW QUESTIONS

18 Discuss the characteristics displayed by a group suffering from groupthink.
19 Describe how work group moods can affect a work group's performance.
20 Outline the work team enablers that help a team to develop efficient workplace practices and cooperative relationships.

DECISION MAKING IN GROUPS OR TEAMS

Decision-making techniques

The purpose of any group existing in business is to achieve a goal or goals. The goals may be short-term and specific, such as planning an advertising campaign for the company, or they may be open-ended and broad, such as the continuing distribution of a company's products by the transport section of the firm. The extent to which the group achieves its goals will depend on the factors discussed above. However, it will also depend on how decisions are made and communicated within the group. There are a number of ways that groups can arrive at decisions—four methods are described below.

DECISIONS BY AUTHORITY

Decisions by authority:
a situation in which the group discusses an issue and then either the leader or an outside supervisor makes the decision.

Decisions by authority, without consultation, exist when decisions are made outside the group or by one member in it and then communicated to the members. Decision by authority after group discussion is one of the most common ways decisions are made in a group. The group discusses the issue, and then either the leader or an outside supervisor makes the decision. This may be the quickest way of reaching a decision, but over the long term it can bring resentment, low morale and lack of purpose in the group.

DECISIONS BY CONSENSUS

Decisions by consensus are decisions made by mutual agreement among group members.

Decisions by consensus occur when a decision is made by agreement among group members. The strength of this method is that members feel they have contributed to the decision-making process and, therefore, will work towards implementing the decision. The disadvantages of decisions arrived at by consensus are that they take time and require well-developed communication skills. The group also needs to believe that the consensus decision is actually the best one. Sometimes, the consensus-decision approach can be a disguised way of authoritarian decision making, or decision by the loudest. In other words, it is very difficult to get real consensus in a group.

DECISIONS BY MAJORITY

Decisions by majority are agreements reached among the majority of group members.

Decisions by majority take place when agreement is reached among the majority of group members. This may be an effective means of group decision if there is insufficient time to get everyone to agree to the decision, or if it is clear they will not all agree. However, a decision made by a majority may leave a minority that is hostile to the decision.

DECISIONS BY COMPROMISE

Decisions by compromise are decisions that appeal to all members of a group without fully satisfying anyone.

Decisions by compromise occur when there are several members of the group who clearly will not agree on anything. The group leader can either make the decision or decide to offer a compromise that might appeal to some without really satisfying anyone.

Facilitating effective decision making

By including all group members when ideas are produced, a greater range of potential solutions and creative decisions is possible than if the ideas of only one person are used. Strategies that include the whole group will avoid some members worrying that their ideas will be rejected. Two useful techniques to stimulate ideas in groups are brainstorming and the nominal group technique.

The *brainstorming* technique encourages members to present ideas spontaneously and without evaluation. All ideas are recorded and no positive or negative evaluation should occur. Members may feel inhibited, however, about calling out loud in a group situation.

The *nominal group technique* lets members work separately from the main group. It often leads to more ideas than working within the group and using a technique such as brainstorming, because anonymity can be maintained and the pressure to conform is not as great. There are, however, disadvantages. Members may feel, for example, that their spontaneity is inhibited and that the situation is too controlled. These two techniques are discussed in Chapter 11, 'Effective Meetings'.

PROCESS PROBLEMS

Whatever the method by which the group reaches a decision, certain process problems can reduce group effectiveness in decision making. Members who feel inhibited in the proposal-of-alternative-solutions stage may also feel inhibited in the solution-evaluation and solution-selecting stage. Their failure to add knowledge and opinions can lead to a 'false consensus', resulting in a lower-quality decision and a lower level of acceptance of the decision. Overcome this problem by encouraging feedback, welcoming constructive criticism, acknowledging diverse opinions and finding alternative solutions.

NORMS

Norms are the shared ideas and expectations about how group members should behave. Some norms are formal and written; others are informal, unwritten expectations that reflect the group's underlying attitudes and preferences. Sometimes, group members will yield their own preferences or beliefs to conform to the norms and expectations of the group.

Norms are the shared ideas and expectations about how group members should behave.

Cruz, Henningsen and Williams (2001) conducted research to examine the influence of group norms and information on group decision making. Participants were presented with either a complete or incomplete set of information relevant to a decision. The information contained transcripts in which the preferences and comments of a group discussing a decision varied. The researchers found that, while the group collectively had the information to make a high-quality decision, normative and informational influences were in conflict and decisions made by group participants conformed to the normative pressures rather than the informational. The group norms also affected perceptions of task difficulty, task attractiveness and decision quality.

PARTICIPATION

A leader can facilitate complete participation by encouraging contributions, discouraging intimidation, and continuing the discussion until all members have had an opportunity to influence the decision. A voting procedure that creates a shortlist of alternatives and ranks the preferred alternatives will ensure that all members influence the selection of the solution. Encourage the group to reach consensus, rather than a majority decision, by agreeing on an alternative that is acceptable to everyone. This may not be the original first choice of every member, but a choice that all members are willing to accept and support.

Good decisions without a detailed action plan of how the decision will be implemented and how to avoid problems may be unsuccessful. An action plan helps the group to anticipate what might go wrong and plan how to prevent or minimise the consequences. It also helps to determine who in the group will be responsible for implementing which tasks, and to delegate accordingly.

CREATIVITY

In the process of group decision making, there is scope and, indeed, a *need* for members to think creatively. The creativity of group members can affect the result of decisions. A greater range of ideas is created and shared between members. Techniques to stimulate creative thinking include brainstorming (see Chapter 11) and attention to 'whole brain function'. Most people are either left-brain or right-brain dominant. This dictates the way they do things. For example, left-brain people tend to be logical, rational, detailed, active and goal-oriented. Right-brain people are more spontaneous, emotional, holistic, nonverbal and visual in their approach. Some organisations are now giving employees 'whole brain training'. Participants learn how to use both sides of the brain and thus improve their creativity. The category that team members fall into will affect their approach to the group and the way they communicate in the group.

Commitment to the group is necessary in an effective decision-making group. A person who feels uncommitted to the group, and sees little value in group membership or in the task, may need to leave the group. Group decision making requires commitment; without it the decision-making process is affected and group effectiveness diminished.

21. Identify four ways of making decisions and the purpose of each.
22. Describe how a team can facilitate effective decision making.
23. How can a team leader facilitate member participation?

APPLY YOUR KNOWLEDGE

WORKING IN GROUPS

1. In groups of five or six, discuss, for about 15 minutes, a topic where a lot of differences of opinion might exist. Choose your own topic or use the topic 'Censorship is an essential part of society'. As a group, come to a decision about the statement, perhaps support or rejection, or any other decision you wish.

   a. During the discussion, each person is to perform a task-related role chosen from Table 10.4 and a maintenance-related role from Table 10.5.

   b. As you work with the group, observe:
      - how decisions are made (authority, consensus, majority or compromise)
      - how often each person speaks and for how long
      - how differences of opinion are settled
      - how often people listen
      - how the task-related roles and maintenance-related roles help or hinder the group.

   c. When the group work is finished, evaluate your contribution by using the checklist on the next page.

2. Work in small groups.

   a. Discuss how the use of good communication techniques, such as supportive communication and responding to others, can improve the way a group performs.

   b. The work team enablers are the key to developing positive and efficient communication and cooperation within the team. In your group, identify work team enablers and evaluate their impact on a work team.

   c. As a large group, brainstorm for two minutes to create a list of the communication skills that help group performance.

3. In small groups:

   a. Recall either a social or work group you belong to, or have belonged to, and discuss whether individual contributions were valued or not.

   b. How would you describe the cohesiveness and climate of the group?

   c. Think of a time when conflict emerged in the group. Discuss the ways in which this conflict was handled.

   d. Which of the four decision-making methods—authority, consensus, majority, compromise—was demonstrated in the group? Give one example.

   e. Discuss how you felt working in the group identified in part (a).

Shrives (2003, p. 33) suggests that the introduction of cooperative and participative practices takes time. 'It requires leaders to thoughtfully lay the groundwork to foster an organic, natural expression of that basic wish in people to express an opinion and influence their own work life.' Outline strategies you would use to support the introduction of teamwork and participative practices.

COMMUNICATING IN GROUPS

Key: VS = Very Successfully, S = Successfully, U = Unsuccessfully

As I work in a group, do I:	VS	S	U
listen?			
give feedback?			
ask questions?			
present ideas?			
influence others?			
handle conflict?			
recognise the stage of development the group has reached?			
contribute to decisions?			
show interest in work and take the initiative?			
communicate positively?			

SUMMARY OF LEARNING OBJECTIVES

1 DESCRIBE THE CHARACTERISTICS OF PROJECT TEAMS, SELF-MANAGED WORK TEAMS, CROSS-FUNCTIONAL TEAMS AND VIRTUAL TEAMS

A project work team is created to complete a particular task or project. Project teams are usually participative, with members contributing to planning and controlling and dealing with issues that arise over the life of the project. Self-managed work teams are either semi-autonomous or autonomous. Members take responsibility for, and monitor, their own work and adapt to changing conditions. Hot groups are created in response to challenging tasks that require speed in planning, creating ideas, making decisions and taking action. Cross-functional team members come from different functional areas and have different specialities, backgrounds, experiences and perspectives. They work together on various tasks and may be responsible for delivering an entire product or service. Cross-functional teams are adaptable and have an intense focus on stakeholder needs. Many people today work in virtual teams, using technologies such as the Internet, intranets and groupware. To maximise team effectiveness, members must pay attention to the use of technologies and how the team communicates, and prepare guidelines to ensure that information is shared and understood.

2 DESCRIBE THE STAGES OF GROUP AND TEAM DEVELOPMENT IN AN ORGANISATION

The work group or team provides a forum where people interact, relationships develop, and a common approach and goals emerge. The stages in group development are forming, storming, norming, performing and adjourning.

3 IDENTIFY COMMUNICATION PRACTICES AND DESCRIBE THEIR IMPACT ON TEAMWORK

Teamwork is based on collaboration and communication through a variety of mediums, including face-to-face, paper-based, and electronic, such as the Internet, intranet, databases, mobile telephony, teleconferencing, email, voice mail, blogs and podcasts. Good speaking and listening skills, feedback and responding skills enable members to treat one another with confidence and empathy as they work together. Team communication purposes include dissemination of information, setting goals and agreeing objectives, establishing a climate of trust, and striking a balance between empowerment and accountability.

 OUTLINE THE ADVANTAGES AND DISADVANTAGES OF GROUP DECISIONS

A group offers the advantages of providing more information than one person, sharing a greater range of attitudes and experiences, promoting new ideas, and offering greater job satisfaction than working alone. The disadvantages include taking a long time to make a decision, facing pressures to conform, being dominated by one or two members, and difficulties in allocating responsibility.

 DISCUSS THE ROLES THAT CAN EMERGE WITHIN A WORK GROUP OR TEAM

The four general roles operating within a work group or team are task-related roles, maintenance-related roles, defensive roles and dysfunctional roles. These roles may be taken by any or all of the members at different times in the group's life cycle. In successful groups, task behaviours and socioemotional behaviours interact to achieve goals while maintaining harmonious relations. Members have the skills to attend to one another and to share information.

They are able to set the 'ground rules' to be used in working together. Individuals are able to identify with the group and have their needs for inclusion, control and acceptance met. Generally, team members are in favour of teamwork when their role in the team provides them with varied, skilled and responsible jobs.

 IDENTIFY AND EXPLAIN FACTORS THAT INFLUENCE WORK GROUP AND TEAM PERFORMANCE

The size of the group, style of leadership, and members' skills, qualifications and attitudes affect group performance. The way a team functions is also affected by its structure, the amount of group cohesion, the climate or group atmosphere, and the physical conditions or environment. The work team enablers—power, accountability, capability, direction and transparency—influence a team's performance. They are vital not only to team output, but also to communication and collaboration. Groups perform well when the organisation, the team(s) and individual team members all communicate with one another to get the job done and build cooperative relationships.

 DESCRIBE SEVERAL GROUP DECISION-MAKING TECHNIQUES

Types of decisions include decisions by authority, by consensus, by majority and by compromise. Decision-making techniques include brainstorming and the nominal group technique. On occasions there will be a need to think creatively. There is always a need to encourage contributions and to share ideas. Action plans are a useful way to detail the activities that will put the decisions into practice.

KEY TERMS

ACTIVITIES AND QUESTIONS

1. In small groups, discuss questions (a) and (b):
   a. Why do task-related and maintenance-related roles have a positive impact on a group?
   b. Why do defensive and dysfunctional roles have a negative effect on a group?
   c. Prepare (by yourself) a 1000-word essay on the topic, 'The impact of task, maintenance, defensive and dysfunctional roles on group performance'.

2. In small groups:
   a. Think about the way the group completing this course with you interacts.
   b. Discuss the group's membership, leadership and study environment, and the impact of each of these on the group's performance.
   c. Estimate the level of cohesiveness and the climate of the group.
   d. Small groups are commonly used to make decisions in business and in organisations. How can knowledge of the factors that affect the way a group performs improve the quality of the decisions made within the group?

3. Work in small groups.
   You are asked to present a keynote speech to the annual conference of a business association. The conference organisers have asked you to speak on the topic, 'Specific techniques that facilitate participation in a group and the impact of creativity on group decision making' and to prepare an abstract for prepublication. Use your small group as an advisers group and develop the topic and an abstract of not more than 500 words. In your abstract, show how participation and creativity can lead to high-quality decisions.

4. Work in small groups.
   A new financial product development cross-functional team was launched by a major international banking group. Team members were selected from around the world. As team members began to feel more confident and their work together accelerated, the newly appointed Deputy Vice-President, who had no previous involvement with the process, added new expectations, challenged the established set of priorities, and made negative comments publicly about the team's interactions with senior functional managers. The team's work suddenly slowed down, morale dropped and expectations of success disappeared. Team members' inability to meet face-to-face at this critical time to work through the changes added to their frustration.
   a. Discuss and identify the problems caused by the Deputy Vice-President's approach to the financial product development team.
   b. Brainstorm strategies you could use to reinvigorate the cross-functional team.
   c. Assume you are the team leader. Prepare a list of guidelines about how the Deputy Vice-President should interact with any cross-functional team in the future. The guidelines will be used in discussion with the Deputy Vice-President. He will be asked to refine the guidelines and engage in a future feedback session about the guidelines with the team leader.

5. Work in small groups.
   a. Discuss this statement:
      Communication is one of the unique challenges for virtual team members at every stage of their development and performance cycle.
   b. In your discussion, identify and discuss at least three of the communication challenges faced by virtual team members.
   c. In your discussion, identify strategies that meet these challenges effectively.
   d. The 90/10 Rule (Lipnack & Stamps 2000) highlights the fact that people and the relationships they build enable virtual teams to do their work across boundaries. Discuss the types of communication technology and practices that help to overcome the disadvantages caused by a lack of regular, face-to-face social contact and which can be so helpful in accelerating team development and relationship building.
   e. Report your group findings to other groups and compare your findings with theirs.

EXPLORING THE WEB

1. Browse the Quick Find for Team Building Resources at <www.teambuildinginc.com>. Choose two articles on the site and prepare a 250-word evaluative critique for each article.

2. Learn more about groupthink at ChangingMinds. org's 'Groupthink' page <http://changingminds.org/> and at 12 MANAGE, 'Groupthink' <www.12manage. coml>.

a. What causes groupthink to happen?

b. Identify the negative consequences of group-think.

c. Write a brief description of your own experiences of groupthink.

PROJECT WORK

1. Research and write an essay.

Explain the reasons for the growing popularity of work teams and discuss four types of work teams. Your discussion should evaluate factors that contribute to successful team performance.

2. Assume you are required to make a verbal presentation of your essay in a tutorial session. Design a PowerPoint presentation to support your words. Call the verbal presentation 'Creating effective teams'. It should:

- discuss the reasons for the growing popularity of teams in organisations
- specify the characteristics of effective teams

- identify four types of teams and the purpose of each
- identify purposes of team communication and discuss communication practices common to effective teams
- identify a set of criteria an organisation can use to evaluate the success of its teams in performing task behaviours (related to goal achievement) and socioemotional behaviours (related to maintaining harmonious relations among members while they are working to achieve goals).

BIBLIOGRAPHY

Asch, S.E. 1956. 'Studies of independence and conformity: 1. A minority of one against a unanimous majority', *Psychological Monographs*, Vol. 70 (9 whole no. 416).

Bacon, N. & Blyton, P. 2002. 'The impact of teamwork on skills: employee perception of who gains and who loses', *Human Resource Management*, Vol. 13, Issue 2, pp. 13–29.

Baird, J.E. Jr & Weinberg, S.B. 1981. *Group Communication: The Essence of Synergy*, Wm C. Brown, Publishers, Dubuque, Iowa.

Bartel, C.A. & Saavedra, R. 2000. 'The collective construction of work group moods', *Administrative Science Quarterly*, Vol. 45, Issue 2, June, pp. 197–231.

Bartol, K., Tein, M., Matthews, G. & Sharma, B. 2008. *Management: A Pacific Rim Focus*, McGraw-Hill Australia, Sydney.

Bateman, T.S. & Snell, S.A. 2007. *Management: Leading and Collaborating in a Competitive World*, McGraw-Hill/Irwin, New York.

Bertcher, H.J. 1994. *Group Participation: Techniques for Leaders and Members*, Sage Publications, California.

ChangingMinds.org. *Groupthink*, http://changingminds.org/

explanations/theories/groupthink.htm, viewed 11 January 2008.

Cole, K. 2005. *Management Theory and Practice*, 3rd edn, Pearson Education Australia, Sydney.

Combs, W. & Peacocke, S. 2007. 'Leading virtual teams', *Training and Development*, February, pp. 27–28.

Cruz, M.G., Henningsen, D.D. & Williams, M.L.M. 'The presence of norms in the absence of groups? The impact of normative influence under hidden profile conditions', *Human Communication Research*, Vol. 26, Issue 1, pp. 104–24, www3.oup.co.uk/jnls/list/ humcom/hdb/Volume_26/Issue_01/260104.sgm.abs.html, 1 February 2001.

Dewey, J. 1933. *How We Think*, Heath, Boston.

Duarte, D.L. & Snyder, N.T. 1999. *Mastering Virtual Teams*, Jossey Bass, San Francisco.

Duarte, D.L. & Snyder, N.T. 2004. *Mastering Virtual Teams*, 2nd edn, Jossey Bass, San Francisco.

Field, L. & Malver, G. 1996. *Generic Skill Requirements of High Performance Workplaces*, Department of Education and Training, NSW.

Fineman, S. 2003. *Understanding Emotion at Work*, Sage, London.

Golembiewski, R.T. 1962. *The Small Group*, University of Chicago Press, Chicago.

Goodman, P.S., Ravlin, E. & Schminke, M. 1987. 'Understanding groups in organizations', *Research in Organizational Behavior*, Vol. 9, pp. 121–73.

Greene, J. & Grant, A.M. 2003. *Solution-Focused Coaching: Managing People in a Complex World*, Pearson Education, Edinburgh Gate, UK.

Hitchcock, D. 1992. 'Overcoming the top ten self-directed team stoppers', *Journal for Quality and Participation*, December, pp. 42–47.

Hogg, M.A. & Reid, S. 2006. 'Social identity, self categorization, and the communication of group norms', *Communication Theory*, Vol. 16, pp. 7–30.

Hutzel, T. 1992. 'The supervisor's role in self-directed workteams', *Journal for Quality and Participation*, December, pp. 36–41.

Janis, I.L. 1971 .'Groupthink', *Psychology Today*, November, pp. 43–46.

Janis, I.L. 1972. *Victims of Groupthink*, Houghton Mifflin, Boston.

Jordan, P. & Lawrence, S.A. 2005. 'The impact of negative mood on team performance', *Journal of Management and Organization*, Vol. 12, Issue 2, pp. 98–100.

Katzenbach, J.R. & Smith, D.K. 1993. *The Wisdom of Teams: Creating the High-Performance Organization*, Harvard Business School Press, Boston.

Kinicki, A. & Williams, B. 2007. *Management: A Practical Introduction*, 3rd edn, McGraw-Hill, New York.

Larsen, R.J. & Diener, E.E. 1992. 'Promises and problems with the circumplex model of emotion', in M.S. Clark (ed.), *Review of Personality and Social Psychology: Emotion and Social Behavior*, Sage, Newbury Park, CA.

Lencioni, P.M. 2003. 'The trouble with teamwork', *Leader to Leader*, 29 September, pp. 35–40.

Lipman-Blumen, J. & Leavitt, J.J. 1999. 'Hot groups "with attitude": a new organizational state of mind', *Organizational Dynamics*, Spring, pp. 63–72.

Lipnack, J. & Stamps, J. 2000. *Virtual Teams: People Working Across Boundaries with Technology*, 2nd edn, John Wiley & Sons, New York.

Margerison, C. & McCann, D. 1992. *Team Management*, The Business Library Information, Australia.

Moreland, R.L., Levine, J.M. & Wingert, M.L. 1996. 'Creating the ideal group: composition effects at work', in E.H. Witte & J.H. Davis (eds), *Understanding Group Behavior*, Lawrence Erlbaum Associates, New Jersey.

Nasser, D.L. 1988. 'How to run a focus group', *Public Relations Journal*, Vol. 44, pp. 33–34.

Nelson, J. 2006. 'Managing organisational change', *Management Today*, November/December, pp. 40–42.

Parker, G.M. 1994. *Cross-functional Teams: Working with Allies, Enemies, and Other Strangers*, Jossey-Bass, San Francisco.

Parker, G.M. 2003. *Cross-functional teams: Working with Allies, Enemies, and Other Strangers*, 2nd edn, Jossey-Bass, San Francisco.

Paxton, P. & Moody, J. 2003. 'Structure and sentiment: explaining emotional attachment to group', *Social Psychological Quarterly*, Vol. 66, Issue 1, March, pp. 34–37.

Rad, P. & Levin, G. 2003. *Achieving Project Management Success Using Virtual Teams*, J. Ross Publishing, Fort Lauderdale, Florida.

Robbins, S., Bergman, R., Stagg, I. & Coulter, M. 2006. *Management*, 4th edn, Pearson Education Australia, Sydney.

Robbins, S.P., Judge, T.A., Millett, B. & Waters-Marsh, T. 2008. *Organisational Behaviour*, 5th edn, Pearson Education Australia.

Scharf, A. 1989. 'How to change seven rowdy people', *Industrial Management*, Vol. 31, pp. 20–22.

Shaw, J.D., Duffy, M.K. & Stark, E.M. 2000. 'Interdependence and preference for group work: main and congruence effects on the satisfaction and performance of group members', *Journal of Management*, Vol. 26, Issue 2, pp. 259–79.

Sheedy, C. 2006. 'On top of his game', *Management Today*, November/December, pp. 7–11.

Shrives, I. 2003. 'Meaningful cooperation and what it means', *Management Today*, August.

Spreitzer, G.M., Cohen, S.G. & Ledford, G.E. Jr. 1999. 'Developing effective self-managing work teams in service organizations', *Group and Organization Management*, Vol. 24, Issue 3, September, pp. 340–62.

Teambuildinginc.com, *Quick Find for Team Building Resources*, www.teambuildinginc.com/index.html, viewed 11 January 2008.

Tuckman, B.W. 1965. 'Developmental sequence in small groups', *Psychological Bulletin*, May.

12 MANAGE, *Groupthink*, www.12manage.com, viewed 11 January 2008.

Wageman, R. 1997. 'Critical success factors for creating superb self-managing teams', *Organizational Dynamics*, Summer, pp. 49–62.

Wooley, A.W., 1998. 'Effects of intervention content and timing on group task performance', *Journal of Applied Behavioral Science*, Vol. 34, Issue 1, March, pp. 30–46.

Wysocki, R.K. 2001. *Building Effective Project Teams*, John Wiley & Sons, New York.

11

Effective meetings: face-to-face and virtual

1 ▷ distinguish between formal and informal meetings

2 ▷ explain the roles of chairperson, secretary and member

3 ▷ discuss task roles in a meeting, and analyse the skills that support maintenance roles

4 ▷ outline the advantages and disadvantages of virtual meetings

5 ▷ identify communication barriers in face-to-face and virtual meetings

6 ▷ explain the impact of the venue and seating arrangements on the dynamics of a meeting.

VIEWPOINT: HOW ARE UNPRODUCTIVE MEETINGS AFFECTING US?

Statistics from the Meetings Resource Centre show that: 'Most professionals who meet on a regular basis admit to daydreaming (91%), missing meetings (96%) or missing parts of meetings (95%). A large percentage (73%) say they have brought other work to meetings and 39% say they have dozed during meetings. One might be tempted to question these statistics . . . but have you seriously considered how these inefficiencies affect you and your organisation? Some direct effects of unproductive meetings include:

- meetings are longer, less efficient and generate fewer results
- more meetings are needed to accomplish objectives
- with so much time spent in ineffective meetings, employees have less time to get their own work done
- ineffective meetings create frustration at all staff levels
- information generated in unproductive meetings usually isn't managed properly
- inefficient meetings cost organisations billions of dollars each year in otherwise productive employee work time.

The need to improve our meetings is evident. Now the challenge is to communicate, learn and commit to the techniques and technology that will improve our meetings.'

Excerpt from 'How are unproductive meetings affecting us?', *EffectiveMeetings.com*, www.effectivemeetings.com, viewed 12 February 2008.

Face-to-face and online (or virtual) meetings cover three main areas of responsibility. First, the organisation's responsibility is to provide the policy and procedures. Second, the meeting's executive or online facilitator is responsible for organising and running the meeting within its standing orders and formalities. And, third, members are required to participate and take part in the decision making that initiates and implements actions within the meeting's areas of expertise and interest. The meeting's protocols and decision-making procedure should match the organisation's policies and guidelines. When the three areas of responsibility are implemented effectively, meetings provide the participants with the opportunity to create new ideas, solve problems and make democratic decisions.

Effective meetings achieve results.

Meetings can provide and clarify information, give and receive feedback, allow discussion, and enable members to come to some form of agreement or decision. Effective meetings have a clear purpose that participants are informed of in the agenda.

CHARACTERISTICS OF EFFECTIVE MEETINGS

Effective meetings, either face-to-face or virtual, enable people to contribute their points of view and relevant information. This opportunity to contribute increases commitment by members of the work group and other co-workers, who realise that their point of view has been considered as part of any decisions made. Meetings can:

- provide information
- clarify information
- give and receive feedback
- provide training
- allow discussion
- encourage problem solving
- make decisions, plan and take action.

The purpose of any meeting should be clear and the outcomes easy to remember and put into action. Effective meetings are planned carefully and the proceedings structured in an ordered manner appropriate to the purpose and the members. Five basic considerations should be addressed before organising or running a meeting:

1. the characteristics of meetings
2. whether or not to have a meeting
3. the determinants of success
4. the role of the chairperson
5. the need for the agenda to state the purpose and include the key steps to satisfying that purpose.

Advantages and disadvantages of meetings

Meetings are an indispensable business resource, but sometimes they are unnecessary, of negative value, expensive and time-consuming. As well as advantages such as enabling business to be dealt with collectively, providing an opportunity to raise questions and differences, and allowing mutual exchange of ideas, meetings also have disadvantages: they can provide excuses for evading action, become a habit, and be an occasion for self-indulgence or abuse by participants.

A successful face-to-face or virtual business meeting is purposeful, cost-effective and participant-friendly. Without these features a meeting is unsuccessful. The role of the chairperson is crucial in this respect. As well as having facilitation skills to keep members focused on the agenda items and provide direction, the chairperson should have overall control and accept final responsibility. The chairperson should have the status commensurate with the responsibilities and have the authority to lead the meeting.

Clarifying the purpose of the meeting

Issues such as the purpose of the meeting, whether that purpose is justifiable, and whether it could be achieved by different means, need to be resolved objectively. The purpose of the meeting should be identified clearly on the agenda. If there is no purpose, there is no point in holding a meeting.

Saunders (2002, p. 54) makes the comment that being constantly caught up in meetings 'can stop you from doing your job'. Meetings should be 'short, sweet and highly focused—and convened only when face-to-face contact is demanded'. He recommends that before you call a meeting, total up the salaries of the people you think need to be there—'then decide whether it's still worth it' (p. 57). Barnsley (2003, p. 1) agrees that 'for most managers and staff there are too many meetings'. Barnsley quotes David Price of Walk Tall International: 'If you walk into virtually any meeting anywhere in the world and ask what's the purpose of this meeting, most people will answer, "It's Wednesday. We always meet on Wednesday". But they can't tell you the purpose [of the meeting].' Having a purpose to the meeting is one of the keys to a successful meeting, according to David Price.

FACE-TO-FACE MEETINGS

OBJECTIVE **1** ▶
Distinguish between formal and informal meetings

Meetings vary to suit the needs of the organisation and the meeting's purpose. Formal meetings suit a structured situation; informal meetings suit less structured situations. In both types of meeting, certain steps and procedures take place.

FORMAL MEETINGS

Formal meetings are structured, with rules and regulations that follow the British Westminster system of government.

Meeting rules and procedures exist to provide the framework for the business or purpose of the meeting (see Table 11.1). The rules and regulations allow all members to participate. A **constitution** is a document setting out the broad structure and requirements of an organisation. It contains the organisation's name, aims and objectives, rules of administration, membership, office bearers and committee. **Standing orders** set out the specific procedures for conducting formal meetings. In this chapter, only those formal procedures needed to create a structured meeting are discussed.

Even though interaction between members is generally limited by the formal procedures, and the focus is on the leader who manages the meeting and the discussion, the meeting should be conducted in a democratic way. The decision to have a meeting is usually made by the chairperson.

INFORMAL MEETINGS

Informal meetings are less structured than a formal meeting. They are held at work to exchange information, solve problems, make decisions, and set goals for a department or section. A weekly meeting of sales representatives is an example. People are able to use their expertise and contribute in a give-and-take situation.

Members participate. Group discussion, participation, feedback and interaction lead to the final decision and action. This kind of procedure is ideal for the meeting that is oriented towards decision making and problem solving, as it allows the group to become task-oriented. Tasks are defined, plans of action determined and decisions implemented.

Benefits of face-to-face meetings

People come together in a meeting to exchange views, ideas and knowledge. Dollschneider (1997) argues that the business world talks about the need for presentation skills, writing skills and leadership skills, but fails to recognise the need for facilitation skills. Facilitation skills promote group interaction. High-level facilitators are prepared, confident and efficient. They make participants at the meeting feel informed and part of the group process. Quality communication between members leads to an

Formal meetings are structured, with rules and regulations.

A **constitution** is a document that contains an organisation's name, aims and objectives, rules of administration, membership, office bearers and committee.

Standing orders are the rules that govern the manner in which a meeting's business is conducted.

Informal meetings are less structured than formal meetings.

Table 11.1: Examples of formal meetings

Type	Purpose	Example
Annual general meeting	To inform interested parties of the year's progress and the plans for the next year	CSR Limited's Annual General Meeting
Extraordinary general meeting	To inform members of unusual circumstances and any potential advantages and disadvantages to shareholders, other interested parties and the company	A company receives a takeover offer from another company
Board meeting	To provide a forum for management and the board of directors	The board meeting of a Student Association
Departmental meeting	To discuss operations, brief members and discuss assessment methods	Members of the Business Department within a university
Interdepartmental meeting	To discuss common policy with the most senior person from each section or division, and to exchange information	Meeting of Heads of Department within a high school
Operational meeting	To discuss such things as the need for new equipment or new safety procedures	Computer support committee
Briefing	To pass information down through the organisation's channels to save time	Weekly briefing of public relations staff
Private meeting	To provide a forum for members and their invitees	Clubs such as APEX and professional associations
Public meeting	To allow the public to express a point of view or give public support to an issue	Proposed closure of parkland to the general public

effective meeting that enables decisions to be made and actions implemented to achieve successful results. The communication skills needed in the preparation, participation and follow-up stages of a meeting are considered in Table 11.2.

PARTICIPATION

Participation is involvement in the meeting. Participants offer suggestions, take part in the decision making, and accept some of the responsibilities in a way that supports the group's efforts. As members become involved in the discussion, feelings and ideas are shared, and sometimes new ideas and ways of doing things are created. The person leading the meeting should also use effective facilitation skills. By being approachable and supportive of others, a facilitator is able to move the meeting forward. Members are actively engaged in the process of discovering, rather than passively receiving, the information.

Committees

A **committee** has the delegated authority to consider, investigate, and report or act on some matter.

A **committee** is a specific type of meeting. It is a group of people with the delegated authority to consider, investigate, and report or act on some matter. They achieve this by sharing the talents of individual members and sharing responsibility. Many committees are formed to initiate policy making and procedures, but lack the authority for implementation. A number of different types of committees exist and some of them are shown in Table 11.3. Each committee is elected from a larger group or body of people to achieve a particular purpose. The role, function and powers of each committee help the members of that committee to achieve its particular purpose.

Table 11.2: Strategies that aid participation	
Practise courtesy and good meeting manners	• Arrive prepared and on time. • Show readiness to be part of the meeting and involved in the decision making. • Express ideas clearly. • Listen to others and clarify points. • Accept and follow the agenda and the specified time limits. • Avoid causing unnecessary interruptions or distractions. • Cooperate to bring the meeting back to the agenda when others cause interruptions and distractions. • Give an apology to the secretary if leaving early. • Send an apology to the secretary when it is not possible to attend the meeting.
Express your ideas and give feedback	• Participate in the meeting. • Direct comments to all the members. • Summarise your own remarks occasionally. • Ask others for feedback on what has been said in order to check that the ideas have been accurately received and interpreted. • Give feedback that acknowledges and considers the ideas of others.
Ask questions	• Question others when unclear about something. • Avoid questioning in a way that causes unnecessary interruptions. • Aim to increase understanding and speed up the decision making. • Avoid interfering with the time limit or the order of the agenda.
Listen	• Avoid making hasty judgments of other people's ideas. • Seek clarification by paraphrasing the other person's comments. • Think through ideas. • Give others the opportunity to expand or explain the idea.
Match the nonverbal message to the spoken message	• Check that the nonverbal communication is assertive and treats others as equals. • Avoid using body movement that can be interpreted as either aggressive or submissive. • Speak clearly and courteously with open body language. • Consider acceptable styles of clothing and appearance within the meeting. • Use your personal space and the space of others appropriately—formal, informal or belonging.
Follow up	• Check that everyone understands the decisions reached. • Verify who will follow through and complete each of the actions before the meeting concludes. • Take part in the planning for the next meeting. • Offer any contributions to add to the agenda for the next meeting. • Complete any actions before the next meeting.

A committee should represent all the different groups affected by its decisions. The special expertise of members provides a base from which to draw ideas on, for example, public relations, human resource development, or occupational health and safety. A representative committee covers a wide section of the workplace and therefore has more credibility than a very select committee that is seen as representing only the point of view of management or a special interest group. Suggestions and decisions from a representative committee are likely to be easier to implement than a one-sided point of view.

Table 11.3: Types of committees	
Type	**Purpose**
Standing committee	Permanent or recognised committee such as an occupational health and safety committee
Ad hoc committee	Created to consider one specific matter only—once the task is completed the committee is disbanded. A steering committee is an ad hoc committee
Subcommittee	Working party created to examine a particular matter in further detail
Executive committee	Made up of the people elected to office-bearing positions to run the detailed affairs of a club or organisation
Joint committee	Set up by two or more bodies to deal with matters of common interest
Consultative committee	Representative committees set up to offer managers and employees the opportunity to cooperate and consult, and to make recommendations and decisions
Advisory committee	Set up simply to give advice—the committee discusses, explains and makes recommendations to management

REVIEW QUESTIONS

1. Identify the characteristics of effective meetings.
2. Explain the difference between a formal meeting, an informal meeting and a committee. Give an example of each.
3. What is the purpose of an annual general meeting, an extraordinary general meeting and a board meeting?

OBJECTIVE 2 ▶
Explain the roles of chairperson, secretary and member

ROLES AT A MEETING

People within the group may accept an executive role or a membership role. In any role at a meeting, members have two main responsibilities:

1. to prepare for the meeting
2. to participate in the meeting.

Whether taking a leadership or membership role, those members who realise that a group of people meet to complete tasks and, in the process, satisfy their need to belong to the group are likely to make an effective contribution to any meeting.

Duties of the chairperson

The **chairperson** is the presiding officer of a meeting, committee or board.

The **chairperson** is the presiding officer of a meeting, committee or board. He or she should be able to provide leadership to achieve the goals of the meeting, maintain control, exercise impartiality and understand meeting procedures. The chairperson is either elected or appointed and has a twofold responsibility:

1. to prepare and set the scene for the meeting
2. to conduct the meeting according to the standing orders or rules of the organisation, committee or meeting.

The chairperson's role is the most important role in the meeting. It covers those duties carried out by a task leader and a maintenance leader. Thus, an effective chairperson needs a combination of technical skills and human relations skills. A chairperson with these skills is able to prepare the agenda in consultation with the secretary, involve all participants in the meeting, keep the meeting on the order of business presented in the agenda, help the meeting to reach decisions and actions, and promote goodwill among the members. Agendas should be functional. Figure 11.1 shows Tropman's (1996) Agenda Bell, with agenda items allocated within a two-hour meeting. Easy items are discussed in the first third, hard items in the second third and discussion items in the last third. He suggests meetings would be more effective if the typical agenda was replaced by the Agenda Bell.

INCLUDING THE APPROPRIATE PEOPLE

Roebuck (2001, p. 229) comments that the most important decision the chairperson will make about a meeting involves 'whom *not* to invite'. She states that having too many people at a meeting can result in 'confusion, congestion and discontentment'. She recommends inviting 'only those people who need to attend'. In meetings held to develop ideas, the chairperson should invite individuals who have the necessary technical knowledge to assess the feasibility or practicality of the ideas presented. It may be necessary to invite people from other departments to comment on the soundness of the ideas presented, but only a limited number.

In planning meetings, the chairperson should include those people who will be carrying out the plans. These people will be able to warn of problem areas beforehand and save 'time, money and embarrassment' (Roebuck 2001, p. 230). In decision-making meetings, it is important that the chairperson invite only those who have real decision-making power. Roebuck suggests that the chairperson 'gauge the level of authority needed to decide and stop'. In a decision affecting only the chairperson's

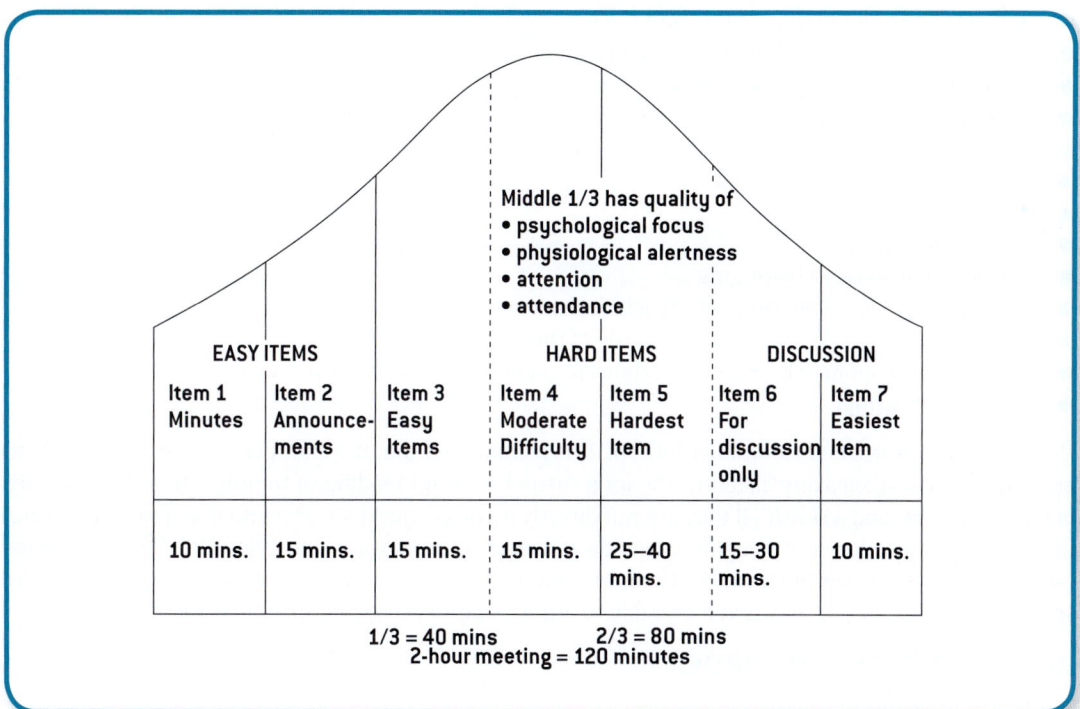

Figure 11.1: Tropman's Agenda Bell

Source: J.E. Tropman, *Effective Meetings: Improving Group Decision Making*, 2nd edn, p. 30. Copyright 1996 Sage Publications, California. Reproduced with permission of Sage Publications.

department, it would not be necessary to include the Chief Executive Officer (CEO) of the organisation, but if it involves a major reconstruction of the division, then the CEO needs to be invited.

MAINTAINING FOCUS

An effective chairperson is able to maintain focus throughout the meeting. Maintaining focus is essential, and the key to this is preparation. Tropman (1996, p. 24) lists five rules to focus the group:

1. *Agenda integrity*: all items on the agenda are discussed; items not on the agenda are not discussed.
2. *Temporal integrity*: begin on time, end on time, and keep to a sensible internal schedule of items within the meeting.
3. *The rule of halves*: provide the person organising the agenda with all the items to be discussed halfway between meetings—that is, if meetings are six weeks apart, by three weeks after the previous meeting.
4. *The rule of thirds*: the agenda scheduler orders the items so that the most important or the most difficult items come in the middle third.
5. *The rule of three-quarters*: three-quarters of the way between the meetings, all relevant material is forwarded to members.

CONDUCTING THE MEETING

The chairperson should:

A **quorum** is the minimum number of people that must be at a meeting for business to be conducted.

- check that a **quorum** (the minimum number needed to conduct the business of the meeting) is present and then declare the meeting open
- welcome people to the meeting and introduce any visitors
- state the aims of the meeting
- indicate the order of the agenda and the time limit for each item
- give priority to the most important items
- sign the minutes when they are confirmed as correct
- allow each item to be dealt with by discussion, presenting information and creating action plans
- manage the moving and seconding of motions and amendments
- delegate when there is a need
- brief members
- give feedback
- create a real sense of belonging
- influence and motivate others to reach decisions
- assign tasks and take action on the basis of the decisions reached
- ensure that responsibilities and timelines for actions are recorded in the minutes
- close the meeting.

Hemphill, McCormick and Hemphill (2001, p. 231) recommend that the chairperson plan the agenda to avoid having guest speakers 'listen to the long (usually boring) reading of minutes, treasurer's report, business matters, and so forth'. If they are not directly involved, guest speakers do not appreciate sitting through these procedures. An organised agenda and meeting procedures that follow timelines encourage guest speakers to accept invitations. Hemphill and colleagues comment that 'word gets around the speakers' circuit, and you may find it possible to attract some who would otherwise not be interested'.

RULING ON POINTS OF ORDER

It is the chairperson's duty to:

A **point of order** asks whether proceedings are in order.

- make a decision on any **points of order** that are raised about whether the proceedings are in order
- make a call to a point of order to allow members to have a say

- acknowledge that members can, at any time in a meeting, point out any improper proceeding or incorrect interpretation of the rules or standing orders that govern the way the meeting is to be conducted
- rule on the point as correct or incorrect after discussion or debate on the point of order
- ask the meeting to vote for a ruling on a dissenting member's point of order—no seconder is needed
- accept the vote and take any necessary action to implement the decision.

FOLLOWING PROCEDURES

The chairperson should:

- allocate enough time for adequate discussion of each item on the agenda
- ensure discussion is completed within the time limits and follow procedures to prevent the meeting degenerating into a 'free for all', a 'gossip' or a 'gripe session'
- follow the rules of the meeting's procedure and keep order
- rule on difficult matters
- focus the discussion on the meeting's objectives
- sum up the main points and ask for a decision or vote
- follow standing orders so as to conduct an orderly and democratic meeting
- deal with any potential conflict before it becomes serious
- be objective and impartial and encourage all members to participate
- ensure that the meeting begins and ends on time
- put to the meeting the motion or proposal that, if all the business is not dealt with in the time limits, the business of the meeting be adjourned to the next meeting
- determine the date and place of the next meeting and close the meeting.

MAINTAINING ORDER

Hemphill, McCormick and Hemphill (2001, p. 230) state that 'maintaining order at the meeting is the responsibility of the leader' and recommend using parliamentary procedures for most meetings, 'since they not only give fair rulings on procedure but tend to smooth out disagreements among members'. They list four basic principles of parliamentary law cited by Marguerite Grumme, parliamentarian:

1. courtesy and justice to all
2. consider one thing at a time
3. the minority must be heard
4. the majority must prevail.

Grumme further commented, 'Parliamentary law is common sense used in a gracious manner.'

Roebuck (2001, p. 233) says that the chairperson must 'encourage, support, and listen' to the participants. She comments: '... by supporting others' right to speak, you do not show agreement. Instead you show your respect for them, accept them, and allow them to express their opinions.' She also warns against the chairperson dominating the meeting, and recommends that the chairperson should:

- avoid interrupting
- not talk for more than a couple of minutes
- keep asking other people to contribute
- allow someone else to present background information
- hold his or her opinions until the end.

MOVING AND SECONDING PROPOSALS, MOTIONS AND AMENDMENTS

A **motion** is a specific proposal for action formally put by a member to the rest of the meeting; for example, 'The motion is put that a pay increase of $30 per week be accepted.' Ideally, a motion should

A **motion** is a proposal for action.

be put in writing and given to the chairperson before the meeting for inclusion in the agenda. At the meeting the proposal is given in writing to the secretary for inclusion in the minutes.

Once the motion is put to the meeting, it must be seconded by another member before it can be discussed and voted on by the meeting. The chairperson asks for a seconder. When the motion is seconded, the chairperson asks the mover of the motion to speak to it; that is, to address the motion. A time limit is imposed by the standing orders or by the chairperson. After the mover of the motion speaks to it, the chairperson asks if anyone would like to speak against the motion. Then discussion on the motion is opened to all members present at the meeting. Throughout the discussion, the chairperson aims to maintain a balance between those speaking to the motion and those speaking against it, by asking alternate speakers to speak to and against the motion.

AMENDMENTS

An amendment to the motion can be suggested by any member. An **amendment** is a proposal to alter the wording to improve and add clarity to the motion by rearranging, removing or adding words. The chairperson asks for a seconder of the amendment and then it is discussed and voted on. If it is accepted, the original motion is amended (changed) before it is put to the vote. An amendment is unable to negate or change the intention of the motion. A member who wants to do this must wait until the motion is discussed and put to the vote and then put their proposal to the meeting as a separate motion.

RIGHT OF REPLY

Once the general discussion on the motion is completed, the chairperson gives the mover of the motion the right of reply. This is the last discussion allowed and an opportunity for the mover of a motion to reiterate and emphasise the main points.

VOTING FOR THE MOTION

The chairperson asks members to **vote** for or against the motion, usually by a verbal 'aye' or 'nay', by a show of hands, or by a ballot. Occasionally, when members feel that the discussion is taking too long, they may pre-empt the chairperson and ask that 'the question be put'; that is, that the motion become the question and that the members' vote for or against the motion be taken. It is more usual for the chairperson to ask for the vote. The simplest way to vote is by asking members to say 'aye' (yes) or 'nay' (no) and to judge by the volume of the voices.

The motion is won or lost by a simple majority. On those occasions when votes for the motion equal those against, the vote is tied. The chairperson then has the **casting vote** to break the tied vote. The chairperson abstains from voting except when the meeting's vote is tied. The chairperson also abstains from the discussion unless he or she leaves the chair and asks someone else to take it.

RESOLUTIONS

A motion put to the meeting and carried becomes a resolution; that is, the discussion on that issue or motion has been resolved to the meeting's satisfaction and the meeting is committed to the action. All motions, whether successful or unsuccessful, should be recorded by the secretary in the minutes.

PROXIES

In a formal meeting such as an annual general meeting, proxies are used to allow absent members to register a vote. A **proxy** is a written authorisation given by a shareholder for someone else, usually the company's management, to cast his or her vote at a shareholders' meeting or at another time. Reid (2001, p. 101) recommends a cut-off time prior to a meeting for the acceptance of proxies. The proxies should be stamped with the date and time of receipt and be entered in a register. The chairperson should have at the meeting all the valid proxy forms appointing him or her to vote on behalf of the absent members. Reid comments that the chairperson should also have 'a statement listing such proxies and the voting power he [sic] has in proportion to total votes. This is useful, psychologically, in establishing his [sic] control if a poll is demanded.'

Table 11.4 explains some of the terms used in connection with meetings.

An **amendment** is a proposal to alter a motion.

At formal meetings members **vote** to make decisions, usually by a verbal 'aye' or 'nay', by a show of hands, or by a ballot.

A **casting vote** is made by the chairperson to decide an issue in the case of a tied vote.

A **proxy** is a written authorisation given by a shareholder for someone else, usually the company's management, to cast his or her vote at a shareholders' meeting or at another time.

Table 11.4: Terminology of meetings

Term	Meaning and purpose
Agenda	A list of the meeting's business, prepared by the secretary in consultation with the chairperson, and distributed before the meeting. It provides participants in the meeting with a brief to prepare information, collect opinions and decide what actions they would like implemented.
Amendment	A proposal to alter a motion in some relevant way. There are four types of amendments: 1 Insert or add certain words. 2 Leave out certain words. 3 Leave out some words in order to insert or add others. 4 Leave out all the words after 'that' and substitute others. An amendment must be debated and voted on before the original motion. If there are several amendments to the motion, each is debated and voted on in turn. An amendment needs a mover and a seconder. The mover and seconder of the original motion, plus anyone else who has spoken in debate on the original motion, may speak to the amendment.
Casting vote	A vote from the chairperson that will decide the issue in the case of a tie. The chairperson may choose not to use this casting vote.
Constitution	The constitution contains the organisation's name, aims and objectives, rules of administration, membership, office bearers and committee.
General business	The heading on the agenda under which 'new' business may be introduced. Any items you wish to raise under this heading are usually mentioned to the secretary beforehand.
Minutes	A record of what happens during the meeting. Minutes may contain records of who was present, motions and amendments passed, decisions taken, action decided on, people responsible for implementing these decisions, and any matters that have been deferred.
Motion	A proposal, placed before a meeting by one of the members, to have action taken. A motion becomes a resolution after it has been agreed to by the meeting. A motion can be classified as substantive or procedural. A substantive motion is any motion of substance to do with the business of the meeting. A procedural motion relates to the rules and regulations of the meeting.
Notice	A notice convening the meeting sent to all members at a time specified by the organisation's rules.
Quorum	The minimum number of people that must be at a meeting in order for business to be conducted. The secretary should check that a quorum is present during voting. The size of the quorum is identified in the constitution.
Standing orders	The rules that govern the manner in which a meeting's business is to be conducted.
Vote	At formal meetings, members vote to make decisions. The vote may be the verbal 'aye' or 'nay', a show of hands, a division, or a secret vote.

Duties of the secretary

The duties of the **secretary**, who assists the chairperson, are numerous. The way in which they are carried out is important to the process of the meeting and its result.

*The **secretary** assists the chairperson.*

AGENDA

The secretary convenes all meetings and prepares the agenda in consultation with the chairperson. The **agenda** clearly states the time, date and place of the next meeting, and the order in which items will be discussed. Agenda items can be separated into two groups:

*The **agenda** lists the order of business. It is prepared by the secretary and distributed before the meeting.*

1. decision items on which action will be taken
2. discussion items.

By dividing the agenda in this way, the chairperson and secretary ensure that the most important items are dealt with either first, or in the middle section (see Figure 11.1). Thus, the agenda lets members know:

- where and when the meeting will be held
- who is invited to the meeting
- what business will be covered
- when each item will be dealt with.

An example of an agenda is given in Figure 11.2. A copy is sent to each member before the meeting, allowing them to think about and prepare for the business to be dealt with at the meeting. An agenda should be prepared and distributed in such a way that members can recognise the problems ahead and have time to analyse possible solutions. The phrase 'other business' indicates discussion of items that are not on the agenda. The agenda may also indicate the time allotted to each item of business.

DOCUMENTATION

The secretary deals with the paperwork associated with a meeting. This includes:

- preparing enough copies of documentation for all members
- sending the agenda for the next meeting with a copy of the minutes of the previous meeting, preferably 14 days after the last meeting (if the meeting is held every four weeks)
- answering requests for information from members.

APOLOGIES

At the meeting, the secretary:

- records the names of those present
- reads **apologies** from absentees and asks the chairperson to call for any other apologies for absentees
- records these apologies.

***Apologies** are the names of people who have apologised for not being present at a meeting.*

CORRESPONDENCE AND MINUTES

The secretary:

- deals with all incoming and outgoing *correspondence*
- keeps clear and accurate **minutes** (Figure 11.3)
- keeps copies of any motions put without notice, records in the minutes the names of those present, apologies, a list of correspondence, a brief summary of any discussion, the conclusions reached and the decisions made
- checks that the minutes clearly identify motions and the person who moves, seconds or amends the motion

*The **minutes** are the official written record of a meeting.*

Date: 4 October 2009

Time: 9am–10am

Location: Suite 11A, Level 2, Australian Institute

Purpose: To plan the annual Christmas function

Order of business

1. Opening of meeting.
2. Apologies.
3. Confirmation of minutes of previous meeting (copy attached).
4. Business arising out of minutes.
5. Correspondence.
6. Business arising out of correspondence.
7. Decision items:
    a. Budget
    b. Type of function
    c. Date and venue
    d. Collection and banking of money.
8. Discussion items:
    a. To invite partners or members only?
    b. Will food and alcohol be provided?
9. Other business.
10. Closing of meeting.

Agenda distribution:

Melissa Baxter	Peter Hill
Penny Baker	Willem Helvi
Colin Kees	Kay Wilson
Cheryl Kerr	Maria Pappas

Figure 11.2: Example of meeting agenda

- identifies in the minutes the actions to be taken and who is to take the action
- checks any doubtful points with the chairperson as soon as the meeting ends and writes up brief, clear and accurate minutes as soon as possible after the meeting, at most within 24 hours
- has the chairperson initial any alterations to the minutes
- records the minutes in a minutes book
- has the chairperson sign these at the next meeting as confirmation that they are correct.

Duties of the members

Productive meetings give results and satisfaction to those who belong to the group. Participants in a meeting can make the meeting more productive by preparing for it and knowing how to conduct themselves in the meeting (see following sections).

Minutes of the Sport and Recreation Social Club Meeting held at Suite 11A, Level 2, Australian Institute, on 4 October 2009

Present: Melissa Baxter (Chair)   Peter Hill (Secretary)
                     Penny Baker   Willem Helvi
                     Cheryl Kerr   Maria Pappas

Apologies: Colin Kees, Kay Wilson

1. Minutes of the previous meeting

   Cheryl Kerr moved and Willem Helvi seconded that the minutes of the previous meeting be accepted. Carried.

2. Business arising out of the minutes of the previous meeting Nil

3. Business arising out of correspondence Nil

4. Purpose of meeting

   The chairperson Melissa Baxter advised that the objective of today's Social Club meeting is to plan and organise the annual Christmas function and that the order of items on the agenda is to be followed.

5. Decision or action items

   Action

   The budget is to be $45 per person.

   Moved: W. Helvi   Seconded: M. Pappas   Carried

   Action

   The function is to be held on 11 December 2009.

   Moved: P. Baker   Seconded: C. Kerr   Carried

   Action

   The Christmas function is to be held at a local restaurant.

   Moved: P. Baker   Seconded: C. Kerr   Carried

   Action C. Kerr

   Determine the price and availability on 11 December 2009 two different venues, Curlin House and the Satay Inn.

   Moved: M. Pappas   Seconded: P. Hill   Carried

   Action W. Helvi

   Money is to be collected from each member of the committee by S. Graham and held in a Credit Union account.

   Moved: P. Baker   Seconded: P. Hill   Carried

   Action S. Graham

6. Discussion items

   Action P. Hill

   To send a memo to all members asking for their preference on:

   a. inviting members and partners, or members only

   b. provide food only, or alcohol and food.

   Moved: C. Kerr   Seconded: W. Helvi   Carried

7. Any other business

   General discussion on the format for next year's Little Athletics presentation night. Members decided to consider different formats and to present their views at the next meeting.

8. Date of next meeting: 5 November 2009

9. Meeting closed: 10.05 am

   Chairperson's signature   Secretary's signature

   Date: Date:

Figure 11.3: Example of minutes of a meeting

REVIEW QUESTIONS

4 *a*   Describe the characteristics of an effective meeting leader.

   b   What makes an effective meeting participant?

5 *a*   Describe the twofold responsibility of the chairperson's role.

   b   How does knowledge of the Agenda Bell help a chairperson?

6 *a*   Explain the role of: the agenda, minutes, decision or action items, discussion items, other business, motion, quorum.

   b   Who opens the meeting?

   c   Who gives the apologies?

   d   Who keeps the minutes or record of the meeting?

   e   Who presents the correspondence in and out?

   f   Who moves and seconds motions?

TASK ROLES AND MAINTENANCE ROLES

Task-related roles

> ◄ OBJECTIVE **3**
> Discuss task roles in a meeting, and analyse the skills that support maintenance roles

Before they attend the meeting, members should read the meeting's agenda and the minutes of the previous meeting. They can then prepare in writing any proposals or motions they wish to put to the meeting and forward these to the chairperson. In readiness to speak about the proposal and to have the right of reply, members should also prepare their oral presentation. The following three steps help with staying on the main point:

1. State the main point to catch the listeners' attention.
2. Give the reason or need for the proposal.
3. Present the relevant background information.

By following these three steps, it is possible to catch members' attention with the main point, give them the reason for the proposal, and present just enough information to persuade them to agree to the proposal—that is, to vote for the motion. Avoid saying too much, as an overload of information may distract members from the main point. Remember to reiterate the main point and its advantages or benefits in the right of reply.

Task-related roles enable the meeting to move through each step or operation in the meeting's process. Goal setting, decision making and problem solving are examples of the tasks that enable the meeting to achieve its purpose.

Task-related roles move the meeting forward.

Once the goals are determined, planning and organising achieve the action to solve the problem. Members of a formal meeting need to indicate to the chairperson their intention to speak and receive the chairperson's call to speak. They then address their remarks to the chairperson before looking at the other members of the meeting. Generally, a member can speak only once when a motion or proposal is being discussed.

Maintenance-related roles

The meeting's leader or chairperson, members of the executive and other members are all responsible for maintenance-related roles within the meeting. **Maintenance-related roles** are the behaviours that are needed in groups or meetings to focus on people and their relationships with one another—for example, to support and encourage member contributions or to resolve disagreements. Use maintenance roles to support and encourage the contributions of members, create a positive atmosphere, reduce tensions and reconcile disagreements. Be willing to negotiate, to modify a position or to admit an error. Open communication channels encourage and facilitate discussion and contributions. Effective use

Maintenance-related roles focus on people and their relationships with one another.

of maintenance skills enables task achievement in a cooperative environment. Maintenance-related roles use the human relations skills of support, encouragement and feedback. Delegating, guiding, influencing and motivating others are all part of the maintenance-related role.

DEFENSIVE AND DYSFUNCTIONAL ROLES

Defensive roles are behaviours that are intended to protect a group from anxiety when it is unable to function effectively.

Dysfunctional roles distract a group from its purpose.

Defensive and dysfunctional roles contrast with task-related and maintenance roles, which facilitate the achievement of a group's goals. People take **defensive roles**—such as tension reliever or scapegoat—to protect other members from the anxiety caused when the meeting is unable to function effectively. People take **dysfunctional roles**—such as show-off, blocker or rebel—to achieve their own hidden agendas and, in doing so, prevent the meeting from achieving its goals. The chairperson has the authority to intervene when a member plays a dysfunctional role by summarising progress, calling the meeting to order or calling an adjournment.

Task-related, maintenance-related, defensive and dysfunctional roles are discussed more fully in Chapter 10. As members develop their communication and message skills in speaking, listening, questioning and encouraging others, they become more productive and self-confident and better prepared to carry out the task-related and maintenance-related roles in a meeting.

PROBLEM PEOPLE IN MEETINGS

Parry (1991, p. 83) says that the impact of problem people should not be exaggerated; however, a chairperson who is aware of the following categories can intervene when necessary. *Abstainers* hold back and include those who are timid, inarticulate or in need of encouragement. Other abstainers are those who are aloof and intimidating, and those who are uncharacteristically silent. *Spoilers* such as ego-trippers, compulsive talkers, snobs, filibusters (monopolisers), snipers and private combatants have to be restrained. *Usurpers* try to take over and start a separate meeting. Any one of the three categories—abstainers, spoilers and usurpers—can cause problems at meetings.

REVIEW QUESTIONS

7 What is the difference between a task-related role and a maintenance-related role?
8 Give two reasons why members might adopt a defensive role in a meeting.
9 How can members encourage others to participate in a meeting?
10 How can a chairperson intervene when a member takes a dysfunctional role in the meeting?

APPLY YOUR KNOWLEDGE

BEHAVIOUR AT MEETINGS

1 In pairs, recall and discuss a meeting one or both of you attended recently.
a What were the seating arrangements for the members? Why do you think they were seated in that way?
b From your observations:
i Was the chairperson effective or ineffective?
ii Identify two ways in which the chairperson or a member helped others to communicate and participate.
iii How can a chairperson maintain control in a meeting?
iv What are two strategies a chairperson can use to create a pleasant environment?
c Who had responsibility to prepare and forward the agenda to members of this meeting?
d Discuss two different ways in which information and items for the agenda could be collected.
e Why should the agenda reach members before the meeting?
f Why did this meeting need to keep minutes?

2 a Next time you participate in a meeting as the chair, the secretary or a member, use the self-evaluation box below to evaluate the meeting and your performance in the meeting.

b Suggest strategies you could use to improve your performance in the items you marked 'poorly'.

c What would you do differently next time?

SELF-EVALUATE YOUR SKILLS

STRUCTURED MEETINGS

Key: VS = Very Successfully, S = Successfully, U = Unsuccessfully

Use this checklist after attending a formal meeting			
Did the chairperson and/or secretary:	VS	S	U
prepare and distribute the agenda?			
organise the venue and seating?			
state the meeting's purpose?			
guide the meeting through the business on the agenda?			
use strategies to complete the tasks?			
focus the discussion on the meeting's objectives?			
enable effective presentation of proposals or motions, discussion and resolution to take place?			
help the meeting to plan appropriate action?			
achieve the meeting's goals?			
use strategies to maintain the group?			
use problem-solving or decision-making strategies?			
involve everyone in the discussion?			
keep accurate minutes?			
use time efficiently?			
identify any follow-up actions?			
start and end according to the agenda?			
Did the members:	VS	S	U
follow structured meeting procedures?			
complete task roles?			
participate in group maintenance roles?			
give motions in writing to the secretary?			
speak logically, clearly and concisely to the motion from a prepared oral presentation?			

Did the members:	VS	S	U
offer their views in a way that supported others in the discussion?			
conform to the problem-solving or decision-making style chosen by the chairperson or meeting?			
show a willingness to commit to the meeting's decisions?			
participate constructively?			

OBJECTIVE 4 ▶
Outline the advantages
and disadvantages of
virtual meetings

VIRTUAL MEETINGS

The ability to communicate inexpensively via desktop computers, the Internet and telephones has resulted in the advent of virtual meetings. They are used effectively to realise organisational goals with a saving of both time and cost. Many people may not attend face-to-face meetings because of the time factor or travel costs.

The definition of virtual meeting varies markedly. According to Walker, Collings and Richards-Smith (2003), it can be any of the following:

- delivery of information to an audience—for example, a broadcast lecture or a document posted on a bulletin board
- an exchange of ideas and opinion, as in an Internet chat session or newsgroup, without any attempt to come to a conclusion
- a meeting with an agenda or a set of objectives that attempts to come to some form of agreement or decision.

In the last category, virtual meetings can be either formal (with a chairperson, an agenda and formal meeting rules) or informal (with a facilitator). In an informal meeting, group participants manage the meeting with possibly one person acting as facilitator to control the meeting. Group members participate from workstations in their own offices without the need of a conference room.

Meetings conducted by electronic conferencing can take many forms:

- webconferencing
- teleconferencing
- videoconferencing
- audioconferencing.

Formal virtual meetings

As with traditional formal meetings, participants require a notice of meeting, an agenda and meeting papers forwarded to them within a stipulated time prior to the meeting. The chairperson presides and acts as the facilitator, and the secretary records those in attendance, apologies, acceptance of the minutes of the previous meeting and reports, as well as the decisions made throughout the meeting. Although virtual meetings obviate the need for participants to be in the same location, managing the meeting requires the chairperson to have specific virtual skills or an assistant conversant with the software.

CONTROL THE DISCUSSION THREADS

Walker, Collings and Richards-Smith (2003) comment that in both informal and formal meetings the primary role of a chairperson or facilitator is controlling discussion threads. These could be related to the formal agenda items or to the many sub-issues that arise. Controlling the discussion in a virtual meeting requires a different approach from that adopted in traditional meetings. Walker and colleagues describe control in a face-to-face meeting as being achieved 'either by participants indicating to the chair that they wish to speak (and the chair then informing them of when it is their turn) or by more informal turn-taking mechanisms, where participants observe others to see if they wish to speak'. Managing 'floor control' is much more difficult in a virtual meeting. Walker and colleagues recommend devising some method of giving participants the 'floor'—for example, by participants sending a private message to the facilitator indicating a wish to contribute, or by the facilitator nominating the next contributor.

In a virtual or electronic meeting, the primary role of the chairperson is to control the discussion threads.

A further problem inherent in formal virtual meetings is the lack of social cues necessary to determine consensus. Body language, such as facial expressions and voice volume, conveys a considerable amount of nonverbal information that is often not apparent in virtual meetings. However, voting in virtual meetings is quick and this can have considerable benefits. Within a few minutes, a quick vote can:

- identify which are the important issues
- establish a consensus on how the meeting should spend its time
- identify which issues already have significant consensus, thus avoiding unnecessary discussion
- identify those issues about which there is little consensus, giving the opportunity for more time to be allocated for discussion. (Web-Meetings Limited 2007)

Walker and colleagues, however, point out that the socialising aspect, the pre-meeting lobbying and caucusing, the important parts of traditional meetings, are not present. They believe that, although assumptions are made that virtual meetings and face-to-face meetings have similar structures, 'in fact the technology used to "host" the meeting by its very nature changes (and limits) the behaviour of electronic meeting attendees'.

Kostner (2007) suggests applying the 80/20 rule to online meetings. 'Spend 80 percent of the meeting time on topics that require all-participant interaction, and 20 percent of the meeting time on information-only topics . . . Reserve the majority of the online meeting time for interaction—identifying issues, brainstorming solutions, making decisions, and building alignment.' She goes on to argue that, because virtual teams collaborate 84% less frequently than traditional same-site teams, online meeting time should not be wasted on anything that can be shared by email or other one-way media.

SYNCHRONOUS MEETINGS

Synchronous meetings—that is, all group members participating at the same time—require forward planning and organisation. Walker and colleagues (2003) recommend the following when running a synchronous meeting using groupware such as AussieMOO or Microsoft NetMeeting.

In a **synchronous virtual meeting**, all group members participate at the same time.

- Make certain the group is not too large. (Four is about the limit.)
- Circulate an agenda to indicate the length of time the meeting should take.
- Appoint a chairperson or facilitator.
- Devise a means of giving the participants the 'floor'.
- Use multiple media that complement each other. For example, in NetMeeting the whiteboard can be used to summarise the main points made in the chat.
- If you have a break, make sure all participants know when the meeting will resume.
- Ensure that everyone has a chance to ask any final questions or make comments before the meeting is closed.

Informal virtual meetings

Teleconferencing, audioconferencing and webconferencing are examples of informal virtual meetings. Each has advantages and disadvantages.

TELECONFERENCING

Teleconferencing is where two or more people in different locations participate in an interactive communications session.

Teleconferencing, where two or more people in different locations participate in an interactive communications session, is the most common form of virtual meeting. Each participant or small groups of participants must have access to a telephone or speaker phone. A designated time for the conference call is circulated and all conference members must be available at that time. Calls can be set up as 'listen-only', where only the moderator speaks, or in a 'question and answer' mode, where each participant is introduced and the moderator controls the interactive discussion.

There are some disadvantages of teleconferencing. Privacy is a major concern, as it is easy for an uninvited person to become part of the meeting if they know the telephone number to call. A moderator introducing and identifying each participant in the meeting can solve this problem. Another disadvantage is that teleconferencing has its own peculiar rhythm and often there is an overlap or delay. Words need to be chosen carefully as without a visual component there is the possibility of misunderstanding.

Participants should identify themselves continually, particularly if they haven't spoken for a while, and order must be maintained. Teleconferences are vulnerable to group actions such as note-passing, grimacing or mocking gestures, as the visual component is absent. Teleconferencing can be inadequate for larger groups or if complex issues are being discussed.

AUDIOCONFERENCING

Audioconferencing enables members who are geographically dispersed to communicate verbally without the expense of meeting face-to-face.

Audioconferencing enables members who are geographically dispersed to communicate verbally without the expense of meeting face-to-face. Audioconferencing takes place via the Internet. Telephone calls are made to any part of the world for the cost of a local connection. The voice is digitised and the digital data is sent to its destination via the Internet. All that is required is a headset with earphones, a microphone and the required software. Savings made on travel costs and long-distance phone calls are the main advantage. The audio quality is sometimes poor, which can be a disadvantage.

WEBCONFERENCING

Webconferencing is used to conduct live meetings or presentations over the Internet. In a web conference, each participant sits at his or her own computer and is connected to other participants via the Internet.

Webconferencing is used to conduct live meetings over the Internet. Each member is connected with other members and able to participate in the meeting. Effective webconferencing involves team building, information sharing and problem solving. A skilled moderator may be necessary to ensure that meetings run smoothly. Applications that offer calendaring and schedule management will assist moderators to:

- schedule the time for meetings
- verify participants are available
- create an agenda.

The disadvantages of webconferencing are the lack of personal contact, the costs involved and the need for participants to be computer-literate. Often, great interest in this technology is shown at first, but interest lapses after a few months.

VIDEOCONFERENCING

Videoconferencing may comprise any number of people communicating in a video session in real time from different locations.

Videoconferencing technology differs from other forms of conferencing in that it allows two or more people in diverse locations to see and hear each other simultaneously. It is often possible for computer applications such as Internet pages and library catalogues to be shared. Bovée and Thill (2005, p. 48) point out: 'Videoconferencing combines audio communication with live video letting team members see each other, demonstrate products, and transmit other visual information.' As the cost of installing videoconferencing systems has fallen considerably over the past few years, videoconferencing will almost certainly become the way of the future. The following strategies improve communication in a videoconference.

- *Introduce each participant.* Give their names and background, or have each participant supply this information to the rest of the group.
- *Get to each point quickly.* Provide only a short introduction. Speak briefly and ask for feedback.
- *Emphasise facial expressions and gestures.* Participants need to see more than a 'talking head'.
- *Avoid busy backgrounds and inappropriate dress.* Busy backgrounds are distracting, as is patterned clothing. Avoid white shirts or blouses unless you can wear a dark jacket over them. If possible, choose colours such as blue or green.
- *Keep all participants on track.* Make certain that the agenda items are followed, and cut short any unnecessary conversations.
- *Seek input from reticent members.* Discourage those who tend to monopolise and encourage input from the less vocal members. As the camera zooms in when a person speaks, it is possible for some members to be overlooked.

Participants should also be aware of the conventions in videoconferencing. DeTienne (2002, pp. 80–81) recommends the following:

- Look at the camera when you want to speak to someone in another location and not at the person's picture on the screen.
- Avoid moving around or having side conversations when another participant is talking, as these actions can be distracting.
- Use the mute function if you find it necessary to cough or to talk to someone in the room. In fact, as videoconferencing systems are generally voice activated, it is a good idea to use the mute function whenever you are not speaking.
- Avoid eating during the conference, as this is unprofessional.
- Speak naturally and be yourself. Pretend that the other participants are sitting in the room with you.

Benefits of virtual meetings

New technology has resulted in a profound change in the way meetings are held. DeTienne (2002, p. 81) lists the following benefits of using the virtual meeting system:

- keeps discussions on track
- engages the participants
- allows all participants to contribute and vote at the same time
- analyses the voting results
- provides a written record of the meeting
- speeds the pace of the meeting
- increases participation from employees at all levels and decreases the impact of the hierarchy
- works well when soliciting input from all participants of a large group.

BENEFITS OF VIDEOCONFERENCING

As an interactive communication medium, videoconferencing has considerably more benefits than those obtained from using email, the telephone or online chat systems. Being able to listen and observe other participants increases understanding and assists in building relationships. The inhibitions often apparent in face-to-face situations, such as a reluctance to disagree with the opinions of others, are not present. In addition, the use of diverse media, such as video, audio clips, graphics, animation and computer applications, can assist with the retention of information and, in a learning situation, accommodate different learning styles. As the costs are far less than those incurred in organising a conference in a physical location, organisations will increasingly be using this mode of conferencing.

DeTienne (2002, p. 79) states that videoconferencing works well when:

- you need the benefit of face-to-face contact and want to save the time and expense associated with travelling to another location
- your goal is to provide information, such as explaining or training
- you are broadcasting presentations and talks to many employees.

DISADVANTAGES OF VIDEOCONFERENCING

The equipment needed for videoconferencing is expensive to purchase and maintain, and staff need to be trained to use it. The fact that the proceedings of videoconferences can be archived and retrieved later can be an inhibiting factor. Participants may be acutely conscious of what they are saying and fear later repercussions. Additionally, there is a lack of immediate feedback as experienced in face-to-face discussions.

DeTienne (2002, p. 79) suggests that videoconferencing should not be used when:

- time-lag difficulties will be distracting or detrimental
- the added social context of face-to-face communication is needed
- short bursts of input are needed from all participants
- sensitive issues are being discussed.

In addition, often the group misses out on the side discussions that can result in creative solutions and ideas. Table 11.5 presents the advantages and disadvantages of videoconferencing.

Table 11.5: Advantages and disadvantages of videoconferencing	
Advantages	**Disadvantages**
Increases understanding	Initial purchase costs
Builds relationships	Maintenance
Heightens communication	Technical training required
Reduces inhibitions	Inhibits spontaneity
Increases connection with the outside world	Lack of immediate feedback
Reduces travelling costs and time	Time-lag difficulties
Proceedings can be archived	Difficulty in discussing sensitive issues
Can bring people together with short notice	Lack of side discussions

REVIEW QUESTIONS

11. What is virtual conferencing?
12. a How can members of virtual meetings develop an identity and a sense of purpose?
    b What are the disadvantages of teleconferencing?
13. a Briefly discuss the problems inherent in formal virtual meetings.
    b Explain how these problems can be overcome.

COMMUNICATION BARRIERS

Communication barriers in face-to-face or virtual meetings result from either poor leadership or poor membership skills, or a combination of the two. Communication barriers interfere with and prevent productive results. They can be caused by poor verbal, nonverbal or listening skills.

Verbal communication barriers are caused by illogical organisation of words, and unclear, ambiguous and discourteous ways of speaking. Jargon, slang and negative language also interfere with the communication flow. Address a person by the wrong name or using the wrong level of formality and there may be an immediate communication barrier.

Nonverbal behaviour also has an effect on the other person. The tone of voice, type of eye contact, gestures, use of space, clothing and appearance all affect communication. Use these in a manner appropriate to the situation to achieve effective communication that matches the needs of sender and receiver and the purpose of the communication. Miscommunication occurs when verbal or nonverbal behaviour is inappropriate to the situation. For example, leaning back, rocking the chair or clasping the hands behind the head sends a message of impatience to other members. Interest in the proceedings is shown by leaning forward and making eye contact with others.

Poor listening because of boredom, lack of interest, a clash of values, jumping to early conclusions, judging the speaker, dislike of the speaker, or distractions in the physical environment raises communication barriers. Part of the message is lost.

◄ OBJECTIVE **5**
Identify communication barriers in face-to-face and virtual meetings

Communication barriers hinder productive results.

Unwillingness to use power

A meeting has access to resources and power. An unwilling, unsure membership is unable to make decisions or to organise and manage the business of the committee or meeting effectively. Communication barriers develop between members. Members realise that the group is ineffective and tend to withdraw or behave in dysfunctional ways. The effectiveness of any meeting or committee is related to the ability of members and the executive to participate, solve problems, organise and manage the business of the committee in a way that achieves results.

Positive verbal and nonverbal feedback to suggestions from other members motivates the group, adds to satisfaction and gives a sense of belonging to a group that is achieving its purpose. In fact, many of the potential barriers to effective communication in a meeting or committee are removed when members use positive verbal and nonverbal feedback and follow through to implement the decisions made.

Communicate using verbal and nonverbal feedback.

Attitudes to meetings

Tropman (1996, pp. ix–xxiii) discusses how decision groups are portrayed as inept. He states: 'Public references, as well as cartoons, repeatedly suggest that groups are collections of the impotent convened to do the impossible. A committee was once defined as a group that takes minutes to waste hours' (1996, p. xix). If we want to improve meetings, he suggests that an understanding of why meetings are so disliked and hard to reform and improve is essential. First, it is cultural: the tendency to support individual action over group action. Second, decision groups are ubiquitous: they appear everywhere. Tropman suggests that the third reason for disliking meetings is the social debits and credit, 'the enmeshing uncertainty of commitment when joining a committee or board' (1996, p. xxi) and the negative, hostile humour encountered, together with the time and energy, commitment, pressure to change views and compromise that is required. Last, the lack of psychological and skill-based training for work in decision groups makes it difficult to reform meetings. Members who have skills in managing and facilitating mutual decision making are effective.

The four elements required for a quality decision group to function, and the four reasons why groups do not work well, are shown in Table 11.6.

Table 11.6: Decision groups	
Functions for a group to work well	**Reasons for group problems**
Setting expectations aimed at accomplishment	Low salience–relatively trivial matters on the agenda
Providing scripts (agendas)	High inertia
Informing participants about position requirements	Burnout
Striving for high-quality decisions	Decision overload

Source: Adapted from J.E. Tropman, *Effective Meetings: Improving Group Decision Making*, 2nd edn, Sage Publications, California, 1996.

Groupthink

'Groupthink', a condition of like-mindedness, is a factor that can influence decisions made in meetings. Bienvenu and Timm (2002, p. 229) believe that this condition arises in groups that are particularly cohesive. When groupthink exists, 'people in the group will exert pressure against any dissenting viewpoints'. Bienvenu and Timm believe that this type of thinking is counterproductive: it stifles creativity and any fresh approaches to solving problems. 'This is especially likely when the group has high enthusiasm and when members' desire for consensus or harmony becomes stronger than their desire for the best possible decision.' (Groupthink is also discussed in Chapter 10.)

OBJECTIVE 6 ▶
Explain the impact of the venue and seating arrangements on the dynamics of a meeting

PLANNING THE ENVIRONMENT

The chairperson and secretary plan the meeting and organise the order of business. They also need to consider the venue, equipment and seating arrangements.

Face-to-face meetings

Seating arrangements influence the kind of interaction that takes place.

Rowan (2003) discusses the impact of seating arrangements on the dynamics in a meeting. 'Simply put, each type of seating arrangement, from a rectangular table or theater style to a circular arrangement without a table, has vastly different ramifications on the participants and thereby the meeting outcome. Each arrangement changes the environment by changing the ways in which participants interact with the speaker and with one another.' She explains how nonverbal communication, particularly eye contact, is used in meetings to control interaction and conversation. Leaders and other key players generally opt for the seats with the best direct eye contact, which are usually at the ends of the table. 'People seated closest to the leader and key players generally minimize their effectiveness because they have the least eye contact with the leader.' Seating arrangements can facilitate communication, encourage formality (or informality), or emphasise power and status.

Round tables are ideal for seeing one another's actions and reactions. Rectangular tables give power to the people at either end. No table creates an informal atmosphere. The person who sits above the rest has more power. Those who sit below others, in a position where they have to look up, lose power.

The ideal seating arrangement, the circular or oval shape illustrated in Figure 11.4, allows everyone to see everyone else. This results in better communication between members and effective control and participation by the chairperson. This type of seating arrangement lessens the possibility of some members of the meeting becoming dominant. The long rectangular table illustrated in Figure 11.4 is less than ideal. It can lead to such problems as 'meetings within meetings'. The members farthest from the chairperson may talk among themselves. The chairperson may find it difficult to maintain control. Board meetings and international meetings often use this layout. It is not as democratic as the circle.

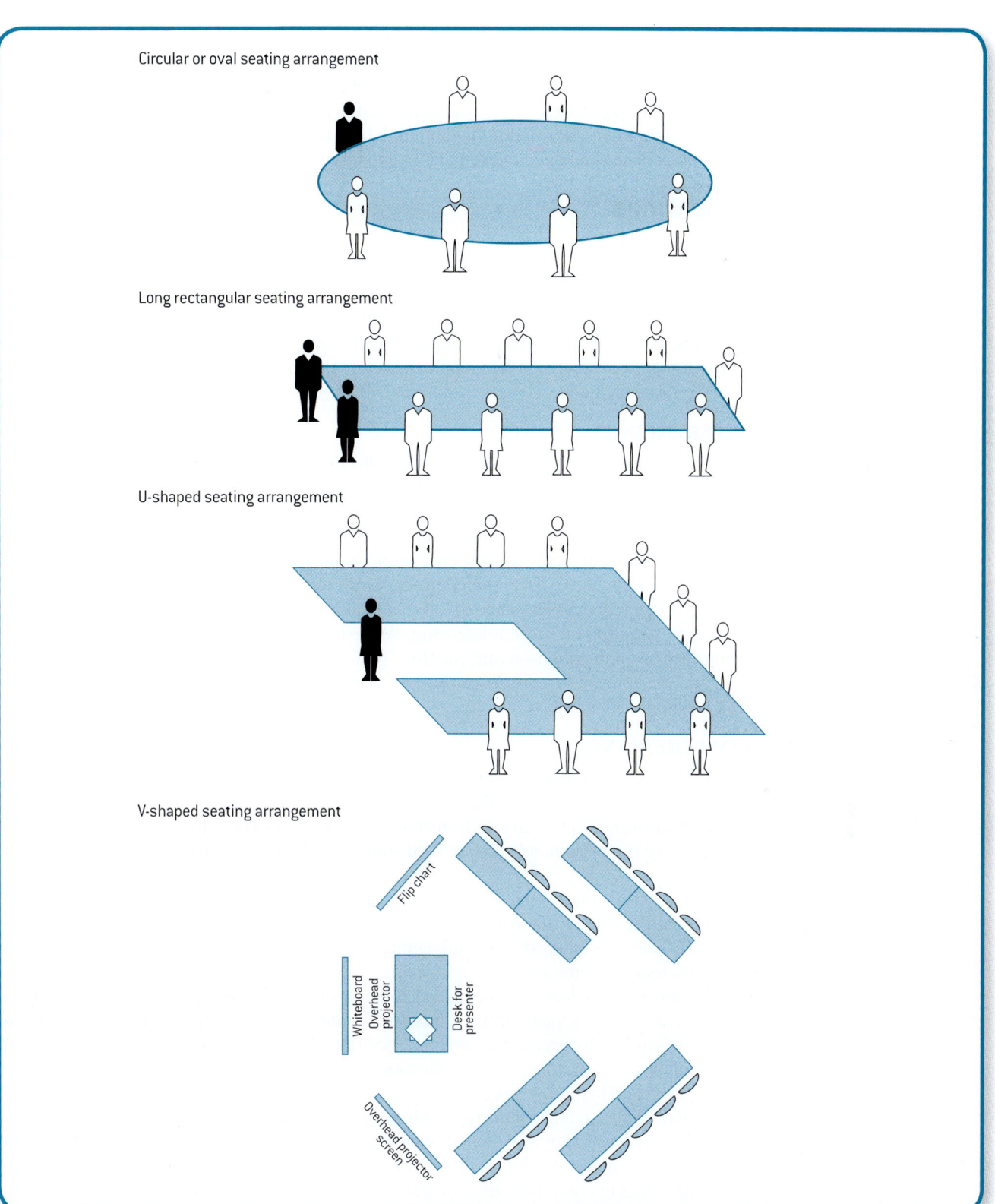

Figure 11.4: *Seating arrangements*

The U-shaped seating arrangement (Figure 11.4) presents similar problems to the long rectangular table. The person on the immediate left of the chairperson will have trouble asserting their presence. The person on the right is easily noticed, as are the members closer to the chairperson. The V-shaped seating arrangement in Figure 11.4 allows a large number of people to receive information at the same time. It is appropriate to an information meeting in which the focus is on the person delivering the information. Members have no need to engage in group discussion and decision making.

Virtual meetings

Virtual meetings are effective when the organiser plans ahead by finding out the names of each participant, their titles if appropriate, and something about each person. Virtual meetings can be impersonal and it is important to create connections between participants. Seek input from participants before the meeting by phone or email. This will ensure that they all have a stake in the process. Ensure that participants are aware of the topics to be discussed and in what order, by distributing agendas, reports or any documents at least one week before the conference. A timing schedule for each agenda item should be included.

WEBCONFERENCING

Webconferencing enables businesses to communicate effectively and quickly. To participate in webconferencing, all that is needed is an Internet link and a Web browser. Participants then log on via a PC and communicate with other members of the group. Functionally, it is easy to navigate and manage. Before the webconference, the dial-in number and conference ID is distributed to participants. Participants are instructed either to dial in on the phone or log in on the Web if visuals are involved, or both. It is not necessary to dial in on the phone if the conference is being broadcast live on the Web. A standard Web browser (version 4.0 or higher of Netscape or Internet Explorer) and a minimum 28.8 kbps connection to the Internet are required for webconferencing. With some applications, a maximum number of 96 participants can be on the phone at any one time. A maximum number of 2048 participants can be logged on to the Web at any given time (Cox Business Services 2003). This can be a cost-effective way to conduct a meeting.

VIDEOCONFERENCING

To be successful, videoconferences need to be highly organised. Table 11.7 identifies three factors to consider as the equipment is organised. Basic videoconferencing equipment, such as monitor, camera, microphone and speaker, is necessary to transmit information between the meeting sites. A more expensive alternative is a broadband satellite with studio capabilities that can produce a full-motion video connection.

Renting basic videoconferencing equipment is a cheaper option than purchasing it. However, trends indicate that the cost of this equipment will fall as time goes on. This will encourage organisations to install their own videoconferencing equipment in order to be competitive. There are two common systems, room systems and desktop systems.

A *room system* involves having a dedicated room permanently set up. A large screen at the front of the room shows participants in their different locations. Also set up in the room are special cameras, hardware and high-speed Integrated Services Digital Network (ISDN) lines. High bandwith Internet access allows Web graphics to be loaded quickly on Netscape and ensures that the picture and sound will be clear. This is the more expensive option for organisations. SBS Pacific Bell (2003) states that the broadband satellite connection with studio-quality equipment can produce an excellent full-motion video connection, but that 'the equipment and transmission expense is huge'. Because of the expense, SBS Pacific Bell believes that the Internet may eventually replace ISDN as the medium of choice. Recent advances in computer and telecommunications technology have resulted in increased interest in compressed video systems which squeeze vast amounts of information into a fraction of its former bandwidth by a codec. The compressed video can be transmitted via the Internet or telephone

Table 11.7: Factors to consider in videoconferencing

Factor	Reasons
Stick to the schedule.	• You may have booked the conference room only for the time scheduled for the meeting and indicated on the agenda. • Other groups may have the conference room booked for the next hour. • If you have hired the conference room, the extra cost involved may put you over budget.
Ensure that the videoconferencing equipment is working properly.	• Arrive at the location early and make certain that there will be no failure with the equipment. • If you are transmitting documents through the computer software, check that the resolution will be adequate for participants in other locations. Being confident with operating the equipment will also mean that you are able to concentrate on the conference.
Position your cameras in advance.	• Preset the cameras/keypad with several views, such as a wide-angle view of all the participants and a zoom-in for the presenters. • Ensure that everyone is visible so that there will be no distractions such as hidden voices and disembodied hands.

network. Although picture and sound quality may be diminished through loss of information, it is a more economical proposition (SBC Pacific Bell 2003).

Desktop systems differ from the room system in that participants use their own individual computer. Each computer has videoconferencing software and a webcam (webcamera). A much cheaper option than the room system, the desktop system uses local area network (LAN) lines or regular telephone lines. The images are generally transmitted over the Web. Many desktop systems have document-sharing software that allows participants at various locations to view and edit the same computer document. The disadvantages are that these systems are not as smooth because of the reduced bandwidth—that is, the amount of information that can be transmitted in an information channel—and they are also inadequate for showing fine detail such as the writing on a whiteboard. DeTienne (2002, p. 78) points out that they can be an attractive alternative because they are a fraction of the cost of the room system and 'are good for geographically dispersed employees in small offices without conference rooms'.

REVIEW QUESTIONS

14 Briefly describe three different seating arrangements suited to a meeting.
15 How does each of these arrangements influence the interaction between the members of a meeting?
16 Which seating arrangement do you prefer in a formal meeting? Give reasons for your answer.

BEHAVIOUR AT MEETINGS

1 Work in groups of four.

    a   Discuss the difference between task and maintenance behaviours in a meeting.

    b   From the list of duties carried out by the chairperson (see pages 320–4), nominate three task behaviours. From the list of duties carried out by the secretary (see pages 326–7), nominate three task behaviours.

    c   Briefly explain the following statement: 'As a task leader and a maintenance leader, the chairperson should have both the technical skills and the human relations skills to be an effective task and maintenance group leader.'

2 In groups of four, role-play a scene at a meeting in which Keith, the chairperson and senior member of staff, removes Ellen from a position in which she controlled the number of staff employed and the payment of part-time staff. Keith does this by announcing in front of all staff, including Ellen, without any prior consultation, that from next Monday Lee will be taking over responsibility for employing and paying staff. Keith looks pompous and defiant, Ellen objects vehemently, Lee looks smug, and others at the meeting visibly stiffen.

    a   Three people play the roles of Ellen, Keith and Lee, while the fourth person watches the disagreement and records the nonverbal behaviour displayed. In this role play, you are not allowed to speak as you express your disagreement—just use nonverbal behaviour.

    b   Then the group of four uses this record of the nonverbal behaviour of Ellen, Keith and Lee to decide, in each case, whether the behaviour was aggressive, assertive or submissive. You might like to repeat the task, giving each person a chance to play each role.

    c   List four different types of nonverbal behaviour that could be displayed by Keith and could lead to communication barriers in this meeting.

    d   What strategies could Keith have employed before and at the meeting to minimise the tensions and communication barriers caused in the meeting?

    e   Identify three nonverbal behaviours that could reduce or even remove the communication barriers between Keith, Ellen and Lee.

3   a   Give some examples of virtual meetings in a business you know.

    b   What were the main reasons for holding a virtual meeting rather than a face-to-face meeting?

    c   What are the advantages and disadvantages of virtual meetings?

4 Assume you have been allocated the role of 'organiser' for your company's next videoconference.

    a   Briefly explain the tasks you will need to complete *before* the conference and *during* the conference.

    b   What are the advantages and disadvantages of videoconferencing?

5   a   How does the availability of videoconferencing affect the traditional roles of chairperson and secretary in formal virtual meetings?

    b   Briefly explain the role undertaken by the facilitator in an informal virtual meeting.

6 Next time you attend a videoconference, use the checklist on the following page to evaluate the effectiveness of the meeting.

SELF-EVALUATE YOUR SKILLS

VIDEOCONFERENCING

Did the videoconference facilities and organisation:	Yes	No	Unsure
allow participants at each of the different locations to have equal access and opportunity to participate?			
enable participants to see each other on the screen clearly?			
enable the television to show a small 'picture in picture' of what was happening in your own location so that you could see how you appeared to the other participants and ensure you avoided moving out of sight of the camera?			
provide participants at each location with a remote control so they could control the camera, picture quality and volume?			
discourage those participants who like to play with the remote, making pointless fine adjustments that are irritating to others?			
allow people to zoom in on the person speaking?			
allow participants at round-table discussions to zoom the camera out so that all participants are on camera at once?			
use voice recognition technology that detects which participant is talking and projects them on to the big screen?			
enable participants to work from formal agendas and take minutes?			
avoid unstructured rambling conversations?			
encourage participants to apply the discipline required by the situation and avoid: – side conversations? – talking over another speaker? – fast movements and heavily patterned clothing?			
provide a forum at which participants were able to come to some form of agreement or decision?			

SUMMARY OF LEARNING OBJECTIVES

 1 ▷ DISTINGUISH BETWEEN FORMAL AND INFORMAL MEETINGS

Formal meetings follow structured proceedings and are usually held in a setting that supports the organisation holding the meeting. Formal face-to-face and virtual meetings have an agenda and meeting papers forwarded to participants within a stipulated time prior to the meeting. Informal meetings are less structured. The leader or organiser is usually determined by the group and the roles are worked out by the participants.

Face-to-face meetings allow people to come together to exchange views, ideas and knowledge. Members use their verbal and nonverbal communication skills to participate, give feedback and make decisions. The chair, secretary and members receive immediate feedback on decisions made and suggestions offered. There is often a sense of belonging to the group.

2 ▷ EXPLAIN THE ROLES OF CHAIRPERSON, SECRETARY AND MEMBER

The chairperson's position is one of authority. The chairperson prepares for the meeting, conducts the meeting, rules on points of order and implements follow-up actions. Many of the duties completed before a meeting are done in consultation with the secretary. The secretary prepares the agenda, organises the documentation for the meeting, accepts the apologies and correspondence, and takes the minutes. Members complete task-related roles such as participating and passing motions and amendments. They also attend to the maintenance-related roles to keep the group together and maintain a feeling of belonging.

3 ▷ DISCUSS TASK ROLES IN A MEETING, AND ANALYSE THE SKILLS THAT SUPPORT MAINTENANCE ROLES

Before the meeting the secretary prepares the agenda, which lets members know where and when the meeting will be held, what business will be covered and when each item will be dealt with. The agenda is distributed at least seven days before the meeting. The secretary prepares the minutes as the official written record of the meeting. They must be confirmed by the members at the next meeting as a true and accurate record.

The executive and members of a meeting use a number of different communication tools. Speaking, listening, negotiation, conflict resolution, and verbal and nonverbal skills are all used in meetings. Maintenance-related roles enable the group to stay together as a group.

4 ▷ OUTLINE THE ADVANTAGES AND DISADVANTAGES OF VIRTUAL MEETINGS

The advent of conference telephone calls, webconferencing and videoconferencing means that it is no longer necessary for groups to meet physically in one location. Travel time and costs are reduced and participants around the globe can communicate with each other.

Virtual meetings can deliver information to a large audience, exchange ideas or allow members to formally work together to an agenda or set of objectives in order to come to some form of agreement or decision. Technological problems can cause barriers to communication. In a formal virtual meeting, task-related roles move the meeting forward. It may be harder for maintenance roles to evolve because of the lack of face-to-face contacts.

5 ▷ IDENTIFY COMMUNICATION BARRIERS IN FACE-TO-FACE AND VIRTUAL MEETINGS

Communication barriers occur as a result of misunderstanding or misinterpretation of the message. Illogical organisation of words or unclear, ambiguous ways of speaking can cause barriers in face-to-face and virtual meetings. Trivial matters on the agenda, lack of interest in the meeting, too many items on the agenda, or a poor attitude to meetings and their objectives can lead to ineffective meeting outcomes. A leader who is unwilling to use his or her legitimate power to implement decisions can lead to dissatisfaction.

6 ▷ EXPLAIN THE IMPACT OF THE VENUE AND SEATING ARRANGEMENTS ON THE DYNAMICS OF A MEETING

Careful consideration should be given to the venue and seating arrangements for meetings. Choose the one that best suits the meeting's purpose. Seating arrangements can facilitate communication, encourage formality (or informality) or emphasise power. Participants in online meetings should be able to see one another clearly on screen. Communication and interaction at meetings are affected by the use of physical space and the surroundings.

KEY TERMS

ACTIVITIES AND QUESTIONS

1   Work in small groups.
    'Meetings are usually thought of as producing ideas, suggestions or recommendations.'
    a   Brainstorm the strategies you could use when chairing a meeting to ensure the meeting achieved these outcomes.
    b   Discuss the main barriers to effective meetings.
    c   Explain how nonverbal communication can impact on the development of maintenance-related roles in a meeting. Give examples.
    d   'There is a strict code in operation at meetings and people ignore it at their peril.' Outline the reasons for having strict codes in operation at meetings.

2   Work in a small group to critically evaluate the following statement:
    Some organisations rotate the position of chairperson. Although not all people perform equally successfully, the advantages outweigh the disadvantages.

3   Compare the Agenda Bell in Figure 11.1 with the agenda shown in Figure 11.2. What are the strengths and weaknesses of each?

4   Briefly explain the following statement:
    The agenda sets the tone and substance for a meeting and helps to eliminate time-consuming and costly digressions.

5   Consider the following statement:
    Meeting policy and procedures that are developed carefully and followed consistently offer the executive and members strategies that enhance the quality and effectiveness of meetings.
        Nominate two strategies a chairperson can use to guide a meeting through the items of business.

6   'As an interactive medium, videoconferencing has considerably more benefits than obtained from using email, telephone and online electronic systems.'

    a   Briefly explain the statement.
    b   When does videoconferencing work well?

7   a   How does the availability of videoconferencing impact on decision making in a global company?
    b   What decision-making technique would you prefer to use in a videoconference? Justify your choice.

8   Assume that the Society of Business Communicators is to hold its annual conference. The title is 'Communication: Not Always Simple'. You are the secretary of the committee planning the conference. In groups of six or seven, plan and conduct a committee meeting following meeting procedures and the agenda. Work through the following tasks:
    a   Prepare a memorandum and draft agenda for the initial planning meeting for the conference, which will be held at the Adelaide Hilton Hotel. Invent the details for the place, time and date of the meeting. Follow the agenda format for the Australian Institute's Christmas Function meeting shown in Figure 11.2. In your agenda, include tasks (b), (c) and (d) below as items of business.
    b   In the meeting, conduct a brainstorming session to create a range of ideas for the sessions to be offered during the conference. Before you brainstorm, clearly define the problem. Use each of the six steps in the brainstorming process. In the last step, you are creating a tentative list of topics for the sessions at the conference. As you brainstorm, keep in mind that conference participants will be from large and small businesses in the private sector, and from large government departments. Many are from public relations departments and all

consider themselves to be communicators within a business or organisational context.

c Also in the meeting, delegate a member to create a checklist that will help the committee check that the proposed venue, the Adelaide Hilton Hotel, meets the committee's requirements for a highly professional venue.

EXPLORING THE WEB

1 View an example of the Standing Orders for General Meetings ASSTA at <www.assta.org>.
   a What is the purpose of the standing orders?
   b How is general business to be conducted?
2 Learn more about meeting protocols through an Internet search of the following strings: 'meeting + constitution', 'meeting + standing orders', 'meeting + formal', 'meeting + chairperson', 'meeting + secretary', 'meeting + agenda'.

3 Visit Internet Conferencing – Advantages at <http://ezinearticles.com/> to find out more about webconferencing.
   a What are the advantages of Internet conferencing?
   b What, in your view, are the disadvantages of webconferencing?
   c What do you think the future will hold for webconferencing and why?

PROJECT WORK

In groups of six or seven, plan and conduct a meeting. The meeting's members are three librarians, two marketing specialists and two small-business managers. The local council has asked the meeting to investigate the feasibility of establishing a new library in the municipality. The purpose of the meeting is to discuss the provision of new library facilities.

a Decide on the procedures to follow in the meeting.
b Nominate or vote one person to the role of chairperson and one person to the role of secretary.
c The secretary and chairperson create the agenda and distribute it to each member of the meeting. The items for *decision* or *action* are the suitability of the proposed building, library opening and closing times, print materials, audiovisual materials and loan periods. The items for *discussion* are photocopy services, research facilities, floor plan, additional services, the availability of public transport, and any other items your group may suggest.

d The chairperson conducts the meeting, following the agenda.
e The secretary takes the minutes.
f Members:
   i   participate in the meeting
   ii   choose one of the items from the agenda and prepare a written proposal or motion to hand to the secretary and a five-minute oral presentation on the motion
   iii vote on each motion
   iv   decide who will take the action.
g The chairperson organises the time and date of the next meeting and closes the meeting.
h After the meeting, use the checklist on page 343 to evaluate the group's competency in planning, conducting and participating in a meeting.

BIBLIOGRAPHY

Association Inc. *Standing Orders for General Meetings ASSTA*, www.assta.org/, viewed 28 November 2007.

Barker, A. 2002. *How to Manage Meetings*, Kogan Page, London.

Barnsley, J. 2003. 'Meeting of minds', *Sydney Morning Herald*, Weekend 7, My Career, 22–23 February, p. 1.

Bienvenue, S. & Timm, P.R. 2002. *Business Communication: Discovering Strategy, Developing Skills*, Prentice Hall, Upper Saddle River, New Jersey.

Blackmore, J. 'Technology: Why use electronic conferencing in distance education?', www.cyg.net, viewed 26 March 2003.

Boddy, D., Boonstra, A. & Kennedy, G. 2002. *Managing Information Systems: An Organisational Perspective*, Pearson Education, England.

Bovée, C.L. & Thill, J.V. 2005. *Business Communication Today*, 8th edn, Pearson Education International, USA.

Cox Business Services. *Webconferencing: Frequently Asked Questions*, www.educause.edu, viewed 27 March 2003.

DeTienne, K.B. 2002. *Guide to Electronic Communication: Using Technology for Effective Business Writing and Speaking*, Pearson Education, New Jersey.

Dewey, J. 1933. *How We Think*, Heath, Boston.

Dollschneider, S. 1997. 'You may be a good communicator, but are you a good facilitator?', *Communications World*, Vol. 14, Issue 3, February, pp. 44–46.

EffectiveMeetings.com. How are unproductive meetings affecting us?, www.effectivemeetings.com, viewed 12 February 2008.

Hemphill, P.D., McCormick, D.W. & Hemphill, R.D. 2001. *Business Communication*, 6th edn, Prentice Hall, Upper Saddle River, New Jersey.

Indiana University. 'Effectively using electronic conferencing', www.indiana.edu, viewed 23 March 2003.

Kostner, J. *Eight Steps to Better Online Meetings*, http://ezinearticles.com, viewed 3 December 2007.

Parker, D. 'Internet conferencing: advantages', http://ezinearticles.com, viewed 3 December 2007.

Parker, G.M. & Hoffman, R. 2006. *Meeting Excellence: 33 Tools to Lead Meetings That Get Results*, Jossey Bass, California.

Parry, H. 1991. *Management Skill Guide: Meetings*, Croner Publications, Surrey, England.

Peacock, T. 'Educating teachers on new frontier', *Weekend Australian*, www.theaustralian.news.com.au, viewed 20 February 2003.

Pease, A. & Pease, B. 2007. *The Definitive Book of Body Language: The Hidden Messages Behind People's Gestures and Expressions*, Bantam, New York.

Putnis, P. & Petelin, R. 1999. *Professional Communication: Principles and Applications*, 2nd edn, Pearson Education, Sydney.

Reid, M. 2001. *Get What You Want from a Meeting*, Crown Content, Melbourne.

Renton, N.E. 2005. *Guide for Meetings and Organisations*, Vol. 2, Guide for Meetings, 8th edn, Law Book Co., Melbourne.

Roebuck, D.B. 2001. *Improving Business Communication Skills*, 3rd edn, Prentice Hall, Upper Saddle River, New Jersey.

Rowan, J.M. 'Seating arrangements should support goal of meeting', www.bizjournals.com, viewed 28 November 2007.

Saunders, A. 2002. 'Meetings: would you miss them?', *Management Today*, October, pp. 54–57.

SBC Pacific Bell. *Videoconferencing for Learning: Introduction, Knowledge Network Explorer*, www.kn.pacbell.com, viewed 26 March 2003.

Scannell, E.E. 1992. 'We've got to stop meeting like this', *Training and Development*, Vol. 46, Issue 1, January, pp. 70–71.

Smart Technologies ULC, 'Effective Meetings', www.effectivemeetings.com/,viewed 28 November 2007.

Tropman, J.E. 1996. *Effective Meetings: Improving Group Decision Making*, 2nd edn, Sage Publications, California.

Wainwright, G.R. 1987. *Meetings and Committee Procedure*, Hodder & Stoughton, UK.

Walker, D.W., Collings, P. & Richards-Smith, A. 'Electronic conferencing', http://simnotes.canberra.edu.au/synch.nsf, viewed 25 March 2003.

Web-Meetings Limited. 'Meetings across the web: introduction', www.web-meetings.ltd.uk, viewed 28 November 2007.

12

Knowledge management and decision making

Photo: Steve Vanh

1 ▷ describe the role of knowledge workers

2 ▷ describe how knowledge management develops people and organisations

3 ▷ describe typical knowledge-management processes and practices

4 ▷ describe the key concepts underpinning knowledge management and the seven levels of knowledge

5 ▷ discuss the role of communities of practice in the valuing and sharing of tacit knowledge

6 ▷ describe four problem-solving and decision-making techniques.

OUTLINE

The role of knowledge workers

Knowledge management

Key knowledge-management concepts

Communities of practice

Decision making and problem solving

VIEWPOINT: KNOWLEDGE MANAGEMENT

'Knowledge management is the process of improving the job performance of knowledge workers by eliminating relevant ignorance and inability as quickly and inexpensively as possible AND providing the proper environment, motivation and role models.

This simple definition encompasses a very broad range of worthy activities, including:

- identifying internal or external best practices and adopting them as standards
- making sure that useful innovations move quickly throughout the organisation
- useful training efforts
- internal communication and journalism
- managing, coaching and mentoring.

Knowledge management is simply management—of people and of processes—in any organisation that is predominantly made up of knowledge workers. Because knowledge resides in people, knowledge management is people management—and must address the hearts as well as the brains of the workforce.'

Excerpt from KM-Experts. *Collaboration + Innovation = Results: Definitions*, http://km-experts.com, viewed 23 April 2008.

Today's global economy is a knowledge economy interconnected through Web-based and digital technologies. Expertise and intellectual property resources are as essential to growth and development as land, natural resources, buildings and equipment. The knowledge economy has changed how people work, how corporations are valued and how people earn an income.

Knowledge—data, information and intelligence that can be used to act—is fast becoming the most important capital, because it drives the ongoing development of the knowledge economies and societies. Current Web-based and digital technologies enable knowledge to be transported anywhere around the globe almost instantaneously and consequently offer enormous opportunities for sharing, archiving and retrieving knowledge. The success of any organisation, society or nation lies in harnessing knowledge. Knowledge is more than information. Drucker (2003, p. 287) argues that 'Knowledge is not impersonal like money. Knowledge does not reside in a book, a database, or a software program; these contain only information. Knowledge is embodied in a person; applied by a person, taught and passed on by a person; used or misused by a person.'

Competitive, progressive organisations apply and manage knowledge to improve business relationships and performance. McGee and Prusak (1993), two early researchers in the knowledge management field, state: 'In an information economy, organisations compete on the basis of their ability to acquire, manipulate, interpret and use information effectively. Organisations that master this information competition will be big winners in the future, while organisations that don't will be quickly overtaken by their rivals.' Successful organisations align their knowledge-management strategies to business objectives and manage knowledge to achieve business goals. They value and apply knowledge to strategic and day-to-day operational activities.

THE ROLE OF KNOWLEDGE WORKERS

Drucker (1959) used the phrase **knowledge worker** to describe a person who works primarily with information, or develops and uses knowledge in the workplace. Knowledge work (Drucker 1973) is a category of work performed by subject-matter specialists in all areas of an organisation. Knowledge work is information-based rather than materials-based and covers the range of tasks performed by individuals within an organisation through to tasks performed across global networks of people. A big-picture approach to knowledge work is shown in the seven-level hierarchy in Table 12.1. The hierarchy provides a useful context for planning, developing and implementing organisation-wide knowledge-management programs and projects.

Knowledge management thrives in knowledge organisations. The culture in a knowledge organisation:

- values knowledge
- encourages knowledge sharing
- applies knowledge to all activities
- empowers people to make decisions relating to work activities
- encourages networks and recognises the efforts of knowledge workers.

Knowledge organisations achieve organisational goals, and improve business relationships and performance, by using systems and processes to generate, transform, manage and transfer knowledge-based products and services.

Knowledge workers create knowledge and have know-how about customer expectations, sales trends, production methods and strategic directions. Their knowledge of factors affecting the business leads to better decision making across the organisation. **Know-how** is intellectual property and confidential information such as designs, drawings, procedures, methods, and the accumulated expert knowledge, skills and experience of staff used by an organisation in its strategic and operational activities. **Intellectual capital** is the human capital held in the minds of individuals: knowledge, competencies and experience; structural capital in the form of information systems, databases and processes; relationship capital in the form of relationships with customers, brands, trademarks and other intellectual property.

Knowledge is data, information and intelligence that can be used to act.

A **knowledge worker** works primarily with information, or develops and uses knowledge in the workplace.

OBJECTIVE 1 ▶
Describe the role of knowledge workers

Know-how is intellectual property and confidential information such as designs, drawings, procedures, methods, and the accumulated expert knowledge, skills and experience of staff used by an organisation in its strategic and operational activities.

Intellectual capital is the collective knowledge (whether or not documented) of the individuals in an organisation or society that can be applied to work to add value.

Table 12.1: A hierarchy of knowledge work	
Level	**Description**
1 *Knowledge work* (Drucker 1973) performed by subject-matter specialists in all areas of an organisation	Includes: • writing • analysing • advising
2 *Knowledge functions* (McGee & Prusak 1993) performed by technical staff, to support knowledge processes and projects	Includes: • capturing • organising • providing access to knowledge
3 *Knowledge processes* (Mumford 1961) performed by professional groups as part of a knowledge-management program	Includes: • preserving • sharing • integrating • reviewing know-how
4 *Knowledge-management programs* (Leonard 1993) performed by in-house knowledge-management professionals or outside consultants	Includes: • linking the generation of knowledge with its use in policies • analysing and reporting program and project outcomes • facilitating organisational learning • adapting existing knowledge to emerging situations in an organisation
5 *Knowledge organisations* (Davenport & Prusak 1998) with a culture and strategies that enable knowledge workers to make things happen	Includes: • viewing knowledge as a key asset • acknowledging that knowledge workers add value • converting knowledge into solutions, innovations, products and services • solving problems and providing knowledge services for others to use
6 *Knowledge services* (Simard et al. 2007) performed by subject-matter specialists, technical staff and knowledge-management professionals	Includes: • using knowledge to create new knowledge • extracting benefits from existing knowledge bases • supporting other organisational services • providing benefits and new services for industry • transferring benefits of new knowledge to society and the community
7 *Social networks* (Tapscott & Williams 2007) developed across communities of practice	Includes: • learning and reflecting on practice collectively • collaborating across and between organisations to co-produce knowledge outputs • leveraging internal organisational capacity with social networks

Tacit and explicit knowledge

Tacit knowledge is the knowledge people carry in their minds and, hence, is difficult to access. **Explicit knowledge** is knowledge that has or can be articulated and stored, and can easily be transferred to others.

Effective communication is the key to the sharing of tacit and explicit knowledge within and between organisations. The work of knowledge workers depends to a large extent on tacit knowledge as well as explicit knowledge.

Tacit knowledge is knowledge that people carry in their minds, and which is thus difficult to access.

Explicit knowledge is knowledge that has been articulated and stored, and can easily be transferred to others.

Tacit knowledge can be difficult to communicate to the rest of an organisation because it is known only by an individual; in many cases, people do not realise they have tacit knowledge that is valuable to others. Tacit knowledge can be embedded in an organisation's culture in the 'know-how' gained through experience. Both types of tacit knowledge (that within an individual and that within an organisation) can be learned through personal experiences, practice, and facilitated activities such as coaching, mentoring and training. Explicit knowledge is easier to communicate because it is articulated in procedures, manuals, and paper-based and electronic documents. Transforming tacit knowledge into explicit knowledge is one of the challenges facing an organisation.

REVIEW QUESTIONS

1. *a*   Define the terms 'knowledge' and 'knowledge worker'.
   b   How would you describe a knowledge-aware organisation?
2. Briefly explain the levels in the hierarchy of knowledge work.
3. *a*   Distinguish tacit and explicit knowledge.
   b   Why is tacit knowledge more valuable than explicit knowledge?

OBJECTIVE 2 ▶
Describe how knowledge management develops people and organisations

KNOWLEDGE MANAGEMENT

Knowledge management is the process through which organisations generate value by gathering, organising and sharing their intellectual and knowledge-based assets. It encompasses the range of practices used by organisations to identify, create, represent and distribute knowledge for reuse, awareness and learning across the organisation. Effective knowledge-management practices supply the right information to the right people at the right time. The creation, management and use of knowledge is an essential part of the decision-making process undertaken by employees at every level in an organisation, including leaders, and managers, supervisors, team leaders, newly appointed and experienced staff.

Knowledge management is the process through which organisations generate value by gathering, organising and sharing their intellectual and knowledge-based assets.

Two factors are critical to the successful implementation of knowledge-management practices across an organisation:

1. *A knowledge-sharing culture.* Effective knowledge-management programs and practices impact on the culture of the organisation and change the behaviour of employees.
2. *Continuous learning and application of knowledge by people.* Effective knowledge management builds stronger relationships among key staff, and between staff and customers and suppliers.

Both factors highlight the importance of communication and human interactions in the knowledge-management process.

Effective knowledge management improves performance and organisational competitiveness.

Knowledge management and its effective deployment improve an organisation's competitiveness. Well-designed knowledge-management practices enable an organisation to:

- apply continuous cost, time and quality improvements
- have a better understanding of the needs and preferences of customers
- develop strong relationships with its suppliers
- retain key employees and their knowledge
- improve its competitive position in the market
- gain a reputation as innovators and thought leaders in their industry.

Knowledge-management strategies go well beyond the need for new tools and processes or formal strategies. Technology and people are central to knowledge management. The tacit and explicit knowledge carried by people is a key component of value in a knowledge-based company. Technology is the means by which information flows globally, nationally and within a company. Communication is the key to information flows.

Organisation culture

Good knowledge-management practices are supported by long-term behaviour that reflects trust among an organisation's employees. A **knowledge champion** is a knowledge leader who actively drives the knowledge agenda and creates commitment and support. Appointment of a knowledge champion shows that top management recognises the importance of knowledge management and actively supports the ongoing creation of personal and corporate knowledge. Good knowledge champions communicate. They listen, choose the appropriate medium, and position the knowledge-management message in the wider context to make it relevant to the organisation and its people. They convey the knowledge-management message thoughtfully, clearly and concisely.

Team spirit and collaboration enhance the turning of personal knowledge into corporate knowledge that can be widely shared and applied throughout an organisation. A relatively stable organisational and cultural environment supports both organisational and personal knowledge-management strategies. The organisation allows individuals to apply knowledge-management practice to themselves, their role in the organisation and their career development.

Knowledge management is about a set of new sources of competitive advantage that enables companies and economies to compete through:

- generating
- gathering
- organising
- sharing
- using, and
- exploiting distinctive sources of know-how.

> A **knowledge champion** is a knowledge leader who actively drives the knowledge agenda and creates commitment and support.

Knowledge-management strategies

A knowledge organisation encourages learning by promoting exchange of information among employees, thus creating a more knowledgeable workforce. The organisation becomes a **learning organisation**, with the capacity to learn, adapt and change continuously in response to its experiences, successes and mistakes.

In a knowledge organisation, leaders and managers must be able to challenge traditional ways of doing things, manage the organisation's knowledge bases, lead people and encourage continuous improvement. They are responsible for the introduction and maintenance of knowledge-management strategies across an organisation. Their roles require them to champion and implement systems and processes to use, share, promote, exploit and celebrate knowledge transfer and learning. Three critical success factors in any knowledge-management program are knowledge leadership, clearly identified business benefits, and communication across the organisation.

Generally, organisations take one of two broad approaches to applying knowledge management:

1. sharing existing knowledge better by making implicit knowledge more explicit and putting in place mechanisms to move the knowledge more rapidly to where it is needed
2. using the innovative processes to create and convert new knowledge and then share the newly created knowledge through facilitation activities, training, mentoring, coaching and other knowledge-sharing processes.

As well as formalising methods for collecting and distributing knowledge, effective knowledge management and leadership involves the design, implementation and review of activities and processes to improve the creation, sharing and application of knowledge within an organisational framework. Effective knowledge management:

- leads to better information and insights
- applies an organisation's internal resources effectively
- improves creativity and productivity within an organisation
- makes for better connections between people.

> ◄ OBJECTIVE 3
> Describe typical knowledge-management processes and practices

> A **learning organisation** has the capacity to learn, adapt and change continuously in response to its experiences, successes and mistakes.

Knowledge-management programs

Organisations establish knowledge-management programs to provide consistency in good practice that leads to better customer experiences and a consequent competitive advantage in the market. The outcomes from an effective knowledge-management program are the ability to:

- access useful and relevant knowledge resources quickly
- manage the proliferation of data and information overload in the complex and changing environment
- facilitate learning about the organisation's existing knowledge base, intellectual capital and know-how
- leverage the expertise of people across the organisation
- use tacit and explicit knowledge to innovate and develop improved products or services
- increase the number of connections between staff to increase the quality of information
- participate in formal and informal networking to increase the flow and quality of information
- collaborate, share and reflect on best practice
- share tacit knowledge held by key individuals with others to prevent loss of know-how as key employees resign or retire.

Knowledge workers require access to efficient and effective information and communication technologies that:

- are people-friendly and easy to access
- have a strong link to business needs
- have processes that integrate with work procedures
- are supported by an internal management information service (MIS) that fixes problems
- enhance reliability and accessibility of service for users.

Effective knowledge-management tools:

- map and communicate tacit and explicit knowledge across the organisation
- develop new knowledge
- address underlying knowledge drivers
- address barriers to creating, sharing and applying knowledge.

Typical characteristics of organisations that implement knowledge-management practices successfully, and those that are unsuccessful, are set out in Table 12.2.

REVIEW QUESTIONS

4 Describe the characteristics of a knowledge-sharing culture.
5 Name two factors critical to the successful implementation of knowledge-management practices across an organisation.
6 How does positive team spirit and collaboration enhance knowledge management?
7 What is the role of managers and leaders in knowledge management?
8 Explain two broad approaches organisations can take to applying knowledge-management principles.

OBJECTIVE **4** ▶
Describe the key concepts underpinning knowledge management and the seven levels of knowledge

KEY KNOWLEDGE-MANAGEMENT CONCEPTS

While information and communication technology has an important role to play in knowledge management, it is not the end in itself. It is simply one of the tools used to exploit the distinctive sources of know-how in each industry and organisation. Effective deployment of the knowledge-

Table 12.2: Implementation of successful and unsuccessful knowledge management

Successful practices	Unsuccessful practices
• Demonstrate good teamwork, often in cross-functional and virtual teams • Have an open culture that supports innovation and learning • Introduce incentives and personal development programs to change behaviour • Interact effectively to build internal and external networks and knowledge • Foster innovation by encouraging the free flow of ideas • Apply effective communication strategies across all levels of the organisation	• Have teams working in isolation, rather than in collaboration with others • View technology alone as the driver of knowledge management • Downsize or outsource without evaluating the impact of the loss of tacit and explicit knowledge • Focus on the 'bottom line' so strongly that interaction and reflection are impossible • Are closed to new ideas and believe the organisation already has all the answers • Forget to communicate the purpose and knowledge-management approach

management tools supports a knowledge-sharing culture and facilitates people as they engage in continuous learning across the levels of knowledge in an organisation.

Levels of knowledge in an organisation

Leaders and managers are expected to champion knowledge management and to lead by example. A knowledge-management program has a better chance of impacting successfully on an organisation's culture when the seven levels of knowledge in the organisation are identified clearly (see Table 12.3). Rather than trying to leverage change across all seven levels, an organisation should choose to apply knowledge-management practices, tools and techniques to two or three levels at a time. By focusing on two or three levels only, successes can be tracked and reported, and new measures developed to address issues and challenges.

Table 12.3: Levels of knowledge in an organisation

Area	Leadership and management role
1 Organisational memory	To draw on lessons from the past or elsewhere in the organisation
2 Knowledge assets	To ensure measurement and management of intellectual capital
3 Knowledge in relationships	To ensure that the organisational and cultural environment enhances collaboration and supports knowledge transfer
4 Knowledge in people	To ensure that processes nurture and harness brainpower and encourage knowledge sharing
5 Knowledge in processes	To support the application of the best know-how to core tasks across the organisation
6 Knowledge in products and services	To encourage smarter solutions customised to the users' needs
7 Customer knowledge	To apply knowledge to provide products and services that meet and exceed customer expectations

Key concepts

Knowledge management is a set of activities with its own tools and techniques. Some of the key strategies and concepts underpinning knowledge-management activities are listed in Table 12.4.

Knowledge-management enablers

The **knowledge-management enablers** in Figure 12.1 (on page 358) are examples of:

- technologies (knowledge bases, intranets and document-management systems) that support knowledge management
- organisational enablers (communities of practice, **after-action reviews** (the systematic extraction of learning from an event or activity), coaching, mentoring, meetings, webconferencing and podcasts) that support people's access to tacit and explicit knowledge.

As other chapters in this book deal with these areas, they are only mentioned here in terms of their capacity to enable the organisation to implement knowledge management effectively (see Chapters 9, 10, 11 and 21).

While enablers support the sharing of knowledge, common obstacles to knowledge management are lack of time and too much focus on detail rather than the big picture. Organisational introversion, based on fear of exposing internal operations to others, can limit innovation and organisational learning. Power plays can prevent the collaboration so necessary to the introduction, implementation and review of knowledge-management practices.

> **Knowledge-management enablers** are the technologies and organisational strategies that support knowledge-management practices.

> **After-action review** is a systematic process used to extract the learning from an event or activity. It addresses the questions: What should have happened? What actually happened? What lessons are there for the future?

REVIEW QUESTIONS

9 Identify the seven levels of knowledge in an organisation.

10 Identify three knowledge-management strategies, and explain their purpose.

11 Define the term 'knowledge-management enablers'.

12 List three common obstacles to knowledge management.

> **OBJECTIVE 5 ▶**
> Discuss the role of communities of practice in the valuing and sharing of tacit knowledge

> A **community of practice** is a group that promotes social learning and builds relationships over an extended period of time.

COMMUNITIES OF PRACTICE

A **community of practice** is a group of people joined by a common theme, interest or affiliation who engage in a process of social learning and collaboration over an extended period to share ideas, find solutions and build innovations. The social structure in a community of practice builds relationships and encourages collective learning. Members engage in discussions and joint activities, help each other, share information and learn from each other.

A community of practice provides a forum in which knowledge is acquired through situated learning in the context of social relationships (Lave & Wenger 1991). It is not so much that learners acquire structures or models to understand the world, but they participate in frameworks that have a social structure. Wenger (1998) states: 'A community of practice defines itself in the doing, as members develop among themselves their own understanding of what their practice is about . . . the boundaries of a community of practice are more flexible than those of an organizational unit. The membership involves whoever participates in and contributes to the practice . . . It is defined by knowledge rather than by task.'

The basic objective of members of a community of practice is to learn and exchange what they know. Communities of practice are:

- associated with knowledge management and learning that focuses on specific knowledge assets

Table 12.4: Key knowledge-management strategies and concepts

Strategy	Purpose
Communicating, encouraging, sharing knowledge	To share knowledge effectively by: • choosing the appropriate medium • expressing thoughts clearly and concisely • positioning the message in its wider context and adapting the message to the receiver's knowledge and needs • being a good listener.
Valuing, collecting and sharing tacit and explicit knowledge to benefit organisational goals	To collaborate and share: • the tacit knowledge carried in people's minds that is often difficult to access • explicit knowledge codified and articulated as information in databases and documents.
Valuing, building on and exploiting organisational and individual know-how	To measure intellectual capital and know-how: • increase tacit and explicit knowledge • develop new and grow existing know-how.
Personal knowledge management (PKM)	To apply knowledge-management practices to: • your career development • your role in the organisation • promote lifelong learning.
Knowledge-sharing mechanisms	To facilitate practices and events that: • encourage greater sharing of knowledge than normally takes place in an organisation • enable collaboration within sections and across the organisation • encourage participation in communities of practice, after and during action reviews, peer reviews • support access to information taxonomies, coaching and mentoring programs.
Social networking analysis (SNA)	To enable companies to: • identify key leaders and knowledge management practitioners • set up mechanisms, such as communities of practice, to enable leaders to pass on their knowledge to colleagues.

• seen as one of the channels through which knowledge flows
• seen as ways of developing social capital—Putnam (2000) defines social capital as 'the collective value of all social networks and the inclinations that arise from these networks to do things for each other'
• seen as forums with four types of pivotal knowledge sharers:
  — central connectors, who are not formal leaders but have the expertise and strong connections within the organisation to link most people in an informal network with one another
  — boundary spanners, who connect one network with another in different parts of the organisation or externally
  — information brokers, who are acknowledged sources of expertise or subject-matter experts

Pivotal knowledge workers are the central connectors, boundary spanners, information brokers and peripheral specialists that interact within a community of practice to share, discuss and reflect on practices in areas of shared interest.

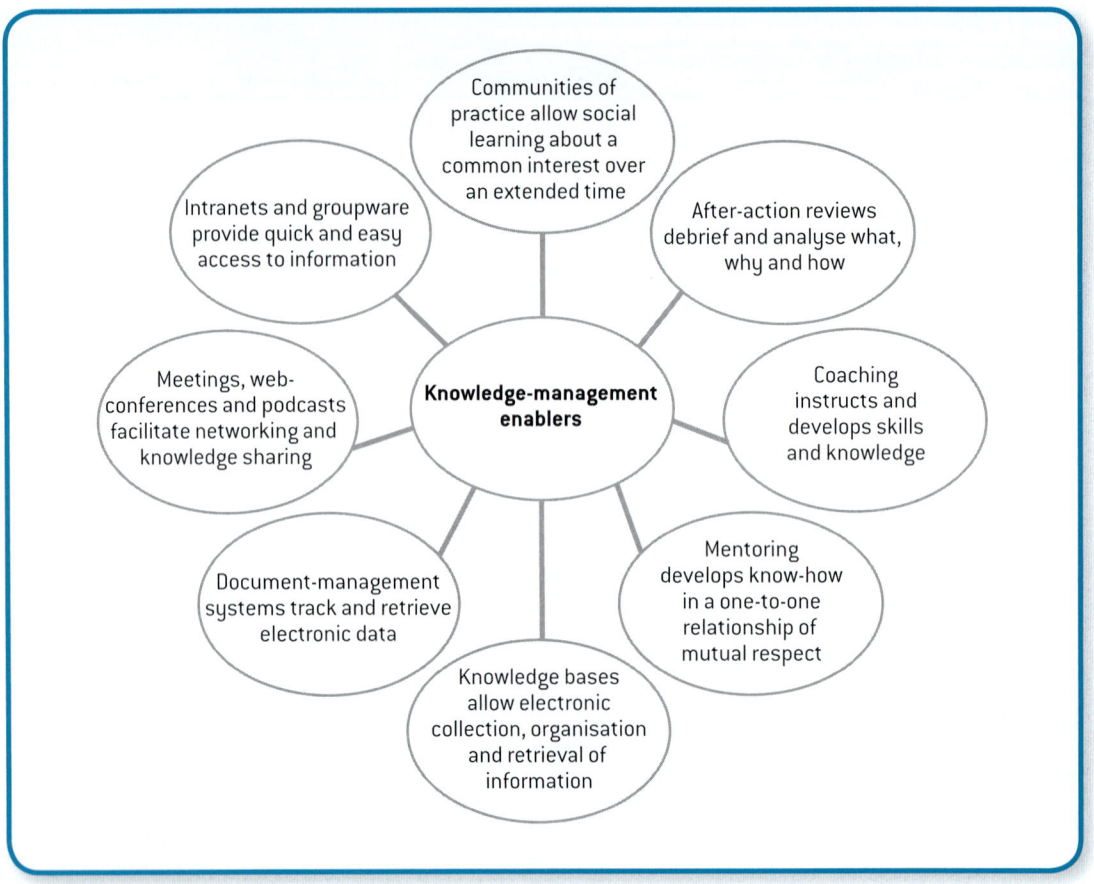

Figure 12.1: Knowledge-management enablers

— peripheral specialists, who provide expertise as required and usually have a high turnover rate (Coakes & Smith, 2007)

- recognised as forums that provide the personal contact and trust needed to nurture new knowledge, stimulate innovation and share existing valuable tacit knowledge
- accepted as an organisational development practice that enables newcomers to access the expertise of experienced and key personnel—a practice that develops the organisation's internal capacity to manage knowledge and improve business relationships and performance.

Smith (2003) suggests: 'For a community of practice to function it needs to generate and appropriate a shared repertoire of ideas, commitments and memories. It also needs to develop various resources such as tools, documents, routines, vocabulary and symbols that in some way carry the accumulated knowledge of the community.' The interaction in a community of practice enables members to discuss new developments in their area of shared interest. They build know-how through sharing experiences, information, strategies and ways of addressing issues. The community of practice provides an opportunity to reflect on practice.

Coakes and Smith (2007) suggest that 'communities of practice are the place where innovation takes place in organisations'. They argue that innovation leaders and opinion leaders are found by analysing the trust-tagged social networks in organisations. 'The trust networks support the development of this capability by building and sustaining the Social Capital necessary for innovation and opinion leaders to develop, flourish, and support their communities.'

Robertson (2004) states: 'One of the key elements of a community of practice is that the group takes on the responsibility for the stewardship of the knowledge within their domain. This often involves the creation of some form of knowledge base, or content repository.' Captured knowledge can be shared across other areas of the organisation that may face the same challenge, or be stored for future use. He suggests a knowledge base may be constructed using these technologies:

- content-management systems
- collaborative environments
- wikis
- specialised community of practice tools.

A corporation may establish a community of practice. An industry or sector may establish a community of practice—for example, a professional association. A community of practice is more than a network of relationships. There is mutual engagement between members of a community of practice as they share, create, organise, and review practices and knowledge. As well as face-to-face communication, technologies such as email, podcasts, electronic conferences and instant messaging support interaction among members of a community of practice.

REVIEW QUESTIONS

13 What is a community of practice?
14 What makes a community of practice different from a network?
15 List the basic objectives of a community of practice.

APPLY YOUR KNOWLEDGE

EFFECTIVE KNOWLEDGE MANAGEMENT

1 DeTienne (2002, p. 4) says: 'The basic goal of knowledge management is to leverage and reuse knowledge resources to achieve a competitive advantage and to improve the bottom line.'

Choose one company you believe is a knowledge organisation and answer the following questions.

  a Identify knowledge you believe is crucial to this organisation's business success.

  b Who is likely to have this knowledge, and how are key personnel able to access the knowledge?

  c Assume you are the knowledge champion. How would you assess how well the organisation develops, manages and exploits new knowledge?

  d In your role as knowledge champion, how would you communicate the knowledge-management program's purpose and intended outcomes across the organisation? Give examples of the type of communication strategies you would use.

2 Compare and contrast two knowledge-management enablers. Describe their purpose and how they facilitate knowledge creation and sharing.

3 Use the checklist on the following page to evaluate the success of an organisation's approach to knowledge management.

KNOWLEDGE MANAGEMENT

Key: VS = Very Successfully, S = Successfully, U = Unsuccessfully

Does the organisation:	VS	S	U
value and apply knowledge?			
encourage knowledge sharing?			
empower people to make decisions?			
encourage teamwork and networking?			
supply knowledge bases, intranets and document-management systems?			
encourage communities of practice?			
offer coaching and mentoring opportunities?			
apply communication strategies across all levels of the organisation?			
provide incentives that support knowledge?			

DECISION MAKING AND PROBLEM SOLVING

> **OBJECTIVE 6** ▶
> Describe four problem-solving and decision-making techniques

People working at every level in the knowledge hierarchy solve problems and make decisions. An organisation that values knowledge provides knowledge workers with opportunities to engage in problem solving and decision making. First, people are encouraged to engage in critical thinking and questioning in order to analyse, evaluate and create new ideas from the facts and existing knowledge bases. Second, support is provided to implement the decisions taken and the procedures or plans of action developed in the thinking process. Case-based reasoning, the nominal group technique, brainstorming and Dewey's reflective thinking process are four useful decision-making and problem-solving techniques.

Case-based reasoning

Case-based reasoning is the process of solving new problems based on the solutions to similar past problems.

Our general knowledge about situations is recorded as internal scripts that allow us to set up expectations and make inferences (Schank & Abelson 1977). Previous scripts are the basis of **case-based reasoning**, which is the process of solving new problems based on the solutions to similar past problems. Schank and Abelson (1995) argue that the knowledge people use is encoded in language and stories and that knowledge is utilised as 'people answer questions, people make plans and inform others of them, people comprehend what others are saying, people inform other people of events that have taken place, people give advice to other people'.

Harrison (1997) states: 'In case-based reasoning (CBR) systems expertise is embodied in a library of past cases, rather than being encoded in classical rules. Each case typically contains a description of the problem, plus a solution and/or the outcome. The knowledge and reasoning process used by an expert to solve the problem is not recorded, but is implicit in the solution.' In case-based reasoning, past experiences are used to solve a current problem. The process to follow is:

1. Match the problem against similar cases.
2. Apply critical thinking and questioning to similar cases (what, why and how), suggest a solution, and use and test it for success.
3. Review and improve the solution (if necessary).
4. Retain the current case and its final solution as a new case.

Knowledge gained from past cases is transferred to the current situation. Case-based reasoning is a useful process to apply when decisions must be made about a complex problem. People often seek solutions in analogous problems. Knowledge organisations realise that remembering and learning from previous experiences is useful. Records of previously solved problems are kept for future reference and knowledge acquisition. Case-based reasoning applies in business, legal, medical and other professions because it allows for incremental development of the case base. Past experience is adapted to new situations.

Nominal group technique

The **nominal group technique** enables the members of a group to work as individuals and to think about and present new ideas. 'Nominal' means a group in name only. The main advantage offered by this technique is the opportunity to think independently of others. A disadvantage in the nominal group technique is that members may feel their spontaneity is inhibited and that the situation is too controlled. Once the thinking process and presentation of ideas is finished, members work together again as a group to consider and evaluate the ideas. Table 12.5 outlines the steps of the nominal group technique.

The **nominal group technique** enables the members of a group to work as individuals and to think about and present new ideas.

Brainstorming

When people in a group need to generate new ideas to reach a decision or to solve a problem, brainstorming can quickly and effectively involve all members in the decision. **Brainstorming** is a process suited to stimulating innovative ideas and creative solutions. Table 12.6 explains the process of brainstorming. In the brainstorming process, each person contributes to the problem solving and feels part of the process that leads to the result. Brainstorming is a quick and easy method to use with groups. It leads to new ideas and includes everyone.

Brainstorming is a group process for generating ideas and creative solutions.

Table 12.5: The nominal group technique	
Step	**Process**
1 Discuss and clarify the situation	As a group, members listen, ask questions about the problem, and clarify the issue and the way in which the nominal group process will work.
2 Work as individuals	Group members think quietly about the issue or problem; they write down all their ideas and possible solutions individually, without discussing them. Time: 15–20 minutes.
3 Present and record the ideas	A 'round robin' contribution of ideas takes place. The leader records a contribution from each person until all the ideas are listed on a flip chart or board. No evaluation or discussion occurs at this time. Members may suggest further ideas to add to those listed.
4 Clarify and evaluate	Once all the ideas are recorded, the group discusses, analyses and evaluates them.
5 Rank the ideas	Each member of the group independently assigns a rank to the ideas. (If 20 ideas are presented, each person considers each idea and then gives the best one a score of 20, the next best 19 and so on until the least-favoured idea receives a score of one.)
6 Choose the most preferred option	Each person's ranking for each idea is recorded on the flip chart next to the idea. (If there are eight people in the group, each idea will have eight scores.) If members prefer to maintain anonymity, the ideas can be voted on by ranking them on cards. The leader collects the voting cards and records the votes. The scores are then totalled and divided by eight to give the average score. The idea with the highest average score is the preferred option.

Table 12.6: The brainstorming process

Step	Process
1 Define the problem or issue to be considered	Clarify for all members the issue to be considered—e.g. a financial group may want to decide on ways to improve its superannuation services. The facilitator states the problem: to 'identify ways to improve superannuation services' and briefs the group on the brainstorming process.
2 Brief the meeting	Tell everyone that for two minutes the group is to suggest ways in which the defined problem can be tackled. As the list is created, no one is to interrupt, comment on or evaluate another person's contribution. It is important that no one speaks except to add new ideas to the list.
3 Encourage all members to participate	Urge everyone to participate and feel part of the group. As ideas are offered, they are written on a large sheet of paper or board that everyone can see. Simply throw ideas forward for two minutes. A timekeeper calls time at the end of two minutes.
4 Evaluate the ideas	All members of the group evaluate the list to determine which ideas are a possibility and which to discard.
5 Choose the action	The possible ideas are considered further until a decision is made on which to implement. At this point the brainstorming exercise is complete.

Sutton and Hargadon (1996, pp. 685–718) conducted experimental research that indicated 'People in face-to-face brainstorming meetings are less efficient at generating ideas than when working alone . . . when brainstorming sessions are viewed in an organisational context and the "effectiveness at what" and "effectiveness for whom" questions are asked, efficiency at idea generation may deserve no special status as an effectiveness outcome' (1996, p. 685). They point out that, in general, 'effectiveness and performance are not objective truths that exist independently of the people who monitor, measure and report the outcomes' (1996, p. 716). Thus the labels may reflect more about the monitors than the measurements. The effectiveness of brainstorming as a tool to create new ideas for products and business systems should be considered in context. Factors in the context, such as organisation culture, cohesiveness, harmony or disharmony, affect the willingness of members to engage in brainstorming.

Once ideas are created, through either the nominal group technique or brainstorming, the group must decide on a course of action that will ensure the ideas are acted upon. A plan of action is needed.

Reflective thinking process

Dewey's reflective thinking process offers an agenda for problem solving.

A useful method to use in problem solving is Dewey's reflective thinking process. The process has five stages and is a creative problem-solving method. Participants understand the reasons for the decision and are willing to discuss the results with others. Problem solving is a useful way of creating new ideas on an issue that concerns everyone. Table 12.7 outlines the process.

FACILITATING EFFECTIVE PROBLEM SOLVING

A function of task forces, committees, networks, communities of practice and other groups is to share knowledge, solve problems and make decisions. The group is established so that experiences and ideas can be shared, rather than using the ideas of only one person. These guidelines may be helpful in the problem-solving process. State the problem in terms of the situation in order to avoid threatening behaviour towards group members and making them defensive. Ask for help in solving a mutual

Table 12.7: Dewey's reflective thinking process

Stage	Process
1 Define the problem	Define and clarify the group's understanding of the problem or issue to be addressed. Encourage each person to contribute ideas and opinions.
2 List all the possible alternatives	Brainstorming is a relatively easy technique for listing all the alternatives to solve the problem. Follow the brainstorming steps in Table 12.6.
3 Discuss and analyse the possible solutions	Work through the list with everyone until it is narrowed down to a few possible alternatives. This process of group participation draws everyone into the decision making and brings a commitment to the decision reached.
4 Choose a solution	Limits need to be set, and acceptable and unacceptable results identified. There is no point agreeing to a solution that is unacceptable or impossible to implement. This simply wastes time. (You would not use problem solving on an issue that requires only a quick decision.)
5 Plan the course of action	Ask group members for ideas so that people participate. Planning is directed at the task of implementing the action decided by the group. As planning takes place, some members may ask to be involved in implementing the plan. If this arises from interest, these volunteers will probably be willing to follow through until the task is finished.

problem. For example, 'How can we increase productivity in our section?' State the problem in a way that encourages discussion of a variety of causes and possible solutions. State only one objective. Having two objectives can become confusing and cause uncertainty about the priority.

Be aware of common mistakes that can occur in diagnosing and analysing a problem:

- confusing facts with opinions or assumptions
- confusing symptoms with causes
- looking for someone to blame
- evaluating solutions immediately rather than waiting until all solutions have been offered
- proposing solutions before the problem is clearly understood
- defining the problem in a way that implies there is only one solution, or that a choice must be made between two solutions
- focusing on the past instead of what can be done in the present
- discussing solutions outside the control of the group.

Avoiding these problems calls for clear thinking and an alertness to what is happening in the problem-solving process. The supporting facts and the logic behind the ideas should be explained.

REVIEW QUESTIONS

16 Briefly explain the process of case-based reasoning.

17 How does the nominal group technique allow members to think independently?

18 Identify the steps in Dewey's reflective thinking process.

KNOWLEDGE MANAGEMENT AND DECISION MAKING

1 a What does effective knowledge management do?

b What are the likely outcomes from effective knowledge-management programs?

c Describe the characteristics of effective knowledge-management tools.

d Describe the features common to organisations that implement their knowledge-management programs and practices ineffectively.

2 Which of the four ways to solve problems and make decisions in a group do you prefer to use? Why?

3 a List five mistakes that may occur when a group diagnoses or analyses a problem.

b How can these problems be overcome?

4 How does case-based reasoning transfer past knowledge to the current situation?

SUMMARY OF LEARNING OBJECTIVES

 1 ▷ **DESCRIBE THE ROLE OF KNOWLEDGE WORKERS**

Knowledge work is information-based, rather than materials-based. A hierarchy of knowledge work crosses seven levels. These are knowledge work, knowledge functions, knowledge processes, knowledge-management programs, knowledge organisations, knowledge services and social networks. The role of knowledge workers is to work primarily with information, or to develop and use knowledge in the workplace.

 2 ▷ **DESCRIBE HOW KNOWLEDGE MANAGEMENT DEVELOPS PEOPLE AND ORGANISATIONS**

Effective knowledge management develops a knowledge-sharing culture that allows people to learn and change behaviour. Continuous learning and application of knowledge builds stronger relationships between people and between the organisation and its staff, customers, suppliers and public.

 3 ▷ **DESCRIBE TYPICAL KNOWLEDGE-MANAGEMENT PROCESSES AND PRACTICES**

Communication is the key to effective knowledge-management practices and programs. Sharing existing knowledge and using innovative practices creates new knowledge. The result is greater insight, better knowledge and stronger connections between people. While information technology has an important role to play in knowledge management, it is not the end in itself. It is simply one of the tools used to exploit the distinctive sources of know-how in each industry and organisation.

 4 ▷ **DESCRIBE THE KEY CONCEPTS UNDERPINNING KNOWLEDGE MANAGEMENT AND THE SEVEN LEVELS OF KNOWLEDGE**

The seven levels of knowledge are organisational memory, knowledge assets, knowledge in relationships, knowledge in people, knowledge in processes, knowledge in products and services, and customer knowledge. Communication encourages knowledge sharing, and valuing and building know-how at both the personal and organisational levels. Knowledge-sharing tools enable collaboration and participation across an organisation. Another key concept is communicating the knowledge and having it flow through an organisation. Innovation, improvements and growth are based on knowledge management. People with knowledge-management skills are able to adapt to the impacts of rapid change.

 5 ▷ **DISCUSS THE ROLE OF COMMUNITIES OF PRACTICE IN THE VALUING AND SHARING OF TACIT KNOWLEDGE**

'Community of practice' refers to the process of social learning in a social structure that builds relationships over an extended period of time. The community generates a shared repertoire of ideas, commitments and memories. It must also develop various tools, documents, routines and vocabulary to carry the accumulated knowledge of the community. The social interaction and structure supports the sharing and transfer of tacit knowledge as well as explicit knowledge. Members engage in discussions and joint activities, help each other, share information and learn from each other. The community of practice provides a forum in which tacit knowledge is acquired through situated learning in the context of social relationships.

6 ▷ **DESCRIBE FOUR PROBLEM-SOLVING AND DECISION-MAKING TECHNIQUES**

Case-based reasoning, the nominal group technique, brainstorming and Dewey's reflective thinking process are used to think critically about issues and problems. These techniques enable a group to think creatively and share ideas and knowledge. Action plans are a useful way of detailing the activities that will put the decisions into practice. Common errors in analysing a problem can be identified and avoided.

KEY TERMS

after-action review	356	know-how	350	knowledge worker	350
brainstorming	361	knowledge	350	learning organisation	353
case-based reasoning	360	knowledge champion	353	nominal group technique	361
community of practice	356	knowledge management	352	tacit knowledge	351
explicit knowledge	351	knowledge-management			
intellectual capital	350	enablers	356		

ACTIVITIES AND QUESTIONS

1 Work in small groups to identify typical knowledge-management processes. Many large business organisations are making tangible efforts to improve their knowledge-management practices using the processes shown in Table 12.8, column 1.
   a In column 2, suggest the type(s) of context appropriate to each process.
   b In column 3, give specific examples of knowledge-management practices appropriate to each process in column 1.

2 Your manager has asked you to prepare your professional development plan for the next five years. Design a professional development plan that identifies:
   a your personal knowledge-management goals
   b the activities you will undertake to achieve the goals
   c the timelines for implementation and completion.

3 a What does this statement (DeTienne 2002) mean? 'Managers are now responsible for making knowledge productive, not for producing products.'
   b List two strategies a manager can use to encourage team members to use knowledge effectively?

c Should the knowledge champion be the Chief Executive Officer? Justify your answer.

4 Coakes and Smith (2007) say, 'Social networks are frequently used in organisations to analyse the relationships among employees in search of knowledge. They identify where knowledge flows to and from and show who asks questions and who they ask for the answers. Analysing these social networks identifies the people within a network and asks questions about their relationships with others within the network. Thus it can find the pivotal knowledge sharers.'
   a Identify and explain the role of four types of pivotal knowledge sharers.
   b How can an organisation develop and support its pivotal knowledge sharers to interact and share their repertoire of ideas, commitments and memories with a community of practice?
   c 'Organisations should do everything they can to encourage knowledge workers to share experiences in communities of practice.' Do you agree or disagree with this statement? Support your position.

Table 12.8: Typical knowledge-management processes

Process	Appropriate context	Appropriate knowledge-management practices
Traditional knowledge-sharing devices		
Current, innovative knowledge-sharing devices		
Sharing knowledge and working collaboratively on projects with external organisations		

EXPLORING THE WEB

1 Review these chapter-related websites to learn more about knowledge sharing.

   a Visit *Intranets and knowledge sharing* by Robertson (2004), <www.steptwo.com.au>, for a discussion of knowledge sharing in communities of practice and intranets, staff directories and expertise finders, and collaborative environments.

   b Visit the Knowledge Sharing World Bank Institute site at <http://go.worldbank.org> to view knowledge-sharing initiatives.

   c Visit <www-ksl.stanford.edu> to browse a comprehensive range of papers on knowledge sharing.

   d Visit 'I Heard it Through the Grapevine', <www.hymncds.com/>, to gather ideas about making knowledge management work by learning to share knowledge, skills and experience.

   e Visit @brint.com, *The Biztech Network*, <www.brint.com/>, and follow the link to 'Knowledge management' to access a number of articles related to knowledge management.

2 Learn more about communities of practice by reading Wenger (1998), 'Communities of practice learning as a social system,' <www.co-i-l.com/>.

   a What makes a community of practice different from a community of interest?

   b Describe the five stages of development in a community of practice.

   c List and describe five types of interaction between a community of practice and the organisation as a whole.

   d Why should leaders nurture and support communities of practice?

PROJECT WORK

Work in small groups.

1   The phenomenon of the knowledge economy has created new winners and losers in the global marketplace. Knowledge champions need to plan and implement effective knowledge-management and decision-making strategies for their organisations to thrive.

   a   Assume the role of a knowledge champion for your own workplace or a workplace of your choice.

   b   Design an action plan to manage knowledge and make decisions in each of the seven strategic areas identified in Table 12.9, 'Strategies for organisational development'. The ability to *act*

on knowledge will often determine success, so focus on actions to develop personal knowledge management.

   c   Identify knowledge-sharing mechanisms and tools for each strategic area.

   d   Use Table 12.9 to brainstorm appropriate actions. You may use the suggested goals or customise your own.

2   Prepare a group oral business presentation that demonstrates how personal and organisational knowledge management develops people and organisations.

3   Deliver the presentation.

Table 12.9: Strategies for organisational development

Strategic area	Suggested goal	Actions/tools required
Customer knowledge	Understand what the customer wants	
Knowledge in processes	Have performance know-how	
Knowledge in products (and services)	Customise competitive, smarter solutions to meet users' needs	
Knowledge in people	Nurture and harness brainpower	
Organisational memory	Draw on lessons from the past or elsewhere in the organisation	
Knowledge in relationships	Use deep personal knowledge to underpin successful collaboration	
Knowledge assets	Measure and manage intellectual capital and know-how	

BIBLIOGRAPHY

@brint.com. *The Biztech Network*, www.brint.com/, viewed 26 November 2007.

Choo, C.W. & Bontis, N. 2002. *The Strategic Management of Intellectual Capital and Organizational Knowledge*, Oxford University Press, New York.

Coakes, E. & Smith, P.A.C. 2007. 'Supporting innovation: communities of practice and change', *Journal of Management Practice*, Vol. 8, Special Issue 1, May, www.tlainc.com/articlsi3.htm.

Cook, P. *I Heard it Through the Grapevine: Making Knowledge Management Work by Learning to Share Knowledge, Skills and Experience*, www.hymncds.com/creative/grapevine.htm, last updated 1 April 2005.

Davenport, T.H. & Prusak, L. 1998. *Working Knowledge*, Harvard Business School Press, Boston.

DeTienne, K.B. 2002. *Guide to Electronic Communication: Using Technology for Effective Business Writing and Speaking*, Pearson Education, New Jersey.

Dewey, J. 1933. *How We Think: A Restatement of the Relation of Reflective Thinking to the Educative Process*, Heath, Boston.

Drucker, P.F. 1959. *Landmarks of Tomorrow*, Harper, New York.

Drucker, P.F. 1973. *Management: Tasks, Responsibilities, Practices*, Harper & Row, New York.

Drucker, P.F. 2003. *The Essential Drucker*, HarperBusiness, New York.

Edvinsson, L. & Malone, M.S. 1997. *Intellectual Capital: Establish Your Company's True Value by Finding its Hidden Brainpower*, HarperCollins Publishers, New York.

Gruber, T. (compiled directory of) *Knowledge Sharing Papers*, www-ksl.stanford.edu/, viewed 22 November 2007.

Haag, S., Cummings, M., McCubbrey, D., Pinsonneault, A. & Donovan, R. 2006. *Management Information Systems for the Information Age*, 3rd edn, McGraw-Hill, Canada.

Harrison, I. *Case Based Reasoning*, www.aiai.ed.ac.uk/links/cbr.html, last updated 30 May 1997, viewed 21 November 2007.

Heller, F., Pusic, E., Strauss, G. & Wilpert, B. 1998. *Organisational Participation: Myth and Reality*, Oxford University Press.

Lave, J. & Wenger, E. 1991. *Situated Learning: Legitimate Peripheral Participation*, Cambridge University Press.

Leake, D. (ed.) 1996. *Case-Based Reasoning: Experiences, Lessons, and Future Directions*, AAAI Press/MIT Press, USA.

Leonard, D. 1993. *Wellsprings of Knowledge*, Harvard Business School Press, Boston.

McGee, J. & Prusak, L. 1993. *Managing Information Strategically: Increase Your Company's Competitiveness and Efficiency by Using Information as a Strategic Tool*, John Wiley & Sons, New York.

Mumford, L. 1961. *The City in History: Its Origins, Its Transformations, and Its Prospects*, Harcourt, Brace and World, USA.

Nickols, F. 2000. '*What Is*' *in the World of Work and Working: Some Implications of the Shift to Knowledge Work*, http://home.att.net/~nickols/shifts.htm, last updated 12 September 2004.

Putnam, R. 2000. *Bowling Alone: The Collapse and Revival of American Community*. Simon & Schuster, New York.

Robertson, J. *Intranets and Knowledge Sharing* (see 'Exploring the Web'), last updated 5 May 2004, viewed 22 November 2007.

Schank, R.C. & Abelson, R.P. 1997. *Scripts, Plans, Goals, and Understanding: An Inquiry into Human Knowledge Structures*. Lawrence Erlbaum, Hillsdale, NJ.

Schank, R.C. & Abelson, R.P. 1995. 'Knowledge and memory: the real story', in R.S. Wyer (ed.), *Knowledge and Memory: The Real Story*, Lawrence Erlbaum Associates, USA.

Simard, A., Broome, J. Drury, M. Haddon, R. O'Neil, R. and Pasho, D. 2007. *Understanding Knowledge Services*, Natural Resources, Canada.

Smith, M.K. 2003. 'Communities of practice', *The Encyclopedia of Informal Education*, www.infed.org/. Last updated 23 October 2007.

Story, M. 2008. 'Storming knowledge', *Management Today*, March.

Sutton, R.I. & Hargadon, A. 1996. 'Brainstorming groups in context: effectiveness in a product design firm', *Administrative Science Quarterly*, Vol. 41, Issue 4, December, pp. 685–718.

Tapscott, D. and Williams, A.D. 2007. *Wikinomics*. Penguin Group, New York.

Wenger, E. 1998. 'Communities of practice: learning as a social system', published in *The Systems Thinker*, June, www.co-i-l.com, viewed 20 November 2007.

World Bank Institute. *Knowledge Sharing*, http://go.worldbank.org/8U1SZCCEE0, viewed 22 November 2007.

World Internet Property Organisation. *Encouraging Creativity and Innovation*, www.wipo.int/, viewed 20 November 2007.

Part 4

Finding and Communicating Information

13 Researching and processing information

Photo: Günay Mutl

LEARNING OBJECTIVES

After studying this chapter you should be able to:

1 ▷ describe an effective process for conducting research

2 ▷ discuss academic honesty and describe how to maintain ethics and etiquette in your research

3 ▷ distinguish primary, secondary and tertiary sources of information

4 ▷ discuss how to use search engines, web directories and databases effectively

5 ▷ discuss different approaches to notations, citations and referencing

6 ▷ prepare a bibliography and list of references.

VIEWPOINT: BOOLEAN SEARCH

'Most search engines allow you to utilise one of the more effective advanced search techniques, using so-called "Boolean Operators" to refine your search. These Operators are the discriminators AND, OR and NOT and the proximity locators NEAR and FOLLOWED BY. Using these Operators allows you to refine your search much more effectively than just using keywords.

AND means that all the terms you input must appear in any document.

OR means that at least one of the terms you use must be included in any document retrieved.

NOT means that at least one of the terms you have entered must not appear in any document. Some search engines simply use the symbols + and − instead of the Boolean operators to include and exclude search terms.

NEAR means that the terms you have entered must be within a certain number of words to each other. FOLLOWED BY means that the first term must directly be followed by the next.'

Extract from 'How to use search engines', *Sensei.com.au WEB GUIDE*, www.sensei.com.au/, viewed 19 February 2008. © Telstra Corporation (ABN 33051 775 556) 2008. ™ Telstra Corporation.

Before writers can prepare effective essays, reports, papers, theses and dissertations they must research well, organise relevant information, identify the document's purpose and present it in a way that suits the context. In the university context, writers must research from credible sources and use the format, writing and citation styles recommended by their faculty.

Sound research enhances the power of an argument, its conclusions and recommendations. Begin an effective research process by identifying and describing the issue, writing the thesis or purpose statement clearly, limiting the scope and determining the sources of information.

THE RESEARCH PROCESS

OBJECTIVE **1** ▶
Describe an effective process for conducting research

Primary research is research undertaken for the first time. Secondary research already exists in paper and online media. Tertiary research contains information from a variety of secondary sources. Each of the three sources provides information and evidence. Experienced researchers evaluate the objectivity and credibility of their information sources by asking questions and using critical thinking skills (see Chapter 14).

Research skills

The skills used to produce a solidly researched business or academic document are set out in Table 13.1. Throughout your academic and business careers you may be required to gather and research information about government regulations, the environmental impact of a new development, financial trends and many other areas of interest.

Research tools include indexes and abstracts, periodicals and serials, general and specialised directories, general reference documents (including government publications) and online search engines, web directories and online databases. Public and university libraries have professional reference librarians who can assist students to use these tools, and to locate resources and access online information. Most have trained searchers who can assist with accessing current online information and a large range of databases in subject areas not provided through the library's online information system.

Planning the document

Effective planning involves having clear ideas about selected topics and intended audiences.

Effective planning is the key to good writing. Cantor (1993, p. 17) states: 'Successful writers will undoubtedly agree that their most fruitful efforts began with clear ideas about their selected topics and intended audiences.' He suggests asking the following questions:

- What expertise do I have to share?
- With whom do I wish to share it (the audience)?
- What is the best medium through which to do so (journal, book, conference paper)?

Writers should stay abreast of the current state of literature in the area in which they are working, particularly as 'referee panels usually insist on comprehensive reviews of the literature, thus ensuring that the new material is discussed, described, analysed, composed, or contrasted within an existing body of knowledge' (1993, p. 17). Cantor suggests that, as well as reading current journals in their field, writers should attend conferences, serve as referees or editors of journals and newsletters, get on to a computer bulletin board and share ideas with others.

Thesis statement

Gibaldi (1995, p. 30) defines a thesis statement as 'a single sentence that formulates both your topic and your point of view'; writing this statement will assist you to see where you are heading and keep you on a productive path. Anderson and Poole (1994, p. 22) define a thesis as 'an idea or theory that is expressed as a statement, a contention for which evidence is gathered and discussed logically'; they say that '[s]ince a thesis is a sustained argument, often detailed and quite complex, considerable

Table 13.1: Research skills

Skill	Purpose
Choose a manageable topic	• To focus your search
Find relevant sources	• To become familiar with the subject
Evaluate the sources by reading and thinking critically	• To evaluate the objectivity, accuracy and currency of sources • To avoid fallacious argument and reasoning • To verify inferences are not overgeneralised • To identify any information gaps
Process the sources consulted	• To comprehend and analyse numerical and statistical data • To analyse and judge the quality of arguments presented • To form an argument around the thesis statement
File the information (paper-based and electronic)	• To be able to retrieve the information easily • To be able to access and refer to the sources in the future
Develop a thesis, premise or position statement	• To identify the premise or position to be developed • To test the premise's validity • To focus the research around the thesis, premise or position statement
Take detailed notes and prepare an outline	• To gather material that addresses the thesis • To create a framework for the document • To organise the material into an outline that addresses the thesis
Write and revise the first draft	• To structure content into introduction, body or findings, conclusions and recommendations (if any) • To draw valid conclusions based on sound research • To make realistic, achievable recommendations that provide solutions • To add any visual material to strengthen the argument (trend lines, photographs, tables, other) • To check spelling and grammar
Document the sources of information in the notes and bibliography	• To attribute quotes, paraphrasing or summaries of other people's work accurately • To enable others to access the sources and authorities
Type the final draft and proofread	• To format and improve the document's readability • To submit a professional-looking document

preparation and planning are necessary before the initial research can begin' (1994, p. 19). As the selection of a topic is often the most difficult task, they suggest the following criteria:

- Does the topic really interest you?
- Can the topic be completed in the required time?
- Is the necessary equipment available?
- Are subjects available?
- Are travel funds available to locate data sources?
- Are library facilities sufficient?
- Is the study achievable?
- Is the problem a significant one?

The Writing Tutorial Services of Indiana University (2004) believe that people 'look early in an essay for a one- or two-sentence condensation of the argument or analysis that is to follow'. They contend that the essay should contain a thesis statement, for the following reasons:

- to test the ideas by distilling them into a sentence or two
- to better organise and develop the argument
- to provide the reader with a 'guide' to the argument.

A good thesis statement, they say, will usually include the following four attributes:

- takes on a subject about which reasonable people would hold different opinions
- deals with a subject that can be adequately treated given the nature of the assignment
- expresses one main idea
- asserts the writer's conclusions about a subject.

Designing the study

Anderson and Poole (1994, p. 24) state: 'Choosing a design for a study essentially involves selecting the most appropriate methods or techniques to solve the particular problem under investigation. It is a crucial step in a thesis, because, if a wrong decision is made, the whole study may be criticised on the grounds of inappropriate design or, even worse, as being unscientific or illogical.' Researchers should identify the key and emerging issues in their field of study and evaluate the adequacy of existing research studies in their area of interest. By identifying the principal issues, they are able to determine the significance of their proposed thesis statement. The ability to write a thesis statement and to conduct a literature review are two of the skills required of an effective researcher.

Levine (2007) lists the following steps in the 'thinking about it stage' of thesis writing:

1. Be inclusive with your thinking—don't try to eliminate ideas too quickly.
2. Write down your ideas—this will allow you to revisit them later and perhaps modify or change them.
3. Try not to be overly influenced at this time by what you feel others expect from you—for example, your colleagues, your profession or your academic department.
4. Don't begin your thinking by assuming that your research will draw international attention to you—be realistic in setting your goal.
5. Be realistic about the time that you are willing to commit to your research project.
6. Try a small preliminary study to clarify your research.

Cantor (1993, p. 19) says: 'Once the writing topic is formulated and a publishing medium is identified, a literature search can begin.' Gibaldi warns that '[n]ot all sources are equally reliable or of equal quality'. The writer should check that the material is not 'based on incorrect or outdated information, on poor logic, or on narrow opinions held by the author' (1995, p. 24). Gibaldi also warns against plagiarism, which he defines as using 'another person's idea or expressions in your writing without acknowledging the source' (p. 26).

Conducting a literature review

A *literature review* is an extensive search of the information available on a topic, resulting in a list of references to books, periodicals and other materials on the topic. Notations and citations credit the work to the original source. In a literature review, you research secondary and tertiary sources of information. An effective review of the literature enables you to:

- test the appropriateness of your thesis, purpose statement or proposition
- evaluate your approach, structure and framework
- provide background information and become familiar with the subject or topic
- locate and demonstrate your familiarity with significant and up-to-date research
- develop valid arguments supported by up-to-date and credible sources of information.

A visual representation (called a Mind Map®) of the tasks completed in a literature review is shown in Figure 13.1. The tasks are identified in the key concepts or words—descriptors, sources, titles

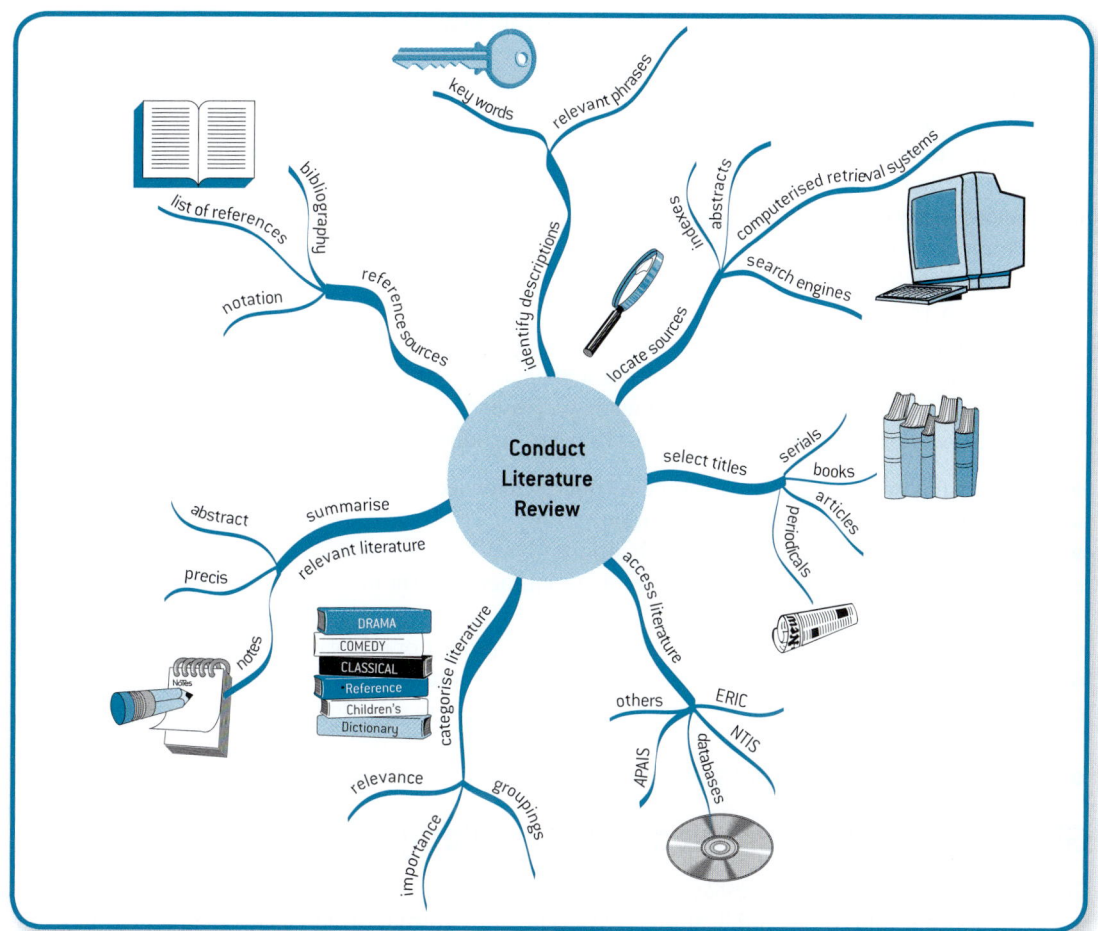

Figure 13.1: A Mind Map® of tasks completed in a literature review

Source: Created using mind mapping principles identifed by T. Buzan, *Make the Most of Your mind*, Pan Books, London, 1988.

and literature—linked to one another around the central image. Other concepts flow from each of these concepts. The Mind Map® orders and sorts the information. From this map an essay could be written on the topic, 'Outline the Main Tasks Completed in a Literature Review'.

REVIEW QUESTIONS

1 Briefly explain the steps in the research process.
2 How can writers stay abreast of the current state of literature in the area in which they are working?
3 What does the thesis or purpose statement do?

ETHICS AND ETIQUETTE

◄ OBJECTIVE 2
Discuss academic honesty and describe how to maintain ethics and etiquette in your research

Why is research ethics and etiquette important? By working in accordance with ethical principles as you research information in your studies and business career you build a reputation as someone to know and respect in your field of work. In your university studies, academic honesty is essential. Refer to your *Student Handbook* for acceptable standards of conduct and the conduct your university views as unacceptable. Academic honesty is ethical behaviour in all academic work, including acknowledging all sources correctly, presenting your own work, gathering objective and reliable data, and working in accordance with the university's guidelines.

The purpose of scholarship and academic discourse is to develop knowledge by making discoveries and adding to them through further investigation, correction, modification or expansion. The academic process of attributing and citing sources as academics and other researchers analyse, evaluate, agree, disagree or modify existing knowledge has built a cooperative international research community. The cooperation is based on acknowledgment of who discovered, interpreted or created the original and emerging knowledge.

Attention to academic honesty improves not only your writing but also your reputation and credibility. Citations and referencing show the extent of your research and your capacity to present ideas, paraphrase, develop an argument, and evaluate and balance viewpoints. They also show the reliability of the sources you use, particularly important when you research from the Internet which allows anyone to publish ideas without evaluation from editors or peers. Academically honest behaviour avoids:

Ethical research documents sources, gives appropriate credit, and respects the intellectual property and digital rights of others.

- plagiarising by copying from a source without acknowledgment
- making errors in paraphrasing or citation
- contriving data in survey and research reports
- using the same paper for two different assignments without permission from the tutors or lecturers
- buying, selling or borrowing someone else's essay, project or other work
- obstructing or interfering with another person's work intentionally
- cheating by submitting other people's work as your own in examinations, group projects or work placement
- breaching copyright for print and electronic materials.

Giving appropriate credit and acknowledgment

Research for a university paper, essay or thesis sources the ideas of experts and authorities published in books, journals and other publications. The source of information must be documented to avoid plagiarism. The word 'plagiarism' is derived from the Latin *plagiarus* (kidnapper). Writers should avoid **plagiarism**—that is, presenting the ideas and expressions of others gathered in research as their own.

Plagiarism is the presentation of ideas and expressions of others as one's own.

A verbatim quote is taken directly from an author's work. Putnis and Petelin (1999, p. 349) comment: '[T]he advantage of the verbatim (direct) quote is that you use the author's exact words.' They recommend using a direct quote when 'it illustrates a point more compellingly and authoritatively than you can through a summary or paraphrase; and you want to share it with the reader before analysing or critiquing it'.

Intellectual property is the property of your mind or intellect.

Plagiarism and breach of intellectual property and digital rights are two major illegitimate uses of the ideas of others. Intellectual Property Australia's (2008) definition is: '**Intellectual property** represents the property of your mind or intellect. It can be an invention, trade mark, original design or the practical application of a good idea.' Respect the intellectual property and digital rights of others. Their rights are protected by law. Appropriate credit and acknowledgment should be given for all authors in a co-authored work. Acknowledgment should also be given for the contribution of good ideas, helping with word processing, research or any other useful contribution.

Digital rights are the rights of copyright holders of digital works, devices or documents intended to prevent unauthorised duplication of their work to ensure 'fair play' from continued revenue streams.

Maintaining credibility

It was suggested earlier that you focus your research around the thesis, premise or position statement. When doing this, avoid skewing the research to force the specific outcome, thesis or position statement. Rather than simply setting out to prove or disprove your thesis, your aim is to clarify and test the thesis. Avoid referring only to information that supports your view and overlooking contradictory information.

If you gather information from primary sources, respect the privacy of the individuals, businesses or organisations you observe or interview. Avoid giving misleading information about the purpose and intent of your research. Don't observe or record observations without consent from the people you will be observing.

Overgeneralising, using fallacious arguments and presenting misleading information will damage your credibility. Check your visuals and graphics to ensure they present the information accurately and show both advantages and disadvantages. Any insights, conclusions and recommendations should not stretch the truth. There is no point in preparing and presenting a business plan and financial projections that far exceed the organisation's current resource capability. Acceptance of the plan will only lead to failure to meet the projections and the consequent loss of your credibility.

REVIEW QUESTIONS

4 *a*   Define the term 'academic honesty'.
    b   What advantages do you gain by paying attention to academic honesty?
5 *a*   What is intellectual property? Give an example.
    b   What are digital rights? Give an example.
6   What do you need to do to build your credibility as a researcher and writer?

FINDING INFORMATION

◄ OBJECTIVE 3
Distinguish primary, secondary and tertiary sources of information

The handling of information is a large part of the research process. Successful researchers are able to collect, store and retrieve information from primary, secondary and tertiary sources. **Primary sources of information** are the people or organisations that take the action or cause the events that become part of society's store of information. Those who review and write about the direct action taken by the primary sources of information prepare the secondary sources of information. *Secondary sources of information* are published and stored after the event has taken place. *Tertiary sources of information* are compiled from secondary sources. Anderson and Poole (1994, p. 23) state that 'in surveying a field initially, it is useful to work from the general to the specific, or from tertiary and secondary sources to primary sources'.

Primary sources of information

There are many ways of obtaining primary sources of information. Some of these are summarised in Table 13.2.

Secondary and tertiary sources of information

Libraries collect and store information on many areas of interest. Their special expertise in collecting and storing information in a form that can be easily found makes them an invaluable source of secondary information. Each library has an online information system that provides access to its networked information resources and services. University libraries have online catalogues, bibliographic citations and indexing databases to thousands of periodicals, full-text journals and information services across a variety of academic disciplines. University libraries also provide access to information on the Internet from their campuses, through the university's network and remotely through computers connected to the Internet.

Secondary sources are summaries of information gathered from primary sources. They include handbooks, dictionaries, encyclopaedias, translations, reviews of research, abstracts, books and other publications. Some of the many sources of secondary information are presented in Table 13.3. Table 13.4 lists specific examples of secondary sources of information.

Primary sources of information are the people or organisations that take the action or cause the events that become part of society's store of information.

Primary sources of information are generally unpublished information gathered first hand.

It is essential to put citations into your first draft, rather than trying to remember where to put them when you are writing the second and third drafts.

Secondary sources are summaries of information gathered from primary sources.

Table 13.2: Methods of gathering primary information

Source	Strategy	Purpose
Observation	• Observe the event a number of times. • Check that the observation is of a typical event rather than an atypical or unusual event. • Interpret the observations objectively. • Set up the observation in such a way that background, particular work experience or attitude to others cannot cause the evaluation to be subjective.	Collect information and make an objective evaluation of the data.
Experiment	• Try a number of alternatives; e.g. a researcher has ideas that may lead to a better environment for staff, such as screens between desks in an open-plan office. • A careful researcher will try out each idea and measure the results; e.g. experts such as Occupational Health and Safety Officers could be called in to measure the results. • Offer evidence on the basis of the results of the experiments.	Provide more reliable and accurate information than observation.
Interviews	• Prepare the questions and their order of presentation before the interview. • Conduct the interview by asking questions and recording the answers. • Compile the results after the interview.	Gather facts and opinions that can be analysed and evaluated.
Questionnaires and surveys	• Plan the questions. • Focus on the issue and your purpose. • Administer the survey and collect the information. • Extract and compile the information. • Analyse and interpret the information.	Gather valid facts and information from within small groups, larger organisations or the community at large.
Human resources	• Interview and/or administer surveys or questionnaires with primary sources such as Adult Community Education, Working Women's Centre or Workers' Health Centre. • Design the questions. • Conduct the interview or administer the survey or questionnaire. • Analyse the information and draw conclusions.	Gather information through direct contact with the source of information.
Files and records	• Focus on a particular company. • Use office files and records to gather current information. • Search background information. • Follow up any expertise on the organisation that is relevant to your information needs.	Collect information on a particular industry or company.
Professional associations	• Contact professional associations, their support services, trade associations or trade unions. • Interview your own business and professional contacts.	Gather professional information relevant to the purpose and information needs.

Tertiary sources of information are compiled from secondary sources.

Tertiary sources, such as textbooks, contain information from a variety of secondary sources. As libraries collect and store information on many different areas of interest in a form that can be easily found, they are an invaluable source of tertiary information.

New members of a library should ask for a complete library tour or join a conducted group tour to help them become familiar with the different sections of the library and the whereabouts of the various indexes. You can also ask for an interlibrary loan if a book you need is not in the library.

Table 13.3: Secondary sources of information

Type	Examples
Library catalogues are databases that list information found through the reference services of a library	• Reference books, periodicals, journals, newspapers and audiovisual material, fiction and non-fiction books. • Libraries hold their subject, author and title indexes in online computer information systems and on microfiche. • Libraries can access the catalogues of other institutions.
Online computer information systems held in libraries	• A full list of titles available online can be found in the title and subject lists of databases such as the Clann Database. • The entire Clann Database is updated quarterly. • The Clann Database can be searched by title, author, author/title, subject or keyword.
Compact disc read-only memory (CD-ROM) uses a variety of information-handling software	• CD-ROM is used to find the library's catalogue disc, the *Grolier's Encyclopaedia* disc and the *McGraw-Hill Encyclopaedia of Science and Technology*. • CD-ROM also supplies abstract-only services such as the Educational Resources Information Centre (ERIC). A two-to-three paragraph summary of each publication is supplied as an abstract. It makes it possible to decide if the material is relevant to your purpose. • Library staff also use online searching services to find Australian and international electronic databases, such as Aussinet, an Australian database.
Periodicals and journals relevant to a particular topic can be found using the periodicals index in the library	• The Australian Public Affairs Information Service (APAIS), created by the National Library of Australia in Canberra, is a subject index to current literature in the humanities and social sciences. Search key words in the index to find current literature for your purpose.
Audiovisual and other services	• Libraries provide audiovisual facilities to view videos and films or listen to tapes. • A photocopier is provided at a price per copy as a service to members and borrowers. • Information can also be gathered from teletext and videotext.
Archives store historic and public information	• The Commonwealth and each state government has non-current records or documents relating to their activities. • Many large corporations, such as national and global banks, have their old records and documents filed away. • It is possible, although time-consuming, to find information stored in organisations and government departments.
Mass media	• The media produce information in newspapers, magazines, television, radio and film. Information presented in this way is up to date. • Approach the media critically to separate and identify facts from opinions.

Advantages and disadvantages of print and electronic media

Print media include books, journals, reference books, newspapers and other paper-based documents. They are tangible, portable and a permanent record. The quality of published print media is high because of the editorial and publishing processes applied to published documents. However, there are at least three disadvantages. The first is that print media have to be held in a physical space such as a library that can only be accessed during opening hours. Second, paper-based sources of information take up a lot more space than electronic sources. Third, conducting large-scale searches and cross-referencing is time consuming.

Table 13.4: Specific examples of secondary sources of information

CD-ROM	Handbooks or guides	Dictionaries and encyclopaedias
• EBSCO General Science • Computer Select • Engineering and Applied Science • Film Index International • Humanities Index • Heritage and Environment Index • Austrom • Australian Business Index • Business Periodicals Index • Australian Encyclopaedia • Acel Occupational Health and Safety Index • Computer Law Services • Austlii • Social Sciences Index	• Australian Business Handbook • Business Who's Who in Australia • Commonwealth and State Year Books • Australian Parliamentary Handbook • Telephone Directories • Australian Postal Commission Postal Guide • Universal Business Directory (UBD) • Style Manual for Authors, Editors and Printers	• The Science Dictionary in Basic English • Concise Oxford Dictionary • Macquarie Dictionary • Webster's Geographical Dictionary • Australian Commercial Dictionary • Black's Medical Dictionary • A Dictionary of Acronyms and Abbreviations

Electronic media include the Internet, online databases and CD-ROMs. These are accessible from any location and at any time. It is easy to conduct a large-scale electronic search and to cross-reference through hyperlinks. However, there are disadvantages. First, the material is intangible and not permanent unless printed out. Second, computer technology must be available to access the information and the technology can fail. Third, the quality of the information is not always credible because of the ease and almost instantaneous uploading of new information. The quality imposed by effective editing and publishing services is often missing.

Evaluating sources

Evaluate the information gathered in research to sort the good from the bad. Bovée and Thill (2004, pp. 306–7) identify nine criteria for evaluating the credibility of source information: honesty and reliability, lack of bias, purpose of the material, credibility of the author, where did the source get its information, can the material be independently verified, is the material current, is the material complete and do the source's claims stand up to scrutiny. Critical evaluation of the source material ensures you are able to use the material with confidence.

There are legal and ethical constraints to be taken into account when using material from the Internet. Lehman and Dufrene (2002, p. 335) warn researchers to be cautious in using information found on the Internet, for the following reasons:

● Internet resources are not always accurate. Some are reliable and credible, and some are not.
● Certain uses of Internet sources may be illegal. Some material is copyright protected and cannot be incorporated into documents that have commercial use unless permission is granted by the copyright holder (and perhaps a fee paid).
● Internet resources are not always complete. Selections of articles and documents may be available, but the full text may be obtainable only in published form.
● Electronic periodicals are not always subjected to a rigorous review process. Most traditional magazine or journal articles are reviewed by either an editorial board or peer reviewers, but this is not necessarily the case for articles available on the Internet.

REVIEW QUESTIONS

7 *a* Why should you critically evaluate your source material?

b Identify five criteria you can use to evaluate the credibility of source information.

8 Briefly discuss the legal and ethical constraints to be taken into account when using the Internet as a source of information.

9 Journal articles are credible sources of information. Identify two reasons for this credibility.

10 What are the advantages and disadvantages of print and electronic media?

APPLY YOUR KNOWLEDGE

RESEARCH SKILLS

Work in small groups.

1 a Briefly describe the difference between primary, secondary and tertiary sources of information.

b Give an example of each and describe their purpose.

2 Assume that the local council has commissioned your consultancy firm to compile a report titled, 'Beach Front Amenities and Developments: Council's Responsibilities'. The finished report is to be presented to local resident action groups.

a Name three organisations that could provide information in the initial research stage. Are these primary, secondary or tertiary sources of information?

b List three words that could be used in a library search for secondary sources of information.

3 a Compile a list of four search terms.

b Use the library's catalogues to find a book, an article in a journal, and a relevant magazine or newspaper article.

c Prepare an email to other students explaining how to maintain ethics and etiquette in the research process.

4 Lehman and Dufrene (2002) warn researchers to be 'cautious in using information found on the Internet'. Outline the reasons for carefully evaluating sources of information found on the Internet.

SEARCH ENGINES, WEB DIRECTORIES AND DATABASES

◄ OBJECTIVE **4**
Discuss how to use search engines, web directories and databases effectively

Search engines, web directories and databases provide online access to secondary source material. A **search engine** is a computer program that searches the collection of pages on the Web. Search engines identify individual web pages by specific key word. The creator of a web page and site should inform the search engines of its existence and use key words in the titles on the web pages to make it easier for researchers to find sites of interest. The search engine receives a request from a researcher, looks for the key words, compares that request with the index created by the 'robot' or 'web crawler', and returns the results of the search to the researcher.

A **search engine** is a computer program that searches the collection of pages on the Web.

The role of search engines

Search engines usually provide more responses than directories. Bovée and Thill (2004, pp. 310–11) point out that 'search engines don't actually search the web when you submit a query; doing so would be painfully slow. Instead, they search through an index of pages that the search engine updates periodically.' The best way to conduct a search is to try several search engines because different parameters, or ways of finding the information, exist on different search engines. A simple search can be conducted by entering words or a phrase and pressing 'enter'. Some engines will require you to enclose the phrase in quotation marks or to identify the 'exact phrase' from a menu. Ryrie (2001, p. 49) adds: 'More complex search syntax can usually be found on a search engine in the section called "Advanced" which is nearly always next to the search window.'

Meta Crawler is a search facility that searches search engines. Meta Crawler accesses many search engines such as Google, Yahoo! Search, MSN Search, Ask Jeeves, About, MIVA, LookSmart and more at the same time. The search results come from a combined pool of search engines.

Unless the specific URL is known, there is no way to find the information other than to search the World Wide Web. One of the disadvantages of web searching is that it tends to return too many responses. Web searching is simple and fast, but it returns a great number of results. The process becomes more effective if you can narrow the search terms.

Web directories and online databases

A team of editors prepare web directories. Researchers use web directories for specific searches.

- Yahoo! <www.yahoo.com> is a useful directory for mainstream information or requests and has good business links.
- About <www.about.com> is a good general directory with featured articles, videos and other useful information.
- Galaxy <www.galaxy.com> has broad coverage over many topics with excellent links in the business section.
- InfoSeek <www.go.com> is geared towards commercial users and has a large commercial database and a quick response time.
- Highbeam <www.highbeam.com> is an online database of newspapers and magazines geared towards individual, student and small business users.

Bookmarking

A **bookmark** (or favourite) is a saved link to a web page.

Once researchers find their areas of interest, the practice is to bookmark the site through a web browser (e.g. Netscape browser). The **bookmark** is a saved link to the URL visited. Later, it is easy to go back to the bookmark menu and click on the URL to go directly to the site. The bookmark file can be ordered into a hierarchy of folders of your own choice within areas of interest. A folder labelled 'Corporations', for example, would contain every bookmarked site about corporations. This folder could be subdivided into 'Retail Corporations', 'Legal Corporations', 'Mining Corporations', and each of these subdirectories would contain the sites of interest in that category. Microsoft Explorer refers to 'bookmarking' and 'favourites'. Favourites are organised into a hierarchical order of choice.

Boolean logic customises a research request.

Searching online can yield thousands of results. By using Boolean logic, the research request can be customised with the operators AND, OR and NOT. For example, a search for studies on the relationship between 'empathy' and 'self-disclosure' could use the words 'empathy' alone and 'self-disclosure' alone. The search would give a list of all works on each word. A Boolean search using 'empathy and self-disclosure' excludes works that are not about both. A Boolean search is a useful tool to use when searching online sources of information.

REVIEW QUESTIONS

11. Distinguish between search engines and web directories. Provide two examples of each.
12. What is bookmarking?
13. What does an online database do? Give two examples.

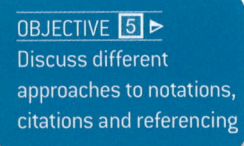
OBJECTIVE 5 ▶
Discuss different approaches to notations, citations and referencing

NOTATIONS

Writers of academic documents, reports, assignments and workplace documents must acknowledge their sources (primary, secondary and tertiary) by using **notations**. Notations can be inserted in one of three places in the document:

① as citations within the text
② as footnotes at the bottom of the page
③ as endnotes placed at the end of the document and before the list of references or bibliography.

Notations acknowledge the sources of information.

Lehman and Dufrene (2002, p. 343) state: 'A crucial part of honest research writing is documenting or referencing sources fairly and accurately. Although time consuming and tedious, meticulous attention to documentation marks you as a respected, highly professional researcher.' They list (pp. 343–4) the following reasons for documentation:

- Citations give credit where it is due—to the one who created the material.
- They protect writers against accusations of plagiarism.
- They support your statements.
- They aid future researchers pursuing similar material.

Gibaldi (1995, p. 4) says: 'While you must fully document the facts and opinions you draw from your research, the documentation should only support your statements and provide concise information about the sources cited; it should not overshadow your own ideas or distract from them.'

Citations in the text

Any factual statement substantiated by the findings of another author's work, or a quotation from another author's work, must be acknowledged (cited), as shown in the examples in Figure 13.2. The **citation** must appear in two places. The first is as a shortened in-text reference in the report, assignment or essay. The second is a full reference in the reference list or bibliography at the end of your report, assignment or essay.

Citations acknowledge the work of others.

When citing an interview, so that your source can be verified or additional information obtained, Bienvenu and Timm (2002, p. 311) recommend providing the following information:

- whether the information was conducted face-to-face or on the telephone
- name of the person interviewed (and their position, if applicable)
- location of the interview
- date of the interview.

Examples:

- Personal interview with Dr John Marlborough, Chief Executive Officer, Pseudo Company, Melbourne, 17 January 2008.
- Telephone interview with Professor Jennifer Adamson, Dean of Studies, Somewhere University, NSW, 20 March 2008.

The author-date (or Harvard) system is widely accepted because it is easy to use and economical in terms of time and space. In this system, someone else's work is identified instantly by giving, in brackets, the author's name and year of publication. An example of a shortened in-text reference is (Browne & Keeley 2007). Sometimes it is useful to give the page or volume numbers as well: for example (Browne & Keeley 2007, pp. 56–57).

In the list of references or bibliography at the end of the document, give full publication details of the works cited: author's surname and initials or given name, year of publication, title, publisher and place of publication. For example, the full reference is Browne, M.N. & Keeley, S.M. 2007. *Asking the Right Questions: A Guide to Critical Thinking*, 8th edn, Pearson Prentice Hall, New Jersey.

Note: The ampersand character (&) is used instead of the word 'and' in the Harvard Method.

Figure 13.2: Example of the author-date (Harvard) system of referencing

If you are citing material obtained from class or lectures, Bienvenu and Timm recommend the following format:

- circumstances
- name of source
- name of course (if appropriate)
- location
- date.

Examples:

- Guest lecture, Professor Carol Merriman, Somewhere University, 3 May 2008.
- Class lecture, Dr Patrick Burns, Business Communication 101, Somewhere University, Rural Campus, 15 April 2008.

For unpublished documents (Bienvenu & Timm, p. 312) the citation should include:

- name of document's writer
- title (if available)
- an indication that it is 'unpublished'
- organisation name (if relevant and available)
- a date (if available).

Example:

- Manning, Serge, 'Population Movements to Urban Areas, 1950–2010', unpublished thesis, 10 November 2012.

Putnis and Petelin (1999, p. 347) make the comment: 'The fact that a book or article has been published is no guarantee that it is of high quality.' They recommend that you become familiar with the respected scholars in your particular field.

FOOTNOTES

A **footnote** is a comment at the foot of the page giving extra information about a point in the text.

Superscripts are used to number **footnotes**, which are comments at the foot of the page giving extra information about a point in the text. Superscripts are small numbers placed in the main body of the text slightly above the line at the end of the sentence—for example, 'The results of the meeting were unavailable.[1]' Footnote 1 would give the details of the source of this statement or supply further information about the meeting.

The traditional place for a footnote is at the bottom of the page. However, unless you are using a word processing program with a facility for footnotes, it is easier to place the reference at the end of the document rather than trying to insert footnotes correctly at the bottom of each page.

ENDNOTES

Endnotes comprise supplementary material placed at the end of a chapter or article.

Superscripts are also used to number **endnotes**, which are supplementary material placed at the end of a chapter or article. Word processing packages have this capability. Number the superscripts in sequence throughout a document and list the notations in numerical order at the end of the document before the list of references, as in the examples in Figure 13.3.

Check the method of notation and documentation preferred by the lecturer/instructor or organisation. If no one method is preferred, writers may use their own judgment and decide how to document and place the references. Consistency is important.

REVIEW QUESTIONS

14. What is 'notation'?
15. a Explain the difference between a footnote, a citation and an endnote.
    b What information is required in an endnote?
16. Differentiate between the note (or traditional) style of referencing and the author–date (or Harvard) style.

The information required for the first reference to a work in a footnote or endnote is the same as that required for the author–date system list of references, but it is presented in a slightly different order: author's initials or given name and surname, title, publisher, place of publication, year of publication and page number(s). For example:

1 M. Neil Browne and Stuart M. Keeley, *Asking the Right Questions: A Guide to Critical Thinking*, 8th edn, Pearson Prentice Hall, New Jersey, 2007, pp. 56–57.
2 Kathryn Bartol, Margaret Tein, Graham Matthews and Bishnu Sharma, *Management: A Pacific Rim Focus*, 5th edn, McGraw-Hill, Sydney, 2008, p. 186.

Second and subsequent references to a source in a footnote or endnote do not have to be as detailed as the first reference. The simplest way is to abbreviate the first reference; for example:

3 Browne et al. (1997), p. 102.

Figure 13.3: Examples of the note (or traditional) system of referencing—footnote or endnote

BIBLIOGRAPHY AND LIST OF REFERENCES

In academic writing, it is standard practice to reference or cite the sources of information. By referencing well, you not only show your ability to acknowledge the work of others; it also allows you to show the range of ideas and approaches to the topic that you have found, analysed and evaluated. The three main rules of referencing are given here. Apply them consistently.

1 Include a reference every time someone else's ideas or information are used or referred to.
2 Include a reference when:
  - someone's ideas are expressed in your own words—*paraphrased*
  - someone else's ideas are expressed in your own words in a reduced from—*summarised*
  - someone else's idea is copied in their exact words—*quoted*
  - someone else's graphic (diagram, table, chart) is reproduced—*copied*.
3 Reference in at least two places—a shortened in-text reference and a reference with full details in the list of references or bibliography at the end of the essay or assignment.

Referencing systems

A list of references gives details only of those works cited in an assignment, report or essay. A **bibliography** gives details of works cited in the text, as well as other relevant material you read when writing the report or further recommended reading. These works may include primary sources, such as interviews or responses to surveys, and secondary and tertiary sources, such as books, journals, newspapers and government publications.

A list of references or bibliography is arranged in alphabetical order by authors' surnames. There are two main methods of presenting a list of references or a bibliography: the author–date (Harvard) system, and the note (or traditional) system. The main difference between the two systems is the order of information. The **author–date (or Harvard) system of referencing** involves acknowledging work written by someone else by identifying it in the following order: the author's surname and initials or given name, year of publication, title, publisher and place of publication. The **note (or traditional) system of referencing** identifies work written by someone else in the following order: author's given name or initials, author's surname, title, publisher, place of publication and year of publication. For each of the two methods, the same presentation is used for both a bibliography and a list of references. Examples of both are given in Figures 13.2, 13.3 and 13.4.

◄ OBJECTIVE 6
Prepare a bibliography and list of references

A **bibliography** is a list of all the sources of information used in a report, as well as further recommended reading.

The **author–date (or Harvard) system of referencing** involves acknowledging work written by someone else by identifying it in the following order: the author's surname and initials or given name, year of publication, title, publisher and place of publication.

The **note (or traditional) system of referencing** identifies work written by someone else in the following order: author's given name or initials, author's surname, title, publisher, place of publication and year of publication.

A. THE AUTHOR–DATE (OR HARVARD) METHOD

Information is presented in the following order:

Books: Print media

1. Author's surname and initials or first name
2. Year of publication
3. Title of book in italics or underlined
4. Name of publisher
5. Place of publication

Bartol, K., Tein, M., Matthews, G. & Sharma, B. 2008. *Management: A Pacific Rim Focus,* 5th edn, McGraw-Hill, Sydney.

Browne, M.N. & Keeley, S.M. 2007. *Asking the Right Questions: A Guide to Critical Thinking*, 8th edn, Pearson Prentice Hall, Upper Saddle River, New Jersey.

Journal articles: Print and online media

1. Author's surname followed by initials or first name
2. Year of publication
3. Title of article in single quotation marks
4. Title of journal in italics or underlined
5. Volume number and issue number, if applicable
6. Page numbers

Madlock, P.E. 2008. 'The link between leadership style, communicator competence and employee satisfaction', *Journal of Business Communication*, Vol. 45, Issue 1, pp. 61–78.

World Wide Web page: Online media

1. Author of webpage
2. Last update or copyright date
3. Title of web page
4. Available: URL
5. Access date

The Internet Public Library. 25 February 2008. *About the Internet Public Library*, www.ipl.org/div/about/, viewed 5 April 2008.

B. THE NOTE (OR TRADITIONAL) METHOD

Information is presented in the following order.

Books: Print media

1. Author's initials or first name followed by surname
2. Title of book in italics or underlined
3. Name of publisher
4. Place of publication
5. Year of publication

K. Bartol, M. Tein, G. Matthews and B. Sharma. *Management: A Pacific Rim Focus*, 5th edn, McGraw-Hill, Sydney, 2008.

M.N. Browne and S.M. Keeley, *Asking the Right Questions: A Guide to Critical Thinking*, 8th edn, Pearson Prentice Hall, Upper Saddle River, New Jersey, 2007.

Figure 13.4: Example of a list of references or bibliography

Articles: Print media

1 Author's initials or first name followed by surname
2 Title of article in single quotation marks
3 Title of journal in italics or underlined
4 Volume number and issue number, if applicable
5 Date of publication
6 Page numbers

L. Crisp, 'Time to go', *Financial Review Boss*, Vol. 9, January 2008, pp. 52–55.

Journal article: Online media

1 Author's initials or first name followed by surname
2 Title of article in single quotation marks
3 Title of journal in italics or underlined
4 Volume number and issue number, if applicable
5 Page numbers, if applicable
6 Available on URL—i.e. protocol/site/path/file
7 Access date

J.L. Bower. 'Solve the succession crisis by growing inside-outside leaders', *Harvard Business Review*, November 2007, www.hbr.org, viewed 1 December 2007.

World Wide Web page: Online media

1 Author/editor's initials or first name followed by surname (if known)
2 Title of page
3 Revision or copyright date (if available)
4 Page publisher (if known)
5 Available on URL—i.e. protocol/site/path/file
6 Access date

Australian Broadcasting Commission. *ABC Online*, 2008, www.abc.net.au, viewed 6 April 2008.

Note that, in both methods, references are listed in alphabetical order. Careful documentation assists the reader and adds to the writer's credibility.

About.com (2007) defines electronic publishing as 'the process of creating and disseminating information via electronic means including email and via the Web'. Any non-print-based material that can be electronically delivered, sorted and manipulated by the user is classed as electronic publishing. Referencing of online documents needs to happen with as much care and attention to detail as the referencing of paper-based documents. Standards have been established and continue to evolve in response to the needs of the creators of online information, writers and those who use the information.

Wright (1998, p. 1) comments that an electronic document may not have an equivalent in paper form, or another form, and that it is necessary for writers 'to create references to these electronic resources in order to document their research'. She cites the draft standard for bibliographic references to electronic documents ISO 690 Part 2, *Information and documentation—Bibliographic references—electronic documents or parts thereof*, ISO/FDIS 690-2, published by the International Standards Organisation. Wright also recommends printing and filing the reference so that you can later produce it as evidence of authenticity, particularly in view of the changes that can occur to online documents and even web addresses after you have accessed them.

The formats and examples given here offer models for online references that are included in the bibliography of a business writer's research paper, assignment or report.

For print material downloaded from the Internet and online sources, Australian students are likely to follow the traditional (note) method or the Harvard (author–date) system of referencing and add the URL details. For United States and Canadian students, the *Modern Language Association Style Guide* is widely used for referencing professional and university papers. It is best to check with the lecturer for the preferred style within any particular faculty.

REVIEW QUESTIONS

17 Identify two rules of referencing.

18 What is the difference between a shortened in-text reference and an end-of-text reference?

19 Why do writers include a bibliography in their documents?

20 A researcher has found some information online that they use in a report. The source of the information needs to be acknowledged in the bibliography. What details should the researcher include?

APPLY YOUR KNOWLEDGE

PROCESSING AND EVALUATING INFORMATION

1 a   Conduct a complex web search for one of your assignments in any subject by following the guidelines provided by Ryrie (2001, p. 49):

Boolean search expressions (AND, OR, NOT) are the mainstay, or you can use + and – symbols in front of keywords to indicate which ones should or should not appear in a search. You can then refine your search by, for example, changing the order in which keywords appear and including more complex conditions . . . more and more search engines are using the menu approach to searches, such as 'Exact phrase', 'Match All Words' or 'Match Any Words'.

  b   Organise the results of your search into a bibliography.

  c   Add two books and an article from a journal to your bibliography. Include the author's name, title, publisher, place and date of publication following the note or traditional method.

2 Work in small groups.

  a   Discuss the reasons for referencing sources from any medium fairly and accurately.

  b   Discuss the three rules of referencing.

  c   What makes paraphrasing different from plagiarism?

  d   Find your Institution's policy on plagiarism on its website. What are the consequences of plagiarism?

  e   Prepare a set of rules any student could use to avoid plagiarism. The set of rules should include a brief introduction that defines the term 'academic honesty'.

3   Next time you are doing research, use the checklist below to evaluate the sources of information.

SELF-EVALUATE YOUR SKILL

EVALUATING INFORMATION SOURCES

I have:	Yes	No
Verified the accuracy of a document by asking: • who wrote the page? • what is the purpose of the document? • why was it produced? • does the author have the qualifications to write the document?		

I have:	Yes	No
Verified the source's reputation by asking: • is the author respected for their honesty and objectivity? • does the author present evidence for and against their argument? • has the author presented useful new information?		
Evaluated the objectivity of the document by asking: • what objectives does the document meet? • how detailed is the information? • what opinions are given and inferences drawn by the author? • do the claims in the document withstand critical analysis?		
Checked the currency of the document by asking: • when was it produced? • when was it updated?		

SUMMARY OF LEARNING OBJECTIVES

 DESCRIBE AN EFFECTIVE PROCESS FOR CONDUCTING RESEARCH

Planning is the first step in the research process. Plan well and you will locate relevant sources of information efficiently. Critical thinking is essential as you analyse, evaluate and process the sources of information. Preparation of a thesis or purpose statement and an outline is an essential part of the process. The thesis focuses your research, and the outline sorts and organises the research information and your ideas. Develop a well-reasoned argument with supporting conclusions and recommendations (if required). Document the sources following the rules of referencing. Revise and proofread.

 DISCUSS ACADEMIC HONESTY AND DESCRIBE HOW TO MAINTAIN ETHICS AND ETIQUETTE IN YOUR RESEARCH

Academic honesty is ethical behaviour in all academic work, including acknowledging all sources correctly, presenting your own work, gathering objective and reliable data, and working in accordance with the university's student guidelines. Ethical research documents sources, gives appropriate credit, and always avoids plagiarism by referencing sources in the shortened in-text reference and the full reference in the bibliography or list of references at the end of the essay, assignment or report.

Respect the right to privacy of anyone you interview or observe to gather primary sources of information.

 DISTINGUISH PRIMARY, SECONDARY AND TERTIARY SOURCES OF INFORMATION

Sources of information are used by researchers. Primary sources are usually unpublished information gathered first hand. Secondary sources are published in print form or online, and tertiary sources are compiled from secondary sources. Primary, secondary and tertiary sources provide information and facts and opinions. The information is then weighed up or evaluated against the researcher's own findings. Researchers analyse the existing information and add to the body of knowledge from their own research.

Ask questions to verify the accuracy of the source material, the source's reputation, the objectivity of the document and its currency. Check for any bias and fallacious reasoning. Source material can have different purposes: to inform, persuade, entertain or advertise. The purpose influences the type of information used and how it is presented.

One of the most important questions to ask is: 'Do the source's claims stand up to scrutiny?' If they don't, discard the source material. The purpose of the research process is to gather and use relevant, factual, current and objective information that enables you to build an argument and maintain your reputation by presenting a well-researched and effective document.

DISCUSS HOW TO USE SEARCH ENGINES, WEB DIRECTORIES AND DATABASES EFFECTIVELY

Search engines receive a request from a researcher, look for key words, compare that request with the index created by the 'robot' or 'web crawler', and return the results of the search to the researcher. A team of editors prepare the web directories, which are used for specific searches. Online databases give access to journal articles, magazines and newspapers.

 DISCUSS DIFFERENT APPROACHES TO NOTATIONS, CITATIONS AND REFERENCING

Citations and notations acknowledge the work of another author at one of three places in the document:

as citations within the text, as footnotes or as endnotes. The most commonly used methods of referencing are the author–date (Harvard) system and the note (or traditional) method.

 PREPARE A BIBLIOGRAPHY AND LIST OF REFERENCES

A bibliography covers all sources (quoted or unquoted) on a topic. The list of references identifies materials cited in the report, essay or project that are not the writer's original work. The list of references acknowledges the original writer and contains enough information to locate the source easily: for example, the author's name, title of the publication, publisher, place and date of publication. The references are listed alphabetically by author's family name.

KEY TERMS

ACTIVITIES AND QUESTIONS

1. a   Name two library catalogues used in a library search.
   b   List three resources or services that libraries offer.
2. a   List three sources of information to use as you research an essay topic. Briefly explain why each of them is useful.
   b   Why are dictionaries and encyclopaedias used?
   c   Why would you use APAIS?
   d   Why would you use a CD-ROM catalogue?
   e   Why would you use a search engine, web directory or online database?
3. a   Gather the relevant information for an essay or a business report you are writing
      • by using a search engine such as AltaVista, Google or MSN to find at least two documents to use as source data

      • by using an online database such as Highbeam or Infoseek to find at least two documents to use as source data
      • by using a web directory such as Internet Public Library or Galaxy to find two sources of information relevant to the essay or business report.
   b   Place the six documents from (a) into the bibliography using the traditional (note) method of referencing.
4. Work in small groups.
   a   Brainstorm the reasons for evaluating your sources of information.
   b   Discuss the likely consequences of accepting all source information without thinking critically about it.
   c   Create a 'Tips list for applying ethical principles and etiquette in your research'. The tips list will

be used by first-year university students.

5   Work in small groups to design a survey for first-year students titled 'Academic Honesty'.

    a   Create a set of 6–10 questions you could use in a survey seeking opinions about academic honesty.

    b   Prepare a brief introduction that identifies why students should observe academic honesty in their studies.

    c   Include three Internet sites after the survey questions that survey respondents could access to identify academically honest and dishonest behaviours.

    d   Identify anything else that might be useful to include in the survey for first-year students.

EXPLORING THE WEB

1   Complete the free tutorial *Internet Detective* <www.vts.intute.ac.uk> on the Information and Communication Technology site to help develop the critical thinking skills required for any Internet research.

    a   Name some common mistakes that people make when they search the Internet.

    b   What are the three main types of Internet search tools?

    c   How can you develop a search strategy?

    d   Why should you think critically about the information you find on the Internet?

    e   What advantages do you gain by creating a links basket?

2   Visit the National Library of Australia's website <www.nla.gov.au/>.

    a   Write a procedure for accessing journal articles.

    b   Choose a topic and use it as an example of 'how to' throughout your procedure.

PROJECT WORK

Assume you work in a newly established consulting firm. The firm's focus is on strategic planning and compliance with government regulations. Your manager has asked you to prepare a short information report titled 'Web searching tips' for the newly appointed team of business development managers. A major function in the business development role is accessing new clients and building relationships.

In the report, you are required to explain how the business development managers can use search engines, web directories and online databases to source information about existing small, medium and large companies. You are also required to explain how to search the Web efficiently. Relate your conclusions to the needs of the business development managers. The information report should start with a clear purpose statement. Prepare an outline and use appropriate headings throughout the report. Recommendations are not needed in an information report.

Start your research on the Web by visiting 'Web searching tips' at the Internet Public Library <www.ipl.org/div/websearching>.

a   Compare how search engines and web directories work by viewing the IPL's Search Engine Directory collection and Web Directories collection.

b   List five criteria for evaluating the information on web pages.

The findings from (a) and (b) should be included in your information report.

BIBLIOGRAPHY

About.com. 2007. 'Electronic publishing search', *About.com*, www.about.com/, viewed 3 December 2007.

Allen, K.L. 2005. *Study Skills: A Student Survival Guide*, John Wiley & Sons, United Kingdom.

American Psychological Association. 1994. *Publication Manual of the American Psychological Association*, 4th edn, APA, Washington DC.

Anderson, J. & Durston, B.H. 1988. *Thesis and Assignment Writing*, John Wiley & Sons, Brisbane.

Anderson, J. & Poole, M. 1994. *Thesis and Assignment Writing*, 2nd edn, John Wiley & Sons, Brisbane.

Andrew, M. 1999. 'Editing publications for the higher education sector', *Stylewise*, Vol. 5, Issue 2, pp. 1–2.

Bernard, J.R.L. (ed.) 1986. *The Macquarie Thesaurus: The Book of Words*, Macquarie Library, Macquarie University, Sydney.

Bienvenu, S. & Timm, P.R. 2002. *Business Communication: Discovering Strategy, Developing Skills*, Pearson Education, Upper Saddle River, New Jersey.

Bovée, C.L. & Thill, J.V. 2004. *Business Communication Today*, 8th edn, Pearson Prentice Hall, Upper Saddle River, New Jersey.

Browne, M.N. & Keeley, S.M. 2007. *Asking the Right Questions: A Guide to Critical Thinking*, 8th edn, Pearson Prentice Hall, Upper Saddle River, New Jersey.

Byrne, G. 1999. 'Information from the Net—plagiarism v. sharing', *Stylewise*, Vol. 5, Issue 2, p. 3.

Cantor, J.A. 1993. *Guide to Academic Writing*, Praeger Publishers, USA.

Delbridge, A. (ed.) 1997. *The Macquarie Dictionary*, 3rd edn, Macquarie Library, Macquarie University, Sydney.

DeTienne, K.B. 2002. *Guide to Electronic Communication: Using Technology for Effective Business Writing and Speaking*, Pearson Education, New Jersey.

Eagleson, R.D. 1990. *Writing in Plain English*, AGPS, Canberra.

Elliott, G.R. 1998. 'Australian management research: prospects for the new millennium', *Journal of the Australian and New Zealand Academy of Management*, Vol. 4, Issue 2, pp. 18–26.

Gibaldi, J. 1995. *MLA Handbook for Writers of Research Papers*, 4th edn, Modern Language Association of America, USA.

Gibaldi, J. 1998. *MLA Style Manual and Guide to Scholarly Publishing*, 2nd edn, Modern Language Association, New York.

Gibaldi, J. 2003. *MLA Handbook for Writers of Research Papers*, 6th edn, Modern Language Association of America, New York.

Guffey, M.E. 1997. 'Formats for the citation of electronic sources in business writing', *Business Communication Quarterly*, Vol. 60, Issue 1, March, pp. 59–76.

Intellectual Property Australia. *What is Intellectual Property?* www.ipaustralia.gov.au/about/index.shtml, viewed 3 April 2008.

Lehman, C.M. & Dufrene, D.D. 2002. *Business Communication*, 13th edn, South-Western, Ohio.

Levine, J.S. *Writing and Presenting Your Thesis or Dissertation*, Michigan University, www.learnerassociates.net/, last updated 1 August 2007, viewed 17 November 2007.

McLean, N. & Cook, J. 1993. 'Report of Commission of European Communities on Opportunities for Publishers in the Information Services Market', *Electronic Publishing: Technical Standards*, www.adfa.oz.au/, viewed 14 February 2001.

Meyer, M. 1982. *The Little, Brown Guide to Writing Research Papers*, Little, Brown & Company (Canada), USA.

National Office for the Information Economy. 2002. *Keeping Government Publications Online: A Guide for Commonwealth Agencies*, July, www.nla.gov.au/, viewed 3 December 2007.

Putnis, P. & Petelin, R. 1999. *Professional Communication: Principles and Applications*, 2nd edn, Pearson Education Australia, Sydney.

Radford, M.L., Barnes, S.B. & Barr, L.R. 2005. *Web Research*, 2nd edn, Allyn & Bacon, USA.

Ryrie, T. 2001. 'Search engines', *Charter*, September, p. 49.

Sensei.com.au. 'How to use search engines', *Web Guide*, www.sensei.com.au/web-guide/how-to-use-search.php, viewed 19 February 2008.

Style Manual for Authors, Editors and Printers, 6th edn, John Wiley & Sons, Brisbane, 2002.

The Chicago Manual of Style, 15th edn, University of Chicago Press, Chicago, 2003.

Turabian, K.L. 1996. *A Manual for Writers of Term Papers, Theses and Dissertations*, 6th edn (rev. by J. Grossman & A. Bennett), University of Chicago Press, Chicago.

Wright, M. 1998. 'Citing references to electronic sources', *Stylewise*, Vol. 4, Issue 1, pp. 1–2.

Writing Tutorial Services. *How to Write a Thesis Statement*, Indiana University, www.indiana.edu/, last updated 27 April 2004, viewed 17 November 2007.

14

Critical thinking: argument, logic and persuasion

Photo: Andrew Prokhorc

LEARNING OBJECTIVES

After studying this chapter you should be able to:

1 ▷ Explain the role of critical thinking in academic work

2 ▷ Evaluate the logic in an argument by identifying the relationship between the premise (position or purpose statement) and conclusion

3 ▷ Identify common fallacies and describe their impact on reasoning

4 ▷ Distinguish quality evidence from poor evidence

5 ▷ Discuss how techniques of persuasion influence others to change attitudes or take action.

VIEWPOINT: WHY CRITICAL THINKING?

'Everyone thinks. It is our nature to do so. But much of our thinking, left to itself, is biased, distorted, partial, uninformed, or downright prejudiced. Yet, the quality of our life and that of what we produce, make or build depends precisely on the quality of our thought. Shoddy thinking is costly, both in money and in quality of life. Excellence in thought, however, must be systematically cultivated.

Critical thinking is that mode of thinking—about any subject, content, or problem—in which the thinker improves the quality of his or her thinking by skilfully analysing, assessing, and reconstructing it. Critical thinking is self-directed, self-disciplined, self-monitored, and self-corrective thinking. It presupposes assent to rigorous standards of excellence and mindful command of their use. It entails effective communication and problem-solving abilities, as well as a commitment to overcome our native egocentrism and sociocentrism.'

Excerpt from 'Our concept of critical thinking', *The Critical Thinking Community*, www.criticalthinking.org/, viewed 19 February 2008.

The examination and testing of propositions about any subject or problem requires critical thinking. Critical thinking is defined by Dewey (1933, p. 118) as 'active, persistent, and careful consideration of any belief or supposed form of knowledge in the light of the grounds that support it and the further conclusions to which it tends'. Rather than accepting passively the views of another party, critical thinkers raise questions, find information, evaluate evidence, and think about the reasons for any conclusions or beliefs and their likely implications.

A widely accepted definition presented by Norris and Ennis (1989) states: 'Critical thinking is reasonable reflective thinking that is focused on deciding what to believe or do.' This definition includes decision making as part of critical thinking. Fisher and Scriven (1997, p. 21) state: 'Critical thinking is skilled and active interpretation and evaluation of observations and communications, information and argumentation.' This presents critical thinking as a skilled activity involving questioning and metacognition (thinking about your own thinking).

A recent definition is by Browne and Keeley (2007, p. 3): 'Critical thinking consists of an awareness of a set of interrelated critical questions, plus the ability and willingness to ask and answer them at appropriate times.' In their view the process involves questioning, thinking and a desire to use critical questions actively. Critical thinking and questioning enables you to examine and test propositions of any kind that are offered for acceptance, in order to find out whether the reasons and conclusions equal the argument.

Persuasion is the process of convincing another to change their beliefs or behaviour through moral or logical argument. Successful persuasive strategies focus on speaker credibility, logical arguments and psychological appeals. The sender's credibility incorporates trustworthiness, competence and dynamism. An effective persuasive message creates the balance of emotional and logical appeals appropriate to its purpose.

Business and related academic studies are concerned with identifying problems and solutions, relating theories to practice, making comparisons and contrasts. When reading academic documents you need to question critically and think rationally about your response to the theory or article by developing an understanding of the content and evaluating it. In your studies, read and evaluate what others have said in order to find out what is already known and to understand the main arguments put forward by authoritative writers and scholars in the field.

THE ROLE OF CRITICAL THINKING

OBJECTIVE 1 ▷
Explain the role of critical thinking in academic work

Critical thinking is about making good judgments. **Critical thinking** considers possible viewpoints and results in interpretation, analysis and evaluation of evidence, and the conclusions inferred from the evidence. It is purposeful, self-regulatory judgment that occurs when an issue is raised, a problem needs to be solved, opinions are reconsidered or experiences carefully reflected upon. Critical thinking is more than personal opinion. It involves making judgments based on research and evaluations by:

Critical thinking considers possible viewpoints and results in interpretation, analysis and evaluation of evidence, and the conclusions inferred from the evidence.

- distinguishing between fact and opinion
- evaluating the validity of information sources
- evaluating the validity of particular theories and their application to particular situations.

A **critical thinker** is skilled at articulating and evaluating arguments, and understanding how evidence supports or opposes a claim.

A **critical thinker** is skilled at articulating and evaluating arguments, and understanding how evidence supports or opposes a claim.

Critical thinking activities

Critical thinking applies to a number of activities undertaken in your academic work, including those shown in Table 14.1.

The purpose of critical thinking is to question, rather than taking everything you read at face value. Its purpose is not to 'criticise'. Critical thinking is used to critique academic papers, reports, and other written and oral presentations. It is a desirable skill in all aspects of university work—note making, assignment writing, tutorial presentations, and the practical component of professional practice or

Table 14.1: Critical thinking activities

• Making connections between ideas, texts, frameworks and theories	• Drawing inferences and making generalisations
• Identifying assumptions	• Establishing cause and effect
• Making links between ideas	• Comparing and contrasting
• Forming opinions and arguments	• Identifying problems and solutions
• Making and supporting a claim	• Analysing and classifying
• Asking questions and challenging ideas	• Problem solving, evaluating and weighing up
• Observing facts, and comparing them with hypotheses and assumptions	• Questioning and judging the validity of the source and the worth of evidence

placement—as it enables you to expand your knowledge and skills. As you read, think about and question the structure, purpose, audience and author of the text.

Critical reading and questioning

An **argument** is a claim or assertion that may be believed or disbelieved. The position taken in the argument is the starting point for presenting a convincing case. It is usually presented as a position statement in the introduction of the essay. The argument is presented in stages throughout a document or oral presentation to build the case. The aim is to convince or persuade the reader or listener to accept the argument.

An **argument** is a claim or assertion; a convincing argument shows the relationship between the premise and the conclusion.

Documents based on an argument make a claim (an opinion, proposal, evaluation or interpretation) about a topic and justify this claim with specific evidence. The argument is based on the evidence and aims to convince the receiver the claim is true. Critical reading enables you to identify the relationship between the premise (the position or purpose statement) and the conclusion.

The conclusion is inferred or derived from the reasoning presented in the argument.

Academic writers are expected to develop and substantiate an analytical argument or position through the use of evidence. The argument is usually based on inductive or deductive reasoning and should avoid fallacious reasoning at all times. As you research and gather evidence for an essay, assignment or academic paper, read critically by completing the broad steps in Table 14.2.

The first step in the critical reading process is to identify the premise, claim or assertion.

Critical questions are the key to critical thinking. Browne and Keeley (2007, p. 3) suggest that critical questions will assist you to:

- react critically to an essay or to evidence presented in a textbook, a periodical or on a website
- judge the quality of a lecture or speech
- form an argument
- write an essay based on a reading assignment
- participate in class.

Typical critical questions include 'What if . . .?', 'How could . . .?' and 'What does this mean for . . .?'. Examples of questions asked by critical readers of academic papers and research articles include:

- Are the sources of evidence credible?
- Do the inferences drawn overgeneralise?
- Is opinion presented as fact?
- Are the results verifiable?
- Are the points made in the study supported by evidence?
- Is the sample size big enough to fulfil the aim of the study?
- Is the sample representative of the wider population?
- Do the criteria for inclusion in the population sample result in an unrepresentative group?

Table 14.2: Read and question the evidence critically

Read critically	Ask questions to verify that the writer has:
Step 1 Has the writer gathered, read and understood the evidence?	• developed a position, understood the topic and chosen a position • presented the position to the reader and justified the position through the use of evidence • convinced the reader to accept the position, argument and conclusion.
Step 2 Does the writer recognise and acknowledge the different positions taken in the readings?	• gathered sufficient evidence from various sources, some of which will take different positions towards the topic • improved understanding by analysing and evaluating the different approaches • compared and contrasted different conflicting views, particularly in controversial areas.
Step 3 Has the writer developed an argument out of the evidence to support his or her chosen position?	• developed the chosen position • evaluated each position and decided why one is more valid than another • verified his or her chosen position and established the starting point of the argument • determined the relevance of the points to the argument.
Step 4 Has the writer presented and supported his or her position and conclusion clearly and concisely?	• matched evidence with different stages of the argument • prepared a position statement and introduction • identified the stages in the body of the paper to see how the writer has developed the argument to support the position • asked critical questions about the development and completeness of the argument and the quality of the evidence (Are there any gaps?) • substantiated his or her position by developing the argument, rather than simply summarising the evidence • related the conclusion clearly to the premise.

REVIEW QUESTIONS

1. a What is the purpose of critical thinking?
   b Identify three critical thinking activities you have undertaken in the past week.
2. How do critical questions help you in your academic work?
3. Identify the four broad steps in the critical reading process.

APPLY YOUR KNOWLEDGE

CRITICAL THINKING AND READING

1. Work in small groups.
   a Explain the difference between merely summarising the evidence, and using it to substantiate your position and develop your argument.
   b Explain why you need the support of experts in academic writing.
   c Assume a lecturer has made these comments on your essay:
      • 'You have made some good points but you have not substantiated them.'
      • You need to show me that you have done the reading on this topic.'
      • 'Your argument here contradicts your starting position.'

Discuss the strategies you could use to avoid these comments on future essays.

2 a   Find a journal article relevant to your next essay or project. Critically read the article and use the checklist below to rate your critical reading skills.

   b   How will you improve your skills in any area you identified as unsuccessful?

SELF-EVALUATE YOUR SKILL

THINK CRITICALLY AS YOU READ

Key: VS = Very Successfully, S = Successfully, U = Unsuccessfully

I have read critically by:	VS	S	U
identifying the main points of this document or text			
thinking about and analysing the relevance of the examples used			
identifying the 'school of thought' the author belongs to and any particular bias or framework			
analysing the quality of the reasoning to identify any fallacies			
thinking about the logic and steps of the presented argument			
checking that the main ideas in the text are supported by well-researched, non-emotive, logical evidence			
checking for bias or distortions in the evidence			
evaluating the conclusion against the argument presented			
making connections between this and other texts			
agreeing or disagreeing with the author			
evaluating the evidence supporting the message			
thinking about the wider implications			

LOGIC AND ARGUMENT

An argument consists of one or more premises and one conclusion. A **premise** is a proposition or claim on which an argument is based or from which a conclusion is drawn. The premise may be written as a purpose or position statement. A conclusion is the claim being made by the writer or speaker. A conclusion is based on the reasoning and evidence presented in the argument. It is the message that the writer or speaker wants you to accept. A conclusion may be either true or false, believed or not believed. An argument is presented in support of the premise. Until tested a premise may be either true or false. A good argument is based on sound premises and reasoning; a poor argument is based on unsound and inaccurate reasoning.

Deductive and inductive arguments

The difference between a deductive and inductive argument comes from the sort of relation the writer or speaker presents between the premises and the conclusion. A **deductive argument** is an argument based on logical necessity, where the premises provide (or appear to provide) complete support for the conclusion. The argument is deductive when the truth of the premises establishes the truth of the

◄ OBJECTIVE 2
Evaluate the logic in an argument by identifying the relationship between the premise (position or purpose statement) and conclusion

A **premise** is a proposition or claim on which an argument is based or from which a conclusion is drawn.

conclusion. A common form of deductive argument is a syllogism. The argument contains a major and minor premise leading to a conclusion. **Syllogisms** are made up of a sequence of statements. They may be valid or invalid. An example of a valid syllogism is: 'All animals breathe oxygen. Camels are animals. Therefore, camels breathe oxygen.'

An **inductive argument** is an argument where the premises provide (or appear to provide) some degree of support (but less than complete support) for the conclusion. The argument is inductive when the writer or speaker thinks that the truth of the premises does not definitely establish the truth of the conclusion, but provides good reason to believe the conclusion is true. Both inductive and deductive logic are used in arguments. They are differentiated in Table 14.3.

Generalisations

Speakers and writers use research reports and findings to support their generalisations. **Generalisations** are claims about events in general. The statement 'Funding grants raise literacy standards' is a generalisation. By contrast, the statement 'The funding grant was effective in raising literacy standards for the target group in the study' is not a generalisation because it provides evidence about the specific group in the study.

General statements or opinions based on a few cases or incomplete knowledge must be tested for accuracy. Jumping to conclusions, or making hasty generalisations, occurs when a broad conclusion is based on the statistics of a survey of a small group that fails to represent the whole population. The inductive generalisation is a logical fallacy based on insufficient evidence. Test an inductive generalisation by critical questioning, discussions, agreement, disagreement, comment, and further gathering and investigation of evidence.

SAMPLING

Sampling is a widely accepted research tool. **Sampling** is the analysis of a group by determining the characteristics of a significant percentage of its members chosen at random. The quality of the generalisations from research findings depends on the representative nature of the sample: the number, breadth and randomness of the people or events studied by the researchers. Check that the sampling is random—that is, that it gives each member of the target population an equal chance of selection in the sample. The number to include in the sample depends on the nature of the population, the type of investigation, the degree of accuracy required and the available funds. An unbiased sample covers the breadth and diversity of people in the total population. For example, a study into the literacy rates of new arrivals wishing to gain Australian citizenship would include a sample of people from all the nationalities entering the country, rather than only those from the United Kingdom. The sample should represent the study's target group. An unrepresentative sample causes problems because the researchers may overgeneralise their findings.

The **deductive argument** is based on logical necessity—if you can accept the premise, you must also accept the conclusion.

Syllogisms contain at least two premises—a major and minor premise—leading to a conclusion

An **inductive argument** is based on probability—what conclusion is most likely to be expected or believed from the available evidence.

A **generalisation** gives a general, rather than a specific, character to a subject.

Sampling is the analysis of a group by determining the characteristics of a significant percentage of its members chosen at random.

Table 14.3: Deductive and inductive logic	
Deductive logic	**Inductive logic**
<ul><li>Applies general principles to reach specific conclusions</li><li>Enables predictions to be made about future events</li><li>Enables fast decision making on the basis of experience and existing knowledge</li><li>Restricts thinking by discounting conclusions drawn from other types of thinking (e.g. lateral and creative)</li><li>Leads to false conclusions when the premises are incorrect</li></ul>	<ul><li>Examines specific information to derive a general principle</li><li>Creates predictive models of truth based on personal observation and experience</li><li>Allows for sampling of a large target audience to save time and money</li><li>Produces wrong conclusions about the target population if the sampling methodology is weak</li><li>Invites overgeneralisation, particularly if data contradict the researcher's premise</li></ul>

ARGUMENT

Regardless of whether the writer or speaker is using inductive or deductive reasoning, you need to check whether the argument is based on fact, opinion, belief or prejudice. Question the quality and quantity of the research to avoid basing a decision on insufficient evidence and fallacious reasoning such as faulty generalisations. A **fallacy** is an argument in which the premises given for the conclusion do not provide the needed degree of support. There is an error in the reasoning. Fallacies are discussed in the following pages.

A **fallacy** is a type of logical error that leads to a false statement or belief.

Browne and Keeley (2007, p. 25) state: 'Reasons are beliefs, evidence, metaphors, analogies and other statements offered to support or justify conclusions. They are the statements that together form the basis for creating the credibility of a conclusion.' The use of one or more ideas to support another idea is described by two interchangeable terms—'argument' and 'reasoning'. The characteristics of arguments are shown in Table 14.4.

Assumptions and evidence

Analyse the assumptions and evidence underpinning the argument. **Assumptions** are unstated beliefs that support the explicit reasoning. Browne and Keeley (2007, p. 54) suggest that assumptions are:

An **assumption** is an unstated belief that supports the explicit reasoning.

- hidden or unstated (in most cases)
- taken for granted
- influential in determining the conclusion
- potentially deceptive.

Critical thinkers question in order to assess, clarify and validate assumptions. They avoid jumping to conclusions on the basis of invalid assumptions. *Prescriptive or value assumptions* are those taken-for-granted and often unstated beliefs about the way we think things should be. *Descriptive assumptions* are explicit beliefs about the way the world is. Browne and Keeley (2007, p. 104) state: 'Almost all reasoning we encounter includes beliefs about the way the world is, was, or is going to be that the communicator wants us to accept as "facts". These beliefs can be conclusions, reasons or assumptions. We can refer to such beliefs as factual claims.'

Critical thinkers ask questions about the quality and quantity of the evidence. **Evidence** is anything used to determine or demonstrate the truth of an assertion. It is explicit information used by the writer/speaker to justify the dependability of a factual claim. The main kinds of evidence include research studies, case examples, definitions, scientific facts, and findings from surveys and question-naires.

Evidence is anything used to determine or demonstrate the truth of an assertion. It is explicit information used by the writer/speaker to justify the dependability of a factual claim.

When evaluating an argument, apply the following criteria:

- the logical soundness of the argument
- its consistency with other knowledge.

Table 14.4: Characteristics of arguments	
Characteristic	**Explanation**
• Must have intent • Must exemplify and provide evidence • Must have three identifiable parts: premise (or thesis), reasons and conclusion	• To convince or persuade the reader or listener to accept and respond to the conclusion • To present a quality argument and support the likelihood of the proposal identified in the thesis or premise • To enable the writer or speaker and his or her audience to identify the premise, think critically about the reasons, and either accept or reject the conclusion.

Inference and conclusions

Read or listen critically to determine what the writer or speaker is trying to prove. The basic structure of an argument is: 'This because of That . . .' 'This' refers to the conclusion, and 'That' refers to the support for the conclusion. This structure enables the writer to infer the conclusion.

Inference is the act or process of inferring, or passing from one premise, proposition, statement or judgment considered as true to another whose truth is believed to follow from that of the former. Inferences are drawn from statistical sample data and applied as generalisations about the whole population. Conclusions are inferred and derived from the reasoning presented in the argument. The conclusion is the outcome of this reasoning. A valid deductive inference is true if the premises are true.

Conclusions are ideas that require other ideas to support them. Thus, whenever someone claims something is true or ought to be done but provides no statements to support the claim, that claim is not a conclusion because no evidence has been offered. The unsupported claim is simply an **opinion**.

Fallacies—false arguments

Curtis (2007) explains fallacies as mistakes in reasoning. 'However, not just any type of mistake in reasoning counts as a logical fallacy. To be a fallacy, a type of reasoning must be potentially deceptive, it must be likely to fool at least some of the people some of the time. Moreover, in order for a fallacy to be worth identifying and naming, it must be a common type of logical error.'

Fallacious reasoning may be conscious or unconscious. While conscious errors are deliberate 'tricks' in reasoning, unconscious errors are caused by faulty assumptions and uncritical thinking. Some common fallacies are illustrated in Table 14.5.

Inference is the process of deriving a conclusion.

Conclusions are ideas that require other ideas to support them.

An **opinion** is a belief held with confidence but not substantiated by positive knowledge or proof.

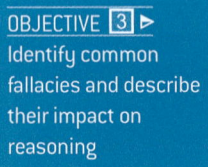

OBJECTIVE 3 ▶
Identify common fallacies and describe their impact on reasoning

REVIEW QUESTIONS

4 Differentiate between deductive reasoning, inductive reasoning and opinion. Define the terms 'syllogism' and 'generalisation'.
5 Identify the characteristics of an argument.
6 Explain the relationship between the premise and the conclusion.
7 Define the term 'fallacy' and give three examples of common fallacies.
8 Explain the difference between conscious and unconscious fallacious reasoning.

OBJECTIVE 4 ▶
Distinguish quality evidence from poor evidence

QUALITY OF THE EVIDENCE

Academic studies, propositions and arguments must be based on research, credible sources of information and argument built on evidence. **Propositions** are claims on which an argument is based or from which a conclusion is drawn. As you read academic documents, you must apply critical thinking because you are required to evaluate and respond to the propositions and arguments presented in the documents. The written assignments, essays, projects and oral presentations you prepare demonstrate your understanding, evaluation and critique of the content. Like appeals to any source, appeals to research evidence must be considered thoughtfully. The fact that research has been applied to a problem may mean the research evidence is dependable and that the interpretation of the meaning of the evidence is accurate. By contrast, poor research may mean the evidence and interpretation of its meaning is not dependable. Think about the evidence supporting the main ideas. Is the evidence well researched, reliable, non-emotive and logical? An affirmative answer verifies the quality of the research. A negative answer suggests poor-quality research.

A **proposition** is a claim on which an argument is based or from which a conclusion is drawn.

Quality evidence is well researched, reliable, credible, non-emotive and logical.

Table 14.5: Fallacies	
Type	**Purpose**
Ad hominem (to the man)	To imply that an idea is unreliable because of the person holding it; to debate the person, not the issue
Non-sequitur (it does not follow)	To assume that one thing follows from another, and to show that the conclusion follows logically from the initial statement when this is not so
Ad populum (appeal to popularity)	To justify a claim by appealing to sentiments that large groups of people have in common, and thereby assuming falsely the desirability of anything favoured by the large group
Post hoc ergo propter hoc (after this therefore because of this)	To confuse cause and effect by making the assumption that, because one event occurred after the other, the first event caused the later event
Confusion of 'some' and 'all'	To make too broad a generalisation or an assertion that needs qualification—the most common error of all
Slippery slope	To assume that the proposed action will set off a chain of unwanted or undesirable events even when procedures exist to prevent them happening
Either/or thinking	To reduce a problem to only two possibilities when there are more than two
Searching for perfect solutions	To assume a solution should not be adopted because part of a problem would remain after the solution is tried
Oversimplification	To propose very simple solutions and answers to difficult and complex issues
Appeals to questionable authority	To cite an authority without the required expertise to support the argument and its conclusion
Ignoring the question	To avoid addressing the question and wander off into other areas
Wishful thinking	To make the faulty assumption that because we wish 'A' were true or false, then 'B' is indeed true or false
Appeals to emotions	To distract receivers from relevant reasons and evidence by using emotionally charged language
Fallacy of exclusion	To exclude relevant evidence that would undermine the inductive argument
False analogy	To ignore significant differences and avoid verifying that the two things being analogised are in fact comparable
Begging the question	To assume the conclusion in the reasoning or make the assumption that something has been agreed or established when this is not the case; often occurs when the reasoning is circular (the conclusion merely restates the opening assertion)
Red herring	To present an irrelevant topic that diverts attention from the original issue and helps to win an argument by shifting attention and the argument on to another issue

Problems with research findings

Browne and Keeley (2007, pp. 120–1) highlight the following eight points about research findings.

1. Research varies greatly in quality.
2. Research findings often contradict one another.
3. Research findings *do not prove* conclusions.
4. Like all of us, researchers have expectations, attitudes, values and needs that bias the questions they ask, the way they conduct their research and the way they interpret their research findings.

5. Speakers and writers often distort or simplify research conclusions.
6. Research 'facts' change over time, especially claims about human behaviour.
7. Research varies in how artificial it is. Often, to achieve the goal of control, research loses some of its 'real-world' quality.
8. The need for financial gain, status, security and other factors can affect research outcomes.

Evaluating research evidence

Research findings can only be generalised to people and events that are like those in the research target group.

Question any research findings critically before embracing them. Determine whether different conclusions could be drawn from the argument presented, and evaluate the wider implications of the findings for you and for the discipline. Table 14.6 provides clues for evaluating research results.

Table 14.6: Clues for evaluating research studies

Apply these questions to research findings to determine whether the findings are dependable evidence.

1 *What is the quality of the source of the report?* Usually the most dependable reports are those published in peer-reviewed journals, in which a study is not accepted until it has been reviewed by a series of relevant experts. Usually—but not always—the more reputable the source, the better designed the study. So, try to find out all you can about the reputation of the source.

2 *Are other clues included in the communication suggesting the research was well done?* For example, *does the report detail any special strengths of the research?*

3 *Has the study been replicated?* Has more than one study reached the same conclusion? Findings, even when 'statistically significant', can arise by chance alone. For example, when an association is repeatedly and consistently found in well designed studies, like the link between smoking and cancer, then there is reason to believe it, at least until those who disagree can provide persuasive evidence for their point of view.

4 *How selective has the communicator been in choosing studies?* For example, have relevant studies with contradictory results been omitted? Has the researcher selected only those studies that support their point?

5 *Is there any evidence of critical thinking?* Has the speaker or writer showed a critical attitude towards earlier research that supports their point of view? Most conclusions from research need to be qualified because of research limitations. Has the communicator demonstrated a willingness to qualify?

6 *Is there any reason for someone to have distorted the research?* We need to be wary of situations in which the researchers need to find certain kinds of results.

7 *Are the conditions in the research artificial and therefore distorted?* Always ask, 'How similar are the conditions under which the research study was conducted to the situation the researcher is generalising about?'

8 *How far can we generalise, given the research sample?*

9 *Are there any biases or distortions in the surveys, questionnaires, ratings or other measurements that the researcher uses?* We need to have confidence that the researcher has measured accurately what they wanted to measure. The problem of biased surveys and questionnaires is very pervasive in research.

Source: M.N. Browne & S.M. Keeley, *Asking the Right Questions: A Guide to Critical Thinking*, Pearson Prentice Hall, Upper Saddle River, New Jersey, 2007, pp. 122–3. Reproduced with permission.

REVIEW QUESTIONS

9. Contrast the features of quality evidence and poor evidence.
10. Describe four problems with research findings.
11. Discuss at least six clues you would look for when evaluating research results.

THE ROLE OF PERSUASION

◀ OBJECTIVE 5
Discuss how techniques of persuasion influence others to change attitudes or take action

Persuasion is the process of convincing another person or party to change his or her beliefs or behaviour by employing appeals to both feelings and intellect. Through persuasion, we affect others and they affect us. For example, two different types of persuasive speeches—speeches of conviction and speeches of actuation—aim to influence the listeners for different purposes. In a speech of conviction, the speaker attempts to convince the listener to believe as the speaker does. In a speech of actuation, the speaker aims to have listeners take the action proposed by buying a product or service, signing a petition, agreeing to a change or accepting a proposal.

A persuasive, logical argument convinces someone to change or take action because they believe it is the appropriate thing to do. Changes brought about by persuasion rather than coercion are likely to continue. Successful persuasion influences the other person to change a point of view or take some action and is often based on commonly held beliefs and values. By contrast, persuasion based on coercion influences in a way that leaves the receiver no desirable alternative but to adopt the change of attitude or behaviour proposed by the speaker.

Any type of persuasive message has at least three common components—a receiver, the message and the sender. As persuasion is about the receivers' needs and the benefits any change will have on them, it is important to realise that not all people reach conclusions in the same way and consequently may react differently to the same evidence and appeals. As you prepare a persuasive message, focus on the receiver by:

- identifying the group standards, habits of thinking and norms of a particular group to help you develop arguments that cross boundaries such as culture, gender and organisational differences
- determining the individual standards held by those people within a group who have influence over other members and what motivates them
- thinking critically to establish criteria that will influence them
- matching the solutions or proposals in the message with the criteria and the needs of the receiver.

Persuasion is the process of convincing another to change his or her beliefs or behaviour through moral or logical argument.

Techniques of persuasion

Successful persuasive messages flow from the credibility of the sender, logical arguments and psychological appeals. The basic process of persuasion requires that the person making a claim supports it in such a way that the receiver accepts the claim. Three persuasive techniques are discussed here.

RHETORICAL MIX

The rhetorical mix of oral language, written language and visuals used in persuasive messages is designed to convince the audience to take action. Winn and Beck (2002) used a three-part rhetorical model to evaluate websites to examine how the design elements on an e-commerce website carried out the rhetorical function of persuasion. The three-part model included the rhetorical mix of:

1. *Logos*, or the appeal to logic (price, variety, product information)
2. *Pathos*, or the appeal to the emotions (entertainment potential of the website, sensory appeal through audiovisuals, intuitiveness of navigation, and the extent to which the website can be personalised for users)
3. *Ethos*, or appeal to credibility (privacy and security, corporate image and branding).

Winn and Beck concluded that understanding how design elements appeal to a shopper's logic, emotions and assessment of credibility gives designers a set of tools to maximise the persuasive power of a website.

FEATURES–BENEFITS MIX

The features–benefits mix is a technique of persuasion that incorporates a mixture of a product or service's features and benefits into the message to show the audience the real benefits. The message must stress the benefits in order to focus on the receiver's need and enable the receiver to see the relevance of the features and benefits to them. The message has two essential components:

1. features of a product or service, and a clear and concise illustration of how to apply these features
2. linkage of the features with the benefits to enable the receiver to understand 'what's in it for me' (WIFM).

PSYCHOLOGICAL APPEALS

Psychological appeals include appeals to the need for companionship, adventure, power, authority, humour and loyalty, or appeals to feelings such as fear, love, boredom or curiosity. Fulfilment of these needs is a powerful motivator.

Abraham Maslow's hierarchy of individual needs, shown in Figure 14.1, provides a useful way to categorise types of needs from lower-level to higher-level needs. The hierarchy progresses through the five levels of need: physiological needs, safety needs, acceptance needs, esteem needs, self-actualisation needs.

The hierarchy of needs developed by Maslow suggests that an unsatisfied need provides the motivation to act in order to satisfy that need. Table 14.7 gives an example of how persuasive messages can be designed to meet each of the needs described by Maslow.

Maslow's model of human motivation identified five levels of need.

Emotional and logical appeals

Most persuasive appeals have a balance between logic and emotion. While logic without emotion may disengage the receiver, too much emotion creates the impression that the real issues are hidden or the sender has done too little research. An optimum balance between logic and emotion enhances the credibility of the speaker and captures the audience's attention. Consideration of the four factors in Figure 14.2 provides an optimum balance in persuasive communication (Olderman 1997). Logical appeals balanced by little emotion are appropriate when persuading the receiver to make a significant change, accept a complex idea or make an important decision. Emotional appeals balanced by some logic are appropriate when selling a product or service.

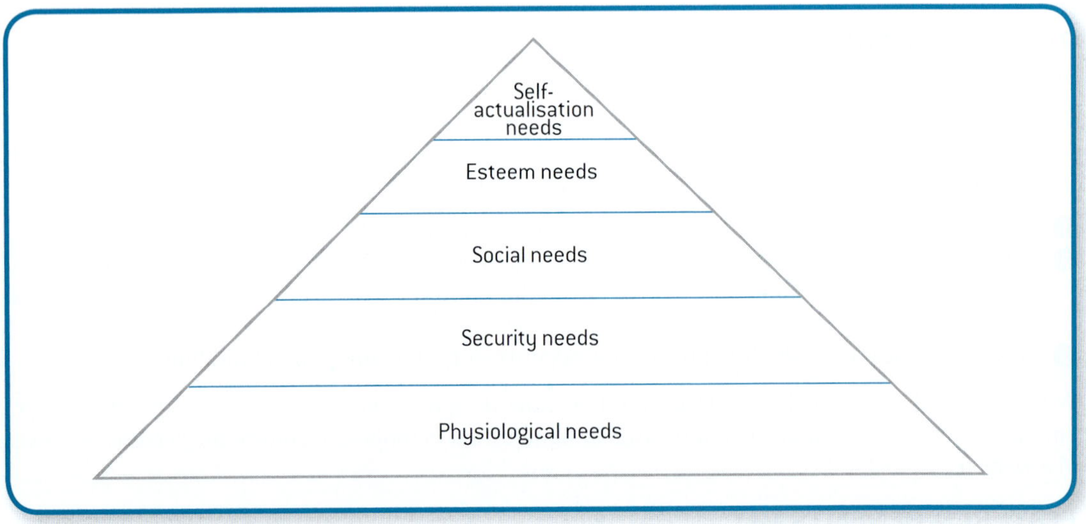

An effective persuasive message balances logic and emotion in its appeal.

Figure 14.1: Maslow's hierarchy of needs

Table 14.7: Maslow's five levels of human needs applied to an advertising campaign for a luxury apartment	
Human needs	**Wording in advertising campaign**
Physiological needs	Single-level comfortable apartment, air-conditioned, gymnasium and swimming pool, easy street access
Safety and security needs	Facilities include security entrance, fire alarms throughout the building and secure parking
Belonging needs	Facilities include common room, gymnasium, swimming pool and tennis courts, with opportunities to meet with friends and other residents
Esteem and status needs	Ownership of property with panoramic views to ocean and hinterland in prestigious location and building
Self-actualisation needs	Live the lifestyle of your choice in outstanding surroundings

Credibility

Several factors contribute to a persuasive speaker's or writer's credibility, including education, profession, personality, physical appearance, standard of dress, respect for others, general awareness and knowledge of the problem or issue, and personal and social competence. A credible sender combines ethos, logos and pathos to build a logical persuasive message. He or she avoids reasoning fallacies such as hasty generalisation, faulty analogical reasoning and ignoring the issue. Rather than using powerless styles of communication such as 'ums', 'ahs', qualifiers and hesitations, his or her presentation is assertive and convincing. An aware receiver evaluates the sender and the message by observing the sender's verbal, nonverbal and questioning techniques, and responding to the identified benefits.

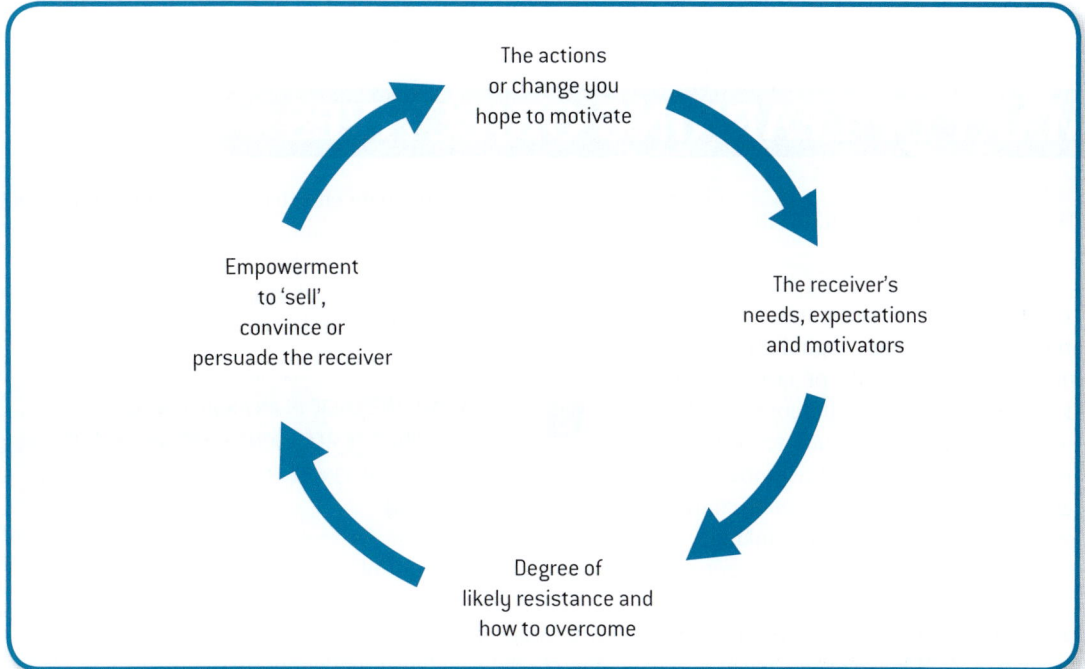

Figure 14.2: Optimum balance in persuasive appeals—four factors

REVIEW QUESTIONS

12 Describe the process of persuasion. What do persuasive messages appeal to?

13 Identify three techniques of persuasion.

14 *a*   Discuss the reasons for achieving a balance between emotional appeals and logical appeals in a persuasive message.

   b   Identify four factors that help you to achieve this balance.

APPLY YOUR KNOWLEDGE

ARGUMENT AND PERSUASION

1   Work in small groups.

    a   Brainstorm the pitfalls of relying on personal observation to support an argument.

    b   Discuss how the application of critical thinking avoids many of the built-in biases evident in our personal observations and intuition.

    c   Report your findings to the larger group.

2   Work in small groups.

    a   Explain how understanding the nature of a conclusion is an essential step in critical reading, writing and listening.

    b   Find and critically read a journal article.

        •   Identify the inferences drawn and comment on their validity.

        •   Does the article present enough information about how the study was carried out to reach a conclusion?

        •   Is the evidence sufficient and from credible sources?

        •   What critical questions would you ask of the author to improve your understanding of the article and its conclusion?

3   'Logical appeals should always be balanced by emotion.' Do you agree or disagree? Give reasons for your answer.

SUMMARY OF LEARNING OBJECTIVES

 EXPLAIN THE ROLE OF CRITICAL THINKING IN ACADEMIC WORK

Critical reading allows you to enquire into existing material and analyse the ideas, arguments, and supporting evidence in order to verify or critique the existing body of knowledge. Thoughtfully consider the writer's purpose and use critical questioning to evaluate the issues, assumptions, argument, reasoning and conclusion. Critical thinking is a process for taking charge of and accepting responsibility for your own thinking.

Critical questions are an essential part of the critical thinking process. Critical questions are not criticism. They are an active response to a journal article or essay. 'What if . . .?', 'How could . . .?', 'What does this mean . . .?' questions help you to judge the quality of a lecture, form an argument or participate effectively in a group discussion. Critical reading and questioning enables you to analyse the quality of the reasoning, check for distortions or bias in the evidence, evaluate the conclusion against the argument presented, and think about the wider implications.

 EVALUATE THE LOGIC IN AN ARGUMENT BY IDENTIFYING THE RELATIONSHIP BETWEEN THE PREMISE (POSITION OR PURPOSE STATEMENT) AND CONCLUSION

The basic structure of an argument is 'This because of That'. 'This' refers to the conclusion, while 'That' refers to the support for the conclusion. A valid argument is based on credible evidence that supports the premise or claim. The logic in an argument may be deductive or inductive.

A deductive argument applies general principles to reach specific conclusions. An inductive argument examines specific information to derive a general principle.

IDENTIFY COMMON FALLACIES AND DESCRIBE THEIR IMPACT ON REASONING

Fallacies are errors in reasoning. They may oversimplify, exclude information, make appeals to authority or power, attack the person, ignore the question, make false analogies and include a range of other errors in reasoning. Fallacies in an argument demonstrate flawed logic and lead to invalid or flawed conclusions.

DISTINGUISH QUALITY EVIDENCE FROM POOR EVIDENCE

Check the credibility of the sources of evidence. The evidence should be sufficient to build a sound argument to support the conclusion. Critical questions enable you to find any biases or distortions in the research methodology, identify the strengths and weaknesses of the evidence, and verify that inferences and generalisations are valid. Quality evidence leads to sound conclusions. Poor evidence leads to unsound and invalid conclusions.

DISCUSS HOW TECHNIQUES OF PERSUASION INFLUENCE OTHERS TO CHANGE ATTITUDES OR TAKE ACTION

Successful persuasive strategies centre on speaker credibility, logical arguments and psychological appeals. A speaker's credibility incorporates trustworthiness, competence and dynamism. Effective use of psychological appeals requires careful analysis of the receiver's needs. Techniques of persuasion include rhetorical mix, features–benefits mix and psychological appeals. Effective persuasive messages have a balance of emotional and logical appeals appropriate to the type of message, its context and the receiver.

KEY TERMS

argument	397	evidence	401	persuasion	405
assumption	401	fallacy	401	premise	399
conclusion	402	generalisation	400	proposition	402
critical thinker	396	inductive argument	400	sampling	400
critical thinking	396	inference	402	syllogism	400
deductive argument	399	opinion	402		

ACTIVITIES AND QUESTIONS

1 Work in small groups to discuss the meaning of the following statement: 'A convincing argument is sound, thoughtful and logical.'

2 Find a journal article you may want to use as a reference for an essay or paper in your course and prepare a short critique. (Make judgments or show the relative merits of the argument.) In the critique, give enough information for the reader to know what the article is about and enough analysis and evaluation to help you decide whether or not you will use the article in your essay or paper.

Use these guidelines in the critique:

- Filter the information by creating a list of the headings and subheadings. (If the article has no headings, list the main ideas.)
- Define the premise or purpose of the argument *and* the reasoning strategy used.
- Provide a brief reasoned appraisal or assessment of the facts or argument presented in the article.
- Identify the article's main strengths and weaknesses.

3 Work in small groups.
   a What types of evidence are likely to be presented in a political broadcast?
   b How would you evaluate the quality of the evidence?
   c Design a set of questions you could use to evaluate the broadcast critically?

4 Choose two key terms from the list above to give

yourself broad topics to investigate. Find two articles on the topics and prepare a 200- to 300-word evaluative critique for each article. Prepare a brief introduction that identifies the two terms and why you chose them.

5 Write a persuasive essay by choosing a topic. It must be something debatable rather than a fact—for example, if you were to choose as your topic 'Sharks are dangerous', there would be no need for persuasion. However, if you chose the topic 'Sharks should be eliminated from our coastline', you have a topic that can be debated.

The persuasive essay will focus on only one side of the argument—your chosen side. It should not be a pros-and-cons essay or a personal opinion essay. A suggested outline for the persuasive essay is:

* Introduction to state the issue.

* State the facts surrounding the situation.
* State your case by discussing why your way is the best way, and by sharing evidence and expert opinions to support your position.
* Examine and refute the opposition by presenting negatives of the opposing view. If there are positive aspects of the opposing view, point them out, but compare them with the overall benefits of your case.
* Reconfirm your position by reviewing the main points of your argument.
* Conclude that your position is the preferred position based on all the information provided in the essay.
* You must back up your logic with evidence collected in research that supports your position.

EXPLORING THE WEB

1 Research critical thinking and reading by viewing the resources at Critical Thinking on the Web, <www.austhink.org/>.
   a Typical responses to a document or text are restatement, description and interpretation. Differentiate the three responses.
   b Why should academic readers take responsibility for their own assertions, rather than simply restating what an author has said?
   c Describe the process of inference.
   d Follow the link to 'Great Critical Thinkers'. What do great critical thinkers have in common?

2 Learn more about fallacies in reasoning. Visit Logical Fallacies: The Fallacy Files, <www.fallacyfiles.org>, to view examples of fallacies. View a collection of classic fallacies at The Fallacy Zoo, <www.goodart.org/fallazoo.htm>. Visit 'The Nizkor Project', <www.nizkor.org/features/fallacies/> for a description and examples of fallacies.
   a What is an argument?
   b Define the term 'fallacy' and give examples of fallacious arguments.

PROJECT WORK

Your task is to prepare either an inductive or deductive argument supporting a current controversial issue. Complete the following steps.
1 Research a current controversial issue.
2 Choose your position on that issue and write the premise, purpose or position statement.
3 Develop the argument (with an appropriate balance between logical and emotional appeals).

4 Write your conclusion and relate it to your original premise.
5 Analyse your project critically by asking questions that evaluate the type of reasoning in the argument, the quality of the evidence and your conclusion.
6 Make any corrections or improvements, and submit your project.

BIBLIOGRAPHY

Austhink. *Critical Thinking on the Web: A directory of quality online resources*, www.austhink.org/critical/index.htm, viewed 15 November 2007.

Browne, M.N. & Keeley, S.M. 2007. *Asking the Right Questions: A Guide to Critical Thinking*, 8th edn, Pearson Prentice Hall, Upper Saddle River, New Jersey.

Cottrell, S. 2003. *The Study Skills Handbook*, 2nd edn, Palgrave, New York.

The Critical Thinking Community. *Our Concept of Critical Thinking*, www.criticalthinking.org/, viewed 19 February 2008.

Curtis, G. *Logical Fallacies: The Fallacy Files*, www.fallacyfiles.org/, viewed 20 November 2007.

de Bono, E. 1990. *The Use of Lateral Thinking*, Penguin, Harmondsworth.

Dewey, J. 1933. *How We Think*, Heath, Boston.

Fisher, A. 2001. *Critical Thinking: An Introduction*, Cambridge University Press.

Fisher, A. & Scriven, M. 1997. *Critical Thinking: Its Definition and Assessment*, Centre for Research in Critical Thinking, UK.

Kurland, D. *Critical Reading*, www.criticalreading.com/, viewed 20 November 2007.

Labossiere, M.C. 'Fallacies' *The Nizkor Project*, www.nizkor.org/features/fallacies/, viewed 20 November 2007.

Maslow, A. 1954. *Motivation and Personality*, Harper & Row, New York.

Norris, S.P. & Ennis, R.H. 1989. *Evaluating Critical Thinking*, Midwest Publications, Pacific Grove, California.

Olderman, R.M. 1997. *10-Minute Guide to Business Communication*, Macmillan Spectrum/Alpha Books, New York.

Osland, D., Boyd, D., McKenna, W. & Salusinszky, I. 1991. *Writing in Australia: A Composition Course for Tertiary Students*, Harcourt Brace Jovanovich, Sydney.

Paul, R. & Elder, L. 2001. *Critical Thinking: Tools for Taking Charge of Your Learning & Your Life*, 2nd edn, Prentice Hall.

Petelin, R. & Durham, M. 1992. *The Professional Writing Guide: Writing Well and Knowing Why*, Longman Cheshire, Melbourne.

Seiter, J.S. & Gass, R.H. 2003. *Perspectives on Persuasion, Social Influence and Compliance Gaining*, Allyn & Bacon, USA.

Winn, W. & Beck, K. 2002. 'The persuasive power of design elements on an e-commerce web site', *Technical Communication*, Vol. 49, pp. 17–35.

Yoder, B. *The Fallacy Zoo*, www.goodart.org/fallazoo.htm, viewed 20 November 2007.

15

Oral business presentations

Photo: © lofoto | Dreamstime.com

1	▷	distinguish several approaches to oral business presentations and explain the purpose of each
2	▷	select, organise and shape relevant information, and explain the impact of different patterns of organisation on the audience
3	▷	describe the purpose of each part of an oral business presentation
4	▷	deliver an effective oral business presentation
5	▷	explain how to deal with challenging audience members.

OUTLINE

Types of business presentations

Planning the presentation

Preparing the presentation

Delivering the presentation

Managing challenging audience members

VIEWPOINT: IN BUSINESS: MEMORABLE END-OF-YEAR SPEECHES

Executive Speaking consultant Darren Fleming says the secret of a memorable [end-of-year] speech is keeping it short and focused on a purpose—whether it is to congratulate employees for good work, prepare employees for an upcoming product launch that requires team focus, or inspire them to meet next year's targets. He recommends that managers recap the year's highlights, drawing on the successes of team members present. Appropriate anecdotes of how the team dealt with a difficult client or how a task was completed can inspire pride and reward top performers. But make sure every statement and anecdote relates to the core purpose of the speech . . . .

End-of-year functions are one place where emotive language is appropriate because it is the most powerful language to inspire people and leave a lasting impression, Fleming says. Logical arguments may leave employees feeling uninvolved.

Adapted from D. Fleming, 'Points in business', *Business Review Weekly*, 30 November 2006, p. 54.

Within the workplace there are a number of occasions when staff members will need to speak on a work-related issue in a public forum. The oral presentations they may be asked to make include introductions, instructions, team briefings, brief oral reports, speeches of welcome and long formal presentations. Usually such presentations in the workplace aim to inform, persuade or entertain the audience. To achieve these aims, speakers need to plan well and present their material confidently.

TYPES OF BUSINESS PRESENTATIONS

OBJECTIVE 1 ▶
Distinguish several approaches to oral business presentations and explain the purpose of each

Several different approaches to speaking in public are available to you. The approach you choose depends on the occasion and the purpose of your presentation. In this chapter, seven different approaches to speaking in public are discussed:

1. prepared speeches
2. impromptu speeches
3. manuscript speeches
4. memorised speeches
5. oral briefings
6. team briefings
7. podcasts.

Using these approaches, ideas are presented for others to think about and consider. The intention is to have the audience respond in a certain way, so the speaker needs to prepare carefully and focus on the presentation's purpose. Regardless of the method you choose, you need to design a presentation that is relevant to the specific task and audience. In achieving this relevance the presentation will be designed to achieve one, or a combination, of three objectives: to inform, persuade or entertain (see Table 15.1).

A business presentation is designed to inform, persuade or entertain.

Hooke and Phillips (1996, p. 113) believe that no particular style is to be preferred; however, they regard the manner of delivery, visual presentation and building audience rapport as important factors. They list three factors in an effective style of presentation.

The first is the manner of delivery. The style of delivery is enhanced by using appropriate language, choosing words carefully, using plain English, aiming for clarity, and adopting suitable volume, pace and tone of voice. They also suggest using humour if appropriate, but not too much, and using repetition for emphasis. The second factor is visual presentation. Nonverbal behaviour such as maintaining eye contact and using gestures to add to the message, but not detract from it, improve the style of delivery. Using visual aids (that complement, rather than distract) to simplify complex points, and avoiding the tendency to rely on notes, has a positive visual impact on the audience. The third factor, building audience rapport, is enhanced by the use of personal stories and self-deprecation, if appropriate.

Table 15.1: Objectives and strategies	
Objective	**Strategies**
1 To inform	An informative speech conveys factual information, using clear examples and supporting material. It aims to develop ideas, pass on information, or show how something works or can be done. Balance the content and discussion to achieve an unbiased, objective presentation.
2 To persuade	A persuasive speech establishes a need in the audience and explains the action required to satisfy the need. A persuasive speech aims to influence the audience, to change their attitude, or to bring them round to a particular point of view.
3 To entertain	An entertaining speech uses a variety of techniques, such as humour, anecdotes, examples and quotations around a common theme, so that the audience enjoys the presentation. As a speaker, you may decide to combine informative or persuasive elements with entertainment.

Humour can maintain interest and help you to build rapport with the audience. It allows the audience to identify with the presenter. When building audience rapport, it is worth remembering that humour is a double-edged sword. It can unite or divide the audience. While one person may enjoy your humour, another may take offence. The best way to develop rapport with your audience is to use humour that is inclusive. Avoid jokes that are sexist, racist or likely to divide your audience.

The prepared speech

The **prepared speech** is planned and organised before the time of presentation. An outline is created, and notes that will act as prompts are prepared from the outline. A speaker who uses prompts well will appear spontaneous and relaxed throughout the delivery. In the preparation stage, note important ideas, phrases, quotations and statistics. While it is not essential to write down every word, some speakers who are really nervous may prefer to do so. More experienced and relaxed speakers try to choose some words at the time of presentation in order to increase spontaneity.

Try not to talk from a complete set of notes: it is too easy to lose the place or be tempted to read it word for word. This can bore the audience. A speaker who can address the audience without reading the prepared speech can maintain eye contact with them. Eye contact holds the audience's interest and allows the speaker to note their response to the presentation. Two of the most useful aids for those making a prepared speech for the first time in public are:

1. PowerPoint presentation
2. palm or cue cards.

PowerPoint presentations are discussed in Chapter 16.

Prepare **palm cards** by noting your main points and supporting information on them, then hold them in the palm of your hand as you deliver your speech. Cue cards and notes help the speaker to stay with the topic. They keep the outline and main points clear and ensure that the speaker's statements are accurate. A recommended size for palm cards is 75 mm by 130 mm. Avoid notebook-sized sheets because they are obvious to the audience and difficult to use.

The impromptu speech

The **impromptu speech** is unexpected and delivered without time for preparation. Some impromptu speeches are special occasion or courtesy speeches, such as welcomes, introductions and acknowledgments. As this style of speech usually takes the speaker by surprise, it is important to think clearly, analyse the situation quickly, and speak briefly and to the point. A successful formula used by many speakers for an impromptu speech is the PREP formula.

P   the main point
R   the reason
E   the example
P   the main point restated.

Speakers following this formula would start with the main point and then state the reason for talking about that point—for example, a longstanding commitment to an environmental issue. State the reason clearly. Follow with an example to illustrate the main point, draw the picture and involve the audience. Examples that add interest may come from the speaker's experience, someone else's experience, or a past experience common to the group. Alternatively, the speaker may use statistics or a relevant quotation. Conclude by restating the main point in different words. This reinforces the main point and gives strength and continuity to the delivery. This formula enables both speaker and audience to reach the main point quickly.

A **prepared speech** is planned and organised before the time of presentation.

Prompts help a speaker to appear spontaneous.

Palm cards are small cards bearing the main points and supporting information of a speech, which are held in the palm of the hand during the speech.

An **impromptu speech** is unexpected and delivered unprepared.

The manuscript speech

A **manuscript speech** is read.

The **manuscript speech** is researched and structured. It is suited to longer, more technical and difficult business presentations at meetings or conferences. A legal presentation, a parliamentary address, a press release, or a speech that is to be reported or quoted will use this speaking style. It is usually read.

Devices such as wide margins, large type and double spacing help the speaker to read while maintaining some eye contact with the audience. Experienced speakers avoid reading the entire speech word-for-word because they want to speak *to* the audience, rather than *at* them. This means involving them through use of the speaker's facial expression and eyes.

The memorised speech

A **memorised speech** is learned and recalled.

The **memorised speech** is suited to short talks. Aim to memorise the ideas and concepts without trying to recall every word. Experienced speakers memorise the introduction carefully. They are then able to sound relaxed and confident. You should rehearse, not only the words, but also the style of delivery so that it sounds natural. Practise maintaining eye contact with your audience to avoid that 'unfocused look' (looking upward) as you try to recall (visualise) your memorised text. Memorising the introduction is a useful strategy for any type of speech. Trying to memorise a long talk can cause problems: speakers may forget their place and panic.

The briefing

A **briefing** is a short oral report.

A **briefing** is a short, accurate summary of the details of a plan or operation. It is an oral report that aims to inform or persuade the listeners. Briefings are used to instruct, inform, propose or justify solutions, or to persuade the audience to act in a certain way. An oral briefing that invites the audience to participate is usually more effective than a long speech. Very few people enjoy sitting for a half-hour or more listening to one person. In planning and delivering this type of speech, remember:

- Prepare the briefing to achieve its specific purpose.
- Present background information.
- Discuss the available options or alternatives.
- Analyse the advantages and disadvantages of a particular course of action.
- Outline the positive impacts of the instructions or planned change.
- Encourage participation, questions and suggestions.
- Show interest in the responses.

The team briefing

Briefings by several members of a team are becoming more common. The members of the team consider as a group the purpose of the team presentation and the nature of the audience. Once the purpose is decided, the team designs the overall structure of the presentation and breaks it into logical sections. A particular part of the message is then allocated to each speaker. The team aims for a unified and coherent message, rather than a series of presentations from individual speakers. Hence, it is important to decide which member of the team will:

- present the introduction and beginning of the main body
- develop the main body and provide the supporting details
- reinforce the ideas in the main body and present the conclusion.

Consider also the techniques you will use to tie the ideas together into a whole presentation, and the audiovisual aids that will support the main ideas. Take care to speak to the audience rather than to other members on the team. When appropriate, refer to the ideas presented by other members of the team and link your content to theirs.

Throughout a briefing—regardless of whether it is an individual or team briefing—define the main terms and restate the main ideas in different words. Repetition emphasises the main points, helps understanding and reinforces the message.

The most frequent use of briefings is in staff meetings, in customer contacts, and in oral reports to supervisors and managers on potential successes or problems. Whatever the purpose of the briefing, it is often appropriate to leave a short memo report with the audience. People are more likely to remember a communication that combines both a spoken and written message.

The podcast

Podcasts are replacing or supplementing conference calls, training courses, briefings and other group communication activities. Podcasts aim to facilitate collaboration and sharing between users. In an effective podcast the presenter connects well with the audience and provides value. A clear purpose and pattern of organisation enables the audience to understand and become receptive to the ideas in the message.

A **podcast** is different from its face-to-face counterparts. Rather than a combination of spoken words and nonverbal communication in a shared physical space, the electronic message is a digital presentation at a distance. Instead of responding immediately as in a face-to-face interaction, time delays may happen before receivers log on to an electronic presentation. The shared experience of members of a podcast or blog happens in a virtual world rather than in a shared physical space. In the virtual world the receiver responds to elements such as language, ideas, structure and the presenter's nonverbal communication, voice pitch, pace, pausing and inflection.

> A **podcast** is a digital presentation distributed over the Internet for playback on portable media players and personal computers.

A simple structure provides a clear pathway for the receivers. Three clear points are more effective than ten. Any message sent electronically should have a strong opening to gain attention and a strong closing that receivers will remember easily.

Familiar, unambiguous language that moves straight to the point is easy to understand. Long phrases, redundancies and fillers used to 'fill in time' show that the presenter has not taken the time to think through his or her ideas or plan and structure the presentation. Ideas structured around a central point or main theme show the audience the progression of ideas and the relationship between them. Personal experiences, examples, illustration, facts and statistics add interest and catch the audience's attention. Effective podcasts emphasise common ground in terms of experiences, interests, values and goals between the presenter and the audience. The characteristics common to effective podcasts are presented in Chapter 21.

REVIEW QUESTIONS

1. List seven different approaches to public speaking.
2. a   Briefly explain the difference between an impromptu speech, a prepared speech and a team briefing.
   b   How is a podcast different from its face-to-face counterparts?
3. A business presentation is designed to achieve one of three objectives. Name the three objectives.

APPLY YOUR KNOWLEDGE

IMPROMPTU SPEECHES AND BRIEFINGS

1. Work in groups of six.
   a   Each person writes two topics for a speech on a piece of paper. Your topics can be your favourite subject (e.g. a favourite leisure activity, a pet hate, the impact of newspapers on public opinion) or any other suitable subject.
   b   Shuffle the pieces of paper and place them face down. Each member of the group selects one of the pieces of paper in turn

and gives an impromptu speech on one of the topics for a maximum of two minutes. As you speak, follow the PREP formula on page 415. You could take turns by alphabetical order of family name, or by age from oldest to youngest.

② What is the PREP formula? Use it to indicate the main points or structure you might use in giving an impromptu speech on the environment or physical fitness, or a toast to an unexpected guest at a function.

PLANNING THE PRESENTATION

OBJECTIVE **2** ▷
Select, organise
and shape relevant
information, and explain
the impact of different
patterns of organisation
on the audience

No matter which style of business presentation you make—prepared, impromptu, manuscript, memorised, briefing or podcast—it must be planned and prepared in a way that is relevant to the audience. In this preparation stage of a presentation, six steps are completed:

① Define the purpose.
② Analyse the audience.
③ Consider the context and setting.
④ Identify the main ideas.
⑤ Research and find supporting material for the message.
⑥ Plan and organise the material.

Each step will help the speaker to achieve a confident, well-paced delivery that engages and holds the audience's interest.

Defining the purpose

Define the presentation's purpose, intended aim or desired result. Communicate directly to the audience. Aim to catch the audience's attention and interest. It is important to define your objective, because communication without a clear objective is likely to wander and accomplish little (Hooke & Phillips 1996, p. 27). To define your objective, they suggest that it is important to 'picture what success looks like . . . be specific rather than general about your objectives'. Once the purpose is defined, develop the presentation to help the listener understand the message. It is also important to be clear about the nature of your intended message (Hooke & Phillips 1996). If you want to persuade, be clear on whether it is the whole group or only a few decision makers. If it is to inform, present in a way that differentiates between the facts and a point of view. When the purpose of your presentation is to inspire, the way or style in which you communicate is usually more important than the information in the message. Appearing natural and spontaneous is important in an entertaining presentation.

Analysing the audience

Consider your audience.

When the audience create in their minds the message the speaker intended to convey to them, the speaker has been successful. The audience's experience, age, interests and reasons for listening greatly influence the meaning they receive from the message. Analyse the audience so you know these details and can pitch the presentation to meet the needs, interests and level of knowledge of the receivers. If these details about the audience are not known, the speaker may make the mistake of delivering material that is too difficult or too basic, or that entirely misses the audience's needs and interests. It is easier to analyse a group of people with similar levels of skills or background; a diverse group of people requires more detailed analysis.

Lane (1987, pp. 242–4) suggests four basic questions be answered when analysing the audience:

① How much does the audience know about the topic?
② How involved is the audience in the topic or issue?

3 How controversial will the topic be for the audience?

4 How can the topic be related to audience interests?

Hooke and Phillips (1996, p. 50) comment that the more you know about your audience, the more effective you will be. Pitch the message at the audience's needs and wants, not your own. Know what they respond to and tailor your presentation accordingly.

Considering context and setting

Acknowledge the **context**, or situation, and deliver the presentation in a manner appropriate to that situation. The context may be an informal gathering of colleagues or a very formal public presentation or formal teleconference. Consider the number of people you will address. A presentation to the Chief Executive Officer and senior managers in the boardroom will be different from a briefing about a new project to a group of international colleagues via a podcast or a presentation of product details to a number of people at a trade show. The situation or context will impact on the preparation and delivery of the material. It is important to take it into account.

Context is the setting within which the presentation takes place.

Identifying the main ideas

In the planning stage, define your main idea. Decide the one message you want the members of the audience to remember. Prepare a one-sentence statement that links your subject and purpose to the audience's frame of reference. As the audience has only one chance to hear spoken ideas, the main idea and any supporting ideas need to be ordered logically and in a way that is easy to understand.

Focus attention on the central purpose of the presentation.

Consider the supporting ideas in terms of the message. Check that they link together and that they cover all the areas the audience needs to hear in order to understand the presentation's purpose. Structure the presentation into an outline that highlights the main ideas and organises them clearly and logically for the audience.

Research and investigation

Research and investigation are necessary to find facts, evidence and supporting documentation. Use the research to present an objective, impartial point of view that supports and develops the ideas in the outline. Chapter 13 discusses research more fully, identifying both primary and secondary sources.

Research from a variety of sources.

Choosing a pattern of organisation

In the outline the focus is on the presentation's main purpose. Organise the presentation to suit this purpose and the needs of the audience. This helps the speaker to present the material clearly, and makes it easy for the audience to understand the presentation. A clearly organised plan and a thorough understanding of the main ideas to be covered enable the speaker to appear relaxed and confident.

Organise the main ideas into a clear and logical outline.

Hooke and Phillips (1996, p. 51) comment that 'without an appropriate structure, a speech, a presentation, or even a conversation is just a collection of random thoughts. Your thoughts may be brilliant, but without an appropriate structure to tie them together, they will be unintelligible.' They list the following key points:

- Keep it simple: three points rather than 12; be concise.
- Prepare a strong opening and closing: the opening is crucial to gain attention and the closing is what the audience will remember.
- Present a transparent structure: signposting makes it easier to follow the presentation and take notes.
- Use notes effectively: notes eliminate the need to memorise; bullet points help to maintain structure and highlight key points; stage directions help with style of presentation.

LOGICAL PATTERNS OF ORGANISATION

The outline or pattern of organisation in an oral presentation is more than an exercise in logic. An effective pattern helps the audience to make sense of your presentation, follow your ideas, make connections between ideas and remember them. There are five basic logical patterns of organisation for oral presentations.

1 *Chronological order*. Three common chronological patterns are historical development, step-by-step patterns, and past–present–future patterns of development. For example, a step-by-step outline for the topic 'How to apply the PREP formula in an impromptu speech':

   a   Begin by stating the main point.

   b   State the reason for talking about the main point.

   c   Follow with an example to illustrate the main point and involve the audience.

   d   Conclude by restating the main point in different words to reinforce that point.

2 *Spatial order*. Geographical location is the most common use of this pattern. For example, a spatial order pattern for the topic 'Growth in employment':

   a   Employment rates in Queensland.

   b   Employment rates in New South Wales.

   c   Employment rates in the Australian Capital Territory.

3 *Cause–effect order*. This pattern is suited to a presentation where the goal is to achieve understanding or agreement. This order presents a causal relationship. For example, a cause–effect pattern for the topic 'Increase in housing costs':

   a   There has been a sharp increase in housing costs over the last decade [as a result]

   b   It is extremely difficult for a single-income family to purchase a house.

   The cause–effect pattern may be reversed to an *effect–cause sequence*, for example:

   a   It is extremely difficult for a single-income family to purchase a house. [this is because]

   b   There has been a sharp increase in housing costs over the last decade.

4 *Problem–solution*. This pattern is suited to persuasive presentations that propose a new policy or a specific course of action. For example, a problem-solution pattern for the topic 'Financing dental health':

   a   The current system of financing dental health nationally is inadequate. [to remedy this]

   b   A system of national dental health subsidies would provide access to dental care for all citizens.

5 *Topical*. Different topics require different structures, but one that applies to almost any topic is the inductive sequence. For example, an inductive pattern for the topic 'City council cuts to community services':

   a   The city council continues to cut budgets [and]

   b   Sporting fields and parks are poorly maintained [and]

   c   Inner-city garbage services have been cut [and]

   d   City library and art gallery services are reduced [therefore, logical conclusion]

   e   Our local government is not providing adequate services to local citizens.

PERSUASIVE PATTERN OF ORGANISATION: MONROE'S MOTIVATED SEQUENCE

Monroe's motivated sequence is a pattern of organisation appropriate to a presentation that is designed to persuade the audience to accept and respond to the speaker's message.

An accepted organisational pattern for persuasive oral presentations is the **Monroe's motivated sequence**, set out in Table 15.2. A persuasive oral presentation is required when you present a new idea, a proposal for change or a new project. When presenting a proposal to your manager, colleagues or clients, your intention is to:

- convince those who are undecided about the proposal or change
- convert any opposition to acceptance and sponsorship of your proposal.

Although the motivated sequence may be adapted to almost all speaking situations, Alan Monroe originally designed it to motivate and produce action on the part of the audience. The pattern works well when your presentation has a persuasive purpose, because the sequence of ideas motivates the audience to respond.

Step	Purpose	Strategies
Table 15.2: Monroe's motivated sequence		
1 Attention step	• To gain the attention and interest of the audience • To secure goodwill and respect	• Personal greeting • Rhetorical question • Startling statement/statistics • Quotation • Humorous anecdote • Illustration • Reference to a subject, event or occasion
2 Need step	• To describe the problem • To show the reason for improving the problem	• Statements supported by evidence • Illustration • Show ramifications • Be graphic • Pointing to help the audience understand the connection between them and the problem
3 Satisfaction step	• To offer solutions for the need described in the need step	• Support statements with evidence • Explanation • Theoretical demonstration • Practical experience • Meet objections and potential counterarguments
4 Visualisation step	• To increase audience's desire to adopt the solution and proposed action • To help the audience visualise results	• Take a positive approach to show what will happen on adoption • Take a negative approach to show what will happen if not adopted • Contrast to compare the outcome from adopting or not adopting your solution or proposed action
5 Action step	• To motivate the audience to act • To convey a sense of completion	• Inducement • Challenge • Illustration • Quotation • Summary

REVIEW QUESTIONS

4 What six steps would you take in planning a presentation?

5 Why is it important to consider the nature of your audience? Justify your answer.

6 Identify five basic logical patterns of organisation for oral presentations.

7 Explain the steps in Monroe's motivated sequence.

OBJECTIVE **3** ▶
Describe the purpose
of each part of an oral
business presentation

PREPARING THE PRESENTATION

After considering the purpose, audience and context, clearly identifying the main ideas, researching for supporting evidence and organising the material, the speaker must write the presentation. There are four steps to complete in this stage:

① Write the presentation.
② Rewrite for the ear.
③ Practise and revise the content.
④ Organise the visual aids.

At this stage, the aim is to order the information logically and to use clear, concise language. While the primary aim is to prepare a presentation suited to the needs of the audience, wise speakers will also prepare the material in a way that suits their own particular needs as a speaker. They will also think about their own credibility as a speaker and the credibility of their sources.

Lane (1987, p. 264) emphasises the need for speaker credibility and states that 'whatever the speaker's actual claim to expertness, trustworthiness, or dynamism, it is what the audience believes about the speaker that determines his or her credibility'. Initial credibility is based on the audience's knowledge of the speaker's background and reputation. A positive audience response during the presentation elicits additional credibility for the speaker. Credibility rises and falls as the audience responds to elements such as language usage, ideas and structure. Lane (1987, pp. 267–9) suggests the following ways of developing speaker credibility:

● communicating positive attitudes about self, the message and the audience
● finding and emphasising common ground (see Figure 15.1) in terms of experiences, interests, values, goals or cultural assumptions mentioned in the presentation
● preparing every presentation with care to allow the speaker to demonstrate confidence, clear reasoning and extensive knowledge.

Writing the presentation

Once a clear outline of the key or main ideas is prepared, the next step is to write the presentation. While the outline identifies the main ideas and their structure, each part of the presentation shows the

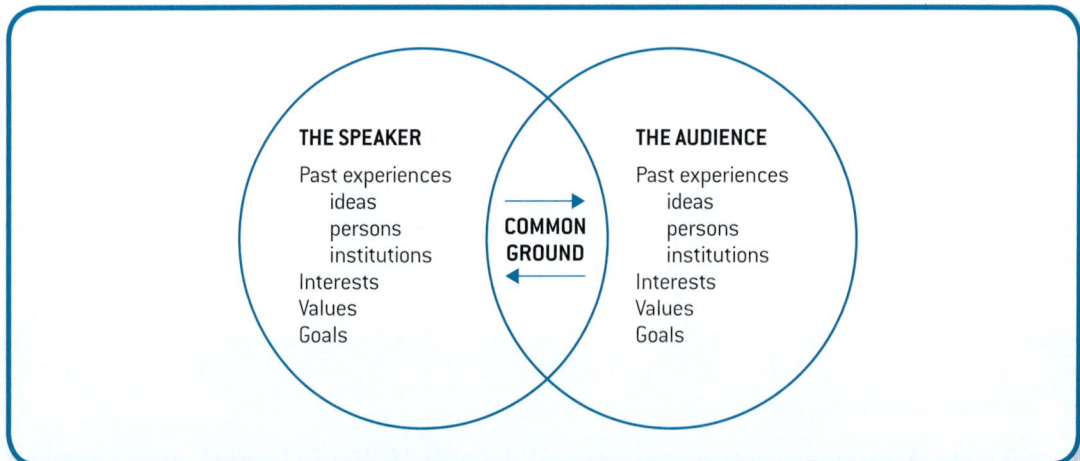

Figure 15.1: Diagram showing common ground between speaker and audience

Source: L.L. Lane, *By All Means Communicate*, Prentice Hall, New Jersey, 1987, p. 268. Reproduced with permission.

audience the progression of ideas and the relationship between them. An oral presentation has three main parts: introduction, body and conclusion (Table 15.3).

INTRODUCTION

The **introduction** is usually brief and leads into the main ideas in the body of the talk. It identifies the aim or main theme. The theme is the central issue that is discussed or developed in the body. As well as identifying the main theme, the introduction gains the audience's attention and establishes a relationship or rapport between speaker and audience. Strategies to use in the introduction are to:

- pose a question
- use humour appropriate to the audience and relevant to the topic
- relate a short **anecdote**
- present an interesting fact.

Identify the main theme clearly, followed by a preview of how your presentation is structured.

*The **introduction** should create interest.*

*An **anecdote** is a brief story or an example from past experience.*

BODY

The **body** contains the information. An experienced presenter acknowledges a typical listener's span of attention by having no more than three or four ideas in the talk. Organise these under headings and subheadings. Emphasise the main points and expand on these with supporting material. Examples of supporting material include:

- personal experiences
- examples
- illustrations
- facts
- statistics.

*The **body** develops the central theme.*

Refer to the strategies for planning and organising information in Chapter 13. These can be used to organise and sequence the information in the body of your presentation.

Add personal interest to the presentation by including anecdotes and experiences. A relevant personal story or example can make the difference between a dry presentation and an interesting, enjoyable and memorable talk. Compile or collect examples from friends, business associates, newspapers, television and radio. Table 15.4 gives examples of techniques to use to enliven a presentation. It indicates the speaker's motivation for using them and the audience's likely response to the strategy.

When choosing the words to use in a talk, be sure they are appropriate. When in doubt about the exact meanings of words, use a dictionary. A thesaurus can provide the best word or an alternative. Other reference material, such as an encyclopaedia, will give factual information, while a dictionary of quotations is a useful source of material that will make introductions and conclusions more interesting.

Table 15.3: Parts of an oral presentation	
Part	**Function**
1 Introduction	The introduction aims to catch the audience's attention and clearly identify the topic. It should be presented in a manner that stimulates interest and includes a preview of the presentation.
2 Body	The body develops the theme and provides supporting information. The body is the central part of the presentation. This section informs, persuades or entertains the audience.
3 Conclusion	The conclusion summarises the main ideas. The summary, or conclusion, is a brief overview of the key points. It reinforces the main ideas, giving the listeners a second chance to hear ideas presented earlier, and concludes by reminding the audience of your purpose.

Table 15.4: Techniques for enlivening a presentation

Technique	Audience response	Speaker's motivation
Defining a term	Clearer understanding	To sharpen understanding
Relating an experience	Interest	To arouse interest
Asking a question	Thinking through the answer	To allow audience to try out this information
Making an announcement	Attending	To catch audience's attention
Offering an explanation	Clearer understanding	To increase audience's understanding
Presenting different views on the subject	Thinking, questioning alternative	To raise curiosity
Making a request	Considering own response	To receive cooperation or funding
Providing a summary	Expecting end of talk	To reinforce ideas presented
Using a visual aid	Understanding and interest	To illustrate, enhance or support

CONCLUSION

The **conclusion** reinforces the main idea or presents an overview.

The **conclusion** is based on the arguments or information in the main body of the presentation. As a rule, it contains no new material. It should be the most memorable part of the presentation. To make an impact, use:

- a relevant anecdote
- a quotation
- an example
- a recommendation.

Speakers indicate that they are about to end the talk by using signalling words, such as:

- in conclusion
- to summarise
- in closing.

Your conclusion summarises the main ideas. In a long presentation it may be easier to review or summarise each section separately. The main point of your summary is to remind the audience of the purpose of the talk and its importance. Speakers may conclude by inviting their audience to take some action, by challenging them, or by asking for their cooperation or support. They also thank them for their interest.

Once the first draft of the presentation is written, practise the presentation, perhaps with a tape-recorder. Then replay it and prepare to rewrite for the ear.

Rewriting for the ear

Writing for the ear prepares the presentation as a spoken, rather than a written, channel of communication. Read the presentation aloud and listen for:

- a simple structure that is easy to follow
- an active voice with simple tenses
- words that are easy to hear and understand
- concise words with a clear meaning
- words that sound right together
- breathing spaces that add impact to the message

- words that help to move the listener through the introduction, body and conclusion.

This technique refines the presentation to meet the needs of a live audience who are listening to, rather than reading, the message.

Rehearsing and revising

Rehearse and revise by reading the content several times to become familiar with the main ideas and establish the delivery time. Most presenters have a time limit and it is important to stay within the limit. Rewrite parts that sound awkward. Allow for audience participation, especially in training sessions, seminars or instructions to staff.

Be ready to answer questions.

By practising the talk in front of a mirror, with someone listening or with a video- or tape-recorder, you are able to hear your voice and see your nonverbal communication. As you practise, you can decide how loudly or softly you want to speak, what parts of the presentation to emphasise and where to pause. You can also check the time it takes to make the presentation. Listening to yourself allows you to pick up all the 'you knows', 'ums' and 'ers', and any errors in pronunciation.

Be willing to answer questions from the audience: this creates an open exchange between an active audience and the speaker. Before they begin the talk, experienced speakers indicate when they will handle questions. This may be throughout the talk, at breaks between the main ideas or at the end of the presentation. An active audience responding to questions, or involving themselves in discussions and small group exercises, is more likely to remember the content. An active audience also provides the speaker with valuable feedback.

At this stage, organise visual aids to catch the interest of the audience and reinforce the ideas presented. Visual material is an important signal to people, so use it to improve any presentation. The term 'multi-sense' recognises that people receive messages in several different ways. This means that a delivery with a variety of communication channels will have a stronger impact than a delivery that depends only on voice and body movement.

Each visual aid should be simple and present only one idea; too much detail can distract from the main point. Chapter 21 discusses visuals and the use of technology in presentations.

REVIEW QUESTIONS

8 What is the role of the introduction? List two strategies you can use to make the introduction more effective.

9 Identify three techniques for enlivening the body of a presentation.

10 What is the role of the conclusion? Why do you think it is often seen as one of the most important sections of the presentation?

11 a What is meant by 'rewrite the presentation for the ear'?

b Why should you rehearse and revise the presentation?

12 What functions do audiovisual aids play in a presentation?

APPLY YOUR KNOWLEDGE

PLAN AND PREPARE THE PRESENTATION

1 As an active member of the Small Business Association, you have been outspoken about your concern at the decline in business activity in the Central Business District (CBD). You have been asked to address a gathering of interested parties that will include key representatives of state and local government bodies. The purpose of your presentation is to generate discussion about the recovery of the CBD and propose joint local and state-funded ventures to achieve this.

a   What speaking approach would be appropriate?

b   Outline the six steps you would take in preparing this presentation.

c   How would you investigate the plans and actions of other groups and individuals interested in the revival of the CBD?

d   Indicate three techniques you might employ in delivering the presentation to influence the audience's response, and two types of visual or graphic aids that might be useful.

2   In groups of three, prepare and deliver a team briefing to the large group. Assume you are a team of salespeople for a firm, Carp, a wholesale distributor of electrical retail goods. The purpose of your presentation is to introduce the audience, a group of buyers from a retail store, to a new product you would like them to order and sell through their retail store. You may need to emphasise:

- the product's features
- the benefits the store gains by purchasing from your team and by selling the product
- the advantages that this product has over other products.

The team's intention is to instruct and show the audience how to use, demonstrate and sell the electrical goods to the public. Evaluate the delivery using the self-evaluation checklist at the end of the chapter (page 432).

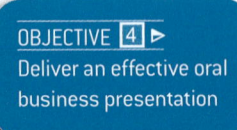

OBJECTIVE 4 ▶
Deliver an effective oral business presentation

Establish and maintain a relationship with the audience.

DELIVERING THE PRESENTATION

As there is no opportunity for the two-way give and take offered in conversations and group discussions, it is harder for public speakers to establish and maintain a relationship with the audience, and to engage their attention. A public speaker delivers one continuous message. Thus, to be effective, an oral presentation must combine the content, explanation and supporting information, visual aids, choice of words, vocal qualities, body movement and nonverbal communication in a way that catches the audience's attention. An effective oral presentation is relevant and accessible to the audience, allowing the speaker to establish and maintain a relationship with them throughout the delivery.

Involving the audience

Hooke and Phillips (1996, p. 160) believe that encouraging an audience to ask questions adds to the presentation. They state that a willingness to answer questions enhances credibility and keeps the audience interested. Answers to predictable questions can be prepared beforehand. It is important to 'listen intently for any underlying meaning in the question'. It is also necessary to treat the questioner with respect and to 'try to refer back to your presentation when answering the question'.

Casting

Jay and Jay (2000) believe that it is often better for more than one person to make the presentation, particularly if the audience is aware that the second presenter has the skill, experience or knowledge in that area. If a less senior person is a better presenter, Jay and Jay suggest that the senior person only introduce and close the presentation, especially a large one. By opening and closing the presentation, the senior person is publicly giving support to the presentation and is seen as the sponsor of the occasion. It is unwise for a senior person to take part in a presentation if they want to contribute to the discussion raised by the presentation, as it will be much more difficult to give advice or criticism.

Nonverbal behaviour includes movement of the hands, head, feet and legs, posture, eye movements, facial expressions, vocalisations and voice qualities.

Nonverbal communication

Speaking well not only requires careful planning and preparation; it also involves choosing an approach that suits the natural communication style of the speaker. The speaker is then able to match his or her verbal and **nonverbal behaviour** to the presentation.

The content of the talk and the physical and vocal behaviours of the speaker all communicate information to the audience. Aim to establish and maintain a confident, well-paced delivery that looks natural and comfortable. The first few times anyone gives a business presentation or speech they will probably feel nervous. Experience and good preparation are the best strategies for overcoming stage fright.

Nonverbal behaviours modify or change the spoken words in the presentation by repeating, contradicting, substituting, complementing or accenting the words. Some of the behaviours that impact on the presentation are:

- posture
- facial expressions
- appearance and dress
- gestures or movements of the hands, arms, shoulders and head
- voice quality
- volume
- articulation
- variation in the rate of speech.

An upright but not rigid posture with feet apart, knees slightly flexed, hands at side or holding palm cards allows you to look relaxed and confident. Speaking in public gives the audience only one opportunity to hear and understand the message. Hence, public speakers must talk clearly and at a suitable pace. A relaxed expression with an occasional smile reduces nerves, makes contact with the audience and helps them to understand the message they are hearing. Big and confident gestures release your nervous energy, reinforce the verbal message and enliven the presentation. Gestures keep your hands occupied and prevent you fiddling with keys or pens.

Refer to the sections on body movement and vocal qualities (paralanguage) in Chapter 4 for more information about voice quality, volume and the pace of presentation. Decide how to use these to project yourself as a confident speaker. Remember to dress appropriately. Look the part and you will catch the audience's attention.

A confident speaker appears natural and comfortable.

Handling anxiety or stage fright

Anxiety is a normal response to any situation that involves risk. Nervousness can be positive if it provides the extra emotional or physical energy necessary to deliver the presentation successfully. However, if the fear of speaking becomes distressing, it has reached the stage where the stress needs to be managed. Thorough preparation and research reduce anxiety and *stage fright*. Speakers who prepare their presentations thoroughly know their subject well and feel confident and secure in their knowledge. Thorough preparation also helps them respond to any questions and challenges offered by the audience.

Careful preparation and a practised delivery reduce anxiety.

Before the presentation, check all equipment to make sure that projectors, digital equipment, electrical outlets, seating arrangements, pens, paper and anything else needed are available and in working order. As an exercise for increasing breath control, breathe deeply, concentrating on the diaphragm rather than the lungs. Upright posture allows deep breathing. Movement while waiting and during the presentation can ease muscle tension and assist breathing.

Relaxation can help anxiety, but speakers need to find a method they feel comfortable with. Some people focus on their positive and competent aspects. Others choose to breathe deeply. Smile at the audience and someone is likely to smile back. This increases confidence and gives a feeling of empathy between speaker and audience. Move around during the talk and plan to use some type of visual aid, as this gives you 'something to do' physically. This can help to take away some of the nervousness.

Most people are more critical of their own performance than the audience is. An audience appreciates your preparation, knowledge and willingness to deliver the oral presentation. The key to overcoming stage fright is to know your subject and the content of the presentation. The more opportunities you have to practise, to speak at meetings, to instruct staff or to give a presentation to a group of clients, the more your confidence and skill will increase. Consider joining a public speaking group, a drama society or a professional association to gain experience, confidence and skills to use in public speaking.

REVIEW QUESTIONS

13 Explain two strategies a presenter can use to establish and maintain a relationship with the audience.

14 Describe nonverbal behaviours that impact on an oral presentation.

15 Identify two nonverbals that detract from a presentation and describe how to improve them.

16 Outline three strategies for reducing stage fright.

OBJECTIVE 5 ▶
Explain how to deal with challenging audience members

MANAGING CHALLENGING AUDIENCE MEMBERS

Whenever you stand in front of an audience as a manager, trainer, specialist or guest speaker, members of that audience may ask questions to seek more information, clarify ideas or state their own views. Some of the questions may be difficult or intimidating.

Before you begin the question and answer part of your presentation, announce the time limit for the question period and the question limit per person. These ground rules help to maintain control, avoid heated exchanges, and prevent one or two people from dominating the question period.

Establish the ground rules upfront to help maintain control during the question and answer period.

Fielding intimidating or difficult questions

Irrespective of the purpose or intent of an intimidating question, you must still answer it. Diplomacy and politeness are the key words in this situation. Avoid being drawn into an irrelevant argument, discussion or side issue. Stay with the relevant issue and address the question in a constructive manner. An intimidating question can be:

- critical of your research
- highlight an error of fact or judgment.

Whenever an intimidating question is asked, take a moment to reflect on the question while considering the following:

- Is the question relevant to what is being presented?
- Is the question out of context?
- Is the question simply a comment on what is being said?
- Is the question too controversial?
- Is the question simply promoting that person to the group?

Think carefully about the question and the questioner. The person who asks the question may be one of the types shown in Table 15.5.

Table 15.5: Types of people who question	
Questioners	**Proposed solution**
Digressors from the issue or topic	Remind them politely that we are discussing a different issue or topic.
Dominators of the discussion	Draw others in the audience into the discussion by asking, 'What do the rest of you think?'
Promoters of hidden agendas	Remind them politely to stay with the context of the presentation and discussion.
Self-promoters	Involve others in the discussion by asking general questions of the audience without dismissing the self-promoter.
Poor articulators	Rephrase the question back to them by saying, 'You mean . . .?' This avoids a 'putdown' and encourages the questioner to remain involved.

Some useful remarks to use as you handle difficult or intimidating questions are:

Respond honestly and assertively to hostile questions without anger or defensiveness.

- 'Let's deal with that question later.'
- 'We will be dealing with that issue later, so can we keep that question until then?'
- 'I simply do not know the answer. I will research it and get back to you.'
- 'This question does not seem to really apply to the topic, so shall we move on?'
- 'Can anybody else comment on this question?' (This response involves the audience and provides you with a moment to ponder the question.)

Avoiding panicking and engaging in defensive arguments

If you are asked a challenging question, avoid panicking or engaging in a defensive argument. The situation can be handled by not taking on your challenger. In a situation where you may know you are right, informing your challenger that they are wrong, or belittling them, is likely to inflame the situation. It is preferable to use the strategies set out in Table 15.5 to 'manage' your challenger and encourage further discussion with other audience members. You are then in the position of a moderator for this particular issue, rather than in conversation with the individual. This strategy means you are seen as being involved with the group and sharing information.

Some tips for handling challenging questions:

- Avoid panicking; take a moment to reflect on the question.
- If you don't know the answer, say you will research the question and get back to them.
- Involve the audience along the lines of: 'This is an excellent question. What do you think?'
- When a critical question is asked, agree with the questioner on some level, however small, as it helps to establish rapport and shows you are open-minded.
- Try to anticipate tricky or critical questions; this strategy will help you to develop appropriate responses that will reflect well on you.

Irrespective of how a question is asked, always be assertive, clear and polite with your answer. You may feel you are under attack, but remaining calm and courteous at all times will help to defuse what could become a volatile situation and prevent matters from deteriorating. The assertion skills in Chapter 6 provide a number of strategies you can use. Questioning and feedback skills are particularly useful.

REVIEW QUESTIONS

17 List two techniques that would provide a focus and maintain attention on the presentation's most important point.

18 What can presenters do to maintain control during a question-and-answer period of a presentation?

19 Briefly describe two strategies you can use to manage challenging or difficult questions.

APPLY YOUR KNOWLEDGE

DELIVERING A PRESENTATION

1 a Working in groups of three, choose *one* of the following topics. Each person in the triad is to prepare a three-minute presentation on that one topic (i.e. the same topic) but one member will aim to inform the audience, another to persuade and the third to entertain.

- Sexual equality
- A current business issue
- Competition is necessary
- We have too much leisure time
- My favourite music

- Charities are necessary
- The benefits of technology.

b   In your presentation outline, clearly distinguish between the introduction, main body and conclusion. As you prepare, include at least one of the strategies suggested in this chapter for the introduction, body and conclusion.

c   Prepare a set of palm cards.

d   Practise your presentation in front of the other two members of your group. The two observers should complete the self-evaluation on page 432 and discuss the evaluation once the speaker has finished.

e   After the discussion, list two ways to improve your nonverbal communication.

f   Deliver the presentations to the large group. Ask them to identify which of the three presentations is designed to inform, persuade or entertain.

2 View a television speech by a politician or public figure.

a   How did the speaker gain the audience's attention in the introduction?

b   'Both the meaning and feeling are conveyed by your voice.' Briefly explain this statement. Then explain how your speaker used their voice to make their presentation.

c   Comment on the speaker's nonverbal communication.

d   What strategy did the speaker use to conclude the speech?

SUMMARY OF LEARNING OBJECTIVES

 1 ▷ DISTINGUISH SEVERAL APPROACHES TO ORAL BUSINESS PRESENTATIONS AND EXPLAIN THE PURPOSE OF EACH

The six types of business presentations are: prepared speeches, impromptu speeches, manuscript speeches, memorised speeches, oral briefings, team briefings and podcasts. Successful speakers consider the advantages and disadvantages of each approach, and present their ideas in the style suited to the occasion.

 2 ▷ SELECT, ORGANISE AND SHAPE RELEVANT INFORMATION, AND EXPLAIN THE IMPACT OF DIFFERENT PATTERNS OF ORGANISATION ON THE AUDIENCE

The information selected should suit the speaker's needs as the sender of the message, and the needs of the receiver. To meet these needs, decide on the purpose of the talk, complete an analysis of your audience, and consider the context or situation. The chosen pattern of organisation must focus the audience's thoughts on the main purpose of the presentation. Without a structure the presentation is just a collection of random thoughts. The pattern identifies what you are talking about, why and in what order. Logical patterns include chronological, spatial, cause–effect, problem–solution and topical. A persuasive

pattern of information is used to convince the audience to accept your proposal.

Careful planning allows speakers to develop the aim of their presentation clearly. Experienced speakers research and find support for their main ideas and develop a logical structure for them. They organise the ideas to give an interesting introduction, a body that develops the main ideas and an effective conclusion.

 3 ▷ DESCRIBE THE PURPOSE OF EACH PART OF AN ORAL BUSINESS PRESENTATION

The introduction creates interest, establishes your credibility and leads into the main ideas in the body. The body develops the central theme. In the body, connect the ideas and provide a clear pathway for your audience to follow. Your aim is to hold their attention and enable them to understand your topic. The conclusion reinforces the main idea and describes the next steps. It points the way ahead.

 4 ▷ DELIVER AN EFFECTIVE ORAL BUSINESS PRESENTATION

As you gain experience and confidence in speaking in public you will need fewer notes and an outline that is reduced to key words and phrases. Speak directly to your audience and make eye contact in particular. A friendly voice and a smile create a feeling of interest. Enthusiasm, humour, gestures and facial expression all attract the audience's attention and interest. Use a high level of energy to avoid a monotonous tone in delivery.

Relate your subject to your audience's needs. Pose a question, use humour (when appropriate), give examples and illustrations. Explain the relationship between your subject and ideas that are familiar to the audience. Illustrate your ideas with relevant and clear visuals.

Convey the content in clear language that signals and links new ideas. Encourage participation, questions and suggestions, and listen to and acknowledge this feedback. Effective speakers show their interest nonverbally with a smile, a nod, a hand gesture or a forward movement of the body.

5 ▷ EXPLAIN HOW TO DEAL WITH CHALLENGING AUDIENCE MEMBERS

Avoid being drawn into side issues by irrelevant arguments or questions asked by any digressors, dominators or self-promoters in the audience. Respond honestly and assertively to hostile questions without anger or defensiveness. Diplomacy and politeness will help you to manage any challenger, and encourages discussion and involvement from others in the audience.

KEY TERMS

anecdote	423	impromptu speech	415	nonverbal behaviour	426
body	423	introduction	423	palm cards	415
briefing	416	manuscript speech	416	podcast	417
conclusion	424	memorised speech	416	prepared speech	415
context	419	Monroe's motivated sequence	420		

ACTIVITIES AND QUESTIONS

1   Hooke and Phillips (1996) list the manner of delivery, visual presentation, and building audience rapport as important factors in an effective public speaking style. Prepare a self-evaluation tool to evaluate the style of delivery in an informative prepared presentation. Each statement in the self-evaluation tool should use the imperative tone (start with a verb). Ensure the self-evaluation covers the three factors listed by Hooke and Phillips.

2   Assume you work in a supervisory position in a large organisation. The organisation has recruited ten new people to start work in clerical positions in a fortnight. You have been asked to conduct the orientation session for the new employees. Your aim is to welcome and introduce them to the organisation and raise their awareness of their role in the firm. You are also to instruct them in their hours of work, working conditions, pay periods, and the company's expectations of performance.

Prepare and deliver a presentation suited to this orientation session. Invent the necessary details.

3   **Speaking in public**

a   Choose a topic or issue. Write a memo report (see Chapter 18) on your chosen topic.

b   Research, plan, practise and deliver a five- to eight-minute presentation on the same topic. Follow these steps.

i   Use the self-evaluation checklist below to check and evaluate the planning of your presentation.

ii   Use the audience analysis chart in Table 15.6 to help you choose and focus your topic.

iii   Then decide on the following. Do you want to design a presentation that:
   • informs
   • persuades
   • entertains or
   • uses a combination of these?

iv   Plan the presentation. As you plan, use a format similar to Table 15.7 to evaluate your audience. Decide on the following in relation to your audience:
   • what they already know
   • things they need to know
   • what they want to know.

v   Practise the presentation with one other person. As you speak, your partner is to complete the self-evaluation, below. Use this feedback to make refinements to your presentation.

vi Deliver the presentation to the large group.

SELF-EVALUATE YOUR SKILL

PLANNING AND DELIVERING THE PRESENTATION

In the planning stage, have I:	Yes	No	Unsure
decided on the purpose?			
analysed the audience?			
chosen the most appropriate speaking approach?			
researched effectively?			
listed and ordered the main ideas logically?			
prepared an introduction?			
prepared the main body?			
listed some examples to illustrate the main point?			
prepared suitable audiovisual material?			
prepared a conclusion?			
provided supporting ideas?			
practised the presentation?			
In the delivery stage, did I:	**Yes**	**No**	**Unsure**
identify the presentation's purpose?			
use language suited to the audience?			
use suitable strategies in the introduction, body and conclusion?			
show progression and relationships between each part of the presentation?			
use different forms of suitable support material?			
make effective use of my voice?			
have eye contact with the audience?			
handle any stress or anxiety?			
demonstrate confidence?			
establish and maintain a relationship with the audience?			
finish within the time limit?			

Table 15.6: Audience analysis chart

Name	Age group	Workplace	Interests	Plans for the future
1				
2				
3				
4				
5				
6				
7				

Table 15.7: Evaluation/summary of audience

In general, the audience . . .
My relationship to the audience is that of . . .
What topics from the workplace or the general topics would be of interest to the audience?
What topics from the workplace or the general topics interest me?
The audience's attitudes to the topic are likely to be . . .
What similarities exist between members of the group?
What differences are obvious in the group?

EXPLORING THE WEB

1 The 'Creative quotations' site, <www.creative quotations.com/>, offers over 50 000 quotes. Browse the site to find relevant quotes that will add interest to your presentations.

2 Find three websites that deal with the use of humour in public speaking or presentations. How effective is humour, and why? How can it be used successfully? What are the pitfalls?

3 Visit the 'Speech tip' site, <www.speechtips.com>, to gather ideas about planning, writing and delivering oral presentations.

4 Visit 'Art of speaking in public: tips, techniques, training, famous speeches, humour and quotes', <www.angelfire.com/ab/speakers/main.htm>. It has 60+ tips on effective public speaking.

PROJECT WORK

Imagine you have been asked to sell the idea of a daily exercise program to improve fitness and motivation in a particular workplace.

a Identify your objectives in making the presentation.

b Plan and work successfully towards achieving your presentation objectives by:
   • defining your presentation objectives clearly

   • analysing your audience strategically in terms of demographics, motivations, values and 'hot buttons'

   • preparing content strategically with a focus on audience benefits, and using delivery tactics to meet your goals

- developing your central idea or thesis so that you can get your point across in 30 seconds or less
- conducting research and consulting experts to

boost your credibility, ensure your currency, and identify differing perspectives for your topic.

c   Then write and deliver your presentation.

BIBLIOGRAPHY

Ehninger, D., Gronbeck, B., McKerrow, R. & Monroe, A. 1992. *Principles and Types of Speech Communication*, HarperCollins, New York.

Hahner, J.C. 2002. *Speaking Clearly: Improving Voice and Diction*, McGraw-Hill, New York.

Henderson, J. & Henderson, R. 2007. *There's No Such Thing as Public Speaking: Make Any Presentation or Speech as Persuasive as a One-on-One Conversation*, Prentice Hall, Upper Saddle River, New Jersey.

Hooke, J. & Phillips, J. 1996. *Getting Your Message Across*, Simon & Schuster, Sydney.

Jay, A. & Jay, R. 2000. *Effective Presentation*, Prentice Hall, New Jersey.

Lane, L.L. 1987. *By All Means Communicate*, Prentice Hall, New Jersey.

Lucas, S. 2003. *The Art of Public Speaking*, 8th edn, McGraw-Hill, New York.

Maes, J., Weldy, T.G. & Icenogle, M.L. 1997. 'A managerial perspective: oral communication competency is most important for business students in the workplace', *Journal of Business Communication*, Vol. 34, Issue 1, January, pp. 67–80.

Robinson, O. 2003. 'Speak easy, my career', *Sydney Morning Herald*, 19–20 July.

Seiler, W.J. & Beall, M.L. 2007. *Communication: Making Connections*, 7th edn, Allyn & Bacon, USA.

16

Communicating through visuals

Photo: iStockphoto

VIEWPOINT: VISUAL ORGANISATION

'Visual communication can be thought of as two intertwined parts: personality, or look and feel, and visual organization. The personality of a presentation is what provides the emotional impact. Creating an appropriate personality requires the use of colors, type treatments, images, shapes, patterns, and more, to "say" the right thing to your audience.

Visual organization is how we see visual relationships. Whenever we attempt to make sense of information visually, we first observe similarities and differences in what we are seeing. These relationships allow us to not only distinguish objects but to give them meaning. For example, a difference in:

- color implies two distinct objects (or different parts of the same object)
- scale suggests one object is further from us than the other
- texture (one is more blurry) enforces this idea and so on.

Once we have an understanding of the relationships between elements, we can piece together the whole story and understand what we are seeing.'

Excerpt from L. Wroblewski, 'Visible narratives: understanding visual organization', *User Interface Engineering*, Originally published 20 January 2003, www.uie. com/articles/visible_narratives/, viewed 12 February 2008. Reproduced with permission.

No matter how good a report or written or oral presentation is, it can be further improved by the use of graphics or visuals: a picture is worth a thousand words. By using visuals at the appropriate points the presenter captures the audience's attention and maintains interest. Visual aids can help to simplify complex ideas and lead to more reader or audience involvement. After a presentation the words may be forgotten. The visuals that went with it are the more memorable part of the message.

Graphics organise information, such as percentages, numbers or rates of change. They show relationships, highlight trends, and help to sort, classify and group data. Graphics also clarify technical ideas and emphasise important points. The information in graphics should be accurate, descriptive and up to date.

Lane (1987, p. 242) defines an **audience** as 'an assembly of people related by a common purpose to hear one or more speakers. Every audience has needs and expectations that it wants the speaker to meet.' An audience analysis in the planning stage allows presenters to adapt the content in the message and choose the appropriate visuals and technology to meet the needs of the particular audience as they prepare the presentation. Chapter 15 discusses ways to analyse the content needs of the audience.

Studies conducted by Mehrabian (1971) showed that only 7% of what an audience believes and understands comes from the text, 38% comes from what it hears and 55% from what it sees.

The purpose of an oral business presentation is to inform, persuade and engage the audience. Appropriate visual aids add interest and enhance the message. Leeds (2003, p. 20) comments: 'Visual aids used badly are not aids: they cost you 90% of the audience's attention. Used well, you gain 90% of their attention.'

Before choosing the technology and visual support materials, decide how comfortable the audience will be with the technology; how the technology will aid their understanding of the unknown, the unfamiliar or the unclear; and how it will enhance the presenter's ability to meet the audience's needs and expectations.

INCORPORATING GRAPHICS

OBJECTIVE **1** ▶
Explain how visual aids enhance written and oral business presentations

Graphics can be used for a variety of purposes:

- to reinforce and complement the ideas in the text
- to clarify complex material, particularly figures and statistics
- to show the total picture
- to emphasise the written ideas
- to link and unify ideas
- to catch the reader's attention
- to help the reader remember the information.

As presenters plan and structure the content for their oral presentations they rely on left brain thinking. The left side of the brain controls many of the intellectual processes, such as logic, speech and language. By adding visual aids to the spoken presentation the presenter is able to engage right brain functions in the audience, such as perceptual insight and feelings. Visuals can balance the audience's left and right brain thinking.

Maintaining audience attention

By varying the texture in the presentation a presenter is able to enliven it. 'Change—whether in the voice level, pace of presentation, body movement, supporting materials—is the most important agent for maintaining attention,' state Putnis and Petelin (1999, p. 191). The average **attention span** for adults is about 20 minutes. An experienced presenter stages his or her presentation to cater for this attention span.

A number of factors compete for the audience's attention. Distractions in the venue, such as external noise and excessive heat or cold, or internal factors such as tiredness, hunger and personal

Graphics convey information visually.

An **audience** is a group of readers or listeners of a particular piece of writing, or oral or visual presentation.

Attention span is the time the average adult can attend to and process the information in a speaker's presentation.

problems, can distract the audience. An audience may pay more attention to the presenter's poor use of technology and visuals than to the message.

Presenters who analyse their audience well use the appropriate level of complexity in their presentations to meet the perceptual capabilities of the audience. They provide enough stimulation to capture the audience's attention. While a message that is below the audience's level will bore them, one that is too complex will lose them. Presenters who want to hold the audience's attention for more than 20–25 minutes must vary the texture of the presentation by using their voice and nonverbals well, and by introducing variety into their presentation through the use of visuals and technology.

Enhancing the message

One of the challenges facing presenters is how to make their presentations live for their audience(s). The various **visual aids** and technology a presenter can use to facilitate a presentation include:

- whiteboards (interactive, electronic and standard)
- prepared flip charts
- physical objects
- working models
- DVDs and videos
- PowerPoint presentations
- video and teleconferencing

Visual aids are graphics and visual devices used by a speaker to improve the audience's understanding.

Regardless of the type of aid or technology, use the three criteria—simplicity, clarity and visibility— to evaluate the technology and visuals. There is no point in using poor-quality visuals. An audience should not be confused by a complicated visual. Visuals that are too small or prepared in messy, illegible handwriting can irritate and confuse the audience. Any visual should simplify and clarify the ideas in the presentation. A visual should not distract from the presentation.

Staging the presentation

A message is more powerful and interesting when it is communicated visually as well as verbally. The visuals add another dimension that improves the presentation. The best presenters realise their audience(s) are active rather than passive receivers.

As a general rule, presenters should provide a change of pace, medium or subject every ten minutes or so to maintain the audience's attention and interest. Audio or visual aids provide the change of pace needed to add texture, maintain attention, let the audience know what is coming and make an impact. Jay and Jay describe seven key areas to address in a presentation, as set out in Table 16.1.

Selecting graphics

Graphics that misrepresent information mislead the reader. Once this is realised, the credibility and value of the writing is likely to be questioned. Be careful not to give a false impression by exaggerating similarities or differences. Graphics of substance show complex ideas clearly and concisely, giving the reader the greatest number of ideas without cluttering the page. Successful graphics explain, simplify and emphasise the main relationships. Select the graphics with these criteria in mind.

Select graphics that present a true and accurate picture.

REVIEW QUESTIONS

1. What percentage of what an audience believes and understands comes from the text, from what the audience hears and from what the audience sees (Mehrabian 1971)?
2. What does a successful graphic do?
3. Identify three criteria you can use to evaluate the technology and the visuals.

Table 16.1: Key areas to address in a presentation

Key area	Strategy
1 Texture (refers to different ways of addressing the audience)	One person talking alone for two hours, without aids, represents monotony rather than a sufficiently varied texture. Presenters need to analyse what the audience is getting: • Is there too much solid talk at any point? • Will they be punch drunk with slide sequences? • Are the demonstrations wasted by being too close? Could they be split up? • Does it get too jumpy and bitty? Drop dull patches. Make cuts and changes without losing hold of the main purpose.

2 Attention curve	In a 40-minute period, psychologists have identified the response of an audience: it starts high, drops fairly shallowly in the first ten minutes, then drops more steeply, reaching the lowest point after about 30 minutes; it starts again to rise steeply and is high for the last five minutes. Jay and Jay (2000, pp. 19–21) state that from this analysis:
	• 'a shorter "period"—say 25 to 30 minutes—contains a higher percentage of high attention'
	• 'the most important points for an audience to remember must be at the beginning and the end' and 'in particular the last picture and sentence or phase of each period, which stay in the mind a little longer before new words and images are piled on top, are especially important'.
	  • after the first 10 minutes, 'the greatest attention must be paid to texture variation and all other devices to revive and retain attention'.
	   Let the audience know when the session is ending, so that their attention will rise.

3 Breaks and session lengths	Realise that breaks are a high point. Have two-minute breaks rather than one of 20 minutes. Try to end each session on a high note.
4 A peep behind the curtain	Use in smaller presentations rather than larger ones with printed programs. Indicate to the audience what is coming. Give the audience something to look forward to.
5 Audience participation	Involve the audience. Jay and Jay point out that a joke is an obvious example—the audience's laughter means they are participating—however, 'a joke that is not laughed at is a major disaster'. Give the audience something to hold, even to keep, perhaps a sample or an example, which can be passed along each row.
6 Impact	Identify three categories of visual aids: explanatory, corroborative and impact. Use explanatory visuals such as pictures, diagrams and models to describe and explain key concepts and ideas. Use corroborative visuals to back up the argument and lift interest. Answer the question posed, premise or purpose of the presentation with a visual impact. Ask yourself: 'What pictures do I want the audience to carry away in their minds?' Place the impact visuals in key positions such as first or last thing in the session. Leave on show through the break.
7 Casting (refers to who should deliver the presentation)	Decide to use more than one presenter to add variety or to combine the knowledge and skill of two or more people in the one presentation. Allocate appropriate time to different presenters; e.g. a senior person may open and close the proceedings and the expert in a particular area makes the main presentation. Make arrangements for an understudy for an important presentation; e.g. a large international conference cannot be left without a speaker. Use a technical assistant if the technology is complicated.

Source: Adapted from A. Jay & R. Jay, *Effective Presentation*, Prentice Hall, New Jersey, 2000, pp. 17–25.

GRAPHICS IN REPORTS AND WRITTEN PRESENTATIONS

◄ OBJECTIVE 2
Identify the features of graphics suited to reports and written presentations

Fardell (1998, pp. 1–2) comments that although graphs and charts can be the most effective way to convey statistical data, 'they often impede information transfer because they have not been designed for the reader's needs'. Research by the Australian Bureau of Statistics suggests that the effectiveness of any graph or chart can be tested by the following questions:

- Does it show data clearly without distorting the facts?
- Is too little or too much information presented in the available space?
- Does it convey an unambiguous message about the data?
- Is the reader encouraged to analyse the data?
- Are large quantities of data made coherent?
- Are there any superfluous decorative design elements?

Concepts, related information, trends, movement and changes in time, comparisons and spatial distributions can all be shown graphically. Some of the main types of graphics used in report writing are tables, line graphs, column graphs, bar graphs, dot graphs, pie charts, diagrams, photographs, illustrations and maps. Each has particular strengths and weaknesses. Table 16.2 compares the advantages and disadvantages of several kinds of graphics.

When they are used effectively, the ideas and information are complemented by the visual or graphic aid and are more easily understood by the reader.

Table 16.2: Comparison of different kinds of graphics

Graphic	Advantage	Disadvantage
Table	Offers comprehensive detail and allows clear comparisons between large amounts of quantitative data	Difficult to read quickly and hard to recognise relationships
Diagram	Allows emphasis to be placed on the details of interest by presenting a simple representation; can show a cross-section	Easy to miss the main point if the diagram becomes too cluttered with detail
Line graph	Indicates the movement and trends in the data clearly	Inappropriate labels and scales can make it difficult to interpret the information
Column or vertical bar graph	Offers clear comparisons between items or from one period to the next	Difficult for the eye to interpret size and proportions
Horizontal bar graph	Allows clear and direct comparisons in size	Difficult to read when there are too many grouped or stacked bars in one graph
Dot graph	Enables the eye to pick up the values more quickly	Awkward to read unless the order of presentation moves down from the largest to the smallest figure
Pie chart	Shows relative proportion and the importance of each part to the unit	Difficult to judge area and size differences
Photograph or illustration	Shows subject as it appears; has immediate impact	Difficult to see the point because of detail
Map	Shows a large amount of detail in one representation	Difficult to read unless the scales, legends and labels are concise and easy to read

Presenting data, facts and figures

Tables, line graphs, bar graphs, dot graphs and pie charts present facts and figures. They provide evidence and support for arguments in written and oral presentations. Browne and Keeley (2007, p. 155) suggest: 'Statistics are evidence expressed as numbers. Such evidence can seem quite impressive because numbers make evidence appear to be very scientific and precise, as though it represents "the facts". Statistics, however, can and often do lie! They do not necessarily prove what they appear to prove.'

Think critically to identify and avoid misleading facts and figures, fallacious arguments and invalid conclusions.

Apply your critical thinking skills when gathering and compiling facts and figures into graphics. Ask critical questions. Are the statistics deceptive? Are they omitting information to deceive? Are they biased or confusing? Protect your reputation by providing useful objective information and avoiding the misuse of facts and figures.

TABLES

Tables present facts and figures.

Tables are used to present precise data, facts and figures. Clear comparisons of a large amount of quantitative data can be given in a way that is easy to understand. A table emphasises similarities or differences in the data. Tables present related information in parallel lists or columns (see Table 16.3). As a result, relationships are shown more clearly and less space is needed than for a long description interspersed with figures. It is also easier to locate specific figures from a table than from a string of sentences. The data in tables should be right-hand justified in each column, as this positioning is easier for the eye to follow down the column. When the data in a table are graphed, the information and relationships are further simplified. As a result, the graph gives a clearer representation of the information.

LINE GRAPHS

Line graphs show trends over time for variables that have a continuous relationship.

Line graphs show movement. Their main purpose is to indicate trends over time. Whenever information on quantities is presented visually in a line graph, there is a beginning point; that is, a point of origin. A vertical and a horizontal line are drawn at right angles from this point. Each point on the graph that shows the relationship between the two variables portrayed in the graph is projected into the two-dimensional space created by the axis and plotted at the point where the two variables meet.

Line graphs can have one line, known as a simple line chart, or a number of lines, called a multi-line chart. Multi-line charts should be limited to three or four lines. Line charts or graphs are used when one factor in time is compared with another over a period of time (see Figure 16.1). Line charts show clearly the rate of change in a given value or item over time. The data are plotted as points connected by segments of a line that becomes the line graph or chart.

Table 16.3: Table showing Company XYZ overheads by category and year						
Overheads	2004	2005	2006	2007	2008	2009
Advertising and promotion	11 000	10 000	7 000	10 000	12 000	14 000
Premises	33 000	30 000	22 000	28 000	61 000	63 000
Motor vehicles	5 000	4 000	3 000	6 000	6 000	7 000
Communications	15 000	11 000	10 000	12 000	17 000	20 000
Finance	5 000	4 000	3 000	10 000	14 000	18 000
Equipment	9 000	8 000	6 000	15 000	22 000	24 000
Employees	261 000	210 000	176 000	210 000	239 000	250 000
Administration	101 000	95 000	69 000	70 000	74 000	76 000
Total overheads	440 000	372 000	296 000	361 000	445 000	472 000

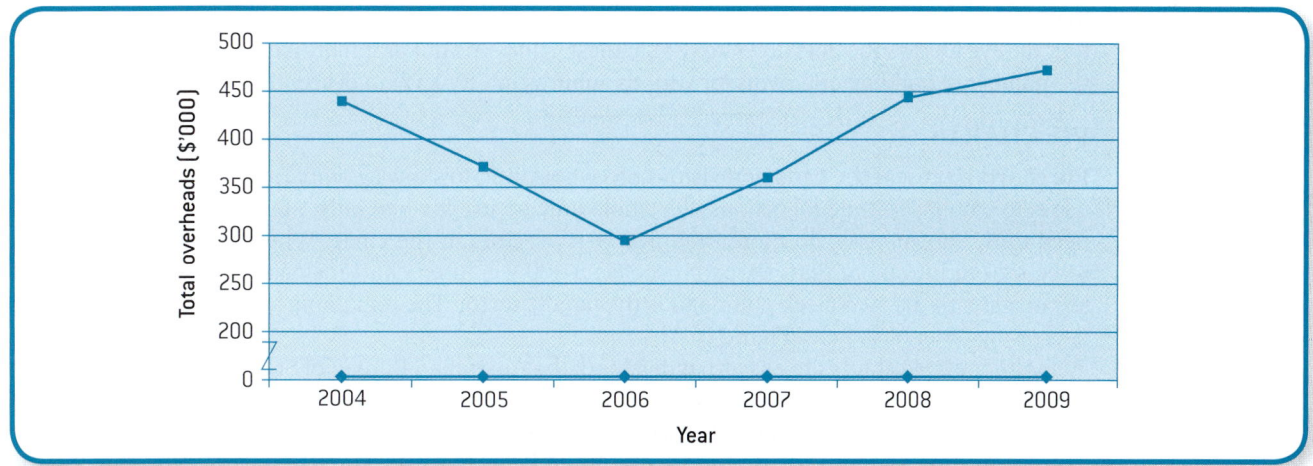

Figure 16.1: A line graph showing total overheads for Company XYZ by year

COLUMN OR VERTICAL BAR GRAPHS

Column graphs or **vertical bar graphs** are used to show changes from one time period to the next, or to compare one item with another. The columns in the graph can be single, grouped or stacked to show the relative size of sections when a whole unit is broken up into several parts. This kind of information is best shown in grouped columns, as it is more difficult for the eye to interpret size and proportions on a stacked bar graph.

Vertical bar graphs usually show five or six items at a maximum. The vertical bar graph in Figure 16.2 is a column graph showing the percentage of a company's turnover applied to various expenses and the percentage of business turnover remaining as net profit for the quarters ending June and September 2009.

A **column** or **vertical bar graph** is a graphic that uses vertical columns to show change over time or to compare amounts/items.

Bar graphs make comparisons.

DOT GRAPHS

A **dot graph** is used when there are six or more variables. The Australian Bureau of Statistics now tends to use dot charts instead of bar charts because the eye picks up the value more quickly, making dot charts easier to interpret. The dot graph makes it easy to visually connect the graphed point back

A **dot graph** is used when there are six or more variables.

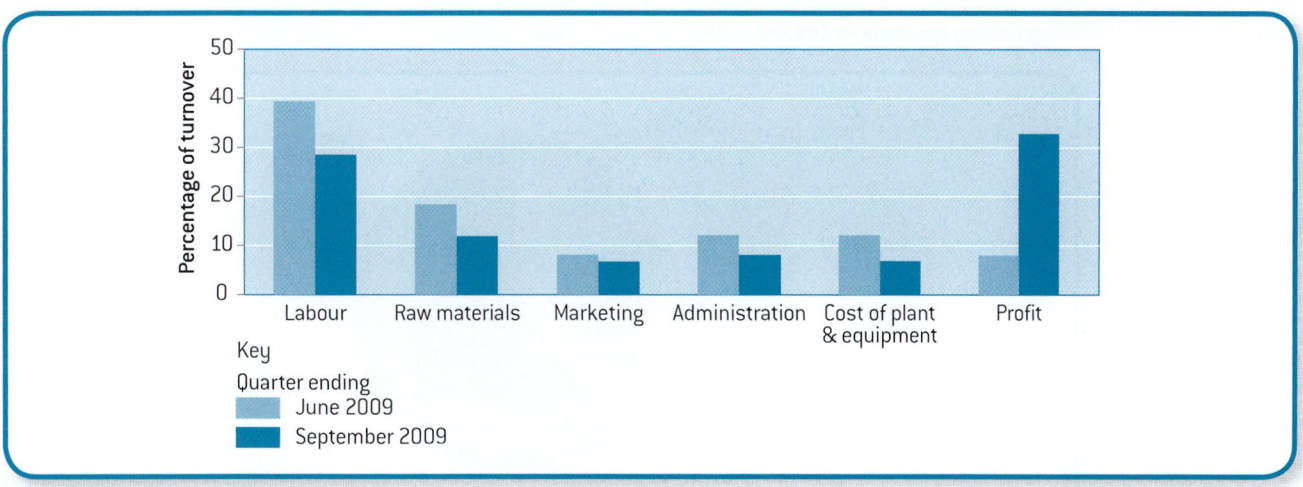

Key
Quarter ending
June 2009
September 2009

Figure 16.2: The percentage of turnover applied to certain expenses and the percentage of turnover remaining as net profit for the period for Specialty Ice Cream Retail Outlet

to its label on the vertical axis. The information is easier to read when plotted in descending order so that the eye follows the dots down to the smallest value. The dot graph presented in Figure 16.3 shows the number of building approvals for various suburbs in City XYZ, in descending order.

PIE CHARTS

A **pie chart** compares the parts of a unit.

Pie charts represent the parts or divisions of a whole unit, to show a comparison. The pie chart's main use is to emphasise the proportions of a whole unit, so use it when only a few elements of the whole need to be shown—say, no more than five or six sectors in the circle. When the whole unit needs to be broken into more than six parts, choose a 100% column chart instead of a pie chart. The first sector starts at the 12 o'clock point and is the largest sector. The remaining segments are arranged in decreasing order of size (see Figure 16.4).

Although pie charts are easy to understand, the Australian Bureau of Statistics prefers not to use them because it is difficult to judge the areas and size differences accurately. The areas can be distorted if the graph is tilted slightly, and a pie graph cannot show negative values.

Tables, line graphs, bar graphs, dot graphs and pie charts are standard visual aids. They can be used to present facts and figures in oral presentations as well as in written reports. The next section discusses visuals that present information, concepts and ideas.

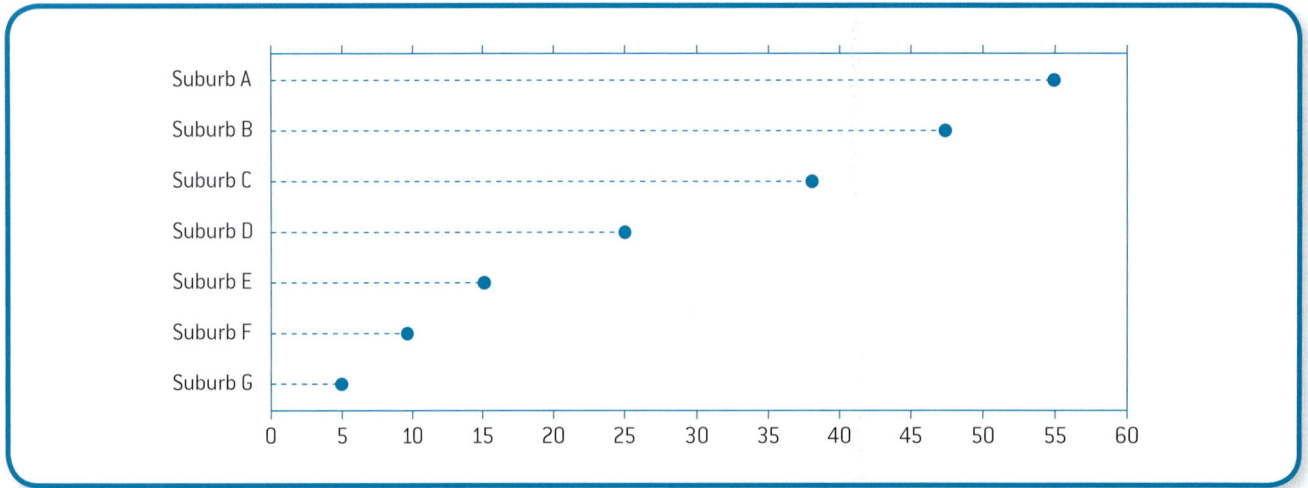

Figure 16.3: Dot graph showing building approvals for City XYZ

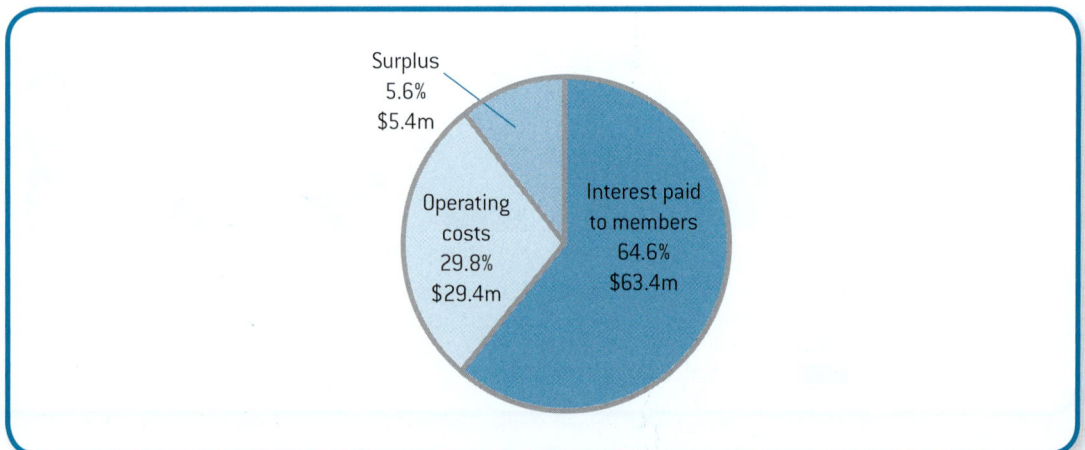

Figure 16.4: A pie chart showing distribution of annual income from XYZ Credit Union to members

Presenting information, concepts and ideas

The most common types of visuals for presenting spatial relationships, abstract ideas and other information are diagrams, photographs, illustrations, drawings, maps, flow charts, organisation charts, animation and digital video.

DIAGRAMS

A **diagram** is a form of chart that is used to compare structures. It provides a visual representation of the elements and their relationship to one another. The organisation chart and flow chart are often used as report graphics, although any kind of structure can be shown in a diagram. Diagrams are particularly helpful when showing and reinforcing technical details. They are also useful for advertising promotions, for selling, and for setting a mood or tone.

A **diagram** compares structures.

PHOTOGRAPHS AND ILLUSTRATIONS

Photographs are easily understood, have an immediate impact and show the physical appearance of the subject. Often a photograph can replace a lengthy description. For example, site descriptions in a valuation report are more easily understood if photographs of the property and site are included. Centrepoint Tower in Sydney is easier to visualise if the written description is accompanied by a photograph of the building.

Photographs are used to show the physical appearance of the subject.

A photograph should be placed as close as possible to the part of the text in a report, essay or article to which it refers. Sometimes it is more convenient to place the photograph before the relevant text and this is acceptable practice. A photograph will have more impact if it is placed on the right-hand page. Enlarging and cropping a photograph is acceptable to emphasise the important details.

Photographs have three main disadvantages: they are expensive; they are often visually busy, with lots of detail; and they are unable to show a cross-section (that is, what is inside the subject that makes it work).

The disadvantages of photographs mean that many report writers prefer to use **drawings** to emphasise the details of interest. The drawing can simplify the real-life situation, highlight important points, and give the reader an impression of the idea or concept.

A **drawing** is a graphic used to emphasise details of interest.

The illustration in Figure 16.5 shows potential hazards in a workplace. It is much easier to comprehend these from an illustration than words.

MAPS

A **map** is a specific type of diagram that uses scale, grids, symbols, lines, colours, legends, titles, figures and text to show the location of landforms, cities, towns, roads, and so on. Maps make clever use of graphics in a way that transfers a large amount of detail on to the page. If you decide to use a map, ensure that it is simple and easy to reproduce, either as an enlargement or a reduction.

Maps use scale, grids, symbols, lines, colours, legends, titles, figures and text to show the location of landforms, cities, towns, roads, etc.

Maps use many **symbols** as a means of conveying information in a small space. For example, a street directory may use a red cross to represent a hospital and a solid red dot for traffic lights. Successful and accepted symbols are clear, simple, instantly recognised, and easy to enlarge, reduce or reproduce.

A **symbol** is a shorthand form of writing.

Graphics and text should be integrated and project an accurate image.

FLOW CHARTS AND ORGANISATION CHARTS

Flow charts illustrate a sequence of actions or steps using special shapes and arrows to indicate the relationships. Flow charts are diagrams that map out and communicate a process visually. The step-by-step picture of the process enhances analysis and makes it easier to talk about it. The flow chart in Figure 16.6 shows the sequence of activities taken to report an occupational health and safety (OHS) accident or incident.

A **flow chart** illustrates the steps in a process, procedure, system or model.

An **organisation chart** illustrates the relationships between the functions, units and positions in an organisation (see Figure 16.7). It is the framework linking the functions and employees in an organisation. An organisation chart also shows the formal upward and downward channels of communication.

An **organisation chart** illustrates the relationships between the functions, units and positions in an organisation.

Figure 16.5: An illustration showing potential hazards

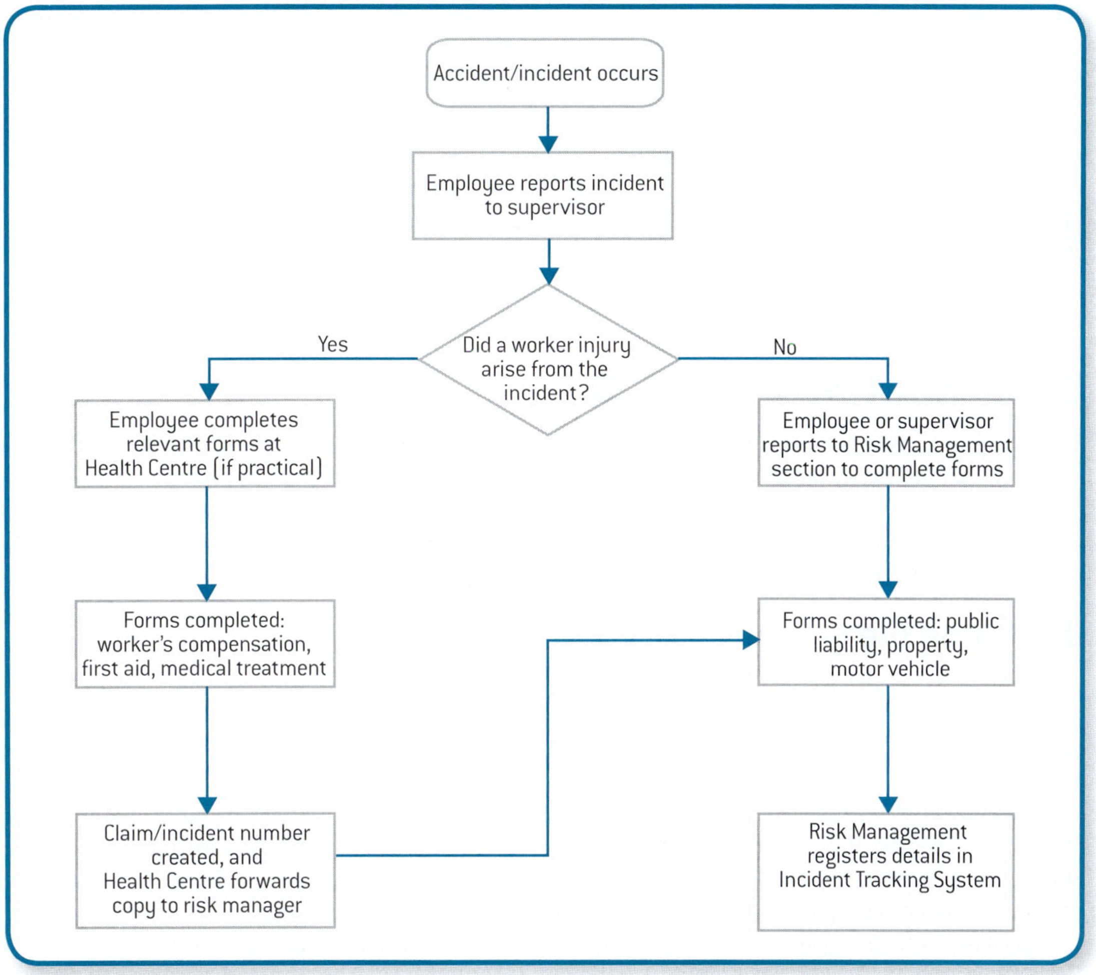

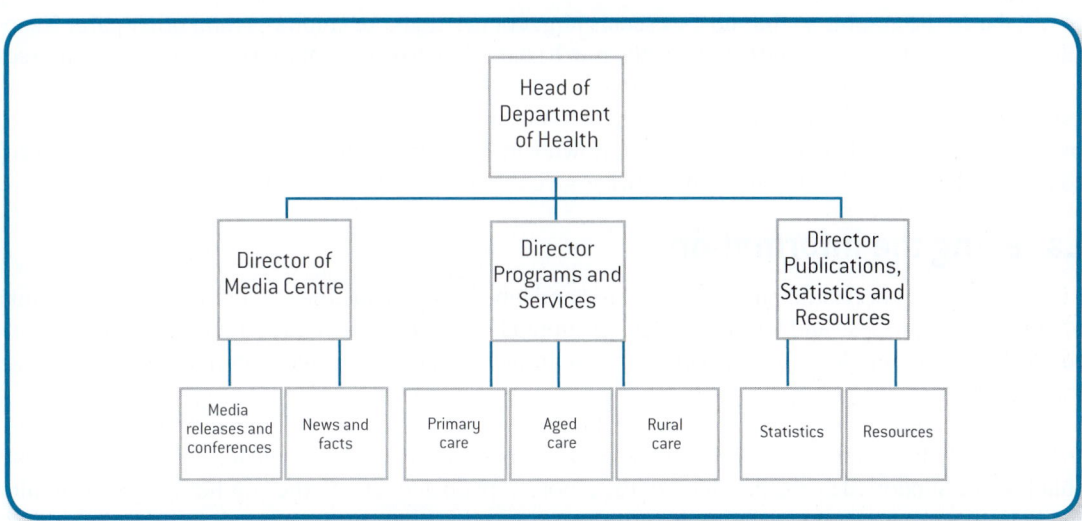

Figure 16.6: A flow chart showing accident/incident reporting and investigation

Figure 16.7: An organisation chart showing ADY Department of Health

REVIEW QUESTIONS

4 **a** List five main types of graphics.

b Why are graphics used in reports?

5 **a** Name three elements that should be included in a table.

b Which graph or chart is used to represent the parts of a whole unit in order to compare them?

6 **a** What sorts of graphs are used in Figures 16.2 and 16.3?

b Briefly explain the difference between these two types of graphs.

OBJECTIVE 3 ▶
Explain the importance of design consistency in visuals

CONSTRUCTING GRAPHICS

Some graphics are obtained from other sources—for example, photographs, maps, flow charts, organisation charts and diagrams by planners—while others are constructed from information gathered in research—for example, tables, graphs and pie charts. Graphics should be formatted in a consistent style. The background design, colour, artwork, fonts and type styles of a presentation's visuals should be consistent and create an attractive layout. Design inconsistencies confuse and annoy audiences.

A successful graphic can be enlarged or reduced without losing the message.

Designing the graphic

Sometimes you may design the graphic to give particular emphasis to one element. Another time you may wish to relate the elements in the graph to one another; for example, to compare similarities, differences or dependencies between the elements. Simplicity in design helps; too much detail is confusing. Organise the graphic to make it simple and easy to read.

Kienzler (1997) raises the issue of **visual ethics** and comments that visuals have an emotional impact, are seen by those who simply skim a document, and are remembered for longer than the written word. Hence, distortions and intentional ambiguity should always be avoided. Ethical business communicators design graphics that are clear, honest and objective.

Visual ethics is concerned with ethical issues involved in the production of visual images.

Lesikar, Pettit and Flatley (1998, p. 273) comment that graphics are supplementary to words. Their role is to help the words communicate the report content. 'They help to give emphasis to the key points of coverage. Also, they serve to improve the report's physical appearance, making the report more inviting and readable.'

Balance the graphic so that no part seems larger or carries more emphasis than other parts. Keep the spacing consistent. It is better to have too much space than to use a diagram or map that is cluttered with too much information. Ensure that each part of the graphic is labelled clearly (see below). It is essential to use a scale that covers the range of data. As a general rule, the breadth of a graph should be twice its height. When a key is used, it is shown within the frame around the graph. Writing placed to either side of a graphic is distracting. Always give the source of your information.

Labelling the information

An effective graphic has an explanatory title or heading and clear units of measurement, with the source of information and the specific focus easily identified.

The main concept or relationship is highlighted and labelled to enable the reader to identify and think about the aid's purpose and ideas. Clear labels should be placed on each line and piece of information to identify the main ideas. To avoid cluttering a graph too much, identification may be made in the form of a key.

When more than one graphic is used in a report, each one should be numbered. Set out the facts in the written document and then place the graphics as close as possible to the information in the text that is being supported by the graphics. In the report, explain and refer to the graphics. The text should lead up to and away from each graphic, thus ensuring that they are integrated into the discussion rather than left as optional pieces of artwork.

REVIEW QUESTIONS

7 Describe the features of an effective visual.
8 What do effective visuals do?
9 Contrast the characteristics of ethical and unethical visuals.

APPLY YOUR KNOWLEDGE

GRAPHIC COMMUNICATION

1 a In preparation for your next session, break into groups of three. Your first task in the next session will be to analyse a variety of graphs. Each person in your group of three should collect six different types of graphics between now and the next session.
  b When you meet as a group in the following session, analyse each of the graphics individually, then:
  - compare your findings with the others in your group
  - evaluate your findings against the checklist below.

2 As a group, prepare a set of instructions titled 'How to construct an effective graphic'.

3 In your group, discuss the following statement: 'It is possible to prove anything with statistics; therefore, in our next report we should bend our data to suit our own findings.'
  a Do you agree or disagree with the statement?
  b Comment on the effect on the report writer's credibility and the likely result if action is taken on the basis of misinformation.

SELF-EVALUATE YOUR SKILL

RATE YOUR UNDERPINNING KNOWLEDGE OF GRAPHICS

Before you decide to keep a graphic in your report, ask the following.

Does this graphic:	*Yes*	*No*	*Unsure*
have a title?			
have labelled axes (if relevant)?			
give a clear and accurate representation of the subject?			
have a definite purpose?			
illustrate only one subject?			
add interest to the report?			
support the findings?			
use titles, captions and legends appropriately?			

VISUAL AIDS AND TECHNOLOGY IN ORAL PRESENTATIONS

◄ OBJECTIVE 4
Explain the use of visuals and technology in oral presentations

Technology enables presenters to incorporate animation, video clips, photo slideshows and web-based resources into presentations. Video and movie files or animated clips can be inserted into software packages such as PowerPoint to provide visual support for an oral business presentation. Insert the file or animated clips into the PowerPoint presentation and play them either automatically or manually at

Visuals make an oral presentation more memorable, increasing the chances that the message will be remembered.

the right moment. Recent advances in communications and information technology allow speakers to download graphs, drawings and figures from the Internet. The Internet is a rich source of visual aids.

Oral presentations using visuals are more interesting and persuasive. The use of visual aids in oral presentations is similar to their use in written presentations. Any visual aid—diagrams, pie charts, flow charts, graphs, tables and illustrations—should reinforce the meaning and enhance the presentation. Prepare an effective visual by avoiding too much detail and too many words. Any visual supporting an oral presentation should be easy to read and understand.

Maintaining the flow and rhythm

Visuals can maintain the flow and rhythm of an oral presentation and reinforce the key concepts. The intention is to enhance the audience's perception and comprehension of the total message by making what the presenter says more memorable, more intelligible and more enjoyable. Four principles underpin the use of technology in a presentation. It must:

1. support the presentation's purpose
2. be pertinent to the subject matter
3. be suited to the audience
4. blend with and supplement the presentation, rather than dominate it.

No matter how good a verbal presentation is, it can be improved by good visual presentation and the support of technology. Long after many of the ideas from a presentation have been forgotten, the visuals remain in the memory. The use of technology visually supports a spoken presentation and can tap into the audience's senses, improve their satisfaction with the presentation, and ensure that the message the presenter imparts is the intended message. The term 'multi-sense' recognises that people receive messages in several different ways. According to Malouf (1988, p. 81), total input through our five senses is divided into the percentages shown in Table 16.4.

Audience interactivity

Multimedia is more than one concurrent medium; for example, text, sound and video images.

Multimedia means the use of more than one presentation medium concurrently; for example, the message is sent as a combination of text, sound and motion video. A presentation by a speaker, together with sound, images and motion video, is a multimedia presentation. The variety of media gains the attention of the audience through a number of senses. The audience can interact with a multimedia presentation by voice command, mouse manipulation, touch screen, text entry and group participation.

Multimedia presentations in any form keep the listener and speaker active and enhance the learning and understanding process through variety. They are effective when they:

Match the technology to your purpose and audience.

- capture the audience's attention
- attract and arouse interest
- assist the presenter to arrange the content in an orderly manner
- reduce the listener's confusion

Table 16.4: Percentage of input received through different senses	
Sense	**Percentage**
Smell	3%
Taste	4%
Touch	7%
Hearing	11%
Sight	75%

Source: Adapted from D. Malouf, *How to Create and Deliver Dynamic Presentations*, Simon & Schuster, Sydney, 1988, p. 81.

- give additional impact to increase the listener's motivation
- highlight an important point
- support the point
- emphasise relationships
- clarify and summarise
- aid memory and the retention of ideas.

Choose carefully before deciding to use visual aids and technology. The budget available, the cost of equipment, the time available to prepare and present, and the speaker's preference and ability to use different types of technology and equipment all have an impact on the decision. Any problems in using the equipment may distract the audience. It is also worth considering whether it is easy to carry or arrange the equipment.

Characteristics of technology

Projector panels, video players, computers, presentation software such as PowerPoint, and video-conferencing all have different characteristics appropriate to different contexts and types of speeches and presentations. Factors in the context, such as size of venue, audience numbers, lighting, budget, projection surface and the distance the image has to be projected, all affect the choice of technology.

Lane (1987) highlights the need to select and design aids to enhance the message, not the reverse. The aids and technology should be integrated with the message and other support materials. Plan in advance how to display aids for the receivers, check all aids before using them to ensure their readiness for use, and make certain that the audience can see the aids.

Generally, audiences are comfortable with new technology if presenters can use it correctly. Twomey (2000) highlights the readiness of Australians to participate in one particular type of online technology: the Internet. In November 1999, 25% of Australian homes were connected to the Internet. By November 2000, the number had risen to 35%. By 2006, the number of Australian households with a broadband Internet connection was 2.3 million (ABS 2007).

Australians are comfortable with and willing to use technology. They expect presenters to incorporate relevant technology into their presentations. Presenters can create visuals or whole presentations on multimedia programs or live video images, and deliver them worldwide over the Internet for the audience to revisit after a face-to-face presentation. Podcasts, for example, are used to reach a wider audience or to allow analysis and evaluation of the presentation's content by keynote conference speakers, university lecturers, and corporate presenters of company annual reports.

In traditional channels of communication the information is sender-based. The sender decides what to send, to whom to send it, and how and when to send it. When the message is sent via a technology channel such as the Internet, anyone with a computer, iPhone or portable media device can receive the message directly, without the involvement of others. Regardless of whether the sender sends the message to only one receiver, to a number of authorised receivers with login names and passwords, to a network, or to anyone who has the software to connect to the Internet, the receiver can decide what to receive and when to receive it. The implication is that the communication model is receiver-based, not sender-based.

Although new technology provides a wide range of graphic and visual supports for presenters, there are challenges to incorporating the technology into presentations. The rule when using technology in a presentation is to stay within the confines of the presentation's purpose, the needs of the sender to convey information and the needs of the audience. The technology must be appropriate to the audience, the occasion, the location and the presenter. It should also be cost effective, available and easy to use.

WHITEBOARDS (INTERACTIVE, ELECTRONIC AND STANDARD)

A presentation to a small group (up to 20–25 people) is enhanced by the use of interactive whiteboards, electronic boards, standard whiteboards and flip charts. They can be used spontaneously to write key words, capture brainstorming ideas, and draw diagrams, mind maps and flow charts. The presenter can use an interactive whiteboard to encourage audience participation. An electronic whiteboard can be scrolled through to a clean section and the information on the screen can be printed out. While the flip chart is not really a piece of technology, it is a visual that is still widely used in presentations, particularly those with audience participation.

POWERPOINT PRESENTATIONS

Avoid overusing PowerPoint.

Good practice requires the presenter to keep the intended audience in mind and think about presentation software such as PowerPoint and Harvard Graphics. The content, style and format of an oral presentation are decided and outlined in the planning stage. Presentation software has built-in slide designs, and the presenter can easily choose a built-in design and key in the words. Clip art is also easy to insert and will have a greater impact than a presentation that uses only words.

The date should always be inserted as a reference point, particularly in terms of retrieving the file. Once the presentation is saved, it can be run as a slide show by using either the keyboard on a laptop computer or the mouse, or set on automatic. Software applications make it easy to prepare high-quality visuals on PowerPoint. As Word, Excel and PowerPoint are designed to share information, data can be moved between the applications. Table 16.5 provides useful hints for using a PowerPoint presentation.

PowerPoint should be used only to reinforce what a presenter says.

- Practise and memorise speeches.
- Present a slide after making a point.
- Limit the number of words used on a slide.
- Restrain use of animation and sound for impact.

VIDEOCONFERENCING AND PODCASTS

A videoconference is a live connection via audio, text and video between people in separate locations.

The increasing use of digital technology has implications for presenters. As capabilities expand and prices drop, a presentation can be delivered all over the country or, indeed, around the world. Presentations using satellite linkups and the Internet are now close to television broadcasting and studio productions, moving away from conference auditoriums and other face-to-face venues. The technology in these presentations is more complex than verbal presentations accompanied by supporting materials conveyed by technology from a stage. It may be necessary to engage professionals for lighting, sound, presentation and other components. Distance education, annual meetings,

---

Table 16.5: Hints for using PowerPoint

- Create the content in outline form.
- Determine the page set-up and size of the page before the slides are formatted.
- Keep the style and format consistent throughout the presentation.
- Avoid flicking backwards and forwards through the PowerPoint slides.
- Insert relevant clip art to gain the audience's attention and interest.
- Design the presentation to focus on the audience's need to understand; i.e. a receiver-based message, rather than a sender-based one.
- Sequence the slides.
- Build up a complex concept by using a simple slide and then overlay with additional details.
- Rehearse the software presentation.
- Avoid having too much light on the screen.
- Avoid standing between the audience and the screen.
- Look at the audience, rather than the screen.
- Keep the slides clear and concise.
- Avoid tripping on cables and wires.
- Have back-up transparencies for use with an overhead projector in case of system failures.

Table 16.6: Hints for videoconferencing and teleconferencing

- Have appropriate technology and equipment.
- Know how to use the controls.
- Test the equipment and practise its operation.
- Use language suited to the audience.
- Show progression and relationships.
- Use different forms of support material if appropriate.
- Make effective use of your voice.
- Use nonverbals well.
- Be willing to contribute.
- Handle any anxiety, nervousness or stress.
- Demonstrate confidence.
- Finish within the time limit.

Additional hints for teleconferencing

- Book and schedule appropriate resources.
- Make sure participants know the time of the call.
- Check international times.
- Establish protocols to avoid talking over one another.
- Make sure all participants have an opportunity to contribute.
- Thank participants for their contribution before finishing the conference.

company-wide announcements, product announcements and staff meetings can all happen in a tele-conference or videoconference. Table 16.6 provides hints for videoconferencing and teleconferencing.

Digital technologies allow teleconferencing, videoconferencing and audio conferencing sessions for people at different locations. Podcasts are replacing or supplementing video and teleconferencing. Podcasts facilitate collaboration and sharing between the presenter and the audience. Podcasts are discussed in Chapter 15, 'Oral Business Presentations'.

The new technologies allow people in different locations to be part of an audience for a presentation and to interact as a group.

Many lecture theatres and conference centres are provided with computers in the form of laptops and computer software, and network connections. These broadcast PowerPoint and other forms of presentation. While the technology provides the presenter with benefits, it is not infallible. There will be occasions when the technology lets presenters down. The rule of thumb is always to have a fall-back position. If the technology does not work, presenters cannot ask the audience to come back at another time. They must still present.

A podcast is a digital media file, or a related collection of such files, that is distributed over the Internet for playback on portable media players and personal computers.

REVIEW QUESTIONS

10 Discuss four principles underpinning the use of technology in an oral presentation.

11 a   List four types of supporting material appropriate to an oral presentation.

  b   Describe how and why you might use these in a presentation.

12 Explain the purpose of a multimedia presentation.

13 a   What are the benefits of using an electronic board?

  b   When should a flip chart be used?

14 'Good presentation requires the presenter to keep the intended audience in mind when preparing PowerPoint presentations.' Comment.

15 What type of visuals would you use in a podcast?

VISUALS IN BUSINESS PRESENTATIONS

Work in small discussion groups.

1. a   Identify the characteristics of visuals and technology that enliven an oral presentation.
   b   Describe the advantages and disadvantages of PowerPoint.
   c   Prepare a tips list for using PowerPoint effectively.
2. a   What are the seven key areas to address in an oral presentation (Jay & Jay 2000)?
   b   How can you vary the texture in your presentation (Putnis & Petelin 1999)?
   c   In which segment of your presentation should you make the most important point?
   d   Describe factors that can compete for an audience's attention in a podcast.
3. a   Prepare an oral presentation entitled 'All technology should be seen as part of a receiver-based communication model rather than a sender-based model'.
   b   Prepare visual aids to support the presentation.
   c   Use the checklist below to evaluate your visual aids.

SELF-EVALUATE YOUR SKILL

VISUALS IN ORAL BUSINESS PRESENTATIONS

Before you decide to use a visual in your presentation, ask the following:

Will this visual:	Yes	No	Unsure
support the presentation's purpose?			
add variety to the presentation?			
gain the attention of the audience through a number of senses?			
direct the audience's attention to the main points?			
help to keep the listener/audience active?			
emphasise the main points?			
distract the audience?			
simplify the ideas?			
clarify the ideas?			
make the presentation memorable?			
be easy to use?			
improve the presentation?			
be appropriate to the context?			

SUMMARY OF LEARNING OBJECTIVES

1 ▷ EXPLAIN HOW VISUAL AIDS ENHANCE WRITTEN AND ORAL BUSINESS PRESENTATIONS

Visual aids improve the quality and impact of written and oral presentations. Visuals enliven a presentation and send a more powerful and interesting message. Successful visuals explain, simplify and emphasise the main relationships.

The visual aids should underline the main message, be simple, and add variety to illustrate and reinforce the message. They explain, corroborate and add impact to the message.

2 ▷ IDENTIFY THE FEATURES OF GRAPHICS SUITED TO REPORTS AND WRITTEN PRESENTATIONS

Always aim for honesty when presenting information in graphs or charts. If the reader detects a misrepresentation or the distortion of information, the credibility of the whole document may be questioned. Add clarity to the graphic by using an appropriate size, quality and location of information in the graphic. Construct the graphic in a way that emphasises important points and adds meaning to the written words by showing the data and relationships clearly.

Each graphic should have a clear purpose, catch the reader's interest, and encourage the reader to think about the ideas or data presented. By choosing the graphic most suited to the message, the writer is able to use it to focus the reader's attention. The graphic makes the information more intelligible and interesting.

3 ▷ EXPLAIN THE IMPORTANCE OF DESIGN CONSISTENCY IN VISUALS

Devise visual aids to assist in the presentation of the message. Consistency in the background design, colour, artwork, fonts and type styles of a presentation's visuals is essential.

Apply design components consistently, and match the visuals to the presentation's purpose and subject matter for effective visuals. They must blend with and supplement, rather than dominate, the presentation. Their purpose is to capture the audience's attention, give additional impact, support points, emphasise relationships, clarify, and make the presentation memorable.

4 ▷ EXPLAIN THE USE OF VISUALS AND TECHNOLOGY IN ORAL PRESENTATIONS

The essence of oral presentations, whether they be given using traditional face-to-face methods or the most recent multimedia technology, is communication.

Technology, when used effectively, enhances a presentation. It allows the presenter to visually explain or add to what is being said. Animation, video and film can help to illustrate ideas, and a PowerPoint presentation can supplement the presenter's words. Visuals leave an impression on the audience, whether it is good or bad. The criteria to use when selecting a visual for any medium are relevance, simplicity, legibility and ease of use.

KEY TERMS

ACTIVITIES AND QUESTIONS

1 a Construct a line graph and a column graph from the information in Table 16.7.

The figures represent the annual profit and share prices over six years for a large corporation. As you plot the graphs, show the profit against time as a line graph, and the share price for each year as a series of columns on the same graph. Use years as the scale on the horizontal axis, A$ million on the left-hand vertical axis and $ share price on the right-hand axis.

   b What advantages does the visual representation have over the table?

   c Briefly discuss two relationships shown on the graph.

Table 16.7: Profit and share prices

Year	Profit (A$ million)	Share price
2004	185	$1.809
2005	220	$3.40
2006	315	$5.00
2007	375	$6.00
2008	410	$7.80
2009	580	$9.50

2 a Summarise the following data by placing it in a table.

The superannuation fund's portfolio covers a wide range of assets. The largest proportion, 40%, is in Australian shares, followed by 20% in international shares. Liquidity needs to be part of the fund, so 5% cent of the portfolio is held in liquid assets; because profitability is important, property shares make up another 15%. Safety is provided by fixed interest shares, so the fund has placed another 15% of its assets in Australian fixed interest and 15% in international fixed interest holdings.

   b To enable a visual comparison to be made, place the information from the six percentages in the table into a pie chart.

3 Consider the graphs you have plotted in Question 1 above.

   a Identify which of the graphs shows the following:
      i   changes over time
      ii   relative size
      iii comparison between items.

   b Decide which graph is the most or least successful.

   c Justify your answer by briefly outlining what is communicated by the graph.

4 Work in small groups.

   a Analyse the following quote.
      Good practice requires a presenter to prepare the content, style and format to meet their needs as a presenter, the needs of the audience and the limits of the technology.

   b Use the data from your analysis to prepare a PowerPoint presentation or overhead projector presentation supporting the statement.

   c Make the presentation as a group project.

5 Analyse this statement in an essay.
   Presenters who use technology well apply the principles of instructional design, educational psychology and graphic design to organise their information into an effective communication process and make their presentation and use of technology more audience friendly.

6 Faults in the design and content of supporting materials are barriers to communication. How can presenters avoid these barriers to communication in their presentations?

7 Work in small groups.
   It is claimed that visual aids can add to the effectiveness of your presentation.
   Explain how this happens.

8 *Modern presentation technologies slow the pace of a presentation below that which is required for total audience involvement.*
   Critically evaluate this statement.

9 Find out about trends in the use of videoconferencing for reasons other than presentations. What are the common uses? What types of organisations are embracing this technology? What does the future hold for videoconferencing?

EXPLORING THE WEB

1. Check out the resources at <www.ruf.rice.edu/>.
   a. What are the benefits of using visuals in oral presentations?
   b. Prepare a set of guidelines for using visuals in an oral presentation.
   c. What is the key to using visual aids effectively?
2. Learn more about symbols by visiting 'Online Encyclopedia of Western Signs and Ideograms' at <www.symbols.com/>.

3. Visit the Australian Bureau of Statistics site at <www.abs.gov.au>.
   a. What services are provided by the Australian Bureau of Statistics? Search the site to find the answers to parts b and c of this question.
   b. What was the size of the Australian population in the latest projected figures?
   c. What is a population pyramid? How is the data for the pyramid collected?

PROJECT WORK

Work individually.

1. Use the Web to search for ways in which presenters who want to do more with technology in their presentations can use the new capabilities. In your search, use a combination of search tools—for example, a directory such as Yahoo!; or, for more general information, Google. Narrow down the search results by using key words and a Boolean search with AND, OR and NOT. Also consider the 'exact phrase' options provided on search engines such as Anzwers.
2. Collate your research results into a presentation for Toastmasters International. Your presentation can be supported by any technology of your choice.
3. Deliver your presentation.

BIBLIOGRAPHY

Australian Bureau of Statistics. *Home Page*, www.abs.gov.au/, viewed 1 December 2007.

Australian Bureau of Statistics. 2007. *8146.0—Household Use of Information Technology, Australia, 2006–07*, ABS, Canberra, December.

Australian Government Department of Communications, Information Technology and the Arts. *Communications and Technology for Business*, www.dcita.gov.au/communications_for_business, viewed 14 November 2007.

Browne, M.N. & Keeley, S.M. 2007. *Asking the Right Questions: A Guide to Critical Thinking*, 8th edn, Pearson Prentice Hall, Upper Saddle River, New Jersey.

Cant, S. 2004. 'Powerful software', *Sydney Morning Herald*, 27 January.

Fardell, L. 1998. 'Presenting statistical and tabular information', *Stylewise*, Vol. 4, Issue 4, p. 1.

Hooke, J. & Phillips, J. 1996. *Getting Your Message Across*, Simon & Schuster, Sydney.

Jay, A. & Jay, R. 2000. *Effective Presentation*, Prentice Hall, New Jersey.

Kienzler, D.S. 1997. 'Visual ethics', *Journal of Business Communication*, Vol. 34, Issue 2, April, pp. 171–87.

Koppi, T. & Pearson, E. 2005. 'The COERSEA model for interactive presentations', *Journal of University and Teaching and Learning Practice*, Vol. 2, Issue 2, pp. 4–89.

Lane, L.L. 1987. *By All Means Communicate*, Prentice Hall, New Jersey.

Leeds, D. 2003. *PowerSpeak: Engage, Inspire and Stimulate Your Audience*, Career Press, USA.

Lesikar, R.V., Pettit, J.D & Flatley, M.E. 1998. *Basic Business Communication*, 8th edn, McGraw-Hill, USA.

Lucas, S. 1995. *The Art of Public Speaking*, 5th edn, McGraw-Hill, New York.

McMillan, C. 2001. 'Why you need presentation skills', *Australian Business News*, Vol. 22, March.

Malouf, D. 1988. *How to Create and Deliver Dynamic Presentations*, Simon & Schuster, Sydney.

Mehrabian, A. 1971. *Silent Messages*, Wadsworth, Belmont, California.

Putnis, P. & Petelin, R. 1999. *Professional Communication Principles and Applications*, Prentice Hall, Sydney.

Springston, J.K. 2001. 'Public relations and new media technology: the impact of the Internet', in Robert. L Heath (ed.), *Handbook of Public Relations*, Sage Publications, London.

Symbols.com. 'Explore a world of symbols', *Online Encyclopedia of Western Signs and Ideograms*, www.symbols.com/, viewed 1 December 2007.

The Rice On-Line Writing. *Lab Designing Effective Oral Presentations*, www.ruf.rice.edu/~riceowl/oral_presentations.htm, viewed 1 December 2007.

Tufte, E.R. 1983. *Visual Display of Quantitative Information*, Graphics Press, Cheshire, Connecticut.

Tufte, E.R. 2004. *Visual Display of Quantitative Information*, Graphics Press, Cheshire, Connecticut.

Turk, C. & Kirkman, J. 1989. *Effective Writing: Improving Scientific, Technical, and Business Communication*, 2nd edn, E. & F.N. Spon, London.

Twomey, P. 2000. 'The current state of play: Australia and the Information Economy', Presentation to AFMA Technofuture 2000, 17 May, National Office for the Information Economy, www.noie.gov.au/ publications/ speeches/twomey/presentations/presentation _AFMA_ Technofuture2000_170500/, viewed 23 February 2001.

Wroblewski, L. 'Visible narratives: understanding visual organization', *User Interface Engineering*, Originally published: 20 January 2003, www.uie.com/articles/visible_narratives/, viewed 12 February 2008.

Part 5

Writing for Results

17 The business writing process

Photo: Arne Trau

OUTLINE

Business messages in plain English

The seven elements of plain English

Appropriate language

Coherent sentences and paragraphs

Rhythm, tone, order and format

Editing according to the principles of plain English

1 ▷ describe three advantages gained from writing in plain English

2 ▷ use language appropriately in a business context

3 ▷ use sentences and paragraphs appropriately in a business context

4 ▷ apply rhythm, tone, order of information and format appropriately in business documents

5 ▷ identify the types of errors to look for when editing written business messages.

VIEWPOINT: WHAT'S PLAIN ENGLISH? DEPARTMENT OF EDUCATION SCIENCE AND TRAINING

DEST (2007) states: 'Plain English is good, clear writing which communicates as simply and effectively as possible.' DEST suggests these documents should be in plain English:

- forms of all kinds, including applications for government payments, loan and credit card applications, taxation forms and hospital admission forms
- documents explaining government policies and laws, such as copyright law, Equal Employment Opportunity legislation, and occupational health and safety legislation
- insurance policies and renewal forms
- brochures, leaflets and booklets
- letters from banks, government departments and other organisations
- bills, such as phone and gas bills
- instructions for using products such as electrical appliances
- information for patients about drugs and medicines
- legal documents, including legislation, contracts and leases
- corporate rule books and policy guidelines
- tenders and specifications
- internal documents such as training materials, memos, procedures and quality assurance manuals
- annual and other reports
- newsletters
- notices and signs
- airline and public transport timetables.

Department of Education Science and Training (DEST) site, 'What's plain English'? www.dest.gov.au/sectors/training_skills/publications_resources/plain_english_at_work/whats_plain_english.htm, viewed 31 October 2007.

Effective writers apply a three-stage process to their writing: planning, writing and editing. In the planning stage, they identify the purpose, consider the needs of the receiver, define the writing purpose, and order the content in a logical and appropriate sequence. In the writing stage, the writer's tools are the words, sentences, paragraphs and layout of the message. A writer who uses these tools well is able to convey the message's meaning concisely, courteously and confidently. In the editing stage, experienced writers evaluate the structure, content and writing quality before they send their work to the intended audience. They also proofread for correctness and clarity.

The receiver of any document wants to understand what should happen, why it should happen and how to go about making it happen. Consequently, the main purpose in any writing task is to get the message across. An effective writer follows the grammatical conventions and develops a clear writing style that presents information to meet the reader's need to understand. His or her writing style conveys the message easily and quickly, and readers are given the best possible chance of understanding the message.

BUSINESS MESSAGES IN PLAIN ENGLISH

OBJECTIVE **1** ▶
Describe three advantages gained from writing in plain English

A clear, concise and coherent message written in plain English helps readers to understand and thereby make decisions and take actions on the basis of the information and so exercise their democratic rights as citizens.

The most important principle of plain English is that documents are created and written from the receiver's viewpoint. The structure and purpose of the document are decided by answering these four questions:

1. What does the reader need to know?
2. How much do they understand about the subject?
3. What is the best way to organise ideas so that they make sense to the reader?
4. Is the document really necessary, or would another method of communication work better?

Plain English is a readable writing style that uses the 'you' approach, positive language, clear expression, and an assertive, courteous tone.

Plain English involves the use of clear, straightforward expression that avoids obscurity, inflated vocabulary and convoluted sentence construction. Plain English makes the process of giving information and receiving feedback easier. A document written in plain English has three advantages:

1. equity
2. efficiency
3. effectiveness.

These advantages of a plain English writing style have a significant impact on your organisation and your receiver.

Equity

Documents and forms are one of the main means of communication in the workplace, and between organisations and their clients. It is important to write in plain English so that people are able to understand the content, how the information applies to them, and whether it is necessary to take any further action.

Access to information is a right for people living in a democratic society. A great deal of the information received in written form affects people's lives—for example, a contract for the purchase of a home, or information on social security benefits.

Language can be used to exercise power over people. Language that is clear and easily understood can empower people, while language that is unclear and obscure can disempower people by denying their right to take action on the basis of the information. It is important to people that they understand the meaning of laws, rules and contracts, as a lack of information, or a misunderstanding, can cause problems and even hardship. People need, therefore, to understand written forms and documents because those without accurate, complete and clear information can be placed at a disadvantage.

How often have you heard someone say, 'We didn't read the fine print' with reference to some mistake in interpretation of a complex document?

Efficiency

A plain English writing style is easier to read and understand. As a result, more people can understand the message and the number of enquiries from clients who cannot understand the message is reduced. The use of plain English also reduces the number of incorrectly completed forms and so saves clerical time in processing or returning incomplete or incorrectly completed forms.

Wainscott (2003) comments, 'Plain English makes good business sense . . . Plain English is the best way to ensure that your managers, staff, suppliers, customers and the wider public understand your message.' Benefits for staff and customers include:

- reduced time spent training staff to understand and use documents
- fewer customer questions and complaints
- fewer misunderstandings and disputes.

Effectiveness

An effective document has a clear purpose and meets the needs of the receiver. A document written in plain English has an order or sequence of information that is easy to understand and a tone that is appropriate to the document's purpose. It will create an effective message that is clear and easily understood by the receiver. In addition, an effective document is one written to match the way the *receiver* thinks, rather than the way the writer thinks. Writers who put themselves in the place of the receiver and focus on the receiver's need to know and understand the information will write more effectively.

The 3 × 3 writing process

Plain English writers plan the structure and write and review the document to achieve their writing purpose and increase its readability for the receiver. All documents (formal and informal) are created and written from the receiver's point of view. Guffey (2003, pp. 130–1) comments that the **3 × 3 writing process** 'provides you with a systematic plan for developing all your business communications from simple memos and informational reports to corporate proposal and oral proposals'. The main elements of the 3 × 3 writing process are: phase 1, prewriting; phase 2, writing; and phase 3, revising. In phase 1, you analyse, anticipate and adapt your approach. In phase 2, you research, organise and compose. Phase 3 is the editing stage, when you revise, proofread and evaluate your document.

The **3 × 3 writing process** provides a systematic plan for developing all business communication (written and spoken).

Guffey comments that the time you spend on each phase will vary. The rough guide given by one expert for scheduling a project is:

- 25% worrying and planning (phase 1)
- 25% writing (phase 2)
- 45% revising and 5% proofreading (phase 3).

Some steps, however, may be compressed, as in the case of writing short, routine messages. Prewriting may take only a few moments of reflection. Longer, more detailed documents will require more attention to all phases.

Although it may appear that you perform each phase in sequence, 'most business writing is not that rigid . . . the steps may be rearranged, abbreviated, or repeated' (Guffey 2003). Writers differ in their approach. Some writers revise every sentence and paragraph as they go, while others rewrite and rethink as new ideas occur during the writing stage. Experienced writers tend to 'alter, compress and rearrange the steps as needed' (p. 132). The chapters in this part of the book, 'Writing for Results,' present strategies for applying the 3 × 3 process in your paper-based and online written communication.

REVIEW QUESTIONS

1 Define the term 'plain English'.
2 How does writing in plain English advantage the reader?
3 Describe the three phases in the 3 × 3 writing process.

THE SEVEN ELEMENTS OF PLAIN ENGLISH

In choosing words that will work in a business context, business writers are guided by the current emphasis on plain English—the use of words that are familiar and friendly to the receiver—because they create effective workplace documents. (Academic writers will need to use more formal, specialist, technical language: this writing style is presented in Chapter 20.) Correct choice of words, clear structuring of sentences and paragraphs, logical ordering of ideas, and developing an appropriate tone ensure an effective writing style in any writing context. Regardless of the type of writing task, every document will contain seven components of writing style:

1 the words or language
2 the sentences
3 the paragraphs
4 the rhythm or flow
5 the tone
6 the order of information
7 the layout or format.

We look at these seven components in the next three sections of the chapter.

APPROPRIATE LANGUAGE

OBJECTIVE 2 ▶
Use language appropriately in a business context

Words are the communication tool that exposes or expresses meaning and gives a form to ideas, feelings and events. These words have been assigned meanings through use and convention. Familiar, unambiguous words that move straight to the point simplify the reader's task and ensure that the message is clear immediately. A writer who chooses words that are appropriate to the writing purpose and the audience is more likely to be understood. As far back as 320 BC, Aristotle stated: 'One must consider also the audience . . . the reader is the judge.' In the 21st century the same rule applies: always think of the effect of the writing on the audience. Good writing communicates clearly to the other person what is in the writer's mind. Poor writing confuses the other person and leads to misunderstanding and mistakes.

Vocabulary is the stock of words in a language.

The **vocabulary** of business includes all the words of a language and the common words and phrases relating to business knowledge and activities. Business words that are over-used become jargon. Jargon obscures a message's meaning—for example, the word 'incentivise' instead of 'encourage'. Appropriate business language helps the receiver to understand a message's content, how it applies to them, and what action, if any, they need to take.

Murphy (2001), in her *Stylewise* article 'Plain English—style of choice', comments that 'all the structural care in the world falls apart if we don't take care of the words'. Carefully choosing active or passive sentence constructions, or ensuring suitable sentence lengths, can be negated if the words used are not carefully selected.

Murphy criticises the use of long phrases, redundancies and fillers. Some people, she says, use 'extra words as written throat clearing'. The extra words are used to fill in time while they decide what they want to say. She recommends planning what you want to write and getting to the point quickly. Redundancies occur when an idea is repeated. Fillers, in contrast, are words that 'creep into sentences while the writer is still thinking'. They are usually vague—for example, 'it would seem that' or 'as we can plainly see'—and should not be used.

George Orwell, in his essay 'Politics and the English Language' (1946), wrote about the prevalence of pompous phrases that were designed to sound weighty. According to Jones (2003), Orwell lamented the corruption of the English language and used as an example the use of Latin- and Greek-based words where simpler words would do (for example, 'ameliorate' for 'improve', 'clandestine' for 'secret'). Murphy concurred with Orwell, saying that pompous words get in the way of the message and should be replaced with unpretentious words. For example, words such as 'cognisant of' or 'instantaneously' should be avoided (use 'know' and 'now' instead).

An Australian Government publication, <www.detya.gov.au/publications/plain_en/pepubs. htm>, warns that '50 per cent of adult Australians can't cope with a level of writing more complex than that found in a popular newspaper'. They recommend pitching writing at this level.

AVOID UNNECESSARY WORDS, CLICHÉS AND MIXED METAPHORS

The use of more words than are necessary to convey the meaning irritates the reader, who may decide to read no further. Some examples of the use of too many words, and suitable alternatives, are given in Table 17.1. One of the characteristics of good writing is economy of style. Achieve this by removing unnecessary words and any repetition. In the words of Strunk and White (2000): 'Vigorous writing is concise. A sentence should contain no unnecessary words . . . for the same reason that a drawing should have no unnecessary lines and a machine no unnecessary parts.'

Clichés are words that have been so overused they have lost meaning and impact. Examples of clichés that are used in official documents are given in Table 17.2. Avoid them. Readers realise that writers who use clichés are simply offering a mechanical response, rather than putting in the effort to add individuality and clarity to their writing.

Clichés are words that have been so overused they have lost meaning and impact.

Avoid using mixed metaphors—for example, 'as clear as mud'—because they confuse the reader. A metaphor is a description of an object or an action that is imaginative but not literally

Table 17.1: Too many words	
Poor use	**Better use**
in the event that	if
precedes before	before
reverse backward	reverse
subsequent to	after
actual fact	fact
the majority of	most
progress forward	progress
despite the fact that	although
on the occasion of	on
I personally	I
wise words of wisdom	wise words
completely eliminate	eliminate
because of the fact that	because
in point of fact	the fact

Table 17.2: Clichés	
raising the ante	a spanner in the works
the bottom line	full steam ahead
at this point in time	to really take off
the object of the exercise	snail mail
viable alternative	hard copy
back to the drawing board	real time
head hunting	firing on all cylinders
conservative estimate	number crunching
the writing on the wall	bite the bullet
at the end of the day	the too-hard basket

Source: Reprinted by permission of Waveland Press, Inc. from Raymond L. Gorden, *Instructor's Manual to Accompany Basic Interviewing Skills,* Waveland Press Inc., Prospect Heights, Illinois, 1992 (reissued 1998). All rights reserved.

applicable—for example, 'as clear as crystal'. On those occasions when a metaphor is used, the writer should pay particular attention to the literal meaning of the figure of speech in order to make it easy for the reader to visualise and understand the writer's meaning. A mixed metaphor scrambles the message.

CHOOSE CONCRETE LANGUAGE

Concrete language uses specific words that are easy to understand.

Concrete language describes details precisely. It is easier to understand and has more impact than abstract, vague or general language. The receiver may interpret an abstract term quite differently from the writer's intended message. Concrete language sends a clear and specific image that is easy to interpret. Garner (1991) suggests: 'Use concrete terms and your readers will have a clearer idea of your meaning. You enhance your words when you allow readers to visualise what you say.'

The phrase 'increased profits', for example, has a much clearer message for the reader than 'apparent significant financial gains'.

USE TECHNICAL TERMS WHEN APPROPRIATE

Technical terms have a precise meaning specific to a particular subject or organisation. A writer who writes to an informed audience that understands the precise meaning of the terms will find them useful. On the other hand, an uninformed receiver may simply 'turn off' or become worried by the information. A salesperson, for example, who writes to a potential customer, 'It's a GDK-34e with features such as OnRamp 2 (ETSI) ISDN and DISA' without an explanation of the technical terms or the acronyms will surely fail to communicate.

Technical terms used in an inappropriate context can exclude the reader from understanding and sharing important ideas. Technical terms are used to help the reader understand the message, rather than to show the reader the cleverness or superiority of the writer. Whenever possible, avoid jargon such as 'distributive bargaining' or 'sub-prime mortgages' in non-technical documents.

ACTIVE VOICE

In the **active voice**, the subject of the sentence is placed before the action to show who completes the action.

The **active voice** communicates vividly and clearly and lets the reader know who is performing the action—for example, John drives the car. An effective writer places the subject before the action to give a stronger link between them, and to show who or what is doing the action. The active voice gives strength and immediacy. It emphasises the subject as completing or doing the action. The sentence 'John washed the clothes at the laundromat' is in the active voice. John is the person doing the action of 'washing the clothes'. Both the doing of the action and the emphasis in the sentence are placed on

'John'. This technique creates a stronger feeling that something is happening, because the subject and the action are held together in the structure of the sentence.

PASSIVE VOICE

The sentence 'The clothes were washed at the laundromat by John' is passive voice; that is, the subject of the sentence, 'clothes', is the passive receiver of the action 'were washed'. When the subject of a sentence *receives* the action instead of taking the action, the sentence is in the **passive voice**. Emphasis is placed on the subject, 'clothes', rather than on 'John' who is doing the action. Passive voice is less direct than the active voice. It often leaves out the important information of who or what is performing the action; for example, 'The doors were closed at midnight.'

In the **passive voice**, the subject of the sentence is acted upon.

Extended use of the passive voice has the effect of slowing down your writing, and even creating a sense of sluggishness. In contrast, the active voice creates a sense of immediacy and energy. It also reduces distance and formality, as in 'I enclose a cheque', rather than 'A cheque is enclosed'.

The passive voice with the agent omitted exists in a sentence that omits the person or thing doing the action; for example, 'The flat had been thoroughly cleaned.' In this kind of usage, it is assumed that the actor is unimportant. The reader does not need to know who cleaned the flat. The fact that it has been cleaned is the important point. The passive voice is useful if the writer wants to avoid identifying or blaming someone; for example, 'The broken mirror was discovered after the girls had left.'

There are times when the use of the passive voice is appropriate because it allows a more diplomatic tone to emerge; for example, 'Your payment has not been received' rather than 'You have not sent payment'. It is also useful when giving bad news.

Table 17.3 gives examples of the active and passive voice.

USE PERSONAL PRONOUNS

Personal pronouns (I, she, he, you, they) help the reader to understand the message, because they speak directly to the reader and show what applies to the reader and what applies to the writer. Personal pronouns are part of everyday language. They help writers to avoid abstractions and keep sentences short, and encourage them to use concrete language. Since first and second person pronouns include both the male and female gender, they help the writer to avoid the awkward use of he/she with words such as they/their/theirs, we/us, our/ours and you/your/yours. Personal pronouns complement the 'you' approach.

THE 'YOU' APPROACH

The **'you' approach** in writing speaks personally to the receiver by addressing them directly as 'you' throughout the document. The sentence 'Thank you for your enquiry' is an example of this approach. The 'you' style of writing projects an empathetic tone, is personal, and includes both male and female readers. It is an example of plain English. Sometimes the word 'you' can be linked to the word 'us' to create a positive relationship between the writer and the reader. However, in workplace writing it is

The **'you' approach** is a writing style that speaks personally to the reader.

Table 17.3: Active and passive voice	
Active voice	**Passive voice**
The business reached the highest sales figures for the year this month.	Record sales figures for the year were reached by the business this month.
Ling completed the assignment.	The assignment was completed by Ling.
The third-year Management students prepared the project.	The project was prepared by the third-year Management students.
Barbara completed the work.	The work was completed by Barbara.
I submitted the assignment late.	The assignment was late.

usual to focus on the document's purpose and the needs of the receiver, rather than on the needs of the organisation or the writer. The 'you' approach in writing helps to do this and to create a more personal, reader-friendly document.

NON-DISCRIMINATORY, INCLUSIVE LANGUAGE

The choice of language often carries hidden meaning. Some words carry sexist or racist messages. These can give positive or negative characteristics to others on the basis of sex or race, and can be offensive and demeaning to those who are discriminated against. Table 17.4 gives examples of some discriminatory techniques and their purpose. The need to offer Australia's diverse population equality of access to opportunities in education, jobs and promotion makes the use of communication strategies such as plain English and inclusive communication an essential part of workplace communication.

Sexist language gives one gender more prominence and importance in a written document. Three strategies for removing sexism in language are suggested here.

1. Avoid the use of male-dominated terms to describe occupations or roles that are shared by both men and women; for example, 'chairman' (use 'chair' or 'chairperson').
2. Eliminate the unnecessary mention of a person's gender, as in 'lady doctor' or 'female engineer'.
3. When using a pronoun to refer to an individual whose gender is not specified, avoid simply using the male pronoun 'he'. Either restructure the sentence to avoid the pronoun, or make the sentence plural; for example, 'All students are responsible for submitting their projects on time.' Others suggest the use of the plural pronoun even when a single pronoun is required. The *Macquarie Student Writer's Guide* suggests this approach.

While stylists continue to discuss ways around the problem, strategies to avoid discriminatory, exclusive language must be found by the individual writer (see Table 17.5).

Inclusive language includes all readers.

Non-discriminatory, **inclusive language** includes all readers. It invites the reader to take action on the basis of the information provided. Even if an organisation is currently female-dominated, such as nursing, or male-dominated, such as engineering, changing attitudes and trends in education mean that women and men are working in all industries. Resentment and communication barriers can occur when language is addressed exclusively to one sex. It is discriminatory.

Because both men and women are involved in business communication, there is an increasing trend to encourage the use of language that includes both groups. To write an engineering job description that says 'The best man for the job will have the following characteristics . . .' ignores women engineers.

Table 17.4: Communication strategies		
Discriminatory communication technique	**Purpose**	**Inclusive communication technique**
Derogatory labelling	To put down people from another culture or group.	Refuse to use derogatory labels.
Stereotyping people belonging to a particular group	To isolate or exaggerate certain factors and generalise these to all people in a group.	Recognise and avoid the use of language that applies fixed images or stereotypes to groups of people.
Invisibility	To subsume one group into another by label, name or term.	Use inclusive language and language preferred by the minority group.
Imposed labelling	To reinforce the majority group's view because the minority lacks the power to define themselves.	Avoid the use of one single generic name for a number of different groups of people.
Extra visibility	To place emphasis on a difference such as sex, race or ethnic background.	Avoid emphasis on differences such as sex, race and ethnic background.

Successful writers use words that are appropriate to the setting in which the writing takes place. The emerging global economy means businesses and organisations operate within a global society that has a wide cultural diversity. As part of their planning, good writers consider this cultural diversity and make sure that they use non-discriminatory, inclusive language.

USE PARALLEL LANGUAGE

Achieve a tighter link between related ideas by expressing them in **parallel language**; that is, an equivalent grammatical form. The words 'sitting' and 'walking', for example, are parallel; but 'sitting' and 'walked' are not parallel. Also, use words that give the same weight or emphasis to two different but equally important characteristics. The phrase 'the man and the woman' is an example of parallelism, while 'the man and the lady' is not. The phrase 'the gentleman and the lady' is parallel, though outdated.

> **Parallel language** uses the same parts of speech to give balanced phrases that add flow and rhythm to a piece of writing.

A sports commentator who says, 'The men are really holding their strength' and then describes the female event by saying 'The girls will need to hold their strength' is not using parallel language. There are two uses of non-parallel language in this example. The difference between the terms 'men' (adults) and 'girls' (children) gives less weight to the women and therefore can be interpreted as patronising or discriminating. Also, the actions 'holding their strength' and 'hold their strength' are of non-parallel grammatical form.

Effective writers make words work for them by using simple, familiar, concrete language, free of jargon, repetition and clichés. They are prepared to work at achieving competency in word use so that words work well for them and their readers.

A dictionary and a thesaurus are both useful. When choosing words, a quick check in the dictionary will ensure that the spelling is correct, while the thesaurus will offer a range of words suitable for the writing purpose. The word processor is another useful aid to writing. Some packages have a thesaurus, spell check, grammar check and dictionary included in the software.

Table 17.5: Discriminatory language

Sexist	Non-sexist
Each student must submit his assignment by August.	Each student must submit the assignment by August.
When a person is employed, he must contact Personnel.	When people are employed, they must contact Personnel.
My girl will answer the telephone.	My assistant will answer the telephone.
You and your wife are invited to the Christmas party.	You and your partner are invited to the Christmas party.
Lady lawyer	Lawyer
Actress	Actor
Manpower	Staff or workforce
Workman	Worker, employee
Foreman	Supervisor

REVIEW QUESTIONS

4 What is the difference between active and passive voice?
5 a Describe the 'you' approach in writing.
  b What is its purpose?
6 Why is it important to use inclusive language in business writing?

COHERENT SENTENCES AND PARAGRAPHS

OBJECTIVE **3** ▶
Use sentences and paragraphs appropriately in a business context

The sentence is a string of words in which written ideas are presented. These patterns are then interpreted by the receiver. Successful writers aim to send information in sentences that are easy to understand.

Since the natural word order of English speakers is subject–verb–object, a sentence written in this order is clear and easy to understand. While modifiers such as adjectives and adverbs give additional information about a word, too many will make the sentence difficult for the reader to understand. Clarity and coherence in writing are a result of carefully and correctly constructed sentences.

Types of sentences

There are three main types of sentences. Each uses a particular structure or pattern of words.

A **simple sentence** contains one idea in a main clause that stands alone.

❶ A **simple sentence** contains only one idea, expressed in one clause. It thus has only one finite verb; that is, one verb with a subject. The sentence 'James carried the baby' is a simple sentence containing one clause, one finite verb—'carried'—and its subject, 'James'.

A **compound sentence** has two main clauses; each could stand alone.

❷ **compound sentence** contains two or more main ideas, expressed in two principal clauses. A 2 compound sentence has at least two finite verbs; that is, two verbs with subjects. 'James carried the baby and Mary pushed the stroller' is a compound sentence containing two verbs and their subjects, 'James carried' and 'Mary pushed'. A compound sentence is made up of two simple sentences, usually joined by a connecting word such as 'and' or 'but'.

A **complex sentence** has one main clause and one or more subordinate or dependent clauses.

❸ A **complex sentence** contains more than one idea. Apart from the main idea, contained in the principal clause, a complex sentence has at least one other idea that relates to or depends on the main clause. Thus the sentence 'James carried the baby, who was crying' is a complex sentence containing the main idea—namely, that James carried the baby—but also the additional idea (in a subordinate clause) that the baby was crying.

The value of understanding these basic facts about sentences is that the writer can avoid two of the most common errors in writing sentences: writing fragments instead of whole sentences, and writing sentences that lack unity.,

SENTENCE FRAGMENTS

A sentence fragment is incapable of standing alone and making complete sense. An example of an incomplete sentence or fragment is: 'Writing to the clients.' Clearly, the reader needs the writer to finish the thought; for example, 'Writing to the clients was an important task of the manager.' The cause of the incompleteness in the sentence fragment is the absence of a finite verb; that is, a verb with a subject. Beware of treating sentence fragments as whole sentences. They are not, and their presence both confuses the reader and suggests that the writer is unaware of the demands of correct English usage.

Sentence sprawl

Sentence sprawl occurs when a sentence contains separate ideas.

A second, very common fault is the development of a sentence that lacks unity because it contains two quite separate ideas that need separate sentences. Writers often try to cover too much in one sentence, using too many words. Once the meaning of the sentence becomes unclear, sentence sprawl has crept into the writing. It often confuses the reader because there are:

- too many related ideas for the reader to remember
- too many qualifications and modifications to a simple idea for the reader to interpret.

A document is more readable when overly long sentences are broken into two or three sentences clustered into a paragraph. Variety in sentence length also helps to keep the reader's interest.

If a sentence looks awkward, read it aloud. If it sounds too long, or the ideas tangle together, the sentence is a poorly constructed, complex sentence. Eagleson (1990) offers the following guidelines to ensure sentence unity and clear, uncomplicated sentences:

- Sort out the different ideas.
- Include only one or two ideas in each sentence.
- Break a sentence with too many qualifications and modifications of ideas into two or three separate sentences.
- Put conditions attached to the main ideas into separate sentences.
- Put explanations into separate sentences.

If the writing sounds choppy and interrupted, the sentences may be too short. In this case, join two sentences with words such as 'or', 'and', 'nor', 'but', 'so', 'because', 'unless', 'although' and 'otherwise'.

Grammar provides order in written and spoken language. Correct use of grammar adds to the sentence structure and the flow of ideas, and lets the reader understand the writer's intention and information. Effective grammar uses the conventions on which the expectations of the writer and reader meet. Accordingly, the reader relies on the writer to use them and the writer relies on the reader to expect them.

This book does not aim to explain correct grammatical usage or punctuation. However, it is suggested that you develop competence and confidence in dealing with the mechanical details of spelling, grammar and punctuation in your writing. Refer to Fowler (2007) for useful information on grammar.

SENTENCE LENGTH

The general rule when writing in plain English is to keep sentences short and compact to ensure that they are correct, coherent and easy to read. Overly long and involved sentences can be difficult to read and understand. On the other hand, too many short sentences can be just as difficult to read because the connections between the ideas are unclear. Hence, good writers read their sentences to check that the ties or connections in the sentences are straightforward and lead the reader along through the ideas without causing confusion. Variety in sentence length improves the flow of ideas.

Readability

Readability is the measure of the ease with which a written document may be read. In business correspondence, it is advisable to keep sentences short and compact so that the meaning is conveyed clearly.

Readability is the ease or difficulty with which a sentence can be read.

THE FOG INDEX

By applying a simplified version of Gunning's Fog index (a mathematical formula designed in the late 1940s) to a piece of writing, it is possible to gain an indication of its readability. A sentence with eight or fewer words is very easy to read. An average reader would have no trouble with a sentence of 17 words. In this classification, the 17-word sentence is defined as the standard sentence. A sentence of 29 words or more is very difficult to read. However, variety in sentence length can increase the reader's interest.

Even writers with a writing style so good they can correctly construct complex sentences of 30 words or more will think of alternatives. The average reader—who will make up the greatest part of their readership—may only be able to read and understand a simpler construction with an average sentence length of about 17 words. Writers who always use complex sentences are likely to cause their readers to have problems in understanding.

The Fog index is applied by choosing a piece of writing of about half a page to one page in length. The number of words of three syllables or more is counted. Exceptions to the 'three or more syllable' rule are topic words and proper nouns, verb tense endings and plural words. These are not counted. Once the number of words of three syllables or more is counted, the number of sentences is counted.

Then the number of words with three or more syllables is divided by the number of sentences to determine the Fog index. A Fog index of 2–3 is a reasonable average for business writing, while an index of 4–5 is rather too heavy for business writing. An index of 6+ is typical of much academic and technical writing.

In general, the lower the Fog score the greater the number of people who can read and understand the document. While a low Fog score does not guarantee good writing, a score of 5 or more warns the writer that the document is difficult to read and comprehend. To reduce a high score, omit words that are unnecessary, replace long words with shorter words and divide long sentences into shorter sentences. In other words, use a plain English writing style.

PUNCTUATION

Punctuation in sentences gives a flow to the written version of the English language. It creates an impression of the correct sound in the reader's mind. This helps understanding. Punctuation achieves for written communication what pauses and inflection achieve for spoken communication. Writers who use it correctly keep their message clear and their credibility intact. Remember, the starting point in punctuation is to use a capital letter to start a sentence and a full stop to complete it. A comma is used to mark a pause, or to give the remainder of the sentence equal weight with the earlier section.

AVOID OVERCAPITALISATION

Although a tendency to overcapitalise still persists in some forms of business writing, the use of capitals is being seen increasingly as old-fashioned. The Department of Education, Employment and Workplace Relations website gives the following example of the sort of sentence written by many public servants: 'When the Department issued its Annual Report, the Minister tabled it in Federal Parliament.' The department recommends using the more modern and readable style: 'When the department issued its annual report, the minister tabled it in federal parliament.'

Structuring paragraphs around one idea

The coherence and rhythm of any piece of writing depends not only on word choice and sentence structure, but on the unity and coherence of the paragraphs. A **paragraph** is a clustering of sentences built around one main idea or point. The most important function of the paragraph is to help the reader understand the writing. To make paragraphs work in this way, writers must ensure that the focus and writing of each paragraph stand out sharply. Some strategies that will help in this are the use of a topic sentence and a structure that ties the information together.

A **paragraph** is a group of sentences dedicated to one main idea.

PARAGRAPHS IN THE INTRODUCTORY SECTION

In an opening or introductory paragraph, organise the ideas or thoughts around:

- a statement of the subject
- a statement of the intention in the piece of writing
- background information
- a question
- an anecdote
- an opinion.

The first three of these devices are used most often in workplace documents because of their objective nature.

PARAGRAPHS IN THE BODY

Within the main body of a piece of writing, a **topic sentence**—that is, a statement of the main idea in the paragraph—is a useful device. It usually occurs at the beginning of a paragraph but is sometimes used at the end. When the main idea is presented in a topic sentence at the beginning of the paragraph,

A **topic sentence** is a statement of the main idea in the paragraph.

follow it with comment sentences to explain, discuss or analyse the paragraph's main idea. Alternatively, a writer may discuss the supporting information in the comment sentences first, and then present the main idea in the last sentence of the paragraph. Either way, the topic sentence identifies for the reader the central issue of that paragraph.

PARAGRAPHS IN THE CONCLUDING SECTION

In a closing or concluding paragraph, writers may organise the content around:

- a course of action
- a recommendation
- a summary
- a quotation
- a question or challenge
- a restatement of the introduction.

GROUPING SENTENCES

The structure of a paragraph is important if writers want their writing to be readable and the meaning to emerge clearly. Group the sentences within the paragraph to provide a logical progression of information. Linking words such as 'therefore', 'consequently' and 'however' are used to tie all the sentences together and carry the reader comfortably from point to point. Always aim to order the sentences within a paragraph in a way that will make the content approachable and easy to read.

In achieving this sort of coherence, attention to punctuation and such techniques as parallel structure are very important. Information and exercises are available in the references listed at the end of the chapter. Fowler's *Little Brown Handbook* is particularly useful.

PARAGRAPH LENGTH

In business writing, the usual rule is to have at least two sentences in a paragraph. However, a sentence can stand alone as a paragraph, as a special device to add emphasis to a particular point. Short paragraphs are easier and clearer to read. Consider varying paragraph length to provide variety. Remember that paragraphs provide relief to the eye. White space is important as it breaks up blocks of printed material that could otherwise overwhelm or discourage the reader.

An effective writing style presents information in a way that is correct, concise, clear and complete. Since paragraphs rarely stand alone, writers must be able to link them to one another to produce a piece of writing that is clear, coherent and unified. They write their paragraphs to show the reader the development of ideas within the paragraph, to follow ideas from one paragraph to the next, and to progress logically to the concluding comments. Writers who do this make it easy for their readers to comprehend the purpose and meaning of their communication.

PARAGRAPH UNITY

Kane (1988, pp. 71–78) states: 'Paragraph unity involves two related but distinct concepts: coherence and flow. *Coherence* means that the ideas fit together. *Flow* means that the sentences link up so that readers are not conscious of gaps.' Kane says that two criteria are necessary for a paragraph to be coherent: *relevance* ('every idea must relate to the topic') and *effective order* ('ideas must be arranged in a way that clarifies their logic or their importance'). Additionally, there is a negative criterion—*inclusiveness*—'that nothing vital must be omitted'.

Kane states that 'relevance alone is not enough to establish coherence'. If ideas, even if relevant, are poorly arranged, then the paragraph will lack coherence. Arrangement is often inherent in the subject—for example, sequencing a story or detailing a recipe—and often there is an implicit logical structure. One solution Kane offers is 'to arrange ideas in order of relative importance, either climactically, placing the most important last, or anti-climactically, putting it first'.

7 Define the terms 'simple sentence', 'compound sentence' and 'complex sentence'. Write an example of each type of sentence.

8 Define the term 'sentence sprawl'. Briefly discuss three ways of removing sentence sprawl from your writing.

9 *a* Describe two techniques that help to organise information into a paragraph.

   b Identify three techniques that can be used to emphasise a point.

APPLY YOUR KNOWLEDGE

SENTENCE CONSTRUCTION

1 Divide the following sentence into at least three shorter sentences using Eagleson's guidelines presented earlier. A few of the words may need to be changed to give more clarity to the writing.

My strong interest in your organisation and in the field of publishing is based on a long-term involvement with data and people and I am writing to offer multi-faceted employable skills to meet your well-reputed organisation's needs.

2 Make these two simple sentences into a compound sentence.

Marie and Jaryk attended the conference. Charles decided to stay at home.

3 Identify the main clause and the subordinate clause in the following complex sentence.

The child who is wearing the Collingwood sports jumper is my cousin.

4 Reorganise the following long, involved sentence into a paragraph of shorter sentences, so that it can be read quickly and understood at once.

Like many other ways of writing, a piece of persuasive writing uses a number of different strategies to persuade the reader including gaining the reader's attention, interest, desire for the product or service and the willingness to take the action although there are two general strategies underlying any type of writing; that an effective piece of writing will consider its purpose and the needs of the receiver and persuasive writing also uses these two strategies.

5 Reorganise the following passage by combining short statements into longer ones wherever you think the expression can be improved.

Seating arrangements can affect communication between members in a meeting. Round or oval tables are ideal. People see one another's actions and reactions. Rectangular tables are less ideal. They give power to the people at the other end of the table. No tables give informality. Sit above the rest and you have more power. Sit below other people and they have the power.

Suggestion for beginning the first sentence:

Different seating arrangements . . .

Suggestions for making the connections between sentences:

- because . . .
- as . . .
- while . . .

Use 'or when' to connect two short sentences into the concluding sentence.

Suggestion for beginning the concluding sentence:

In any one of the arrangements above . . .

6 Divide into pairs to prepare student profiles for inclusion in a newsletter.

   a Interview your fellow student and create a profile showing name, age, school background, previous academic and school achievements, work experience, and hobbies or interests.

   b Discuss the reasons for using active voice, parallel language and an appropriate layout.

   c Write the profile.

   d Work together to evaluate your profiles for a writing style appropriate to the audience, information structured to highlight the main points, accuracy of information, and presentation appropriate to the writing purpose.

RHYTHM, TONE, ORDER AND FORMAT

A positive tone, the rhythm in a piece of writing, and the order of information all have an impact on the reader. Writers who are able to use a plain English writing style and organise the information into a format that achieves a professional appearance are able to produce effective business documents.

◄ OBJECTIVE 4
Apply rhythm, tone, order of information and format appropriately in business documents

Rhythm

As people read, there is a measured flow or **rhythm** that lets the reader follow a movement in the words. Rhythm in language is used by the writer to emphasise the flow of ideas or to provide pauses that halt the flow to emphasise a point. Techniques that writers can use to create breaks in the rhythm and to emphasise a point they want noticed include:

- a full stop
- a new paragraph
- a topic sentence
- a simple sentence
- a longer complex or compound sentence.

Rhythm is a measured flow of words.

Many experienced writers read their work aloud to listen for the rhythm, and ask themselves the following questions: Does it flow? And does it provide variety? Rhythm in writing is important because it helps to create a style that makes the writing both readable and interesting.

A positive and courteous tone

Tone is the mood or feeling expressed in a piece of writing. Tone is an important part of the meaning of the message. The reader, like the listener, interprets meaning not only from the words but from the tone in which those words are conveyed. The tone of a piece of writing is a factor of the words used and the way in which the writer arranges the words. Courteous, confident and assertive tones are acceptable in business writing and are used when offering an opinion, stating a fact or asking a question. Angry, aggressive, belittling or patronising tones are unacceptable.

Tone is the mood of the writing.

IMPERATIVE TONE

When a command or direction is given, the imperative mood or tone is used—for example, 'Pass the ball to the left-winger' or 'Leave the computer turned on'. The imperative tone leaves out the understood subject 'you'.

POSITIVE TONE

Often a message that contains negative information can be softened and made more acceptable by positive phrasing. For example, you would substitute 'It is possible to commence work on the project early in October' for 'We regret that we are unable to commence work on your project before the beginning of October'.

The first sentence uses a positive tone to create a positive relationship between the writer and the receiver. The second message carries negative and apologetic overtones that are likely to irritate the receiver and create a poor image of you and your organisation. Positive terms help to achieve an assertive, positive and courteous tone. Empathy for the position of the reader can help to build relationships and personalise a piece of writing.

A sentence with a positive beginning—'It is possible . . .'—is likely to be more effective than one with a negative beginning: 'It is not impossible . . .' Each has the same meaning, but the first example works better because it tells the receiver what is possible, in a positive manner. In business writing, use positive language. Try to avoid double negatives, as they are very difficult for the reader to understand.

Writers who are bored, uninterested or in a hurry will reveal this attitude in the tone of their written communication. Take care to write in a way that avoids giving the impression that you are bored, uncertain, pompous, lacking in interest, or are in a hurry to complete the writing task. Tone reflects the writer's attitude towards the receiver and the subject. Writers can improve their writing by taking the time to place themselves in the receiver's position and writing courteously and positively.

Ordering and structuring information

Sequence the information to achieve the writing purpose.

Order of information is the sequence in which the information is presented. In business writing this is usually direct, indirect or problem-solving. A discussion of different ways to order information to achieve the objective of the document is presented in Chapter 13.

The order in which ideas are presented must suit the communication purpose. Some of the communication purposes at work are to inform, to persuade and to instruct. It is vital to choose a method of ordering that suits the analysis, the purpose of the written communication, the content to be presented and the needs of the receiver. Organise written documents to suit the content and the discussion.

ORDER OF PRESENTATION

In a document that uses vertical channels of communication—that is, one that is directed to a supervisor or others at different levels within the organisation—the following order of presentation is appropriate:

- State the problem.
- Present the information related to this problem or issue.
- State the action to be taken.
- Discuss the intended outcomes or implications of this action.
- Request acknowledgment of the message and point the way ahead.

This order of information clearly leads the reader to the action required and invites the reader to provide feedback, to acknowledge successful work or to take further action. Conclude by pointing the way ahead, stating any action to be taken, or requesting information or help. Order of information is discussed more fully in Chapters 13 and 19.

The order suggested above encourages the reader to give feedback that lets the writer know if the message is successful or if reinforcement of the message and a continuation of the communication is necessary. Format uncomplicated business writing with standard headings to provide a useful framework for the written ideas. The headings in common use are:

- issue
- background
- implications for policy
- implications for budgeting
- necessary action.

To develop the content in business writing, the rule, as in any writing, is to place the points in emphatic positions.

Achieving a professional layout

Layout is the arrangement of information on a page or screen.

Layout is the arrangement or presentation of information on a page or screen. It creates the first impression of the message in the mind of the reader and makes the important information stand out. Therefore, set out any document to:

- give maximum impact
- achieve the communication purpose
- enable the reader to find detailed information easily
- improve readability.

Large organisations usually have a style manual that defines the desired design features and gives guidelines so that a consistent image is presented to the organisation's public.

Documents that use formal channels of communication—for example, a submission or a short report—will have a formal layout, whereas a handwritten note will suit communication in the informal channel. As a rule, internal channels of communication have a less formal presentation than external channels.

Appropriate professional layout of any communication is an integral part of an effective style of writing.

BASIC DESIGN PRINCIPLES

Business documents use a wide variety of layouts. The first step is to match the type of document with the communication purpose and channel. The next is to use the basic design principles shown in Table 17.6.

The Department of Education, Training and Youth Affairs website makes the assertion that 'Clear design is just as important as good writing' and gives the following design tips.

1. *Give visual cues.* Headings, subheadings, initial capitals and even numbered paragraphs can act as important signposts.
2. *Break up slabs of type.* Break the document into smaller chunks with short headings or even small graphics.
3. *Use lots of white space.* Use wide margins and plenty of room at the top and bottom of the page.
4. *Choose a typeface for readability.* Most of the typefaces designed for maximum legibility are serif typefaces, but some popular sans-serif typefaces (Gill Sans, Frutiger, Stone Sans and Optima) are also very legible. Choose clear typefaces; use quirky or unusual typefaces only to add character to covers and headings. A typeface's 'x-height' is also important in readability. It is easier to read typefaces with a large x-height. (The x-height is the height of letters such as 'x', 'a' and 'e'.)
5. *Don't shout.* Don't overuse **bold** or *italics*. Never use CAPITAL LETTERS for a whole sentence or paragraph.
6. *Use colour wisely.* The easiest to read is black type on a white background. In the design of forms, type on a shaded background has an important role. Headings and highlighted quotes can be effective on a coloured background.
7. *Reading between the lines.* Four interrelated factors affect the legibility of body text:
   a   the line length (if it is too long, readers tend to lose track; if it is too short, reading flow is interrupted too often)
   b   the type size
   c   the space between lines of type (generous space increases legibility)
   d   the alignment of the right-hand side (the left-hand side alignment increases legibility, but justification—where both sides of the column or page of type are straight—creates uneven gaps which interrupt the reading flow).

Source: Department of Education, Training and Youth Affairs, *Design Tips*, <www.detya.gov.au/archive/publications/ plain_en/design.htm>, viewed 4 September 2003. Copyright Commonwealth of Australia. Reproduced by permission.

Table 17.6: Basic design principles	
Principle	**Purpose**
1 Hierarchy	To rank levels of information (usually no more than four or five levels)
2 Typeface	To improve appearance (usually serif, such as Times New Roman or Book Antiqua, or sans serif, such as Arial or Helvetica, in different point sizes; the most common sizes are 10, 11 or 12 point)
3 Layout	To improve readability (includes use of white space, right- and left-hand margins, line spacing and paragraph depth)
4 Graphics	To illustrate the information and make it easier to understand
5 Colour	To highlight information (usually black and white, and shading)

HIGHLIGHT THE MAIN POINTS

Outline and order the information to help the reader follow ideas through the document's structure. Achieve this by highlighting the main points with:

- headings
- a numbering system
- underlining
- indenting
- shading
- white space.

REVIEW QUESTIONS

10 Contrast a positive tone with a negative tone and give an example of each.

11 Briefly describe the design elements that make up the layout of a document.

12 Describe an order of information suited to a document that uses vertical channels of communication.

EDITING ACCORDING TO THE PRINCIPLES OF PLAIN ENGLISH

OBJECTIVE 5 ▶
Identify the types of errors to look for when editing business documents

Edit for clarity, correctness and appropriateness.

In the final stage, have the courage to edit the work critically and from the point of view of the receiver. This is your chance to ensure that what you have written is not only clear, but also correct and appropriate to the receiver. An editor's role is to ensure that what writers set out to say is indeed what they have said, and that the result is clear, correct and appropriate to the receiver. Editors check that the language highlights the important information, that no information is missing, and that any redundant information and repetition is removed.

The introduction should be inviting and lead the reader to the information in the body of the document. Avoid information overload in the introduction. Too many definitions or too much new and unnatural vocabulary will overwhelm the reader. When editing a summary, ask the following questions: Does it highlight the most important points? Does it orient the reader towards future action?

Writers who edit for clarity, correctness and appropriateness evaluate the document against the seven characteristics of an effective writing style (Table 17.7). Check that the document has each of these characteristics and that it is written at a level the audience can understand.

Proofread for grammar, usage and punctuation. Spellcheck the document to find typos, misspellings and repeated words. Most computerised style checkers will also analyse the style of writing and comment on the ratio of active to passive voice.

Table 17.7: Seven characteristics of an effective writing style

Characteristic	Features
1 Clear	Readable, coherent and unambiguous
2 Complete	Containing all necessary detail
3 Concise	Having no more detail than is necessary
4 Considerate	Aware of the receiver
5 Courteous	Tactful and sensitive
6 Concrete	Not vague or abstract
7 Correct	In detail, grammar, punctuation and spelling

13 Describe three common errors in writing.

14 What should writers avoid in a document's introduction?

15 Contrast the features of a good and poor summary.

APPLY YOUR KNOWLEDGE

WRITING

1. a List six words about the public transport system.

   b Create a topic sentence around one of these words.

   c Prepare a draft paragraph by using the other words in clear sentences that discuss, explain or outline the topic. Take care to vary the length of your sentences.

   d Reread the draft paragraph and highlight the topic sentence. If the topic sentence is placed other than as the first sentence in the paragraph, rewrite the paragraph in an order that places the topic sentence first and order the other three comment sentences appropriately.

2. Assume you are preparing a pamphlet on the topic 'The harmful effects on skin of an excessive amount of sun'. Your task is to write a paragraph that summarises in general terms the effects of excessive sun on human skin.

   a Start the paragraph with a topic sentence that contains the words 'skin cancer'.

   b Follow the topic sentence with two or three comment sentences.

   c Conclude with a sentence that repeats at least one of the key words from your topic sentence.

3. In a reply to a request from a new employee for information about the Social Club, write a four-paragraph account of the activities of the club. Prepare each paragraph so that it begins with a topic sentence followed by comment sentences that build upon the idea in the topic sentence. Repeat a key word from the topic sentence in the last sentence of at least one of the paragraphs.

4. Consider the sentence: 'A number of different strategies can be used to construct paragraphs in a way that makes their content approachable and easy to read, rather than unapproachable and difficult to read.' Briefly explain two different strategies that make a paragraph easy to read.

5. Work in small groups to discuss the following.

   a How do sentences and paragraphs organise information and help the reader through a piece of writing?

   b List two techniques that help to organise information in a paragraph to make it easy to read.

   c List three techniques that can be used to emphasise a point.

   d What is an appropriate tone to use in a set of instructions to employees?

   e What is the difference between a negative and a positive tone? Give examples of two negative and two positive phrases.

   f Define the term 'layout'.

6. Apply the Fog index by choosing a half- to one-page piece of your own writing.

   a Count the number of words of three or more syllables. Do not count the topic words and proper nouns, such as Melbourne, or verb tense endings such as -ing and -ed, or plural words.

   b Count the number of sentences.

   c Divide the number of words with three or more syllables by the number of sentences to give you the Fog score.

   d Compare the readability of your writing against the scores explained on pages 471–2.

   e Why should you be interested in the readability of your document?

   f Should all writing have a low Fog score? Give reasons for your answer.

7. Use the points in the checklist below to self-evaluate your competence in paragraph construction in the questions above.

EFFECTIVE PARAGRAPHS

Does each paragraph:	Effectively	Satisfactorily	Ineffectively
present an idea or thought?			
discuss, explain or develop?			
express clearly the ideas, thoughts or facts as intended?			
use a strategy suited to an introductory, main body or concluding paragraph?			
place the main points in emphatic positions?			
use an order within the paragraph that leads the reader through the idea?			
contain connections to link the sentences?			
relate to and achieve the writer's purpose?			

SUMMARY OF LEARNING OBJECTIVES

 1 ▷ DESCRIBE THREE ADVANTAGES GAINED FROM WRITING IN PLAIN ENGLISH

A plain English writing style is reader-friendly writing that makes it easy to understand business information and ideas. A plain English writing style has three advantages: increased efficiency, equity and effectiveness in communicating the message.

 2 ▷ USE LANGUAGE APPROPRIATELY IN A BUSINESS CONTEXT

Language appropriate to the audience that is courteous and inclusive is more likely to achieve its intended result. Choose clear, concise words for enhance readability. Use technical terms when writing for an informed audience; however, avoid using clichés. The active voice holds the subject and action together. Parallel language links your ideas, balances phrases, and leads the reader through your ideas. Use the 'you' approach to connect with the receiver and to make the document reader-friendly.

 3 ▷ USE SENTENCES AND PARAGRAPHS APPROPRIATELY IN A BUSINESS CONTEXT

Carefully structured sentences and paragraphs built around one idea are easy to read and understand. Avoid sentence fragments by including a subject and action in every sentence. Sentence sprawl, caused by too many ideas in one sentence, is a common fault that makes business documents difficult to understand. The average number of words per sentence for a business document that is easy to read and understand is 20. An effective paragragh has a logical flow, and organises ideas and information around one main idea, thus making it easier for the reader to understand its content.

 4 ▷ APPLY RHYTHM, TONE, ORDER OF INFORMATION AND FORMAT APPROPRIATELY IN BUSINESS DOCUMENTS

Effective business writing uses a courteous, confident and assertive tone complemented by an appropriate rhythm or flow of ideas to add interest and improve the readability of the document. Information is usually sequenced in a direct, indirect or problem-solving order. The main points are placed in empathic positions. The format of the document creates the first impression. Format any business document professionally to give maximum impact, achieve the communication purpose, highlight the main points and improve its readability.

5 ▶ IDENTIFY THE TYPES OF ERRORS TO LOOK FOR WHEN EDITING WRITTEN BUSINESS MESSAGES

Writing in plain English helps to prevent misunderstanding by removing the communication barriers caused by ambiguity, wordiness, obscure and archaic language, technical jargon and officialese. The message is written in a confident manner that conveys a clear and complete message to the receiver. The types of errors to look for when editing written business messages are typos, misspellings and repeated words. Edit to achieve a plain English style in your business writing.

KEY TERMS

ACTIVITIES AND QUESTIONS

1   Prepare a written response to this question: 'Is plain English too simple for a business audience?'

2   Define the terms 'topic sentence' and 'comment sentence'. The topic sentences of four different paragraphs are given here. Copy the topic sentence and construct a paragraph of four more comment sentences in each case.

   a   Tennis should receive radio and television coverage.

   b   A large four-wheel-drive vehicle can be an expensive purchase.

   c   The family are looking forward to taking a holiday in New Zealand.

   d   Speaking before a business audience requires special skills.

3   Write a sentence in the active voice and then a sentence in the passive voice on each of the following topics:

   a   the winner of the men's singles at Wimbledon

   b   the current rate of interest on credit cards

   c   motivation and its impact on a person's work performance

   d   alcohol.

4   Describe the tone of the following response to a customer, and rewrite the document using a more appropriate tone.

Dear Sir

Your allegations of an alleged delay in processing your credit claim have been considered by this section and dismissed.

Please consider the needs of an overworked staff before you put pen to paper and write to this organisation again.

5   Consider the first draft presented below.

A computing system is a useful tool for the report writer. A powerful word-processing package that is easy to use is highly recommended. The features of a word-processing package are not always easy but make it easy to format, edit and rewrite the document. The main advantage for staff is the freedom to vary the information and format of the report without the need to key in the information again. Once the text is keyed in, it is there to stay until it is moved or deleted. Word processors allow the writer to move the text to different locations in the document and to change the layout. Sometimes the operators make mistakes. Layout is part of the business message.

After reading the first draft, the writer decided that the content was vague in its wording, had a tendency towards negative attitudes, and failed to emphasise the positive benefits of training all staff in the special features of word processing. Assume you are the writer of the first draft. Rewrite it to remove the irrelevancies, and specify the main points in a list to clarify and emphasise their importance.

6   In each of the following sentences, identify and correct the fault.

   a   I apologise for the way our product reached you and it seems the panels have broken through insufficient packaging.

    b   Mrs Jones, the attractive wife of the manager, opened the new store.

    c   We must repeat again and again, Mrs Jackson, how deeply apologetic we are that our service to you has been so very poor.

    d   We beg to acknowledge receipt of your gracious letter of the 16th instant.

    e   You have not sent your cheque for payment of this month's account.

    f   We regret that we are unable to commence work on your contract until July.

    g   Thank you for your letter regarding delivery of your order and we suspect damage was caused in transit.

7   Prepare a flyer for a newly published book titled *Communication in Today's Business Environment*.

    a   Use a plain English writing style.

    b   Apply the five basic design principles set out in Table 17.6 and the Department of Education, Training and Youth Affair's design tips on page 477.

    c   Edit your flyer according to the principles of plain English.

8   A member of your staff has produced the following document. You are not happy with the language or the sentence structure.

Dear Sir/Madam

It has come to our attention that your account is currently in arrears, due perhaps to an oversight on your part or alternatively to some temporary pecuniary difficulty that you may be experiencing. It is the long held policy of this company that clients responsible for bad debts should be denied further access to credit until such time as the overdue amount has been received. In view of this, it would appear imperative that you attend to this matter without further loss of time. Should payment not have been received at the above office, or indeed have been posted to same, within a month of the date hereon, continued credit in this store will be impossible.

    a   Identify three errors in language and one in sentence structure.

    b   Rewrite the document.

9   Work in small groups to develop a list of design features for five different business documents.

    a   Identify five different business documents.

    b   Discuss each document, and define its purpose and audience.

    c   List the design features of each document.

    d   Prepare a thumbnail sketch of the design for each document on flip chart paper.

    e   Present your thumbnail sketches and a group summary of your discussion to the large group.

EXPLORING THE WEB

1   a   Access the Department of Human Services' 'Writing style guide' at <www.health.vic.gov.au/>. It provides a concise and clear guide to business writing.

    b   Find another writing style guide for any organisation or business. What is the target audience of each guide? Why is it important that the information in each of these guides is easily understood by its audience? In your opinion, will the guide help employees to write business messages more efficiently or effectively? Give reasons for your answer.

2   Practise writing in plain English by visiting the Invesco 'Oxford Dictionary of Australian Investment Terms' at <www.invesco.com.au>. Choose eight of the terms and write a short précis of each term in plain English. Put the term in context by giving an example of an industry, company or situation where the term could be used appropriately. Format the content in your précis to make it reader-friendly.

3   Research style and usage to make sure your business messages use an effective style by visiting the 'Grammar slammer', <http://englishplus.com/grammar>, to learn the basics of writing style and usage. Find the link 'Style and usage' to browse and click on the topic(s) of your choice.

PROJECT WORK

Your project for this chapter is to edit a business document. Select a business document you have received or read in the recent past (from a journal, business or organisation).

1 Find all examples of:
- topic sentences
- simple sentences
- complex or compound sentences
- linking phrases
- repetition of key words.

2 Find any other places in the document where these devices could have been used successfully.
3 Make any editorial changes that will add to the clarity of the business message.
4 Comment on the effectiveness of the document in achieving its purpose of meeting the sender's need to convey information clearly and identifying the needs of the audience correctly.

BIBLIOGRAPHY

Aristotle, *Rhetoric* (transl. W. Rhys Roberts), http://classics.mit.edu/Aristotle/rhetoric.html, viewed 27 June 2008.

Bovée, C.L. & Thill, J.V. 2005. *Business Communication Today*, 8th edn, Pearson Education International, USA.

Department of Education, Employment and Workplace Relations. 'Avoid overcapitalisation', *Writing Tips*, 5 February 2004, www.dest.gov.au/sectors/training_skills/publications_resources/plain_english_at_work/writing_tips.htm#Avoid_overcapitalisation, viewed 27 June 2008.

Department of Education, Science and Training. 'What's plain English site', www.dest.gov.au/sectors/training_skills/publications_resources/plain_english_at_work/whats_plain_english.htm, viewed 31 October 2007.

Department of Education, Training and Youth Affairs. 'Design tips', www.detya.gov.au/archive/publications/plain_en/design.htm, viewed 4 September 2003.

Department of Education, Training and Youth Affairs. 'Some useful publications', www.detya.gov.au/publications/ plain_en/pepubs.htm, viewed 4 September 2003.

Eagleson, R.D. 1990. *Writing in Plain English*, AGPS, Canberra.

Flesch, R. 1990. *How to Write, Speak and Think More Effectively*, A Signet Book, New York.

Flesch, R. *How To Write Plain English*, www.mang.canterbury.ac.nz/courseinfo/AcademicWriting/Flesch.htm, viewed 4 September 2003.

Fowler, H.R. 2007. *Little Brown Handbook*, 10th edn, Longman, USA.

Garner, B.A. 1991. *The Elements of Legal Style*, Oxford University Press, Oxford.

Gordon, R.L. 1992. *Instuctor's Manual to Accompany Basic Interviewing Skills*, Waveland Press Inc., Prospect Heights, Illinois (reissued 1998).

Guffey, M.E. 2003. *Business Communication: Process and Product*, 4th edn, South-Western, Ohio.

Hywood, G. 2003. 'The bottom line we face when language won't work for us', *Sydney Morning Herald*, 6 November.

Invesco. *Oxford Dictionary of Australian Investment Terms*, www.invesco.com.au/web/webdict.nsf/pages/index, viewed 31 October 2007.

Jones, P. 2003. 'Talk the talk and lose the thought', *The Australian*, Higher Education Supplement, 25 June.

Kane, T.S. 1988. *The New Oxford Guide to Writing*, Oxford University Press, New York.

McAlpine, R. 'From plain English to global English', *Quality Web Content*, www.webpagecontent.com/arc_archive/139/5/, updated 2006, viewed 1 July 2008.

Murphy, E.M. 2001. 'Plain English—style of choice', *Stylewise*, Vol. 7, Issue 3.

Orwell, G. 1946. 'Politics and the English language', www.resort.com/~prime8/Orwell/patee.html.

Putting it Plainly: Current Developments and Needs in Plain English and Accessible Reading Materials, published by the National Board of Employment, Education and Training, England, 1996.

Strunk, W. Jr & White, E.B. 2000. *Elements of Style*, 4th edn, Longman.

Style Manual for Authors, Editors and Printers, 6th edn, John Wiley & Sons Australia, 2002.

Victorian Government, Department of Human Services. 2005. *Writing Style Guide*, Melbourne, viewed 31 October 2007.

Wainscott, J. 'Plain English', *Workwrite: A Process for Communicating*, www.goodwriting.co.nz/plainenglish.html, viewed 4 September 2003.

Watson, D. 2003. *Death Sentence: The Decay of Public Language*, Knopf.

18 Writing business letters, memos and short reports

Photo: Dr Heinz L

LEARNING OBJECTIVES

After studying this chapter you should be able to:

1 ▷ plan and write effective business letters and adapt the style for international business correspondence

2 ▷ recognise good news/neutral letters and apply the direct order of information

3 ▷ write considered bad news letters using the indirect order of information

4 ▷ write effective persuasive letters and understand the AIDA formula

5 ▷ plan and write effective memos

6 ▷ plan and format short reports so as to effect the efficient transfer of information

7 ▷ write justification, progress, periodic and incident reports, and understand the uses of these forms of report.

OUTLINE

Business letters

Direct order of information: writing strategy for good news or neutral letters

Indirect order of information: writing strategy for bad news letters

Writing persuasive letters

Memos

Short reports

Four types of short report

VIEWPOINT: CLARITY AND FORTHRIGHTNESS IN BUSINESS LETTERS

A sample insurance company form letter before it is rewritten in plain English:

'We have recently implemented an enhancement to our computer system that will enable us to provide better service to our valued customers. This has resulted in a slight delay in the processing of your renewal. The difference you will notice is in the payment schedule. Your annual policy premium has been divided over 11 (eleven) months, and as a result your monthly payment will have increased due to the reduced number of monthly instalments.'

Rewritten in plainer language:

'We are a little late in sending your renewal documents because we have made a change in our computer system in order to provide better service. Your annual premium will now be divided over 11 months instead of 12, so the monthly payment will increase slightly.'

The great American 19th-century fiction writer Mark Twain highlights the need for conciseness: 'I am sorry this is such a long letter, but I did not have the time to write a short one.'

Excerpt from Plain Language Association International website, www.plainlanguagenetwork.org/Samples/#business, viewed 12 February 2008.

Business letters are written for many reasons: to initiate action, to inform, to request and to persuade.

Business letters are written for many reasons. Some are written to initiate a business contact or to reply to a contact made by someone else; others are written to give directions or make requests. Some are written to persuade a potential customer to buy or to encourage a customer to pay an overdue account.

A successful business letter is one that elicits the expected response. A letter-writing style that is clear, direct and courteous, used with the correct format, will create a positive first impression and help to influence the reader to accept the writer's ideas.

The three main types of business letters are good news letters, bad news letters and persuasive letters. Each has a different purpose and requires a structure suitable for that purpose.

The term *memo* (or *memorandum*) is used to describe the standard format of communication within an organisation. Memos (or *memorandums* or *memoranda*) are used to communicate information, explain new procedures, announce changes or make requests, confirm results and advise on decisions needed. They are rarely sent between people working in different organisations, although government departments may use memos to communicate with other government departments or authorities.

Short reports communicate information to a variety of people within and outside an organisation. Their main purpose is to provide objective information to justify ideas or proposals, give information on the progress of a project, or present information periodically. Short reports collect and move information through the organisation.

PRINTED MESSAGES RATHER THAN ELECTRONIC?

Paper-based business documents make a more formal impression than online written documents.

While advances in technology mean increasing numbers of business messages are forwarded online, there are still many reasons to use printed paper-based business letters, memos and short reports. The paper-based format is more formal than online media, gives legal or official status, and can be stored for future reference.

Business letters are an appropriate format for special messages such as commendations, condolences, apologies, warnings about legal action, references, or acceptance of an offer of employment. The business letter has more presence than an email, makes a more formal impression, and adds a personal touch through the handwritten signature. It is likely to be treated more seriously by the receiver than an email. Written communications may have greater impact than email and other online media because of the information overload caused by excessive amounts of email.

Applications for credit, rental agreements, employment contracts, sales agreements, and certificates of accomplishment on an official company letterhead are formal documents. Business letters, memos and short reports are more acceptable for formal messages than email or fax, because the status of paper-based documents is often seen as more official than online messages. Legal requirements mean that business agreements, contracts and other documents must be paper-based, signed and witnessed. They must also be filed for future reference.

BUSINESS LETTERS

OBJECTIVE 1 ▶
Plan and write effective business letters and adapt the style for international business correspondence

The **layout** of the letter is the frame for the body of your letter. It consists of eight parts that are regarded as essential, plus other optional parts. The essential parts are listed in Table 18.1 and on the website <www.business-letters.com/business-letters.htm>. The site also suggests five main steps—identify your aims, establish the facts, know the recipient of the letter, create a sample copy and decide on the physical layout of the letter—to follow as you write a business letter.

Functions of the parts

Layout is the arrangement of information on a page.

Each part of a business letter is used for a particular purpose. The parts and their purpose are illustrated using the business letter from Castle's Realty (Figure 18.1 on page 488). The purpose of this letter is to acknowledge the request for new office space. It is a good news letter and, therefore, follows the writing strategy set out in in Table 18.7 on page 494.

Table 18.1: Essential parts of a business letter layout

Essential parts	Optional parts
Writer's name and address	Attention line
Date	Reference initials
Inside address	Enclosure
Greeting or salutation	File number
Subject line	Sender's telephone extension
Body of the letter	Email address
Complimentary close	Company web address
Writer's signature and job title or designation	

LETTERHEAD

The **letterhead** identifies the writer and their address and telephone number. Most business organisations use company stationery with a letterhead that includes the company name, address, email address, and telephone and fax numbers. Some companies also include a reference (Our Ref. or Your Ref.) and telephone extension.

A **letterhead** displays the official name, address, telephone, fax, email address and logo, usually at the top of the page.

DATE

The date is placed between the letterhead and the inside address; for example:

- 7 August 2011
- August 7, 2011

Short forms of dates can be misleading in your international business letters. For example, 7/8/11 will be read as 8 July in the United States, but as 7 August in Australia. Always spell out the month in words.

INSIDE ADDRESS

The inside address is the reader's address. It is placed between the date and the salutation, two lines below the date.

ATTENTION LINE

Some organisations such as local government councils ask that all correspondence be directed to the general manager. In a situation such as this, identify in an **attention line** the specific person who is to attend to the letter's contents. It is placed two lines below the inside address.

The **attention line** names the person who is to attend to a letter's contents.

SALUTATION

The **salutation** is the writer's greeting to the reader. It is placed two lines below the inside address or the attention line. When the writer knows the receiver's name, it is used in the salutation or greeting rather than 'Dear Sir' or 'Dear Madam'. If the writer knows the person well enough to use their first name, this makes the letter more personal. In this case, the writer should also sign the letter with his or her first name.

The **salutation** is the writer's greeting to the receiver.

On many occasions, writers will need to use 'Mr', 'Ms', 'Mrs' or 'Miss' in the salutation. 'Mr' and 'Ms' distinguish between people on the basis of gender. 'Mrs' and 'Miss' distinguish between people on the basis of marital status. If a woman prefers to be addressed as 'Mrs' or 'Miss', then use this form of address. The convention these days is to use 'Ms' if you do not know a woman's preference.

CASTLE'S REALTY

18 High Street
HALE NSW 2640
Telephone (02) 5923 4680
Facsimile (02) 5923 4681
Email castles@ocean.com.au

7 August 2011

Mr Nick Scrubs
The Manager
Good Health Medical Centre
21 Well Street
HALE NSW 2640

Order of information   Dear Nick

Subject line   **OFFICE SPACE**

Acknowledgment   Thank you for the opportunity to submit our proposals to you for more appropriate office space for the Good Health Medical Centre.

Clear yes   We are delighted to be able to offer you the option of leasing the Florence Nightingale Building adjoining Central Park. The previous lessee, New Face Beauty, bought an office block in High Street two months ago.

Details   New Face Beauty renovated the Florence Nightingale Building extensively and we believe you will find the layout an ideal fit for your needs. The building is located at 6 Park Street and I will be pleased to organise an inspection for you. A bus stop is outside the building.

New Face Beauty will vacate the premises next week. We can offer you a five-year lease on the building for a monthly rental of $5000, with an option to extend the lease for a further five years. If this building is not suitable, we can suggest some excellent alternatives.

Actions to be taken   Please advise me if you wish to inspect the Florence Nightingale Building or discuss alternative sites.

Courteous close   Thank you for your interest in my good health. My golf has improved to the stage where I think I should challenge you to a match.

Yours sincerely

Tom Castle

Tom Castle

Manager

Figure 18.1: Effective letter of acknowledgment in full block layout—a good news letter

SUBJECT LINE

The **subject line** identifies the letter's subject or purpose. It should be no more than six to ten words. It is placed below the salutation.

The **subject line** identifies a letter's subject or purpose.

BODY OF THE LETTER

The writing style suited to the body of the letter is the '*you*' *approach*, because it speaks personally to the reader. As it has a direct impact on the reader, the 'you' approach is likely to be understood easily and to achieve the intended action. Each part of the body has the particular purpose shown in Table 18.2. A successful combination of opening and closing paragraphs in the body of the letter catches the reader's attention and interest and prompts the response you seek.

The 'you' approach is a writing style that speaks personally to the reader.

COMPLIMENTARY CLOSE

The **complimentary close** should match the form of address used in the salutation. For a business letter that opens with 'Dear Sir' or 'Dear Madam', close with 'Yours faithfully' followed by your signature, name, and job title or designation. When you write to someone you have met, a specific person in the organisation or a person who has corresponded with you before, their name is used in the salutation or opening and 'Yours sincerely' in the complimentary close. The usual rule is to use 'Yours faithfully' when the receiver's name is unknown and 'Yours sincerely' when the person's name is known and used in the salutation (Table 18.3). Type the complimentary close two lines below the last line of the letter.

The **complimentary close** is the formal (yours faithfully) or less formal (yours sincerely) closing.

Hyslop (1997, p. 2) comments on the closing of business letters: '[N]owadays usage is less strict and it seems that there is a preference for *Yours sincerely* in all cases. Of course when writing to a business organisation you can avoid this dilemma altogether by using the memorandum form, that is without salutation or complimentary close.'

Table 18.2: The body of a letter		
Part	**Purpose**	**Strategy**
Beginning	The beginning has two purposes: to open courteously and, when appropriate, to link the letter to previous transactions.	In the opening paragraph, aim to catch the reader's attention, interest and desire to read further. State your intentions. Explain the situation. Present the alternatives and related information. Use original opening statements that are relevant to the rest of the letter, rather than clichéd openings that use a group of words routinely, such as: 'We are pleased to inform you . . .'
Middle or body	The body of a letter contains content appropriate to the purpose of the letter. The message puts the reader in a position to take action on the basis of the document.	The middle or body of the letter presents details and information. The writer's aim is to create a clear, concise and complete message that is easy for the reader to understand. The style uses the 'you' approach.
Ending	The ending has two purposes: to indicate future action and to close courteously.	The closing paragraph states the actions to be taken by the reader. The final sentence concludes with the same courteous tone used throughout the letter. This tone maintains goodwill between the writer and the reader.

Table 18.3: Salutation and complimentary close		
Dear Sir	Dear Mr Johnson	Dear James
Yours faithfully	Yours sincerely	Yours sincerely

SIGNATURE BLOCK

The writer's signature and name follow the complimentary close. It may be appropriate to place the position or job title of the writer under the signature and typewritten name.

Types of layout

The effect of any letter is improved by the choice of a suitable and correct layout. The parts of a business letter can be arranged in different ways. There are two main types of layout:

1. full block layout
2. modified block layout.

The parts and content of both these layouts are arranged to create a positive first impression.

FULL BLOCK LAYOUT

Full block layout places each part of the letter against the left-hand margin of the page: the sender's address, the date, the inside address and the salutation are all placed against the left margin. Each paragraph is started against the left margin, as are the complimentary close and the signature block. Supplementary parts, such as enclosures, file numbers and copy notations, are also blocked. Full block layout is an attractive and modern layout that is easy to read (see Figure 18.1 on page 488).

MODIFIED BLOCK LAYOUT

Modified block layout centres the sender's address or blocks it to the right margin. The date is placed directly below and in line with the sender's address or blocked to the right. The inside address and the salutation are placed against the left-hand margin, and each paragraph is blocked against the left-hand margin. The complimentary close and signature block are centred in line with the writer's address and the date. Modified block layout is a more conservative style of layout (Figure 18.5 on page 504).

PUNCTUATION STYLES

Two different punctuation styles for business letters are the open style and the mixed style. Open style omits punctuation throughout each part of the letter except the body. No punctuation is used in the salutation or the complimentary close. In mixed style, a comma is placed after the salutation and after 'Yours faithfully' or 'Yours sincerely' in the complimentary close. The example in Figure 18.3 on page 496 uses the open style.

Planning the business letter

It is the responsibility of the letter writer to know the purpose in writing and to send this message clearly and courteously to the receiver. By completing the following seven steps in a business letter, you are able to achieve this. Skilful letter writers complete many of these steps automatically and avoid the ten common errors listed in Table 18.4.

1. Decide on the purpose of the letter.
2. Decide what is to be said.
3. Write all the ideas in point form.
4. Order these ideas into a sequence appropriate to the type of letter.
5. Write the first draft using correct business writing style.
6. Read the letter to ensure that the purpose is likely to be achieved.
7. Rewrite if necessary.

The 3 × 3 writing process

The 3 × 3 writing process is a systematic plan for developing business letters, memos and short reports. The process has three parts:

Table 18.4: Ten common errors to avoid

1	Obscure, unfamiliar words and jargon	6	Traditional routine openings that sound insincere
2	Lengthy sentences and very long paragraphs	7	Negative, pessimistic content
3	A discourteous or too familiar tone	8	New ideas in the closing paragraph
4	Long sections of unbroken text	9	A closing that omits the actions or desired results
5	An order of information unsuited to the letter's purpose	10	A poor and untidy format

1 Phase 1: prewriting—analyse, anticipate and adapt your approach.
2 Phase 2: writing—research, organise and compose.
3 Phase 3: revising and editing—revise, proofread and evaluate your document.

When writing short, routine messages, you may take only a little time to reflect and plan. Longer, more detailed documents will require more time to select, organise, shape, write and edit.

Applying a plain English style to business documents

A **plain English** writing style uses positive language, clear expression and a courteous tone. Combine these features with a logical structure to create a letter that is easy to read and understand. Plain English is discussed more fully in Chapter 17. Some of the key elements in an effective letter-writing style are set out in Tables 18.5 and 18.6. As well as following these rules, improve the readability of your letters by using short sentences (15–20 words in length).

Plain English is a readable writing style that uses the 'you' approach, positive language, clear expression, and an assertive, courteous tone.

Alley (1996, p. 170) states: 'Unlike a telephone conversation, correspondence presents the audience with a contract that is dated and can support a claim in court.' He points out that if the information to be conveyed is difficult to phrase, correspondence allows you to revise the message until it is correct. Alley emphasises four aspects of business letter-writing style: organisation, emphasis, clarity and forthrightness. In his view, it is important to get to the main point as quickly as possible—in the first paragraph or first sentence. Important details should be in the first or last sentence of the paragraph. These are two emphatic points because of their position and the white space before and after the paragraph.

As the receiver reads a business letter faster than larger documents, clarity of expression aids the reader's understanding and adds conviction to the writing. Present new ideas clearly and the reader is likely to accept them. Arrange ideas in a logical sequence and the reader will be able to follow the flow of thoughts. Alley points out that people often seem to change their personality when they write letters and, instead of using plain English, they resort to such phrases as 'per your request' or 'enclosed please find'. In his view, 'the goal of being forthright is important because in correspondence, more than other types of documents, tone is difficult to control' (1996, p. 176). The appropriate tone in a business letter displays courtesy towards the reader and confidence in the correspondence.

International business letters

Communicate successfully with people all over the world by making your business letters easy for readers of English as a foreign language to read and understand. The ability to create appropriate business letters for an international audience not only contributes to more efficient business transactions, but also demonstrates that you are knowledgeable and culturally sensitive. Lehman and Dufrene (2002, p. 182) suggest the following strategies when writing messages for an international audience:

● Write naturally but avoid abbreviations, slang, acronyms, technical jargon, sports and military analogies, and other devices. Many of these may be confusing and unfamiliar to those whose English is a second language.
● Avoid words that trigger emotional responses such as anger, fear or suspicion.
● Use simple terms, but attempt to be specific as well. Avoid pompous words such as 'pursuant to your request' or superlatives such as 'fantastic' or 'terrific'.

Table 18.5: Elements in a plain English writing style

Key element	Purpose	Strategies
Clarity	Clarity in expression aids the reader's understanding and adds conviction to your writing.	• Present new ideas clearly. • Arrange ideas in a logical sequence. • Avoid jargon and technical terms unless you are certain that the reader will understand the terms. • Remove ambiguous and unnecessary words.
Readability	Readability makes your information accessible to an average reader.	• Use 15–20 words per sentence. • Limit each sentence to one idea. • Use complex sentences of 25–35 words sparingly, as they require a high level of reading skill. • Vary the length of sentences to add rhythm and interest to your writing. • Avoid slang.
Positive language (see Table 18.6)	Positive language creates a positive first impression.	• Use direct and courteous language. • Project your desire to communicate with the reader. • Use a courteous and tactful tone. • Choose positive words rather than negative words.
Active voice	The active voice shows who or what took the action.	• Present a positive and enthusiastic impression by using the active voice (see pags 466–7 in Chapter 17). • Examples are: 'Tony reports to . . .'; 'I act as Manager . . .' • Frequent use of passive voice produces a sluggish effect. • Active voice creates an energetic image.
The 'you' approach	The 'you' approach addresses the readers and their interests.	• Focus on the readers. • Speak directly to them and address their needs. • Open a letter with a sentence that reflects an awareness of the needs of the reader. • Show consideration for the readers and how the content affects them. • Remember to focus on the document's purpose.
Punctuation	Punctuation helps understanding.	• Use a capital letter to start. • End a sentence with a full stop to break an idea into parts and separate ideas from one another. • Decide whether you need to use a comma by reading the sentence aloud. • Check that the sentences are not too long. • Apply the general rule: always use more full stops than commas.
Paragraphs	Paragraphs organise information around one idea.	• Use the average paragraph length in a business letter—about six lines. • Avoid breaking an idea that should be presented as a complete unit in one paragraph into two paragraphs just to achieve the average paragraph length. • Occasionally, let a sentence stand alone as a paragraph to add emphasis.

Table 18.6: Positive and negative language

Negative sentences	Positive sentences
'It is not unlikely that . . .'	'Possibly this can . . .'
'Company policy does not allow . . .'	'Company policy prevents . . .'
'I see no reason why . . .'	'I see . . .'
'Do not use the telephone for personal calls . . .'	'Use the telephone only for business calls . . .'

- Follow the same techniques for increasing readability as you would use in writing to someone fluent in English. Write short, simple sentences containing only one idea and construct short paragraphs that focus on developing one idea.
- Consider the subtle differences in the ways specific cultures organise messages. Asians, for example, typically use indirect patterns of writing, even when conveying good news.
- Use graphic visual aids and forms whenever possible, to simplify the message.
- Use figures for expressing numbers to avoid confusion.
- Be aware of differences in the way numbers and dates are written. For example, the American date form puts the month before the day.
- Write out the name of the month in international correspondence to avoid misunderstandings.
- Become familiar with the traditional format of letters in the country of the person to whom you are writing, and adapt your format as much as possible.

Source: From Pkg. Himstreet and Baty's *Business Communication Handbook,* 13th edn, by Lehman/DuFrene. © 2002. Reprinted with permission of South-Western, a division of Thomson Learning, <www.thomsonrights.com>.

REVIEW QUESTIONS

1. List the eight basic components of a business letter.
2. List the features of the full block layout for a letter. What are the advantages of the full block layout?
3. Identify at least three errors you should avoid when writing a business letter.
4. Why must you always identify the purpose of a letter before you begin writing?
5. Briefly explain the 'you' approach in writing and justify its use.
6. How can cultural differences impact on a written message? Give examples.

DIRECT ORDER OF INFORMATION: WRITING STRATEGY FOR GOOD NEWS OR NEUTRAL LETTERS

◄ OBJECTIVE 2
Recognise good news/ neutral letters and apply the direct order of information

In a **good news** or **neutral letter**, the writer and reader share positive, favourable or neutral information. Good news or neutral letters are common at work. Some uses of good news or neutral letters are to grant a loan or extend credit, make an inquiry or a request, introduce your organisation to potential customers, inform members of an organisation's activities, extend an agreement or create goodwill. A good news letter uses the order of information set out in Table 18.7. This strategy creates the direct order of information and a structure suitable for any good news, positive or neutral letter.

The subject line helps to focus the reader's attention on the letter's content. It should be six to ten words in length. A writer may choose to omit the subject line and identify the letter's purpose and good

Good news or **neutral letters** present positive or neutral information by using the direct order of information.

- Identify the letter's purpose in the subject line or opening paragraph.
- Place the good news in the opening paragraph.
- State the details that support the favourable or good news in the middle paragraphs.
- Close with a statement of goodwill.

news in the opening paragraph. This gives the reader the positive answer, information or good news at the outset. This immediately catches the reader's attention and creates the desire to read further.

In the middle paragraphs, give details and information. A positive letter is neutral or of benefit to the writer and reader; there are no existing or expected problems. Provide all necessary information clearly and logically. Use the closing paragraph to state any action to be taken by the reader and close on a positive note. The effective letter of request in Figure 18.2 is an example of a good news letter.

Four types of good news letter

The writing strategy outlined in Table 18.7 is suitable for preparing any positive or neutral business letter. It enables you to apply the appropriate order of information for a good news letter. The content of different types of positive or neutral letters will vary. This section offers specific guidelines for planning four different types of good news letter:

1. an inquiry
2. a request
3. an acknowledgment
4. a letter of introduction.

A letter of inquiry seeks information.

A **letter of inquiry** asks others to share information and ideas. Most inquiries are routine; for example, an inquiry about the availability of a product or the details of a service. The information will be used when making a decision on completing orders or providing a service, or passed to someone else. The good news order of information is used for a letter of inquiry. A writer who needs specific information may open with a question. On occasions, more than one question may be asked. In this case, open with a summary statement. Then in the body, list and number the questions from most important to least important. Indicate the action to be taken by the reader and close courteously.

A letter of request seeks specific action.

A **letter of request** is different from an inquiry in that it seeks a specific action. Figure 18.2 is a letter of request. The good news order of information is used for a letter of request.

A purchase order is an example of a specific request. A purchase order is usually made by ordering face-to-face from the sales representative, by telephoning the company or by filling out an order form. On the occasions when a letter is written, authorise the purchase in the first sentence. The reader is then able to identify the letter as an order rather than simply a request for information. Include all relevant details, particularly the order number and the quantity. Give the price and date of delivery and describe the item in detail. State how you would like to have the product delivered: by rail, post or private transport carrier. In the conclusion, specify the method of payment.

A letter of acknowledgment recognises the actions of another.

A **letter of acknowledgment** acknowledges requests for information, confirms orders, supplies information and thanks the reader. An effective acknowledgment letter maintains goodwill. The writing plan for a letter of acknowledgment follows the good news order of information set out in Table 18.7.

It is courteous and helpful to acknowledge orders immediately. If a delay in delivery is likely, send an interim acknowledgment letter thanking the customer for the order. Give the reasons for the delay so that the customer knows what is happening and when to expect delivery. Close the letter courteously. Figure 18.3 presents a letter acknowledging an inquiry about training facilities.

GOOD HEALTH MEDICAL CENTRE

21 Well Street HALE NSW 2640

Telephone (02) 5923 1987 Facsimile (02) 5923 1997 Email goodhealth@mednet.com.au

5 August 2011

Mr Tom Castle
The Manager
Castle's Realty
18 High Street
HALE NSW 2640

Order of information	Dear Tom
Subject line	
Identify the request	**OFFICE SPACE**

The Good Health Medical Centre requires a larger rental property urgently and I hope you can suggest a number of suitable options. The centre now has four full-time and three part-time doctors practising at the centre. However, our current office space is cramped and inadequate.

Background details

Our doctors need:

- five consulting rooms
- three treatment rooms
- off-street parking
- a large reception and waiting area
- a staff recreational area
- adequate space for storing our medical files.

We would like to operate within walking distance of Central Park and on a bus route.

Our response

Our current lease will expire at the end of September. We would want to begin a long-term lease for our new rooms at this time. Prompt attention to our needs would be appreciated.

Courteous close

I hope your good health continues and that your golf game continues to encourage improved performances on the Hale Golf Course.

Yours sincerely

Nick Scrubs

Nick Scrubs
Manager

Figure 18.2: Letter of request (good news letter)

Tavern
Function Centre
42 The Esplanade
New Beach NSW 2111
Phone (02) 1111 1111 email tav@function.com.au

30 April 2010

Mr Mathew Lloyd
Management Institute
PO Box 444
Havenville NSW 2222

Order of information

Dear Mathew

Acknowledgment

Thank you for the opportunity to submit a proposal for an all-day seminar.

Naturally we would be delighted to hold your function at the Tavern Function Centre and to help out in any way to make the seminar a great success.

Details

Mathew, based on your needs I would like to offer you use of the 'Boardroom' and the 'Saloon Room'.

For an all-day seminar we can offer you:

Hire of function room (each)	$200.00
Complimentary 'cuppa' on arrival	
Morning tea, coffee & biscuits	$7.00 per guest
Substantial morning tea, including cakes and biscuits	$8.00 per guest
Light conference luncheon, including gourmet sandwiches, fruit platters, tea, coffee and orange juice	$20.00 per guest
Afternoon tea	$7.00 per guest

Any other beverages can be charged to you on a consumption basis. Alternatively, guests can purchase their own drinks.

Any equipment required during the seminar, such as PowerPoint, smartboards, videos and screens, will be available to hire on the day at a cost of $40.00 per unit. A microphone and lectern will be set up at no additional charge.

Courteous close

I look forward to helping you organise the function. If you have any questions, please call me any time.

Yours sincerely

Francene Lee

Francene Lee
Functions Coordinator

Figure 18.3: Effective letter of acknowledgment

Some letters of acknowledgment will be in answer to a request for service or help. The same writing strategy applies:

- Begin with an acknowledgment: 'Thank you for your invitation to address your students.'
- Clearly say yes: 'I will be delighted to do so.'
- Supply necessary information: 'I am available on the date you nominate but, because of work commitments, would prefer the later time of 8 pm.'
- Close courteously: 'Please contact my secretary to confirm these details. I look forward to seeing you.'

A successful **letter of introduction** will reach the reader at a time when there is a need for the type of service offered in the introduction. By using correct business letter format and each of the basic parts of a business letter, the letter will make a positive first impression on the reader. The letter of introduction aims to maintain contact and create goodwill and the opportunity for future sales. Real estate agents and car salespeople often use letters of introduction. Reminder letters from doctors and dentists are another version of a letter of introduction.

A **letter of introduction** seeks to create a link between sender and receiver.

Personalise the letter with the reader's name. Write in a courteous tone and with the 'you' approach to show an interest in the reader's needs. Provide details of interest with believable information. Close with a paragraph that lets the reader know what you can do for them. State or point the way to the action they can take to make contact with you.

A successful introduction letter creates a communication link between the writer and the potential client. Some letters of introduction almost cross the line between a good news letter and a persuasive letter because they can have persuasive elements. It is an unrequested letter, so try to keep it short, complete and courteous to avoid irritating the reader.

Each of the four good news letters presented above has its own writing plan, but each one uses the same writing strategy: the direct order of information. A type of letter that uses a different writing strategy, the indirect order of information, is the bad news letter. The writing strategy for conveying bad news and four types of bad news letters are discussed in the next section.

REVIEW QUESTIONS

7. Briefly explain the order of information in a good news letter.
8. Identify four types of good news letters.
9. Explain how a letter of introduction creates a link between the sender and receiver.

APPLY YOUR KNOWLEDGE

WRITING BUSINESS LETTERS

1. In a business letter, what is the function of the following?
   a. letterhead
   b. salutation
   c. subject line
   d. body
   e. complimentary close
   f. signature block.
2. In small groups, discuss the following:
   a. How does block layout differ from modified block layout?

b Where do you place supplementary parts such as enclosures, file numbers or copy notations in a letter using modified block layout?

c Why is it important to format your business letter well?

3 Some examples of poor letter-writing technique and phrases to avoid are listed below. Correct and rewrite the sentences.

a 'I am pleased to inform you that you are required to attend the next meeting.'

b 'For all practical purposes, time could be saved if you used the new terminals.'

c 'It is important here to take into account the fact that prices will increase in May.'

d 'In most cases, goods are delivered within 14 days of the date on the order form.'

e 'I desire to inform you that our representative is unable to call next week.'

f 'You are advised for your information that we will not agree to your proposal.'

g 'Due to the fact that State Rail will be repairing the lines tomorrow, train travel will be unavailable between 10 and 12 pm next Friday.'

h 'Before examining the reasons for this, I should state that all staff are expected to use electronic mail.'

i 'We demand payment of the outstanding amount owed to us: $340 within the next 48 hours otherwise your service will be disconnected.'

j 'In this, comparatively the most fragmented, most competitive media market in Australia (four commercial television networks, five commercial radio stations, three weekly community newspapers and one daily newspaper), the rates charged are already the most competitive possible, consistent with the standards demanded by our advertising clients.'

4 Assume that you are Azhar Hayat. You are writing in response to an advertisement offering MP3 players at $100 below normal retail price. You want information about the brand name, the availability of service and repairs, delivery times and method of payment. Write the letter using full block layout and the seven basic parts of a letter. In the opening paragraph, present a clear courteous request.

5 Consider the following ineffective opening for a letter of request.
'I received a brochure outlining the details of the Great New Zealand Ski Holiday for 17 days at $3995. Since I want to travel with my family sometime within the next 12 months, I would like to know the dates of departure and any other details. Could you please send me specific details?'
Rewrite the request as a clear direct opening to the letter.

6 What is the main purpose of a letter of acknowledgment? Briefly explain the writing strategy used in a letter of acknowledgment.

7 Assume you are Allen Reiffel, a council development officer. You have been asked to draft a letter of acknowledgment thanking people for their donations or help after recent floods. Assume you are writing on behalf of the Lord Mayor's Appeal. Format the letter in blocked layout and use a writing strategy to achieve the order of information suited to a good news or neutral letter. (Invent the council's address.)

8 Write a letter of inquiry to your bank asking for information on the different types of accounts and interest rates suited to a new account you wish to open. Assume you are interested in savings accounts, fixed-term accounts and cheque accounts. You also want to know the minimum amounts needed in each account to receive the best interest rate. Follow the writing plan suited to a letter of inquiry. Start the letter with the inquiry and explain why you are making the inquiry. Close with a neutral, courteous paragraph.

9 Assume you are Amanda Brown, secretary of a local service club. Write a letter of acknowledgment to members thanking them for their participation and support in the activities of the club during the past year. You might mention activities the club has been involved in, such as fundraising to provide extra sporting equipment for the local Police and Citizens Youth Club. Club members have also organised an exchange study scheme between Australian and European 16- to 18-year-olds. Invent details for your address and a member's address.

INDIRECT ORDER OF INFORMATION: WRITING STRATEGY FOR BAD NEWS LETTERS

◄ OBJECTIVE 3
Write considered bad news letters using the indirect order of information

A **bad news letter** gives the reader unwelcome news; it is therefore likely to disappoint the reader. It is a difficult letter to write successfully, because the writer must offer the bad news yet keep the goodwill of the receiver. This means that the letter should be structured so that the reader has every chance of understanding the explanation and accepting the decision.

A **bad news letter** gives unwelcome news, using the indirect order of information.

In business, bad news letters are written for many different reasons. Some uses of bad news or negative letters are to refuse credit, refuse a request, decline to speak at a function, decline to donate time or money to an organisation, notify an unsuccessful job applicant, explain why an order cannot be filled, and refuse a requested adjustment.

Someone who receives bad news in the first part of the letter may read no further. The writer needs to guide the reader gradually through the letter, so that he or she sees and reads any reasons and explanation for the refusal before reaching the bad news. The writing strategy set out in Table 18.8 achieves this indirect order of information. It leads the reader through the relevant information and explanation to the bad news towards the end of the letter.

Open with a sentence that acknowledges the original request, as this gives information on which both the writer and reader agree. It is a neutral opening paragraph. If the refusal is stated in the opening paragraph, the customer may simply stop reading. As the writer wants the reader to read the whole letter, this neutral paragraph is used to lead the reader to the main purpose of the letter. Examples of neutral openings are:

- 'Thank you for your order No. 18-652.'
- 'Your inquiry for vacation employment is appreciated.'

In the middle paragraphs, present a positive explanation of the situation with courteous and clear reasons for the refusal. It is unacceptable and discourteous to sound sarcastic, patronising, insulting or angry. Explain the reasons before giving the refusal. Lead the reader to the bad news tactfully.

State the refusal clearly, because the reader needs to know the organisation's decision. Write the letter with conviction and confidence so that the reader understands the reasons for the refusal. Never place the refusal in the last sentence of the letter. Close in a neutral way with a sentence or paragraph that is courteous and pleasant. Avoid referring again to the bad news, apologising repeatedly or using clichés. Instead, close the letter in a positive way.

Four types of bad news letter

This section offers specific guidelines for planning four different types of bad news letter:

1. order refusals
2. saying 'no' to a request for credit
3. refusing an adjustment
4. declining invitations and requests for favours.

Table 18.8: Writing strategy for a bad news letter

- Open with a neutral buffer.
- Explain the situation.
- Give the refusal or negative news.
- Close with a positive paragraph.

Sometimes, orders are refused because buyers have overextended their credit level or are poor or slow payers. Alternatively, your organisation may not deal with the requested line of stock. The writing plan or order of information for an **order refusal** follows the bad news order of information set out in Table 18.8.

Some of the reasons for refusing credit could be that the applicant has spent too little time at one address or in current employment, has too few assets or too low a level of income. The most usual request for credit, and therefore the most usual **credit refusal**, is for a loan or a credit card. The writing plan or order of information when refusing credit is the bad news order of information.

A genuine adjustment is a justified request to change, replace or make an adjustment to a transaction that has already taken place. Examples may include requests to replace damaged goods or missing parts, to replace an incomplete order, or to correct an error on an account. An **adjustment refusal** is given when the organisation believes that the request for an adjustment is unjustified, that the problem was not caused by the organisation or that a problem does not exist. The bad news order of information is used when refusing an adjustment. By giving valid reasons for the refusal, you are able to soften the bad news.

The bad news order of information is also used when declining invitations and requests. Invitations and requests often come from other business people or community groups. To maintain goodwill, it is necessary to write the refusal in a manner that expresses an interest in the reader. This order of information helps the writer to achieve this goodwill.

In each of these bad news letters, the writing strategy is the indirect order of information. The part of the letter most important to the reader is the decision, in this case the refusal. The indirect order of information leads the reader to this decision, so that all the contents—the reasons as well as the decisions—are written in an attempt to maintain the reader's goodwill. A successful bad news letter will maintain a positive relationship with the reader (see Figure 18.4).

An **order refusal** declines a request.

A **credit refusal** rejects a request for credit.

An **adjustment refusal** is given when the organisation believes that the request for an adjustment is unjustified.

REVIEW QUESTIONS

10 Why is the indirect order of information used in bad news letters?

11 What is the purpose of the neutral closing in a bad news letter?

12 How can a company soften an adjustment refusal?

OBJECTIVE **4** ▷
Write effective persuasive letters and understand the AIDA formula

WRITING PERSUASIVE LETTERS

A **persuasive letter** is written to influence the reader to change an attitude or take some action to satisfy a need. In business, this may mean persuading the reader to buy a product, to pay an overdue account or to consider an application for work. Clearly, the motivation to respond comes from within the reader; the suggestion that stirs that motivation comes from the letter writer. The writing strategy or order of information for a persuasive letter is set out in Table 18.9.

Persuasive letters aim to influence the reader to change an attitude or take some action to satisfy a need.

Table 18.9: Writing strategy for a persuasive letter

- Open with a sentence or paragraph that catches the reader's attention.
- In the next paragraph, develop an idea that interests the reader or shows how the idea serves the reader's interest.
- Use the middle paragraphs to develop the desire to have the product or service, or to respond to your letter.
- State in the concluding paragraph the action to be taken.

Morjo & Morjo

1 Smart Place | Wellington | New Zealand | Ph/Fax: (04) 472 7213
Email: morjo@morjo.net.nz

8 May 2011

Mrs A Ridge
The Manager
Paramount Events Management
22 Main Street
Moonee Ponds VIC 3039
Australia

Order of information   Dear Adele

Subject line   **Keynote Address**

Neutral buffer   Thank you for asking me to be the keynote speaker at your motivational conference 'Marketing Success Made Simple'. I have always enjoyed your conference sessions and am flattered that you think I could stimulate the imaginations of your delegates.

Explanation   However, my staff has me on a tight schedule this year. I have been lucky enough to be invited to deliver the Hobson International Lecture Series for the Global Bankers Network. This requires constant travel in America, Australasia, Europe and Africa. I continue to give my Open University Lectures and fulfil my commitments to the International Advertising Association, but at the expense of family and leisure time.

Refusal   I would love to support you with this conference and I am honoured that you would consider me for your keynote speaker. But I cannot accept any more engagements this year.

Positive close   I value our relationship and hope I can offer my services at another time. Good luck with the conference. I know it will make a difference to the life and work of your delegates.

Yours sincerely

Jo Nikita

Jo Nikita
Senior Partner

Figure 18.4: Effective bad news letter declining an invitation

Order of information: the AIDA formula

The **AIDA formula** aims to catch the attention and interest of a customer, and to spark their desire and willingness to take action.

The **AIDA formula** describes the process suited to persuasive writing. It aims to catch the attention and interest of the reader, and to spark their desire and willingness to take action. AIDA stands for:

- **A**ttention
- **I**nterest
- **D**esire
- **A**ction

It is not enough just to catch the reader's attention, and to create interest in and desire for the product or service. The reader must also be *willing to take action* to fulfil this desire. Throughout the letter, be enthusiastic and interested in the reader. Put the reader in the picture. Conclude by speaking directly to the reader's needs with a clear and direct message. Use the 'you' approach in writing.

Interest and desire stimulate action.

At the beginning of the letter, capture **A**ttention by focusing on the reader in a positive way. Then, in the second paragraph, to create **I**nterest, give the appeal in the form of direct or indirect benefits; for example, comfort, popularity, economic benefit, self-interest, distinctiveness, prestige, reputation, quality of life, or convenience. In the **D**esire section, suggest the central reason, giving complete information to answer the reader's questions. Again, emphasise the benefits the reader will receive. In the concluding section, following the persuasive arguments, indicate the **A**ction the reader needs to take. Close positively, pointing to future contact.

Persuasive letters are written when the writer expects resistance, or wants to change an attitude or influence the reader to take some action. Catch the reader's attention immediately, follow with the reasons and explanatory details that create interest and desire, then provide any additional information in a logical way. This provides the foundation for the actions the writer wants to persuade the reader to take.

Types of appeals

The *appeals* most often in use in persuasive letters are emotional appeals, informative appeals and appeals to authority. Emotional appeals relate to the senses, while objective appeals relate to the intellect. Appeals to authority relate to feelings of status and esteem. The main characteristics of each are presented in Table 18.10.

Before beginning to write a persuasive letter, decide on the best assurance that the appeal can offer the reader. Then decide on the sort of information and type of appeal that will best support this assurance. If you wish to persuade people to visit the local art gallery, the appeal is likely to be objective, whereas if you wish to persuade women to buy the latest line in perfume, the appeal is likely to be emotional. Figure 18.5 shows an effective letter of persuasion.

Persuasive techniques

Persuasive letters aim to influence the reader to change an attitude or take some action they would not normally take. When planning and organising a persuasive letter, the writer decides on the type of appeal and the channel to use to achieve the appeal's purpose. Catch the reader's interest with the subject line or first paragraph. Identify the main benefit and create the rest of the appeal around the benefits and advantages to the reader. Often writers use conversational language to give a less formal, more friendly tone to the letter.

As you write, catch the reader's attention and interest immediately by using attention-getting devices such as:

- making an offer
- using a startling statement
- telling an anecdote

Table 18.10: Persuasive messages

Types of appeal	Main characteristics
Emotional appeal	• indirect rewards often outweigh the direct rewards • generalisations are used • comparisons between unlike events are made • appeal to feelings is emphasised • appeal to the subconscious part of the mind is made.
Objective appeals	• direct rewards outweigh indirect rewards • advantages and disadvantages are presented • comparisons are made between two like events • statistics and facts are presented • logic is used and appealed to • appeal to the conscious part of the mind is made.
Appeals to authority	• suggests security and safety • suggests trust in the authority figure • offers prestige • invites the customer to enjoy the product also • implies that the buyer will become the person they would like to be.

- offering a bargain
- asking a question.

Table 18.11 gives examples of writing techniques that have been used by a variety of businesses to catch the attention and interest of potential customers. The examples are taken from newspapers, journals, pamphlets and magazines.

Create interest and desire by appealing to the reader's self-interest with such techniques as:

- making the reader feel part of the event
- highlighting something of interest
- suggesting some course of action
- discussing the new features of a product and the benefits to the reader
- emphasising the central selling point
- highlighting the benefits to be gained by the reader
- explaining the advantages.

As a persuasive writer, you should be thoroughly familiar with the subject matter. This knowledge enables you to understand the product and the need it can fulfil. You can then identify the need and explain how the product meets that need. Encourage the reader to take action by making the action clear and easy. Place the emphasis on the word 'you'. You might also offer the reader some inducement to use the service; for example, a special price or gift. Some examples of the ways in which a piece of writing can stimulate action are set out in Table 18.11.

Persuasive writing is also used in sales letters, credit communications, collection letters, job applications and cover letters to résumés.

Sales letters

Sales letters use the same technique and order of information as other persuasive letters. They aim to motivate the reader to act by gaining their attention and interest, which leads to desire and action. To achieve this, the writer needs to know the product or service, the nature of the people who will buy

Sales letters aim to influence the reader.

74 Lambton Quay
Wellington New Zealand
Phone: (04) 472 6111

17 October 2011

Ms Maureen Talbot
93 Port Street
Lower Hutt

Order of information

Dear Ms Talbot

Attention

Congratulations! You have been chosen to receive the XYZ Credit Card, which establishes your ability to pay and your reliability as a desirable customer in selected stores throughout the world.

Focus on interests

The use of your credit card means you will no longer be worried about carrying extra cash around with you when travelling. As well, if you should become stranded overseas or run out of money, our nearest office will provide you with cash immediately, up to $1000.

Desire

There are no hidden costs for users of this prestigious credit card and only a small interest charge for extended repayments.

Action

Fill in the enclosed application form and slip it into the supplied postage paid envelope today. You will soon be enjoying the freedom, prestige and courteous attention this card will give you.

Yours sincerely

James Mason

James Mason
Marketing

Figure 18.5: An effective letter of persuasion (modified block layout)

the service or product (that is, the market) and the competitors. The writer then decides on the type of appeal that will influence the reader to buy. The AIDA formula is useful in ordering the information in a sales letter, as set out in Table 18.12.

An unusual opening statement, a sample, photographs or sketches, a solution to a problem or even gimmicks may attract attention. Interest is further developed with a description and explanation that highlight the features and benefits. Offers of proof to support the claims include samples, trial offers, statistics and guarantees.

The persuasive sales letter shows readers what is in it for them. Although a product may have many features, pay particular attention to just one or two of the best. By listing all the features, you may confuse the reader. Instead, place all the features into an attachment such as a brochure.

To motivate the reader to take action, the writer needs to relate the benefits of the product directly to the reader's needs; for example, 'with free child care'. The action the writer wants the reader to take is then stated clearly; for example, 'Come in and test drive today' or 'Telephone your order today'.

Table 18.11: Techniques to catch attention and interest, raise desire and encourage action

Techniques to catch attention

- Rent or buy—What's best for you?
- Be part of the holiday action!
- Heard the news? We are still only $10 an item.
- Win one of five.

Techniques to catch interest

- Every purchase over $10 goes into the draw.
- Bonus free offer this month only.
- After all, the roof is the largest area of the house.

Techniques to raise desire

- What it can do for your home is limited only by your imagination.
- It comes in a large range of colours.
- So if you're looking for quality that's practical, Worth is for you.
- Available in either blue or white, the Harmony is as easy on the eye as it is on the pocket.

Techniques to encourage action

- To find out more, post or fax this advertisement to Enterprise Corporation today.
- Ring now for an obligation-free measure and quote.
- You can invest now through any branch of the bank or through your financial adviser.
- For full details and itineraries for the holiday of your lifetime, call your travel agent Denise now.
- Register your business today.
- Inquire now at Lin Ngu's restaurant.

Table 18.12: Writing strategy for a sales letter

- Catch the reader's attention in the subject line or introductory paragraph.
- Use the introductory paragraph to focus on the reader's self-interest—the benefit to them.
- In the middle paragraphs, emphasise the central selling point, create a desire and give the price.
- Close with the actions to be taken by the reader.

Concrete words and objective language give a clearer image of the product than abstract language and overstatement. Effective sales letters are usually short (up to one page in length) with any extra information included as enclosures or attachments. Figure 18.5 is an example of a sales letter that uses the AIDA formula.

Credit communications

Most businesses operate on a credit basis. Hemphill, McCormick and Hemphill (2001, p. 175) comment that credit 'is a way of life'. It is important to be able to communicate effectively with customers requesting credit. They refer to the '4Cs' of credit:

1. *Character*: a person's basic ethics, such as honesty, dependability and sense of moral values, indicated by a past credit record and/or satisfactory answers in a credit application.
2. *Capital*: for example, cash, securities or real estate to which the applicant has access.

3. *Capacity*: earning potential of the applicant, such as income, royalties or investment income.
4. *Conditions*: any problem conditions that could affect the applicant's credit application, such as regional economic conditions or employment conditions in a specific industry, business or profession.

It is usually on the basis of these '4Cs' that credit is given or refused. Most credit applications are made by filling in a form provided by the business. On occasions, however, a written request will be made. For trade customers, the chief sources of information regarding a person's capacity to pay are obtained from:

- the customer
- credit card agencies and/or firms with whom the customer has previously dealt
- employers
- local retail credit associations (Hemphill, McCormick & Hemphill 2001, p. 177).

All business correspondence needs to be handled promptly; however, as Lehman and Dufrene (2002, p. 172) comment, 'it is especially important when communicating about credit'. They recommend the following guidelines for writing when extending credit to a customer:

- Open by extending credit and acknowledging shipment of an order. Because of its importance, the credit aspect is emphasised more than the acknowledgment of the order.
- Indicate the basis for the decision to extend credit, and explain the credit terms. For example, refer to the applicant's prompt paying habits with present creditors.
- Present the organisation's credit policies. For example, explain credit terms, authorised discounts and payment dates, and include any legally required disclosure documents.
- Communicate a genuine desire to build a strong business relationship.

If the decision is made not to extend credit, 'your primary writing problem is to refuse credit so tactfully that you keep the business relationship on a cash basis' (Lehman & Dufrene 2002, p. 257). The main part of the message should be an explanation of the refusal. Lehman and Dufrene believe that 'both writers and readers benefit from the explanation of the reasons behind the refusal'. It helps establish fair-mindedness and shows that the decision was not arbitrary. For the reader, the explanation is useful as a guide to how they might qualify for credit purchases at a later date.

Collection letters

Collection letters use persuasion to collect money from those who are slow to pay.

The types of appeals suited to **collection letters** are appeals to fair play, cooperation, reputation, pride and self-interest. Each of these demonstrates that the desired action is reasonable and in the best interests of the reader. Positive appeals focus on cooperation, fair play and pride, while negative appeals focus on self-interest; for example, losing a credit rating. In all communication, the aim is to develop positive relationships with others and to maintain goodwill. The positive appeal is the one most likely to get the desired response and lead to effective relationships between the organisation and the reader.

A number of letters may be written to collect money from those who are slow to pay. Some organisations break the collection process into four stages:

1. reminder stage
2. strong reminder stage
3. inquiry stage
4. urgency stage.

Others break the collection process into three stages by combining the reminder and strong reminder into one stage.

The time taken for the process to develop from a reminder to the urgency stage depends on the type of credit account, the company's knowledge of the debtor and the organisation's collection policies. All collection letters, regardless of the collection stage, should specify the amount owing and the account number. The writing strategy to be followed throughout the collection process is set out in Table 18.13.

Table 18.13: Writing strategy for a collection letter

- Identify the letter's purpose in the subject line or introductory paragraph.
- Use the introductory paragraph to focus the reader's attention on the issue.
- In the middle paragraphs, give details and state the actions to be taken by the reader.
- Close with a neutral statement.

THE REMINDER

In the first stage, the organisation gives the customer a reminder. The assumption is that the customer has forgotten to pay, so the letter is a courteous reminder of the need to pay. This stage is usually 30 days after the purchase.

THE STRONG REMINDER

In this stage, the writer still assumes the customer has forgotten to pay. This stage is only offered to an established customer or someone the writer feels has a valid reason for not paying. For other customers, move straight into the inquiry stage, usually when the account is 60 days overdue.

INQUIRY

By the time this stage is reached, the situation is serious. The writer believes something is wrong. The persuasive letter becomes a direct request to the customer to reply, either by letting the organisation know the problem or taking immediate action to correct the problem. The letter also appeals to the customer's self-interest, reputation or sense of fair play. By this stage, the account is usually 90 days overdue.

The inquiry asks the reader why the overdue account has not been paid; that is, it asks for an explanation and payment if possible. If the writer can influence the customer to respond with a reason for the non-payment, there is a reasonable chance of working out a payment plan.

URGENCY

By this stage, the account is at least 200 days overdue. The need to collect the money is urgent and you assume there is a reason for not paying. In this stage, the writer clearly states the action to be taken by the customer. The tone of the letter suggests the payment must be made; it is more demanding but still courteous. Figure 18.6 shows a collection letter appropriate to the urgency stage of the process.

If, as a result of non-payment, the organisation is going to take some other action, let the customer know what will happen if the urgent request is ignored. The account may, for example, be placed in the hands of a collection agency, or legal action may be initiated.

In the first stages of the collection process, it is best to assume that the customer has simply forgotten to pay. In the third and fourth stages, it is easier to write courteously if the writer still assumes that the customer wants to pay but has some problem that is preventing payment.

REVIEW QUESTIONS

13 a   Why is the AIDA formula used?

b   What do persuasive letters aim to do?

14 a   List four different ways of gaining attention in the first sentence or paragraph of a sales letter.

b   Describe one way of creating desire for the product in a sales letter.

15 What are the four stages in the collection process?

19 March 2010

Mr James Roberts
52 Corona Avenue
Somewhere Ville VIC 9999

Dear Mr Roberts

Order of information

Identify the letter's purpose

Subject: Payment of Outstanding Rent

TRS Rental Agency is writing to request urgent payment of the outstanding rent of $2400.

Focus the reeder's attention

Non-payment of the outstanding rent will seriously affect your credit rating and opportunities for future rentals from any registered rental agency.

State the action to be taken by the reader

Please pay the full balance of the outstanding rent today by:

- electronic transfer
- cheque or
- cash at our office at the address above.

State what will happen if the request for payment is ignored

Payment of the outstanding rent is urgent, as we will place the account in the hands of a debt collection agency on Friday of this week if you have not made payment or contacted us.

Close with a neutral statement

If you cannot pay the full balance today, please contact us to discuss your current situation. We will do what we can to help you.

Yours sincerely

Maria Rufo

Maria Rufo
State Rental Manager

Figure 18.6: A collection letter—urgency stage

APPLY YOUR KNOWLEDGE

PERSUASIVE LETTERS

1 Working in pairs, assume you have received a request from the careers adviser at the local high school to place a Year 10 pupil for work experience.

    a Discuss the difference between the writing strategy for a good news letter and a bad news letter. List two differences between the two types of letter.

b   Decide who will write a letter accepting the pupil for work experience and who will write a letter refusing the place for work experience.

c   Discuss and evaluate the effectiveness of each letter using the following checklist.

2   Work in pairs to complete the following tasks. A client asks that you replace a faulty appliance outside warranty conditions. The appliance's problem is clearly the result of misuse and abuse. You feel the request is unjustified.

a   Outline the writing plan for this letter.

b   Discuss and prepare an opening statement that acts as a neutral and relevant buffer.

c   Prepare a concluding statement that avoids referring to the bad news, apologising or using clichés.

d   Write the letter declining to replace the appliance.

3   a   Assume you have a customer with an account that is outstanding for an amount of $2400. Write the first reminder letter informing the customer of this amount and the need to pay. The customer does not pay for three months. Write a letter suited to the fourth stage.

b   What is the main difference between the first and fourth stages in a collection campaign?

SELF-EVALUATE YOUR SKILL

GOOD NEWS, BAD NEWS AND PERSUASIVE LETTERS

Review and edit your business letters.

	Very Successfully	Successfully	Unsuccessfully
In a good news letter, have I:			
• used the direct order of information?			
• identified clearly the letter's purpose in the introduction?			
• closed with a statement of goodwill?			
In a bad news letter, have I:			
• used the indirect order of information?			
• opened with a neutral buffer?			
• concluded with a positive statement?			
In a persuasive letter, have I:			
• gained the reader's attention?			
• aroused the reader's interest and desire?			
• concluded with an action statement?			

MEMOS

◄ OBJECTIVE 5
Plan and write effective memos

The parts of a memo parallel those of a business letter. However, they are fewer and simpler, dispensing with some of the courtesies of the letter. **Memos** (or **memorandums**) are usually used for day-to-day routine information. They are relatively brief documents, typically half, one or two pages, although memos about formal issues can be longer. Memos are less private than business letters because they are delivered by inter-office mail or email. (Refer to Chapter 21 for email-writing strategies.)

A **memorandum** (or **memo**) is a standard format for internal written communication

Assume that a memo, whether paper-based or electronic, is permanent. It may be archived for years on disk, to reappear later in formal or informal print media in a situation unrelated to its original purpose. While some receivers store emails electronically, others print the email messages they receive and file and index them for ease of retrieval and reference later.

As the memo is an internal means of communication and less formal than a letter, there is no need to include an inside address, greeting, complimentary close or full signature. The four headings indicated in the instruction memo in Figure 18.7 are normally included.

The headings 'To' and 'From' clearly identify the receiver and sender of the memo. 'To' usually precedes 'From' as a courtesy to the receiver. The subject line indicates the topic of the memo; for example, 'Delivery Schedules for March'. Keep the title informative but brief. The body of the memo is a clearly structured message, which is often written in short, numbered paragraphs. The content in the body, including the first sentence in a paragraph, should be blocked to the margin. To achieve a clearly structured message, use a plain English writing style (see Chapter 17) and an objective description of the topic supported with factual content.

A memo is often written in short, numbered paragraphs.

Advantages of a memo

As a memo is a written form of communication, it has four advantages over the spoken word:

1. It reaches a large number of people at the same time.
2. It provides a written record to refer to at any time, or to place on file.
3. It allows detailed or difficult information to be logically and accurately relayed.
4. It can indicate, through the use of a company letterhead, that the information it contains is part of the organisation's procedures.

Memos are a useful way to summarise information and forward the same message to a number of people within an organisation. The memo should be objective, unbiased, and have a courteous and confident tone.

MEMORANDUM

To: All Staff

From: Elaine Thomas, Administrative Officer

Date: 14 May 2011

Subject: Operating Instructions for New Copying Machines

Introduciton   A new photocopier has been installed in the general office.

All staff are welcome to use it.

Main point   To ensure the copier's survival, it is important to keep the following procedures in mind:

Secondary information
- Use the machine for no longer than 30 minutes at a time.
- After use, allow the machine to cool for at least five minutes.
- Make sure the switch is turned off after use.

Action   Please speak to me if you have any questions about the machine.

Figure 18.7: Instruction memo

Disadvantages of memo writing

Bienvenu and Timm (2002, p. 32) comment, 'Disadvantages of written media include high cost and the lack of immediate feedback. In most cases, writing a document is harder work—and more costly—than just talking.' They provide some interesting facts about the expense of writing memos (p. 33):

> The cost of writing memos has a high price tag, according to a recent study by IWCC Training in Communications, a Toronto consulting firm. Planning, composing, and editing a routine memo takes an average of 54 minutes. This means that writing a memo costs almost $82, based on an annual employee salary of $35,000. And the annual cost of writing one memo per week? $4258.60.

Lehman and Dufrene (2002, p. 202) suggest that before writing a memo you ask yourself the question: Could you communicate this information by telephone or in person? Unless a written record is necessary, the memo or email 'cannot replace the personal interaction so essential in today's team-based work environments'. The authors also warn against using a written communication tool as an avoidance mechanism.

Four steps to effective memos

Memos vary enormously in length and complexity. Some are brief routine announcements; others present complicated and sensitive information. Any memo, paper-based or email, warrants the following four steps.

1. Identify the subject.
2. Select and order information.
3. Write simply.
4. Use a suitable tone.

Six types of memo

Memos are used for a number of purposes: to make requests, give instructions, provide authorisation, offer acknowledgment or document decisions. In each instance, the nature of the message and the writer's purpose will have an effect on the structure of the memo. Six routine memos are identified in Table 18.14.

Table 18.14: Six types of memo	
Type	**Purpose**
1 Instruction memo	The object of the instruction memo is to provide the receiver with all the information they need to be able to carry out the directions confidently.
2 Request memo	The request memo asks the receiver to provide certain information or to take certain action. The writer expects the receiver to take action and communicate that action.
3 Announcement memo	The announcement memo provides information and is usually for more than one receiver. The message may be for everyone in the organisation.
4 Transmittal memo	The transmittal memo is the cover note for a more formal, lengthy message.
5 Authorisation memo	The authorisation memo gives the receiver permission or authority to take action.
6 Confirmation memo	The confirmation memo confirms in writing what has been agreed between the sender and the receiver. It contains specific details, such as dates, venues, goals, anticipated outcomes and other details.

SHORT REPORTS

OBJECTIVE 6 ▶
Plan and format short reports so as to effect the efficient transfer of information

A report, whether long or short, is a document containing comprehensive information on a specific subject. Its function is to provide information and, sometimes, expert opinion, which offers management a basis on which to check on progress, plan for the future or make decisions.

The key to success in developing a document that is both easy to read and effective lies in careful planning. A report has a more powerful effect and will be easier to read when it has:

Effective planning ensures efficiency.

- a clear indication of the purpose
- accurate and objective information
- suitable headings
- a suitable order of information that highlights the main points and leads logically to the conclusions.

Short reports communicate written, objective information within and outside an organisation.

Lehman and Dufrene (2002, p. 427) comment that, while **short reports** incorporate many of the organisational strategies of long reports, they differ in that they 'include only the minimum supporting materials to achieve effective communication. Short reports focus on the body—problem, method, findings and conclusion.' Short reports, they state, might also incorporate the following features:

- personal writing style using first or second person
- contractions when they contribute to a natural style
- graphics to reinforce the written text
- headings and subheadings to partition portions of the body and to reflect organisation
- memorandum and letter formats, when appropriate.

When faced with the task of producing a short report, the six-step approach below will be helpful. This approach is developed more fully in Chapter 19, 'Writing Long Reports'. The principles apply to most writing tasks.

Six-step approach to planning a short report

In the investigation and planning stages of developing the short report, consider the following six steps:

1 *Identify the purpose.* Take time to clarify the task precisely.
2 *Consider the readers.* Their needs, knowledge level and familiarity with jargon should be identified at the beginning, as these will affect both the content and language of the report.
3 *Identify the information needs.* List these as well as the sources that will provide the information. In accomplishing this step, create ideas by brainstorming, consulting co-workers or considering previously successful examples.
4 *Gather the information purposefully.* Keep the task clearly in mind and avoid being side-tracked. Sometimes, it may be necessary to research information from both primary and secondary sources (see Chapter 13).
5 *Sort the information.* Discard any irrelevant material and organise what is important into sections under suitable headings.
6 *Arrange the sections* in a suitable, logical sequence.

Creating a logical outline will enable you to work swiftly to produce a complete but concise report.

Order of information in short reports

In deciding the order of information for a short report, it is useful to consider the following three ways of ordering the content:

1. indirect order of information
2. direct order of information
3. routine order of information.

The purpose of each order of information is given in Table 18.15. Figures 18.8, 18.9 and 18.10 summarise the details of each order of information.

Table 18.15: Purpose of each order of information

Indirect order of information	Direct order of information	Routine order of information
A problem-solving order of information for a reader unfamiliar with the content (see Figure 18.8)	A problem-solving order of information for a reader familiar with the content (see Figure 18.9)	A decision-making or routine order of information suited to a reader who needs to make decisions on the basis of the information (see Figure 18.10)
The indirect order moves the reader through the short report. The criteria, facts, options and alternatives are logically developed to enable the reader to understand the information.	The direct order leads the reader from the solutions to the problem, then to the reasons for suggesting the solutions, and finally to the facts on which these conclusions are based.	The routine order of information is presented within the context of an overview—each main idea is presented with the related secondary ideas in order to give accurate information on which to base decisions or to communicate information to others in the organisation.

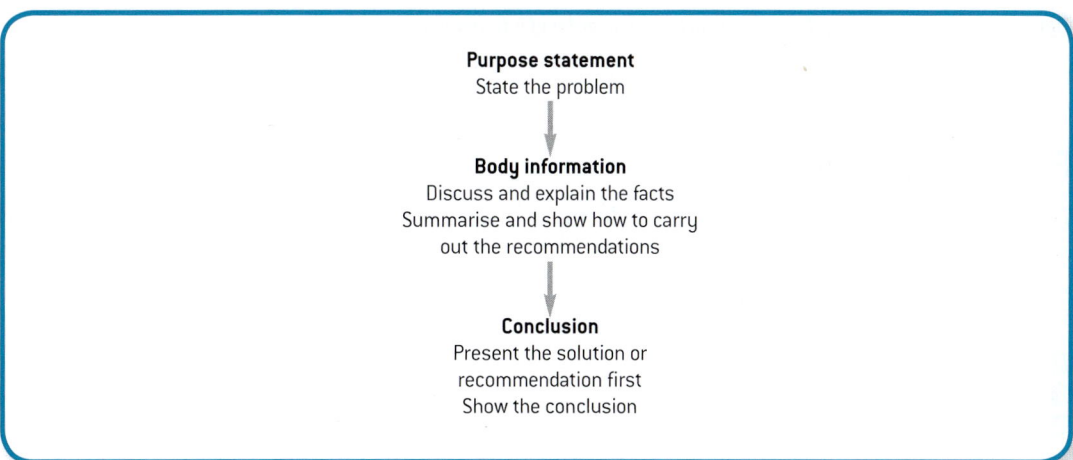

Purpose statement
State the problem

↓

Body information
Discuss and explain the facts
Summarise and show how to carry
out the recommendations

↓

Conclusion
Present the solution or
recommendation first
Show the conclusion

Figure 18.8: Plan for writing the short report: Indirect order of information

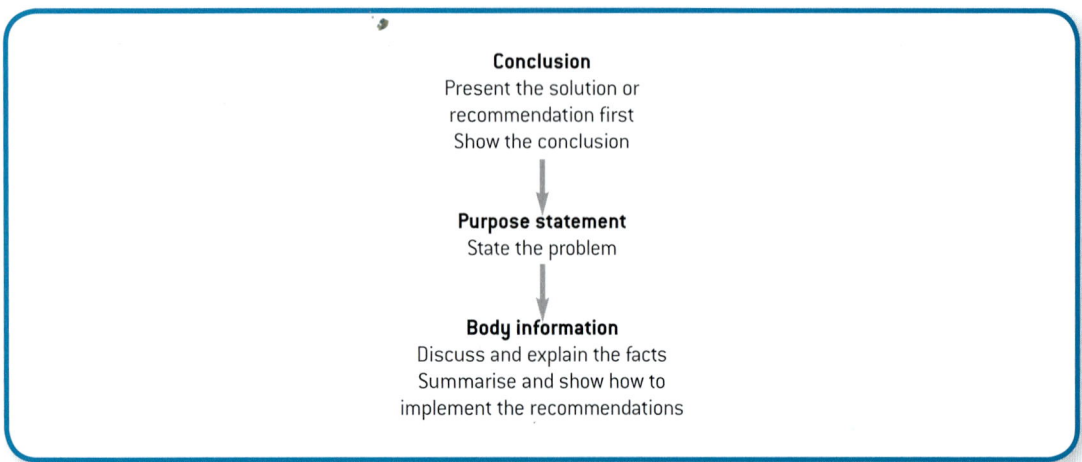

Figure 18.9: Plan for writing the short report: Direct order of information

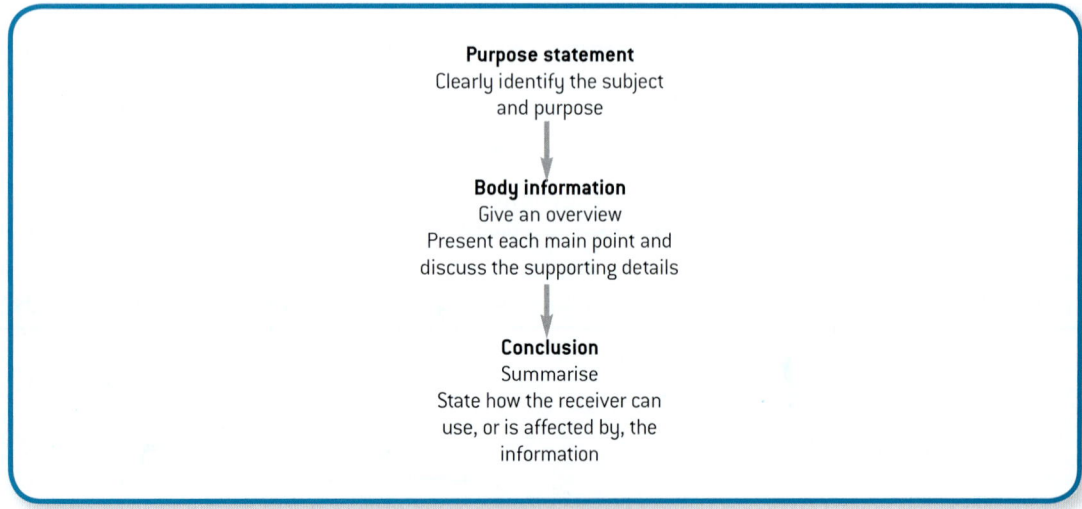

Figure 18.10: Plan for writing the short report: Routine order of information

Formatting short reports

Short-report formats used in business are formal, letter and memo.

The short report format is very efficient for placing information on the page in a way that is easy to read and understand. Writers have developed this format over time as a particular way to convey certain types of information. Use each part of a short report correctly. Several different formats are used in short reports. Discussion here is limited to three typical short report formats:

1. the formal short report
2. the letter report
3. the memorandum report.

Table 18.16 summarises the details. Table 18.17 lists the characteristics of poor short report writing.

Table 18.16: Minimum acceptable report formats

Formal short report	Letter report	Memorandum report
1 A title page	1 The writer's address	1 Reader's name
2 An introduction	2 The date	2 Writer's name
3 Sections with headings in the body	3 Inside or reader's address	3 Date
4 Conclusions	4 Salutation	4 Subject line or title
5 Recommendations (when required)	5 Subject line	5 Body
Attachments are included if the information is useful.	6 Body	
	7 Complimentary close	
	8 Signature block	

Table 18.17: Characteristics of poor short reports

- Omission of significant information
- Inclusion of irrelevant detail
- Illogical structuring of information
- Overuse of jargon
- Poor use of white space
- Inappropriate choice of format
- Addition of irrelevant attachments

REVIEW QUESTIONS

18 Define the term 'short report'.

19 List the six steps in planning a short report.

20 . Differentiate the indirect, direct and routine order of information in short reports.

APPLY YOUR KNOWLEDGE

MEMOS AND SHORT REPORTS

1 Assume you are the manager of a chain of natural health food stores. As you check the stock of breakfast cereals, you notice the seal is broken on more than half the packages. You decide to return all the new delivery of breakfast cereal to the manufacturer.

Write a request memo to the stores officer, asking her to prepare the stock for return to the supplier. Use the checklist below to evaluate your memo.

2 Plan the short report.

Assume you are to prepare a short report asking for new computer technology. You are given the following instructions on the order of information to use in the report.

- Open by stating the proposed changes and then go straight into the current problems of computing software being inadequate for the size of the company. This is your introduction.
- Start the body of the report with some concrete examples of the advantages of the new software. Briefly explain the advantages. Remember to be clear and not to overload your short report with technical information that would be more

easily understood by word processor operators than management. Then present the problems of the existing system, the advantages and any disadvantages of the new proposal.

- Place the conclusions and recommendations at the end of the report.
a Place the information above into the correct order for report writing.
b Prepare an outline that clearly identifies the headings for the short report.
c Create a title for the short report.

SELF-EVALUATE YOUR SKILL

WRITING A MEMO

Read your first draft and ask yourself these questions:

Have I:	Yes	No	Unsure
decided the memo's purpose?			
used correct memo layout?			
used a subject line?			
written a clear message?			
ordered the information?			
closed with the action to be taken or a positive statement?			

OBJECTIVE 7 ▶
Write justification, progress, periodic and incident reports, and understand the uses of these forms of report

FOUR TYPES OF SHORT REPORT

There are four widely used types of short report that follow the memorandum report format but may, of course, be written using the letter report format or short formal report format:

1. justification reports
2. progress reports
3. periodic reports
4. incident reports.

These short reports have different purposes and different orders of information and suit different situations. The purpose and order of information for justification, progress and periodic reports are shown in Table 18.18. The various situations covered are set out in Table 18.19.

The direct order of information is used when the conclusion or recommendation serves as the basis for action. Lesikar and Pettit (1998, p. 197) suggest that short reports tend to use direct order. '[B]ecause they usually are more goal oriented, shorter, more informal reports are likely to use the direct order of presentation.' Short reports usually start with a purpose statement rather than introductory material, because the receivers are usually aware of the subject matter. A short report should be brief and simple. By following the orders of information set out in Table 18.18, the subject matter is arranged to suit the purpose and is logical and easy to read and comprehend.

A **justification report** presents an idea or proposal and then uses evidence to justify it.

Justification report

As the justification report seeks approval for change and the resources to initiate the changes proposed by the writer, it is usually sent upwards in the organisation. **Justification reports** give the reasons for

Table 18.18: Order of information in short reports

Justification report: Indirect order of information	Progress report: Direct or indirect order of information	Periodic report: Direct or indirect order of information
1 Purpose statement • Identify the report's purpose with a subject line or purpose statement.	1 Purpose statement • Identify the report's purpose with a subject line or purpose statement.	1 Purpose statement • Identify the report's purpose with a subject line or purpose statement.
2 Body of information • Describe the current situation. • Describe the change. • Describe the cost factors. • Discuss the advantages or disadvantages.	2 Body of information • Open the body of the report with the current status, work or goals completed. • Follow with the positive features of the operation. • Present any problems, and state how they were resolved or will be resolved.	2 Body of information • Open the body of the report with the facts and figures. • Present objective information on achievements and problems.
3 Conclusion • Draw or make a conclusion. • Close with the recommendation/s.*	3 Conclusion • Point to the future.	3 Conclusion • Summarise the findings. • Close with the recommendation/s.*

* The recommendation can be placed at either the beginning or end of the report. The position depends on your needs as a writer and the needs of the receiver.

Table 18.19: Situations suited to different types of short reports

Situations suited to justification reports	Situations suited to progress reports	Situations suited to periodic reports
• a change of procedures • a change in accommodation • a change in operating times • a drop in sales • a need to change from the existing computer software to a more powerful package • an increase in budget for a particular department • a change to a switchboard • a discount policy on the price of a product.	Short progress reports are used to: • check the rate of work on a new building • discuss future goals, their time frame, and forecasts for completion of the project • report on office renovations • report on a rezoning application lodged with council • report to union members on wage negotiations • provide daily medical reports on a patient's progress.	Short periodic reports may deal with: • monthly staff absenteeism • annual figures on unauthorised leave from each section • monthly revenue reports • audit reports • weekly sales figures • outstanding accounts.

change and explain clearly why the change is necessary. The proposed changes are placed in the body of the report or in the recommendations.

Information that achieves a balance between the advantages and disadvantages of the current situation and the proposed changes allows for clear conclusions and recommendations. If there is a need to follow up, review or check on progress, state this as a recommendation.

Always use facts as the basis for the justification report and emphasise these to support the request for approval or change.

Achieve the correct emphasis by using the *indirect order of information* set out in Table 18.18. A short report asking for a change to normal procedures may meet with some resistance. Open with a neutral statement that leads the reader through the problem and the details supporting the change. It is essential to remind or persuade the reader that there is a problem, rather than assume that they are familiar with the information. Close by pointing the way ahead or using a neutral statement or a goodwill statement. One of the advantages of writing a justification report is that the information and the written approval are on file for future reference. Justification reports can be written to argue for, or offer an explanation for, the situations listed in Table 18.19.

Progress report

A **progress report** informs management of the rate of progress in relation to a schedule, identifies the goals for subsequent time periods, or provides a forecast.

Progress reports are written on request or according to need.

A **progress report** informs management of the rate of progress in relation to a schedule, identifiies the goals for subsequent time periods, or provides a forecast. Progress reports are written on request or need, rather than at regular intervals. They are part of an organisation's management information system and usually move upwards through the organisation. Organisations often compare the current report with previous progress reports on file, as this gives a clear overview of progress on the project.

The progress report can vary from formal to informal, depending on the context. Positive language is used to present the report's findings, and an emphasis is placed on achievements and progress. Aim to maintain balance by reporting on successes and evaluating any problems encountered or anticipated.

A progress report may be used to introduce a new system or to check current movements or progress. Note that conclusions or recommendations, or both, are used in a progress report only when needed; for example, to provide comment on performance or a recommendation regarding a change in plans.

The *order of information* set out in Table 18.18 emphasises the main points in a progress report. Progress reports often compare actual results against the anticipated or intended results. They suit the situations listed in Table 18.19.

COMPLETION REPORT

A completion report complements the progress reports that have been provided during the life of a project. It is the last report prepared and is written to say that the project has been finalised. A completion report is a courteous way of saying the project is finished and thanking management for the opportunity to work on the project.

Periodic report

A **periodic report** provides objective information on a regular basis.

A periodic report is the most common report prepared in business. A **periodic report** is prepared and circulated at regular intervals, perhaps daily or monthly. An accounts receivable clerk may, for example, prepare monthly reports on debtors, showing accounts overdue and long overdue, with an explanation of the steps taken to recover the debts. On the basis of this information, management makes decisions to pursue the debt with a collection letter, telephone call or legal action. A real estate agent may prepare a monthly report for management on the percentage of listed houses sold each month.

Many periodic reports are prepared using standard pre-printed forms, which are easy to complete, read and file. Others are produced following the same format each time that particular periodic report is written. This allows easy comparison of the information in the report from one period to the next.

Emphasise the most important points in the body of the report. Place similar information under the same heading. Use tabulation or indenting, listings or point form to make it easier for your reader to understand and to find information. To structure a periodic report, use the order of information set out in Table 18.18. The situations listed in Table 18.19 suit periodic reports because the information is collected and reported on regularly.

Incident report

An incident report is an example of a form report (a report with a standard format). The **incident report** offers management a clear factual account of an incident that is non-routine, such as an accident or any other unusual occurrence. It offers the receiver factual details, rather than a comprehensive analysis or justification of the event.

An **incident report** deals with non-routine matters.

Incident reports may be written on:

- incidents involving client/staff interaction
- unusual delays in normal procedures
- accidents
- special events.

The *order of information* for an incident report is a short general statement about the incident and its results, followed by a description of the circumstances that led up to the incident, an outline of what happened in appropriate detail, and an indication of the outcome or the effect that the incident had or is having.

ACCIDENT REPORTS

Accident reports are an example of an incident report. An accident is investigated to establish the facts and to determine any omissions or inadequacies that may have led to the accident and any action(s) that should be taken.

The accident report describes the organisation's health and safety system and how the organisation can prevent the accident happening again. The report should also identify the procedures that were in place at the time of the accident. The adequacy of the safety procedures and any problems identified in the investigation are presented in the body of the report. Recommendations should focus on improvement and prevention strategies in order to improve safety procedures and systems. The actions taken as a result of the recommendations aim to prevent any future accidents.

FORM REPORTS

A form report is a cost-effective way to collect information. The standard layout provided by the form enables information to be gathered in a consistent manner from a number of different sources. Headings and subheadings let the writer place like information into the same section, and the layout predetermines the order of information. The time spent planning the order of information is eliminated.

Lehman and Dufrene (2002, p. 427) comment, 'Form reports meet the demand for numerous, repetitive reports.' They list the following benefits of form reports:

- When designed properly, form reports increase clerical accuracy by providing designated places for specific items.
- Forms save time by telling the preparer where to put each item and by pre-printing common elements to eliminate the need for any narrative writing.
- In addition to their advantages of accuracy and time saving, forms make tabulation of data relatively simple. The value of the form is uniformity.

Accurate and up-to-date records are easy to maintain from pre-printed forms that allow the receiver to interpret, analyse and compile the information quickly. It is for this reason that periodic and incident reports are often prepared on pre-printed forms.

Effective business letters, memos and short reports produce the desired response. Writers who are clear about their objective when writing a business letter, memo or report are aware of their receivers and ready to spend time selecting and arranging information in a message that is easy to read and likely to produce action.

REVIEW QUESTIONS

21 Define the terms 'justification report', 'progress report' and 'periodic report'.

22 Briefly discuss three differences between a progress report and a periodic report.

23 When is an incident report written?

APPLY YOUR KNOWLEDGE

APPLYING THE 3 × 3 WRITING PROCESS TO SHORT REPORTS

1 Assume you are a holiday employee with a large accounting firm. Your employment next holiday depends on successful completion of current course work. The accounting firm has asked you to write a short report on your progress in your studies and to include your anticipated subject choice for the next year of study.

   Write this report with details on the number of subjects, your performance in these, and any further subjects needed to complete your studies.

2 Assume you work in the nursery of a large mining organisation. This nursery regenerates areas affected by the mining operations. As manager of the nursery, you have to prepare a monthly report. Use the following statistics to report to the general manager.

   • number of plants in the nursery—6000
   • number of plants planted in the field—4500
   • number of work hours on the job—120
   • number of hectares cleared—10 000

   Write the report in memorandum report layout.

3 Prepare a letter report on one of the following topics:

   a How to use the AIDA formula in a piece of persuasive advertising for a new brand of joggers that have just been released on the Australian market. The potential market is seen as 20- to 35-year-old men and women who play sport. Assume you are writing to business students.

   b Three pieces of technology used by accountants.

   c Five job functions performed by the Human Resources Officer.

   d Why marketing is so important to the organisation.

   e Three different services usually provided by any welfare agency of your choice.

4 Review and edit the first draft of your letter report by ticking your responses in the checklist below.

SELF-EVALUATE YOUR SKILL

WRITING SHORT REPORTS

Have I:	Very Successfully	Successfully	Unsuccessfully
prepared a purpose statement?			
followed the six-step approach when planning the report?			
organised information in an order suitable for the type of report?			
used a format suitable for the type of report?			
produced a high-quality short report?			

SUMMARY OF LEARNING OBJECTIVES

 1 ▷ PLAN AND WRITE EFFECTIVE BUSINESS LETTERS AND ADAPT THE STYLE FOR INTERNATIONAL BUSINESS CORRESPONDENCE

The language and writing style most appropriate to workplace correspondence is a plain English writing style. Readability, positive language, active voice and the 'you' approach produce a style that maintains the readers' goodwill, encourages them to read to the end of the letter and identifies the action, if any, to be taken. The order of information in the body is influenced by the letter's purpose, the needs of the receiver and the type of news conveyed in the letter. Take the time to identify the reader and purpose before writing the letter and it will be more likely to achieve its intended result.

The globalisation of business means an increasing number of written business messages are directed to international receivers, many of whom are readers of English as a foreign language. Apply plain English guidelines as you write business documents to allow your international readers to understand the content, how the information applies to them, and whether it is necessary to take any further action. Avoid using abbreviations, technical jargon and acronyms unless you are writing to an international receiver who understands them. Avoid using words that trigger emotional reponses.

2 ▷ RECOGNISE GOOD NEWS/NEUTRAL LETTERS AND APPLY THE DIRECT ORDER OF INFORMATION

Good news letters use the direct order of information to present positive or neutral information. A good news letter places a positive answer, information or good news in the opening paragraph to catch the reader's attention. The middle paragraph states the details supporting the favourable news. The final paragraph closes on a positive note.

3 ▷ WRITE CONSIDERED BAD NEWS LETTERS USING THE INDIRECT ORDER OF INFORMATION

Bad news letters use the indirect order of information to give the reader unwelcome news. A bad news letter is likely to disappoint the reader; therefore, it uses the indirect order of information—a neutral buffer, explanation of the situation, statement of the refusal or negative news, and a positive closing paragraph—to guide the reader through the relevant information and explanation to the bad news.

4 ▷ WRITE EFFECTIVE PERSUASIVE LETTERS AND UNDERSTAND THE AIDA FORMULA

Persuasive letters use the four-step AIDA process—attention, interest, desire and action—to catch the attention and interest of the readers and persuade them to take action. The persuasive letter attracts attention and interest, emphasises the need, and states the action to be taken. The attention focused on the need creates the desire for the service and an awareness of the rewards. The last stage is to persuade the person to take action.

5 ▷ PLAN AND WRITE EFFECTIVE MEMOS

As a quick and simple way to send information, requests and instructions within an organisation, the internal memo is particularly useful. It deals with information and action in a consistent simple format. The standardised format, concise statement of fact, and matter-of-fact tone of the memo speed up the flow of information essential to the organisation's efficiency. Plan and write your memos to ensure they contribute to better communication and greater efficiency.

6 ▷ PLAN AND FORMAT SHORT REPORTS SO AS TO EFFECT THE EFFICIENT TRANSFER OF INFORMATION

Aim to construct and produce a readable report that offers clear, accurate and complete information. The six-step approach enables the writer to produce a logical outline. When the report is written around this outline, it is better able to achieve its purpose; that is, to provide information that will enable the reader to make a decision, check progress or plan for the future. Format the document correctly using one of three formats—short formal report, letter or memo report—regarded by convention as acceptable.

WRITE JUSTIFICATION, PROGRESS, PERIODIC AND INCIDENT REPORTS, AND UNDERSTAND THE USES OF THESE FORMS OF REPORT

A short report is written to inform, advise or persuade. The writer's task is to provide a document that is easy to read and that allows the reader to consider, analyse or evaluate new information quickly. Aim to provide a balanced view. Base interpretations, conclusions and recommendations on the facts, and avoid reporting from bias or a subjective position.

Choose an order of information suitable for the type of report, its purpose and distribution. Adopt a functional order of content such as those suggested for the four types of short reports most frequently used: the justification report (indirect order of information), progress report (indirect order of information), periodic report (routine order of information) and incident reports. Incidents such as accidents are non-routine and are usually reported in a form report. The standard layout of the form report allows information to be arranged consistently.

KEY TERMS

ACTIVITIES AND QUESTIONS

1   'Writing is not only knowing what you want to say and why; it is also knowing how to write.' How does this influence the way you write a letter?

2   a   How can format influence the reader's attitude to what you have written?

   b   If inadequate formatting can detract from the clarity of a message, can over-formatting also distract the reader?

3   As the Human Resources Officer at Larkin Organisations you are asked to write a letter inviting members of staff to participate in a conference entitled 'Improving the Quality of Work'. The conference is to be held over two days, 19 and 20 August, from 9 am to 4.30 pm each day. Larkin Organisations is willing to pay the conference fee of $400 per person to cover travel, accommodation and breakfast. Any member participating in the conference is expected to pay for his or her own lunch and dinner. The purpose of the conference is to present strategies by which individuals can improve the quality of their working life.

   Write a letter inviting staff to attend the conference, following the writing strategy for a good news letter.

4   A customer has written a letter of complaint asking for an adjustment of 20% discount off their latest order of building supplies because of the inconvenience caused by late delivery. You feel that this demand for a 20% discount, which represents $250, is unwarranted as you arranged to have the materials delivered on time and the delay was caused by the transport company. As Sales Manager, Maria Carlton, write a letter to the customer acknowledging the complaint and refusing the request for the 20% discount. Follow the writing plan for an adjustment refusal. Address your letter to Mr J. Rogers, 62 Lynch Avenue, Enmore NSW 2042. Your address is 45 Belmore Road, St Peters NSW 2056.

5   Think of a new product or service you would like to buy. Write a sales letter to yourself using the features listed below:

   a   blocked letter format

b   seven basic parts of a business letter plus two additional parts

c   correct order of information following the AIDA formula

d   an appropriate opening

e   appeal focused around one or two central selling points.

6   Assume you are the senior lecturer of a group of students. Write a memo asking the students to indicate their first and second choice of subjects for the next semester. Use correct memo format.

7   Assume you are head of the administrative division in a large government department. You supervise 25 staff in the division. A new training program, 'An Introduction to Management', is to be offered on two separate dates to all staff in the administrative division.

a   List three advantages of using a memo in this situation instead of a spoken message.

b   Write an announcement memo to staff.

c   In your position as head of the administrative division, write an authorisation memo to the training manager, stating that funds are available for the program. Create the extra details you may need for times, dates, venue and content.

8   You work as an accountant and branch manager for your organisation, Simpson and Taylor Financial Consultants. A senior member of staff, Sandy Thompson, will conduct an interview next month to select a new trainee accountant. Prepare a memo of instruction to Sandy Thompson outlining the steps she needs to complete before the interview takes place.

9   Find an example of a short report in the library, or obtain a company report. Write a memorandum report to your lecturer discussing the following:

•   Is the purpose of the report clear?

•   Can the organisation of the report be improved?

•   Is the information relevant, clear and readable?

•   Can you identify information that has been repeated?

•   Do the conclusions summarise and draw together the ideas in the report?

10   Assume you are employed by the local council as the manager of the local ocean baths. The Christmas and New Year high tides are a hazard to swimmers. Heavy seas break into the pool and cause a back swell that can drag swimmers over the northern promenade and into the ocean.

As baths manager, you have taken the following precautions:

•   placed warning signs in prominent positions

•   installed a safety chain across the northern area

•   installed a loudspeaker system

•   stored safety and rescue equipment in an accessible position.

This year the situation is particularly dangerous. The north-easterly swell and winds have created a heavy surf. It is the last Saturday in December. You have clearly announced over the loudspeaker system that waves breaking on to the pool are very dangerous. Everyone is to leave the northern end of the pool.

Three people have refused to move from the northern end of the pool. As you walk towards them, a large wave drags them back into the dangerous surf. You radio the surf and rescue helicopter, then use your own rescue equipment to try to save the three swimmers. Two of them are rescued unharmed. The third person is seriously injured.

a   Write a memorandum report to the council, based on the information provided above.

b   Ensure that each section of the short report is used correctly.

c   Place headings throughout the body of the report. You may place the conclusion and recommendations at either the beginning or end of your report. The checklist, 'Writing Short Reports', on page 520 can be used to check that each step in the task has been completed to a suitable standard.

EXPLORING THE WEB

1   Visit 'Writing the basic business letter', <http://owl.english.purdue.edu/>. Navigate to 'Business letters: accentuating the positives' and answer these questions.

a   What are the disadvantages of using negative words?

b   How can you soften bad news?

c   How does the use of space affect the impact of bad news?

d   Navigate to 'Revision in business writing'. Create a list of five tips you can use to revise your business writing efficiently.

e   Explain the statement, 'Revision requires a shift in your perspective'.

2   The site <www.writing.eng.vt.edu/> discusses what information to present in a progress report. Read the advice provided and answer the questions here.

   a   Briefly explain the essential components in a progress report.

   b   View the sample laboratory report and design report. What is the purpose of each report?

c   What features are common to both short reports?

d   What are the differences between them?

e   Find a business report online and identify the features common to the business report and the sample technical laboratory and design reports.

PROJECT WORK

You have been employed as a consultant to improve the writing of workplace documents. You are required to submit a report on your recommendations for improvement. You may use a case study approach and create a company, or you might base your project on the company you work for.

1   Provide a brief description of the organisation you will use in your project.

2   You decide to commence with research on the six types of memos. Memos are the standard format of internal communication an organisation uses for its own staff.

   a   Describe six examples of routine memos and set out some guidelines for producing them.

   b   Write a sample of each memo to use as quality examples in your report.

3   The next step is to research the four types of short reports that the company produces. The reports have different purposes and suit different situations.

   a   Describe the four examples of short reports and set out guidelines for producing them.

   b   Collect an example of each of the reports and evaluate them using the headings in Table A. You will use the data in your report.

4   You are now ready to research how to improve the writing of workplace documents. The data collected under the headings in Table A will form the basis of your recommendations.

Table A: Headings to use in evaluation

- Purpose has been stated clearly
- Objective and accurate information used
- Headings were suitably applied
- Information was organised to highlight main points
- Report was structured logically to reach a conclusion

   a   Analyse how the 3×3 writing process is used to write memos and short reports.

   Phase 1

   Phase 2

   Phase 3

   b   Develop a game plan or a course of action to improve the writing of workplace documents for your chosen organisation.

5   a   Write your report to the company.

   b   Format your report professionally.

   c   Use the checklist on page 520 to evaluate your short report.

   d   Submit your working papers and your completed report.

BIBLIOGRAPHY

Alley, M. 1996. *The Craft of Scientific Writing*, Springer-Verlarge, New York.

Atherton, A. *Report Writing—How to Format a Business Report*, http://ezinearticles.com/?Report-Writing-How-to-Format-a-Business-Report, viewed November 2007.

Bienvenu, S. & Timm, P.R. 2002. *Business Communication: Discovering Strategy, Developing Skills*, Pearson Education, Upper Saddle River, New Jersey.

Bovée, C.L. & Thill, J.V. 2005. *Business Communication Today*, 8th edn, Pearson Education International, USA.

Business-Letters.Com, *Business Letters: How to Write Them*, www.
business-letters.com/business-letters.htm, viewed
27 September 2007.

Byrne, G. 1999. 'Information from the Net—plagiarism v. sharing?,
Stylewise, Vol. 5, Issue 2, p. 3.

Guffey, M.E. 2003. *Business Communication: Process and Product*,
4th edn, South-Western, Ohio.

Hemphill, P.D., McCormick, D.W. & Hemphill, R.D. 2001. *Business
Communication*, 6th edn, Pearson Education, Upper Saddle
River, New Jersey.

Hyslop, R. 1997. 'Ever more sincerely', *Stylewise*, Vol. 3, Issue 2.

Junket Studies. *Eleven Rules of Writing*, www.junketstudies.com/
rulesofw/, viewed 7 February 2001.

Lehman, C.M. & Dufrene, D.D. 2002. *Business Communication*, 13th
edn, South-Western, Ohio.

Lesikar, R.V. & Pettit, J.D. Jnr. 1998. *Report Writing for Business*, Irwin/
McGraw-Hill, USA.

Locker, K.O. 1995. *Business and Administrative Communication*,
3rd edn, Richard D. Irwin, USA.

Osland, D., Boyd, D., McKenna, W. & Salusinszky, I. 1991. *Writing
in Australia: A Composition Course for Tertiary Students*, Harcourt
Brace Jovanovich, Sydney.

Plain Language Association International, *Sample Webpage*, www.
plainlanguagenetwork.org/Samples/#business, viewed
12 February 2008.

Purdue University, *Writing the Basic Business Letter*, http://owl.english.
purdue.edu/owl/resource/653/01/, viewed 31 October 2007.

Stasko, N. 1992. 'Standard letters: How standard are they/ What
do they really say?', *Designing Information for People*, Proceedings
from the Symposium, pp. 155–73.

Style Manual for Authors, Editors and Printers, 6th edn, AGPS,
Canberra, 2002.

Virginia Tech. *Writing Guidelines for Engineering and Science Students*,
www.writing.eng.vt.edu/workbooks/prog.html, viewed
31 October 2007.

Yahoo! Directory *Business Letters*, http://dir.yahoo.com/
Social_Science/Communications/Writing/Correspondence/
Letter_Writing/Business_Letters/, viewed 12 September 2007.

19

Writing long reports

Photo: Christine Bald

OUTLINE

Analytical and informational reports

Effective planning

Writing the long report

Sample report

Editing the long report

LEARNING OBJECTIVES

After studying this chapter you should be able to:

1 ▷ differentiate analytical and informational reports and give examples of each

2 ▷ plan a report, and gather and order information

3 ▷ using an appropriate writing style, write the front matter, body and end matter of a long report

4 ▷ format and edit a long formal report.

VIEWPOINT: REPORT WRITING

'You should start writing your report when you have drawn some conclusions from your work. Write your conclusions first—until your conclusions have been written down there is nothing to be reported. A report written in this way will have a clear sense of direction because the remainder of the report will aim to justify your conclusions. In general terms:

- The introduction poses the question
- The conclusion is a suggested answer
- The remainder of the report is a route of evidence and arguments along which the reader will travel as they journey from the introduction to your conclusion and recommendations.

Finally, your aim is to convince the reader that your conclusions are valid.'

Extract from Bournemouth University. 'Writing business reports', *Academic Support*, www.bournemouth.ac.uk/study_support/writing_business_reports.html, viewed 18 February 2008.

Formal reports are major documents written for specific purposes.

Like other communication activities, long report writing takes place within the rapidly changing business context. Comprehensive information and knowledge is the key to meeting the demands of the current business environment. Long formal reports provide accurate, objective and complete information to support business decision making.

An effective long report is a major structured presentation that defines its purpose clearly, identifies the main issues, and organises material according to purpose, audience and context; it has an objective report writing style and is formatted professionally. A long analytical report develops logical arguments, presents solutions based on evidence, evaluates solutions objectively, and recommends appropriate, specific and realistic actions.

ANALYTICAL AND INFORMATIONAL REPORTS

OBJECTIVE **1** ▷
Differentiate analytical and informational reports and give examples of each

The two main types of formal reports are analytical reports and informational reports. Analytical reports are written by experts, often working in teams. The **analytical report** assesses opportunities and recommends action. Critical thinking skills are required to evaluate the findings and reach conclusions. The writer must ask critical questions about what has happened, what is likely to happen and how. **Informational reports** present the evidence gathered and the work already done in the area of investigation. Informational reports do not analyse or persuade. They convey factual information.

An **analytical report** assesses a situation or problem and recommends a course of action.

An **informational report** delivers data and information without making recommendations.

Characteristics

An analytical report will be read by the person who ordered the study. The analysis must always be balanced and objective. Informational reports may be positive (increased customer satisfaction), neutral (occupational health and safety incidents at zero over the last three reporting periods) or negative (a decrease in sales). The characteristics of analytical and informational reports are set out in Table 19.1.

Table 19.1: Characteristics of analytical and informational reports

Analytical reports	Examples	Informational reports	Examples
• Examine a problem or issue • Analyse information • Answer questions • Interpret • Assess risk, threats and opportunities • Explore consequences • Justify past decisions or actions • Draw conclusions • Make recommendation(s)	• Reports with proposals to solve problems: — analysis of failures — analysis of specific issues — risk mitigation reports • Reports to support decisions: — justification reports — feasibility studies • Reports to assess opportunities: — due diligence reports — market analysis reports • Reports to examine change and its impacts: — continuous improvement reports — standard reports	• Offer data and information • Provide feedback about sales, inventories, expenses, occupational health and safety • Provide information without: —analysis —conclusions —recommendations • Establish expectations and guidelines • Show compliance with government regulations • Focus on facts and figures	• Reports to monitor and control operations: —plans —operating reports —activity reports —periodic reports • Reports to implement policies, procedures or processes • Reports to document progress: —project status reports —building progress reports • Reports to demonstrate compliance: —registration bodies —environmental bodies —financial bodies

The writer of an informational report must organise and present the information in a format and sequence appropriate to the report's purpose, content and audience. Good report writing skills are required to prepare an appropriate outline, decide the order of presentation, write clearly and concisely, and use headings and numbering systems to help the receiver understand the information.

In an analytical report the reader's interest will focus on the significance of the problem identified in the report, and the practicality of the solution in terms of cost, duration and effect on other operations. The person who commissioned the report is likely to ask other experts to validate the scope of the report, the evidence collected, the methodology used, and the practicality of the conclusions and recommendations. The focus of this chapter is long analytical reports.

REVIEW QUESTIONS

1. Briefly explain the difference between an analytical report and an informational report, and provide business examples of each.
2. What is the purpose of an informational report?

EFFECTIVE PLANNING

◀ OBJECTIVE 2
Plan a report, and gather and order information

The *planning* stage of a long analytical or information report is the most time-consuming and, in one sense, the most important stage. Better planning leads to easier writing and editing, and to a better report. There are seven steps in planning a report:

The planning of a long report is crucial to its success.

1. Define the problem and purpose.
2. Consider the reader.
3. Determine the ideas to include.
4. Collect the information.
5. Sort and evaluate the information.
6. Organise the information.
7. Prepare the outline.

Complete each of these seven planning steps before you start writing the long formal report.

Defining the problem and purpose

Analyse the task (or the problem, where relevant) and then decide clearly what the purpose of the report is. If, for example, a report writer has been asked to develop a Local Traffic Management Plan, the writer will first need to determine whether the task is to identify and correct an existing problem or to provide a forward plan that will prevent problems arising. Alternatively, if the writer is examining the feasibility of opening a new office in the city, the purpose will be to evaluate the site against the range of criteria seen as essential in an acceptable site; for example, access to public transport or availability of parking. In this case, the report writer's task is to investigate an option, rather than define and solve a problem.

Define the task or problem.

Once the task is determined and the purpose defined, the report should be developed to help the reader solve the problem or make a decision. If the purpose is clearly defined, the writer will be more able to prepare a long report that the reader will understand.

Considering the reader

Consider the needs of the reader.

Think about who will read the long report. Is the reader a supervisor, fellow worker, client or government department? The answer to this question will affect how the problem is defined, and the way in which arguments are developed, problems analysed and solutions presented. Report writers should do more than write. They should also consider the readers' point of view, their need for detail, their preference for a particular order of information, and their experience and understanding of technical terms. The content, structure and language of a long report may all be influenced by the needs and preferences of the reader. Table 19.2 identifies the needs of the writer and of the reader.

In many cases a report is written in response to a request from another person. That person will have expectations about the final document, its purpose and what it will achieve. Consider these expectations early in the planning stage and the report writing task will be easier and more likely to achieve its purpose. McMurrey (2007) suggests that audiences must be analysed in terms of characteristics such as background knowledge, experience and training, needs and interests, and other demographic factors. Effective report writers adapt their writing to meet the needs, interests and background of the audience.

Determining the ideas to include

Establish the issues or topics to be addressed. For example, if a traffic management plan is proposed, the report writer will need to explore such issues as the effect on the environment, the availability of parking and the effect on residents. From the list of issues to be addressed, create a preliminary plan or outline of headings. Any hypotheses, assumptions or propositions should be formulated and tested to check their accuracy and relevance to the report's purpose.

Collecting the information

After identifying the relevant issues, find sources of information on each one. Gather information from primary and secondary sources, checking that they are credible and reliable. Review Chapter 13 for further details on researching primary and secondary sources of information.

Sorting and evaluating the information

Once information has been gathered, review the material. In the review process it is useful to highlight key words and ideas that relate to the purpose of the report. These highlighted sections will be part of the report's findings: place them in a working file. Put irrelevant information into a file to be checked later; it is unwise to throw out any research information until the report is finished.

Organising the information/preparing the outline

Organise the material according to the headings created. The report writer's next task is to create a suitable structure or outline for the report. Determine this by considering the whole picture. How do ideas link together? Are there any gaps in the information? What issues and headings are the most important? If the writer is dissatisfied with the initial outline it should be revised, new topics included and those that are no longer relevant deleted. The outline is the preliminary draft or plan of the long report.

Classify the information under appropriate headings. Then see if any section needs to be broken into subsections with subheadings. For example, a major section may be 'Current traffic problems'. Within that section there may be a subsection 'Peak hour congestion'.

Turk and Kirkman (1989, pp. 61–62) state that 'most reports and papers . . . will be best organised in a pyramid structure, in order of importance, with a summary at the top and a gradual expansion into

Table 19.2: The different needs of writer and reader	
The writer needs to know	**The reader needs**
• the purpose of the long report	• information and evidence
• its scope and limitations	• an analysis of the information
• any existing information	• conclusions
• the use to which the long report's findings will be put	• recommendations

greater detail within the body of the paper. The base of the pyramid will be your appendices containing the most detailed information.'

The sequence or order of information varies according to whether the report is good news, bad news or persuasive. However, in each case it must provide a logical order or outline for your data. Order of information is discussed in Chapter 13.

Some of the ways to order the information logically are:

- chronological sequence (by time)
- order of importance (most important to least important, or least important to most important)
- geographical identity (e.g. by capital city)
- inductive order (from the particular to the general)
- deductive order (from the general to the specific)
- cause to effect
- problem solving.

An outline prepared for the Local Traffic Management Plan, for example, may use the chronological sequence, identifying the emergence of problems in each of the last five years by order from the first year to the last year. Alternatively, the problem-solving order may be used to identify the nature of the problem, its causes and possible solutions.

The outline provides the writer with the structure of the **body**—or main part—of the report. It enables the writer to present information in this crucial section of the report logically and clearly.

The **body** is the main part of the report.

Another aspect of ordering or sequencing the text requires consideration. It is the order in which the introduction, body, conclusion and recommendations are presented. This sequence is largely determined by the purpose and nature of the message. It is a decision taken after the body is written, but the reasons for sequencing these parts differently need to be considered. How the report is organised affects how it is received and whether action is taken. A writer who is trying to persuade a reluctant reader that restructuring in the workplace is essential will choose a different sequence from the one used if the findings endorse a proposal to which the reader is committed.

The sequence in which information is presented can be either direct or indirect.

INDIRECT SEQUENCE

Long reports are usually ordered with an introductory section first, followed by the centre section and then the final section. However, the sequence can be varied to achieve different purposes. In an analytical report the most common order is:

Use the indirect sequence for a reader outside that area of expertise.

1. introduction
2. body
3. conclusion
4. recommendations.

In the indirect sequence, the reader is introduced to what the writer is about to do and why, and to the limits of the report. The reader is then led through the body and on to the conclusion and recommendations. (Note: an informational report does not make recommendations.)

DIRECT SEQUENCE

There may, however, be occasions when the direct sequence is more appropriate. An analytical report may start with the introduction and follow immediately with an overview of the long report's findings and the answer to the problem. Then present the body or findings of the report after the conclusion and recommendations. Achieve this with the following sequence or order of presentation:

1. introduction
2. conclusion
3. recommendations
4. body.

When writing to an informed person, there is an alternative way to use the direct presentation of information. Present an overview and the suggested answers or conclusion first. Then follow with the recommendations, the introduction and the body of information that supports the conclusion and recommendations. This use of the direct sequence in an analytical report focuses the reader's attention on the conclusion and recommendations first. Achieve this with the following sequence:

1. conclusion
2. recommendations
3. introduction
4. body.

Choose a sequence or order of presentation that suits the purpose and the reader's needs. Once an appropriate outline and order of presentation is developed, the planning of the text is complete. The task now is to write the full text and to prepare the additional components of the long report.

REVIEW QUESTIONS

3. What is the purpose of effective planning in long report writing?
4. Identify at least three different needs of the report writer and those who read the report.
5. Explain at least four ways to order information in a long report.
6. a. Discuss two ways in which you can sequence the introduction, body, conclusion and recommendations in a long report.
   b. Briefly explain the reasons for using different orders when presenting information.
7. What advantages do you gain by ordering information to suit the report's purpose, task and audience?

OBJECTIVE 3 ▶
Using an appropriate writing style, write the front matter, body and end matter of a long report

WRITING THE LONG REPORT

The focus throughout the rest of the chapter is on writing an analytical report. In the writing stage of preparing a long analytical report, the first task is to produce the text: the central part of the document that contains the body of the findings, an introduction to the findings, and the conclusions and recommendations. A range of additional parts, which appear either before or after the main text, will be prepared later. Details about the content of each of these parts are given below, in the order in which they appear in a report.

Writing style

Report-writing style
avoids personal pronouns and emotional language.

The principles of an appropriate **report-writing style** apply to all sections of the report. 'Writing style' is the term used to describe how the report writer uses words, sentences, paragraphs and layout to present ideas and connect with the reader. A person's report-writing style may be described as crisp and clear, verbose, academic and theoretical, or factual and business-like.

Although plain English is suitable for most writing at work, the 'you' approach is unsuitable for long reports because the language in a report should be impersonal. A report presents facts and information on events and situations, rather than on people, so avoid using 'I', 'you', 'he', 'she' and 'we'.

In avoiding the use of personal pronouns in writing a report, writers will find they use the passive voice more often. Instead of saying, for example, 'I undertook research', they will write 'Research was undertaken'. In the passive voice, the subject of the sentence does not perform the action; it receives the action. Take care, however, to limit the use of the passive voice as it can make the document sound sluggish.

The long report format

Organisations and individuals have trialled and adjusted report formats over a number of years. The only definitive formatting rule to have emerged is to vary the format to suit the purpose and nature of the report. In the final packaging and presentation, follow the in-house style of the organisation and formal report-writing conventions to achieve a professional appearance and an effective transfer of information.

Sussams (1993, p. 37) states: 'Every organisation which produces reports should establish a set of rules as to their layout. These rules are required (a) to ensure that all reports project the same "brand image" (e.g. thorough professionalism or whatever is appropriate to the organisation), (b) to assist the author, the typist and the reader, all of whom will be able to work more easily and more efficiently if they get used to a particular style.' Three basic factors are suggested to establish a set of rules: clarity, appearance and convenience. Sussams stresses the need for consistency in layout.

Fardell (1998, p. 1) states: 'Presenting complex data is not easy. The final presentation should be the result of an iterative process taking into account the content of the publication, the objectives to be met and user expectations.' She suggests organising information to reflect the relative importance and structure of the data by using bold to emphasise totals and distinguishing the importance of the various levels of heading by using different fonts and formatting.

The parts of a long report can be grouped into three broad sections: front matter, text (or body) and end matter. Plan and write the long report around these groupings and the task will be completed more efficiently. You will have less need to write and rewrite if you focus continually on the three sections identified in Table 19.3 and place information in the correct section as the task progresses. All the possible parts of a long formal report are presented in Table 19.4.

A long report has three main sections—front matter, body and end matter.

Table 19.3: The structure of a long report

Broad section	Parts in each section	
	Essential	**Optional**
The front matter or preliminaries	• title page • letter of transmittal • table of contents	• list of tables • list of figures • abstract or synopsis or executive summary • authorisation document
The centre, text or body of the report	• introduction • discussion and analysis of the report's findings • development of ideas • conclusion • recommendations	• tables • graphics
The end matter or supplementary material	• bibliography • glossary • index	• appendix

Table 19.4: Parts of a long formal report

Part	Purpose
Title page	Identifies the report's title, the receiver's name and title, the writer's name and title, and the date.
Letter of transmittal	Indicates in the form of a formal covering letter the person who authorised or requested the report, the terms of reference, the scope of the report and the problems addressed. It serves as a record of transmittal, identifies the writer, and acknowledges others who contributed.
Terms of reference	States clearly and concisely the scope of the report.
Acknowledgments	Lists the names of persons and institutions who assisted in preparing the report.
Table of contents	Records the name of each part of the report and the name of each first- and second-order heading within the body, and the page on which each occurs.
List of figures or tables	Records titles and page numbers of tables, illustrations and diagrams.
Executive summary, preface, abstract or synopsis	Mentions briefly the report's purpose, findings, conclusion and recommendations. It gives the starting point and directions of the report.
Introductory section of the body	Defines the research task and problem, and includes: • the purpose statement • background information • scope, aims and limits of the report • authorisation for the report.
Centre section of the main body	Presents factual, objective information. Findings are analysed and discussed, and evidence is presented. Headings and a numbering system are used to signal to the reader when new ideas are to be introduced and developed.
Conclusion	Summarises the report's findings and evaluates the main facts.
Recommendations	Offers solutions or courses of action.
Signature block	Contains the signature, name and job title of the writer, usually placed after the recommendations and before the appendices and bibliography.
Appendices and attachments	Present additional material such as charts and tables that are relevant to the report.
References and bibliography	References include the information quoted in the text. List in the bibliography recommended reading material on the subjects covered in the report or other relevant subjects. The two terms have in the past been used to distinguish between the different functions of a list of references and a bibliography. However, these days the list of references and further reading are often presented together and titled as either references or bibliography.
Glossary	Defines and explains technical words.

LONG REPORTS

1 The way in which the words are used creates an expression and flow of ideas and makes a connection with the reader. The units of expression in a report create a report-writing style. They are:

- words
- phrases
- sentences
- paragraphs
- sections under headings
- parts of the report.

  a   Explain the phrase 'creates an expression'. Define each of the units of expression listed above.

  b   What writing style is most appropriate to report writing?

  c   Explain the phrase 'writing in plain English'. Can you incorporate a plain English style into your report writing?

2 Work in small groups. First, read this paragraph:

The purpose statement is the most important component of the introductory section of the report. It aims to convey the report's purpose to the reader. Other words that can be substituted for the term purpose statement are goal, aim or objective. It is one sentence or paragraph that describes what the report aims to do.

  a   Each person in the group is then to write a purpose statement for a long report that aims to investigate student amenities provided at your college or university.

  b   Compare your purpose statement with those of the other members of the group.

3 a   Work in small groups to brainstorm a list of the characteristics of a good report.

  b   As a group, prepare a list of report-writing tips a trainer could use as part of an introductory report-writing training session for a newly employed group of graduates.

Writing the front matter

In the long report format, the parts placed before the main text are the title page, letter of transmittal, letter of authorisation, table of contents, list of tables and executive summary. These are classified as the **front matter** and are all numbered with Roman numerals except for the title page, which is usually not numbered.

TITLE PAGE

The **title page** includes the long report's title, the name of the person who authorised the report, and the name and designation of the report writer (see the sample title page in the report 'Proposed New Watering System for Fairways Golf Club' on page 540). Create a title that indicates the purpose and nature of the report. Place the name of the organisation, the person to whom the report is submitted and the date of submission on the title page. For a report that is to be distributed to other sections or people in the organisation, also place the name of these sections on the title page.

LETTER OF TRANSMITTAL

A **letter of transmittal** is formatted in block business letter layout and addressed to the person who authorised or requested the report (see the covering letter in the report on page 541). It is the formal way of stating that the report has been completed within the **terms of reference** and by a certain date.

Bovée and Thill (2005, p. 445) suggest the following: 'Open [the letter of transmittal] by officially conveying the report to your readers and summarizing its purpose . . . The rest of the introduction includes

The **front matter** contains the preliminary parts that appear before the text of the report.

The **title page** is the first page of a report. It includes the report's title, the name of the person who authorised the report, and the name and designation of the report writer.

The **letter of transmittal** is the covering letter for a report. It should state who authorised the report, when it was authorised, and its purpose and scope.

The **terms of reference** define the scope of a report.

information about the scope of the report, the methods used to complete the study, and the limitations that became apparent.' In the body of the letter of transmittal, mention any points of special interest in the report, point out any additional research that is necessary, and provide any supporting details that will help the reader to understand and use the report. The recommendations then follow unless the reader is likely to find them difficult to understand. In this case, the findings and conclusions should be summarised before the recommendations. Finally, thank the reader for the opportunity to do the work and offer to answer any questions. Remember that the letter of transmittal may be the first part of the report to be read, so use it to impress. Also acknowledge and thank others who worked on the project.

TABLE OF CONTENTS

The **table of contents** lists the main sections and subsections of a report.

Include the main sections and subsections of the report in the **table of contents**. Check that the numbering system for the main sections of the long report and for headings and subheadings within the body is easy to use. Indicate the number of the page on which each main heading appears. In a formal report, the page numbers for the front matter are shown in Roman numerals. The page numbers for the remainder of the report are shown as Arabic numerals. An example of a table of contents for a report is shown in the report on page 543.

LIST OF ILLUSTRATIONS

When only a few figures or tables are used, the list of figures and/or tables is placed under the table of contents. If a large number have been included, list them on a new page. List the number of each figure or table, its title, and the page on which it appears (see the report on page 544).

PREFACE, ABSTRACT, SYNOPSIS OR EXECUTIVE SUMMARY

The **preface, abstract, synopsis** or **executive summary** is the part of a proposal or report that summarises the contents and findings.

In a **preface**, **abstract**, **synopsis** or **executive summary**, state the intentions in writing the report. Give a brief outline, half to one page in length, of the report's scope, purpose, methods, findings and conclusions (see the executive summary in the report on page 544).

The executive summary is the part of the front matter that sets the framework and helps readers outside the area of expertise to recognise the starting point and the direction to be taken by the report. Therefore, to help focus the reader's thoughts on the topic, the *purpose statement* should be repeated in the executive summary. The purpose statement identifies the document's theme.

REVIEW QUESTIONS

8 What writing style would you use in a long analytical report?

9 Name the parts of the report that belong in the front matter.

Writing the body or text

The largest part of a long report is the body or text. The pages of the text of a long report are numbered with Arabic numerals (1, 2, 3 and so on). Plan and write the body or text of a long formal report in three main sections:

1 the introductory section of the body
2 the centre section of the body
3 the final section of the body.

Set out the sections of the body for clarity and understanding.

The task is to present the ideas so that they emerge clearly for the reader. For this reason, use headings and subheadings to create manageable and readable information, and use spacing to add clarity. Never cramp the information to save space, because the material on the page will become too dense and therefore more difficult to read.

INTRODUCTORY SECTION

The **introduction** defines the research task and problem, so it makes sense to begin it with the purpose statement. It is helpful to think clearly about the goals to be achieved in the final report and to state these in the next part of the introduction. Then present the terms of reference. As they are the instructions for writing the report, they should be available to both the writer and the reader. Then follows the methodology.

Finally, state the report's scope and limits. For example, the writer may decide that a report on 'Business Management in Australia' is too broad for the purpose and will need to limit the scope of the long report. Let the reader know this by writing the terms of reference in the introduction: for example, the terms of reference may limit the report to 'Small Business Management in the Retail Sector in New South Wales'.

Table 19.5 lists the parts of the introductory section.

> The **introduction** identifies the report's purpose, scope, methodology and terms of reference.

CENTRE SECTION

The *centre section* expands and develops the material. It is the main section of the report. When the body or centre section of the long report is being produced, focus on the report's purpose by continually asking the question, 'What is it that I am reporting on?' With this focus in mind, write according to the outline and to the order of information decided on. If the outline is causing difficulties—for example, by giving undue weighting to a particular issue, or introducing issues that are not central to the long report—revise it. Do this by reconsidering the purpose, limits, terms of reference and findings of the report.

> The centre section contains a detailed discussion of the long report's findings.

Objectivity

In long reports, take care to remain *objective*. Information should be factual, relevant and up to date. Present the argument in a way that analyses and interprets the information objectively. By using sound reasoning techniques and an objective approach, the writer can argue convincingly for and against the case being presented.

> Objectivity is based on thinking, rather than emotion.

Findings

The centre section of the body or text conventionally investigates and analyses the **findings**, and identifies and develops solutions about the issue or problem. In this section, aim to present a balanced and comprehensive view and substantiate the content and findings with documented evidence.

> **Findings** are the facts and information presented in a document.

Table 19.5: Parts of the introductory section of a long report	
Part	**When it is used**
Authorisation	In every case, except when the writer decides to prepare the report of his or her own accord.
Problem	In every case where the report addresses a problem.
Purpose	In every case.
Scope	In every case.
Methodology	In every case.
Sources	In every case, except when the writer is writing the report on the basis of his or her own experience.
Background	Only when it is necessary for the reader to have this information in order to understand the findings presented in the report.
Definition of terms	Only when technical or ambiguous terms are used in the report. Even then, it may be better to place the definitions in a glossary.
Limitations	In every case where a limitation, such as available information, research assistance, time or money, has affected the extent of research.
Brief statement of the results	Only when the conclusion and recommendations are placed at the end of the body of the report.

Readers will expect to see how the ideas develop throughout the body of the report. Use analytical and thinking skills well. Show clearly how the argument or analysis develops by using signalling devices and linking words to show the connections between ideas, and by providing headings and a numbering system that reflect the structure of the argument.

Headings

Headings highlight the main ideas and give order to the information in a way that is suited to the purpose of the report and helpful to the reader. Effective headings divide the centre section (or body) of the report into well-defined sections and lead the reader through the document's structure so that he or she can identify the content and order of the long report easily. In this book, the headings are divided into three orders. The first-order heading is blocked to the margin, larger than the other headings and in upper case. The second- and third-order headings are blocked to the margin in decreasing size and are in lower case. The intention is to signal to the reader that a completely new section is beginning, with subsections and then perhaps sub-subsections.

A heading should be used each time a new aspect of the content is presented. The use of headings breaks the text into sections that are readable. Pages of information without headings become unwieldy, dense and difficult to understand.

Numbering systems

Choose a numbering system that suits the document. The purpose of the numbering system (and headings) is to give an outline that is easy to understand and read.

Graphics

Graphics can be used in the centre section to add meaning and emphasis to the findings. However, if they detract from the argument or interfere with the logical progression of ideas, place them in an appendix. Any graphic in the main text should focus the reader's attention by using the following four-step method:

1. Explain the idea in writing.
2. Discuss how the graphic relates to the information presented.
3. Place the graph or diagram straight after this explanation and discussion.
4. Number the graphic and put a reference to it in the body of the text.

Only use graphs or diagrams that add meaning and interest to the findings of your report.

Notations

Notations identify the sources of information.

In the centre section of the report, use author–date references, endnotes or footnotes to direct the reader to extra sources of information or to present different views on the topic. Document the evidence and findings in your footnotes and endnotes accurately. The sources of information should be fully acknowledged in the list of references or bibliography. If the information cannot be traced and checked, your results may be questioned or even disbelieved. Refer to Chapter 13 for more ideas on notations.

FINAL SECTION

The *final section* of the body of the long report contains the conclusion and recommendations. Set these out as separate subsections of the final section. An example of the final section of a report is shown in the report on page 551.

The placement of conclusions in the final section is, in practice, a matter for the report writer to decide. It is often preferable to place the conclusions before the body of the report or, in some cases, even before the introduction. The sequence of introduction, body and conclusion is discussed above in the 'Effective Planning' section of this chapter.

Conclusion

The report's **conclusion** is usually short: half a page to one page. Avoid writing new ideas or findings in the conclusion. If the purpose of the report is to investigate and analyse findings, it may be enough to use a conclusion to summarise the findings. Winckel and Hart (1996, p. 12) state: 'The conclusion(s) of a report must be related to, and resulting from, the material which appears in the report. The content of the Conclusion will be linked to the Introduction.'

*The **conclusion** must be related to and result from the material in the report.*

Recommendations

Recommendations should aim to solve the problem or provide the answers to questions asked in the report's terms of reference. Always base the recommendations on the research findings, analysis and discussion, so that they flow logically and obviously from the information in the body or text of the report. Then the reader can evaluate the solutions objectively against the report's purpose; that is, what the report aims to do and why it was put together.

***Recommendations** are the actions proposed as a result of the findings.*

Present each recommendation in a separate point or paragraph. Clearly state the actions to be taken. For example, if you recommend that a new building worth $1.8 million is to be bought, you need to justify this recommendation with supporting evidence in the centre section of the long report. Supporting tables are placed either in the body of the report or in the appendix, not in the final section. In the body, include figures on items such as total outlay, borrowings and period of repayment in relation to projected earnings and cash flow, to support the recommendation.

The imperative voice is used for recommendations. Begin the recommendation with a verb. The subject 'you' is assumed in the recommendation. Another useful strategy is to write the recommendations as an action plan that is specific and achievable. Then, if the reader agrees with the recommendations, the action can be carried out easily and quickly.

Signature block

Report writers usually place their signature, name and job title in a **signature block** at the end of the final section of the main text. This is usually after the recommendations and before the appendices and bibliography.

*The **signature block** contains the report writer's signature, name and job title.*

An effective long report provides comprehensive information and expert opinion. As well as collecting and analysing information, the writer has to apply time, thought and effort to each stage of the process. Table 19.6 suggests a sequence to follow as you prepare a long report.

Writing the end matter

The **end matter** is the last part of the report. It includes the appendix, bibliography and glossary of terms, and is placed after the body of the text. Facts and findings relevant to the report, but which would interfere with the flow of ideas if included in the body, are placed in an **appendix**. Information that is too long or too technical is also placed here. Readers are referred to the appendix from the body of the report and can use the information if they want to follow the idea further.

***End matter** is the final part of a report or book and contains the appendix, bibliography, glossary of terms and index.*

*An **appendix** contains useful information unsuited to the body of a report.*

Examples of the types of information that can be placed in appendices are statistics, surveys or questionnaires used in research, additional graphs, and extracts from journals and newspapers that are supplements to the text in the body of the report. Each separate appendix should be lettered: Appendix A, Appendix B and so on. The Arabic numbering used in the text of the report can continue into the appendix, or the appendices can be numbered internally. For Appendix A with three pages the pages are lettered A1, A2, A3. For a two-page Appendix B, B1, B2.

It is acceptable to use the **bibliography** to list all the references and sources of information used, as well as further recommended reading. A reference list contains only the sources of information referred to in the report. Gather information on bibliographies from Chapter 13, or use the in-house style of the organisation. The Citation Styles Online site, <www.bedfordstmartins.com/online/citex.html>, presents a number of different citation styles for electronic information. Note that some report writers still prefer a separate list of references for all the sources and references used in the report and a bibliography for suggested further reading.

*The **bibliography** is a list of all the sources of information used in a report, as well as further recommended reading.*

Table 19.6: The long report writing sequence review

You will complete a number of steps when you compile a long report.

1 Receive the instruction and clarify the terms of reference and the reader's expectations.

2 Gather the data or information from primary or secondary sources.

3 Interpret the data objectively on the facts, not your attitudes or feelings towards the topic.

4 Organise the data to suit the report's purpose. A report written for people who understand the technical details will include more technical and difficult language than a report that is written for people outside that area of expertise.

5 Write the report as a link between the writer and the reader. The report format and report-writing style are used to communicate the report's findings, conclusions and recommendations. Reports that do this effectively are clear, concise, readable and easy to understand.

6 Compile the report in a way that invites respect for your findings. Unfortunately, not every report is read. Aim to have the final product, the report, used in the organisation's decision making by offering a clear presentation and a balanced evaluation of the evidence and research findings. At the very least, you will want the summary, introduction, conclusions and recommendations to be read and acknowledged. Correct report layout helps to achieve this.

7 Present the completed report in a professional manner, using a layout and style that makes it easy to find information and interesting to read.

The decision to read the report is the reader's. Ensure that the report is read by gaining the reader's interest, attention and desire to read further. Present a report that fills a need and that is perceived as relevant.

SAMPLE REPORT

The report that follows illustrates the material discussed in this chapter.

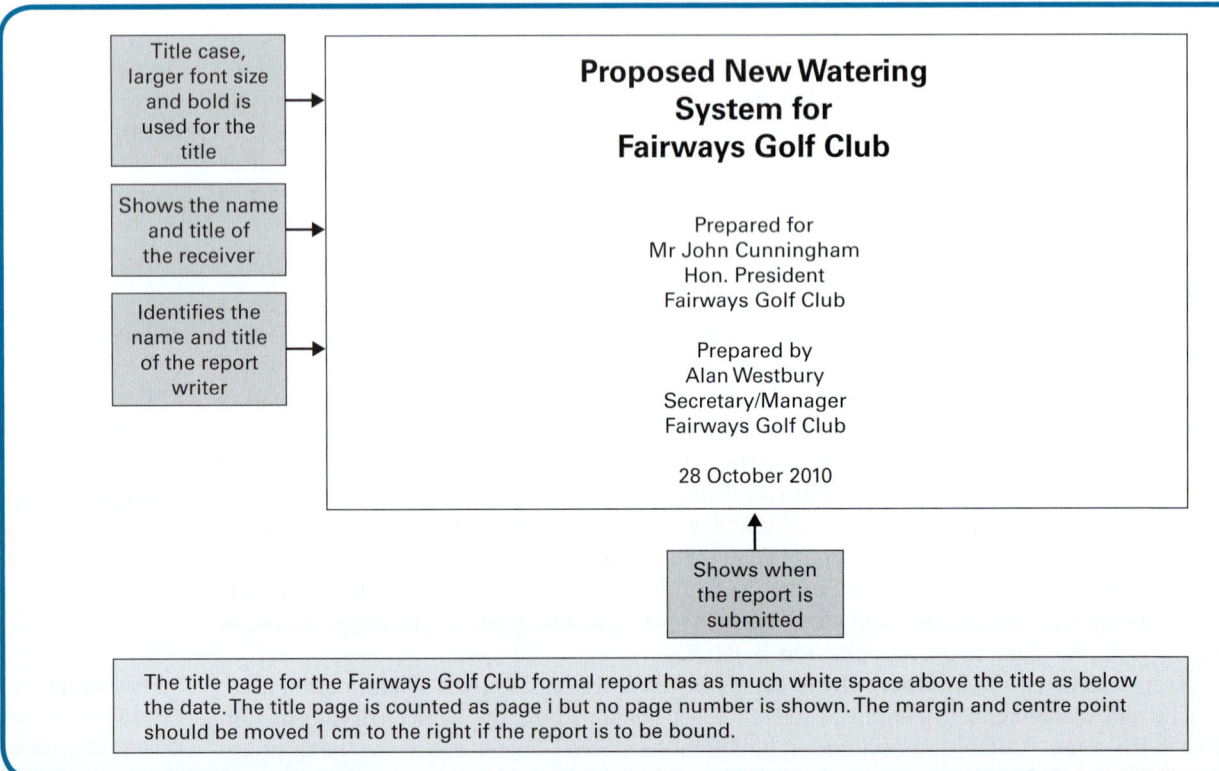

Figure 19.1 Example: Fairways Golf Club formal report

Source: Dwyer, J. *The Business Communication Handbook* , 7th edn, Pearson Education Australia, Sydney, 2006. Reproduced with permission.

FAIRWAYS GOLF CLUB
Driveway Avenue, Merrylands VIC 3055
Tel/Fax: (03) 6653 2948 Email: fairgolf@blue.com.au

28 October 2010

Mr John Cunningham
Hon. President
Fairways Golf Club
Driveway Avenue
MERRYLANDS VIC 3055

Dear John

Here is the report you requested on 3 July on the proposed new watering system for the golf club.

I have detailed in this report an examination of the differences between the existing watering system and the proposed system. I have included a cost-effectiveness analysis, as well as a detailed comparison of the physical and engineering differences of the two systems.

Additionally, I have included an analysis of the possible effect on golfers and the results of a survey of golf club staff, golfers and nearby residents. The City Council's requirements and the results of an inspection of the new watering system in operation at the Riverview Golf Club are also detailed.

My recommendation is that the Golf Club should postpone implementation of this system until other options are considered.

Please contact me if you have any questions regarding this report.

Yours sincerely

Alan Westbury
Secretary/Manager

ii

Highlights the report's purpose and refers to the research, analysis and the findings

Points to the report's recommendations

Letter of transmittal for the Fairways Golf Club formal report uses full block format with centred letterhead and open punctuation. The letter of transmittal page is numbered by the lower-case roman numeral ii, centred at the bottom of the page. The margin and centre point should be moved 1 cm to the right if the report is to be bound.

Figure 19.1 *continued*

Identifies who is authorising the report and when

Identifies the subject to be investigated

The scope of work is identified

Identifies when the report is due

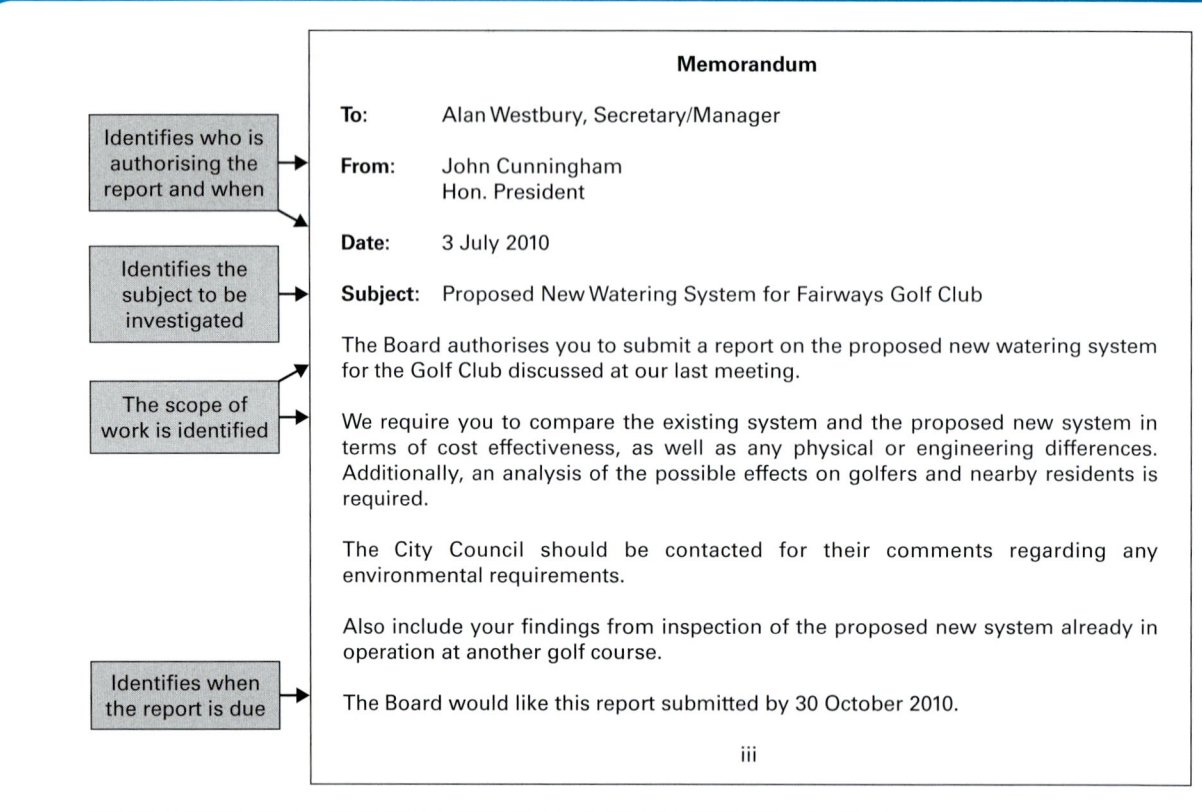

Memorandum

To: Alan Westbury, Secretary/Manager

From: John Cunningham
Hon. President

Date: 3 July 2010

Subject: Proposed New Watering System for Fairways Golf Club

The Board authorises you to submit a report on the proposed new watering system for the Golf Club discussed at our last meeting.

We require you to compare the existing system and the proposed new system in terms of cost effectiveness, as well as any physical or engineering differences. Additionally, an analysis of the possible effects on golfers and nearby residents is required.

The City Council should be contacted for their comments regarding any environmental requirements.

Also include your findings from inspection of the proposed new system already in operation at another golf course.

The Board would like this report submitted by 30 October 2010.

iii

The authorisation document identifies the scope of the report. The memo of authorisation page is numbered by the lower-case roman numeral iii, centred at the bottom of the page.

Figure 19.1 ***continued***

Page numbers for front matter are lower-case roman numerals and for the remainder of the report Arabic numerals

Table of Contents

iv

Highlights outline by indenting secondary heading

Figure 19.1 *continued*

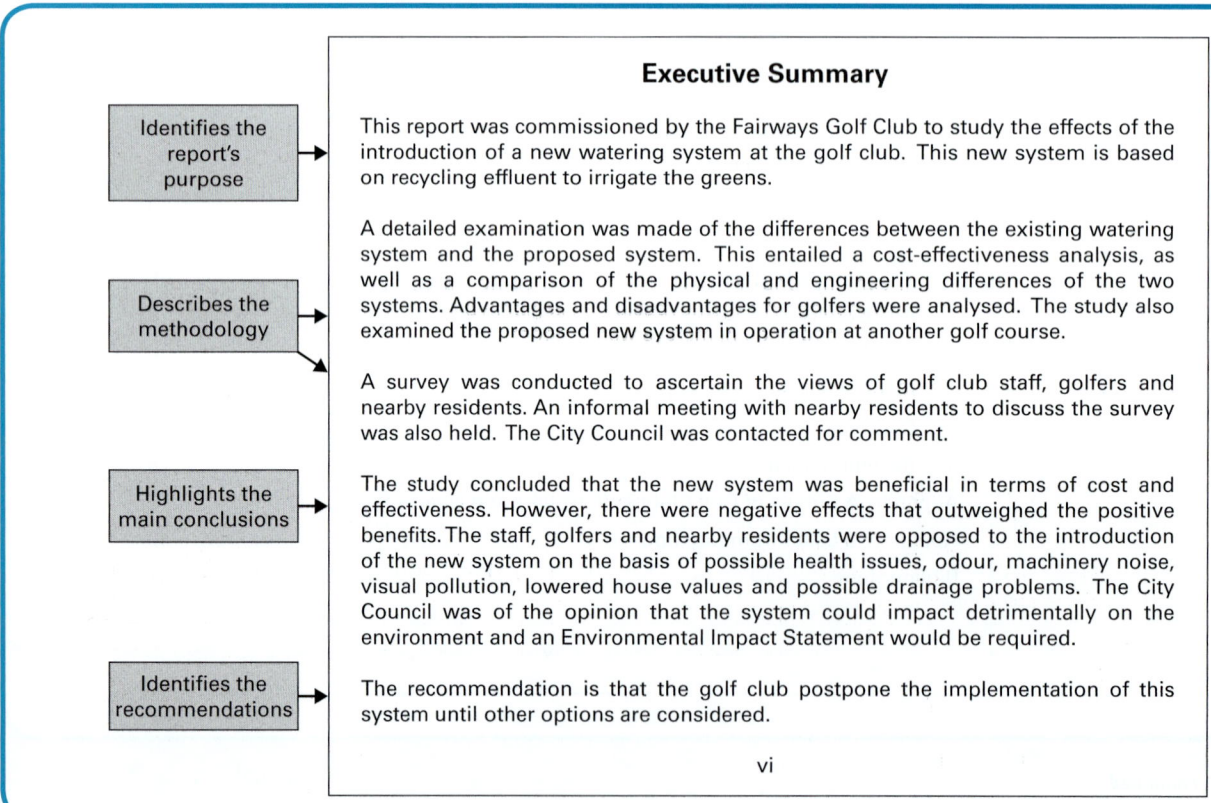

List of Illustrations

v

The list of illustrations is placed on a separate page from the table of contents for the Fairways Golf Club report. When a report's table of contents is shorter, you may place them on the same page. The writer uses title case to parallel the style within the report. Remember to use formatting styles on your report's headings and you will be able to generate a contents page automatically using your software package.

The executive summary on the next page gives readers a quick overview or picture of the report. It states the reasons for writing the report and identifies the scope, research methods used, findings and conclusions. It is an essential component of a long business report.

Figure 19.1 *continued*

Executive Summary

Identifies the report's purpose

This report was commissioned by the Fairways Golf Club to study the effects of the introduction of a new watering system at the golf club. This new system is based on recycling effluent to irrigate the greens.

Describes the methodology

A detailed examination was made of the differences between the existing watering system and the proposed system. This entailed a cost-effectiveness analysis, as well as a comparison of the physical and engineering differences of the two systems. Advantages and disadvantages for golfers were analysed. The study also examined the proposed new system in operation at another golf course.

A survey was conducted to ascertain the views of golf club staff, golfers and nearby residents. An informal meeting with nearby residents to discuss the survey was also held. The City Council was contacted for comment.

Highlights the main conclusions

The study concluded that the new system was beneficial in terms of cost and effectiveness. However, there were negative effects that outweighed the positive benefits. The staff, golfers and nearby residents were opposed to the introduction of the new system on the basis of possible health issues, odour, machinery noise, visual pollution, lowered house values and possible drainage problems. The City Council was of the opinion that the system could impact detrimentally on the environment and an Environmental Impact Statement would be required.

Identifies the recommendations

The recommendation is that the golf club postpone the implementation of this system until other options are considered.

vi

Figure 19.1 *continued*

The introductory section of the main text of the Fairways Golf Club report contains the report's title and has one major heading and two subheadings

Proposed New Watering System for Fairways Golf Club

1.0 Introduction

Fairways Golf Club has endeavoured to ensure that the most efficient and cost-effective watering system has been used to keep the golf course in the best condition for golfers.

Recent drought conditions have resulted in the greens requiring more water to maintain their current condition. However, increased Water Board charges have necessitated the club limiting the amount of water required for the greens. This has led to detrimental conditions for the golfers and golfer dissatisfaction. The club's aim is to make certain that the greens are maintained to golfers' satisfaction. To ensure this under present conditions would incur additional Water Board costs. This would result in an increase in fees.

In the light of these anticipated increased costs, the Board of the Golf Club has requested an investigation into the effects of the introduction of a proposed new watering system at the golf club. This proposed system would reduce the amount of water necessary to irrigate the greens by incorporating recycled treated effluent.

This report details the results of these investigations. The results show that, although the new system would be beneficial in terms of cost and effectiveness, there are negative effects that outweigh the positive benefits.

1.1 Purpose, Scope and Limitations

The purpose of this report is to analyse the differences between the existing system and the proposed system, the effects on golf club staff, golfers and nearby residents, and to determine whether the proposed new system should be introduced.

1.2 Sources and Methods

In preparing this report, a cost-effectiveness analysis, as well as a detailed comparison of the physical and engineering differences between the two systems, was made.

A survey was conducted to ascertain the views of golf club staff, golfers and nearby residents. An informal meeting was also held with the nearby residents to discuss the survey.

An analysis was made of the advantages and disadvantages to golfers. The City Council was contacted for comment and possible objections.

Inspection was made of the proposed new system in operation at Riverview Golf Club for comparison purposes.

1

Continued

The title is placed on the first page of the introductory section 5 cm from the top of the page. The Fairways Golf Club report introduction presents a brief background statement, and defines the report's task in a purpose, scope and limitations statement. It also describes the sources and methods used to gather and analyse information. Table 19.5 (see page 537) describes other parts you may choose to include in the introductory section of a long report.

Figure 19.1 *continued*

The content in the central section of the body of the Fairways Golf Club report contains six main headings

2.0 Cost Comparison of Existing and Proposed Watering Systems

Costs of both the existing and proposed new watering systems were investigated. Initially, there would be the cost of installing the new system and additional landscaping. However, results showed that over subsequent years there would be considerable cost benefits in installing the new system that would compensate for the cost of installation.

The important difference is that the recycled treated effluent would considerably reduce Water Board charges, resulting in a large cost saving.

Since the commissioning of this report, advice has been received that a large engineering works is being closed. As the Water Board will not be supplying water on a large scale to this site, it is possible that the Water Board may consider supplying additional water to the golf course at a reduced rate.

2.1 Costs of Existing System

The existing system has been in operation for more than 30 years. Currently, the overall costs of the existing system amount to $86,690 annually. This includes depreciation of equipment ($15,500) as well as the day-to-day operating costs listed below.

2.1.1 Current operating costs

2.1.1.1	Greenkeeping Includes replacement of turf and fertilising, also petrol for mowers	2,505.00
2.1.1.2	Water Board usage charges Includes increased charges this year	11,685.00
2.1.1.3	Electricity	5,000.00
2.1.1.4	Maintenance Includes lawnmower repairs and pumping equipment service calls	1,300.00
2.1.1.5	Staffing Includes salary of one greenkeeper and one apprentice	50,200.00
		$70,690.00

2.2 Costs of Proposed System

The central section investigates and analyses the report's findings

The proposed system would incur initial costs of installing the pump machinery, cables, pipes, and housing for the machinery, as well as landscaping. The existing sprinkler system would be incorporated into the new watering system. The club presently has this amount available, so it will not be necessary to obtain a loan. However, loss of interest on this amount should be taken into account.

Depreciation of equipment would be marginally higher. The anticipated operating costs are based on quoted figures from the Water Board and the installing company.

2.2.1 Installation costs

2.2.1.1	Installing pump machinery, cables and housing	200,000.00
2.2.1.2	Landscaping	3,000.00
		$20,3000.00

2.2.2 Anticipated operating costs

2.2.2.1	Greenkeeping	1,000.00
2.2.2.2	Water Board charges (costs reduced using the recycling process)	2,000.00
2.2.2.3	Electricity	5,500.00
2.2.2.4	Maintenance (costs reduced owing to new equipment installed)	800.00
2.2.2.5	Staffing	50,900.00
		$60,200.00

2

Continued

Figure 19.1 *continued*

3.0 Comparison of Physical and Engineering Differences

There are considerable physical and engineering differences between the two systems. These are detailed below.

3.1 Physical Differences

The major physical differences would be in the installation of the plant to treat the effluent and the construction of plant housing. This would be situated near the tenth dam behind the sixth tee.

The housing for the new machinery would differ markedly from the present plant housing, which is small and unobtrusive. The new housing, a recycled shed, would be covered with treated pine lattice cladding to blend into the landscape. The housing roof cover would be Caulfield Green Colorbond zincalume custom orb roof cladding. (A sketch of the housing is shown in Figure 1.)

Landscaping would be required to ensure minimal visual effect from the housing. A 'buffer' of native plantings would need to be created.

Graphics improve the report's readability and create interest

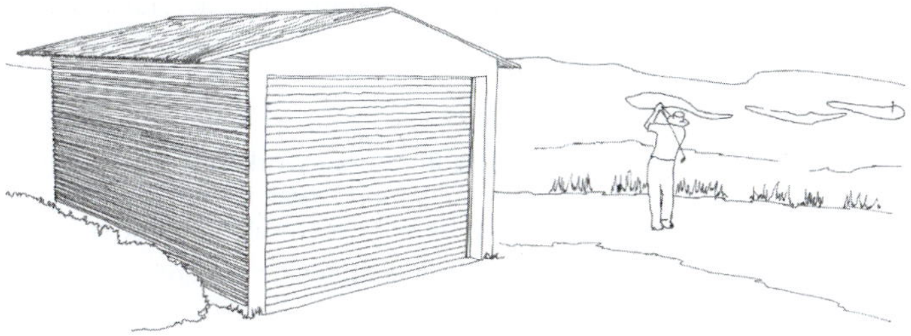

Figure 1 Sketch of Machinery Housing

3.2 Engineering Differences

The main engineering difference between the two systems is in the transfer system to recycle the sewerage water. Cables would be laid underground from an access shaft in Salisbury Street and the effluent pumped to a plant on the golf course. The effluent would be treated by ozone to separate the contaminants. The contaminants would be discharged back into the sewer. The clean, treated water would then be pumped to the main storage dam before being distributed to other dams on the course. The treated effluent would be of a high quality, but marginally lower than the World Health Authority standard for drinking water.

The new system differs from the existing system in that the pumps would be in operation during night hours. Watering of the greens, however, would occur on the same cycle as presently exists.

4.0 Advantages and Disadvantages for Golfers

There are considerable advantages for golfers with the introduction of the proposed system. However, there are also some disadvantages that could affect golfers. Perceived advantages and disadvantages are listed below.

4.1 Advantages

The main benefit for golfers would be the improved condition of the greens, both in summer and winter. Additionally, the saving on Water Board charges would mean that fees could remain at their present level.

The savings made by the golf club would also result in the club being able to improve the clubhouse and its facilities. This would give golfers better amenities without the need to increase fees.

3

Continued

Figure 19.1 *continued*

4.2 Disadvantages

There would be some disruption during the installation of the cables and machinery and the creation of new ponds. Attempts would be made to keep this at a minimum.

There may be some opposition from golfers to increased operating noise; however, as most of the operations will be confined to evening hours, this should be minimal. The company supplying the new system has given assurance that the noise level will be within acceptable decibel levels.

The golfers may be opposed to treated effluent being used to water the greens. Signs will be erected advising golfers of this fact.

5.0 The Proposed New System in Operation at Riverview Golf Club

The Secretary/Manager and head greenkeeper inspected the proposed system in operation at the Riverview Golf Club during August and September.

They also consulted the greenkeeper and manager of Riverview Golf Club regarding financial advantages for the club. They asked for comments or objections the club may have received from golfers and nearby residents relating to the new system.

5.1 Inspection Results

The irrigation of the golf course worked well. The greens were regularly watered and were of a high quality and a lush green.

There appeared to be no discernible noise effects from machinery operation.

This section presents data gathered from primary sources

5.2 Manager's and Greenkeeper's Comments

5.2.1 Financial savings

The manager reported that there had been considerable saving on water costs since the installation of the new system. The recycling had greatly increased the club's ability to maintain the greens in an acceptable condition at much lower cost.

5.2.2 Golfers' and nearby residents' comments and/or objections

5.2.2.1 Golfers

According to the manager, there had been some adverse comments from golfers during the installation period. Golfers were at first reluctant to have treated effluent used as irrigation. However, golfers now appreciate the improved condition of the greens. They also appreciate the removal of the water levy imposed during the earlier drought period.

5.2.2.2 Nearby residents

Riverview Golf Club differs from Fairways Golf Club in that a large proportion of the green is adjacent to a river. As a result of this, only a very small number of residents adjoin the golf course.

The machinery and housing is located near the riverbank away from any residential property.

The only objections from residents were in relation to run-off from the dams during a recent heavy rainfall and the fear of possible health problems from the treated effluent. Over four years of operation, there have been no health issues.

6.0 Survey Results

Surveys were made of golf club staff, golfers and nearby residents. Additionally, an informal evening meeting was held to inform nearby residents of the reasons for the survey.

There was a 100% return from golf club staff. Of the golfers, the return was 20%. A very high percentage (89%) of the residents of the four streets adjoining the golf club returned completed surveys.

4

Continued

Figure 19.1 *continued*

Overall, results showed that golf club staff and golfers were in favour of a new watering system. They appeared to have few objections to the proposed system. The main objection was in respect of the machinery housing.

Nearby residents, however, raised very strong objections to the introduction of this proposed watering system. They were concerned about possible odour and drainage problems. A particular concern was the likelihood of health risks if there was run-off from the golf course into their properties. Noise levels were also a problem, particularly as the machinery would operate mainly during evening hours. Visual pollution from the proposed machinery housing construction was an added concern. At the informal evening meeting, they also expressed concerns about possible devaluation of their properties. Many had already lodged objections to the construction of the proposed new watering system directly to the City Council.

Survey results from the different groups are listed below and shown in the graphs.

6.1 Golf Club Staff (n=14)

6.1.1 A majority of the staff (78.6%) were in favour of the introduction of a new watering system.

6.1.2 A small number (21.4%) were in favour of increasing fees and retaining the existing system.

6.1.3 Numbers were equally divided on the possibility of increased noise from the machinery of the proposed watering system.

6.1.4 A small majority (56.4%) were concerned with possible health problems.

6.1.5 A majority (85.7%) felt that the introduction of new clubhouse facilities and the improved condition of the greens would attract new members.

6.1.6 A large percentage (92.85%) considered that the machinery housing located near the ninth tee would be visual pollution.

Survey data gathered is objective and factual. It provides evidence and facts that are analysed and presented in the body of the report

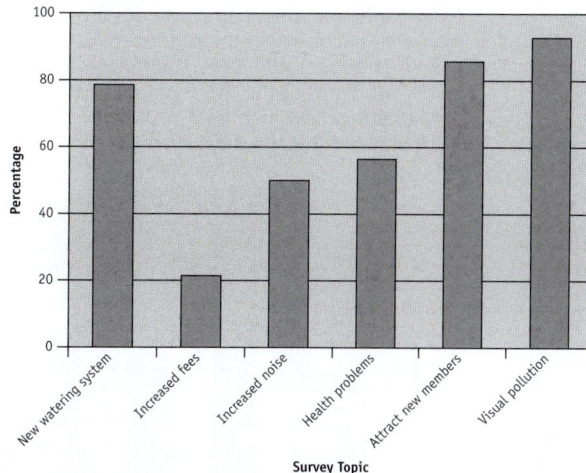

Figure 2 Survey Responses from Golf Club Staff (n=14)

6.2 Golfers (n=223)

6.2.1 A majority of the golfers (89.2%) were in favour of the introduction of a new watering system.

6.2.2 A very low percentage (10.3%) was in favour of increasing fees and retaining the existing system.

6.2.3 A slight majority (53.36%) felt that there could be noise pollution.

6.2.4 A significant number (78.4%) felt that there was a health risk.

Figure 19.1 *continued*

6.2.5 Similar to golf club staff, the golfers (89.6%) felt that the introduction of new clubhouse facilities and the improved condition of the greens would attract new members.

6.2.6 Similar to golf club staff, 99% of the golfers felt that the machinery housing would be visual pollution.

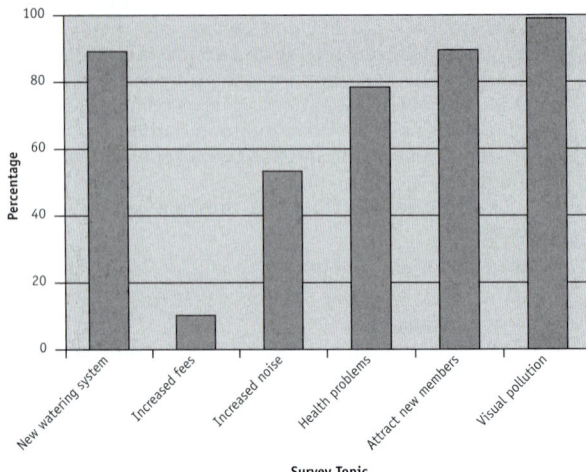

Figure 3 Survey Responses from Golfers (n=223)

6.3 Nearby Residents (n=98)

6.3.1 96% of residents were opposed to the introduction of the new system.

6.3.2 100% were in favour of increasing the fees.

6.3.3 Numbers were equally divided on the possibility of increased noise from the machinery of the proposed watering system.

6.3.4 A large majority (96%) felt there was a health risk.

6.3.5 75% felt that the introduction of new clubhouse facilities and greens would attract new members.

6.3.6 90% felt that the machinery housing would be visual pollution.

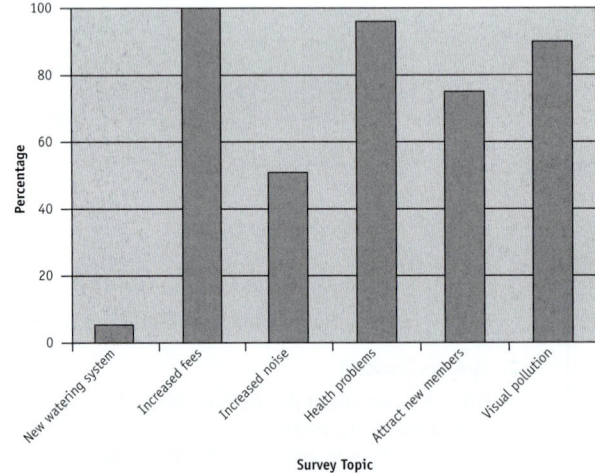

Figure 4 Survey Responses from Residents (n=98)

Responses are compiled into column graphs and interpreted

6

Continued

Figure 19.1 *continued*

7.0 City Council Requirements

The City Council was contacted to ascertain if there were any objections to the implementation of the proposed new watering system based on recycling treated effluent. Detailed plans of the proposed system were submitted.

The City Council's engineers inspected the golf course and consulted golf club management.

After the inspection, a letter was received from the City Council stating that there were concerns about the introduction of this system. They were of the opinion that there could be detrimental effects. They have requested an Environmental Impact Statement before any consideration of the implementation of the proposed watering system.

7

The central section of the Fairways Golf Club report is factual and objective. The central section has six sections identified by headings. The sections are further divided by subheadings that make it easier for the receiver to understand the report's analysis and findings. The Fairways Golf Club report develops an argument in writing by analysing, illustrating, comparing, interpreting and evaluating information.

8.0 Conclusions

Although the new system is beneficial in terms of cost and effectiveness, the negative effects outweigh the positive benefits.

8.1 There is strong opposition from golf club staff, golfers and nearby residents that could lead to a loss of goodwill and long-term revenue on the basis of:

- possible odour
- health risk
- machinery noise
- possible drainage problems
- lowering of land values.

8.2 The City Council requires an Environmental Impact Statement and this would have an impact on costing. Additionally, the City Council might impose conditions that would make the introduction of this system cost-prohibitive.

9.0 Recommendations

9.1 That installation of the proposed new system be postponed.
9.2 That other options be explored:

9.2.1 Approaching the Water Board for a reduction in rates (closure of the large engineering works may make this a feasible option).
9.2.2 Reviewing other watering systems currently available.

Alan Westbury

Alan Westbury
Secretary/Manager
Fairways Golf Club
28 October 2010

8

The final section of the main text of the Fairways Golf Club report contains the conclusions, recommendations and signature block

The conclusions and recommendations are clear and suggest postponement of the new system until further options are explored. They are the most important part of the long report and suggest the actions to be taken. Management decisions will be made on the basis of the conclusions and recommendations. Note that an example of a bibliography is shown at the end of each chapter of this book.

Figure 19.1 *continued*

Bibliography

City Council. *City of Ballarat Annual Report 2006–2007*, www.ballarat.
vic.gov.au/Your_Council/Publications/Annual_Reports/AnnualReport2006–2007.

Evans, I. 'Water efficiency given a sporting chance', Australian Government
Department of Agriculture, Fisheries and Forestry, www.nht.gov.au/
publications/case-studies/irrigation2004/sporting.html, viewed
28 November 2007.

Fairways Golf Club. 2008. *Annual Report 2007–2008*, Regional Publishers,
Somecity.

Pira, E. 1997. *A Guide to Golf Course Irrigation Systems, Design and Drainage*, John
Wiley & Sons, New Jersey.

11

The bibliography lists references and sources of information in alphabetical order by author surname.

Figure 19.1 *continued*

REVIEW QUESTIONS

10 Differentiate between a long report's conclusions and its recommendations.

11 Explain this statement: 'A long report's conclusions are more than a summary.'

12 What is the difference between a long report's synopsis and its conclusion?

13 How are recommendations presented?

OBJECTIVE **4** ▶
Format and edit a long
formal report

EDITING THE LONG REPORT

Once the long report is read, the writer wants the reader to take action on the basis of the report's findings, conclusion and recommendations. Any blocks in the communication flow between writer and reader can prevent this happening. Peterson (2001) identifies issues of subject, style, organisation and presentation. She suggests that work be edited carefully and any problems removed before the document is sent to the receiver.

The editing stage gives the writer the opportunity to remove these problems. The six steps in Table 19.7 give the writer a systematic approach to the editing task. The checklist on pages 554–5 is a useful guide to editing a formal report.

Table 19.7: A six-step approach to editing a long report

Step	Purpose	Strategy
1 Eliminate communication blocks such as unclear, obscure or abstract words, sexist language, unfamiliar jargon and abbreviations.	To create a more concise and readable report	• Remove irrelevant information and unnecessary repetition. • Rewrite any sentences that are too long and verbose. • Avoid exaggeration as it irritates the reader and distorts the message. • Remove any conversational language such as 'a terrific result'. It is much more accurate to say 'the percentage changes are high' or 'the figures and impact of the results are significant'. • Place figures and complex information in a graph or table in the body, or as an appendix.
2 Correct any errors in spelling, punctuation, grammar or sentence structure.	To ensure that sentences are understandable and unambiguous at the first reading	• Rewrite sentences that are poorly structured and unclear. • Check that the language used is clear, concise and concrete. • Check that each paragraph has a topic sentence, that it is short and clear, and that the ideas stay with the paragraph's main point. • Restructure paragraphs that lack coherence or unity. • Check that each paragraph follows on logically from the previous one.
3 Edit to clarify the report's purpose and focus in the introduction.	To ensure that the reader can find the purpose of the report in the first paragraph	• Check that the terms of reference are clearly identified in the introduction. • Verify that the objectives in preparing the report are clearly identified in the introduction. • Check that the focus of the report is consistent with the terms of reference and within the limits of the report.
4 Remove any subjective opinions.	To present factual and objective information	• Check for and remove any subjective opinions, as these will cast doubt on the credibility of the report's findings. • Ensure that the information has clear and accurate references. • Check that the arguments are logical. • Check the correctness of the information presented.
5 Remove irrelevant information.	To remove any information that is not central to the main argument or needed to develop the findings and discussions	• Place information that is not central to the argument in an appendix or endnotes. • Check that information and facts are developed in their order of importance. • Remove any information that interrupts the logical progression of ideas.
6 Edit the layout or format.	To present a professional report	• Consider the order of information, the numbering of sections and the sequence of ideas in the body. • Check that each component of a long report is included and that all achieve their purpose.

14 List the six steps in the editing process.

15 Peterson (2001) identifies the issues of subject, style, organisation and presentation addressed in the editing stage. What is the outcome when these issues are ignored?

16 Describe strategies you could use to verify that:
- the reader can understand the report's purpose
- the information is factual and objective
- communication blocks are eliminated.

APPLY YOUR KNOWLEDGE

PREPARE THE REPORT

Assume you are the Assistant Human Resources Manager with the Australian Bank. The bank is established in the capital city of each state in Australia. The bank plans to expand by establishing a branch network. Branches will be located in the capital cities, and in every city and major town within every state in Australia.

The Human Resources Manager has authorised you to investigate the effect of the expansion on staff training needs. You are to write a report titled 'Expansion: The Impact on Staff Professional Development and Training'. The purpose of the report is to determine the number of new staff needed to create the branch network, to investigate the professional development and training needs of staff, and to make recommendations on the needs of new staff and existing staff.

You will submit the completed report to the Human Resources Manager and forward a copy to the General Manager of the Australian Bank by 31 August.

1 Write the report title page.

2 Create a table of contents that lists each of the basic parts of a long report and the main headings within the body of this report. Start with the introduction and move through to the bibliography.

3 Write the introduction to the report as follows:
  a Prepare the purpose statement and place it as the first sentence in the introduction. In the purpose statement, indicate your specific objective and what you hope to achieve.
  b State the name of the organisation, the position of the person who authorised the report, the limits of the report and the date by which the report is to be submitted.

4 Prepare the report's letter of transmittal and set it out in block letter format.

SELF-EVALUATE YOUR SKILL

EDITING A LONG FORMAL REPORT

Have I:	Yes	No	Unsure
clarified the report's purpose?			
fulfilled the terms of reference?			
used correct long formal report format?			
used an introduction that: — explains the report's purpose? — defines the problem? — guides the reader into the centre section of the report?			

Have I:	Yes	No	Unsure
used a centre section that: — has headings and perhaps subheadings? — uses language appropriate to the report's purpose, content and readers? — uses paragraphs that aid the flow and analysis of the findings? — presents factual and objective information? — analyses the findings?			
used a conclusion that: — draws the ideas together? — summarises the content and findings?			
prepared recommendations that offer solutions to any problems in the body?			

SUMMARY OF LEARNING OBJECTIVES

 1 ▶ **DIFFERENTIATE ANALYTICAL AND INFORMATIONAL REPORTS AND GIVE EXAMPLES OF EACH**

Analytical reports examine a problem or issue, analyse information, explore consequences, draw conclusions and recommend actions. Some examples are problem-solving reports, reports assessing opportunities, and feasibility studies. Informational reports provide data, information and feedback without analysis, conclusions or recommendations. Examples are reports to demonstrate compliance with government regulations and project progress reports.

 2 ▶ **PLAN A REPORT, AND GATHER AND ORDER INFORMATION**

The seven steps to follow as you plan a report are: define the problem and purpose; consider the needs of the reader; determine the ideas to include; collect the information; sort and evaluate the information; organise the information; and prepare the outline. Gathering the relevant information occurs after you have identified the relevant issues. Primary and secondary sources of information are used in business reports. Verify that your sources are credible and reliable.

Logical ways to order the information include: chronological sequence, geographical identity, inductive order, deductive order, cause to effect, and problem solving. Sequence the information in order of importance, with a summary at the top followed by a gradual expansion into greater detail in the body of the report.

 3 ▶ **USING AN APPROPRIATE WRITING STYLE, WRITE THE FRONT MATTER, BODY AND END MATTER OF A LONG REPORT**

The way a report writer uses words, sentences, paragraphs and layout to present ideas and to connect with the reader determines the report's writing style. A person's report-writing style may be described as crisp and clear, verbose, academic and theoretical, or factual and businesslike.

A long formal report has three main sections—front matter, body and end matter. The front matter contains the preliminary parts that appear before the text of the report. These are the title page, letter of transmittal, table of contents, list of tables, preface, abstract, synopsis or executive summary.

The body or text of a long formal report is its longest part. The body of the report has three main sections—the introductory section of the body, the centre section of the body and the final section of the body. The introductory section identifies the report's purpose, scope, methodology and terms of reference. The centre section contains a detailed discussion of the long report's findings. The final section of the body contains the conclusion and recommendations.

The end matter is the final part of a report and contains the appendix, bibliography, glossary of terms and index.

 4 ▶ **FORMAT AND EDIT A LONG FORMAL REPORT**

Three broad sections are used in the standard long report format. These are: the front matter; the centre, text or body; and the end matter. The reader of a long report would expect the writer to follow this format.

The long report's content should be edited for accuracy, objectivity and completeness. Edit the structure and writing style for logic, clarity and conciseness. A long report is a formal document and, as such, needs to be professionally packaged in a format that suits its purpose.

KEY TERMS

ACTIVITIES AND QUESTIONS

1 a Briefly explain why your long-report writing style should be factual and objective, presenting a balanced view of the findings.

   b Consider the following statement:

   The 'you' approach is suggested as suitable for most business writing tasks because it speaks directly to the reader and creates a personal connection between the writer and reader.

   Why, then, is it inappropriate to use the 'you' approach in long formal reports?

2 Discuss three ways in which outlining, and using headings and a numbering system, can improve a report's capacity to communicate.

3 a Using report-writing principles and guidelines, develop an outline for a comparison report on a product or service suited to your area of study or workplace. For example, you might like to compare different accounting principles, computer software packages or personnel procedures. Organise the material. Keep major topics and subtopics specific.

   b Prepare a title page for the outline you developed above.

   c Assume you have been asked by your manager, Sofia Madison, of Integrity Corporation, to undertake the above report. Write the letter of transmittal that you would prepare for the report in block letter layout. Invent any necessary details.

   In the opening paragraphs of the letter, identify the report's purpose. Refer to the report's contents and findings in one or two paragraphs. Assume you had help from the purchasing department within Integrity Corporation in preparing the report. Write a paragraph thanking those involved. In the final paragraph, close courteously and offer help to the reader.

4 Find a long report in the library or in your organisation. Evaluate the report by answering these questions:

   a What improvements could you make to the title page?

   b Does the report use an abstract or synopsis, preface or executive summary?

   c Is the table of contents well constructed?

   d How many levels of headings does the report have? Are they suitable?

   e What is the order of presentation?

   f Is the report written in the active or passive voice, or both?

   g Is the conclusion well written and convincing?

   h Can you suggest any changes or improvements?

5 Write a short guide for a report-writing novice.

EXPLORING THE WEB

1   Visit the Online Technical Writing Audience Analysis page <www.io.com/>, and answer the following questions.

   a   What are the consequences of a lack of audience analysis and adaptation?

   b   McMurrey (2007) identifies three typical audiences for technical reports. Identify three typical audiences for formal business reports.

   c   According to this website, what characteristics should you consider when analysing your audience?

2   Review these chapter-related websites to improve your formal report-writing skills.

   a   *How to Write a Formal Report* <www.articleclick.com/> discusses the purpose of each part of a formal long report.

   b   The site *Report Writing—How to Format a Business Report* has some good advice on formatting business reports.

   c   Identify the components in the front, middle and back sections of a long formal report by visiting the *Better Business Report Writing . . . How to Write a Formal Report* site, <www.pro-technical-writing.com/>.

   d   Learn about the elements you should monitor as you edit your report writing by visiting the site *Writer, Edit Thyself* <www.poewar.com/>. Review the ten most common problems encountered by the editors, book doctors and contest judges polled by Lois Peterson.

PROJECT WORK

Assume that a report has been authorised by the President of the Chamber of Commerce. The report's findings are to be used by the Chamber of Commerce in its efforts to lobby the local government council to zone more land for retail use in order to extend the size of the existing shopping complex.

a   In groups of two or three, discuss the different sources of information available for research to prepare a report on the topic, 'Services Offered in a Large Suburban Shopping Complex'. Choose a shopping complex with which you are familiar.

b   Place these sources of information into a table with the headings 'Primary Sources of Information' and 'Secondary Sources of Information'.

c   In your group of two or three, brainstorm to generate a list of ideas to include in the report.

d   Then, as an individual, place these ideas into an outline that identifies the main headings and subheadings for the report.

e   Present your report in long report format, including all the appropriate components (refer to Table 19.4) and an appropriate report-writing style.

f   Edit your report, and evaluate its completeness and effectiveness by using the checklist on pages 554–5.

BIBLIOGRAPHY

American Psychological Association. 2001. *Publication Manual of the American Psychological Association*, 5th edn, Washington.

Articleclick, *How to Write a Formal Report*, www.articleclick.com/creating-formal-documents.html, viewed 16 November 2007.

Atherton, A. *Report Writing—How to Format a Business Report*, http://ezinearticles.com/?Report-Writing-How-to-Format-a-Business-Report, viewed 16 November 2007.

Bournemouth University. 'Writing business reports', *Academic Support*, www.bournemouth.ac.uk/study_support/writing_business_reports.html, viewed 18 February 2008.

Bovée, C.L. & Thill, J.V. 2005. *Business Communication Today*, 8th edn, Pearson Education International, USA.

Brown, R. 1999. 'Welcome to 1999 Stylewise', *Stylewise*, Vol. 5, Issue 1.

Fardell, L. 1998. 'Presenting statistical and tabular information', *Stylewise*, Vol. 4, Issue 4, p. 1.

Goodworth, C. 1991. *The Secrets of Successful Business Report Writing*, Butterworth-Heinemann, Jordan Hill, Oxford.

Guffey, M.E. 2005. *Business Communication: Process and Product*, Thomson South Western.

Harnack, A. & Kleppinger, E. 'Citation styles online', *Online A Reference Guide for Electronic Sources*, www.bedfordstmartins.com/online/citex.html, viewed 16 November 2007.

Lesikar, R.V. & Pettit, J.D. Jnr. 1998. *Report Writing for Business*, Irwin/McGraw-Hill, USA.

McMurrey, D. *Online Technical Writing Audience Analysis*, www.io.com/~hcexres/textbook/resource.html, viewed 16 November 2007.

Ober, S. 2006. *Contemporary Business Communication*, 6th edn, Houghton Mifflin Publishing Company.

Peterson, L.J. 2001. *Writer, Edit Thyself*, www.poewar.com/writer-edit-thyself, viewed 16 November 2007.

Pro Technical Writing. *Better Business Report Writing . . . How to Write a Formal Report*, www.pro-technical-writing.com/business-report-writing.html, viewed 16 November 2007.

Raynolds, N. 1988. 'What investors want from the annual report', *Wall Street Journal*, 18 January, p. 10.

Reinsch, N.L. Jnr. 1990. 'Ethics research in business communication: the state of the art', *Journal of Business Communication*, Vol. 27, pp. 251–72.

Riley, K. 1993. 'Telling more than the truth: implicature, speech acts, and ethics in professional communication', *Journal of Business Ethics*, pp. 179–96.

Style Manual for Authors, Editors and Printers, 6th edn, John Wiley & Sons, Brisbane, 2002.

Sussams, J.E. 1993. *How to Write Effective Reports*, Gower Publishing, England.

Tixana, A. 2000. *The Knowledge Management Toolkit*, Prentice Hall, New Jersey.

Turk, C. & Kirkman, J. 1989. *Effective Writing: Improving Scientific, Technical, and Business Communication*, 2nd edn, E. & F.N. Spon, London.

Winckel, A. & Hart, B. 1996. *Report Writing Style for Engineering Students*, Faculty of Engineering and the Flexible Learning Centre, University of South Australia, Adelaide.

20 Academic writing

Photo: Lisa Klumpp

VIEWPOINT: BEING CRITICAL

'As an academic writer, you are expected to be critical of the sources that you use. This essentially means questioning what you read and not necessarily agreeing with it just because the information has been published. Being critical can also mean looking for reasons why we should not just accept something as being correct or true. This can require you to identify problems with a writer's arguments or methods, or perhaps to refer to other people's criticisms of these. Constructive criticism goes beyond this by suggesting ways in which a piece of research or writing could be improved.

. . . being against is not enough. We also need to develop habits of constructive thinking. Edward de Bono

Introducing questions, problems and limitations (theory)
One question that needs to be asked, however, is whether . . .
A serious weakness with this argument, however, is that . . .
One criticism of much of the literature on X is that . . .
The key problem with this explanation is that . . .'

Extract from The University of Manchester. 'Being critical', Academic Phrase Bank, www.phrasebank.manchester.ac.uk/critical.htm, viewed 19 February 2008.

Academic writers read and evaluate what others have said in order to find out what is already known and to understand the main arguments being put forward by authoritative writers and scholars in the field. Academic writers not only read and inquire into existing material, but also analyse the ideas in order to verify or critique the existing body of knowledge. Hence it is important for them to think clearly as they solve problems and develop arguments in writing. Thinking clearly before they write enables them to present more valid and convincing arguments.

Students sitting for an examination or preparing an essay question or assignment must read the question carefully and identify its purpose. When the question asks for an analysis, the writer should examine each of the parts. If the question asks for a comparison, then the writer should discuss similarities and relationships. Marks will be awarded not only for the content but also for the way in which the writer determines the writing purpose and then uses careful reasoning to support an argument.

THREE TYPES OF THINKING

OBJECTIVE 1 ▶
Compare three types of reasoning

Three widely accepted types of thinking are inductive, deductive and lateral thinking. An awareness of the principles of clear thinking makes it possible to check your point of view and to differentiate between valid arguments, based on fact and clearly established propositions, and invalid arguments, based on beliefs and prejudice. A **proposition** is the point to be discussed or maintained in argument, usually stated as a sentence near the outset of the document. A **belief** is the mental acceptance of and conviction in the truth or validity of something. Beliefs are not always based on facts. Refer to Chapter 14 for more information on the critical thinking process.

A **proposition** affirms or denies something.

A **belief** is a personal conviction, not necessarily based on fact.

Inductive thinking examines specific information to derive a general principle.

Generalisation gives general rather than specific character to a subject.

Inductive thinking

Inductive thinking considers the known data or evidence, makes a rule or generalisation, and assumes this applies in all cases. Inductive thinking leads the reader through the information, facts or reasons to the result. As information and evidence are accumulated, a conclusion is drawn and the generalisation is made on the basis of the findings. Inductive thinking enables you to think from experience by:

- using information or data based on observation and experience
- checking that the data collected is accurate, valid and able to be checked
- basing observations on a large enough sample to support the conclusions
- examining a sample that is representative and typical of the whole group
- acknowledging and analysing items of information that do not fit the pattern
- generalising the conclusion from the specific items of information or data.

Deductive thinking

In deduction the assumption is that we can move from some general known truth to new knowledge about certain particulars or individuals. **Deductive thinking** gives the general rule or overview and then applies this rule to a specific or particular case to reach a conclusion. This reasoning process moves from the general rule to the particular case. Using deductive thinking allows you to think by:

Deductive thinking applies general principles to reach specific conclusions.

- proposing a general or universal statement
- applying the universal statement to a particular case
- reaching a conclusion about the particular case.

A **fact** is something that can be shown to be true.

An **opinion** is a personal judgment.

This type of thinking asks the receiver to accept the original assumption. To make the original statement acceptable, base the argument as far as possible on **fact**, rather than **opinion**. The results or answers created from deductive thinking depend on the accuracy and objective nature of the original assumption.

At the most basic level there are two ways to reason; inductive and deductive reasoning. In the inductive reasoning process you detail the specific information, examples and evidence to derive a general principle or conclusion based on the evidence. Alternatively, in deductive reasoning you start with the product of the reasoning—that is, the general premise or claim. The implications and justification of the thesis, premise or claim are then explored and explained before returning to it in the conclusion.

Trochim (2006) states: 'Inductive reasoning, by its very nature, is more open-ended and exploratory, especially at the beginning. Deductive reasoning is more narrow in nature and is concerned with testing or confirming hypotheses.' Regardless of the type of reasoning, critically think about the reasoning and argument, and test the evidence. Look for bias in the evidence, and check its reliability, relevance and currency. In academic writing, avoid 'jumping' too quickly to generalisations that may be invalid.

Lateral thinking

Lateral thinking acknowledges intuition and unconscious reasoning. It is useful in providing new ideas and suggestions. Using lateral thinking allows you to think by:

- recognising dominant polarising ideas
- searching for different ways of looking at things
- relaxing the rigid control of vertical thinking
- using chance
- analysing the ideas to establish relationships
- determining the new information is valid and logical.

To establish relationships and determine that the new information is valid and logical, apply a process of **rationalisation** to the solution created from the lateral thinking process. Rationalisation can be used with lateral thinking by:

- taking up a new and arbitrary position
- working backwards to create a logical path between the position and the starting point
- finding a possible new path that is useful in this situation
- testing the path with logic.

In all three types of thinking, valid and reliable conclusions are based on evidence and a way of thinking that is free of personal bias, prejudice or attitudes. Conclusions based only on past experience and personal perception, rather than on facts, have a high probability of being inaccurate.

> **Lateral thinking** acknowledges intuition and unconscious reasoning.
>
> De Bono (1990) presents lateral thinking as a strategy for thinking creatively.
>
> **Rationalisation** applies logic to test the solution.

TECHNIQUES FOR SOUND REASONING

Whether you are developing your argument as a written or spoken presentation, you must support it with evidence. In your effort to present information logically and to argue soundly, you may find the kinds of evidence and strategies shown below helpful.

> ◀ OBJECTIVE **2**
> Discuss techniques for sound reasoning

DISTINGUISH BETWEEN FACTS, OPINIONS, BELIEFS AND PREJUDICE

As you research sources of information:

- keep in mind that the source of information is presenting a case or a point of view
- analyse the point of view to determine whether it is based on fact or opinion
- check the facts for accuracy
- identify opinions or points of view
- check that conclusions drawn from the argument are based on facts supported by credible evidence
- challenge any conclusions drawn from personal beliefs unsupported by facts
- check for prejudice based on:
  —prejudgment without a thorough examination of the facts and evidence
  —beliefs unsupported by facts.

FORM OBJECTIVE OPINIONS

Use facts whenever possible. If you need to present opinions, base them on factual information. Avoid emotional statements and subjective opinion influenced only by past experience, values and beliefs.

PRESENT ADVANTAGES AND DISADVANTAGES

Give balance to your work and point of view by presenting both the advantages and disadvantages. Include relevant information, rather than omitting unpleasant information or ideas that may go against your point of view. Move to a new conclusion on the basis of the findings. Avoid presenting only that part of the information that suits your point of view, as this is misleading. Analyse the issue or problem from all angles to allow for greater understanding and possible new insights.

AVOID EXAGGERATION

Avoid exaggeration and present a balanced, rather than a biased, view. This will improve the credibility of your argument. Exaggeration is quickly recognised by the perceptive reader.

CHECK STATISTICS

Check statistics for relevance and authority. Statistics collected by the Australian Bureau of Statistics (ABS) carry more authority than those collected by personal observation, because they are factual and objective figures. Sort and evaluate your data and organise it into an understandable format. Draw conclusions based on the evidence presented in the data.

REVIEW QUESTIONS

1. Briefly explain the difference between inductive reasoning and deductive reasoning.
2. What are the key features of lateral thinking?

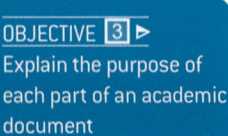
OBJECTIVE 3 ▶
Explain the purpose of each part of an academic document

STRUCTURING THE CONTENT

Academic writers should use the researching and planning strategies outlined in Chapter 13. Writers research to gather information already in existence, and plan in order to structure the large volume of information into a logical sequence. Create a working outline and keep all the ideas on one issue together. Gibaldi (1995, p. 31) advises that you can transform your working outline into a final outline once you have a satisfactory thesis statement, and that step 'will help you organise your ideas and the accumulated research into a logical, fluent, and effective paper'. Wolfe (2006) states: 'If you make a plan of each chapter and section before you sit down to write, the result will probably be clearer and easier to read.'

You should spend about 50% of your time on researching, investigating, organising and planning, and only 30% of your time on writing. The remaining 20% goes on editing, rewriting and proofreading. Writers who plan well and structure their content before they start to write are able to create a logical path through the document. The reader (or marker) is then able to filter the information and understand and evaluate or appraise the piece of writing easily. They are also able to find a clear pathway through the parts of the document.

Parts of the document

The various parts of business documents are discussed in Chapters 17, 18 and 19. This section presents the parts of a major research paper. Turabian (1996, pp. 1–13) lists the various parts of a paper (set out in Table 20.1) and how these parts should be organised. She recommends that the relevant department should be consulted to determine any special requirements before beginning on a research paper. All academic papers should be typed double-spaced, although indented block quotations may be single-spaced.

Papers have three main sections: the front matter or preliminaries; the text; and the end matter or reference matter. In long papers such as doctoral theses, each of these parts may consist of several pages and must begin with a new page.

INTRODUCTION

Good **introductions** say what the writer is going to do in the document. Students who receive high gradings are those who take the time to determine the document's purpose—compare, illustrate, analyse, justify, summarise, evaluate, or some other purpose—and then use writing strategies that achieve that purpose. Table 20.2 sets out the strategies used to achieve each purpose.

> The **introduction** prepares the reader by identifying the aim or main theme.

THESIS STATEMENT

The problem is stated in the form of a **thesis statement** that identifies the issue, problem, gap in knowledge, or some other goal to be addressed in the paper, essay, assignment or report. A successful statement of the problem has two parts: first, the writer poses the problem or issue; and, second, he or she identifies the benefits gained by addressing the issue.

> A **thesis statement** is a claim, an assertion or a point.

Table 20.1: The parts of a major research paper	
Title page	Follow the style of title pages at your university or college exactly.
Blank page or copyright page	Count the blank page in the pagination.
Dedication	Keep it brief.
Epigraph	This is a quotation placed at the beginning of a work or of one of its parts.
Table of contents	List all the parts except the title page and the table of contents.
List of illustrations	Give figure numbers in Arabic numerals.
List of tables	Give table numbers in Arabic numerals.
Preface	Explain the motivation, background, scope and purpose of the study or paper.
Acknowledgments	Thank mentors/colleagues. List the individual or institution that supported the project, and give credits to works cited for which permission to reproduce was granted.
List of abbreviations	Give a spelled-out version the first time a term appears, followed by the abbreviation in parentheses.
Glossary	Define unfamiliar words or technical terms.
Editorial method	Include as a separate section but keep remarks short. Comments about capitalisation and punctuation that have been modernised may be included in the preface instead.
Abstract	Use to briefly summarise the thesis and contents of the paper.
Text	Separate into well-defined divisions and also include parenthetical references keyed to a reference list, or superscript numbers keyed to footnotes or endnotes. The text usually begins with an introduction and is divided into chapters.
Appendix	Place in the end matter (if needed).
Endnotes	Number consecutively throughout the paper and group them under the heading 'Notes' in the end matter.
Bibliography or reference list	Place in the end matter as the last part of the document.

Table 20.2: Strategies in academic writing	
Purpose	**Strategy**
Analyse	Examine each of the elements.
Compare	Show similarity or relationships.
Differentiate	Discriminate between two or more factors.
Illustrate	Make clear by written examples, drawings, pictures or other devices.
Contrast	Show differences between two or more factors.
Critically evaluate	Articulate the arguments on both sides of an issue by arguing for and against.
Criticise	Make a judgment or show the relative merits of an argument.
Interpret	Explain or bring out the particular meaning.
Evaluate	Give a reasoned appraisal or assessment of the facts or argument presented.
Summarise	Provide a brief account or an abridged version.
Justify	Demonstrate or show a satisfactory reason for the argument.

A common mistake in writing complex documents is to rush ahead and write before defining and interpreting each part of the question or problem. Once the purpose is determined and identified in the introductory part, both writer and marker know what the writer is trying to do.

BODY

The body of a written document is the main section and contains the ideas being presented. Good writers write according to their outline and the order of information prepared in the planning stage; however, at the same time they give themselves the freedom to revise the order of information if it causes them difficulties in the writing stage. They also focus on the essay's purpose and present the argument in a way that achieves this purpose. Their essays summarise major developments, explore relationships and explain how principles apply in a particular situation.

The body of a document contains the research findings and develops the argument. The techniques for sound reasoning discussed earlier are used to form objective opinions. The practice of distinguishing between facts, opinions, beliefs and prejudices is a good way of avoiding one of the main weaknesses in essays: sweeping statements. Statements supported by factual evidence present a stronger case, because readers are able to verify the information.

The main focus in the body is the writing purpose identified in the purpose statement. The important points should be easy to identify throughout the body of the essay. The signalling devices presented later in this chapter help to identify the main points.

CONCLUSION

The **conclusion** links the argument and evidence to the original premise, claim or proposition.

The **conclusion** is more than a summary of the main points in the argument or the essay's findings. It links to the original premise, claim or proposition, and shows that the position taken throughout the argument is a convincing and valid one. An effective conclusion shows that the writer has understood the question and developed an argument to achieve the particular writing purpose. A conclusion is a response to an issue.

Levine (2008) suggests:

If you are including a Conclusions/Implications section in your dissertation make sure you really present conclusions and implications. Often the writer uses the conclusions/implications section to merely restate the research findings . . . I want you to help me understand what it all means . . . think of conclusions/implications as the 'So what' statements. In other words, what are the key ideas that we can draw from your study to apply to my areas of concern.

Make your conclusion easy to find by using indicator words such as 'consequently', 'therefore', 'it is highly probable that', 'thus', 'shows that'. The conclusion is presented as a statement or statement(s) drawn from the reasoning. Make the conclusion easily identifiable, and make sure it is a direct response to your stated issue or premise.

ABSTRACT, PRÉCIS OR SUMMARY

Academic papers and essays usually contain either an **abstract**, a **précis** or a **summary** placed at the beginning of the essay or paper. The choice is determined by the writer's preference. The purpose of an abstract is to identify the essential argument in the document without passing any opinion or critical comment. It isolates the central theme and may show the main subsidiary themes. The purpose of a précis is to condense the material. As a result, the précis leaves out the examples, illustrations and comparisons in the essay and presents the main points only. It is usually the last part of the essay to be written. A summary gives an overview of the main theme and sub-themes.

An **abstract**, **précis** or **summary** highlights the main ideas in an essay.

A well-written introduction and conclusion can make a useful framework for the précis, abstract or summary. By rewriting and combining the ideas in the introduction and conclusion, the writer can prepare a smooth-flowing abstract, précis or summary.

REVIEW QUESTIONS

3　What do good introductions do?
4　Why should you take the time to determine an essay's purpose?
5　Why do academic writers state the problem in the form of a thesis statement?
6　Differentiate between the abstract and the body of an essay.

Developing the argument

◀ OBJECTIVE 4
Analyse the strategies used to develop an argument

For academic writers, it is not enough simply to gather and recall information. They must also present an argument by thinking about the information and showing in writing the relationships between the ideas. The reader is asked to accept the writer's reasoning and to consider a proposition or course of action on the basis of the **argument** in the document. (See Chapter 14 for more information about the process of reasoning and argument.) When you use reasoning in your writing, your aim is to convince the reader to accept your thesis, claim or point of view. The *Internet Encyclopedia of Philosophy* (2004) defines argument as '. . . a connected series of statements or propositions, some of which are intended to provide support, justification or evidence for the truth of another statement or proposition. Arguments consist of one or more premises and a conclusion.' An effective argument provides support or evidence and demonstrates a clear connection between the original premise and the conclusion.

Argument is a process of reasoning that shows the relationship between ideas, and aims to convince others of the truth of something.

PROBLEMS IN DEVELOPING AN ARGUMENT

Browne and Keeley (2007, p. 10) state: 'Critical thinking can be used to either (1) defend *or* (2) evaluate and revise your initial beliefs . . . Weak-sense critical thinking is the use of critical thinking to defend your current beliefs. Strong-sense critical thinking is the use of the same skills to evaluate all claims and beliefs, especially your own.' They comment that defensive weak-sense critical thinking tries to 'annihilate opinions and reasoning different from yours . . . we run the strong risk of making mistakes we could otherwise avoid'. Weak-sense critical thinking causes problems, including oversimplifica-tion, slippery-slope, false analogy, begging the question and others (see Chapter 14). Strong-sense critical thinking helps to protect against self-deception and conformity. By asking critical questions as they gather, analyse and evaluate evidence, writers are able to build strong arguments to support their premise or claim. They avoid the problems caused by presenting flawed information and invalid conclusions.

Petelin and Durham (1992, p. 49) comment: 'Critical thinking, by providing you with information that is complete, accurate and fair, helps you to write logically. Despite this, logical writing is sometimes difficult to achieve. Unwarranted assumptions may crop up in a document when the writer has not sufficiently considered the issue or readers. An argument which sounds good may sway readers by emotion, misuse of the language, or faulty reasoning.' Pitfalls in developing a logical argument, they say, are false assumptions, fallacies and insidious fallacies. In this last category they include a barrage of objections, card stacking, engineered suspicions, inappropriate humour and the red herring.

They suggest evaluating the main message by asking the following questions:

- Is my main message clear?
- Is it stated early enough in the document to direct readers?
- Have I given the opposing view and raised relevant questions?
- Have I chosen convincing reasons and main points?
- Have I provided evidence?
- Have I made realistic assumptions?

Lewis and Slade (1994, p. 77) state that 'reasoning and critical thinking skills underlie all human activity'. These skills are necessary to connect and organise ideas, whether they are spoken or written. Lewis and Slade classify them into three components—analysis, inference and evaluation—and assert that most reasoning 'involves all components simultaneously'.

Analysis involves:

- identifying what is being said
- distinguishing what is relevant from what is not
- seeing connections between different strands of thought
- recognising vagueness and ambiguity, then clarifying terms if necessary
- identifying members of a class, in terms of likenesses
- identifying counter-instances as different in some respect
- identifying analogies.

Inference involves passing from one proposition, statement or judgment considered as true to another whose truth is believed to follow from that of the former. A generalisation is made in response to the argument and its evidence. The inference process involves:

- identifying underlying assumptions
- generalising from particular instances—that is, abstracting
- recognising cause-and-effect relationships.

Evaluation involves:

- giving reasons for beliefs and decisions and then choosing how to act
- criticising and questioning ideas constructively
- modifying ideas in response to criticism.

Using clear and objective language

Clear and objective language should be used throughout the body of the essay, thesis or assignment. Effective sentence construction and coherent paragraphs allow the argument to be developed logically and give clarity to the presentation. Objective language that gives clear meaning to the piece of writing makes it easy for the reader to follow the argument. Refer to Chapter 17, 'The Business Writing Process', for the elements of writing style: language, sentences, paragraphs, tone, rhythm, order of information and layout. The principles presented in that chapter also apply to academic writing. Some additional writing techniques that are useful in essay and thesis writing are included in the 'Writing techniques' section later in this chapter.

Writers show they are competent when they write in a way that is thoughtful and coherent, and demonstrate the amount of work they have done in gathering information and thinking about the ideas. Their writing is objective and their readers are able to follow their ideas easily.

ACRONYMS AND ABBREVIATIONS

'One aspect of higher education publications which causes headaches for editors is the extensive use of acronyms and abbreviations' (Andrew 1999, p. 2). It is the editor who has to judge whether to accept these or spell them out, keeping in mind the target audience. Andrew believes the best solution is a compromise: spelling out an abbreviation at least the first time it is used, and including in every report a glossary of abbreviations and **acronyms** that are used extensively. She is convinced, however, that 'spelling terms out always helps the reader and improves the readability of a report'.

Citations

The sources of information should always be acknowledged in the form of **citations**, endnotes or references, or in the **bibliography**. An academic paper presented without appropriate and accurate citations leaves the writer open to allegations of plagiarism. Two common standards for citations and bibliographies, the Harvard system and the traditional note method, are presented in Chapter 13. Either style is acceptable if it is used consistently throughout the paper.

Objectivity is based on thinking, rather than emotional reaction.

An **acronym** is a word formed from the initial letters of other words.

Citations acknowledge the work of others and allow the reader to find the original source of information.

A **bibliography** is a list of the sources of information used, as well as further recommended reading.

REVIEW QUESTIONS

7 List some signs that could indicate a writer is using 'weak-sense' critical thinking to defend his or her current beliefs.

8 Identify three pitfalls in developing a logical argument.

9 Briefly discuss the three components of reasoning and critical thinking skills.

APPLY YOUR KNOWLEDGE

DEVELOPING IDEAS

1 Work in small groups.
   a Create a table with the three headings: 'inductive', 'deductive' and 'lateral' thinking.
   b Discuss the strategies used to achieve each of these types of thinking and list them in the table.
   c Think about the purpose of each type of thinking and then, as a group, prepare a summary statement identifying the purpose of each type of thinking.
   d Come together as a large group and brainstorm to create a list of situations suited to lateral thinking. (Brainstorming is described on pages 361–2.)

2 Consider these topics.
   a Digital technology provides great opportunities for businesses to work better.
   b Golf is now a carefully marketed commodity.
   c Communication is the key to business success.
   d Flexible work practices are a crucial issue for managers.
   e Corporate mentoring programs give back to the corporation.
      Choose one of the topics. Interpret the topic and prepare, in about one page, a convincing argument that supports or refutes the claim made in the topic.

3 Work in small groups.

    a   Brainstorm the characteristics of an effective academic document.

    b   Brainstorm the characteristics of an effective piece of business writing.

    c   List the main differences between academic and business writing.

    d   Report your findings to the large group.

WRITING TECHNIQUES

OBJECTIVE 5 ▶
Describe writing techniques that identify the main point and indicate connections between ideas

This section discusses techniques that help to make a piece of academic writing easy to read and understand. Their use enables sentences in a paragraph and a longer piece of writing to move forward clearly, rather than circling back on the same idea. The three techniques discussed here are:

1 signalling devices
2 linking devices
3 transitional expressions.

Each of these techniques helps to give effective structure and organisation to a document.

Signalling devices

Signalling devices identify the main point and indicate the connections.

Signalling devices help the reader to follow the flow of ideas through the document. Signals should be used to:

- identify the main point
- indicate the connections between the main point and any supporting points
- indicate the connections between all the main points in the document.

HEADINGS

One of the most important signalling devices is headings. Headings at the beginning of a document, and subject headings and subheadings throughout the document, help to:

- signal the next section or idea
- give a brief survey of the information to follow
- give the reader a place to stop and think
- let the reader select the sections of interest or most importance.

TOPIC SENTENCES

Topic sentences identify the main point of the paragraph.

Topic sentences signal the main point in the paragraph. It may not be possible to use a topic sentence in every paragraph; however, whenever a paragraph contains a new idea or new information, signal the new idea with a topic sentence. The paragraph must fulfil the topic sentence to prevent the writer wandering away from the topic.

Table 20.3 shows four types of topic sentences. The first type places the specific information first (small businesses) followed by the general information (small-business sector). The second presents the general information (the Australian economy) first, followed by the specific information (the unemployment rate). The third type of topic sentence (spatial order) describes the situation as it is seen from above. Other sentences in the paragraph describe what is happening below and to the left. In the last example, the topic sentence identifies the starting time of the aerobics class as 10.30 am. The rest of the paragraph describes the activities in the class by chronological order.

Type	Example
Table 20.3: How different types of topic sentences organise a paragraph	
Specific to general	'The result is bankruptcy in local small businesses, which leads to a failure in the Australian small-business sector of more than 50 000 firms.'
General to specific	'The Australian economy is moving into a recession; as a result, the unemployment rate is increasing.'
Spatial order	'From above, the demonstration in the square below suddenly changed from a peaceful scene to chaos. Armed tanks were moving in from the left and the few demonstrators who first saw them began running. The panic was contagious and within seconds all the demonstrators were trying to run away from the tanks. The scene below was chaotic.'
Chronological order	'Today at 10.30 am I attended a beginner's class in aerobics. The instructor started with warm-up exercises and then moved on to the group of power exercises for the greater part of the hour. In the concluding section, the instructor led us through the wind-down exercises. Then the session was finished, and we all retreated gratefully to the showers.'

Linking devices

Linking phrases and bridge words make logical connections between ideas and give continuity to the writing. An example of a bridge between sentences is evident in the following sentences about local parks:

> Many local parklands are overgrown. As local government elections take place soon, the council is becoming more conscious of public opinion.

The word 'local' is used to make a logical bridge from the conversation about parkland to mention of the council.

Linking phrases form logical connections between ideas.

REPETITION OR KEYNOTING

Repetition of key words and phrases can link the sentences in a paragraph. Usually the topic sentence contains the key words used later in the paragraph. For example:

> The information asked for is collected in a manner that ensures the confidentiality of the information supplied. Your cooperation is sought in completing and returning the enclosed form by 2 March 2010. Please ensure that the information sought is returned by that date.

In this paragraph, the key words 'information' and 'returned' are repeated in the last sentence. This strategy is known as 'keynoting'.

PARAGRAPH FLOW

The visible sentence links that create flow can be established, Kane (1988, p. 73) suggests, in two basic ways:

1. Establish a master plan at the beginning and introduce each new idea by a new linking word or phrase; for example, 'There are three main banks in Australia . . . The first, . . . , The second, . . .' and so on.
2. Concentrate on 'linking sentences successively as the paragraph develops, making sure that each statement connects with the one preceding it'.

Kane suggests repeating key words; using conjunctive adverbs (such as presently, meanwhile, afterwards, therefore, however); and using syntactic patterning (repeating the same basic structure in successive or near successive sentences; for example, 'In Newcastle, the people are mainly Labor supporters. In Sydney, the politics of the people cannot be easily described.'). He comments: 'While reusing the same sentence pattern often involves repeating some words, the similar grammatical structure is in itself a strong connective device' (1988, p. 77).

SUBSTITUTING PRONOUNS FOR NOUNS

Sentences can be linked to one another by substituting pronouns for nouns. In the following example the pronouns 'her' and 'she' refer to 'Hannah', who is mentioned in the topic sentence:

> When Hannah, a long-time associate and member of the Society of Business Communicators, suggested we attend the society's Bi-Annual Conference in 2009, I agreed. The society has asked her to deliver a paper on the topic 'Fashioning the Communication Strategy'. She agreed to deliver the paper and we both agreed to complete the research together.

USING PHRASES TO LINK PARAGRAPHS

A paragraph discusses a thought or idea and should follow on logically from the previous paragraph. Paragraphs rarely stand alone. Therefore, writers need to recognise different linking strategies and be able to use them. Examples of linking phrases that lead from one paragraph into the next argument or change of idea are given in Table 20.4.

Transitional expressions

Transitional expressions connect ideas within and between sentences. Transitions help the reader follow your ideas from one place to another, from one time to another, or from one subject to another; for example, 'On the other hand . . .' makes the connection between two ideas. A transitional expression is also used to show the relationship between what has just been described and what is to come next; for example, 'After the Black and White Ball . . .'

A transition in place can be made by writing, for example, 'Back at the beach . . .', which moves the reader from the present place to a scene at the beach. 'One year later . . .' or 'In May 2010 . . .' are both examples of a transition in time. Table 20.5 lists more transitional expressions.

Transitional words or word groups join ideas and show their relationship with connecting words and phrases. They are used deliberately to provide variety and add to readability and understanding. Effective use of transitions and connections allows the paragraph to develop and extends the topic sentence logically.

Signalling devices help the reader to follow the flow of ideas; topic sentences signal the main point in a paragraph; and linking phrases help the reader to make logical connections between ideas. Each of these writing techniques attracts the reader's attention, interest and desire to read further.

Transitional expressions make connections between ideas or subjects.

Table 20.4: Linking a paragraph to the preceding paragraph

- However, it has . . .
- On the other hand . . .
- It is intended now to . . .
- Following on from . . .
- Associated with . . .
- Another cause of . . .
- Alternatively, a document may . . .
- Contradictory evidence suggests . . .
- In the case of . . .

Table 20.5: Transitional expressions

Expression	Purpose
In addition, last, next, and, in the first place, again, also, equally important, another, besides	To add or show sequence
Similarly, in the same way, likewise, in this manner	To compare
In contrast, whereas, but, although, and yet, even so, on the other hand, regardless	To contrast
For instance, to illustrate, in this way, for example, truly, specifically	To give examples
Accordingly, with this object, hence, because, as a result, consequently, since, for this reason	To show cause and effect
To the north, to the right, below, above, nearby, behind, before, elsewhere, on the other side	To indicate place
Soon, now, when, lately, after a while, as soon as, later, meanwhile, then before, a week later	To indicate time
In summary, that is, in brief, to summarise, in conclusion, finally, hence, of course, in different terms	To summarise or conclude

REVIEW QUESTIONS

10 Contrast signalling devices and linking devices and give an example of each.

11 Identify three techniques you can use to improve paragraph flow.

12 Explain the purpose of three different types of transitional expressions and provide an example of each.

WRITING AN ARGUMENTATIVE ESSAY

An argumentative essay makes a claim or premise, investigates the topic, establishes a position on the topic and draws a conclusion. Argumentative essays require:

- a clear thesis, premise or chosen position
- presentation of different points of view
- evidence to support the premise
- critical and analytical reasoning to reach a convincing conclusion.

◄ OBJECTIVE 6
Write an argumentative essay

An argumentative essay aims to convince the reader to accept the thesis statement, premise or claim by presenting an argument with supporting and opposing credible and current evidence.

Planning the structure

A process you can use to plan, structure and write an argumentative essay is shown in Table 20.6. An example of an argumentative essay is given in Figure 20.1. As you build the argument, its focus should shift from the opposing to the supporting evidence. An argumentative essay should include supporting and opposing arguments. By including both sides of the argument, you:

- demonstrate you have evaluated both sides of the argument
- are able to anticipate and counter any opposing arguments.

A useful strategy to organise your supporting material is:

1st main point
    evidence/support (author, referencing details)
    evidence/support (author, referencing details)
2nd main point
    evidence/support (author, referencing details)
    evidence/support (author, referencing details)

Table 20.6: The argumentative essay process

Steps	Strategy
1 Prepare a clear, concise and defined thesis statement or premise in the first paragraph of the essay	By: • presenting the thesis statement or premise in either the first or last sentence of the first paragraph • using the first paragraph to set the context by reviewing the topic in a general way • explaining why the topic is important or why readers should care about the issue
2 Make clear and logical transitions between the introduction, body and conclusion	By: • using signalling devices to help the reader follow the flow of ideas through the essay • using transitional expressions to connect ideas within and between the introduction, body and conclusion and help the reader follow the essay's argument
3 Build effective paragraphs in the body	By: • making a logical connection to the premise in the opening paragraph of the body of the essay • using some paragraphs to support the thesis statement directly with evidence collected during research • using some paragraphs to explain how and why the evidence supports the premise • writing at least one or two paragraphs that discuss conflicting opinions on the topic • limiting each paragraph to the discussion of one general idea to improve clarity and flow of thoughts • improving readability by using topic sentences
4 Provide factual, logical, current and credible evidential support	By: • gathering and presenting well-researched, accurate, detailed and current information to support the premise statement and consider other points of view • ensuring evidence supporting the premise is factual and logical • applying critical thinking to the different points of view in the evidence • explaining how opposing evidence may not be up to date or well informed
5 Write the conclusion that links to the thesis statement or premise	By: • focusing on the original premise and showing how the argument and evidence supports it • synthesising the information presented in the body of the essay • avoiding the introduction of any new information

3rd main point
    evidence/support (author, referencing details)
    evidence/support (author, referencing details)

Sample essay

The following model argumentative essay presents arguments for and against allowing fringe test cricket players to play for any nation. The *italicised words or phrases* highlight the connections between ideas and contrast the opposing ideas. They lead the reader from the thesis statement in the introduction through the argument in the body to the conclusion. The conclusion links to the thesis statement.

Fringe Test Cricket Players

Introduction contains thesis statement and sets the context

Fringe test cricket players (those up and coming and players close to test selection) should be able to play cricket for any nation at any location globally. The issue has been widely and hotly debated in the major national newspapers and talkback radio. It is an important issue because it concerns fundamental moral, emotional and economic issues that impact on the capacity of fringe cricketers to earn an income from their sporting abilities. A variety of arguments have been canvassed in letters to the editors of major national newspapers and comments on talkback radio.

Body
Arguments for

Arguments for allowing fringe test cricketers to play for any country *contend that* restricting cricketers or, for that matter, any sportsperson from gaining financial rewards for their sporting skills is unfair, anachronistic and anti free trade. *Furthermore*, the time span for earning money in a sportsperson's life is very limited. *In addition*, there is no financial reward for the many hours of dedication.

Denial of earning rights through sport restricts basic human freedom. Australia produces a wealth of highly skilled professional cricketers. *As a result,* some will never have the opportunity to play for Australia. Fringe test cricketers should have similar opportunities to other professional sporting people. *Moreover*, there is little amateur sport left anywhere in the world. Most sports are fully professional where participants are paid for their work. Fringe test cricket players should be allowed to play test cricket for any country *in order to* increase their earning capacity and contribute to the standard of cricket internationally.

Allowing these fringe test cricketers to play for any country would recognise the professionalism of modern sport and at the same time take the skills around the world. The success of Australian cricketers overseas has a 'ripple effect'; their earning capacity has a stimulating effect on producing more and better cricketers on the home front while, at the same time, improving the skills and standards in cricket-playing countries. Increased professionalism will augment the size of the international cricketing audience and deepen cricketing traditions over the longer term.

Arguments against

It has been argued that sportspeople should be loyal, patriotic and, above all, tribal and indebted to their country, and much of the public expects this. Many Australians, *so this argument goes*, love their cricket and spend a great deal of their summer leisure time watching it. They love their heroes, especially their local heroes, and would be horrified to see some of their best young cricketers playing for another country.

One prominent retired test cricketer, writing to a daily newspaper, *contends that to* play for your district, state or country is reward in itself. He further argues that it is not Australia's problem to save world cricket by bringing it up to Australia's standard and *asserts that* cricket is based on tradition. Other correspondents *explain* you need history and tradition to build the mystique of cricket. *Indeed*, tradition is the very 'meat' of cricket.

Argument for

It is the contention of many of the correspondents on this subject that we should continue to go our usual way in the context of 'If you are good enough you will play cricket for Australia'. This position goes on to assert that it has worked well in the past. Why should we change it?

Conclusion

However, Australians playing cricket in other countries has lifted standards and cricket morale. *Furthermore*, comments by returning Australian cricketers are very positive about improvements they noted on tour. *In addition*, those cricketers returning from overseas tours emphasise in the daily press the need for promoting the skills of cricket.

In conclusion, fringe test cricketers should be allowed to play for any side anywhere in the world. Our society is now multicultural and global. We trade globally, we work globally and now our sporting people play globally.

Figure 20.1: Model argumentative essay

Avoiding plagiarism

The *Merriam-Webster Online Dictionary* defines 'plagiarise' as 'to steal and pass off (the ideas or words of another) as one's own, to use (another's production) without crediting the source, to commit literary theft, present as new and original an idea or product derived from an existing source'. Within universities, **plagiarism** is viewed as academic dishonesty.

The Plagiarism.org website (2007) states: 'All of the following are considered plagiarism:

- turning in someone else's work as your own
- copying words or ideas from someone else without giving credit
- failing to put a quotation in quotation marks
- giving incorrect information about the source of a quotation
- changing words but copying the sentence structure of a source without giving credit
- copying so many words or ideas from a source that it makes up the majority of your work, whether you give credit or not (see our section on "fair use" rules).'

The most direct way to avoid plagiarism is to acknowledge and cite the source. (See Chapter 13 for different citation styles.) Plagiarism has serious consequences, such as immediate failure in a subject. Any person or company using commercial written materials illegally could be sued by the owner.

In your essays and other academic writing you will be expected to reach the accepted standards and to follow established protocols. Use the checklist below before you submit your essay. The lecturers assessing your work will be marking against these accepted standards.

> **Plagiarism** is the act of stealing and passing off the ideas or words of another as your own.

SELF-EVALUATE YOUR SKILL

STANDARD ESSAY CONVENTIONS

Key: VS = Very Successfully, S = Successfully, U = Unsuccessfully

I have:	VS	S	U
used a thesis statement or premise			
clarified the issues to be covered			
used accepted essay structure—introduction, body and conclusion and any additional components (if requested)			
used topic sentences and built paragraphs around one idea			
used linking devices and transitional expressions to make logical connections between ideas			
researched reputable, credible sources and peer-reviewed material			
applied critical thinking to understand and evaluate research			
cited quotations correctly			
used an accepted academic referencing style consistently			

REVIEW QUESTIONS

13 What are the main features of a good argumentative essay?

14 Outline a process you can follow to plan, structure and write an argumentative essay.

15 *a* Identify at least four behaviours that are considered plagiarism.

b What is the most direct way to avoid plagiarism?

EDITING

Good writers leave enough time to edit their work. They edit methodically by looking at different aspects such as spelling, structure and content at different passes through the manuscript. A booklet written by Van Buren and Buehler (1980) presented the levels of edit approach developed by the staff of the Jet Propulsion Laboratories (JPL) in Pasadena, California, in the late 1970s. The JPL approach has been influential in helping editors define ahead of time the type of editing that is to be done.

Levels of editing

The nine types or levels of editing are:

1 *Coordination edit*—primarily concerned with handling and controlling the manuscript.

2 *Policy edit*—to ensure the document reflects the policies of the organisation.

3 *Integrity edit*—to ensure the parts of the document match and verify, and that there are no gaps or repetitions in numbering systems.

4 *Screening edit*—to identify and correct aspects of the text, including spelling and artwork.

5 *Copy clarification*—to ensure the copy used in the publishing process is legible, with clear instructions for final preparation.

6 *Format edit*—to verify that the document conforms to established layout, typographic designs and standards.

7 *Mechanical style edit*—to ensure that the mechanics of text and figures conform to the specified style.

8 *Language edit*—to provide an in-depth review of the way ideas are expressed.

9 *Substantive edit*—to verify that the content of the document is meaningful, and that the individual parts of the document are coherent.

When editing material, Beer (2003, pp. 474–5) believes: 'Three levels seem to provide the most widely used framework . . . level three deals with the big picture . . . level two aims at improving the clarity and cohesion of the prose . . . level one is concerned with clarity and conciseness.' These three levels are the minimum standard to use as you edit your essays, assignments, reports, projects and other academic documents. Levine (2008) suggests using the table of contents to help improve your manuscript. He comments: 'Use it to see if you've left something out, if you are presenting your sections in the most logical order, or if you need to make your wording a bit more clear.'

The levels of edit concept provides a systematic approach to the editing task. An editing checklist that includes each of the levels is a useful editing tool. Typical headings you can use to check your work are:

- *Structure*—how the document is organised
- *Content*—what the document says
- *Style*—how you say what you say
- *Format*—the physical arrangement and appearance of the document
- *Mechanics*—checking for grammar, sentence structure errors, punctuation, spelling and typographic errors.

Proofreading is the final step in the writing process. Strategies to assist in the final proofreading include spell checking, reading aloud, allowing time to elapse between writing and proofreading, and getting others to proofread.

Use standard authorities, such as the Department of Finance and Administration's *Style Manual for Authors, Editors and Printers* and *The Macquarie Dictionary*, to determine issues of spelling or style.

REVIEW QUESTIONS

16 What does revising require a writer to do?

17 How is editing different from revising?

18 Identify at least five levels of editing.

19 Prepare an editing checklist to use in your future essays.

APPLY YOUR KNOWLEDGE

TECHNIQUES USED IN A JOURNAL ARTICLE

Find a journal article in the library that is relevant to your area of study.

1 Write down the article's thesis or purpose statement.

2 Explain the type of argument developed in the article.

3 Examine the strategies used to develop the argument and evaluate their effectiveness.

4 a List all examples of:
   - signalling devices
   - topic sentences
   - linking phrases
   - transitional expressions.

   b Choose three of these devices and analyse their effectiveness in making the information in the journal article easier to read and understand.

5 a Analyse the structure of the journal article by creating an outline of the order of information.

   b Explain why the order of information is effective or ineffective.

6 What do you believe is likely to be the greatest problem in writing a journal article effectively?

SUMMARY OF LEARNING OBJECTIVES

1 ► COMPARE THREE TYPES OF REASONING

Inductive reasoning leads the reader through the information, facts or reasons to the end result. Deductive reasoning gives the main point or overview and then presents the information or facts to support the argument. Lateral thinking is a creative process in which the thinker explores an idea from many different points of view.

2 ► DISCUSS TECHNIQUES FOR SOUND REASONING

Techniques include questioning critically to distinguish between facts, opinions, beliefs and prejudice; forming objective opinions; presenting advantages and disadvantages; avoiding exaggeration and checking statistics.

EXPLAIN THE PURPOSE OF EACH PART OF AN ACADEMIC DOCUMENT

The introduction states the problem as a thesis statement that identifies the issue, problem, gap in knowledge or some other purpose. It lets both writer and reader know what the writer is trying to do. The body contains the research findings and presents a thoughtful and coherent argument based on accurate and relevant evidence. The conclusion is more than a summary of the main points. It links the argument back to the thesis statement or premise. The abstract, précis or summary highlights the main ideas in a condensed form.

 ANALYSE THE STRATEGIES USED TO DEVELOP AN ARGUMENT

Some of the strategies used to inquire into existing knowledge and to develop an argument are analysis, comparison, differentiation, illustration, contrast, critical evaluation, criticism, interpretation, summary and justi-fication. Academic writers need to do more than present a case. They also need to show they have thought about a large number of facts and events from a number of different perspectives, and that their argument is informed, thoughtful, balanced and convincing.

5 ▷ **DESCRIBE WRITING TECHNIQUES THAT IDENTIFY THE MAIN POINT AND INDICATE CONNECTIONS BETWEEN IDEAS**

Techniques that identify the main point and indicate connections between ideas are signalling devices (headings, topic sentences), linking devices (bridges, keynoting, paragraph flow, pronouns) and transitional expressions.

 WRITE AN ARGUMENTATIVE ESSAY

Argumentative essays aim to convince the reader to accept the thesis statement, premise or claim by presenting an argument with supporting and opposing credible and current evidence. Writing an argumentative essay requires you to apply the higher-order analytical and critical thinking skills to verify, critique and extend the existing body of knowledge. The writer creates a thesis statement or makes a claim, assertion or point. Credible sources such as authorities, scholars and study results are researched and presented as evidence. In an effective argumentative essay the conclusion is supported by the evidence and argument, and links back to the original thesis statement.

7 ▷ **IDENTIFY THE LEVELS OF EDITING TO APPLY TO AN ACADEMIC DOCUMENT**

A systematic approach to editing requires the writer to edit the document's structure, content, style, format and mechanics. Editing, rewriting and proofreading should take at least 20% of the time spent in creating a document.

KEY TERMS

ACTIVITIES AND QUESTIONS

1. Work in small groups to discuss the following statement:

   A convincing argument is sound, thoughtful and logical.

   a. Discuss the meaning of this statement.

   b. Prepare an individual written analysis of the statement (about 750 words).

2. Find a journal article you may want to use as a reference for an essay or paper in your course and prepare a short critique (make judgments or show the relative merits of the argument) (500–750 words). In the critique, give enough information for the reader to know what the article is about and enough analysis and evaluation to help you decide whether you will use the article in your essay or paper.

   Use these guidelines in the critique:

   - Filter the information by creating a list of the headings and subheadings. (If the article has no headings, list the main ideas.)
   - Define the thesis or purpose of the argument *and* the strategy used. (The strategy could be to analyse, compare, illustrate, contrast or other.)
   - Provide a brief, reasoned appraisal or assessment of the facts or argument presented in the article.
   - Identify the article's main strengths and weaknesses.

3. Work in small groups.

   You and your fellow group members have been asked to present a paper to a university business faculty enquiry entitled 'An investigation into plagiarism in major essays submitted for assessment'. The specific issues the faculty wants you to address are:

   - the ways in which a student can plagiarise the work of another
   - the strategies students should use to avoid plagiarism

   - the consequences for a student who engages in plagiarism
   - the consequences for a faculty that ignores allegations of plagiarism.

4. Work in small groups.

   a. Read the statement.

      Inductive reasoning, by its very nature, is more open-ended and exploratory, especially at the beginning. Deductive reasoning is more narrow in nature and is concerned with testing or confirming hypotheses.

   b. Discuss the writer's meaning and give examples of situations appropriate to each type of reasoning.

5. Write the following comparison/contrast essay (about 1500 words).

   Compare and contrast life in Australia in the decade 1980–1990 with life in Australia in the decade 2000–2010.

   Use the checklist on page 581 in this chapter as the steps to follow as you research, plan and write the essay.

   a. In the introduction, present a thesis statement, premise, claim or assertion.

   b. In the body, the usual rule is to compare and then contrast by:

      - presenting the similarities between lifestyle in the two time periods gathered in your research (compare);
      - presenting the differences in lifestyle in the two time periods gathered in your research (contrast).

   c. In the conclusion, restate the thesis and show how you have proved it.

   d. Prepare an abstract or précis.

COMPARISON/CONTRAST ESSAY

Key: *VS = Very Successfully, S = Successfully, U = Unsuccessfully*

In this comparison/contrast essay, have I:	VS	S	U
identified clearly the two subjects I will be comparing and contrasting?			
made a list of the similarities between the subjects?			
made a list of the differences between the subjects?			
prepared an outline that organises the essay?			
identified the similarities and differences the reader would expect?			
identified any surprising, puzzling or contradictory points?			
posed a problem (or thesis) in the introduction?			
discussed what causes the similarities or differences?			
outlined the effects of these on the subject?			
drawn conclusions?			

EXPLORING THE WEB

1   Learn more about reasoning on 'The reasoning page', <http://pegasus.cc.ucf.edu>, by browsing a comprehensive range of argumentation/critical thinking/informal logic resources.

2   Learn more about essay writing by visiting *Guide to Basic Essay Writing*, <http://members.tripod.com>. The site identifies the basic structure of an essay and offers strategies to use as you plan, structure and write an essay.

3   Learn more about citation styles by visiting *Welcome to Essay Centre*, <http://essayinfo.com>, and following the link to 'Citation styles'.

4   Visit *English Works Essays* at <http://depts.gallaudet.edu/>, and answer the following questions.
a   Differentiate between three common types of essay.
b   What is the purpose of an argumentative essay?
c   How is an argumentative essay structured?
d   Decide how you will structure the essay in your project work for this chapter.

PROJECT WORK

Your project for this chapter is to write an argumentative essay. The purpose of an argumentative essay is to convince the reader of the validity of your premise, evidence, argument and conclusion.

Search for a topic that interests you in your major field. The topic should be one that is open to opposing views. Alternatively, your lecturer or tutor may provide you with the topic.

Ensure your essay:

- has a clear thesis, premise or chosen position
- presents different points of view
- provides evidence to support the thesis, premise or chosen position
- applies critical thinking and analytical skills to the argument
- presents a convincing conclusion.

Submit your essay.

BIBLIOGRAPHY

Anderson, J. & Poole, M. 2002. *Assignment and Thesis Writing*, 4th edn, John Wiley & Sons, UK.

Andrew, M. 1999. 'Lecturing publications for the higher education sector', *Stylewise*, Vol. 5, Issue 2, pp. 1–2.

Bailey, S. 2003. *Academic Writing: A Practical Guide for Students*, Routledge, Taylor & Francis, London.

Beer, D.F. (ed.). 2003. *Writing and Speaking in the Technology Professions*, 2nd edn, Wiley-IEEPress, USA.

Bradley, M. *Resources for Technical Writers*, www.techpubs.com/resources.html, last updated 19 July 2004.

Browne, M.N. & Keeley, S.M. 2007. *Asking the Right Questions: A Guide to Critical Thinking*, 8th edn, Pearson Prentice Hall, Upper Saddle River, New Jersey.

Department of Finance and Administration. 2002. *Style Manual for Authors, Editors and Printers*, 6th edn, John Wiley & Sons, Brisbane.

de Bono, E. 1990. *The Use of Lateral Thinking*, Penguin, Harmondsworth.

Dewey, J. 1933. *How We Think*, Heath, Boston.

Essay Info. *Welcome to Essay Centre*, essayinfo.com, viewed 16 November 2007.

Gibaldi, J. 1995. *MLA Handbook for Writers of Research Papers*, 4th edn, Modern Language Association of America, USA.

Gibaldi, J. 1998. *MLA Style Manual and Guide to Scholarly Publishing*, 2nd edn, Modern Language Association, New York.

Internet Encyclopedia of Philosophy, www.iep.utm.edu/a/argument.htm, last updated 2004.

Jansz, B.B. *The Reasoning Page*, http://pegasus.cc.ucf.edu/~janzb/reasoning/, last updated 16 October 2007.

Kane, T.S. 1988. *The New Oxford Guide to Writing*, Oxford University Press, New York.

Levine, J.S. *Writing and Presenting Your Thesis or Dissertation*, www.learnerassociates.net/dissthes>, last updated 24 January 2008.

Lewis, G. & Slade, C. 1994. *Critical Communication*, Prentice Hall Australia, Sydney.

Livingstone, K. *Guide to Basic Essay Writing*, http://members.tripod.com/~lklivingston/essay, last updated 5 September 2007.

Merriam-Webster Online Dictionary, viewed 20 November 2007.

Peck, J. & Coyle, M. 1999. *The Student's Guide to Writing: Grammar, Punctuation and Spelling*, Palgrave, New York.

Petelin, R. & Durham, M. 1992. *The Professional Writing Guide: Writing Well and Knowing Why*, Longman Cheshire, Melbourne.

Plagiarism.org. 'What is plagiarism?', *Learning Centre*, www.plagiarism.org/learning_center/what_is_plagiarism.html, viewed 18 November 2007.

Trochim, W.M.K. 'Deduction & induction', *Research Methods Knowledge Base*, www.socialresearchmethods.net/kb/dedind.php, last updated 20 October 2006.

Turabian, K.L. 1996. *A Manual for Writers of Term Papers, Theses and Dissertations*, 6th edn (rev. by John Grossman & Alice Bennett), University of Chicago Press, USA.

University of Manchester. 'Being critical', *Academic Phrase Bank*, www.phrasebook, manchester.ac.uk/critical.htm, viewed 19 February 2008.

Van Buren, R. & Buehler, M.F. 1980. *The Levels of Edit*, 2nd edn, JPL Publication 80-1, January.

Van Leunen, M.C. 1992. *A Handbook for Scholars*, Oxford University Press.

Watson, G. 1987. *Writing a Thesis: A Guide to Long Essays and Dissertations*, Longman, London.

Wolfe, J. 'How to write a PhD thesis', Science@unsw.www.hhys.unsw.edu.au/~jw/thesis.html, last modified 2 November 2006.

21 Business messages via electronic media

LEARNING OBJECTIVES

After studying this chapter you should be able to:

1 ▷ discuss the characteristics of electronic media appropriate to business messages

2 ▷ apply the 3 x 3 writing process as you write business messages for electronic media

3 ▷ create effective email messages

4 ▷ explain the role of instant messaging (IM) and text messaging in business communication

5 ▷ discuss the role of blogging in the workplace

6 ▷ adapt the 3 x 3 writing process to podcasts

7 ▷ explain the role of syndication

8 ▷ discuss the effects of information overload.

VIEWPOINT: FUTURE BECKONING

Martin North, Managing Consulting Director of Fujitsu Australia, contends in an interview with Cameron Cooper that '. . . a radical transformation of business thinking is required . . . to appropriately apply new technologies . . . A more strategic approach to innovation and how you can apply new technologies over a period of time is a fundamental capability that organisations need.'

North cites Web 2.0, the second generation of web-based communities and hosted services, social networking sites and 'wikis' that facilitate collaboration and sharing. 'There's a huge challenge there to break out of the mould of the old static content and one-way communication, and into much more collaborative, information sharing, web-as-a-platform thinking . . . Innovative sectors in this area include financial services and community-based operations, although in Australia there is a long way to go . . . There's a need to raise awareness of what's feasible and possible, so it's not just a conversation about technology, but it's the applications of technology to business things.'

Source: C. Cooper, 'Future beckoning', *Management Today*, November/December 2007, pp. 12–18.

The World Internet Project (WIP) is a long-term longitudinal study of the social, political and economic impact of computer and Internet technology. It is a major international, collaborative project based at universities and research institutes around the world. The WIP (2007) '. . . believes that the Internet's influence will ultimately be far greater than television'. A major impact of computer and Internet technology for business has been the rapid increase of universally standardised, accessible electronic media. Business organisations pushing for competitive advantage have responded flexibly and quickly to the increasing variety of electronic media and formats.

The Internet offers business organisations a universally accessible network of low-cost, speedy communication tools, publication tools and resources that connect individuals, organisations and communities across time zones and geographical boundaries. The Internet can be used 24 hours a day to send or find information, rather than having to work only within the hours that workplaces and libraries are open. The Internet's move to mobile devices will trigger the next great online advance. Mobile means we can go online anywhere.

Continuous improvements in web platforms mean that people can now upload as well as download information. Users are able to create and distribute content, often with the freedom to share and reuse. A significant outcome for business is the capacity to send, through a combination of multimedia, a greater number and variety of messages online. In your business career you will need to use a range of existing and new electronic media professionally.

CHOOSING ELECTRONIC MEDIA FOR BUSINESS MESSAGES

OBJECTIVE **1** ▶
Discuss the characteristics of electronic media appropriate to business messages

Recently the options for sending messages via electronic media have expanded rapidly. Progressive businesses apply the electronic media to maintain and improve business communication and performance.

Many electronic communication applications—for example, entries in databases, calendar and contacts software, web page creation and email—require you to write effectively (see Table 21.1). People can chat, be seen on the computer screen, take part in instant messaging (IM) sessions, or communicate through business blogs and communities of practice.

Types of media

Messages conveyed electronically often combine text, sound and motion. The multimedia keeps the sender and receiver active and enhances the sense of community. Multimedia adds interest by increasing perceptual insight and feelings about the ideas presented. Simplicity, clarity and visibility make the message easy to understand.

Electronic interaction is different from its face-to-face counterpart. Rather than a combination of spoken words and nonverbal communication in a shared physical space, the electronic message is often simply written words or an audio or video presentation at a distance. Instead of the immediate response of a face-to-face interaction, there may be time delays before receivers log on to an electronic message. The shared experience of members of an email mailing list, podcast or blog happens in a virtual world, rather than in a shared physical space. In the virtual world the receiver responds to elements such as language use, ideas and structure conveyed through a combination of multimedia.

A simple structure provides a clear pathway for the receivers. In an IM or podcast, three points are more effective than ten. Any message sent electronically should have a strong opening to gain attention and a strong closing that receivers will remember easily. Familiar, unambiguous language that moves straight to the point is easy to understand. Long phrases, redundancies and fillers show that the sender has not taken the time to think through his or her ideas, or plan and structure the message. Ideas structured around a central point or main theme show the audience the progression of ideas and the relationship between them. Personal experiences, examples, illustration, facts and statistics add interest and catch the receiver's attention. Effective electronic messages emphasise common ground in terms of experiences, interests, values and goals between sender and receiver.

Table 21.1: Electronic media for business communication

Media	Purpose
Email	Email is faster and more efficient than regular mail. It is a low-cost, attractive alternative to printed messages. Most companies use email for internal and external communication. Disadvantages include junk mail, spam and viruses.
Instant messaging (IM)	IM is increasingly used as an effective business communication tool. It enables users to discuss interactively via chat boards or voice over IP. Changes in a document can be seen as they are made. Collaboration in personal and flexible ways is possible through IM. It is faster than email and simple to use. Another advantage is the fewer problems with security, privacy and unwanted messages (spam).
Text messaging	Text messaging is a phone-based medium with the added advantage of mobility and portability. It is less convenient than computer-based IM because of the small screen and phone pad size.
Blogs	Blogs are online journals on which users post thoughts, comments or news in a chronological format. An effective blog has a clear focus and is updated regularly. Businesses are increasingly using blogs for small-team communication, communication between executives, and communication with others outside the organisation.
Podcasts	Podcasts are replacing or supplementing conference calls and training courses and other group communication activities. They are the online equivalent of recorded radio or video broadcasts. Podcasts allow businesses to publish and broadcast audio or video messages.

Regardless of the medium, business communicators need to pay special attention to planning, presenting and reviewing their message, rather than simply 'dashing off' a message. The need to respond immediately and pressure of time can cause you to forget to complete one or more of these steps. Often, the result is a poorly structured and unprofessional message that is unlikely to achieve its intended purpose.

REVIEW QUESTIONS

1. Cooper (2007) states: 'A more strategic approach to innovation and how you can apply new technologies over a period of time is a fundamental capability that organizations need.' Consider an organisation of your choice and suggest the capabilities that it will require in five years.
2. Discuss five electronic media choices that are becoming increasingly important in business communication.

APPLYING THE 3 × 3 WRITING PROCESS

◄ OBJECTIVE 2
Apply the 3 × 3 writing process as you write business messages for electronic media

This section looks at the skills needed when writing messages for electronic media. Effective online writing skills affect the efficiency and management of businesses. For example, entries in databases need to be suitable for retrieval at any time by anyone. Comments in the remarks section of the database must be easy to understand. These comments are an ongoing record for use in different ways across a number of different processes—for example, billing on invoices. A database of heritage properties may be posted and stored on the Web for ready access by national or international visitors to the site. Information should always be cited accurately so that other users can trace the original source.

Specific software packages are designed to manage contacts and communication with contacts. The packages bring together electronically a number of applications that used to be separate—for example, calendars, contacts and email. Features such as the tasks, journal and note sections allow users to communicate in writing. Regardless of whether the written message is sent internationally or to the person at the next desk, the message still needs to be clear, readable and easy to understand.

A systematic approach to developing business messages effectively is the 3 × 3 writing process.

- Phase 1 is prewriting—analyse, anticipate and adapt the approach to meet your purpose, the information you need to convey and the audience's needs.
- Phase 2 is writing—select, organise, shape and write your message.
- Phase 3 is editing—revise, proofread and evaluate the document.

Skilful writers use these steps automatically and avoid the ten common errors set out in Table 21.2.

Phase 1: Prewrite

In online writing, consider the purpose of the message and the effect it will have on the receiver. By keeping the main objectives in mind, the writer is able to convey a clear message and retain the goodwill of the reader. In the prewriting stage, when sending an email, plan and complete the following four steps:

1. Decide on the purpose.
2. Decide on the content.
3. Write all the ideas in point form.
4. Order these ideas into a sequence appropriate to the purpose.

In replying to an email message, or contributing to a blog, respondents can create a structure for their message by asking themselves the following questions:

- What is the writer's relationship with me?
- Why are they writing to me?
- What do they want?
- How can I help?

Phase 2: Write

No matter how sophisticated the computer software and networks, people must still do the actual composing of the message. Words, sentences and paragraphs send the written message from one person to another. A plain English writing style is recommended because it uses positive language,

Table 21.2: Ten common errors to avoid
1 Hasty responses under the pressure of time, rather than reasoned responses
2 Responses that are insensitive to the level of computer knowledge of the receiver
3 A rude and discourteous or overly familiar tone
4 Traditional routine openings that sound insincere
5 Obscure, unfamiliar words and jargon
6 Lengthy sentences and very long paragraphs or long sections of unbroken text
7 Negative, pessimistic content
8 A closing that omits the actions or desired results
9 An assumption that the receiver checks for email as regularly as the sender does
10 A sender who forgets to give a name and is identified only by the email address, e.g. xyz@abc.net

clear expression and a courteous tone. Combine these features with a logical structure to create a message that is easy to read and understand. Plain English is discussed more fully in Chapter 17. Some of the key elements in an effective online writing style are set out in Table 21.3.

Three basic composition techniques—topic sentences, transitions and logical order—improve any piece of online writing because they build solid paragraphs. A simple paragraph contains a *topic sentence* followed by sentences containing information to support the topic sentence. Sometimes, a simple paragraph contains a summary or concluding sentence. The general-to-specific order of information is used when the topic sentence is placed at the beginning of the paragraph. The topic sentence makes a claim and the supporting sentences amplify, compare and present details to back up the claim.

> A topic sentence contains the main idea in a paragraph.

Transitional words and phrases mark a path for the reader. Transitional expressions show sequence, compare or contrast, give examples, indicate time, and summarise or conclude. Their purpose is to join ideas and show relationships.

> Transitional words or phrases make connections between two or more ideas.

In emails and blogs, highlight the main points with headings. These guide the reader through the message and make the information more accessible. In business messages the content should be objective. If an opinion is given, separate it clearly from the objective content. Arrange the information in short paragraphs and use lists where appropriate to make the information easy to read.

Table 21.3: Elements in an effective online writing style

Key element	Purpose	Strategies
Clarity	To aid the reader's understanding and add conviction to the writing	• Create single-subject messages whenever possible. • Open the email message with a sentence that: — makes a connection to previous correspondence — identifies the document's purpose, or — reflects an awareness of the needs of the reader. • Focus on the subject and purpose. • Show the reader how the content affects them. • Present new ideas clearly. • Arrange ideas in a logical sequence.
Readability	To make information accessible	• Use 15–20 words per sentence. • Limit each sentence to one idea. • Show who or what took the action by using the active voice. • Avoid slang. • Remove ambiguous and unnecessary words. • Avoid jargon and technical terms unless the reader is a technical expert.
Positive language	To create a positive first impression	• Use direct and courteous language. • Choose positive words rather than negative words.
Punctuation	To help understanding	• Use a capital letter to start a sentence and end with a full stop. • Apply the general rule: always use more full stops than commas.
Paragraphs	To organise information around one idea	• Create short paragraphs that are easy to read, unless a longer paragraph is needed to contain an idea. • Let a sentence stand alone as a paragraph sometimes, to add emphasis.
Tone	To establish the communication climate	• Avoid inflaming emotional responses. • Use a courteous and tactful tone. • Use an appropriate level of formality.

EMOTICONS

An **emoticon** is a symbol, or combination of symbols, used to convey emotional content that supplements the written message.

An **emoticon** (sometimes referred to as a 'smiley') is a symbol, or combination of symbols, used to convey emotional content that supplements the written message. It is usually made from a short sequence of keyboard letters and symbols. Examples of emoticons are shown in Table 21.4. In formal messages and messages to senior members of an organisation, it is unwise to use emoticons. They are appropriate only in informal messages between colleagues and friends.

Phase 3: Edit

Because dense documents are difficult to read and understand, check that you have used a paragraph for each new point and lists or bullet points appropriately. This signals a new idea to the reader and leaves some white space between ideas.

Check that the tone of the message is courteous and confident, and use the spell check. In order to remove any rude or hostile comments created on the spur of the moment, and any criticism or insult of others or their views, always read a written message before it is forwarded online. The term 'flaming' describes emotions expressed in an electronic message. Experienced users read their email messages and, if they feel that the words 'Flame! Flame!' should be inserted to label emotion, they know they must edit out the emotional words by rewriting that section. In this way, they remove the emotional content and send only objective, factual content and carefully reasoned arguments.

According to Barwell (1995–1996), '. . . electronic publications need to be subject to the same kind of quality-control procedures as happen with their print counterparts'. All communication, regardless of whether it is electronic or print, should be clear, easy to understand and appropriate to its context. The receiver should not have to 'wrestle' with the message to understand its meaning.

Table 21.4: Examples of emoticons

Emoticon	Meaning
:-] ☺	Smiley face
;-)	Wink (light sarcasm)
:-(☹	Sad face or frown (anger or displeasure)
8-)	Eye-glasses
:-D	Shock or surprise
:-/	Perplexed
:-P	Wry smile
;-}	Leer
:-Q	Smoker
:-e	Disappointment
:-@	Scream
:-0	Yell
:-*	Drunk
:-	Male
>-	Female

REVIEW QUESTIONS

3 Discuss the phases in the 3 × 3 writing process.

4 Describe three key elements in an effective online writing style.

CREATING EFFECTIVE EMAIL MESSAGES

Electronic mail (email) is the transmission of messages from computer to computer through electronic transmission devices such as modems, telephone lines, mail servers and other telecommunications services. An electronic mail system allows sender and receiver to create, send, receive, file, copy, print and delete electronic messages. Email is the most widely used application on the Internet. It is important that you consider your audience and the situation before deciding whether email is the right medium. Corporations can lose considerable amounts of money and time as a result of ineffective email management.

Purpose and layout

Email messages are used for a number of purposes—to make requests, give instructions, provide authorisation, offer acknowledgment and document decisions. In each instance, the nature of the message and the writer's purpose will have an effect on the structure of the email message. It is useful to look at some examples of routine email messages and establish some guidelines for producing effective messages.

The layout of an email message forms the frame for the message contained in the body of the email. The minimum acceptable layout parts in an email message are:

- receiver's name
- sender's name
- subject
- date
- body
- email address
- one other way, apart from the email address, to contact the sender.

Five common types of email

In business there are five types of email that are routinely sent to people who are both internal and external to the organisation. These mirror the types of internal memos that can be sent (as detailed in Chapter 18) and include:

1 instruction emails
2 request emails
3 announcement emails
4 transmittal emails
5 authorisation emails.

INSTRUCTION EMAIL

The objective of the instruction email is to give your receivers all the information they need to carry out the instructions confidently. The instructions should be logically arranged so that what has to happen stands out clearly. An order of information suited to an instruction email is introduction, main point, secondary information and action. This order enables the reader to understand what has to happen

Electronic mail (email) is the transmission of messages from computer to computer through electronic transmission devices such as modems, telephone lines, mail servers and other telecommunications services.

◄ OBJECTIVE 3
Create effective email messages

and who has responsibility for making it happen. The tone should be pleasant and the message should include all necessary details.

REQUEST EMAIL

The aim of the request email is to ask the receiver for certain information or action. The request email tells the receiver clearly and precisely what is required. It is arranged in the following way: the main point, the secondary idea or details, then the action required.

ANNOUNCEMENT EMAIL

The announcement email provides information. It follows the order suggested for writing good news letters. The announcement comes first, followed by the secondary details or information and then the required action.

TRANSMITTAL EMAIL

The transmittal email is a cover note that accompanies a more formal or lengthy message. An order of information suited to a transmittal email is to start with the main point, then present the secondary details and identify the required action. The tone should be confident and courteous, and all necessary details should be included.

AUTHORISATION EMAIL

The authorisation email gives someone permission or authority to do something. It presents the background information first, then the main points, and finally the secondary details and action.

Tips for effective use

DeTienne (2002, p. 34) advises using email when you need to:

- contact someone who is not available
- send the same message to several people instantaneously
- deliver your message inexpensively
- send a forwardable message
- transfer sounds, video clips, programs or pictures.

In addition, she recommends using email when you need to communicate written information that is:

- detailed: conveys detailed information such as lists, phone numbers
- not private: the information is not confidential
- fast: a quick response is required
- recorded: a record of the communication is required
- easy to distribute: especially when a soft copy is required for editing.

It is important that email is not used when the information you want to convey is sensitive or should be delivered personally, such as bad news. It should not be used when immediate feedback is necessary or if you are concerned about the format or look of your message.

Email messages vary enormously in length and complexity. Some are brief, routine announcements; others present complicated and sensitive information. Any email message, however, warrants the following four steps:

1. Identify the subject.
2. Select and order the information.
3. Write simply.
4. Use a suitable tone.

Other important points to remember when writing email messages are:

- Be concise, and use a conversational, professional tone and not a casual writing style (although this is permissible in a personal email).
- Be aware that different people may use email differently. (Many do not open their email every day.)
- Use capital letters sparingly, to emphasise or highlight. (The use of capital letters is associated with 'flaming'—that is, shouting or yelling.)
- Do not assume that everyone appreciates or understands emoticons or abbreviations.
- Review your messages before you send them, and remember that they are not private; ensure that your emails are not just unnecessary gossip.
- Refrain from including anything personal, because your business emails may be accessible to others.
- Ensure that your messages are sent to the correct audience and have been received. (In most cases, you will be advised if your email has not been delivered.)
- Avoid sending big files or adding too many attachments. These can tie up connections and cost companies considerable time and money.
- Close your emails with an automatic professional signature that includes your full name, title, address and phone number at the end of your emails. This assists recipients who choose to reply by post or telephone, rather than email.

EMAIL SECURITY

A general guideline is to view all email as insecure unless it is encoded or encrypted. The content of emails stored on mail servers can be read by system administrators and others who may access the system. Emails are a permanent record because they are backed up electronically and can be recovered. Deleting them from the email inbox or sent box does not destroy them. As part of the routine maintenance and management of networks and systems, logs (records of transmissions) are kept of email messages sent and received, the email addresses of senders and receivers, and the time of transmission. Web server logs also record information on the sites that people visit. These records are compiled by, and stored on, the software used to operate networks, including web servers, mail servers and gateways.

JUNK MAIL

Adding to information overload is junk email (**spam**). Strategies to deal with junk mail are continually being devised. However, as most Internet users don't have the time or the knowledge to deal with spam, they have to rely on their Internet service provider and a handful of products to deal with the influx of unwanted mail.

Spam is junk email.

Reader access techniques

Effective reader access can be achieved by using the following techniques.

- Write informative subject lines that tell the reader what, when, where and other important information—for example, *Confined Spaces OHS Meeting 8 June in Staff Room 3*. Refer to Table 21.5 for examples of effective and ineffective subject lines.
- Present your key ideas quickly in the first few paragraphs. Many people do not read more than the first page.
- Use displayed lists with bullets or dashes.
- Use shorter sentences and paragraphs than in other documents.

Table 21.5: Subject lines	
Ineffective subject line	**Effective subject line**
Introduction of New Technology	New Instant Messaging (IM) Service from 1 May
Employee Amenities	Schedule for Upgrade of Staffroom Amenities
Project Report	Business Systems Redesign Ahead of Schedule
Next Week's Marketing Meeting	Bring Quarterly Core Market Statistics

DOCUMENT MANAGEMENT

The proliferation of online documents, particularly those worked on by more than one person, requires the users to manage their documents. Studying online requires careful thought about record keeping. Items such as projects, and ideas gathered from email, blogs, podcasts or the Web, all need to be stored for future reference. Documents need to be classified by content ready for filing. Natural classification systems based on similarity—for example, News, Business, Entertainment, Social Sciences, Law—are the easiest to use. Classification of information and storage in online directories and files that are easy to access improve personal efficiency.

Advantages and disadvantages of email

The advantages and disadvantages of email are outlined in Table 21.6.

Table 21.6: Advantages and disadvantages of email	
Advantages	**Disadvantages**
• Is a faster channel than regular mail (sometimes referred to as 'snail mail')—most messages worldwide arrive within minutes of being sent	• Noncontrollability of those who will see a message—may appear later in a variety of printed forms—lack of privacy and confidentiality
• Can be sent to a number of different receivers and opened at convenient times	• Possible time lag if the receiver chooses not to open and read their email for a few days
• Can be used to access databases and file libraries	• Difficulty in accessing the system for those who are computer illiterate
• Can be stored and sent at off-peak telephone rates	• Lack of nonverbal communication cues to add meaning
• Saves paper	• Can cause information overload
• Enables a message to be written and edited by a number of people before it is forwarded to the receiver and can be used to avoid telephone tag	• Overuse of jargon and email abbreviations; e.g. IMHO (in my humble opinion), BTW (by the way), ROFL (roll on the floor laughing)
• Can use combinations of text, pictures and diagrams	• Can be used to send 'spam' (junk mail) to unsuspecting users
• Documents or files can be attached and *cc* or *bcc* copies forwarded at the same time as the original	• Difficulty in distinguishing between casual and formal messages because of their similar layout

Email mailing lists

An **electronic mailing list** allows for widespread distribution of information by email to many Internet users. It is a list of names and email addresses of subscribers, similar to a traditional mailing list, used for sending publications to an organisation's customers. The email messages are sent to the subscribers' email addresses. A single designated email address known as the *reflector* receives the message and sends a copy of it to all subscribers on the list. There are two main types of email mailing lists.

1. An announcement list, used primarily as a one-way flow of information that can only be posted by selected people.
2. A discussion list enables any subscriber to use the mailing list to send messages to all the other subscribers, who may answer in similar fashion. The actual discussion and information exchanges build a sense of community. Discussion mailing lists are usually topic-oriented (e.g. politics, educational groups, business discussions, cultural groups). To keep discussions focused on areas of interest and to eliminate spam, some discussion lists have a moderator who must approve every message before it is sent to the rest of the subscribers.

> An **electronic mailing list** is a list of names and email addresses of subscribers used for sending publications to an organisation's customers.

Netiquette

Netiquette is used to maintain and promote goodwill between the writer and the receiver. There are many do's and don'ts to consider when writing an email. Although netiquette is a set of guidelines only, following these guidelines can help to raise your profile and make it more likely that your email is treated as high priority.

A professional email message is courteous and confident. Writers using netiquette not only consider their own needs as a writer and the writing purpose, but also the receiver's need to understand and take action on the basis of the message.

> The term '**netiquette**' describes the conventions and accepted standards used by senders of a message online.

INTERNET ADDRESSES

Each part of an Internet address has a specific purpose. The minimum acceptable format is the least a writer can use to make his or her email message readable; extra parts can be used for specific purposes.

The Internet postal system works in a similar manner to letter postal services. The header on the piece of email is the equivalent of a postmark on a letter. The date and time the message is sent and received (and the difference between it and Greenwich Mean Time) is shown in the header.

Internet addresses must be accurate. One incorrect digit and the email will go to the wrong location. Although Internet addresses are usually upper- and lower-case insensitive, the general rule is to use lower case. An Internet address contains the user ID at a site or domain. The domain identifies the organisation running the site and the kind of site. The organisation suffix at the end of the email address identifies the type of organisation. Examples are shown in Table 21.7.

Table 21.7: Examples of organisation suffixes in email addresses	
Suffix	*Used for*
com	Commercial businesses
org	Non-profit organisations
gov	Government organisations
net	Companies or organisations that run large networks
mil	Government and military organisations
edu	Educational institutions

Giving the receiver several ways to make contact is helpful. This information can be placed under the complimentary close and signature block. Add the web page address and the receiver can quickly go to their browser and find it.

Internet addresses and the layout of email addresses now follow a standard that may change in response to future demands by users. As happens with any new development, it takes time to determine new standards and to have them accepted as conventions.

USING COMPUTER TECHNOLOGY

Software programs also contain special features that allow you to write more effectively. These include outlining/headings, cut and paste, microediting, footnotes, page numbers, and tools such as thesaurus, spell check and grammar check. You can also improve your documents by adding sounds to emphasise, add interest and clarify points. It is possible to add background music, colour pictures and video clips. However, it is important to consider your audience before deciding what to include.

DRAFS email management system

Arnold (2002) developed the acronym DRAFS—delete, reply, act, forward, save—as an efficient strategy for managing email. Table 21.8 describes the purpose of each part of the acronym.

Table 21.8: DRAFS email strategy

Acronym	Strategy
D: Delete	• Delete unwanted and out-of-date messages • Install spam filters to delete junk mail before it appears on your screen • Avoid responding to senders of junk email
R: Reply	• Reply as soon as possible • Send a brief response to let the sender know you are working on your reply when the response is complicated or you do not have the time to respond within the first working day of receiving the email • Use a subject line that identifies the message clearly or refers to previous interactions on the topic • Use the Out of Office tool as a courtesy to tell those sending you emails when you will return
A: Act	• Allocate time to the actions you must take in response to emails—high-priority tasks now, less important jobs as soon as possible • Avoid procrastination and the need to open and handle your emails more than once
F: Forward	• Forward and *cc* emails only to those who need to know, to avoid overloading others with excessive email • Respect privacy by ensuring your emails do not breach confidentiality
S: Save	• Organise those emails you need to keep into folders and subfolders • Archive the emails you wish to keep on your hard drive.

REVIEW QUESTIONS

5. Email is an integral part of an organisation's internal and external communication. Why?
6. What is the purpose of an email subject line?
7. What is the purpose of an email mailing list?
8. What are the advantages and disadvantages of email? How can the disadvantages be avoided?

INSTANT MESSAGING AND TEXT MESSAGING

Instant messaging (IM) allows easy collaboration in real time. It is a faster and simpler communication channel than email. It presents fewer security and privacy issues and fewer unwanted messages than email. Most IM systems allow the user to display an online status message to notify others they are available, busy, or away from the computer.

Instant messaging conveys information quickly and efficiently. It allows instantaneous communication between a number of parties. Continuous improvements in technology enable sender and receiver to see one another by using web-cams and talk directly for free over the internet. IM conversations can be saved for later reference. People are not forced to reply immediately to incoming messages, so instant messaging is less intrusive than communication via phone. In contrast to email, the parties know whether others are available, and mobile communication devices allow users to send and receive IM anywhere.

IM at work is a business form of communication and the conventions are expected. Present a professional image by avoiding poor grammar, incorrect spelling, the use of informal language, emoticons, and the shortening of longer or commonly used words. Conversations in the workplace are more formal and serious than social conversation. Incorrect use or abuse of IM can:

- increase security risks—for example, infecting computers with viruses or worms
- increase compliance risks
- lead to theft of intellectual property and breach of copyright.

IM capabilities can mimic conversation, display documents, or allow people to interact simultaneously by keying information, questions, answers and comments. The capabilities include automated newsfeeds from blogs and websites, and basic chat and presence awareness. IM services are available on PCs, mobile phones and PDAs.

If emailing is not possible, a cheap alternative to telephoning is the increasingly popular **text messaging** using a mobile phone. For a moderate cost, short messages can be left for the recipient. In addition to cost savings, a significant benefit is being able to make contact without interrupting the recipient. Disadvantages include the disruption caused by the loud beep or tone that indicates receipt of the message and the limited number of characters that can be sent. Text messaging, because of its space limitations, has given rise to an abbreviated form of communication called neticisms that needs to be read in context (see Tables 21.9 and 21.10).

> ◀ OBJECTIVE 4
> Explain the role of instant messaging (IM) and text messaging in business communication

Instant messaging (IM) offers the benefits of rapid response, lower cost and wide availability.

Text messaging refers to sending short text messages from a mobile phone to other mobile phone users using the SMS standard. It usually means messaging that takes place between two or more mobile devices.

Table 21.9: Examples of abbreviations in text messaging

Abbreviation	Meaning
r	are
u	you
b4	before
attg	attending
\gr8	great
4	for
nite	night
pls	please
ty	thank you
wtg	waiting
2day	today

Table 21.10: Examples of common neticisms

BTW	By the way
FWIW	For what it's worth
IMHO	In my humble opinion
OTOH	On the other hand
ROTFL	Rolling on the floor laughing
RTFM	Read the ————— manual
TTFN	Ta ta for now

Source: Kristen Bell DeTienne, *Guide to Electronic Communication: Using Technology for Effective Business Writing and Speaking*, Pearson Education, New Jersey, 2002, p. 46. Reprinted by permission of Pearson Education, Inc.

In addition to written text messages, MMS picture messaging makes it possible to send and receive messages with text, pictures and attached sounds. Although the cost is greater, this new visual way of messaging is expected to complement and perhaps eventually supersede the present text messaging.

REVIEW QUESTIONS

9 What are the benefits of text messaging to an organisation?

10 What are the differences between instant messaging and text messaging?

APPLY YOUR KNOWLEDGE

EFFECTIVE EMAIL MESSAGES, IM AND TEXT MESSAGES

1 Work in small groups.

   a Brainstorm the advantages businesses have gained by replacing traditional memos with email.

   b Discuss the impact of the overuse of email in business.

   c Identify strategies to prevent the overuse of email.

   d Report back to the large group and compare your answers.

2 Work in small groups to discuss the following:

   • the relative importance of electronic communication channels

   • the impacts of communication via these channels

   • how these electronic channels of communication have changed the way people communicate.

   Prepare, as a group, an email message to your lecturer detailing your conclusions.

3 Complete the following checklist. For any 'No' response, decide how you will fill that knowledge gap.

4 Compare and contrast email and instant messaging as channels for business messages.

5 Participate in an IM session. Use the following checklist to evaluate your performance.

EMAIL PROTOCOLS

I am able to:	Yes	No
alphabetise recipients' addresses to avoid sending signals of hierarchy		
use special features to hide other readers if i don't want these known		
check that the email has been delivered		
refrain from sending copies to other recipients if it is not necessary		
refrain from sending an email when angry or upset		
check that the correct attachments are included and that they translate to other servers		
work within requirements of different time zones, particularly if an immediate response is required		
send a short reply to acknowledge receipt if i need to take time to consider my response		
delete unwanted messages immediately, to minimise clutter and clear disk storage space		
check the system for viruses, especially when downloading from other systems		
check my mailbox's limit and delete unwanted messages immediately to make the inbox easier to use		
understand and follow my company's email policy		

RATE YOUR UNDERPINNING KNOWLEDGE OF IM

Do I:	Yes	No
start by always asking if the person I am IMing is available and if it is a good time to chat?		
communicate briefly and clearly? IM generally only allows 512 characters (79 words) per message.		
avoid using IM for confidential messages, complex messages or personal messages?		
use the features of the IM program, such as Busy and Away messages, to let those trying to communicate know my availability?		
never IM under an alias?		
avoid using IM slang?		
send quality messages that are professional, use business language and maintain good business etiquette?		
control IM to avoid continual interruptions to my work flow?		
observe security and privacy issues?		
follow organisational IM guidelines and legal requirements?		

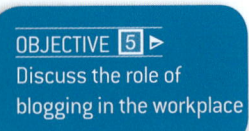

OBJECTIVE 5 ▶

Discuss the role of
blogging in the workplace

A **blog** is a website where
messages are written and
can be combined with
music, audio, photographs
and video.

THE ROLE OF BLOGGING

Business blogs are used as both internal and external communication. **Blogs** send information quickly within the organisation to improve communication and the organisation's culture. Blogs are used externally as a mass communication channel to deliver marketing information about new products and to gather feedback from existing clients. Blogs designed for public relations purposes deliver messages about the latest company news and successes with the general public. Lemay (2008, p. 65) states: 'Dell also runs an online blog associated with IdeaStorm, Direct2Dell, where it publishes articles and videos to customers, responds to feedback, and generally interacts in a more focused way than it can through IdeaStorm.'

Blogs support collaboration by multiple contributors on specific topics or even specific development projects. Some blogs are interesting, factual and informative. Others are simply thoughts and opinions, many without substance or proof. Critically evaluate the information on business blogs.

Fitzgerald (2006) suggests: 'Blogs provide a quick way to publish on the Web and even create an online version of a water cooler discussion.' He presents the following three ground rules for blogging: '1. Know why you're blogging. 2. Know your reader . . . know who you would like to have read your blog, and why. 3. Know the drill . . . the time commitment . . . it's OK to post occasionally, as long as you're up front about your likely frequency.' Business blogs are used to:

- spread the corporate culture
- seek feedback from clients
- help teams collaborate
- help sell products or services
- encourage interaction between geographically dispersed staff
- provide up-to-date information during an emergency
- correct misinformation and rumours across the company.

The tone of a blog is usually informal and written in a conversational style. However, for business blogging, always parallel the culture of your organisation. Remember that blogs at work are a business form of communication and the conventions are expected. Criticism of an employer, a competitor, supplier or staff member on a blog is unacceptable.

Fitzgerald (2006) gives the following five tips for writing blogs:

Keep it short. And skimmable.
Get thick skin. Know that your blog will generate comments you might not want to hear . . .
Blogs are forever, or reasonably close to it. Remember that blogs are permanent and searchable . . .
Check grammar and spelling . . . sloppiness reflects poorly on me and my company.
The rules can be broken . . .

Copyright is a type of legal protection for people who express ideas and information in certain forms. The most common forms are writing, visual images, music and moving images. Copyright of any published material, including web-published material, is usually held by the writer, their employer or publisher. To take someone's work without their permission to reproduce that work is plagiarism. Plagiarism of other people's work is unethical and illegal.

For web-based forms of communication, links are an accepted and convenient way to access related information. Instead of copying substantial portions of work from other sites, provide a link. Readers are diverted away from your page by links, but there are advantages you may not consider at first. Advantages include:

- linking to authoritative sources is likely to improve credibility
- keeping up to date is the responsibility of the link site
- opportunities arise to build a business relationship with the linked sites.

Netiquette requires you to make contact with the web manager or other contact person before linking to their site. This is usually done by email to provide a written record of the request and response.

Those requesting links often offer a reciprocal link. Never create a link without seeking permission, because the host site may do a web search of phrases and key words to see if its text is being copied. Alternatively, they could do an Internet search for their URL to check if their content is being copied.

REVIEW QUESTIONS

11 *a* What is the role of blogging in the workplace?

b Discuss three ground rules for blogging.

12 Identify three advantages gained by using links to other websites, rather than copying substantial portions of work from other sites to your blog.

THE ROLE OF PODCASTS

A **podcast** is a digital media file, or related collection of such files, distributed over the Internet for play back on portable media players and personal computers. The entertainment world uses podcasts to present trailers as downloads, to allow movie and music fans to view these new 'teaser trailers' on the way to work or at home in order to create interest in an upcoming movie or album due for release.

A podcast is an effective medium for advertising because it can be downloaded at any time, anywhere. New smartphones—for example, iPhones—have wireless capability and special computer-enabled features not previously associated with telephones. Features including wireless email, Internet, web browsing, fax, local and remote data transfer between phone set and computers, and online banking provide numerous business opportunities. A podcast can be directly downloaded to an iPhone anywhere at any time.

Global companies are able to hold their half-yearly financial meetings and beam them internationally across a website. A podcast can then be created of this to allow the media and stakeholders of the meeting to take the board members' speeches away for further analysis. As the podcast is multimedia capable, PowerPoints and slide shows can be added to give the stakeholders even more relevant information.

Universities use podcasts as tools to educate students by providing lectures as downloads for further analysis. Lecturers can set up a podcast with a right-hand slide PowerPoint presentation and a left-hand video of them talking about the slides in a previous lecture to jog students' memory.

Podcasts and blogs are appropriate channels of business communication whenever there is a continuing flow of information to share with the receivers. Podcasts can be transcribed into blogs and vice versa. The 3 × 3 writing process provides a systematic approach to creating the content of podcasts. In phase 1 of the process, decide the purpose and scope of the podcast. In this phase, analyse the audience and anticipate their needs. In phase 2, write the podcast. Create a specific descriptive title to capture the audience's attention.

Prepare a written outline. The written outline serves two purposes. It organises the ideas and can be used to provide a summary of the episode in the form of **show notes**. Some writers prefer to write one or two paragraphs to use as the show notes, or summary, of the episode. The show notes let people see as well as listen to the podcast. The show notes should include enough information to catch attention without telling the whole story. Aim to add interest and attract the eye by including relevant images.

Incorporate *transitional* words and phrases to mark a path for the reader. Transitional expressions indicate sequence, compare or contrast, give examples, indicate time, and summarise or conclude. Their purpose is to join ideas and indicate relationships.

Some of the audience will access podcasts through audio indexing and search. Key words or phrases relevant to each episode should be included in the show notes to help bring those who search

◄ OBJECTIVE **6**

Adapt the 3 × 3 writing process to podcasts

A **podcast** is a digital media file that is able to be taken off a website and added to a portable media device.

Show notes are an outline of the contents of each episode of a podcast.

the Web for podcasts of interest to a site. The show notes should also display addresses, phone numbers, email addresses, or other details that are difficult to remember.

In phase 3 of the 3 × 3 process, edit, revise, proofread and evaluate the message in the podcast. Review the approach and the recording of the podcast episode for a clear introduction, middle section and conclusion. Bovée and Thill (2005) say: 'Finally, consider integrating your podcasting efforts with a related blog. Not only can you provide additional information, but you can use the commenting feature of the blog to encourage feedback fron your audience.'

Characteristics of effective podcasts

Podcasting provides the opportunity for collaboration across a general mass audience or for specific peer-to-peer interaction about a relevant issue or topic. Effective podcasts have a theme that captures enough interest to sustain audience participation and reward the effort put into establishing the podcast. The characteristics common to effective podcasts are:

- identifying the purpose and scope of the podcast to ensure it meets the needs of the audience
- planning and ordering the information to avoid meandering around the topic and confusing the audience
- communicating with a personal style, a good clear voice, and introducing new information briefly and clearly
- presenting content that provides a clear pathway by using introductions, previews, transitions from one segment to another, conclusions and reviews to prevent the audience 'switching off'
- encouraging others in the session to join the conversation in order to maintain interest and provide the opportunity for ongoing collaboration and sharing
- participating professionally by using business language and maintaining good business etiquette and ethics
- observing security and privacy issues
- following organisational guidelines and legal requirements
- syndicating the podcast if required via the RSS process.

The **syndication** process distributes, through web feeds, the content of blogs, podcasts and other digital communication channels to subscribers who receive it via aggregators.

A **web feed** (or news feed) is a data format used for providing users with frequently updated content via content distributors who syndicate a web feed, thereby allowing users to subscribe to it.

REVIEW QUESTIONS

13 When are podcasts appropriate channels of business communication?

14 Discuss the characteristics of effective podcasts.

15 How do transitional expressions help a podcast audience?

OBJECTIVE 7 ▶
Explain the role of syndication

THE ROLE OF SYNDICATION

The **syndication** process enables content owners to publish content updates from web pages, blogs, podcasts and other kinds of digital media. Summaries, précis or headlines, rather than full content, are published in the web feed. Common sources for web feeds are blogs, podcasts and news websites. Web feeds provide users with frequently updated content. A **web feed** is a document that contains content items with web links to longer versions.

Owners of content syndicate a web feed to which users can subscribe. Selected information is then distributed through the web feed. Web feeds are operated by many news websites, weblogs, podcasters and other digital communication media. A collection of web feeds can be aggregated or made accessible in one spot by software programs known as **aggregators**. Aggregators are scheduled to check for new content periodically. Really Simple Syndication (RSS) is another common web feed format.

An **aggregator** is a web application that makes a collection of syndicated web content such as news headlines, blogs and podcasts accessible in a single location for easy viewing.

One problem for the content owner is 'scraping'. Scraping occurs when an unknown third party creates a feed from a website, blog or podcast without the content owner's knowledge. The result is lack of confidentiality and unauthorised distribution of the content.

Syndication enables business users to access content such as latest company policies, news and stock quotes on their personal page. Additional feeds can be used to add content from other sites to personalised pages. Exposure to threats associated with email—spam, viruses, phishing and identity theft—is minimised when subscribing to a feed because users do not disclose their email address. Organisations verify compliance with guidelines about the use of digital channels by using a web feed server behind their firewall to distribute, manage and track the use of internal and external web feeds by users and groups.

One of the challenges for those syndicating a podcast or blog is to connect with the intended audience. Web feeds that are easy for potential subscribers to find will be readily accessed. Content owners can list in any of the Webmaster Directories that specialise in the relevant digital medium for publication to provide access to a wider audience. The sites VOISD Webmaster Directory <www. Voisd.com> and Best of the Web Blogs <http://blogs.botw.org> provide services for creators of blogs, industry news and a range of other digital mediums. **Tagging** uses one-word descriptors to highlight content and points of interest to potential subscribers. Sites such as 'del.icio.us social bookmarking' <http://del.icio.us> help audiences to locate sites for research, collaboration or specific content. The use of directories and tagging benefits both content owners and receivers.

> **Tagging** is a popular way to locate, classify, rank and share Internet resources through the use of shared lists of user-created Internet bookmarks.

REVIEW QUESTIONS

16 Define the terms 'syndication' and 'aggregators'.

17 What does the syndication process let content owners do?

18 *a* Identify a problem for the content owner.

   b How can the threat posed by this problem be minimised?

MANAGING INFORMATION OVERLOAD

> ◄ OBJECTIVE 8
> Discuss the effects of information overload

One of the biggest problems in today's technological world is the amount of information that can be accessed and the ongoing number of interactions with others. There are increasing amounts of data available via the Internet, an increasing number of phone calls, emails, voicemails, items by post, inter-office memos, faxes, mobile phone calls and meetings to handle.

> Information overload can cause continuous partial attention.

The main difficulty is discriminating between what is necessary and useful, and what is useless. Bovée and Thill (2005, p. 13) comment: 'Email traffic alone is mushrooming toward an estimated 60 billion messages a day.' The heavy reliance on email messages by organisations has led to a massive amount of information being communicated daily. The increasing use of blogs and podcasts has led to more opportunities for interruptions and distractions from the prime activities in any job.

Continuous partial attention

Linda Stone, Vice-President of Corporate and Industry Initiatives at Microsoft, has coined the term '*continuous partial attention*' to describe the way people are coping with the barrage of communication. She states: 'With continuous partial attention, we're scanning incoming alerts for the one best thing to seize upon: "How can I tune in, in a way that helps me sync up with the interesting or important opportunity?"' She says that it is crucial for CEOs to break free from continuous partial attention and recommends they pause to reflect, focus, think a problem through, and then take steady steps forward in an intentional direction (cited in Maxwell 2002). Some companies have dealt with information overload by introducing various measures, including:

- restricting times for email use by shutting down the system for periods of time
- encouraging employees to send fewer emails
- discouraging the use of the word 'urgent'
- putting company news, manuals and minutes on company databases to be accessed at times convenient to employees.

Reuters (1996) conducted a worldwide study called 'Dying for Information', and found that information overload was a problem in the information age. Managers suffer from increased tension, and one-third from ill-health, because of information overload. The symptoms include anxiety, poor decision making, difficulties in memorising and remembering, and reduced attention span. Information overload adds to the individual stress caused by the need for managers to adapt to a rapidly changing environment. Too much information leads not only to stress, but also to decreasing effectiveness and productivity in the business world.

Reed (1995) highlights the need to manage information and make decisions about version control: how to review and change documents, and how to identify who added, deleted, updated or approved amendments. 'At present in our long transition from a paper-based society to an electronic society, forms of communication are in flux and we are all participating in the development and mutation of currently accepted forms into new ones suited to the digital era'.

The current move is to 'just-in-time' publishing. Information in its most up-to-date form is printed quickly when requested, rather than being printed ahead of time. The Australian Vice-Chancellors Committee (2001) discusses a number of issues relating to information technology, including the change in emphasis from libraries as collection-based services to access-based information services and the need to establish common interfaces and standards for information access. Privacy and copyright protection present challenges for online content creators. The Australian Government Information Management Office (2007) provides comprehensive information about intellectual property, copyright and privacy issues.

More research is necessary to successfully manage the explosion of information, which can only worsen as more and more people gain access to online technology. People are being flooded with more information (often useless trivia) than they can effectively process. Being able to manage this information flow and convert it into knowledge is an important skill to develop.

Data and information must be translated into knowledge.

Actions based on the management of knowledge make an organisation more competitive than those who simply respond to changes in the environment. Organisations need people who can use the new technologies and understand, interpret and manage information to meet customer and other stakeholder expectations. Those who manage knowledge well are able not only to create new ways of doing things, but also to recognise existing problems and discover emerging and potential problems. They are able to transform the knowledge into creative ideas that can be used to solve problems.

APPLY YOUR KNOWLEDGE

BLOGS AND PODCASTING

1. Some blogs focus on a particular subject, such as politics, travel, fashion, specific projects or legal issues.
   a. Choose a subject of interest to you. Assume you already have a blog site on that subject. Decide whether your blog is to inform, persuade or entertain.
   b. Prepare four blog entries on your subject to post sequentially on the blog. Identify the headings and sections clearly.
   c. Use the checklist below to review and edit your blog. Make any corrections and post the blog entries over the next week.

2. Analyse three podcasts:
   a. create the criteria you will use to rate the podcasts
   b. view the podcasts and rate them as best, medium, worst
   c. decide how to improve the podcast you rated worst.
3. What is the purpose of syndication?
4. Read the statement: 'The challenge from the current information overload is to get the most relevant, meaningful, contextualised information so that we can turn that into useful knowledge and wisdom.'
   a. Identify three strategies to deal with information overload.
   b. Describe the advantages gained by breaking away from a continuous partial attention span.

SELF-EVALUATE YOUR SKILL

RATE YOUR UNDERPINNING KNOWLEDGE OF BLOGGING

Am I able to:	Yes	No
use blogging to provide information, feedback and the opportunity to collaborate with a specific interest group or audience about ongoing issues?		
identify the purpose and scope of the blog to ensure it meets my communication purpose and the needs of the audience?		
communicate with a personal style, a good clear voice and careful writing?		
present topics of interest to the audience?		
introduce new information briefly and clearly?		
encourage others in the session to join the conversation in order to maintain interest and provide the opportunity for ongoing collaboration and sharing?		
participate professionally by using business language and maintaining good business etiquette and ethics?		
offer a newsfeed option so that subscribers have access to automatic updates?		
observe security and privacy issues?		
follow organisational blogging guidelines and legal requirements?		

REVIEW QUESTIONS

19. Briefly describe the concept of 'information overload' and its effects.
20. Give examples of ways in which companies have tried to deal with information overload.
21. What is *continuous partial attention,* and how does it help people to cope with information overload?

SUMMARY OF LEARNING OBJECTIVES

1 ▷ DISCUSS THE CHARACTERISTICS OF ELECTRONIC MEDIA APPROPRIATE TO BUSINESS MESSAGES

Email is a low-cost, widely available and fast way to communicate. Disadvantages include overuse, spam, lack of privacy and security issues. Instant messaging is faster than email but requires sender and receiver to be online at the same time. Text messaging has the advantage of mobility and portability, but the small screen and phone pad size can be difficult for some users. Blogs are used for communication between teams or individuals within an organisation, and also to communicate new information and issues to those outside the organisation. Businesses use podcasts to publish and broadcast messages to their internal and external audiences.

Regardless of the type of media used to convey a message electronically, three criteria apply—simplicity, clarity and visibility. Language, ideas and structure should be audience-centred and appropriate to the purpose.

2 ▷ APPLY THE 3 × 3 WRITING PROCESS AS YOU WRITE BUSINESS MESSAGES FOR ELECTRONIC MEDIA

The 3 × 3 writing process follows three phases. Phase 1 is prewriting—you analyse, anticipate and adapt the approach to meet your purpose, the information you need to convey and the audience's needs. Phase 2 is the writing stage. Clear and positive language enables the receiver to understand the message, the required actions and who is to take the action. Select, organise and shape the message as you write. Phase 3 is editing, when you revise, proofread and evaluate the message.

3 ▷ CREATE EFFECTIVE EMAIL MESSAGES

Before writing an email, decide on your writing purpose and then select and organise the content into the most appropriate sequence. Build coherent paragraphs, or use bullet points or numbering when appropriate. Before you send the email, review and edit it to check that the purpose is clear and the message is appropriate to the receiver's needs. Is it courteous and confident or rude and abrupt? Is the information accurate? Would you be happy for the email to be forwarded to others and kept in records, or is it poorly written and formatted? Does the email follow organisational email guidelines and respect the chain of command? The DRAFS email management system stands for delete/reply/act/forward/save.

4 ▷ EXPLAIN THE ROLE OF INSTANT MESSAGING (IM) AND TEXT MESSAGING IN BUSINESS COMMUNICATION

IM is a quick and cost-effective way for businesses to communicate. IM capabilities can mimic conversation, display documents, and allow people to interact simultaneously by keying information, questions, answers and comments. The capabilities include automated newsfeeds from blogs and websites, and basic chat and presence awareness. IM services are available on PCs and mobile phones. Text messages are written, but using MMS picture messaging makes it possible to send and receive messages with text, pictures and attached sounds.

5 ▷ DISCUSS THE ROLE OF BLOGGING IN THE WORKPLACE

A blog is the appropriate form of business communication whenever there is a continuing flow of information to share with the receivers. Business blogs are used to spread the corporate culture, seek feedback from clients, help teams collaborate, help sell products or services, encourage interaction between geographically dispersed staff, provide up-to-date information during an emergency, and correct misinformation or rumours.

6 ▷ ADAPT THE 3 × 3 WRITING PROCESS TO PODCASTS

The three phases in the writing process provide a system that podcasters can use to complete the prewriting, writing and editing activities. Attention-grabbing headlines and show notes attract visitors to the podcast.

7 ▷ EXPLAIN THE ROLE OF SYNDICATION

The syndication process makes available a section of a website, blog, podcast or other digital communication medium for others to use. Syndication involves subscribing to a web feed for information in the form of headlines, précis or summaries of recently added content.

Currently, millions of online publishers, including newspapers, commercial websites and blogs, publish their latest news headlines, product offers or blog postings in standard-format newsfeeds.

► **DISCUSS THE EFFECTS OF INFORMATION OVERLOAD**

The Internet generates a massive amount of information daily. It can be difficult to discriminate between what is useful and what is not when browsing the Web or receiving email. A contributing factor is the increasing amount of junk email being received. This explosion of information has led to information overload. The practice of continuous partial attention has been one response. Efforts are being made to manage the problem of information overload, but more research into ways of dealing with it is required.

KEY TERMS

aggregator	602	instant messaging (IM)	597	syndication	602
blog	600	netiquette	595	tagging	603
electronic mail (email)	591	podcast	601	text messaging	597
electronic mailing list	595	show notes	601	web feed	602
emoticon	590	spam	593		

ACTIVITIES AND QUESTIONS

1 a If you are short of time when writing an email at work, you may be tempted not to plan the email, to rush the writing of it and to fail to read it over before sending. Why is this bad practice? What could be the consequences?

   b What differences in tone, style and format might you notice between an email from the staff social club about next Friday night's river cruise, and an email from an external customer enquiring about order delivery times?

   c You are starting a small business that sells specialised horticultural equipment. You are drafting some text to give to your web designer for your new promotional website. What tone, style and format should your text and the website feature?

2 'Web-based communities and hosted services such as social-networking sites, blogs and podcasts aim to facilitate collaboration and sharing between users.'

   a Why are more and more businesses using blogs and podcasts to communicate with their clients and publics?

   b Find an example of a business blog and describe the characteristics that make it effective (or ineffective).

3 a Find an example of a successful podcast.

   b Identify the characteristics that make it successful.

   c Briefly explain the purpose and scope of the podcast.

4 a An email list is an email-based facility to which individuals subscribe. Once subscribed, the individual will automatically receive any messages that are 'posted' to the list. Some lists archive their messages on a web page. Locate the archive pages from two different lists. Determine the nature of the online community that uses each list. What function does the list serve for these communities?

   b Discuss the role of an email list as a communication tool.

5 Find three articles that discuss use of the Internet in the workplace and its effect on productivity. Summarise each article and write a brief concluding overview of your research findings.

6 a Work in small groups to analyse this statement: 'A discussion about the Internet is also about the revolution in the lives of ordinary people that it has brought in a remarkably short period of time. So who's benefiting, who isn't and what are we going to do about it?' Brainstorm to create a list of the benefits of the Internet.

   b Create a three-column table. In column 1 identify at least six typical groups in society—for example, business, community, family and others. Place in column 2 the benefits the Internet provides to each group. In column 3 identify any disadvantages for each group.

   c Visit the *World Internet Project* home page, <www. worldinternetproject.net>, to access relevant and up-to-date information about the World Internet Project's research, publications and annual conferences, which look at the impact of new technologies.

7   Find out more about information overload. What is it? What are its effects on people and productivity? What solutions or management techniques are being suggested for information overload?

EXPLORING THE WEB

1   Visit the *Copyblogger* site <www.copyblogger.com/>, and read the advice you find about 'Introducing the A*I*D*A Formula for Blogging' (Clark 2007).
    a   What makes the AIDA formula the copywriter's best friend?
    b   How can the AIDA formula help a blogger?
    c   What advantage does a blogger gain by 'tacking' an E on to the end of the AIDA formula?
    d   Use the AIDA formula to prepare a blog entry on any topic of your choice.
2   a   The Office of the Privacy Commissioner site, <www.privacy.gov.au/>, provides 'Guidelines on workplace email, browsing and privacy (30/2/2000)' to assist organisations to create a policy or improve their existing policy. Search the Web and find other examples of email policies.
    b   Evaluate two of the policies by preparing a written response to each of the following questions.

    •   What are the main topics each policy covers?
    •   Is the onus on the employee to take a commonsense approach to use, or on the organisation to continually monitor emails?
    •   What disciplinary action is taken for a breach of policy? Give your opinion of the fairness of the policy and any possible disciplinary action.
    c   Conclude your written evaluation by comparing and contrasting the effectiveness of each email policy.
3   a   Expand your knowledge of netiquette rules by visiting the site 'RFC 1855 Netiquette guidelines', <www.dtcc.edu/>. It has a comprehensive set of for mail and talk online and for administrators.
    b   Conduct an Internet search to define the rules of netiquette.
    c   Write an appropriate set of rules for a small business with three networked offices.

PROJECT WORK

1   You are given two principles for ethical conduct by bloggers.
    Principle 1: I will never engage in deceptive conduct online.
    Principle 2: I will fully disclose who I am and who I work for (my identity and affiliations) when communicating on a blog.

Suggest another three principles.
2   Choose two blogs and use your five principles for ethical conduct to write a critical evaluation of each blog's application of ethical principles.
3   Identify strategies for effective participation in a podcast. In the following table, list practical ways to develop or improve each skill.

Table 21.11: Seven skills for participation in podcasts

Skill	Practical strategy
1 To think better	
2 To plan better	
3 To research better	
4 To organise better	
5 To create better content	
6 To collaborate better	
7 To network better	

BIBLIOGRAPHY

Arnold, K.J. 2002. 'Email basics: practical tips to improve communication', in E. Biech (ed.), *The 2002 Annual Handbook, Vol. 1. Training*, Jossey-Bass, San Francisco.

Australian Government Department of Finance and Deregulation. *Web Publishing Guide*, http://webpublishing.agimo.gov.au, viewed 22 February 2008.

Australian Government Information Management Office. *Web Publishing Guide*, Department of Finance and Administration, http://webpublishing.agimo.gov.au, viewed 26 October 2007.

Australian Vice-Chancellors Committee. *Exploiting Information Technology in Higher Education: An Issues Paper*, AV-CC Publications, www.avcc.edu.au/news/public_statements/publications/eitihe/sec4.htm#4.3, 14 February 2001.

Barwell, G. 1995–1996. 'Electronic publishing: a measure of success', *Key Issues In Australian Electronic Publishing*, Australian Vice-Chancellors Committee, Electronic Publishing Working Group, www.adfa. oz.au/Epub/key/Opening.html, viewed 14 February 2001.

Best of the Web Blogs, Home Page, http://blogs.botw.org, viewed 14 October 2007.

Bovée, C.L. & Thill, J.V. 2005. *Business Communication Today*, 8th edn, Pearson Education, New Jersey.

Clark, B. 'Introducing the A*I*D*A formula for blogging', *Copyblogger*, www.copyblogger.com/aida-formula-for-blogging, viewed 26 October 2007.

'Conferencing: talk is cheap with Internet telephony', www.learnthenet.com/english/html/64teleph.htm, 27 March 2003.

Cooper, C. 2007. 'Future beckoning', *Management Today*, November/December, pp. 12–18.

Cramond, B. 1998. 'Framing the future web forum', Advisor Network & Staff Development, www.tafe.sa.edu.au/institutes/para/ftf/home.htm, 1 July.

del.icio.us social bookmarking, Home Page, http://del.icio.us, viewed 26 October 2007.

DeTienne, K.B. 2002. *Guide to Electronic Communication: Using Technology for Effective Business Writing and Speaking*, Pearson Education, New Jersey.

Diffuse. 'Guide to Internet privacy', www.diffuse.org/privacy.html, 23 February 2003.

Dollschneider, S. 1997. 'You may be a good communicator but are you a good facilitator?', *Communications World*, Vol. 14, Issue 3, February, UMI ProQuest ABI/INFORM, March 1998.

Fitzgerald, M. 2006. 'Welcome to my blog', *CIO Magazine online*, www.cio.com.au/index.php/, posted 3 July, viewed 31 October 2006.

Greengard, S. 1997. 'Extranets linking employees with your vendors', *Workforce*, November, pp. 28–34.

Hambridge, S. *RFC 1855 Netiquette Guidelines*, www.dtcc.edu/cs/rfc1855.html.

Lemay, R. 2008. 'Dell resurfaces', *AFR Boss Magazine*, Vol. 9, April, p. 65.

Maxwell, J.H. 2002. 'Stop the Net, I want to get off', *Inc. Magazine*, Vol. 24, Issue 1, January, p. 7.

Office of the Privacy Commissioner. *Guidelines on Workplace Email, Browsing and Privacy (30/2/2000)*, www.privacy.gov.au/internet/email, viewed 30 October 2007.

Price, R.P. 1997. 'An analysis of stylistic variables in electronic mail', *Journal of Business and Technical Communication*, Vol. 11, Issue 1, January, pp. 5–23.

Reed, B. 1995. 'A recordkeeping critique of document management systems', *Record Keeping Systems Publications*, www.recordkeeping.com.au/pub_docmgt3.html, viewed 10 April 2008.

Reuters. 1996. *Dying for Information*.

Schramm, R.M. & James, M.L. 1992. 'The impact of e-mail in today's organizations', *Office Systems Research Journal*, Vol II, Issue 1, pp. 3–13.

Sharman J.C. & Wilshire, C. 2007. 'Fighting plagiarism in Australian universities: why bother', *Australian Journal of Political Science*, Vol. 42, Issue 3, September, pp. 503–8.

SOFWeb, 'Discussion Groups—Using the Internet', www.sofweb.vic.edu.au/internet/discuss.html, viewed 6 March 2003.

VOISD. Webmaster Directory, Home Page, www.Voisd.com, viewed 24 October 2007.

World Internet Project, Home Page, www.worldinternet project.nets, viewed 24 October 2007.

Zorn, T.E. & Violanti, M.T. 1996. 'Communication abilities and individual achievement in organizations', *Management Communication Quarterly*, Vol. 10, Issue 2, November, CD-ROM Business Periodicals online.

Part 6

Employment Communication

22

Finding, applying and being interviewed for a position

Photo: Zimmytws/Dreamstime

LEARNING OBJECTIVES

After studying this chapter you should be able to:

1 ▷ locate employment market information

2 ▷ discuss the characteristics of effective résumés

3 ▷ choose the appropriate résumé (basic, functional or targeted) for the position and your qualifications

4 ▷ prepare an electronic résumé to align your qualifications to the needs of the position

5 ▷ write an effective application letter

6 ▷ differentiate between types of employment interviews

7 ▷ evaluate the stages in an employment interview

8 ▷ identify and discuss post-interview activities

9 ▷ discuss how to deal with problem interviews.

VIEWPOINT: MAKING THAT FIRST IMPRESSION COUNT

A well-written résumé can mean the difference between securing a job interview and ending in the recycling bin, John Dagge writes.

The résumé is your foot in the door, the first impression a potential employer has of you. It can be the difference between gaining an interview and getting a 'thanks but no thanks' letter.

Margot Scott, Centre for Career Development, advises clients to list duties and career achievements under two separate headings. 'What people tend to do is mix their achievements and responsibilities . . . It's important to show that you can improve the workplace . . . Your résumé needs to be written for every job, it's not a static document.'

In an increasingly litigious employment environment, Jacqueline Allen, from DBM, says: 'Résumés should not include any personal details about your age, marital status, gender or religion.' Allen recommends including a profile statement—a 150-word summary of what you want from your career and what you can offer a prospective employer—on the front page.

Adapted from J. Dagge. 'Making that first impression count', My Career, *The Sun Herald*, 11 January 2004, p. 8.

A **résumé** is an informative, comprehensive document about your qualifications, experience and achievements.

Careful preparation is the key to a successful search for a position. Success in finding the right position depends on your ability to market yourself. A key component in the marketing process is the résumé. It should be a powerful document, whether for a first job, a move to another position, a change in career, a promotion or a consultant position.

The application is the only source of information a potential employer can use to decide whether you should be invited to an interview. Applicants are short-listed and called for interview because of the quality of their written application, so it is important to make it interesting, informative and persuasive. An electronic résumé is a targeted résumé with keywords.

At the interview your role is to demonstrate your interest in, and suitability for, the job. Your responses will focus on your capabilities, interests and expertise in order to secure the desired position.

OBJECTIVE **1** ▶
Locate employment market information

SEARCHING FOR A POSITION

When searching for a position, you have the option of consulting various established services, or using contacts and your own initiative. Examples of ways to find a position are set out in Table 22.1.

Why have a résumé?

A variety of reasons for having a **résumé** are set out in Table 22.2.

Table 22.1: Finding a position	
Strategy	**Purpose**
Online opportunities	The Internet lets you search quickly for vacant positions. A job search website, such as those listed below, allows you to search for vacancies by location (including international, national, state, region or capital city), by occupation, industry or advertiser. The jobs published in many newspapers are also available through job search websites which provide a wide variety of career resources—information on job seeking, sample résumés, career networking, training and skills, company research, employment news. • www.careerone.com.au • www.seek.com.au • www.positionsvacant.com.au • www.mycareer.com.au • www.jobsearch.gov.au • www.monsterboard.com.au—for international job opportunities
Newspapers	A common way of finding a position is to check the 'Positions Vacant' section in newspapers. • National, metropolitan and local newspapers advertise jobs, particularly on Mondays, Wednesdays and Saturdays. • The national papers advertise professional positions throughout their pages as well as in their 'Positions Vacant' sections. • Government organisations advertise as early as August or September for the general intake of employees for the next year. • Some private employers advertise around October or November. School leavers and TAFE and university graduates apply for many of these positions.

Employment agencies	• Many employers avoid advertising in the press because such large numbers of people apply for each position.
	• It can be too time-consuming to sort through all the applications and choose the best applicants to interview. Instead of advertising, these employers use the services of a private employment agency which matches the skills and qualifications of people on its register with the requirements of the position.
	• Entering the words 'employment agencies' or 'recruitment agencies' into a search engine will give you links to agency websites. Often you can register and store your profile and résumé with an employment agency via the Internet. The agency not only lists positions vacant but may also email you suitable job vacancies on a daily basis, provide potential employers with your details, and make your résumé available on their website for recruiting employers to access.
Networking	Employers fill the position through their own networks of professional and business contacts, or social and family contacts.
	• Create your own network of friends, neighbours, sporting and social clubs, and contacts at work.
	• Let people in your network know that you are in the market for a job or change of employment. Ask someone to be your personal or professional referee. If they agree, tell them about the kind of work and position you are looking for. This way, people in your network can pass on information and may even recommend you for a position.
Publications	Most professional associations publish journals and many of these carry advertisements for positions.
	• Use the computer facilities at the library to find journals published by companies and potential employers.
	• The library also files government gazettes, such as the 'Public Service Notices', which list government positions.
	• Information about organisations and potential contacts for employment can be found in: —the business news section of local and national newspapers —the latest version of the Yellow Pages telephone directory —industry publications, which also report on current developments and trends in industry —company brochures and annual reports, which outline the company's history, size and activities —employer directories such as *The Business Who's Who* and *Kompass*.
Direct mail campaign (cold canvassing)	When looking for a job, you may decide to go one step further and seek opportunities through cold canvassing, or a direct mail campaign. Applying for unadvertised positions widens your opportunities.
	• Determine the skills you have and the type of position suited to them.
	• Decide which companies might offer employment that matches your qualifications and aspirations.
	• Search for your targets.
	• Forward your résumé and letter of application.
Temping and freelancing	• Temping is a growing part of the job market. Register your availability as a temporary worker by contacting recruitment agencies directly, or via their Internet websites. Agencies will interview, test for competency in communication skills, and cross-check with the details on your résumé before placing you on their register.
	• As well as searching on the Internet, you can apply directly to an organisation either by email or by letter, offering your services and requesting an interview. Emphasise the benefits that freelancing has for an employer—for example, flexibility, contract rates and reduced overheads.

Table 22.2: Reasons for having a résumé	
Reason	**Strategy**
To clarify your direction and career goals	• Identify qualifications and accreditations. • Highlight strengths and boost your confidence. • Commit to finding a job or making a career change.
To pass the employer's screening process	• Present facts that might favourably influence the employer. Show how you can meet the specific job requirements. • Provide contact information: an up-to-date address and a telephone number that will always be answered during business hours. • Highlight transferable skills and experiences.
To establish you as a professional person	• Demonstrate high standards by using business writing style. • Organise the content into sections that focus on skills and abilities. • Format the résumé professionally. • Use good-quality paper and printing for a professional appearance.
To have something to give to potential employers	• Give the résumé to your job-hunting contacts and professional referees to provide background information. • Give out your résumé in *informational interviews* with a request for a critique (a creative way to cultivate the support of a new contact). • Send as a follow-up to any informal initial contact about a position.
To use as an appendix or attachment	• Provide as part of a grant or contract proposal. • Submit as an accompaniment to a college or university application. • Provide as part of a tender submission. • Keep in human resource records such as personnel files.

Highlighting your experience, skills and qualities

Networking is a positive way of building relationships, often to mutual advantage.

When you have found a position you want, give yourself the best chance of gaining the attention of an employer or recruitment agency by:

- assessing your qualifications, skills, interests, values and attitudes
- matching them to the requirements of the position
- writing a persuasive and powerful résumé.

Widen your job search by using a direct mail campaign.

Evaluate all your experiences and interests to reveal your main strengths and weaknesses and any talents or skills you may have overlooked or considered unimportant. People who feel they have little or no work experience relevant to an advertised position, or who have been out of the workforce for some time, may underrate their skills and abilities. For example:

Align your qualifications and experience to the position.

- University graduates entering the workforce should highlight their qualifications and use keywords to align these to the requirements of the position.
- Many graduates have developed their planning skills by organising school functions or by leadership and teamwork in sporting activities. School leavers also know how to manage time, set goals and work under pressure.
- Women returning to the paid workforce after being full-time homemakers have developed skills in stock control, budget management, organisation, planning, and getting along with others.

In voluntary social and welfare work, even though the work is unpaid, you gain valuable contacts, experience and skills that can be useful in other positions. Identify these strengths, then prepare the best résumé you can to showcase them and command the interest of potential employers and recruiters. Prepare a powerful résumé that tells the employer why you suit their position.

REVIEW QUESTIONS

1. Briefly outline three ways of finding a position in the employment market. Which way do you prefer? Why?
2. What are the main services offered on an online recruitment site?
3. What are the advantages and disadvantages of conducting a job search online?
4. Outline three reasons for having a résumé.

WRITING YOUR RÉSUMÉ

The purpose of your résumé is to win an interview. Command attention and impress those who read your résumé by:

◀ OBJECTIVE 2
Discuss the characteristics of effective résumés

- identifying the specific direct benefits you offer to fill the position
- showing how you match the needs of the employer, selection panel or recruitment agency
- choosing the type of résumé that suits your particular qualifications and experience
- using a writing style that makes the information in the résumé accessible and interesting to read
- using keywords that relate to the position requirements.

Using power action words to command attention

A résumé targeted to your goal and supported by action words has a powerful impact on the reader. Power words are *verbs*. They highlight your accomplishments and show the reader you have what it takes to be successful. Some examples are given in Table 22.3.

Power words highlight your accomplishments.

Table 22.3: Power action words for hard-copy résumés			
Communicating	**Managing**	**Creating**	**Administration**
Persuaded	Solved	Planned	Arranged
Mediated	Produced	Shaped	Achieved
Consulted	Reviewed	Designed	Organised
Developed	Analysed	Prepared	Prioritised
Cooperated	Initiated	Invented	Accomplished
Led	Implemented	Motivated	Wrote
Facilitated	Instituted	Tackled	Issued
Recommended	Tackled	Published	Selected
Presented	Targeted	Set up	Updated

Note that, for an electronic or keyword résumé, you will need to use stand-alone nouns as keywords to allow search engines to find (hit) your résumé. The keywords are used to match your skills to the computer search keyword or phrase. (Keyword résumés are discussed in the electronic résumé section of this chapter.) As you write the résumé, incorporate the power words and keep the guidelines in Table 22.4 in mind.

Writing style

In a résumé, write action-oriented short statements that are direct and easy to understand. Avoid sprawling sentences with too many points or ideas to grasp, or too many qualifications to each point. They only confuse the reader.

Punctuation achieves for your résumé what pauses and inflection do for spoken communication. Use it correctly to keep your points distinct and your message clear.

KEYWORD SECTIONS

Use a section of keywords, placed early in the résumé, to help recruiters sort your résumé into the pile for invitation to an interview. **Keywords** match the requirements of the position and motivate employers

Keywords are the words searchers type into search engines to find what they want.

Table 22.4: Writing guidelines	
Guideline	**Description**
Use clear language	• Familiar, unambiguous words that move straight to the point to make an immediate impact on the potential employer or recruiter. • Choose words that are appropriate to the recruitment situation and the position you are applying for.
Use keywords	• Keywords (buzz words) are generally nouns (however, they can also include verbs). Use keywords that fit the essential, compulsory, advantageous or desirable categories in the position. • Use keywords to identify crucial skills and experience required of a successful candidate.
Remove unnecessary words	• Use no more words than needed to convey the meaning. • Edit carefully to avoid repetition.
Avoid clichés	• Meaning and impact are lost when hackneyed expressions or clichés are overused.
Use specific language	• Describe details precisely to aid understanding. • Make more impact by using concrete language that conveys a specific image that is easy to interpret. • Avoid general or theoretical language unless it is needed to add meaning.
Use technical terms carefully	• Technical terms (jargon) have a precise meaning and are useful when you write for those who are familiar with them. • Avoid them when you write for those who are unfamiliar with the technical meaning.
Use the active voice	• Lets the reader know exactly who does or did what. • Uses the subject-and-verb sequence to link the subject directly to the action in the structure of the sentence. • Active voice creates a sense of energy—passive voice slows the message down.
Choose non-discriminatory, inclusive language	• Sexist or racist messages carry hidden meanings that are offensive or demeaning to others. Avoid using them in your résumé or any other document.
Use parallel language	• Equivalent grammatical form links related ideas.

or recruiters to invite you to interview. Show you are results-oriented by using words that highlight the results of work done and your accomplishments. Use figures or percentages wherever possible.

A paragraph is dedicated to one main idea. To make your paragraphs work, you must ensure that the main point of each one stands out sharply. Some strategies that will help you with this are listed in Table 22.5. By the end of your résumé, the reader should realise that you are a strong candidate.

A courteous, confident tone is appropriate for a résumé. Humour and flowery expressions are not suitable.

Headings and layout

The order in which you present your information in the résumé is critical to its success. The rule is to use skill headings and to place the important points in positions that will draw the reader's attention to them. Think about your headings. Experience usually goes before education. 'Professional History' or 'Professional Experience' sound more impressive than 'Employment' or 'Work History'. Use skill headings and subheadings that match your résumé's career goal or objectives. Table 22.6 suggests suitable headings.

The way you lay out the information on the page affects the first impression of your résumé. Project a professional image and set out your résumé to:

- make maximum impact
- convince the reader you are an ideal candidate
- gain you an invitation to interview.

Organise your information so that the reader can follow its progress through the document. Highlight the main points with:

- headings
- numbered lists or sections

Table 22.5: Paragraphs	
Strategy	**Purpose**
Use a topic sentence	To place the keyword or main idea at the beginning or end of the paragraph.
Have at least two sentences in a paragraph	To make the idea easier to comprehend. In a résumé the general rule is no more than three sentences in a paragraph.
Use a stand-alone sentence as a paragraph	To emphasise a particular point—this strategy is suited to a résumé.
Vary paragraph length	To give variety to your writing.
Use verbs (action words)	To start bullet points and phrases that highlight: • actions • results or • achievements.
Give examples of accomplishments	• to demonstrate what you have done in the past and • show your strengths.
Use white space to avoid a cluttered page	To break up blocks of printed material that could otherwise overwhelm or discourage the reader.

Table 22.6: Headings that gain attention

Heading	Items to include
Experience	• List jobs in reverse chronological order from most recent to earliest. • Focus on the most recent or relevant jobs (summarise a number of the earliest jobs in one line or short paragraph). • Decide which is more impressive for the position—your job titles or the names of the organisations you worked for; present the most impressive of the two first and use boldface type if appropriate. • Describe the organisation in a phrase, put dates at the end of the job, to de-emphasise them. • Include volunteer roles that add weight to your résumé.
Education	• List education in reverse chronological order. • Place degrees or licences first (set degrees apart so they are easily seen) followed by certificates and in-house professional development programs. • Put in boldface whatever will be most impressive and include any major distinctions. • List selected course work if this will help convince the reader of your qualifications for the targeted job. • Include advanced training, summarising the information and including only what will impress the reader. • Include ongoing degree work and bracket the expected date of completion: e.g. B. Comm. (expected 2010).
Awards	• Place school awards in the Education section and state what the award was for. • Place commendations or praise under Awards and Commendations and quote the source. Include civic or community leadership awards.
Professional memberships	• Include those that are current, relevant and impressive. • Include leadership roles if appropriate. • Show how your membership in an association enhances your appeal as a prospective employee.
Publications	• Include if published. • Summarise if there are many.
Activities and interests	• Indicate a skill, knowledge or interest related to the employment goal, such as photography for someone in journalism. • Show well-roundedness, good physical health and knowledge of a subject relating to the position. • Include hobbies if you wish.
References	• State 'References available upon request' at the end of your résumé. • Bring photocopies of references to the interview, to be given to the employer upon request.

- underlining
- indenting
- shading
- white space.

Set out the material clearly and use space to make it easy to understand; the reader will welcome the break provided by white space. Table 22.7 provides some guidelines to help you create a professional layout.

Double-check to make sure your résumé is accurate and honest. Stretching the truth in a résumé may catch up with you at the interview. When your current job title is unrelated to your current career

Table 22.7: The key to success—a professional layout

- Use bold caps for your name on page 1.
- Put your name at the top of page 2.
- Put section headings, skills headings and important ideas in boldface.
- Spell out numbers up to and including ten; use the numerical form for numbers more than ten (as a general rule), unless they are the first words in a sentence.
- Spell out abbreviations unless they are unquestionably obvious.

goals, consider using skill headings rather than job title. Highlight and emphasise your strengths and accomplishments. The purpose of your résumé is to catch readers' attention, interest them and create the desire to invite you to an interview.

REVIEW QUESTIONS

5 Why should you use power words in your résumé?
6 Create a list of résumé-writing guidelines.
7 In a résumé, keywords are essential. Why?

APPLY YOUR KNOWLEDGE

MATCH YOUR ATTRIBUTES TO THE POSITION

1 Access a copy of one of the major newspapers for your state's capital city.
    a   Identify the main headings in the Positions Vacant section.
    b   Which sections would you look in if you were seeking a job that matched your current experience, qualifications and interests?
2 On the Internet, enter 'recruitment agencies', 'employment agencies' or 'job search' into a search engine. Following the links to three of the resulting websites listed.
    a   Describe the features of each website.
    b   Which sector of the job market does each website seem to target?
    c   Assess each website for its usefulness and decide if you will post your résumé on it.
    d   What benefits does the site offer to candidates?
    e   What services does the site offer to employers?
    f   How do employers and candidates register on the site?
    g   How can an employer:
        - add a job registration to the site?
        - search a current candidate list according to specific job criteria?
    h   What keywords would you use to search the Web for a position as a:
        - management accountant
        - web designer
        - temporary professional desktop publisher?

i   What are three items you could discuss on a recruitment agency's chat page?

j   Explain the differences (if any) between an online national recruitment website and an online global recruitment website.

k   Visit a generalist site such as a newspaper website and key in the words 'temporary' + 'jobs'. Prepare a résumé suited to one of the positions you find in this search.

3 a   Select a vacant position that interests you and that you are qualified for from a newspaper, publication or online.

b   What are the attributes that the employer considers essential and desirable in the successful candidate?

c   What are the headings you would use in a résumé to help you secure an interview for this position?

4 a   Brainstorm to create a list of facts about what a good résumé does.

b   Brainstorm to create a list of common fallacies about what a résumé does.

THREE TRADITIONAL TYPES OF RÉSUMÉ

OBJECTIVE 3 ▶
Choose the appropriate résumé (basic, functional or targeted) for the position and your qualifications

Format and order the information in the résumé skilfully to demonstrate personal standards of excellence and good written communication skills.

A résumé is the summary of your personal data: education, skills, qualifications, work experience, references, hobbies and interests. It is also referred to as a curriculum vitae, or CV. The résumé should make it easy for the employer, recruiter or selection panel to identify your strengths by showing them how your qualifications match the job requirements. In a résumé, concentrate on the attributes that are essential and desirable for the job.

A résumé is divided into two broad sections and further divided into subsections, each with a heading. Think about the two broad sections as the first half and the second half. The first half contains personal details and your employment objective. The second half contains assertions about how you fit the position, with objective evidence and supporting facts. Place evidence of your professional experience, accomplishments, affiliations and other factors in the second half of the résumé. The subsections in the first and second half of the résumé could be headed as shown in Table 22.8. You may want to vary the order of the subsections, or change them to suit a specific application or to highlight your particular strengths.

It is no longer necessary to mention your marital status or age in a résumé. If either of these personal details is necessary for the position, the interviewer will ask for them. If age and marital status have nothing to do with your ability to do the job, these questions should not be asked.

The three most common types of résumé are basic (general), functional and targeted. They are described in Table 22.9.

For each style of résumé, you must ensure that it:

- provides detailed, relevant information about your background, abilities and experience
- is written in an effective style using short, descriptive phrases in bullet-point form rather than lengthy sentences and paragraphs
- has a clear format with distinctive headings and subheadings
- uses a logical order of information.

Table 22.8: The two main sections of a résumé, with subsections	
First half	**Second half**
• personal details—place your name at the top so it is easy to find • employment objective	• professional experience • education • achievements • activities and interests • referees

Table 22.9: Three types of résumé

Type	Description
Basic résumé	• Includes all the usual parts of a résumé with appropriate headings, but is simpler and shorter than the functional résumé. • Suits those who have just left school or have little work experience. The headings shown in Figure 22.1 will help you to organise it.
Functional résumé	• Uses a different order of presentation from the basic résumé to make the most of a wide range of skills and work experience (see Figure 22.2). • As most employers are interested in seeing how your most recent experience matches their needs, present your work experience first, starting with most recent, and put the rest in reverse chronological order. • Develop subheadings that highlight the job functions in which you have demonstrated expertise—for example, supervisory, marketing, training, or sales skills and responsibility. • Use the advertisement as a guide for highlighting specific functions.
Targeted résumé	• Is targeted to your career goal. • Identifies the key skills, areas of expertise and body of experience the employer will be looking for. • Builds the résumé structure and content around the target.

A résumé is prepared to show how you fit the position, so great emphasis is placed on those aspects of the document that demonstrate skills or experience relevant to the job. Plan the résumé to suit the position, highlight your strengths and win an interview.

Basic résumé

The **basic résumé** suits those who have just left school or have little work experience. The headings shown in Figure 22.1 will help you to organise a basic résumé.

A **basic résumé** includes all the usual parts of a résumé with appropriate headings, but is simpler and shorter than the functional and targeted résumés.

Functional résumé

In a **functional résumé**, each skill or work experience should be highlighted according to its relevance to the essential and desirable qualifications of the position. A functional résumé suits a public sector position. The third type of résumé, a targeted résumé, can also be used to address the selection criteria used by most public sector agencies. It is essential to make a careful study of the advertisement as you prepare your résumé so that you can present your experiences in terms of the criteria listed for the position.

Make it easy for the selection panel, or the person responsible for the cull, to identify your strengths. There is no point in writing your whole life history if, in the process, you bury the attributes that are essential and desirable for the job. Information that is irrelevant to the job makes it difficult for the panel or interview to find what is relevant. Figure 22.2 shows the layout of a functional résumé.

The **functional résumé** places emphasis on skills and experience gained through previous employment, particularly those that are significant for the position(s) you are applying for.

Targeted résumé

A **targeted résumé** is also known as a *specific résumé* because it emphasises relevant skills and experience for a specific job. When preparing your targeted résumé, bear in mind that prospective employers cull applicants when deciding who to call for an interview. The cull takes place before the

A **targeted résumé** emphasises skills and experiences relevant to a specific job; it focuses on skills and capabilities, rather than history.

Patrick Bennett

43 Scane Street
SOMEWHERE VIC 0000
00 0000 0000
patbennett@telemail.com.au

Employment objective
Open with a sentence or paragraph stating your reasons for wanting this position. Write with a clear and confident style that shows you have something to offer the potential employer.

Educational qualifications	List all your certificates, the subjects they cover, the year each was completed, and the name of the institution that awarded each one.
	Attach copies of subject transcripts to support your application, with the most recent one on top and the rest in reverse chronological order.
Professional experience	Mention all work experience, including voluntary, part-time and student vacation work.
	Highlight your particular strengths.
Achievements	Identify any special achievements from school or other organisations—for example, school captain, prefect or local club leader.
	Highlight special communication skills (such as public speaking or debating) as these are essential to most positions.
Activities and interests	Present your most recent activities first, with the rest following in reverse chronological order. The employer likes to know about your interests and special skills.
Referees	Nominate people who have agreed to recommend your skills and recent work. Or you can give the names of referees at the interview.

Figure 22.1: Layout and function of the parts of a basic résumé

interview. It eliminates, on the basis of the applications, those people considered unsuitable because of lack of qualifications, experience, ability or motivation for the position.

INDIVIDUALLY TAILOR THE RÉSUMÉ

The targeted résumé is a variation of the functional style. Individually tailor it to the position. It makes a statement to the employer about the relevance of your skills and capabilities to their company and the available position. The targeted style requires you to write an individually tailored résumé for each position. A targeted résumé draws on examples of specific skills, in contrast to a functional résumé which provides examples of a more general nature. Preparation of a targeted résumé can be time-consuming if you are applying for a number of positions because it is targeted to each position. The targeted résumé is directed towards a particular job and is designed to demonstrate how you meet the specific job requirements. The targeted résumé style is popular because it is effective in most situations. It suits experienced professionals who have developed an extensive range of abilities in positions unrelated to the position they are applying for. They highlight and target the skills and abilities that address the requirements of the position, rather than the traditional ones of education,

<table>
<tr><td colspan="2" align="center">**Patrick Bennett**
43 Scane Street
SOMEWHERE VIC 0000
00 0000 0000
patbennett@telemail.com.au</td></tr>
<tr><td colspan="2">**Employment objective**
State your reason for wanting the position.</td></tr>
<tr><td>**Employment experience**</td><td>Present your employment history, starting with the most recent position, proceeding in reverse chronological order to your first position. Your most recent job functions and achievements are of the greatest interest to the employer.
Give the title of each position, then briefly describe each job function, particularly those relevant to the position you are applying for.
Indicate any specific achievements or initiatives you accomplished in your previous positions.</td></tr>
<tr><td>**Meet the essential and desirable criteria**</td><td>Use headings that reflect the words of the:
• essential criteria
• desirable criteria.</td></tr>
<tr><td>**Educational qualifications**</td><td>Fully identify your qualifications, the institutions where they were gained and the details of course subjects. Present these in reverse chronological order, starting with the most recent. Emphasise any that are particularly important to your potential employer.</td></tr>
<tr><td>**Activities and interests**</td><td>Offer potential employers evidence of your ability to mix with others and mention any special skills that may be relevant—for example, community involvement or sporting interests.</td></tr>
<tr><td>**Professional memberships**</td><td>List any memberships of professional associations, as these indicate that you are keeping up with the latest developments in your industry or occupation.</td></tr>
<tr><td>**Referees**</td><td>Present at least one who is professional and work-related, and one who will provide a character reference. An academic reference could also be useful.</td></tr>
</table>

Figure 22.2: Layout of a functional résumé

work and interests Present within each of these specific skills categories the range of experiences that demonstrates your strengths in the area.

Figure 22.3 shows the sequence of information in a targeted résumé. The headings suggested make it easy to record your positions from latest to earliest, and to describe the responsibilities and achievements in each. Highlight particular strengths with action verbs such as *design, audit, adapt, initiate, prepare, negotiate, report, research, supervise, inspect* or *promote*. These action words, or power words, add strength to your writing and show that you have the responsibility and ability to follow projects through to completion.

Name
Address
Telephone
Date

Employment objective (or profile statement)	
Educational qualifications	You may present these in reverse chronological order, or you may choose to present the qualifications most relevant to the position, such as degree, diploma or trade certificate. Include other qualifications in order of importance to the position.
Professional experience	

Position held	Duties and responsibilities	Achievement	Date
A brief description of the job, job title	A brief outline of your duties and the job title of the person you were responsible to	Indicate special capacities and abilities; emphasise any authority held	2005–09
Achievements	List any significant achievements from your employment experience. These will emphasise your strengths and the skills you can bring to the workplace.		
Personal interests and hobbies	List interests or hobbies that indicate your ability to mix with other people. Other interests may show that you are capable of working alone. Decide whether these will help in your application for the position. This section should be informative, simple and clear.		
Referees/References	Provide the names and contact numbers of two referees. Seek the approval of these people before you give their names as referees. Take the originals of references for the interview and photocopies to leave with the interviewers.		

Figure 22.3: Layout and function of parts of a targeted résumé

The main advantages of a targeted résumé are the opportunity to:

- link your experiences closely with the employer's specific needs
- ensure that the focus is on your skills and capabilities, rather than your work history
- conduct background research into the employer's needs and whether you have interpreted those needs accurately.

Remember, an employer will spend on average only one or two minutes scanning your résumé. Make it professional, concise and powerful. Take the initiative and be proactive. How will the other person know you are a self-starter, team player or independent unless you tell them in the résumé? As the targeted résumé is for a particular position, highlight any common threads or relationships between, for example, your communication skills, customer service, enthusiasm and flexibility that highlight your capacity to interact and lead positively.

REVIEW QUESTIONS

8 Distinguish between basic, functional and targeted résumés.
9 Describe the contents of each broad section of a résumé.
10 Explain the main advantages of each type of résumé—basic, functional and targeted.

ELECTRONIC RÉSUMÉS

Many employers and recruitment agencies prefer to collect, sort and file **electronic résumés** in preference to hard-copy résumés. Electronic résumés differ from traditional hard-copy résumés. There are four common ways of presenting electronic résumés:

1 scanned résumés
2 email résumés
3 Internet résumé posting banks
4 home page résumés.

Placing your résumé online is a much faster process than posting traditional hard-copy résumés, because the Internet lets you:

- collect the application form and company information quickly
- fill out the form and submit the job application almost immediately.

The factors underpinning a successful electronic résumé are careful preparation, good organisation, an effective business writing style and professional layout. In an online résumé:

- content is the primary feature
- uniform presentation is essential
- keywords are essential.

Employers and recruiters increasingly rely on electronic résumés, résumé posting boards and job banks to find job candidates. Any paper-based résumés should be in a scannable format, as résumés are either being scanned or inputted directly into keyword-searchable databases. When you submit your résumé online to sites such as <www.monster.com> or <www.careerbuilder.com>, for example, your résumé is electronically inputted into their databases. The résumés are then accessed when an employer or recruiter inputs a keyword list of requirements to describe the position they are seeking to fill.

The database searches for keywords describing:

- job titles, responsibilities and descriptions
- educational requirements, including certificates, diplomas and degrees
- technical and computer knowledge
- abilities and personality traits.

The software scans through thousands of résumés and identifies those that most closely match the inputted keywords. Those résumés with the most *hits* by the software (keywords) are likely to be read by the employer or recruiter.

Many recruiters now scan applicant résumés into a computerised screening database system to simplify the screening and selection process. An effective scannable résumé has:

- content that is impressive and distinguishable from the other competitors for the position
- keywords that are used extensively to secure a large number of hits and the corresponding high ranking during the computer-based search
- a format with simple, conservative fonts that OCR (Optical Character Recognition) software can recognise as it attempts to match characters scanned from your résumé with standard letter shapes.

◄ OBJECTIVE 4
Prepare an electronic résumé to align your qualifications to the needs of the position

Electronic résumés are placed on a database and searched by keywords.

Keyword résumés

Keyword résumés are uploaded into a computer database and retrieved by a keyword search.

Keywords are nouns or noun phrases that identify skills unique to a specific profession or industry.

There are differences between a traditional résumé prepared in hard copy and a keyword résumé. **Keyword résumés** are uploaded into a computer database. The only way they are retrieved is by conducting a keyword search. Keywords are the words searchers type into search engines to find what they want. If you fail to include the right keywords, or misspell them, your résumé is unlikely to be selected in a search.

There are differences between a traditional résumé prepared in hard copy and a keyword résumé. Keyword résumés are uploaded into a computer database. The only way they are retrieved is by conducting a keyword search. Keywords are the words searchers type into search engines to find what they want. If you fail to include the right keywords, or if you misspell them, your résumé is unlikely to be selected in a search.

The use of key words of the noun or noun phrase type (*operational management*, *SANTIX*, *business process improvement*, *commercial leadership*), as opposed to power action verbs often found in traditional résumés (*developed*, *mediated*, *designed*, *organised*), is one of the main differences between a keyword résumé and a traditional paper-based résumé. The emphasis is on stand-alone nouns that enable your résumé to be located by the computer search facility

Phrases are used to describe personality traits, such as *good communication skills*, *excellent time management*, *works well under pressure* and *pays attention to detail*, as well as professional experience, education and other skills. For example, an applicant asked to demonstrate a customer service perspective and focus skills could include phrases such as the following: 'Excellent interpersonal communication and relationship management skills, as evidenced by a 20% increase in winning contracts over a 12-month period.'

Keyword résumés are a little longer than traditional résumés because they include more detail, as well as a keyword section.

Rule: The more skills and facts you provide, the more opportunities or hits you will match or generate on the computer search program. The keywords are the most important element of the résumé. Always check the spelling of your keywords.

A quick way to find the most common keywords for a position is to look up a variety of advertisements and be aware of commonly used industry words. The likely keywords in the advertisement in Figure 22.4 are in bold typeface. By including a keyword section *towards the front of your résumé* as well as using keywords throughout it, you will optimise your résumé's ranking with search engines and computer tracking systems. The keywords should be in headings, phrases or sentences that make sense, rather than casually scattering them about your résumé.

Help the recruiter or employer to find your résumé and include it among the highest-ranked résumés by making it keyword rich and scanner friendly. Use keywords that:

- are industry or job specific
- include job titles, relevant skills, industry jargon
- include necessary educational and academic achievements
- relate to what a recruiter or potential employer would be looking for in a suitable job applicant.

Although active verbs have long been essential for building a successful résumé, now the noun or noun phrase that follows an active verb is equally important. It is the keyword. For example:

- self-directed Customer Service Manager with a strong work ethic and problem-solving abilities
- talented Architectural Project Manager with strong coordination and communication skills applied to design teams and consultants on construction projects over the areas of budget, scheduling and quality control
- accomplished in public relations, media and advertising activities
- nominated by the National Group for the Relationship Manager of the Year Award.

Applications are invited from suitably qualified persons committed to quality **customer service** for a position in **Library Services** in new media production areas. The library operates a busy service with 15 000 active members and a circulation of 300 000 loans per annum.

Key responsibilities

Supervise reference Information Services. Maintain and **develop services** for **special client groups**. Maintain the **Professional Information Service**. Coordinate the provision of **film**, **television**, **radio** and new **media services** to client groups. Undertake c**ollection management**. Undertake **library promotions**. Maintain **film** and **video archives**.

Essential criteria

- **Tertiary qualifications** in **Library** and **Information Science**.
- High-level customer service skills and excellent interpersonal and public relations skills.
- Excellent **supervisory**, **organisation**, **time management** and **team-building skills**.
- Superior **research** and **reference skills**. Experience with **automated library systems**.

Desirable criteria

- Five years recent experience as **librarian**.
- Detailed knowledge of **information technologies**, including the Internet.
- Experience with the **Horizon Library System**.
- Experience in the **development** of **library policies** and **procedures**.

Figure 22.4: Sample job advertisement with probable keywords highlighted

Keywords can be generated from these resources:

- job descriptions or person specifications
- job postings—either printed or online—for example, <www.nnsw.com.au/regional/jobsearch.html> or <http://au.dir.yahoo.com/Business_and_Economy/Business_to_Business/Education/Job_and_Employment_Resources>
- Industry association websites, printed or online
- Yellow Pages, either printed or online
- job-related publications (including the *Occupational Outlook Handbook*), <www.careersonline.com.au/Links/Jobs-Careers_Advice_and_Counselling.html>
- résumé and career exploration books, paper-based or online—for example, <www.quintcareers.com/career_exploration.html>
- corporate websites (including the ones of interest to you)
- other résumés posted online.

An example of a keyword section for Paula's résumé, an Occupational Health and Safety specialist, is shown in Figure 22.5. Paula placed the keyword section strategically near the front of her résumé. She also included similar keywords throughout the body of her résumé to enhance its ranking by the computer applicant screening system or Internet search. To ensure she had included sufficient keywords and presented them consistently in her résumé, Paula scanned through it and marked the keywords with a highlighting pen. She then posted the résumé online.

The specific terminology used in positions must be used as keywords. They are the necessary experience and skills. Keywords are also found in educational degrees and diplomas, job descriptions and titles, software requirements, names of companies and professional organisations, and personality attributes. A word need only be used once for it to be a hit in a keyword search. Use synonyms wherever possible to increase your number of hits.

Occupational Health and Safety specialist, Workers Compensation Claims Coordinator, OHS Audits, Contribution to Occupational Health and Safety Policy, Injury Management, Risk Assessment, Risk Management, Report to Directors, OHS Committee Chairperson, OHS Training and Development, Customer Relations and Support, Leadership, Collaboration and Teamwork, Analysis, Problem Solving and Decision Making, Public Presentations, Negotiation and Conflict Resolution, Bilingual, fluent English and Cantonese.

Figure 22.5: Paula's OHS keywords

SUMMARY AREA

In the summary area of your electronic résumé:

- highlight your most important qualities, achievements and abilities with several short statements, each containing a keyword
- tailor every word in the summary to your targeted goal
- make this area of your résumé keyword rich.

The most common features of a well-written summary are shown in the checklist below. Next time you create a résumé, use the checklist to assess the summary area.

SELF-EVALUATE YOUR SKILL

SUMMARY AREA OF A RÉSUMÉ

The summary area of my résumé:	Yes	No
has a sentence describing my profession		
identifies my level of expertise		
makes two or three statements about my:		
— unique mix of skills, and/or		
— range of environments in which I have experience, and/or		
— particular or special documented professional accomplishments, and/or		
— history of awards, promotions, commendations, and/or		
— specific professional or personal characteristics.		
concludes with a sentence that describes my professional objectives or interests		

Design your résumé to meet the needs of the web search engines because recruiters search the Web for résumés. Often it is more effective for them than posting a job opportunity because it is free of charge.

Scannable résumés

A *scannable résumé* is posted by mail and then scanned by the employer or recruiter into a computer database using Optical Character Recognition (OCR). The database program will sort the résumés by:

- keywords
- industry-specific words

- areas of experience
- education and qualifications.

Scanning, particularly with older software, can change the appearance of your résumé dramatically because scanners can have difficulty reading words or special characters such as: bullets, underlining and italics.

Next time you prepare a scannable résumé, follow the recruiter's or employer's guidelines. Use the checklist below to check the quality of your résumé before you send it.

SELF-EVALUATE YOUR SKILL

CONTENT AND DESIGN GUIDELINES FOR ONLINE AND SCANNABLE RÉSUMÉS

Have I:	Yes	No
used high-quality A4, white or off-white paper?		
printed on one side of the paper only?		
kept the format simple and conservative?		
avoided the use of italics, bold, underlining, bullets or lines?		
used Times, Palatino, Arial, Courier, Verdana or similar plain font?		
used no more than two fonts in sizes between 10 and 12 points?		
printed the résumé at the highest resolution possible?		
avoided faxing a scannable résumé?		
used a minimal amount of punctuation given that it can confuse OCR?		
given my name and contact information at the top of each page?		
used margins and line spacing to give white space and keep the résumé from looking crowded?		
left justified the text?		
used major headings such as 'Professional History' or skill headings?		
formatted headings with either bold text or all capitals?		
ensured capitalisation, punctuation and date formats are consistent and there are no spelling errors?		
used headings sparingly but consistently to structure and shape the information?		
used horizontal lines to separate sections of my résumé?		
made dates of employment easy to find and formatted them consistently?		
used keywords and industry-specific words?		
used consistent verb tenses: that is, current job in present tense, past employment in past tense?		
avoided repetition by checking that each entry highlights a capability or accomplishment?		
avoided the use of graphics, vertical lines and shaded boxes that may confuse the OCR software?		
used a keyword-rich summary area to highlight my best assets such as education, experience and skills?		
used paper clips rather than staples?		
mailed the résumé flat in a large envelope to prevent creases or folds?		

Newer scanners can take snapshots of your résumé and print it. To ensure your résumé scans well on older or newer scanning software, make it computer friendly by converting it into an ASCII file or plain text format with line breaks. Use the *save as* option to remove formatting commands such as bullets, bolding, centring and graphic lines. The résumé will then print as a plain document. Proofread it for keywords and accuracy. When you send a scannable résumé by mail, also include a professionally formatted résumé. Put a Post-it note on each with the words *Scannable Résumé* and *Visual Résumé*.

Some scanning systems will rank and score résumés on the total number of keywords in them. Identify the keywords listed in advertisements and position descriptions for the positions that interest you. Then ensure you use these keywords in headings and the text in your résumé.

Email résumés

An *email résumé* is simply a résumé sent using electronic mail. Email résumés are a preferred method of electronic résumé, more than scannable résumés, because they are already in an electronic format that is easily scanned into database systems. To prepare an email résumé you may have to use a combination of word processing programs, text editors and email programs. Always follow the recruiter's instructions regarding the format of the email. For example, it may need to be saved in a particular word processing format such as Microsoft Word; or it may need to be saved as HTML plain text or an ASCII file.

An employment application consists of a résumé and a covering letter.

The cover letter should form the first part of your email résumé, followed by the résumé itself. Any position reference numbers and titles that describe the position you are applying for should be included in the cover letter. Also include your telephone number and email address.

As in all résumés—hard copy or electronic—include keywords in a keyword section or summary. The keyword section should be targeted to the key skills for the position you are interested in. Before sending an email résumé, find out whether it is to be entered straight into a database or used as a regular résumé. If it is to be included in a database it will also need to be a keyword résumé. Email the résumé to your own email address before you send it to check for any formatting problems.

Internet résumé posting banks

Internet résumé posting banks provide online forms for you to use to input your résumé into their databank.

Many of these résumé builders are laid out in a chronological format, rather than a targeted résumé format. When your current position title does not match the requirements of the advertised position, try using a skill heading with a keyword from the advertisement first and then your position title in brackets—for example, Corporate Support (Coordinator Internal Services).

One of the disadvantages of online applications is the temptation to fill them out quickly and send them off without reading and editing for detail and accuracy. Electronic applications are usually placed straight into a database. This highlights the importance of keywords that will be picked up in a search.

QUESTIONS TO ASK

Before you post a résumé on an Internet site, read the information and then ask the recruiter the questions set out in Table 22.10.

Home page résumés

Home page résumés are written in Hypertext Markup Language (HTML) and placed on the World Wide Web. They are found and indexed by search engines. While it is unusual for employers and recruiters to ask for this type of résumé, some online job banks offer it as an option or service. People hoping to be headhunted for a position, or people in the computing or information technology industry, often use an HTML résumé. The Web résumé bank on the Nerdworld server, for example, lets those working in the computing industry demonstrate their information technology skills to a prospective employer.

When you prepare a home page résumé, realise that employers and recruiters will not spend time and effort searching for your résumé on a personal website. Avoid having a dark background with

Table 22.10: Questions to ask before using an Internet posting bank

- Is a keyword résumé required?
- How is the résumé to be used?
- Is it to apply for a specific vacant position, to answer a recruiting drive, or for submission to a database in the hope of being headhunted at some later date?
- Will it go to a local, national or global database?
- If applying in a country other than Australia, are there any work restrictions?
- How long will it be held on the database?
- Can I remove it from the database? How secure is the database?
- Who has access to it?

light-coloured letters, as it will be difficult to read when printed. It is your responsibility to post your résumé into potential recruiters' websites, into their online résumé bank or to email it. Make it easy for them to reply to your home page résumé by including your URL and email address. Table 22.11 gives further hints.

Anyone can access a résumé directly when it is placed on a web server. Security concerns mean that you may prefer to use an email address or to lodge a résumé directly with an online employment agency, rather than place your personal details online. Ask who will have access to your personal details and how long your résumé will remain active. This information is usually provided with the instructions on applying for positions.

Table 22.11: Hints for reader-friendly home page and HTML résumés

Hint	Purpose
Place the most important information, such as your personal details and a skill heading, at the top of each screen.	To maximise your résumé's impact and alignment to the position
Use skill headings and titles of keywords that match the employer's needs and requirements of the position, because employers use search engines that sort by page title and the words or phrases in the résumé.	To help the recruiter or employer find applicants with the skills and qualifications required in the position
Create an additional link or page from your home page that includes an ASCII or plain text version of your résumé with all HTML coding removed.	To make it easy for employers or recruiters to copy and paste your résumé into their database
Break your home page résumé into several pages and use hyperlinks to enable recruiters to jump from one page or section to the next without having to scroll through the résumé.	To make it easy for recruiters to use small pages or anchors to jump within the résumé

REVIEW QUESTIONS

11 Describe the differences between a traditional résumé prepared in hard copy and a keyword résumé.

12 Identify four common ways to present electronic résumés.

13 a What does a database search for in an electronic résumé?

b Where should keywords be located in an electronic résumé?

c What should be included in the summary section of an electronic résumé?

RÉSUMÉS

1 a What type of résumé would best suit your experience, education and background?

   b What are some of the areas you would emphasise in your résumé?

2 Think about a position you would like.

   a Write a career objective suited to this position.

   b What sections or headings would you use when preparing a résumé for this position?

   c Prepare the second half (evidence section) of the résumé. Draft the 'Professional Experience' or 'Professional History' section, using at least six of the action words below.

expand	obtain	communicate
initiate	evaluate	interpret
report	operate	supervise
maintain	program	analyse
install	print	interpret
solve	create	analyse
design	liaise	delegate

   d Complete your résumé in the basic, functional or targeted résumé format.

   e If you were placing your résumé with an online recruitment agency, list at least six keywords that would make it easy for an online employer to determine whether you suit the position they want to fill.

3 This activity is designed to highlight the fact that your résumé must command attention and match the needs of employers and recruiters. Headlines and subheadings like those used in Mitch's résumé in Figure 22.8 do this quite powerfully yet use limited space. This activity uses only part of Mitch's résumé. By the end of the chapter you will prepare a full résumé.

   The primary criteria or requirements for the position of Marketing and Communications Manager are shown in Figure 22.6. Mitch decides to apply for this position. Your task is to analyse the primary criteria for the position and decide if the rewritten part of Mitch's résumé fits the primary criteria (Figure 22.8).

   a The first half of any résumé contains personal details and the employment objective. The second half is the evidence section. Read part of the evidence section of Mitch's résumé in Figure 22.7 to see how well it markets his best skills, achievements and experience for the Marketing and Communications Manager position.

   b Use the checklist below to determine quickly whether Mitch's skills match the primary criteria and requirements listed in Figure 22.6.

   Résumé checklist

Does Mitch's résumé:	Yes	No
start off with a broad overview of his vast experience?		
give in to the temptation to communicate all areas of experience?		
assume that the employers and recruiters will take the time to wade through such descriptions?		
describe the specific experience being requested or required?		
customise and target the résumé to the exceptional communications and influencing skills mentioned in Item 5 of the advertisement?		

   c Assume you have given feedback to Mitch and he rewrites that section of his résumé. Now look at the rewritten section of Mitch's new résumé, shown in Figure 22.8 .

Marketing and Communications Manager

1 Individual will lead the organisation's marketing strategy and continue to drive growth
2 Responsible for the overall PR strategy, customer communication, brand management and corporate social responsibilities
3 Experience in a business-to-business environment within financial services on both a strategic and tactical level
4 A proven track record in building brand equity through PR, media and advertising activities
5 Exceptional communication and influencing skills
6 MBA required.

Figure 22.6: Primary criteria or position requirements

Marketing and Communications Manager

Executive qualifications summary: Former owner and manager of small to medium-sized international companies in international trade and project management, management consulting; advertising, marketing and building brand equity.

Project work consulting in: International finance, Acquisitions, Strategic planning, Operations, Marketing, Advertising, Public relations, and Training.

Skills: Strong written, oral and computer communications capabilities. Strategic planning; analysis; decision making; budgeting; operations. Resourceful and competitive. **Special expertise in:** Opportunity identification and capitalisation; idea generation; leadership; goal setting; public speaking; and successful project completion

Objective: Executive position utilising my varied expertise and skills in finance, general management, international sales, advertising, communications, planning, operations, sales, distribution and corporate social responsibilities.

Figure 22.7: Part of the evidence section of Mitch's résumé

Marketing and Communications Manager

Offers:

Extensive, Seasoned Expertise in Financial Services Product and Brand Development for Major International Financial Products
Extensive Experience in PR Strategy Development, Customer Communication and Brand Management

Proven ability

Capture New and Emerging Markets and Implement Multi-Million Dollar Advertising Campaigns proven by:

• Managing Domestic & Worldwide Marketing Operations generating up to $46 million annually with responsibility for brand development and strategic planning of Finprod, advertising and international public relations programs.
• Researching and identifying innovative customer communication and brand management to achieve revenues of $75 million within four years for a new start-up division in a financial service category.
• Managing marketing's contribution on dollar budgets.
• Overseeing key relationships with public relations and external advertising firms and managing Corporate Social Responsibilities.
• Holding a Masters in Business Administration from an internationally recognised Australian university.

Figure 22.8: Mitch's rewrite

Decide:

  i   What makes it more powerful?

  ii   Does the opening heading present Mitch's top qualifications at a glance?

  iii What makes it more convincing?

  iv   Comment on the effectiveness of Mitch's approach in making specific, achievement-oriented statements in the new résumé, rather than broad, general statements.

 d   Which résumé do you think will have a greater chance of grabbing the attention of employers and recruiters?

 e   Which one will help Mitch position himself effectively and pave the way to negotiating a top salary? Justify your answer.

4 a   Print the online forms from one of the large online recruitment groups. How can you input your résumé into the online form?

 b   What is the difference between keyword, online, HTML and scannable résumés?

5 a   Surf a number of home page résumés. Critique those you find by analysing their design, content and keyword sections.

 b   Discuss any strengths and weaknesses you find in the résumés.

THE APPLICATION LETTER

OBJECTIVE **5** ▶
Write an effective application letter

A **letter of application** is a brief, specific covering document for a traditional written résumé designed to persuade the receiver to read the accompanying résumé.

The **letter of application** is the persuasive part of the application. It should make a positive impression and focus attention on the relevance of your qualifications to a specific job. It is a covering letter and should be brief (about one page) and specific. Use it to draw attention to those qualifications or experiences listed in the résumé that equip you for the job. The aim is to achieve a balance between your perception of your suitability for the job and the potential employer's needs. It should persuade the reader to consider your application carefully, as someone potentially well suited to the advertised position.

The steps involved in writing a persuasive letter are discussed in Chapter 18. An example of a letter of application is given in Figure 22.10. The covering letter, or letter of application, should contain three main parts.

1 The introduction expresses interest in the job and applies for the position.

2 The body points out specific qualities, qualifications and experiences mentioned in your résumé and states your interest in the organisation.

3 The conclusion indicates where and how you can be reached for interview.

Write the letter of application using the AIDA formula.

The *AIDA formula* is a helpful strategy to use in the covering letter or letter of application. (Chapter 18 gives more details.) A well-planned letter of application is likely to arouse the potential employer's interest and attract attention to your application. Table 22.12 shows how to apply the AIDA formula to a covering letter. The desire to call you for an interview and the action of inviting you to an interview will be made on the basis of your letter and résumé.

The advertisement in Figure 22.9 is for the position of Accounts Clerk in the accounts payable section of a large accounting office in the CBD. The person must have experience in accounts payable, good communication skills, experience with data entry in a computerised accounts system, and the ability to work with a high degree of accuracy. Desirable qualifications are typing or word processing skills.

If you applied for this job, you could include some of the words in the advertisement in your covering letter, then refer the reader to your résumé for more information. Figure 22.10 is an example of a covering letter for the position of clerk shown in Figure 22.9.

Table 22.12: Applying the AIDA formula to a covering letter

AIDA formula	Purpose
Attention	A covering letter with a positive opening has an impact on potential employers. It states your interest in the position, aims to catch readers' attention and invites them to read further.
Interest	In the body of the letter, use positive language and signal your ability to do the job by showing how your qualifications and experience equip you for the position. The aim is to arouse the interest of potential employers. One of the easiest ways to do this is to start one or two of the paragraphs in the body of the letter with a topic sentence that includes some of the words in the advertisement that describe the job essentials.
Desire	Refer the reader to the particular part of the résumé that supports your special strengths for the position. As readers reach this part of the letter, you want them to recognise your value and feel the desire to call you for interview.
Action	The conclusion invites the reader to take action. As you want an interview, use the closing paragraph to state that you are interested in the position and are available for interview.

Credit Control

Melbourne Location

Circa $56 000

This exciting opportunity currently exists within a dynamic company.

Reporting to the Finance Manager, your key duties will include:

a   High-volume telephone and written collections

b   Weekly reporting on overdue debts

c   Providing cash flow projections to the Finance GM

d   Daily allocation of payments received

e   Daily download of transactions from the bank and depositing received

You will be able to work independently in a stand-alone environment. Deadlines will create pressure. The position requires outstanding communication skills. Applicants with experience in a similar role will be highly regarded.

Please apply in writing to:

Mr J Johnson

Finance Manager

GPO Box 000

MELBOURNE VIC 3000

Your interest will be treated in the strictest of confidence.

Figure 22.9: Example of a 'Positions Vacant' advertisement

Ms Jane Coulton
28/210 Smith Street
COLLINGWOOD VIC 3066

20 August 2010

Mr J Johnson
Finance Manager
GPO Box 000
MELBOURNE VIC 3000

Dear Mr Johnson

Position: Credit Control

I wish to apply for the position of Credit Control advertised in the *Melbourne Age* on 13 August 2010.

My qualification of Bachelor of Commerce is supported by my extensive experience in the accounts department of a large telecommunications company. These experiences include accounts payable, accounts receivable, bank reconciliations, cash flow projections and general accounting functions.

I am very keen to secure the advertised position with your company. My qualifications and experience are outlined in the accompanying résumé.

The duties of my present position range from the daily reconciliation of payments received to weekly reporting on overdue debts. Part of my role is to download daily the transactions from the bank and depositing received. I also conduct a high volume of telephone and written collections.

Implementing the duties in my current position requires effective communication skills (both interpersonal and written). Effective communication skills and contact with relevant personnel help to remove potential problems before they occur.

I have developed the skills identified in the advertisement in previous positions over the past five years. The enclosed references attest to my achievements in these positions.

I look forward to discussing my application at an interview. I can be contacted on (03) 0000 0000 or at the address above.

Yours sincerely

Jane Coulton

Figure 22.10: Example of letter of application or covering letter

In the covering letter, take care to use new information rather than duplicate details in the résumé. Interpret and target the information to the position you want. The employer is trying to achieve two things in the employment process:

1. identify the person with the personal attributes to suit the job specification
2. ensure that the person chosen has the qualifications, experience and motivation to be able to do the job, or to be trained for the job.

About two weeks after you have mailed a job application, if you haven't received an acknowledgment, it is appropriate to make an inquiry either by letter or telephone call. The inquiry aims to determine what has happened to the application and to state again, courteously and clearly, your interest in the organisation and the fact that you are available and would like the opportunity to present supporting evidence of your capabilities at an interview.

Effective references

It is important to include in the résumé the names of *referees* or people prepared to speak in support of your professional competence and experience. References relevant to the position support the claims in your résumé. Reference checks are usually made by a potential employer to establish an applicant's stability, loyalty, capabilities, personality, and ability to take instructions and act accordingly. Work-related **references** are documents that highlight and support certain skills and experiences you have gained. They are usually written by your immediate supervisor, manager or employer.

A **reference** highlights your skills and work experiences.

When you plan to offer someone's name as referee, or present a written reference, telephone them in advance to warn them of your actions. This can result in a more positive report when they receive a telephone call about you. Prospective employers rarely accept a written reference at face value. They prefer to check by telephone with the named referees to establish the character and work history of a potential employee. In the job application, you may choose to include photocopies of references. However, be prepared to present the originals at the interview. Some positions require at least one personal and one academic reference. Each reference should comment favourably on your abilities and come from a credible source. It should also be professional in appearance.

Before you leave a position, think about who you will ask to be a referee. The referees should be willing and able to write fluently and be enthusiastic about your abilities. Good verbal references are invaluable when it comes to being offered a position. References from previous employers can give credibility to the claims in your résumé, particularly references that highlight experience or skills relevant to the position you are applying for.

An employment interview is conducted to select the best applicant for the position.

REVIEW QUESTIONS

14. a The résumé demonstrates your skills, experience and qualifications. What does the covering letter do?
    b What kind of action does a covering letter, or letter of application, attempt to achieve?
15. a Identify the purpose of each of the main parts of a letter of application.
    b Why must the covering letter be a persuasive letter?
    c Explain how the AIDA formula is used in a covering letter.
16. Compare the advantages and disadvantages of written and oral references.

EMPLOYMENT INTERVIEWS

◀ OBJECTIVE 6
Differentiate between types of employment interviews

The *employment interview* uses a question-and-answer format to exchange information between interviewer and applicant. The process follows five stages—pre-interview, the opening of the interview, the body, the close and the post-interview stage. In each stage, interviewer and applicant have responsibilities to make the exchange of information successful and to ensure that the content of the interview matches its type and objectives.

Types of job interview

There are three main types of job interview:

1. single interview
2. series interview
3. panel interview.

The **single interview** is conducted by a single interviewer responsible for interviewing all applicants and selecting the new staff member. It can be open to interviewer bias. The series interview and the panel interview help to remove bias and subjectivity because more than one interviewer assesses applicants' abilities.

The **series interview** is conducted in turn by a number of interviewers. Each interviewer is looking for a particular area of expertise and evaluates each applicant in this area of expertise. The interviewers meet after the interviews to consult and make a group selection. The process in a series interview and the result of the interview are not very different from the panel interview. In each case, a group of interviewers assesses the quality of the applicants.

The **panel interview** is conducted by a group of interviewers. Each member on the panel asks specific questions relevant to their specialised experience. This range of experience gives a wider selection of questions and answers and helps to remove personal bias from the interview. The panel works together to assess the applicant.

The principles of Equal Employment Opportunity are supported when at least one woman and one man sit on an interview panel. Members of an interview panel should know how to conduct and participate in an interview. They should also avoid the tendency to be subjective or to allow bias to affect the quality of the decision.

Lehman and Dufrene (2002, p. 580) describe the **computer-assisted interview**, which is used by companies in the United States. These companies have found that computer-assisted interviews are 'a reliable and effective way to conduct screening interviews'. Lehman and Dufrene also cite L.C. Marion's 1997 research showing that 'applicants prefer computer interviews to human interviews' and that applicants 'respond more honestly to a computer, feeling less need to give polite, socially accepted responses' (p. 580). The overall quality of the selection process improves, as typical human errors such as forgetting to ask important questions, talking too much or forming unjustified negative impressions are overcome.

Thornburg (1998) comments: 'Coopers & Lybrand, which uses an Aspen Tree product, is the first company to put its computer-assisted interviewing system on the Internet, using a web site called Springboard'. Business students in accounting, auditing and computers complete an employment application and initial screening interviews online at their convenience by accessing the website.

'E-mail Print Link a major clothing manufacturer used computer-assisted interviewing to conduct the first round of interviews and screen out inappropriate applicants. The company saved $2.4 million during a three-year period by reducing turnover from 87 to 51 percent. Interactive voice response technology (IVR), which has been in use for a long time, is being used along with other database technologies in computer-assisted interviews to capture information about potential employees, giving the company more flexibility and speeding hiring decisions' (Thornburg 1998).

Another type of interview is the **stress interview**. This is designed to 'place the interviewee in an anxiety-producing situation so an evaluation may be made of the interviewee's performance under stress' (Lehman & Dufrene 2002, p. 581). The authors comment that 'understanding that interviewers sometimes deliberately create anxiety to assess your ability to perform under stress should help you to handle such interviews more effectively'.

Many large companies in the United States are using the **virtual interview**, which allows candidates from remote locations to be screened. This type of interview saves time and money, but it is not considered as good as a 'live interview' for important final interviews. Lehman and Dufrene comment: 'Because of the additional stress of functioning under the glare of a camera, videoconferencing is an excellent method

Series interview: several interviews conducted in turn by a number of interviewers.

Single interview: a job interview conducted by one interviewer responsible for interviewing all applicants and selecting a new staff member.

Series interview: several interviews conducted in turn by a number of interviewers.

A **panel interview** is conducted by a group of interviewers.

A **computer-assisted interview** is used to screen the applicants.

A **stress interview** places the interviewee in an anxiety-producing situation.

A **virtual interview** is conducted via videoconferencing technology.

to screen out candidates who cannot work under pressure' (pp. 582–3). They recommend the following tactics to prepare for a successful video interview.

- Suggest a preliminary telephone conversation with the interviewer to establish rapport. Arrive early and acquaint yourself with the equipment; know how to adjust the volume and brightness, and become familiar with other camera functions.
- Concentrate on projecting strong nonverbal skills: speak clearly but do not slow down; make certain you are centred in the frame; sit straight; look up, not down; and use gestures to communicate energy and to reinforce points, while avoiding excessive motion.
- Realise that voices might be out of sync with the pictures, so adjust the timing of your responses to avoid interrupting the interviewer.

Interviews may be either structured or unstructured. A structured interview, say Lehman and Dufrene (2002, pp. 580–1), is generally used in the screening process. The interviewer follows 'a predetermined agenda, including a checklist of items or a series of questions and statements designed to elicit the necessary information or interviewee reaction'. This type of interview gives the interviewer comparable data with which to evaluate the interviewees. The unstructured interview (which has decreased in popularity) allows the interviewer to explore diverse areas. It is used to determine the applicant's ability to speak confidently on a wide range of topics.

REVIEW QUESTIONS

17 Identify the main differences between the single interview, series interview and panel interview.
18 What is the purpose of a stress interview?
19 Why do you think the unstructured interview has decreased in popularity?

THE INTERVIEW PROCESS

◄ OBJECTIVE 7
Evaluate the stages in an employment interview

From the employer's point of view, the purpose of an employment interview is to attract and choose the best applicant for the position. From the applicant's point of view, the purpose is to demonstrate by their responses to the questions and by their behaviour in the interview that they are the best person for the position. Some of the goals of an interview that will select the best applicant for the position are to:

- gather information from interviewees to help predict their future performance
- inform applicants about the job and the organisation
- determine applicants' ability to work with others and 'fit' into the organisational culture
- allow applicants to use the interview's structure to present themselves well.

Robbins and colleagues (2008, p. 148) assert that interviews are poor predictors of competent performance in a job. 'Because interviews usually have so little consistent structure and interviewers vary in terms of what they are looking for in a candidate, judgments about the same candidate can vary widely.' A few of the factors that cause interviews to be poor predictors of job performance are an interviewer with a stereotyped view of what represents a good applicant; favouritism for those who hold similar views to the interviewer; undue emphasis given to negative information; and the likelihood that the interviewer will forget much of the interview's content soon after its conclusion.

The pre-interview stage

Interviewers usually receive more applications for a position than the number of applicants they are willing to interview. So, before the interview, they prepare a short list and interview only those

A **cull** is the elimination of
unsuitable applicants.

who best suit the position. Each application is assessed for suitability. This **cull**, or sorting, of applications into two groups—those to be called for an interview and those not to be interviewed—is made by comparing the information in the applications against the essential and desirable qualifications for the position. Applicants who have prepared an application that demonstrates they have the required skills are called to an interview; those who have not are not called to an interview. A courteous interviewer (or selection panel) informs all applicants, whether successful or not, of the result of their application.

By examining the applications closely, interviewers should be able to minimise the bias caused by forming impressions in the early stages of an interview. Some interviewers may search for information consistent with their first impression, instead of information that verifies the alignment of the applicant's skills and qualifications to the position description. Tucker and Rowe (1977, p. 287) identify the importance of the early stages of an interview to the outcome. They say that 'the application form is an essential and valuable component of the personnel selection model. When consulted prior to the interview, it provides the recruiter with information that is not likely to be obtained from any other source and cues the interviewer to probe certain areas of an applicant's background.' In their view, the application form and the interview provide the most complete information. Both are important contributors to the final decision.

In the pre-interview stage, experienced interviewers determine the style and structure of the interview. Is it a directive or non-directive style of interview? *Directive interviews* are controlled and organised by the interviewer. *Non-directive interviews* involve the participants and the organisation in setting the goals and process of the interview. Employment interviews are usually directive interviews.

In the pre-interview stage, interviewers should take the time to verify that each part of the process set out in Table 22.13 has happened or will be able to happen. At this stage, applicants should prepare for the interview. Judy Barnsley, in the *Sydney Morning Herald* (2002), quotes Anne Silver of Training and Development Studies: 'A successful interview starts long before you arrive at the interviewer's office, and preparation, research and practise, practise, practise are the key to performing well when you get there.' Silver further comments that research is perhaps the area where most applicants are underprepared. Researching the company 'is essential in order to tailor your specific skills to the job at

Table 22.13: The interview process: Actions of interviewers	
Stage	**Activities**
1 Pre-interview	• obtaining the position specification that lists the essential and desirable qualifications • meeting legislative requirements such as Equal Employment Opportunity • preparing the questions (open, closed, mirror and probing) to provide consistency and fairness • selecting the interview panel • reading the job applications with the panel • culling those applicants whose specifications do not meet the job requirements • short-listing the candidates following a cull • checking references
2 Conducting the interview through the opening, body and close of the interview	• creating an open, friendly and welcoming environment in the opening stage • introducing all the interviewers • asking questions from a prepared list • patterning questions during the body of the interview • using good listening and speaking skills • taking notes to jog memory

hand'. Silver also recommends working out answers to possible questions and then practising them in front of a mirror, a friend or even the dog!

Applicants who are familiar with the interview process shown in Table 22.13 are able to plan well and perform competently throughout the interview and follow-up activities. Before the interview, applicants should also verify details such as the time, location, and the documents that should be brought to the interview.

Applicants who study the job advertisement in the planning stage are able to prepare questions specific to the position. Two examples are:

- 'What are the key requirements of this position?'
- 'What do you see as the highest priorities for someone in this position?'

A probing question could be added to the first question; for example:

- 'Are you saying the key requirements will be . . .?'

Well-prepared applicants also think about the common themes that interviewers may use to plan their questions. They are then able to answer questions in the body of the interview in a way that shows they can do the job, accept responsibility and complete major tasks.

Conducting the interview

Applicants should be aware of the expected behaviours in the three types of interview (single, series and panel) and in each stage of an interview. While preparing your résumé, you established your own preferences and career goals. As you think about the sorts of questions that are likely to be asked in the interview, plan your answers to show how your past experience, interests, qualifications and strengths fit you for the position.

An effective interviewer may use a combination of directive and non-directive techniques. Non-directive techniques involve using minimal questions, creating a conversational tone, and adopting positive nonverbal cues to encourage the applicant to speak. The interviewer needs a thorough knowledge of the selection criteria, adequate planning and effective communication skills.

In her advice to interviewers, Cole (2005, p. 742) says: 'Bear in mind that you are seeking behavioural examples of a candidate's past performance and conduct.' The single best predictor of future job performance is past job behaviour. Hence, questions should be behaviour-based in order to gather information about past performance. To prepare to answer these questions, applicants should ask for the **job specification** or **description** before the interview. You are then able to respond in terms of what you have done and are capable of doing. Prepare appropriate answers and use your communication skills to show you can speak, listen, give feedback and interact appropriately.

In the opening stage of the interview, an impression of the other person is formed. Applicants show the interviewers how well they can speak and relate to others in the interview situation. Applicants who enter the room courteously and confidently create a positive first impression. Nonverbal communication, such as a firm handshake, upright posture and direct eye contact, shows confidence. Nodding, smiling and open nonverbal behaviours are assertive and courteous. Create a positive first impression by dressing and grooming yourself in a manner appropriate to your chosen profession.

The interviewer's purpose throughout the interview is twofold: to obtain specific information from the applicant, and to achieve an interview process that is comfortable for the applicant. Rather than being intimidated by interviewers taking notes, remember that the notes will jog their memory. The notes are used in the post-interview stage when the interviewers must make a choice from among the applicants. Good interviewers take care to maintain eye contact with, and interest in, the applicant.

Training consultant Anne Silver says there are two types of questions an applicant can expect: behavioural questions that probe past experience, and hypothetical questions that test how you handle a scenario. To answer hypothetical questions, Silver suggests that interviewees should explain three things: what the situation was, how they responded to it, and what the outcome or result was.

Directive interview techniques focus on a specific topic and seek further information.

Non-directive interview techniques use minimal questions, create a conversational tone, and adopt positive nonverbal cues to encourage the applicant to speak.

The **job specification** or **description** is the basis for the essential desirable qualities listed in the advertisement, as well as the basis for questions in the interview.

During the body of the interview, interviewers should ask open questions that relate to past behaviour to enable applicants to relax and talk about how they have used their skills and abilities in the past. Some examples of open questions are:

- 'I see from your résumé that you are currently working in retail management. Please summarise your main responsibilities.'
- 'I see you are currently employed as an accounts clerk. What does that job involve?'
- 'Would you please summarise your main responsibilities in your job as an accounts clerk?'

For applicants with little or no work experience, interviewers may begin with interests or previous training and education. They will ask such questions as:

- 'I notice that your course included a major project. What skills did you require to complete the project?'
- 'You've had experience as a volunteer in a welfare agency. In what ways did you find work as a volunteer to be satisfying?'

Some applicants' responses may be inadequate, irrelevant, poorly organised or inaccurate. An interviewer who listens carefully and with empathy may decide to vary the type of question, to clarify information or to allow the applicant to elaborate. This enables the applicant to give more information and provide accurate feedback to the interviewers. By summarising what an applicant has said, the interviewer can check understanding. For example:

Interviewee: 'As well as liaising with wholesalers and suppliers regarding stock control, I was also responsible for controlling finances.'

Interviewer: 'So your main responsibilities were to keep stock inventory, deal with day-to-day problems with suppliers, and ensure deliveries from suppliers. You also controlled all finances for the company?'

Writing in the *Sydney Morning Herald* (2003), Natasha Wallace warns job applicants to 'Beware the killer question in your next job interview'. The killer question (KQ) can be daunting, as in 'Tell me something about yourself you've never told anyone before' or 'What would you do if I told you I thought you weren't interviewing very well?' It might even be as abstruse as 'How many planes do you think are flying over Sydney right now?' She quotes Ed Suttle, director of Professional Career Strategies: 'They're designed for shock effect to enable them (the interviewers) to get behind the résumé. You get an opportunity to get a look at the interviewee's personality and see how they handle pressure.' According to Wallace, one of Britain's largest office support recruitment consultancies says that 90% of employers pose a killer question during the interview. A survey in 2002 showed that '66 per cent thought the ability to answer KQs distinguished an interviewee from other candidates when their IQs and experience were equal'.

The closing stage

In the closing stage of the interview, applicants should take the opportunity to ask questions about the position and the company. If they do not, experienced interviewers will encourage them to ask questions by making statements such as:

- 'Are there any points you would like clarified?'
- 'Do you have any questions for the panel?'
- 'Can we give you more information about . . .?'

The questions you ask should be appropriate. It is the applicant's responsibility to come to the interview prepared and to have the confidence to ask questions courteously and confidently. Skilful interviewers anticipate the questions that may be asked and have the relevant information available, perhaps as written summaries of policies or guidelines. It is the interviewer's responsibility to give applicants accurate job information, to answer their questions and to allow scope to discuss their abilities. The interviewer should also thank the applicant for attending the interview. The applicant should thank the interviewer for the opportunity to present at an interview.

The post-interview stage

In the post-interview stage, follow up with a letter of inquiry if you have not heard from the company within two weeks. The letter of inquiry is a follow-up letter that expresses thanks while at the same time reinforcing your application and performance in the employment interview. The **follow-up letter** follows the order of information for a good news letter outlined in Chapter 18. It should be courteous and concise and no more than one page in length. The follow-up letter confirms again your interest in the position by:

- thanking the interviewers for their time
- adding any points of information you may have overlooked
- confirming your interest in the position.

A follow-up telephone call can be made if you have not received a reply to your letter within seven days. Call the interviewer, express your interest again and ask when you are likely to hear the result. The interviewer will explain the delay or let you know whether you were successful or unsuccessful.

Sometimes, the job is offered by telephone; at other times, it is offered in writing. An offer in writing is preferable. It should set out the conditions of employment, such as hours of work and salary. Once you decide to accept the job, telephone the contact person and let them know. Then write a **letter of acceptance** that:

- thanks the employer for the job offer
- states your pleasure in accepting the position
- identifies the position fully
- clarifies the duties it requires and names the person who will be your supervisor
- acknowledges the salary and the conditions
- states how much you are looking forward to the new challenge and opportunity to contribute to the organisation.

If you choose not to accept the position, write a letter declining the offer. The bad news order of information is suited to this type of letter. Open with a neutral buffer, give the reasons for refusing, decline the offer clearly and courteously, and close with an expression of thanks for the offer.

◄ OBJECTIVE 8
Identify and discuss post-interview activities

Follow up the interview with a letter of inquiry.

A **letter of acceptance** is a courteous letter stating acceptance of an offer of employment.

Accept or decline an offer of employment in writing.

REVIEW QUESTIONS

20 Identify the stages in an employment interview and describe what interviewers do in each stage.

21 How should interviewees use each stage in an employment interview?

22 *a* What does a follow-up letter do?

    b How long should you wait before making a follow-up telephone call?

23 *a* Why should you accept an offer of employment in writing?

    b What should you include in the acceptance letter?

PROBLEM INTERVIEWS

Interviews are not always effective in choosing the best person for the job. Problems include:

- poor planning by the interviewer or the applicant
- too much attention given to negative or irrelevant information
- lack of objectives
- lack of structure in the interview

◄ OBJECTIVE 9
Discuss how to deal with problem interviews

- little knowledge by the interviewer of the job under discussion
- lack of knowledge about the position and the company by the applicant
- lack of knowledge about the applicant by the interviewer
- judging the applicant on inappropriate criteria
- poor listening by the interviewer or applicant, resulting in their hearing only part of the answers
- the influence of personal attitudes, stereotypes and bias.

Avoid these problems by planning the interview's content carefully, interacting courteously in the interview and demonstrating you can get the job done. Knowledge of potential problems and some of the traps in hiring, bias in employment interviews, and the validity of employment interviews can help you counter their effects when you are in an employment interview.

While the panel interview can be daunting, it can more easily avoid the ten traps in hiring identified by Fernandez-Araoz (1999, pp. 111–14) and listed in Table 22.14. A panel takes the perceptions of two or three interviewers into account.

Table 22.14: Traps in hiring

Trap	Outcome
1 The reactive approach	Focuses the search on the familiar personality and effective competencies of the previous person who held the position, rather than on the job's requirements.
2 Unrealistic specifications	Limits the potential number of candidates.
3 Evaluating people in absolute terms	Requires answers to absolute questions, such as 'What are your strengths and weaknesses?' The answers are opinions given without any evidence to support them.
4 Accepting people at face value	Takes candidates' answers as accurate and truthful. Executives and interviewers often readily believe candidates' answers to questions and their résumé information.
5 Believing references	Omissions are ignored. References are of limited value. 'A recent survey of 854 executives conducted by the Society of Human Resource Management found that only 19% would reveal to reference-seekers why a candidate left their company, and only 13% would describe a candidate's work habits' (1999, p. 112).
6 The *just like me* bias	Creates a 'halo' effect in which one positive characteristic can eclipse all others; reinforces the tendency to rate highly people who are just like you.
7 Delegation gaffes	Delegates the initial interviews to others who are ill-prepared, or asks human resources staff to create a job description without proper briefing.
8 Unstructured interviews	Produces unreliable predictions of performance. The interviewer with a list of well-prepared questions is more reliable in predicting performance.
9 Ignoring emotional intelligence (self-awareness, self-regulation, motivation, empathy)	Ignores the idea that 'emotional intelligence is a critical predictor of professional success' (1999, p. 113) and more important than intellect and experience.
10 Political pressures	Chooses people for the wrong reasons. People like to hire friends; senior executives like to get their candidate selected so they will have an ally; others prefer someone inferior to get the job so that it does not jeopardise their own promotion chances.

Equal Employment Opportunity

Equal Employment Opportunity (EEO) policies and programs have been created in response to legislation. They are aimed at bringing about fairer representation in employment of all groups in the community. EEO applies the merit principle. For the merit principle to operate, the best and most efficient person must be selected. As a result, no person should be discriminated against on the basis of:

- sex
- marital status
- membership of an ethnic or racial minority group
- physical handicap
- intellectual impairment
- sexual preference.

In addition, the compulsory age of retirement no longer exists. Equal opportunity exists when people's chances of employment, promotion, training, or obtaining any other benefit or opportunity related to their employment are neither reduced nor increased on the basis of the characteristics listed above.

Equal employment opportunity has become a part of management practice in both the public and the private sector. It aims to avoid discrimination. **Discrimination** in the workplace means denying people equal treatment for reasons other than those relating directly to the job. One of the purposes of this legislation is to ensure that recruitment and selection for jobs in an organisation is based on merit. The person with the relevant skills, experience and qualifications best suited to the job should get the job.

Equal Employment Opportunity (EEO) is a policy that aims to achieve fairer representation in employment of all groups in the community.

The merit principle selects the best person for the position.

Discrimination in the workplace denies people equal treatment for reasons other than those relating directly to the job.

Bias in job interviews

Cash, Gillen and Burns (1977, p. 309) state that 'despite objectively equivalent qualifications, job applicants may encounter different employment opportunities that are dependent upon their sex, physical attractiveness, and the sex role characteristics of the opportunities they seek'. Research has demonstrated that biases limit the interview's validity and reliability as a technique of personnel selection. Research into sex-role stereotypes has shown that an applicant's gender and the omission or inclusion of a photo on a résumé depicting the applicant as physically attractive or unattractive can affect interviewers' recommendations for employment. Sex and physical attractiveness biases were also demonstrated in the research of Dipboye, Arvey and Terpstra (1977), which showed that bias occurred independently of the sex of the interviewer.

It has also been shown that nonverbal visual cues, such as eye contact, smiling, posture, inter-personal distance and body orientation, affect interviewers' judgments (Imada & Hakel 1977). DeGroot and Motowidlo (1999) show from their study that, as well as visual cues, some vocal cues such as pitch, range, rate, pauses and loudness displayed in the employment interview can affect interviewers' judgments. They suggest this results from the personal reactions (liking, trust, attributed credibility) that interviewers form towards individuals who display these visual and vocal cues.

Attempts to overcome biased judgments by way of organisational diversity training programs have also come under scrutiny. A study by Kulik, Perry and Bourhis (2000) involved raters who were either preoccupied or not and who were shown three training videos: one that recommended they try to suppress age-related thoughts; a second that provided information about age, sex, race and ethnic diversity and recommended trying to suppress demography-related thoughts; and a third that contained no suppression information. The results showed that those who were instructed to suppress age-related thoughts and who were preoccupied 'evaluated an older applicant less favourably than raters in other conditions' (p. 589). From these results, the researchers suggest that 'organisational diversity training including instructions to suppress stereotypic thoughts may have detrimental effects on evaluations of non-traditional job applicants if raters are cognitively busy when they implement these instructions' (p. 589).

Natasha Wallace (2002) says: 'Cultural practices can hinder migrant applicants in job interviews.' She asks, 'Does avoiding someone's eyes in an interview *really* mean you're lying about your qualifications? Or if you're softly spoken, do you *really* lack confidence?' Even though Australia is culturally diverse, 'considering a person's ethnic and cultural background and being aware of your own assumptions when assessing individuals for a job . . . is a concept barely known here'. Often managers are pressured to make decisions quickly and to rely on first impressions, usually to the detriment of the migrant applicant.

Wallace recommends being mindful of the following when interviewing people from a culture other than your own:

- Be aware of your own assumptions and judge others accordingly.
- Don't place undue emphasis on body language or tone of voice.
- Learn about the candidate's ethnic background and culture.
- Avoid using jargon and metaphors.
- Speak slowly, clearly and in simple language.

Employment interview validity

Research analysing the relationships between four interviewer-related factors and employment interview validity (Huffcutt & Woehr 1999, p. 549) suggests that:

- training should be provided to interviewers regardless of whether the interview (i.e. the questions and rating scales) is structured
- the same interviewer should be used across all applicants, especially when the interview is not highly structured
- using a panel of interviewers does not contribute to validity and may actually have a detrimental effect.

Results for the fourth interviewer factor, taking notes during the interview, were inconclusive. The researchers found a fairly high correlation between note taking and interview structure and hence were unable to isolate the note-taking factor. They consider that taking notes has the potential to improve both the quantity and quality of the information used in the evaluation of applicants and should be further investigated.

Ethics in job interviews

Wilson and Goodall (1991, p. 131) list four established ethical guidelines for employment interviews:

1. Interviewers should not ask illegal questions.
2. Interviewers should not use any discriminatory information that comes out in the interview.
3. Interviewers should not intentionally misrepresent themselves or their company.
4. Interviewers should not intentionally deceive the interviewee with respect to the employment decision.

Lehman and Dufrene (2002, p. 591) advise candidates to be knowledgeable about interview questions that might lead to discriminatory hiring practices. They comment: 'A recent survey indicated that more than one-third of applicants [in the United States] have been asked an illegal interview question pertaining to race, age, marital status, religion, or ethnic background.' Listed below are some of the questions they consider should not be asked of an applicant.

- 'What religious holidays will require you to miss work?'
- 'Could you provide a copy of your birth certificate?'
- 'Do you have a disability that would interfere with your ability to do the job?'
- 'How many days were you sick last year?'

- 'How much alcohol do you consume each week?'
- 'Are you married?'
- 'Who is going to watch your children if you work with us?'

Lehman and Dufrene suggest that you can answer these questions in three different ways. First, you could refuse to answer and inform the interviewer that the question is improper. (With this approach, you might embarrass or offend the interviewer.) Second, you could compromise your principles and answer the question. Third, you could give a low-key response, such as: 'How does this question relate to how I will do my job?' Or you might give an answer that shows you understand the legitimate concern behind the question. For example, in answer to the question, 'Do you plan to have children?', you might respond: 'I plan to pursue a career regardless of whether I decide to raise a family.'

REVIEW QUESTIONS

24. a Identify three 'traps in hiring'.
     b Explain how you can minimise or even avoid these traps.
25. a What does equal employment policy aim to achieve?
     b Describe two causes of bias in employment interviews.
26. Discuss four established ethical guidelines for employment interviews.

APPLY YOUR KNOWLEDGE

GOOD PRACTICE IN INTERVIEWS

1. Assess your communication skills when applying for jobs by using the following table to evaluate your job search products—résumé and letter of application.

A. Résumé		
Good practice	Yes	No
Do your words express results you have achieved, problems you have dealt with, or important learning experiences you have had?		
Is your résumé clearly set out, concise, well organised, persuasive and positive in tone?		
Have you shown and discussed your final draft with at least two people?		
B. Letter of application		
Good practice	Yes	No
Is the letter well planned and does it use the AIDA formula?		
Does the letter address all the requirements of the position?		
Does the letter name the position in the first paragraph and express the wish for an interview in the concluding paragraph?		
Is the letter persuasive and does it use the AIDA formula?		
Does the letter show genuine interest in the company based on thorough research?		
Does the letter identify purpose in the first paragraph and invite a response in the concluding paragraph?		

2. Evaluate your job search actions—collecting information on employment opportunities, making inquiries about a position and following up to obtain feedback—in the following tables.

A. Collecting information on employment opportunities		
Good practice	*Yes*	*No*
I have evaluated my experience, qualifications, skills, interests, values and attitudes, and identified the type of work that suits my abilities.		
I use online recruitment websites to search for jobs.		
I use at least five different ways to find a job.		
B. Making inquiries about a position		
Good practice	*Yes*	*No*
I always contact the advertising company for more information about the position.		
I research the company using the Internet/library.		
I notify my referees before applying for the position.		
C. Following up to obtain feedback		
Good practice	*Yes*	*No*
I make inquiries by telephone or mail two weeks after sending job applications or cold canvassing applications.		
I ask for feedback on my applications and make changes to my résumé and/or letter.		
I record my job search activities in a well-organised manner.		

3. Find an online recruitment site and locate a job that suits your skills and qualifications. Prepare an employment application for this position in a format that can be posted on to a web recruitment site.

4. Organise an interview for yourself from the following suggestions:
    - Mock interview conducted by one of your referees or a person in your network.
    - Role-play interview organised and conducted with your student group.

5. a   Finish the mock interview by obtaining feedback from the interviewer using the interview checklist below.
    b   Document the results of the feedback you obtained in the interview checklist. Use the table below.

Interview performance results		
Action	Suggestions for improvement	Action interviewer's feedback

    c   Analyse the strengths and weaknesses in your interview performance.
    d   Outline how you will improve your weaknesses and focus on your strengths for your next interview.

SELF-EVALUATE YOUR SKILL

RATE YOUR COMPETENCE IN INTERVIEWS

INTERVIEW CHECKLIST				
Position title:				
Date interview conducted:				
Key: A = Acceptable, NI = Needs Some Improvement, CI = Needs Concentrated Improvement, NA = Does Not Apply				
	A	NI	CI	NA
Arrives on time and dresses appropriately				
Introduces self and creates a good first impression				
Maintains good eye contact and posture				
Speaks in an audible voice				
Enthusiasm noted in voice				
Describes self in positive terms				
Responds concisely, but adequately, to questions				
Relates work skills and abilities to position				
Gives positive responses to questions about				
— work history and experience				
— education/qualifications				
— career direction				
Seems motivated to work				
Asks questions relevant to the job				
Presents necessary documents/work samples				
Concludes interview with summary of strengths				
Thanks interviewer at the end				
Asks if and when interviewer could be contacted regarding decision				

SUMMARY OF LEARNING OBJECTIVES

1 ▷ LOCATE EMPLOYMENT MARKET INFORMATION

Sources of information include newspapers, employment agencies, professional publications, the Internet and your personal networks. Many positions are filled through contacts and networking. Recruitment via the Internet is increasing rapidly. Regardless of where you access information, locating it takes time and effort. The reward is the position you want. Employers look for applicants who are results-oriented, can get things done, and have personal standards of excellence and good communication skills.

2 ▷ DISCUSS THE CHARACTERISTICS OF EFFECTIVE RÉSUMÉS

Effective résumés highlight the value of your experience, qualifications and qualities. They contain power action words and keywords that command attention. The content is organised by the use of headings and a professional layout.

3 ▷ CHOOSE THE APPROPRIATE RÉSUMÉ (BASIC, FUNCTIONAL OR TARGETED) FOR THE POSITION AND YOUR SKILLS AND QUALIFICATIONS

A résumé must be specific to the tasks and responsibilities of the position you are applying for. Highlight your strengths and achievements. The résumé should contain a profile statement or employment objective, educational qualifications, skills, employment experience and achievements. The résumé may be organised as a basic, functional or targeted résumé.

4 ▷ PREPARE AN ELECTRONIC RÉSUMÉ TO ALIGN YOUR QUALIFICATIONS TO THE NEEDS OF THE POSITION

A large number of organisations are now requesting applicants for positions to post their résumés online. The databanks of résumés held online are searched by keywords that match the requirements of the position. Successful online résumés have clear content that relates the applicant's skills, experience and accomplishments to the position. The format is uniform and easy to read. Keywords are essential.

5 ▷ WRITE AN EFFECTIVE APPLICATION LETTER

The letter of application is a persuasive letter that aims to attract the reader's attention and interest. It also aims to create (in the potential employer) the desire to take action—in this case, to call you for an interview. It has three main parts: introduction, body and conclusion. The covering letter should be short, no more than one page in length.

6 ▷ DIFFERENTIATE BETWEEN TYPES OF EMPLOYMENT INTERVIEWS

The three main types of employment interview are the interview conducted by a single interviewer; the series interview, conducted in turn by a number of interviewers; and the panel interview, conducted by a group of interviewers.

7 ▷ EVALUATE THE STAGES IN AN EMPLOYMENT INTERVIEW

There are five main stages in an employment interview— pre-interview, the opening of the interview, the body, the close and the post-interview stage. While interviews can be stressful, an understanding of the activities in each stage makes it easier to demonstrate your ability to do the job.

8 ▷ IDENTIFY AND DISCUSS POST-INTERVIEW ACTIVITIES

Before you leave the interview, make sure you know what the next step is so that you can follow up if the expected response does not take place. A courteous and concise follow-up inquiry letter or telephone call enables you to express thanks and reinforce your interest in the position. Respond to an offer of the position with a letter of acceptance or a letter declining the offer.

9 ▷ DISCUSS HOW TO DEAL WITH PROBLEM INTERVIEWS

Interviewers who do not plan often fall into the 'traps in hiring'. An applicant may have to take part in an interview without clear objectives and structure. By preparing well in the pre-interview stage and by using good speaking, listening and questioning skills, applicants can show their capacity to work well and to interact effectively even when the situation is not ideal.

Interviewers who plan well are able to select the best person for the position. They apply Equal Employment Opportunity principles to avoid discrimination, and select the person with the skills, experience and qualifications that best match the requirements of the position. Effective interviewers avoid bias caused by discriminatory responses to an applicant's age, sex, ethnic background, religion or other characteristics unrelated to performance. They also avoid the bias caused when interviewers make decisions based on their personal reactions or responses to the interviewees, rather than on objective evidence provided in the interview.

Effective interviewers are ethical. They do not ask illegal questions that discriminate, do not intentionally misrepresent themselves or their company, and do not intentionally deceive the interviewee with respect to the employment decision. Interviewers who plan well and behave ethically are the key to achieving valid and reliable outcomes from employment interviews.

KEY TERMS

ACTIVITIES AND QUESTIONS

1 Read the case study below.

Case study: Writing a traditional basic résumé

The following comments were made in an interview with a member of an employment agency.

The purpose of the résumé and the covering letter is to get an interview for a job. The covering letter should be structured so that it encourages the interviewer(s) to read your résumé. The covering letter should be a one-page part of your résumé and should briefly address each of the points in the job description. It should relate your experience to the key qualifications in the job advertisement.

The résumé should be a simple statement of your background and should include your name, address, school records, post-school qualifications, membership of any professional organisations, and hobbies and personal interests.

When summarising your experiences, make it easy for the interviewer(s) by arranging your job experiences in reverse chronological order, beginning with your current position. State who you worked for, and how long you worked for them; give a brief description of the organisation, in bullet points. Do

not be reticent about your particular achievements, and be prepared to discuss these at the interview. You may, if you wish, state your reasons for leaving an organisation; for example, 'resigned to gain further experience in another company'.

A résumé should be concise, to the point and not more than four pages in length. There is always a risk that anything longer than four pages will not be read. This would disadvantage you, as you would attend the interview assuming that the interviewers know all about you.

a What is the purpose of the résumé and covering letter?

b What is the appropriate length of each document?

c The summary of your job experience should be listed in reverse chronological order. Why?

2 a Choose from a newspaper a position suited to your qualifications and interests.

b Prepare a suitable résumé for this position in the format most suited to your qualifications, abilities and experience.

3 Work individually.
  a Make a bulleted list of your own accomplishments where you can give specific examples of outstanding or improved performance.
  b Write a 150-word statement summarising what you want from your career and what you can offer a prospective employer. Where would you place this statement in your résumé?
  c Prepare a page for your résumé listing your career achievements. Avoid making the mistake of confusing your achievements with your responsibilities, and remember to leave enough white space on the page so that prospective employers can read it easily.

  d Visit <www.careerone.com.au> or any other online site to find a position you would like to apply for. Prepare a résumé for that position.
4 Work in small groups.
  a Discuss the advantages and disadvantages of the virtual interview for the interviewer and the interviewee.
  b Brainstorm to create a list of strategies the interviewee could use to communicate well in a virtual interview.
  c Report your findings to the large group.

EXPLORING THE WEB

1 Learn more about résumé writing by visiting:
  • 'Résumés ACPeople',
  • 'Résumé writing tips and examples', <www.provenrésumés.com>
  • 'Résumé writing', .
2 Practise an interview by visiting:
  • Graduate Careers Australia, *Interviews and Beyond*

  Practice Interviews,
  • 'Preparing for tomorrow's interview today', <www.perfectinterview.com>.
3 Find out more about interview questions by visiting 'Sample job interview questions', .

PROJECT WORK

Work in small groups. Read the following passage, answer the questions, and conduct a role-play interview.

The Public Relations and Marketing Department has a new and exciting opportunity for a highly motivated Marketing Coordinator. This is a new initiative and the successful applicant will have the opportunity to be involved 'hands on' in all aspects of implementation. The Marketing Coordinator must have excellent communication, research and project management skills and have proven professional experience in strategic marketing. The successful applicant will demonstrate:
  • *sharp intellect and analytical capabilities*
  • *excellent interpersonal and communication skills (written, oral, presentation and negotiation)*
  • *business acumen and strong customer focus.*
The Marketing Coordinator will be responsible for implementing marketing strategies that will raise the profile of the City Council and its community. This position

has been classified as a Grade 16 with a salary range of $80 000 p.a. to $90 000 p.a. and a fully maintained vehicle, and will be dependent upon relevant skills, competencies and experience.

An information package for the position containing a Job Description and a Person Specification can be obtained. Written applications addressing the criteria as set out in the job description and person specification, with the contact details of two recent referees, should be forwarded by Monday, 23 April 2010 to: . . .

Work in groups of three or four. Assume you are the interviewer preparing the questions for the position of Marketing Coordinator.

a Create two questions to open the interview and two questions to close the interview.
b Create five questions that will help you to evaluate the ability of the applicant to complete the essential and desirable tasks identified in the advertisement.

c Check that you have included at least one open, one closed and one probing question. If any type of question is missing, change one of the questions into that type of question.

d Create an evaluation sheet to help you evaluate and compare the answers given by each interviewee.

e Conduct the interview as a panel interview—two people interviewing a third for the Marketing Coordinator position. A fourth person observes and uses the checklist below to evaluate the performance of the two interviewers.

Checklist: Behaviour as an interviewer			
Did you:	Very Successfully	Successfully	Unsuccesfully
define the interview's purpose?			
show interest and involvement?			
prevent interruptions?			
prepare questions?			
prepare answers?			
prepare an evaluation sheet?			
listen carefully?			
show empathy for the interviewee?			
show courtesy in the interview?			
assess your own behaviour?			
respect the interviewee's personal space?			
achieve the interview's purpose?			
dress appropriately?			
complete each stage of the interview?			

BIBLIOGRAPHY

ACPeople. *Résumés*, www.acpeople.com.au/résumé, viewed 21 November 2007.

Australia's Careers Online. *Careers Advice and Counselling*, www.careersonline.com.au/Links/Jobs-Careers_Advice_and_Counselling.html, viewed 22 November 2007.

Barnsley, J. 2002. 'Show and tell time', My Career, *Sydney Morning Herald*, 21–22 September, p. 1.

Bullock, G. 2000–01. 'Finding the right stuff', in *Your Business: Telstra's Magazine for Business Owners*, December–January, pp. 20–22.

Career Builder Home Page, www.careerbuilder.com, viewed 21 November 2007.

Cash, T.F., Gillen, B. & Burns, D.S. 1977. 'Sexism and "beautyism" in personnel consultant decision making', *Journal of Applied Psychology*, Vol. 62, Issue 3, pp. 301–10.

CICA Career Industry Council of Australia Home Page, www.cica.org.au, viewed 13 February 2008.

Cole, K. 2005. *Management Theory and Practice*, Pearson Education Australia, Sydney.

Culwell-Block, B. & Sellers, J.A. 1994. 'Résumé content and format—do the authorities agree?', *Bulletin of the Association for Business Communication*, Vol. 57, Issue 4, pp. 27–30.

Dagge, J. 2004. 'Making that first impression count', My Career, *The Sun Herald*, 11 January, p. 8.

DeGroot, T. & Motowidlo, S.J. 1999. 'Why visual and vocal interview cues can affect interviewers' judgments and predict job performance', *Journal of Applied Psychology*, Vol. 62, Issue 3, pp. 288–94.

Dipboye, R.L., Arvey, R.D. & Terpstra, D.E. 1977. 'Sex and physical attractiveness of raters and applicants as determinants of résumé evaluations', *Journal of Applied Psychology*, Vol. 62, Issue 3, pp. 288–94.

Fernandez-Araoz, C. 1999. 'Hiring without firing', *Harvard Business Review*, July–August, pp. 109–24.

Graduate Careers Australia. *Interviews and Beyond Practice Interviews*, www.graduatecareers.com.au/content/view/full/178, viewed 21 November 2007.

Graduate Careers Australia. 2007. *Graduate Outlook 2007*.

HealthPost.com. *Résumé Writing*, www.healthposts.com.au/résumé/writing.asp, viewed 21 November 2007.

Huffcutt, A.I. & Woehr, D.J. 1999. 'Further analysis of employment interview validity: a quantitative evaluation of interviewer-related structuring methods', *Journal of Organizational Behavior*, Vol. 20, pp. 549–60.

Imada, A.S. & Hakel, M.D. 1977. 'Influences of nonverbal communication and rater proximity on impressions and decisions in simulated employment interviews', *Journal of Applied Psychology*, Vol. 62, Issue 3, pp. 295–300.

Job Seeking Sites, www.nnsw.com.au/regional/jobsearch.html, viewed 22 November 2007.

Keats, D.M. 2000. *Interviewing: A Practical Guide for Students and Professionals*, University of NSW Press, Sydney.

Kelly Services. *Sample Job Interview Questions*, www.kellyservices.com.au/web/au/services/en/pages/careers_sample_interview_questions.html, viewed 21 November 2007.

Kulik, C.T., Perry, E.L. & Bourhis, A.C. 2000. 'Ironic evaluation processes: effects of thought suppression on evaluations of older job applicants', *Journal of Organizational Behavior*, Vol. 21, pp. 689–711.

Lehman, C.M. & Dufrene, D.D. 2002. *Business Communication*, 13th edn, South-Western, Ohio.

Marion, L.D. 1997. 'Companies tap keyboards to interview applicants', *News and Observer*, 11 January, p. B5.

Monster Home Page, www.monster.com, viewed 12 October 2006.

Mycareer. *Job Search Page*, www.mycareer.com.au, 21 November 2007.

Perfect Interview. *Preparing for Tomorrow's Interview Today*, www.perfectinterview.com, viewed 21 November 2007.

QuintCareers.Com. *Career Exploration Tools and Resources*, www.quintcareers.com/career_exploration.html, viewed 22 November 2007.

Robbins, S., Judge, T.A., Millett, B. & Waters-Marsh, T. 2008. *Organisational Behaviour*, 5th edn, Pearson Education Australia, Sydney.

Thornburg, L. 1998. 'Computer-assisted interviewing shortens hiring cycle', *HR Magazine*, February, http://findarticles.com/p/articles/mi_m, viewed 10 April 2008.

Tucker, D.H. & Rowe, P.M. 1977. 'Consulting the application form prior to the interview: an essential step in the selection process', *Journal of Applied Psychology*, Vol. 62, Issue 3, pp. 283–7.

Wallace, N. 2002. 'First impressions', My Career, *Sydney Morning Herald*, 19–20 October, p. 1.

Wallace, N. 2003. 'Knockout blow', My Career, *Sydney Morning Herald*, 18–20 April, p. 1.

Weekend Australian. 2003. 'Job-seekers' one-stop shop', Weekend CareerOne, 2–3 August, p. 1.

Wilson, G.L. & Goodall, H.L. Jr. 1991. *Interviewing in Context*, McGraw-Hill, USA.

Glossary

abstract *See* executive summary.

academic honesty Ethical behaviour in all academic work, including acknowledging all sources correctly, presenting your own work, gathering objective and reliable data, and working in accordance with the university's student guidelines.

accommodation A negotiation style in which one party is willing to oblige or adapt to meet the needs of the other party.

acculturation The process of adjusting to the host culture by adopting its values, symbols and/or behaviour.

acronym A word formed from the initial letters of other words.

action plan A working document for the implementation of chosen options.

active listening A listening technique in which the listener works at paying attention to the whole message—that is, the content and the feeling.

active voice A writing style in which the subject is placed before the action to give a stronger link between them and to show who or what is doing the action.

adaptors Nonverbal acts performed unconsciously in response to an inner desire.

adjourning stage Stage of group development when the group is restructured, the committee is wound up or the task force is dissolved after completing its objectives.

adjustment refusal A refusal given when an organisation believes that a request for an adjustment is unjustified.

advertising Activities that aim to sell a product.

affect displays Changes in facial expressions that display emotion.

after-action review A systematic process used to extract the learning from an event or activity. The process addresses the questions: What should have happened? What actually happened? What lessons are there for the future?

agenda A list of a meeting's business prepared by the secretary in consultation with the chairperson and distributed before the meeting.

aggregator A web application that makes a collection of syndicated web content such as news headlines, blogs and podcasts accessible in a single location for easy viewing.

aggressive behaviour When one person seeks to dominate others.

agreement chart Differentiates between three different outcomes: the negotiated agreement, the BATNA and the WATNA.

AIDA formula A formula describing the process suited to persuasive writing. It aims to catch the attention and interest of the customer and to create desire and a willingness to take action.

amendment A proposal to alter a motion in a formal meeting.

analytical report Assesses a situation or problem and recommends a course of action in response.

anecdote/story Example from past experience.

announcement memo A memo that provides information.

apologies The names of people who have apologised for not being present at a meeting.

appeals Emotional messages that appeal to the senses.

appendix Information relevant to a report but which would interfere with the flow of ideas if included in the body; usually attached at the end of the report.

argument A claim or assertion that may be believed or disbelieved; a process of reasoning that shows the relationship between ideas and aims to convince others of the truth of something.

argumentative essay Aims to convince the reader to accept the thesis statement, premise or claim by presenting an argument with supporting and opposing credible and current evidence.

artefacts Objects used to convey nonverbal messages about self-concept, image, mood, feelings or style.

assertion Behaviour that acknowledges your rights as an individual and the rights of other people.

assertive behaviour A constructive style of behaviour, based on high self-esteem and an acceptance of self.

assertive statements Used to make people aware of your rights while respecting theirs.

assumption An unstated belief that supports the explicit reasoning.

attending listening Focusing on the speaker by giving physical attention.

attention line Names the person who is to attend to a letter's contents.

attention span The time the average adult can attend to and process the information in a speaker's presentation.

audience An assembly of people related by a common purpose to hear one or more speakers.

audioconferencing Enables members who are geographically dispersed to communicate verbally without the expense of meeting face-to-face.

audiovisual aids Aural and visual devices used by a speaker to improve the audience's understanding.

author-date (or Harvard) system of referencing Acknowledging work written by someone else by identifying it in the following order: the author's surname and initials or given name, year of publication, title, publisher and place of publication.

authorisation memo A written statement giving the reader authority to take some action.

authoritarian leader A leader who determines the policies and work of the team, with little discussion or input from other group members.

authority The characteristic given to a person with the accepted source of information or the right to determine actions, or the respect or acceptance that commands influence.

autonomous or **semi-autonomous work groups** Sections or groups in an organisation that are provided with general objectives and targets by senior managers and then left to decide the work process.

bad news letter Gives unwelcome news, using the indirect order of information.

barriers These occur when the message received is not necessarily the same as the message sent.

basic résumé Includes all the usual parts of a résumé with appropriate headings, but is simpler and shorter than functional and targeted résumés.

BATNA The best alternative to a negotiated agreement.

belief A personal conviction, not necessarily based on fact.

bibliography A list of all the sources of information used in a report, as well as further recommended reading.

blog A website where messages are written; can be combined with music, audio, photographs and video.

body The main part of a spoken or written presentation.

bookmark A saved link to a web page, added to a list of saved links.

boundary spanners People who work at the interface of the organisation and in their work cross organisational and/or national boundaries.

brainstorming A group process for generating ideas and creative solutions.

briefing A short, accurate summary of the details of a plan or operation, given orally.

B2B Business-to-business interactions between businesses, government departments and other organisations, rather than with individual customers.

B2C Business-to-customer interactions one-to-one between two or more people.

bureaucracy An organisational system characterised by division of labour, a clearly defined hierarchy, and detailed rules and regulations.

case-based reasoning The process of solving new problems based on the solutions to similar past problems.

casting vote A vote by the chairperson that decides an issue in a meeting in the case of a tied vote.

centralisation The degree of decision-making power located at the highest level.

chairperson The presiding officer of a meeting, committee or board.

channel The vehicle of communication.

citations Acknowledgment of the work of others, allowing the reader to find the original source of information.

clarifying statement A communication technique that aims to bring accuracy to an area of confusion. The listener explains how they have interpreted the message.

clichés Words that have been so overused they have lost meaning and impact.

client records Information about the type and level of service expected and received by a customer.

climate The atmosphere created by the cohesiveness of the group or team.

closed question A question that is designed to limit the response.

coaching A method of directing and instructing people with the aim of achieving some goal or developing specific skills that produce results.

code of ethics A formal statement of an organisation's values and ethical rules.

co-destiny relationships Built when buyers, sellers, customers and providers partner in strategic alliances.

coercive power Power based on force or punishment.

cohesion A sense of belonging and inclusion that allows team members to satisfy their needs and objectives.

cohesiveness A level of common purpose and commitment to the team among members.

collaboration People cooperating to produce a solution satisfactory to everyone.

collection letter Uses persuasion to collect money from those who are slow to pay.

column (vertical bar) graph A graphic that uses vertical columns to show changes over time, or to compare amounts/items.

committee A group of people who have the delegated authority to consider, investigate, and report or act on some matter.

communication Any behaviour—verbal, nonverbal or graphic—that is perceived by another.

communication barriers Anything that distorts or interrupts the message and its meaning.

communication channel The means or techniques that are used to send a message.

communication climate The tone of a relationship, as expressed by the verbal and nonverbal messages between people.

communication model A simplified representation of the main elements in the communication process.

communication networks Patterns of communication established among employees who work closely together in a small group.

communication process A two-way exchange of information between two or more people.

communications The plural form of the word refers to the technology and machines that carry messages.

communication structure The pattern of interaction among people who comprise the organisation.

community of practice A group that promotes social learning and builds relationships over an extended period of time.

competency The ability to complete a task to the standard required by industry.

competition A situation in which one party negotiates to maximise its results at the expense of the other party's needs.

complexity A factor of the number of sections, departments, individual job functions and titles in an organisation.

complex sentence A sentence that contains one main clause and one or more subordinate or dependent clauses.

complimentary close The formal or less formal closing.

compound sentence A sentence that contains two or more main ideas expressed in two main clauses, each of which is able to stand alone.

compromise The settlement of differences by mutual concessions.

computer-assisted inverview Used to screen applicants.

conclusion A summary of the findings and an evaluation of the main facts discussed in a report; a closing overview of the main points of a presentation; must be related to and result from the material in the report.

concrete language Definite and specific words that are easy to understand.

confidence The ability to feel comfortable with other people and situations.

conflict A clash of opinions, values, needs or goals.

conflict management A process in which the parties attempt to manage the conflict and move towards a solution without escalating the conflict or giving away their interests.

conflict map A tool used to find the cause of a conflict.

conflict resolution A process that seeks to resolve the problem, even though this requires change.

confrontation A situation where people are in opposition or feel antagonistic towards one another.

connotation The association placed on a word by past experience, attitudes, values or context.

consensus An agreed position.

constitution A document that contains an organisation's name, aims and objectives, rules of administration, membership, office bearers and committee.

consultative power Power that is based on a capacity to seek information, consider advice from others and make plans with others.

consulting The action of gathering information from customers (or others) about their needs and expectations.

context The situation or setting within which communication takes place. Contains three dimensions: physical, social–psychological and temporal.

conversational listening Involves both surface and in-depth listening skills.

correspondence A meeting's incoming and outgoing mail.

counselling interview An interview that aims to provide support for employees dealing with emotional problems.

cover page Part of a proposal that includes the name of the proposing organisation or person, their contact address and telephone number, title of the project, the name of the person to whom the project is submitted, and the date.

credit refusal Rejects a request for credit.

crisis A level of conflict where behaviour and normal functioning are affected.

critical thinker A person skilled at articulating and evaluating arguments, and understanding how evidence supports or opposes a claim in order to make good judgments.

critical thinking The ability to ask and answer critical questions, and the desire to use the critical questions actively.

cross-cultural communication Communication between people from different cultural backgrounds.

cross-functional teams Members with complementary skills, knowledge and experience to accomplish the team purpose and task.

cull Elimination, on the basis of the job application, of those people considered unsuitable because of lack of qualifications, experience, ability or motivation for the position.

cultural nonverbal communication Rule-governed nonverbal behaviour learned unconsciously by observing others in the society or group.

cultural relativism The recognition of cultural differences and acceptance that each social group has its own set of cultural norms.

cultural sensitivity Awareness of the common rules and patterns of behaviour in other countries.

culture An integrated system of learned behaviour patterns that are characteristics of the members of a group or organisation; learned social behaviours that develop over time.

customer A person who purchases and/or seeks goods or services from another person or organisation.

customer complaint A customer's expression of dissatisfaction with a good or service supplied by another.

customer enquiry A customer's seeking of information, usually by questioning about a good or service provided by another.

customer experience The perception customers gain from their interactions with an organisation's products, services, people and processes.

customer relations management (CRM) A combination of strategy, process and technology used to manage customer interactions.

customer service Meeting the needs and expectations of the customer as defined by the customer.

customer value package The range of strategies designed to give customer service based on the things that customers value.

customer values The four types of customer values are basic, expected, desired and unanticipated value.

decision block The space provided for the receiver of a submission to give written approval.

decision by authority A situation in which a group discusses an issue, and then either the leader or an outside supervisor makes a decision.

decision by compromise A decision that appeals to all members of a group without fully satisfying anyone.

decision by consensus A decision made by mutual agreement among group members.

decision by majority An agreement that is reached among the majority of group members.

decision-making agenda A nine-stage process that encourages all members of a team to participate in planning the actions to be taken to complete a task.

decode To interpret a message to achieve understanding.

deductive argument Argument based on logical necessity—if you can accept the premise, you must also accept the conclusion.

deductive reasoning Argues from the general to the particular.

defensive roles Behaviours that are intended to protect a group from anxiety when it is unable to function effectively.

delegate To give someone else the authority and responsibility for carrying out a task while retaining accountability.

demographic details Personal details asked for in a survey, such as age, gender and place of residence.

denotation The literal meaning of a word.

diagram A graphic that is used to compare structures.

digital rights The rights of copyright holders of digital works, devices or documents to prevent unauthorised duplication of their work to ensure 'fair play' from continued revenue streams.

directive interview An interview that is controlled and organised by the interviewer.

directive techniques Used in interviews to focus on a particular topic and gain further information.

direct or inductive order of information Identifies information chronologically in the sequence in which it occurs.

discipline or reprimand interview An interview that aims to discuss unacceptable or inappropriate behaviour and to create and discuss the plans to take action to change the situation.

discomfort A level of conflict where things do not feel right or you feel uncomfortable in a situation.

discrimination In the workplace, discrimination means denying people equal treatment for reasons other than those relating directly to the job.

diversity A context that covers gender, age, language, ethnicity, cultural background, sexual orientation, religious belief and family responsibilities.

docking station A way to 'plug in' a portable laptop computer to common computer peripherals, enabling the laptop to become a substitute for a desktop computer.

dot graph A graph that is used when there are six or more variables.

drama triangle An illustration of non-assertive behaviour in which people play the role of victim and behave in a helpless manner.

drawing A graphic used to emphasise details of interest.

dysfunctional roles Behaviours that distract a group from its purpose or inhibit its progress towards its goals.

edit To revise and correct a piece of writing.

editing The final stage in writing that involves checking and correction.

effective listening Using listening skills to understand the sender's intended message.

electronic communication Any message created and sent along electronic channels (e.g. email).

electronic mail (email) The transmission of messages from computer to computer through electronic transmission devices such as modems, telephone lines, mail servers and other telecommunications services.

electronic mailing list A list of names and email addresses of subscribers used for sending publications to an organisation's customers.

electronic résumé Placed on a database and searched by keywords.

emblems Nonverbal acts that are learned through imitation (e.g. nodding the head).

emoticon A symbol, or combination of symbols, used to convey emotional content that supplements the written message.

emotional appeals Appeal to needs such as companionship, adventure, power, authority, humour and loyalty, or appeals to feelings such as fear, love, boredom or curiosity.

emotional awareness Knowing specifically how you feel.

emotional competence The capacity to manage self and relationships effectively.

emotional intelligence The capacity to reason with emotion.

empathy The ability to understand and feel as the other person feels.

empathy blockers These have a negative impact on communication and may cause barriers between the sender and receiver of a message.

employment agency A broker of jobs—a middle person between employers and job applicants.

employment interview An interview that aims to attract and choose the best applicant for a position.

empowerment Allows people to make decisions, accept responsibility, and become more self-directed members of a team.

encode To put a message into words, pictures or actions so that it can be sent.

encouraging listening Invites speakers to disclose their thoughts and feelings.

enculturation The process of learning or absorbing one's own culture.

end matter The final part of a report or book containing the appendix, bibliography, glossary of terms, and index.

endnotes Supplementary material placed at the end of a chapter or article.

environment Surrounding circumstances, conditions or influences.

Equal Employment Opportunity (EEO) A policy that aims to achieve fairer representation in employment for all groups in the community.

equity The quality of being fair or impartial.

esteem The regard or favourable opinion in which a person is held by others.

ethical research Documents sources, gives appropriate credit, and respects the intellectual property and digital rights of others.

ethics The principles of right and wrong that guide decision making when faced with conflicting responsibilities.

ethnocentrism The belief that one's cultural norms are superior to those of other social groups.

evaluative listening Used to accept or reject an idea.

evidence Material used to determine or demonstrate the truth of an assertion. It is explicit information used by the writer or speaker to justify the dependability of a factual claim.

executive summary, preface, abstract or **synopsis** Part of a proposal or report that summarises the contents and findings.

expertise power Power that is held because of a person's knowledge, aptitude and ability.

explicit knowledge Knowledge that has been articulated and stored, and can easily be transferred to others.

external channels of communication Means of sending messages to people outside the organisation.

external conflict Conflict between people.

extranet Software that links organisations in intercompany relationships.

facilitation A process in which a facilitator seeks to help the parties arrive at a common definition of their relationship, define their separate goals, facilitate analysis and discover options that meet the needs of all.

fact Something that can be shown to be true.

fallacy An error in reasoning that leads to a false statement or belief.

false analogy A faulty form of reasoning in which false similarities are inferred.

feedback The receiver's response to a sender's message. It tells the sender how the message is being interpreted and helps the receiver to confirm whether their perception of the message is correct.

feedforward Information sent before the main message, often nonverbally.

fight response Used in a conflict situation to control or defend a position.

findings Facts and information presented in a document.

flight response Used in a conflict situation to escape the situation and avoid the results.

flow chart Illustrates the steps in a process, procedure, system or model.

flow response Used in a conflict situation to acknowledge the situation and respond appropriately.

footnote A comment at the foot of the page giving extra information about a point in the text.

formal group A group established by management that is usually regulated through formal or contractual processes.

formal meetings Meetings that are structured, with rules and regulations; unchanging proceedings.

formal outline Contains headings and subheadings identifying the main ideas and supporting information in a document to be written.

formal short report The minimum acceptable format for a short report includes a title page, introduction, sections with headings in the main body, conclusions and recommendations (when required).

formalisation In an organisation, the existence of firmly structured lines of communication, authority and control.

format Layout and appearance of a document.

forming stage Stage of group development when group members may be uncertain about the group's membership, leadership and goals, so great importance can be attached to the group's leader as members look for support, guidance and direction.

form report A standard layout enabling information to be gathered in a consistent manner from different sources.

framing The way in which a party describes, explains or defines a conflict.

free-form structure The situation when an individual or group is given almost total freedom by top management, usually to complete a given task.

front matter The first part of a report, containing title page, letter of transmittal, table of contents, abstract or synopsis, and authorisation document.

functional résumé Places emphasis on skills and experience gained through previous employment, particularly those that are significant for the position(s) you are applying for.

general business The section of the agenda under which new business may be introduced.

generalisation To give a general, rather than a specific, character to a subject.

globalisation The process of growing world interdependence caused by changes in global economies and communications technology.

glossary Defines and explains technical terms.

goal An aim or end towards which effort is directed.

good news letter or **neutral letter** Presents positive, favourable or neutral information, using the direct order of information.

goodwill The reputation of a business and its relations with its customers.

grapevine The way gossip travels through the workplace.

graphic Visual representation that organises information, shows relationships, highlights trends, and helps to sort, classify and group data.

graphic communication Represents ideas, relationships or connections visually with shapes, diagrams and lines.

ground rules Statements about how the parties will treat one another in a conflict negotiation.

group cohesiveness The level of common purpose and commitment to the group among members.

groupthink A situation in which a high level of group cohesiveness prevents disagreement, constructive criticism and full assessment of alternatives.

Harvard (or author-date) system A way of referencing quoted works.

hierarchical subject index Search engine that places subjects into a graded order within a directory.

hierarchy An organisational system that moves through a number of levels.

high-transparency organisation An organisation with effective flows of information upwards, downwards and horizontally.

horizontal bar chart A graphic that emphasises the differences or similarities between two or more items at a certain point in time.

horizontal channel Communication channel that operates between colleagues at the same level within the organisation's structure.

hot groups Groups that share an attitude for dedication to the task and are goal-focused.

'I' messages Assertive statements that help to send a clear message.

immediacy The sense of contact the receiver gets from the person communicating.

impromptu speech An unexpected speech that is delivered without preparation.

incident level A level of conflict where some short, sharp exchange has occurred and caused a slight irritation.

incident report Offers a clear factual account of something that happens which is non-routine, e.g. an accident.

inclusion The use of language that does not exclude a group of people on the basis of gender, race or some other factor.

inclusive language Includes all readers.

indirect or deductive order of information Emphasises the problem at the beginning and end of the document. Starts with the result or action needed, then provides detailed evidence and discussion, and concludes with the main point.

inductive argument An argument based on probability—what conclusion is most likely to be expected or believed from the available evidence.

inductive reasoning Argues from the particular to the general.

inference The process of deriving a conclusion.

inference theory Proposes that classifications and drawing conclusions about people is based on an unconscious internalised set of general propositions.

informal group A group that is not formally established within the structure of the organisation.

informal meeting A meeting that is less structured than a formal meeting.

informal networks Communication links between individuals and sections that bypass the formal structures in an organisation.

informal organisational structure The links between individuals, groups and whole sections of the company that are not legitimised by management.

informational listening Used when the listener wants to understand the content, thoughts and ideas in the message.

informational report Delivers data and information without making recommendations.

information overload Excessive amounts of information.

information power Power that results from having access to, and control over, the distribution of important information about organisational operations and future plans.

in-house Done within the organisation without seeking outside help.

inquiry A letter that asks others to share information and ideas.

inside address The receiver's address in a business letter.

instant messaging (IM) One of the web 2.0 capabilities that helps users share and collaborate through basic chat, presence awareness, automated newsfeeds, blogs and other media.

instruction memo A memo that gives directions.

intellectual capital The collective knowledge (whether or not documented) of the individuals in an organisation or society that can be applied to work to add value.

intellectual property The property of your mind or intellect.

intentional message The message the sender means to send.

interaction management The balance between sender and listener as they interact with one another.

intercultural communication The interpersonal interaction between members of different cultural groups that differ from each other in the knowledge shared by their members and in their linguistic forms of symbolic behaviour.

intercultural conflict A real or perceived incompatibility of goals, values, expectations, process or outcomes between two or more interdependent individuals or groups from different cultures.

interdependent behaviours Task behaviours related to goal achievement and socioemotional behaviours related to harmonious relations.

internal channels of communication Means of communicating to people within the organisation.

internal conflict Conflict within a person caused by an unsatisfied need or an unresolved experience or emotion.

Internet Worldwide cooperative public telecommunications network accessible to anyone with suitable equipment.

interpersonal communication Interaction between two people on a one-to-one basis or in small groups.

interpersonal concerns The three interpersonal concerns in teams are the need for inclusion, the need to know who has control, and the need to be accepted.

interview An exchange of information that has a purpose and is planned, structured and controlled by the interviewer.

interviewee The person being interviewed.

interviewer The person conducting the interview.

intracultural communication Shared communication between members of the same cultural group.

intranet A private version of the Internet used by individual enterprises to share computer resources and company information.

intrapersonal communication Communication with oneself through the process of thinking and feeling.

introduction The first part of a presentation that prepares your audience for what you are going to say and identifies the aim or main theme.

jargon The language peculiar to a trade or profession.

job description Lists the objectives of the position and the duties completed by a person in the position.

job interview An interview conducted to choose the best applicant for a position.

job specification An outline of duties and responsibilities.

Johari window This theory explains the parts that make up each person's self-concept in two broad divisions: the areas of yourself known to you, and the areas of yourself known to others.

justification report Presents an idea or proposal and then uses evidence to justify it.

justified customer complaint A valid and reasonable complaint from a customer.

keynoting Restatement and repetition of key words.

keyword résumé Uploaded into a computer database and retrieved by a keyword search.

keywords The words searchers type into search engines to find what they want.

kinesic behaviour Movement of the torso, hands, head, feet or legs; posture; eye movement such as blinking; and facial expressions such as smiles.

know-how Intellectual property and confidential information such as designs, drawings, procedures, methods, and the accumulated expert knowledge, skills and experience of staff used by an organisation in its strategic and operational activities.

knowledge Data, information and intelligence that can be used to act.

knowledge champion A knowledge leader who actively drives the knowledge agenda and creates commitment and support.

knowledge management The process through which organisations generate value by gathering, organising and sharing their intellectual and knowledge-based assets.

knowledge-management enablers The technologies and organisational strategies that support knowledge-management practices.

knowledge organisations Organisations that use systems and processes to generate, transform, manage and transfer knowledge in order to achieve goals and improve performance.

knowledge worker Works primarily with information, or develops and uses knowledge in the workplace.

laissez-faire leader A leader who has a policy of non-interference and lets the group run itself.

lateral thinking A creative thinking technique in which the thinker explores a situation or idea from different points of view, by making out-of-the ordinary connections.

layout The arrangement of information on a page or screen.

leader A person who achieves the organisation's goals through the work of others without relying on his or her position power. Leaders have the ability to influence others.

leadership The process of influencing groups and individuals towards the achievement of an organisation's vision and objectives.

leadership style Consistent pattern of behaviour adopted by a leader.

leading question A question so worded that it suggests the desired answer.

learning A sequence of recall, comprehension, application, analysis, synthesis and evaluation.

learning organisation An organisation with the capacity to learn, adapt and change continuously in response to its experiences, successes and mistakes.

legitimate power Power held because the organisation has given authority to that position.

letterhead Displays the official name, address, telephone, fax, email address and logo, usually at the top of the page.

letter of acceptance A courteous letter stating acceptance of a job offer.

letter of acknowledgment A letter that acknowledges requests for information, confirms orders, supplies information and thanks the receiver.

letter of application The persuasive part a job application. It is a covering letter and should be brief (about one page) and specific.

letter of inquiry A letter that seeks information.

letter of introduction A letter that aims to maintain contact and create goodwill and the opportunity for future sales.

letter of request A letter that seeks specific action.

letter of transmittal The covering letter for a report.

letter report A report that includes the seven basic parts of a business letter plus a subject line.

line graphs Diagrams that show movement. Their main purpose is to show trends over time in a situation in which there is a continuous relationship.

linking phrases Phrases that make logical connections between ideas and give continuity to a piece of writing.

listening Involves both hearing and striving to understand the other person's message.

list of references Gives details only of those works cited in the report or essay.

logical appeals Use of logic to influence the receiver to change attitudes or behaviour.

logical order A sequential flow of ideas.

long report A formal document written to provide comprehensive information and expert opinion.

lose-lose situation A situation in which both parties are dissatisfied with the negotiated result.

lose-win strategy A situation in which one party withdraws or makes too many concessions, while the other party wins.

low-transparency organisation An organisation with an ineffective flow of communication upwards, downwards and horizontally; as a result, there are strong internal and external grapevines.

maintenance-related functions Behaviours that focus on what is happening in the group, the way members listen and relate to each other, and the behaviour developments within the group.

maintenance-related roles The behaviours that are needed in groups or meetings to focus on people and their relationships with one another—e.g. to support and encourage the contributions of members or to resolve disagreements.

management The process of planning and coordinating work activities and tasks so that they are completed efficiently and effectively with and through other people.

manager A person who achieves the organisation's goals through the work of others.

manuscript speech A written speech suited to technical and/or complicated information. It is often read.

map A type of graphic that uses scale, grids, symbols, lines, colours, legends, titles, figures and text to show the location of land forms, cities, towns and roads. *See also* conflict map.

Maslow's hierarchy of needs Maslow identified five levels of human needs: physiological, safety and security, belonging, esteem and status, and self-actualisation.

mass communication Communication with an organisation's public.

matrix A hierarchical, functional, departmentalised structure where people report through two chains of command.

mechanistic organisation An organisation that operates in a stable, highly structured environment, rather like a machine.

media Communication channels that reach large numbers of people—e.g. television, radio, newspapers, magazines.

media release A statement issued to the media by a company, giving details of a newsworthy event.

mediation A process in which a third party is engaged to help disagreeing parties to move to an agreement.

meeting A forum or group of people that provide and clarify information, give and receive feedback, encourage problem solving and allow discussion.

memorandum or **memo** The standard format of internal written communication within an organisation.

memorandum proposal A proposal that uses a standard memorandum layout.

memorandum report A report in memorandum format for circulation within an organisation.

memorised speech A speech that is learned and recalled.

memory The capacity to recall or recognise something that has been previously experienced.

mentoring A relationship in which those with experience and knowledge facilitate and support those with less experience and knowledge.

message The idea or feeling transmitted from the sender to the receiver to achieve understanding.

Mind Map® A problem-solving technique that begins with the main idea as the focus. Key concepts then project out from the main idea.

minutes The official written record of what happened during a meeting.

mirror question A question that restates the interviewee's previous answer and invites them to add further information.

misunderstanding level A level of conflict where motives and facts are often confused or misperceived.

Monroe's motivated sequence A pattern of organisation appropriate to a presentation that is designed to persuade the audience to accept and respond to the speaker's message.

motion A proposal for action put by a member to the rest of the meeting.

motivation A process that directs individual action or behaviour towards a goal.

multicultural society A society that consists of people of diverse cultural, racial, religious and ethnic backgrounds.

multimedia More than one concurrent medium; e.g. text, sound and video images.

needs Major requirements that people have.

negotiation A process in which two or more parties try to resolve differences, solve problems and reach agreement.

netiquette The conventions and accepted standards used by a sender of messages online (made up of Inter*net* and et*iquette*).

network A group of people who exchange ideas and information with one another.

network analysis Identifies patterns of interaction, cliques, and the connectedness and openness of groups.

networking The process of building and maintaining interpersonal and professional contacts.

neutral letter *See* good news letter.

'new' network A network that is empowered to make decisions and where knowledge is shared along all channels of communication.

newsgroup An association (formal or informal) of computer users with a special interest who form a network for distributing electronic messages.

news value The term used to describe the criteria for making news.

noise or **interference** An interruption to the message or communication flow between the sender and receiver that can lead to misunderstanding.

nominal group technique A technique enabling members of a group to work as individuals and to think about and present new ideas.

non-assertive behaviour Described as aggressive or submissive behaviour that ignores our own rights by failing to express honest thoughts and beliefs.

non-directive interview An interview technique that involves the participants and the organisation in setting the goals and process of the interview.

non-directive techniques Use minimal questions, create a conversational tone, and adopt positive nonverbal cues to encourage the applicant to speak.

nonverbal behaviour Movement of the hands, head, feet, legs, posture; eye movements, facial expressions, vocalisations and voice qualities.

nonverbal communication Communication that is sent by any means other than words or graphics. It modifies, changes or complements the verbal communication.

nonverbal learning The extralinguistic transmission of cultural knowledge, practices and lore.

norming stage Stage of group development when group norms, or acceptable behaviour, attitudes, work patterns and related behaviour, emerge.

norms The shared ideas and expectations about how members of a group or society should behave.

notation Acknowledgment of sources of information.

note (or traditional) system of referencing A way of referencing quoted works, using the following order: author's given name or initials, author's surname, title, publisher, place of publication and year of publication.

notice of meeting A document convening a meeting that is sent to all members at a time specified by the organisation's rules.

objective Based on rational thought, rather than emotional reaction.

online information Information that is generated by, transmitted by or accessed via a computer system or network.

openness The inclination to respond frankly and spontaneously to people and situations; the ability to acknowledge personal feelings and thoughts as one's own.

open question A question that is designed to encourage the interviewee to speak freely and to provide a range of information.

operations Actions taken to reach goals.

opinion A personal judgment; a belief held with confidence but not substantiated by positive knowledge or proof.

options The range of alternatives from which the appropriate choice can be made.

order of information The sequence in which information is presented.

order refusal Declines a request.

organic organisation An organisation operating in a dynamic, flexible environment.

organisation chart Illustrates the relationships between the functions, units and positions in an organisation.

organisational culture A pattern of shared assumptions and beliefs; members learn about appropriate behaviours and share them with new members.

organisational structure The framework of an organisation, showing the specialisation of functions and the levels, or hierarchy.

organisational writing The writing developed for and within the organisation.

other-orientation The ability to attend to and focus on the other person in an interpersonal interaction.

P2P Peer-to-peer interactions without direct mediation of an organisation or business.

palm cards Small cards bearing the main points and supporting information of a speech, which are held in the palm of the hand during the speech.

panel interview An interview conducted by a group of interviewers.

paragraph A clustering of sentences built around one main idea.

paralanguage How something is said.

parallel language Use of the same parts of speech to give balanced phrases that add flow and rhythm to a piece of writing.

paraphrasing Expressing the meaning of what was said, using different words from the original.

participative leader A leader who encourages members of the group to take an active role in decision making.

passive voice A form of the verb in which the subject of the sentence is acted upon. Often used in technical and scientific writing.

perception The process by which people select, organise and interpret data in order to give meaning to a message.

performance interview An interview that seeks to evaluate employees' performance and provide feedback on the organisation's perception of that performance.

performing stage Stage of group development when a group has formed its identity and structure.

periodic report A report that keeps management informed by providing, at regular intervals, information on some aspect of the organisation's operation.

permissive leader *See* laissez-faire leader.

persecutor A role from the drama triangle played by those who put the other person down or bully them into action.

personal nonverbal communication The use of nonverbal actions in a way that is personal or unique to a person.

persuasion The process of influencing another to change his or her beliefs or behaviour through moral or logical argument.

persuasive letter A letter that is written to influence the reader to take some action.

persuasive writing Writing that aims to influence the reader to change an attitude or take some action to satisfy a need.

photograph A graphic used to show the physical appearance of the subject.

pie chart A circular graphic representing the parts or divisions of a unit; gives a comparison of the parts.

plagiarising To steal and pass off the ideas or words of another as one's own; to use another's production without crediting the source; to commit literary theft, present as new and original an idea or product derived from an existing source.

plain English A writing style that is easy to read and understand; uses positive language, clear expression and an assertive, courteous tone.

podcast A digital media file, or a related collection of such files, distributed over the Internet for playback on portable media players and personal computers.

point of order A question raised (usually at a meeting) as to whether proceedings are in order.

positional bargaining An approach to negotiation that negotiates from positions, rather than interests.

positiveness The ability to communicate in a confident way while acknowledging the other person.

post-interview stage The time immediately after the interview(s) when the interviewer or panel evaluate the applicants and the results of the interviews.

power The capacity to influence, the possession of delegated authority, or an ability to act.

précis A condensed version of a piece of writing, highlighting the main ideas.

preface *See* executive summary

pre-interview stage Preparation for an interview when the purpose of the interview is defined, details of time and location are decided, and research is undertaken to establish the responses required and the questions to be asked.

prejudice A preconceived opinion or feeling, favourable or unfavourable.

premise A proposition or claim on which an argument is based or from which a conclusion is drawn.

prepared speech A speech that is planned and organised before the time of presentation.

presentational codes Give messages, such as gestures and eye movements, about what is happening now.

pre-testing A pilot of the questions prepared for a survey to remove any potential problems before the survey is given to the chosen population.

primary activities Activities that produce the most important results.

primary sources of information The people or organisations who take the action or cause the events that become part of society's store of information.

principled bargaining A negotiation method made up of four elements: people, interests, options and criteria. The negotiating purpose is to satisfy the underlying interests of the parties.

priorities The most important things.

probing question A question that follows on from the last response of the interviewee.

problem-solving order of information Used to focus the reader's thoughts on the problem. Start with the problem. Provide a detailed discussion of the factors that caused the problem, and conclude with the solution.

problem-solving process A five-stage process to create new ideas and/or solve problems.

process models of communication Contain seven main elements—sender, receiver, message, feedback, channel, content or setting, and noise or interference.

progress reports Reports that are part of the organisation's management information system.

proposal A plan or scheme sent to a decision maker in the form of a well-organised and persuasive document. *See also* motion.

proposition A claim on which an argument is based or from which a conclusion is drawn.

protocol The special set of rules of communication used by the terminals/nodes (and related software) in a telecommunications network as they send and receive messages.

proximity Nearness in place.

proxy A written authorisation given by a shareholder for someone else, usually the company's management, to cast his or her vote at a shareholders' meeting or at another time.

public communication When an organisation communicates with a number of receivers at the same time.

public relations Activities concerned with the presence or image of an organisation and the positive public acceptance of this image.

public relations crisis An abnormal situation or public perception that is beyond the scope of everyday business and threatens the operation, safety and reputation of an organisation.

public relations issue Cause for concern when an organisation's stakeholders form into groups because its actions impact on them.

publics Those groups that have actual or potential interest in, or impact on, an organisation's ability to achieve its objectives.

purpose statement A sentence identifying a document's theme or subject.

quality management An approach to client service that involves everyone in the organisation in quality improvement.

quality service The act of providing a good or service to the expected, desired or unanticipated level of service.

questionnaire Form used by participants in a survey to record their opinions.

quorum The minimum number of people that must be at a meeting for business to be conducted.

rationalisation Applies logic to test the solution.

readability How easy a document is to read. To improve the readability of business writing, keep sentences short and logical.

reading A physical and intellectual exercise that involves identifying and understanding what is written.

realistic conflict Conflict that can be resolved if people are willing to use effective strategies and negotiation skills.

receiver The receiver decodes or interprets the sender's message to achieve understanding.

recommendations The actions proposed as a result of the findings of a report or proposal.

reference A document written to highlight and support the skills and experiences of a person going for a job interview.

referent power Power that flows from being respected, admired, liked or personally identified with by others.

reflective listening Restates to the speaker the feeling and content in the message.

reflective statement Lets the speaker know that the listener understands the underlying feelings.

reframing The process of changing the way a thought is presented.

regulators Nonverbal acts, such as head nods and movements, that regulate communication between people by maintaining and controlling the flow of speaking and listening.

reliability In a survey, gives the same results under the same conditions at different times.

report writing conventions Accepted guidelines that ensure the expectations of the writer and the reader of the report are in agreement. The conventions cover the report's structure, format, writing style and content.

report-writing style An objective form of writing.

request memo A memo that asks for information.

rescuer A role from the drama triangle played by people who offer help and support while denying their own needs.

resolution A process that develops from an analysis of the total situation by the concerned parties to meet all their needs. A motion put to the meeting and carried.

résumé An informative, comprehensive document about your qualifications, experience and achievements.

reward Something given or received in return for taking some action.

reward power Power held by a person in authority who has control over resources desired by others—they can influence or manipulate the behaviour of others who want the reward.

rhythm A measured flow of words that is used to emphasise the flow of ideas or to provide pauses that halt the flow in order to emphasise a point.

role A way of behaving in a particular situation; a set of expected behaviours associated with a position.

role repertoire The number of roles constantly and competently performed at home, work, leisure and in other contexts.

routine order of information Factual information that is presented in the context of an overview of the complete picture.

routing information The list of signatures or initials on a memo, usually prepared in alphabetical order or in order of seniority of position.

sales letter A persuasive letter that follows the order of information in the AIDA formula.

salutation The writer's greeting to the receiver.

sampling The analysis of a group by determining the characteristics of a significant percentage of its members chosen at random.

search engine A computer program that receives requests from Internet researchers, compares them with the index created by the 'robot' or 'web crawler', and returns the results of the search to the researcher.

secondary sources of information Material published and stored after an event has taken place; summaries of information gathered from primary sources.

secretary Assists the chairperson; conducts correspondence, prepares the minutes, keeps records and completes other duties for a meeting.

self-actualising person Someone who realises their own potential.

self-concept The mental image that people have of themselves.

self-disclosure Involves showing how you react to and feel about a situation.

self-image A person's view of themselves.

self-monitoring Manipulationof the image that each person presents to others in their interpersonal interactions.

self-presentation The way you choose to present yourself in a specific context.

self-managed work teams Semi-autonomous or autonomous teams with a high level of control over their work.

self-monitoring Manipulation of the image that each person presents to others in their interpersonal interactions.

self-presentation The way you choose to present yourself in a specific context.

self-referential messages Statements that refer to the speaker.

semi-autonomous work groups *See* autonomous work groups.

sender The sender encodes an idea or feeling in words or signs that the receiver will recognise and transmits this message to the receiver.

series interview Several interviews conducted in turn by a number of interviewers.

service culture The way in which service is offered across an organisation.

service strategy The techniques used to offer service.

settlement A process arrived at by a mediator offering a compromise that differs from a resolution.

short messaging service (SMS) A means of sending short messages to and from mobile phones, often called text messaging.

short report Communicates written, objective information within and outside an organisation.

short report format The three main short report formats used in business are the formal, letter and memo format.

show notes An outline of the contents of each episode of a podcast.

signalling devices Subject headings, introductory paragraphs, prefaces or summaries all signal that the flow of ideas, the importance of ideas, or the emphasis in the document is about to change.

signature block The letter writer's signature, name and job title.

simple sentence A sentence that contains only one idea expressed in one clause.

single interview A job interview that is conducted by a single interviewer responsible for interviewing all applicants and selecting a new staff member.

Situational Leadership® model A model that considers the interaction of leadership style, the characteristics of the followers, the relationship between task and relationship behaviour, and the situation.

SMART approach A goal-setting technique in which goals are specific, measurable, achievable, relevant, and timely or time-bounded.

social network service Provides a forum for communities of people who share interests to interact online.

social networking analysis (SNA) The mapping and measuring of relationships and flows between people and groups within an organisation.

spam Junk email.

stage fright Anxiety or fear about making a presentation before an audience.

stakeholders Individuals or groups affected by an organisation's actions.

standing orders The rules that govern the manner in which a meeting's business is to be conducted.

stereotype A set of beliefs about the personal attributes shared by an entire group.

storming stage Stage of group development when conflict that clarifies ideas and is resolved is a positive force in the group as the team moves through the conflict and becomes more cohesive.

stress Any pressure or demand, physical or psychological, that creates a state of tension.

stress interview Places the interviewee in an anxiety-producing situation.

subject line Identifies a letter's subject or purpose.

submission A request for funds or approval for a course of action.

submissive behaviour Accepting the opinions of others without asserting one's own point of view; based on low self-esteem.

success triangle An illustration of the flow response, or assertive behaviour, in a conflict situation.

summarising Restating in a condensed way the most important points.

summary An overview of the main themes and sub-themes in a document.

supportive communication Genuine, spontaneous and non-evaluative communication.

supportiveness The ability to supply descriptive and spontaneous feedback to another person in a provisional manner.

survey A research technique used to gather information that is not otherwise available.

syllogism Contains at least two premises—a major and minor premise—leading to a conclusion.

symbols A shorthand form of writing—e.g. the international stop sign.

synchronous virtual meeting All group members participate at the same time.

syndication process Distributes through web feeds the content of blogs, podcasts and other digital communication channels to subscribers who receive it via aggregators.

synopsis *See* executive summary.

table A graphic in which related information is presented in parallel columns.

table of contents Lists the main sections and subsections of a report.

tacit knowledge Knowledge that people carry in their minds, or knowledge embedded in an organisation's culture ('know-how'), and which is thus difficult to access.

tagging A popular way to locate, classify, rank and share Internet resources through the use of shared lists of user-created Internet bookmarks.

targeted résumé Emphasises skills and experiences relevant to a specific job; it focuses on skills and capabilities, rather than history.

task-related functions Behaviours that focus on the task to be achieved.

task-related roles The behaviours needed to focus on the specified goals to be completed as a group or meeting achieves its purpose—e.g. goal setting, decision making and problem solving.

tautology Unnecessary repetition of an idea.

team A group with a charter or reason for being.

team briefing A presentation designed and delivered by team members.

team structure The elements that make up the whole team as it moves through the stages in the development of a team.

teamwork When trust, cooperation and compatibility exist between the leader and members; cooperative effort by the members of a group or team to achieve a common goal.

teleconference A telephone meeting between two or more people in different locations, involving sophisticated communications technology.

tender document A bid or offer to provide a product or service in exchange for a fee.

tension A level of conflict where relationships are weighed down by negative attitudes and fixed opinions.

terms of reference Statements that define the scope of a report.

tertiary sources of information Material compiled from secondary sources.

text The main body of matter in a document.

text messaging Sending short text messages from a mobile phone to other mobile phone users using the SMS standard.

thesis statement A sentence in a document making a claim, an assertion or a point.

thinking The process by which new concepts or representations of information are created in the mind.

3 × 3 writing process A systematic plan for developing all business communication (written and spoken).

title page The first page of a report; includes the report's title, the name of the person who authorised the report, and the name and designation of the report writer.

tone The mood of the writing.

topic sentence Signals the main point of a paragraph.

total message The words, the nonverbal behaviour and their meaning.

total quality management The process by which everyone in the organisation focuses on providing quality customer service.

traditional written outline A way to prepare for writing a report in which the main ideas and their supporting information are listed.

transactional leaders Leaders who clarify role and task requirements to guide or motivate their followers to achieve goals at the desired level of performance.

transactional leadership A style of leadership linked to goal achievement in which leaders motivate followers to perform at expected levels, agree on goals, focus on compliance, achievement and rewards, and engage in rational problem solving.

transformational leaders Leaders who have the ability to evoke strong emotions such as trust, admiration and respect in their followers. They are able to influence others and provide inspiration and motivation.

transformational leadership A style of leadership that motivates followers to perform beyond normal expectations by taking people beyond self-interest, and raising motivation and moral commitment to concentrate on higher-level goals.

transitional expressions Words or phrases that make connections between two ideas or subjects.

transmittal memo The cover note for a more formal lengthy message.

tree diagram A way to prepare for writing a report in which the general points are organised as branches on a tree.

triangle A visual plan for a document that shows the main ideas as a contained unit.

undercurrent message The hidden part of the message that may contain feelings and/or content.

unintentional message The meaning placed on the message by the receiver is different from the sender's intended message.

universal nonverbal communication Body movements common to humankind, such as a smile or tears.

unrealistic conflict Conflict that cannot be resolved because the people involved are unwilling to change their attitudes.

unrelated nonverbal communication Random nonverbal behaviour, such as a sneeze, that is unrelated to the verbal message.

validity The soundness or authority of research.

verbal communication Communication between two or more people in the form of spoken or written words.

verbal following The listener follows on from what the speaker has said by asking questions related to the speaker's message, giving feedback to follow up on the meaning of the message in order to gain a shared understanding.

verbosity The use of too many words.

vertical bar graph See column (vertical bar) graph.

vertical channel The channels that move communication up and down between different levels in the organisation.

victim A role played in the drama triangle in which a person who is not a real victim plays the role of a victim in order to have someone else rescue or persecute him or her.

videoconferencing May comprise any number of people communicating in a video session in real time from different locations.

virtual interview Conducted via videoconferencing technology.

virtual team A physically dispersed group working across distance, time, organisational and national boundaries, using information technology to interact.

vision A clear view of what a team or organisation is doing and will do in the future.

visual aids Graphics and visual devices used by a speaker to improve audience understanding.

visual ethics Concerned with ethical issues involved in the production of visual images.

vocabulary The stock of words in a language.

vocal characterisers Nonverbal vocal behaviour, including laughing, crying, sighing, yawning, clearing the throat, yelling, whispering.

vocalisations Vocal characterisers, qualifiers and segregates such as sighing, pitch height, and 'uh-huh' or 'um' sounds that give clues to the meaning of the spoken message.

vocal qualifiers How something is said—e.g. intensity and pitch.

vocal segregates Nonverbal sounds such as 'uh-huh','um', 'uh', 'ah'; silent pauses and intruding sounds.

vote At formal meetings, members vote to make decisions. The vote is usually by a verbal 'aye' or 'nay', by a show of hands, or by a ballot.

WATNA The worst alternative to a negotiated agreement.

webconferencing Used to conduct live meetings or presentations over the Internet.

web feed A data format used for providing users with frequently updated content via content distributors who syndicate a web feed, thereby allowing users to subscribe to it.

web page A page on a website made up of a related collection of web files.

win-lose strategy A situation in which one party is satisfied and one is dissatisfied with the settlement negotiated.

win-win approach Aims to satisfy the needs and interests of both parties in the situation.

win-win strategy A situation in which both parties are satisfied with the settlement negotiated.

withdrawal A negotiation style in which one party retracts their point of view or backs away from the situation.

work team enablers The key to developing positive and efficient communication and cooperation within and between teams.

World Wide Web All the resources and users on the Internet that are using the hypertext transport protocol (HTTP).

writing style The way a writer uses words, sentences, paragraphs, tone, rhythm, order of information and layout to present ideas.

'you' approach A writing style that speaks personally to the reader by addressing them directly as 'you' throughout the document.

Index

Pages in **bold** indicate a key term/glossary definition; *italics* indicate a graphic.